THE ENCYCLOPEDIA OF
SERIAL KILLERS

Second Edition

Michael Newton

Facts On File
An imprint of Infobase Publishing

The Encyclopedia of Serial Killers, Second Edition

Facts On File, Inc.
An imprint of Infobase Publishing
132 West 31st Street
New York NY 10001

ISBN 978-0-7394-7249-1

Text and cover design by Cathy Rincon

Printed in the United States of America

For Janice Gail Knowlton,
survivor and friend.
(1937-2004)

I did it all for me. Purely selfish. I worshiped the art and the act of death, over and over. It's as simple as that. Afterwards it was all sexual confusion, symbolism, honoring the "fallen." I was honoring myself. I hated the decay and the dissection. There was no sadistic pleasure in the killing. I killed them as I would like to be killed myself, enjoying the extremity of the death act itself. If I did it to myself I could only experience it once. If I did it to others, I could experience the death act over and over again.

—Dennis Nilsen

Contents

Preface to the Second Edition

I appreciate the opportunity to update and expand *The Encyclopedia of Serial Killers*. Much has happened in the field since I completed the original work in early 1999, as evidenced by the increased volume of cases reported. The first edition included data on 1,621 specific serial murder cases; this edition contains 2,309 (a net increase of 42 percent in the span of five years). Not all of those cases and killers are "new," however, since expanded study of serial crime has shed light on many older cases that were unrecognized or poorly reported when the first edition went to press. Accordingly, while the previous edition dated records of the first known serial killer from the first century A.D., we now know that compulsive predators were active in ancient Rome as early as 331 B.C. In time, older cases will no doubt emerge.

With so much new material from which to choose, a volume many times the size of the original might easily have been prepared. Instead, as in the first edition, Facts On File has placed a premium on user-friendly format and economy. The new edition differs from its predecessor in three ways: (1) New entries and updated information have been added throughout the main text, while revisions and corrections have been undertaken based on new research and sources; (2) 689 cases have been added to the work's appendixes on solo killers, team killers, and unsolved crimes, while certain errors in the supplementary material have also been corrected; (3) The bibliography has been extensively updated, listing 686 English-language sources (compared to 276 in the first edition). In short, the revised *Encyclopedia of Serial Killers* represents the most complete source on the subject presently available.

Thanks are due to various individuals who provided supplementary material for this volume and/or suggested corrections from the first edition. First and foremost, I owe thanks to David Frasier at Indiana University—friend and fellow author, researcher par excellence—for his continuing assistance and support. The work in hand would literally not exist without his generous help. Others unsung when the first edition went to press include Barry Baldwin, Kimba D'Michi, Michael Kingman, Alan and Lenore Locken, Heather Newton, Rod Poteet, and Stan Reid.

As in the first edition, every effort has been made to ensure the timeliness and accuracy of this work. Readers possessing additional data on any aspect of serial murder are invited to contact the author via the publisher, or at his Web site (http://www.michaelnewton. homestead.com).

Preface to the First Edition

In recent years it has become routine—indeed, almost obligatory—for authors of studies on serial murder to describe the phenomenon as "elusive," "mysterious," even "baffling." It is not entirely clear why that should be the case—except, perhaps, that "normal" minds rebel at understanding those who kill repeatedly outside the law, either for profit or the simple, atavistic pleasure of the act.

It is the purpose of this volume to demystify, as far as possible, those predators in human form who have been with us since the dawn of history, their numbers multiplying exponentially within the past four decades. Understanding of the problem and development of workable solutions is important both in the United States (which, with less than 5 percent of the world's population, has produced some 84 percent of all known serial killers since 1980) and in nations ranging from Australia to South Africa and Russia, where a new wave of serial murder bids fair to reach crisis proportions in the next millennium.

The entries in this work are alphabetically arranged, including both case histories of individual serial killers and essays on general topics (e.g., motives for serial murder, etc.) Cross-referenced items may be listed at the end of a specific entry or signified by use of SMALL CAPITAL LETTERS in the body of the text. The large number of serial killers on record—more than 1,500 at this writing—renders comprehensive coverage of each and every case unfeasible in any single volume. Thus, case histories presented in the main text were selected as examples of specific serial killer types, motivations, nationalities, and so forth. The remainder of cases known at this writing are presented in a detailed appendix, further subdivided into sections for solo killers, those who murder with accomplices, and cases presently unsolved.

Many people have assisted in the preparation of this work, particularly with the details of lesser-known cases. They include: David Frasier, reference librarian at the University of Indiana in Bloomington; A. M. Barmer, at the Jacksonville (Fla.) Public Library; Becky Clark, at the Lincoln (Nebr.) Public Library; M. Collin, at the Santa Barbara (Ca.) Public Library; Virgil Dean, with the Kansas Historical Society; Nijole Etzwiler, at the Baraboo (Wisc.) Public Library; Elizabeth Fitzgerald, at the Providence (R.I.) Public Library; Marcia Friddle, at the Chicago Public Library; Sally Fry, with the Orange County (Fla.) Library System; Merle Groce, with the Morgan City (La.) Archives; Sandra Hancock, at the West Florida Regional Library in Pensacola; C. Jones, reference librarian at the Public Library of Nashville (Tenn.); Donald Langlois, reference librarian for the Arizona Department of Library, Archives and Public Records; Catherine Larsen, at the Kalamazoo (Mo.) Public Library; David Meeks, at the Palatka (Fla.) Public Library; Antonio Mendoza, of the Internet Crime Archives; the Oakland Public Library, Oakland History Room; Mary Lou Rothman, at the Indian River County (Fla.) Main Library; Mark Schreiber; Steve Stangle, with the St. Johns County (Fla.) Public Library System; Warren Taylor, at the Topeka and Shawnee County (Kans.) Public Library; Elizabeth Thacker, at the San Francisco Public Library; Vivian Turner, at the Sacramento (Ca.) Public Library; Katherine Turton, with the Chattahoochee Valley (Ga.) Regional Library System; Sharon Van Dorn, at the Dallas Public Library; Carolyn Waters, at the St. Petersburg (Fla.) Public Library.

Every effort has been made to ensure the timeliness and accuracy of the work in hand. Inevitably, by the time it goes to press there will be more new cases in the media and fresh developments in some of those reported here. Readers possessing additional information on any aspect of the serial murder phenomenon are encouraged to write the author, in care of Facts On File.

Entries A-Z

ALLEN, Howard Arthur

An African-American serial killer with a taste for elderly victims, Howard Allen never strayed far from hometown Indianapolis in his search for prey. In August 1974, at age 24, he invaded the home of 85-year-old Opal Cooper, beating her to death in the course of a petty robbery. Convicted on a reduced charge of manslaughter, Allen received a term of two to 21 years in state prison. Paroled in January 1985, he returned to Indianapolis and found work in a car wash, biding his time before he resumed the hunt.

On May 18, 1987, a 73-year-old Indianapolis woman narrowly escaped death when a prowler choked and beat her in her home. Two days later, Laverne Hale, 87, was attacked in a similar fashion, dying of her injuries on May 29.

The raids continued on June 2, when a burglar ransacked the home of an elderly man five blocks from the Hale murder scene. This time, the tenant was absent. The prowler vented his anger by setting the house on fire.

On July 14, Ernestine Griffin, age 73, was murdered in her Indianapolis home, stabbed eight times with a 10-inch butcher knife, a kitchen toaster smashed repeatedly against her skull. Grieving relatives estimated that the killer had escaped with $15 and a camera belonging to his victim.

The case broke on August 4, 1987, with Howard Allen's arrest on multiple charges. Witnesses linked him to the May 18 attack, leading to Allen's indictment on charges of burglary, battery, and unlawful confinement. He was also charged with arson and burglary (from the June 2 incident), as well as the murder of Ernestine Griffin.

Police were not finished with their suspect, however. As it happened, Laverne Hale had been a neighbor of Allen's, living directly behind his house, and he became a suspect in her murder, based on her killer's modus operandi. In early August, detectives announced that Allen was a prime suspect in eleven other cases, each involving robbery or assault of elderly victims in their homes around Indianapolis.

In the spring of 1988, Allen was convicted of burglary and felony battery in the May 18 assault, plus an additional count of habitual criminal behavior. He was sentenced to 88 years on those charges, but the worst was yet to come. On June 11, 1988, he was convicted of murder and robbery in the slaying of Ernestine Griffin, with the jury recommending CAPITAL PUNISHMENT. At this writing, Allen awaits execution on Indiana's death row.

"ANGEL Makers of Nagyrev"

Little is known of Julia Fazekas before 1911, when she suddenly appeared in the Hungarian village of Nagyrev, 60 miles southeast of Budapest on the River Tisza. She was pushing middle age, a widow by her own account, but no one seemed to know exactly what had happened to her husband. Between 1911 and 1921, midwife Fazekas was jailed 10 times for performing illegal abortions, but sympathetic judges acquitted her in each case. Meanwhile, apparently unnoticed by police, she had inaugurated one of Europe's most bizarre and deadly murder sprees.

The rash of homicides is traceable to World War I, when able-bodied men from Nagyrev were drafted to fight for the Austro-Hungarian Empire. At the same time, rural Nagyrev was deemed an ideal site for camps containing Allied prisoners of war—a circumstance that catered to the wildest fantasies of women suddenly deprived of men. The prisoners most likely enjoyed a limited freedom within the village, and it soon became a point of pride for lonely wives in Nagyrev to boast a foreign lover, sometimes three or four. An atmosphere of rampant promiscuity prevailed, and husbands straggling home from combat found their women strangely "liberated," frequently dissatisfied with one man in the marriage bed.

As wives began to voice complaints of boredom and abuse, midwife Fazekas offered them relief: supplies of arsenic obtained by boiling flypaper and skimming off the lethal residue. Peter Hegedus was the first known victim, in 1914, and other husbands followed over time before the poisoning became a fad, the casualty list expanding to include parents, children, aunts, uncles, and neighbors.

By the mid-1920s, Nagyrev had earned its nickname as "the murder district." During that period an estimated 50 women used arsenic to trim their family trees. Julia Fazekas was the closest thing the village had to a physician, and her cousin was the clerk who filed all death certificates, thereby subverting homicide investigations in the embryonic stage. The final toll of victims is still unknown, but most reports suggest 300 as a reasonable estimate for 15 years of wholesale murder.

The "angel makers" saw their world unravel in July of 1929, when a choir master from neighboring Tisza-kurt accused Mrs. Ladislaus Szabo of serving him poisoned wine. A stomach pump saved his life, and detectives were still pondering the charge when a second victim complained of being poisoned by his "nurse"—the same Mrs. Szabo. In custody, seeking leniency for herself, Szabo fingered a friend, Mrs. Bukenoveski, as a fellow practitioner. Bukenoveski, in turn, was the first to name Julia Fazekas. In 1924, she said, Fazekas had provided the arsenic used to kill Bukenoveski's 77-year-old mother, after which the old woman was dumped in the Tisza to simulate an accidental drowning.

Fazekas was hauled in for questioning and staunchly denied everything. Without solid evidence, police were forced to release her, but they mounted a roving surveillance, trailing Fazekas around Nagyrev as she cautioned her various clients, arresting each woman in turn. Thirty-eight were jailed on suspicion of murder, and police descended on the Fazekas home to seize the ringleader. They found her dead from a dose of her own medicine, surrounded by pots of flypaper soaking in water.

Twenty-six of the Nagyrev suspects were held for trial at Szolnok, where eight were sentenced to death, seven to life imprisonment, and the rest to lesser prison terms. The condemned included Susannah Olah, a self-styled witch who boasted of training venomous snakes to attack her victims in bed, competing with Fazekas in sales of "Aunt Susi's inheritance powders"; Olah's sister Lydia, a septuagenarian whose flat denials of guilt failed to impress the jury; Maria Kardos, who murdered her husband, a lover, and her sickly 23-year-old son, persuading the young man to sing her a song on his deathbed; Rosalie Sebestyen and Rose Hoyba, condemned for the murder of "boring" husbands; Lydia Csery, convicted of killing her parents; Maria Varga, who confessed to buying poison from Fazekas to kill her husband—a blind war hero—when he complained about her bringing lovers home; Juliane Lipke, whose seven victims included her stepmother, an aunt, a brother, a sister-in-law, and the husband she poisoned on Christmas Eve; and Maria Szendi, a true liberationist who told the court she killed her husband because "he always had his way. It's terrible the way men have all the power."

"ANGELS of Death"

Built in 1839, Lainz General Hospital is the fourth largest medical facility in Vienna, Austria, with some 2,000 persons on staff. Pavilion 5 at Lainz is typically reserved for problem cases—patients in their seventies and older, many of them terminally ill. In such a setting, death is no surprise. If anything, it sometimes comes as a relief . . . but there are limits, even so. Beginning in the spring of 1983 and lasting through the early weeks of 1989, Death got a helping hand at Lainz. Officially, the body count stands at 42, but educated guesses put the final tally closer to 300 victims for the hospital's hard-working "Angels of Death."

Waltraud Wagner, a nurse's aide on the graveyard shift at Pavilion 5, was 23 years old when she claimed her first victim in 1983. As later reconstructed for authorities, she got the notion of eliminating patients when a 77-year-old woman asked Wagner to "end her misery." Waltraud obliged the lady with a morphine overdose, discovering in the process that she enjoyed playing God and holding the power of life and death in her hands. It was too much fun to quit, too nice to keep from sharing with her special friends.

Over time, Wagner recruited three accomplices, all working the night shift in Pavilion 5. Maria Gruber, born in 1964, was a nursing school dropout and unwed mother. Irene Leidolf, two years older than Gruber, had a husband at home but preferred hanging out with the girls. Stephanija Mayer, a divorced grandmother 20 years Waltraud's senior, emigrated from Yugoslavia in 1987 and wound up at Lainz, soon joining ranks with Wagner and her murderous cronies.

As described by prosecutors at her trial, Wagner was the sadistic Svengali of the group, instructing her disciples on the proper techniques of lethal injection, teaching them "the water cure"—wherein a patient's nose was pinched, the tongue depressed, and water was poured down the throat. The victim's death, while slow and agonizing, appeared "natural" on a ward where elderly patients frequently die with fluid in their lungs. In the police view, "Wagner awakened their sadistic instincts. Soon they were running a concentration camp, not a hospital ward. At the slightest sign of annoyance or complaint from a patient, they'd plan the patient's murder for the following night."

"Annoyances," in Waltraud's book, included snoring, soiling sheets, refusing medication, or buzzing the nurse's station for help at inconvenient times. In such cases, Wagner would proclaim, "This one gets a ticket to God," executing the murder herself or with help from one of her accomplices.

Even with four killers working the ward, it took some time for the deadly game to accelerate. Most of the homicides linked to Wagner and company occurred after early 1987, when Mayer rounded out the team, but Waltraud remained the leader and head executioner for what was soon nicknamed "the death pavilion." Rumors of a killer at large on Pavilion 5 were widespread by 1988, and Dr. Xavier Pesendorfer, in charge of the ward, was suspended in April 1989 for failure to launch a timely investigation.

Ultimately negligence among the killers led to their downfall. Wagner and her cohorts liked to have a few drinks after work, reliving special cases that amused them, chuckling over one victim's dying expression or another's convulsions. In February 1989, they were giggling over the death of elderly Julia Drapal—treated to the "water cure" for refusing medication and calling Wagner a "common slut"—when a doctor seated nearby picked up snatches of their conversation. Horrified, he went to police, and a six-week investigation led to the arrest of all four suspects on April 7.

In custody, the "death angels" confessed to 49 specific murders, Wagner allegedly claiming 39 as her own. "The ones who got on my nerves," she explained, "were dispatched directly to a free bed with the good Lord." It was not always simple, she allowed: "Of course the patients resisted, but we were stronger. We could decide whether these old fogies lived or died. Their ticket to God was long overdue in any case."

There was immediate speculation on a much higher body count, and Wagner's accomplices pointed fingers at their mentor in a bid to save themselves. Alois Stacher, head of Vienna's health department, quoted Irene Leidolf as being "convinced that 100 patients were killed by Wagner in each of the past two years."

Stephanija Mayer admitted helping Wagner out on several homicides that Waltraud managed to forget.

Indeed, as the case progressed to trial, Wagner became increasingly reluctant to discuss her role in the murders. By late 1990, she had backed off her original boast of 39 victims, claiming a maximum of 10 patients killed "to ease their pain." Chancellor Franz Vranitzky was unimpressed with the turnabout, calling the Lainz murder spree "the most brutal and gruesome crime in Austria's history."

Nor were judge and jury sympathetic when the four defendants went to trial in March of 1991. Prosecutors failed to sell their case on 42 counts of murder, but they proved enough to do the job. Waltraud Wagner was convicted of 15 murders, 17 attempted murders, and two counts of aggravated assault, drawing a sentence of life imprisonment. Irene Leidolf also got life, on conviction of five murders and two bungled attempts. Stephanija Mayer earned 15 years for a manslaughter conviction and seven counts of attempted murder, while Maria Gruber received an identical term for two murder attempts.

See also MEDICAL MURDERS

ARCHER-GILLIGAN, Amy

Little is known about the early life of the woman who would later commit, in the words of her prosecutor, commit "the biggest crime that ever shocked New England." Born in 1873 and married to James Archer in her early twenties, Amy Archer produced her only child—a daughter, Mary—in 1898. Three years later, billing herself as a nurse, without apparent qualifications, she opened a nursing home for the elderly in Newington, Connecticut. Despite "Sister Amy's" relative lack of experience, there were no complaints from her clients, and Newington was sad to see her go in 1907, when she moved to Windsor, 10 miles north, and opened the Archer Home for the Elderly and Infirm.

For the first three years, it was business as usual in Windsor. Twelve of Amy's clients died between 1907 and 1910, a predictable mortality rate that brought her no unusual profit. The surprise casualty of 1910 was James Archer, his death ascribed to natural causes. Amy waited three years before she remarried, to Michael Gilligan, and her second husband lasted a mere 12 months. The family physician, Dr. Howard King, saw no reason for alarm, nor was he concerned by the deaths of 48 clients at Amy's rest home, lost between 1911 and 1916. The number might have seemed excessive for a home with only 14 beds, but Dr. King accepted Sister Amy's diagnoses in the deaths, his negligence and senility combining to short-circuit suspicion.

In fact, Amy had devised what seemed to be the perfect get-rich scheme, inducing new clients to pay $1,000 in advance for "lifetime care," then cutting short their days with poison or a smothering pillow, blaming each successive death on old age or disease. With Dr. King's obliging death certificates in hand, authorities were loathe to cast aspersions, but ugly rumors began to circulate around Windsor by 1914. Two years later, surviving relatives of elderly Maude Lynch took their suspicions to police, and an undercover officer was planted in the rest home, collecting evidence that led to Sister Amy's arrest in May 1916. Postmortem examinations found traces of poison in Michael Gilligan and five deceased patients, leaving Amy charged with six counts of murder and suspected of numerous others. (Physicians calculated a "normal" resident death toll for 1911–16 at eight patients, compared to Amy's *forty-eight*.)

Dr. King came out swinging, his shaky reputation on the line, describing Sister Amy as a victim of foul persecution. Poison had been planted in the several bodies, he maintained, by "ghouls to incriminate Mrs. Gilligan." Prosecutor Hugh Alcorn responded by calling the case "the worst poison plot this country has ever known." Objections from Amy's lawyer winnowed the charges to one murder count—in the May 1914 death of patient Frank Andrews—and she was convicted in July 1917. Amy's life sentence was successfully appealed on technical grounds, but a second jury returned the same verdict, leaving her caged in Weathersfield Prison. In 1923, a rash of "nervous fits" produced a diagnosis of insanity, and Amy was transferred to a state asylum where she died in 1962, at age 89.

ARCHERD, William Dale

Born in 1912, William Archerd cherished a lifelong fascination with medicine. Lacking the cash and self-discipline required for medical school, he sought work as a hospital attendant, learning what he could of drugs and their effects through practical experience. During 1940 and '41, Archerd worked at Camarillo State Hospital, in California, serving in departments where insulin shock therapy was used to treat mental illness. In 1950, he pled guilty to illegal possession of morphine in San Francisco, receiving five years' probation. A second offense revoked his probation, and Archerd was confined to the minimum-security prison at Chino; escaping in 1951, he was quickly recaptured and transferred to San Quentin. By October 1953, he was free on parole.

Archerd's "bad luck" extended into other aspects of his life, as well. Married seven times in 15 years, he lost three wives to mysterious illnesses between 1958 and 1966. If that were not enough, his friends and relatives were also dying under unusual circumstances.

William Dale Archerd talks to journalists in court. (Wide World API)

On July 27, 1967, Archerd was arrested in Los Angeles and charged with three counts of first-degree murder. The victims included his fourth wife, Zella, who collapsed two months after their marriage, on July 25, 1956; a teenaged nephew, Burney Archerd, dead at Long Beach on September 2, 1961; and wife number seven, author Mary Brinker Arden, who died on November 3, 1966. As charged in the indictment, Archerd was suspected of injecting each victim with an overdose of insulin, thereby producing lethal attacks of hypoglycemia.

At least three other victims were suspected in the murder series. Archerd's first known victim, according to police, was a friend named William Jones, who died in Fontana, California, on October 12, 1947. Archerd's fifth wife, Juanita, had also displayed classic symptoms of hypoglycemia at her death, in a Las Vegas hospital, on March 13, 1958. Another of Archerd's friends, Frank Stewart, died in the same hospital two years later, on March 17, 1960.

On March 6, 1968, William Archerd was convicted on three counts of murder, the first American defendant convicted of using insulin as a murder weapon. His death sentence was affirmed by California's state supreme court in December 1970, then reduced to life imprisonment two years later, when the US Supreme Court described existing death-penalty statutes as "cruel and unusual punishment."

ARSON and Serial Murder

Often labeled "fire-setting" when committed by juveniles, arson is ranked by all experts as a major childhood WARNING SIGN of future violent behavior. It is also a crime unique in itself, and some serial killers pursue sidelines in arson throughout their adult lives. As with homicide, the FBI's *Crime Classification Manual* (1992) divides arson into various categories by motive, several of which apply to known serial slayers.

The first category, *vandalism-motivated* arson, is most likely to be seen in children or adolescents, though adults are by no means immune to the urge. The subcategory most applicable to serial stalkers in this field is *willful and malicious mischief,* often targeting schools, churches, and similar institutions.

The next category, *excitement-motivated* arson, is subdivided by the FBI into groups labeled *thrill seeker, attention seeker, recognition (hero),* and *sexual perversion,* all of which apply to known serial killers. DAVID BERKOWITZ kept a detailed log of fires he set and false alarms he telephoned to New York City fire stations. In England, BRUCE LEE could only reach orgasm while lighting and watching residential fires, a quirk that claimed 22 lives before he was captured. Serial arsonist John Orr, himself a captain and arson investigator with the Glendale, California, Fire Department, was convicted and sentenced to prison in 1992 for setting various brush and house fires around the Los Angeles area during 1990 and 1991, including one fire that destroyed 67 hillside homes; six years later, in June 1998, Orr was convicted of setting the 1984 blaze that killed four persons in a Pasadena hardware store. Curiously, Orr set fires most often after attending seminars with fellow arson investigators.

Revenge-motivated arson may include fires set for *personal retaliation, societal retaliation, institutional retaliation, group retaliation* (as by gangs and cults), or *intimidation.* David Berkowitz once tried setting fire to the apartment of a total stranger whom he thought was somehow "plotting" against him. David Wayne Roberts killed three persons when he torched the home of a salesman who reported him for stealing auto tires.

Crime-concealment-motivated arson is another type that fits some serial offenders. In New York, sadistic slayer Richard Cottingham set fire to a hotel room where the headless corpses of two women he'd killed were recovered from the ruins. Russia's ANATOLY ONOPRIENKO, with 52 kills charged against him, massacred whole families with his favorite shotgun, then burned their houses down in an attempt to destroy evidence. Similar motives are seen in cases of bodies left in burning cars (though torching a car is not legally classified as arson).

Profit-motivated arson is a favorite pastime of certain BLACK WIDOWS and other serial killers driven by desire to collect insurance payoffs. BELLE GUNNESS and Virginia Rearden both collected insurance payments from multiple fires before they turned to killing for profit. (Belle also faked her own death, leaving another woman's headless corpse in the ashes of her Indiana home before she fled to parts unknown.)

Extremist-motivated arson, in FBI parlance, is subdivided into arson as a tool of *terrorism, discrimination,* or *riots and civil disturbance.* A prime case in point is racist nomad JOSEPH FRANKLIN, who torched synagogues between his deadly sniper attacks on blacks and interracial couples.

Serial arson rates a category of its own in the FBI manual, once again defined (as with SERIAL MURDER) as "three or more firesetting episodes, with a characteristic emotional cooling-off period between fires." Predictably, the cooling-off period remains undefined but "may last days, weeks, or even years." No allowance is made in the FBI's taxonomy for arsonists arrested after their second fire, but again, those deemed to act without the undefined hiatus are dubbed *spree* arsonists. Finally, *mass arson* is defined by the Bureau as the setting of multiple fires at a single location, as on several floors of a high-rise hotel. No explanation is offered for how this may differ from, say, the profit-motivated burning (with multiple ignition points) of a large building torched for insurance.

See also BOMBING; MOTIVES; PARAPHILIA

ARTWORK and Memorabilia Related to Serial Murder

Considering the celebrity status conferred on infamous criminals in modern society, it comes as no surprise that some of them become "collectible" through such media as portraits and autographed photos, personal mementos, model kits, trading cards, comic books, and sundry other items ranging from tawdry curiosities to the bizarre. This fascination with felons in general—and serial killers in particular—is viewed by some critics as a symbol of societal decadence (even imminent apocalypse), while others dismiss it as a passing fad. On balance, given the apparent declining interest in such items since the mid-1990s, the latter view would seem to be correct.

Serial killer art, as noted by authors Harold Schechter and David Everitt, may be conveniently divided into two categories: art *depicting* serial murderers, and art created *by* the killers themselves. The former category includes everything from formal portraits and life-sized sculpture to weird, abstract sketches on cheaply produced trading cards and the sometimes graphic scenes depicted in various comic book "biographies" of notorious slayers. The several sets of trading cards and comics sparked heated controversy in the early 1990s, as parents and conservative religious leaders blamed them for "corrupting" modern youth. Producers of the cards and comics countered with reminders that their goods were plainly marked "for sale to adults only" and were not intended for a younger audience—an argument which critics viewed as somewhat disingenuous. (Nassau County, New York, legally banned the sale of one card set to minors; by the time that law was voided on appeal, the company in question had gone bankrupt.)

Generally speaking, collectors of serial killer art are more interested in work produced by the murderers themselves, and there has been no shortage of product from the 1980s onward. Prison inmates have tons of spare time, and some unlikely artists have emerged from America's captive population of recreational killers. JOHN GACY was easily the most famous, known worldwide for his paintings of clowns, skulls, and other subjects, sold from death row in a marketing scheme so controversial that the state of Illinois would later sue Gacy's estate, seeking to recover room and board expenses for the years he spent in prison. As with many other artists, Gacy's work has grown more pricey since his death in 1994, one outraged critic purchasing a block of paintings and burning them publicly, to prevent them reaching "the wrong hands."

One of John Wayne Gacy's clown paintings (Wide World API)

While Gacy hogged headlines in the war of words surrounding killer art, other notorious predators were quietly at work, including Richard Speck (wildlife watercolors), "Night Stalker" RICHARD RAMIREZ (ballpoint doodles), MANSON "FAMILY" alumnus Bobby Beausoleil (paintings), and Charles Manson himself (sketches and toy animals fashioned from socks). "Quiet" hardly describes the case of "Gainesville Ripper" Danny Rolling, whose pen-and-ink drawings were sold by his publicist and one-time fiancée, Sondra London, until the state of Florida filed suit to shut the business down. Elmer Wayne Henley, accomplice and slayer of Houston's DEAN CORLL, has emerged as another prison artist of note, his paintings displayed at two Texas galleries in 1998. Predictably, the showings drew more anger than acclaim, picketers at one gallery arriving with signs that read "hang Henley, not his art." New York inmate Arthur Shawcross sparked a similar furor in September 1999, when prison administrators learned that he had retained agents to sell his paintings on the Internet auction site eBay. Shawcross spent nine months in solitary confinement for that transgression of prison policy and lost all art privileges for an additional five years. On May 16, 2001, eBay announced a ban on further sales of "murderabilia."

Other collectible items in the serial murder genre include T-shirts emblazoned with portraits of various killers, autographs from sundry slayers, a scale model of EDWARD GEIN (complete with shovel and lantern, preparing to rob a fresh grave), and similar items. An Internet website markets scores of "killer fonts," allowing persons so inclined to print computer-generated documents in the (simulated) handwriting of various psychopaths ranging from "JACK THE RIPPER" to more recent specimens. By 1995, several mail-order catalogs offered a wide range of murderous memorabilia and accessories—fake skulls and severed limbs, etc.—for collectors with money to burn. An easy winner in the poor-taste category (and impossible to authenticate without DNA tests) was the offer of fingernail clippings from LAWRENCE ("Pliers") BITTAKER, awaiting execution at San Quentin. In February 1999, the Back Bay Brewing Company named a new brand of ale for alleged "BOSTON STRANGLER" Albert DeSalvo, declaring: "It's probably one of our best."

As with FICTION AND FILM treatments of serial murder, the sale and collection of killer art and memorabilia invites protests that vendors and buyers alike are somehow "glorifying" human monsters, transforming them into "heroes." And, while it is undeniable that certain infamous killers—notably Manson and Ramirez—enjoy literal cult icon status with some pathological characters on the lunatic fringe, most casual collectors of murder memorabilia seem slightly eccentric, at worst. As the majority of baseball card collectors never pitch a big-league game, so there has been no case to date of any "killer art" collector emulating Gacy, Speck, or Manson with a series of atrocious crimes. The controversy surrounding such items generates income for vendors and critics alike (as when religious groups hold rallies and sell pamphlets or collect donations to oppose the latest "sinful" fad), but otherwise, the impact of serial murder collectibles on American society seems no more significant or lasting than the Nehru jacket or the hula hoop.

In September 1999, French authorities suggested that art might be a motivating factor in a series of unsolved murders around Perpignan. The first victim, 19-year-old Moktaria Chaib, was found stabbed to death and mutilated near Perpignan's railway station in December 1997. Police arrested Dr. Andres Barrios, a Peruvian-born surgeon whom reporters quickly dubbed "a Latin JACK THE RIPPER," and detectives linked him tentatively to the 1995 disappearance of 17-year-old Tatiana Andujar in the same vicinity. Then, with Barrios still in custody, the slayer struck again in June 1998, killing 22-year-old Marie-Hélène Gonzalez, escaping with her severed head and hands. Barrios was then released on bond, while officers compared the mutilations suffered by Chaib and Gonzalez to portraits of disfigured women painted by surrealist Salvador Dalí. The link was strengthened, some said, by the late artist's comment that he "sprang to attention with joy and ecstasy" when he passed Perpignan's railway depot. The crimes in France remained unsolved when this work went to press.

See also GROUPIES

ATLANTA "Child Murders"

The curious and controversial string of deaths that sparked a two-year reign of terror in Atlanta, Georgia, has been labeled "child murders," even though a suspect—ultimately blamed for 23 of 30 "official" homicides—was finally convicted only in the deaths of two adult ex-convicts. Today, nearly two decades after that suspect's arrest, the case remains, in many minds, an unsolved mystery.

Investigation of the case began, officially, on July 28, 1979. That afternoon, a woman hunting empty cans and bottles in Atlanta stumbled on a pair of corpses, carelessly concealed in roadside undergrowth. One victim, shot with a .22-caliber weapon, was identified as 14-year-old Edward Smith, reported missing on July 21. The other was 13-year-old Alfred Evans, last seen alive on July 25; the coroner ascribed his death to "probable" asphyxiation. Both dead boys, like all of those to come, were African-American.

On September 4, Milton Harvey, age 14, vanished during a neighborhood bike ride. His body was recovered three weeks later, but the cause of death remains officially "unknown." Yusef Bell, a nine-year-old, was last seen alive when his mother sent him to the store on October 21. Found dead in an abandoned school November 8, he had been manually strangled by a powerful assailant.

Angel Lenair, age 12, was the first recognized victim of 1980. Reported missing on March 4, she was found six days later, tied to a tree with her hands bound behind her. The first female victim, she had been sexually abused and strangled; someone else's panties were extracted from her throat.

On March 11, Jeffrey Mathis vanished on an errand to the store. Eleven months would pass before recovery of his skeletal remains, advanced decomposition ruling out a declaration on the cause of death. On May 18, 14-year-old Eric Middlebrooks left home after receiving a telephone call from persons unknown. Found the next day, his death was blamed on head injuries, inflicted with a blunt instrument.

The terror escalated that summer. On June 9, Christopher Richardson, 12, vanished en route to a neighborhood swimming pool. Latonya Wilson was abducted from her home on June 22, the night before her seventh birthday, bringing federal agents into the case. The following day, 10-year-old Aaron Wyche was reported missing by his family. Searchers found his body on June 24, lying beneath a railroad trestle, his neck broken. Originally dubbed an accident, Aaron's death was subsequently added to the growing list of dead and missing blacks.

Anthony Carter, age nine, disappeared while playing near his home on July 6, 1980; recovered the following day, he was dead from multiple stab wounds. Earl Terrell joined the list on July 30, when he vanished from a public swimming pool. Skeletal remains discovered on January 9, 1981, would yield no clues about the cause of death.

Next up on the list was 12-year-old Clifford Jones, snatched off the street and strangled on August 20. With the recovery of his body in October, homicide detectives interviewed five witnesses who named his killer as a white man, later jailed in 1981 on charges of attempted rape and sodomy. Those witnesses provide details of the crime consistent with the placement and condition of the victim's body, but detectives chose to ignore their sworn statements, listing Jones with other victims of the "unknown" murderer.

Darren Glass, an 11-year-old, vanished near his home on September 14, 1980. Never found, he joins the list primarily because authorities don't know what else to do with his case. October's victim was Charles

Wayne Williams (Wide World API)

Walker, was strangled on February 19 and found the same day. Joseph Bell, 16, was asphyxiated on March 2. Timothy Hill, on March 11, was recorded as a drowning victim.

On March 30, Atlanta police added their first adult victim to the list of murdered children. He was Larry Rogers, 20, linked with younger victims by the fact that he had been asphyxiated. No cause of death was determined for a second adult victim, 21-year-old Eddie Duncan, but he made the list anyway, when his body was found on March 31. On April 1, ex-convict Michael McIntosh, age 23, was added to the roster on grounds that he, too, had been asphyxiated.

By April 1981, it seemed apparent that the "child murders" case was getting out of hand. Community critics denounced the official victims list as incomplete and arbitrary, citing cases like the January 1981 murder of Faye Yearby to prove their point. Like "official" victim Angel Lenair, Yearby was bound to a tree by her killer, hands behind her back; she had been stabbed to death, like four acknowledged victims on the list. Despite those similarities, police rejected Yearby's case on grounds that (a) she was a female—as were Wilson and Lenair—and (b) that she was "too old" at age 22, although the last acknowledged victim had been 23. Author Dave Dettlinger, examining police malfeasance in the case, suggests that 63 potential "pattern" victims were capriciously omitted from the "official" roster, 25 of them *after* a suspect's arrest supposedly ended the killing.

In April 1981, FBI spokesmen declared that several of the crimes were "substantially solved," outraging blacks with suggestions that some of the dead had been slain by their own parents. While that storm was raging, Roy Innis, leader of the Congress of Racial Equality, went public with the story of a female witness who described the murders as the actions of a cult involved with drugs, pornography, and Satanism. Innis led searchers to an apparent ritual site, complete with large inverted crosses, and his witness passed two polygraph examinations, but by that time police had focused their attention on another suspect, narrowing their scrutiny to the exclusion of all other possibilities.

On April 21, Jimmy Payne, a 21-year-old ex-convict, was reported missing in Atlanta. Six days later, when his body was recovered, death was publicly attributed to suffocation, and his name was added to the list of murdered "children." William Barrett, 17, went missing May 11; he was found the next day, another victim of asphyxiation.

Several bodies had, by now, been pulled from local rivers, and police were staking out the waterways by night. In the predawn hours of May 22, a rookie officer stationed under a bridge on the Chattahoochee River

Stephens, reported missing on the ninth and recovered the next day, his life extinguished by asphyxiation. Capping off the month, authorities discovered skeletal remains of Latonya Wilson on October 18, but they could not determine how she died.

On November 1, nine-year-old Aaron Jackson's disappearance was reported to police by frantic parents. The boy was found on November 2, another victim of asphyxiation. Patrick Rogers, 15, followed on November 10. His pitiful remains, skull crushed by heavy blows, were not unearthed until February 1981.

Two days after New Year's, the elusive slayer picked off Lubie Geter, strangling the 14-year-old and dumping his body where it would not be found until February 5. Terry Pue, 15, went missing on January 22 and was found the next day, strangled with a cord or piece of rope. This time, detectives said that special chemicals enabled them to lift a suspect's fingerprints from Terry's corpse. Unfortunately, they were not on file with any law enforcement agency in the United States.

Patrick Baltazar, age 12, disappeared on February 6. His body was found a week later, marked by ligature strangulation, and the skeletal remains of Jeffrey Mathis were discovered nearby. A 13-year-old, Curtis reported hearing "a splash" in the water nearby. Above him, a car rumbled past, and officers manning the bridge were alerted. Police and FBI agents halted a vehicle driven by Wayne Bertram Williams, a black man, and spent two hours grilling him and searching his car, before they let him go. On May 24, the corpse of Nathaniel Cater, a 27-year-old convicted felon, was fished out of the river downstream. Authorities put two and two together and focused their probe on Wayne Williams.

From the start, he made a most unlikely suspect. The only child of two Atlanta schoolteachers, Williams still lived with his parents at age 23. A college dropout, he cherished ambitions of earning fame and fortune as a music promoter. In younger days, he had constructed a working radio station in the basement of the family home.

On June 21, Williams was arrested and charged with the murder of Nathaniel Cater, despite testimony from four witnesses who reported seeing Cater alive on May 22 and 23, *after* the infamous "splash." On July 17, Williams was indicted for killing two adults—Cater and Payne—while newspapers trumpeted the capture of Atlanta's "child killer."

At his trial, beginning in December 1981, the prosecution painted Williams as a violent homosexual and bigot, so disgusted with his own race that he hoped to wipe out future generations by killing black children before they could breed. One witness testified that he saw Williams holding hands with Nathaniel Cater on May 21, a few hours before "the splash." Another, 15 years old, told the court that Williams had paid him two dollars for the privilege of fondling his genitals. Along the way, authorities announced the addition of a final victim, 28-year-old John Porter, to the list of victims.

Defense attorneys tried to balance the scales with testimony from a woman who admitted having "normal sex" with Williams, but the prosecution won a crucial point when the presiding judge admitted testimony on 10 other deaths from the "child murders" list, designed to prove a pattern in the slayings. One of those admitted was the case of Terry Pue, but neither side had anything to say about the fingerprints allegedly recovered from his corpse in January 1981.

The most impressive evidence of guilt was offered by a team of scientific experts, dealing with assorted hairs and fibers found on certain victims. Testimony indicated that some fibers from a brand of carpet found inside the Williams home (and many other homes, as well) had been identified on several bodies. Further, victims Middlebrooks, Wyche, Cater, Terrell, Jones, and Stephens all supposedly bore fibers from the trunk liner of a 1979 Ford automobile owned by the Williams fam-

ily. The clothes of victim Stephens also allegedly yielded fibers from a second car—a 1970 Chevrolet—owned by Wayne's parents. Curiously, jurors were *not* informed of multiple eyewitness testimony naming a different suspect in the Jones case, nor were they advised of a critical gap in the prosecution's fiber evidence.

Specifically, Wayne Williams had no access to the vehicles in question at the times when three of the six "fiber" victims were killed. Wayne's father took the Ford in for repairs at 9:00 A.M. on July 30, 1980, nearly five hours *before* Earl Terrell vanished that afternoon. Terrell was long dead before Williams got the car back on August 7, and it was returned to the shop next morning (August 8), still refusing to start. A new estimate on repair costs was so expensive that Wayne's father refused to pay, and the family never again had access to the car. Meanwhile, Clifford Jones was kidnapped on August 20 and Charles Stephens on October 9, 1980. The defendant's family did not purchase the 1970 Chevrolet in question until October 21, 12 days *after* Stephen's death.

On February 27, 1982, Wayne Williams was convicted on two counts of murder and sentenced to a double term of life imprisonment. Two days later, the Atlanta "child murders" task force officially disbanded, announcing that 23 of 30 "List" cases were considered solved with his conviction, even though no charges had been filed. The other seven cases, still open, reverted to the normal homicide detail and remain unsolved to this day.

In November 1985, a new team of lawyers uncovered once-classified documents from an investigation of the Ku Klux Klan, conducted during 1980 and '81 by the Georgia Bureau of Investigation. A spy inside the Klan told GBI agents that Klansmen were "killing the children" in Atlanta, hoping to provoke a race war. One Klansman in particular, Charles Sanders, allegedly boasted of murdering "List" victim Lubie Geter, following a personal altercation. Geter reportedly struck Sanders's car with a go-cart, prompting the Klansman to tell his friend, "I'm gonna kill him. I'm gonna choke the black bastard to death." (Geter was, in fact, strangled, some three months after the incident in question.) In early 1981, the same informant told GBI agents that "after twenty black-child killings, they, the Klan, were going to start killing black women." Perhaps coincidentally, police records note the unsolved murders of numerous black women in Atlanta in 1980–82, with most of the victims strangled. On July 10, 1998, Butts County Superior Court Judge Hal Craig rejected the latest appeal for a new trial in Williams's case, based on suppression of critical evidence 15 years earlier. Judge Craig denied yet another new-trial motion on June 15, 2000.

"AX Man of New Orleans"

In the predawn hours of May 23, 1918, New Orleans grocer Joseph Maggio and his wife were murdered in bed by a prowler who chiseled through their back door, used Joseph's ax to strike each victim once across the skull, then slit their throats with a razor to finish the job. Maggio's brothers discovered the bodies and were briefly held as suspects, but police could find no evidence of their involvement in the crime and both were soon released.

A few blocks from the murder scene, detectives found a cryptic message chalked on the sidewalk. It read: "Mrs. Maggio is going to sit up tonight just like Mrs. Toney." Police could offer no interpretation, so the press stepped in. An article in the *New Orleans States* cited a "veritable epidemic" of unsolved ax murders in 1911, listing the victims as Italian grocers named Cruti, Rosetti (allegedly killed with his wife), and Tony Schiambra (whose spouse was also reportedly slain). Over nine decades, half a dozen authors have accepted that report as factual, relying on the "early" crimes to bolster this or that supposed solution in the case. Unfortunately, the initial report was so garbled that it bore little resemblance to fact.

Local records reveal that a victim named Cruti was murdered at home in August 1910, followed one month later by a vicious ax assault on Joseph and Conchetta Rissetto. (Joseph survived his wounds and blamed the crime on an unidentified burglar.) The only coroner's report on a Rosetti in 1911 involved Mary Rosetti, a black woman whose death was ascribed to dysentery. Meanwhile, New Orleans journalists ignored the June 1911 ax attacks on a couple named Davi. (The wife survived in that case.) Anthony Sciambra and his wife Johanna were murdered at home in May 1912, both shot at close range and thus divorced entirely from the Ax Man crimes. Ironically, there were other unsolved ax murders in Louisiana during 1911, claiming a total of 16 lives, but the victims were all black and none were killed in New Orleans.

On June 28, 1918, a baker delivering bread to the grocery of Louis Besumer found a panel cut from the back door. He knocked, and Besumer emerged, blood streaming from a head wound. Inside the apartment, Besumer's "wife"—Anna Lowe, a divorcée—lay critically wounded. She lingered on for seven weeks, delirious, once calling Besumer a German spy and later recanting. On August 5 she died, after naming Besumer as her attacker, prompting his arrest on murder charges. (Nine months later, on May 1, 1919, a jury deliberated all of 10 minutes before finding him innocent.)

Returning late from work that same evening—August 5—Ed Schneider found his pregnant wife unconscious in their bed, her scalp laid open. She survived to bear a healthy daughter, but her memory of the attack was vague, at best. A hulking shadow by her bed, the ax descending—and oblivion.

On August 10, sisters Pauline and Mary Bruno woke to sounds of struggle in the adjacent room occupied by their uncle, Joseph Romano. They rushed next door to find him dying of a head wound, but they caught a glimpse of his assailant, described in official reports as "dark, tall, heavy-set, wearing a dark suit and a black slouch hat."

The rest of August 1918 was a nightmare for police, with numerous reports of chiseled doors, discarded axes, and lurking strangers. Several of the latter were pursued by vengeful mobs but always managed to escape. At last, with time and the distraction of an armistice in war-torn Europe, the hysteria began to fade.

On March 10, 1919, the scene shifted to Gretna, across the river from New Orleans. A prowler invaded the home of Charles Cortimiglia, helping himself to the grocer's own ax before wounding Charles and his wife and killing their infant daughter. From her hospital bed, Rose Cortimiglia accused two neighbors, Iorlando Jordano and his son Frank, of committing the crime. Despite firm denials from Charles, both suspects were jailed pending trial.

Meanwhile, on March 14, the *Times-Picayune* published a letter signed by "The Axeman." Describing himself as "a fell demon from the hottest hell," the author announced his intention of touring New Orleans on March 19—St. Joseph's Night—and vowed to bypass any home where jazz was playing at the time. "One thing is certain," he declared, "and that is that some of those people who do not jazz it (if there be any) will get the axe!" On the appointed night, already known for raucous celebration, New Orleans was even noisier than usual. The din included numerous performances of "The Axman's Jazz," a song composed for the occasion, and the evening passed without a new attack.

The Jordano trial opened in Gretna on May 21, 1919. Charles Cortimiglia did his best for the defense, but jurors believed his wife and convicted both defendants of murder on May 26. Frank Jordano was sentenced to hang, while his elderly father received a term of life imprisonment. (Charles Cortimiglia divorced his wife after the trial, and Rose was arrested for prostitution in November 1919. She recanted her testimony on December 7, 1920, explaining to police that spite and jealousy prompted her accusations. The Jordanos were pardoned and released from custody.)

And still the raids continued. Grocer Steve Boca was wounded at home on August 27, 1919, his door chiseled through, the bloody ax discarded in his kitchen.

On September 3 the Ax Man or an imitator entered Sarah Laumann's bedroom through an open window, wounding her in bed and dropping his weapon on the lawn outside. Eight weeks later, on October 27, grocer Mike Pepitone was murdered at home; his wife glimpsed the killer but offered detectives no helpful description. There the crime spree ended as it had begun, in mystery.

Author Robert Tallant proposed a solution to the Ax Man riddle in 1953, in his book *Murder in New Orleans*. According to Tallant, a man named Joseph Mumfre was shot and killed in Los Angeles on December 2, 1920, while walking on a public street. Mumfre's assailant, a veiled woman dressed in black, was identified as the widow of Mike Pepitone. At her murder trial, which resulted in a 10-year prison sentence, she named Mumfre as her husband's killer—and, by implication, as the Ax Man of New Orleans. Tallant reports that New Orleans detectives checked Mumfre's record and found that he was serving time in jail for burglary during the Ax Man's hiatus from August 1918 to March 1919.

Other authors seized upon Tallant's solution, reporting that Joseph Mumfre was imprisoned between 1911 and 1918, thus implying a connection to earlier New Orleans homicides (though he would still be excluded as a suspect from the 1912 Sciambra attack). Author Jay Robert Nash "solved" the case in his book *Bloodletters and Badmen* (1973), calling Mumfre a Mafia hit man who was allegedly pursuing a long vendetta against "members of the Pepitone family." The explanation fails when one recalls that only one of the Ax Man's 11 victims—and the last, at that—was a Pepitone. Likewise, speculation on a Mafia extortion plot against Italian grocers ignores the fact that four victims were not Italian, and several were completely unconnected to the grocery business.

Still, there is a more deadly flaw in the Tallant-Nash solution to the Ax Man mystery: the Joseph Mumfre murder in Los Angeles never happened!

Ax Man researcher William Kingman has pursued the Mumfre tale and received formal notice from California's State Registrar of Vital Statistics on September 10, 2001, that no person named Joseph Mumfre died anywhere in the Golden State between 1905 and 2000. The story of Mumfre's murder in Los Angeles and Mrs. Pepitone's subsequent trial is, in short, a complete fabrication. Robert Tallant is beyond interrogation on this or any other subject, having died in New Orleans on April 1, 1957. As for the Ax Man of New Orleans, his case remains a tantalizing mystery.

"BABY Farming": Infanticide for profit

Each historical era spawns its own peculiar types of crime, from piracy and slave trading to the modern age of "wilding" and computer "hackers." The occupation known as "baby farming" was a product of the Victorian era, when sex was equivalent to sin and illegitimate birth meant lifelong shame for mother and child alike. In that repressive atmosphere, the "baby farmer"—usually a woman—was prepared to help an unwed mother through her time of trial . . . but only for a price.

In most cases, the "farmer" provided room and board during a mother's confinement, allowing embarrassed families to tell the neighbors that their daughter had gone "to study abroad" or "stay with relatives." Facilities ranged from humble country cottages to the likes of LILA YOUNG's spacious Ideal Maternity Home, where hundreds of infants were born between 1925 and 1947. Unwed mothers went home with their reputations and consciences intact, secure in the knowledge that their babies would be placed in good homes through black-market adoptions.

It was a no-lose proposition for the "baby farmer," paid by those who left a child and once again by those who came to pick one up. If certain laws were broken in the process, it was all the better reason for increasing the adoption fees. Most unwed mothers and adoptive parents doubtless viewed the "baby farmer's" occupation as a valuable public service, never mind prevailing law.

It was not uncommon, however, for "baby farmers" to repeatedly use criminal negligence or deliberate murder as a shortcut to profit in the maternity game. Over time there have been several headline cases, and not

even the United States has been exempt from lethal "baby farming," illustrated by the New York City case of 14 infant murders reported in 1915. That case remains unsolved, but other practitioners were brought to book for their crimes in England and Canada, with one case broken as recently as the late 1940s.

"BAD Seeds": "Natural-born" killers

The notion of inherited criminal traits is nothing new. Indeed, the first scientific system of criminal identification was crafted by French anthropologist Alphonse Bertillion in 1879, based on a complex system of bodily measurements, including those of the skull and facial features. While the Bertillion system was eventually discredited, the belief in hereditary "criminal types" persisted in some quarters—and has lately garnered support, albeit conditional, from the medical and psychiatric professions.

The label of "bad seeds" derives from William March's 1954 novel of the same title, which told the story of a homicidal eight-year-old, her violent tendencies inherited from a murderous mother she never knew. By 1954, of course, it was well known that many—if not most—violent criminals emerged from homes where CHILDHOOD TRAUMA and abuse were routine. At the same time, however, occasional aberrant cases (or those with incomplete histories of the offender) challenged supporters of environmental causes in the "nature vs. nurture" argument.

In the 1960s, some researchers ardently pursued the "XYY syndrome," so called after individuals born with a surplus Y—or male—chromosome. An estimated

100,000 males come so equipped in the United States annually, and it has been suggested that the extra dash of "maleness" makes them more aggressive, even violent, with a greater tendency toward criminal activity. The theory got a boost in 1966, when random killer Richard Speck was diagnosed—mistakenly, as it turned out—as one such "supermale." Eager researchers cited his stature and facial acne as sure-fire symptoms of XYY syndrome, but genetic tests failed to bear out their suspicion. In the meantime, it was noted that XYY males comprise a larger percentage of the nation's prison population than of the male population at large, but such figures are easily skewed. As authors Jack Levin and James Fox point out in *Mass Murder* (1985), the XYY males who wind up in prison or mental institutions accused of violent crimes constitute a minuscule segment of the overall group.

Another proponent of the "bad seed" theory, the late Joel Norris, cites 23 symptoms of genetic damage found in a select listing of modern serial killers. The WARNING SIGNS range from bulbous fingertips and curved fifth fingers to crooked teeth and "electric-wire hair that won't comb down." Unfortunately, the list of "killer symptoms" is so broad, and ultimately vague, that it is rendered next to useless.

With various serial killers reporting convulsions or seizures from childhood, it is logical to ask if epilepsy plays a role—however minor—in cases of episodic violence. Without indicting epileptics as a class, it is worth noting that electroencephalogram (EEG) tests reveal "spiking" patterns of random, uncontrollable electrical discharges during seizure activity. Their source, the limbic brain, controls primitive emotions like fear and rage, triggering the "fight-or-flight" response when we are frightened or surprised. Some analysts now speculate that similar disorders may produce unpredictable violent outbursts in specific individuals.

Another target of modern research into episodic violence is the hypothalamus, sometimes described as the brain's "emotional voltage regulator." Dr. Helen Morrison, a Chicago psychiatrist whose interview subjects include JOHN GACY, PETER SUTCLIFFE, and "Mad Biter" Richard Macek, cites damage to the hypothalamic region of the brain as a potential cause of violent crime. The hypothalamus regulates hormone production, including the adrenal and thyroid glands, with corresponding influence on individual response to real or perceived threats. In essence, Dr. Morrison contends that damage to the hypothalamus may prevent an individual from growing toward emotional maturity. When threatened or insulted, even if the threat is mere illusion, individuals with hypothalamic damage may respond with childish tantrums . . . and the grown-up weapons of adults.

Chemical imbalance may also affect human attitude and behavior, whether that imbalance results from brain damage, glandular dysfunction, environmental contaminants, or the deliberate ingestion of drugs and alcohol. Manic-depression, schizophrenia, and some forms of psychosis are treatable with medication to varying degrees, since they originate within the body, rather than within the mind. Today, we know that such conditions may also be hereditary, handed down through many generations of a single family—in which case, certain schizophrenic or psychotic killers may indeed be the proverbial "bad seeds."

There are, of course, substantial risks involved in trying to predict an individual's adult behavior from specific childhood symptoms, and it must be granted the vast majority of children from "tainted" families—or from abusive homes—do not go on to kill for sport. Predictive theories are often based on tiny samplings, sometimes on a single case, and subjects chosen for review have typically drawn much attention to themselves by their bizarre behavior. In practice, some of the worst serial killers—including the likes of CHARLES MANSON and HENRY LUCAS—present histories of both severe abuse and genetic, inherited dysfunction. Frequently the offspring of alcoholic, drug-abusing parents with criminal backgrounds, tortured and molested from infancy, such human monsters may in fact be born *and* made.

See also CROSS-DRESSING; MOTIVES; PARAPHILIA

BAI Baoshan

Described in official dispatches as China's most prolific serial killer to date, with 15 known victims (compared to 13 for LI WENXIAN), Bai Baoshan apparently committed his first murder in the early 1980s, during a poorly planned holdup. Convicted of murder and robbery in that case, he served 13 years in prison and emerged with a brooding desire for revenge against society at large.

Bai's payback rampage began in March 1996, when he attacked a police sentry in Beijing and stole a semi-automatic weapon, later used to kill one person and wound six others (including four patrolmen). Authorities believe he also robbed and killed a Beijing cigarette vendor before leaving town and traveling to the northern Chinese province of Hebei. There, Bai killed another policeman and stole his automatic rifle, moving on to Urümqi, the capital of Xinjiang province. In Urümqi, authorities say Bai and two accomplices murdered 10 persons—including police officers, security guards, and civilians—while stealing 1.5 million yuan (about $180,000). Unhappy with the prospect of sharing his loot, Bai killed one of his cohorts and kept all the money for himself. By that time, Bai had earned the dubious honor of being labeled China's "Public Enemy No. 1."

Returning to Beijing in October 1997, the 39-year-old gunman was traced by police and arrested on October 16, charged with 14 homicides and various related felonies. A local newspaper reported his confession, and he was returned to Xinjiang province for trial, where most of his victims were slain. Convicted on all counts and sentenced to death, Bai Baoshan was executed on May 6, 1998.

BALL, Joe

Born in 1892, Joe Ball was a one-time bootlegger and tavern owner in Elmendorf, Texas, near San Antonio. In the 1930s, he ran the Sociable Inn, distinguished by its lovely waitresses and alligator pit out back, where Ball would daily entertain his patrons with the ritual of feeding time. He seemed to have a problem keeping waitresses—and wives—but the variety was part of what made Joe's establishment so popular.

Ball possessed a darker side, however, and according to reports from other residents of Elmendorf, he sounded anything but sociable. One neighbor, a policeman named Elton Crude, was threatened with a pistol after he complained about the stench emitted by Joe's alligator pond. (The smell, Ball normally explained, was due to rotting meat he used for 'gator food.) Another local was so terrified of Ball that he packed up his family one night and fled the state, without a word of explanation.

In September 1937, worried relatives reported Minnie Gotthardt's disappearance to authorities in Elmendorf. The missing 22-year-old had been employed with Ball before she dropped from sight, but under questioning the tavern keeper said that she had left to take another job. Police were satisfied, until another waitress—Julia Turner—was reported missing by her family. Ball's answer was the same, but this time there were problems with his story, since the girl had left her clothes behind. Joe saved himself by suddenly remembering an argument with Julia's roommate; Turner had been anxious to get out, he said, and Ball had given her $500 for the road.

Within a few short months, two other women joined the missing list; one of them, Hazel Brown, had opened up a bank account two days before she disappeared, then "left" without retrieving any of the cash. Texas Rangers entered the case, compiling a roster of Ball's known employees over the past few years. Many were found alive, but at least a dozen were permanently missing, along with Joe's second and third wives. Ball stood up well under questioning, but his elderly handyman cracked, reporting that he had helped Ball dispose

of several female corpses, acting under threat of death when he fed their dismembered remains to the alligators. From the safety of his new location, Joe's ex-neighbor joined the litany, describing an evening in 1936 when he had seen Ball chopping up a woman's body and tossing the fragments to his hungry pets.

The Rangers had enough to indict Ball, but they needed solid evidence for a conviction. On September 24, 1938, they dropped by the Sociable Inn to examine Joe's meat barrel, and Ball realized the game was up. Stepping behind the bar, he rang up a "no sale" on the cash register, drew a pistol from the drawer, and killed himself with one shot to the head. His handyman was jailed for two years as an accessory after the fact, while Joe's alligators were donated to the San Antonio zoo.

BÁTHORY, Erzsebet

Born in 1560, Erzsebet (or Elizabeth) Báthory was the daughter of an aristocratic soldier and the sister of Poland's reigning king. Her family, in fact, was one of the oldest noble houses in Hungary, its crest bearing the draconic symbol incorporated by King Sigismund into the Order of the Dragon. The Báthory clan included knights and judges, bishops, cardinals, and kings, but it had fallen into decadence by the mid-16th century, the royal bloodline marred by incest and epilepsy, with later family ranks including alcoholics, murderers and sadists, homosexuals (considered criminally deviant at the time) and Satanists.

Though physically beautiful, Erzsebet was clearly the product of polluted genetics and a twisted upbringing. Throughout her life, she was subject to blinding headaches and fainting seizures—probably epileptic in nature—which superstitious family members diagnosed as demonic possession. Raised on the Báthory estate at the foot of the brooding Carpathian Mountains, Erzsebet was introduced to devil worship in adolescence by one of her Satanist uncles. Her favorite aunt, one of Hungary's most notorious lesbians, taught Erzsebet the pleasures of flagellation and other perversions, but young Erzsebet always believed that where pain was concerned, it was better to give than to receive.

When Erzsebet was barely 11, her parents contracted her future marriage to Count Ferencz Nadasdy, an aristocratic warrior. Their wedding was postponed until Erzsebet turned 15, finally solemnized on May 5, 1575. The bride retained her maiden name as a sign that her family possessed greater status than Nadasdy's clan.

The newlyweds settled at Csejthe Castle, in northwestern Hungary, but Count Nadasdy also maintained other palatial homes around the country, each complete with a dungeon and torture chamber specially designed to meet Erzsebet's needs. Nadasdy was frequently

Erzsebet Báthory (Author's collection)

nipples of her victims, sometimes ramming needles beneath their fingernails. "The little slut!" she would sneer, as her captive writhed in pain. "If it hurts, she's only got to take them out herself." Erzsebet also enjoyed biting her victims on the cheeks, breasts, and elsewhere, drawing blood with her teeth. Other captives were stripped, smeared with honey, and exposed to the attacks of ants and bees.

Count Nadasdy reportedly joined Erzsebet in some of the torture sessions, but over time he came to fear his wife, spending more and more time on the road or in the arms of his mistress. When he finally died in 1600 or 1604 (accounts vary), Erzsebet lost all restraint, devoting herself full time to the torment and sexual degradation of younger women. In short order, she broadened her scope from the family staff to include nubile strangers. Trusted employees scoured the countryside for fresh prey, luring peasant girls with offers of employment, resorting to drugs or brute force as pervasive rumors thinned the ranks of willing recruits. None who entered Erzsebet's service ever escaped alive, but peasants had few legal rights in those days, and a noblewoman was not faulted by her peers if "discipline" around the house got out of hand.

By her early forties, Erzsebet Báthory presided over a miniature holocaust of her own design. Abetted by her aging nurse, Ilona Joo, and procuress Doratta Szentes— aka "Dorka"—Erzsebet ravaged the countryside, claiming peasant victims at will. She carried special silver pincers, designed for ripping flesh, but she was also comfortable with pins and needles, branding irons and red-hot pokers, whips and scissors . . . almost anything at all. Household accomplices would strip her victims, holding them down while Erzsebet tore their breasts to shreds or burned their vaginas with a candle flame, sometimes biting great chunks of flesh from their faces and bodies. One victim was forced to cook and eat a strip of her own flesh, while others were doused with cold water and left to freeze in the snow. Sometimes, Erzsebet would jerk a victim's mouth open with such force that the cheeks ripped apart. On other occasions, servants handled the dirty work, while Erzsebet paced the sidelines, shouting, "More! More still! Harder still!" until overwhelmed with excitement, she fainted into unconsciousness on the floor.

One special "toy" of Erzsebet's was a cylindrical cage, constructed with long spikes inside. A naked girl was forced into the cage, then hoisted several feet off the floor by means of a pulley. Erzsebet or one of her servants would circle the cage with a red-hot poker, jabbing at the girl and forcing her against the sharp spikes as she tried to escape. Whether she cast herself in the role of an observer or active participant, Erzsebet was always good for a running commentary of suggestions

absent for weeks or months at a time, leaving his bride alone and bored, to find her own diversions. Erzsebet dabbled in alchemy, indulged her sexual quirks with men and women alike, changed clothes and jewelry five or six times a day, and admired herself in full-length mirrors by the hour. Above all else, when she was angry, tense, or simply bored, the countess tortured servant girls for sport.

One major source of irritation in the early years of marriage was Erzsebet's mother-in-law. Eager for grandchildren, Nadasdy's mother nagged Erzsebet incessantly over her failure to conceive. Erzsebet would finally bear children after a decade of marriage, but she felt no maternal urges in her late teens and early twenties. Young women on her household staff soon came to dread the visits of Nadasdy's mother, knowing that another round of brutal assaults would inevitably follow the old lady's departure.

Where torture was concerned, the bisexual countess possessed a ferocious imagination. Some of her tricks were learned in childhood, and others were picked up from Nadasdy's experience battling the Turks, but she also contrived techniques of her own. Pins and needles were favorite tricks of the trade, piercing the lips and

and sick "jokes," lapsing into crude obscenities and incoherent babble as the night wore on.

Disposal of her lifeless victims was a relatively simple matter in the Middle Ages. Some were buried, others were left to rot around the castle, while a few were dumped outside to feed the local wolves and other predators. If a dismembered corpse was found from time to time, the countess had no fear of prosecution. In that place and time, royal blood was the ultimate protection. It also helped that one of Erzsebet's cousins was the Hungarian prime minister and, another served as governor of the province where she lived.

Erzsebet finally overplayed her hand in 1609, shifting from hapless peasants to the daughters of lesser nobility, opening Csejthe Castle to offer 25 hand-picked ingenues "instruction in the social graces." This time, when none of her victims survived, complaints reached the ears of King Matthias, whose father had attended Erzsebet's wedding. The king, in turn, assigned Erzsebet's closest neighbor, Count Gyorgy Thurzo, to investigate the case. On December 26, 1610, Thurzo staged a late-night raid on Csejthe Castle and caught the countess red-handed, with an orgiastic torture session in progress.

A half-dozen of Erzsebet's accomplices were held for trial; the countess was kept under house arrest while parliament cranked out a special statute to strip her of immunity from prosecution. The resultant trial opened in January 1611 and lasted through late February, with Chief Justice Theodosius Syrmiensis presiding over a panel of 20 lesser jurists. Eighty counts of murder were alleged in court, though most historical accounts place Erzsebet's final body count somewhere between 300 and 650 victims. Erzsebet herself was excused from attending the trial, held in her apartment under heavy

guard, but conviction on all counts was a foregone conclusion. The "bloody countess" had run out of time.

Erzsebet's servant-accomplices were executed, Dorka and Ilona Joo after public torture, but the countess was spared, sentenced to life imprisonment in a small suite of rooms at Csejthe Castle. The doors and windows of her apartment were bricked over, leaving only slits for ventilation and the passing of food trays. There, she lived in isolation for three and a half years, until she was found dead on August 21, 1614. The exact date of Erzsebet's death is unknown, since several meals had gone untouched before her corpse was found.

Bizarre as it is, the Báthory legend has grown in the telling, most recent accounts incorporating tales of vampirism and ritualistic blood baths supposed to help Erzsebet "stay young." Erzsebet's sanguinary fetish is usually linked to the spilling of some unnamed servant girl's blood, with the countess accidentally spattered, afterward impressed that her skin seemed more pale and translucent than usual—traits considered beautiful in those days, before discovery of the "California tan." In fact, extensive testimony at Erzsebet's trial made no mention of literal blood baths. Some victims *were* drained of blood from savage wounds or by design, but deliberate exsanguination was linked to Erzsebet's practice of alchemy and black magic, rather than any design for a warm bath. In any case, Erzsebet's murder spree began when she was in her teens or twenties, long before the threat of aging ever crossed her mind.

BERKOWITZ, David Richard

New Yorkers are accustomed to reports of violent death in every form, from the mundane to the bizarre. They take it all in stride, accepting civic carnage as a price of living in the largest, richest city in America. But residents were unprepared for the commencement of an all-out reign of terror in July 1976. For 13 months, New York would be a city under siege, its female citizens afraid to venture out by night while an apparent homicidal maniac was waiting, seeking prey.

The terror came with darkness on July 29, 1976. Two young women, Donna Lauria and Jody Valenti, had parked their car on Buhre Avenue in Queens, remaining in the vehicle and passing time in conversation. If they saw the solitary male pedestrian at all, they didn't take note of him. In any case, they never saw the pistol that he raised to pump five shots through the windshield. Donna Lauria was killed immediately; her companion survived and got off "easy," with a bullet in one thigh.

The shooting was a tragic incident, but in itself was not unusual for New York City. There was scattered sympathy but no alarm among the residents of New York's urban combat zone . . . until the next attack.

One of Báthory's several castles, where hundreds of girls were tortured or killed (Author's collection)

On October 23, Carl Denaro and Rosemary Keenan parked outside a bar in Flushing, Queens. Again, the gunman went unnoticed as he crouched to fire a single bullet through the car's rear window. Wounded, Carl Denaro survived. A .44-caliber bullet was found on the floor of the car, and detectives matched it to slugs from the Lauria murder.

Just over one month later, on November 26, Donna DeMasi and Joanne Lomino were sitting together on the stoop of a house in the Floral Park section of Queens. A man approached them from the sidewalk, asking for directions, but before he could complete the question he had drawn a pistol, blasting at the startled women. Both were wounded, Joanne paralyzed forever with a bullet in her spine.

Again the slugs were readily identified, and now detectives knew they had a random killer on their hands. The gunman seemed to favor girls with long, dark hair, and there was speculation that the shooting of Denaro in October may have been an "accident." The young man's hair was shoulder length; a gunman closing on him from behind might have mistaken Carl Denaro for a woman in the darkness.

Christmas season passed without another shooting, but the gunman had not given up his hunt. On January 30, 1977, John Diel and Christine Freund were parked and necking in the Ridgewood section of New York, when bullets hammered out their windshield. Freund was killed on impact, while her date was physically unscathed.

Virginia Voskerichian, an Armenian exchange student, was walking toward her home in Forest Hills on March 8, when a man approached and shot her in the face, killing her instantly. Detectives noted that she had been slain within 300 yards of the January murder scene.

On April 17, Alexander Esau and his date, Valentina Suriani, were parked in the Bronx, a few blocks from the site of the Lauria-Valenti shooting. Caught up in each other, they may not have seen the gunman coming; certainly they had no time to dodge the fusillade of bullets that killed them both immediately, fired from point-blank range.

Detectives found a crudely printed letter in the middle of the street, near Esau's car. Addressed to the captain in charge of New York's hottest manhunt, the note contained a chilling message.

I am deeply hurt by your calling me a weman–hater [sic]. *I am not. But I am a monster. I am the Son of Sam. . . . I love to hunt. Prowling the streets looking for fair game—tasty meat. The weman* [sic] *of Queens are the prettyest* [sic] *of all. . . .*

The note described "Sam" as a drunken brute who beat the members of his family and sent his son out

David Berkowitz (Wide World API)

hunting "tasty meat," compelling him to kill. There would be other letters from the gunman, some addressed to newsman Jimmy Breslin, hinting at more crimes to come and fueling the hysteria that had already gripped New York. The writer was apparently irrational but no less dangerous for that, and homicide investigators had no clue to his identity.

On June 26, Salvatore Lupo and girlfriend Judy Placido were parked in Bayside, Queens, when four shots pierced the windshield of their car. Both were wounded; both survived.

On July 31, Robert Violante and Stacy Moskowitz parked near the Brooklyn shore. The killer found them there and squeezed off four shots at their huddled silhouettes, striking both young people in the head. Stacy died instantly; her date survived, but damage from his wounds left Violante blind for life.

It was the last attack, but homicide detectives didn't know that yet. A woman walking near the final murder scene recalled two traffic officers writing a ticket for a car parked close to a hydrant; moments later, she had seen a man approach the car, climb in, and pull away with squealing tires. A check of parking ticket records traced an old Ford Galaxy belonging to one David Berkowitz, of Pine Street, Yonkers. Staking out the address, officers discovered that the car was parked outside; a semiautomatic rifle lay in plain view on the seat, together with a note written in the "Son of Sam's" distinctive, awkward style. When Berkowitz emerged from his apartment, he was instantly arrested and confessed his role in New York's reign of terror.

The story told by Berkowitz seemed tailor-made for an INSANITY DEFENSE in court. The "Sam" referred to in his letters was a neighbor, one Sam Carr, whose Labrador retriever was allegedly possessed by ancient demons, beaming out commands for Berkowitz to kill and kill again. On one occasion he had tried to kill the dog, but it was useless; demons spoiled his aim, and when the dog recovered from its wounds, the nightly torment had redoubled in intensity. A number of psychiatrists described the suspect as a paranoid schizophrenic, suffering from delusions and therefore incompetent to stand trial. The lone exception was Dr. David Abrahamson, who found that Berkowitz was sane and capable of understanding that his actions had been criminal. The court agreed with Abrahamson and ordered Berkowitz to trial. The gunman soon pled guilty and was sentenced to 365 years in prison.

Ironically, Berkowitz seemed grateful to Dr. Abrahamson for his sanity ruling and later agreed to a series of interviews that Abrahamson published in his book *Confessions of Son of Sam* (1985). The interviews revealed that Berkowitz had tried to kill two women during 1975, attacking them with knives, but he turned squeamish when they screamed and tried to fight him off. ("I didn't want to hurt them," he explained, confused. "I only wanted to kill them.") A virgin at the time of his arrest, Berkowitz was prone to fabricate elaborate lies about his bedroom prowess, all the while intent upon revenge against the women who habitually rejected him. When not engaged in stalking female victims, Berkowitz reportedly was an accomplished arsonist: a secret journal listed details of 300 fires for which he was allegedly responsible around New York. In his conclusion, Dr. Abrahamson described his subject as a homicidal exhibitionist who meant his crimes to be a public spectacle and harbored fantasies of "dying for a cause."

There is another side of David Berkowitz, however, and it surfaced shortly after his arrest, with allegations of his membership in a satanic cult. In letters mailed from prison, Berkowitz described participation in a New York cult affiliated with the lethal "Four P Movement," based in California. He revealed persuasive inside knowledge of a California homicide, unsolved since 1974, and wrote that "There are other Sams out there—God help the world."

According to the story told by Berkowitz in prison, two of neighbor Sam Carr's sons were also members of the killer cult that specialized in skinning dogs alive and gunning victims down on darkened streets. One suspect, John Charles Carr, was said to be the same "John Wheaties" mentioned in a letter penned by Berkowitz, containing other clues that point to cult involvement in the random murders. Calling themselves "The Children," the cultists operated from a base in Untermeyer Park, where mutilated dogs were found from time to time. Cult members represented the "Twenty-Two Disciples of Hell" mentioned in another "Son of Sam" letter. Suspect John Carr fled New York in February 1979 and "committed suicide" under mysterious circumstances in Minot, North Dakota, two days later. Brother Michael Carr died in a single-car crash in October 1979, and New York authorities reopened the "Sam" case after his death.

Newsman Maury Terry, after six years on the case, believes there were at least five different gunmen in the "Son of Sam" attacks, including Berkowitz, John Carr, and several suspects—one a woman—who have yet to be indicted. Terry also notes that six of the seven shootings fell in close proximity to recognized occult holidays, the March 8 Voskerichian attack emerging as the sole exception to the pattern. In the journalist's opinion, Berkowitz was chosen as a scapegoat by the other cultists, who then defaced his apartment with weird graffiti, whipping up a bogus "arson ledger"—which includes peculiar, out-of-order entries—to support a plea of innocent by reason of insanity.

Berkowitz himself confirmed the occult connection in conversations with fellow inmates and letters mailed from prison. One such, posted in October 1979, reads:

I really don't know how to begin this letter, but at one time I was a member of an occult group. Being sworn to secrecy or face death I cannot reveal the name of the group, nor do I wish to. This group contained a mixture of satanic practices which included the teachings of Aleister Crowley and Eliphaz [sic] Levi. It was (still is) totally blood oriented and I am certain you know just what I mean. The Coven's doctrine are a blend of Druidism, the teachings of the Secret Order of the Golden Dawn, Black Magick and a host of other unlawful and obnoxious practices.

As I said, I have no interest in revealing the Coven, especially because I have almost met sudden death on several occasions (once by half an inch) and several others have already perished under mysterious circumstances. These people will stop at nothing, including murder. They have no fear of man-made laws or the Ten Commandments.

The latest near-death experience for Berkowitz had been a July 10 prison assault that left his throat slashed, requiring fifty-six stitches to close the wound. Less talkative following his narrow escape, Berkowitz still agreed to a January 1982 meeting with attorney Harry Lipsig. In that conversation, he referred to the killer cult as follows:

Q: You had some connection with the Church of Scientology, did you not?
A: It wasn't exactly that. But I can't go into it. I really can't.
Q: Were you connected in any way or an adherent or convert of the Church of Scientology?
A: No, not that way. It was an offshoot, fringe-type thing.
Q: Were John and Michael [Carr] with the Church of Scientology?
A: Well, not really that church. But something along that line. A very devious group.
Q: Did this devious group have a name?
A: I can't disclose it.
Q: Roughly, how large would you say its membership was?
A: Twenty.
Q: Were they all residents of the New York metropolitan area?
A: No.
Q: Were they spread across the nation?
A: Yes.
Q: Did they meet on occasion?
A: Yes, but I really can't say more without counsel.

As Maury Terry noted, both the satanic Process Church of Final Judgment and its spin-off successor, the "Four P" cult, were "offshoot, fringe-type" movements spawned by Scientology. Both groups were also linked to the Charles MANSON FAMILY in California—as was convicted killer William Mentzer, named by Berkowitz in prison interviews as the triggerman in the January 1977 shooting of John Diel and Christine Freund. Investigation of the alleged cult continues, supported by testimony from convicted cannibal-killer Stanley Dean Baker, but no further indictments have been filed to date.

See also CULTS

BIANCHI, Kenneth Alessio, and BUONO, Angelo, Jr.

Born in May 1951 to a prostitute mother in Rochester, New York, Ken Bianchi was given up for adoption as an infant. By age 11, he was falling behind in his schoolwork and was given to furious tantrums in class and at home. He married briefly at 18. Two years later he wrote to a girlfriend, claiming he had killed a local man. She laughed it off, dismissing the claim as part of Ken's incessant macho posturing, but homicide was clearly preying on Bianchi's mind. By 1973, he was cer-

tain that police suspected him of involvement in Rochester's brutal "alphabet murders," though in truth, it took six more years before detective realized his car resembled one reported near the scene of one "alphabet" slaying.

Meanwhile, in January 1976, Bianchi pulled up stakes and moved to Los Angeles, there teaming up with his adoptive cousin, Angelo Buono, in an amateur white-slave racket. Born at Rochester in October 1934, Buono was a child of divorce, transported across country by his mother at age five. By 14, he was stealing cars and displaying a precocious obsession with sodomy. Sentenced for auto theft in 1950, he escaped from the California Youth Authority and was recaptured in December 1951. As a young man, Buono idolized condemned sex offender Caryl Chessman, and in later years he would emulate the so-called red-light rapist's method of procuring victims. In the meantime, though, he fathered several children, viciously abusing various wives and girlfriends in the process. Somehow, in defiance of his violent temperament and almost simian appearance, he attracted scores of women, dazzling cousin Kenneth with his "harem" and his method of recruiting prostitutes through rape and torture.

Kenneth Bianchi (Wide World API)

Two of Buono's favorite hookers managed to escape his clutches during 1977, and Bianchi later marked their departure as the starting point for L.A.'s reign of terror at the hands of Bianchi and Buono. In precisely two months' time, the so-called Hillside Stranglers would abduct and slay 10 women, frequently abandoning their victims' naked bodies in a grim display, as if to taunt authorities.

Rejected for employment by the Glendale and Los Angeles police departments, longing for a chance to throw his weight around and show some "real authority," Bianchi fell in line with Buono's suggestion that they should impersonate policemen, stopping female motorists or nabbing prostitutes according to their whim. Along the way, they would subject their captives to an ordeal of torture, sexual assault, and brutality, inevitably ending with a twist of the garrote.

Yolanda Washington, a 19-year-old hooker, was the first to die, murdered on October 17, her nude body discovered the next day, near Universal City. Two weeks later, on Halloween, police retrieved the corpse of 15-year-old Judith Miller from a flower bed in La Crescenta. Elissa Kastin, a 21-year-old Hollywood waitress, was abducted and slain November 5, her body discovered the next morning on a highway embankment in Glendale. On November 8, Jane King, aspiring actress and model, was kidnapped, raped, and suffocated, her body dumped on an off-ramp of the Golden State Freeway, undiscovered until November 22.

By that time, female residents of Los Angeles were living a nightmare. No less than three victims had been discovered on November 20, including 20-year-old honor student Kristina Wechler, dumped in Highland Park, and two classmates from junior high school, Sonja Johnson and Dolores Cepeda, discovered in Elysian Park a week after their disappearance from a local bus stop. Retrieval of Jane King's body increased the anxiety, and Thanksgiving week climaxed with the death of Lauren Wagner, an 18-year-old student, found in the Glendale hills on November 29.

By that time, police knew they were looking for dual suspects, based on the testimony of eyewitness including one prospective victim—the daughter of screen star Peter Lorre—who had managed to avoid the stranglers' clutches. On December 9, prostitute Kimberly Martin answered her last out-call in Glendale, turning up nude and dead on an Echo Park hillside next morning. The last to die, at least in California, was Cindy Hudspeth, found in the trunk of her car after it was pushed over a cliff in the Angeles National Forest.

Bianchi sensed that it was time for a change of scene. Moving to Bellingham, Washington, he found work as a security guard, flirting once more with the police work he craved. On January 11, 1979, Diane Wilder and

Angelo Buono led from court in handcuffs (Wide World API)

Karen Mandic were raped and murdered in Bellingham, last seen alive when they went to check out a potential house-sitting job. Bianchi had been their contact, and inconsistent statements led police to hold him for further investigation. A search of his home turned up items stolen from sites he was paid to guard, and further evidence finally linked him to the Bellingham murders. Collaboration with L.A. authorities led to Bianchi's indictment in five of the Hillside murders in June 1979.

In custody, Bianchi first denied everything, then feigned submission to hypnosis, manufacturing multiple personalities in his bid to support an insanity defense. Psychiatrists saw through the ruse, and after his indictment in Los Angeles, Ken agreed to testify against his cousin. His guilty plea to five new counts of homicide was followed by Buono's arrest in October 1979, and Angelo was charged with 10 counts of first-degree murder. A 10-month preliminary hearing climaxed in March 1981, with Angelo ordered to stand trial on all counts.

Bianchi, meanwhile, was desperately seeking some way to save himself. In June 1980, he received a letter from Veronica Lynn Compton, a 23-year-old poet, playwright, and aspiring actress, who sought Ken's opinion of her new play (dealing with a female serial killer). Correspondence and conversations revealed her obsession with murder, mutilation, and necrophilia, encouraging Bianchi to suggest a bizarre defense strategy. Without a second thought, Veronica agreed to visit Bellingham, strangle a woman there, and deposit specimens of Bianchi's sperm at the scene, thus leading police to believe the "real killer" was still at large.

On September 16, 1980, Compton visited Bianchi in prison, receiving a book with part of a rubber glove inside, containing his semen. Flying north to Bellingham, she picked out a female victim at random but bungled the murder attempt. Arrested in California on October 3, Compton was convicted in Washington during 1981 and received a life sentence. She published a memoir (*Eating the Ashes*) from prison in 2002.

As Buono's trial date approached, Bianchi issued a series of contradictory statements, leading prosecutors to seek dismissal of all charges in July 1981. A courageous judge, Ronald George, refused to postpone the trial, which ultimately ran from November 1981 to November 1983. Convicted on nine counts of murder—oddly excluding Yolanda Washington's—Buono was sentenced to nine terms of life imprisonment without parole. His cousin was returned to Washington State for completion of two corresponding life terms in the Bellingham case. Buono died at Calipatria State Prison, in California's Imperial County, on September 21, 2002.

BITTAKER, Lawrence Sigmund, and NORRIS, Roy Lewis

Lawrence Bittaker was serving time for assault with a deadly weapon in 1978, when he met Roy Norris at the California Men's Colony in San Luis Obispo. A convicted rapist, Norris recognized a soul mate in Bittaker, and they soon became inseparable. While still confined, they hatched a grisly plot to kidnap, rape, and murder teenage girls "for fun," as soon as they were freed. If all went well, they planned to kill at least one girl from each "teen" age—13 through 19—while recording the events on tape and film.

Paroled on November 15, 1978, Bittaker began making preparations for the crime spree, obtaining a van that he dubbed "Murder Mack." Norris was released on June 15, 1979, after a period of observation at Atascadero State Hospital, and he hurried to Bittaker's side, anxious to implement their plan.

Nine days later, on June 24, 16-year-old Linda Schaeffer vanished following a church service, never to be seen again. Joy Hall, 18, disappeared without a trace in Redondo Beach on July 8. Two months later, on September 2, 13-year-old Jacqueline Lamp and 15-year-old Jackie Gilliam were lost while thumbing rides in Redondo Beach. Shirley Ledford, 16, of Sunland, was the only victim recovered by authorities, abducted on

October 31 and found the next morning in a Tijunga residential neighborhood. Strangled with a wire coat hanger, she had first been subjected to "sadistic and barbaric abuse," her breasts and face mutilated, arms slashed, her body covered with bruises.

Detectives got their break on November 20, when Bittaker and Norris were arrested on charges stemming from a September 30 assault in Hermosa Beach. According to reports, their female victim had been sprayed with Mace, abducted in a silver van, and raped before she managed to escape. The woman ultimately failed to make a positive ID on Bittaker and Norris, but arresting officers discovered drugs in their possession, holding both in jail for violation of parole.

Roy Norris started showing signs of strain in custody. At a preliminary hearing in Hermosa Beach, he offered an apology "for my insanity," and he was soon regaling officers with tales of murder. According to his statements, girls had been approached at random, photographed by Bittaker, and offered rides, free marijuana, jobs in modeling. Most turned the offers down, but others were abducted forcibly, the van's radio drowning out their screams as they were driven to a remote mountain fire road for sessions of rape and torture. Tape recordings of Jacqueline Lamp's final moments were recovered from Bittaker's van, and detectives counted 500 photos of smiling young women among the suspects' effects.

On February 9, 1980, Norris led deputies to shallow graves in San Dimas Canyon and the San Gabriel Mountains, where skeletal remains of Lamp and Jackie Gilliam were recovered. An ice pick still protruded from Gilliam's skull, and the remains bore other marks of

Lawrence ("Pliers") Bittaker takes the stand at his murder trial. (Wide World API)

cruel mistreatment. Charging the prisoners with five counts of murder, Los Angeles County Sheriff Peter Pitchess announced that Bittaker and Norris might be linked to the disappearance of 30 or 40 more victims. By February 20, the stack of confiscated photographs had yielded 19 missing girls, but none were ever traced, and Norris had apparently exhausted his desire to talk.

On March 18, Norris pled guilty on five counts of murder, turning state's evidence against his confederate. In return for his cooperation, he received a sentence of 45 years to life, with parole possible in the year 2010.

Bittaker, meanwhile—nicknamed "Pliers," for his favorite instrument of torture—denied everything. At his trial, on February 5, 1981, he testified that Roy Norris first informed him of the murders after their arrest in 1979. A jury chose not to believe him, returning a guilty verdict on February 17. On March 24, in accordance with the jury's recommendation, Bittaker was sentenced to die. The judge also imposed an alternate sentence of 199 years and four months in prison, to take effect in the event that Bittaker's death sentence is ever commuted on appeal.

"BLACK Widows": Female serial-killer type

Borrowed from the venomous spider that devours its mate after sex, this label is applied in criminology to female murderers who prey on their own husbands, relatives, or lovers. Monetary gain, through life insurance or inheritance, is frequently a motive in such crimes, although it may not be the *only* motive. NANNY DOSS, according to her own confession, killed successive husbands in search of true romance, as she had seen that state of bliss portrayed in women's magazines. When mothers kill their children—most particularly when the victims' lives are not insured—there is clearly some psychological motive for the crimes. South African Daisy De Melker murdered her stepchildren in a misguided effort to gain more attention from her husband. Other maternal child killers, like MARYBETH TINNING, apparently suffer from MUNCHAUSEN'S SYNDROME BY PROXY—essentially a pathological craving for the attention and sympathy they receive during tragic times.

Like their web-spinning namesake, black widows frequently use poison to dispatch their mates and parents, siblings, and assorted other relatives. Where children are concerned, asphyxiation is a killing method favored by the "gentle" sex. Of course, there are exceptions to the rule. Gunshot wounds defy classification as death from natural causes, but a shooting may be staged to look like suicide or accidental death, a tactic favored by Barbara Stager in North Carolina. Burly BELLE GUNNESS not only bludgeoned, but sometimes

Louise Peete was a classic black widow, motivated by profit. (Author's collection)

dismembered her victims, while Velma Barfield set one of her husbands on fire as he slept. In Texas, Betty Beets preferred to make her husbands disappear entirely, waiting for a legal declaration of death to free up life insurance benefits.

Black widows, finally, for all the ink and paper spent describing their murders as "quiet" and "gentle," rank among the most cold-blooded killers on record. The very calculation of their crimes may help explain why three of the four women executed in America since 1976 are ranked in this category. Others are presently sentenced to death in North Carolina and Texas.

See also "BLUEBEARD" KILLERS; MODUS OPERANDI; MOTIVES; WEAPONS

"BLUEBEARD" Killers: Male serial-killer type

A generic term for any man who murders a series of wives or fiancées, this subgroup of serial murder ironically derives its popular nickname from a 15th-century slayer of children. French nobleman GILLES DE RAIS was the original "Bluebeard," so called after the blue-black color of his facial hair, but any link between this kind of murder and sadistic pedophilia has long since been lost. Years after Gilles was executed, a popular folk tale hung the nickname on the fictional Chevalier Raoul, whose seventh wife found the corpses of his six murdered predecessors in a room her husband forbade her to enter.

Most real-life Bluebeards, in the mold of JOHANN HOCH and HENRI LANDRU, woo and slay their female victims in pursuit of some material reward, such as inheritance or life insurance. Frequently, they practice bigamy and fraud, along with other mercenary crimes, before they ultimately find the nerve to kill. It would be rash to

rule out any sexual or psychological motive in such cases, however. Prolific Bluebeard Harry Powers told authorities in West Virginia that watching victims die in his homemade gas chamber "beat any cat house I was ever in." Another American Bluebeard who murdered at least seven wives, James Watson, was discovered on arrest to be a hermaphrodite (possessing both male and female genitalia). We can only imagine what impact the deformity had on his numerous wedding nights, but it surely distorted his outlook on women and sex.

See also "BLACK WIDOWS"; MOTIVES

BOLBER-PETRILLO-FAVATO Murder Ring

America's most prolific team of killers-for-profit were active in Philadelphia, Pennsylvania, during the 1930s, claiming an estimated 30 to 50 victims before the ring's various members were apprehended. Students of the case, in retrospect, are prone to cite the gang's activities as evidence that modern homicide statistics may be woefully inaccurate. If 20,000 murders are reported in a given year, they say, it is entirely possible that 20,000 more go unreported, overlooked by the authorities.

The basic murder method was conceived in 1932, by Dr. Morris Bolber and his good friend, Paul Petrillo. After one of Bolber's female patients aired complaints about her husband's infidelity, the doctor and Petrillo planned for Paul to woo the lonely lady, gaining her cooperation in a plan to kill her wayward spouse and split $10,000 in insurance benefits. The victim, Anthony Giscobbe, was a heavy drinker, and it proved a simple matter for his wife to strip him as he lay unconscious, leaving him beside an open window in the dead of winter while he caught his death of cold. The grieving widow split her cash with Bolber and Petrillo, whereupon her "lover" promptly went in search of other restless, greedy wives.

It soon became apparent that Italian husbands, caught up in the middle of the Great Depression, carried little life insurance on themselves. Petrillo called upon his cousin Herman, an accomplished local actor, to impersonate potential victims and apply for heavy policies. Once several payments had been made, the husbands were eliminated swiftly and efficiently through "accidents" or "natural causes." Dr. Bolber's favorite methods included poison and blows to the head with a sandbag, producing cerebral hemorrhage, but methods were varied to fit circumstances. One victim, a roofer named Lorenzo, was hurled to his death from an eight-story building, the Petrillo cousins first handing him some French postcards to explain his careless distraction.

After roughly a dozen murders, the gang recruited local faith healer Carino Favato, known as the Witch in

Gilles de Rais, the original "Bluebeard" (Author's collection)

her home neighborhood. Favato had dispatched three of her own husbands before going into business full-time as a "marriage consultant," poisoning unwanted husbands for a fee. Impressed by Dr. Bolber's explanation of the life insurance scam, Favato came on board and brought the gang a list of her prospective clients. By the latter part of 1937, Bolber's ring had polished off an estimated 50 victims, at least 30 of whom were fairly well documented by subsequent investigation.

The roof fell in when an ex-convict approached Herman Petrillo, pushing a new get-rich scheme. Unimpressed, Petrillo countered with a pitch for his acquaintance to secure potential murder victims, and the felon panicked, running to police. As members of the gang were rounded up, they "squealed" on one another in the hope of finding leniency, their clients chiming in as ripples spread throughout a stunned community. While several wives were sent to prison, most escaped by testifying for the state. The two Petrillos were condemned and put to death, while Dr. Bolber and Carino Favato each drew terms of life imprisonment.

BOMBING and Serial Murder

A favorite tool of terrorists since the mid-19th century, bombs are built and detonated for all the same reasons that people set fires. On an individual basis, serial bombing is less common than serial ARSON, but several striking cases have been logged in modern times. "Mad Bomber" George Metesky operated in New York through the late 1940s and early 1950s, nursing an explosive grudge against the corporation (and one-time employer) he blamed for infecting him with tuberculosis. More recently, "Unabomber" Theodore Kaczynski—once dubbed the "scariest criminal in America" by *Playboy* magazine—detonated 16 bombs in eight states between May 1978 and April 1995, killing three persons and wounding at least 20 others.

As with any other serial crime, the MOTIVES in repeated bombings may vary over time, from one incident to the next. Walter Moody's first mail bomb, in 1972, was addressed to car dealer who had repossessed his vehicle; 19 years later, he was sentenced to life without parole in federal prison for mailing bombs to judges and lawyers supportive of black civil rights, including two victims who died. Diagnosed as schizophrenic in 1968, Moody saw high explosives as the cure for all the grudges he held against individuals and society at large.

Extremists of both left and right have made their mark with bombs in recent times. During the 1960s, a splinter faction of the Ku Klux Klan called Nacirema—

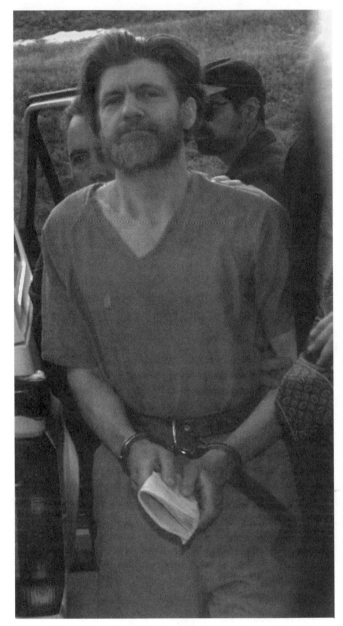

"Unabomber" Theodore Kaczynski being escorted to court (Wide World API)

American spelled backwards—trained its members in the art of demolition and was deemed responsible (though never prosecuted) for more than 100 racist bombings in the southern states. A similar, if less well-traveled, clique was the so-called Silver Dollar Group that drew its membership from Klansmen in southeastern Louisiana and some nearby Mississippi counties. Each member of the group carried a silver dollar minted in the year of his birth, and they specialized in car bombs, crippling one NAACP leader in 1965 and killing another in 1967.

While bombs are used most often in extremist-motivated crimes or criminal enterprise cases (including attacks by organized crime), there may also be a sexual motive in bombing. The Metesky case presents the first well-known application of psychological PROFILING, in which Dr. James Brussel divined the offender's sexual angst from the phallic shape of his pipe bombs. At the same time, sex was not the *sole* motive for Metesky's bombings, as he clearly nursed a hunger for revenge against his past employers. There may also be a craving for attention in such cases, demonstrated by Metesky's (and Kaczynski's) correspondence with the media.

Italian police have pursued a "Unabomber" of their own since October 2000, when pipe bombs and explosive charges disguised as packaged food injured several victims. One woman lost several fingers after a booby-trapped tube of tomato paste exploded in her hand. By November 21, 2000, the authorities blamed the unknown bomber(s) for planting 21 devices. Unlike the case of Theodore Kaczynski, no communication with the media had been attempted as of April 2003, when a booby-trapped pen maimed a nine-year-old girl at San Biagio di Callalta. That marked the bomber's last attack (as of press time for this work), and the case remains unsolved.

Likewise, in Los Angeles, police have no suspects in the May 2001 case of three traffic cones rigged with gasoline bombs and left near local schools, set to explode if passersby removed plastic flowers from the apex of the cones. Authorities described the bombs as being meant for children, but none exploded and the unknown saboteur apparently tired of his twisted game. Farther north, on San Francisco Bay, nine "low-powered bombs" exploded in Fremont, California, between May 18 and June 4, 2001. Three other unexploded bombs were found in the same vicinity, but the bomber eluded detection. Police sergeant Dennis Madsen told reporters, "I think whoever's doing it is getting a lot of notoriety. This guy's sitting at home reading the papers and enjoying it." (Another Fremont local, Rodney Blach, was arrested in October 1999 and convicted in December 2001 for a series of bombings in 1998. Those blasts, apparently intended to kill local officials, were unrelated to the explosions in 2001.)

Chinese bomber Jin Ruchao was a fugitive from murder charges in Yunnan, where he allegedly murdered a woman on March 6, 2000. Ten days later, in the northern city of Shijiazhuang, Jin allegedly set explosive charges that demolished several buildings, killing 108 persons in a series of blasts. Arrested on March 31, he was tried and sentenced to death on April 18, 2001. Amnesty International condemned the sentence as a product of hasty and incomplete investigation.

No such claim can be made for David Copeland, the notorious "London Nailbomber" whose devices killed three victims and wounded at least 116 in April 1999. Copeland, an outspoken neo-Nazi, targeted gays and ethnic minorities with his lethal charges, planted at bars and bus stops. Convicted of murder on June 30, 2000, Copeland received six terms of life imprisonment.

See also PARAPHILIA; WEAPONS

BONIN, William George   *See* "FREEWAY MURDERS"

"BOSTON Strangler"

A decade before the term "serial killer" entered popular usage outside of Great Britain, Boston was terrorized by an elusive killer who claimed at least 11 female victims between June 1962 and January 1964. In every case the victims were raped—sometimes with foreign objects—and their bodies laid out nude, as if on display for a pornographic snapshot. Death was always caused by strangulation, though the killer sometimes also used a knife. The ligature—a stocking, pillowcase, whatever—was invariably left around the victim's neck, tied with an exaggerated ornamental bow.

Fifty-five-year-old Anna Slessers was the first to die, strangled with the cord of her bathrobe on June 14, 1962. A nylon stocking was used to kill 68-year-old Nina Nichols on June 30. Helen Blake, age 65, was found the same day, with a stocking and bra knotted around her neck. On August 19, 75-year-old Ida Irga was manually strangled in her home, "decorated" with a knotted pillowcase. Jane Sullivan, age 67, had been dead a week when she was found on August 20, strangled with her own stockings, slumped over the edge of a bathtub with her face submerged.

The killer seemed to break his pattern on December 5, 1962, when he murdered Sophie Clark, a 20-year-old

Albert DeSalvo in custody (Author's collection)

African American. Another shift was seen with 23-year-old Patricia Bissette, strangled on her bed and covered with a blanket to her chin, in place of the usual graphic display. With 23-year-old Beverly Samans, killed on May 6, the slayer used a knife for the first time, stabbing his victim 22 times before looping the traditional stocking around her neck. Evelyn Corbin, age 58, seemed to restore the original pattern on September 8, strangled and violated by an "unnatural" assault, but the killer went back to young victims on November 23, strangling 23-year-old Joann Graff and leaving bite marks on her breast. The final victim, 19-year-old Mary Sullivan, was found on January 4, 1964, strangled with a scarf.

Ten months later, on November 3, 1964, police arrested 33-year-old Albert Henry DeSalvo for questioning on rape charges. It was not his first brush with the law. While serving in the U.S. Army, in January 1955, DeSalvo was accused of molesting a nine-year-old girl, but the child's mother declined to press charges and DeSalvo had been honorably discharged in 1956. Four years later, in March 1960, he confessed a series of assaults committed by Boston's "Measuring Man," a smooth-talking culprit who poses as a door-to-door scout for a fictitious modeling agency, fondling scores of women while he took their "vital statistics" for future reference. The confession earned DeSalvo a two-year prison term for assault and lewd conduct, but he was paroled after 11 months, his obsession undiminished.

Next, DeSalvo told police, he became the "Green Man," a home-invading rapist nicknamed for the green work clothes he wore. Detectives suspected DeSalvo of 300 rapes, but he astonished them by confessing nearly 2,000. In one hectic day, he raped six women in four different towns, with two of the attacks unreported prior to his confession. Those admissions sent DeSalvo to Bridgewater State Hospital, confined for psychiatric evaluation. There, he befriended George Nassar, a convicted murderer awaiting trial for his second robbery-slaying since 1948. Their private discussions were interspersed with visits from police, climaxed by DeSalvo's claim that he was the "Boston Strangler."

In his latest confession, DeSalvo added two "new" victims to the body count, both previously overlooked by homicide investigators. One, 85-year-old Mary Mullen, was found dead in her home of apparent heart failure on June 28, 1962. DeSalvo claimed that Mullen had collapsed from shock when he invaded her apartment, whereupon he left her body on the couch without pursuing the traditional assault. Mary Brown, age 69, was stabbed and beaten in her home on March 9, 1963, again without a showing of the famous "strangler's knot."

It seemed like an open-and-shut case, but numerous problems remained. The strangler's sole surviving victim, assaulted in February 1963, failed to pick DeSalvo from a lineup. Witnesses from the Graff and Sullivan crime scenes likewise failed to recognize DeSalvo. Several detectives, meanwhile, had focused their aim on an alternate suspect, fingered by "psychic" Peter Hurkos, but their man had voluntarily committed himself to an asylum soon after the last murder. Finally, if DeSalvo was driven to kill by a mother fixation, as psychiatrists claimed, why had he chosen young women as five of his last seven victims?

Legal maneuvers swept those problems under the rug in 1967, when celebrity lawyer F. Lee Bailey negotiated an unusual plea bargain for DeSalvo. In lieu of homicide charges, DeSalvo pled guilty to the Green Man rapes and received a sentence of life in prison. A fellow inmate fatally stabbed him on November 26, 1973, and while the murder silenced DeSalvo, it did not erase the doubts surrounding his confession.

More than a quarter-century after DeSalvo's last arrest, forensic scientists revisited the Boston Strangler case in an effort to solve the nagging mystery. DeSalvo's corpse was exhumed in October 2001, for extraction of DNA material to use in tests unknown to pathologists in the 1960s. Two months later, on December 6, James Starrs—a professor of law and forensic science at George Washington University—announced "blockbuster results" in the case. Specifically, DNA samples from two individuals were found on the corpse of a victim, neither traceable to DeSalvo. Starrs told the press, "It's indicative, strongly indicative, of the fact that Albert DeSalvo was not the rape-murderer of Mary Sullivan. If I was a juror, I would acquit him with no questions asked." Sullivan's nephew, Casey Sherman, had an even more emphatic message for reporters: "If he didn't kill Mary Sullivan, yet he confessed to it in glaring detail, he didn't kill any of these women."

Retired Massachusetts prosecutor Julian Soshnick disagreed, replying, "It doesn't prove anything except that they found another person's DNA on a part of Miss Sullivan's body." Seeming to ignore the import of that evidence, Soshnick stood firm: "I believe that Albert was the Boston Strangler." Another retired investigator, former Boston homicide detective Jack Barry, cited DeSalvo's detailed confessions as proof of guilt. "He just knew so much," Barry said, "things that were never in the paper. He could describe the wallpaper in their rooms." Dr. Ames Robey, supervisor of Bridgewater State Hospital in the 1960s and the chief psychiatrist who evaluated DeSalvo, found the confessions less persuasive. "He was a boaster," Robey told reporters. "I never believed it for a minute."

In any case, the DNA discovery stopped short of solving Boston's most famous murder mystery. Professor Starrs believes that at least one of the DNA samples recovered from Sullivan's body belongs to her killer, but he admitted in December 2001, "We cannot tell you the $64,000 question as to whose it is."

Some students of the case believe the answer may be found at Bridgewater, where killer George Nassar conferred with DeSalvo through long days and nights. It is possible, critics maintain, that Nassar may have been the strangler, briefing DeSalvo on the details of his crimes in hope of sending authorities off on a wild goose chase. DeSalvo, already facing life imprisonment for countless rapes, admittedly struck a cash bargain with Nassar, whereby Nassar would pocket part of the outstanding reward for turning in DeSalvo, afterward passing most of the money on to DeSalvo's wife. As a clincher, the strangler's lone survivor favored Nassar as a suspect, rather than DeSalvo. Other theories postulate the existence of two Boston Stranglers, one for the young and one for the elderly victims. Journalist Hank Messick added a new twist in the early 1970s, quoting a Mafia hit man (now deceased) to the effect that DeSalvo had been paid by members of organized crime to "take a fall" for the actual, still unidentified Boston Strangler.

BRUDOS, Jerome Henry

Born in South Dakota during January 1939, Brudos moved to California with his family as a child. He grew up with a deep, abiding hatred for his domineering mother and a strange, precocious fetish for women's shoes. Discovering a pair of high heels at the local dump, he brought them home, where they were confiscated and burned by his mother. By the time he entered first grade, Brudos was stealing shoes from his sister; at age 16, now living in Oregon, he branched out into burglary, making off with shoes from neighboring homes, sometimes snatching women's undergarments from clotheslines.

In 1956, at 17, Brudos beat up a girl who resisted his crude advances on a date, winding up in juvenile court. Ordered to visit the state hospital in Salem as an outpatient while continuing his high school education, Brudos apparently gained nothing from therapy. Joining the army in March 1959, he was troubled by dreams of a woman creeping into his bed at night. A chat with an army psychiatrist led to Jerome's discharge on October 15, 1959, and he went home to live with his parents in Salem, moving into their toolshed.

Unknown to members of his family, Brudos had begun to prey on local women, stalking them until he found a chance to knock them down or choke them unconscious, fleeing with their shoes. Still virginal in 1961, he met his future wife and quickly made her preg-

nant, trooping to the altar from a sense of obligation. By 1967, settled in the Portland suburb of Aloha, Brudos began complaining of migraine headaches and "blackouts," relieving his symptoms with night-prowling raids to steal shoes and lacy underwear. On one occasion, a woman awoke to find him ransacking her closet and Brudos choked her unconscious, raping her before he fled.

On January 26, 1968, 19-year-old Linda Slawson was selling encyclopedias door-to-door when she called on Jerry Brudos. Bludgeoned and strangled to death in his basement, she became the first of five known victims killed by Brudos in Oregon. The second, 16-year-old Stephanie Vikko, disappeared from Portland in July. A third, student Jan Whitney, 23, vanished on November 26 during a two-hour drive from Eugene to McMinnville, her car found abandoned north of Albany, Oregon.

So far, authorities were working on a string of disappearances, with no hard proof of homicide. That changed on March 18, 1969, with the discovery of Stephanie Vikko's remains in a wooded area northwest of Forest Grove. Nine days later, 19-year-old Karen Sprinker vanished from a Salem parking garage, leaving her car behind. Two witnesses reported same-day sightings of a large man, dressed in women's clothing, loitering in the garage.

As the police were searching for their suspect, Brudos faced a minor crisis in his own backyard. While cleaning house, his wife had turned up photographs of Jerry dressed in drag, and she had also found a "plastic" breast, described by Brudos as a paperweight. (In fact, it was a hunting trophy, treated with preservative.) She missed the other photographs, depicting Brudos with his victims, posing with their bodies, dressing them in frilly underwear like life-sized dolls, but dark suspicion had begun to fester, all the same.

On April 23, 1969, Brudos claimed his final victim, picking off 22-year-old Linda Salee at a Portland shopping mall. Her body, weighted down with an auto transmission, was pulled from the Long Tom River on May 10. Two days later and 50 feet downstream, a team of divers turned up victim Karen Sprinker, weighted with an engine block. The second body wore a brassiere several sizes too large, padded with paper towels to conceal the fact that her breasts had been amputated.

Interviews with local coeds yielded several stories of an aging, self-described "Vietnam veteran" who frequently approached girls on campus, asking for dates. Police staked out the scene of one such rendezvous in Corvallis on May 25, questioning Jerry Brudos closely before they let him go. Picked up on a concealed weapons charge five days later, Brudos broke down and confessed to the murders in detail, directing authorities to evidence that would cinch their case. On June 27, 1969, Brudos pled guilty on three counts of first-degree murder and was sentenced to a term of life imprisonment. His popularity with fellow inmates is recorded in a string of prison "accidents," including one that left him with a fractured neck in 1971.

"BTK Strangler"

Residents of Wichita, Kansas, were ill prepared to cope with monsters in the early days of 1974. Their lives were by and large conservative, well-ordered, purposeful. They had no previous experience to help prepare them for the coming terror, and it took them absolutely by surprise.

On January 15, four members of the Otero family were found dead in their comfortable suburban home, hog-tied and strangled with cords cut from old Venetian blinds. Joseph Otero, 38 years old, lay face down on the floor at the foot of his bed, wrists and ankles bound with samples of the same cord that was wrapped around his neck. Close by, wife Julie lay on the bed she had once shared with her husband, bound and strangled in similar fashion. Joseph II, age nine, was found in his bedroom, mirroring his father's placement at the foot of the bed, with a plastic bag over his head. Downstairs, 11-year-old Josephine Otero hung by her neck from a pipe in the basement, clad only in a sweatshirt and socks. None of the victims had been sexually assaulted, though police found semen at the crime scene.

Aside from the killer's ritualistic MODUS OPERANDI, police knew the crime had been planned in advance. Phone lines were cut outside the house, and the killer had brought ample cord from some other source for binding and strangling his victims. Several neighbors filed reports of a "suspicious-looking" stranger in the area, but published sketches of the unknown subject led police nowhere. A local teenager confessed to the murders, naming two accomplices, but none had any knowledge of the crimes beyond stark details published in the press. Still, their arrests served a purpose, prompting the killer to clamor for credit.

In October 1974, Wichita's bogeyman penned the first of several letters to the media, placed in a book at the public library. A phone call directed an editor of the *Wichita Eagle* to the hidden letter, filled with numerous misspellings, which advised police: "Those three dude[s] you have in custody are just talking to get publicity for the Otero murders. They know nothing at all. I did it by myself and no one[']s help." The slayer proved his point by describing the murder scene in detail, down to the color of each victim's clothing. He added a clincher, informing detectives of a fact they had

not recognized—the theft of Joseph Otero's wristwatch. "I needed one so I took it," the killer explained. "Runs good." Signing himself the "BTK Strangler," the killer provided his own translation in a postscript. He wrote: "The code words for me will be . . . Bind them, Torture them, Kill them."

Police released their young suspects while requesting that the letter be suppressed against the possibility of further false confessions in the case. No one came forward. No new evidence materialized. Twenty-nine months elapsed before the killer showed his hand again.

On March 17, 1977, 26-year-old Shirley Vian was murdered in her home, stripped, bound and strangled on her bed, left with a plastic bag over her head and the familiar cord wrapped tight around her neck. Vian's three children, locked in a closet by the armed intruder who had invaded their home, managed to free themselves and called police. Again, the crime was clearly premeditated: the killer had stopped one of Vian's sons on the street that morning, displaying photographs of an unidentified woman and child, asking directions to their home.

On December 9, 1977, 25-year-old Nancy Jo Fox was found murdered in the bedroom of her Wichita apartment, left with a nylon stocking tied around her neck. Unlike previous victims, she was fully clothed. An anonymous caller directed police to the crime scene, and officers traced the call to a downtown phone booth, where witnesses vaguely recalled "someone"—perhaps a blond six-footer—using the booth moments earlier.

The killer mailed a poem to the *Wichita Eagle* on January 31, 1978, but it was routed to the advertising department by mistake and lay undiscovered for days. Disgruntled by the absence of publicity, the slayer shifted targets, firing off a letter to a local television station on February 10. "How many do I have to kill," he asked, "before I get my name in the paper or some national attention?"

In his latest note, the BTK Strangler claimed seven victims, naming Vian and Fox as the latest. That left one still unaccounted for, as he closed with a taunting punch line: "You guess the motive and the victims." Unable to prove their correspondent's latest claim, authorities still took him at his word, announcing theoretical acceptance of the body count. The killer's last letter in 1978 was addressed to an elderly Wichita woman who eluded him by staying out late on the night he had chosen to kill her. "Why didn't you appear?" he asked.

Alternately blaming his crimes on "a demon" and a mysterious internal "Factor X," the strangler compared his work to that of London's "JACK THE RIPPER," New York City's "Son of Sam," and the "Hillside Strangler" in Los Angeles. "When this monster enter[ed] my brain," he wrote, "I will never know. But, it [is] here to stay. Maybe you can stop him. I can't. It seems senseless but we cannot help it. There is no help, no cure except death or being caught and put away." Psychiatrists who analyzed the letters felt the killer saw himself as part of some nebulous "grand scheme," but they were unable to pinpoint his motive or predict his next move.

In fact, there would be none for 26 years, until the *Wichita Eagle* received another BTK letter on March 19, 2004. The envelope contained a one-page letter in familiar style, together with a photocopy of murder victim Vicki Wegerle's driver's license and three snapshots of her corpse, each with the clothing arranged in slightly different positions. Police informed the media that no official photos had been taken of Wegerle's body in situ, when she was found on September 16, 1986, thus proving that her killer was the cameraman. Predictably, the letter's return address—from a fictitious *Bill Thomas Killman*—led detectives to a long-vacant apartment house in Wichita.

Another BTK letter arrived in early May 2004, this one posted to Wichita television station KAKE, Channel 10. It was delivered to police, who passed it on to the FBI laboratory for handwriting analysis. G-men confirmed the killer's authorship of that communication on June 28, after a third letter arrived at Wichita police headquarters. Authorities were mum on the contents of the last two notes, but Lieutenant Ken Landwehr told reporters, "I'm 100 percent sure it's BTK. We do believe that BTK is in Wichita. We truly feel that he is trying to communicate with us. We are specifically interested in talking to anyone who was approached at their residence between 1974 and 1986 by a man presenting himself as an employee of a school or a utility company. Obviously we are not interested in legitimate encounters. We want to know about situations where a man attempted to get into your house under suspicious circumstances."

Thousands of fruitless tips followed announcement of the latest BTK correspondence, and all were tracked by police to frustrating dead ends. Meanwhile, detectives staked their hopes on modern DNA technology (unavailable during the killer's crime spree in 1977–86) and on the content of his cryptic letters. "I don't think they're just ramblings," said retired captain Bernie Drowatzky. "I've always thought there was a key in there. I just never was able to find it."

Eleven months after the final rash of letters, on February 25, 2005, Wichita police announced the arrest of a BTK suspect. Dennis L. Rader was a 59-year-old city employee, married father of two, a popular Cub Scout leader and longtime deacon at Christ Lutheran Church. Friends and relatives were stunned on February 27, when authorities announced that

Rader had confessed six murders, doubly amazed when he was charged with 10 slayings on March 1. While only seven homicides were previously linked to the BTK series, detectives now listed three more victims, including:

- *Kathryn Bright,* age 21, bound and stabbed to death in her home on April 14, 1974. Her brother Kevin, shot and left for dead in the same incident, was a coworker of Rader's at a local camping-gear factory.
- *Marine Hedge,* age 53, kidnapped from her suburban Park City home on April 27, 1985, later found strangled with a pair of pantyhose and discarded on a rural road. At the time of her murder, Hedge lived on the same street as Rader.
- *Delores Davis,* age 62, snatched from her home outside Park City on January 19, 1991. When found beneath a bridge on February 1, she had been bound and strangled with pantyhose.

Police remain tight-lipped about their means of targeting Rader after three decades. Some reports mention a computer disk enclosed with one of the BTK letters in March 2004, which police allegedly traced back to Rader's church. All accounts include mention of DNA samples obtained from Rader's 26-year-old daughter, but details surrounding that evidence were hopelessly confused at press time for this volume. Some stories claim Rader's daughter was suspicious of him and approached police; others say she volunteered DNA in an effort to clear her father's name; yet a third version states that DNA samples were subpoenaed by FBI agents over the daughter's objections. In any case, the physical evidence and Rader's supposed confessions were enough to see him held in lieu of $10 million bond, pending trial. Ironically, detectives noted that during the height of the BTK panic, from 1974 to 1988, Rader worked for a local security firm, installing home-intrusion alarms throughout Wichita. On June 27, 2005, after several refusals by local prosecutors, Rader was finally permitted to plead guilty on 10 murder counts. In a chilling, deadpan open-court confession, he described the slayings in detail, explaining that he murdered his victims to satisfy sexual fantasies. At the Otero massacre, because he wore no mask, Rader declared, "I made a decision to go ahead and put 'em down." He kept Polaroid snapshots of his "projects" as TROPHIES, and planned "potential hits" with care. "If one didn't work out," he explained, "I just moved on to another one." At the end of Rader's recitation, prosecutors recommended a sentence of 175 years to life, thus making sure that Rader would die before attaining eligibility for parole. On August 19, 2005, he was sentenced to 10 life terms.

Theodore Bundy being led back to prison in handcuffs
(Wide World API)

BUNDY, Carol   *See* CLARK, DOUGLAS

BUNDY, Theodore Robert

Ted Bundy is a striking contrast to the general image of a "homicidal maniac": attractive, self-assured, politically ambitious, and successful with a wide variety of women. But his private demons drove him to extremes of violence that make the gory worst of modern "slasher" films seem almost petty by comparison. With his chameleon-like ability to blend, his talent for belonging, Bundy posed an ever-present danger to the pretty, dark-haired women he selected as his victims.

Born Theodore Robert Cowell in November 1946 at a home for unwed mothers in Vermont, Ted never knew his father, described vaguely by Louise Cowell as a serviceman she dated several times. Poverty forced Louise and her newborn son to live with her strict Methodist parents in Philadelphia, where Ted spent the first four years of his life pretending Louise was his sister. He would later paint a sunny picture of those years, professing love for grandfather Sam Cowell, but other family members describe Sam as a bitter racist and wife

beater, who also enjoyed kicking dogs and swinging cats through the air by their tails.

Whatever the truth, it is clear that *something* troubled Ted in those days. Early one morning, when he was barely three, Ted's 15-year-old aunt awoke to find him lifting her blankets, slipping butcher knives into the bed beside her. "He just stood there and grinned," she recalled. "I shooed him out of the room and took the implements back down to the kitchen and told my mother about it. I remember thinking at the time that I was the only one who thought it was strange. Nobody did anything."

In 1950, Louise and Ted moved to Tacoma, Washington, where she met and married John Bundy in May 1951. Despite good grades in school, Ted's file was filled with notes from his teachers alluding to his explosive and unpredictable temper. By the time he finished high school, Ted was a compulsive masturbator and a night-prowling voyeur, twice arrested by juvenile authorities on suspicion of burglary and auto theft. In 1970, he seemed to shift gears, winning a commendation from the Seattle Police Department for chasing down a purse-snatcher. A year later, Ted was enrolled at the University of Washington, working part-time on a suicide hot line. Behind the new civic-minded facade, however, Ted's morbid fantasies were building toward a lethal flash point.

Linda Healy was the first fatality. On January 31, 1974, she vanished from her basement lodgings in Seattle, leaving bloody sheets behind, a bloodstained nightgown hanging in her closet. Several blocks away, young Susan Clarke had been assaulted, bludgeoned in her bed a few weeks earlier, but she survived her injuries and would eventually recover. As for 21-year-old Lynda Healy, she was gone without a trace.

Police had no persuasive evidence of any pattern yet, but it would not be long in coming. On March 12, Donna Gail Manson, 19, disappeared en route to a concert in Olympia, Washington. On April 17, 18-year-old Susan Rancourt vanished on her way to see a German-language film in Ellensburg. On May 6, 22-year-old Roberta Parks failed to return from a late-night stroll in her Corvallis neighborhood. On June 1, 22-year-old Brenda Ball left Seattle's Flame Tavern with an unknown man and vanished as if into thin air. Ten days later, 18-year-old Georgeann Hawkins joined the list of missing women, lost somewhere between her boyfriend's apartment and her sorority house in Seattle.

Now detectives had their pattern. All the missing women had been young, attractive, with their dark hair worn at shoulder length and parted in the middle. In their photos, laid out side by side, they might have passed for sisters, some for twins. Homicide investigators had no corpses yet, but they refused to cherish false illusions of a happy ending to the case. There were so many victims, and the worst was yet to come.

On July 14, a crowd assembled on the shores of Lake Sammamish to enjoy the sun and water sports of summer. When the day was over, two more names would be appended to the growing list of missing women: 23-year-old Janice Ott and 19-year-old Denise Naslund had each disappeared within sight of their separate friends, but this time police had a tenuous lead. Passersby remembered seeing Ott in conversation with a man who carried one arm in a sling, and he was overheard to introduce himself as "Ted." With that report in hand, detectives turned up other female witnesses who were themselves approached by "Ted" at Lake Sammamish. In each case, he had asked for help securing a sailboat to his car. The lucky women had declined, but one had followed "Ted" to where his small Volk-

swagen Beetle was parked. There was no sign of any sailboat, and his explanation—that the boat would have to be retrieved from a house "up the hill"—had aroused her suspicions, prompting her to put the stranger off.

Police now had a fair description of their quarry and his car. The published references to "Ted" inspired a rash of calls reporting suspects, one of them in reference to college student Ted Bundy. The authorities checked out each lead as time allowed, but Bundy was considered "squeaky clean," a law student and Young Republican active in law-and-order politics, complete with commendations from the Seattle PD. So many calls reporting suspects had been made from spite or simple overzealousness that Bundy's name was filed away with countless others, momentarily forgotten.

On September 7, hunters found a makeshift graveyard on a wooded hillside several miles from Lake

Police and scent-trained dogs search for Bundy victims. (Wide World API)

Sammamish. Dental records were required to finally identify remains of Janice Ott and Denise Naslund; the skeleton of a third woman, found with the others, could not be identified. Five weeks later, on October 12, another hunter found the bones of two more women in Clark County. One victim was identified as 20-year-old Carol Valenzuela, missing for two months from Vancouver, Washington, on the Oregon border; again, the second victim would remain unknown, recorded in the files as a "Jane Doe." Police were optimistic, hopeful that discovery of victims would eventually lead them to the killer, but they had no way of knowing that their man had given them the slip already, moving on in search of safer hunting grounds and other prey.

The terror came to Utah on October 2, 1974, when 16-year-old Nancy Wilcox disappeared in Salt Lake City. On October 18, 17-year-old Melissa Smith vanished in Midvale; her body, raped and beaten, would be unearthed in the Wasatch Mountains nine days later. Laura Aimee, 17, joined the missing list in Orem on October 31 while walking home in costume from a Halloween party. A month would pass before her battered, violated body was discovered in a wooded area outside of town. A man attempted to abduct attractive Carol Da Ronch from a Salt Lake City shopping mall on November 8, but she was able to escape before he could attach a pair of handcuffs to her wrists. That evening, 17-year-old Debbie Kent was kidnapped from the auditorium at Salt Lake City's Viewmont High School.

Authorities in Utah kept communications open with police in other states, including Washington. They might have noticed that a suspect from Seattle, one Ted Bundy, was attending school in Utah when the local disappearances occurred, but they were looking for a madman rather than a sober, well-groomed student of the law who seemed to have political connections in Seattle. Bundy stayed on file and was again forgotten.

With the new year, Colorado joined the list of hunting grounds for an elusive killer who apparently selected victims by their hairstyles. Caryn Campbell, 23, was the first to vanish, from a ski lodge at Snowmass on January 12; her raped and battered body would be found on February 17. On March 15, 26-year-old Julie Cunningham disappeared en route to a tavern in Vail. One month later to the day, 18-year-old Melanie Cooley went missing while riding her bicycle in Nederland; she was discovered eight days later, dead, her skull crushed, with her jeans pulled down around her ankles. On July 1, 24-year-old Shelly Robertson was added to the missing list in Golden; her remains were found on August 23, discarded in a mine shaft near the Berthoud Pass.

A week before the final grim discovery, Ted Bundy was arrested in Salt Lake City for suspicion of burglary. Erratic driving had attracted the attention of police, and an examination of his car revealed peculiar items such as handcuffs and a pair of pantyhose with eyeholes cut to form a stocking mask. The glove compartment yielded gasoline receipts and maps that linked the suspect to a list of Colorado ski resorts, including Vail and Snowmass. Carol Da Ronch identified Ted Bundy as the man who had attacked her in November, and her testimony was sufficient to convict him on a charge of attempted kidnapping. Other states were waiting for a shot at Bundy now, and in January 1977 he was extradited to Colorado for trial in the murder of Caryn Campbell at Snowmass.

Faced with prison time already, Bundy had no patience with the notion of another trial. He fled from custody in June and was recaptured after eight days on the road. On December 20 he tried again, with more success, escaping all the way to Tallahassee, Florida, where he found lodgings on the outskirts of Florida State University. Suspected in a score of deaths already, Bundy had secured himself a new hunting ground.

In the small hours of January 15, 1978, he invaded the Chi Omega sorority house, dressed all in black and armed with a heavy wooden club. Before he left, two women had been raped and killed, a third severely injured from the blows he rained upon her head. Within the hour, he had slipped into another house, just blocks away, to club another victim in her bed. She, too, survived. Detectives at the Chi Omega house discovered bite marks on the corpses of 20-year-old Lisa Levy and 21-year-old Margaret Bowman, appalling evidence of Bundy's fervor at the moment of the kill.

On February 6, Ted stole a van and drove to Jacksonville, where he was spotted in the act of trying to abduct a schoolgirl. Three days later, 12-year-old Kimberly Leach disappeared from a schoolyard nearby; she was found in the first week of April, her body discovered near Suwanee State Park.

Police in Pensacola spotted Bundy's stolen license plates on February 15 and were forced to run him down as he attempted to escape on foot. Once Bundy was identified, impressions from his teeth were taken to compare with bite marks on the Chi Omega victims, and his fate was sealed. Convicted on two counts of murder in July 1979, he was sentenced to die in Florida's electric chair. A third conviction and death sentence was subsequently obtained in the case of Kimberly Leach.

It would take almost a decade to see justice done. Ted stalled his execution with repeated frivolous appeals that went as far as the US Supreme Court in Washington. Between legal maneuvers, he passed time with media interviews, jailhouse small talk with fellow sadis GERARD SCHAEFER, and brief consultation with Washington authorities on the still unsolved case of the "GREEN RIVER KILLER." Ted's luck and life ran out on January 24, 1989, when he was executed in the state of Florida. Before his execution, Bundy confessed to 20 or 30 murders (published reports vary). The earliest murder admitted by Bundy was that of an unidentified hitchhiker killed near Olympia, Washington, in May 1973. Two years later, Bundy said, he had killed 12-year-old Lynette Culver, abducted from a junior high school in Pocatello, Idaho.

In addition to those named above, authorities believe him responsible for at least seven other murders, committed between 1973 and 1975. Victims in those cases include: 17-year-old Rita Jolly, from Clackamas County, Oregon; Vicki Hollar, 24, from Eugene; 14-year-old Katherine Devine, of Seattle; Brenda Baker, another Seattle 14-year-old; Nancy Baird, 21, from Farmington, Utah; 17-year-old Sandra Weaver, killed in Utah; and yet another Utah victim, 17-year-old Sue Curtis. Some investigators believe Bundy may have killed 100 or more victims in all, perhaps beginning when he was an adolescent, but evidence is sparse to nonexistent in those cases. Bundy took the secret to his grave.

BUNTING, Jon   *See* SNOWTOWN

BUONO, Angelo   *See* BIANCHI, KENNETH

CANNIBALISM and Serial Murder

Throughout history, many cultures have sanctioned and ritualized the consumption of human flesh, but cannibalism is generally banned today, since its practice requires either homicide or desecration of corpses (a criminal offense in most American jurisdictions). Still, as bizarre as it seems in modern society, cannibalism is not particularly rare among serial killers, particularly those driven by sexual or sadistic MOTIVES.

Indeed, it has always been so. In ancient Mexico, where Aztecs sacrificed and cannibalized an estimated 15,000 victims yearly, Emperor Moctezuma was said to prefer dining on the same young boys he chose to share his bed. Cannibal killer ALBERT FISH also preferred the flesh of children, while California's EDMUND KEMPER devoured parts of at least two female victims, later terming the act a means of "possessing" them forever. The "CHICAGO RIPPERS," four young Satanists, habitually severed and devoured the breasts of women they abducted, raped, and killed.

Cannibalism is not always a sexual act. For some, it may be a survival technique. Millions starved to death in Russia during the 1930s while Josef Stalin communized the nation's agricultural system, and the tragedy was repeated 20 years later under Mao Zedong in the People's Republic of China. In both countries, many cases of cannibalism were reported (including parents who devoured their own children), but authorities responded in very different ways. Soviet officials executed an unknown number of cannibals, while sentencing some 350 others to life imprisonment; Chinese leaders, on the other hand, sometimes applauded acts of homicide and cannibalism, especially where the victims were members of the "reactionary" old guard. In Russia, at least one case of serial murder and cannibalism was also reported from Leningrad during the long Nazi siege, but details are elusive thanks to Soviet censorship. (Perhaps significantly, Russian slayer ANDREI CHIKATILO blamed his own forays into cannibalism on childhood stories concerning his older brother, allegedly murdered and eaten during the famine of the 1930s.)

There is at least one case on record of serial murder and cannibalism committed as acts of revenge. Embittered at the murder of his wife by members of the Crow Indian tribe, trapper John Johnston waged a ruthless vendetta in the Colorado Rockies, killing scores of tribesmen and devouring their still-warm livers, raw, as a gesture of contempt. When Hollywood tackled his story a century later, handsome Robert Redford took the lead as *Jeremiah Johnson*, a romantic hero, with no trace of "Liver-eating Johnston" to be found on-screen.

Reports of cannibalism flourished in the 1990s, perhaps because of the subject's sensational nature. In October 1997, Ugandan police arrested Ssande Sserwadda, accused by his wife of cannibalism. In custody, Sserwadda freely admitted the charge, reporting that he learned the practice from his parents. He told the court, "We are a family of cannibals, we always have been, and I feel queasy if I go too long without tasting human meat. But just because we like to eat human flesh, does that mean we're bad people?" Sserwadda admitted eating seven corpses in the past year, then added that his brother "is the really greedy one. He's eaten dozens." Presuming that Sserwadda dined on corpses without committing murder, the court sentenced him to three years in prison. He shocked the judge by asking if he could take a human leg, introduced as evidence at trial in 2001, to prison with him for a snack. "It's still got plenty of meat on it. It's a shame to let it go to waste."

In Nigeria, authorities jailed two alleged cannibals at Lagos, in February 1999. The suspects, identified as Clifford Orji and Tahiru, lived beneath a local bridge and were accused by neighbors of supplying human organs to black-magic practitioners. Raiders found the pair grilling parts of a fresh corpse, and seized the flesh and various bones as evidence. A police spokesman accused Orji and Tahiru of murdering women, and claimed they preferred "young, fine girls with long hair." No disposition for that case was available at press time, but new reports of widespread cannibalism emerged from the neighboring Congo region in 2003. There, dwindling tribes of pygmies complained to the United Nations that rural guerrillas regularly killed and devoured members of their race, driving their people toward extinction. Reports published in Europe, during August 2003, described mobile armies of "child soldiers" dragooned by their elders to fight in a long-running civil war, subsisting on flesh from their slain enemies as they prowled the countryside.

Modern Asia has no shortage of cannibalism reports. In January 2001, Western journalists revealed that human flesh (dubbed *saram hoki*) was sold in the marketplace at famine-blighted Hoeroung, North Korea. Films and photographs supported the claim, depicting parts of a dismembered child in one cooking pot. Reporter Carla Garapedian told the world, "All of the North Koreans we interviewed knew about it." North Korean officials declined to comment. A year later, in March 2002, authorities in Hyderabad, India, alleged that members of "a nameless sect" consumed human flesh as part of a *puja* ritual designed to help them find hidden treasure. No charges were filed in that case, but several alleged cannibals were reportedly slain by their neighbors on suspicion of practicing evil magic.

Eastern Europe has produced its share of cannibals in recent years. Ilshat Kuzikov, a 37-year-old resident of St. Petersburg, Russia, was convicted in March 1997 of killing and devouring at least three male acquaintances since 1992. Officers who raided his home found dried ears hanging on the walls and soft-drink bottles filled with human blood. Four years later, in April 2001, authorities in Chisinau, Moldova, arrested two women for selling human organs in the city's marketplace. A full-scale investigation was announced, but its results are presently unknown. Four Ukrainians were jailed at Kiev in July 2002, charged with killing a teenage girl and devouring her body. Police claimed that the prisoners, including three men and a woman, had killed at least six victims for their flesh. The latest kidnapping

had also involved an abortive $3,000 ransom demand. Detectives found "several books on black magic" at one suspect's home, suggesting that the murders sprang from Satanism. Once again, no disposition of the case has been reported.

Across the Atlantic, accused cannibal Dorangel Vargas was arrested by police in San Cristóbal, Venezuela, in February 1999. A former mental patient who was briefly held on similar charges in 1995, Vargas confessed to murdering and eating 10 men over the past two years. "Sure I eat people," he told reporters. "Anyone can eat human flesh, but you have to wash and garnish it well to avoid diseases." Notwithstanding those admissions and the reported discovery of human remains at his home, some observers defended Vargas as a hapless "scapegoat," allegedly framed by illicit organ-traffickers. No judgment in the Vargas case had been announced by press time for this volume.

On April 14, 2001, police in Kansas City, Kansas, charged 21-year-old Marc Sappington with murdering and cannibalizing three men over the past week. Dismembered remains of one victim, 16-year-old Alton Brown, were found in Sappington's basement. Held in lieu of $2 million bond, Sappington was examined for psychiatric abnormalities by analysts who reported his fascination with Milwaukee cannibal-killer JEFFREY DAHMER. After being certified as sane, Sappington faced trial in July 2004. Jurors convicted him across the board, on three counts of murder plus one count each of kidnapping and aggravated burglary.

In 2004, European authorities announced their discovery of an Internet cannibal network that "links maneaters from Austria to America." That revelation emerged from the murder trial of German defendant Armin Meiwes, a cannibal who advertised online for a "young well-built man who wants to be eaten" and thus met Bernd-Jurgen Brandes, whom he killed and devoured in 2001. Defense attorneys for Meiwes submitted that he should be freed because Brandes volunteered to be slain and consumed. Jurors convicted Meiwes on a reduced charge of manslaughter, sending him to prison for eight and a half years, but police were more concerned with evidence that two more victims may have been eaten in Europe. German criminologist Rudolf Egg told reporters, "There are several hundred people with cannibalistic tendencies in Germany alone, and many thousands around the world." Inspector Isolde Stock announced that Meiwes's e-mail correspondence with members of various "cannibal forums" would fill two large trucks if it were printed out. The haul included several thousand photos of nude men, downloaded from the prisoner's computers, in addition to scenes of torture.

See also JOACHIM KROLL; PARAPHILIA; VAMPIRISM

CAPITAL Punishment and Serial Killers

Always controversial in America, imposition of the death penalty for murder (or other serious crimes) remains a constant point of heated debate. Serial killers, whose multiple murders frequently incorporate brutal torture and sexual assault, are often described as "poster children" for capital punishment, but abolitionists would spare all felons, without regard to the nature or number of their crimes. Arguments range from the moral ("All killing is wrong"; "All lives are precious") to the economic ("Life imprisonment is cheaper than lengthy death-sentence appeals"), but results of every published poll to date suggest that a majority of those surveyed support execution in cases of first-degree (premeditated) murder.

The 1960s saw a sharp decline in American executions, with seven inmates executed in 1965 (down from 152 in 1947), and only one in 1967. No more had been dispatched by 1972, when the US Supreme Court ruled that all American death penalty statutes, as currently written, were unconstitutional under the Eighth Amendment's ban on cruel and unusual punishment. Across the country, 648 condemned inmates—including such notorious serial killers as Richard Speck and six members of the MANSON FAMILY—saw their sentences commuted overnight to life imprisonment with possible parole (though few of the repeat offenders have been freed to date). By 1976, a groundswell of public opinion induced the high court to revise its opinion, permitting execution in the case of certain felonies specifically defined by law. Multiple murder (or murder accompanied by torture and/or sexual assault) is among those crimes authorized for capital punishment in all 38 death-penalty states. Texas was the first state to specifically list serial murder as a capital offense.

The first condemned inmate to die in America after a nine-year hiatus in executions was serial slayer Gary Gilmore, shot by a Utah firing squad in January 1977. Between that event and September 2004, at least 81 other serial killers were executed in 19 American states. In retrospect, there seems to be no statistical validity for the abolitionist argument that suicidal slayers migrate to death-penalty states in search of an "easy" death. New York, as a prime example, has consistently ranked among the top five U.S. states in cases of serial murder reported, although the state banned capital punishment for more than 20 years, from 1972 to 1994.

See also GEOGRAPHY

CARIGNAN, Harvey Louis

By all rights, Harvey Carignan should never have become a serial killer. Sentenced in Alaska to be hanged for murdering a woman in 1949, the hulking killer might have been eliminated early on had the judicial system not intervened. An overzealous sheriff had elicited confessions from the suspect with assurances that Carignan would not be executed, a condition that appeals courts found disturbing. Carignan's death sentence was overturned in 1951, and after serving nine more years for attempted rape, he was paroled in 1960. There would be more arrests, for burglary, assault, and other crimes; in 1965, Carignan was sentenced to a term of 15 years in Washington, but with time off for good behavior, he hit the street again in 1969, consumed with an abiding rage against society in general and women in particular.

Harvey married a Seattle widow shortly after his parole, but their relationship was doomed from the beginning. Sullen and uncommunicative, Carignan would frequently get up at night and drive long distances "to be alone and think." When he refused to share his thoughts or name his destinations on the long nocturnal drives, his marriage fell apart. Remarrying another widow in 1972, Carignan showed no improvement. His lascivious attentions to a teenage stepdaughter finally forced the girl to run away from home, and he was faced with yet another failing marriage in the spring of 1973.

That May, young Kathy Miller answered Harvey's advertisement for employees at a service station that he leased. The girl was missing for a month before two boys discovered her remains while hiking on an Indian reservation north of Everett, Washington. Nude and bundled in a sheet of plastic, Kathy had been bludgeoned with a hammer, knocking holes the size of nickels in her skull.

Detectives in Seattle were aware of Harvey's record, and they hounded him with such intensity that he departed from their city shortly after Kathy Miller's body was discovered. Later a speeding ticket from Solano County, California, on June 20 placed Carignan in the vicinity where a half-dozen women had been murdered in the past two years, but there was nothing solid to connect him with the crimes, and he continued on his way cross-country, seeking sanctuary in his old, familiar haunts in Minneapolis.

On June 28, Marlys Townsend was assaulted at a bus stop in that city, clubbed unconscious from behind. She woke in Harvey's car, still groggy from the blow, but when he tried to make her masturbate him, she found strength enough to save herself by leaping from the speeding vehicle. Police made no connection with the human time bomb ticking in their midst.

Jewry Billings, age 13, was thumbing a ride to her boyfriend's house in Seattle on September 9 when Carignan pulled up and offered her a ride. Inside the car, he threatened Jewry with a hammer and forced her to perform sexual acts on him while he assaulted her with the hammer's handle. When he finished with her, Carignan released his battered captive, but the incident was so humiliating that the girl maintained it as a closely guarded secret for a period of several months.

A year would pass before detectives witnessed Harvey's handiwork again. On September 8, 1974, he picked up Lisa King and June Lynch, both 16, while they were hitching rides in Minneapolis. He offered money if the girls would help him fetch another car that had been stranded in a rural area. Once out of town, however, Harvey stopped the car and started beating June about the head and face. When Lisa ran for help, he sped away and left his latest victim bleeding on the roadside.

A month before, on August 10, another romance had collapsed for Harvey, ending no less tragically for his intended. Eileen Hunley was a woman of the church who looked for good in others. She had looked for good in Harvey Carignan when they began to date, but there was none to be found. She had informed her friends of her intent to terminate the sour relationship, but Eileen Hunley disappeared on August 10. Her corpse was found in Shelbourne County five weeks later, her skull imploded by the force of savage hammer blows.

An engine failure on September 14 almost cost Gwen Burton her life. When Harvey Carignan appeared to offer her a ride, she had no inkling that the trip would turn into a waking nightmare. Once they were alone, he ripped her clothing, choked her into semiconsciousness, and raped her with his hammer, finally slamming her across the skull before he dumped her in a field to die. Miraculously, she survived and crawled to a nearby highway, where a passing motorist arrived in time to save her life.

On September 18—the same day Eileen Hunley's body was recovered—Harvey picked up Sally Versoi and Diane Flynn. He used the old ruse about fetching another car, then began to make lewd propositions, assaulting both girls when they failed to respond on command. They escaped when he ran short of fuel and was forced to stop at a rural service station.

Two days later, 18-year-old Kathy Schultz did not return on schedule from her college classes, and a missing-person bulletin was issued by police. Her corpse was found next day, by hunters, in a cornfield forty miles from Minneapolis. As in the other cases, Kathy's skull had been destroyed by crushing hammer blows.

Police in Minneapolis were talking to their counterparts in Washington by now, and within days, survivors started picking Harvey out of lineups as the man who had abducted and assaulted them throughout the past two years. A search of his possessions turned up maps with some 181 red circles drawn in isolated areas of the United States and Canada. Some of the circles yielded nothing, others indicating points where Harvey had applied for jobs or purchased vehicles, but others seemed to link him with a string of unsolved homicides and other crimes involving women. One such cryptic circle marked the point where Laura Brock had disappeared, near Coupeville, Washington. Another, at Medora, North Dakota, coincided with discovery of a murdered girl in April 1973. Yet another had been drawn around the very intersection in Vancouver where a woman, waiting for a city bus, had been assaulted from behind and beaten with a hammer.

An ill-conceived INSANITY DEFENSE involving messages from God did not impress the jury at Carignan's trial for attempted murder (of Gwen Burton) in March 1975. He was convicted and received the maximum of 40 years in prison. Since no criminal in Minnesota may be sentenced to a term exceeding 40 years, the other trials and sentences were merely window dressing: 30 years for the assault of Jewry Billings; 40 years for Eileen Hunley's murder; 40 years for killing Kathy Schultz. One hundred fifty years in all, of which the killer may be forced to serve no more than 40, with the usual potential for time off for "good behavior."

CATOE, Jarvis R.

At 6:00 A.M. on August 4, 1941, 26-year-old Evelyn Anderson left her home in the Bronx, walking to her job as a waitress in a nearby restaurant. She never punched the clock that day, and it was 9:00 P.M. before her lifeless body was discovered in an alley off Jerome Avenue. She had been strangled by a powerful assailant, marks of fingernails embedded in her throat, but she had not been sexually abused.

A few days later, Anderson's watch was recovered from a New York City pawnshop, hocked by one Charles Woolfolk. Under questioning, Woolfolk swore that he received the watch from a lady friend, Hazel Johnson, who in turn pointed an accusing finger at suspect Mandy Reid. Hauled in for interrogation, Reid said she got Anderson's handbag—containing the watch—from her friend Jarvis Catoe, a resident of Washington, D.C. A background check on Catoe revealed two arrests for indecent exposure in 1935, after which he worked part-time as a taxi driver, supplementing his income by selling information as a police informant.

Catoe, a 36-year-old black man, was arrested by authorities in Washington. On August 29, he confessed to the murders of seven women in Washington and one in New York City; four others had been raped but left alive, and he reportedly had failed in efforts to abduct

Jarvis Roosevelt Catoe confesses to strangling 10 women with "these hands." (Wide World API)

two more. Another slaying in the District of Columbia was added to the list on September 1. Corroborating his confession, Catoe told police where they could find one victim's lost umbrella, and he knew that 20 dollars had been stolen in another case—a fact known only to detectives, members of the victim's family, and her killer.

Catoe named Evelyn Anderson as his New York victim, but the rampage had started years earlier in Washington. Florence Darcy was the first to die, raped and strangled in 1935, but the case had been "closed" a year later with the conviction of an innocent man. Josephine Robinson was next, murdered on December 1, 1939. Lucy Kidwell and Mattie Steward were killed two months apart in September and November 1940. Ada Puller was the first victim of 1941, murdered on January 2.

Thus far, all of Catoe's victims had been black, but things heated up for Washington police, when the strangler shifted to Caucasian prey. Rose Abramovitz, a bride of one month, hired Catoe to wax some floors on March 8 and was murdered for her trouble, left sprawled across her bed while Catoe scooped up 20 dollars and escaped.

It rained in Washington on June 15, and Jesse Strieff, a pretty secretary at the War Department, was relieved when Catoe stopped to offer her a lift. Mistaking his car for a taxi, she climbed in and was driven to a nearby garage, where Catoe raped and strangled her, hiding her umbrella and stuffing her clothes in a trash bin. Strieff's nude body was discarded in another garage, 10 blocks away, her death provoking congressional investigations and a personnel shakeup in the Washington Police Department. Still, the case remained unsolved until Catoe got careless in New York.

At once, police from several eastern jurisdictions sought to question Catoe in a string of unsolved murders. Officers from Lynn, Massachusetts, suspected a connection with a homicide recorded in July of 1941, and detectives in Garden City, Long Island, were curious about the death of a patrolman in 1940. Authorities from Hamilton Township, New Jersey, questioned Catoe about a series of shotgun murders, between 1938 and 1940, later cleared with the arrest of Clarence Hill. Spokesmen for the NYPD requested that Catoe be questioned about the February 1940 strangulation death of Helen Foster. For all the circus atmosphere, the final tally stands, as far as anyone can tell, at nine murdered women.

Brought to trial in late October 1941, for killing Rose Abramovitz, Catoe sought to recant his confessions, claiming that police had tortured him while he was "sick and weak." A jury failed to buy the act, deliberating only 18 minutes before returning a verdict of guilty, with a recommendation of death. Catoe was executed in the capital's electric chair on January 15, 1943.

"CHICAGO Rippers"

It was a case with all the grisly melodrama of a Hollywood production. A serial slayer, predictably dubbed "Jack the Ripper" by newsmen, was stalking young women in Chicago and environs, discarding their mutilated corpses like cast-off rubbish. Homicide detectives had no inkling of the killer's motive or identity; they couldn't even manage to agree upon a final body count. The speculation published daily in Chicago's press was bad enough; the truth, when finally exposed, was infinitely worse.

On May 23, 1981, 28-year-old Linda Sutton was abducted by persons unknown from Elmhurst, a Chicago suburb. Ten days later, her mutilated body— the left breast missing—was recovered from a field in Villa Park, adjacent to the Rip Van Winkle Motel. The evidence suggested Sutton had been kidnapped by a sadist, but police had no solid clues to his identity.

A year passed before the next acknowledged victim in the series disappeared. On May 15, 1982, 21-year-old Lorraine Borowski was scheduled to open the Elmhurst realtor's office where she worked. Employees turning up for work that morning found the office locked, Borowski's shoes and scattered contents from her handbag strewn outside the door. Police were called at once, but five more months elapsed before Borowski's corpse was found, on October 10, in a cemetery south of Villa Park. Advanced decomposition left the cause of death a mystery.

Two weeks later, on May 29, Shui Mak was reported missing from Hanover Park, in Cook County, her mutilated body recovered at Barrington on September 30. On June 13, prostitute Angel York was picked up by a "john" in a van, handcuffed, her breast slashed open before she was dumped alive on the roadside. Descriptions of her attacker had taken police nowhere by August 28, when teenage hooker Sandra Delaware was found stabbed and strangled to death on the bank of the Chicago River, her left breast neatly amputated. Rose Davis, age 30, was in identical condition when police found her corpse in a Chicago alley on September 8. Three days later, 42-year-old Carole Pappas, wife of a Chicago Cubs pitcher, vanished without a trace from a department store in nearby Wheaton, Illinois.

Detectives got the break they had been waiting for on October 6. That morning, prostitute Beverly Washington, age 20, was found nude and savaged beside a Chicago railroad track. Her left breast was nearly severed the right deeply slashed, but she was breathing, and emergency surgery saved her life. Hours later, in a seemingly unrelated incident, drug dealer Rafael Torado was killed, and a male companion wounded when the occupants of a cruising van peppered a street-corner phone booth with gunfire.

Two weeks later, on October 20, police arrested unemployed carpenter Robin Gecht, a 28-year-old former employee of contractor JOHN GACY, and charged him with the cruel assault on Beverly Washington. Also suspected of slashing prostitute Cynthia Smith before she escaped from his van, Gecht was an odd character, once accused of molesting his own younger sister.

Authorities immediately linked him to the "Ripper" slayings, but they had no proof, and he made bail on October 26.

Meanwhile, detectives had learned that Gecht was one of four men who had rented adjoining rooms at Villa Park's Rip Van Winkle Motel several months before Linda Sutton was murdered nearby. The manager remembered them as party animals, frequently bringing women to their rooms, and he surprised investigators with one further bit of information. The men had been "some kind of cultists," perhaps devil worshipers.

Two of the Rip Van Winkle tenants, brothers Andrew and Thomas Kokoraleis, had left a forwarding address for any mail they might receive. Police found 23-year-old Thomas at home when they called, and his inconsistent answers earned him a trip downtown. The suspect promptly failed a polygraph examination, cracking under stiff interrogation to describe the "satanic chapel" in Gecht's upstairs bedroom, where captive women were tortured with knives and ice picks, gang-raped, and finally sacrificed to Satan by members of a tiny cult including Gecht, the Kokoraleis brothers, and 23-year-old Edward Spreitzer. As described by the prisoner, cultic rituals included severing one or both breasts with a thin wire garrote, each celebrant "taking communion" by eating a piece before the relic was consigned to Gecht's trophy box. At one point, Kokoraleis told detectives, he had counted 15 breasts inside the box. Some other victims had been murdered at the Rip Van Winkle, out in Villa Park. He picked a snapshot of Lorraine Borowski as a woman he had picked up, with his brother, for a one-way ride to the motel.

Robin Gecht (Author's collection)

Andrew Kokoraleis (Author's collection)

Edward Spreitzer (Author's collection)

Police had heard enough. Armed with search and arrest warrants, they swept up Robin Gecht, Ed Spreitzer, and 20-year-old Andrew Kokoraleis on November 5, lodging them in jail under $1 million bond. A search of Gecht's apartment revealed the satanic chapel described by Tom Kokoraleis, and lawmen came away with a rifle matched to the recent Torado shooting. Satanic literature was also retrieved from the apartment occupied by Andrew Kokoraleis. With their suspects in custody, authorities speculated that the gang might have murdered 18 women in as many months.

Tom Kokoraleis was charged with the slaying of Linda Borowski on November 12 and formally indicted by a grand jury two days later. Brother Andrew and Edward Spreitzer were charged on November 14 with the rape and murder of victim Rose Davis. When the mangled body of 22-year-old Susan Baker was found on November 16 at a site where previous victims had been discarded, police worried that other cult members might still be at large. No charges were filed in that case, however, and authorities now connect Baker's death to her background of drug and prostitution arrests in several states.

Facing multiple charges of rape, attempted murder, and aggravated battery, Robin Gecht was found mentally competent for trial on March 2, 1983. His trial opened on September 20, and Gecht took the witness stand next day, confessing the attack on Beverly Washington. Convicted on all counts, he received a sentence of 120 years in prison.

Tom Kokoraleis had suffered a change of heart since confessing to murder, attorneys seeking to block the reading of his statements at forthcoming trials, but on December 4, 1983, the confessions were admitted as evidence. Four months later, on April 2, 1984, Ed Spreitzer pled guilty on four counts of murder, including victims Davis, Delaware, Mak, and Torado. Sentenced to life on each count, he received additional time on conviction for charges of rape, deviant sexual assault, and attempted murder.

On February 6, 1985, a statement from Andrew Kokoraleis was read to jury in his trial for the Rose Davis murder. In his confession, the defendant admitted he was "cruising" with fellow cultists Gecht and Spreitzer when they kidnapped Davis, with Andrew stabbing her several times in the process. Convicted on February 11, he received a death sentence on March 18, 1985. Kokoraleis was executed by lethal injection on March 16, 1999.

On March 4, 1986, Edward Spreitzer was convicted of murdering Linda Sutton and formally sentenced to death on March 20. Authorities declared that Spreitzer had agreed to testify against Gecht in that case, but no further charges have been filed to date in Chicago's grim series of cannibal murders.

CHIKATILO, Andrei Romanovich

A native of the Ukraine, born October 16, 1936, Andrei Chikatiko was a late-blooming serial killer who traced his crimes back to early childhood. His family had suffered greatly during Joseph Stalin's forced collectivization in the 1930s, Chikatilo said. Apart from knowing poverty and hunger, he had lost an older brother, allegedly murdered and cannibalized by neighbors during the famine that claimed millions of Russian lives. Whether the tale was true or not, young Andrei's mother drilled it into him with frequent repetition, and his later deeds would replicate the act.

While most serial murderers kill for the first time in their teens or early twenties, Chikatilo was a slow starter. With a university degree, a wife and two children, he presented the appearance of a meek family man, but dark urges were brewing behind that pacific facade. Employed as a school dormitory supervisor, Chikatilo was fired over allegations that he had molested male students. A new job, as a factory supply clerk in Rostov-on-Don, required frequent travel by bus or train, and Chikatilo turned the circumstance to his advantage, trolling for victims in bus depots and railway stations.

The self-described "mad beast" and "mistake of nature" committed his first murder on December 22, 1978, in the town of Shakhty. The body of his victim, a nine-year-old girl whom Chikatilo strangled, raped, and stabbed repeatedly, was pulled from the Grushevka River days later. Chikatilo was one of many suspects questioned in the case, but police soon focused on 25-year-old Alexander Kravchenko, an ex-convict who had served time for murder and rape. In custody, Kravchenko was beaten by police until he confessed, whereupon he was sentenced to death and shot by a firing squad. The "solution" looked good on paper, but it naturally failed to deter the real killer from striking again.

The terror began in earnest nearly three years later, in September 1981. Over the next nine years, dozens of corpses would be found in wooded areas adjacent to train or bus depots, grossly mutilated by a phantom who was quickly dubbed the "Rostov Ripper." The victims included young women and children of both sexes, raped and stabbed repeatedly in a pattern of grisly overkill. Some victims had their tongues bitten off; others were disemboweled, sometimes with organs missing that suggested the killer might be indulging in CANNIBALISM. (Chikatilo later confessed to occasionally nibbling on internal organs but denied consuming human flesh.) Repeated stab wounds to the face were a specific trademark of the killer, but the mutilations he inflicted otherwise appeared to follow no set pattern.

Chikatilo may have come late to the murder game, but he was making up for lost time. At the peak of his

Andrei Chikatilo at trial (Author's collection)

homicidal frenzy, in 1984, eight victims were found in the month of August alone. Chikatilo was held for questioning again that year and released for lack of evidence after Communist officials intervened on his behalf, lamenting the "persecution" of a loyal party member.

It would take another six years, with some 25,000 suspects interrogated, before police came back to Chikatilo a third time and finally bagged their killer. Part of the problem was communist mythology, maintaining that such "decadent Western crimes" as serial murder never occurred in a "people's republic." State censorship forbade police from broadcasting descriptions of their suspect—or even admitting his crimes had occurred—and homicide investigators were thus reduced to the same cloak-and-dagger routine that had retarded investigation of earlier, similar cases. Propaganda aside, however, there seemed to be mayhem aplenty in Rostov-on-Don: before it ended, the Ripper investigation would disclose 95 additional murders and 245 rapes committed by *other* human predators in the district.

Chikatilo finally ran out of luck in November 1990, when he was spotted in a Rostov railway station, sporting bloodstains on his face and hand. While he was not arrested at the time, his name was taken down, and the discovery of another victim near the depot two weeks later prompted his arrest on November 20. After eight days of interrogation, Chikatilo confessed a total of 55 murders, leading police to several corpses they had not discovered yet. His recitation of atrocities—illustrated by demonstration on mannequins—included sadistic mutilation of several victims while they were still alive.

Charged with 53 counts of murder, Chikatilo went on trial in June 1992; four months later, on October 15, he was convicted on all but one count and sentenced to death. A last-minute appeal for clemency was rejected by President Boris Yeltsin in February 15, 1994, and Chikatilo was executed that same day, with a pistol shot to the back of his head. Alexander Kravchenko, meanwhile, was posthumously pardoned for the slaying of Chikatilo's original victim.

CHILDHOOD Trauma as Precursor of Serial Murder

Before physicians can eradicate a plague, the sources of contagion must be recognized and understood. The same is true of aberrant behavior on the part of human beings. There can be no cure without a recognition of the cause. What prompts a man or woman to adopt a predatory lifestyle, stalking human prey for motives that may be incomprehensible to others? Are such monsters born complete with killer instincts, "BAD SEEDS" with an insatiable genetic taste for blood, or are they shaped and educated over time? If we determine how such predators are made, can we disrupt the process soon enough to save their lives and those they will eventually destroy?

It is unusual for psychiatric "experts" to agree on anything beyond vague generalities, but a review of current literature suggests resounding unanimity on the significance of early childhood to the physical and mental health of an adult. The crucial element is variously labeled "bonding" or "attachment" and refers to the emotional connection formed between an infant and its parents, starting virtually from the moment of its birth. That bonding is achieved by stages, and while experts disagree on how much time is needed to complete the process—published estimates range from two weeks to six years—all agree that disruption of bonding may produce a child (or an adult) incapable of feeling sympathy, affection, or remorse. As pediatrician Selma Fraiberg writes in *Every Child's Birthright* (1977), "If we take the evidence seriously, we must look upon a baby deprived of human partners as a baby in deadly peril. These are babies being robbed of their humanity."

In the worst-case scenario, detachment may produce an individual suffering from antisocial personality disorder (APD). Once commonly described as "psychopaths," such individuals are now more often labeled "sociopaths," to distinguish their affliction from the separate—and more severe—condition of psychosis. In essence, while there are degrees of relative severity in APD, its victims are essentially devoid of conscience: they are chronic liars, cheats, and thieves, self-centered, frequently incapable of empathy with other human beings. Some "adjust" and manage to live out their lives behind what one psychiatrist has called a "MASK OF SANITY"—as "crafty" businessmen, "slick" politicians, and the like. For others, though, the lies and petty thefts of childhood lead to lifelong criminal careers, and some of those are little more than brutal predators in human form.

In some cases, trauma begins in the womb, with critical damage incurred by a fetus from the moment of conception. Malnutrition during pregnancy, for instance, may result in abnormal brain development, with teenage mothers especially at risk. Likewise, maternal alcoholism or drug abuse is another hazard to fetal development; recent studies suggest that habitual used of cocaine may also damage the genetic code of sperm. Physical birth defects aside, the children of alcoholics and addicts are likely to enter the world with damaged brains or nervous systems, limiting the child's—and future adult's—ability to control violent, impulsive behavior. Indeed, it appears from modern studies that even an unwanted or unhappy pregnancy, without physical damage, may jeopardize the future of an unborn child, as maternal anxiety results in secretion of hormones detrimental to the fetus.

Environment kicks in at the moment of delivery, and nothing breaks the childhood bonding cycle quite like parental abandonment. As noted by author John Bowlby (*The Making and Breaking of Affectional Bonds* [1979]), "In psychopaths the incidence of illegitimacy and the shunting of the child from one 'home' to another is high. It is no accident that [Ian] Brady of the 'Moors' murders was such a one."

That said, the children given up to foster care or the adoption system may be luckier than some who stay at home. Dysfunctional families are potential crucibles of crime, as indicated by the FBI's three-year study of 36 sexually motivated killers, including 29 with multiple victims. When the Bureau's sampling of killers were quizzed on their family backgrounds, 69 percent reported histories of alcohol abuse, 53 percent listed relatives with psychiatric problems, 50 percent noted criminal histories, 46 percent admitted family sexual problems, and 33 percent detailed histories of familial drug abuse. The FBI study points out certain common factors in the killers' early lives, including: (1) trauma, often in the form of physical or sexual abuse; (2) developmental failure stemming from that trauma; and (3) interpersonal failure on the part of caretaking adults to serve as positive role models for the child.

Some childhood trauma may be accidental, and various serial killers report childhood histories of severe head injury. More often than not, however, the damage suffered by future criminals is deliberately inflicted during their formative years. When the FBI quizzed its sampling of captive murderers, 42 percent reported incidents of physical abuse in childhood, while 74 percent harbored memories of psychological abuse; 43 percent of those surveyed reported incidents of sexual abuse; and 28 percent had medical histories of sexual injury or disease. An overwhelming 73 percent reported childhood involvement in unspecified "sexually stressful events." In that context, it is curious—perhaps instructive—to note that at least seven male serial killers are known to have been dressed as girls during childhood by their parents or adult caretakers. Two of those—HENRY LUCAS and CHARLES MANSON—were actually sent to school in dresses as a bizarre form of "lesson" or punishment.

Childhood abuse frequently results in social isolation, learning disabilities (47 percent of the FBI's surveyed killers were high-school dropouts), symptoms of neurological impairment (29 percent suffered persistent headaches; 19 percent were subject to seizures), problems with authority or self-control, precocious or bizarre sexual activity, substance abuse, even self-destructive behavior. Overall, the recurring theme of childhood abuse and trauma among criminals—and "recreational killers" in particular—serves as persuasive evidence that serial murderers are made, not born.

CHRISTIE, John Reginald Halliday

Yorkshire-born in April 1898, John Christie endured a stern childhood, with little or no visible affection from his parents. Developing chronic hypochondria in a bid for attention, he also ran afoul of police as a juvenile, resulting in beatings at home. Christie left school at 15 to become a police clerk but was fired for petty theft. Next, he went to work in his father's carpet factory but was caught stealing again and banished from home.

Wounded and gassed in World War I, Christie was blind for five months and suffered hysterical loss of his voice spanning three and a half years. Marriage, in 1920, seemed to hold his bad luck at bay for a time, but in 1934 Christie was struck by an automobile, suffering serious head injuries along with other, lesser wounds. Briefly employed at the post office, he spent seven months in jail for stealing money orders. In 1938,

Christie and his wife moved into a flat at 10 Rillington Place, in London. A year later, he joined the War Reserve Police, earning a bully's reputation for throwing his weight around and punishing neighbors for minor blackout offenses.

Christie's several homicides were all committed in the flat on Rillington Place, with the early crimes occurring in the midst of wartime. His initial victim was Ruth Fuerst, an Austrian immigrant who called on Christie while his wife was visiting relatives. He strangled her while having sex and buried her that evening in his garden. Number two was Muriel Eddy, one of Christie's coworkers at a London radio factory. Stopping by the flat with Christie's wife away, Muriel complained of feeling ill. Her host prescribed a "cure" which consisted of inhaling lethal gas, and Eddy joined Ruth Fuerst in Christie's busy garden.

In late November 1949, a neighbor, illiterate truck driver Timothy Evans, approached police and said, "I would like to give myself up. I have disposed of the body of my wife." Following his directions, police searched the drains below Rillington Place, but in vain. A second visit found the corpse of Beryl Evans in a shed behind the house, together with her strangled infant daughter, Geraldine. (During the search, Christie stood talking with two detectives in his garden, while a dog rooted around their feet and turned up a skull. Christie shooed the animal away and trod the skull back under, with his official visitors none the wiser!)

Upon recovery of the bodies, Evans first confessed to killing both his wife and daughter, later altering his statement to blame Christie. In his second affidavit, the trucker claimed that his wife died during an abortion performed by Christie, after which Christie offered to arrange for the "unofficial adoption" of baby Geraldine. Detectives and a jury chose to believe Christie, described by prosecutors in court as "this perfectly innocent man." Convicted of strangling his daughter only, Evans was sentenced to death and eventually hanged.

By that time, married life was wearing thin for Christie. On the night of December 14, 1952, he strangled his wife with a stocking and wedged her body under the floorboards, afterward claiming that she had suffered spontaneous convulsions and he "could not bear to see her suffer."

With the nuisance of a live-in spouse removed, Christie's murder schedule escalated. On January 2, 1953, he brought home Rita Nelson, a London prostitute, plying her with liquor before he induced her to sit in a deck chair, covered with a canopy, which he had planted above an open gas pipe. When Nelson fell unconscious, Christie strangled her and raped her

corpse before concealing it in a cupboard. The method worked so well that he repeated it with prostitute Kathleen Maloney on January 12 and with Hectorina McLennan on March 3.

Christie left Rillington Place on March 20, 1953, and the new tenants began renovations four days later. They found his cupboard, hidden by a layer of wallpaper, with three female corpses inside. Police responding to the call soon found his wife beneath the floor and unearthed Christie's first two victims in the garden. Searchers found a human femur propping up the fence out back and in the flat a tin was found containing pubic hair removed from four different women. (Curiously, the hair matched none of Christie's known victims.).

Arrested on March 31, Christie soon confessed to the series of murders, contending that Beryl Evans traded sex in return for his help in committing suicide. At his trial, in June, the jury rejected Christie's INSANITY DEFENSE, and he was sentenced to die. He mounted the gallows on July 15, 1953.

CIUDAD JUÁREZ, Mexico: "Serial killer playground"

Ciudad Juárez lies just across the border from El Paso, Texas, in northern Chihuahua. Long recognized as a center of violent crime and a major source of narcotics, the city of 2 million residents emerged during the 1990s as a "serial killers' playground," where women are raped and murdered with alarming frequency. In 2003, the *El Paso Times* reported that "nearly 340" victims had been slain during the past decade, while Amnesty International placed the total at 370. Some cases have been solved, but unnamed "experts" speculate that "90 or more" may be serial murder victims. No one claims a single killer is responsible—in fact, police have jailed more than a dozen suspects—but one fact is uncontested: All females are in danger on the streets of Ciudad Juárez.

The first to die, officially, was Alma Chavira Farel, found beaten, raped, and strangled in the Campestre Virreyes district on January 23, 1993. In fact, she may not have been the year's first victim, since local disappearances exceed known homicides. Still, Chavira remains the first acknowledged victim of a predator whom the media would later dub "the Juárez Ripper" or "El Depredador Psicópata." No mutilations were recorded in Chavira's case, but many subsequent victims suffered "similar" slashing wounds to their breasts. Police acknowledged 16 more murders of women in Ciudad Juárez by year's end, with the last recorded on December 15. That case was solved, along with four others. In the dozen cases still open from 1993, five victims remain unidentified today. Cause of death in those cases includes four strangulations, four stabbings (one stabbing victim was set afire afterward), one beating, and one gunshot. Advanced decomposition ruled out a determination in two other cases.

In 1994, police recorded eight unsolved murders of women in Ciudad Juárez. "Possible culprits" were named in three other cases, but none were arrested. Three of the dead are still unidentified; the others ranged in age from 11 to 35. In cases where the cause of death is known, six were strangled, two stabbed, one bludgeoned, and one burned alive. Before that brutal year ended, criminologist Oscar Maynez Grijalva warned local police that some of their unsolved murders might be the work of a serial killer. Maynez later said that his warning was ignored.

The year 1995 was worse yet, with at least 19 women slain by mid-September. Eight of the victims remain unidentified, with one case solved and "probable suspects" named (but not convicted) in two others. Where cause of death could be determined, six were strangled, one stabbed, and one shot. Three of the four victims found in September presented police with an obvious pattern: On each, the right breast was severed and the left nipple bitten off. It thus appeared that a serial killer was stalking Ciudad Juárez, linked by a similar MODUS OPERANDI to three of the most recent crimes, but authorities were not overly concerned. In October 1995, detectives claimed the case was solved. They had charged a suspect—a foreigner—with one of the city's brutal sex murders.

Abdel Latif Sharif was born in Egypt in 1947. Decades later, he claimed to have been sexually abused as a child, allegedly sodomized by his father and other male relatives. He emigrated to the United States in 1970, settling first in New York City, where he soon established a reputation for drunken promiscuity, fixated on young girls. Fired from his job for suspected embezzlement in 1978, Sharif moved to Pennsylvania. A friend, John Pascoe, recalled a deer-hunting expedition with Sharif, where the Egyptian reportedly wounded a buck and then tortured the dying animal. Pascoe also claimed that girls "often" disappeared in Sharif's company, though none of the alleged victims were identified. Pascoe says he ended the friendship in 1980, after finding various possessions of an unnamed "missing" girl in Sharif's home, and a mud-caked shovel on the porch.

By 1981, Sharif had settled in Palm Beach, Florida, working as a chemist and engineer for Cercoa, Inc. His talents were sufficiently impressive that the company created a department just for him. On May 2, 1981, he took a 23-year-old woman home, beat and raped her repeatedly, then suddenly turned solicitous and drove her to a hospital. Cercoa bankrolled Sharif's defense in

that case, and again in August 1981, when he attacked a second woman in West Palm Beach. Sharif received probation for the first rape and served only 45 days for the second. Cercoa finally fired Sharif in 1982, tired of paying his mounting legal bills.

Resettled in Gainesville, Sharif was married briefly, then divorced after he beat his bride unconscious. He advertised for a live-in housekeeper on March 17, 1983, then beat and repeatedly raped a young woman who answered the ad, telling her, "I will bury you out back in the woods. I've done it before, and I'll do it again." Held without bond pending trial in that case, Sharif escaped from the Alachua County jail in January 1984 but was soon recaptured. On January 31, 1984, Sharif received a 12-year sentence for rape. Prosecutor Gordon Gorland told reporters that on the day Sharif was released he would be "met at the prison gates and escorted to the plane" for deportation to Egypt, but it was an empty promise.

When Sharif was paroled in October 1989, he moved to Midland, Texas, and a job with Benchmark Research and Technology. The U.S. Department of Energy singled him out for praise in his new position, and Sharif was photographed shaking hands with Senator Phil Gramm. News of a 1991 drunk-driving arrest alerted a former acquaintance from Florida, now living in Texas, who reported Sharif to the Border Patrol as a fugitive from deportation proceedings. A long series of hearings ensued, and the matter was still unresolved two years later, when Sharif held a woman captive in his home and repeatedly raped her. Sharif's attorney then offered the government a deal: If the latest charges were dismissed, Sharif would voluntarily leave the United States forever.

Federal prosecutors accepted the bargain, and Sharif moved to Ciudad Juárez in May 1994, working at one of Benchmark's maquiladoras (factory sweatshops producing goods for export, where workers earn an average of five U.S. dollars per day). In October 1995, a young female employee accused Sharif of raping her at his home in the exclusive Rincónes de San Marcos neighborhood. She also said that Sharif had threatened to kill her and dump her corpse in Lote Bravo, a desert region south of town where several other victims had been found. Those charges were later withdrawn, but detectives learned that Sharif had dated 17-year-old Elizabeth Castro García, who was raped and murdered in August 1994. After many delays, Sharif was convicted of that crime in March 1999 and received a 30-year sentence (reduced to 20 years in February 2003, when an appellate court found "problems with the evidence"). Police called him a serial killer, yet his conviction did not solve the grisly mystery of Ciudad Juárez. One month after Sharif's arrest, police acknowledged that 520 locals had vanished in the past 11 months and that "an important percentage of them are female adolescents."

Between Sharif's arrest and the first week of April 1996, at least 14 more victims ranging in age from 10 to 30 were slain in Ciudad Juárez. Where cause of death was known, 10 had been stabbed, one shot, and one strangled. At least four suffered unspecified mutilations after death, and one victim—15-year-old Adrianna Torres—fit the pattern of three other slayings, with her right breast severed and her left nipple bitten off. The ongoing slaughter belied official reports that the city's homicide wave had ended with Abdel Sharif's arrest. Police needed an explanation for the murders, but one that would not exonerate their prime suspect.

They got their wish on April 8, 1996, when 18-year-old Rosario García Leal was found raped and mutilated outside Ciudad Juárez. One suspect questioned in that case was Hector Olivares Villalba, a member of a local street gang called Los Rebeldes ("The Rebels"). In custody, Olivares claimed he had participated in García's murder on December 7, 1995. Half a dozen Rebels were involved, he said, including gang leader Sergio Armendariz Díaz (AKA "El Diablo"). Armed with Olivares's confession (later recanted as a product of police torture), officers raided several nightclubs and detained 300 persons. From that mob, they winnowed out nine Rebels, including Armendariz, Juan Contreras Jurado ("El Grande"), Carlos Hernández Molina, Carlos Barrientos Vidales, Romel Cerniceros García, Fernando Guermes Aguirre, Luis Adrade, Jose Juárez Rosales, and Erika Fierro.

The nine, plus Olivares, were accused of plotting with Abdel Sharif to free him from prison by murdering local women and making it seem like the original "Ripper" was still at large. Police claimed that some of the Rebels had visited Sharif in jail and were paid for their "copycat" crimes. Juan Contreras told detectives that Armendariz had sent him to collect $4,000 cash from Sharif in prison. Later, Contreras claimed, he had joined Armendariz and other Rebels in the rape-murder of a young woman known only as Lucy. Contreras subsequently recanted his statement, and all charges were dropped against suspects Cerniceros, Fierro, Guermes, Hernández, and Olivares. The remainder are still awaiting trial (a slow process in Mexican courts), and El Diablo earned a separate six-year prison term for leading the February 1998 gang-rape of a 19-year-old fellow inmate. The other Rebels claim they were tortured by police, some displaying burn scars from cigars and cigarettes. Authorities stand by their charges, blaming Sharif and the Rebels for 17 murders. Chihuahua's medical examiner maintains that dental casts from Armendariz "identically" match bite marks

found on the breasts of at least three victims. Nonetheless, in 1999 a Mexican court found insufficient evidence to charge Sharif as a conspirator in any additional slayings.

Even before that ruling, police admitted that their conspiracy theory was defective. The Rebels roundup changed nothing in Ciudad Juárez. Brutal murders continued, while community groups accused police of negligence or worse. At least 16 victims were slain between April and November 1996, with eight still unidentified today. Five were stabbed, three shot, and one was found in a drum of acid. As usual, advanced decomposition left the cause of death unknown in several cases. In 1997, police recorded 17 unsolved murders of females aged 10 to 30, with seven of the dead unidentified. While rape was confirmed in only four cases, the posture and nudity of several other corpses suggested sexual assault. In cases where a cause of death could be determined, five were stabbed, three strangled, three shot, and two beaten.

Statistically, 1998 was the worst year so far, with 23 unsolved murders logged by December. Authorities described the January death of 20-year-old Rosalina Veloz Vasquez as "similar to 20 other murders in the city." Six of the year's victims remain unidentified. The killings reflected the usual mix of stabbings, stranglings, gunshots, and immolation. Victim Rocio Barrazza Gallegos was killed on September 21, strangled in a patrol car parked outside the local police academy, by an officer assigned to the open investigation.

By 1998 the long-running investigation had become a fruitless numbers game. In May, Associated Press (AP) reports listed "more than 100 women raped and killed" in Ciudad Juárez. A month later, AP raised the body count to 117. In October 1998, another AP report placed the official body count at 95, while a woman's advocacy group called Women for Juárez estimated the total somewhere between 130 and 150. Mexico's Human Rights Commission issued a scathing condemnation of the police in 1998, but politicians suppressed the report to avoid any adverse impact on impending state elections. Still clinging to suspect Abdel Sharif, Attorney General Arturo Chávez told Reuters on June 10, 1998, that "police think another serial killer may be at work due to similarities in three crimes this year." At year's end, on December 9, the AP reported: "At least 17 bodies show enough in common—the way shoelaces were tied together, where they were buried, how they were mutilated—that investigators say at least one serial killer is at work. And 76 other cases bear enough similarities that investigators say one or more copycats may be at work."

The first quarter of 1999 witnessed the unsolved murders of at least eight victims. Abdel Sharif's trial for the Castro murder, beginning on March 3, brought no respite from carnage. In the predawn hours of March 18, a 14-year-old girl staggered up to the door of a stranger's home on the city's outskirts. Bloody and sobbing, she told a story of rape and near-murder, naming her attacker as maquiladora bus driver Jesús Guardado Marquez (AKA "El Dracula" or "El Tolteca"). A background check on Guardado revealed a prior conviction for sexual assault. By the time police went looking for him, he had vanished with his pregnant wife, but Durango authorities captured him several days later. Guardado allegedly confessed to multiple murders and named four accomplices: Victor Moreno Rivera ("El Narco"), Augustin Toribio Castillo ("El Kiani"), Bernardo Hernando Fernández ("El Samber") and Jose Gaspar Cerballos Chavez ("El Gaspy"). All were bus drivers, collectively dubbed Los Choferes ("The Chauffeurs"). Police named Moreno as the ringleader of the rape-murder team, collaborating with Abdel Sharif in another copycat scheme intended to spring Sharif from prison. Charged with a total of 20 murders, all suspects denied any role in the crimes. Guardado soon recanted his confession, claiming police torture, while Sharif maintained his innocence and denied any contact with Los Choferes.

Mexican authorities defended their latest conspiracy theory, but statistics were against them. Media reports published in May 1999 claimed that "nearly 200 women" had been murdered since 1993—a substantial jump over October 1998's estimate of 117. Retired FBI agent ROBERT RESSLER had no luck PROFILING the killer(s) or Ciudad Juárez, and a team of active-duty G-men likewise returned from the border city empty-handed. Press reports from the summer of 1999 offered body counts ranging from 180 to 190, coupled with reminders that "at least 95 women" were still missing. Chihuahua authorities claimed that FBI leaders had endorsed their conviction of Abdel Sharif, while bureau headquarters denied it.

Conflicting opinions came from Candice Skrapec, a Canadian-born instructor at California State University in Fresno, billed in the press as a "world-renowned expert on serial killers." In July 1987 Skrapec told the *Toronto Star* that "Railway Killer" Angel Maturino Reséndez, lately posted to the FBI's Ten Most Wanted list on suspicion of multiple murders in the United States, was also a suspect in the slaughter around Ciudad Juárez. A month later, Skrapec told the *Toronto Star* that she believed "at least three serial killers are involved in the unsolved murders of 182 women in Juárez" since 1993. Skrapec went on to say that "there may be even more murders that could be tied to the three suspected serial killers, and [. . .] they were operating in 1992." Skrapec spent the summer of 1999

advising Mexican authorities on the case, telling reporters that "of the 182 total deaths, 40 to 75 [victims] had been sexually violated."

A new mystery surfaced in December 1999, with discovery of a mass grave outside Ciudad Juárez, initially thought to contain as many as 100 corpses. In fact, it yielded only nine, including three U.S. citizens. Inclusion of Americans among the dead prompted a new line of inquiry. "Still a mystery," the *Dallas Morning News* declared, "is what happened to nearly 200 people, including 22 U.S. citizens who, in many cases, vanished after being detained by men with Mexican police uniforms or credentials." Those vanished persons, collectively dubbed Los Desaparecidos ("The Disappeared"), are still missing today, despite joint investigations by U.S. and Mexican authorities. Some were presumably casualties of the drug wars that periodically rock Ciudad Juárez, but apparent police involvement in the kidnappings rekindled dark suspicions. An El Paso–based organization, the Association of Relatives and Friends of Disappeared Persons, keeps pressure on Chihuahua authorities to recover the missing, so far without result.

The advent of a new millennium did not relieve the ordeal of Ciudad Juárez. On November 6 and 7, 2001, skeletal remains of eight more women were found in a vacant lot 300 yards from the Association of Maquiladoras headquarters, a group representing most of the city's U.S.-owned factories. Police announced the creation of a special task force to investigate the murders, with a $21,500 reward offered for capture of the killer(s), but the new display of energy consoled no one. The latest victims, ranging in age from 15 to 20, were allegedly identified on November 10, shortly after police arrested two 28-year-old bus drivers, Javier García Uribe and Gustavo González Meza. Prosecutors blamed García and González for the latest slayings, claiming that both men "belong to a gang whose members are serving time for at least 20 of the rape-murders." The suspects proclaimed that any jailhouse statements issued in their names were the product of torture, their lawyers received death threats, and one attorney—Mario Escobedo Jr.—was killed by police on February 5, 2002, after officers "mistook him for a fugitive." Eleven weeks later, on April 22, police grudgingly confessed that DNA tests had failed to support any of their November victim identifications. Waffling again on November 5, 2002, prosecutors declared that new tests had confirmed the identity of victim Veronica Martínez, while yielding no results on the other seven. Gustavo González died on February 8, 2003, allegedly from complications after jailhouse surgery. Javier García was still awaiting trial when this volume went to press.

The García and González arrests—bringing the total of suspects in custody to 51, by some reports—had no effect on the local murder rate. Ten days after the new suspects were jailed, another young woman was found stripped and beaten to death in Ciudad Juárez. On February 11, 2002, the Inter-American Commission for Human Rights dispatched Marta Altolaguirre to investigate reports that would-be protesters were harassed and threatened by police. That claim moved Mexican president Vicente Fox to order a new investigation by "federal crime specialists." Local prosecutors, resentful of that order, protested to the *Dallas Morning News* that "27 of the 76 cases" were solved, while "the other killings involving women have been isolated incidents."

Global publicity only shortened tempers in Ciudad Juárez. On March 9, 2002, Texas state legislators joined in a binational protest march through El Paso. Jorge Campos Murillo, a deputy attorney general in Mexico City, sparked controversy when he claimed that some of the slayings were committed by "juniors"— sons of wealthy Mexican families whose money and connections spared them from prosecution. (Shortly after making those remarks, Campos was transferred to another job and declined further interviews.) FBI agents resumed their investigation in October 2002, but profiling efforts so far have been fruitless. Civic leaders in Ciudad Juárez remain keenly focused on business. After a large wooden cross was erected near the border as a memorial to the murdered and missing women, Mayor Jesús Delgado received protests from the Association of Business Owners and Professionals of Juárez Avenue, complaining that the display was "a horrible image for tourism." On the same day that protest was filed—September 23, 2002—police found two more women's corpses in Ciudad Juárez. One victim was strangled and partially disrobed; detectives claimed the other had died of a drug overdose, but special investigator David Rodríguez was openly skeptical of that verdict. Yet another young victim was found on October 8, apparently beaten to death.

The year 2002 ended badly for image-conscious merchants in Ciudad Juárez. Mexico's first lady, Sahagun de Fox, publicly called for an end to the murders on November 25, as more than a thousand black-garbed women marched to protest the sluggish investigation. In January 2003, after three more victims were found at Lomas de Poleo, published estimates of the body count ranged from "nearly 100" to 370. On February 17, 2003, two boys walking their dogs in the desert northeast of town found three more corpses, and police responding to the scene unearthed a fourth. The latest victims, all teenagers, had vanished from downtown Ciudad Juárez between September 23, 2002, and February 4, 2003.

On April 1, 2004, the United Nations Committee on the Elimination of Discrimination Against Women publicly condemned Mexican officials for their mishandling of the Chihuahua murder spree. The U.N. report suggested that drug trafficking "lies at the heart of the murders," while official corruption and incompetence render solution of the case impossible. Mincing no words, the panel said that "the investigation has been tempered by passiveness and illegality seen in the obstruction of studies, the slowness in investigating disappearances, falsification of evidence, harassment of the victims' families and the use of torture to obtain confessions."

Special prosecutor María López Urbina, appointed to investigate the crimes in February 2004, issued a preliminary report four months later. She found "grave deficiencies" in the 11-year manhunt, citing 81 specific individuals for negligence or incompetence. The report denounced specific police officers, state investigators, forensic experts, and investigative supervisors, but spared elected officials from public criticism. López announced plans to study 50 open cases at a time, with new reports published at four-month intervals until all the crimes were reviewed. President Fox promptly declared, "We have accepted the challenge, considering that it's our moral duty to clarify the circumstances that have given rise to the homicides and to punish the guilty parties."

The murders continue.

Individual suspects in the Ciudad Juárez slayings, identified in media reports but still uncharged at press time for this work, include the following:

Angel Maturino Reséndez: Condemned and awaiting execution in Texas, he remains a suspect in some of the murders, according to profilers Robert Ressler and Candice Skrapec. No charges have been filed in Mexico.

Armando Martínez: Arrested in 1992 for the murder of a Chihuahua City woman, he was "accidentally" released and subsequently vanished (along with his police file). Murder defendant Ana Benavides, accused in 1998 of killing and dismembering a Ciudad Juárez couple and their child, claims Martínez committed the triple murder and framed her for his crime.

Carlos Cardenas Cruz and Jorge García Paz: Former Mexican federal agents turned fugitives, they are sought for questioning in the 1998 disappearance of 29-year-old Silvia Arce and 24-year-old Griselda Mares, who were allegedly killed by corrupt police in a "mistaken" dispute over stolen weapons.

Pedro Valles: An ex-police officer, he was assigned to investigate the Ciudad Juárez murders when he strangled girlfriend Rocio Barrazza Gallegos at the state police academy, in September 1998. He remains a fugitive.

Dagoberto Ramírez: Another Ciudad Juárez policeman, fired in 1999 after he was accused of murdering his lover. Ramirez was freed upon claiming that the woman committed suicide, but his superiors declined to reinstate him.

Julio Rodríquez Valenzuela: A former police chief of suburban El Sauzal, accused in April 1999 of attempting to rape a 16-year-old girl near the site of two previous murders. Chihuahua authorities report that he fled "to El Paso or New Mexico," and he remains at large.

Sergio Hernández Pereda: A Chihuahua state police officer until 1997, he has been a fugitive from murder charges since his wife was slain in 1998.

Melchor Baca: A former federal police officer who has been a fugitive since 1995, sought on charges of killing his wife's alleged lover at the courthouse where both were employed.

Conspiracy theories also persist in Ciudad Juárez. The most popular targets include:

Rogue police officers: At least 10 women have accused local police officers of kidnapping and sexual assault since 1998. No charges have been filed in those cases, but investigators say they suspect an unnamed police officer in the 1995 murders of 29-year-old Elizabeth Gómez and 27-year-old Laura Inere.

Drug cartels: Authorities suspect that some of Chihuahua's murdered and missing women were addicts or small-time smugglers, executed because they "knew too much." An FBI report from November 2002 blamed unnamed narco-traffickers for the February 2001 torture slaying of 17-year-old Lilia García, found 100 yards from the spot where eight other victims were discovered in 2002.

High-society sadists: Taking their cue from Jorge Campos Murillo, some police and reporters blame the murders on "a cabal of rich and powerful men" whose wealth makes them untouchable. No suspects have been named.

Satanic cults: Reviving memories of the drug-cult murders committed by followers of ADOLFO DE JESUS CONSTANZO at Matamoros in the 1980s, some Chihuahua residents profess to see an occult hand at work in local homicides.

Organ harvesters: An urban myth echoed in films and novels has a grisly resonance in Ciudad Juárez. Rumors claim that vital organs were removed from several victims. During 2003 and 2004, federal police announced plans to prosecute 18 separate cases of illegal organ trafficking in northern Chihuahua, but none have yet gone to trial.

While the search for a one-size-fits-all solution continues, authorities occasionally discover new viable suspects. On October 13, 2004, defendant Javier García Uribe received a 50-year prison term for the rape-murders of eight women in Ciudad Juárez, committed during 2000 and 2001. At the same time, Mexican authorities ruefully admitted that most of city's maquiladora murders—recalculated at 341 since 1993—remain officially unsolved.

As this volume went to press, Mexican courts closed the books on 12 maquiladora murders in Ciudad Juárez. On January 6, 2005, four bus drivers described as members of Los Toltecas gang were convicted of raping and murdering six young women. Their prison terms ranged from 40 to 113 years. That same afternoon, another judge pronounced six members of Los Rebeldes, confined since 1999, guilty of six additional murders. Leader Jesús Manuel Guardado received a 113-year sentence, and his codefendants drew 40-year terms.

CLARK, Douglas Daniel, and BUNDY, Carol Mary

Born in 1948, the son of a retired navy admiral turned international engineer, Douglas Clark had lived in 37 countries by the time he settled in southern California. He liked to call himself "the king of the one-night stands," supplementing his machinist's income through affairs with frowzy matrons, reserving his leisure time for kinky liaisons with underaged girls and young women. In his private moments, he cherished dark fantasies of rape and murder, mutilation and necrophilia, yearning for the moment when his dreams could graduate to grim reality.

At age 37, Carol Bundy was typical of Clark's conquests. A diabetic vocational nurse, the obese mother of two had left her abusive husband in January 1979, quickly falling in love with the manager of her new apartment building. A native of Australia, 45-year-old John Murray sang part-time at a local country-western bar, Little Nashville, but he was never too busy to help out a tenant in need. Noting that Bundy suffered from severe cataracts, Murray drove her to a Social Security office and had her declared legally blind, thus bringing in $620 each month for Carol and her sons. Next, he took her to an optometrist, where she was fitted for glasses, enabling her to discard her white cane. Enraptured, Carol began deliberately clogging the toilets and drains in her apartment, anything at all to bring the manager around. Soon they were lovers, but Murray was married, refusing to give up his family. In October

1979, Carol approached his wife, offering $1,500 if the woman would disappear, but the effort backfired, with Murray berating her and coldly suggesting that she find other lodgings.

Three months later, in January 1980, Carol was pining away in Little Nashville when she met Doug Clark, and he immediately swept her off her feet. Clark moved into her home the same night, working by day in the boiler room of a Burbank soap factory, devoting his nights to exercises in depravity that made Carol his virtual slave. She swallowed her pride when he brought younger women home for sex, dutifully snapping photographs on command. One of his conquests was an 11-year-old, picked up while roller skating in a nearby park, but Carol made no complaint as kinky sex gave way to pedophilia, increasingly spiced with discussions of death and mutilation.

On June 11, 1980, half-sisters Gina Narano, 15, and Cynthia Chandler, 16, vanished from Huntington Beach, en route to a meeting with friends. They were found the next morning beside the Ventura Freeway near Griffith Park, in Los Angeles; each had been shot in the head with a small-caliber pistol. At home, Clark gleefully confessed the murders to Bundy, regaling her with how he had forced the girls to perform sexual acts on him, shooting each in the head as they were completed.

In the predawn hours of June 24, Karen Jones, a 24-year-old prostitute, was found behind a Burbank steakhouse, murdered by a single gunshot to the head. Later that morning, police were summoned to Studio City, where another female victim—this one headless—had been found by horrified pedestrians. Despite the missing head, she was identified as Exxie Wilson, 20, another veteran streetwalker.

That afternoon, while Carol Bundy's sons were visiting relatives, Clark surprised her by plucking a woman's head from the refrigerator and placing it on the kitchen counter. He ordered Carol to make up the twisted face with cosmetics, and she later recalled, "We had a lot of fun with her. I was making her up like a Barbie with makeup." Tiring of the game, Clark took his trophy to the bathroom for a shower and a bout of necrophilia.

Newspaper headlines were already touting the crimes of a new "Sunset Slayer" by June 27, when Exxie Wilson's head was found in a Hollywood alley, stuffed inside an ornate wooden box. Authorities noted that it had been thoroughly scrubbed before it was discarded by the killer. Three days later, a group of snake hunters near Sylmar, in the San Fernando Valley, turned up a woman's mummified corpse, identified as Sacramento runaway Marnette Comer. Last seen alive on June 1, the 17-year-old prostitute had been dead at least

three weeks when she was found. Like other victims in the series, she was known to work the Sunset Strip.

And the murders continued. On July 25, a young "Jane Doe" was found on Sunset Boulevard, killed by a shot to the head. Two weeks later, hikers in the Fernwood area, near Malibu, turned up another unidentified corpse, dismembered by scavengers, a small-caliber bullet hole visible in the skull.

Despite her hot romance with Clark, Carol Bundy had continued visiting John Murray at Little Nashville, where he performed by night. She did not hold her liquor well, and after dropping several hints about her new lover's criminal activities, she was appalled by Murray's comment that he might report Doug Clark to the police. On August 5, she kept a midnight rendezvous with Murray in his van, parked two blocks from the bar, and she killed him there. Found days later, the singer had been stabbed nine times and slashed across the buttocks, his head severed and missing from the murder scene.

It had become too much for Carol Bundy. Two days after Murray's body was discovered, she broke down on the job, sobbing out to a fellow nurse, "I can't take it any more. I'm supposed to save lives, not take them." Her friend tipped police, and they called on Bundy at home, confiscating three pairs of panties removed from victims as trophies, along with snapshots of Clark and his 11-year-old playmate. Arrested on the job in Burbank, Clark was still in jail four days later when police retrieved a pistol from the boiler room. Ballistics tests would link the gun to bullets recovered from five of the known "Sunset" victims.

At his trial, serving briefly as his own attorney, Clark blamed Carol Bundy and John Murray for the slayings, contending that they had patterned their crimes after the case of THEODORE BUNDY. Jurors saw through the flimsy ruse, and on January 28, 1983, they convicted Clark across the board, including six counts of first-degree murder with "special circumstances," plus one count each of attempted murder, mayhem, and mutilating human remains. Strutting before the jury during the penalty phase of his trial, Clark declared, "We have to vote for the death penalty in this case. The evidence cries out for it." The panel agreed with his logic, and he was sentenced to death on February 15. On death row at San Quentin, he found himself in good company, enjoying daily bridge games with serial slayers WILLIAM BONIN, RANDY KRAFT, and LAWRENCE BITTAKER.

At her own trial for murdering John Murray and one of the unidentified females, Carol Bundy first pled insanity, then reversed herself and admitted the slayings. According to her statement, Murray was shot in the head, then decapitated to remove ballistic evidence. She had also handed Clark the gun with which he shot an unnamed prostitute, found dead along the Sunset Strip in July 1980. Convicted on the basis of her own confession, Bundy received consecutive prison terms of 27 years to life on one count, plus 25 years to life on the other. Bundy died in custody, of heart failure, on December 9, 2003.

COLE, Carroll Edward

A death wish, once in custody, is not unusual among compulsive killers. Carroll Edward Cole, admitted murderer of 13 persons, was securely serving out a term of life imprisonment in Texas, with parole a possibility in seven years, when he elected voluntarily to face new murder charges in Nevada, fully conscious of the fact that he would be condemned to die upon conviction. Once that sentence had been passed, facilitated by his guilty plea, Cole staunchly fended off appeals and efforts of assorted liberal groups to interpose themselves on his behalf. His execution, in December 1985, immediately paved the way for others in the Western states, but Cole's significance lies elsewhere—in the man himself and in the system's failure to prevent his crimes.

When Cole was five years old, his mother forced him to accompany her on extramarital excursions in his father's absence, using torture to extract a pledge of silence, making him a bruised accomplice to her own adultery. As he grew older, Cole was forced to dress in frilly skirts and petticoats for the amusement of his mother's friends, dispensing tea and coffee at sadistic "parties" where the women gathered to make sport of "Mama's little girl." Enrolled in elementary school two years behind his peers, Cole grew up fearing for his masculinity, intensely sensitive to jokes about his "sissy" given name. At nine, he drowned a playmate who made fun of him, avoiding punishment when care-

Carroll Edward Cole (Author's collection)

less officers dismissed the murder as an accident. He had begun to fight habitually at school and once contrived to maim the winner of a yo-yo contest in which Cole had come out second-best: while playing on a piece of road equipment, he engaged the gears and crushed his rival's hand inside the dozer's massive treads.

In adolescence, Cole accumulated numerous arrests for drunkenness and petty theft. He joined the navy after dropping out of high school but was discharged for the theft of pistols, which he used to fire at cars along the San Diego highways. Back at home in Richmond, California, during 1960, he attacked two couples with a hammer as they parked along a darkened lover's lane. Increasingly, he cherished fantasies of strangling girls and women who reminded him of his adulterous mother.

Finally, alarmed by violent fantasies that would not let him rest, Cole flagged a squad car down in Richmond and confessed his urges to police. On the advice of a police lieutenant, Cole surrendered voluntarily and spent the next three years in institutions where he was regarded as an "antisocial personality" who posed no threat to others. Finally discharged in 1963, he moved to Dallas, Texas, and exacerbated matters by immediately marrying an alcoholic prostitute.

The grim relationship was doomed to failure, filled with screaming battles, beatings, and the occasional resort to weapons. Finally, in 1965, persuaded that his wife was servicing the tenants of a motel where they lived, Cole torched the place and was imprisoned on an arson charge. Upon release, he drifted northward, through Missouri and was jailed again for the attempted murder of Virginia Rowden, age 11. Cole had chosen her at random, crept into her room while she was sleeping, and had tried to strangle her in bed. Her screams had driven him away, and he was readily identified by witnesses as her assailant when police arrived.

Missouri offered Cole more psychiatric treatment through assorted inmate programs, but it didn't take. In 1970, he once again surrendered to authorities—this time in Reno, Nevada—confessing his desire to rape and strangle women. Learned doctors wrote him off as a malingerer and set him free on the condition that he leave the state. Cole's file contains the telling evidence of psychiatric failure: "Prognosis: Poor. Condition on release: Same as on admittance. Treatment: Express bus ticket to San Diego, California."

The problem was exported, but it would not go away. Within six months of his return to San Diego, Cole would kill at least three women. (On the day before his execution in Nevada, he suggested that there might have been two others in this period, the details of their murders blurred by massive quantities of alcohol.)

His victims, then and later, shared the common trait of infidelity to husbands, fiancés, or boyfriends; each approached Cole in a bar, accompanied him to lonely roads for sex, and laughed about the skill with which she "put one over" on her regular companion.

Moving eastward, Cole picked off another victim in Casper, Wyoming, in August 1975. Assorted jail terms often interfered with hunting, but he surfaced in Las Vegas during 1977, staying long enough to kill a prostitute and get himself arrested on a charge of auto theft, which was dismissed. A few weeks later, after days of drinking, Cole awoke in Oklahoma City to discover the remains of yet another woman in his bathtub; bloody slices of her buttocks rested in a skillet on the stove.

Returning once again to San Diego, Cole remarried—to another "drunken tramp"—and sought the help of local counselors to curb his drinking. Given the conditions of his home life, it was hopeless, and the urge to murder was consuming him, inevitably fueled by alcohol, a ravenous obsession. During August 1979, he strangled Bonnie Stewart on the premises of his employer, dumping her nude body in an alleyway adjacent to the store. For weeks he had been threatening to kill his wife—the threats reported to an officer in charge of supervising his parole—but when he finally succeeded in September, the authorities refused to rule her death a homicide. Despite discovery of her body, swaddled in a blanket and reposing in a closet of Cole's home, despite Cole's own arrest while drunkenly attempting to prepare a grave beneath a neighbor's house, detectives viewed the death of Diana Cole as "natural," related to her own abuse of drink.

Taking no chances, Cole hit the road. He claimed another victim in Las Vegas, gravitating back to Dallas where, within 11 days in 1980, he would strangle three more victims. Though discovered at the final murder scene, the victim stretched out at his feet, he was again regarded merely as a "casual suspect" by detectives. Weary of the game at last, Cole startled them with his confession to a string of unsolved homicides; at trial, in 1981, his guilty plea insured a term of life with possible parole, and he was counting down the days to freedom when reports of a potential extradition to Nevada changed his mind.

The case of Carroll Edward Cole deserves a place among the classics as a showcase of "The System's" abject failure. As a child, young Eddie Cole was failed by educators who ignored his late enrollment, failed to recognize the signs of chronic child abuse, and dealt with adolescent violence as a problem to be swept away by referral to other agencies. As a potential murderer who sought the help of mental institutions, he was failed by the psychologists and psychoanalysts of half a dozen states, repeatedly discharged as a malingerer, a

harmless fake, "no danger to society." On two occasions, officers in San Diego literally caught Cole in the act of an attempted murder—and on each occasion, they accepted his ridiculous assertion of a lover's quarrel, offering the would-be killer transportation to his home. When violent fantasies became reality, investigators with the same department stubbornly ignored persuasive evidence, rejecting even Cole's confession, passing off two homicides as drunken accidents, and dismissing others as the work of angry pimps. In Texas, Cole might very well have slipped the net again if he had not elected to confess in cases where detectives were inclined to view his homicides as "accidental deaths." In such a case, the system fails not only Carroll Edward Cole; it fails us all.

CONSTANZO, Adolfo de Jesus

Born in Miami on November 1, 1962, Adolfo Constanzo was the son of a teenage Cuban immigrant. He was still an infant when his widowed mother moved to Puerto Rico and married her second husband. There, Adolfo was baptized a Catholic and served the church as an altar boy, appearing to accept the standard tenets of the Roman faith. He was 10 years old when the family moved back to Miami. His stepfather died a year later, leaving Adolfo and his mother financially well-off.

By that time, neighbors in Little Havana had begun to notice something odd about Aurora Constanzo and her son. Some said the woman was a witch, and those who angered her were likely to discover headless goats or chickens on their doorsteps in the morning. Adolfo's mother had introduced him to the Santería religion around age nine, with side trips to Haiti for instruction in Vodun, but there were still more secrets to be learned, and in 1976 he was apprenticed to a practitioner of *palo mayombe*. His occult "godfather" was already rich from working with local drug dealers, and he imparted a philosophy that would follow Adolfo to his grave: "Let the nonbelievers kill themselves with drugs. We will profit from their foolishness."

Constanzo's mother recalls that her son began displaying psychic powers about the same time, scanning the future to predict such events as the 1981 shooting of President Ronald Reagan. Be that as it may, Adolfo had problems foretelling his own future, including two arrests for shoplifting—one involving the theft of a chainsaw. On the side, he had also begun to display bisexual inclinations, with a strong preference for male lovers.

A modeling assignment took the handsome young sorcerer to Mexico City in 1983, and he spent his free time telling fortunes with tarot cards in the city's infamous Zona Rosa. Before returning to Miami, Adolfo collected his first Mexican disciples, including Martín Quintana, homosexual "psychic" Jorge Montes, and Omar Orea, who had been obsessed with the occult from age 15. In short order, Constanzo seduced both Quintana and Orea, claiming one as his "man" and the other as his "woman," depending on Adolfo's romantic whim.

In mid-1984, Constanzo moved to Mexico City full time, seeking what his mother called "new horizons." He shared quarters with Quintana and Orea, in a strange ménage à trois, collecting other followers as his "magic" reputation spread throughout the city. It was said that Constanzo could read the future, and he also offered *limpias*—ritual "cleansings"—for those who felt they had been cursed by enemies. Of course, it all cost money, and Constanzo's journals—recovered after his death—document 31 regular customers, some paying up to $4,500 for a single ceremony. Adolfo established a menu for sacrificial beasts, with roosters going for $6 a head, goats for $30, boa constrictors at $450, adult zebras for $1,100, and African lion cubs listed at $3,100 each.

True to the teachings of his Florida mentor, Constanzo charmed wealthy drug dealers, helping them schedule shipments and meetings on the basis of his predictions. For a price, he also offered magic that would make dealers and their hit men invisible to police and bulletproof against their enemies. It was all nonsense, of course, but smugglers drawn from Mexican peasant stock, with a background in *brujería* (witchcraft), were strongly inclined to believe. According to Constanzo's ledgers, one dealer in Mexico City paid him $40,000 for magical services rendered over three years' time.

At those rates, the customers demanded a show, and Constanzo recognized the folly of disappointing men who carried Uzi submachine guns in their armor-plated limousines. Strong medicine required first-rate ingredients, and Adolfo was well established by mid-1985, when he and three of his disciples raided a Mexico City graveyard for human bones to start his own *nganga*—the traditional cauldron of blood employed by practitioners of *palo mayombe*. The rituals and air of mystery surrounding Constanzo were powerful enough to lure a cross section of Mexican society, with his clique of followers including a physician, a real estate speculator, fashion models, and several transvestite nightclub performers.

At first glance, the most peculiar aspect of Constanzo's new career was the appeal he seemed to have for ranking law enforcement officers. At least four members of the Federal Judicial Police joined Constanzo's cult in Mexico City: one of them, Salvador Garcia, was a commander in charge of narcotics investigations; another, Florentino Ventura, retired from the *federales* to lead the Mexican branch of Interpol. In a country where *mordida* (bribery) permeates all levels of law enforcement and federal officers sometimes serve as triggermen for drug smugglers, corruption is not unusual, but the devotion of Constanzo's disciples ran deeper than cash on the line. In or out of uniform, they worshiped Adolfo as a minor god, their living conduit to the spirit world.

In 1986, Ventura introduced Constanzo to the drug-dealing Calzada family, then one of Mexico's dominant narcotics cartels. Constanzo won the hard-nosed dealers over with his charm and mumbo-jumbo, profiting immensely from his contacts with the gang. By early 1987, he was able to pay $60,000 cash for a condominium in Mexico City and buy himself a fleet of luxury cars that included an $80,000 Mercedes Benz. When not working magic for the Calzadas or other clients, Adolfo staged scams of his own, once posing as a DEA agent to rip off a coke dealer in Guadalajara and selling the stash through his police contacts for a cool $100,000.

At some point in his odyssey from juvenile psychic to high-society wizard, Constanzo began to feed his *nganga* with the offerings of human sacrifice. No final tally for his victims is available, but 23 ritual murders are well documented, and Mexican authorities point to a rash of unsolved mutilation-slayings around Mexico City and elsewhere during the time period, suggesting that Constanzo's known victims may be only the tip of a malignant iceberg. In any case, his willingness to torture and kill total strangers—or even close friends—duly impressed the ruthless drug dealers who remained his foremost clients.

In the course of a year's association, Constanzo came to believe that his magical powers alone were responsible for the Calzada family's continued success and survival. In April 1987, he demanded a full partnership in the syndicate and was curtly refused. On the surface, Constanzo seemed to take the rejection in stride, but his devious mind was plotting revenge.

On April 30, Guillermo Calzada and six members of his household vanished under mysterious circumstances. They were reported missing on May 1, and police noted melted candles and other evidence of a strange religious ceremony at Calzada's office. Six more days elapsed before officers began fishing mutilated remains from the Zumpango River. Seven corpses were recovered in the course of a week, all bearing signs of sadistic torture—fingers, toes and ears removed, hearts and sex organs excised, part of the spine ripped from one body, and two other bodies missing their brains.

The vanished parts, as it turned out, had gone to feed Constanzo's cauldron of blood, building up his strength for greater conquests yet to come.

In July 1987, Salvador Garcia introduced Constanzo to another drug-running family, this one led by brothers Elio and Ovidio Hernandez. At the end of that month, in Matamoros, Constanzo also met 22-year-old Sara Aldrete, a Mexican national with resident alien status in the United States, where she attended college in Brownsville, Texas. Adolfo charmed Sara with his line of patter, noting with arch significance that her birthday—September 6—was the same as his mother's. Sara was dating Brownsville drug smuggler Gilberto Sosa at the time, but she soon wound up in Constanzo's bed, Adolfo scuttling the old relationship with an anonymous call to Sosa, revealing Sara's infidelity. With nowhere else to turn, Sara plunged full-time into Constanzo's world, emerging as the *madrina*—godmother or "head witch"—of his cult, adding her own twists to the torture of sacrificial victims.

Constanzo's rituals became more elaborate and sadistic after he moved his headquarters to a plot of desert called Rancho Santa Elena, 20 miles from Matamoros. There, on May 28, 1988, drug dealer Hector de la Fuente and farmer Moises Castillo were executed by gunfire, but the sacrifice was a disappointment to Constanzo. Back in Mexico City, he directed his drones to dismember a transvestite, Ramon Esquivel, and dump the grisly remains on a public street corner. His luck was holding, and Constanzo narrowly escaped when Houston police raided a drug house in June 1988, seizing numerous items of occult paraphernalia and the city's largest-ever shipment of cocaine.

On August 12, Ovidio Hernandez and his two-year-old son were kidnapped by rival narcotics dealers, the family turning to Constanzo for help. That night, another human sacrifice was staged at Rancho Santa Elena, and the hostages were released unharmed on August 13, Adolfo claiming full credit for their safe return. His star was rising, and Constanzo barely noticed when disciple Florentino Ventura committed suicide in Mexico City on September 17, taking his wife and a friend with him in the same burst of gunfire.

In November 1988, Constanzo sacrificed disciple Jorge Gomez, accused of snorting cocaine in direct violation of *el padrino*'s ban on drug use. A month later, Adolfo's ties to the Hernandez family were cemented with the initiation of Ovidio Hernandez as a full-fledged cultist, complete with ritual bloodletting and prayers to the *nganga*.

Human sacrifice can also have its practical side, as when competing smuggler Ezequiel Luna was tortured to death at Rancho Santa Elena on February 14, 1989; two other dealers, Ruben Garza and Ernesto Diaz, wandered into the ceremony uninvited and were promptly added to the sacrifice. Conversely, Adolfo sometimes demanded a sacrifice without rhyme or reason. When he called for fresh meat on February 25, Ovidio Hernandez gladly joined the hunting party, picking off his own 14-year-old cousin, Jose Garcia, in the heat of the moment.

On March 13, 1989, Constanzo sacrificed yet another victim at the ranch, but he was gravely disappointed when his prey did not scream and plead for mercy in the approved style. Disgruntled, he ordered an Anglo for the next ritual, and his minions went on the hunt, abducting 21-year-old Mark Kilroy outside a Matamoros saloon. The sacrifice went well enough, followed two weeks later by the butchery of Sara Aldrete's old boyfriend, Gilberto Sosa, but Kilroy's disappearance marked the beginning of the end for Constanzo's homicidal cult.

A popular premed student from Texas, Mark Kilroy was not some peasant, transvestite, or small-time pusher who could disappear without a trace or an investigation into his fate. With family members and Texas politicians turning up the heat, the search for Kilroy rapidly assumed the trappings of an international incident, but in the end Constanzo's own disciples would destroy him.

By March 1989, Mexican authorities were busy with one of their periodic antidrug campaigns, erecting roadblocks on a whim and sweeping the border districts for unwary smugglers. On April 1, Victor Sauceda, an ex-cop turned gangster, was sacrificed at the ranch, and the "spirit message" Constanzo received was optimistic enough for his troops to move a half ton of marijuana across the border seven nights later.

And then, the magic started to unravel.

On April 9, returning from a Brownsville meeting with Constanzo, cultist Serafin Hernandez drove past a police roadblock without stopping, ignoring the cars that set off in hot pursuit. Hernandez believed *el padrino*'s line about invisibility, and he seemed surprised when officers trailed him to his destination in Matamoros. Even so, the smuggler was arrogant, inviting police to shoot him, since he believed the bullets would merely bounce off his body.

They arrested him instead, along with cult member David Martinez, and drove the pair back to Rancho Santa Elena, where a preliminary search turned up marijuana and firearms. Disciples Elio Hernandez and Sergio Martinez stumbled into the net while police were on hand, and all four prisoners were interrogated through the evening, revealing their tales of black magic, torture, and human sacrifice with a perverse kind of pride.

Next morning, police returned to the ranch in force, discovering the malodorous shed where Constanzo kept his *nganga,* brimming with blood, spiders, scorpions, a dead black cat, a turtle shell, bones, deer antlers—and a human brain. Captive cult members directed searchers to Constanzo's private cemetery, and excavation began, revealing 15 mutilated corpses by April 16. In addition to Mark Kilroy and other victims already named, the body count included two renegade federal narcotics officers—Joaquin Manzo and Miguel Garcia—along with three men who were never identified.

The hunt for Constanzo was on, and police raided his luxury home in Atizapan, outside Mexico City, on April 17, discovering stockpiles of gay pornography and a hidden ritual chamber. The discoveries at Rancho Santa Elena made international headlines, and sightings of Constanzo were reported as far away as Chicago, but in fact, he had already returned to Mexico City, hiding out in a small apartment with Sara Aldrete and three other disciples. On May 2, thinking to save herself, Sara tossed a note out the window. It read:

> Please call the judicial police and tell them that in this building are those that they are seeking. Tell them that a woman is being held hostage. I beg for this, because what I want most is to talk—or they're going to kill the girl.

A passerby found the note, read it, and kept it to himself, believing it was someone's lame attempt at humor. On May 6, neighbors called police to complain of a loud, vulgar argument in Constanzo's apartment—some said accompanied by gunshots. As patrolmen arrived at the scene, Constanzo spotted them and opened fire with an Uzi, touching off a 45-minute battle in which, miraculously, only one policeman was wounded.

When Constanzo realized that escape was impossible, he handed his weapon to cultist Alvaro de Leon Valdez—a professional hit man nicknamed "El Duby"—with bizarre new orders. As El Duby recalled the scene, "He told me to kill him and Martin [Quintana]. I told him I couldn't do it, but he hit me in the face and threatened me that everything would go bad for me in hell. Then he hugged Martin, and I just stood in front of them and shot them with a machine gun."

Constanzo and Quintana were dead when police stormed the apartment, arresting El Duby and Sarah Aldrete. In the aftermath of the raid, 14 cultists were indicted on various charges, including multiple murder, weapons and narcotics violations, conspiracy, and obstruction of justice. In August 1990, El Duby was convicted of killing Constanzo and Quintana, drawing a 30-year prison terms. Cultists Juan Fragosa and Jorge Montes were both convicted in the Esquivel murder and sentenced to 35 years each; Omar Orea, convicted in the same case, died of AIDS before he could be sentenced. Sara Aldrete was acquitted of Constanzo's murder in 1990 but was sentenced to a six-year term on

conviction of criminal association. Constanzo's *madrina* insisted that she never practiced any religion but "Christian Santería"; televised reports of the murders at Rancho Santa Elena, she said, took her by complete surprise. Jurors disagreed in 1994 when Sara and four male accomplices were convicted of multiple murders at the ranch; Aldrete was sentenced to 62 years, while her cohorts—including Elio and Serafin Hernandez—drew prison terms of 67 years.

CORLL, Dean Arnold

Indiana-born on Christmas Eve of 1939, Dean Corll grew up in a combative home, his parents quarreling constantly. They divorced while Corll was still an infant, then remarried after World War II, but Dean's father provided no stabilizing influence, regarding his children with thinly veiled distaste and resorting to harsh punishment for the smallest infractions. When the couple separated a second time, Corll and his younger brother were left with a series of sitters, their mother working to support the family on her own. Rheumatic fever left Dean with a heart condition, resulting in frequent absence from school, and he seemed to welcome the change when his mother remarried, moving the family to Texas. A part-time business making candy soon expanded to become their livelihood, and Corll was generous with samples as he sought to win new friends.

In 1964, despite his heart condition, Corll was drafted into military service, where he displayed the first signs of homosexuality. On turning 30, in December 1969, he seemed to undergo a sudden shift in personality, becoming hypersensitive and glum. He began to spend his time with teenage boys, like David Owen Brooks and Elmer Wayne Henley, passing out free candy all around, hosting glue- and paint-sniffing parties at his apartment in Pasadena, a suburb of Houston. At the same time, he displayed a sadistic streak, leaning toward bondage in his sexual relationship with young men and boys. On one occasion, during 1970, Brooks entered the apartment to find Corll nude, with two naked boys strapped to a homemade torture rack. Embarrassed, Corll released his playmates and offered Brooks a car in return for his promise of silence. Later, as his passion turned to bloodlust, Corll would use Brooks and Henley as procurers, offering $200 per head for fresh victims.

The date of Corll's first murder is uncertain. Brooks placed it sometime in mid-1970, the victim identified as college student Jeffrey Konen, picked up while hitchhiking. Most of Corll's victims were drawn from a seedy Houston neighborhood known as the Heights, their disappearance blithely ignored by police accustomed to

Elmer Henley (center) in custody (Wide World API)

dealing with runaways. Two were friends and neighbors of Henley, delivered on order to Corll, and sometimes the candy man killed two victims at once. In December 1970, he murdered 14-year-old James Glass and 15-year-old David Yates in one sitting. The following month, brothers Donald and Jerry Waldrop joined the missing list, with Wally Simineaux and Richard Embry slaughtered in October 1972. Another pair of brothers—Billy and Mike Baulch—were killed at separate times, in May 1972 and July 1973, respectively. Corll's youngest known victim was a nine-year-old neighbor, residing across the street from Dean's apartment.

On August 8, 1973, a tearful phone call from Elmer Henley summoned Pasadena police to Corll's flat. They found the candy man dead, six bullet holes in his shoulder and back, with Henley claiming he had killed his "friend" in self-defense. The violence had erupted after Henley brought a girl to one of Corll's paint-sniffing orgies, driving the homosexual killer into a rage. Corll had threatened Elmer with a gun, then taunted his young friend when Henley managed to disarm him. Frightened for his life, Henley insisted that he shot Corll only to save himself. But there was more.

That afternoon, he led detectives to a rented boat shed in southwest Houston, leaving authorities to hoist 17 corpses from their shallow graves in the earthen floor. A drive to Lake Sam Rayburn turned up four more graves, while six others were found on the beach at High Island, for a total of 27 dead. Henley insisted there were at least two more bodies in the boat shed, plus two more at High Island, but police called off the search, content to know that they had broken California's record in the JUAN CORONA case. (Author Jack Olsen, in *The Man with the Candy*, suggests that other victims may have been buried around Corll's candy shop, but authorities show no interest in pursuing the case any further.)

In custody, Brooks and Henley confessed their role in procuring victims for Corll through the years, with Brooks fingering Henley as the triggerman in at least one slaying. "Most of the killings that occurred after Wayne came in the picture involved all three of us," he told police. "Wayne seemed to enjoy causing pain." Convicted of multiple murder in August 1974, Henley was sentenced to life imprisonment, with Brooks drawing an identical term in March 1975. A year later, Houston authorities announced that recent investigations of child pornography had linked other local pedophiles to Corll's murder ring, but no prosecutions were forthcoming. Elmer Henley's conviction was overturned on appeal in December 1978, on the issue of pretrial publicity, but he was convicted and sentenced to prison a second time, in June 1979. Both of Corll's accomplices have been eligible for parole since 1983, but their periodic bids for freedom are routinely rejected. Henley, meanwhile, has emerged as an accomplished artist, his paintings featured at two Houston galleries in March of 1998. One of his favorite subjects: beach scenes.

See also ARTWORK AND MEMORABILIA

CORONA, Juan Vallejo

A native of Mexico, born in 1934, Corona turned up in Yuba City, California, as a migrant worker in the early 1950s. Unlike most of his kind, he stayed on after the harvest, putting down roots and establishing a family, graduating from the role of picker in the fields to become a successful labor contractor. By his mid-thirties, Corona was known to ranchers throughout the county, supplying crews on demand. There was a bit of trouble during 1970 when a young Mexican was wounded—his scalp laid open by a machete—in the café run by Corona's homosexual brother, Natividad. Upon recovery, the victim filed suit against Natividad Corona, seeking $250,000 in damages, and the accused hacker fled back to Mexico, leaving the case unresolved. No one linked Juan to the crime; its violence scarcely seemed to touch his life.

And yet. . . .

On May 19, 1971, a Japanese farmer was touring his orchard when he noticed a fresh hole, roughly the size of a grave, excavated between two fruit trees. One of Corona's migrant crews was working nearby, and the farmer shrugged it off until that night, when he returned and found the hole filled in. Suspicious, he summoned deputies to the site next morning, and a bit of spadework revealed the fresh corpse of transient

Kenneth Whitacre. The victim had been stabbed, his face and skull torn open by the blows of something like a cleaver or machete. Detectives logged the case as a sex crime, after finding pieces of gay literature in Whitacre's pocket.

Four days later, workers on a nearby ranch reported the discovery of a second grave. It yielded the remains of drifter Charles Fleming, but police were still working on identifying him when they found the next burial site, and the next. In all, they spent nine days exhuming bodies from the orchard, counting 25 before the search was terminated on June 4. In Melford Sample's grave, deputies found two meat receipts dated May 21, signed with the name of "Juan V. Corona." On June 4, Joseph Maczak's remains were discovered with two bank receipts, bearing the same signature. Some of the corpses were fresh, while others—like that of Donald Smith—had clearly been in the ground for months. (Medical examiners estimated that the first murders had occurred about February 1971.) Most of the victims were stabbed or hacked to death, with several bearing signs of homosexual assault. Four of the dead were ultimately unidentified; the rest were migrant workers, rootless drifters, with a sprinkling of skid row alco-

holics. None of them had been reported missing by surviving relatives. The bank and meat receipts placed Juan Corona at the murder scenes, and he was held for trial. Defense attorneys tried to blame the murders on Natividad, a known homosexual given to fits of violence, but no one could document his presence in California during the murder spree. Jurors deliberated 45 hours before convicting Corona on all counts in January 1973. A month later, he was sentenced to 25 consecutive terms of life imprisonment.

The case—which set an American record for individual murder convictions at the time—was not completed, yet. Reports issued in December 1973 linked Corona to the death of a 26th victim, but no new charges were filed. In May 1978, an appeals court ordered a new trial for Corona, finding his prior legal defenders incompetent. The retrial was delayed by periods of psychiatric observation and a jailhouse stabbing in 1980, which cost Corona the sight in one eye. Convicted again in the spring of 1982, Corona was returned to prison with a new sentence of 25 life terms.

CROSS-DRESSING and Serial Murder

While frequently used as a plot device in FICTION AND FILM portrayals of serial murder (*Psycho, Dressed to Kill, Silence of the Lambs* etc.), adult transvestism is rare among serial killers. OTTIS TOOLE sometimes donned women's clothes while trolling gay bars for a one-night stand, but when he killed—often without regard to gender—he adopted no particular disguise, as likely to behead a child or run down a hitchhiker as to slay a casual lover.

Perhaps ironically, the point in time when cross-dressing *does* affect the lives of some male serial killers is in childhood, when they have no choice. In fact, it is worth noting that seven unrelated sex killers were subjected to the identical trauma of compulsory cross-dressing during their formative years. In every case but one, the masquerade was orchestrated by a female relative or guardian, and while their stated motives varied, the results were strikingly consistent.

An exception to the rule of torment by a brutal mother figure was CHARLES MANSON, sent to elementary school in a dress by his uncle, with the sage advice that it would teach him "how to fight and be a man." HENRY LUCAS was also sent to school in skirts and dainty curls until administrators filed injunctions to prevent his mother from abusing him in public. It is curious (and possibly irrelevant) that Manson and Lucas both suffered their peculiar torment in Virginia in the early 1940s. Further south and 10 years later, Ottis Toole was dressed in petticoats and lace by an older sister who treated him as a living "doll." (As an adult,

Juan Corona (Wide World API)

ironically, he teamed with Lucas for a murder spree that spanned the continent.) In California, CARROLL COLE was forced to dress as "Mama's little girl" while serving coffee to his mother's friends. Yet another Californian, GORDON NORTHCOTT, was habitually dressed as a girl by his mentally unbalanced mother until age 16. A wicked stepmother was the culprit in Rodney Beeler's case, her favorite dress-up "punishment" producing a serial rapist now sentenced to die for the one murder California authorities are able to prove. And worlds away, in Ecuador, child-killer Daniel Barbosa bitterly recalls the way his mother dressed him as a girl to "keep him out of trouble" in the seedy barrio they occupied.

Children subjected to trauma of this sort are prime candidates for gender confusion and disruption of the "cognitive mapping" that determines future thought patterns, ideally providing control of emotions and linking the individual to his social environment. In the cases noted above, each subject came of age with different personality quirks, but all were prone to sudden, unpredictable violence. Toole and Northcott were openly gay, the former killing indiscriminately, while the latter preyed exclusively on boys. Lucas was another indiscriminate killer, though he favored female victims. Manson was a hard-line career criminal, specializing in auto theft and prison life before an unwelcome parole propelled him into the 1960s drug culture, with youthful runaways ripe for the picking. After one impulsive murder in childhood, Cole restricted his murders to women who reminded him of his drunken, adulterous mother. Barbosa, for his part, killed children—more than 70 in all—preferring a machete as his weapon of choice.

See also CHILDHOOD TRAUMA; WARNING SIGNS

CULTS and Serial Murder

There is no standard, universally accepted definition of what constitutes a "cult." J. Gordon Melton, in his *Encyclopedic Handbook of Cults in America* (1986), defines the term as "a pejorative label used to describe certain religious groups outside the mainstream of Western religion." Six years later, the FBI *Crime Classification Manual* further complicated matters by describing a cult as "a body of adherents with excessive devotion or dedication to ideas, objects, or persons, regarded as unorthodox or spurious and whose primary objectives of sex, power, and/or money are unknown to the general membership." The FBI's definition leaves critical questions unanswered: Who decides when devotion is "excessive" and which ideas (much less persons) are "unorthodox or spurious"? If all members of a religious group—like the self-styled "Death Angels"

responsible for California's "ZEBRA" MURDERS—are aware of the group's illegal aims, does it then cease to be a cult? And if so, what *is* it?

Modern history is rife with examples of cult-related murders, by no means limited to stereotypical practitioners of Satanism or black magic. Ervil LeBaron's polygamous Church of the Lamb of God committed numerous homicides spanning three decades in the United States and Mexico, pursuing the 19th-century Mormon concept of "blood atonement" for sin. The aforementioned "Zebra" killers belonged to a Black Muslim splinter group, while ADOLFO CONSTANZO's disciples mixed "Christian" Santeria with the Afro-Caribbean teachings of *palo mayombe*. Devotees of the antisemitic "Christian Identity" creed have robbed banks and murdered select victims as part of their war against the "Zionist Occupational Government" in Washington, D.C. CHARLES MANSON's followers killed seven persons while attempting to spark the American race war they dubbed "Helter Skelter." In Japan, members of Aum Shinrikyo ("Supreme Truth") unleashed nerve gas on crowded subways in obedience to orders from their mad guru.

As with any other case involving TEAM KILLERS, cult murders may spring from any of the MOTIVES that drive homicidal individuals. Profit, power, sex, revenge—all these and more have mingled with religion throughout history, producing deeds that scandalize mild-mannered sects. Few violent cults have been as flagrantly mercenary as the Persian Assassins or lasted as long as the Kali-worshiping Thugs (responsible for 40,000 ritual murders in the year 1812 alone), but each has done its part to tarnish the name of religion in general and that of "unorthodox" sects in particular.

Despite its social and political advances since the 1960s, Africa remains a "dark continent" in some respects, including cult-related homicides. Nigeria is a grim case in point, with ritual murders reported from the 1930s to the present day. In 1989, Nigerian author Wilson Asekombe claimed that "human sacrifice will soon become the number two cause of death in West Africa, second only to traffic accidents." Although such homicides, like all homicides, are banned by law, blood sacrifices continue in the 21st century. Thirty-three residents of Igboland faced trial in May 2002, on charges of illegally possessing fresh human remains. Three months later, a two-week spate of cult mayhem in Calabar, Nigeria, left 11 victims hacked and shot to death. Police deployed in armored vehicles failed to apprehend the transient killers.

Uganda produced even more shocking revelations in October 1999, as police unearthed 24 corpses at a camp run by Wilson Bushara's Doctrine of Brotherhood sect. If that discovery was not bad enough, a second cult—Gredonia Mwerinda's Movement for the Restoration of the Ten Commandments—fell under scrutiny in March 2000. On March 25, police exhumed 153 bodies from three mass graves at the cult's rural compound, a tally that mounted to 778 by July 7, 2000. While some reports described Mwerinda's sect as a "suicide cult," police reported that some of the victims had been strangled and hacked to death. Media reports indicate that Mwerinda escaped and has thus far eluded police.

South Africa is another hotbed of human sacrifice, where human flesh and organs are prized as *muti* (medicine) in various occult ceremonies. September 2003 brought accusations against a ritual "healer" in Eatonside, after a three-year-old neighbor was slain, his body discarded minus brain, heart and other vital organs. That murder was the third suspected *muti* case in three weeks. On September 9, police in Free State Province arrested six men for trying to sell a human head, hands and feet, genitals, heart, and intestines. On September 20, picnickers found the head of a murdered five-year-old child floating near a dam outside Johannesburg. Few such crimes are solved, and British authorities fear they may have spilled over to London, after a child's dismembered corpse was pulled from the Thames. An African immigrant was charged in that case, and had yet to face trial when this work went to press.

Echoes of the Thug cult sounded from India in July 1997, when Calcutta University professor Bratindra Mukherjee declared that "human sacrifice is once again being practiced in the name of God." A 40-year student of Indian cults, Mukherjee reported a dramatic rise in child abductions during the past 18 months, alleging that many of those snatched from home and the streets had been ritually murdered. Sankarshan Ray, an Indian scientist ostracized by peers after he published a report on child sacrifice, told journalists, "There are things going on, practices and rites, which nobody wants to admit are taking place." That judgment was confirmed in March 2002, when "a nameless sect" of occult treasure-hunters was uncovered at Hyderabad. Members of the cult indulge in CANNIBALISM, police maintain, using human flesh in *puja* rites to help them find hidden wealth.

Halfway around the world, in Brazil, authorities blamed a black magic cult for the mutilation-murders of 20 boys, aged nine to 14, in the decade preceding October 2001. Many of the victims were sexually assaulted prior to death, and most were castrated. Ritual objects, including black ribbons and black candle wax, were found near the bodies. James Cavallaro, spokesman for the human rights group Global Justice, complained to the Organization of American States (OAS), reporting that "[t]he investigation has been abysmal despite the gravity of the cases and the proof is we have 20 corpses and no convictions." The OAS accepted Cavallaro's petition and called upon Brazilian leaders to defend their lack of progress in the case, but no further reports have emerged from the region thus far.

In Honduras, meanwhile, 2001 brought reports that police in Tegucigalpa were investigating local gangs suspected of graduating from satanic animal sacrifices to kidnapping and murdering children. Inspector Florencio Oseguera, chief of Tegucigalpa's gang crime division, reported that the headless corpse of one missing boy had been found in June. "The boy," he said, "as well as being without a head and bloodied, had symbols and markings on his body, in women's eyeliner, just like the cats and hens that were found in areas where the gangs are known to have performed Satanic rites." A specific gang, Los Rockeros (the Rockers), was under scrutiny in that case, but no arrests resulted. Similar charges of satanic activity emerged from Italy in 2004, where police accused cult members of multiple murders committed by the elusive "MONSTER OF FLORENCE." On July 30, 2004, police in Milan jailed eight Satanists on charges of killing five victims since 1998.

DAGLIS, Andonis

Dubbed the "Athens Ripper," this Greek serial slayer raped and strangled three prostitutes between 1993 and 1995, afterward cutting their bodies up with a chainsaw and scattering the bloody pieces along outlying highways. A rather inefficient killer, he also attempted to murder six other women during the same period, but they managed to escape his clutches. One, British national Ann Hamson, talked her way out of danger by persuading Daglis she was not, in fact, a prostitute. Portions of his trial were televised in 1996, including the Ripper's public confession to various crimes charged against him. On January 23, 1997, Daglis was convicted on multiple counts, including three rape-slayings and six attempted murders. He was sentenced to 13 terms of life imprisonment, presumably enough to keep him off the street for the remainder of his life.

DAHMER, Jeffrey Lionel

Milwaukee born in 1960, Jeffrey Dahmer moved to Ohio with his family at age six. In 1968 he was sexually molested by a neighbor boy in rural Bath Township. Unreported at the time, the childhood incident may play a pivotal role in understanding Dahmer's subsequent crimes; likewise, the ferocious arguments between his parents (later divorced) clearly demonstrated to Dahmer that home was no safe haven for a child.

By age 10, Dahmer was "experimenting" with dead animals: decapitating rodents, bleaching chicken bones with acid, nailing a dog's carcass to a tree and mounting its head on a stake. In June 1978, days after his graduation from high school, Dahmer crossed the line from morbid "experimentation" to murder. He was living alone at the time, his parents having separated and fled, neither one thinking to take Jeff along. His victim was hitchhiker Steven Hicks, whom Dahmer took home for a drink and some laughs. When Hicks tried to leave, Dahmer crushed his skull with a barbell, strangled him to death, then dismembered and buried his corpse.

That first slaying shocked Jeffrey back to a semblance of normality. He took a brief shot at college, then signed up for a six-year term of military service, but the army discharged him after barely two years, fed up with his

Jeffrey Dahmer in court (Author's collection)

Forensics experts search for remains of Dahmer victims. (Wide World API)

heavy drinking. (Later speculation on his possible link to several unsolved murders in Germany, committed while Dahmer was stationed there, produced no concrete evidence.) In 1982, he moved into his grandmother's house in West Allis, Wisconsin. That August, Dahmer logged an arrest for indecent exposure at the state fair. Identical charges were filed in September 1986 when two boys accused Dahmer of masturbating in public. Convicted of disorderly conduct in that case, he received a one-year suspended sentence with orders for counseling.

On September 15, 1987, Steven Tuomi vanished in Milwaukee, the mystery unsolved until Dahmer confessed to his murder in 1991. James Doxtator was the next to die, in January 1988, followed by Richard Guerrero on March 24. By September 1988, Jeffrey's odd hours and the stench of his "experiments" had become too much for his grandmother, and he was asked to move out. On September 25 he found an apartment on Milwaukee's North 25th Street.

The next day, Dahmer lured a Laotian boy to his flat, fondled him, and offered cash for a nude modeling session. Police were called, and Dahmer was charged with sexual assault. Convicted in January 1989, he remained free pending a formal sentencing scheduled for May.

Meanwhile, on March 25, Dahmer slaughtered victim Anthony Sears.

Sentenced to one year in jail, Dahmer was released after serving 10 months. The death parade resumed with Edward Smith in June 1990. July's victim was Raymond Smith (no relation to Edward). Ernest Miller and David Thomas were butchered in September. Dahmer bagged Curtis Straughter in February 1991. Errol Lindsey joined the list in April, followed by Anthony Hughes in May.

By that time, Dahmer had conceived the bizarre notion of creating "zombies" who would be his live-in sex toys, obedient to his every whim. Instead of using voodoo, Jeffrey opted for a more direct approach, drilling holes in the selected victim's skull, then dribbling caustic liquids into the wounds in an effort to destroy the subject's conscious will. Needless to say, the weird approach to neurosurgery had a 100 percent failure rate, and none of Dahmer's favored "patients" survived.

One *almost* got away, however. Konerak Sinthasomphone was a brother of the youth Dahmer molested in 1988. Missing from home on May 16, 1991, he was next seen the following day—naked, dazed, and bleeding from head wounds—when neighbors reported his plight to Milwaukee police. Officers questioned Dahmer, who described Konerak as his adult homosexual lover, and since Konerak spoke no English, they returned the youth to Dahmer's custody . . . and to his death. (When news of the blunder broke, following Dahmer's arrest on murder charges, the two patrolmen were briefly suspended from duty, then reinstated when they threatened civil suits against the city.)

The juggernaut rolled on: Matt Turner killed on June 30; Jeremiah Weinberger on July 7; Oliver Lacy on July 15; Joseph Brandehoft four days later. In addition to raping, murdering, and dismembering his victims, Dahmer also sampled CANNIBALISM with at least one corpse, though he denied it was his common practice. Tracy Edwards was lucky, escaping from Dahmer's apartment on July 22 with handcuffs still dangling from one wrist. He flagged a squad car down and led police back to Dahmer's flat at the Oxford Apartments, where the dissected remains of 11 victims were found in acid vats and the refrigerator. In a touch reminiscent of another Wisconsin necrophile, EDWARD GEIN, Dahmer had built a makeshift altar in his bedroom, decorated with candles and human skulls.

By August 22, 1991, Dahmer had been charged with 15 counts of murder. At his trial, beginning on January 30, 1992, Dahmer filed a plea of guilty but insane. Two weeks later, on February 15, jurors found him sane and responsible for his actions. The court imposed 15 consecutive life sentences, thus requiring Dahmer to serve a minimum of 936 years. (He was subsequently charged with the Hicks murder, in Ohio, but was never brought to trial.)

In prison, Dahmer refused offers of protective custody despite the many threats against his life. On July 3, 1994, another convict tried to slash his throat in the prison chapel, but Dahmer emerged from the incident with only minor scratches and refused to press charges. Five months later, on November 28, he was cleaning a bathroom adjacent to the prison gym when another member of the work detail, 25-year-old Christopher Scarver, grabbed an iron bar from a nearby exercise machine and smashed Dahmer's skull, killing him instantly. A second inmate, 37-year-old Jesse Anderson, was mortally wounded in the same attack, dying two days later. A racial motive was initially suspected in the murder since Scarver, like many of Dahmer's victims, was black, but a closer look determined that the killer was deranged, believing himself to be the "son of God," acting out his "father's" command.

DENKE, Karl

A native of Munsterberg, Silesia—now Ziebice, Poland—Denke operated a rooming house in his hometown between 1918 and 1924. His tenants affectionately called him "Papa," and Denke was also well liked in the community at large, serving as the organ blower for his local church. On the side, in three years' time, he also murdered and devoured a minimum of 30 victims.

On December 21, 1924, one of Denke's tenants, a coachman named Gabriel, heard cries for help that seemed to emanate from Denke's downstairs flat. Afraid the landlord might be injured, Gabriel rushed down to help . . . and found a young man staggering along the corridor, blood streaming from his lacerated scalp. Before he fell unconscious on the floor, the stranger blurted out that "Papa" Denke had attacked him with an ax.

Police were summoned and arrested Denke, scouring his flat for evidence. They turned up identification papers for twelve traveling journeymen, plus assorted items of male clothing. In the kitchen, two large tubs held meat pickled in brine; together with the assorted bones and pots of fat they also found, detectives reckoned that it added up to 31 victims, more or less. In Denke's ledger, they found listed names and dates, with the respective weights of bodies he had pickled dating back to 1921. According to that record, Denke seemed to specialize in slaying beggars, tramps, and journeymen who seemed unlikely to be missed around the neighborhood.

No evidence of sexual assault was ever publicized in Denke's case, and homicide investigators were unable to explain his actions. Shortly after his arrest, the cannibal killer hanged himself with his suspenders, in his cell, leaving generations of historians to speculate in vain about his motives.

"DISORGANIZED" Killers

The polar opposite of so-called ORGANIZED KILLERS in the FBI scheme of psychological PROFILING, these offenders appear to have three strikes against them before they begin. They do everything wrong, from the first impulsive act to their desertion of a chaotic, clue-ridden crime scene . . . and yet, some of them still go on to kill and kill again for years on end, if they are ever caught at all.

The "normal" disorganized killer is possessed of average intelligence at best, sometimes mentally retarded, nearly always socially immature. The offender mirrors his father's unstable work record by quitting or losing one job after another, rarely qualifying for a skilled occupation. His (or her) social life is equally barren: the offender typically lives alone and is sexually incompetent, sometimes virginal. (Strangler Harvey Glatman experienced sex for the first time at age 29 when he raped his first murder victim). The disorganized killer rarely drinks to bolster his courage, since his crimes are impulsive and largely unplanned. No serious precipitating stress is seen; rather, the killer strikes at random, almost whimsically, without thinking through his actions. He frequently lives and/or works near the crime scene, perhaps attacking a neighbor, and displays little interest in media coverage of the case. Too distracted or dim-witted to recognize danger, he seldom makes any dramatic changes in lifestyle to avoid detection.

A disorganized crime scene reeks of spontaneity. The victim is often known to his attacker, and perhaps for that reason, the slayer often depersonalizes his prey (as in disfiguring or covering the face). The kill itself is frequently a "blitz" attack with little or no conversation, worlds apart from the "organized" slayer's technique of scripted seduction. Because they are normally killed or disabled in seconds, victims are seldom bound or tortured; any sexual assault is likely to be carried out upon the corpse. Because he gives so little thought to capture, the disorganized slayer rarely transports or conceals his kills, leaving bodies where they fall and are easily found. Little or no effort is made to clean up the crime scene, conceal weapons, or eradicate such evidence as semen stains and fingerprints.

It would appear, from those criteria, that every disorganized killer should be caught after the first or second murder, but such is not always the case. Some, like Sacramento vampire Richard Trenton Chase, embark on such ferocious killing sprees that they outrun investigators for a time through sheer momentum and rack up a fair body count in the process. Others, like Wisconsin's EDWARD GEIN, are blessed by circumstance—remote locations or particularly unobservant neighbors—so that they can kill for years, even decades on end, without being exposed.

See also MODUS OPERANDI; MOTIVES; VICAP

DOUGLAS, John Edward: FBI profiler

A Brooklyn native, born in 1945, Douglas is the first to admit that he was "no academic standout" in high school. Having been rejected by Cornell University, he wound up enrolling at Montana State, in Bozeman, where he struggled to maintain a "D" average. In 1966, with the war in Vietnam heating up, Douglas joined the U.S. Air Force to avoid an army draft and was stationed in New Mexico, where he finished earning his BA. He also became fast friends with a local FBI agent, who urged him to apply for a job with the Bureau after his discharge from military service in 1970.

Douglas was accepted by the FBI and spent his first year as an agent in Detroit, assigned to the Reactive Crimes Unit that investigated kidnappings, bank robberies, and similar federal crimes. A year later, transferred to Milwaukee, he filled a similar position, doubling as a member of the FBI's SWAT team. Recalled to the FBI Academy in 1975 for training in hostage negotiation, Douglas met instructor and fellow agent ROBERT RESSLER, assigned to the Behavioral Science Unit. They hit it off, and Ressler recommended Douglas for a job with BSU in June 1977. Together and separately, they conducted many prison interviews with convicted killers over the next six years as part of the BSU's Criminal Personality Research Project, leading to creation of VICAP, the Violent Criminal Apprehension Program, in 1985. Ressler retired five years later, and Douglas replaced him as the chief of BSU—renamed Investigative Support Services—and held that post until his own retirement in 1995.

Although involved at the periphery of many infamous serial murder cases, often described as the model for fictional G-man Jack Crawford in the novels *Red Dragon* and *The Silence of the Lambs*, Douglas did not pursue and arrest serial killers himself. Still, the job had its dangers, including a schedule so hectic and stressful that it drove Douglas to a near-fatal brain hemorrhage in December 1983 while visiting Seattle to consult on the case of the "GREEN RIVER KILLER."

Although he was interviewed frequently and gave countless lectures while serving with the FBI, true fame found Douglas in retirement, with several best-selling books, countless TV talk-show appearances, and a lucrative sideline in private consultation on criminal cases such as the infamous JonBenét Ramsey murder in Boulder, Colorado. Books coauthored by Douglas in the subject area of serial murder include *Sexual Homicide* (1988); the FBI's *Crime Classification Manual* (1992); *Mind Hunter* (1995); *Unabomber* (1996); *Journey Into Darkness* (1997); *Obsession* (1998); *The Anatomy of Motive* (1999); *The Cases That Haunt Us* (2000), and *Anyone You Want Me to Be* (2003).

Ironically, Douglas's celebrity has evoked public hostility from his one-time mentor, Robert Ressler, criticizing Douglas for his "flamboyance" and denouncing claims that Douglas "went face-to-face with JOHN GACY," when prison records show they never met. (In fairness to Douglas, the claim was apparently made by a press agent, rather than Douglas himself; it appears nowhere in his published books.) When Douglas hired on with the Ramsey defense team in Boulder, announcing his "gut instinct" that the victim's parents were innocent of her murder, Ressler publicly questioned his judgment, describing Douglas in one interview as "a Hollywood type of guy." Douglas, for his part, has thus far declined to participate in public squabbling with his former boss.

DURRANT, William Henry Theodore

At first glance, Theodore Durrant appeared to be what well-placed women and their single daughters would call a "good catch." Still in his twenties, courteous, well groomed, a doctor in training at San Francisco's Cooper Medical College, he was also devoutly religious, serving as assistant superintendent for the regular Sunday school at Emmanuel Baptist Church. Unknown to those around him, though, the young man had a darker side. His dual obsessions were religion and sex, although in the latter field, he would confide to a fellow med student, "I have no knowledge of women."

That didn't stop young ladies from being drawn to Durrant like moths to a flame, however, and one of his strongest admirers was 18-year-old Blanche Lamont, a parishioner at Emmanuel Baptist. On April 3, 1895, they were seen together by numerous witness, making their way toward the church, where Blanche was last seen alive on the sidewalk outside. She had been missing several days, curiously unreported by her family, when Durrant began dropping broad hints that she might have "gone astray." On the side, he was pawning her jewelry and pocketing the cash.

Police were clueless as to Blanche's whereabouts, but another young woman at Emmanuel Baptist, 21-year-old Minnie Williams, was talking her head off, telling friends that she "knew too much" about the case, hinting darkly that Blanche had met with foul play. On April 12, Minnie was seen arguing with Theo Durrant on the street outside the church, but they seemed to patch things up, and she was holding his arm, cuddling close, as they went back inside.

Next morning, a Saturday, members of the church Ladies Society were stunned to find Minnie's lifeless, blood-smeared body wedged inside a church cupboard. Half naked, she had been stabbed in both breasts, her wrists slashed, and her own underwear jammed in her mouth. Police waited a day before searching the rest of the church, thereby disrupting Easter Sunday services, but it was worth the effort. Once they forced the boarded-up door to Emmanuel Baptist's 120-foot belfry, they found Blanche Lamont's body; she was naked, strangled, rape after death, her clothing packed into the belfry rafters. Her corpse had been arranged so neatly, head propped up on wooden blocks, that police immediately cast about for "someone who knows something about medicine."

Theo Durrant was a natural suspect, all things considered, and he was swiftly indicted for Blanche Lamont's murder. Conviction for the "Monster of the Belfry" was even more rapid, jurors setting a new record with deliberations lasting barely five minutes. Durrant was sentenced to die, and while appeals delayed his execution for nearly two years, he was finally hanged on April 3, 1897—the very anniversary of Blanche Lamont's brutal murder.

In 1999, author Robert Graysmith suggested that Durrant was innocent of any wrongdoing, the victim of a frame-up by clumsy police and his own pastor at Emmanuel Baptist, Rev. John Gibson. It was Gibson, Graysmith claims, who murdered Blanche Lamont and Minnie Williams. More startling yet, Graysmith also names Gibson as London's elusive "JACK THE RIPPER." Sadly, for Durrant's supporters, no evidence exists linking "Pastor Jack" Gibson to either crime series, and Graysmith's credibility is undermined by inclusion of fabricated "diary" excerpts, penned while posthumously delving Durrant's private thoughts.

DUTROUX, Marc

No serial killer since London's "JACK THE RIPPER" has produced social and political upheaval on a par with Belgium's Marc Dutroux. A pedophile and alleged child pornographer, Dutroux murdered at least five victims during the period 1995–96, and some reports suggest a final body count that rivals JEFFREY DAHMER's. It was not Dutroux's brutality or the tender age of his victims, however, that sparked public outcry and high-level government resignations in Belgium. Rather, the upheaval stemmed from his claims that he served as "a cog" in a sinister network of rich child molesters whose tentacles spanned western Europe.

The nightmare began on June 24, 1995, when two eight-year-old girls, Julie Lejeune and Melissa Russo, vanished while playing near their homes in Grace-Hollogne, eastern Belgium. Two months later, on August 23, 19-year-old Eefje Lambrecks and 17-year-old An Marchal disappeared on a holiday visit to the seaport town of Ostend. Twelve-year-old Sabine Dardenne went missing on May 28, 1996, while riding her bicycle to school in Kain, southwestern Belgium. Laetitia Delhez, age 14, dropped from sight on December 6, 1995, homeward bound from a public swimming pool in the southeastern town of Bertrix.

Marc Dutroux was well known to police when the girls disappeared. The eldest of five children, born in Brussels in November 1956, he assumed the life of a transient prostitute after his parents (both teachers) separated in 1971. Married for the first time at age 20, Dutroux sired two sons, but flagrant adultery and sporadic wife-beating doomed that relationship in the early 1980s. By then, he had already logged the first in a series of convictions for theft, mugging, drug dealing, and selling stolen cars. Dutroux soon married one of his mistresses, Michelle Martin, and his record went from bad to worse. In 1986, Dutroux and Michelle were arrested for kidnapping and raping five girls.

Both were convicted and sentenced to prison in 1989, but Dutroux's 13-year term was cut short in 1992, parole granted under a government program designed to keep close watch on known sex offenders. Dutroux's own mother opposed his release, warning prison officials, "I have known for a long time and with good cause my eldest's temperament. What I do not know, and what all the people who know him fear, [is] what he has in mind for the future." Nonetheless, Dutroux was freed with a bonus, receiving a monthly invalid's pension of $1,162.

Back on the street, Dutroux returned to his criminal trade and compiled a fortune adequate to purchase and maintain seven homes. In 1993, informer Claud Thirault told detectives that Dutroux had built a concrete bunker under one of his homes, intended as a holding pen for kidnapped girls whom he would sell to pedophiles abroad. Dutroux had offered Thirault $3,500 per head for any victims procured of a certain type—long-haired, slender and prepubescent—but police ignored the warning. Two years later, an internal memo was finally issued, recording the details of Thirault's report. Police called on Dutroux in June 1995, after Julie Lejeune and Melissa Russo disappeared. While searching Dutroux's house, the officers heard muffled screams from somewhere close at hand, but they accepted Dutroux's explanation that the sounds came from children playing outside. Six months later, Dutroux was charged with auto theft and other crimes. Subsequently convicted at trial, he served nearly four months in prison, but emerged in time to snatch Sabine Dardenne from Kain.

The net finally closed on August 13, 1996, when police arrested Dutroux, Michelle Martin (now his ex-wife), and 24-year-old Michel Lelievre in Sars-la-Buissière, southern Belgium. Two days later, Dutroux led detectives to his home in Charleroi, a suburb of Marcinelle, where Sabine Dardenne and Laetitia Delhez were found alive in a makeshift basement dungeon. Both girls were malnourished; both had been drugged and sexually abused. On August 16, soon after police detained a fourth suspect, 54-year-old businessman Jean-Michel Nihoul, Dutroux confessed to kidnapping Eefje Lambrecks and An Marchal. One day later, he admitted murdering both girls and added the name of suspected accomplice Bernard Weinstein to the hit list. That afternoon, Dutroux led police to his Sars-la-Buissière property, where the bodies of Weinstein and two other missing girls—Julie Lejeune and Melissa Russo—were pulled from graves in his backyard. By nightfall, Dutroux and company were charged with kidnapping and murder. On September 2, 1996, police found Eefje Lambrecks and An Marchal buried beneath a garden shed at Weinstein's home, in the Charleroi suburb of Jumet.

Ripples of panic spread swiftly, including media allegations of an international pedophile ring and suspicion that Dutroux might have murdered a fifth girl, reported missing from Slovenia. No charges were filed in that case, or in 12 other slayings mentioned in various media reports, but the charges filed against Dutroux and company were serious enough. Police returned empty-handed from their search of a flooded coal mine on property owned by Dutroux—he had described the site as "interesting"—and Dutroux's attorney complained of death threats and desertion by longstanding clients. Protesters jeered outside Belgium's High Court on October 15, after the five-judge panel removed investigating judge Jean-Marc Connerotte from Dutroux's case on grounds of bias (he had attended a fund-raiser for the victims' families). Two weeks later, 300,000 angry Belgians marched through Brussels, protesting inept police handling of the case.

Confined at Arlon, in southeastern Belgium, Dutroux was swamped with fan mail and cash from strange GROUPIES, even while the general public condemned him as a beast in human form. On December 22, 1996, he recommended that police search the abandoned coal mines once more, but officers demurred, suspecting a practical joke. One lawman told reporters, "I can just imagine that bastard enjoying the television pictures of us digging away in the cold and wet." Formal indictments were issued on February 2, 1997, charging Dutroux with five counts of murder, plus charges of kidnapping, rape, auto theft, and "criminal association." Michel Lelievre faced charges of kidnapping, rape, and drug possession, Michel Nihoul was charged with kidnapping, and Michelle Martin was charged with conspiracy to kidnap.

Controversy continued as the case made its way through Belgian courts with glacial speed. On April 9, 1997, a report from parliament condemned the police investigation of Dutroux as "inhumane, inept, inefficient and ill-equipped." Protest demonstrations marked the second anniversary of the Lejeune-Russo abductions in June 1997. Four months later, parliament's Committee on Legal Affairs and Citizens' Rights demanded the resignation of Belgian judge Melchior Wathelet, who approved Dutroux's parole in 1992, from the European Court of Justice. In February 1998, after parliament rejected claims of an official cover-up, An Marchal's father denounced the report as a whitewash. "The traditional parties in power," he said, "have once again managed to protect themselves. They are laughing at the death of my daughter and the other ones." Dutroux escaped from custody on April 23, 1998, during a trip to the Neufchâteau courthouse, but his stolen car bogged down in mud near Straitmont, and he was soon recaptured. Resignations ensued, beginning with those of Interior Minister Johan Vande Lanmotte and Justice Minister Stefaan De Clerck on the same day, followed by Gendarmerie commander Willy De Ridder on April 28.

Two months later, on June 27, the Belgian Justice Ministry announced that Dutroux's murder trial would not commence before September 2000 "because inquiries into Dutroux's alleged child sex crimes are not complete." That estimate proved wildly optimistic, though Dutroux faced trial for his jailbreak in March 2000. Belgium had no law against escape from custody, but Dutroux faced charges of car theft, assaulting a police officer, and stealing the officer's pistol. Smiling at the outset of those proceedings on March 20, Dutroux listened while his lawyers described his confinement as "inhuman," complaining that Dutroux was no longer "in possession of all of his faculties." An unsympathetic judge convicted Dutroux of theft and threatening behavior on June 19, 2000, slapping Belgium's "most hated man" with a five-year prison sentence.

Legal wrangling postponed Dutroux's murder trial. In early 2003, a grand jury at Neufchâteau dismissed the case against defendant Nihoul, but prosecutors appealed that decision and won a reversal on April 30. Even then, Dutroux and his codefendants did not face trial until March 1, 2004, a delay of nearly eight years. When court finally convened at Arlon, defense attorney Martine Van Praet complained that local hotels denied her a room, while granting free suites to Dutroux's prosecutors. Six hundred witnesses were scheduled to testify before an audience of 300 police and 1,300 journalists, who would beam the gruesome details of the case worldwide. Kidnap survivor Sabine Dardenne described her 80 days in Dutroux's dungeon, where she subsisted on a near-starvation diet while she was raped and otherwise abused. Julie Lejeune and Melissa Russo had starved to death in their basement cell, ignored by Dutroux's wife while Dutroux was imprisoned for auto theft in 1996.

Dutroux seemed unconcerned, dozing off during jury selection and thereby earning rebukes from Judge Stephane Goux. ("He seems to be very tired and had a very bad night," lawyer Ronny Baudewijn explained.) When conscious, Dutroux maintained his pose of wounded innocence, describing himself as a "small cog" in an international sex-slave network. His basement cells were built, Dutroux insisted, to "protect" kidnapped girls from abuse by members of the ring. Blaming "two policemen" for the abductions, Dutroux told the court on March 3, "I didn't even know what pedophilia was. It was all Chinese to me." Michelle Martin changed her tune on the witness stand, insisting that she was "too scared" to feed Lejeune and Russo in captivity while Dutroux served 106 days in prison. She

regarded them as "savage beasts" who might attack her, but insisted that both girls were still alive when Dutroux left jail. The end had been quicker for Eefje Lambrecks and An Marchal, who were drugged, bound, and buried alive.

Judge Jean-Marc Connerotte wept while testifying on March 4, describing death threats and high-level intrigue that obstructed his pursuit of Dutroux's case. "Never before in Belgium," he declared, "has an investigating judge at the service of the king been subjected to such pressure." Upon their release from the dungeon, Connerotte recalled, survivors Dardenne and Delhez "didn't want to come out" until urged by Dutroux. "They thanked Dutroux," said Connerotte. "It was absolutely terrible. They kissed him. That shows how much he had conditioned them." Investigator Jacques Langlois reviewed his 440,000-page dossier on the case, comparing Dutroux's early series of rapes to the later crimes that climaxed in murder. On March 18, guards found a key to Dutroux's handcuffs hidden in a bag of salt in the jailhouse kitchen, but Dutroux expressed "surprise" at charges that he planned a fresh escape. Summarizing his defense on June 10, Dutroux called himself a "scapegoat" in an "organized lynching," insisting to the court that "I am not a murderer." Still, he said, "I don't contest any of my real faults. I am here to be condemned." His chief fault in the deaths of victims Lejeune and Russo, he proclaimed, lay in "abandon[ing] them to the conscience of my wife," who let them starve.

On June 17, 2004, jurors convicted Dutroux on two murder counts (Lambrecks and Marchal), four counts of kidnapping (Dardenne, Delhez, Lejeune, and Russo), and two counts of rape (Dardenne and Delhez). Michelle Martin was convicted of conspiracy, and

Marc Dutroux (right) is led out of the courthouse in Neufchateau, Belgium, on March 20, 2000. (AP Photo/Yves Logghe)

Michel Lelievre was found guilty on charges including abduction, rape, and drug possession. The panel failed to reach a verdict on Jean-Michel Nihoul, charged with kidnapping victim Laetitia Delhez. Many Belgians voiced dissatisfaction with the verdicts, since the trial and eight-year investigation revealed no further evidence against Dutroux's confederates in the alleged international pedophile ring.

EDWARDS, Mack Ray

A native of Arkansas, born in 1919, Edwards moved to Los Angeles in 1941, logging one arrest for vagrancy that April, prior to finding work as a heavy equipment operator. In that role, he helped build the freeways that made L.A. famous, and by early 1970 he was a veteran on the job, married and a father of two, the very model of blue-collar propriety. If people suspected his involvement in a string of brutal murders spanning 16 years, they kept the secret to themselves.

On March 5, 1970, three girls, ages 12 to 14, were abducted by burglars from their home in Sylmar, a Los Angeles suburb. Two escaped from their captors, but one was still missing the next day when Mack Edwards entered a Los Angeles police station, surrendering a loaded revolver as he told the duty officer, "I have a guilt complex." Edwards named his teenage accomplice in the recent kidnapping and directed police to the Angeles National Forest, where the missing girl was found, unharmed. Before authorities could take his statement down, the prisoner informed them there were "other matters" to discuss.

As homicide detectives listened, dumb-struck, Edwards voluntarily confessed to a half-dozen murders dating from the early 1950s. Stella Nolan, eight years old, had been the first to die, in June of 1953. Abducted from her home in Compton, she had never been recovered, and her fate remained a mystery for 17 years until a killer's conscience led him to confess. Mack's second crime had been a doubleheader, claiming 13-year-old Don Baker and 11-year-old Brenda Howell in Azusa, on August 6, 1956. Once again, the bodies were missing, no solution in sight before Edwards surrendered himself to police.

According to the killer's statement, he had sworn off murder for a dozen years, returning with a vengeance in the fall of 1968. Gary Rochet, age 16, had been shot to death at his home in Granada Hills on November 26, and 16-year-old Roger Madison had vanished in Sylmar three weeks later. The last to go was 13-year-old Donald Todd, reported missing from Pacoima on May 16, 1969.

On March 7, 1970, Edwards led officers into the San Gabriel Mountains, seeking the graves of two victims, but altered terrain foiled the search. He had better luck four days later, directing his keepers to a section of the Santa Ana Freeway where the skeletal remains of Stella Nolan were unearthed from an eight-foot-deep grave. Edwards maintained that Roger Madison was buried beneath the Ventura Freeway, but authorities declined to plow the highway up in search of clues. The crimes, Mack said, had all been motivated by an urge for sex.

With Edwards safely under lock and key, police voiced skepticism at the 12-year gap in his killing career, suggesting that there might be other victims unaccounted for—a body count of 22, in all. Responding from his cell, the killer adamantly stuck by his confession. "Six is all there is," he told reporters. "There's not any more. That's all there is." Before his trial, he twice attempted suicide, slashing his stomach with a razor blade on March 30 and gulping an overdose of tranquilizers on May 7.

Charged in three of his six confessed murders, Edwards was convicted and sentenced to die after telling the jury, "I want the chair. That's what I've always wanted." Immediate execution was his goal. As Edwards told the court, "My lawyer told me there are a hundred men waiting to die in the chair. I'm asking the judge if I can have the first man's place. He's sitting there sweating right now. I'm not sweating. I'm ready for it."

Ready or not, Edwards was faced with the prospect of automatic appeals, conscious of the fact that no California inmate had been executed in the past four years. On October 30, 1971, he cut the process short, using an electric cord to hang himself in his death row cell at San Quentin.

See also MISSING PERSONS

ENRIQUETA, Marti

A self-styled witch who made her living through the sale of charms and potions, Enriqueta was arrested by police in Barcelona, Spain, in March 1912 on charges of abducting several local children. Her most recent victim, a young girl named Angelita, was rescued alive from the witch's lair, appalling police with a tale of murder and CANNIBALISM. According to the girl, she had been forced by Enriqueta to partake of human flesh. Her "meal" had been the pitiful remains of yet another child, kidnapped by the murderess a short time earlier.

As ultimately pieced together by authorities, Enriqueta's local crimes had already claimed at least six victims. After murdering the children, she would boil their bodies down for use as prime ingredients in her expensive "love potions." Convicted on the basis of her own confession, coupled with the testimony of her sole surviving victim, Marti Enriqueta was condemned and executed for her crimes.

ERSKINE, Kenneth

At age 24, Kenneth Erskine was diagnosed by court psychiatrists as possessing "a mental age of eleven." A persistent loner, abandoned by his English mother and Antiguan father, he drifted through a milieu of special schools and flophouses, compiling a record of arrests for burglary in London, living on the proceeds of his thefts. Business was good enough for Erskine to open 10 separate bank accounts for his stolen loot, but money isn't everything. Somewhere along the way, the simple-minded youth picked up a taste for homicide.

The first to die was 78-year-old Eileen Emms, strangled in her home during the first week of April 1987. A month later, Janet Crockett, age 67, was killed in identical fashion. The stalker rebounded with a doubleheader on June 28, claiming 84-year-old Valentine Gleime and 94-year-old Zbignew Stabrawa in separate incidents. William Carmen, age 84, was strangled in early July. Two weeks later, 74-year-old William Downes and 80-

year-old Florence Tisdall were found dead on successive mornings.

By then, police were working overtime to find the "Stockwell Strangler," so called after the southwest London neighborhood where five of his victims were slain. There had been petty thefts in several cases, with a television stolen from Crockett's apartment and roughly $900 missing from Carmen's home, but robbery did not appear to be the driving motive. All of the victims were strangled manually, left on their beds with the sheets pulled up to their chins. Five had been sexually molested, but authorities could not determine whether the acts were committed before or after death.

Kenneth Erskine was arrested on July 28 at a social security office for trying to conceal one of his numerous savings accounts. In custody, his palm print matched one lifted from a Stockwell murder scene, and he was picked from a lineup by victim Frederick Prentice, 74, who had survived an attempted strangulation on June 27. Under questioning, Erskine seemed to plead amnesia. "I don't remember killing anyone," he told police. "I could have done it without knowing it. I am not sure if I did."

The court had little difficulty sorting out the problem. Charged with seven counts of murder and one count of attempted murder, Erskine was convicted across the board on January 29, 1988. (Two additional murders, dating from 1986, were eliminated from the list on grounds of insufficient evidence.) The presiding judge sentenced Erskine to seven life terms plus an additional 12 years for attempted murder, recommending that the killer serve a minimum of 40 years before he is considered for parole.

ETHERIDGE, Ellen

A solid family background and religious training did not spare the second wife of Texas rancher J. D. Etheridge from pangs of jealousy. When they were married in the spring of 1912, she thought the wealthy widower admired her for herself. It soon became apparent, though, that he was more interested in finding someone who would cook his meals and clean his large Bosque County home, northwest of Waco. Ellen warmed his lonely bed and tended house, but she began to feel neglected as her husband showered his affection on the children—eight in all—who were the living images of her lamented predecessor.

Over time the jealousy gave way to envy, then to hatred. During June of 1913, Ellen launched her plan to thin the herd, employing poison to eliminate a pair of the offensive children. Two more died on October 2, but the coincidence was too extreme. Authorities were curious, and poison was found in postmortem tests. In custody, the second Mrs. Etheridge confessed her crimes and drew a term of life imprisonment.

See also "BLACK WIDOWS"

EVANS, Wesley Gareth

Slow-witted and hyperactive, Canadian Wesley Evans missed long months of schooling due to erratic behavior that made attendance impossible. Hit by a train at age nine, he suffered severe head injuries that left him comatose for eight days, with temporary paralysis on his left side after he regained consciousness. Released from the hospital after four months of therapy, Evans thereafter walked with a pronounced limp, communicating with slurred speech. Eighteen months later, he was burned over 20 percent of his body while playing with a cigarette lighter. He grew up obsessed with the notion that girls—and later, women—were laughing at his scars. In time, his hidden rage would reach a lethal boiling point.

On November 24, 1984, 27-year-old Lavonne Willems was found dead in a Vancouver home she was watching for friends, then on vacation overseas. She had been murdered in the bedroom, stabbed a total of 25 times, her pants unbuckled and open at the waist. Detectives theorized a sexual motive, but they had no suspect in the case.

On March 31, 1985, realtor Beverly Seto, 39, hosted an open house for potential customers in Matsqui, a Vancouver suburb. When she failed to come home for supper, her husband dropped by the vacant house and found her car outside, the door ajar. Inside the house, a light was burning in the kitchen, though the guests had long since departed. Moving through the silent rooms, he found his wife in the bedroom, her throat slashed, skirt bunched up around her waist. The coroner reported that Seto had been raped, then stabbed a minimum of 20 times.

In late July, police received a tip that named a young man from the Matsqui neighborhood as Seto's killer. He was held for questioning in early August 1985, but officers found nothing to connect him with the murder. Seeking further information on their suspect, they detained one of his friends, 21-year-old Wesley Evans, on marijuana charges, hoping they could pressure him for details on the suspect's movements. What they got, instead, was a surprise confession to the crime.

In custody, the prisoner admitted killing Seto and went on to offer details of the Willems murder. Homicide investigators checked their street maps, startled to find that Evans lived a short four blocks from the location of the Seto slaying and barely eight blocks from the house where Willems died. The opening remarks of Wesley's trial were heard on January 16, 1986. Con-

victed two weeks later, he was sentenced to a term of life imprisonment, required to serve a minimum of 25 years before he would be eligible for parole.

EYLER, Larry W.

A native of Crawfordsville, Indiana, born December 21, 1952, Eyler was the youngest of four children born to parents who divorced when he was young. Dropping out of high school in his senior year, he worked odd jobs for a couple of years before earning his GED. Sporadic enrollment in college between 1974 and 1978 left Eyler without a degree, and he finally pulled up stakes, making the move to Chicago.

Unknown to friends and relatives, Larry Eyler was a young man at war with himself, struggling to cope with homosexual tendencies that simultaneously fascinated and repelled him. Like JOHN GACY and a host of others, he would learn to take his sex where he could find it, forcefully, and then eliminate the evidence of his abiding shame.

On March 22, 1982, Jay Reynolds was found, stabbed to death on the outskirts of Lexington, Kentucky. Nine months later, on October 3, 14-year-old Delvoyd Baker was strangled, his body dumped on the roadside north of Indianapolis. Steven Crockett, age 19, was the victim on October 23, stabbed 32 times with four wounds in the head, and discarded outside Lowell, Indiana. The killer moved into Illinois on November 6, leaving Robert Foley in a field northwest of Joliet.

Police were slow to see the pattern forming, unaware that they had already spoken with one survivor. Drugged and beaten near Lowell on November 4, 21-year-old Craig Townsend had escaped from the hospital before detectives completed their investigation of the unprovoked assault.

The transient slayer celebrated Christmas 1982 by dumping 25-year-old John Johnson's body in a field outside Belshaw, Indiana. Three days later, it was a doubleheader, with 21-year-old John Roach discovered near Belleville and the trussed-up body of Steven Agan, a Terre Haute native, discarded north of Newport, Indiana.

The grim toll continued to rise through the spring of 1983, with most of the action shifting to Illinois. By July 2, the body count stood at 12, with the latter victims mutilated after death, a few disemboweled. Ralph Calise made unlucky 13 on August 31, dumped in a field near Lake Forest, Illinois. He had been dead less than 12 hours when he was discovered, bound with clothesline and surgical tape, stabbed 17 times, his pants pulled down around his ankles.

On September 30, 1983, an Indiana highway patrolman spotted a pickup truck parked along Interstate 65,

Larry Eyler (Author's collection)

victim had been decapitated, and all had their pants pulled down, indicating a sexual motive in the slayings. Another "John Doe" was recovered on December 5 near Effingham, Illinois, and the body count jumped again, two days later, when Richard Wayne and an unidentified male were found dead near Indianapolis.

By that time, police had focused their full attention on Larry Eyler. Survivor Craig Townsend had been traced to Chicago after fleeing the Indiana hospital, and he grudgingly identified photographs of Eyler. Another survivor chimed in with similar testimony, but investigators wanted their man for murder, and the circumstantial case was still incomplete.

Facing constant surveillance in Chicago, Eyler filed a civil lawsuit against the Lake County sheriff's office, accusing officers of mounting a "psychological warfare" campaign to unhinge his mind. His claim for a half-million dollars was denied, and as he left the courtroom, Eyler was arrested for the Ralph Calise murder and held in lieu of $1 million bond. Police were jubilant until a pretrial hearing on February 5, 1984, led to exclusion of all the evidence recovered from Eyler's truck. Released on bail, the killer went about his business while investigators scrambled to salvage their failing case.

On May 7, 1984, 22-year-old David Block was found murdered near Zion, Illinois, his wounds conforming to the pattern of his predecessors, but nothing at the scene clearly linked Eyler to the murder. Police got a break three months later, on August 21, when a janitor's skittish dog led his master to examine Eyler's garbage, in Chicago. Police were swiftly summoned to claim the remains of 15-year-old Danny Bridges, a homosexual street hustler whose dismembered body had been neatly bagged for disposal.

Eyler's arrogance had finally undone him. Experts noted that the Bridges mutilations were a carbon copy of the Derrick Hansen case outside Kenosha in October 1983. Convicted of the Bridges slaying on July 9, 1986, Eyler was sentenced to die. By that time, Mother Nature had already passed her own death sentence on Eyler: he was infected with AIDS and his days were numbered.

In November 1990, bargaining to save himself from execution, Eyler agreed to help Indiana authorities solve a number of his crimes if they would intervene to get him off death row. He confessed to the Agan torture-slaying and surprised investigators by naming an alleged accomplice, 53-year-old Robert David Little, chairman of the Department of Library Science at Indiana State University, in Terre Haute. According to Eyler, Little snapped photos and masturbated while Larry disemboweled the victim. Based on his confession, Eyler received a 60-year prison sentence, and Lit-

with two men moving toward a nearby stand of trees. One appeared to be bound, and the officer went to investigate, identifying Larry Eyler as the owner of the truck. His young companion accused Eyler of making homosexual propositions, then asking permission to tie him up. A search of the pickup revealed surgical tape, nylon clothesline, and a hunting knife stained with human blood. Forensics experts noted that the blood type matched Ralph Calise's, while tire tracks and imprints of Eyler's boots made a fair match with tracks from the field where Calise was discovered. Police held Eyler but released him when the search was ruled illegal.

While the investigation continued, with Eyler still at liberty, the murders likewise kept pace. On October 4, 1983, 14-year-old Derrick Hansen was found dismembered near Kenosha, Wisconsin. Eleven days later, a young "John Doe" was discovered near Rensselaer, Indiana. October 18 yielded four bodies in Newton County, dumped together on an abandoned farm; one tle was arrested on murder charges. That case went to trial at Terre Haute, and in the absence of physical evidence to support Eyler's statement, Little was acquitted of all charges on April 17, 1991. Back in Illinois, Eyler offered to clear 20 murders in exchange for commuta-

tion of his sentence to life imprisonment, but state authorities refused. He died of AIDS on March 6, 1994, after confessing 21 murders to his attorney (including four committed with an accomplice who remains at large).

FALLING, Christine Laverne Slaughter

Christine Falling was born in Perry, Florida, on March 12, 1963, the second child of a 65-year-old father and his 16-year-old wife. Reared in poverty, obese and dull-witted, she required regular doses of medication to control her epileptic seizures. As a child, she showed her "love" for cats by strangling them and dropping them from lethal heights in order to "test their nine lives." At age nine, Christine and her sister were removed for a year to a children's refuge following domestic battles that resulted in police being summoned to their home.

In September 1977, at age 14, Christine was married to a man in his twenties. Their chaotic relationship lasted six weeks and was punctuated by violence, Christine once hurling a 25-pound stereo at her husband in the heat of battle. With the collapse of her marriage, Falling lapsed into a bizarre hypochondriacal phase, logging 50 trips to the hospital in the space of two years. She complained of ailments ranging from "red spots" to vaginal bleeding to snakebites, but physicians rarely found any treatable symptoms.

Rendered virtually unemployable by her appearance and mentality, Christine picked up spending money by baby-sitting for neighbors and relatives. On February 25, 1980, one of her charges—two-year-old Cassidy Johnson—was rushed to a doctor's office in Blountstown, tentatively diagnosed as suffering from encephalitis. The girl died on February 28, an autopsy listing cause of death as blunt trauma to the skull. Christine described the baby "passing out" and falling from her crib, but she was unconvincing. One physician wrote a note to the police, advising them to check the baby-sitter out, but it was "lost" in transit and the case was closed.

Christine moved on to Lakeland, and two months after her arrival, four-year-old Jeffrey Davis "stopped breathing" in her care. An autopsy revealed symptoms of myocarditis, a heart inflammation rarely fatal in itself. Three days later, while the family attended Jeffrey's funeral, Falling was retained to sit with two-year-old Joseph Spring, a cousin of the deceased. Joseph died in his crib that afternoon while "napping," and physicians noted evidence of a viral infection, suggesting it might have killed Jeffrey, as well.

Christine was back in Perry—and back in business—by July of 1981. She had received a clean bill of health from the doctors in Lakeland, but her bad luck was holding. She tried her hand at housekeeping, but 77-year-old William Swindle died in his kitchen her first day on the job. A short time later, Falling accompanied her stepsister to the doctor's office, where an eight-month-old niece, Jennifer Daniels, received some standard childhood vaccinations. Stopping by the market on her way home, the stepsister left Christine in the car with her child, returning to find that the baby had simply "stopped breathing."

Thus far, physicians had sympathized with Christine as an unfortunate "victim of circumstance," but their view changed on July 2, 1982, when 10-week-old Travis Coleman died in Falling's care. This time, an autopsy revealed internal ruptures caused by suffocation, and Christine was hauled in for questioning. In custody, she confessed to killing three of the children by means of "smotheration," pressing a blanket over their faces in response to disembodied voices chanting, "Kill the baby."

"The way I done it, I seen it done on TV shows," Christine explained. "I had my own way, though. **Simple** and easy. No one would hear them scream." Convicted on the basis of her own confession, she was sentenced to a term of life imprisonment, with no parole for the first 25 years.

See also SUDDEN INFANT DEATH SYNDROME

FAZEKAS, Julia *See* "ANGEL MAKERS OF NAGYREV"

FICTION and Film Portrayals of Serial Murder

A volume larger than the work in hand would be required simply to list the novels and short stories, TV shows and movies, plays and operas that incorporate serial murder as a major theme or plot device. Some of those works are justly famous, ranked among enduring classics; others are so poorly executed (or so frankly exploitative) that they linger with the reader/viewer for entirely different reasons. Most, unfortunately, are so crudely imitative of their literary/cinematic forebears that they fail to satisfy on any level and become simply forgettable.

We cannot say with any certainty when random killers first appeared in fiction, but their roots go deep. The Danish "fairy tale" of Hansel and Gretel is one prime example, its child-eating witch of the woods nothing more than a sadistic dabbler in black arts and CANNIBALISM. (Her crimes were mirrored in the real-life case of MARTI ENRIQUETA, a Spanish "witch" executed in 1912 for murdering at least six children, cannibalizing their bodies, and boiling the leftovers down for the love charms she sold on the side.) Likewise, the mythical Chevalier Raoul, better known as "BLUEBEARD," whose seventh wife finds the corpses of her predecessors (or, some versions say, their severed heads) while snooping in a room to which she is forbidden access. Bluebeard may have borrowed his nickname from 15th-century child killer GILLES DE RAIS, but his behavior (and his downfall) prefigures scores of cases wherein killers for profit or passion have murdered a series of wives.

While some vocal critics dwell in fear of life imitating art, blaming this or that film/novel/TV program for the latest incident of carnage in the news, it seems that authors and directors lean more often in the opposite direction, lifting plots and characters (albeit typically in garbled and distorted form) from prior events. It comes as no surprise, therefore, that many real-life murderers have found their way into fiction and film. London's anonymous "JACK THE RIPPER" is the hands-down favorite in that regard, appearing (by a very conservative estimate) in no less than 76 novels, 25 motion pictures, eight stage plays, three short-story anthologies, two poetry collections, one rock opera, and one com-

puter game. Jack has visited the American West, traveled through time, and pursued "Amazon women" on the Moon in the film of that name, while matching wits at least 28 times with master detective Sherlock Holmes. (In one bizarre outing, Holmes *was* the Ripper, plagued by multiple personalities as he chased himself through fog-shrouded London!)

No other real-life serial killer can match Red Jack's tally of fictional works, although quick-trigger William Henry McCarty, AKA "Billy the Kid," has drilled more enemies on screen than he ever did in 19th-century New Mexico. More interesting, in terms of weirdness, is the case of Wisconsin's EDWARD THEODORE GEIN, acknowledged as the inspiration for two movie series (*Psycho* and *The Texas Chainsaw Massacre*, nine films in all), plus at least three other films and four novels. Unlike that of Jack the Ripper, though, Gein's name is rarely mentioned in the works that echo his ghoulish career, which leave the action to such fictional doppelgängers as *Psycho*'s Norman Bates and *Chainsaw*'s Leatherface. (The exceptions are *Ed Gein*, a 2000 film starring Steve Railsback in the title role, and Harold Schechter's novel *Outcry* [1997], set in modern times with Gein long dead and his illegitimate son picking up where the old man left off.) British poisoner Thomas Neill Cream stars in three novels, including *The Gentleman from Chicago* (1973), *The Ripper's Apprentice* (1986), and *Jack* (1988). Herman Mudgett's gruesome 19th-century career is dramatized in *The Scarlet Mansion* (1985).

Cinematic psychos run the full gamut from chilling to childish, their impact based in roughly equal parts on quality of writing and the actor's skill. Low-budget shockers like *Henry: Portrait of a Serial Killer* (1989) may achieve "cult classic" status, but they rarely offer much in terms of insight into the killer's twisted psyche, and the films inspired by real-life crimes almost invariably cite "dramatic license" to explain wholesale revision—if not outright fabrication—of events and characters. (In *Henry*, for example, HENRY LUCAS murders and decapitates crime partner OTTIS TOOLE. In Charles Pierce's film *The Town That Dreaded Sundown* [1976], police wound and nearly capture Texarkana's "MOONLIGHT MURDERER" in a wild chase that never occurred.) *Monster* (2003) avoided most of those pitfalls, and earned actress Charlize Theron an Oscar for her portrayal of condemned killer-prostitute AILEEN CAROL WUORNOS.

Elsewhere in fiction and film, renowned author Joyce Carol Oates has penned a novel and a story inspired by the crimes of JEFFREY DAHMER (*Zombie*, 1995) and Tucson "Pied Piper" Charles Schmid ("Where Are You Going, Where Have You Been?," 1966). Toni Cade Bambara's posthumously published novel, *Those Bones*

Are Not My Child (2000), examines the ATLANTA "CHILD MURDERS." Russian cannibal ANDREI ROMANOVICH CHIKATILO is depicted in the 1995 HBO movie *Citizen X,* and director Spike Lee revisits the panic inspired by DAVID RICHARD BERKOWITZ in *Summer of Sam* (1999). British serial poisoner Graham Young gets a black-comic treatment on screen in *The Young Poisoner's Handbook* (1995). William Friedkin. author of *The Exorcist,* directed *Rampage,* a 1988 film treatment of the "Sacramento Vampire," Richard Trenton Chase. One of the more disturbing fact-based novels currently in print is *Hunter* (1989), a zealous homage to racist serial killer JOSEPH PAUL FRANKLIN written and published by neo-Nazi William Pierce under the name Andrew Macdonald. From death row, Franklin proclaimed that he was "honored" to have *Hunter* dedicated in his name.

Unsolved serial cases have always been fair game for fictional sleuths, with "Jack the Ripper" as a primary example. Author Dan Lees pursued San Francisco's infamous "ZODIAC" slayer in the aptly titled *Zodiac* (1972). Five years later, crime writer Jim McDougall tackled Michigan's child-killing "Babysitter," with *Angel of the Snow.* London's "JACK THE STRIPPER" came alive for Dell Shannon in *Destiny of Death* (1991), while Roderick Thorp unmasked TEAM KILLERS in *River,* his 1996 treatment of Washington's Green River murders (published seven years before the capture of real-life killer GARY LEON RIDGWAY). In such works, fiction may provide at least an illusory closure to cases that have haunted detectives for decades.

The roots of psycho-cinema are traceable to 1915's *Trilby,* and while much of what followed has been wasted celluloid, some outstanding productions have also resulted. One such, loosely based on the real-life case of PETER KURTEN, was *M* (1931), combining Fritz Lang's dark vision with a chilling performance from Peter Lorre as the baby-faced killer. A quarter-century later, Lang scored another hit with *While the City Sleeps,* based on the crimes of Chicago "Lipstick Killer" WILLIAM HEIRENS. Robert Mitchum's performance as a switchblade-wielding preacher distinguished Charles Laughton's directorial debut in *The Night of the Hunter* (1955). Alfred Hitchcock's *Psycho* (1960) made bathtime traumatic for millions of Americans with its infamous shower scene, while the great director's last take on serial murder—*Frenzy* (1972)—offered a new look at the case of London's "JACK THE STRIPPER." More recently, *The Silence of the Lambs* (1991) became the most-honored psycho-film in history, sweeping the Oscars with Academy Awards for best picture, best actor (Anthony Hopkins), and best actress (Jodie Foster).

At the other end of the scale lie such efforts as *Driller Killer* (1979), *Maniac* (1980), *Woodchipper Massacre* (1989), and *Slashdance* (1990), in which the directors' sole purpose seems to be the gratuitous display of ersatz blood and entrails. The result is sometimes unintended comedy, as with *Blue Steel* (1990), wherein a New York stockbroker (Ron Silver) witnesses a violent robbery, deciding on a whim to steal the fallen gunman's pistol and begin killing random strangers on the street.

Suspense is more difficult to maintain on the printed page than on screen, without the potential for visual shocks, but certain novelists succeed admirably in their efforts to make readers squirm, while simultaneously exploring police forensic techniques and the dark side of the human mind. In that respect, Thomas Harris clearly leads the field with 1981's *Red Dragon* (filmed as *Manhunter* in 1986), 1988's *The Silence of the Lambs* (filmed under the same title in 1991), and 1999's *Hannibal,* all of which present the exploits of deranged psychiatrist Hannibal ("The Cannibal") Lecter. Other noteworthy novels in the field include Shane Stevens's *By Reason of Insanity* (1979), Jonathan Kellerman's *The Butcher's Theater* (1988), and Caleb Carr's *The Alienist* (1994). Each offers an unsparing look at the method and madness of serial murder, while preserving the humanity of its characters and transcending the formulaic approach described by some publishers as "slice-and-dice."

A handful of authors and producers have carved enduring niches for themselves in the serial murder genre, managing the "careers" of recurring fictional characters, although the approach differs radically between print and celluloid. On screen, the killers rule, returning time and time again to stalk new victims: Norman (*Psycho*) Bates, Michael Myers (of *Halloween* fame), *Texas Chainsaw*'s "Leatherface," Jason Voorhees (*Friday the 13th*) and scar-faced Freddy (*Nightmare on Elm Street*) Krueger boast 27 titles between them, a record sustained in equal parts by public appetite for sequels and the supernatural ability of each protagonist to survive fatal wounds, regenerate severed limbs—do whatever it takes, in fact, to guarantee one more installment of the series.

The only literary peer of those immortal psychopaths is Daniel ("Chaingang") Bunkowski, the 500-pound "precognate" brainchild of author Rex Miller. Stripped of human feelings by hideous childhood abuse, rescued from prison by a secret military program which unleashed him on a hapless enemy in Vietnam, Chaingang shambles through five novels, chalking up "one victim for each pound of his weight" and somehow evolving from mindless villain to a kind of super-anti-hero in the last three books. He also demonstrates a physical resilience that would make his cinematic peers lime-green with envy, returning for the third installment of the saga after being sliced in half with a samurai sword in part two! On the reverse side of the vigilante coin, rogue FBI agents (or ex-agents) track serial killers with no thought of taking them alive in novels such as A. J. Holt's *Watch Me* (1995) and *Thinning the Predators* (1996) by Daina Graziuna and Jim Starlin. The G-men (or G-women) thus become serial killers themselves, in effect, albeit embarked on a righteous crusade.

A very different series of novels with a serial-killing protagonist concerns Tom Ripley, the affable creation of author Patricia Highsmith. A chameleon-like slayer who assumes the identities of his victims, Ripley debuted in *The Talented Mr. Ripley* (1955), then returned for *Ripley Under Ground* (1970), *Ripley's Game* (1974), *The Boy Who Followed Ripley* (1980), and *Ripley Under Water* (1991). Cinematic treatments of Ripley's lethal adventures include *The American Friend* (1977) and *The Talented Mr. Ripley* (1999), with Matt Damon in the title role.

More typically, series of novels examining serial murder chart the careers of dynamic (and sometimes deeply flawed) investigators. John Sandford's "Prey" series—*Rules of Prey, Silent Prey*, and 13 more—tracks Lucas Davenport, a Minneapolis police detective who suffers from clinical depression. David Wiltse's FBI Agent John Becker (*Prayer for the Dead, Blown Away*, etc.) is himself a borderline psychopath, unleashed by cynical superiors on the Bureau's dirtiest cases, constantly at war with his own urge to kill. James Patterson's Detective Alex Cross (*Kiss the Girls, Jack and Jill*, etc.) is both a psychologist and a black single father, trying desperately to raise gentle children on the mean streets of Washington, D.C., while stalking monsters in human form. Robert Walker's "Instinct" series (*Killer Instinct, Fatal Instinct*, etc.) has an FBI pathologist, Dr. Jessica Coran, bedeviled both by lethal stalkers and by sexist hassles in the old-boy's club of law enforcement. The action moves to Canada and other foreign parts in a series of novels by Michael Slade (*Headhunter, Ripper*, etc.), charting the exploits of the "Special X" squad, assigned to track serial killers for the Royal Canadian Mounted Police. Author Alex Kava follows the trials and triumphs of FBI agent Maggie O'Dell in a series of novels including *Perfect Evil, Split Second, The Soul Catcher*, and *At the Stroke of Madness*.

Debate persists (and doubtless always will) concerning the role—if any—of "psycho" films and novels in promoting real-life violence. As far back as 1927, the sadistic crimes of William Hickman in Los Angeles produced a call for censorship of motion pictures, and the debate has only grown more heated with time, as critics claim "proof" of cause-and-effect between graphic "splatter" films and soaring juvenile crime rates. Specifically, they say, exposure to such violent fare desensi-

tizes adolescent viewers, while the frequent depiction of brutal murders from the killer's point of view (often peering through a mask, to the accompaniment of asthmatic wheezing) allegedly "teaches children to kill." Feminists join the debate with claims that the preponderance of young, half-naked women slaughtered in such films is part and parcel of a "war on women" in America.

In fact, while few would argue that there is an up side to presenting young, impressionable children with a daily dose of blood and gore, there is (at least to date) no evidence that viewing any certain film or reading a specific novel "causes" anyone to kill. The critics got a momentary boost in 1992, when a Maryland suspect detained for beheading his mother identified himself to police as "Hannibal Lecter," but such aberrant antics are nearly always the prelude to a lame INSANITY DEFENSE. In the rare cases where flesh-and-blood killers truly identify with fictional stalkers, they are invariably deranged, with histories of mental illness and weird behavior predating their exposure to any specific entertainment medium.

See also ARTWORK AND MEMORABILIA

FISCHER, Joseph J.

A native of New Jersey, born in 1923, Joe Fischer was raised in Newark and Belleville, later describing his childhood as one of continual conflict and violence. His mother was a prostitute who brought "tricks" home while her husband worked on various construction sites. "I guess what really helped me hate the woman," Fischer later said, "was that she didn't care if me or my brothers were home when she brought her customers in." The strangers sometimes passed out pocket change, urging the children to "get lost," but Joe stayed behind, watching his mother perform with a seemingly endless series of men. His disrespect for her grew over time, provoking frequent arguments that led to beatings, sometimes interrupted when his father waded in to whip them both. "I would have killed her 10 times over," Fischer said, "but I really believed that it would have broken my father's heart."

Enrolled in Catholic school, Fischer was a rebellious student who clashed frequently with police in his adolescent years and was finally sentenced to reform school for robbing St. Peter's Church. Released in 1938, at 15, he lied about his age to join the merchant marine but soon jumped ship, returning to New Jersey. Desertion charges were dismissed when the authorities found out that he was under age, and Fischer had a clean record, more or less, when he joined the Marine Corps, following the Japanese raid on Pearl Harbor in December 1941.

By that time, Fischer was well on his way to full-blown alcoholism, serving 30 days in the brig for drunkenness before he finished boot camp. He later saw combat on Guadalcanal, Kwajalein, and Iwo Jima, before he was posted to mainland China, guarding military trains. His wartime record remains controversial, Fischer variously claiming a Bronze Star, a Silver Star, and two Purple Hearts for various battles, though he could never produce the medals or certificates to verify his alleged heroism. Regardless of the details, it is clear that he saw action and loved every minute of it, remarking years later that "killing felt too good to stop" at war's end. He apparently murdered a number of Chinese civilians under the guise of "protecting" military freight, and while he was never court-martialed, he *was* diagnosed as a dangerous paranoid schizophrenic prior to his discharge from service in 1945.

A series of arrests and committals to mental institutions followed his return to civilian life, climaxed in 1948 by Fischer's conviction for robbery and assault. Paroled in December 1953, he was free for a matter of days before he attacked a 16-year-old boy in New Jersey, beating him to death with a rock on the day after Christmas. That crime sent him away for the next quarter-century. He was paroled in June 1978 to marry a pen pal, 78-year-old Claudine Eggers. The attraction was apparently financial, Claudine picking up the tab for an aimless 13-month jaunt across country that turned into a nonstop murder spree. One of the last to die was Claudine herself, found stabbed to death in the home she sometimes shared with Joe in Wassaic, New York. Fischer surrendered to New York police on July 2, 1979, and freely confessed to the slaying, landing in the Dutchess County jail on a charge of second-degree murder.

That might have been the end for Fischer, but he felt like talking—more specifically, confessing to another 18 homicides. He had set out to kill 25 victims, Joe told detectives, but was still six short of the mark when he grew weary and surrendered. By July 28, authorities in Arizona and Oklahoma had issued warrants for his arrest in the spring 1979 murders of a man in Flagstaff and a female victim, Betty Jo Gibson, in Moore, Oklahoma. Other victims claimed by Fischer in his confessions included "a couple" of deaths in the Bowery, with others in Los Angeles; San Francisco; New Mexico; Cooperstown, New York; Hartford, Connecticut; and Portland, Maine.

Authorities in different jurisdictions often seemed to work at cross-purposes in tracking Fischer's claims. The New Jersey Department of Corrections refused to release his prison psychiatric files, although it was admitted that parole had been granted in 1978 on twin conditions that Fischer join Alcoholics Anonymous and remain subject to "close supervision." A photo found in his possession, meanwhile, was identified as a likeness of 26-year-old Pamela Nolen, missing from Ruidos, New Mexico, since October 30, 1978. (Fischer admitted stabbing a woman to death in New Mexico; he simply didn't catch her name.) Flagstaff police cited evidence confirming Fischer's presence in the motel room where a male victim died on March 31, 1979, but they now called the death accidental; Fischer, for his part, insisted that he beat the man to death. By mid-February 1980, Joe was claiming a total of 32 victims, and police in Norwalk, Connecticut, declared that they had sufficient evidence to charge him in the additional stabbing deaths of two 17-year-old girls, Alaine Hapeman and Veronica Tassielo.

In fact, Joe went to trial in April 1980 only for the murder of his wife. By that time, press reports of his confessions cited "dozens" of victims, one article claiming "up to forty," but Fischer had changed his tune for the moment, denying Claudine's murder when he took the witness stand on April 11. Jurors dismissed his testimony as a self-serving lie, convicting him of second-degree murder on April 23. Three weeks later, on May 16, Fischer received a prison sentence of 25 years to life.

Warrants remained outstanding in Connecticut and Oklahoma, but neither jurisdiction was disposed to extradite Fischer for trial. Confined at Sing Sing, he soon reverted to his early boastful mode, granting interviews to such tabloid TV programs as *Geraldo* and *A Current Affair* in 1989, claiming a body count of "over 100" victims. By February 1991, when Fischer was profiled on *America's Most Wanted,* the number had jumped to "about 150," including allegations of a private graveyard undiscovered by police, with 16 corpses buried in one place, but no one had the interest or the energy to check his stories out. By the time he died in prison seven months later, at age 68, Joe Fischer was largely forgotten, his passing barely noted in the hometown newspaper. Officially, he was responsible for two homicides, suspected of at least three more. His true body count—like that of DONALD GASKINS, HENRY LUCAS, and other boastful killers—will probably never be known.

FISH, Albert Howard

Born Hamilton Fish in 1870, America's most notorious 20th-century cannibal before JEFFREY DAHMER was the product of a respected family living in Washington, D.C. A closer examination, however, reveals at least seven relatives with severe mental disorders in the two generations preceding Fish's birth, including two members of the family who died in asylums. Fish was five years old when his father died, and his mother placed him in an orphanage while she worked to support herself. Records describe young Fish as a problem child who "ran away every Saturday," persistently wetting the bed until his 11th year. Graduating from public school at age 15, he began to call himself Albert, discarding the hated first name which led classmates to tease him, calling him "Ham and Eggs."

As an adult, Fish worked odd jobs, making his way across country as an itinerant house painter and decorator. In 1898 he married a woman nine years his junior, fathering six children before his wife ran away with a boarder named John Straube in January 1917. She came back once, with Straube in tow, and Fish took her back on condition that she send her lover away. Later, he discovered that his wife was keeping Straube in the attic, and she departed after a stormy argument, never to return.

By his own account, Fish committed his first murder in 1910, killing a man in Wilmington, Delaware, but his children marked the first obvious change in Fish's behavior from the date of his wife's initial departure. Apparently subject to hallucinations, he would shake his fist at the sky and repeatedly scream, "I am Christ!" Obsessed with sin, sacrifice, and atonement through pain, Fish encouraged his children and their friends to paddle him until his buttocks bled. On his own, he inserted numerous needles into his groin, losing track of some as they sank out of sight. (A prison X ray revealed at least 29 separate needles in his pelvic region, some eroded with time to mere fragments.) On other occasions, Fish would soak cotton balls in alcohol, insert them in his anus, and set them on fire. Frustrated by agony when he began slipping needles under his own fingernails, Fish lamented, "If only pain were not so painful!"

Though never divorced from his first wife, Fish married three times, enjoying a sex life which court psychiatrists would describe as one of "unparalleled perversity." (In jail, authorities compiled a list of 18 PARAPHILIAS practiced by Fish, including coprophagia—the consumption of human excrement.) Tracing his sadomasochism back to the age of five or six when he began to relish bare-bottom spankings in the orphanage, Fish's obsession with pain was focused primarily on children. Ordered "by God" to castrate young boys, he impartially molested children of both sexes as he traveled around the country. Prosecutors confidently linked him with "at least 100" sexual assaults in 23 states from New York to Wyoming, but Fish felt slighted by their estimate. "I have had children in every state," he declared, placing his own tally of victims closer to 400.

For all that, Fish was careless with his crimes, frequently losing jobs "because things about these children came out." Arrested eight times over the years, he served time for grand larceny, passing bad checks, and violating parole or probation. Obscene letters were another of his passions, and Fish mailed off countless examples to strangers, their addresses obtained from matrimonial agencies of newspaper "lonely-hearts" columns.

In 1928, posing as "Mr. Howard," Fish befriended the Budd family in White Plains, New York. On June 3, while escorting 12-year-old Grace Budd to a fabricated children's party, he took the child to an isolated cottage and there dismembered her body, saving several pieces for a stew which he consumed.

Two years later, with the Budd case still unsolved, Fish was confined to a psychiatric hospital for the first time. After two months of observation, he was discharged with a note reading: "Not insane; psychopathic personality; sexual type." In 1931, arresting Fish once more on charges of mailing obscene letters, police found a well-used cat-o'-nine-tails in his room. He was released after two more weeks of observation in a psychiatric ward.

Compelled to gloat about his crimes, Fish sent a letter to the Budd family in 1934, breaking the news that Grace was dead, oddly emphasizing the fact that "she died a virgin." Traced by police through the letter's distinctive stationery, Fish readily confessed to other

Albert Fish on trial (Wide World API)

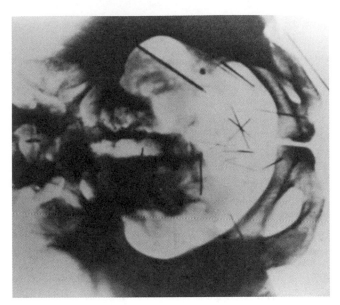

Pelvic X-ray of Albert Fish reveals needles he inserted in his groin. (Wide World API)

homicides, including children killed in 1919, 1927, and 1934.

Authorities disagreed on his ultimate body count, detectives listing at least three more victims in New York City. Arrested for questioning in one case, Fish had been released because "he looked so innocent." On another occasion, a trolley conductor identified Fish as the man he saw with a small, sobbing boy on the day of the child's disappearance. A court psychiatrist suspected Albert of at least five murders, with New York detectives adding three more, and a justice of the New York Supreme Court was "reliably informed" of the killer's involvement in 15 homicides.

At trial, the state was desperate to win a death penalty, overriding Fish's INSANITY DEFENSE with laughable psychiatric testimony. Speaking for the state, a battery of doctors declared, straight-faced, that coprophagia "is a common sort of thing. We don't call people who do that mentally sick. A man who does that is socially perfectly all right. As far as his social status is concerned, he is supposed to be normal, because the State of New York Mental Hygiene Department also approves of that."

With Fish's rambling, obscene confessions in hand, the jury found him sane and guilty of premeditated murder in Grace Budd's case. Sentenced to die, Fish was electrocuted at Sing Sing Prison on January 16, 1936. According to one witness present, it took two jolts before the chair completed its work, thus spawning a legend that the apparatus was short-circuited by all the needles Fish had planted in his body.

"FRANKFORD Slasher"

Philadelphia's Frankford district is the hard-scrabble neighborhood chosen by Sylvester Stallone as the setting for his first *Rocky* film. Rocky Balboa had gone on to bigger, better things by the late 1980s, however, when Frankford earned a new and unwelcome celebrity, this time for the presence of a vicious serial killer who slaughtered at least seven women.

The mystery began on August 28, 1985, when two transit workers reported to their job at a Frankford Avenue maintenance yard, around 8:30 A.M Within moments, they found a woman's lifeless body sprawled between two heaps of railroad ties. She was nude from the waist down, legs splayed, her blouse pushed up to show her breasts. An autopsy report enumerated 19 stab wounds, with a gaping slash along her abdomen nearly disemboweling her. She was identified as Helen Patent, 52, well known in many of the bars on Frankford Avenue.

Just over four months later, on January 3, 1986, a second mutilated corpse was found on Ritner Street in South Philadelphia, 10 miles from the first murder scene. Neighbors were surprised to see the door of 68-year-old Anna Carroll's apartment standing open, and they found her dead inside, on the floor of her bedroom. Like Helen Patent, this victim was also nude below the waist, her blouse pulled up. She had been stabbed six times, her abdomen sliced open from breastbone to pubis.

No more was heard from the slasher for nearly a year—until Christmas night, in fact—when victim number three was found on Richmond Street in the Bridesburg neighborhood, three miles from where Helen Patent was killed. Once again, it was worried neighbors who found the corpse, investigating an open apartment door to find 74-year-old Susan Olzef dead in her flat, stabbed six times in the back. Like Helen Patent, Olzef was a familiar figure on Frankford Avenue, police speculating that her killer may have known her from the neighborhood.

Thus far, Philadelphia's finest had little to go on, and they resisted the notion of a serial killer at large in their town. As Lieutenant Joe Washlick later told reporters in an effort to explain the oversight, "The first three slayings happened in different parts of the city. We could almost give you a different suspect for each job."

Almost . . . but not quite. In fact, there were no leads and had been no arrests by January 8, 1987, when two Frankford Avenue fruit vendors found a woman's corpse stuffed underneath their stand, around 7:30 A.M. The latest victim, 28-year-old Jeanne Durkin, lay facedown and she was nude below the waist, legs spread. She had been stabbed no less than 74 times.

With four corpses and no end in sight, authorities officially linked the Patent and Durkin murders, later connecting all four and creating a special task force to hunt the man Philadelphia journalists were already calling the "Frankford Slasher." For nearly two years, the task force spun its wheels, making no apparent progress until November 11, 1988. That morning, 66-year-old Marge Vaughn was found dead on Penn Avenue, stabbed 29 times in the vestibule of an apartment building from which she was evicted the previous day. She died less than three blocks from the Durkin murder site, a half-mile from the spot where Helen Patent was found . . . and this time, there was a witness of sorts.

A Frankford Avenue barmaid recalled seeing Vaughn around 6:00 P.M. the previous day. Vaughn had been drinking with a round-faced, middle-aged Caucasian man who wore glasses and walked with a limp. Several sketches of the unknown subject were prepared and published, but despite predictable false leads and fingerpointing by uneasy or malicious neighbors, the police appeared no closer to their man than they had been in 1985.

Two months later, on January 19, 1989, 30-year-old Theresa Sciortino left a Frankford Avenue saloon at six o'clock in the evening. She was last seen alive moments later, walking down the street with an unidentified middle-aged man. Around 6:45 P.M., Sciortino's neighbors heard sounds of an apparent struggle inside her apartment, followed shortly by footsteps creeping down the stairs, but they failed to call police, and it was 9:00 P.M. before they spoke to the apartment manager. He, in turn, waited past midnight to check on his tenant, then found Sciortino sprawled on the floor of her kitchen, nude but for socks, stabbed 25 times. A bloody footprint at the scene provided homicide detectives with their best lead yet, and while they initially focused on Sciortino's boyfriend, calling him "a good suspect," he was finally cleared when police checked

his shoes, reporting them "similar, but not identical" to the killer's.

Another 15 months elapsed before the killer struck again. Patrolman Dan Johnson was cruising his beat in the predawn hours of April 28, 1990, when he found a woman's nude, eviscerated corpse in the alley behind a Frankford Avenue fish market. The latest victim had been stabbed 36 times, slashed open from her navel to vagina, and otherwise mutilated. A purse, found nearby, identified the woman as 45-year-old Carol Dowd, and a preliminary canvass of the neighborhood turned up a witness who had seen her walking along Frankford Avenue with a middle-aged white man several hours before she was found.

It looked like another dead end, until detectives got around to questioning employees of the fish market, several days later. One of them, 39-year-old Leonard Christopher, had already spoken to reporters, describing the alley behind his workplace as "a hooker's paradise" and frequent scene of drug deals. Questioned by authorities about his movements on the night Carol Dowd was murdered, Christopher replied that he had spent the evening with his girlfriend. The lady in question, however, denied it, insisting that she spent the night at home, alone. Suspicious now, investigators took a closer look at Leonard Christopher. They found a local mailman who reported seeing Christopher and Dowd together in a bar, the night she died. Another witness—this one a convicted prostitute—allegedly saw Christopher and Dowd walking together down the street. A second hooker told police she saw Christopher emerge from the Frankford Avenue alley around 1:00 A.M. on April 28. According to her report, Christopher had been "sweating profusely, had his shirt over his arm, and a 'Rambo knife' was tucked into his belt."

On the strength of those statements, Christopher—a black man who bore no resemblance to the "Frankford Slasher" sketches or the middle-aged Caucasian seen with Carol Dowd the night she died—was arrested for murder and held without bond, his trial date set for December. A search of his apartment failed to turn up any useful evidence: one pair of slacks had a tiny bloodstain on one leg, but it was too small to be typed or subjected to any tests involving DNA.

While Christopher sat in jail, the Frankford Slasher—or a skillful copycat—struck again in early September. It was 1:00 A.M. on September 8 when tenants of an Arrott Street apartment house complained of rancid odors emanating from the flat occupied by 30-year-old Michelle Martin. The manager used his passkey and found Martin dead on the floor, nude from the waist down, her blouse pushed up to bare her breasts. Stabbed 23 times, she had been dead for roughly two

Police sketches of "Frankford Slasher" suspect (Author's collection)

days, last seen alive on the night of September 6, drinking with a middle-aged white man in a bar on Frankford Avenue.

Ignoring their apparent dilemma, prosecutors went ahead with Leonard Christopher's trial on schedule, in December 1990. Their case was admittedly weak—no motive or weapon, no witness to the crime itself, no evidence of any kind connecting the defendant to the murder scene—but jurors were persuaded by the testimony describing Christopher's "strange" behavior and lies to police. On December 12, he was convicted of murder, later sentenced to life imprisonment. From his cell, Christopher still maintains, "I was railroaded."

And what of the Frankford Slasher, described for years as a middle-aged white man? What of the near-identical murder committed while Christopher sat in jail? Lieutenant Washlick seemed to shrug the problem off, telling reporters, "Surprisingly, we still get phone calls. Leonard Christopher is a suspect in some of the killings, and we have additional suspects as well. Last year, we had 481 homicides in the city, and we solved eighty-two percent of them."

But not the Frankford Slasher case. The perpetrator of those crimes is still at large.

FRANKLIN, Joseph Paul

Born James Clayton Vaughn Jr. in Mobile, Alabama, Franklin was the eldest son of an alcoholic drifter who abandoned his family for months or years at a stretch. Siblings remember that James Vaughn Sr. would celebrate infrequent homecomings by beating his children, with James Jr. absorbing the worst punishment. As a youth, Franklin went for food fads and fringe religions, dropping out of high school after an incident left him with severely impaired eyesight.

The injury was a two-edged sword, exempting Franklin from military conscription, and he married in 1968 at an age when many young men were sweating out the draft lottery, fearful of the war in Vietnam. Soon after their wedding, Franklin's bride noted a change in his personality "like night and day." He began to beat her, emulating the father he hated, and on other occasions she would find him inexplicably weeping. About the same time, their all-white neighborhood was racially integrated, and Franklin began to veer hard right, into the realm of pathological bigotry.

The next few years were marked by ugly racial incidents and sporadic arrests for carrying concealed weapons. Franklin was increasingly drawn to the American Nazi Party, lapsing into the segregationist movement full-time after his mother's death in 1972. Moving to Atlanta, he joined the neo-fascist National States Rights Party, simultaneously holding membership in the local Ku Klux Klan. Franklin began insulting interracial couples in public, and on Labor Day 1976, he trailed one such couple to a dead-end street in Atlanta, spraying them with chemical Mace.

About this time, Franklin legally changed his name, shedding the last links with his "normal" life. Prosecutors allege—and jurors have agreed—that he spent the years from 1977 to 1980 wandering across the South and Midwest, employing 18 pseudonyms, changing cars and weapons frequently, dyeing his hair so often that it came close to falling out. Along the way, he killed more than a dozen persons in a frenzied one-man war against minorities.

According to the FBI, Franklin launched his campaign in the summer of 1977, bombing a Chattanooga synagogue on July 29. Nine days later, investigators say he shot and killed an interracial couple, Alphonse Manning and Toni Schwenn, both 23, in Madison, Wisconsin. On October 8, Gerald Gordon was killed by sniper fire as he left a bar mitzvah in the St. Louis suburb of Richmond Heights.

Harold McIver, the black manager of a fast-food restaurant in Doraville, Georgia, was working the night shift when a sniper took his life on July 22, 1979. On August 8, another black man, 28-year-old Raymond Taylor, was shot and killed through the window of a restaurant in Falls Church, Virginia. Ten weeks later, on October 21, another interracial couple came under attack from the itinerant gunman in Oklahoma City: Jesse Taylor was hit three times with a high-powered rifle before he expired; a single round through the chest killed Marian Bresette as she ran to the aid of her common-law husband.

Franklin struck twice in Indianapolis during January 1980, killing black men with long-distance rifle fire in two separate attacks: 22-year-old Lawrence Reese died in another restaurant shooting, on January 12; two days later, 19-year-old Leo Watkins was killed at a local shopping mall. On May 3, Franklin allegedly killed a young white woman, Rebecca Bergstrom, dumping her body near Tomah, in central Wisconsin. On June 6 he surfaced in Cincinnati, killing black cousins Darrell Lane and Dante Brown from his sniper's perch on a nearby railroad trestle. Nine days later, in Johnstown, Ohio, Franklin shotgunned a black couple—Arthur Smothers and Kathleen Mikula—as they crossed a downtown bridge. On August 20, black joggers Ted Fields and David Martin were cut down by rifle fire in Salt Lake City, Utah.

Arrested in Kentucky on September 25, 1980 (and recaptured a month later after escaping to Florida), Franklin faced a marathon series of state and federal trials with mixed results. In 1982, he was acquitted of federal civil rights charges in the May 1980 shooting that left civil rights leader Vernon Jordan critically injured in Fort Wayne, Indiana (although jurors said they were convinced he shot Jordan and Franklin later confessed). Utah juries subsequently convicted him of two murders *and* civil rights violations; Franklin was serving life on those counts in 1983 when he confessed the 1978 sniping that crippled *Hustler* magazine publisher Larry Flynt in Gwinnett County, Georgia. (Franklin was indicted for that crime but never tried, since he already faced stiffer penalties in other states.)

More convictions followed: for the Chattanooga bombing; for the double murder in Wisconsin, described by prosecutors as "the closest thing to killing for sport"; for the murder of Gerald Gordon, killed leaving a Clayton, Missouri synagogue in 1977 (his first death sentence); for the June 1980 double murder in Cincinnati; for the 1978 murder of William Tatum, shot while talking to a white woman outside a Chattanooga restaurant. Other crimes confessed by Franklin without further convictions include the 1978 shooting of an interracial couple in Atlanta (one victim died, the other remains paralyzed); the separate 1979 murders of a black man and a white woman in Decatur, Georgia; the 1980 murders of two female hitchhikers in West Virginia; the 1980 murder of an interracial couple in Johnstown, Ohio; and the 1980 murder of an interracial couple in Pittsburgh, Pennsylvania. Overall, investigators believe Franklin is responsible for at least 18 murders and five nonfatal shootings in 11 states, plus two bombings and 16 bank robberies. On April 29, 2001, the U.S. Supreme Court rejected Franklin's appeal of his conviction in the George Gordon murder.

One confession with unexpected repercussions was Franklin's admission that he shot 26-year-old Vicki Durian and 19-year-old Nancy Santomero on June 25, 1980, while they were hitchhiking to the Rainbow Festival in West Virginia's Monongahela National Park. Suspect Jacob Beard was convicted of the so-called Rainbow murders in 1993 and received two sentences of life imprisonment without parole. Franklin upset that verdict with his confession that he shot the girls because they favored interracial dating. "One of them told me she had dated blacks and all that," he said. "And the other one told me she would if she had a chance so I just decided to waste them at that time." Beard was released on $150,000 bond, pending retrial of his case, and a second jury acquitted him of all charges on May 31, 2000.

"FREEWAY Murders"

Between December 1972 and June 1980, authorities in seven southern California counties recorded the violent deaths of at least 44 young men and boys, attributing their murders to an unknown "Freeway Killer." Of 11 victims slaughtered prior to 1976, most were known or suspected homosexuals, their deaths lending credence to the notion that the murderer himself was gay. While strangulation was the favored mode of death, some victims had been stabbed with knives or ice picks, and their bodies bore the traces of sadistic torture. Homicide investigators noted different hands at work in several of the murders, but they finally agreed that 21 were almost certainly connected. (Sixteen others would be solved in 1983 with the arrest of "Scorecard Killer" RANDY KRAFT.)

The first "definite" victim was 14-year-old Thomas Lundgren, abducted from Reseda on May 28, 1979, and discarded the same day near Malibu. Mark Shelton, 17, was next, reported missing from Westminster on August 4, his body recovered a week later at Cajon Pass. The day after Shelton's disappearance, 17-year-old Marcus Grabs was kidnapped in Newport Beach, his violated corpse discovered at Agoura on August 6. Donald Hyden, 15, was also found in Agoura, on August 27—the same day he disappeared from Hollywood. On September 7, 17-year-old David Murillo vanished from La Mirada, his body found in Ventura five days later. The remains of Robert Wirotsek were found off Interstate 10, between Banning and Palm Springs, on September 27, but 11 months would pass before he was identified. Another "John Doe" was discovered in Kern County on November 30, with 18-year-old Frank Fox murdered at Long Beach two days later. The killer's last victim for 1979 was another unidentified male, aged 15 to 20, his violated body found on December 13.

The new year began badly for southern California, with 16-year-old Michael McDonald abducted from Ontario on January 1, 1980, found dead two days later in San Bernardino County. Charles Miranda, 14, disappeared from Los Angeles on February 3, his body discarded in Hollywood later that day. On February 5, 12-year-old James McCabe was kidnapped in Huntington Beach, his body recovered three days later in Garden Grove. Ronald Gatlin, 18, disappeared in Van Nuys on March 14, found dead the next day in Duarte. Fifteen-year-old Russell Pugh was reported missing from Huntington Beach on March 21, his body found next day at the Lower San Juan Campground, along with the corpse of 14-year-old victim Glen Barker. Three days later, police found 15-year-old Harry Turner slain in Los Angeles proper.

The killer claimed two victims on April 10, 1980, abducting 16-year-old Steven Wood from Bellflower, rebounding to snatch 18-year-old Lawrence Sharp from Long Beach hours later. Wood's body was found April 11 at Long Beach, but Sharp remained missing until

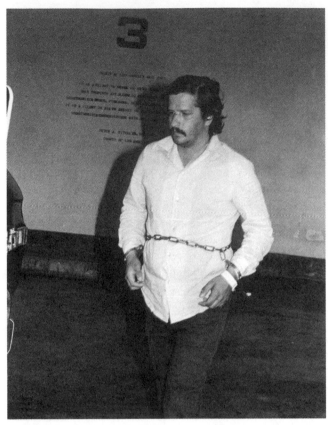

"Freeway Killer" William Bonin in manacles (Wide World API)

May 18 when his remains were discovered in Westminster. Meanwhile, on April 29, 19-year-old Daren Kendrick was reported missing in Stanton, his body recovered from Carson on May 10, with traces of chloral hydrate ("knockout drops") in his system. On May 19, 14-year-old Sean King vanished without a trace in South Gate; he remains among the missing. Eighteen-year-old Stephen Wells, the last to die, was kidnapped in Los Angeles on June 2, his body discovered the next day at Huntington Beach.

Police got their break on June 10 when 18-year-old William Ray Pugh (no relation to Russell Pugh) confessed "inside" knowledge of the murder series. Pugh identified the killer as William George Bonin, a 32-year-old Vietnam veteran and truck driver residing in Downey. A glance at the record revealed Bonin's 1969 conviction in Torrance on felony counts of kidnapping, sodomy, child molestation, and forcible oral copulation. The charges stemmed from four separate attacks between November 1968 and January 1969, with Bonin diagnosed as a mentally disordered sex offender, committed to Atascadero State Hospital. He was released in May 1974 on the recommendation of psychiatrists who found him "no longer dangerous." Two years later, he was back in prison, convicted of kidnap-

ping and raping a 14-year-old boy. Bonin had been paroled in October 1978, seven months before the death of Thomas Lundgren.

Officers established round-the-clock surveillance on Bonin, striking paydirt after 24 hours. On the night of June 11, 1980, their suspect was arrested while sodomizing a young man in his van and was booked on suspicion of murder and various sex charges. Held in lieu of $250,000 bond, Bonin was still in jail when police picked up 22-year-old Vernon Butts on July 25, charging him as an accomplice in six of the "freeway" murders. Between July 26 and 29, Bonin was formally charged with 14 counts of murder, 11 counts of robbery, plus one count each of sodomy and mayhem. Butts, facing six counts of murder and three counts of robbery, soon began "singing" to police, naming more alleged accomplices in the murder ring. James Michael Munro, 19, was arrested in Michigan on July 31 and was returned to California for trial on charges of killing Stephen Wells. Three weeks later, on August 22, 19-year-old Gregory M. Miley was arrested in Texas, waiving extradition on charges of murdering Charles Miranda and James McCabe, plus two counts of robbery and one count of sodomy.

Orange County raised the ante on October 29, 1980, charging Vernon Butts with the murders of Mark Shelton, Robert Wirotsek, and Daren Kendrick, plus 17 other felony counts including conspiracy, kidnapping, robbery, sodomy, oral copulation, and sex perversion. Greg Miley was also charged in another Orange murder, plus seven related felony counts. By December 8, suspect Eric Marten Wijnaendts—a 20-year-old Dutch immigrant—had been added to the roster, charged with complicity in the murder of Harry Turner.

Under California law, a murder committed with "special circumstances"—accompanied by torture, rape, or robbery—may be punished by death. In December, Bonin's playmates started cracking, pleading guilty on various felony charges and drawing life sentences in return for their promise of testimony against Bonin. They spelled out details of the torture suffered by assorted "freeway" victims and the glee with which Bonin inflicted pain. As one remarked, "Bill said he loved those sounds of screams." On January 11, after telling police of Bonin's "hypnotic" control, Vernon Butts hanged himself in his cell, finally successful in the fifth suicide attempt since his arrest. With the new testimony in hand, Orange County indicted Bonin on eight more counts of murder with 25 related counts of robbery and sexual assault.

William Bonin's trial on 12 counts of murder opened November 4, 1981, in Los Angeles. Greg Miley and James Munro testified for the state, describing how Bonin—after his arrest—had urged them to "start going around grabbing anyone off the street and killing them" in a bid to convince authorities that the "Freeway Killer" was still at large. A television reporter divulged contents of a jailhouse interview in which Bonin admitted participation in 21 murders. "I couldn't stop killing," the trucker had said. "It got easier with each one we did."

On January 5, 1982, after eight hours of deliberation, jurors convicted Bonin on 10 counts of murder and 10 of robbery. (He was acquitted in the deaths of Thomas Lundgren and Sean King.) Two weeks later, he was formally sentenced to death, but it took another 14 years to see that sentence carried out. On February 23, 1996, Bonin was finally executed in the gas chamber at San Quentin Prison. It was noted that his passing left bridge partners Randy Kraft, LAWRENCE BITTAKER, and DOUGLAS CLARK one hand short for their next game of cards on death row.

"FREEWAY Phantom"

A puzzling case recorded from the nation's capital, this murder series stands officially unsolved despite conviction of two defendants in one of seven similar homicides. Authorities have speculated on solutions in the case, asserting that "justice was served" by the roundup of suspects on unrelated charges, but their faith was shaken by an outbreak of look-alike murders in Prince Georges County, Maryland, during 1987. At this writing, some students of the case believe the "Phantom" has eluded homicide detectives altogether, shifting his field of operations to a more fertile hunting ground.

The capital stalker's first victim was 13-year-old Carole Denise Sparks, abducted on April 25, 1971, while en route to a neighborhood store in southeast Washington. Her strangled, ravaged body was recovered six days later, a mile and a half from home, lying on the shoulder of Interstate Highway 295, one of several freeways passing through Washington east of the Anacostia River.

Ten weeks passed before 16-year-old Darlenia Denise Johnson disappeared, on July 8, from the same street where Carole Sparks was kidnapped. Strangled to death, she was found on July 19 within 15 feet of the spot where Sparks was discovered on May 1. In the meantime, a third victim, 14-year-old Angela Denise Barnes, had been abducted from southeast Washington on July 13, shot to death, and dumped the same day at Waldorf, Maryland. Brenda Crockett, age 10, disappeared two weeks later, her strangled corpse recovered on July 28 near an underpass on U.S. Highway 50.

The killer took a two-month break in August and September, returning with a vengeance to abduct 12-year-old Nenomoshia Yates on October 1. Familiar marks of strangulation were apparent when her body was found six days later, discarded on Pennsylvania Avenue, near the Maryland state line. At 18, Brenda Denise Woodward was the oldest victim, kidnapped from a Washington bus stop on November 15, stabbed to death, and dumped the next day on an access road leading to Prince Georges County Hospital. A mocking note, its contents still unpublished, was discovered with the body, signed "The Freeway Phantom" in accordance with the nickname coined by journalists. In a macabre twist, FBI experts reported that Woodward had written the note herself, in a steady hand, betraying no hint of tension or fear.

For once, police had ample evidence of pattern, from the victim's race—all African-American—to the peculiar fact that four were named Denise. There also seemed to be a geographical connection both in the abduction and disposal of remains, but speculation brought authorities no closer to their goal of an arrest. The black community in Washington was up in arms, demanding a solution to the case, intent on proving that a white man was to blame, but angry rhetoric did nothing to advance the murder probe.

Ten months elapsed before the Phantom claimed his final victim, abducting 17-year-old Diane Williams on September 5, 1972, Her body was found the next day along I-295, five miles from the point where Carole Sparks was discovered in May 1971. Again, police noted striking similarities with the other crimes—and again, they found no evidence that would identify a suspect in the case.

In late March, Maryland state police arrested two black suspects—30-year-old Edward Leon Sellman and 26-year-old Tommie Bernard Simmons—on charges of murdering Angela Barnes. Both suspects were ex-policemen from Washington, and both had resigned in early 1971 before completion of their mandatory probation periods. Investigators now divorced the Barnes murder from other crimes in the Freeway Phantom series, filing additional charges against both suspects in the February 1971 abduction and rape of a Maryland waitress. Convicted of murder in 1974, both defendants were sentenced to life.

Meanwhile, a federal grand jury probing the Phantom murders focused its spotlight on "a loosely knit group of persons" suspected of luring girls and young women into cars—sometimes rented for the hunt—then raping and/or killing their victims for sport. Suspects John N. Davis, 28, and 27-year-old Morris Warren were already serving life on conviction for previous rapes when a new series of indictments was handed down in December 1974. Warren received a grant of limited immunity in return for testimony against Davis and another defendant, 27-year-old Melvyn Sylvester

Gray. As a government spokesman explained, "The ends of justice can be served just as well if the person is convicted and sentenced to life for kidnapping than if he is jailed for the same term for murder."

Critics questioned the wisdom of that advice 13 years later when a new series of unsolved murders was reported from neighboring Maryland. Again, the female victims were young and black, abducted and discarded in a manner reminiscent of the Freeway Phantom's style. Authorities refuse to speculate upon a link between the crimes, and so both cases are considered "open," officially unsolved.

GACY, John Wayne, Jr.

John Gacy Sr. was an alcoholic tyrant in his home, a crude exaggeration of the famous Archie Bunker TV character with every trace of humor wiped away. He made no effort to conceal his disappointment with the son who bore his name, inflicting brutal beatings for the least offense, occasionally picking up the boy and hurling him across a room. In more pacific moments, he was satisfied to damn John Jr. as a "sissy" who was "dumb and stupid," useless in the scheme of things. In time, the "sissy" portion of his groundless accusations would appear to be a self-fulfilling prophecy.

Born in March 1942 in Chicago, Gacy grew up doubting his own masculinity and taking refuge from sports and other "manly" activities through precocious hypochondria. Struck on the head by a swing at age 11, he suffered periodic blackouts for the next five years until their cause—a blood clot on his brain—was finally dissolved with medication. Thus deprived of one affliction, he developed (or imagined) yet another, settling on the symptoms of a heart ailment that seemed to come and go, depending on his mood.

After graduation from business college, Gacy became a shoe salesman, but he had his sights on better things. He married a coworker whose parents owned a fried chicken restaurant in Waterloo, Iowa, and Gacy stepped into a ready-made role as the restaurant's manager. He was a whiz kid on the job, belying everything his father had to say about his intellect and drive, ascending to a post of admiration and respect among the local Jaycees. His wife and friends were absolutely unprepared for John's arrest in May of 1968 on charges of coercing a young employee into homosexual acts

spanning a period of months. Those accusations were still pending when Gacy hired a teenage thug to beat the prosecution's witness, and more charges were filed. Striking a bargain, Gacy pled guilty to sodomy, and the other charges were dismissed. Sentenced to 10 years in prison, he proved himself a model prisoner and was released in 18 months.

With the state's permission, Gacy moved back to Chicago, where he established himself as a successful building contractor. Divorced while in prison, he soon remarried, settling in a middle-class neighborhood of suburban Des Plaines, where he was popular with his neighbors and hosted elaborate holiday theme parties. On the side, he was active in Democratic politics—once posing for photos with the wife of President Jimmy Carter—and as "Pogo the Clown," performing in full makeup at children's parties and charity events. Few of his new acquaintances knew anything about the Iowa arrest, and those who heard a rumor were assured that John had merely done some time for "dealing in a little porn."

On February 12, 1971, Gacy was charged with disorderly conduct in Chicago, on the complaint of a boy he attempted to rape. The accuser, known to be gay, failed to appear in court for Gacy's hearing, and the charges were dismissed. Parole officers in Iowa were never notified of the arrest or accusations, and Gacy was formally discharged from parole on October 18, 1971.

By his own estimate, the first murder occurred less than three months later, on January 3, 1972. The victim, picked up at a bus terminal, remains unidentified, but his death was typical of Gacy's future approach. In searching for prey, Gacy sometimes fell back on young friends and employees but more often relied on trolling the streets of Chicago for hustlers and runaways. Like the "Hillside Stranglers" in Los Angeles, he would sometimes flash a badge and gun, "arresting" his intended victim. Others were invited to the Gacy home for drinks or a game of pool, and John would show them "tricks" with "magic handcuffs," later hauling out sex toys and the garrote. When he was finished, John would do the "rope trick"—strangulation—and his victim would be buried in a crawl space underneath the house. In later years, as he ran out of space downstairs, he started dumping bodies in a nearby river.

Planting corpses in the crawl space had its drawbacks, notably a rank, pervasive odor that the killer blamed on "sewer problems." Gacy's second wife was also in the way, her presence limiting his playtime to occasions when she left the house or traveled out of town, but when their marriage fell apart in 1976, Gacy was able to accelerate his program of annihilation. Between April 6 and June 13, 1976, at least five boys were slaughtered at Gacy's home, and there seemed to be no end in sight. On October 25 of that year, he killed two victims at once, dumping their bodies in a common grave. As time went by, his targets ranged in age from nine to 20, covering the social spectrum from middle-class teens to jailbirds and male prostitutes.

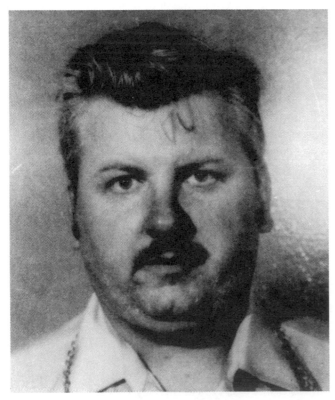

John Wayne Gacy Jr. (Wide World API)

Not all of Gacy's victims died. In December 1977, Robert Donnelly was abducted at gunpoint, tortured, and sodomized in Gacy's house of horrors, then released. Three months later, 27-year-old Jeffrey Rignall was having a drink at Gacy's home when he was chloroformed and fastened to "the rack," a homemade torture device similar to that used by DEAN CORLL in Houston. Gacy spent several hours raping and whipping Rignall, applying the chloroform with such frequency that Rignall's liver suffered permanent damage. Regaining consciousness beside a lake in Lincoln Park, Rignall called police at once, but it was mid-July before they got around to charging Gacy with a misdemeanor. The case was still dragging on five months later when Gacy was picked up on charges of multiple murder.

The end, when it came at last, was solely due to Gacy's carelessness. Fifteen-year-old Robert Piest disappeared from his job at a Chicago pharmacy on October 12, 1978. Gacy's construction firm had lately remodeled the store, and Piest had been offered a job with the crew, informing coworkers of his intention to meet "a contractor" on the night of his disappearance. Police dropped by to question Gacy at his home, and they immediately recognized the odor emanating from his crawl space. Before they finished digging, Gacy's lot would yield 28 bodies, with five more recovered from rivers nearby. Nine of the 33 victims would remain forever unidentified.

In custody, Gacy tried to blame his murderous activities on "Jack," an alter ego (and, coincidentally, the alias he used when posing as a cop). Psychiatrists dismissed the ruse, and Gacy was convicted on 33 counts of first-degree murder in March 1980. Life sentences were handed down in 21 cases, covering deaths that occurred before June 21, 1977, when Illinois reinstated CAPITAL PUNISHMENT. Twelve death sentences were imposed in the cases of victims murdered between July 1977 and December 1978.

Over the next 14 years, Gacy remained a controversial inmate on death row. Abandoning the split-personality defense, he now claimed the bodies unearthed at his home had been planted during his absence by unknown conspirators. He described himself as "the thirty-fourth victim" of an insidious murder plot, with the true killers still at large. By 1993, supporters and the curious could dial Gacy's personal 900 telephone number for a 12-minute "refutation" of the prosecution's case—at a price of $1.99 per minute. Gacy also raised a storm of protest with the paintings—mostly grinning skulls and sad-faced clowns—that he produced and sold from death row. As his appeals ran out and time grew short in early 1994, the killer's portraits were hailed as collector's items, some of them selling at five-figure prices. Brisk sales were also reported for two published volumes of Gacy's prison correspondence with friends on the outside.

Last-minute appeals failed to halt Gacy's execution by lethal injection on May 10, 1994. At the end, there were those who believed Gacy innocent and others who suspect he may have had accomplices in his long-running murder spree . . . who still remain at large. The state of Illinois, meanwhile, was outraged at the murderer's celebrity, announcing plans to sue his estate for reimbursement of costs for room and board, incurred by Gacy during 14 years on death row.

See also ARTWORK AND MEMORABILIA

GALLEGO, Gerald Armand and Charlene

Gerald Armand Gallego never met his father, but he had the old man's temper, all the same. Gerald Senior was serving time in San Quentin when his son was born in 1946, and nine years later he became the first man to die in Mississippi's gas chamber, condemned for the murders of two police officers. Gerald Junior was unaware of the fact, accepting his mother's fiction of an accidental death, but he was already launched on a criminal career of his own. Dozens of minor scrapes with the law climaxed at age 13, with Gerald's incarceration for raping a six-year-old neighbor. His adult record listed 27 felony arrests and seven convictions, with outstanding warrants for incest, rape, and sodomy. By age 32, he had been married seven times—twice to the same woman—with several bigamous unions along the way. The incest charge related to his daughter, Mary Ellen, whom he had repeatedly molested from the age of six.

Despite the overwhelming down side, Gallego could turn on the charm when he chose, and it was running full blast in September 1977 when he met the woman who would share his final years of freedom.

The pampered only child of a supermarket executive in Stockton, California, Charlene Williams was 10 years Gerald's junior, born in October 1956. A certified genius, her IQ tested at 160 in high school, she also possessed a photographic memory and played classical violin well enough to rate an invitation from San Francisco's Conservatory of Music. Despite the early promise, though, she drifted into drug abuse at 12, lost her virginity a year later, and qualified as a borderline alcoholic by age 14. A year later, she was boasting to classmates of her ongoing affair with a black college student—one of the few indiscretions she managed to hide from her doting parents.

Genius IQ notwithstanding, Charlene's extracurricular activities played havoc with her studies at Rio Americano High School, in Sacramento. She squeaked through graduation but washed out of junior college in her first semester. Bent on becoming "a business-

woman," Charlene persuaded her parents to invest $15,000 in a Folsom gift shop, aptly christened "The Dingaling Shop." When that venture went belly-up, she tried her hand at marriage, with equally disastrous results.

Charlene's first husband, an impotent junkie, was discarded for failing to please her in bed. In retrospect, he thought the relationship might have gone better if he had played along with Charlene's plan to hire a prostitute for kinky threesomes, but he preferred to spend his money on heroin. Husband number two shunned drugs; he also shunned his bride, dumping Charlene after several weeks of marriage to live with another woman. On September 10, 1977, Charlene was shopping for dope at a Sacramento poker club when she met Gerald Gallego and fell in love at first sight. A week after their first meeting, the lovebirds moved in together, renting a small house on Sacramento's Bluebird Lane.

Variety was the spice of life for Gallego, and monogamy ran against the grain. Charlene was willing to accommodate his taste for strangers if it kept him home at night, and she made no complaint when he moved a teenage runaway into their love nest. Gerald enjoyed having sex with two women at once, but it was a different story when he came home early one afternoon to find the teenager engaged with Charlene. Enraged, he threw the youngster out an open window and gave Charlene the first of many beatings that would soon become a staple of their turbulent relationship.

The revelation of Charlene's bisexuality turned Gallego's world upside-down. The self-styled "macho man" was suddenly unable to perform in bed, except when forcing himself on Charlene. Violence bred of frustration became a daily event in their home, Charlene sometimes giving as good as she got. In one free-for-all, Gerald broke a finger while punching Charlene in the face; she responded by splitting his scalp with a club, and Gerald was holding her at gunpoint when Charlene's mother interrupted the fracas.

In July 1978, Charlene dreamed up a surprise for Gerald's 33rd birthday, inviting his daughter Mary Ellen and one of her adolescent girlfriends to spend the night on Bluebird Lane. It quickly turned into an orgy, all three females serving Gerald, and his impotence seemed to be cured . . . for the moment. Mary Ellen's departure brought a swift relapse, however, and Charlene conceived the idea of using "disposable sex slaves" to keep her man happy. They spent two months refining the plan, in which Charlene—dressed up to make herself look like a teen—would lure the chosen prey into her "Daddy's" waiting hands.

On September 11, 1978, 17-year-old Rhonda Scheffler and a friend, 16-year-old Kippi Vaught, disappeared from Sacramento on a short walk to a local shopping center. Two days passed before their ravaged, battered bodies were recovered outside Baxter, 15 miles away. Each girl had been sodomized by Gallego and forced to perform oral sex on Charlene, after which Charlene gnawed on their bodies. After the rapes, both victims were bound and beaten to death with a tire iron, and a single bullet was fired into each skull at close range.

Pleased with their experiment, the homicidal lovers celebrated by driving to Reno on September 30, where they were married with Charlene's parents as witnesses. Back in Sacramento, Charles Williams found his daughter a job in a meatpacking plant, thereby satisfying Gerald's demand that she pay her own way.

On June 24, 1979, 14-year-old Brenda Judd and 13-year-old Sandra Colley vanished from the Washoe County fairgrounds in Reno. Wheeling the murder van along a desert highway, Charlene grew so furious at Gerald's starting the rape without her that she swerved off the road and grabbed a gun, intent on killing him. Shots were exchanged, a bullet grazing Gerald's arm before the macho man called for a cease-fire, complaining that the van's abrupt halt had bruised his genitals. Temporarily out of action, Gallego watched Charlene molest both girls before he finished them off with point-blank gunfire.

Judd and Colley were still listed as missing in 1982 when Charlene's jailhouse confession solved the mystery of their disappearance. In the meantime, she suggested the abduction of two black girls on their next outing, but Gerald refused to "contaminate" himself with interracial sex. Finding herself pregnant three weeks after the second double murder, Charlene told her husband the good news. Gallego angrily forced her to go for an abortion—at her own expense, of course.

On April 24, 1980, teenagers Karen Chipman and Stacey Redican disappeared from a Reno shopping mall. Their remains were later discovered near Lovelock, Nevada, on July 27. Both victims had been sexually abused by the Gallegos, separately and in tandem, before they were beaten to death with a blunt instrument.

Five weeks later, on June 1, Charlene's parents joined the killer couple on another drive to Reno, where Gerald and Charlene repeated their marriage vows. This time around, Gallego used the name Steven Robert Feil, a false identity he had secured by stealing a policeman's ID card, using the vital information to request a "duplicate" birth certificate and driver's license for himself. If Charlene's parents questioned the curious move, they kept all doubts to themselves. Charlene was eight weeks pregnant on her wedding day, but this time Gerald took the news well, deciding the baby was "a keeper."

Gerald and Charlene celebrated their second wedding with a fishing trip to Oregon. Linda Aguilar, age 21, was four months pregnant when she disappeared from Port Orford on June 8, 1980. Relatives reported her missing on June 20, and her body was found two days later, planted in a shallow grave south of Gold Beach. Sexually abused by both Gallegos, the victim's skull was shattered, her wrists and ankles bound with nylon cord, but an autopsy revealed sand in her nose, mouth, and throat, indicating that she was buried alive.

Somehow, the latest murder failed to satisfy Gerald and Charlene, perhaps because they only had one victim to abuse. Tension mounted around the Gallego homestead, with neighbors calling police to break up screaming fights on July 12 and 14. Both times, Charlene convinced patrolmen that the sounds of combat emanated from their TV set, denying any conflict with her spouse.

On July 17, 1980, 34-year-old Virginia Mochel was abducted from the parking lot of a West Sacramento tavern, where she worked as a barmaid. For the first time, Gerald and Charlene took their victim back to Bluebird Lane, smuggling her into the house under cover of darkness. Repeatedly sodomized by both Gerald and Charlene, the victim was also flogged with a rope and otherwise abused before Gerald dragged her back to the van and strangled her there. Mochel's skeletal remains, still bound with nylon fishing line, were found outside of Clarksburg, California, on October 30.

Three days later, around 1:30 A.M., 22-year-old Craig Miller left a Sacramento fraternity dance with his date, 21-year-old Beth Sowers. Moments later, friends observed the couple seated in a car outside, a rough-looking stranger sitting up front on the passenger's side. One of Craig's friends was sliding in behind the wheel to make small talk when Charlene Gallego appeared, slapping his face as she ordered him out of the car; she jumped behind the wheel and sped away. Miller's frat brothers memorized the license plate, telling their story to police when Craig was found dead the next day at Bass Lake. Beth Sowers would not be found until November 22, shot three times and dumped in a Placer County ditch.

Officers traced the vehicle to Charlene's parents, recording a flat denial of its involvement in any crime from "Mrs. Steven Feil." The Gallegos promptly skipped town, but Charlene phoned her parents for money a few days later. Police were ready when the next call came, from Omaha, and FBI agents dropped the net on November 17, when Gerald and Charlene called for their money at a Western Union office.

The killer team of man and wife hung tough for eight months, but July 1981 found Charlene shopping for a way to save herself. On July 27, she offered a confession linking Gerald to the Miller-Sowers homicides if only she could be released on bail. Prosecutors ignored her, and Charlene tried again on March 2, 1982, announcing her desire to clear *10* murder cases in exchange for leniency. Police were skeptical until they heard the details, some resisting the plea bargain even then, but the deal was struck by late summer. In return for testimony against her husband, Charlene would receive a maximum sentence of 16 years and eight months in prison.

Gerald Gallego's first trial, in the Miller-Sowers case, opened on November 15, 1982, in Martinez, California. Jury selection took more than a month, with Gallego serving as his own attorney, and the trial dragged on through May. Charlene's self-serving testimony did the trick, and her husband was sentenced to death on June 22, 1983.

Transferred to Nevada for trial in the Chipman-Redican murders, Gerald became the target of an unprecedented public subscription campaign, with California residents donating $23,000 to help defray prosecution expenses. Gallego's second trial opened on May 23, 1984, with Charlene taking the stand on May 24. One June 7, jurors convicted Gallego on two counts of murder and two counts of kidnapping, recommending execution. Gerald received his second death sentence two weeks later, and he was housed at Carson City to await execution.

Charlene, for her part, was also jailed in Nevada for reasons of personal security. "Good time" made her eligible for parole in 1991, but she agreed to serve her full sentence in lieu of facing additional murder and kidnapping charges in California. Her term completed, she was duly released from custody in July 1997. Gerald, meanwhile, clung to hopes of a reprieve in September 1997 after a federal appeals court ordered a new sentencing hearing on grounds that the trial judge issued faulty jury instructions. Nevada's attorney general missed the February 1999 deadline for appealing that decision to the U.S. Supreme Court, and jury selection for Gallego's new penalty hearing began on September 13, 1999. Two months later, on November 17, the new panel condemned Gallego once again. The ink was barely dry on that verdict when, on November 20, 1999, skeletal remains of two Gallego victims were found in Lassen County, California. They were identified in December as Sandra Colley and Brenda Judd. Cancer claimed Gallego's life on July 18, 2002.

GARAVITO, Luis Alfredo

Colombia is one of the world's most violent nations, renowned for its drug wars and narco-terrorism, political upheavals, public assassinations, and random acts of mayhem. Even so, jaded police and journalists were shocked in the 1990s as some unknown predator roamed at will throughout the country, kidnapping and killing scores of children. Most of the victims were boys, although five young girls disappeared from a three-block stretch of Bogotá's Miguelito district between November 1995 and July 1997. The manhunt began during 1997, after 36 decomposed bodies were pulled from shallow graves outside Pereira, 110 miles west of Bogotá. In November 1998, Pereira's mayor announced that 13 more bodies—12 boys and one girl—had been discovered, most beheaded, some with hands bound and bearing signs of torture. None were identified, but police estimated their ages between eight and 13 years.

On December 31, 1998, police arrested suspect Pedro Pablo Ramírez, a paroled sex offender, on suspicion of murdering 29 children. The ink on that story was barely dry when authorities scaled back their estimate, naming Ramírez as a suspect in "at least three" Pereira murders and "possibly three others" in nearby Armenia. No disposition of his case was ever published, but Ramírez was presumably released, when the murders continued despite his arrest. On September 8, 1999, Colombia's police chief, General Rosso Serrano, broadcast a new alarm. "We fear," he told reporters, "that there could be a serial killer or a group of murderers on the loose." All told, Serrano said, 55 bodies had been found since 1994. "The bodies of the children were all similarly mutilated," he declared. "They were buried with hands tied and organs missing." Pereira residents feared a satanic cult at work, while other theorists attributed the crimes to black-market organ traffickers. Most of the victims were homeless street children, and hundreds more were missing nationwide.

In fact, by the time General Serrano sounded the alarm, his quarry was already in custody. Luis Garavito was arrested in April 1999 for attempted rape, and sat in jail thereafter while detectives chased Colombia's child-killer far and wide. Born in 1957 at Genova or Pereira (reports vary), the youngest of seven children in a poor family, Garavito was frequently beaten by his alcoholic father and raped by two male neighbors. He quit school in fifth grade and began drifting aimlessly at age 16, a heavy drinker subject to depression and suicidal urges. In his travels, Garavito worked as a handyman and street vendor, sometimes posing as a monk or spokesman for fictitious groups serving the elderly and children's education. The latter facade gained him entrance to various schools as a "guest speaker," where he basked in attention from children. Acquaintances throughout Colombia knew Garavito by various nicknames—"Goofy," "The Priest," and "El Loco" (madman). Garavito claimed his first victim in 1992, and thereafter recorded his killings in a dog-eared notebook

This mural in Pereira, Colombia, was made in the memory of the children that were killed by Luis Garavito. (AP Photo/Scott Dalton)

that he carried in his pocket. By the time of his arrest, the book contained 140 entries.

On October 30, 1999, prosecutor Alfonso Gómez told assembled reporters that Garavito had confessed his crimes in detail. Police had followed his directions to more graves, Gómez explained, raising the proven body count to 114. While most of the slayings occurred in the western state of Risaralda—with 41 victims unearthed at Pereira and 27 more in neighboring Valle de Cauca—bodies had been found near more than 60 towns, in 11 of Colombia's 32 provinces. While Colombia had suffered 25,000 murders in 1999 alone, many still unsolved, Gómez called the child-murder manhunt "the most important investigation of this type ever carried out" in the country. Apparently forgetting PEDRO ALONZO LÓPEZ, Gómez further claimed that Garavito's rampage "has no precedent in Colombia."

Psychologists examined Garavito in custody, tracing his crimes to vicious CHILDHOOD TRAUMA. Their report described Garavito as "a solitary sadist" who was "suicidal, very depressed, regrets his actions, and is easily angered." Pablo González, chief of Colombia's forensic investigative unit, told reporters, "We aren't looking here at any criminal genius, rather at an individual who has absolutely no qualms about killing." Garavito had lured his young victims with offers of food and drink, then escorted them to isolated areas where they were stripped, raped, killed, and mutilated. As in the case of Pakistan's JAVED IQBAL and Houston's DEAN ARNOLD CORLL, Garavito had preyed on "throwaway" children who lived on the streets and whose disappearance—if reported at all—was ignored by police. Garavito's self-assessment was unsparing. "I was tortured and raped," he declared. "I was tied up and obliged to do things at 12 years of age. I became a monster. There was a superior being inside me."

December 1999 brought the announcement that Garavito's murder tally had been raised from 140 to 182, allegedly including children murdered when he traveled through Ecuador at various times, but prosecutors in that nation filed no charges. On December 17 a Colombian judge sentenced Garavito to 52 years in prison for killing one boy at Tunja in 1996 and raping another at Villavicencio in 1999. On January 31, 2000, he received a 36-year sentence in Pereira, and a judge in Huila Province gave him 55 years for two more murders on February 25, 2000. By May 28, 2000, cumulative sentences in from 11 courts raised his sentence to 835 years, but the pileup had no legal effect, since Colombian inmates serve a maximum of 60 years, regardless of their crimes and sentences.

GARY, Carlton

A black native of Columbus, Georgia, born December 15, 1952, Gary was blessed with a near-genius IQ, but that gift of nature was cruelly balanced by the rigors of childhood and adolescence. Rejected by his father at an early age, Gary was malnourished as a child, and he suffered at least one serious head trauma in elementary school, knocked cold in an accident that left him unconscious on the playground. A heavy drug abuser in his teens, he began logging arrests in 1966, his rap sheet listing charges of robbery, arson, and assault before he reached his 18th birthday.

Gary surfaced in Albany, New York, during the spring of 1970, in time for a series of rape-murders targeting elderly women. In May, Marion Brewer was strangled with a pillow case in her Albany hotel room, followed two months later by 85-year-old Nellie Farmer, slain in a nearby apartment. Gary was arrested as a suspect in the latter case and he admitted being on the scene, but he fingered an accomplice—John Lee Williams—as the killer. Williams was convicted and sentenced to prison on the basis of Gary's testimony, his verdict subsequently overturned after Gary recanted. Escaping prosecution for the murder, Gary was convicted of burglary, receiving stolen property, and possession of drugs, drawing a term in the Onondaga County Correction Institution at Janesville, New York. He escaped from custody on August 22, 1977, and headed home to launch a one-man reign of terror.

On September 16, 60-year-old Ferne Jackson was raped, beaten, and strangled to death at her home in the Wynnton district of Columbus, found with a nylon stocking knotted tight around her neck. The same MO was demonstrated nine days later and a few blocks distant in the slaying of 71-year-old Jean Dimenstein. Florence Scheible, age 89, was killed in identical fashion on October 21, and 69-year-old Martha Thurmond died the same way, two days later. On October 28, 74-year-old Kathleen Woodruff was raped, beaten, and manually strangled at home, her slayer forgetting the traditional stocking in his haste to escape. Ruth Schwob survived the "Stocking Strangler's" attack on February 12, 1978, triggering a bedside alarm, but the killer was determined, traveling a mere two blocks before he raped and strangled 78-year-old Mildred Borom the same morning.

By early March, police knew they were searching for a black man in the string of homicides, and since his victims had been white, a threat of mounting racial violence dogged investigators on the job. They were distracted later in the month by threatening communications from another killer—self-styled "Chairman of the Forces of Evil"—who threatened to murder selected black women if the strangler was not swiftly apprehended. Three deaths would be traced to the Chairman before his arrest on April 4, but prosecution of the Stocking Strangler's competition brought police no closer to their man. On April 20, the killer claimed his final victim in Columbus, strangling 61-year-old Janet Cofer in her home, leaving the usual stocking knotted around her neck.

A week later, on April 27, Greenville, South Carolina, experienced the first in a series of armed robberies by the "Steakhouse Bandit," a gunman who invaded restaurants near closing time. Eight months passed before Carlton Gary was arrested in nearby Gaffney following a similar holdup, and he confessed to the entire series, drawing a sentence of 21 years in prison for armed robbery. Transferred to a minimum-security prison at Columbia four years later, he escaped from custody on March 15, 1983.

Another 14 months would pass before Gary's ultimate arrest, on May 3, 1984, at a motel in Albany, Georgia. Held as a fugitive from South Carolina and linked to an October 1977 burglary in Columbus, Gary was charged with the Scheible, Thurmond, and Woodruff murders on May 4. A jury convicted him on all counts in August 1986, deliberating for three hours before his penalty was fixed at death. He presently awaits execution in Georgia's electric chair.

GASKINS, Donald Henry, Jr.

Few observers would agree with Donald Gaskins's claim that he was "born special and fortunate" in South Carolina on March 31, 1933. The runt of a litter born to an unwed mother named Parrott, Gaskins was known throughout his early life as "Pee Wee" or "Junior Parrott," hearing his true name for the first time as a teenager, in court, when he was convicted of juvenile crimes and sentenced to a state reformatory. By that time, his mother had married one of Donald's numerous "step-daddies," a brutal disciplinarian who beat Donald and his half siblings "just for practice." Pee Wee was "pissed off" at girls from his earliest memory, unable to explain coherently the hatred he felt toward females. Dropping out of school, he joined two adolescent cohorts in a local crime wave that included numerous burglaries and at least one gang rape (of an accomplice's younger sister). The spree ended when a former classmate surprised Gaskins during a burglary and survived a hatchet blow to the head, identifying him for the police.

Sentenced to reform school until his 18th birthday, Gaskins was first gang-raped in the lockup, then "protected" by an older boy who used him sexually and passed him around to friends. Upon release in 1951, he found work on a tobacco plantation, soon deciding there was better money to be made from stealing the crop and torching barns to cover his thefts. Arrested for ARSON and attempted murder in 1952 (after striking a woman with a hammer), he won acquittal on the first charge and bargained the second down to assault and battery. His lawyer promised Gaskins 18 months in jail, but the judge handed down a five-year sentence, plus one more for contempt after Gaskins cursed him. In prison, Pee Wee was soon commandeered for sex by one of the cellblock "power men," until he cut the rapist's throat. Murder charges bargained down to manslaughter earned him another nine years, to be served concurrently with his previous sentence.

Donald Gaskins directs officers to where his victims are buried. (Wide World API)

Gaskins escaped in 1955 but was soon recaptured in Tennessee, now facing federal charges for driving a stolen car across state lines. His three-year sentence on that charge was set to run concurrently with his Carolina prison time, and Gaskins was paroled in August 1961, with 20 dollars and a bus ticket back to Florence. Charged with the statutory rape of a 12-year-old girl in 1962, Gaskins escaped through a courthouse window prior to trial and joined a traveling carnival, but he was soon recaptured and sentenced to eight years in prison. He was paroled in November 1968 on the condition that he not return to Florence for at least two years.

By that time, Gaskins was seething with rage, a blind hatred of society in general and females in particular which, he later said, afflicted him with physical pains "like hot lead" in his stomach and groin. The only release came through violence, and Gaskins committed the first of many random, recreational murders in September 1969, torturing and disemboweling a female hitchhiker he picked up along the Carolina coast, dumping her mutilated body in the ocean south of Georgetown, South Carolina.

Henceforth, Gaskins would mentally divide his slayings into "coastal kills" (committed for sadistic pleasure, victimizing strangers of both sexes) and "serious murders" (involving victims who were personal acquaintances). On death row, decades later, he estimated that he had committed 10 "coastal kills" by October 1970, with his first "serious murders" occurring one month later. The November victims were his own niece, 15-year-old Janice Kirby, and a girlfriend, 17-year-old Patricia Alsbrook, both of whom he raped and murdered at the Sumter mobile-home park where he lived. Gaskins buried them out in the country, revealing Alsbrook's grave in a 1976 bargain with prosecutors to save himself from the electric chair. (Two years later, in another death-row deal, Gaskins pretended to give up Kirby's remains, but he feared discovery of other corpses buried nearby, actually directing searchers to the grave of a victim planted near Columbia in 1973.)

Once Gaskins got the hang of it, his homicides proliferated at a dizzy pace. One murder, the December 1970 torture-slaying of 13-year-old Peggy Cuttino, was blamed on convict William Pierce, serving life for a similar slaying in Georgia; Gaskins admitted the crime in 1977, but embarrassed prosecutors have thus far refused to exonerate Pierce in that case. His "coastal kills" continued on a monthly basis, more or less, while victims of his "serious murders" included criminal accomplices, personal enemies, and neighborhood acquaintances who aroused Gaskins sexually. One of the worst such cases, in 1973, involved the rape-slayings of 23-year-old Doreen Dempsey (eight months pregnant at the time) and her 20-month-old daughter Robin. (Gaskins later described raping the infant as the best sexual experience of his life.) Through it all, Gaskins took comfort in the fact that he was "one of the few that truly understands what death and pain are all about. I have a special kind of mind that allows me to give myself permission to kill."

Gaskins would later describe 1975 as his "killingest" year, climaxed with his arrest for trafficking in stolen cars. An accomplice in several of his "serious murders," Walter Neely, "got religion" that December and turned state's evidence, leading detectives to eight buried victims. Indicted on eight murder charges, Gaskins faced trial in May 1976 on only one count, for the 1975 slaying of Neely's ex-brother-in-law, Dennis Bellamy. Convicted on May 24 and sentenced to die, Gaskins was irate when Neely received a life sentence for the same murder one week later by claiming he had been "controlled" by Pee Wee against his will.

With seven more indictments hanging over him, Gaskins began negotiating for his life, pointing police toward more graves in return for leniency. He need not have bothered, since the U.S. Supreme Court invalidated South Carolina's death penalty statute in November 1976, his sentence automatically commuted to life imprisonment.

A month later, detectives were after Gaskins once again, this time for the murder of Silas Yates, a 45-year-old Carolinian who allegedly offered Gaskins a murder contract in 1975. Pee Wee killed Yates instead, and Gaskins was tried on that charge (with three marginal accomplices) in April 1977, receiving his second life sentence.

South Carolina's death penalty was reinstated by 1978, and Gaskins struck another bargain with prosecutors, agreeing to turn up more bodies and submit to a three-day grilling under sodium pentothal, in return for a signed-and-sealed promise of exemption from the chair. That spring found him sentenced to a total of nine life terms; no charges were filed in the cases of five other murders he confessed, since the existing sentences removed all hope of parole.

That might have been the end for Pee Wee Gaskins, but he couldn't keep his nose clean, even in prison. In 1982 he accepted a contract to kill death-row inmate Randolph Tyner, wiring an explosive charge to Tyner's radio and detonating it with fatal results on September 12. A relative of Tyner's original victim, who arranged the contract, was sentenced to 25 years in prison, but a sympathetic judge made him eligible for parole after 30 months. Gaskins, for his part, was sentenced to die, his final appeal rejected in June 1991. He was electrocuted three months later, on September 6.

Before he died, Gaskins completed work on a gripping (if ungrammatical) autobiography, including an estimate of his final body count. Ignoring his first and last murders committed in prison, Gaskins tabulated 31 "serious murders" (including 14 victims found by police and 17 still buried in three South Carolina counties) and 80 or 90 "coastal kills," for a total in the neighborhood of 110 victims. Since Gaskins never learned the names of his "coastal" victims, remaining deliberately vague on the dates of their murders and locations where their bodies were dumped, the final tally is impossible to verify. By the same token, however, there is no clear reason to dispute his claim, and even if the "coastal" body count was overestimated by 100 percent, Gaskins still qualifies as one of America's most prolific serial killers of modern times.

GECHT, Robin   *See* "CHICAGO RIPPERS"

GEIN, Edward Theodore

Ed Gein may be America's most famous murderer, although his name is seldom heard and barely recognized today. Four decades have passed since he first made headlines, but Gein is still with us in spirit. His crimes inspired the movie *Psycho* and its sequels, spinning off in later years to terrify another generation as *The Texas Chainsaw Massacre*. While other slayers have surpassed Gein's body count, America has never seen his equal in the field of mental aberration.

Gein was born August 8, 1906, at La Crosse, Wisconsin, but his family soon moved to a farm outside Plainfield. His father held jobs as a tanner and carpenter when he wasn't working the farm, and Gein's mother emerged as the dominant parent, settling most family decisions on her own. Devoutly religious, she warned her two sons against premarital sex, but Gein recalled that she was "not as strong" in her opposition to masturbation. Ed's father died in 1940, and his brother Henry was lost four years later while fighting a marsh fire. His mother suffered a stroke that same year, and a second one killed her in 1945 following an argument with one of her neighbors. Alone at last, Gein nailed her bedroom shut and set about "redecorating" in his own inimitable style.

From childhood, Gein had been ambiguous about his masculinity, considering amputation of his penis on several occasions. With pioneer transsexual Christine Jorgenson much in the headlines at the time, Gein considered transsexual surgery, but the process was costly and frightening. There must be other ways, he thought, of "turning female" on a part-time basis.

Edward Gein in custody (Wide World API)

Between 1947 and 1954, Gein haunted three local cemeteries, opening an estimated 40 graves in his nocturnal raids. He might remove whole corpses or settle for choice bits and pieces; a few bodies were later returned to their resting place, but Ed recalled that there were "not too many." Allegedly aided in the early days by "Gus," a simple-minded neighbor, Gein continued excavations on his own when his assistant died. At home, he used the ghoulish relics as domestic decorations. Skulls were mounted on the bedposts, severed skullcaps serving Gein as bowls. He fashioned mobiles out of noses, lips, and labia and sported a belt of nipples around the house. Human skin was variously utilized for lamp shades, the construction of waste-baskets, and the upholstery of chairs.

The choicer bits were specially preserved for Gein to wear at home. For ceremonial occasions, such as dancing underneath the moon, he wore a woman's scalp and face, a skinned-out "vest" complete with breasts, and female genitalia strapped above his own. By "putting on" another sex and personality, Gein seemed to find a measure of contentment, but his resurrection raids eventually failed to satisfy a deeper need.

On December 8, 1954, 51-year-old Mary Hogan disappeared from the tavern she managed in Pine Grove, Wisconsin. Authorities found a pool of blood on the floor, an overturned chair, and one spent cartridge from a .32-caliber pistol. Foul play was the obvious answer, and while deputies recall Ed Gein as a suspect in the case, no charges were filed at the time. (Three years later, the shell casing would be matched to a pistol found in Gein's home.)

On November 16, 1957, 58-year-old Bernice Worden disappeared from her Plainfield hardware store under strikingly similar circumstances. There was blood on the floor, a thin trail of it leading out back where the victim's truck had last been seen. Worden's son recalled that Gein had asked his mother for a date, and on the day before she disappeared Ed mentioned that he needed antifreeze. A sales receipt for antifreeze was found inside the store, and deputies went looking for their suspect. What they found would haunt them all for the remainder of their lives.

Inside a shed, behind Gein's house, the headless body of Bernice Worden hung from the rafters, gutted like a deer, the genitals carved out. A tour of the cluttered house left searchers stunned. Worden's heart was found in a saucepan on the stove, while her head had been turned into a macabre ornament, with twine attached to nails inserted in both ears. Her other organs occupied a box, shoved off to molder in a corner. Deputies surveyed Gein's decorations and his "costumes," counting skins from 10 skulls in one cardboard drum, taking hasty inventory of implements fashioned from human bones.

In custody, Gein readily confessed the Hogan and Worden murders, along with a series of unreported grave robberies. Confirmation of the latter was obtained by opening three graves: in one, the corpse was mutilated as described by Gein; the second held no corpse at all; a casket in the third showed pry-marks, but the body was intact, as Gein remembered.

On January 16, 1958, a judge found Gein incompetent for trial and packed him off to Central State Hospital at Waupun, Wisconsin. A decade later, Ed was ordered up to trial, with the proceedings held in mid-November 1968. Judge Robert Gollmar found Gein innocent by reason of insanity and sent him back to Waupun, where he died of respiratory failure on July 26, 1984.

Gein willingly confessed two murders and was tried for one, but were there others? And if so, how many?

Brother Henry was suggested as a likely victim, by Judge Gollmar, inasmuch as there was no autopsy or investigation of his death. However that may be, there is a stronger case for murder in the disappearance of a man named Travis and his unnamed male companion, last seen at the time they hired Ed Gein to be their hunting guide. One victim's jacket was recovered from the woods near Plainfield, and while Gein professed to know the whereabouts of Travis's body—blaming his death on "a neighbor"—police never followed up on the case.

The search of Gein's home also turned up additional organs, removed from two young women, that could not be matched to existing cemetery records. Judge Gollmar suggests that one likely victim was Evelyn Hartley, abducted from La Crosse on a night when Gein was visiting relatives two blocks from her home. A pool of blood was found in the family garage after she vanished, with the trail disappearing at curbside. Mary Weckler was reported missing a short time later from Jefferson, Wisconsin; a white Ford was seen in the area. When searchers scoured Gein's property they found a white Ford sedan on the premises, though no one in Plainfield could ever recall Ed driving such a car. No other evidence exists to identify Gein's victims, but if he did not dispose of Hartley and Weckler, he at least killed two other young women, their names still unknown.

Gein's burial in Plainfield posed an ongoing problem for local authorities. Vandals repeatedly invaded the local cemetery, chipping fragments from his headstone and defacing it with profane or satanic graffiti. Finally, on June 20, 2000, an unknown thief stole what remained of Gein's marker. The stone surfaced in Seattle, Washington, on June 21, 2001, but no one seemed to know what should be done with it. In Plainfield, Sheriff Patrick Fox told reporters, "We could bring it back and put it in the cemetery, but it would only get stolen again." A proposal to deposit Gein's headstone with the Waushara County Historical Society was flatly rejected. "I brought it up to the group," said board member Ardis Spuhler. "They said, 'No.' They didn't want any part of it. If people are determined to get ahold of this thing, we didn't want them breaking into the museum to get it."

GEOGRAPHY: Distribution of serial killers

No continent except the frozen wasteland of Antarctica has been entirely spared from serial murders, but some regions are clearly safer than others. North America has produced some 80 percent of all known 20th-century serial killers, with the vast majority of those active in the United States. Europe runs a distant second with about 16 percent of the world's total crop: the European leaders are Great Britain (with 28 percent of the continent's total), Germany (with 27 percent), and France (trailing with 13 percent). Third World nations presently spawn 4 percent of the world's known serial killers, but a recent upsurge in reports from South Africa and Latin America threaten to alter those statistics in the new millennium. (The Third World lag, despite huge population blocs, has variously been explained in terms of cultural disparity, poor communication, and news censorship imposed by various totalitarian regimes.)

One thing is clear from any global survey of serial murder: the United States, with 5 percent or less of the world's total population, has produced 76 percent of all known serial killers in the 20th century (closer to 85 percent since 1980). Granted, Americans got a late start in the business of serial murder—the first known predator from ancient Rome had been dead for more than 1,800 years when Columbus found the West Indies; ERZSEBET BÁTHORY died in custody three years after the Jamestown Colony was established in Virginia—but whatever they lacked in timing, the New World settlers made up in zeal.

Serial murder is clearly a national problem in America—none of the 50 states is wholly unaffected—but once again, some districts are more dangerous than others. Georgraphy is another area, as in choice of WEAPONS, where serial killers deviate from the American norm. In an average year, 43 percent of all reported murders are committed in the southern states, while the West, Midwest and Northeast average 20 percent, 19 percent, and 18 percent, respectively. Serial killers are less parochial: 25 percent strike in the South, with the West running a close second at 24 percent; the Midwest and Northeast lag behind with respective figures of 17 and 16 percent. The five most dangerous states in terms of serial murder cases reported are California (with 10 percent of the world total during the 20th century), Florida, New York, Texas, and Illinois.

Crime writer Ann Rule, in U.S. Senate testimony dating from July 1982, suggested that these states (and the Pacific Northwest) may record a disproportionate number of cases because serial killers "run to the borders" in an unconscious physical expression of their mental extremity. The theory sounds intriguing, but there seems to be no evidence of any sort behind it. In fact, if the notion was accurate, states like Montana, North Dakota, and Maine should be overrun with serial killers, instead of ranking near the bottom in reported cases.

In fact, the answer seems to lie in simple logic. The favored hunting grounds of domestic serial killers include five of America's seven most populous states and seven of the nation's 10 most crowded cities. Aside from population density, cities such as New York, Los Angeles, Chicago, San Francisco, and Miami share reputations as the most "liberal" in America, where sex, drugs, and alcohol are concerned; all feature thriving subcommunities of prostitutes and homosexuals who frequently fall prey to random killers. In America's mobile society, those cities draw the vast majority of homeless transients, runaways, and would-be "stars"; they also rank consistently among the worst in terms of violent crime. Warm year-round climates and flourishing agriculture bring thousands (if not millions) of migrant workers and illegal aliens to California, Florida, and Texas every year, providing human predators with yet another ready source of prey. It is impossible to say if these states breed sadistic murderers in greater numbers or attract them as a magnet draws iron filings, from afar, but either way, the evident preponderance of serial killers in the top five states should come as no surprise.

A hunter goes where there is ready game.

Outside of the United States, the past 10 years have witnessed surprising outbreaks of serial murder in the former Soviet Bloc and South Africa; it has even been suggested that South Africa, with a total population less than one-sixth the size of America's, may soon record a higher per capita murder rate than the United States. Explanations for the latest outbreaks vary: both regions have, in fact, recorded cases of serial murder throughout the 20th century, but changing circumstances have apparently increased the incidence (or at least the reporting) of serial murder. Prior to the advent of glasnost in 1987 (and the Soviet Union's official collapse four years later), Communist censors and police worked in tandem to suppress reports of "decadent Western-type crime" in what was supposed to be a socialist Utopia. (The same pattern continues today in China, where at least three serial killers since 1995 have been falsely described in official reports as "China's first.")

South Africa's recent problem with serial murder is rather different from Russia's. While the nation's whites-only government was every bit as brutal as the Soviet regime (to nonwhites, at least), state censorship in South Africa was seldom—if ever—employed to suppress reports of sensational civilian crimes. With the final collapse of apartheid in 1993, some analysts suggest, black rage suppressed for generations has at last found avenues of physical expression. And, while the majority of serial killers in South Africa, as elsewhere, prey on members of their own race, several dozen white farmers have been murdered by roving black slayers in the latter 1990s.

The United States held its statistical lead in serial murders at the start of the 21st century, but authorities in other nations acknowledged a rapid worldwide increase in this typically "Western" crime. Russia set new records at the turn of the millennium, with much of its serial crime concentrated in the southern river city of Rostov-on-Don, where ANDREI ROMANOVICH CHIKATILO once stalked victims in local railway stations. Police report that 29 serial killers and rapists were caught in Rostov during the 1990s, with several others still at large. Some residents vainly sought religious explanations for the plague of predators. In January 1999, a spokesman for the local Orthodox cathedral told *Newsweek* magazine, "The people here are no less God-fearing than anywhere else. Why Satan chooses so many of his servants here is not for us to know." Criminologist Aleksandr Bukhanovsky offered a more plausible explanation. "The problem of serial murder exists everywhere in Russia," he says. "It's just that here we have more practice at catching serial killers, and therefore the statistics are higher."

South Africa faced similar problems in the new century. Since 1990, police have acknowledged 52 serial killers active nationwide, with 16 still at large in November 2003. (By contrast, the years 1936 through 1990 produced only eight verified cases.) Psychologist MICKI PISTORIUS stays busy PROFILING the killers at large, while detective Gerard Labuschagne pursues them with the special 22-member Investigative Psychology Unit. Labuschagne's unit has pioneered in training officers specifically to hunt serial offenders, with the result that detectives from Scotland Yard and other agencies are often sent to hone their skills in South Africa. That focus may also explain why South Africa boasts the world's highest per capita arrest rate for multiple murderers. Statistically, most South Africa predators are captured within six weeks, while the global average is two years.

China, by contrast, says little about its modern rash of serial killings, except when offenders are captured and hastily sentenced to die. Each new outbreak triggers waves of public shock and anger, occasioned at least in part by official news censorship during the course of ongoing investigations. By the time a killer is captured, his score may be well into double digits, and some killers predictably elude arrest. In November 2003, while celebrating the arrest of a man who killed 17 boys lured away from video arcades in Henan, Chinese police reluctantly acknowledged that they had no leads in other cases, including one with 12 female victims and another involving 65 persons slain across four provinces. As for those convicted and executed, Amnesty International complains that Chinese courts and firing squads are sometimes prone to act without sufficient evidence, preferring the appearance of success to actual solution of a crime.

The 21st century also brought startling reports of a murder epidemic in Guatemala, where more than 700 female victims were slain during 2001–03. The year 2003 alone witnessed 383 murders of women; police solved only 11 cases. Many of the victims were brutally tortured, mutilated, beheaded, and/or burned, their bodies discarded in trash bins and along highways. At least two serial killers were involved in the carnage: One smothered prostitutes in Guatemala City and inked messages on their bodies, describing his "pact with Lucifer"; another committed five double murders of young girls within the last six months of 2003, leaving two ravaged corpses together in each case. As in CIUDAD JUÁREZ, MEXICO, human right activists contend—and officials flatly deny—that police are responsible for some of the slayings.

See also HISTORY OF SERIAL MURDER

GOHL, Billy

Nothing of substance is known about Billy Gohl's first 40 years, and the stories he told in response to occasional questions were riddled with holes, contradictions, and some outright lies. By his own reckoning, Gohl was born around 1860, spending most of the next four decades as a laborer and sailor. In 1903 he surfaced in Aberdeen, Washington, as a delegate for the Sailors' Union of the Pacific.

The union office, in those days, functioned as a combination mail drop, bank, and general employment office for its members. Sailors new in port might check for letters, scan the list of vessels needing crewmen, or deposit valuables before they made the rounds at local

Billy Gohl (with saw), the "Ghoul of Gray's Harbor" (Author's collection)

bars. In many cases, sailors just returned from months at sea had large amounts of cash in hand. An honest union delegate would hold the money in a safe until it was reclaimed. In Aberdeen, the spoils belonged to Billy Gohl.

His method was simplicity itself. When sailors turned up individually, Gohl checked the street for witnesses. If it was clear, and if something of substantial value was entrusted to his care, he drew a pistol from his desk and shot his victim in the head. That done, he paused to clean the weapon, then stripped his prey of any extra cash and all identifying documents. Gohl's building had a trapdoor, with a chute extending to the Wishkah River just outside, with currents flowing toward Gray's Harbor and the sea beyond.

Within a few years after Gohl's arrival, Aberdeen acquired a reputation as a "port of missing men." No records exist for his first six years of operation, but authorities pulled 41 "floaters" out of the water between 1909 and 1912, suggesting a prodigious body count. Most of the dead were presumed to be merchant seamen, and Billy Gohl was among the most vocal critics of Aberdeen law enforcement, demanding apprehension of the killers and more protection for his men.

Gohl's downfall was precipitated by a timepiece and his own attempt at cleverness. While rifling the pockets of his latest victim, Billy came upon a watch bearing the engraved name of August Schleuter from Hamburg, Germany. Alert to the potential for incrimination, he replaced the watch and dumped the corpse as usual. When the "floater" came ashore, Gohl was on hand to identify Schleuter as one of his sailors, renewing demands for thorough investigation of the murders.

This time, Billy got his wish. It took some time, but homicide investigators learned the victim was, in fact, a Danish sailor named Fred Nielssen. He had bought the watch in Hamburg from a craftsman who identified each piece he made with an engraving of his name. Gohl's effort to identify the corpse as August Schleuter smacked of guilty knowledge, and detectives finally built a case that brought him into court in 1913 on a double murder charge.

Gohl was rescued from the gallows by Washington's repeal of the death penalty in 1912. Convicted and sentenced to life for two slayings, he rebuffed all efforts to compile a comprehensive list of victims. Even so, publicity surrounding Billy's case was adequate to prompt restoration of CAPITAL PUNISHMENT in 1914. Safe in his prison cell, with no evidence to support further trials and possible execution, Gohl counted the years until his death of natural causes in 1928.

GOODE, Arthur Frederick, III

A native of Hyattsville, Maryland, Arthur Goode was a victim of borderline retardation who still wore his hair in Little Lord Fauntleroy bangs at age 22. In his teens, Goode began making sexual advances to younger boys, quickly becoming notorious in his own neighborhood. Arrested three times for indecent assaults upon minors, he was freed each time when his parents posted bail.

In March 1975, Goode was arrested on five counts of sexual assault, stemming from his abuse of a nine-year-old boy. His parents raised $25,000 to release him from jail, but Arthur wasn't finished yet. While out on bail, he molested an 11-year-old, escaping with five years' probation on the condition that he undergo voluntary psychiatric treatment at Spring Grove State Hospital. The key word was *voluntary,* and no one could stop him when Goode checked out of the hospital 15 weeks later, catching a bus for his parents' new home in St. James City, Florida. Despite warnings and the issuance of a bench warrant for his arrest, no one bothered to go after Goode and bring him back.

On March 5, 1976, Goode lured nine-year-old Jason VerDow away from a school bus stop in Fort Myers, asking the child to help him "find something" in the woods nearby. "I told him he was going to die," Goode later confessed, "and I described how I would kill him. I asked him if he had any last words, and he said, 'I love you,' and then I strangled him."

Police soon recovered the body, nude but for stockings, and Goode was twice questioned as a suspect in the case. Growing nervous, he bused back to Spring Grove and dropped in at the state hospital, spending five minutes there before fleeing, convinced that a receptionist was calling the police. (In fact, the staff professed to have no knowledge of the outstanding arrest warrants.)

Later that day, Goode picked up 10-year-old Billy Arthe, persuading the boy to join him in Washington, D.C., where they spent the next 10 days touring the capital and sleeping in motels. Arthe was still with Goode, unharmed, when they met Kenny Dawson, age 11, and Goode talked the boy into joining them for a bus ride to Tysons Corner, Virginia. There, while hiking in the woods near town, Goode forced Dawson to undress, afterward strangling him with a belt while Billy Arthe looked on, horrified.

Days later, a Falls Church housewife recognized Billy Arthe from newspaper photographs and summoned police. As he was handcuffed, Goode complained, "You can't do nothing to me. I'm sick." A Maryland jury disagreed, finding him sane and guilty of murder, whereupon the court imposed a life sentence. Packed off to Florida for a second trial, Goode was there convicted of first-degree murder and sentenced to die in the electric chair.

While awaiting execution, Goode harassed the parents of his victims with cruel, taunting letters. He, in turn, was frequently abused by other inmates, reviled as "the most hated man on death row." Some convicts threw things at him when he passed their cells; THEODORE BUNDY, more cunning than the rest, contrived to steal cookies from Goode's dinner tray. The sport ended for all concerned when Goode was executed on April 5, 1984. The state denied his last request to be allowed sexual intercourse with "a sexy little boy."

GORE, David Alan, and WATERFIELD, Fred

A Florida native born in 1951, David Gore resembled the stereotypical Southern "redneck," tipping the scales at 275 pounds and was so enamored of firearms that he studied gunsmithing in his free time. He studied women, too, but in a different fashion, losing one job as a gas station attendant after the owner found a peephole Gore had drilled between the men's and women's restrooms. A year younger, cousin Fred Waterfield was another product of Florida's Indian River County, a high-school football star whose ugly temper and taste for violent sex perfectly meshed with Gore's. In 1976, they put their heads together and decided to combine their favorite sports by stalking human game.

Their early efforts were embarrassing. Trailing a female motorist outside Yeehaw Junction, Waterfield flattened her tires with rifle fire, but the intended victim escaped on foot. Later, they followed another woman from Vero Beach to Miami, giving up the pursuit when she parked on a busy street. Their first successful rape took place near Vero Beach, and while the victim notified police, she later dropped the charges to avoid embarrassment in court.

By early 1981, Gore was working days with his father as caretaker of a citrus grove and patrolling the streets after dark as an auxiliary sheriff's deputy. Waterfield had moved north to Orlando, managing an automotive shop, but he made frequent visits home to Vero Beach. Together, they recognized the potential of Gore's situation—packing a badge by night, killing time in the orchards by day—and Fred offered to pay cousin Dave $1,000 for each pretty girl he could find. It was a proposition Gore could not refuse.

On February 19, 1981, Gore spotted 17-year-old Ying Hua Ling disembarking from a school bus and tricked her into his car with a flash of his badge. Driving her home, Gore "arrested" her mother and handcuffed his captives together, phoning Waterfield in Orlando before he drove out to the orchard. Killing time while waiting for his cousin, Gore raped both victims, but Waterfield was more selective. Rejecting Mrs. Ling as too old, Fred tied the woman up in such a fashion that she choked to death while struggling against her bonds. He then raped and murdered the teenager, slipping Gore $400 and leaving him to dispose of the corpses alone in an orchard a mile from the Ling residence.

Five months later, on July 15, Gore made a tour of Round Island Park, seeking a blond to fill his cousin's latest order. Spotting a likely candidate in 35-year-old Judith Daley, Gore disabled her car, then played good Samaritan, offering a lift to the nearest telephone. Once inside his pickup, Gore produced a pistol, cuffed his victim, and called cousin Fred on his way to the orchard. Waterfield was happier with this delivery, writing out a check for $1,500 after both men finished with their victim. Two years later, Gore would spell out Judith Daley's fate, describing how he "fed her to the alligators" in a swamp 10 miles west of Interstate Highway 95.

A week later, Gore fell under suspicion when a local man reported that a deputy had stopped his teenage daughter on a rural highway, attempting to hold her "for questioning." Stripped of his badge, Gore was arrested days later when officers found him crouched in the back seat of a woman's car outside a Vero Beach clinic, armed with a pistol, handcuffs, and a police radio scanner. A jury deliberated for 30 minutes before convicting him of armed trespass, and he was sentenced to five years in prison. Rejecting psychiatric treatment recommended by the court, he was paroled in March of 1983.

A short time after Gore's release, his cousin moved back home to Vero Beach and they resumed the hunt. On May 20, they tried to abduct an Orlando prostitute at gunpoint, but she slipped away and left them empty-handed. The next day, they picked up two 14-year-old hitchhikers—Angelica Lavallee and Barbara Byer—raping both before Gore shot the girls to death. Byer's body was dismembered and buried in a shallow grave, while Lavallee's was dumped in a nearby canal.

On July 26, 1983, Vero Beach authorities received an emergency report of a nude man firing shots at a naked girl on a residential street. Converging on the suspect house, owned by relatives of Gore, offenders found a car in the driveway with fresh blood dripping from its trunk. Inside, the body of 17-year-old Lynn Elliott lay curled in death, a bullet in her skull. Outgunned by the raiding party, Gore meekly surrendered, directing officers to the attic where a naked 14-year-old girl was tethered to the rafters.

As the surviving victim told police, she had been thumbing rides with Lynn Elliott when Gore and another man picked them up, flashing a pistol and driving them to the house, where they were stripped and raped repeatedly in separate rooms. Elliott had managed to free herself, escaping on foot with Gore in pur-

suit, but she had not been fast enough. Gore's companion had left in the meantime, and detectives turned to their suspect in quest of his identity.

Gore swiftly cracked in custody, enumerating crimes committed with his cousin. On March 16, 1984, he was sentenced to die for the murder of Lynn Elliott, Fred Waterfield was convicted in the Byer-Lavallee murders on January 21, 1985, receiving two consecutive life terms with a specified minimum stint of 50 years before parole. Two weeks later, on February 4, cousin Dave received an identical sentence upon his conviction of the Ling, Daley, Byer, and Lavallee homicides.

GRAHAM, Gwendolyn Gail, and WOOD, Catherine May

The deaths at Alpine Manor started as a game. At first, the killers planned to choose their victims alphabetically, with their initials spelling MURDER as a private joke on the police. As luck would have it, though, the aging women first selected still had too much fight left in them, and the plotters had to shift their strategy.

No matter. In the end, they still found easy prey to satisfy their taste for death.

Born in 1963, Gwen Graham was a California native who grew up in Tyler, Texas. She was "quiet and respectful" to her teachers, but she "always had a sad look on her face." In later years she claimed the sadness was occasioned by her father's sexual advances, but the charge—which he denies—was never proved in court. Moving to Michigan in 1986, Graham found work as a nurse's aide at the Alpine Manor Nursing Home in Walker, a Grand Rapids suburb.

Graham's immediate superior at Alpine Manor was 24-year-old Cathy Wood. Wed as a teenager, Wood had ballooned to 450 pounds when her seven-year marriage broke up, leaving her alone and friendless in Grand Rapids. Hired at Alpine Manor in July 1985, she was soon promoted to supervisor of nurse's aides, but her social life remained a vacuum until she met Gwen Graham on the job. Their friendship swiftly crossed the line into a lesbian affair, Wood dieting the pounds away and relishing the social whirl of gay bars, parties, and casual sex. Her chief devotion was to Graham, though, and by late 1986 the two women had pledged undying love to one another, come what may.

Gwen broached the subject of premeditated murder that October, but her lover "thought we were just playing." During sex, Gwen got a kick from tying Cathy down and choking her until she trembled on the verge of blacking out. If Cathy had complaints about the game, she kept them to herself. By slow degrees, she learned that pain and pleasure may be flip sides of the same exciting coin.

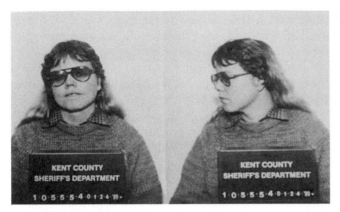

Gwendolyn Graham (Author's collection)

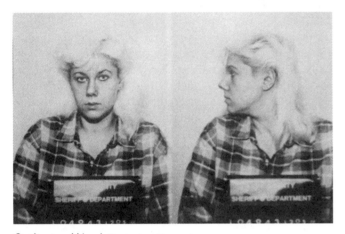

Catherine Wood (Author's collection)

The homicides at Alpine Manor spanned a three-month period, from January to the early part of April 1987. Gwen's first plan, the MURDER game, fell through when her selected targets put up such a fight that she was forced to let them live. Despite her bungled efforts, there were no complaints on file. Both Wood and Graham earned exemplary reports from their superiors and were "well liked by patients" on the ward.

In the future, Gwen decided, she would only pick on women who were too far gone for self-defense. Her lover was the lookout, standing by where she could watch the murder and the nurse's station all at once, diverting any member of the staff who strayed too close while Graham snuffed her chosen victim with a washcloth pressed across the nose and mouth. Sometimes the sheer excitement of a killing was too much, and they retired immediately to an empty room for sex while memories were fresh. In several cases Gwen kept SOUVENIRS—an anklet or a handkerchief, a brooch, a set of dentures.

Murder is a risky business, but the lethal lovers seemed to thrive on danger, boasting of their body count to colleagues who dismissed the comments as "sick jokes." At least three nurse's aides saw the shelf of souvenirs in the house Wood shared with Graham, but none took the gloating tales of murder seriously . . . yet.

By April 1987, the honeymoon was over for Wood and Graham. Cathy balked at personally killing anyone to "prove her love," and she was shortly rescued by her transfer to a different shift. By that time, Gwen was spending time with Heather Barager, another lesbian who ultimately joined her on a trip back home to Texas, leaving Cathy in the lurch. Come August, Cathy spilled the story to her former husband, but Ken Wood stalled another 14 months before he called police. Gwen Graham, meanwhile, had gone to work at Mother Frances Hospital in Tyler, keeping in touch with Cathy on the telephone.

Grand Rapids police were skeptical of Ken Wood's story at first. Some 40 patients had died at Alpine Manor in the first quarter of 1987, all listed as natural deaths, but on reflection eight cases seemed to stand out. Three of those were finally eliminated by detectives, leaving a victim list that included 60-year-old Marguerite Chambers, 89-year-old Edith Cole, 95-year-old Myrtle Luce, 79-year-old Mae Mason, and 74-year-old Belle Burkhard. In no case was there any scientific evidence of murder, but Ken Wood's statement and the second thoughts of staffers at the home were strong enough to make a case.

Both women were arrested in December 1988, Wood held without bond in Grand Rapids on charges of killing victims Cook and Chambers. In Texas, where rumors of the Michigan investigation had already cost Gwen her job, a $1 million bond was sufficient to keep her in jail. A brief extradition fight grew tedious and Graham soon waived the legalities, returning to face charges on her own volition.

The Alpine Manor staff was "overwhelmed" by the arrests, though some remembered Gwen as "unpredictable," remarking casually on Graham's quick temper. Former nurse's aides Deborah Kidder, Nancy Harris, Lisa Lynch, Dawn Male, and Russell Thatcher reevaluated the "sick jokes" and souvenirs they had managed to ignore while lives were on the line. At trial, all five would testify against Gwen Graham for the prosecution, with Cathy Wood emerging as the state's star witness overnight.

A September 1989 guilty plea to charges of second-degree murder spared Wood from life imprisonment, earning her a sentence of 20 to 40 years. In return for that relative leniency, she took the stand against Graham three months later, thereby sealing her ex-lover's fate. Aside from the five victims murdered, said Cathy, Gwen had tried to suffocate at least five others who survived. Wood's ultimate confession to her husband had been prompted less by guilt than fear that Graham would continue killing in her new position at the Texas hospital, this time with infants as her chosen prey.

"When she was killing people at Alpine and I didn't do anything," Wood told the court, "that was bad enough. But when she would call me and say how much she wanted to smash a baby, I had to stop her somehow. I knew she was working in a hospital there. She said she wanted to take one of the babies and smash it up against a window. I had to do something. I didn't care about myself anymore."

Graham's attorney tried to portray Wood as a jealous, vindictive liar, setting his client up as "a sacrificial lamb," but jurors disagreed. They deliberated for seven hours before convicting Gwen on five counts of first-degree murder and one count of conspiracy to commit first-degree murder. On November 2, 1989, Graham was sentenced to six life terms without possibility of parole.

GREENWOOD, Vaughn Orrin

The first of southern California's "Skid Row" slayers launched his one-man war in 1964, taking a decade off before he returned to terrorize Los Angeles with nine more murders committed over the space of two months. Victims were ritually posed by the slasher in death, with salt sprinkled around their bodies and cups of blood standing nearby, their wounds surrounded by markings of unknown significance. Police recruited psychiatric "experts" to create a profile of the killer, publishing assorted sketches of their suspect, but the case was ultimately solved by accident, embarrassing authorities whose profiles of the murderer were sadly off the mark.

The "Skid Row Slasher's" first known victim was an aging transient, David Russell, found on the library steps with his throat cut and numerous stab wounds on November 13, 1964. The following day, 67-year-old Benjamin Hornberg was killed in the second-floor restroom of his seedy hotel, throat slashed from ear to ear, numerous stab wounds marking his head and upper torso.

Police saw a pattern of sorts, but it seemed to lead nowhere, and the early victims were forgotten by December 1974 when the killer returned with a vengeance. On December 1 he murdered 46-year-old Charles Jackson, an alcoholic drifter, on the very spot where David Russell had been slain a decade earlier. Moses Yakanac, a 47-year-old Alaska Native, was knifed to death in a skid row alley on December 8, and 54-year-old Arthur Dahlstedy was slain outside an abandoned building three days later. On December 22, 42-year-old David Perez was found in some shrubbery adjacent to the Los Angeles Public Library. Casimir Strawinski, 58, was found butchered in his hotel room on January 9, and 46-year-old Robert Shannahan had

been dead several days when hotel maid discovered his body—a bayonet protruding from his chest—on January 17, 1975. The final Skid Row victim, 49-year-old Samuel Suarez, was also killed indoors, his body found in a sleazy fifth-floor hotel room.

Inexplicably, the killer switched his hunting ground to Hollywood on January 29, stabbing 45-year-old George Frias to death in his own apartment. Two days later a cash register mechanic, 43-year-old Clyde Hay, was found in his Hollywood home, his body marked by the Slasher's characteristic mutilations.

By that time, L.A. detectives had formed a mental picture of their suspect, described as a white male in his late twenties or early thirties, six feet tall and 190 pounds, with shoulder-length stringy blond hair. A psychiatric profile published on the morning of Clyde Hay's murder described the killer as a "sexually impotent coward, venting his own feeling of worthlessness on hapless derelicts and down-and-outers. . . . He strongly identifies with the derelicts and drifters he kills, and we think he's trying to resolve his own inner conflicts by turning his wrath and hatred outward." The Slasher was further described as a friendless, poorly educated loner, probably homosexual, with an unspecified physical deformity.

On February 2 a prowler invaded the Hollywood home of William Graham, assaulting him with a hatchet before houseguest Kenneth Richter intervened and both men plunged through a plate-glass window. The attacker fled on foot, stopping next at the home of actor Burt Reynolds and carelessly dropping a letter—addressed to himself—in the driveway. Police picked up Vaughn Greenwood, charging him with counts of burglary and assault, their search of his residence netting a pair of cufflinks stolen from victim George Frias. A year later, on January 23, 1976, Greenwood was indicted on 11 counts of murder in the Slasher crimes.

Unfortunately for police, the "suspect profile" was a stumbling block to their solution of the case. For openers, Vaughn Greenwood was a 32-year-old black man, lacking any obvious deformities, and from the testimony of acquaintances he was not impotent. He *was* a loner and a homosexual, who finished seventh grade before he fled his Pennsylvania foster home and thumbed a ride to California. Most of his adult life was spent drifting from Chicago to the West Coast and back again, riding the rails and earning his keep as a migrant farmworker. In Chicago, during 1966, he had demanded cash from 70-year-old Mance Porter following a sexual encounter in the latter's skid row apartment. When Porter refused, Greenwood slashed his throat and stabbed him repeatedly with two different knives, spending five and a half years in prison on conviction for aggravated battery.

While awaiting trial on murder charges, Greenwood was convicted of assaulting William Graham and Kenneth Richter, drawing a prison term of 32 years to life. On December 30, 1976, the defendant was convicted on nine counts of first-degree murder, jurors failing to reach a verdict in the case of victims David Russell and Charles Jackson. Greenwood was sentenced to life on January 19, 1977, the judge recommending that he never be released because "His presence in any community would constitute a menace."

GRETZLER, Douglas, and STEELMAN, William Luther

A native of the Bronx, New York, born in 1951, Doug Gretzler was drifting aimlessly around the country when he met 28-year-old Willie Steelman on October 11, 1973. Once committed to a mental institution,

Steelman had compiled a lengthy record of arrests around Lodi, California, serving prison time on conviction of forgery. He recognized a kindred criminal soul on sight, and soon the men became inseparable, trolling the Southwest in their search for victims, stealing to finance their travels and Steelman's heroin addiction.

On October 28, 1973, they invaded a house trailer near Mesa, Arizona, binding 19-year-old Robert Robbins and 18-year-old Katherine Mestiter, then shooting both victims to death. Drifting into Tucson, they killed 19-year-old Gilbert Sierra and dumped his body in the desert, doubling back to murder Michael and Patricia Sandberg in their Tucson apartment. On the Superstition Desert, Gretzler and Steelman found victim number six, leaving his body in the sleeping bag where he was shot to death. In Phoenix the killers abducted Michael Adshade and Ken Unrein, both 22, dumping

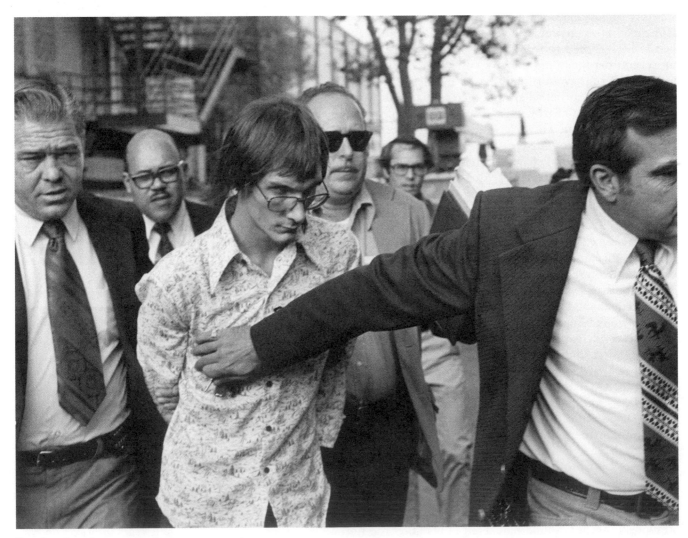

Douglas Gretzler in custody (Wide World API)

William Steelman is arrested (Wide World API)

their nude corpses in a creek bed near Oakdale, California, rolling north in their stolen van.

Authorities in Arizona had already issued warrants for Gretzler and Steelman by the time they reached Victor, California, 40 miles south of Sacramento, on November 6. Walter and Joanne Parkin went bowling that night, leaving their two children—11-year-old Lisa and nine-year-old Robert—in the care of 18-year-old neighbor Debra Earl. In the course of the evening, Debra's parents dropped by to visit, along with brother Richard and Debra's fiancé, 20-year-old Mark Lang. When the Parkins got home, they found a full house—including two strangers with guns.

Carol Jenkins, a houseguest of the Parkins, returned from a date around 3:00 A.M. and went directly to bed, taking the silent house for granted at that hour of the morning. Near dawn she was roused from sleep by two friends of Mark Lang, who had spent the night trying

to find him. Jenkins started a search of her own, stopping short when she found Walter and Joanne Parkin in the master bedroom, shot to death execution-style.

Deputies responding to the call found seven more bodies jammed into the bedroom's walk-in closet. Victims had been gagged with neckties, bound with nylon cord—secured with as many as six knots in places—before they were massacred. In all, medical examiners would remove 25 slugs from nine bodies, plus one stray from Bob Parkin's pillow.

Police published mug shots of Steelman, and Willie was recognized when he checked into a Sacramento hotel on November 8. Officers descended on the scene and both gunmen were swiftly arrested, booked on nine counts of first-degree murder. Gretzler cracked under interrogation, directing police to the scattered bodies of other victims while Steelman kept silent, refusing to enter a plea on the charges. In June 1974 Gretzler pled guilty to nine counts of murder, while Steelman submitted his case to a judge and was promptly convicted. On July 8, both defendants were sentenced to life imprisonment without parole, then returned to Arizona for trial on additional murder charges. A new round of trials saw both killers sentenced to die in Arizona's gas chamber. Willie Steelman died in prison in 1987 with his case still on appeal. Gretzler was executed by lethal injection on June 3, 1998.

GROUPIES: Admirers of serial killers

Despite the brooding atmosphere of violence and perversity that surrounds serial killers, they sometimes have an almost hypnotic effect on the opposite sex, attracting "groupies" in a bizarre twist on the celebrity syndrome. Aging CHARLES MANSON is notorious for the lingering devotion of his female "family" members (and a new generation of fans that staunchly believes he was "framed"), but other random slayers do quite well on their own, without the benefit of preconditioned disciples. Arizona's Charles Schmid—"The Pied Piper of Tucson"—had his own teenage rooting section at the trial which sentenced him to death. THEODORE BUNDY received numerous love letters from attractive young women, many resembling his preferred victims with their long, brown hair parted in the middle; finally choosing one to be his jailhouse bride, Bundy beat the clock and fathered a child from death row, via artificial insemination, before he was executed in 1989. In Nevada, CARROLL COLE received visits and heart-rending poems of love from a woman half his age. JOHN GACY's alleged girlfriend, a twice-divorced mother of eight, wangled a series of TV talk-show appearances, and both "Hillside Stranglers"—KENNETH BIANCHI and ANGELO BUONO—have married since receiving their life prison terms.

One previous Bianchi paramour, Veronica Compton, drew prison time of her own for attempted murder, while trying to free her lover by mimicking the strangler's technique with a random target, complete with a sample of Bianchi's semen smuggled out of jail. In prison, long since soured on Bianchi and his fickle ways, Compton attached herself to "Sunset Slayer" DOUGLAS CLARK. One letter from Compton to Clark, in a classic case of understatement, declared: "Our humor is unusual. I wonder why others don't see the necrophilic aspects of existence as we do."

Ironically, considering his physical appearance and the nature of his crimes, no modern psychopath has drawn more ardent female groupies than "Night Stalker" RICHARD RAMIREZ, the cadaverous devil worshiper sentenced to die for 13 murders in Los Angeles. A regular fan club attended his 14-month murder trial in L.A., some of the young women carrying notebooks and couching their interest in terms of "class projects," while others frankly admitted their attraction for Ramirez and his outspoken Satanism. One such told the press, "Do I love him? Yes, in my own childlike way. I feel such compassion for him. When I look at him, I see a real handsome guy who just messed up his life because he never had anyone to guide him." Two other groupies, one of them a porno model, circulated nude photos of themselves around the county jail, one young woman threatening her rival—and, for reasons still unclear, the president of the United States—in violent fits of jealousy. Finally married to one of his fans, a fellow Satanist, Ramirez also enjoys regular visits from a female juror who sentenced him to die, belatedly convinced that "Richard didn't get a fair trial."

An even more curious case involves HENRY LUCAS and Phyllis Wilcox. Smitten with the one-eyed psychopath after long-running correspondence and several jailhouse visits, Wilcox—a married woman still residing with her husband to this day—became convinced of Henry's innocence and hatched a plot to free him from death row. Obtaining a false driver's license and other ID, Wilcox presented herself to the media as Frieda Powell, the one-time girlfriend Lucas earlier confessed to murdering in 1983 when she was barely 15 years old. "Powell's" sudden reappearance after 13 years was guaranteed to make headlines, and police soon learned the truth from various acquaintances of Wilcox. Phyllis managed to avoid jail time on charges of obstructing justice, but her half-baked effort to liberate Lucas was foiled. Indeed, even had her masquerade been successful, Wilcox would have accomplished nothing: Lucas stands convicted of 10 murders, and Powell's case was not the one that sent him to death row.

See also ARTWORK AND MEMORABILIA

GUNNESS, Belle Paulsdatter

America's first "BLACK WIDOW" of the 20th century was born Brynhild Paulsdatter Storset, on November 11, 1859, in the fishing hamlet of Selbu on Norway's west coast. The daughter of an unsuccessful merchant, Brynhild immigrated to the United States in 1881; three years later, she settled in Chicago, Americanizing her given name to "Belle" (or sometimes "Bella"). In 1884, at age 25, she married a Norwegian immigrant, Mads Sorenson.

The couple opened a confectioner's shop in 1896, but the business was wiped out by fire the following year. Belle told her insurance agents that a kerosene lamp had exploded, and the company paid off on her policy, although no lamp was found in the wreckage. The Sorensens used their found money to purchase a home, but fire leveled the house in 1898, bringing further insurance payments. Bad luck dogged the couple, and a second house burned down before they found a home that met their needs, on Alma Street.

As everything Belle touched was soon reduced to ashes, so her family began to dwindle in the latter 1890s. Daughter Caroline, her oldest child, went first, in 1896. Two years later, Axel, her first son, was laid to rest. In each case, the children were diagnosed as victims of "acute colitis," demonstrating symptoms which—in hindsight—may have indicated they were poisoned.

On July 30, 1900, Mads Sorenson died at home, exhibiting the classic symptoms of strychnine poisoning. Belle admitted giving her husband "a powder," in an effort to "help his cold," but the family physician did not request an autopsy. With Mads under treatment for an enlarged heart, his death was automatically ascribed to natural causes.

The widow Sorenson collected her insurance money and departed from Chicago, settling outside La Porte, Indiana, with three children under her wing. Two were

Belle Gunness (Author's collection)

natural daughters: Myrtle, born in 1897, and Lucy, born in 1899. The new addition, Jennie Olsen, was a foster daughter, passed along to Belle by parents who, apparently, were tired of dealing with the child.

In April 1902, Belle married a Norwegian farmer named Peter Gunness. Less durable than Sorenson before him, Gunness lasted only eight months. On December 16, 1902, he was killed when a heavy sausage grinder "fell" from its place on a shelf, fracturing his skull. A son, named Philip, was born of the brief union in 1903, and Jennie Olsen vanished from the farm three years later. When neighbors inquired, Belle explained that her foster child had been sent "to a finishing school in California."

Widowed for the second time, with only children to assist her on the farm, Belle started hiring drifters who would work for a while and then, apparently, move on. She also started placing "lonely hearts" ads in Norwegian-language newspapers throughout the Midwest, entertaining a series of prospective husbands at her farm. Somehow, none of them measured up to her standards . . . and none of them were ever seen again.

On April 28, 1908, the Gunness homestead was leveled by fire. Searchers, digging through the rubble, found a quartet of incinerated bodies in the basement; three were clearly children, while the fourth—a woman's headless corpse, without the skull in evidence—was taken for the last remains of Mrs. Gunness. The local sheriff arrested handyman Ray Lamphere, employed by Belle from 1906 until his dismissal in February 1908, on charges of arson and murder.

The case became more complicated on May 5, when searchers started finding *other* bodies on the Gunness ranch. Dismembered, wrapped in gunny sacks, and doused with lye, a few reduced to skeletons, the corpses told a graphic tale of wholesale slaughter spanning years. The final body count has been a subject of enduring controversy. Without citing its source, the *Guinness Book of World Records* credited Belle with 16 known victims and another 12 "possibles." The local coroner's report was more modest, listing—in addition to the basement bodies—10 male victims, two females, and an unspecified quantity of human bone fragments. Belle's suitors were buried together in the muck of a hog pen, while her female victims had been planted in a nearby garden patch.

Only six of the victims were positively identified. Jennie Olsen was there, far removed from the mythical finishing school. Farmhands Eric Gurhold and Olaf Lindblom had ended their days in the hog pen, beside farmers John Moo of Elbow Lake, Minnesota, and Ole Budsberg of Iola, Wisconsin. Both of the latter had answered Belle's newspaper ads—and so, presumably, had their six anonymous companions in death. The single

"Jane Doe," buried beside Jennie Olsen, is an anomaly, unexplained to this day.

A coroner's inquest was launched on April 29, and witness depositions taken through May 1 reflect a standard hearing "over the dead body of Belle Gunness." After May 5, with the discovery of new corpses, official documents began describing the headless woman as "an unidentified adult female," assuming that Belle might have faked her own death to escape from the scene. A futile search for the missing skull was begun on May 19, resulting in discovery of Belle's dental bridge, complete with anchor teeth attached. Ignoring the various unanswered questions, the coroner issued his final report on May 20, declaring that Belle Gunness had died "at the hands of persons unknown."

Ray Lamphere, from his cell, was adamant in claiming that Belle was still alive. On April 28, he said, once Belle had set the house on fire, he drove her to the railway station at Stillwell, Indiana. Police initially took his story at face value, arresting an innocent widow, Flora Heerin, en route from Chicago to visit relatives in New York City. Hauled off the train at Syracuse and briefly detained as Belle Gunness, Mrs. Heerin retaliated in a lawsuit charging Syracuse police with false arrest.

Charged with four counts of murder and one count of arson, Ray Lamphere's case went to the jury in November 1908. On November 26, he was convicted on the arson charge alone, suggesting that the jurors felt Belle's death had not been proved "beyond a reasonable doubt." Surviving for two years in prison, Lamphere talked endlessly about the case, crediting Belle with 49 murders, netting more than $100,000 from her victims between 1903 and 1908. The basement victim, he contended, had been found in a saloon, hired for the evening, and murdered to serve as a stand-in. Belle had promised she would get in touch with Lamphere after she was settled elsewhere, but it seemed that she had changed her plans.

The first reported sighting of a resurrected Belle was logged on April 29, six days before the new bodies were found at her farm. Conductor Jesse Hurst was certain Mrs. Gunness went aboard his train at the Decatur, Indiana, station. She was bundled on a stretcher, Hurst recalled, and seemed quite ill.

Perhaps, but what are we to make of the reported sighting at La Porte on April 30? While visiting Belle's closest friend, Almetta Hay, a local farmer claimed he saw the missing woman sitting down to coffee. When Almetta died in 1916, neighbors picking through the litter in her crowded shack retrieved a woman's skull, wedged in between two mattresses. In spite of speculation that it might belong to the decapitated basement victim, the intriguing lead was not pursued.

More "sightings" were recorded through the years. In 1917, a childhood neighbor recognized Belle Gunness on admission as a patient to the South Bend hospital where he was working as a student nurse. He called police, but Belle had slipped away before detectives reached the scene. In 1931, a Los Angeles prosecutor wrote to La Porte's sheriff, claiming that murder defendant Esther Carlson—charged with poisoning 81-year-old August Lindstrom for money—might be Belle Gunness. Carlson carried photographs of three children resembling Belle's, but La Porte could not afford to send its sheriff west in those Depression days, and the suspect died of tuberculosis before trial, leaving the question forever open.

As late as 1935, subscribers to a detective magazine allegedly recognized Belle's photograph as the likeness of a whorehouse madam in Ohio. Confronting the old woman and addressing her as "Belle," one amateur sleuth was impressed by the vehemence of her reaction. Pursuing the matter through friends, he was urgently warned to let the matter rest . . . and so it has.

If Gunness did, in fact, survive her "death," she stands with BELA KISS in that elite society of slayers who—although identified, with ample evidence to win convictions—manage to escape arrest and so live out their lives in anonymity. Her legacy is rumor, and a snatch of tawdry rhyme that reads, in part:

There's red upon the Hoosier moon
For Belle was strong and full of doom;
And think of all those Norska men
Who'll never see St. Paul again.

HAARMANN, Fritz

Born October 25, 1879, in Hanover, Germany, Haarmann was the sixth child of a real-life odd couple. His father, a surly railroad fireman, was dubbed "Sulky Olle" by acquaintances; his mother, seven years her husband's senior, was an invalid. In early childhood, Fritz became his mother's pet and grew up hating his father, preferring dolls to the sports enjoyed by other boys his age. Packed off to a military school at age 16, Haarmann was soon released when he showed symptoms of epilepsy. Back in Hanover, he was accused of molesting small children and was sent to an asylum for observation, but he escaped after six months in custody.

Thereafter, Haarmann earned his way through petty crimes, while molesting children for amusement. Turning over a new leaf in 1900, he became engaged to a local girl but abandoned her for the army when she became pregnant. Honorably discharged in 1903, he returned to Hanover and successfully avoided his father's efforts to have him certified insane. A series of arrests followed for burglary, con games, and picking pockets before Haarmann's father set him up as proprietor of a fish-and-chips shop. Fritz promptly stole the business blind, but he was less successful when he preyed on strangers. Convicted of a warehouse burglary in 1914, he was sentenced to five years in prison. Upon parole, in 1918, he joined a Hanover smuggling ring and prospered, simultaneously working for police as an informer. On occasion he would introduce himself to strangers as "Detective Haarmann."

Wartime Hanover was jammed with homeless refugees, and Haarmann had his pick of boys, enticing them with offers of a place to spend the night. Among the first was Friedel Rothe, age 17, whose parents learned that he had met "Detective Haarmann" just before he disappeared. Police searched Haarmann's flat but came up empty. Six years later, he confessed that Friedel's severed head, wrapped in newspaper, was lying on the floor behind his stove while officers poked through the drawers and cupboards.

Late in 1918 Haarmann was sentenced to nine months in prison on charges of indecency with a minor. On release he found new quarters for himself, falling into company with 24-year-old Hans Grans, a homosexual pimp and petty thief. They became lovers and business associates, Haarmann adding new lines of used clothing and black market meat to the stolen items he sold for a living.

Together, Grans and Haarmann launched a wholesale scheme of homicide for fun and profit. Homeless boys were lured from the railway station, subsequently raped and killed by Haarmann (who informed police that his technique involved the biting of a victim's throat). The corpses were dismembered, sold as beef or pork, and the incriminating portions were dropped into the River Leine. Grans took his pick of the discarded clothing prior to selling off the rest; one victim was reportedly disposed of after Grans expressed a wish to own his trousers.

Hanover police were strangely blind to Haarmann's murderous activities. On one occasion a suspicious customer delivered some of Haarmann's meat to the authorities for testing, and the "experts" wrote it off as pork. "Detective Haarmann" further called attention to himself by visiting the parents of a boy named Keimes, found strangled in a Hanover canal, and subsequently

Fritz Haarmann (center) on his way to trial (Author's collection)

told police that Grans had done the murder. Since the pimp was then incarcerated on another charge, police dismissed the tale and never bothered checking Haarmann's interest in the case.

On May 17, 1924, a human skull was found beside the Leine; another was unearthed May 29, two more on June 13, but Hanover authorities dismissed the matter as a "practical joke." Their attitude changed on July 24 when some children discovered a sack filled with human bones, including another skull, on the riverbank. Panic erupted, with newspapers reporting some 600 teenage boys missing in the past year alone. Dragging the Leine, police recovered more than 500 bones, accounting for an estimated 27 victims.

By coincidence, Fritz Haarmann was arrested during this period and charged with another count of public indecency. A routine search of his flat revealed copious bloodstains, initially dismissed as a result of his unlicensed butcher's operation. Homicide detectives found their first hard evidence when the parents of a missing boy identified a coat, now owned by the son of Haarmann's landlady.

In custody, the suspect suddenly decided to confess his crimes in gory detail. Asked the number of his victims, Haarmann replied, "Thirty or forty, I don't remember exactly." Haarmann's trial opened on December 4 and lasted for two weeks, the defendant grandly puffing on cigars, complaining that there were too many women in the courtroom. Convicted of 24 murders and sentenced to die, Haarmann was beheaded on April 15, 1925. Grans, his accomplice in murder, received a sentence of 12 years in prison.

HAIGH, John George

A British slayer, Haigh was born in 1909 and subjected by his parents to the strict regimen of the Plymouth Brethren, regarding all forms of amusement as sin. As a child, Haigh won a choral scholarship to Wakefield Grammar School, requiring his participation as a choir boy in Anglican services held at Wakefield cathedral. The contrast between those services and the drab Plymouth Brethren rituals confused him, allegedly prompting bizarre visions of forests with trees spouting blood. Whatever the actual source, Haigh displayed early signs of hematomania, the obsession with blood which would ultimately haunt him throughout his life.

Briefly married in 1934, Haigh deserted his wife after serving his first jail term, for fraud, in November of that year. Before the end of World War II he chalked up numerous arrests for theft and minor swindles, completing his last prison term in 1943. Appearing to "go straight" at last, Haigh moved into the respectable Onslow Court Hotel in South Kensington and rented a nearby basement room for use in perfecting his "inventions." The makeshift lab was stocked with tools, a welding set—and a 40-gallon vat of sulfuric acid.

On September 9, 1944, Haigh lured a longtime acquaintance, Donald McSwann, to his basement workshop, killing his prey with a hammer, afterward slashing his throat for the purpose of drinking his blood. The dismembered remains were dissolved in Haigh's acid vat, with the resultant sludge later poured down a manhole. Taking over control of McSwann's nearby pinball arcade, Haigh told the dead man's parents that their son was hiding in Scotland to avoid military conscription. Once a week he went to Scotland, mailing forged letters to the anxious couple, but their suspicions grew over time, even as Haigh's compulsive gambling devoured his stolen income.

On July 10, 1945, Haigh invited McSwann's parents to his lab, bludgeoned them both, and dissolved their remains in acid. Forged documents enabled him to usurp their estate, including five houses and a small fortune in securities, but gambling, poor investments, and a lavish lifestyle left him strapped for cash again by February 1948.

Haigh's next victims were Archie and Rosalie Henderson, touring his new workshop at Crawley, south of London, when they were shot and slipped into an acid bath on February 12. Haigh later told police of sampling their blood, but he was rational enough to execute the forgeries that netted him $12,000 from the dead couple's estate.

A year later, in February 1949, 69-year-old Olivia Durand-Deacon approached "inventor" Haigh with her scheme for marketing artificial fingernails. Invited to the Crawley lab, she was there shot to death, with Haigh allegedly slitting her throat and quaffing a glass of blood before he consigned her to the acid vat. It took a week to finally dispose of her remains, and Haigh had little to show for his effort, selling off her jewelry for $250 to cover some outstanding debts.

Police responding to a missing-person report were suspicious of Haigh's glib answers and his too-helpful attitude, and search warrants were obtained for his basement workshop. Investigators skimmed 28 pounds of human fat from the acid bath, along with bone fragments, dentures, gallstones, and a handbag belonging to

"Acid Bath Murderer" John Haigh in custody (Wide World API)

Mrs. Durand-Deacon. In custody, Haigh confessed everything, playing up the VAMPIRISM angle in his bid for an INSANITY DEFENSE. He confessed two more murders—of victims "Mary" and "Max"—committed solely in the pursuit of fresh blood, but some authorities dismissed the whole story as a theatrical ruse. (Haigh was also observed drinking his own urine in jail.)

Haigh's trial opened on July 18, 1949, with a defense psychiatrist branding him paranoid and describing his acts of vampirism as "pretty certain." Unimpressed, jurors voted him guilty and sane, and the court imposed a sentence of death. Haigh was hanged at Wandsworth Prison on August 6, 1949.

HANCE, William Henry

On September 6, 1977, the nude and lifeless body of an army private, 24-year-old Karen Hickman, was discovered near the women's barracks at Fort Benning, near Columbus, Georgia. Beaten with a blunt instrument, then run over several times with a car, Hickman had been killed elsewhere and her corpse transported to the spot where it was found. Investigators learned that the victim—a white woman—had dated black soldiers exclusively, picking them up in bars near the post. An anonymous call led authorities to her missing clothes a month later, but no new evidence was found. The crime was treated as an isolated incident, almost forgotten in the manhunt for the "Stocking Strangler" who terrorized Columbus between September 1977 and April 1978.

By mid-February the Strangler, described as a black man from evidence found at the crime scenes, had raped and murdered six elderly white women in Columbus. Georgia is Klan country, and racial tension was already mounting when, on March 3, 1978, the chief of police received a letter signed by a self-styled "Chairman of the Forces of Evil." "Since the coroner said the S-Strangler is back," the note read, "we decided to come here and try to catch him or put more pressure on you. . . . From now on black women in Columbus, Ga., will be disappearing if the Strangler is not caught." The first victim, a local black woman named Gail Jackson, had already been abducted by "an organization within an organization," and she was scheduled to die if the Stocking Strangler was not apprehended by June 1. Two more blacks would be killed, the author promised, if the murderer was still at large on September 1.

Police could find no record of a Gail Jackson missing from Columbus, but they did discover that a black prostitute, Brenda Gail Faison, had disappeared from a local tavern on February 28. A second letter to the chief, arriving March 13, suggested that a ransom of $10,000 might secure the hostage's release if homicide

William Hance, "Chairman of the Forces of Evil" (Author's collection)

detectives could not find their man before the deadline. When police made no reply, a third note was delivered two weeks later, claiming that a second hostage named "Irene" had been abducted, scheduled to die on June 1. Detectives learned that 32-year-old Irene Thirkield was indeed missing, last seen on March 16 in the company of an unnamed black soldier.

In the predawn hours of March 30, 1978, an anonymous phone call led MPs to a shallow grave, just off the military reservation, where they uncovered the remains of Brenda Faison, her face and skull crushed into pulp by a savage beating. Four days later, another call directed CID agents to Maertens Range at Fort Benning, and Irene Thirkield's headless body—plus scattered skull fragments—was found hidden behind a pile of logs.

On April 4, an officer reviewing tapes of the anonymous phone calls recognized the distinctive voice, fingering a black 26-year-old private, William Hance, as the caller. An ammunition handler for the 10th Artillery, Hance was arrested that day, charged with

murder and attempted extortion on April 5. He confessed to the murders in custody but later recanted and claimed innocence. A civilian jury convicted him of Brenda Faison's murder on December 16, 1978, voting the death penalty (plus five years on the extortion charge). Convicted of the Hickman and Thirkield murders at a subsequent court-martial, Hance drew a sentence of life imprisonment at hard labor. He was executed in Georgia's electric chair on March 31, 1994.

HANSEN, Robert C.

Born at Pocahontas, Idaho, in 1940, Hansen was the son of a Danish immigrant who followed in his father's footsteps as a baker. In his youth, Hansen was skinny and painfully shy, afflicted with a stammer and a severe case of acne that left him permanently scarred. (In later years he would recall his face as "one big pimple.") Shunned by the attractive girls in school, he grew up hating them and nursing fantasies of cruel revenge.

Hansen was married in 1961 and divorced within the year, following his first arrest on charges of arson. Six years later, he wed another Pocahontas native and she followed him to Anchorage, Alaska, where he opened his own bakery and prospered in a new land, safely removed from the painful memories of childhood and adolescence. Hansen took flying lessons and purchased his own private plane, earning a reputation as an outdoorsman and hunter who stalked Dahl sheep, wolves, and bear with a rifle or bow and arrow.

In 1972 Hansen was arrested twice more, charged with the abduction and attempted rape of a housewife (who escaped his clutches) and the rape of a prostitute (who did not). Serving less than six months on a reduced charge, he was picked up again for shoplifting a chainsaw in 1976. Convicted of larceny, he was sentenced to five years in prison, but the verdict was overturned on appeal, the Alaska Supreme Court regarding his sentence as "too harsh."

Unknown to local authorities, Hansen's visible activities were only the tip of a very lethal iceberg. According to his subsequent confession, Hansen preyed consistently on women in the decade between 1973 and 1983, murdering 17 and raping 30 more who survived. As targets, he selected prostitutes, nude dancers, and the like, transporting them by airplane to the wilderness outside of Anchorage, where they were forced to act out Hansen's private fantasies. "If they came across with what I wanted," he explained, "we'd come back to town. I'd tell them if they made any trouble for me, I had connections and would have them put in jail for being prostitutes." Resistance—or demands for payment after sex—resulted in assorted victims being murdered, sometimes with the ghoulish touch of Hansen stripping them naked and stalking them like animals, making the kill with a hunting knife or his favorite big-game rifle.

The first indication of a killer at large came in 1980, when construction workers unearthed a woman's remains near Eklutna Road. Stabbed to death in 1979, she was never identified and was dubbed "Eklutna Annie" by police assigned to work the case. Later that year, the corpse of Joanna Messina was found in a gravel pit near Seward, and a special task force was organized to probe the killings. Topless dancer Sherry Morrow had been dead 10 months when hunters found her body in a shallow grave beside the Knik River, but the discovery brought authorities no closer to a solution in their case.

In 1983 Hansen decided to save time and energy by bringing his victims home. He called it his "summer project," laying the groundwork by packing his wife and two children off on a European vacation. Next, he began running ads in a local singles newspaper, seeking women to "join me in finding what's around the next bend, over the next hill."

On June 13, 1983, a 17-year-old captive escaped from Hansen en route to his airplane hangar, handcuffs

Robert Hansen poses with a mountain goat he killed with a bow and arrow. (Wide World API)

still dangling from one wrist as she ran for help. Her charges brought Hansen to the attention of task force detectives, and he ultimately confessed to a series of 17 murders, including that of Paula Golding, found by hunters in September 1983. On a flying tour of the wilderness, Hansen began pointing out graves to state troopers and they recovered 11 bodies over the next eight months. Several victims remained anonymous, their names unknown even to Hansen, but others were identified as Rox Easland, Lisa Futrell, Andrea Altiery, Angela Fetter, Teresa Watson, and Delynn Frey—all reported missing from the Anchorage area during Hansen's reign of terror.

On February 18, 1984, Robert Hansen pled guilty on four counts of first-degree murder in the cases of "Eklutna Annie," Joanna Messina, Sherry Morrow, and Paula Golding. Charges were dismissed in the other cases, but it scarcely mattered, as Hansen was sentenced to a term of life imprisonment plus 461 years.

HARVEY, Donald

A homosexual and self-styled occultist, Don Harvey attached himself to the medical profession at age 18, working as an orderly at Marymount Hospital in London, Kentucky, from May 1970 through March 1971. In 1987, Harvey would confess to killing off at least a dozen patients in his 10 months on the job, smothering two with pillows and hooking 10 others up to near-empty oxygen tanks, all in an effort to "ease their suffering." Arrested for burglary on March 31, he pled guilty to a reduced charge of petty theft the next day, escaping with a $50 fine. The judge recommended psychiatric treatment for his "troubled condition," but Harvey chose the U.S. Air Force instead, serving 10 months in uniform before he was prematurely discharged in March 1972, on unspecified grounds.

Back home in Kentucky, Harvey was twice committed to the Veteran's Administration Medical Center in Lexington, from July 16 to August 25 and again from September 17 to October 17. His mother ascribed the committals to mental disorders, with Harvey kept in restraints, and his lawyers would later refer to a bungled suicide attempt. The recipient of 21 electroshock-therapy treatments, Harvey emerged from the VA hospital with no visible improvement in his morbid condition.

Concealing his record, Harvey found work as a part-time nurse's aide at Cardinal Hill Hospital in Lexington between February and August 1973. In June he added a second nursing job, at Lexington's Good Samaritan Hospital, remaining in that position through January 1974. (One of his lovers in Lexington, Harvey later said, was a local mortician's assistant who also enjoyed having sex with corpses after visiting hours at the funeral home.) Between August 1974 and September 1975 he worked first as a telephone operator in Lexington, then moved on to a job as a clerk at St. Luke's Hospital in Fort Thomas, Kentucky. He kept his killing urge in check somehow, but it became increasingly difficult to manage, finally driving him away from home, across the state line to Cincinnati, Ohio.

From September 1975 through July 1985, Harvey held a variety of jobs at the Cincinnati VA Medical Center, working as a nursing assistant, a housekeeping aide, a cardiac-catheterization technician, and an autopsy assistant. In the latter position, he sometimes stole tissue samples from the hospital morgue, taking them home "for study." On the side, he murdered at least 15 patients, supplementing his previous methods with an occasional dose of poison, once joking with ward nurses after a patient's death that "I got rid of that one for you." Nor were Harvey's victims limited to suffering patients. Fuming at neighbor Diane Alexander after a quarrel, he laced her beverage with hepatitis serum, nearly killing her before the infection was diagnosed and treated by physicians.

On July 18, 1985, Harvey was caught leaving work with a suspicious satchel: inside, security guards found a .38-caliber pistol, hypodermic needles, surgical scissors and gloves, a cocaine spoon, two books of occult lore, and a biography of serial killer Charles Sobhraj. Cited by federal agents for bringing a weapon into the VA facility, Harvey was fined $50 and forced to resign from his job.

Seven months later, in February 1986, Harvey was hired as a part-time nurse's aide at Cincinnati's Drake Memorial Hospital, later working his way up to a full-time position. In 13 months, before his ultimate arrest, he murdered at least 23 more patients, disconnecting life-support equipment or injecting them with mixtures of arsenic, cyanide, and a petroleum-based cleanser. Some of the hospital victims, he later admitted, were chosen "by magic," with Harvey chanting over stolen locks of hair or fingernail clippings, arranged on a makeshift altar at his home. Outside of work, he sometimes practiced on his live-in lover, one Carl Hoeweler, poisoning Hoeweler after an argument, then nursing him back to health. Carl's parents were also poisoned, the father surviving, while Hoeweler's mother died.

On March 7, 1987, patient John Powell's death was ruled a homicide, autopsy results detecting lethal doses of cyanide in his system. Donald Harvey was arrested in April, charged with one count of aggravated murder, and held under $200,000 bond when he filed a plea of not guilty by reason of insanity. By August 11, he had confessed a total of 33 slayings, and bond was revoked two days later, with new charges filed.

As Harvey played the numbers game with prosecutors, adding victims to the tune of 52, then 80-plus, his mental state was questioned, and psychiatric tests were performed and scrutinized by experts. A spokesman for the Cincinnati prosecutor's office said, "This man is sane, competent, but is a compulsive killer. He builds up tension in his body, so he kills people." Harvey, for his part, insisted that most of the murders were "mercy" killings, while admitting that some—including attacks on friends and acquaintances outside of work—had been done "out of spite." In televised interviews, Donald discussed his fascination with black magic, pointedly refusing to discuss his views on Satanism, but authorities were treated to a sketch of his makeshift altar.

On August 18, 1987, Harvey pled guilty in Cincinnati on 24 counts of aggravated murder, four counts of attempted murder, and one count of felonious assault. A 25th murder plea, added four days later, earned him a total of four consecutive life sentences, requiring Harvey to serve at least 80 years before he is considered for parole. (For good measure, the court also levied $270,000 in fines against Harvey, with no realistic hope of collecting a penny.)

Moving on to Kentucky, Harvey confessed to a dozen Marymount slayings on September 7, 1987, entering a formal guilty plea on nine counts of murder that November. In breaking JOHN WAYNE GACY's record for accumulated victims, Harvey earned another eight life terms plus 20 years, but he was still not finished. Back in Cincinnati during February 1988, he entered guilty pleas on three more homicides and three attempted murders, drawing three life sentences plus three terms of seven to 25 years on the latter charges. With 37 confirmed murder victims (and confessions nearly tripling that body count), Harvey holds the official record as America's most prolific serial killer.

HAYDON, Mark   *See* SNOWTOWN

HEIDNIK, Gary Michael

Gary Heidnik was two years old when his parents divorced, his mother charging her husband with "gross neglect of duty." Two years later, her chronic alcoholism forced her to send Gary and a younger brother back to live with their father, the unstable pattern of Heidnik's life already well established. Dropping out of high school in October 1961, he joined the army a month later and received medical training at Fort Sam Houston, in Texas. Heidnik was posted to a military hospital in West Germany during May 1962, but he

Gary Heidnik arrives for trial. (Wide World API)

was back in the States by October, committed to a Pennsylvania sanitarium for three months of psychiatric therapy. Honorably discharged from the military with a 100-percent disability rating, his records permanently sealed and classified, he received a monthly pension of $1,355 from the government for his trouble.

Over the next quarter-century, Heidnik was frequently committed to mental institutions at Morristown, Coatesville, and Honesdale, Pennsylvania, sometimes remaining for months at a time. He seemed to profit little from the therapy, professing ignorance about the details of his own condition. "They haven't given me a technical name," he told a judge in 1978, "but it's some kind of schizophrenia."

In February 1964, Heidnik signed up for a practical nursing program in Philadelphia, successfully completing 12 months of training and a six-month internship at Philadelphia General Hospital. By 1967 he had banked enough money from his job and government pension to purchase a three-story house, occupying one floor himself while he rented the others to tenants. On the side, he began hanging around the Elwyn Institute for the retarded, treating female inmates—usually African-American or Hispanic—to picnics, movies, and shopping trips. The "dates" normally wound up at Heidnik's

house for sex, but if anyone objected, their complaints fell through the cracks and were ignored.

In 1971 Heidnik established the "United Church of the Ministries of God," drawing his eight-member congregation from the Elwyn Institute's clientele. His front yard became the repository for a derelict boat and four junk cars, but Gary dismissed the complaints of his neighbors with airy disdain. He preyed on black women for sex but despised their race otherwise, frequently lecturing friends on the imminence of an American "race war."

In autumn 1976, Heidnik barricaded himself in the basement of his home, armed with a rifle and handgun, daring his disgruntled tenants to deliver their complaints in person. One tried to climb through a window and Gary shot him in the face, inflicting a superficial wound. Charges of aggravated assault were later dismissed, and Heidnik soon moved away, selling his house to a university professor. The new owner turned up collections of pornographic magazines, heaps of rotting garbage, and scores of spent .22-caliber cartridges in the attic. Downstairs, in the cellar, he found an 18-inch hole in the concrete floor, with the soil underneath excavated to a depth of three feet.

In 1977 Heidnik invested $35,000 in the stock market, building his fortune up to a half-million dollars over the next decade. He purchased a fleet of luxury cars—including a Rolls Royce, a Cadillac, a Lincoln Continental, and a customized van—dodging legitimate taxes in the guise of a "bishop" in his nonexistent "church." He shared his home with an illiterate retarded woman, and she bore him a daughter in March 1978, the child later turning up in a foster home. On May 7 of that year, Heidnik and his girlfriend drove to a mental institution in Harrisburg, picking up her sister for a day's outing. At age 34, their new companion had the IQ of a three-year-old, and she had been institutionalized for the past 20 years. Authorities found her in Heidnik's filthy basement on May 17, returning her to the home, and Gary was arrested on June 6, charged with rape, kidnapping, deviate sexual intercourse, endangering, unlawful restraint, and interfering with the custody of a committed person.

Hospitalized himself in August 1978, Heidnik was convicted at trial three months later, drawing a sentence of three to seven years in prison. He served four years and four months of the time, dispatched to mental institutions on three occasions after suicide attempts—via pills, carbon monoxide, and by chewing a lightbulb—before he was paroled in April 1983. In December

Police search for evidence outside Gary Heidnik's Philadelphia house. (Wide World API)

1984, Heidnik purchased his last house, on North Marshall Street in Philadelphia, and put up a sign announcing the new location of his one-man "church." Around the same time, he befriended Cyril Brown, a retarded black man employed by Heidnik as a part-time handy man and general "gofer."

In October 1985, Heidnik married a 22-year-old Filipina woman, with whom he had corresponded for the past two years. Almost at once, he began bringing other women home for sexual liaisons, prompting his wife to flee their home in January 1986. She wound up in a shelter for battered women, complaining that Gary frequently raped and assaulted her. Police booked Heidnik on charges of spousal rape, indecent assault, and simple assault, while the courts handed down an injunction barring any form of harassment against his wife. Criminal charges were dropped in March when the complainant failed to appear in court, but her affidavits remain, including descriptions of Heidnik performing with three female partners at once.

On Thanksgiving Day 1985, 26-year-old Josephina Rivera left her boyfriend's apartment following a birthday celebration, bound to do some shopping. A part-time prostitute, she readily accepted Heidnik's offer of $20 for sex and accompanied him to his house, where he choked her unconscious and shackled her to the bed. Later, she was transferred to the basement, dumped in a pit with a weighted board covering the hole. In captivity, Rivera was raped daily by Heidnik, surviving on a diet of bread and water, with an occasional "treat" in the form of dog food or biscuits.

In early December, Heidnik bagged his second captive in Sandra Lindsey, a 25-year-old retarded friend of Cyril Brown. Chained to a beam in the basement, she was subjected to a regimen of torture, rape, and rancid food, Heidnik dividing his time between the two prisoners. Lisa Thomas, 19, was abducted at Christmas, with 18-year-old Jacqueline Askins joining the harem in January 1986. Heidnik began playing the women off against each other, encouraging them to inform on acts of disobedience. Punishments included beatings and electric shocks, with the occasional refinement of a screwdriver jammed into a victim's ears. In his reflective moments, Heidnik regaled them with plans for collecting 10 prisoners and fathering as many children as possible before he died.

In February 1987, Sandra Lindsay died after several days of hanging in chains from the rafters. Heidnik and Rivera, who acted under coercion, bore the corpse upstairs, where it was placed in a tub and dismembered with a power saw. Lindsay's replacement was 23-year-old Deborah Dudley, kidnapped in March, but she proved uncooperative and Heidnik killed her on March 19, hooking electrical wires to her chains as she stood in a pit filled with water. Dudley spent two days in the freezer before Heidnik and Josephina Rivera drove to the Wharton State Forest, near Camden, New Jersey, dumping her corpse in the woods on March 22.

Two days later, Rivera escaped from the basement prison, seeking refuge at her boyfriend's home. He called police, and raiders swept through Heidnik's house on March 25, finding bedroom walls papered with currency, the kitchen decorated with pennies, and Susan Lindsay's chopped-up remains stored in a freezer nearby. The basement was a bona fide chamber of horrors, with three malnourished women chained to the plumbing, nude from the waist down. Foul-smelling pits in the floor had served as their sleeping quarters. Neighbors belatedly recalled a persistent odor of burning flesh emanating from Heidnik's abode. Human remains were retrieved from the drains, and searchers made the drive to New Jersey that afternoon recovering Deborah Dudley's corpse.

Held in lieu of a $4 million bond, Heidnik was hospitalized in April after trying to hang himself in a jail shower stall. Defense attorneys sought to prove their client insane, suggesting that he had been used for military LSD experiments during the 1960s, but jurors rejected the argument, convicting Heidnik of double murder on July 1, 1988. Other charges included six counts of kidnapping, five counts of rape, four counts of aggravated assaults, and one count of deviate sexual intercourse. On July 3 the defendant was sentenced to die by lethal injection, with superfluous prison time totaling 150 to 300 years.

Six months later, on December 31, Heidnik attempted suicide once again, swallowing an overdose of Thorazine in his prison cell. A guard found him comatose on New Year's Day, but Gary soon recovered and returned to death row. The Pennsylvania Supreme Court rejected his automatic appeal on March 7, 1991, whereupon the "Madman of Marshall Street" ordered his attorneys to forego any further appeals. An execution date was ultimately fixed for April 15, 1997, Heidnik insisting that he wanted to die on schedule, but his daughter intervened at the 11th hour, winning an indefinite stay of execution while Heidnik's sanity is reexamined. Heidnik was executed by lethal injection on July 6, 1999, pronounced dead at 10:29 P.M., less than an hour after the U.S. Supreme Court rejected his final appeal.

HEIRENS, William George

On the surface, William Heirens seemed to have every advantage. Born in November 1928, he was the only child of affluent parents in the Chicago suburb of Lincolnwood. His father, a steel company executive, weathered the Great Depression without serious difficulty, and if Heirens had any problems, they came from within. His adolescent sexual repression evolved from parental advice that "All sex is dirty. If you touch anyone, you get a disease." In place of normal outlets, Heirens found release through firesetting and fetish burglaries, reaching orgasm when he invaded homes to steal women's underwear.

In 1942, at age 13, Heirens was arrested for carrying a loaded pistol to the parochial school he attended. His parents were stunned when police came calling, turning up a rifle and three more pistols behind the refrigerator and four more weapons hidden on the roof. In custody, he confessed 11 burglaries and six acts of ARSON, but his youth and family background saved him from serious punishment. Packed off to the Gibault School for Boys at Terre Haute, Indiana, he was released to his parents 11 months later. Back home in Chicago, he resumed his old pattern of night-prowling thefts. According to transcripts of psychiatric interviews, Heirens not only stole women's garments, but sometimes wore them in private while leafing through a scrapbook filled with photographs of ranking German Nazis. A second burglary arrest earned him an 18-month reformatory sentence, but he still managed to enroll as a sophomore at the University of Chicago in 1945 after passing a special entrance exam. At the same time, he continued his career of fetish burglaries.

On June 5, 1945, Heirens was looting the Chicago apartment of 43-year-old Josephine Ross when his victim awoke and caught him in the act. Attacking ruthlessly, he cut her throat and stabbed her several times, relenting at the sight of blood and trying hopelessly to bind her neck with bandages. That done, he spent two hours at the scene, wandering aimlessly from room to room as he experienced multiple orgasms.

Four months later, on October 5, he was surprised once more while prowling the apartment of an army nurse, 27-year-old Lieutenant Evelyn Peterson. Heirens decked her and fled, leaving fingerprints behind, but police failed to match them with the records of his earlier arrests.

On December 10, 1945, 33-year-old Frances Brown emerged from her bathroom to find Heirens rifling her purse. As she began to scream, he shot her twice, then fetched a kitchen knife to finish off the job. Dragging his victim into the bathroom, Heirens tried in vain to wash her blood away, then left her draped across the tub, half-covered with a housecoat. Across one bedroom wall, in Brown's own lipstick, Heirens wrote: "For heaven's sake catch me before I kill more. I cannot control myself."

Chicago police were still seeking the elusive "Lipstick Killer" on January 7, 1946, when Heirens invaded the bedroom of six-year-old Suzanne Degnan, abducting the child and leaving a written demand for $20,000 ransom as a ruse to baffle detectives. Retreating to a nearby basement, Heirens strangled the child and dismembered her body with a hunting knife, wrapping the pieces in paper and dropping them into storm drains as he roamed the streets in early morning darkness.

The case was still unsolved on June 26, when police answered a prowler call on Chicago's north side. Confronted with uniforms, Heirens drew a pistol and squeezed the trigger twice, his weapon misfiring each time. Undaunted, he began to grapple with the officers, struggling fiercely until he was cracked on the head with a flower pot.

In jail, under the influence of "truth serum," the teenage killer blamed his crimes on an alter-ego, "George Murman"—short for "Murder Man." In August 1946, his lawyers cut a deal with the state to save William—s life, accepting three consecutive terms of life imprisonment in exchange for a detailed confession. On the date of formal sentencing, September 5, Heirens tried to hang himself with a bedsheet but bungled the job and escaped without injury. In 1965, Heirens was placed on institutional parole for the Degnan slaying, but he still owed time for the Ross and Brown murders. A federal judge ordered his release in April 1983, citing William's alleged rehabilitation, but the order was overturned on appeal by the state in February 1984. Rejected for parole some 30 times, Heirens remains in custody at this writing and has served more prison time than any other inmate in the history of Illinois. Today, supported by a small but vocal group of friends on the outside, he denies any role in the murders that sent him to prison, insisting that he was framed by corrupt police, pleading guilty to save his own life in the "lynch atmosphere" of the times.

HENLEY, Elmer Wayne   *See* CORLL, DEAN

HISTORY of Serial Murder

In November 1983, *Time* magazine described serial murderers as "a new breed of killer," and while such comments were routine in the 1980s, they were also grossly inaccurate. Some authors with a slightly better grasp of history profess to see the first serial killer in 19th-century London's "JACK THE RIPPER," but even they are off the mark by more than two millennia.

The first recorded case of serial murder dates from 331 B.C., when Roman authorities convicted 170 lethal women of poisoning "countless" male victims and blaming their deaths on the plague. Another Roman defendant, "BLUEBEARD" slayer Calpurnius

Herman Mudgett prepares to kill his last two victims. (Author's collection)

Bestia, killed multiple wives by means of aconite—a poison that he manually inserted into their vaginas during sex. Around the same time, Cicero accused one Oppianicus of murdering victims who included his pregnant wife, two sons, a brother, his father-in-law, and others unnamed. Locusta, a female poisoner for hire, was publicly executed by order of Emperor Galba in 69 A.D. The following year, a defendant named Asprenas was charged with murdering 130 victims. Some 400 years later, in fifth-century Yemen, wealthy Zu Shenatir lured young boys to his home with offers of food and money, sodomizing them before he tossed them to their deaths from an upstairs window. His body count is unknown, but history records that Zu Shenatir was stabbed to death by an intended victim in his home.

An early example of CULT murder was seen in 11th-century Persia (now Iran), where the Assassins, members of a Muslim splinter group, took their name from the descriptive term *hashashin* (users of hashish). Assassins viewed murder as a sacred duty to their god and earthly ruler—the "Old Man of the Mountains"—but their frequent use as mercenary hit men during the Crusades has blurred the lines between slayings considered holy work and those that were strictly business. Inasmuch as killers were dispatched to their assignments with elaborate rituals, including use of sex and psychedelic drugs to generate "visions" of the paradise that awaited faithful servants of the cult, there may have been no real distinction on the part of those who did the killing. The sect was theoretically destroyed in 1256 by Mongol invaders under Hulaku, grandson of Genghis Khan, with some 12,000 members slain, but French observers noted remnants of the group surviving into the early 19th century.

It may be sheer coincidence that the "demise" of the Assassins coincided with the birth of yet another homicidal cult, this time in India. Dating from the early 13th century, the sect called *thag*—Hindi for "deceiver"—saw its members labeled "Thugs" in a corruption of the label they selected for themselves. Cultists were also known as *Phansigars*, after the Hindi word for "noose," since they preferred to strangle victims with the scarf each member wore around his waist. Thugs worshiped Kali, the Hindu goddess of destruction, and aside from random homicide, their rituals also incorporated masochistic elements in which devotees were flogged and mutilated by their priests or hoisted aloft with hooks in their flesh, while the ecstatic audience chanted, "Victory to Mother Kali." It is impossible to say how many victims were annihilated by Thugs in the 600 years before they were suppressed by British military force. Colonial records indicate that some 4,500 Thugs were convicted of various crimes between 1830 and 1848, with at least 110 sentenced to death for murder. One of those, Thuggee Buhram, single-handedly disposed of 931 victims before his arrest in 1840, and British authorities estimated that cultists accounted for some 40,000 murders in the year 1812 alone. Assuming that to be a record year, even 10 times the normal body count, it is apparent that the thugs must still have slaughtered several million victims during their six centuries of active hunting.

In Europe, meanwhile, serial killers emerged from the ranks of nobles and peasants alike. GILLES DE RAIS, the richest man in France and a confidant to Joan of Arc, was executed in 1440 for slaying upward of 100 children in perverted sex-and-magic rituals. Margaret Davey, an English cook, was boiled alive in 1542 for poisoning a series of employers without apparent motive. At least five cannibal killers were prosecuted as "werewolves" in France and Germany between the years 1573 and 1590. In 1611, Hungarian Countess

ERZSEBET BÁTHORY was convicted of torturing young women to death for personal amusement. French poisoner Marie de Brinvilliers practiced her art on invalids before switching to friends and relatives and was executed for her crimes in 1676. Four years later, France was rocked by the *"chambre ardente"* scandal, implicating the king's mistress, a self-styled witch, and a rogue Catholic priest in the ritual murders of several hundred infants. In 1719, Italian authorities executed another female killer, La Tofania, on conviction of poisoning 600 victims.

The European tradition of serial murder continued into the 19th century, with German defendant Gessina Gottfried beheaded in 1828, convicted of poisoning 20-odd victims since 1815. In England, "resurrectionists" Burke and Hare soon tired of robbing graves for medical specimens, killing 11 persons before they were captured in 1828. An Austrian beggar named Swiatek fed at least six murdered children to his hungry family in 1850, and French cook Helene Jegado was executed a year later, accused of poisoning 60 persons over two decades. Joseph Phillipe butchered French prostitutes in the 1860s, and "Jack the Ripper" carried the game to London 20 years later, inspiring a rash of imitators in Moscow, Vienna, Nicaragua—even Texas—by the end of the decade. Amelia Dyer, the British "BABY FARMER," was convicted in 1896 of killing at least 15 infants. The following year, French necrophile JOSEPH VACHER was executed for slaughtering 14 victims over three years' time.

In the United States, the bloodthirsty Harpe brothers terrorized the Wilderness Trail in the 1790s, gutting their victims and dumping the rock-laden corpses into rivers and lakes to avoid discovery. John Dahmen, condemned for two Indiana murders in 1820, confessed several others in Europe and America before he was hanged. New England slayer Samuel Green was credited with "numerous" murders when he went to the gallows in 1822. Four decades later, the Espinoza brothers sought vengeance for the Mexican War by slaughtering 26 Anglos across the Southwest. The murderous Bender clan dispatched at least a dozen Kansas travelers in 1872–73, fleeing the state one jump ahead of vigilante justice. The years 1875–76 brought grim news to Boston, with church sexton Thomas Piper convicted of killing three women, and teenager Jesse Pomeroy sentenced to life for the torture-slayings of neighborhood children. Stephen Richards, the "Nebraska Fiend," murdered at least nine victims before his arrest in 1879. In Chicago, sadist Herman Mudgett built a custom-tailored "murder castle" to dispose of female visitors to the 1893 World's Fair; convicted of one murder, he confessed to 26 others before he was hanged. New England nurse Jane Toppan started poisoning her patients in 1880; at her trial, two decades later, she recited the names of 31 remembered victims, while her prosecutors placed the final tally closer to 100.

Ironically, considering the present state of public anguish over crime, America owes much of its frontier folklore—and a significant part of its modern character—to pathological killers who have been transformed into heroes (or, at least, legends) by a historical twist of fate. Mountain man John Johnston (*Jeremiah Johnson* in the Hollywood rendition) killed scores of American Indians on sight and ate their livers raw as a gesture of contempt. Henry McCarty, aka William Bonney or Billy the Kid, killed less than half the victims claimed for him in 19th-century dime novels, but he was still a remorseless cop-killer and feudist. Alcoholic Clay Allison once murdered a bunkmate for snoring. The truly prolific killers, like Bill Longley and John Wesley Hardin (40 known victims, "not counting Mexicans"), were quick-trigger racists who slaughtered blacks, Hispanics, and Indians at the drop of an imaginary insult, never hesitating to shoot a lawman in the back if the opportunity presented itself. Even those who served sporadically as marshals habitually kept an eye out for "easy pickings" in the form of an unguarded stagecoach or bank. Their latter-day deification through FICTION AND FILM has little or nothing to do with the facts of their everyday lives.

In this century, serial killers have provided the media with some of its gorier headlines. LEONARD NELSON, the Bible-quoting strangler, raped and murdered landladies from coast to coast in the 1920s before a Canadian hangman's rope cut short his career. Cleveland's "MAD BUTCHER" was a 1930s sensation, outwitting Eliot Ness and dissecting his 16 victims so expertly that 10 of the skulls were never found. National Guard units were used to track Charles Starkweather, random slayer of 11 victims in 1957–58, and "Sex Beast" MELVIN REES appalled the nation with his grisly murders of eight victims in Maryland and Virginia two years later. By the time ALBERT DESALVO confessed to a series of 13 murders in Boston, escaping prosecution with a crafty plea bargain in 1967, authorities had recognized the early warning signs of what one FBI spokesman has called "an epidemic of homicidal mania."

And in fact, while serial murder is anything but "new," the numbers of killers and victims *have* increased dramatically in recent years. Between 1900 and 1959, American police recorded an average of two serial murder cases per year nationwide. By 1969, authorities were logging six cases per year, a figure that nearly tripled in the 1970s. By 1985, new serial killers were being reported at an average rate of three per month, a rate that remained fairly constant through 2005. America, meanwhile, was challenged for primacy in the grim competition by Russia and South Africa, where social and political upheavals coupled with relaxation of longstanding news censorship produced a glut of new serial murder reports at the turn of the 21st century.

HOCH, Johann Otto

Born John Schmidt in 1855, at Horweiler, Germany, Hoch immigrated to the United States as a young man and dropped his surname in favor of assorted pseudonyms, frequently taking the name of his most recent victim. At age 51, Chicago police would dub him "America's greatest mass murderer," but statistics remain vague in this puzzling case. We know that Hoch bigamously married at least 55 women between 1890 and 1905, bilking all of them for cash and slaying many, but the final number of his murder victims is a matter of conjecture. Sensational reports credit Hoch with 25 to 50 murders, but police were only certain of 15, and in the end he went to trial (and to the gallows) for a single homicide.

Hoch's first—and only legal—wife was Christine Ramb, who bore him three children before he deserted her in 1887. By February 1895, as "Jacob Huff," he had surfaced in Wheeling, West Virginia, where he won the heart and hand of Caroline Hoch, a middle-aged widow. They were married in April, and Caroline fell gravely ill three months later. Called to her beside, Rev. Hermann Haas watched "Huff" administer a potion that Haas believed to be poison, but the minister took no action and Caroline died days later in agony. "Huff" cleaned out her $900 bank account, sold their house, collected $2,500 in life insurance benefits—and vanished. Suicide was suspected, with his clothing, his watch, and a note found on the bank of the Ohio River, but no body was ever recovered.

Hoch kept his latest victim's surname—described by prosecutors as "a warped keepsake stored in an evil mind"—and moved on to Chicago, finding work in the meat-packing plants when he was not engaged with the business of swindling women. Selecting his victims from newspaper "lonely-hearts" columns, Hoch went merrily about his business until 1898, when he was sentenced to a year in jail for defrauding a used-furniture dealer. Police Inspector George Shippy also suspected Hoch of bigamy, and murder was added to the list upon receipt of a letter from Rev. Haas in West Virginia. Shippy started digging into Hoch's background, turning up reports of dozens of missing or deserted women from San Francisco to New York City, but solid evidence remained elusive. In Wheeling, Caroline Hoch was exhumed in a search for arsenic traces, but surgeons found the body gutted, all her vital organs missing.

Hoch was released at the end of his jail term, chalking up another 15 wives before his ultimate arrest in 1905. Aware that Shippy and others were charting his movements, Hoch killed more often and more swiftly now, relying on primitive embalming fluids—with their high arsenic content—to cover any traces of poison in his victims. On December 5, 1904, he married Marie Walcker in Chicago, killing her almost at once. Wasting no time, Hoch proposed to his new sister-in-law on the night of Marie's death, and they were married six days after the hasty funeral. Amelia Hoch bestowed a gift of $750 on her husband, prompting him to vanish with the cash, and she immediately summoned the police.

Modern science was Hoch's downfall. His late wife's mortician employed a new embalming fluid with no taint of arsenic. Medical examiners found poison in Marie Walcker's system and Hoch was charged with her murder, his photograph mailed to every major American newspaper. In New York City, a middle-aged landlady recognized "Henry Bartels," a new tenant who had proposed marriage to her 20 minutes after renting a room. At his arrest, police seized a revolver, several wedding rings with their inscriptions filed off, and a fountain pen filled with arsenic—which Hoch claimed was intended for himself, a foiled attempt at suicide.

Chicago journalists dubbed Hoch the "Stockyard Bluebeard," trumpeting the speculative details of his criminal career. At trial he whistled, hummed, and twirled his thumbs throughout the prosecution's case, apparently well pleased with his position in the limelight. On conviction of Marie Walcker's murder, he was sentenced to hang, telling the court, "It's all over with Johann. It serves me right." Mounting the gallows on February 23, 1906, Hoch reverted to a claim of innocence, declaring, "I am done with this world. I have done with everybody." As the trap was sprung, a local newsman quipped, "Yes, Mr. Hoch, but the question remains: *What* have you done with everybody?"

Part of the solution was unearthed in 1935 when human bones were found inside the wall of a Chicago house once occupied by Hoch. It was a meager bit of evidence, the victim unidentified, and Johann's body count, the names and number of his murdered wives, will probably remain a mystery forever.

See also "BLUEBEARD"

HOMOSEXUALITY and Serial Murder

Long regarded as a sin or disease in Judeo-Christian society, homosexuality and lesbianism are today widely regarded (at least in liberal circles) as an alternate sexuality, perhaps genetically ingrained, presumably beyond the individual's conscious choice or control. Religious

arguments to the contrary, there is no evidence of elevated insanity rates among homosexuals, nor do they commit a disproportionate number of crimes (except, perhaps, in jurisdictions where homosexual activity is itself criminalized).

That said, homosexuality *does* play a significant role in some cases of serial murder. It is not true, as stated in a *Penthouse* magazine article (March 1998) that some 45 percent of American serial killers in the past quarter-century were identified as homosexuals. The author of that piece based his calculation on "the roughly 80 known serial slayers of the past 25 years in the United States," concluding that 36 of them (all but 10 unnamed) were gay or lesbian. In fact, America produced some *800* serial killers during the decades in question, 90 percent of them ignored by the author in his quest to make a point. Analysis of a more complete sampling indicates that gay serial killers driven by sexual urges account for roughly 5 percent of all known cases where the killers (or their MOTIVES) are identified.

Ironically, while gay serial killers represent a tiny minority of the broader group, their ranks include some of the most prolific slayers in modern times. DONALD HARVEY, convicted of 37 murders (and guilty, by his own admission, of some 50 others), leads in the official body count, closely followed by JOHN GACY (33 convictions), DEAN CORLL (27 dead), JUAN CORONA (25), and PATRICK KEARNEY (28 confessed, 21 convictions). JEFFREY DAHMER seems almost an underachiever in such company, with 17 victims. Convictions lag behind known body counts in other cases: William Bonin was executed for 10 of California's 21 "FREEWAY MURDERS"; "Scorecard Killer" RANDY KRAFT stands convicted of 16 homicides and suspected of 51 more; OTTIS TOOLE was ultimately sentenced for six murders in Florida and one in West Virginia, but police believe he claimed more than 100 victims in company with sidekick HENRY LUCAS; LARRY EYLER was sentenced to die for only one of his 23 murders. In England, gay ex-policeman DENNIS NILSEN slaughtered 15 men and kept their bodies in his home for "company."

Homosexual slayers clearly have no monopoly on violence, but it is true that their crimes often display extremes of "overkill" and mutilation. Dismemberment is almost routine in such cases, exemplified by Kearney's "trash bag" murders in California and the simultaneous "bag murders" committed by Paul Bateson in New York (which inspired the movie *Cruising*, with Al Pacino). On balance, it seems fair to say that while homosexuals sometimes fall prey to "gay bashing" violence by bigoted "straights," they are more likely to be murdered by another homosexual than in a random hate crime.

One myth dispelled by time and weight of evidence is the presumption, common in the West as recently as

World War II, that male homosexuals are somehow more likely to commit sadistic murders of women and children. In fact, while some rare specimens like Ottis Toole kill indiscriminately, without regard to age, race, or gender, gay killers overwhelmingly prefer same-sex victims, while most female victims of serial murder are killed by heterosexual men. Multiple murders of children, meanwhile, are chiefly committed by pedophiles or parents (in which case mothers are predominant).

See also PARAPHILIA; SEX CRIMES

HOSPITAL for Sick Children (Toronto)

Between June 1980 and March 1981, the cardiac ward at Toronto's Hospital for Sick Children experienced a traumatic 616 percent leap in infant mortality, with the number of actual deaths pegged between 21 and 43 babies in various police and media reports. The first "suspicious" death was that of 18-day-old Laura Woodstock, lost on June 30, 1980. Two months later, after 20 deaths, a group of nurses on the ward voiced their concern to resident cardiologists, and a fruitless investigation was launched on September 5, in the interest of resolving "morale problems."

Still, the deaths continued, and on March 12, 1981, a staff physician aired his personal suspicions in a conversation with Toronto's coroner. An autopsy of the latest victim, 27-day-old Kevin Garnett, found 13 times the normal level of digoxin—a drug used to regulate heart rhythm, itself fatal if taken in too large a dose. On March 21, following more deaths and the discovery of elevated digoxin levels in two more corpses, the coroner met with police and hospital administrators in an emergency session. Members of the cardiac nursing team were placed on three days' leave while officers began to search their lockers and compare work schedules to the dates and times of suspicious deaths.

On March 22, with the locker searches under way, another baby died on the cardiac ward at Sick Children. Justin Cook is generally named as the last victim in a bizarre string of slayings, his death attributed to a massive digoxin overdose, inflicted by persons unknown. Three days later, police arrested nurse Susan Nelles on one count of murder, adding three identical charges to the list on March 27. As "evidence" of her involvement in the crimes, officers referred to certain "odd" remarks and facial expressions mentioned by other nurses, noting that 24 of the suspicious deaths occurred on Nelles's shift, between 1:00 and 5:00 A.M.

With Nelles on leave pending trial, bizarre events continued at the hospital. In September 1981, nurse Phyllis Trayner found capsules of propanolol—another heart regulator—in the salad she was eating for lunch, and a second nurse spooned more capsules out of her

soup. Administrators had no explanation for the incident, and rumors flourished of a "phantom" or a "maniac" stalking the hospital corridors.

A preliminary hearing in the case of Susan Nelles opened on July 11, 1982, with prosecutors citing 16 other "carbon copy" murders in addition to the four already charged. Four months later, on May 21, the pending charges were unconditionally dismissed, the presiding judge describing Nelles as "an excellent nurse" with "an excellent record." At the same time, he noted that five of the hospital deaths were apparently murders, committed by persons unknown.

Fresh out of suspects, the state launched its first judicial probe of the case on May 25, requesting assistance from the Atlanta-based Centers for Disease Control four months later. CDC's report on 36 submitted cases called 18 deaths "suspicious," with seven listed as probable homicides; another 10 cases were "consistent" with deliberate digoxin poisoning, but there was insufficient evidence for a definitive conclusion.

A new judicial inquiry was ordered on April 21, 1983, and Gary Murphy, six months old, died on the cardiac ward two days later, his passing notable for "elevated digoxin levels" discovered in postmortem testing. Murphy's death was excluded from the "official" list when hearings began on June 21, with testimony pointing vaguely toward a different suspect on the staff. By February 1984, cardiac nurses were voicing suspicions against Phyllis Trayner, one reporting that she saw Trayner inject infant Allana Miller's IV bottle with an unknown drug three hours before the baby died on March 21, 1981. Trayner flatly denied all charges of impropriety, and the commission left her denials unchallenged, refusing to name a suspect in its January 1985 report. That document describes eight infant deaths as murders, while another 13 are listed as "highly suspicious" or merely "suspicious." Eighteen years down the road, a solution to the case is improbable at best.

See also UNSOLVED MURDERS

HUANG Yong

A native of China's Henan Province, born in 1974, Huang Yong fulfilled his mandatory army service without incident and then returned to farming at Dahuangzhuang. Between September 2001 and November 2003 he prowled neighboring towns, luring boys and young men away from Internet cafés and video arcades with phony job offers. Huang's favorite ruse involved a nonexistent video game, "God Riding on a Wooden Horse," which he allegedly devised and planned to market in the near future. Those who accepted invitations to help Huang perfect the game were conveyed to his home in Dahuangzhuang, then beaten and bound to a noodle-rolling machine for marathon torture sessions before they were finally strangled.

Sixteen-year-old Zhang Liang swallowed Huang's line on November 7, 2003, and followed his new friend home. Over the next four days, Zhang was tortured incessantly and choked three times to the point of unconsciousness while Huang told him, "I've already killed 25. You are the 26th." On November 10, Zhang saved himself with a lie of his own. Pleading for mercy, the youth promised to acknowledge Huang as his godfather and care for Huang in his old age. Huang not only believed the preposterous story, but also gave Zhang money for his journey home. Zhang spent the night with friends, then went home on November 11 and called police the following day. In a raid, Huang was arrested on November 12 and his home was excavated for remains of the dead.

Confusion surrounds the results of that search, with various media reports claiming that police found 17, 18, or 23 corpses on Huang's property. A report from China with the count of 23 states that 16 corpses were unearthed behind Huang's house and seven were extracted from a grave beneath his bed. Yet another report says 18 bodies were found, but that Huang confessed to 25 murders. In any case, Huang was finally charged with 17 murders. He freely admitted to police that he stalked young men in order to "experience the sensation of killing." Huang was convicted on all counts at a three-hour trial on December 9, 2003. He was executed by a firing squad on December 26, but the case still had one more surprise in store.

On March 26, 2004, survivors of Huang's victims found remains of another victim at Huang's home, along with bloodstained kitchen knives that bore traces of human hair. Police followed up the report on April 15 and found yet another corpse at the scene, officially describing the latest unknown dead as "victims 18 and 19."

"I-45 Killer"

In the 15 years from 1982 to 1997, 42 teenage girls and young women were kidnapped from small towns and suburbs along Interstate Highway 45 between Houston and Galveston, Texas. Many of those were later found dead, described by local authorities and FBI agents as the victims of one or more serial killers prowling the 50 miles of wide-open highway. Despite the four-year focus of police attention on a single suspect, no evidence has been found to support an indictment, and by early 1998, it appeared that authorities had been mistaken in their choice of targets all along.

The most recent victim in the murder series was 17-year-old Jessica Cain, last seen alive while performing with a local theater group one night in August 1997. Following the show, she left for home, driving alone down I-45, but she never reached her destination. Jessica's father found her pickup truck abandoned on the shoulder of the highway, and her name was added to the ever-growing victims list.

By that time, police believed they knew the man responsible. Their suspect, Robert William Abel, was a former NASA engineer and operator of a horseback riding ranch near League City, in Brazoria County. Abel first came under suspicion in 1993, when the corpses of four missing girls were found in the desert near his property. FBI agents spent a grand total of two hours with League City police, sketching a psychological profile of the killer based on such traits as "intelligence level" and assumed proximity to the crime scene. Abel's ex-wife pitched in with tales of alleged domestic abuse ("externalized anger," in FBI parlance) and claims that Abel sometimes beat his horses (a charge that he

staunchly denies). The punch line of the federal profile was direct and to the point—"Serial sexual offender: Robert William Abel."

That profile alone was deemed sufficient to support a search warrant, and police moved in, seeking—among other things—a cache of nude photos described by Abel's wife. In fact, they *did* find photographs, some 6,000 in all, of which precisely two depicted naked women, neither of them victims in the murder case. No evidence was found at Abel's ranch connecting him with any sort of criminal activity.

Frustrated in their search for clues, League City police took the unusual step of naming Abel publicly as a suspect in the I-45 murder case. He was "innocent until proven guilty," of course, but in the absence of alternate suspects, his life became a waking hell on earth, with death threats pouring in from neighbors and the relatives of sundry victims. One such, Tim Miller, having lost his daughter Laura to the I-45 killer, launched a personal crusade of daily "reminders" to Abel, including armed visits to his home and threats of murder recorded on Abel's answering machine. League City's finest, still convinced that Abel was their man, took no steps to prevent the harassment and stalled when Abel volunteered to take a polygraph exam. In fact, while League City's assistant police chief publicly "welcomed" Abel's cooperation in the case, said cooperation only made matters worse, since such behavior is common among serial killers.

It was early 1998 before Robert Abel got to take his long-sought polygraph, courtesy of the television show, 20/20. In fact, two tests were administered by a retired FBI agent, with Abel denying any knowledge of the four victims found near his ranch in 1993. He hesitated in responding to one surprise question, dealing with rumors of a young victim's drug use, and was rated "untruthful" in respect to that answer, but a second test, administered without trick questions, found him to be truthful on all counts. FBI agents in Houston called the 20/20 test "extremely significant," admitting that the four-year-old profile of Abel was "poor quality" work on the part of their colleagues. In fact, they told the world, Robert Abel had been eliminated as a suspect in their eyes, and even Tim Miller appeared to repent his harassment of Abel with a televised apology.

Not so the lawmen in League City. Abel may indeed be innocent, they say, but since they have no solid evidence to clear him by their own exacting standards, Abel "is still swimming in the pool of suspects." One is tempted to ask *what* pool, since vague local references to "other suspects" always stop short of naming alternative candidates. Texas courts have barred Abel from filing a lawsuit to clear his name, ruling that League City police are within their rights to publicize him as a suspect, even when the original FBI profile has been retracted.

The *real* I-45 Killer, meanwhile, remains unidentified and presumably still at large. Women added to the tally since the first edition of this work was published include: 39-year-old Jo Ann Sendejas, missing since December 1999 from the San Leon home she shared with her sister (investigators are uncertain whether Sendejas was abducted from the house or climbed out her own bedroom window); 57-year-old Tot Tran Harriman, who vanished with her car while visiting relatives in League City during July 2001; and 23-year-old Sarah Trusty, who vanished while riding her bicycle through Texas City in July 2002. Two weeks later, fishermen pulled her corpse from a local canal.

Texas prison inmate Mark Roland Stallings, serving 489 years for aggravated assault and attempted escape, confessed two of the I-45 slayings in November 2001, further implicating himself in the murders of four other women around Houston. At press time for this volume, no further charges had been filed against Stallings, and his role in the killings (if any) remains uncertain.

INCARCERATION of Serial Killers

Society tends to forget about criminals once they are convicted and sentenced to prison or death. Each new day brings banner headlines of a fresh atrocity, another bogeyman to conjure waking nightmares. Last year's monster is a fading memory, except to his or her surviving victims, grisly details dusted off for special anniversaries and sporadic parole hearings. Who, aside from a handful of aging detectives and crime buffs, remembers

the name of Wisconsin's "Mad Biter"? Montreal's "Vampire Rapist"? The "Peeping Tom" gunman of Washington, D.C.?

Unfortunately, the relief engendered by conviction of a ruthless predator is often premature. In far too many cases, disposition through a prison sentence—even life without parole—is anything but final. Random killers have a way of coming back to haunt society at large beyond the scope of retrospective articles and tabloid TV broadcasts. All too often, they come back against all odds to kill again.

Serial killers, like "normal" felons, respond to confinement in various ways. As natural chameleons, skilled from childhood in the art of covering their tracks, some become model prisoners, following every rule to the letter, working overtime to counsel and encourage other inmates. Many "get religion" and are "born again," as in the case of Charles ("Tex") Watson, a MANSON FAMILY alumnus who runs his own ministry from behind prison walls, receiving regular donations from his flock.

It may be argued (and persuasively) that random killers mind the rules or "find the Lord" with selfserving motives in mind, striving to please their captors and influence future parole boards. Author Joel Norris, on the other hand, describes compliance with authority as a serial killer's natural reflex, induced by imposition of an orderly environment and the removal of those stimuli—drugs, alcohol, pornography, even junk food—which contribute to erratic, aberrant behavior. Whichever theory finally wins out, the fact remains that many random killers never adapt to life in a cage, including 2 percent who wriggle out of custody by means of suicide. At the same time, another 2 percent of America's serial slayers continue to kill behind bars, venting their rage on guards, fellow inmates, even visitors. Another S percent have jailbreaks on their records, and 71 percent of those who escape commit one or more murders before they are run to ground.

Parole is unlikely (though not unknown) for notorious serial killers, but a glance at the record reveals a frightening number who were paroled after their first slaying, sometimes having bargained murder charges down to a lesser offense, such as manslaughter or aggravated assault. HENRY LUCAS was paroled 10 years after killing his mother, free to launch a nationwide murder spree, and at least 30 other serial slayers have been released to kill again in similar circumstances. The problem is worse with JUVENILE KILLERS, since most states demand release of youthful offenders at age 18 or 21, often with their criminal records sealed by court order, thus masking their proven potential for violence. Such cases are the first cited by supporters of CAPITAL

PUNISHMENT, who remind us that no killer to date has returned from the grave to repeat his crimes.

See also INSANITY DEFENSE; TRIAL

"INDEPENDENCE Avenue Killer"

Nicknamed for the street in Kansas City, Missouri, where his female victims plied their trade as prostitutes, this unidentified serial slayer is blamed for 10 murders and the disappearance of three other women since October 1996. The victims found to date have all been pulled from the Missouri River, downstream from Kansas City, suggesting to police that their bodies may have been dropped from various urban bridges. Thus far, aside from an assumption that the killer must be male, nothing is known that would identify a suspect in the case.

The Independence Avenue Killer's first acknowledged victim was 21-year-old Christy Fugate; last seen alive on October 3, 1996, her corpse was pulled from the river in neighboring Lafayette County, east of Kansas City, 12 days later. A month after that grim discovery, on November 19, 20-year-old Connie Wallace-Byas made her last appearance on the Independence Avenue "stroll"; the only black victim, she was missing five months before her body surfaced in Boone County, 90 miles to the east, in April 1997. Meanwhile, the killer had claimed three more victims: 26-year-old Sherri Livingston, vanished on February 14, dragged from the water in Lafayette County on March 29; 41-year-old Linda Custer, missing since February 27, found near Dover in Lafayette County on April 23; and 30-year-old Chandra Helsel, last seen alive on April 5, hauled from the river on May 8 near Booneville in Cooper County, some 70 miles to the east. Tammy Smith was four months shy of her 31st birthday when she vanished from Independence Avenue on December 20, 1997; her corpse was found in the river near Silby, Missouri, on April 2, 1998.

At this writing, police in Kansas City say that four more women's bodies have been found along the river banks, all counted as probable victims of the Independence Avenue Killer. The dead were all alleged or convicted prostitutes, similar in height and weight, all but one of them Caucasian. Advanced decomposition and submersion in the river's swiftly flowing depths have thus far wiped out any useful clues that might have helped identify the slayer, and police are mum on cause of death.

Besides the 10 acknowledged dead, investigators fear that three missing women may also have fallen prey to their local stalker. Alleged prostitute Connie Williams, age 32, was last seen at her mother's home in Kansas City, but police say she was known to strut

for "tricks" on Independence Avenue. If she was murdered, as authorities assume, her disappearance two days prior to Christy Fugate's would make her the killer's first known victim. Forty-year-old Jamie Pankey dropped out of sight on November 1, 1996, and the youngest suspected victim, 19-year-old Cheresa Lordi, was last seen alive on February 24, 1997. The case was profiled on *America's Most Wanted* in spring 1998, but it remains unsolved at this writing. Detectives are at a loss for clues and hope that their quarry makes a critical mistake and is identified before he claims more lives.

INSANITY Defense Used by Serial Killers

In any murder case, the first responsibility of prosecutors and defense attorneys is determination of the suspect's mental state. Our legal system makes allowances for individuals whose aberrant behavior is compelled by mental illness, sparing them from punishment as common criminals. The general public has been outraged in recent years by cases like that of would-be presidential assassin John Hinckley, where verdicts of "not guilty by reason of insanity" spare defendants from execution or prison, instead consigning them to mental institutions for an indefinite term. Surveys of public opinion reveal a consensus that many or most accused felons try to "cop a plea" with bogus insanity schemes, large numbers of them slipping through the cracks and serving "easy time" before they are released once more into society.

In fact, statistics show that only one percent of all American felony suspects plead insanity at trial, and barely one in three of those is finally acquitted. Serial murders, with their bizarre trappings of sadism, necrophilia, and the like, seem ideally suited to insanity pleas, but even here the odds against acquittal are extreme. Since 1900 in America, only 3.6 percent of identified serial killers have been declared incompetent for trial or cleared by reason of insanity.

Unfortunately, there is no firm definition of *insanity* in the United States, beyond the fact that it remains a strictly legal term, divorced from any diagnosis of specific mental illness. Nationwide, the 50 states are free to draft their own peculiar guidelines, chasing abstract terminology around in circles while the individual defendants—and their countless victims—are ignored.

One test of sanity, applied in 16 states, is the M'Naughten rule. Named for a paranoid schizophrenic who murdered the British prime minister's secretary in 1843, this rule is widely favored on the basis of its simple (some would say simplistic) definition of insanity. According to M'Naughten

To establish a defense on the ground of insanity, it must be proved that at the time of committing of the act the party accused was laboring under such a defect of reason from disease of the mind as not to know the nature and quality of the act he was doing; or, if he did know, that he did not know what he was doing was wrong.

A few states supplemented M'Naughten with the so-called irresistible impulse test established by British courts in 1840 and transplanted to America in 1886. As explained by Justice Somerville of Alabama in an early case: "The disease of insanity can so affect the power of the mind as to subvert the freedom of the will, and thereby destroy the power of the victim to choose between right and wrong, though he perceives it." Prosecutors often counter a plea of irresistible impulse with hypothetical arguments of "the policeman at the elbow," seeking admissions that a given defendant could, in fact, restrain himself at chosen times. Today, the question is moot, with a 1984 federal statute abolishing tests for the fabled "irresistible impulse."

In 1954, a judgment from the District of Columbia established the new Durham rule, sometimes called the "products test." In that decision, it was held that "An accused is not criminally responsible if his unlawful act was the product of mental disease or defect." Those terms, in turn, were vague enough to require clarification through a second case in the same jurisdiction, defining "mental disease or defect" as "any abnormal condition which substantially affects mental or emotional processes and substantially affects behavior controls."

Officially unrecognized outside the nation's capital, Durham remained in effect until 1972, when the new Brawner rule—also dubbed the "substantial capacity test"—was inaugurated by the same judge who wrote the Durham decision. Adopted by several states as part of a Model Penal Code, the new rule provides that

1. A person is not responsible for criminal conduct if at the time of such conduct as a result of mental disease or defect he lacks substantial capacity either to appreciate the criminality (wrongfulness) of his conduct or to conform in conduct to the requirement of the law.
2. As used in this Article, the terms "mental disease or defect" do not include any abnormality manifested only by repeated criminal or otherwise antisocial conduct.

Another modern guideline for insanity proceedings, pioneered in Michigan in 1975 and since adopted by seven other states, is the verdict of "guilty but mentally ill." Specifics vary, but in most jurisdictions a defendant convicted under this rule is sent directly to a mental institution, there confined until he or she is deemed healthy enough to begin serving the appropriate prison term. Some critics of this system have denounced it as an underhanded abolition of "insanity," exalting public pressure over human rights, first curing the insane, *then* punishing them for actions beyond their control.

The controversy has not been resolved, by any means, and while it rages, antiquated doctrines like M'Naughten will undoubtedly survive. A fearful public should draw consolation from the fact that in this century, less than 2 percent of all serial killers have been deemed incompetent for trial (one of them an illiterate deaf mute, incapable of communicating with his lawyer) and a comparably small number acquitted on grounds of insanity. At the same time, there *have* been real-life horror stories of insane killers "cured" and released to kill again—EDMUND KEMPER is a shocking case in point—and public fears of such mistakes, while generally exaggerated, are not without basis in fact.

See also CAPITAL PUNISHMENT; INCARCERATION; "MASK OF SANITY"; PARAPHILIA; TRIAL

IONOSYAN, Vladimir M.

In early January 1964, residents of Moscow whispered warnings to their neighbors of a mysterious long-nosed killer prowling the city, knocking on doors at random, and gaining entry to the homes of his victims by posing as a meter-reader for Moscow Gas. It seemed a nearly foolproof gimmick, since the men from Mosgas made their rounds each month and were unlikely to arouse suspicion.

In the absence of reliable reports, with widespread tales of women slain and children mutilated, paranoia took control. By midmonth the authorities reported that at least two Mosgas workers had been violently assaulted on their rounds, roughed up by tenants who were not inclined to scrutinize credentials. It became a standing joke for friends to telephone each other, hanging on the line in silence for a while before they whispered, "Mosgas calling."

On January 16, Moscow police announced the arrest of a suspect in the case. Vladimir Ionosyan, 26, was an unemployed actor fallen on hard times. He had turned to burglary as a source of revenue, reportedly killing in the process. Charged with the ax murders of two boys and a woman in downtown Moscow, Ionosyan was also linked with two similar killings in a suburban district.

Vladimir's arrest resulted from a general police alert to taxi drivers, circulating suspect sketches with instructions to beware of anyone who looked suspicious. Officers were summoned after Ionosyan stopped a trucker on the street and tried to sell a television set—a luxury in Soviet society—at bargain prices.

A three-day trial resulted in Ionosyan's conviction on five counts of murder. Sentenced to death on January 31, 1964, he was shot by a firing squad the next day. Vladimir's female accomplice, former ballerina Alevtina Dmitrieva, received a sentence of 15 years in prison.

IQBAL, Javed

On December 2, 1999, police in Lahore, Pakistan, received a startling letter, dated November 22 and signed by one Javed Iqbal. The note included a confession to the sexual abuse and murder of 100 boys, with directions to Iqbal's three-room rented home in a poor suburb, located 200 yards from the nearest police station. Officers swarmed to the scene, where they found the mutilated remains of three boys dissolving in a vat of acid. Twelve more drums contained chemical cocktails with traces of human tissue. ("In terms of expense," Iqbal wrote, "including the acid, it cost me 120 rupees [$2.40] to erase each victim.") Also found inside the house were sacks of photographs and children's clothing, dozens of small shoes and board games, and a diary detailing Iqbal's gruesome activities.

Detectives knew Iqbal as a 38-year-old chemical engineer and accused child molester, charged three times with sodomy (but never convicted) in the years since 1990. Now, his letter threatened suicide while police offered a reward of 1 million rupees ($19,600) for information leading to Iqbal's arrest. Meanwhile, parents of missing children flocked to view the clothes and photos seized from Iqbal's home. Relics of 69 boys were identified by December 7, though the acid vat victims were burned beyond recognition. In a grim echo of DEAN ARNOLD CORLL's case from the 1970s, provincial governor Mohammed Safdar accused police of ignoring missing-child reports throughout Lahore.

On December 6, 1999, authorities jailed two alleged friends of Iqbal, 19-year-old Zafar Ahmed and 15-year-old Muhammad Sabir. The youths allegedly confessed to raping and murdering 25 children, who were lured to Iqbal's home with promises of food, shelter, and videos. Once there, the victims had been sexually assaulted, drugged, smothered with pillows, and dissolved in acid. Suspect Ishaq Billa, accused by police of selling Iqbal the acid, died on December 7 when he fell from a second-story window of the Crime Investigation Agency (CIA) in Lahore. Detectives called it suicide, but four officers were charged with Billa's murder on December 12. Meanwhile, detectives held Iqbal's wife and daughter "to put pressure on the accused." They also detained former councilor Malik Shaukat for questioning, on grounds that he and Iqbal were both members

of an unnamed "religious militant organization." Fifty persons were injured and 20 arrested on December 9, when police clashed with 300 marchers protesting the manhunt's lack of progress.

Public shock deepened on December 15, when reporters published excerpts from Iqbal's diary, naming 23 persons as "accomplices in the crime." Two of those named were police officers, who soon joined six others in jail. The diary explained that Iqbal's 100 victims were slaughtered between June 20 and November 13, 1999, with the 40th killed on the day of his mother's funeral. Iqbal wrote that some of his alleged accomplices had "forced" him to murder their "rivals," but that assertion clashed with his descriptions and photos of underage victims. While Punjab lawmakers debated a change in the criminal code, mandating police to register missing-child cases, detectives admitted that Iqbal had visited CIA headquarters on November 27 to bail out an alleged accomplice named Shahzad Sajid who was detained on unrelated charges. On that date, agency spokesmen admitted, Iqbal's confession had already been received by police and passed on to the CIA for evaluation. Sheer negligence had permitted Iqbal's escape.

Tired of the chase at last, Iqbal appeared on December 30, 1999 at the office of *Jang,* an Urdu newspaper in Lahore. Wearing a black mask to disguise his face, Iqbal surrendered to reporters and described a near-miss with police that afternoon, when officers had nabbed two more alleged accomplices in Sohawa. Before detectives reached the *Jang* office, Iqbal told the staff, "I could have killed 500; this was not a problem. Money was not a problem. But the pledge I had taken was of 100 children, and I never wanted to violate this.

Javed Iqbal (left) arrives at a court with two children in Lahore, Pakistan, after turning himself in to police on January 6, 2000. (AP Photo/Khalid Chaudary)

I have no regrets. I killed 100 children. I was denied justice." Specifically, he claimed police had beaten him after one of his sodomy arrests, leaving him impotent. "I was so badly beaten that my head was crushed, my backbone broken and I was left crippled," Iqbal said. "I hate this world. My mother cried for me. I wanted 100 mothers to cry for their children." In seeking victims, Iqbal explained, "I went for healthy, strong-looking boys, not frail kids." He had chosen *Jang,* Iqbal said, because "The truth would not have seen the light of day had I surrendered to the police." In conclusion, he declared, "I know my fate. I am ready to face the consequences of my actions."

Making his first court appearance on January 6, 2000, Iqbal told Magistrate Mian Hussain, "I am guilty, I again confess my crime against the nation and I am not afraid of death." Proclaiming himself "the nation's culprit," Iqbal declared that he would not retain a lawyer to defend him. Hussain postponed further hearings until January 13, granting police more time to build their case with a remark that "some progress has been made in the investigation." At the January 13 hearing, Muhammad Sabir confessed to raping and strangling one boy in concert with Iqbal. Iqbal repeated his confession before Judge Allah Ranjha on February 8, saying, "I have killed 100 children. I should be punished." Ranjha ordered a lawyer appointed despite Iqbal's protests. Nine days later, the defendant changed his tune, pleading not guilty on all charges and informing Judge Ranjha, "I have not committed murders. I am not the culprit. I am not mad, though I am regarded as mad." Insisting that he was "only a witness" to the slayings of certain children, Iqbal told the court, "I will expose those people who are involved in this heinous crime."

That plea failed to prevent Iqbal's formal indictment (with Sabir and two other defendants, Shahzad Sajid and a 15-year-old named Nadeem) on February 17, 2000, but the court tightened jailhouse security after Iqbal complained of attempts on his life. Someone had tried to poison him, he said: "I could smell it in my food and in my drink." The 100-page indictment accused all four defendants of kidnapping, sodomizing and murdering 100 boys, dissolving their corpses in acid. Defense attorney Aftab Bajwa sought transfer of the case to a special anti-terrorist court, but his petition was rejected. From jail, Iqbal told reporters that his initial sodomy arrests were frame-ups, stemming from his research on a magazine article on "fake police encounters."

Iqbal's trial began on February 18, with prosecution witnesses including parents of missing children and merchants who sold acid to defendant Sajid on various occasions. On February 28, special prosecutor Berhan Azam named Iqbal as "the most heinous offender" in Pakistan's history. "He is a beast, not a man," Azam proclaimed. Iqbal's diary, complete with photos of his victims and handwritten details of their suffering, made telling evidence against him. He countered by inviting spectators to feel dents in his skull, allegedly inflicted by police truncheons. "I am not a well man," he testified. "My eyesight has been affected and my jawbone was broken. I have problems walking." As for the crimes of which he stood accused, Iqbal said, "I was a witness to the killings but I myself have done nothing. The murders were done in my house by 20 friends of mine. I only confessed because I wanted to bring them to the attention of the authorities. I was broken inside and wanted to die. I felt guilty about what my friends had done." On March 9, Iqbal changed his story yet again, telling the court that none of the missing boys had been slain.

The vacillating statements failed to impress Judge Ranjha. On March 16 he convicted all four defendants of murder. Iqbal stood convicted of all 100 murders, Sajib of 98, Nadeem of 13, and Sabir of three. A second judge, Allah Baksh, sentenced Iqbal to "be strangled 100 times at Minar-e-Pakistan [a Lahore landmark]," after which "his body should be cut in 100 pieces and put in acid, as he did with his victims." Sajid received an identical sentence, while the two condemned inmates also received superfluous prison terms of 700 and 686 years, respectively. Defendants Nadeem and Sabir were spared, after a fashion, sentenced to respective prison terms of 253 and 63 years for their crimes.

While Iqbal's eye-for-an-eye death sentence captured international attention, it was hollow theater. Pakistan's interior minister instantly challenged the verdict as "barbaric," while human rights activists noted that few condemned prisoners are actually executed in Pakistan. "Police inconsistencies" overturned most death sentences on appeal, and execution was commonly waived for defendants convicted of religious homicides. Iqbal appealed his verdict on March 22, and Pakistan's Islamic Council rejected the court-ordered mode of execution five days later, deeming it contrary to the tenets of Islam.

On October 8, 2001, authorities announced that Iqbal and Shahzad Sajid had been found dead in separate cells at the Kot Lakhpat jail. Guards described both deaths as suicides, but reports conflicted as to whether the men were hanged or had died from ingesting "some poisonous substance." Newspapers termed the deaths "mysterious," reporting that "circumstantial evidence and the condition of the two bodies belied the official claim." Mindful of the murder charges filed in Ishaq Billa's "suicide," jail superintendent Mian Farooq told the press, "We are investigating the matter and nothing has so far been ascertained." Another prison official, Abdussattar Ajiz, compounded the mystery by claiming that a guard, Iftikar Husain, found the two men hanging in their cells but failed to report it. Instead, he allegedly "untied the knots of the bed sheets, laid the bodies on the floor to create the impression that they were asleep. He did so to save his own skin." Both corpses were dispatched to the city morgue for autopsies, which reportedly found signs that Iqbal and Sajid had been beaten prior to death. Officially, both deaths were classified as suicide.

IRELAND, Colin

Known in the tabloid press as London's "Gay Slayer," Colin Ireland was a serial murder "WANNA-BE" who made the leap from morbid daydreams to multiple murder as a conscious, deliberate choice of lifestyle. While his final body count lagged far behind those of prolific British slayers BRUCE LEE, DENNIS NILSEN, and PETER SUTCLIFFE, Ireland still deserves mention here for the sheer determination he displayed in pursuing his lethal "career" choice.

Born in 1954, the illegitimate child of a news agent's assistant, Ireland was raised by his mother and maternal grandparents in Dartford, Kent. He would recall himself in childhood as "a thin, lanky little runt, always getting the worst of it" from schoolyard bullies. By adolescence, Ireland was constantly in trouble of his own making, logging convictions for theft, burglary, and blackmail while still in his teens. He served two terms in Borstal reformatory, after which he was rejected in a bid to join the French Foreign Legion. No longer a runt at six feet two, Ireland had developed a taste for paramilitary garb and survivalist training, frequently camping out on the Essex moors. Twice married and divorced, he volunteered to manage a homeless shelter in London, but an explosive temper cost him the job in December 1992. A colleague at the shelter recalled that Colin was "troubled, frustrated, and didn't know what to do with his life."

The answer, as Ireland divined it, was serial murder.

He selected gay sadomasochists as his preferred victims on the theory that they would be easy targets, freely submitting to bondage at a stranger's hands. (In Ireland's view they were also less likely to arouse public sympathy.) Filling a knapsack with his murder gear—rope, gloves, a knife, a change of clothing (in case his got bloody)—Ireland found his first victim, 45-year-old theater director/choreographer Peter Walker, at a London gay bar called The Coleherne. Invited back to Walker's flat, Ireland tied Walker to his bed, beat and whipped him, then killed him. (Reports differ on whether Walker was strangled or suffocated with a plastic bag.) Lingering to watch TV and tidy up the

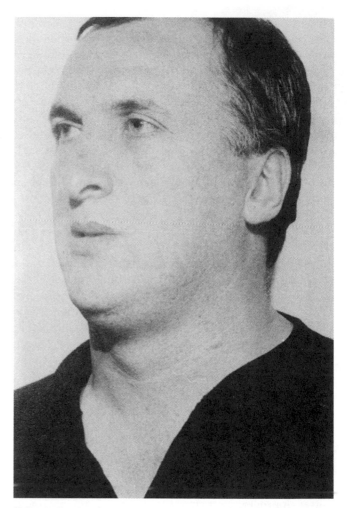

Colin Ireland (Author's collection)

crime scene, Ireland left the body with knotted condoms jammed into the mouth and nostrils and two teddy bears arranged on the bed in a sex position.

Walker's body was still undiscovered two days later, on March 5, 1993, when Ireland telephoned a London tabloid newspaper, the *Sun,* to say he was concerned about the dead man's dogs, left unattended in the flat. He also said, "It was my New Year's resolution to murder a human being."

Police had no evidence of any substance, and their manhunt was further hampered by a March 6 judicial ruling that acts of sadomasochistic sex were illegal for consenting British adults. Potential victims were thus extremely reluctant to cooperate with authorities, and autopsy results were inconclusive as to whether Walker's death had been deliberate or accidental. On balance, police knew little more than that the dead man was HIV-positive.

In late May, Ireland returned to The Coleherne and picked up 37-year-old librarian Christopher Dunn.

Dunn's body, bound and gagged, nude but for a leather bondage harness, was found at his northeast London home on May 30, police recording his death as a probable accident. No link was made to Walker's death, three months earlier. The "accident" theory took a hit soon after Dunn's death when cash was removed from his bank account, the thief using Dunn's ATM card. A few days later, police received an anonymous call from Dunn's killer, taunting them for their failure to link the two crimes.

On June 7, authorities found the corpse of 35-year-old Perry Bradley III, an American businessman and closet homosexual, in his Kensington apartment. Once again, the victim was naked and bound, apparently strangled, his credit cards missing. A plastic doll was left atop the body, posed to simulate a sex act. When the killer telephoned police again days later, he told them, "I did the American. You've got some good leads on my identity from clues at the scene." Detectives were inclined to disagree, but they worried more about the anonymous caller's stated desire to become a serial killer. He had studied "the FBI manual" for details of technique and the minimum required body count. "I have got the book," he said. "I know how many you have to do."

Mention of "the FBI manual" prompted transatlantic phone calls to ex-FBI Agent ROBERT RESSLER, coauthor of the textbooks *Sexual Homicide* (1988) and the FBI *Crime Classification Manual* (1992), as well as a recent memoir of his own career PROFILING serial killers for the Bureau's Behavioral Science Unit. (For the record, none of Ressler's books were ever found in Ireland's possession, though all of them were readily available through public libraries and bookstores.) Ressler cooperated with Scotland Yard on a profile of the elusive Gay Slayer, but as usual, police would need a lucky break to place their man in custody.

By the time Perry Bradley's corpse was found, Ireland later told authorities, he realized that he was losing control. "I was reaching a point where I was just accelerating," he said. "It was just speeding up, getting far worse. It was just like a roller-coaster effect." His next anonymous call to police was almost a plea for detectives to catch him. "Are you still interested in the death of Peter Walker?" he asked. "Why have you stopped the investigation? Doesn't the death of a homosexual man mean anything? I will do another. I have always dreamed of doing the perfect murder."

A few hours later, still on June 7, Ireland was back at The Coleherne, picking up 33-year-old Andrew Collier. Upon returning to the victim's flat, Ireland handcuffed and tied him to the bed, then strangled Collier. He also choked the life from Collier's cat, arranging its carcass atop Collier's corpse with the tip of its tail in Collier's mouth, the cat's mouth fastened on Collier's penis. Both the tail and the penis were fitted with latex condoms. This time, while he was cleaning up the crime scene, Ireland missed one fingerprint, found by police on a window frame.

On June 15, Ireland met Emanuel Spiteri, a 41-year-old Maltese chef, and went back to Spiteri's southeast London flat for sex. Once there, he bound and strangled his victim, then spent the night watching television, eating Spiteri's food. Ireland set fire to the apartment before he left, but the flames went out after causing only minor damage. Police were unaware of the crime when he telephoned them next day, asking, "Have you found the body in southeast London yet, and the fire?"

By that time, authorities were finally prepared to admit they had a serial killer at large in London. Before they could make the announcement, though, their quarry telephoned again. "I have read a lot of books on serial killers," he said. "I think it is from four people that the FBI classify as serial, so I may stop now I have done five. I just wanted to see if it could be done. I will probably never reoffend again."

Ireland was half-right: the "FBI manual" actually specified *three* victims for a bona fide serial killer, but he had claimed his last victim. Spiteri's killing prompted Scotland Yard to launch a mass-publicity campaign, including televised pleas for the killer to give himself up. Detectives learned that Spiteri had traveled by train with another man to Catford on the night he was killed, and a British Rail security camera yielded blurry photos of the victim with an unidentified heavyset man. The photos were published, and several London gays reported meetings with a man matching the suspect's description.

On July 19, 1993, Ireland approached his solicitor, admitting that he was the man in the photo, claiming that Spiteri was alive at his home with another unidentified man when they parted company. Police soon matched his fingerprint to the Collier crime scene, but Ireland hung tough until August 19 when he finally "crumbled," in the words of one investigator, and confessed to all five homicides. On December 20, after pleading guilty on all counts, he was sentenced to five terms of life imprisonment. The judge who sentenced him declared, "To take one human life is an outrage; to take five is carnage. In my view, it is absolutely clear you should never be released."

But Ireland was not finished killing yet—at least, if rumors emanating from Wakefield Prison, Yorkshire, are accurate. The stories—officially unconfirmed at this writing—claim that Ireland strangled his cellmate, a convicted child-killer, but no charges were filed against him, since he was already serving life without parole and no harsher penalty is available under British law.

Two weeks after the reported killing, Ireland was transferred to maximum-security lodgings at Whitemoor Prison, Cambridgeshire, where he is presumably kept under closer watch, with a private cell of his own.

"IVAN the Ripper"

In 1974, a decade after VLADIMIR IONOSYAN sparked a local panic with the "Mosgas" murders, residents of Moscow circulated rumors of another homicidal maniac at large. According to reports, the slayer was a fair-haired, handsome young man, armed with a cobbler's bodkin or similar instrument, who trailed his female victims from the city's ornate subway stations, stabbing them to death in nearby streets and alleys.

Manhunting is doubly difficult in a society that admits no crime problem, but Moscow police indirectly confirmed at least some of the reports. By October 19, extra police and militia patrols were at large, their activity officially explained as preparation for the annual celebration of the Bolshevik revolution on November 7. At the same time, posters bearing sketches of a suspect surfaced in the city's 17 taxi garages, enlisting cab drivers as lookouts in the search.

By October 21, police confirmed that they were searching for the killer of "a woman." Inside sources put the body count at seven, with the latest murder five days earlier. An eighth intended victim had survived her wounds, providing homicide investigators with the likeness reproduced in suspect sketches. Five days later, on October 26, authorities reported they were holding a suspect in a series of stabbings who had killed at least 11 Moscow women. The unnamed prisoner had been arrested on the evening of October 24, after three victims were slain in a period of 24 hours.

Police maintained their news blackout as the suspect was shuffled off for psychiatric evaluation, and the disposition of the case remains unknown, but this time the official silence backfired. On the streets, a population starved for solid news fell back on rumor, doubting that the slayer had been captured. "They caught one, but there is a second killer," one woman confided to a Western journalist. "They still have not caught the main one."

"JACK the Ripper"

Arguably the world's most infamous serial killer, Victorian London's unidentified slasher of prostitutes remains an object of study—some say obsession—for thousands of students today. If we may trust the faceless experts on *Jeopardy,* more books, plays, articles, and movie scripts have been written about Red Jack than about any other murderer in history, except Adolf Hitler. At that, Der Führer had to kill some 20 million people just to break the tie, while Jack the Ripper slaughtered only five. Still, his (or her) identity remains an active topic of debate, with new works on the subject published every year.

Because he got away.

The mystery of Jack the Ripper opens on August 31, 1888, with the discovery of a woman's lifeless body on Buck's Row, in the heart of London's Whitechapel slum. The victim was Mary Nichols, known as Polly to her friends, and she had earned her meager living as a prostitute before a presumed final client showed a taste for blood. Her throat was slashed, with bruises found beneath the jaw suggesting that she had been punched or choked unconscious before the killer plied his blade. Upon undressing Polly at the morgue, the medical examiner found deep postmortem slashes on her abdomen, with stab wounds to the genitals.

The murder of an East End prostitute was nothing new to Scotland Yard. Detectives had two other cases on the books for 1888 already. Emma Smith had been attacked on April 2, by a gang of four or five assailants, living long enough to describe her killers. Martha Tabram was found in Whitechapel on August 7, stabbed 39 times with a weapon resembling a bayonet.

Neither crime had anything in common with the death of Mary Nichols, and detectives had to wait for further slayings to reveal a pattern.

On September 8, the police found their link with the discovery of Annie Chapman's corpse a half mile from Buck's Row. The victim, yet another prostitute, had first been choked unconscious, after which her throat was cut and she was disemboweled. Her entrails had been torn away and draped across one shoulder; portions of the bladder and vagina, with the uterus and ovaries, were missing from the scene. *The Lancet* quoted Dr. Bagster Phillips, medical examiner, on the proficiency of Chapman's killer. "Obviously," Dr. Phillips said, "the work was that of an expert—or one, at least, who had such knowledge of anatomical or pathological examinations as to be enabled to secure the pelvic organs with one sweep of the knife."

The first of several letters allegedly penned (in red ink) by the killer was written on September 25 and mailed three days later, addressed to London's Central News Agency. It read:

Dear Boss,

I keep on hearing the police have caught me but they won't fix me just yet. I have laughed when they look so clever and talk about being on the right track. That joke about [unnamed suspect] Leather Apron gave me real fits. I am down on whores and shan't quit ripping them till I do get buckled. Grand work the last job was. I gave the lady no time to squeal. How can they catch me now. I love my work and want to start again. You will soon hear of me and my funny little games. I saved some of the proper red stuff in a ginger beer bottle over the last job to write with but it went thick like glue and I can't use it. Red ink is fit enough I hope ha ha. *The next job I do I shall clip the lady's ears off and send to the police officers just for jolly wouldn't you. Keep this letter back till I do a bit more work, then give it out straight. My knife is nice and sharp I want to get to work right away if I get the chance. Good luck.*

Yours truly,
Jack the Ripper

Don't mind me giving the trade name. Wasn't good enough to post this before I got all the red ink off my hands curse it. They say I am a doctor now ha ha.

The Ripper claimed two more victims on September 30. The first, Elizabeth Stride, was found in a narrow court off Berner Street at 1:00 A.M. Her throat was slashed, but there had been no other mutilation, indicating that her killer was disturbed before he could complete his grisly task. Three-quarters of an hour later, Catherine Eddowes was found by a constable in Mitre Square. According to the officer, she had been gutted "like a pig in the market," with her entrails "flung in a heap about her neck." The murderer (or someone else) had chalked a cryptic message on a nearby wall: "The Juwes are not the men that will be blamed for nothing."

Medical examination of the corpse from Mitre Square revealed that Eddowes had been slashed across the face, her throat was cut, and she was disemboweled. The killer had removed a kidney, which was not recovered at the scene. One final bit of evidence, a superficial wound beneath one ear, suggested that the killer had attempted to fulfill his promise of a trophy for police.

That morning, while police were scouring the streets of Whitechapel, someone mailed another message to the Central News Agency.

I was not codding dear old Boss when I gave you the tip. You'll hear about Saucy Jack's work tomorrow. Double event this time. Number one squealed a bit. Couldn't finish straight off. Had no time to get ears for police. Thanks for keeping last letter back till I got to work again.

Jack the Ripper

A third communication was mailed on October 16 to George Lusk, head of the newly organized Whitechapel Vigilance Committee. It read:

From hell

Mr. Lusk

Sir I send you half the Kidne I took from one woman prasarved it for you tother piece I fried and ate was

Letter written by "Jack the Ripper" to the Central News office in London (Wide World API)

very nise I may send you the bloody knif that took it out if you only wait a whil longer

[signed] Catch me when you can Mister Lusk

Examining the partial kidney that accompanied the letter, Dr. Openshaw, pathological curator of the London Hospital Museum, pronounced it "ginny," of the sort expected from an alcoholic. It showed symptoms of Bright's disease, as (allegedly) did the kidney left to Catherine Eddowes by her killer. Dr. Openshaw also noted that the renal artery is normally three inches long: two inches had remained with Eddowes; one inch was attached to the repulsive trophy sent to Lusk.

(Another pathologist, Dr. Sedgwick Saunders, reported that Eddowes's remaining kidney was perfectly healthy; he believed the kidney sent to Lusk was a prank by medical students.)

London's panic had begun to fade by Halloween, but Jack the Ripper was not finished yet. Police were summoned on the morning of November 9 to Miller's Court in Spitalfields to view the sad remains of Mary Kelly, former prostitute. Discovered by her landlord's errand boy, inquiring after tardy rent, she was the only victim killed indoors, Jack taking full advantage of the opportunity to sculpt a grisly piece of butcher's art.

As usual, the victim had been murdered with a slash across the throat, this time so deep that she was nearly decapitated. Jack had skinned her forehead, slicing off her nose and ears. Her left arm had been nearly severed at the shoulder, while both legs were flayed from thighs to ankles. Kelly had been disemboweled, one hand inserted in her gaping abdomen, her liver draped across one thigh. Her severed breasts lay on the nightstand with her kidneys, heart, and nose. Police found strips of flesh suspended from the nails of picture frames, and blood was spattered on the walls. Examination showed that she was three months pregnant, but her killer claimed the uterus and fetus for himself.

So closed the Ripper's reign of terror as it began, in mystery . . . or, did it? The private papers of Sir Melville Macnaghten, former chief of CID for Scotland Yard, named three prime suspects, while insisting that the Ripper "had *five* victims and five only." However, other students of the case are not so sure. A number of them reckon two more victims in the tally, thus raising the body count and expanding the Ripper's career from 10 weeks to three years.

Prostitute Alice Mackenzie, found dead on July 17, 1889, is the first "extra" victim normally ascribed to Jack. With her throat slashed and familiar gashes to her abdomen, Mackenzie seemed a likely new addition to the Ripper's list. One medical examiner, Dr. Thomas Bond, openly credited Jack with the crime, while Dr. Bagster Phillips disagreed. (Dr. Phillips also thought two separate killers were responsible for the established Ripper crimes in 1888). While hesitating to connect Mackenzie's murder to the Ripper, Phillips *did* believe it was related to a second crime, discovered nearly two years later.

On February 13, 1891, a prostitute named Frances Cole was found in Spitalfields, throat slashed, her abdomen ripped open. Merchant seaman James Sadler was arrested for the homicide and several times remanded prior to his release for lack of evidence. An alcoholic prone to violent rages, Sadler had been seen in Whitechapel the day Mackenzie died and shipped out to the Baltic two days later. Satisfied, albeit off the record, of his guilt in two sadistic murders, some investigators treated Sadler as a suspect in the Ripper crimes, but he was never charged.

Suspects abound in this intriguing case, with anyone and everyone fair game for one dramatic theory or another. In the absence of conclusive evidence (no fingerprints, no witness to the crimes, no DNA), the list of suspects grows with every passing year. Those on record to date include:

Montague John Druitt (1857–88), a London barrister first on Macnaghten's suspect list, whose body, weighted with stones in an apparent suicide, was dredged from the Thames on December 1, 1888. Macnaghten wrote that "From private information I have little doubt but that his own family suspected this man of being the Whitechapel murderer." An alternative theory paints Druitt as both killer and victim, murdered by affluent Oxford associates to avert potential scandal.

PROBLEMS: Macnaghten misidentifies Druitt as a 41-year-old doctor; no evidence links Druitt to the crimes; his apparent suicide note does not mention the murders.

Aaron Kosminski (1864/65–1919), a Polish Jew employed in London as a hairdresser, the second of Macnaghten's three suspects, allegedly driven insane by masturbation, confined to a lunatic asylum in 1891.

PROBLEMS: No evident link to the murders; no proven Ripper crimes between November 1888 and February 1891 while he was still at large.

Michael Ostrog (born c. 1833), the third official suspect, described by Macnaghten as "a mad Russian doctor & a convict & unquestionably a homicidal maniac." A known thief and con man, paroled from his last prison term in 1904, he thereafter vanished from the public record.

PROBLEMS: Ostrog was not a doctor (though he sometimes posed as one); no evidence connects him to the murders.

"Jill the Ripper"—Nickname for an unknown female suspect, allegedly an abortionist concealing her crimes with mutilation, proposed in 1888.

PROBLEM: No real-life candidate identified.

Severin Antoniovitch Klosovksi (1865–1903), aka "George Chapman," a Polish barber-surgeon and resident of Whitechapel in 1888; poisoned three common-law wives after 1895 and was hanged for the third offense. At his arrest, Inspector Frederick Abberline supposedly remarked, "So you've caught Jack the Ripper at last!"

PROBLEMS: No evidential link to the crimes; sadistic slashers rarely (if ever) switch to poisoning.

Dr. Thomas Neill Cream (1850–92), poisoner of four Lambeth prostitutes in 1891–92; supposedly cried, "I am Jack the—" when he was hanged.

PROBLEM: Cream was imprisoned in Illinois at the time of the murders.

Prince Albert Victor Christian Edward (1864–92), the Duke of Clarence and Heir Presumptive to the throne of England, first named as a Ripper suspect in 1962. Most "Royal Ripper" theories describe the prince as a woman-hating homosexual, driven mad by syphilis, whose deer-hunting experience taught him to gut corpses.

PROBLEMS: No evident links to the murders; no proof of syphilis; official records place him far from London on the dates of all five murders; gay serial killers typically seek same-sex victims.

James Kenneth Stephen (1859–92), a tutor (some say gay lover) of Prince Albert Victor, first publicly named as a Ripper suspect in 1972. Allegedly suspected by Inspector Abberline (based on a diary, possibly forged, that surfaced in 1988), Stephen supposedly hated women in general and prostitutes in particular. Some students of the case regard his handwriting as similar (or identical) to that of several "Ripper" notes.

PROBLEMS: No evident links to the crimes (or to a homosexual affair with the prince); many "Ripperologists" believe *all* correspondence from the killer was a hoax, authored by newsmen or cranks.

Prince Albert Victor and *James Stephen,* named as TEAM KILLERS by Dr. David Abrahamson in *Murder and Madness* (1992).

PROBLEMS: Same as above for both suspects; numerous historical errors; Scotland Yard denies Abrahamson's claim that he based his theory on information from police files.

Dr. Alexander Pedachenko (1857?–1908?), Russian doctor who emigrated to Britain, alleged (in 1928) to have committed the murders in connivance with the Czarist secret police "to discredit the Metropolitan Police."

PROBLEMS: Dubious sources; no evident link to the crimes.

Sir William Gull (1816–90), physician in ordinary to Queen Victoria who treated Prince Albert Victor for typhus in 1871, first linked to the Ripper case in 1970. Gull is accused of leading a conspiracy to silence those with knowledge of Prince Albert Victor's illegal marriage to a Catholic commoner, mutilating the victims in accordance with Masonic ritual.

PROBLEMS: No evident link to the crimes;

Gull was partially paralyzed by the first of several strokes in 1887; prevailing law would have annulled the alleged marriage; subsequent research indicates the woman in question was not Catholic.

Walter Richard Sickert (1860–1942), a major British artist, described in various theories since 1976 as either the lone Ripper or a participant in Dr. Gull's Masonic plot. One graphologist claimed (in 1993) that the Ripper's "Dear Boss" note was written in Sickert's disguised handwriting. Novelist Patricia Cornwell revived the Sickert case in 2002 (strangely omitting any mention of authors who plowed the same ground before her) and reportedly spent $4 million pursuing her suspect. DNA testing of various "Ripper" letters proved fruitless, and the "case closed" verdict ultimately rests on amateur psychoanalysis of Sickert's paintings.

PROBLEM: No proven link to the murders.

Robert Donston Stephenson (b. 1841), aka "Dr. Roslyn D'Onston," first named as a Ripper suspect in 1987. Stephenson allegedly committed the murders as part of a black magic ritual.

PROBLEM: No evident link to the crimes.

James Maybrick (1838–89), a Liverpool cotton broker, allegedly the author of the "Ripper diary" published amidst great controversy in 1993.

PROBLEMS: No evidence besides the "diary" connects him to the crimes; several analysts brand the "Ripper diary" a forgery dating from the 1920s.

Dr. Francis Tumblety (1833?–1903), an Irish-American "herb doctor" arrested in London on November 7, 1888, on multiple counts of assault (against four men) dating back to July; released on bail, he fled to America before trial. Obituaries named him as a Ripper suspect, but the case against him was first publicized in 1995.

PROBLEMS: No proven link to the crimes; differed greatly in appearance from alleged descriptions of the Ripper.

Joseph Barnett (1858–1926), a London fish porter who lived with Mary Kelly until two weeks before her death, first named as a suspect in 1995.

PROBLEMS: Cleared by police in 1888; no proven link to the murders.

James Kelly (d. 1929), a London resident confined to an asylum after killing his wife in 1883; he escaped in January 1888 and remained at large until his voluntary surrender in February 1927. Deceased two years later, he was first named as a suspect in 1986.

PROBLEMS: No proven link to the murders; no explanation for their brief duration, while Kelly remained at large for another 39 years.

Rev. John George Gibson (?–?), a Canadian preacher who left his Scottish parish in 1887, whose whereabouts are unknown until he surfaced in the United States in December 1888. In 1992, author Robert Graysmith named Gibson as the Ripper and as the slayer of two women murdered at Gibson's San Francisco church in April 1895. WILLIAM HENRY THEODORE DURRANT was convicted of the latter crimes and hanged in April 1897, in what Graysmith calls a miscarriage of justice.

PROBLEMS: No evidence links "Pastor Jack" to any of the London murders, and Graysmith's resort to fiction (including a fabricated "diary" from Durrant) weakens his case in the California slayings.

"JACK the Stripper"

Seventy years after "JACK THE RIPPER" murdered and disemboweled prostitutes in London's East End, a new generation of hookers learned to live with the ever-present fear of a lurking killer. This "Jack" carried no knife and penned no jaunty letters to the press, but he was every bit as lethal (claiming eight victims to the Ripper's five) and possessed of far greater longevity (operating over nearly six years, compared to the Ripper's 10 weeks). At the "conclusion" of the case, both slayers shared a common attribute: despite a wealth of theories and assertions, neither "Jack" was ever captured or identified.

On June 17, 1959, prostitute Elizabeth Figg, 21, was found floating in the Thames, clad only in a slip, her death attributed to strangulation. Four and a half years passed before discovery of the next murder, with the skeleton of 22-year-old Gwynneth Rees unearthed during clearance of a Thames-side rubbish dump, on November 8, 1963. The cause of death was difficult to ascertain, and homicide investigators later tried to disconnect both murders from the "Stripper" series, but today the better evidence suggests that these were practice runs, the early crimes committed by a killer who had yet to hit his stride.

Thirty-year-old Hannah Tailford was the next to die, her naked corpse discovered in the Thames by boatmen on February 2, 1964. Her stockings were pulled down around her ankles, panties stuffed inside her mouth, but she had drowned, and the inquest produced an "open" verdict, refusing to rule out suicide, however improbable it seemed.

On April 9, 1964, 20-year-old Irene Lockwood was found naked and dead in the Thames, floating 300 yards from the spot where Tailford was found. Another drowning victim, she was four months pregnant when she died. Suspect Kenneth Archibald confessed to the murder later that month, then recanted his statement, blaming depression. He was subsequently cleared at trial.

Helen Barthelemy, age 20, was the first victim found away from the river. On April 24, her naked body was discovered near a sports field in Brentwood, four front teeth missing, with part of one lodged in her throat. Traces of multicolored spray paint on the body suggested that she had been kept for a while after death in a paint shop before she was dumped in the field.

On July 14, 21-year-old Mary Fleming was discarded, nude and lifeless, on a dead-end London street. Witnesses glimpsed a van and its driver near the scene, but none could finally describe the man or vehicle with any certainty. Missing since July 11, Fleming had apparently been suffocated or choked to death—as opposed to strangled—and her dentures were missing from the scene.

Margaret McGowan, 21, had been missing a month when her nude corpse was found in Kensington on November 25, 1964. Police noted the familiar traces of paint on her skin, and one of her teeth had been forced from its socket in front. The last to die was 27-year-old Bridget O'Hara, last seen alive on January 11, 1965, her body found on February 16 hidden in some shrubbery on the Heron Trading Estate in Acton. Her front teeth were missing, and pathologists determined that

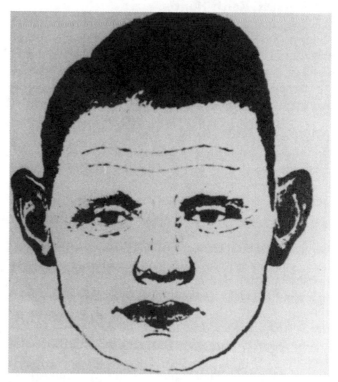

Police sketch of "Jack the Stripper" (Author's collection)

135

she had died on her knees. The corpse was partially mummified, as if from prolonged storage in a cool, dry place.

Despite appeals to prostitutes for information on their "kinky" customers, police were groping in the dark. Inspector John Du Rose suggested that the last six victims had been literally choked to death by oral sex, removal of the teeth in four cases lending vague support to the hypothesis. A list of suspects had supposedly been narrowed down from 20 men to three when one of those committed suicide, gassing himself in his kitchen and leaving a cryptic note: "I cannot go on." It might mean anything—or nothing—but the murders ended with the nameless suspect's death, and so police seem satisfied, although the case remains officially unsolved.

Who *was* the Stripper? Suspects range from a deceased prize fighter to an unnamed ex-policeman, but Du Rose favored a private security guard on the Heron Trading Estate, his rounds including the paint shop where at least some of the victims were apparently stashed after death. The only "evidence" of guilt is the cessation of similar crimes after the suspect's suicide, but numerous serial killers—from the original Ripper to the ZODIAC and "Babysitter"—have "retired" once they achieved a certain body count. The best that we can say for Scotland Yard's solution is that it is plausible . . . but unconfirmed.

JESPERSON, Keith Hunter

The convoluted case of Keith Jesperson, nicknamed the "Happy Face Killer," officially began in Oregon on January 22, 1990. A student from Mt. Hood Community College was bicycling along the Old Scenic Highway, north of Portland, when she spied a woman's corpse lying off to one side. The victim had been strangled with a rope, still tied around her neck; her bra was pulled up to expose her breasts, pants bunched around her ankles. An autopsy revealed the woman had been sexually assaulted. The victim was identified, through sketches broadcast in the media, as 23-year-old Taunja Bennett, last seen alive by her parents a week before her body was found.

Detectives scoured the bars and truckstops where Bennett was known to spend much of her time. In one café, employees recalled frequent customer John Sosnovske boasting that he had murdered a woman he met in a bar. "He was laughing," a waitress told police. "He thought it was a big joke." Already on probation for drunk driving and driving with a suspended license, Sosnovske was a notorious drinker whose girlfriend—Laverne Pavlinac—had a habit of reporting him to the police on phony charges every time they quarreled. Eight months before the murder, in the spring of 1989,

she had telephoned the FBI and falsely accused John of robbing banks. When the G-men cleared him, she repeated the accusation to local police.

Pulled in for questioning, Pavlinac accused her husband of Taunja Bennett's murder, and police obtained a search warrant for the couple's home. None of Bennett's missing personal effects were found, as searchers hoped, but they *did* turn up an envelope addressed to Sosnovske, with "T. Bennett—a Good Piece" written on the back. Sosnovske, for his part, denied killing Taunja or writing the message.

Laverne Pavlinac, meanwhile had radically changed her story. In the first version, John had merely boasted of the murder, spilling enough details that she was convinced of his guilt. In the new tale, Pavlinac admitted watching him rape and kill Taunja on the night of January 21. It was enough for the authorities; Sosnovske was promptly charged with murder, and Laverne was indicted for aiding him in the crime.

There were problems with the story, even so. Most critically, police had several witnesses who reported seeing Taunja Bennett at a bar in Gresham the night she died, 25 miles from the restaurant where Sosnovske allegedly met her. Taunja had been playing pool, the witnesses said, with two unidentified men—neither of them John Sosnovske. It made no difference to the jurors who tried Laverne Pavlinac in early 1991: she was convicted and sentenced to 10 years in prison for her alleged role in the crime. Sosnovske still maintained his innocence, but Laverne's conviction unnerved him, and he soon cut a deal with the state, pleading "no contest" to felony murder and kidnapping, accepting a life sentence with parole eligibility after 15 years.

Case closed . . . or was it? By the time Sosnovske copped his plea, investigators had already hit another snag. In January, while Laverne Pavlinac was on trial, a message was found written on a men's room wall at the Greyhound bus depot in Livingston, Montana. It read: "I killed Taunja Bennett January 21, 1990, in Portland, Oregon. I beat her to death, raped her and loved it. I'm sick but I enjoy myself too. Two people took the blame and I'm free." A few days later, in a truckstop men's room in Umatilla, Oregon, a second message was found: "I killed Taunja Bennett in Portland. Two people got the blame so I can kill again."

Both messages were signed with a "happy face"—a circle with two dots for eyes and a broad crescent smile.

Detectives in Portland theorized that some unknown friend of Sosnovske's wrote the graffiti in an effort to spring John from prison, but the author was untraceable. Then, in 1994, the Portland *Oregonian* received a letter in the same awkward handwriting, signed with the same smiling face. This time, the author claimed a total of six victims, including five more in Oregon and one in California. "I feel bad," he wrote, "but I will not turn myself in. I am not stupid." The letter went on:

In a lot of opinions I should be killed and I feel I deserve it. My resposiblity [sic] is mine and God will be my judge when I die. I am telling you this because I will be responsibil [sic] for these crimes and no one else. It all started when I wondered what it would be like to kill someone. And I found out. What a nightmare it has been.

Despite that indication of remorse, the letter closed on an ominous note: "Look over your shoulder. I'm closer than you think."

The apparent author of the "Happy Face" notes was identified in March 1995, shortly after the remains of 41-year-old Julia Ann Winningham were found at a scenic outlook near Washougal, Washington. A former resident of Salt Lake City, Winningham had lately resided in nearby Camas, Washington, before she dropped out of sight; her body was found on March 11. Homicide investigators learned that she had left Utah in the company of 39-year-old Keith Jesperson, a truck driver employed by Systems Transport out of Cheney, Washington. Picked up for questioning, Jesperson soon confessed his role in a series of murders around the Pacific Northwest—including Taunja Bennett's. Authorities were skeptical until Jesperson led them to Bennett's missing purse. On November 3, 1995, he pled guilty to Bennett's murder and two other Oregon slayings and subsequently sentenced to life imprisonment. Media reports claim Jesperson wept with joy when John Sosnovske and Laverne Pavlinac were released from custody on November 27.

By that time, however, Jesperson—or "Face," as he liked to sign his letters from prison—had more pressing matters to worry about. His string of confessions had a price tag attached in the form of subsequent indictments and convictions. A new case had also been opened since his arrest with the September 1995 discovery of a woman's badly decomposed remains along Interstate Highway 80 in Nebraska. A tattoo and X rays identified the woman as 21-year-old Angela Subrize, an Oklahoma City native last seen alive in Wyoming with Jesperson in January 1995. The trucker, for his part, admitted killing Subrize in Wyoming, afterward tying her corpse beneath his truck and dragging it for "10 or 12 miles" before he finally dumped it after crossing into Nebraska.

Part of the problem for investigators was the ever-changing list of Jesperson's confessions. At one point, he allegedly confessed 160 murders, describing his victims as "piles of garbage" dumped on the roadside, but he soon recanted most of the stories. One case he backtracked on was that of Angela Subrize, doubtless influenced by Wyoming's expressed intent to indict him on capital charges. He still admitted *knowing* Angela, even sharing her bed on occasion, but now insisted they had parted company while on the road, Subrize continuing eastward on her own to meet her fate at someone else's hands.

Wyoming prosecutors didn't buy the revised version, filing extradition papers with the governor of Oregon in 1997. Jesperson's next ploy was a new confession, this time to the slaying of a fourth Oregon woman, Bend resident Bobbi Crescenzi, killed in 1992. Jack Crescenzi was already serving time for his wife's murder, but Jesperson seemed bent on springing him from custody, as he had done with Sosnovske and Pavlinac in the Bennett case. He hit a snag this time, however, when police tracking his movements were able to rule out any contact between "Face" and the victim. In fact, they charged, a former cellmate had been running interference between Jesperson and Jack Crescenzi, supplying Keith with details of the crime, Crescenzi offering $10,000 (payable to Jesperson's children) for a confession that would lead to his release.

Exposure of the jailhouse plot led some authorities to question Jesperson's confession in the Bennett case, but his real problem lay in Wyoming. Extradited in December 1997, Jesperson initially boasted of his plan to demolish the prosecution's case by exposing his own prior lies, then switched to yet another angle of attack, confessing once again to the Subrize homicide. One difference: he had actually killed Subrize in *Nebraska,* Jesperson now claimed, contesting Wyoming's right to try the case at all. When all else failed, he copped another plea on June 3, 1998, admitting the Subrize murder in exchange for another life sentence.

Ever the manipulator, "Face" had barely filed that plea before telling the press he had lied about killing Taunja Bennett. It was good for filler in the papers, but if Jesperson believed it would reverse the Oregon sentence, he was destined for grave disappointment. Formally sentenced in four cases, he is suspected by authorities of at least four more slayings, including one from 1994 in Okaloosa County, Florida. Closer to home, prosecutors in Riverside County, California, have announced their intent to try Jesperson for a 1992 murder near Blythe, if he ever seems likely to win parole.

JOHNSON, Milton

An Illinois native, born in 1951, Johnson was convicted at age 19 of raping a Joliet woman, torturing his victim with a cigarette lighter in the process. The charge carried a sentence of 25 to 35 years in prison with a consecutive term of five to 10 years added on conviction of burglary.

Even with "good time," Johnson should have been confined until April 1986, but authorities saw fit to release him more than three years prematurely on March 10, 1983. Their generosity would cost at least 10 lives.

For two long months, between June and August 1983, Joliet and surrounding communities were terrorized by a series of random "weekend murders" marked by savage violence. Law enforcement officers were mobilized to sweep Will County in a search for suspects, but the killer managed to elude them, slaughtering his victims with impunity, while residents stocked up on guns and ammunition in their own defense.

The crime spree started with the death of two Will County sisters on Saturday, June 25. A week later, on July 2, Kenneth and Terri Johnson were shot to death without apparent motive, the woman's body discarded in southwestern Cook County. Five persons—including two deputy sheriffs—were killed on Saturday, July 16, in what authorities termed a "random wholesale slaughter." The next evening, 18-year-old Anthony Hackett was shot to death, his fiancée raped and stabbed by a black assailant.

The violence escalated a month later. On Saturday, August 20, four women were found shot and stabbed to death in a Joliet pottery shop, their handbags dumped nearby with money still inside. Once more, police were left without a solid clue in the slayings of proprietor Marilyn Baers, 46, and her three customers: 75-year-old Anna Ryan, 29-year-old Pamela Ryan, and 39-year-old Barbara Dunbar. On August 21, the killer shifted to Park Forest in Cook County, binding 40-year-old Ralph Dixon and 25-year-old Crystal Knight before slashing their throats in Dixon's apartment and stabbing the woman 20 times. The murder of 82-year-old Anna Johnson broke the pattern, falling on a Thursday, and a suspect was swiftly apprehended in that case, leaving 17 murders unsolved.

On March 9, 1984, Milton Johnson was arrested while visiting his parole officer, charged with aggravated battery and deviate sexual assault in the rape of Anthony Hackett's fiancée. Officers focused on Johnson after repeated complaints of a black pickup driver harassing Joliet women over the past two weeks, ending when one victim memorized Johnson's license number. Evidence collected at various murder scenes—including fibers, fingerprints, and a sales receipt bearing the name of Johnson's stepfather—linked Milton to 10 of the Will County murders, including Hackett's, the pottery shop massacre, and the carnage of July 16. (The receipt had been found beneath one of the murdered officers.) In addition to those cases, police saw a "strong possibility" of Milton's participation in the July 2 murders of Ken and Terri Johnson.

Granted a change of venue on grounds of pretrial publicity, Johnson waived his right to trial by jury in the Hackett case. Convicted on all counts in September 1984, he was sentenced to die. Four months later, on January 23, 1986, Johnson was convicted of quadruple murder in the ceramic shop massacre, a second death sentence pronounced five days later. Prosecution in five other murders was deferred indefinitely, and Johnson remains on death row at this writing.

JONES, Genene Ann

In February 1983, a special grand jury convened in San Antonio, Texas, investigating the "suspicious" deaths of 47 children at Bexar County's Medical Center Hospital over the past four years. A similar probe in neighboring Kerr County was focused on the cases of eight infants who developed respiratory problems during treatment at a local clinic. One of those children also died, and authorities were concerned over allegations that deaths in both counties were caused by deliberate injections of muscle-relaxing drugs.

Genene Jones, a 32-year-old licensed vocational nurse, was one of three former hospital employees subpoenaed by both grand juries. With nurse Deborah Saltenfuss, Jones had resigned from Medical Center Hospital in March 1982, moving on to a job at the Kerr County clinic run by Dr. Kathleen Holland. By the time the grand juries convened, Jones and Holland had both been named as defendants in a lawsuit filed by the parents of 15-month-old Chelsea McClellan, lost en route to the hospital after treatment at Holland's clinic in September 1982.

On May 28, 1983, Jones was indicted on two counts of murder in Kerr County, charged with injecting lethal doses of a muscle relaxant and another unknown drug to deliberately cause Chelsea McClellan's death. Additional charges of injury were filed in the cases of six other children, reportedly injected with drugs including succinylcholine during their visits to the Holland clinic. Facing a maximum sentence of 99 years in prison, Jones was held in lieu of $225,000 bond.

An ex-beautician, Jones had entered nursing in 1977, working at several hospitals around San Antonio over the next five years. In early 1982, she followed Dr. Holland in the move to private practice, but her performance at the clinic left much to be desired. In August and September 1982, seven children suffered mysterious seizures while visiting Dr. Holland's office, their cases arousing suspicion at Kerr County's Sip Peterson Hospital, where they were transferred for treatment. Holland fired Jones on September 26, after finding a bottle of succinylcholine reported lost three weeks earlier, its plastic cap missing, the rubber top pocked with needle marks.

(In retrospect, Dr. Holland's choice of nurses seemed peculiar, at the very least. Her statements to authorities admit that hospital administrators had "indirectly cautioned" her against hiring Jones, describing Genene as a suspect in hospital deaths dating back to October 1981. Three separate investigations were conducted at Bexar County's hospital between November 1981 and February 1983, all without solving the string of mysterious deaths.)

On November 21, 1983, Jones was indicted in San Antonio on charges of injuring four-week-old Rolando Santos by deliberately injecting him with heparin, an anticoagulant, in January 1982. Santos had been undergoing treatment for pneumonia when he suffered "spontaneous" hemorrhaging, but physicians managed to save his life. Their probe continued, authorities branding Jones a suspect in at least 10 infant deaths at Bexar County's pediatric ward.

Genene's murder trial opened at Georgetown, Texas, on January 15, 1984, with prosecutors introducing an ego motive. Jones allegedly sought recognition as a hero for "saving" children in life-or-death situations. Nurses from Bexar County also recalled Genene's plan to promote a pediatric intensive-care unit in San Antonio, ostensibly by raising the number of seriously ill children. "They're out there," she once told a colleague. "All you have to do is find them."

Jurors deliberated for three hours before convicting Jones of murder on February 15, fixing her penalty at 99 years in prison. Eight months later, on October 24, she was convicted of injuring Rolando Santos in San Antonio and sentenced to a concurrent term of 60 years. Suspected in at least 10 other homicides, Jones was spared further charges when Bexar County hospital administrators shredded 9,000 pounds of pharmaceutical records in March 1984, thus destroying numerous pieces of evidence then under subpoena by the local grand jury.

See also MEDICAL MURDERS

JOUBERT, John J.

On August 22, 1982, 11-year-old Richard Stetson disappeared while jogging near his home in Portland, Maine. A motorist found his body the next morning, lying beside a rural highway, and while he was initially believed to be the victim of a hit-and-run, autopsy results showed that Stetson had been strangled, then stabbed several times in the chest. Bite marks on his body were inflicted by a set of human teeth.

Investigators had no solid evidence to work with, and a year elapsed before a suspect, 24 years old, was booked for Stetson's murder. Charges were dismissed in February 1984, by which time there were two more victims on the list some 1,500 miles away.

Danny Joe Eberle, age 13, was delivering newspapers in Bellevue, Nebraska, when he vanished on the morn-

ing of September 18, 1983. His bicycle and papers were found inside a gate at the fourth house on his route, but Eberle remained missing until September 21 when searchers pulled his body from a roadside ditch. Partially stripped, he had been stabbed repeatedly and then dumped where he was found. Detectives noted bite marks on the body, and his ankles had been bound before he died.

On December 2, 12-year-old Christopher Walden disappeared while walking to school in Papillon, Nebraska, three miles from the scene of the Eberle murder. Stabbed repeatedly, his corpse was found by pheasant hunters two days later, hidden in a grove of trees outside of town.

Six weeks later, on January 11, 1984, a suspicious young man was seen loitering around a Bellevue preschool. Challenged by a staff member, he shoved her, threatened her with death, then ran to a nearby car, and sped away. The woman memorized his license number, and the rented vehicle was traced to 20-year-old John Joubert, an enlisted man at nearby Offutt Air Force Base. A search of Joubert's quarters turned up rope identical to Danny Eberle's bindings; more rope and a hunting knife were found in his car when Joubert was arrested that night.

In custody the suspect confessed to both local murders, warning detectives that he might kill again if released. Charged with two counts of murder on January 12, Joubert was held in lieu of $10 million bond pending trial. He pled guilty to both counts on July 3, 1984, and a panel of three judges fixed his sentence at death.

A native of Portland, Maine—reportedly obsessed from childhood with fantasies of CANNIBALISM—Joubert had also been making headlines at home. Detectives noted similarities between the two Nebraska murders and the Stetson case, instantly bumping Joubert to the head of their short suspect list. Hair samples and dental impressions were obtained from Joubert in February 1985, and he was indicted for Richard Stetson's murder on January 10, 1986. Convicted nearly five years later, in October 1990, Joubert was sentenced to a term of life without parole, then returned to Nebraska to await execution. Appeals prolonged his life for another five years and nine months before he was executed on July 17, 1996.

JUVENILE Serial Killers

Unlike "normal" murderers, who commit their first and only homicide as adults in a conflict with relatives or friends, serial killers often start young, graduating to murder from a childhood pattern of violence directed toward animals, siblings, playmates—even adults.

About 1 percent of identified serial slayers—including CARROLL COLE, PETER KURTEN, and Herman Mudgett—are known to have claimed their first victim before the age of 10. Another 26 percent kill for the first time while still in their teens. Conversely, the older a potential killer becomes, the less likely he or she is to act out homicidal fantasies: 44 percent of known serial murderers began killing in their twenties, 24 percent in their thirties; a mere 4 percent killed for the first time in their forties, and only two individuals committed their first murder beyond age 50. (Age at first kill is disputed or unknown for the remainder of identified serial slayers.)

Juvenile killers present a special problem for society, since nearly all American jurisdictions limit the length of time a youthful offender may be detained for any crime, regardless of the charge. In general, statutes mandate unconditional release by age 18 or 21, and juvenile records are frequently sealed (even to police scrutiny) when the offender becomes an adult, thus effectively erasing criminal records that include convictions for multiple murders, rapes, and other felonies. The dramatic increase in violent juvenile crime—including a rash of sensational schoolyard shootings in 1997–98—has prompted some states to lower the legal age at which offenders may be tried and sentenced as adults. Of 38 states with CAPITAL PUNISHMENT statutes in place, eight specify no minimum age for execution, but U.S. Supreme Court rulings have effectively barred the death penalty for defendants under 16. Twelve states permit execution at that age, four more at 17, while 13 (and the federal government) bar capital charges below 18 years of age. (New York requires a death row candidate to be at least 19.)

Harsh punishment for juvenile offenders, even multiple murderers, remains a subject of heated debate in American society. On balance, it appears that a majority of citizens believe defendants who commit "adult crimes"—murder, rape, and so on—should face adult penalties. Even some hard-liners rebel at the thought of executing killers younger than 16, but serial killers are recidivists by definition, and the tiny number of successful paroles in such cases—four of 1,500-plus offenders released to date without (apparently) killing again—is a telling argument against the view that "anyone can be reformed."

See also INCARCERATION; TRIAL

KALLINGER, Joseph Michael

Born December 11, 1936, in Philadelphia, Joseph was surrendered for adoption as an infant, finding a home with Austrian immigrants Stephen and Anna Kallinger in October 1938. His childhood was bizarre, to say the least, marked by parental abuse in the form of floggings with a cat-o'-nine-tails, beatings with a hammer, and repeated threats of emasculation. In the summer of 1944, Kallinger was sexually abused at knifepoint by a gang of older boys, prompting subsequent episodes in which he masturbated while clenching a knife in his fist.

Kallinger married his first wife at age 17, the stormy relationship producing 10 children before she abandoned their home for another man in September 1956. A year later, Joseph was hospitalized with a suspected brain lesion, but tests revealed a "psychopathological nervous disorder." Married a second time in April 1958, Kallinger soon torched his own home for amusement, reaping a fringe benefit of $1,600 from fire insurance. Committed to a state hospital in July 1959 following a suicide attempt, Kallinger would set fire to the family's second home on four separate occasions— twice in May 1963, once in August 1965, and again in October 1967.

By 1972 the Kallingers had six children at home, including two from his failed first marriage. On January 23 of that year, Joseph branded his oldest daughter's thigh with a hot iron as punishment for running away. Arrested a week later, he was found incompetent for trial, held for 60 days' mental evaluation, and ultimately ruled fit for trial in June. Conviction on child abuse charges earned him four years' probation with a provision for mandatory psychiatric treatment.

By 1974, Kallinger was reportedly hallucinating constantly, holding animated discussions with a disembodied head (dubbed "Charlie") and receiving personal "orders from God." The divine orders included demands that Kallinger murder young boys and sever their genitals, an urge that he confided to his son, 13-year-old Michael, on June 26. When Joe requested Michael's help, the boy responded with enthusiasm: "Glad to do it, Dad!" Eleven days later, they murdered José Collazo, a Puerto Rican youth, in Philadelphia, first torturing their victim and then cutting off his penis.

Kallinger next set his sights on one of his own children, Joseph Jr. In his first attempt Joe tried to make the boy back off a cliff, cartoon-style, while posing for photographs. Failing in that, he took both boys along on a July 25 arson run, bungling an attempt to trap Joe Jr. in a burning trailer. Finally, three days later, Kallinger and Michael drowned their victim at a demolition site; the body was recovered by authorities on August 9, 1974. Questioned as a suspect in the murder, Kallinger was not arrested due to lack of evidence.

That autumn, the father-son team began ranging farther afield in their search for victims. On November 22, they burglarized a house in Lindenwold, New Jersey, but no one was home. At their second stop, victim Joan Carty was tied to her bed and sexually assaulted by Joe Kallinger. Eleven days later, in Susquehanna Township, Pennsylvania, five hostages were bound and robbed at knifepoint, the Kallingers making off with $20,000 in cash and jewelry after slashing one woman's breast. Striking next in Homeland, Maryland—a Baltimore suburb—father and son held a woman captive in her home, forcing her to fellate Joe at gunpoint. On January

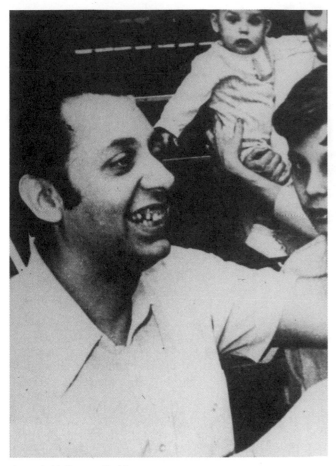

Joseph Kallinger (left) (Author's collection)

Kallinger received a mandatory life sentence to run consecutively with his time in Pennsylvania.

Kallinger's violent outbursts continued in prison, with Joseph setting himself on fire in March 1977. A month later, he assaulted a fellow inmate before lighting a fire on his cell block. In March 1978, he slashed another convict's throat in an unprovoked attack, but his victim survived. Ten years later, in televised interviews, Kallinger expressed his continuing desire to slaughter every person on earth, after which he hoped to commit suicide and "become God."

By that time, Kallinger had been tried and convicted (in January 1984) of murdering José Collazo and his own son Joseph Jr., drawing two more consecutive life sentences. Briefly transferred to Pennsylvania's Fairview State Hospital for the Criminally Insane in 1990, after a new spate of suicide attempts and "religious" hunger strikes, Kallinger was back in state prison on March 26, 1996, when he choked to death on his own vomit in the prison infirmary.

KEARNEY, Patrick Wayne

On July 5, 1977, authorities in Riverside, California, announced the confessions of two male suspects in a grisly series of "trash bag" murders, thought to include 15 victims in five different counties since 1973. The suspects, Patrick Kearney and David Douglas Hill, were charged in only two cases—both victims slain in March 1977—but on the same day, Kearney led detectives to six alleged body-dumping sites in Imperial County. Evidence recovered from Kearney's home, where Hill resided as a live-in lover, included fibers matched to those found on several corpses, plus a bloody hacksaw used in the dismemberment of certain victims.

The California "trash bag" case officially began on April 13, 1975, when the mutilated remains of 21-year-old Albert Rivera were discovered near San Juan Capistrano. By November, five more bodies had been found in Los Angeles, Orange, Riverside, and San Diego counties. The discovery of two more victims in March 1977 raised the body count to eight, and by that time police had their pattern. All the identified victims were gay; each was found nude, shot in the head with a similar weapon; several were dismembered or otherwise mutilated, their remains packaged in identical plastic garbage bags.

The final victim was 17-year-old John LaMay, last seen by his parents on March 13 when he left home to visit a friend named "Dave." Police entered the case five days later, after LaMay's dismembered remains were found beside a highway south of Corona. Friends of the victim identified "Dave" as David Hill, supplying homicide detectives with an address. Warrants were issued

6, the ritual was repeated in Dumont, New Jersey, with another female victim.

Two days later, on January 8, Kallinger and son invaded another home in Leonia, New Jersey, holding eight captives at gunpoint while they ransacked the house. Nurse Maria Fasching was stabbed to death for refusing Joe's order to bite off a male victim's penis, but Kallinger got careless on the getaway, discarding a bloody shirt near the scene. Officers traced the shirt to its owner and the Kallingers were arrested on January 17 by a joint raiding party of federal and state authorities. Two months later, Michael Kallinger was ruled delinquent but "salvageable," with murder charges dismissed in return for his guilty plea on two counts of robbery. He was placed on probation until his 25th birthday, in December 1982.

Joe Kallinger's first trial in Pennsylvania ended with a hung jury in June 1975. Three months later, at his retrial, he was convicted on nine felony counts and sentenced to prison for 30 to 80 years by a judge who called him "an evil man . . . utterly vile and depraved." Convicted of the New Jersey murder in October 1976, for Hill and his roommate, but the lovers remained at large until July 1 when they entered the Riverside County sheriff's office, pointed to their posters on the wall, and smilingly announced, "That's us."

A high school dropout from Lubbock, Texas, David Hill joined the army in 1960 but was soon discharged on diagnosis of an unspecified personality disorder (possibly related to his HOMOSEXUALITY). Back in Lubbock, he married his high school sweetheart, but the romance was short-lived. In 1962, he met Patrick Kearney, stationed with the air force in Texas, and the attraction was mutual. Hill divorced his wife in 1966 and moved to California with Kearney a year later. They were living together in Culver City, a Los Angeles suburb, when the long string of murders began. (The first victim, known only as "George," was buried behind Kearney's Culver City duplex in September 1968; detectives following the killer's directions unearthed his skeleton in July 1977.)

On July 14, 1977, Patrick Kearney was formally indicted on two counts of murder, including that of John LaMay. David Hill was released the same day, his charges dismissed as Kearney shouldered full responsibility for the slayings, telling police that he killed because "it excited him and gave him a feeling of dominance." By July 15, Kearney had signed confessions to 28 murders, with 12 of the cases confirmed by police. On December 21, he pled guilty on three counts of first-degree murder, receiving a sentence of life imprisonment.

Prosecutors launched the new year by charging Kearney with another 18 counts of murder in February 1978. Nine of those charges disposed of the first dozen victims in Kearney's confession; the others included two children, ages five and eight, along with four victims whose bodies were never recovered. On February 21,

"Trash Bag Killer" Patrick Kearney (right), with David Hill (Author's collection)

Kearney pled guilty on all counts, receiving another life sentence. If his original confessions were truthful, at least seven victims remain unidentified today.

KEMPER, Edmund Emil, III

The product of a broken and abusive home, belittled by a shrewish mother who occasionally locked him in the basement when he failed to meet her standards of behavior, Edmund Kemper grew up timid and resentful, nursing a perception of his own inadequacy that gave rise to morbid fantasies of death and mutilation. As a child he often played a "game" in which his sisters took the part of executioners, with Kemper as their victim, writhing in imaginary death throes as they "threw the switch." Preoccupied with visions of decapitation and dismemberment, he cut the heads and hands off of his sister's doll—a MODUS OPERANDI that he would repeat, as an adult with human victims.

Before the age of 10, Kemper graduated to living targets, burying the family cat alive and subsequently cutting off its head, returning with the gruesome trophy to his room, where it was placed on proud display. Despite his tender age, he brooded over fantasies of love and sex, with violence playing an inevitable role. Unable to express affection in a normal way, he showed the WARNING SIGNS of latent necrophilia. One afternoon, discussing Edmund's childish crush upon a grade-school teacher, Kemper's sister asked him why he didn't simply kiss the woman. Kemper answered, deadpan, "If I kiss her, I would have to kill her first." A second family cat fell victim to his urges, this one hacked with a machete and the pieces hidden in the closet until they were accidentally discovered by his mother.

Branding her son "a real weirdo," Kemper's mother first packed him off to live with her estranged husband, and then—after running away—the boy was delivered to his paternal grandparents, dwelling on a remote California ranch. There, in August 1963, 14-year-old Kemper shot his grandmother with a .22-caliber rifle, afterward stabbing her body repeatedly with a kitchen knife. When his grandfather came home, Kemper shot the old man as well, leaving him dead in the yard.

Interrogated by authorities, Kemper could only say that "I just wondered how it would feel to shoot Grandma." He regretted not stripping her corpse, and that statement, along with the motiveless violence displayed in his actions, got Kemper committed to the state's maximum-security hospital at Atascadero. In 1969, a 21-year-old behemoth grown to six-feet-nine and some 300 pounds, Kemper was paroled to his mother's custody over the objections of state psychiatrists.

During Ed's enforced absence, his mother had settled in Santa Cruz, a college town whose population

"Coed Killer" Edmund Kemper (Author's collection)

boasted thousands of attractive coeds. For the next two years, through 1970 and 1971, Kemper bided his time, holding odd jobs and cruising the highways in his leisure time, picking up dozens of young female hitchhikers, refining his "line" until he knew that he could put them totally at ease. Some evenings, he would frequent a saloon patronized by off-duty policemen, rubbing shoulders with the law and soaking up their tales of crime, becoming friendly with a number of detectives who would later be assigned to track him down.

On May 7, 1972, Kemper picked up two 18-year-old roommates from Fresno State College, Mary Ann Pesce and Anita Luchessa. Driving them to a secluded culdesac, he stabbed both girls to death, then took their bodies home, and hid them in his room. Delighted with his "trophies," Kemper took Polaroid snapshots, dissected the corpses, and sexually assaulted various organs before tiring of the game. Bundling the remains into plastic bags, he buried the truncated bodies in the Santa Cruz mountains, tossing the heads into a roadside ravine.

Four months later, on September 14, Kemper offered a ride to 15-year-old Aiko Koo. Suffocating her with his large hands, Kemper raped her corpse on the spot and then carried it home for dissection. Koo's severed head

was resting in the trunk of Kemper's car next morning when he met with state psychiatrists who pronounced him "safe," recommending that his juvenile record be sealed for Kemper's future protection. Following the interview, he buried Koo's remains near a religious camp located in the mountains.

Another four months passed before the "Coed Killer" struck again, on January 9, 1973. Picking up student Cindy Schall, Kemper forced her into the trunk of his car at gunpoint, then shot her to death. Driving back to his mother's house, he carried the corpse to his room and there had sex with it in his bed. Afterward, Kemper dissected Schall's body in the bathtub, bagging the remains and tossing them over a cliff into the sea. Schall's head was buried in the backyard of his mother's home, facing up toward the house, and Kemper would later remark to his mother that "people really look up to you around here."

By this time, various remains of Kemper's victims had been found and officers were on the case. Apparently, none of them had the least suspicion that their friend, Ed Kemper, was the man they sought, and some felt comfortable enough in Kemper's company to brief him on the progress of their ongoing investigation. Smiling, often buying the next round, Kemper was all ears.

On February 5, 1973, Kemper picked up 23-year-old Rosalind Thorpe and another hitchhiker, Alice Lin. Both young women were shot to death in the car, then stacked in the trunk like so much excess luggage. Driving home, Kemper ate dinner and waited for his mother to retire before stepping outside and decapitating both corpses as they lay in the trunk. Unsatisfied, he carried Lin's body inside and raped it on the floor. Returning to the car, he chopped off her hands as a casual afterthought.

With spring's arrival, Kemper's frenzy escalated, coming back full circle to his home and family. He toyed with the idea of killing everybody on his block as "a demonstration to the authorities" but finally dismissed the notion. Instead, on Easter weekend, Kemper turned on his mother, hammering her skull in as she slept. Decapitating her, he raped the headless corpse, then jammed her severed larynx down the garbage disposal. ("It seemed appropriate," he told police, "as much as she'd bitched and screamed and yelled at me over so many years.") Her head was propped up on the mantle for use as a dart board.

Still not sated, Kemper telephoned a friend of his mother, Sally Hallett, and invited her over for a "surprise" dinner in his mother's honor. Upon her arrival, Kemper clubbed her over the head, strangled her to death, then decapitated her. The headless body was deposited in bed, while he wandered off to sleep in his mother's room.

On Easter Sunday, Kemper started driving east with no destination in mind. He got as far as Colorado before pulling over to a roadside telephone booth and calling police in Santa Cruz. Several attempts were necessary before his friends would accept his confession and local officers were dispatched to make the arrest while Kemper waited patiently in his car.

In his detailed confessions, Kemper admitted slicing flesh from the legs of at least two victims, cooking it in a macaroni casserole, and devouring it as a means of "possessing" his prey. He also acknowledged removing teeth, along with bits of hair and skin from his victims, retaining them as grisly keepsakes, TROPHIES of the hunt. Described as sane by state psychiatrists, Kemper was convicted on eight counts of murder. Asked what punishment he considered fitting for his crimes, the defendant replied, "Death by torture." Instead, he was sentenced to life imprisonment with the possibility of parole. Confined at Vacaville, he joined an inmate volunteer group recording books for the blind, and by January 1987 had completed more books than any other prisoner, with some 5,000 hours of recordings behind him. He remains incarcerated at this writing, with six parole bids rejected to date.

KISS, Bela

A family man and amateur astrologer, Hungarian Bela Kiss began his career as a serial murderer relatively late in life. In February 1912, at 40 years of age, Kiss moved to the village of Czinkota with his wife Marie, some 15 years his junior. Within a matter of weeks, Marie had found herself a lover, one Paul Bikari, and in December 1912, Kiss sadly told his neighbors that the couple had run off together, leaving him to pine alone. In place of his wife, Kiss hired an elderly housekeeper. She, in turn, learned to ignore the parade of women who came to spend time with Czinkota's newly eligible bachelor.

About that same time, Kiss began collecting large metal drums, informing the curious village constable that they were filled with gasoline, expected to be scarce with the approach of war in Europe. Budapest authorities, meanwhile, were seeking information on the disappearance of two widows, named Schmeidak and Varga, who had not made contact with their friends or relatives for several weeks. Both women had last been seen in the company of a man named Hoffmann, said to live near the Margaret Bridge in Budapest, but he had also disappeared without a trace. Czinkota's constable was generally aware of the investigation, but he saw no reason to connect Herr Hoffmann with the quiet, unassuming Bela Kiss.

In November 1914, Kiss was drafted into military service, leaving for the front as soon as he was sworn into the ranks and issued gear. Another 18 months would pass before officials in Czinkota were informed that Kiss had died in combat, one more grim statistic for the casualty rosters in that bloody spring of 1916. He was forgotten by the townsfolk until June when soldiers visited Czinkota in a search for stockpiled gasoline.

The village constable remembered Kiss and his cache of metal drums and led a squad of soldiers to the dead man's home. Inside the house, the searchers turned up seven drums . . . but they contained no gasoline. Instead, each drum contained the naked body of a woman, strangled and immersed in alcohol. The drawers of Kiss's bureau overflowed with cards and letters from women responding to newspaper advertisements, purchased by Kiss in the name of Hoffmann, a self-described "lonely widower seeking female companionship."

Czinkota's constable recalled that there had been more drums—and many more, at that. A search of the surrounding countryside revealed another 17, each with a pickled corpse inside. Authorities from Budapest identified the missing widows, and Marie Kiss occupied another drum; her lover, Paul Bikari, was the only male among the 24 recovered victims.

Police theorized that Bela Kiss had slain his wife and her clandestine lover in a jealous rage, disposing of their bodies in a fashion that—he thought—eliminated any possibility of subsequent discovery. The crime apparently unleashed some hidden mania, and Kiss spent the next two years pursuing lonely women with a passion, bilking several of their savings prior to strangling them and sealing them inside his makeshift funeral vaults. It was a grisly case, but Kiss had gone to face a higher court.

Or had he?

In the spring of 1919, Kiss was sighted on the Margaret Bridge in Budapest, "Herr Hoffmann's" antebellum stomping ground. Police investigation proved that Kiss had switched his papers with a battlefield fatality, assuming the dead man's identity to make good his escape. That knowledge brought detectives no closer to their man, however, for Kiss has slipped the net again.

The futile search went on. In 1924, a deserter from the French Foreign Legion told officers of the Sûreté about a fellow legionnaire who entertained the troops with tales of his proficiency with the garrote. The soldier's name was Hoffman, and he matched descriptions of Bela Kiss, but the lead was another dead end. By the time Hungarian police were informed, legionnaire "Hoffman" had also deserted, vanishing without a trace.

In 1932, a New York homicide detective, Henry Oswald, was convinced that he had sighted Bela Kiss, emerging from the Times Square subway station. Nicknamed "Camera Eye" by colleagues because of his uncanny memory for faces, Oswald was unshakable in his belief that Kiss—who would have been approaching 70—was living somewhere in New York. Unfortunately, Times Square crowds prevented Oswald from pursuing Kiss, and he could only watch in helpless rage as his intended quarry disappeared.

In 1936, a rumor spread that Kiss was working as a janitor in an apartment building on New York's Sixth Avenue. Again, he managed to evade police—if he was ever there at all—and there the trail grew cold. Whatever finally became of Bela Kiss remains a mystery, beyond solution with the passage of more than six decades. In Hungary, he is remembered as the one who got away.

KNOWLES, Paul John

A Florida native, born in 1946, Knowles logged his first arrest at 19, spending roughly six months of each year thereafter in jail on various convictions for burglary and auto theft. He was serving time in Raiford when he began corresponding with California divorcée Angela Covic, and she visited the prison long enough to accept his proposal of marriage, shelling out money for lawyers to win his release. Parole came through in May 1974, and Knowles flew directly to San Francisco for the nuptials, but Covic had changed her mind, warned off by a psychic who foresaw the entry of a new, dangerous man in her life. The night she dumped him, Knowles allegedly went out and killed three people on the streets of San Francisco, but his claim has not been verified.

Back home in Jacksonville, Knowles was jailed after a bar fight, but he picked a lock and escaped on July 26, 1974. That night, he invaded the home of 65-year-old Alice Curtis, leaving her bound and gagged as he ransacked her house for money, finally taking off in her car. She choked to death on the gag, but Knowles hung around town for a few days, using her vehicle, until police connected him with the crime and his picture began turning up on TV. Preparing to drop the hot car on a quiet residential street, he spied 11-year-old Lillian Anderson and her seven-year-old sister Mylette, recognizing them as friends of his mother. Convinced the girls had seen him and would notify police, he kidnapped both of them and dumped their strangled bodies in a swamp outside of town.

The next day, in Atlantic Beach, Florida, Knowles broke into the home of Marjorie Howe, strangling her with a nylon stocking and stealing her television set. His next victim was a teenage "Jane Doe" hitchhiker, raped and strangled for sport as he drifted aimlessly, working his way north. On August 23, he invaded the home of Kathie Pierce at Musella, strangling her with a telephone cord while her three-year-old son looked on but leaving the child unharmed.

On September 3, Knowles met businessman William Bates at a tavern in Lima, Ohio, sharing a few drinks before he strangled Bates and dumped his body in some nearby woods, where it would be discovered in October. Stealing money, credit cards, and Bates's car, Knowles made his way to Sacramento, California, then doubled back through Utah, pausing at Ely, Nevada, long enough to murder campers Emmett and Lois Johnson on September 18.

Three days later, passing through Sequin, Texas, he spotted a female motorist stranded at roadside and stopped "to help," raping her before he strangled her to death and dragged her body through a tangled barbed-wire fence. On September 23, he met beautician Ann Dawson in Birmingham and instantly caught her fancy; they traveled together, at her expense, until Knowles tired of the game and killed her on September 29. Her body has never been found.

Knowles drifted on through Oklahoma, Missouri, Iowa, and Minnesota, apparently keeping his nose clean, leaving no bodies behind. By October 19, he needed a "fix," and he found it in Woodford, Virginia, barging into the home of 53-year-old Doris Hovey, shooting her dead with her own husband's rifle, then wiping his prints from the gun and placing it beside her

Paul Knowles in custody (Wide World API)

body. Afterward, police could find no signs of sex or robbery to offer them a motive in the case.

Still driving William Bates's stolen car, Knowles picked up two hitchhikers in Key West, planning to kill them both, but his scheme went awry when a policeman stopped them for traffic violations. The careless officer let Knowles go with a warning, but the experience had shaken Paul. Dropping his passengers off in Miami, Knowles phoned his lawyer for advice. Rejecting the suggestion of surrender, he met the attorney long enough to hand over a taped confession, then slipped out of town before police were informed of his presence.

On November 6, in Macon, Georgia, Knowles befriended Carswell Carr and was invited home to spend the night. Over drinks, he stabbed Carr to death and then strangled Carr's 15-year-old daughter, failing in his attempt to have sex with her corpse. In the wake of his flight from Macon, Knowles was also suspected in the November 2 murder of hitchhiker Edward Hilliard, found in some nearby woods, and his companion Debbie Griffin (still among the missing).

Barhopping in Atlanta on November 8, Knowles met British journalist Sandy Fawkes, impressing her with his "gaunt good looks." They spent the night together, but Knowles was unable to perform in bed, and he failed repeatedly at sex over the next two days, suggesting possible impotence with a willing companion. They separated on November 10, but Knowles picked up one of Sandy's friends, Susan MacKenzie, the next day, demanding sex at gunpoint. She escaped and notified police, but when patrolmen tried to stop him, Knowles brandished a sawed-off shotgun and made his escape.

A short time later in West Palm Beach, he invaded the home of invalid Beverly Mabee, abducting her sister and stealing their car, dropping his hostage off in Fort Pierce, Florida, the following night. A police officer recognized the stolen car next morning and pulled Knowles over, but Knowles was faster on the draw. Taking the officer hostage, he drove away in the patrol car, using its siren to stop motorist James Meyer, switching cars a second time. Burdened with two prisoners now, Knowles handcuffed both men to a tree in Pulaski County, Georgia, and shot each one in the head at close range.

A short time later, Knowles tried to crash through a police roadblock, losing control of his car and smashing into a tree. A chaotic foot chase ensued, with Knowles pursued by dogs and helicopters; he was finally cornered by an armed civilian on November 17. In custody, he claimed 35 murders, but only 18 could be verified. On November 18, while being transferred to maximum security, Knowles made a grab for the sheriff's revolver, and FBI Agent Ron Angel shot him dead in his tracks.

KODAIRA Yoshio

Arguably Japan's most prolific serial killer of modern times, Kodaira Yoshio, born in 1905, was the son of a violent alcoholic and was described by his first-grade teacher as "inattentive and listless; gets into fights on a daily basis." The pattern continued throughout elementary school, Kodaira further handicapped by a severe stutter, scraping by with low grades and graduating—barely—with the rank of 21st in a class of 23 students. Apprenticed to a Tokyo metalworks in lieu of higher education, he drifted through a series of blue-collar jobs, none lasting more than a few months. An unwed father at age 18, he joined the Imperial Japanese Navy to escape his parental obligations.

As a seaman of the Japanese fleet, Kodaira soon became accustomed to the low-rent brothels in various ports of call. By 1927, he was involved in Japanese actions against mainland China, participating in various atrocities that included the rape and murder of helpless civilians. As he later described one incident, "Four or five of my comrades and I entered a Chinese home, tied up the father, and locked him in the closet. We stole their jewelry and raped the women. We even bayoneted a pregnant woman and pulled out the fetus from her stomach. I also engaged in those depraved actions."

And loved every minute of it.

Back in civilian life by 1932, Kodaira married the daughter of a Shinto priest over her father's objections. The union was a stormy one and climaxed when Kodaira settled one argument by beating his father-in-law to death with an iron bar, injuring six other family members in the process. Sentenced to 15 years at hard labor, he was released in the general amnesty of 1940 and found work as a civilian employee at a naval facility in Tokyo. Most of his subordinates were female, and Kodaira made a habit of spying on them as they bathed after work. On May 25, 1945, he raped and strangled one of them, 19-year-old Miyazaki Mitsuko, and hid her corpse behind an air raid shelter on the premises.

Japan was under frequent air attack by that time, her island fortresses in the Pacific falling to amphibious invaders, and Kodaira's crime went undiscovered while the chaos of the war distracted the police from his crimes. Encouraged by his success, he raped and strangled 30-year-old Ishikawa Yori on June 22. Three weeks later, on July 12, he repeated the procedure with 32-year-old Nakamura Mitsuko. A fourth victim, 22-year-old Kondo Kazuko, died on July 15. Matsushita Yoshie, age 21, was killed on September 28; 17-year-old Shinokawa Tatsue followed on October 31; and 19-year-old Baba Hiroko on December 30.

Kodaira took a six-month breather after that, claiming his next victim—15-year-old Abe Yoshiko—on June

30, 1946. Two more would follow before he was finally caught by police.

With no more female employees to victimize, Kodaira had worked out a new approach for himself, loitering in public places, offering to help young women purchase food or other items on Tokyo's thriving black market. So it was that Kodaira met 17-year-old Midorikawa Ryuko on July 10, striking up a friendship that included visits to her home, where he foolishly gave his real name to the young woman's parents. Ryuko disappeared on August 6, leaving home to meet Kodaira for an alleged job interview; her nude corpse was found at Tokyo's Zojoji Temple a few days later. A second body, found nearby, was identified as Shinokawa Tatsue, reported missing by her parents in Shibuya.

Police went looking for Kodaira after they obtained his name from Ryuko's parents, and he freely confessed his crimes with no plea for leniency and was sentenced to death on August 20, 1947. (In addition to the murders, he confessed to 30 or more rapes where the victims survived.) Two years and two months later, on the morning of October 5, 1949, Kodaira was hanged at Miyagi Prison.

In the wake of his execution, Japanese author Edogawa Rampo tried to make sense of the case. "The type of crime he committed was not particularly unusual," Edogawa wrote, "but to have repeated it, using the same methods, was definitely unusual. This incident can be attributed to the relaxation of morals that has occurred since the end of the war. This is because all of us—the criminal, his victims, and society at large—all bear some guilt. Moreover, the atmosphere of social neglect brought on by Japan's defeat has brought out the beast in such individuals, particularly men who have returned from battle."

Edogawa did not not seem to think that "the beast" had been *deliberately* evoked by Japanese wartime tactics reflected in such incidents as the Rape of Nanking, where at least 300,000 unarmed civilians were murdered in cold blood, girls and women raped by the tens of thousands in an orgy of violence officially condoned—and shared—by superior officers. It was, perhaps, more comforting to share the blame among Kodaira's victims than to recognize the truth, namely, that Imperial Japan had deliberately, consciously produced a generation of pitiless rapists and killers.

KOKORALEIS, Andrew and Thomas *See*
"CHICAGO RIPPERS"

KORDIYEH, Gholomreza Khoshruy Kuran

An Iranian serial killer born in 1969, Gholomreza Kordiyeh logged his first arrest at age 24 on charges of kidnapping and rape. He escaped from custody en route to trial and remained at large for another four years, graduating to murder in February 1997. Over the next five months, he killed at least nine women, impersonating a cab driver as he cruised Tehran's streets by night, in search of victims. The women who entered his "taxi" were raped and stabbed repeatedly, then doused with gasoline and set on fire in an effort to disguise Kordiyeh's crimes. Some of the bodies were imperfectly consumed by flame, allowing investigators to count up to 30 stab wounds on a single corpse.

Police dubbed their quarry the "Tehran Vampire" after his night-prowling habits but were confounded in their search for the slayer until Kordiyeh got careless, allowing two victims to slip through his grasp. The women helped authorities prepare a suspect sketch, and they swiftly identified Kordiyeh following his June arrest for acting suspicious at a Tehran shopping mall. Confronted with the evidence—including human bloodstains in his car—Kordiyeh duly confessed to the murders. His trial was broadcast live on state-run television for a fascinated audience, and the vampire was sentenced to hang.

Befitting the occasion, Kordiyeh's execution on August 12, 1997, was a public spectacle. Twenty thousand spectators turned out for the event, chanting "Allahu Akbar" ("God is great") while Kordiyeh received a flogging of 214 lashes from relatives of his victims. That ritual complete, the semiconscious stalker was hanged from a bright yellow construction crane, erected near the scene of his crimes. His last words, before the crane hoisted him aloft, were: "I borrowed money from no one, and I owe none to anyone. I ask God for forgiveness for what I did."

Iranian authorities, meanwhile, were less than satisfied with the result of the public display, fearing that Kordiyeh's example might inspire lethal copycats. Before year's end, another Tehran cabbie was arrested for attempting to molest a female passenger. According to press reports, the would-be rapist boasted to police, "I'm going to be the next Tehran Vampire."

KRAFT, Randy Steven

Shortly after 1:00 A.M. on May 14, 1983, highway patrol officers in Orange County, California, stopped a weaving motorist suspected of intoxication. The driver, Randy Kraft, immediately left his vehicle, all smiles as he approached the cruiser to conduct his business. Growing more suspicious by the moment, the officers walked Kraft back to his car, where they found Terry Gambrel, a 25-year-old marine, slumped dead in the passenger's seat. He had been strangled with a belt, and Kraft was booked on suspicion of murder and held in lieu of $250,000 bail.

"Scorecard Killer" Randy Kraft in court (right) (Wide World AP)

A background check on Kraft revealed a 1966 arrest for lewd conduct in Huntington Beach, with charges dismissed. He graduated from college a year later with a degree in economics and spent a year in the air force before he was discharged on grounds related to HOMOSEXUALITY. In 1975, Kraft was arrested in Long Beach for lewd conduct with another man; on conviction he spent five days in jail and paid a $125 fine.

The search of Kraft's impounded auto turned up 47 color photographs depicting several young men, some of them naked, some apparently unconscious—or worse. A briefcase in the trunk contained a notebook filled with more than 60 cryptic messages in some sort of personal code. A tour of Kraft's home uncovered further evidence, convincing the authorities they had a most prolific killer on their hands. Kraft's photographs depicted three young men whose deaths were still unsolved in southern California. Robert Loggins, a teenage marine, had been found dead in September 1980; now, police had snapshots of his naked body stretched out on a couch in Kraft's home. Roger De Vaul, age 20, was last seen alive while hitchhiking with a friend, Geoffrey Nelson, on February 12, 1983. Nelson's body was found in Garden Grove that afternoon; De Vaul's had turned up the following day. Eric Church, another chronic hitchhiker, was found dead in Orange County on March 27, 1983.

And the body count kept rising. Fibers from a rug in Kraft's garage matched those recovered from the corpse of 18-year-old Scott Hughes, discarded along the Riverside Freeway in April 1978. Personal items recovered from Kraft's home included property stolen from three murder victims in Oregon, plus two items belonging to a man found dead near Grand Rapids, Michigan, in December 1982. Investigators learned that Kraft had worked for a Santa Monica—based aerospace firm between June 1980 and January 1983, visiting company offices in Oregon and Michigan at the times of unsolved murders in both states.

As names were added to the list of victims, prosecutors cracked the code in Kraft's notebook. Thus, "2 in 1 Hitch" referred to the double murder of Nelson and De Vaul. "Marine Carson" was a reference to Richard Keith, a young marine last seen in Carson, California, whose strangled body was found in Laguna Hills in June 1978. "Jail Out" described the case of Ronald Young, found stabbed in Irvine hours after his release from the Orange County jail on June 11, 1978. "Parking Lot" recalled memories of an eight-year-old case in which Keith Crotwell had vanished on March 26, 1975. Fishermen found his severed head days later, off the coast of Long Beach, and his skeleton was finally recovered in October. Kraft was briefly questioned in that case, and while he admitted meeting Crotwell *in a parking lot* the day he vanished, officers had not considered him a suspect in the crime. "Euclid" stood for another young marine, Scott Hughes, discarded on the Euclid Street freeway ramp in Anaheim.

The list went on and on, with each notation matched to yet another unsolved homicide. A prosecutor working on the case gave Kraft his nickname, remarking to journalists that "What we have here is a true *scorecard killer.*"

Eventually charged with 16 murders—and strongly suspected of 51 others—Kraft delayed his trial for five years with various legal maneuvers. The trial itself set a new record for Orange County, dragging on for 13 months, but Kraft was finally convicted on all counts in May 1989. The penalty phase of his trial took another four months, with the jury recommending death on August 11, and Kraft was formally condemned on November 29. Confined on death row at San Quentin, he whiles away the hours playing bridge with fellow serial killers DOUGLAS CLARK, LAWRENCE BITFAKER, and (until his 1996 execution) WILLIAM BONIN. Another occasional pastime of Kraft's is frivolous litigation: in 1993 he filed a $60 million libel suit against the publisher and author of a book about his case, claiming the volume had unfairly portrayed him as a "sick, twisted man," thereby scuttling his "prospects for future employment"! The lawsuit was dismissed by California's Supreme Court in June 1994.

KROLL, Joachim

A nomadic German sex killer, Kroll lived in the vicinity of Duisburg, filling his bachelor apartment with electronic gadgets and inflatable sex dolls, frequently strangling the latter with one hand while he masturbated with the other. Too nervous and shy for sex with conscious partners, he turned to rape and murder at age 22, killing so often over the next two decades that he lost count of his victims. In the 1960s Kroll tried CANNIBALISM on a whim, enjoying it so much that he kept up the practice, stalking "tender" victims in an effort to reduce his grocery bills.

Kroll's first remembered victim was 19-year-old Irmgard Strehl, raped and murdered in a barn near the village of Walstede during February 1955. Twelve-year-old Erika Schuletter was the next to die, raped and strangled at Kirchhellen in 1956. Three years later and miles away, he killed Klara Jesmer in the woods near Rheinhausen on June 17, 1959. Sixteen-year-old Manuela Knodt was raped and murdered near Bredeney, south of Essen, with slices cut from her buttocks and thighs in the first slaying publicly attributed to the man police would dub the "Ruhr Hunter."

On April 23, 1962, 13-year-old Petra Griese was raped and killed at Rees, near Walsum, both buttocks sliced off along with her left forearm and hand. The Hunter was still stalking Walsum on June 4 when 13-

Joachim Kroll, the "Ruhr Hunter" (Author's collection)

year-old Monica Tafel vanished on her way to school. Searchers found her body in a nearby rye field, steaks carved from her buttocks and the back of her thighs.

Kroll sometimes seemed to change his pattern in an effort to confuse police. No meat was taken when he murdered 12-year-old Barbara Bruder in Burscheid during 1962. In August 1965 at Grossenbaum, he crept up on a pair of young lovers, stabbing a tire on their car, then fatally knifing the driver, Hermann Schmitz, when he stepped out to investigate the noise. In Marl, Kroll raped and murdered Ursula Rolling on September 13, 1966, rebounding three months later to kill five-year-old Ilona Harke at Wuppertal, slicing steaks from her buttocks and shoulders.

Kroll's luck nearly ran out in 1967 when he settled briefly in Grafenhausen, befriending local children who began to call him "Uncle." Luring a 10-year-old girl into a nearby field one afternoon, he promised to "show her a rabbit" but produced obscene photos instead, hoping the child might become sexually aroused. Instead, she was horrified, bolting for safety as Kroll made a grab for her throat, and he fled Grafenhausen the same day before police could begin asking troublesome questions.

On July 12, 1969, Kroll invaded the home of 61-year-old Maria Hettgen in Hueckeswagen, strangling her to death and raping her corpse in the front hall. Reverting to children on May 21, 1970, he waylaid 13-year-old Jutta Ranh in Breitscheid, discarding her strangled body after he had satisfied his lust. In 1976, 10-year-old Karin Toepfer was raped and strangled on her way to school, in Dinslaken Voerde.

Kroll's arrogance defeated him in July 1976 when he claimed his next victim in his own neighborhood of Laar, a Duisburg suburb. Four-year-old Marion Ketter was reported missing from a nearby playground, and police were asking questions door-to-door when they heard a curious story from one of Kroll's neighbors. According to their witness, Kroll had warned them that the upstairs toilet in their block of flats was clogged "with guts." A plumber quickly verified the statement, flushing a child's lungs and other organs out of the pipe, and detectives went calling on Kroll. In his apartment they discovered plastic bags of human flesh stored in the freezer; on the stove, a tiny hand was boiling in a pot with carrots and potatoes.

Convinced that they had bagged the Hunter, officers were stunned by Kroll's long-running litany of rape and murder. He remembered 14 victims, but he really couldn't say if there were more, a circumstance that left detectives free to speculate upon his final body count. With CAPITAL PUNISHMENT abolished in Germany after World War II, Kroll received the maximum possible punishment of life in prison.

KURTEN, Peter

Born in Koln-Mulheim, Germany, in 1883, Peter Kurten was the product of a violent, abusive childhood. Thirteen members of his family existed in a single room, the atmosphere heavily charged with sexual tension. Kurten's father, a brutal alcoholic, frequently compelled his wife to strip for sex in front of the assembled children, and he later went to prison for attempting to rape his own daughter. Peter likewise molested his sisters on occasion, and he was further influenced by a sadistic dogcatcher who lived in the same building. As a child, Kurten frequently watched the man torture his dogs and was instructed in the art of masturbating animals for sport.

Kurten committed his first murders at age nine when he pushed a playmate from a raft on the banks of the Rhine. A second boy jumped in to help the first, and Kurten managed to push them both under the raft, where they drowned. As in the case of CARROLL EDWARD COLE a half-century later, these youthful murders were dismissed by negligent authorities as "accidental" deaths.

About age 12, Kurten moved with his family to Dusseldorf. Already twisted in his view of sexuality, he masturbated compulsively, attempting intercourse with his sisters and various schoolgirls. From age 13 he also practiced bestiality with sheep, pigs, and goats, deriving special satisfaction when he stabbed sheep to death during intercourse.

In his early teens Kurten ran away from home to live as a nomadic robber, choosing girls and women as his prey. Back home in Dusseldorf at age 16, he briefly worked as an apprentice molder, but his master proved abusive, and Kurten absconded with cash from the till, settling in Coblenz with a prostitute who thrived on violence and perversion. Kurten logged his first arrest in Coblenz, one of 17 indictments that would land him in jail for a total of 27 years over the course of his life. Released in 1899, he learned his parents had divorced and Kurten promptly moved in with another masochistic hooker twice his age.

Kurten claimed his first adult murder in November 1899, strangling a girl during sex in the Grafenberger Wald outside Dusseldorf, but no body was found and his victim may have survived. He was jailed twice for fraud in 1900, then received another two years for attempting to shoot a girl with a rifle. Theft charges kept him behind bars until 1904, where he occupied his time with fantasies of violent sex and vengeance on society.

Drafted by the military on release from prison, Kurten soon deserted. He had started setting fires by that time, drawing sensual excitement from the flames. His targets normally were barns and hayricks, torched

Peter Kurten, the "Vampire of Dusseldorf" (Author's collection)

in hopes that sleeping tramps might be burned alive. Sentenced to seven years on a theft charge in 1905, Kurten later claimed to have poisoned several inmates in the prison hospital. On release in 1912, he raped a servant girl and shortly after that was found accosting women in a local restaurant. A waiter tried to intervene and Kurten drove him off with pistol fire, earning another year in prison for his trouble.

On May 25, 1913, Kurten broke into a pub in Koln-Mulheim while the owners were away. Creeping up to their quarters, he found their 13-year-old daughter, Christine Klein, asleep in bed. He cut her throat and raped her with his fingers, dropping a handkerchief with his initials at the scene, but luck was with him. The victim's father, Peter Klein, had recently quarreled with his brother Otto, the latter threatening to do something Klein "would remember all his life." Otto Klein was indicted and tried for the murder, finally cleared for lack of evidence, while Kurten followed the proceedings with amusement.

Stepping up his schedule, Kurten found another sleeping victim but was frightened off by members of her family. In separate incidents he struck a man and woman with a hatchet, reaching climax at the sight of blood. He also torched another haystack and attempted strangulation of two women, prior to drawing eight more years in jail on unrelated charges.

Freed in 1921, he moved to Altenburg, informing new acquaintances that he had been a prisoner of war in Russia. Kurten met his future wife in Altenburg, a woman who had served five years in jail for shooting her fiancé. She initially rejected his proposals but agreed to marry Kurten when he threatened her with murder.

Settling down to a peculiar version of domestic bliss, Kurten endured a "normal" life for several years before he had a relapse and was charged with sexually assaulting servant girls on two occasions. Moving back to Dusseldorf in 1925, he was delighted by a blood-red sunset on the night of his arrival. Kurten took it as a sign. He was preparing to launch his final reign of terror.

Based upon his subsequent confessions, Kurten bore responsibility, by 1928, in four attempted strangulations (all of women) and a rash of fires that claimed two homes and 15 other targets. Still, he did not hit his stride until the early weeks of 1929. On February 3 he stabbed a woman 24 times and left her lying in the street, but she recovered after months of care. Ten days later, Kurten scored his first fatality of the new campaign, stabbing a mechanic 20 times at Flingern.

On March 9, eight-year-old Rose Ohliger was found at a construction site in Dusseldorf; she had been raped, stabbed 13 times, and efforts had been made to burn the corpse with paraffin. Comparing notes, detectives found their last three victims had been marked by stab wounds to the temples, but the choice of victims—first a woman, then a man, and now a child—apparently ruled out a pattern in the case.

In April 1929, police picked up a simple-minded transient for assaulting local women, but they found no evidence connecting him with homicide, and he was sent to an asylum. Kurten rested from his labors, meanwhile, dallying with servant girls at home and "playfully" attempting strangulation after sex. Returning with a vengeance during August, Kurten later claimed that he had choked a woman by the name of "Ann" and dumped her body in the river, but no trace of her was ever found. Before the month was out, three other victims—one a man—were stabbed in hit-and-run

attacks in Dusseldorf, but all survived. On August 24, two children—five-year-old Gertrude Hamacher and 14-year-old Louise Lenzen—were found dead near their homes, both strangled, with their throats cut. One day later, Gertrude Schulte was accosted on her way to see the fair, at Neuss. Confronted with a crude demand for sex, she said that she would rather die. "Well, die, then," Kurten answered, stabbing Gertrude several times before he fled. She lived and gave police a fair description of her would-be rapist, but detectives still rejected the suggestion of a single man behind their recent crime wave.

Kurten tried to strangle three more women in September, hurling one victim into the river for good measure, but all survived. Ida Reuter was less fortunate, her skull crushed with a hammer near the end of the month. Another hammer victim, Elizabeth Dirries, was killed at Grafenbery on October 12. On the 25th, two more women were bludgeoned in separate attacks, but both recovered from their wounds.

Five-year-old Gertrude Alberman was reported missing in Dusseldorf on November 7, her body recovered two days later after Kurten sent directions to a local newspaper. The child had been strangled, then stabbed 36 times. Following Kurten's instructions, police also unearthed the remains of Maria Hahn, stabbed 20 times, raped after death, and buried in mid-August.

Kurten's luck ran out on May 14, 1930, when he picked up Maria Budlick and took her home for a meal, thereafter strolling through the woods with sex and strangulation on his mind. Maria fought him off, and Kurten unaccountably released her after she assured him that she had forgotten his address. Police were summoned and, in custody, their suspect launched into a marathon confession that would send him to his death.

Kurten's trial opened on April 13, 1931, and ended eight days later. Jurors needed only 90 minutes to convict him on nine counts of murder, sternly rejecting Kurten's INSANITY DEFENSE. Sentenced to death by beheading, Kurten informed a psychiatrist that his greatest thrill of all time would be hearing the blood spurt from his own severed neck. He went to the guillotine, all smiles, on July 2, 1931.

LAKE, Leonard, and NG, Charles Chitat

A native of San Francisco, Leonard Lake was born July 20, 1946. His mother sought to teach him pride in the human body by encouraging Lake to photograph nude girls, including his sisters and cousins, but the "pride" soon developed into a precocious obsession with pornography. In adolescence, Lake extorted sexual favors from his sisters, in return for protection from the violent outbursts of a younger brother, Donald. By his teens, Leonard displayed a fascination with the concept of collecting "slaves." Lake joined the Marine Corps in 1966 and served a noncombatant tour in Vietnam, as a radar operator. He also underwent two years of psychiatric therapy at Camp Pendleton for unspecified mental problems before his ultimate discharge in 1971.

Back in civilian life, Lake moved to San Jose and got married, developing a local reputation as a gun buff, "survivalist," and sex freak. His favorite high was filming bondage scenes, including female partners other than his wife, and he was soon divorced. In 1980, Lake was charged with grand theft after looting building materials from a construction site, but he got off easy with one year's probation. Married a second time in August 1981, he moved with his wife to a communal ranch at Ukiah, California, where a "Renaissance" lifestyle was practiced—complete with period costumes and surgical alteration of goats to produce "unicorns." A few months after his arrival in Ukiah, Lake met Charlie Ng.

Hong Kong–born in 1961, Charles Chitat Ng was the son of wealthy Chinese parents. Forever in trouble, Ng was expelled from school in Hong Kong and then from an expensive private school in England, where he was caught stealing from classmates. A subsequent shoplifting arrest drove him to California, where he joined the Marine Corps after a hit-and-run incident, falsely listing his birthplace as Bloomington, Indiana. An expert martial artist and self-styled "ninja warrior," Ng talked incessantly of violence to his fellow leathernecks. In October 1979, he led two accomplices in stealing $11,000 worth of automatic weapons from a marine arsenal in Hawaii and found himself under arrest. During psychiatric evaluation, Ng boasted of "assassinating" someone in California, but he never got around to naming the victim. He escaped from custody before trial and was listed as a deserter when he answered Lake's ad in a war gamer's magazine, in 1981.

The two men hit it off at once, in spite of Lake's racism, which seemed to encompass only African Americans and Hispanics. They began collecting automatic weapons from illegal sources, and a team of federal agents raided the Ukiah ranch in April 1982, arresting Lake and Ng for firearms violations. Released on $6,000 bond, Lake promptly went into hiding, using a variety of pseudonyms as he drifted around northern California. His second wife divorced him after the arrest, but they remained on friendly terms. As a fugitive, Ng was denied bail, and he struck a bargain with military prosecutors in August, pleading guilty to theft in return for a promise that he would serve no more than three years of a 14-year sentence. Confined to the military stockade at Leavenworth federal prison, Ng was paroled after 18 months, avoiding deportation with a reference to the phony birthplace shown on his enlistment papers. On release from prison, he returned to California and again teamed up with Leonard Lake.

By that time, Lake had settled on two and a half acres of woodland near Wilseyville in Calaveras County, enlisting the help of neighbors to construct a fortified bunker beside his cabin, where he stockpiled illegal weapons and stolen video equipment. His every thought was recorded in various diaries, including details of "Operation Miranda," entailing the collection of sex slaves to serve his needs after the anticipated nuclear holocaust. On the subject of females, Lake wrote: "God meant women for cooking, cleaning house and sex. And when they are not in use, they should be locked up." An oft-repeated motto in the diaries advised, "If you love something, let it go. If it doesn't come back, hunt it down and kill it." On February 25, 1984, shortly before his reunion with Ng, Lake described his life as "Mostly dull day-to-day routine, still with death in my pocket and fantasy my major goal." If authorities are correct, the first death in Lake's pocket may have claimed his brother Donald, reported missing by their mother—and never seen again—after he went to visit Lake in July 1983.

On June 2, 1985, employees of a lumberyard in South San Francisco called police to report a peculiar shoplifting incident. An Asian man had walked out of the store with a $75 vise, placed it in the trunk of a Honda auto parked outside, and then escaped on foot

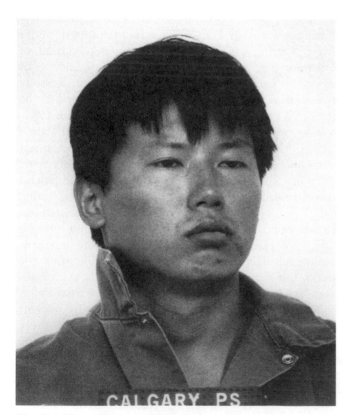

Charles Chitat Ng (Wide World API)

before they could detain him. The car was still outside, however, and officers found a bearded white man at the wheel. He cheerfully produced a driver's license in the name of "Robin Stapley," but he bore no resemblance to its photograph. A brief examination of the Honda's trunk turned up the stolen vise, along with a silencer-equipped .22-caliber pistol. Booked on theft and weapons charges, "Stapley" evaded questions for several hours, then asked for a drink of water, gulping a cyanide capsule removed from a secret compartment in his belt buckle. He was comatose on arrival at the hospital, where he would linger on life-support equipment for the next four days, finally pronounced dead on June 6.

A fingerprint comparison identified "Stapely" as Leonard Lake, but the driver's license was not a forgery. Its original owner was also the founder of San Diego's Guardian Angels chapter—and he had not been seen at home for several weeks. The Honda's license plate was registered to Lake, but the vehicle was not. Its owner of record, 39-year-old Paul Cosner, was a San Francisco car dealer who had disappeared in November 1984, after leaving home to sell the car to "a weird guy."

Lake's auto registration led detectives to the property in Wilseyville, where they discovered weapons, torture devices, and Lake's voluminous diaries. Serial numbers on Lake's video equipment traced ownership to Harvey Dubs, a San Francisco photographer reported missing from home—along with his wife Deborah and infant son Sean—on July 25, 1984. As detectives soon learned, the stolen equipment had been used to produce ghoulish "home movies" of young women being stripped and threatened, raped and tortured, at least one of them mutilated so savagely that she must have died as a result. Lake and Ng were the principal stars of the snuff tapes, but one of their "leading ladies" was quickly identified as the missing Deborah Dubs.

Another reluctant "actress" was Brenda O'Connor, who once occupied the cabin adjacent to Lake's with her husband, Lonnie Bond, and their infant son Lonnie Jr. They had known Lake as "Charles Gunnar," an alias lifted from the best man at Lake's second wedding (and another missing person, last seen alive in 1983). O'Connor was afraid of "Gunnar," telling friends that she had seen him plant a woman's body in the woods, but rather than inform police, her husband had invited a friend—Guardian Angel Robin Stapely—to share their quarters and offer personal protection. All four had disappeared in May 1985.

Another snuff tape victim, 18-year-old Kathleen Allen, made the acquaintance of Lake and Ng through her boyfriend, 23-year-old Mike Carroll. Carroll had served time with Ng at Leavenworth and later came west to join him in various shady enterprises. Allen abandoned her job at a supermarket after Lake informed her that Carroll had been shot and wounded "near Lake Tahoe," offering to show her where he was. Her final paycheck had been mailed to Lake's address in Wilseyville.

Aside from videocassettes, authorities retrieved numerous still photos from Lake's bunker, including snapshots of Lake in long "witchy" robes, and photos of 21 young women captured in various stages of undress. Six were finally identified and found alive; the other 15 have remained elusive, despite publication of the photographs, and police suspect that most or all of them were murdered on the death ranch.

Gradually, the search moved outward from Lake's bunker into the surrounding woods. A vehicle abandoned near the cabin was registered to another missing person, Sunnyvale photographer Jeffrey Askern, and police soon had a fair idea of what had happened to Lake's vanishing acquaintances. On June 8, portions of four human skeletons were unearthed near the bunker, with a fifth victim—and numerous charred bone fragments, including infant's teeth—discovered on June 13. Number six was turned up five days later and was the first to be identified. A 34-year-old drifter, Randy Jacobson had last been seen alive in October 1984 when he left his San Francisco rooming house to visit Lake and sell his van. Two of Jacobson's neighbors, 26-year-old Cheryl Okoro and 38-year-old Maurice Wok, also on the missing list, were linked to the Wilseyville killers by personal contacts and cryptic notes in Lake's diary.

Three more skeletons were sorted out of scattered fragments on June 26, and authorities declared that Lake and Ng were linked to the disappearance of at least 25 persons. One of those was Mike Carroll, who reportedly agreed to dress in "sissy" clothes and lure gays for Ng to kill, then died himself when Charlie tired of the game. Donald Giuletti, a 36-year-old disc jockey in San Francisco, had offered oral sex through published advertisements, and one of the callers was a young Asian man who shot Giuletti to death in July 1984, critically wounding his roommate at the same time. Lake's wife recalled that Ng had boasted of shooting two homosexuals, and the survivor readily identified Ng's mug shot as a likeness of the gunman.

Two other friends of Ng—and occasional coworkers at a Bay Area warehouse—were also missing. Clifford Parenteau, age 24, had vanished after winning $400 on a Superbowl bet, telling associates that he was going "to the country" to spend the money with Ng. A short time later, 25-year-old Jeffrey Gerald dropped from sight after he agreed to help Ng move some furniture. Neither man was seen again, and Ng was formally charged with their deaths in two of the 13 first-degree murder counts filed against him. Other victims named in the indictment include Mike Carroll, Kathleen Allen, Lonnie Bond and family, Robin Stapely, Don Giuletti,

and three members of the Dubs family. (Remains of Stapely and Lonnie Bond were found in a common grave on July 9, bringing the official body count to 12.) Ng was also charged as an accessory to murder in the disappearance of Paul Cosner.

On July 6, 1985, Ng was arrested while shoplifting food from a market in Calgary, Alberta. A security guard was shot in the hand before Ng was subdued. Charges of attempted murder were reduced to aggravated assault, robbery, and illegal use of a weapon, with Ng sentenced to four and a half years' imprisonment upon conviction. On November 29, 1988, a Canadian judge ruled that Ng should be extradited to the United States for trial on 19 of the 25 felony counts filed against him. Ng's appeal of that decision was rejected on August 31, 1989, but further legal maneuvers stalled his extradition until 1991.

Even that was not the end, however, as Charlie Ng pulled out all the stops, using every trick and legal loophole in the book to postpone his trial for another seven years. He fired attorneys, challenged judges, moved for change of venue (granted, to Orange County), lodged complaints about jailhouse conditions—in short, used the cumbersome California legal system to hamstring itself. In October 1997, Ng's stubborn refusal to cooperate with his latest court-appointed attorney won yet another delay in his trial, with jury selection pushed back to September 1, 1998. Police in San Francisco, meanwhile, grudgingly admitted "accidentally" destroying vital evidence in one of the 13 murder counts filed against Ng, but 12 more still remained for his trial. In May 1998, Judge John Ryan permitted Ng to fire his lawyers and represent himself, with a stern warning that the trial would begin on September 1, whether Charlie liked it or not. On July 15, Ng tried for yet another postponement, claiming that his glasses were "the wrong prescription" and his personal computer was not fully programmed, thus hampering his defense. Judge Ryan, unmoved, denied the motion and scheduled pretrial hearings to begin on August 21. Ng's trial was the longest, most expensive criminal proceeding ever in a state notorious for courtroom marathons, finally ending on May 3, 1999, when Ng was convicted and the jury recommended death. He was formally condemned on June 30, 1999.

LANDRU, Henri Désiré

Born in Paris during 1869, this future "BLUEBEARD" was a bright student who studied mechanical engineering at age 16. He served four years in the army, rising to the rank of sergeant before his discharge in 1894. During the same period, Landru seduced his cousin and she bore him a daughter in 1891, becoming his wife two years later. On discharge from the service he enlisted with a Paris firm requiring cash deposits from its new employees, but the owner soon absconded with the money, leaving Landru bitter at society in general.

He logged the first of seven felony arrests in 1900 and was sentenced to a two-year term for fraud. He drew another two years in 1904, 13 months in 1906, and three years in 1908. While still imprisoned on the latter term he was returned to Lille for trial on charges of swindling 15,000 francs from a middle-aged widow he met through a newspaper lonely-hearts ad. That conviction earned him another three years, but Landru accepted his punishment philosophically, fathering three more children during his brief vacations from prison.

Free on parole in 1914, Landru was suspected by police of various offenses and convicted in absentia, sentenced to a four-year prison term and lifelong deportation to New Caledonia, to be imposed upon his apprehension. He had nothing left to lose except his life, and by the outbreak of the war in Europe he was risking that, as well.

In 1914, posing as "Monsieur Diard," he struck up an acquaintance with a widow, Madame Cuchet, and her 16-year-old son. Despite warnings from her family, the lady furnished a villa at Vernouillet and the three of them set up housekeeping. The Cuchets disappeared in January 1915, with Landru pocketing 5,000 francs on the deal and presenting his wife with the woman's gold watch as a gift.

In early June 1915, Landru began courting another widow, Madame Laborde-Line. She sold off her furniture on June 21, telling friends she was going to live with her future husband at Vernouillet. Madame Laborde-Line was last seen alive on June 26, after which Landru sold her securities and other belongings for cash.

Meeting his victims through lonely-hearts ads had become a routine, and by the time he disposed of his second mark Landru had two more waiting in the wings. A Madame Guillin, 51, joined him at Vernouillet on August 2, and Landru sold off her securities a few days later. By December, a series of forged documents had siphoned 12,000 francs from the missing woman's bank account.

Calling himself "Dupont," Landru rented a villa at Gambais, south of Paris, in December 1915. His latest paramour, Madame Héon, joined him there on December 8 and was never seen again. Her friends were briefly pacified by notes from Landru, each explaining that the woman could no longer write herself because of failing health.

Victim number six, Madame Collomb, had corresponded with Landru since May 1915, accepting his pledges of true-blue affection. She moved into his Gam-

bais villa in November 1916, but their romance was short lived, and the lady vanished on Christmas Day.

In January 1917, Landru met a young servant girl, Andrée Babelay, at a railway station, offering her a place to stay while she looked for work. On March 11, Andrée told her mother she was engaged, and she moved in with Landru full-time on March 29. Penniless, she had nothing to offer in terms of financial rewards, but her days were still numbered. By April 12, she had vanished without a trace.

In July, after more than two years of running correspondence, Landru began courting Madame Buisson. They boarded the train for Gambais on August 19, and she was seen no more. Suspicious relatives launched their own investigation in the face of police indifference and began comparing notes with the family of Madame Collomb.

Landru, meanwhile, continued his courting apace. Madame Jaume met her husband-to-be through a matrimonial agent, moving to Gambais on November 25, 1917. Five days later, Landru cleaned out her bank account. Madam Pascal joined the list on April 5, 1918, her furniture sold as an afterthought. Madame Marchadier accepted Landru's proposal on New Year's Day 1919; she moved to Gambais two weeks later . . . and vanished.

Pressure from the Buisson and Collomb families eventually forced police to arrest Landru on April 12, 1919. A notebook was found, bearing cryptic notations on each of his victims, but excavations at the villa unearthed only the remains of three dogs. No trace of his human prey was ever found, and Landru remained uncooperative, certain that he would go free in the absence of bodies.

Prosecutors disagreed, and his trial at Versailles in November 1919 became a sensation. Neighbors from Gambais recalled the rancid smoke sporadically produced by Landru's chimney, most likely the result of bodies burning in his incinerator, and the court was satisfied. Convicted of murder, he was sentenced to die in spite of the jury's recommendation for clemency. Taking his secrets to the grave, Landru was guillotined on February 23, 1922.

LEE, Bruce

Born Peter George Dinsdale in 1960, Britain's most prolific serial killer of modern times was the son of a prostitute and afflicted from birth with epilepsy, partial paralysis, and a deformed right arm. Until the age of three, he lived with his maternal grandmother, afterward joining his mother and her common-law husband until their relationship disintegrated. Until the age of 16, Dinsdale attended a school for the physically handicapped and was there introduced to homosexual practices that, in the words of his prosecutors, "eventually led to his downfall and discovery." At age 19, Dinsdale legally changed his name to Bruce Lee, in emulation of the kung fu movie star he idolized.

A classic pyromaniac, Lee would explain in his confessions that a tingling in his fingers signaled him that it was time to light a fire. His first act of ARSON, at age nine, caused more than $30,000 damage to a shopping center. Lee's normal technique involved dumping paraffin through a mail slot, followed by a match to light the fuel.

Lee scored his first fatality in June of 1973. On January 5, 1977, 11 elderly men were killed and six rescuers injured when he torched a nursing home. Slapped by an old man in an altercation over Lee's disturbing some pigeons, Bruce threatened to kill his assailant. Later, the birds were all found with their necks wrung, and the man was burned to death in his armchair at home. The death was ruled an accident until, years later, Lee confessed that he had found the man asleep and set his clothes afire with paraffin.

In 1980, a house fire on Selby Street in Hull killed Edith Hastie and her three sons. Police found paper soaked in paraffin near the front door, but the Hasties were so unpopular with their neighbors that everyone in the vicinity was suspect. Some 18,000 persons were questioned before police discovered that Charles Hastie, one of the victims, was acquainted with various homosexuals who patronized public restrooms near his home. A group of suspects was rounded up, including Lee, who confessed to a series of fires spanning the past 11 years. In all, 26 persons had died by his hand, and multiple manslaughter charges were filed.

Pleading guilty on all counts, Lee was sentenced to an indefinite term in a mental hospital. As his prosecutor remarked, "The sad fact is that this is his only real accomplishment in life, and something he had expressed himself as being proud of." Lee described his motive more compellingly. "I am devoted to fire," he said. "Fire is my master, and that is why I cause these fires."

LEWINGDON, Gary James and Thaddeus Charles

Between February and December 1978, residents of Columbus, Ohio, were panicked by a string of random, senseless murders, characterized by nocturnal ambushes and home invasions, during which victims were shot numerous times at close range. Police were stymied in their search for the ".22-caliber Killer" and only a clumsy mistake by one gunman prevented the crimes from continuing indefinitely.

On February 12, 1978, a prowler invaded the home of nightclub owner Robert McCann, executing him, his mother Dorothy, and live-in girlfriend Christine Herd-

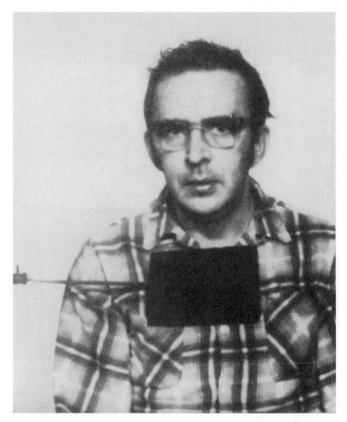

Gary Lewingdon (Author's collection)

man with multiple shots to the head. Robbery appeared to be the motive, but police were less certain on April 8 when 77-year-old Jenkin Jones was gunned down in his home, shot six times in the head, his four dogs killed nearby.

The same gun was used in both crimes, and ballistics tests matched again on April 30 when Rev. Gerald Fields was killed in Columbus while working part-time as a security guard. Three weeks later, on May 21, the gunman cornered 47-year-old Jerry Martin and his wife Martha in their home, snuffing both victims with close-range shots to the head.

Police played a hunch, dusting off their files on an unsolved shooting from December 1977. Joyce Vermillion and Karen Dodrill had been ambushed on December 10, gunned down after work at a Newark, Ohio, restaurant, and detectives examined the nine slugs retrieved from their bodies. Again the bullets matched, and that made nine dead in a little over five months' time.

The final victim, 56-year-old Joseph Annick, was robbed of his wallet and shot nine times in his own garage on December 4, 1978. A different .22 was used, but homicide investigators recognized the classic style of overkill, and none of them had any doubts when Annick joined the victims list as number 10.

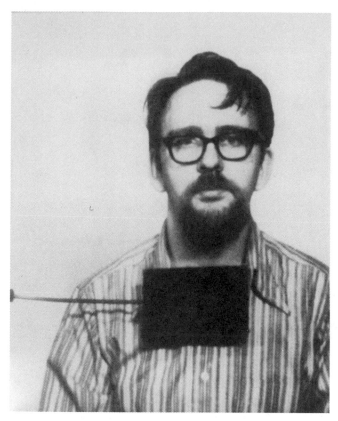

Thaddeus Lewingdon (Author's collection)

The case broke on December 9 when 38-year-old Gary Lewingdon presented Annick's stolen credit card to a clerk in a local department store. Arrested on the spot, he was detained on suspicion of murder while detectives examined his rap sheet. Discharged from the air force in 1962, Lewingdon had lived with his mother until 1977 when he married one of victim Robert McCann's night-club waitresses. Along the way, he had logged arrests for petty larceny, possession of criminal tools, indecent exposure, and carrying a concealed weapon. None of the charges had led to conviction, but this time detectives were sure that they had their man cold.

In custody, Lewingdon swiftly confessed to his role in the ".22-caliber murders," fingering his brother Thaddeus as the other triggerman. Search parties recovered the murder weapons, stolen from a gunshop in November 1977, and the brothers were indicted on December 14, Gary facing 20 felony counts, while Thaddeus was hit with 17.

On February 19, 1979, Thaddeus Lewingdon was convicted of the Vermillion, Dodrill, and Jones homicides. A month later, on March 26, he was convicted of the McCann-Martin murders and sentenced to six terms of life imprisonment. Brother Gary went to trial for all 10 homicides on May 14; 12 days later, the jury

convicted him on eight counts, failing to reach a verdict on two others. His sentence was fixed at eight consecutive life terms, plus a $45,000 fine.

LI Wenxian

Hard-line communist societies face a built-in disability in dealing with serial killers, since state propaganda denies the existence of crime in a "workers' paradise." Russian authorities learned the grim truth over a span of two decades from butchers like GENNADIY MIKHASE-VICH (33 victims), ANDREI CHIKATILO (55 dead), ANA-TOLY ONOPRIENKO (at least 52 slain), and "IVAN THE RIPPER" (never publicly identified), but the notion of serial killers was still new to Red China in 1991 when a faceless stalker surfaced in Guangzhou (formerly Canton).

The slasher's first victim was reportedly found on February 22, 1991, described vaguely as a woman in her early twenties. Her genitals were carved out with a knife, but the mutilation did not prevent police from finding unspecified "evidence of sexual intercourse." Five more slayings followed in the next six months, each victim reportedly subjected to a sexual assault, then smothered, stabbed, or strangled, after which the bodies were dismembered, stuffed in rice bags, and dumped on rubbish heaps in the bleak suburbs where Guangzhou's "floating population" lives in dismal squalor. And then, the murders stopped.

Thus far, there had been no press coverage of the crimes in China, marking the case as a "success" in terms of propaganda, even though the murderer remained at large. Chinese authorities ran out of luck in March of 1992 when a seventh victim washed ashore in the nearby British colony of Hong Kong. As described in the *South China Morning Post*, number seven had been slit from throat to stomach, then crudely stitched shut again, her fingers severed almost as an after-thought. Because no women were reported missing from Hong Kong, it was assumed the corpse had floated in from mainland China, and thus the "Guangzhou Ripper" was belatedly exposed.

Even then, it was impossible for homicide investigators, reared from childhood under Communism, to believe that their system would spawn such a monster. Zhu Minjian, head of Guangzhou's provincial Criminal Investigation Department, told reporters, "In all my thirty years with the force, I have never come across anything like this. Perhaps he copied from the West." Zhu said there had been "progress" in the case, but he was not pre-pared to share the details. "We're putting a lot of effort into this case," he declared. "We've got to solve it."

Still, the murders continued for another four years, some victims bludgeoned with a hammer in addition to being choked and stabbed repeatedly. Thirteen women were dead by November 1996 when the Ripper made his first mistake, leaving his latest victim alive. The woman identified her attacker as Li Wenxian, a one-time farmer from southern Guangdong province who had migrated to Guangzhou in 1991 and found work with a construction team. In custody, Li confessed to the attacks, telling police that he was motivated by revenge against all prostitutes, since one of them had cheated him a short time after his arrival in Guangzhou. Convicted by the Intermediate People's Court on charges of murder, rape, and robbery, Li was sentenced to death on December 18, 1996.

"LINKAGE Blindness": Law enforcement problem

A phrase coined by Dr. Steven Egger in 1984, "linkage blindness" describes the frequent inability (or deliberate refusal) of some police departments to recognize links between the several crimes committed by a serial killer at large. The problem is exacerbated by nomadic killers who cross jurisdictional lines and by the often bitter rivalry between law enforcement agencies. (In Los Angeles, for instance, relations between the city police and county sheriff's office were so strained that the local FBI field office maintained duplicate teams to investigate bank robberies, one each for coordination with LAPD and the sheriff's department.) That rivalry intensifies in jurisdictions where state or local police are at odds with the FBI over prior conflicts, and some departments withhold cooperation from federal programs such as VICAP. Sadly, the net result of such squabbling is seen in the handiwork of criminals who might be apprehended earlier if all concerned in tracking them were able to cooperate.

LONG, Robert Joe

A distant cousin of HENRY LUCAS on his mother's side, born October 14, 1953, at Kenova, West Virginia, Long may be the classic case of someone "destined" to become a serial killer. With other members of his family, he suffered from a genetic disorder characterized by an extra X chromosome, causing his glands to produce abnormal amounts of estrogen in puberty, with the result that his breasts began to enlarge. Surgery removed six pounds of excess tissue from his chest, but the resultant gender confusion remained, perhaps exacerbated by his mother, who shared Long's bed until he reached age 13. (Long's mother, twice divorced, denies his allegations that he watched her entertain numerous male "visitors" in their one-room apartment.)

Aside from genetic and family problems, Long also suffered a series of grievous head injuries beginning at age five, when he was knocked unconscious in a fall from a swing and one eyelid was skewered on a stick. The following year he was thrown from his bicycle, crashing headfirst into a parked car, with injuries including loss of several teeth and a severe concussion. At age seven, he fell from a pony onto his head, remaining dizzy and nauseous for several weeks after the accident.

At age 13, Long met the girl who would become his wife and simultaneously gave up sleeping with his mother. Various accounts agree that he was dominated by his girlfriend almost from the moment of their meeting, but his mother kept her hand in, too, the females in his life apparently cooperating rather than competing.

Long enlisted in the army prior to marriage, and he crashed a motorcycle six months later, shattering his helmet with the impact of his skull on asphalt. Convalescing in the hospital, he was alternately stricken by blinding headaches and unpredictable violent rages, and he discovered a new obsession with sex. While still in a cast, Long masturbated five times a day to relieve himself, continuing the practice at home despite twice-daily

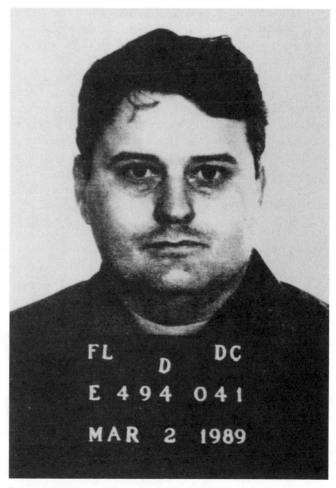

Robert Joe Long (Wide World API)

intercourse with his wife. Still it was not enough, and soon he began to search for prey.

Between 1980 and 1983, Long terrorized the communities of Miami, Ocala, and Fort Lauderdale as the "Classified Ad Rapist," answering "For Sale" ads in newspapers and in midday attacks preying on housewives who had placed them. Dropping by while their husbands were working, Long typically pulled a knife, bound his victims, raped them violently, and robbed their homes before he fled. Convicted of rape in November 1981, Long was cleared on appeal through discovery of "witnesses" alleging the victim's consent, and so the attacks continued, with murder shortly added to his list of crimes.

Unlike the 50 women raped by Long, his murder victims were selected from the ranks of prostitutes, nude dancers, or other women whom he viewed as "tramps." Between May and November 1984, he strangled, stabbed, and shot at least nine victims, with a 10th suspected by police but never charged against him. In early November, he snatched a 17-year-old girl off the Street and raped her, sparing her life out of pity when she described acts of incest performed by her father. In releasing a victim capable of describing him and his car, Long sealed his own fate, but police were too slow to save victim Kim Swann, murdered two days later in a final frenzy.

Arrested on November 17, 1984, Long was charged with nine counts of first-degree murder plus felony counts of abduction, rape, and sexual assault on his surviving victim. Convicted at trial in early 1985, he was sentenced to die and remains on death row at this writing, still awaiting execution.

LOTTI, Giancarlo   *See* "MONSTER OF FLORENCE"

LÓPEZ, Pedro Alonzo

Pedro López was the seventh child of 13, born in squalor to a prostitute in the village of Tolima, Colombia. Exiled from the family hovel at age eight after his mother caught him fondling a younger sister, Pedro was picked off the street by a pedophile who offered him food and a place to stay. Instead, the boy was taken to a derelict building and raped, a trauma that apparently did irreparable damage to his already twisted psyche.

Homeless, terrified of strangers, Pedro slept in alleys and empty market stalls, drifting from town to town and living hand-to-mouth on the streets. In Bogotá, an American family took López in, providing him with free room and board and enrolling him in a day school for orphans. At age 12, Pedro ran away after stealing money from the school, his flight allegedly precipitated by a teacher's sexual advances.

Six years passed before the future "Monster of the Andes" left another mark on public records, this time charged and sent to prison for theft of an automobile. On his second day behind bars, 18-year-old Pedro was gang-raped by four older inmates, a risk run by young men in jails the world over. Instead of reporting the crime, López fashioned himself a crude knife and went out for revenge, killing three of his assailants in the next two weeks. Authorities described the homicides as self-defense and tacked a token two years onto Pedro's sentence.

On release from prison, López started stalking young girls with a vengeance; by 1978 the killer estimated he had raped and slain at least 100 in Peru. His specialty appeared to be abducting children from Indian tribes, but the technique backfired when he was captured by a group of Ayachucos in northern Peru while attempting to kidnap a nine-year-old girl. López was beaten by his captors, stripped, and tortured. The Ayachucos were about to bury him alive when a female American missionary intervened, convincing Pedro's captors that they should deliver him to the police. They grudgingly agreed and López was deported within days, Peruvian authorities declining to waste valuable time on Indian complaints.

Once more at liberty, López began traveling widely in Colombia and Ecuador, selecting victims with impunity. A sudden rash of missing girls in three adjacent nations was ascribed to the activity of slavery or prostitution rings, but the authorities had no firm evidence and no suspects. The case broke in April 1980 when a flash flood near Ambato, Ecuador, uncovered bodies of four missing children. Days later, Carvina Poveda observed López leaving the Plaza Rosa marketplace with her 12-year-old daughter. Summoning help, she pursued him and López was captured by townspeople and held for police who began to suspect that they might have a madman in custody.

In the face of Pedro's stubborn silence, police tried a new stratagem. Dressing a priest, Father Córdoba Gudino, in prison garb, they placed him in a cell with López, leaving Gudino to win the suspect's confidence, swapping stories of real or imagined crimes late into the night. At length, when the padre had heard enough, López was confronted with the evidence of his own admissions and he broke down, making a full confession. Liaison with authorities in Peru and Colombia substantiated parts of the prisoner's grisly, almost incredible story.

According to Pedro's best estimate, he had murdered at least 110 girls in Ecuador, perhaps 100 in Colombia, and "many more than 100" in Peru. "I like the girls in

160

Ecuador," he told police. "They are more gentle and trusting. They are not as suspicious of strangers as Colombian girls."

In the course of his confessions, López made an effort to invest his crimes with philosophical trappings. "I lost my innocence at age eight," he told interrogators, "so I decided to do the same to as many young girls as I could." Trolling village markets for selected targets with "a certain look of innocence," López first raped his victims, then stared into their eyes as he strangled them, deriving sadistic pleasure from watching them die. Hunting by daylight, so darkness could not hide their death throes, López allegedly sought out one victim immediately after another, his bloodlust becoming insatiable over time.

Police were initially skeptical of their suspect's grandiose claims, but doubts evaporated after López led detectives to 53 graves in the vicinity of Ambato, standing by in chains as they unearthed the remains of girls aged eight to 12. At 28 other sites, searchers came up empty in the wake of raids by predatory animals, but the police were now convinced. Originally charged with 53 murders, López saw the ante boosted to 110 as a result of his detailed confessions. As Major Victor Lascano, director of the Ambato prison, explained: "If someone confesses to fifty-three you find and hundreds more you don't, you tend to believe what he says." Lascano also told reporters that "I think his estimate of 300 is very low, because in the beginning he cooperated with us and took us each day to three or four hidden corpses. But then he tired, changed his mind, and stopped helping."

The change of heart came too late to let the "Monster of the Andes" off the hook. Convicted on 57 murder counts in Ecuador, López was sentenced to life imprisonment—a penalty that normally amounts to 16 years in custody, since consecutive terms are forbidden by law. Few observers believed that parole would ever liberate the man billed by the *Guinness Book of World Records* as the world's most prolific serial killer, but justice was blind. Authorities released López in 1996 and deported him to Colombia. He is presumed to be at large today, living under a pseudonym.

LUCAS, Henry Lee

America's most controversial murderer was born August 23, 1936, at Blacksburg, Virginia. The Lucas family home was a two-room dirt-floor cabin in the woods outside of town, where Henry's alcoholic parents brewed bootleg whiskey, his mother doing occasional turns as the neighborhood prostitute. Viola Lucas ran her family with an iron hand, while husband Anderson—dubbed "No Legs" after his drunken

encounter with a freight train—dragged himself around the house and tried to drown his personal humiliation in a nonstop flow of liquor.

The Lucas brood consisted of nine children, but several were farmed out to relatives, institutions, and foster homes over the years. Henry was one of those "lucky" enough to remain with his parents, and Viola appears to have hated him from the moment of birth, seizing every opportunity to make his life a hell on earth. Both Anderson and Henry were the targets of her violent outbursts, man and boy alike enduring wicked beatings, forced to witness the parade of strangers who shared Viola's bed. Sickened by one such episode, Anderson Lucas dragged himself outside to spend a night in the snow, there contracting a fatal case of pneumonia.

Henry survived, after a fashion, but his mother's cruelty knew no restraint. When Lucas entered school in 1943, she curled his stringy hair in ringlets, dressed him as a girl, and sent him off to class that way. Barefoot until a kindly teacher bought him shoes, Henry was beaten at home for accepting the gift. If Henry found a pet, his mother killed it, and he came to understand that life—like sex—was cheap. When Henry's eye was gashed, reportedly while playing with a knife, Viola let it fester until doctors had to surgically remove the withered orb, replacing it with glass. On one occasion, after he was beaten with a piece of lumber, Henry lay semiconscious for three days before Viola's live-in lover, "Uncle Bernie," took him to a hospital for treatment.

Bernie also introduced the boy to bestiality, teaching Henry to kill various animals after they were raped and tortured. At age 15, anxious to try sex with a human being, Lucas picked up a girl near Lynchburg, strangled her when she resisted his clumsy advances, and buried her corpse in the woods near Harrisburg, Virginia. (The March 1951 disappearance of 17-year-old Laura Burnley would remain unsolved for three decades until Lucas confessed the murder in 1983.)

In June 1954, a series of burglaries around Richmond earned Lucas a six-year prison term. He walked away from a road gang on September 14, 1957, and authorities tracked him to his sister's home in Tecumseh, Michigan, three months later. A second escape attempt, in December 1957, saw Lucas recaptured the same day, and he was discharged from prison on September 2, 1959.

Back in Tecumseh, Henry was furious when his 74-year-old mother turned up on his doorstep, nagging him incessantly with her demands that he return to Blacksburg. Both of them were drinking on the night of January 11, 1960, when she struck him with a broom and Henry struck back with a knife, leaving her dead on the floor. Arrested five days later in Toledo, Ohio,

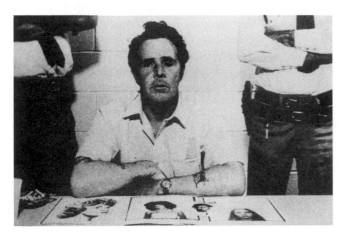

Henry Lee Lucas, with sketches of several victims (Author's collection)

Lucas confessed to the murder and boasted of raping his mother's corpse, a detail he later retracted as "something I made up." Convicted in March 1960, he drew a term of 20 to 40 years in prison. Two months later, he was transferred to Ionia's state hospital for the criminally insane, where he remained until April 1966. Paroled on June 3, 1970, Lucas went back to Tecumseh and moved in with relatives.

In December 1971, Henry was booked on a charge of molesting two teenage girls. The charge was reduced to simple kidnapping at his trial, and Lucas went back to prison at Jackson. Paroled in August 1975 over his own objections, Henry found brief employment at a Pennsylvania mushroom farm, then married Betty Crawford—the widow of a cousin—in December 1975. Three months later they moved to Port Deposit, Maryland, and Betty divorced him in the summer of 1977, charging that Lucas molested her daughters from a previous marriage.

Meanwhile, according to Henry's confessions, he had already launched a career in random murder, traveling and killing as the spirit moved him, claiming victims in Maryland and others farther afield. In late 1976 he met 29-year-old OTTIS TOOLE at a Jacksonville, Florida, soup kitchen. The homosexual Toole was an arsonist and serial killer in his own right, and they hit it off immediately, swapping grisly tales of their adventures in homicide. Over the next six and a half years, Lucas and Toole were fast friends, occasional lovers, and frequent traveling companions, taking their murderous act on the road.

A bachelor again by 1978, Lucas moved in with Toole's family in Jacksonville. There, he met Toole's niece and nephew, Frieda and Frank Powell, falling slowly in love with the 10-year-old girl who called herself Becky. In 1979, Lucas and Toole were hired by a Jacksonville roofing company, Southeast Color Coat, but they often missed work as they answered the call of the highway. Two years later, after Toole's mother and sister died a few months apart, Becky and Frank were placed in juvenile homes. Lucas helped spring them both, and they made a quartet on the road, Frank Powell witnessing deeds that would drive him into a mental institution by 1983.

Authorities came looking for Becky Powell in January 1982, and she fled westward with Lucas. In Hemet, California, they met Jack and O'Bere Smart, spending four months with the couple as house guests and hired hands, refinishing furniture to earn their keep. In May, O'Bere Smart had a brainstorm, dispatching Lucas and Powell to care for her 80-year-old mother, Kate Rich, in Ringgold, Texas.

Henry and Becky arrived on May 14, spending four days with Rich and cashing two $50 checks on her bank account before relatives booted them out of the house. Thumbing their way out of town, they were picked up by Ruben Moore and invited to join his religious commune—the All People's House of Prayer—near Stoneburg, Texas. Becky grew homesick in August and they set off, hitchhiking, on August 23. Camped out that night in Denton County, they began to quarrel. Becky made the grave mistake of slapping Lucas, and he stabbed her on the spot, dismembering her corpse and scattering its parts in the desert.

Back in Stoneburg next morning, Lucas explained that Becky had "run off" with a trucker. Kate Rich dropped from sight three weeks later, on September 16, and police grew suspicious when Lucas left town the next day. His car was later found abandoned in Needles, California, on September 21. An arsonist burned Kate Rich's home on October 17, and deputies were waiting when Lucas surfaced in Stoneburg the following day. Held on a fugitive warrant from Maryland, he was released when authorities there dropped pending charges of auto theft.

Chafing under surveillance, Lucas huddled with Ruben Moore on June 4, 1983, declaring an intent to "clear his name" by finding Powell and Rich, wherever they might be. He left a pistol with Moore for safekeeping and rolled out of town in a wheezing old junker. Four days later, Moore was summoned to fetch him from San Juan, New Mexico, where his car had given up the ghost. Returning to Stoneburg on June 11, Lucas was jailed as an ex-con possessing a handgun. Four nights later he summoned the jailer, pressing his face to the bars of his cage as he whispered, "I've done some bad things."

Over the next 18 months, Lucas confessed to a seemingly endless series of murders, bumping his estimated body count from 75 to 100, then from 150 to 360, tossing in murders by friends and associates to reach a total "way over 500." Ottis Toole, then serving time on a Florida ARSON charge, was implicated in many of the crimes, and Toole chimed in with more confessions of his own. Some of the crimes, said Lucas, were committed under orders from a nationwide satanic cult, the "Hand of Death," that he had joined at Toole's request. Toole sometimes ate the flesh of victims they had killed, but Lucas abstained. His reason: "I don't like barbecue sauce."

Detectives from around the country gathered in Monroe, Louisiana, in October 1983, comparing notes and going home convinced that Toole and Lucas were responsible for at least 69 murders. A second conference at Monroe in January 1984 raised the total to 81. By March 1985, police in 20 states had "cleared" 90 murders for Lucas alone, plus another 108 committed with Toole as an accomplice. Henry stood convicted in nine deaths, including a death sentence for the slaying of an unidentified female hitchhiker, and he was formally charged with 30 more across the country. Dozens of officers visited Lucas in jail, and he also toured the nation under guard, visiting crime scenes, providing details from memory. A California tour in August 1984 "cleared" 14 cases. Five months later, in New Orleans, Lucas solved five more. In the first week of April 1985 he led a caravan through Georgia, closing the books on 10 murders.

Lucas was barely home from that trip when the storm broke on April 15. Writing for the Dallas *Times-Herald,* journalist Hugh Aynesworth prepared a series of headline articles blasting the "massive hoax" that Lucas had perpetrated, misleading homicide detectives and the public, sometimes with connivance from the officers themselves. According to Aynesworth, overzealous detectives had prompted Lucas with vital bits of information, coaching him through his confessions, deliberately ignoring evidence that placed him miles away from various murder scenes at the crucial moment. From jail, Lucas joined in by recanting his statements across the board. Aside from his mother, he claimed to have slain only two victims—Powell and Rich—in his life. By April 23 he was denying *those* crimes, despite the fact that he led police to Becky's remains, while Rich's bones were recovered from his stove at Stoneburg. His mother's death, Lucas proclaimed, had been a simple heart attack.

From the beginning, officers had been aware of Henry's penchant for exaggeration. One of his first alleged victims, a Virginia schoolteacher, was found alive and well by police. Some of his statements were clearly absurd, including confessions to murders in Spain and Japan, plus delivery of poison to the People's Temple cultists in Guyana. On the other hand, there were also problems with Henry's retraction. Soon after the Aynesworth story broke, Lucas smuggled a letter to author Jerry Potter, claiming that he had been drugged and forced to recant. A local minister, close to Lucas since his 1983 "conversion," produced a tape recording of Henry's voice, warning listeners not to believe the new stories emerging from prison.

The most curious part of Henry's new tale was the role of Hugh Aynesworth, himself. In his newspaper series, Aynesworth claimed to have known of the "hoax"—hearing the details from Henry's own lips—since October 1983. A month later, on November 9, Aynesworth signed a contract to write Henry's biography. In September 1984, he appeared on the CBS *Nightwatch* program, offering no objections as videotapes of Henry's confessions were aired. As late as February 1985, Aynesworth published a Lucas interview in *Penthouse* magazine, prompting Henry with leading remarks about Lucas "killing furiously" and claiming victims "all over the country" in the 1970s. Through it all, the *Times-Herald* maintained stony silence, allowing the "hoax" to proceed, while dozens (or hundreds) of killers presumably remained free on the basis of Henry's "false" confessions.

In retrospect, the Aynesworth series smells strongly of sour grapes. A clue to the author's possible motive is found in his first article, with a passing reference to the fact that Lucas had signed an exclusive publishing contract with a Waco used-car dealer shortly after his 1983 arrest. The prior existence of that contract scuttled Aynesworth's deal, concocted five months later, and prevented him from winning fame as Lucas's biographer. The next best thing, perhaps, would be to foul the waters and prevent competitors from publishing a book about the case. (It is worth noting that Aynesworth omits all mention of his own contract with Lucas, while listing various other authors who tried to "cash in" on the "hoax.")

Aynesworth produced an elaborate time line to support his story, comparing Henry's "known movements" with various crimes to discredit police, but the final product is riddled with flaws. Aynesworth rules out numerous murders by placing the Lucas-Toole meeting in 1979, while both killers and numerous independent witnesses describe an earlier meeting in late 1976. (In fact, Lucas was living with Toole's family in 1978, a year before Aynesworth's alleged "first meeting.") The reporter cites pay records from Southeast Color Coat to prove that the killers seldom left Jacksonville, but office manager Eileen Knight recalls that they would often "come and go." (At the same time, Aynesworth places Lucas in West Virginia while he was working in Florida, the same error of which he accuses police.) According to Aynesworth, Lucas spent "all the time" between January and March 1978 with girlfriend Rhonda Knuckles, never leaving her side, but that version ignores the testimony of a surviving witness, tailed by Lucas across 200 miles of Colorado and New Mexico in February of that year. The woman remembers Henry's face and she recorded his license number for police, but her story is lost in Aynesworth's account. At one point, Aynesworth is so anxious to clear Henry's name that he lists one victim *twice* on the time line, murdered on two occasions, four days apart in July 1981.

Authorities reacted in various ways to Henry's turnaround. Arkansas filed new murder charges against him on April 23, eight days after his change of heart, and other jurisdictions remain unimpressed by his belated claim of innocence. In Marrero, Louisiana, relatives of victim Ruth Kaiser point out that Lucas confessed to stealing a stereo after he killed the 79-year-old woman, a theft that was never reported and therefore could not have been "leaked" by police. As they recalled, "He described things that we had forgotten about, details that never appeared in the paper and that we never put in the police report."

Investigator Jim Lawson, of the Scotts Bluff County sheriff's office in Nebraska, questioned Lucas in September 1984 regarding the February 1978 murder of schoolteacher Stella McLean. "I purposely tried to trick him several times during the interview," Lawson said, "but to no avail. We even tried to 'feed' him another homicide from our area to see if he was confessing to anything and everything in an effort to build a name for himself, but he denied any participation in the crime."

Commander J. T. Duff, intelligence chief for the Georgia Bureau of Investigation, describes Henry's April 1985 tour thus: "Lucas was not provided with any information or directions to any of the crime scenes but gave the information to law enforcement. When a crime scene was encountered, Lucas voluntarily and freely gave details that only the perpetrator would have known."

By November 1985, police in 18 states had reopened 90 "Lucas cases," but what of the other 108? And what of the November 1983 telephone conversation between Lucas in Texas and Toole in Florida, monitored by police? At the time, Henry and Ottis had not seen or spoken to each other in at least seven months, deprived of any chance to draft a script, but their dialogue lends chilling support to the later confessions.

LUCAS: *Ottis, I don't want you to think I'm doing this for revenge.*

TOOLE: *No. I don't want you to hold back anything about me.*

LUCAS: *See, we got so many of them, Ottis. We got to turn up the bodies. Now, this boy and girl, I don't know anything about.*

TOOLE: *Well, maybe that's the two I killed my own self. Just like that Mexican that wasn't going to let me out of the house. I took an ax and chopped him all up. What made me—I been meaning to ask you. That time when I cooked some of those people. Why'd I do that?*

LUCAS: *I think it was just the hands doing it. I know a lot of the things we done, in human sight, are impossible to believe.*

Indeed. And yet, the victims *were* dispatched, if not by Toole and Lucas, then by someone else. The truth may never be revealed, but in the meantime, Lucas remains in prison, authorities convinced of his involvement in at least 100 homicides. His death sentence was commuted to life imprisonment on June 26, 1998. Lucas died in prison on March 12, 2001, but controversy followed him beyond the grave. Two months after his death, DNA tests eliminated Lucas as a suspect in the November 1978 murder of Lisa Martini, a Kennewick, Washington, teenager whose slaying he confessed to in 1984.

LUPO, Michele

A former choir boy in his native Italy, Michele (or Michael) Lupo discovered his homosexual tendencies while serving with an elite military unit in the early 1970s. Commando training taught him how to kill bare-handed, and he took the knowledge with him when he moved to London in 1975. Starting out as a hairdresser, Lupo worked his way up to ownership of a stylish boutique, buying himself a $300,000 home in Roland Gardens, South Kensington. Along the way, he boasted of liaisons with some 4,000 male lovers, recording the intimate details in numerous journals. The consequence for his promiscuity was revealed in March 1986 when he tested positive for the AIDS virus. After this Lupo ran amok, indulging his taste for sadomasochism in a brutal campaign of revenge against the gay community.

On March 15, 1986, 37-year-old James Burns was prowling leather bars in search of a companion for the night, undeterred by his own diagnosis of AIDS two weeks earlier. Vagrants found his body in a London basement, mutilated with a razor, sodomized, and smeared with human excrement, his tongue bitten off in the frenzied attack that took his life. Three weeks later, on the afternoon of April 5, AIDS victim Anthony Connolly was found by children playing in a railroad shed, his body slashed and smeared with human offal in a carbon-copy homicide.

Lupo was leaving a gay bar on the night of April 18 when he met an elderly tramp on Hungerford Bridge and something inside of him suddenly "screamed out at the world." Assaulting the stranger, Lupo kicked him in the groin and strangled him on the spot, afterward dumping his body into the Thames. The following day, Lupo met Mark Leyland at Charing Cross, and the men made their way to a public restroom for sex. Once there, Leyland changed his mind, whereupon Lupo pulled an iron bar and attacked him. Escaping with his life, Leyland reported the incident as a mugging, later telling the truth to police after Lupo's arrest. (He has since disappeared.) Victim Damien McClusky was last seen alive in a Kensington tavern on April 24, 1986. His body—strangled, raped, and mutilated with a razor—was discovered some time later in a basement flat.

On the night of May 7, Lupo picked up another gay partner, attempting to strangle him with a black nylon stocking, but once more his prey escaped. This time, police received a full report and escorted the victim on a tour of gay bars to identify the culprit, finally spotting Lupo on the night of May 15. A search of Lupo's home revealed one room converted to a modern torture chamber, and his confiscated diaries were reported to contain the names of many prominent connections. Convicted at his trial in July 1987, Lupo received four life sentences and two terms of seven years each (for attempted murder), with the judge's assurance that in his case, "life meant life." Interpol investigated other mutilation deaths in Amsterdam, West Berlin, Hamburg, Los Angeles, and New York City, seeking connections to Lupo and his various trips abroad, but no further charges were filed.

"MAD Butcher of Kingsbury Run"

The gully known as Kingsbury Run lies like a scar across the face of downtown Cleveland, Ohio. Sixty feet deep in places, the ancient creek bed is lined with more than 30 pairs of railroad tracks serving local factories and distant cities, bearing cargo to Pittsburgh, Chicago, or Youngstown or whisking commuters to posh bedroom communities like Shaker Heights. During the Great Depression, Kingsbury Run was also a favorite camp site for hoboes and a playground for children with time on their hands. In the latter 1930s, it became the focal point of America's most fascinating murder mystery—a puzzle that endures to this day—though, in fact, the case had its origins elsewhere, on the shores of Lake Erie.

On September 5, 1934, a driftwood hunter found the lower portion of a woman's torso buried in sand at Euclid Beach, eight miles east of downtown Cleveland. The victim's legs were severed at the knees, her skin discolored by the application of a chemical preservative. A coroner extrapolated height and age from the pathetic evidence available, but victim number one did not resemble any of Cleveland's known missing women. She was never identified, police adding insult to injury by their stubborn refusal to count her as an "official" victim once a pattern of crime became apparent.

A year later, on September 23, 1935, boys playing in Kingsbury Run found two headless male bodies, nude but for stockings worn by the younger victim. Both had been emasculated, and their severed heads were found nearby. The older victim, unidentified, had died at least five days before the younger, and his skin possessed a reddish tinge from treatment with a chemical preserva-

tive. The younger man, identified as 29-year-old Edward Andrassy, was a bisexual ex-convict with a long record of petty arrests in Cleveland. Retraction of the neck muscles on both corpses pointed to decapitation as the likely cause of death.

On January 26, 1936, a Cleveland butcher was alerted to the presence of "some meat in a basket" behind his shop. Investigating, he was stunned to find two human thighs, one arm, and the lower half of a woman's torso. The upper torso, lower legs, and missing arm were found behind a vacant house on February 7 several blocks away, but fingerprints had already identified the victim as Florence Polillo, a 41-year-old prostitute. Her head was never found.

Four months later, on June 5, two boys found the severed head of a man in Kingsbury Run, a mile from the spot where Andrassy and his nameless companion were found in September 1935. Railroad workers found the matching body on June 6, but victim number five remained anonymous, despite publication of numerous distinctive tattoos. His fingerprints were not on file in Cleveland, and he had not been reported missing.

On July 22, 1936, the naked, headless body of an unknown man was found beside Big Creek in the suburb of Brooklyn, across town from Kingsbury Run. The only victim slain on Cleveland's southwest side, this new "John Doe" would also be the only victim killed where he was found. Decomposition foiled all efforts to identify the corpse.

A hobo spotted number seven—or a portion of him—in Kingsbury Run on September 10, 1936. The dismembered remains were floating in a stagnant pond, and police divers were called to retrieve two halves of the torso, plus the lower legs and thighs. The severed head, along with arms and genitals, was never found. Decapitation had not been the cause of death, but medical examiners could not identify another cause.

Soon after the discovery of victim number seven, Detectives Peter Merylo and Martin Zalewski were assigned to the "torso" case full-time. Over the next two years, they investigated hundreds of leads, cleared scores of innocent suspects, jailed dozens of perverts and fugitives—all without bagging their man. The press, meanwhile, ran banner headlines on the futile search for Cleveland's "Mad Butcher," speculating endlessly on motives, the identity of the victims, and the killer's supposed surgical skill.

On February 23, 1937, the upper half of a woman's torso was found at Euclid Beach, almost precisely where the first (still unacknowledged) victim was discovered in September 1934. The lower trunk was found in Lake Erie, off East 30th Street, on May 5, while the head, arms, and legs remained forever missing.

On June 6, the skeleton of a black woman—missing one rib, plus the bones of arms and legs—was found beneath the Lorain-Carnegie Bridge. The victim was decapitated, and Coroner Samuel Gerber placed her death sometime in early June of 1936. In April 1938, the son of Rose Wallace "identified" his mother's remains on the basis of dental work, but problems remained. Wallace had disappeared in August 1936, two months after the victim's estimated date of death, and her Cincinnati dentist was deceased, his files destroyed, rendering positive identification impossible. Detective Merylo accepted the shaky ID, but it brought him no closer to the arrest of a suspect.

Exactly one month after number nine was found, the lower torso of a man was sighted in the Cuyahoga

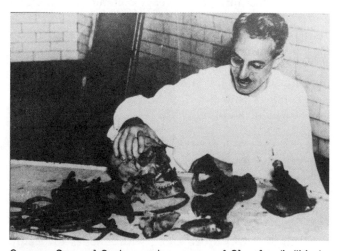

Coroner Samuel Gerber with a victim of Cleveland's "Mad Butcher" (Author's collection)

River, underneath the Third Street Bridge. Police retrieved the upper trunk and severed thighs that afternoon, but other pieces surfaced in the days to come. By July 14, authorities had everything except the nameless victim's head, and that was never found.

On April 8, 1938, a woman's lower left leg was fished out of the Cuyahoga, behind Public Square. The missing left foot, both thighs, and two halves of the torso were hauled ashore, wrapped in burlap, on May 2, but the victim's head, right leg, and arms remained at large.

The last "official" victims—male and female, killed at different times—were found on August 16, 1938, by workmen at a lakeside rubbish dump. The new "John Doe" was nothing but a skeleton, decapitated in familiar style, missing two ribs, plus both hands and feet. Murdered no later than February 1938, he may have died as early as December 1937. The female victim was cut into nine pieces, but all were accounted for. She had been killed sometime between February and April 1938, her identity forever disguised by advanced decomposition.

In January 1939, the Cleveland *Press* reprinted the following letter, mailed from Los Angeles:

Chief of Police Matowitz:

You can rest easy now, as I have come to sunny California for the winter. I felt bad operating on those people, but science must advance. I shall astound the medical profession, a man with only a D.C.

What did their lives mean in comparison to hundreds of sick and disease-twisted bodies? Just laboratory guinea pigs found on any public street. No one missed them when I failed. My last case was successful. I know now the feeling of Pasteur, Thoreau and other pioneers.

Right now I have a volunteer who will absolutely prove my theory. They call me mad and a butcher, but the truth will out.

I have failed but once here. The body has not been found and never will be, but the head, minus the features, is buried on Century Boulevard, between Western and Crenshaw. I feel it my duty to dispose of the bodies as I do. It is God's will not to let them suffer.

"X"

No buried heads were found in Los Angeles, and the manhunt shifted back to Cleveland. On July 5, 1939, sheriff's deputies arrested a Slavic immigrant, 52-year-old Frank Dolezal, and launched a marathon interrogation of their suspect. Dolezal eventually confessed to murdering Andrassy and Polillo, flubbing many details that were "corrected" in later confessions. He later retracted all statements, charging detectives with third-degree tactics, and suspicious stains found in his flat were identified as animal blood. On August 24, Dolezal "committed suicide" in his cell, found hanging from a wall hook shorter than he was, and the autopsy revealed four ribs broken by beatings in jail. Today, no one regards him as a serious suspect in the "torso" case.

On May 3, 1940, three male corpses were discovered in abandoned boxcars at McKees Rocks, Pennsylvania, outside Pittsburgh. All had been decapitated, and the heads were missing; one was otherwise intact, while two had been dissected at the hips and shoulders. Killed in the cars where they lay, the men had been dead from three to six months, and all three bodies had been scorched by fire. The most "complete" victim was identified as 30-year-old James Nicholson, a homosexual ex-convict from Wisconsin. The killer had carved the word "NAZI" on Nicholson's chest, inverting the "Z" by accident or by design. Authorities unanimously blamed the crimes on Cleveland's butcher, tracing the movements of the boxcars to pinpoint the murders in Youngstown, Ohio, during December 1939.

Journalist Oscar Fraley, in his book *4 Against the Mob,* contends that Eliot Ness—then Cleveland's director of public safety—not only identified the Mad Butcher in 1938, but also brought him to a semblance of justice. Tagged with the pseudonym of "Gaylord Sundheim," the suspect was described as a homosexual premed student and member of a prominent Cleveland family. Interrogated by Ness in autumn 1938, "Sundheim" allegedly escaped prosecution by committing himself to a mental hospital, where he died around 1940 or '41. In the interim, he tormented Ness with a barrage of obscene, menacing notes, which terminated with his death.

The tale deserves consideration, inasmuch as Ness preserved the "greeting cards"—all carefully anonymous—and they are viewable in Cleveland archives. But do taunting notes provide a viable solution to the torso murders? Why did experts on the case insist the Butcher claimed three victims in December 1939, when "Sundheim" had been out of circulation for a year or more? If Ness was certain of the killer's whereabouts, why did he allow "suspect" Frank Dolezal to be abused (and possibly murdered) by sheriff's officers in 1939? If the case was solved in 1938, why did Detective Merylo pursue the Butcher into retirement, blaming his elusive quarry for more than 50 murders by 1947? Tantalizing as it is, the Fraley story falls apart on close examination, failing every test of common sense.

There is a grisly postscript to the Butcher's story. On July 23, 1950, a man's headless body, emasculated and dismembered, was found in a Cleveland lumberyard, a few miles from Kingsbury Run. The missing head turned up four days later, and the victim was identified as Robert Robertson. Coroner Samuel Gerber, responsible for handling most of the Butcher's "official" victims, reported that "The work resembles exactly that of the torso murderer."

In retrospect, it is clear that the Mad Butcher murdered at least 16 victims between 1934 and 1939. He may have slaughtered the 1950 victim as well, and speculation links the same elusive suspect with a series of "headless murders" around New Castle, Pennsylvania, between 1925 and 1939. No firm connections were established in that case, and the number of New Castle victims has been wildly inflated by sensational journalists, but the crimes *were* committed in close proximity to rail lines serving Cleveland and Youngstown. None of the New Castle victims were ever identified, and the identity of their killer—like the whereabouts of the Mad Butcher's eight trophy heads—remains a mystery.

In 2002, author James Badal identified Eliot Ness's prime suspect as Dr. Francis Edward Sweeney, a Cleveland physician born in May 1894. Sweeney served in World War I and was discharged from the U.S. Army with a notation that he was "25% disabled." He studied medicine in St. Louis, returned to Cleveland following his 1928 graduation, and was licensed to practice in Ohio on January 8, 1929. Sweeney's wife committed him for treatment of alcoholism in December 1933, and he was discharged a month later. The court dismissed a second petition to have him committed, and Mrs. Sweeney filed for divorce in September 1934 (granted in 1936). Court-ordered psychiatric examinations performed in February and April 1938, at the behest of a medical colleague and Sweeney's sister, found Sweeney sane. Ness's description of his unnamed suspect matched Sweeney in some respects—married to a nurse, related to a congressman—but nothing connects him directly to the murders. Sweeney committed himself to a veteran's hospital in August 1938, emerged briefly in 1939, then returned to custodial care in August 1939. He proved a bothersome patient, described by an FBI file as "constantly in trouble" with hospital authorities until his death in July 1964. Perhaps significantly, that date conflicts with Ness's public claims that his nameless suspect died in the 1940s.

MALVO, Lee Boyd, and MUHAMMAD, John Allen

In the wake of terrorist attacks that claimed nearly 3,000 victims on September 11, 2001, residents of Washington, D.C., and environs were naturally frightened by the prospect of further attacks. That nightmare came to life in October 2002, with a series of deadly sniper attacks that panicked the U.S. capital and spread ripples of fear nationwide.

The killing spree began, ironically, with a wild shot that struck no one. At 5:20 P.M. on October 2, 2002, a rifle bullet drilled the display window of a Michael's craft store in Aspen Hill, Maryland, without hitting any shoppers. Forty-four minutes later, 55-year-old James Martin was killed in the parking lot of a Shoppers Food Warehouse in Wheaton, Maryland, 15 miles north of Washington. Officers rushed from the Wheaton police station, directly opposite the shooting scene, but Martin was already dead, his killer nowhere in sight.

The sniper rested overnight, then returned to action at 7:41 A.M. on October 3. His next shot killed 39-year-old landscaper James Buchanan while he was mowing grass at the Fitzgerald Auto Mall in White Flint, Maryland. At 8:12 A.M., another rifle slug killed Premkumar Walekar, a 54-year-old taxi driver, while he filled his cab's tank at a gas station in Aspen Hill, Maryland. Twenty-five minutes later, the gunman shot and killed 34-year-old Sarah Ramos outside a post office in Silver Spring. Twenty-five-year-old Lori Ann Lewis-Rivera was killed at 9:58 A.M. while pumping gas at a station in Kensington, Maryland. The day's last victim, 72-year-old Pascal Charlot, was gunned down on a Washington street corner, near the Montgomery County (Maryland) line, shortly before 10 P.M. The sniper's first survivor, Caroline Seawell, was wounded on October 4 in the parking lot of a Michael's craft store outside Fredericksburg, Virginia.

Ballistics experts soon reported that the same .223-caliber rifle was used in five of the shootings, but that revelation brought police no closer to the gunman. A late-night alert for a burgundy Chevrolet Caprice led officers to one such car, abandoned and burned on the outskirts of Washington, but detectives never determined whether the vehicle had any link to the shootings. At day's end, Montgomery County police chief Charles Moose could only say, "We do have someone that so far has been very accurate in what they are attempting to do. We probably have a skilled shooter and that heightens concern." Hasty attempts at PROFILING described the shooter as a random "thrill seeker" devoid of rational MOTIVES.

Concern moved closer to panic on October 7, when 13-year-old Iran Brown was shot outside his school in Bowie, Maryland. Brown survived his chest wound to become the sniper's second "failure." Patrolmen found the death card from a tarot deck lying near a spent rifle cartridge in a patch of woods 150 yards from the school. Inscribed on the card was a handwritten message: "Dear policeman, I am God." Chief Moose wept as he told reporters, "All of our victims have been innocent and defenseless, but now we're stepping over the line. Shooting a kid—it's getting to be really, really personal now." Moose invoked a new federal statute on

serial murder to request FBI assistance on the case, but G-men had no magic recipe for capturing the killer. An unnamed suspect "of previous interest" was detained for questioning on October 9, but the sniper struck again while he was still in custody.

The latest victim was 53-year-old Dean Meyers, killed with a single shot while he pumped gas at a filling station outside Manassas, Virginia. Prince William County police chief Charles Deane initially told reporters that the crime "appears to be consistent with the other shootings in the region," then declared on October 10 that ballistics had scored another match to the elusive sniper's weapon. At the same time, FBI agents released their first composite drawing in the case, depicting a white minivan or "box truck" allegedly seen near the site of the shooting. Chief Deane appealed in vain for the killer to desist, airing a plea that "There's enough damage been done."

The sniper obviously disagreed. On October 11, 53-year-old Kenneth Bridges was killed by a single gunshot while filling his car's gas tank at a station near Fredericksburg, Virginia. Three days later, the killer struck again. Linda Franklin, a 47-year-old employee of the FBI's National Infrastructure Protection Center, was killed by a single shot at 9:15 A.M. on October 14 outside a Home Depot store near Falls Church, Virginia. After that murder, state authorities told reporters, "There's some pretty decent eyewitness information that maybe we haven't had in some of the previous shootings." Specifically, bystander Matthew Dowdy described an "olive-skinned" gunman fleeing the scene in "a cream-colored Chevrolet Astro van with a burned-out taillight," but the lead proved false. On October 18, police jailed Dowdy for filing a false report.

On October 18, retired FBI profiler ROBERT K. RESSLER appeared on Larry King's CNN talk show, predicting that the sniper might travel as far south as Richmond, Virginia, and perhaps "down to Ashland [Virginia]." One day later, a 37-year-old man was shot and wounded outside a Ponderosa restaurant in Ashland, 90 miles south of Washington, D.C. While critics raged against the media for "giving a madman ideas," Chief Moose released a cryptic message via the media in Maryland: "To the person who left us a message at the Ponderosa last night. You gave us a telephone number. We do want to talk to you. Call us at the number you provided. Thank you." The plea brought a response by telephone, but it was garbled. On October 21, Chief Moose again used television cameras to address the killer: "The person you called could not hear everything you said. The audio was unclear and we want to get it right. Call us back so that we can clearly understand." That same afternoon, police arrested two passengers of

An FBI visual information specialist (center) gestures as he testifies in front of a model of the Chevrolet Caprice trunk in which sniper John Allen Muhammad was captured. The model shows the modifications that were made so that the sniper could shoot while undetected in the trunk. (AP Photo/Tracy Woodward, Pool)

a white van in Henrico County, Virginia, but they proved to be illegal immigrants with no connection to the case.

A note found near the Ashland shooting scene raged at "incompetent" police and warned: "Your children are not safe anywhere at any time." That threat prompted authorities to close 10 Richmond-area schools on October 22, and while that move relieved some local parents, it failed to stop the sniper. At 5:56 that morning, Conrad Johnson, a 35-year-old bus driver, was shot and killed at a bus stop in Aspen Hill, Maryland. Ballistics confirmed the same gunman at work. Police found another note at the scene, demanding that $10 million be wired to a domestic bank account. Chief Moose convened a press conference, advising the killer that his request was not "electronically possible," but he welcomed further negotiations. "We remain open and ready to talk to you about the options you have mentioned," Moose said. "It's important we do this without anyone else getting hurt. You indicated that this is about more than violence. We are waiting to hear from you."

On October 22, authorities in Tacoma, Washington, seized a bullet-riddled tree stump from the backyard of a rented home, announcing that they wished to run ballistics tests related to the sniper case. That same day, a call to the sniper hotline claimed credit for a September 21 shooting that killed 52-year-old Claudine Parker and wounded 24-year-old Kellie Adams at a liquor store in Montgomery, Alabama. A magazine found at that crime scene bore fingerprints identified as those of 41-year-old John Allen Muhammad (né Williams). On October 23 police in Maryland issued an arrest warrant for Muhammad, citing federal weapons charges. A frequent traveling companion was identified as 17-year-old Lee Boyd Malvo, a Jamaican citizen. The two were spotted at 1 A.M., sleeping in a car at a highway rest stop in Frederick County, Maryland, and police swarmed the scene to arrest them at 3:19 A.M. Ballistics tests matched a .223-caliber Bushmaster rifle, found in Muhammad's car, to various bullets recovered from victims.

Investigation of Muhammad's background identified him as a Louisiana native who converted to Islam and changed his name in 1985. He subsequently served in the U.S. Army from November 1985 to April 1994, including foreign service in the 1990 Gulf War. Muhammad was trained as a mechanic and truck driver, but he also won an expert marksmanship badge with an M-16 rifle. Twice divorced and a father of four, Muhammad was embroiled in bitter custody disputes with both ex-wives, including allegations that he abducted his children from their "infidel" mothers. His second wife received a permanent restraining order against Muhammad in March 2000, which legally barred him from owning firearms.

After serving at Fort Louis, near Tacoma, Muhammad had remained in Washington State upon his return to civilian life. There he met Malvo, born in Jamaica on February 18, 1985. Malvo and his mother entered the U.S. illegally, in January 2001, and settled in Bellingham, where Malvo attended high school. He soon met Muhammad and appeared to idolize the older man, who often introduced Malvo as his son or stepson. Malvo's mother called police on December 19, 2001, in an effort to separate her son from Muhammad, but the effort backfired when officers discovered her alien status. Immigration agents detained mother and son for a month, until Malvo's mother posted $15,000 bond for their release. A deportation hearing was scheduled for November 20, 2002, but Malvo vanished in the meantime, fleeing across country with Muhammad. They lived at various addresses, including one in New Jersey where Muhammad shared title with co-owner Nathaniel Osbourne for the car in which Muhammad and Malvo were arrested. That vehicle, a blue 1990 Chevrolet Caprice, had a hole cut in its trunk lid that allowed a rifleman to shoot unobserved while lying inside.

Muhammad was initially detained on charges of violating his ex-wife's protection order (by owning a gun) and illegally transporting a weapon across state lines. Malvo was held as a material witness to the murders while forensic experts sifted evidence from various crime scenes. At one point, Malvo tried to escape

Lee Boyd Malvo listens to court proceedings during the trial of fellow sniper John Allen Muhammad. (AP Photo/Martin Smith-Rodden, Pool)

Sniper John Allen Muhammad is led into a Prince William County courtroom in Manassas, Virginia. (AP Photo/Mike Morones, Pool)

through a ceiling panel in a police interrogation room, but he was soon recaptured. On October 24, police noted "some very good similarities" between Malvo and a composite sketch of a suspect in the Alabama shooting. One day later, Maryland authorities charged Malvo and Muhammad with murder in six of the sniper attacks. Alabama filed charges of murder and attempted murder in Montgomery. Maryland statutes barred capital punishment for Malvo, as a minor, but Muhammad was fair game for death row. On October 26, police in Tacoma announced that Muhammad was suspected of murdering Isa Nichols, a 21-year-old business partner of Muhammad's ex-wife, who was shot at a relative's home on February 16, 2002. On October 27, police upgraded Malvo from willing bystander to triggerman in several of the recent shootings. October 28 saw Muhammad indicted for capital murder and five other charges, for the Meyers shooting in Virginia. On November 1, ballistic tests linked Malvo and Muhammad to the wounding of a Silver Spring, Maryland, liquor store clerk on September 14, 2002, and the murder of 45-year-old Hong Im Ballenger (shot outside a Baton Rouge, Louisiana, beauty parlor on September 23, 2002). The pair's itinerary also placed them in Tucson, Arizona, in March 2002, when 60-year-old Jerry Taylor was killed on a golf course two miles from the home of Muhammad's sister.

By November 10, 2002, Malvo had confessed responsibility for three of the sniper shootings, and police identified him as the triggerman in most (if not all) of the slayings. Muhammad, they alleged, had served as Malvo's mentor, lookout, and getaway driver. Aside from confessions, Malvo's DNA was found on a half-eaten grape at the scene of one shooting; his fingerprints were lifted from paper found at a second crime scene. The Chevrolet's small trunk also suggested that Muhammad could not have performed the shootings from inside it. U.S. Attorney General John Ashcroft dismissed federal charges against the defendants in Maryland, clearing the way for transfer to Virginia, where execution of minors was not banned by law. At the same time, legal experts feared that naming Malvo as the sniper might defeat efforts to execute Muhammad.

Those fears had no basis. On November 17, 2003, jurors in Virginia Beach convicted Muhammad of capital murder in the Dean Meyers killing. The panel sentenced him to death on November 24. A second jury rejected Malvo's claim that he had been "brainwashed" by Muhammad, convicting the teenager of capital murder (in the death of Linda Franklin) on December 19, 2003. Some three months later, on March 10, the judge sentenced Malvo to a term of life imprisonment without parole. A second trial for Malvo, delayed pending a U.S. Supreme Court ruling on execution of minors, had not convened when this volume went to press. No charges have thus far been filed against the killers in Alabama, Louisiana, or Washington State.

Lee Malvo received a second life sentence on October 26, 2004, after entering a plea bargain to save his life. Capital punishment was waived in return for Malvo's plea of "no contest" in the death of victim Kenneth Bridges, the attempted murder of Caroline Seawell, and two related firearms charges.

MANSON Family

Born "no name Maddox" in Cincinnati, Ohio, on November 12, 1934, Charles Manson was the illegitimate son of Kathleen Maddox, a 16-year-old prostitute.

His surname was derived from one of Kathleen's many lovers, whom she briefly married, but it signified no blood relationship. In 1936, Kathleen filed a paternity suit against one "Colonel Scott" of Ashland, Kentucky, winning the grand monthly sum of five dollars for the support of "Charles Milles Manson." Scott instantly defaulted on the judgment, and he died in 1954 without acknowledging his son.

In 1939, Kathleen and her brother were sentenced to five years in prison for robbing a West Virginia gas station. Charles was packed off to live with a strictly religious aunt and her sadistic husband, who constantly berated the boy as a "sissy," dressing him in girl's clothing for his first day of school in an effort to help Manson "act like a man." Paroled in 1942, Maddox reclaimed her son, but she was clearly unsuited to motherhood. An alcoholic tramp who brought home lovers of both sexes, Kathleen frequently left Charles with neighbors "for an hour," then disappeared for days or weeks on end, leaving relatives to track the boy down. On one occasion she reportedly gave Charles to a barmaid as payment for a pitcher of beer.

By 1947, Kathleen was seeking a foster home for her son, but none was available. Charles wound up in the Gibault School for Boys in Terre Haute, Indiana, but

Charles Manson at a parole hearing (Wide World API)

fled after 10 months, rejoining his mother. She still didn't want him, so Manson took to living on the streets, making his way by theft. Arrested in Indiana, he escaped from the local juvenile center after one day's confinement. Recaptured and sent to Father Flannigan's Boy's Town, he lasted four days before his next escape, fleeing in a stolen car to visit relatives in Illinois. He pulled more robberies en route and on arrival, leading to another bust at age 13. Confined for three years in a reform school at Plainfield, Indiana, Manson recalls sadistic abuse by older boys and guards alike. If we may trust his memory, at least one guard incited other boys to rape and torture Manson, while the officer stood by and masturbated on the sidelines.

In February 1951, Manson and two other inmates escaped from the Plainfield "school," fleeing westward in a series of stolen cars. Arrested in Beaver, Utah, Manson was sentenced to federal time for driving hot cars across state lines. Starting off in a minimum-security establishment, Manson assaulted another inmate in January 1952, holding a razor blade to the boy's throat and sodomizing him. Reclassified as "dangerous," Manson was transferred to a tougher lockup, logging eight major disciplinary infractions—including three homosexual assaults—by August 1952. He was moved to the Chillicothe, Ohio, reformatory a month later and suddenly turned over a new leaf, becoming a "model" prisoner almost overnight. The cunning act was rewarded with parole in May 1954.

Arrested a second time for driving hot cars interstate, in September 1955, Manson got off easy with five years' probation. He celebrated by skipping a court date in Florida on pending charges of auto theft, and his probation was promptly revoked. Picked up in Indianapolis on March 14, 1956, he was sent to the federal prison at Terminal Island, California, winning parole on September 30, 1958. Seven months later, on May 1, 1959, he was jailed in Los Angeles on charges of forging and cashing stolen US Treasury checks. Once more, he escaped with probation, swiftly revoked with his April 1960 arrest for pimping and transporting whores interstate. Entering the lockup at McNeil Island, Manson listed his religion as "Scientologist"; his IQ was tested at 121. Paroled on March 21, 1967, over his own objections, Manson was drawn to San Francisco and the teeming Haight-Ashbury district.

It was the "Summer of Love," when thousands of young people flocked to the banner of drugs and "flower power," heeding Timothy Leary's advice to "tune in, turn on, drop out." The streets and crash pads overflowed with teenage runaways and drifters, seeking insight on the world and on themselves. Behind the scenes, a minor army of manipulators—gurus, outlaw bikers, pushers, pimps, and Satanists—stood ready to squeeze a grim profit from the Age of Aquarius.

In San Francisco, Manson displayed a surprising charisma, attracting young dropouts of both sexes, drawn from all strata of white society. Some, like Mary Brunner, were college graduates. Others, like Susan Atkins and Robert Beausoleil, were involved with satanic cults. Most were hopelessly confused about their lives, adopting Manson as a combination mentor, father figure, Christ incarnate, and the self-styled "God of Fuck." They drifted up and down the state in fluctuating numbers, with the "family" topping 50 members at its peak. From Mendocino and the Haight to Hollywood, Los Angeles, and Death Valley, Manson's nomads followed their leader as the Summer of Love became a nightmare. Along the way, they rubbed shoulders with the Church of Satan, the Process Church of Final Judgment (worshiping Satan, Lucifer, and Jehovah simultaneously), the Circe Order of Dog Blood, and—some say—the homicidal "Four P Movement." Manson grew obsessed with death and the Beatles song "Helter Skelter," which he interpreted as predicting race war in America. In Manson's view, once "blackie" had been driven to the point of violence, helpless whites would be annihilated, leaving Manson and his family to rule the roost.

On October 13, 1968, two women were found beaten and strangled to death near Ukiah, California. One, Nancy Warren, was the pregnant wife of a highway patrol officer. The other victim, Clida Delaney, was Warren's 64-year-old grandmother. The murders were ritualistic in nature, with 36 leather thongs wrapped around each victim's throat. Several members of the Manson "family"—including two later convicted of unrelated murders—were visiting Ukiah at the time.

Two months later, on December 30, 17-year-old Marina Habe was abducted outside her West Hollywood home; her body was recovered on New Year's Day, with multiple stab wounds in the neck and chest. Investigators learned that Habe was friendly with various "family" members, and police believe her ties to the Manson group led directly to her death.

On May 27, 1969, 64-year-old Darwin Scott—the brother of Manson's alleged father—was hacked to death in his Ashland, Kentucky, apartment, pinned to the floor by a long butcher knife. Manson was out of touch with his California parole officer between May 22 and June 18, 1969, and an unidentified "LSD preacher from California" set up shop with several young women in nearby Huntington, around the same time.

On July 17, 1969, 16-year-old Mark Walts disappeared while hitchhiking from Chatsworth, California, to the pier at Santa Monica to do some fishing. His battered body, shot three times and possibly run over by a

Left to right: Susan Atkins, Patricia Krenwinkel, and Leslie Van Houten en route to the Sharon Tate murder trial. (Wide World API)

car, was found next morning in Topanga Canyon. Walts was a frequent visitor to Manson's commune at the Spahn movie ranch, and the dead boy's brother publicly accused Manson of the murder, though no charges were filed.

Around the time of Walts's death, a "Jane Doe" corpse was discovered near Castaic, northeast of the Spahn ranch, tentatively identified from articles of clothing as Susan Scott, a "family" member once arrested with a group of Manson girls in Mendocino. Scott was living at the ranch when she dropped out of sight, and while the Castaic corpse remains technically unidentified, Susan has not been seen again.

In the month between July 27 and August 26, 1969, Manson's tribe slaughtered at least nine persons in southern California. Musician Gary Hinman was the first to die, hacked to death in retaliation for a drug deal gone sour, "political" graffiti scrawled at the scene in his blood, as Manson tried to blame the crime on "blackie." On August 9, a Manson hit team raided the home of movie director Roman Polanski, slaughtering Polanski's wife—pregnant actress Sharon Tate—and four of her guests: Abigail Folger, Jay Sebring, Voytek Frykowski, and Steven Parent. The following night, Manson's "creepy crawlers" killed and mutilated another couple, Leno and Rosemary LaBianca, in their Los Angeles home.

An atmosphere of general panic gripped affluent L.A., the grisly crimes demonstrating that no one was safe. On August 16, sheriff's deputies raided the Spahn ranch, arresting Manson and company on various drug-related charges, but Charles was back on the street by August 26. That night, he directed the murder and dis-

memberment of movie stunt man Donald ("Shorty") Shea, a hanger-on who "knew too much" and was suspected of discussing family business with police.

Ironically, Manson's downfall came about through a relatively petty crime. On the night of September 18–19, 1969, members of the family burned a piece of road-grading equipment that was "obstructing" one of their desert dune buggy routes. Arson investigators traced the evidence to Manson, and he was arrested again on October 12. A day later, Susan Atkins was picked up in Ontario, California, and she soon confided details of the Tate-LaBianca murders to cellmates in Los Angeles. Sweeping indictments followed, but even Manson's removal from circulation could not halt the violence.

On November 5, 1969, family member John Haught—aka "Zero"—was shot and killed while "playing Russian roulette" in Venice, California. Eleven days later, another "Jane Doe"—tentatively identified as family associate Sherry Cooper—was found near the site where Marina Habe's body had been discovered in 1968. On November 21, Scientologists James Sharp, 15, and Doreen Gault, 19, were found dead in a Los Angeles alley, stabbed more than 50 times each with a long-bladed knife. Investigators learned that Gaul had been a girlfriend of Bruce Davis, a family member subsequently convicted of first-degree murder in L.A.

And Manson's arm was long. Joel Pugh, husband of Mansonite Sandra Good, flew to London in late 1968, accompanied by Bruce Davis. Their mission included the sale of some rare coins and the establishment of connections with satanic orders in Britain. Davis returned to the United States in April 1969, but Pugh lingered on, and his body was found in a London hotel room on December 1, his throat slit with razor blades, his blood used to inscribe "backwards writing" and "comic books drawings" on a nearby mirror. (Despite the impossible scribbling, his death was ruled a suicide.)

Charged with the seven Tate-LaBianca murders, Manson and three of his female disciples—Susan Atkins, Patricia Krenwinkel, and Leslie Van Houten—went to trial in June 1970. The defense rested its case on November 19, and attorney Ronald Hughes disappeared eight days later, after he was driven to Sespe Hot Springs by two family associates called "James" and "Lauren." The lawyer's decomposing corpse was found in Sespe Creek five months later, around the time Manson's death sentence was announced, and positive identification was confirmed through dental X rays.

Prosecutor Vincent Bugliosi believes that he has traced the fate of "James" and "Lauren," suspected of guilty knowledge in Hughes's death. On November 8, 1972, hikers found the body of 26-year-old James Willett, shot-gunned and decapitated, in a shallow grave near Guerneville, California. Three days later, Willett's station wagon was spotted outside a house in Stockton, and police arrested two members of the Aryan Brotherhood inside, along with three Manson women. Lauren Willett, wife of James, was buried in the basement, and an initial tale of "Russian roulette" was dropped in April 1973 when four suspects pled guilty to murder charges.

Meanwhile, the Manson trials continued in Los Angeles. Triggerman Charles "Tex" Watson was convicted and sentenced to die for the Tate-LaBianca murders in 1971. During August of that year, six family members—including original disciple Mary Brunner—tried to steal 140 weapons from a Hawthorne gun shop, planning to break Manson out of jail, but they were captured in a shootout with police. All were subsequently convicted, and Brunner was also sentenced for participation in the Hinman murder. Robert Beausoleil and Susan Atkins picked up additional death sentences for that slaying, while Manson, Bruce Davis, and Steve Grogan were convicted in both the Hinman and Shea murders. Various death sentences were overturned by the US Supreme Court's 1972 ruling against CAPITAL PUNISHMENT, and all of the family hackers are now technically eligible for parole. In Manson's absence, Lynette "Squeaky" Fromme held the family reins, corresponding with Charlie in prison and spreading his gospel on the streets, forging new alliances with sundry cults and racist groups. In September 1975, she tried to assassinate President Gerald Ford, but her pistol misfired and Squeaky was sentenced to life imprisonment.

As for the family patriarch, commutation of his death sentence launched Manson on a seemingly endless tour of the California prison system—from San Quentin to Vacaville, on to Folsom, back to San Quentin, and so on. Wherever he went, the pattern was identical: conflicts with authority and other inmates, various beatings and murder attempts (to date, he has been poisoned, set on fire, and badly beaten several times), half-hearted hunger strikes, and raving television interviews. In March 1974, Manson was diagnosed as an "acute psychotic"; two months later he assaulted a guard; two months after that, he was caught passing notes about a planned escape attempt. The Aryan Brotherhood, once Manson's de facto prison bodyguard, soon turned against him, one member sexually assaulting him at San Quentin, others beating him up at Folsom, another team slipping rat poison into his favorite soft drink. Still, there were rumors of Charlie orchestrating payback: one of his AB tormentors was stabbed to death at Folsom, while another was shotgunned by the proverbial persons unknown, shortly after his parole. Both crimes were probably related to the Brotherhood's traffic in drugs or continual feuding with blacks, but Manson was pleased to take credit for the murders with a wink and a grin.

While eligible for parole since 1972, no convicted "family" killer has yet been released. Susan Atkins and Tex Watson claim to have "found God" in prison, Watson founding his own ministry with a small but loyal cadre of disciples in the free world. Krenwinkel and Van Houten insist they have changed, matured, but no public official mindful of his future in elective office is prepared to take them at their word. As for Manson himself, his yearly parole hearings—those he deigns to attend—have been converted into a theater of the grotesque, with Manson rambling incoherently, sometimes for hours on end, on topics ranging from the Brazilian rain forest to his "frame-up" by an unjust society. Sometimes he doesn't show at all: in 1979, for example, he passed on the hearing and sent the parole board a "Get Out of Jail Free" card from his Monopoly set.

And there is always more trouble waiting for Manson, wherever he goes. In August 1997, he was sentenced to serve seven months at California's "super-max" Pelican Bay State Prison, after he was convicted of selling drugs to other inmates. He completed that sentence in June 1998 and was transferred to yet another lockup. March 1999 brought a surprise announcement that Manson would assist Professor Robert Beattie of Newman University in teaching a class on the U.S. legal system. Sandi Gibbons, a spokesperson for the Los Angeles district attorney's office, noted that it was not Manson's first foray into academia. "He likes to interact with young people," she said. "He thinks he can pass along something to them." As Manson told Professor Beattie in a tape-recorded conversation, "I have 50 years of experience in incarceration. I pretty much have a leg up on the law from an underworld perspective."

At press time for this volume, all parole bids from Manson and his homicidal followers have been rejected by California authorities.

See also ARTWORK AND MEMORABILIA; GROUPIES

"MASK of Sanity": Psychological defense mechanism

Most serial killers—indeed, most psychopaths (or sociopaths)—are consummate chameleons, able through years of practice to conceal their brooding rage behind a civilized, even charming, facade. Psychiatrist Hervey Cleckly dubbed this disguise the "mask of sanity" in his book of the same title (1982) and went on to explain:

It must be remembered that even the most severely and obviously disabled psychopath presents a technical appearance of sanity, often one of high intellectual capacities, and not infrequently succeeds in business or professional activities for short periods, some for considerable periods. . . . Although they occasionally appear on casual inspection as successful members of the community, as able lawyers, executives, or physicians, they do not, it seems, succeed in the sense of finding satisfaction or fulfillment in their own accomplishments. Nor do they, when the full story is known, appear to find this in any other ordinary activity.

The annals of modern serial murder are replete with examples of killers who passed unnoticed as the boy or girl next door. THEODORE BUNDY was a Boy Scout in his youth, later a well-liked political activist who presented the image of a successful law student despite slumping grades. Repeat killers Arthur Bishop, Richard Angelo, and JOHN JOUBERT were all Eagle Scouts in their teens. JOHN GACY was famous for his holiday theme parties, performing as a clown at children's hospitals when he was not immersed in local politics. DEAN CORLL was another charmer, luring young victims and accomplices alike with gifts of homemade candy. Rape-slayer ALBERT DESALVO frequently posed as a talent scout, persuading dozens of women to open their doors and submit to intimate fondling while he recorded their measurements for nonexistent modeling assignments. Despite a life style of CANNIBALISM and "unparalleled perversity," ALBERT FISH was bland enough to win the trust of total strangers, waltzing off with their children to "birthday parties" from which they would never return. Even crazy EDWARD GEIN was known around his hometown as a simple-minded handyman and local "character"; no one suspected he was also killing, robbing graves, and crafting household decorations out of human body parts.

It comes as no surprise, therefore, when the arrest of a serial killer is met with dismay from his neighbors, the media recording statements of surprise that a "nice, quiet fellow" could perform such grisly deeds. In part, that shock is due to ingrained images from Hollywood, where random killers are portrayed as scar-faced, heavy-breathing hulks who roam the streets in bloodstained aprons, armed with power tools. Such specimens exist, of course, but they are rare exceptions to the rule. The psychopathic killer's "mask of sanity" conceals a multitude of sins and often makes his victims easy prey when he—or she—turns on the charm.

See also INSANITY DEFENSE; PARAPHILIA

"MASS Murder": Defined

Prior to introduction of the term *SERIAL MURDER* in the mid-1960s, most slayers of multiple victims were referred to indiscriminately as mass murderers. Today, thanks largely to the FBI, *mass murder* is defined as any killing of four or more victims at one time and place. The Bureau's

Crime Classification Manual further divides mass murder into "classic" and "family" subsets: the classic case "involves one person operating in one location at one period of time"; the family scenario involves murder of four or more relatives and may be dubbed a "mass murder/suicide" if the perpetrator also kills himself.

Unfortunately, there are several problems with the Bureau's definition, first and foremost of which appears to be the exclusion of any multiple murder committed by two or more killers. Taken at face value, the FBI definition seemingly fails to include such events as the St. Valentine's Day massacre of 1929 (with seven dead) and Seattle's Chinatown massacre of February 1983 (13 dead) on grounds that multiple gunmen were involved. Conversely, FBI Agents ROBERT RESSLER and JOHN DOUGLAS in their book *Sexual Homicide* (1988) refer to a case of "mass murder" in which only three victims were killed. Further problems arise with the introduction of SPREE MURDER, which—depending on the circumstances of the case—may be indistinguishable from either "mass" or "serial" murder. Published references to "serial mass murder" also needlessly confuse an already complicated issue.

MATHURIN, Jean-Thierry   *See* PAULIN, THIERRY

MEDICAL Murders

A disturbing number of serial killers are found in the medical profession, making victims of the very patients who entrust the twisted healers with their lives. The reasons for their choice of a career in medicine (and murder) are admittedly complex, but one advantage is the ready-made supply of victims—often weak and helpless, sometimes even comatose—who are presented daily to the medical professional. Those who select their victims from among the patients of a major hospital or nursing home are sheltered from suspicion by their Hippocratic oath and by the fact that death—particularly of the old and gravely ill—is taken more or less for granted. Only when a slayer grows too arrogant or careless, leaving telltale clues behind or killing too voraciously within a short time span, is he (or she) exposed.

Medical killers are found in the ranks of licensed physicians and dentists, of registered nurses, and of lower-ranked employees such as orderlies and nurse's aides. They are both male and female, black and white (although Caucasians dominate this group). As in their training, race, and gender, so they are diverse in MOTIVES, although certain major themes repeat themselves time after time.

One common motive in medical murder is the so-called mercy killing, wherein the slayer allegedly seeks to end the suffering of selected patients by ending their lives. The FBI *Crime Classification Manual* (1992) presents nurse's aide DONALD HARVEY as an example of a "mercy killer" in action, although his techniques smacked of sadism (and his selection of victims, at least in some cases, was achieved through satanic rituals).

A second type of medical killer is the would-be "hero," precipitating life-or-death emergencies with the intent of stepping in to save a patient at the penultimate moment, thus earning kudos from his peers or members of the victim's family. These operators—theoretically, at least—may not intend to kill at all but may instead fall short in their attempts to "rescue" patients they have driven to the brink of death. The FBI presents baby-killer GENENE JONES as an example of the "hero" type; identical motives have been ascribed to male nurse Richard Angelo in New York and to various others around the world.

Some medical slayers, of course, kill for profit. In the 1930s, Dr. Morris BOLBER organized a murder-for-insurance ring in Philadelphia that claimed an estimated 50 lives. Most practitioners operate on a more modest scale, but some—like Connecticut's AMY ARCHER-GILLIGAN—open their own clinics or rest homes with murder in mind. Another profit-motivated killer, Missouri dentist Glennon Engelman, made no use of his medical skills when it came down to murder, preferring dynamite and firearms as his tools.

Finally, as some "healers" sexually abuse their patients, so we cannot rule out sexual or sadistic motives in some medical murders. Lesbian lovers GWENDOLYN GRAHAM and CATHERINE WOOD made a brutal "game" of murder at a Michigan rest home, so excited by the death throes of their victims that they often had to find an empty room for hasty bouts of sex when they were finished smothering a patient in her bed. Likewise, it is undoubtedly significant that all three patients killed by Dr. Tony Protopappas in his dental chair with anesthetic overdoses were attractive females under 35 years old.

The most frightening aspect of medical murder is the apparent ease with which some practitioners evade detection, sometimes forever, while running up prodigious body counts. A review of modern unsolved cases reveals seven hospitals—including five in the United States and one each in Canada and France—where unknown slayers claimed 320 victims with complete impunity. In one case where a killer on the ward *was* brought to book, a hospital administrator also pled guilty to destroying evidence illegally in a misguided effort to protect the hospital's "good name." The most prolific medical slayer since World War II is Britain's Dr. HAROLD FREDERICK SHIPMAN, convicted of 15 murders in January 2000 and officially blamed for the deaths of at least 215 patients between 1977 and 1998.

See also MODUS OPERANDI; WEAPONS

MIKHASEVICH, Gennadiy

The first Russian serial killer acknowledged by the state-controlled Soviet news media, Gennadiy Mikhasevich was born in 1947, in the territory of Byelorussia (present-day Belarus). Details of his crimes remain sparse: the February 3, 1988, Tass announcement of his execution simply states that Mikhasevich had "savagely killed" 33 women over the past 15 years. Some Western reports cite a body count of 36, with the first death recorded in 1971, but the reliability of those accounts is still unclear.

We know that Mikhasevich was employed as a factory worker in Saloniki, serving for a time as chief of the state motor vehicle repair works, volunteering as an auxiliary policeman in his spare time. In the latter capacity, he helped "investigate" his own crimes, questioning various suspects and sometimes stopping drivers of cars that resembled the elusive slayer's vehicle. Through it all, he continued to kill, with 14 victims murdered in the peak year of 1984.

Soviet police might not admit to a killer at large, but they were aware of his crimes, all the same. Regrettably, as Tass admitted years later, "the investigation veered from the right track," with a dozen defendants convicted and sentenced for various crimes they did not commit, following "breaches of law" by Byelorussian homicide investigators. Four innocent suspects were actually framed and convicted on murder charges: one of them was executed, another killed himself in custody, and a third innocent defendant went blind in prison. Officials responsible for the frame-ups were belatedly punished, according to Tass, but once again the details are unavailable.

No matter who they sent to jail, the murders continued; the elusive slayer picked women up in his small, red Zaporachet car and strangled them with a scarf. A letter was sent to police at one point, signed "Patriot of Vitebsk," which attributed the slayings to "revenge against adulterous women." Detectives knew the letter was authentic when similar notes were left with the killer's last two victims in 1985. Meanwhile, Detective Nikolai Iquatovich was slogging through mountains of paperwork, checking out the owners of some 200,000 red cars and the holders of 312,000 interstate passports. It was reportedly the latter approach which led to Mikhasevich's arrest, sometime in 1985. He confessed to the murders in custody and was sentenced to death by firing squad.

MILAT, Ivan Robert Marko

Australia's worst serial killer of modern times, Ivan Milat was the son of Croat immigrants, born in 1945. A nonsmoker who also shunned liquor, Milat worked as a highway construction worker and devoted his leisure time to motorcycle riding, off-road touring in a four-wheel-drive vehicle, and hunting. Friends assumed that his passion for stalking game was restricted to four-legged targets, but they were mistaken. Today, Milat stands convicted of seven murders committed between 1989 and 1992 and suspected of more dating back to the late 1970s.

Australia's two-year manhunt for the vicious "Backpack Killer" began in September 1992 when hikers found the decomposed remains of two women in the Belanglo State Forest, near Sydney, at a point called Executioner's Drop. The corpses were identified as 21-year-old Caroline Clarke and 22-year-old Joanne Walters, British tourists last seen alive in Sydney on April 18, 1992, while thumbing rides to Adelaide. Autopsies revealed that both young women had been sexually assaulted; Walters had been gagged and stabbed to death, and Clarke was shot 12 times in the head.

The discovery of two corpses prompted a wider search, and police soon found a shallow grave a few miles distant from the first site that contained the skeletal remains of Australians James Gibson and Deborah Everist. The two 19-year-olds had disappeared somewhere between Liverpool and Goulburn while hitchhiking to a conservation festival on December 9, 1989. Gibson's pack and camera were found beside a rural highway two months later, as if thrown from a passing car.

The search continued. In October, authorities found the remains of 21-year-old Simone Schmidl, a German visitor who disappeared on the same stretch of road between Liverpool and Goulburn, hitchhiking to Melbourne on January 21, 1991. Her glasses and camping equipment had later been found in the brush near Wangatta, a small town in Victoria. According to the medical examiner's report, Simone had been bound, gagged, and stabbed repeatedly.

The corpses of two more German tourists, 21-year-old Gabor Neugebauer and 20-year-old Anja Habschied, were found on November 4, 1992. The couple had last been seen alive 10 months earlier, on December 26, 1991, when they set off hitchhiking from King's Cross to Darwin and vanished without a trace. Their deaths bore all the signs of another sexual attack: Neugebauer was apparently strangled, then shot six times in the head; his girlfriend was nude below the waist and she had been decapitated, her head missing from the scene.

By that time, Australian police knew they had a serial killer at large. Published photos of the victims brought calls pouring in from locals who had seen them hiking through the countryside or thumbing rides, but none apparently had seen the killer—except, perhaps, for Paul Onions. A British subject from Birmingham, Onions heard about the "backpack murders" on television and recalled his own near miss with death outside Sydney in January 1990. Onions had been thumbing rides when he was picked up by the driver of a silver Nissan four-wheel-drive truck, who introduced himself as "Bill." A half mile north of the Belanglo State Forest, Bill had stopped and pulled a gun, declaring, "This is a robbery!" Onions had run for his life through the bush, bullets whizzing past his head, and managed to escape after a hectic chase. He recalled the gunman well enough to help police prepare a sketch, including the would-be killer's handlebar mustache.

Investigators, meanwhile, were reviewing their files on old sex crimes—including a December 1974 rape allegation filed against Ivan Milat, known to use the nickname "Bill." On May 22, 1994, a flying squad of 50 officers raided the property in Eagle Vale, a Sydney suburb, where Milat lived with a girlfriend. The raiders caught their man in bed, and a search of his home turned up evidence including firearms linked to the murders and camping gear stolen from the victims. (A sword, reportedly used to behead Anja Habschied, was found in a later search at the home of Milat's mother.) Detectives suggested that Milat sometimes killed his victims and then used their skulls for "target practice" after they were dead, thus accounting for multiple head wounds.

On May 31, 1994, Milat was formally charged with seven counts of murder, plus the attack on Paul Onions and various weapons charges. (Two of his rifles, as well as a homemade silencer found by police in his possession, were banned by Australian law.) At his four-month trial in 1996, Milat's attorney tried to undermine the prosecution's case by fingering alternate suspects, including two of Milat's own brothers, Richard and Walter. Jurors rejected the ploy, convicting Ivan of all seven murders on July 27, but presiding Justice David Hunt did tell the court, "In my view, it is inevitable that the prisoner was not alone in that criminal enterprise." In the absence of further indictments, however, Milat was the lone recipient of six life sentences, plus an additional six-year term for the attempted murder of Paul Onions.

Milat echoed Justice Hunt's opinion in February 1997 when he appealed his conviction on the unusual grounds that he did not act alone in the murder. No action has been taken to date on that appeal, but Milat was placed under tight security three months later after prison guards foiled a "meticulously planned" escape by Ivan and three other inmates. By November 1997,

Milat had fired the attorney who fingered his brothers as suspects, representing himself in a new—and futile—appeal to the New South Wales Supreme Court.

Authorities in New South Wales believe that they have only scratched the surface of Milat's homicidal rampage. On March 22, 1998, detectives announced a new investigation into Milat's movements dating back to the late 1970s. According to press reports, he is suspected in the disappearances of six Newcastle women and an equal number of tourists, including visitors from Europe and Japan. One rare survivor, a 41-year-old Newcastle resident, has told police she was abducted and raped by Milat in 1978. A second rape victim, attacked the following year, has also been reinterviewed in an effort to link Milat to the crime. The Newcastle disappearances—long presumed murders—date back to 1979 when Milat was employed on a road crew working in the area.

In October 1999 Milat offered to help Queensland investigators solve the cases of three missing women. He failed to turn up the bodies, but authorities named him as the prime suspect in three disappearances occurring between December 1978 and April 1979. Nineteen months later, in May 2001, Milat was hospitalized after a bungled suicide attempt, in which he swallowed a spring mechanism from his prison toilet. Later that year, he tried again, gulping 24 staples, three razor blades, and the chain from a pair of nail clippers. From those adventures, he proceeded to a hunger strike, designed to overturn rejection of his various appeals. It failed. October 2002 brought news that Milat might receive $40,000 compensation for violation of his privacy, after X-rays from his second 2001 suicide attempt were illegally released to the media. That payment never came through, and Milat received his final disappointment on May 29, 2004, when Sydney's High Court decreed that he should never be released from prison.

MISSING Persons as Potential Victims

Any discussion of serial murder, and particularly UNSOLVED MURDERS, ultimately touches on the subject of missing persons in America. One reason why it is impossible to estimate the number of unknown serial killers at large—much less to calculate the number of their victims—is because police across the nation have no standard method of recording missing-person reports. Too often, it appears that such reports are simply filed away and instantly forgotten by authorities who have their hands full dealing with the criminals and victims they can see.

It took DEAN CORLL and his accomplices three years to murder 27 boys in Houston, Texas, but the crimes were not revealed until Corll's death in August 1973. JOHN GACY spent the best part of seven years planting bodies in the crawl space underneath his home in a Chicago suburb before simple negligence led police to his doorstep. California's JUAN CORONA was more energetic, claiming 26 lives in three months, but none of his transient victims were even reported missing until a Yuba City farmer stumbled on the first of many shallow graves.

It is alarming to discover that we often don't know who is dead or missing in America today. In 1984, the US Department of Health and Human Resources estimated that 1.8 million children vanish from home every year. Ninety-five percent are listed as runaways, and 90 percent of those return home within two weeks, leaving a "mere" 171,000 children at large on the streets. Five percent of the missing—some 90,000—are identified as abductees, with 72,000 reportedly kidnapped by parents involved in bitter custody disputes. The other 18,000 children are simply gone.

The FBI cast doubt on those statistics three years later, reporting that the Bureau investigated only 150 "stranger abductions" of children between 1984 and 1986, but what did that disclaimer really prove? Federal agents normally remain aloof from kidnap cases in the absence of ransom demands or concrete evidence of interstate flight, and they take no notice whatsoever of runaways. Indeed, the statistics themselves are suspect, since FBI spokesmen radically changed their tune in 1995, admitting reports of some 300 stranger abductions *per year*—an average of one every 29 hours throughout America.

The case of vanishing adults is even more obscure, with no statistics readily available from any source. A published estimate from 1970, no doubt conservative, suggested that at least 100,000 adults disappear in the United States each year. Again, the vast majority are tagged as runaways—from debt or broken marriages, increasing numbers of the homeless traveling in search of jobs and warmer climates—but the fact remains that some undoubtedly fall prey to human predators. Five victims of Juan Corona's 1971 murder rampage remain unidentified to this day. Outside Chillicothe, Missouri, Ray and Faye Copeland paid their transient farmhands off with bullets in the head, and no one gave the missing men a second thought.

A corollary of the missing persons problem is the yearly glut of unidentified remains discovered in America each year. Scarcely a day goes by without announcements that a corpse or a skeleton has been recovered somewhere, from the littered alleys of New York, Chicago, or Los Angeles to the southwestern deserts or southern marshlands, in New England's piny woods, or on the rugged mountain slopes of

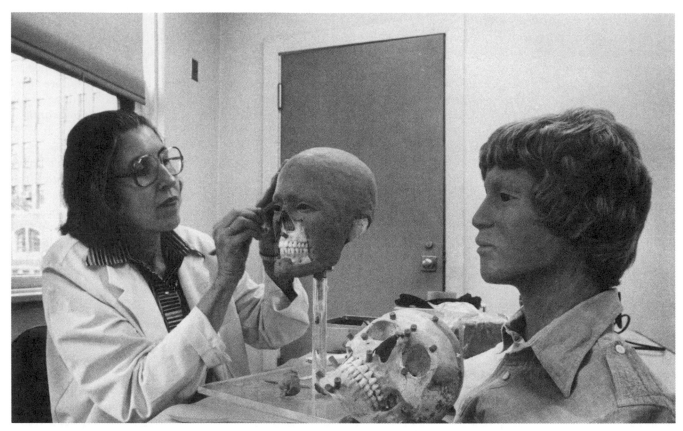

Bones of John Gacy's victims were reconstructed in an attempt to identify them. (Wide World API)

Washington and Oregon. Decomposition frequently prohibits any cause of death from being diagnosed, and scores (if not hundreds) of persons are consigned to nameless paupers' graves each year, logged in police records as John or Jane Doe.

It should not be supposed, of course, that every missing person in America and each set of unidentified remains denotes some superpredator at large and killing with impunity. At the same time, it is naive to think that every missing child (or adult) in the country simply "ran away" in search of greener pastures or that every sun-bleached skeleton discovered off the beaten track is merely one more careless hiker who fell prey to hunger or the elements. The truth, no doubt, lies somewhere in between, and it may never be revealed without concerted efforts on the part of law enforcement officers from coast to coast.

See also VICTIMOLOGY

MODUS Operandi of Serial Killers

For all their widely varied MOTIVES, regardless of race or gender, serial killers generally stalk and kill their human prey in one of three ways, referred to hereafter as nomadic, territorial, or stationary methods. On rare occasions, most particularly when at risk of capture, a killer may change his or her technique, but such deviations are rare and never seem to last for long.

Nomadic killers are the travelers, moving frequently—often compulsively—from one location to another, killing as they go. Such hunters are the prime beneficiaries of "LINKAGE BLINDNESS," drifting from one jurisdiction to another before police in one area recognize a pattern of behavior. It is not uncommon for nomadic killers such as HENRY LUCAS and OTTIS TOOLE to kill in several different states—or even, like "The Serpent," Charles Sobhraj, to kill in several different countries. A victim found hitchhiking in Texas may be murdered in New Mexico and discarded in California, thus confounding homicide investigators (if, indeed, the corpse is ever found at all).

Territorial killers are by far the most common of serial slayers, staking out a particular hunting ground that varies greatly in size from one case to the next. Some, like "Son of Sam" DAVID BERKOWITZ, stalk a particular city or neighborhood. Others range farther afield, as when the "GREEN RIVER KILLER" trolled for victims on the highway between Seattle and Tacoma, Washington. Others are more strictly localized, driven by personal compulsion to haunt a particular location. Lester Harrison, for instance, committed all but one of his murders in close proximity to Chicago's Grant Park. In theory, territorial killers should be easier to catch, since they offer homicide investigators frequent opportunities to view their handiwork, but some still manage to remain at large for years—or to escape entirely, as with London's "JACK THE RIPPER."

Stationary killers are the rarest of all, claiming most (if not all) of their victims at one location. Offenders in this group are evenly divided between those who kill at home and those who murder in the workplace. "Home" killers include most "BLACK WIDOWS" who prey on their own families, plus others like JOHN GACY who bring strangers back to their lair (and often hide their corpses on the premises). Killers in the workplace include a majority of the doctors and nurses responsible for MEDICAL MURDERS in rest homes and hospitals, plus aberrant specimens like Calvin Jackson, a New York janitor who raped and killed nine women in the hotel he was hired to clean. A case apparently unique in history is that of Jerry Spraggins, who apparently returned three times within as many years to one apartment in Montclair, New Jersey, killing female tenants who had no connection to each other or to him.

A stationary killer may be forced to move from time to time, for reasons unrelated to his crimes, but he—or she—will normally maintain established hunting patterns. Likewise, there is often speculation in the case of unsolved murders that the killer may have shifted to another town or state—again, Green River comes to mind, with speculation that the unknown killer may have moved to San Diego, Kansas City, or some other locale with a nameless predator at large—but without convincing evidence (a fingerprint, ballistics matches, DNA), no such conclusion is supportable in unsolved cases.

See also MOTIVES; WEAPONS; VICTIMOLOGY

"MONSTER of Florence"

The countryside surrounding Florence, Italy, has long been favored as a prime vacation spot for campers, hikers, and other nature lovers. In the summer months, warm breezes, starry skies, and rolling meadows make the district a perfect trysting spot for lovers, honeymooners, or couples seeking to rekindle a romantic flame in their relationships. In the latter half of the 20th century, however, Florence acquired a different sort of reputation, as the preferred hunting ground of a serial killer who preyed exclusively on couples. Nearly four decades after the terror began, many details of the case remain in doubt—and some think the killer(s) are still at large.

The Florence slayer's first appearance was recorded on August 21, 1968, when Barbara Locci and her adulterous lover, one Antonio Lo Bianco, were shot to death as they lay on the front seat of a car parked beside a rural lane. In the backseat, Locci's six-year-old son slept through the double murder undisturbed, suggesting to police that the killer may have used a silencer. Despite a paucity of evidence, the crime appeared routine to local homicide investigators, and Locci's husband was convicted of the murders at trial. Six years elapsed before his innocence was proven, when the killer struck again.

The second set of victims, 19-year-old Pasquale Gentilcore and 18-year-old Stefania Pettini, were slain on September 14, 1974, with the same .22-caliber Beretta automatic pistol used in 1968; once more the gunman used distinctive copper-jacketed Winchester bullets, manufactured in Australia in the 1950s. Unlike the first crime, however, this time the female victim was sexually mutilated after death, a grim addition that would become the Florence slayer's trademark.

Another long hiatus in the murders followed, broken on June 6, 1981, when the unknown gunman killed 30-year-old Giovanni Foggi and 21-year-old Carmela Di Nuccio. Di Nuccio was stabbed more than 300 times, with a severed grape vine thrust into one of her wounds. Breaking his pattern, the killer struck again on September 22, 1981, claiming the lives of 26-year-old

Police sketch of the "Monster of Florence" (Author's collection)

Stefano Baldi and 24-year-old Susanna Campi. Again, the female victim was mutilated, Cambi's genitals excised as Stefania Pettini's had been in 1974.

The murders continued with numbing regularity over the next four years. On June 19, 1982, 22-year-old Paolo Mainardi and 20-year-old Antonella Migliorini were shot with the familiar pistol, Migliorini posthumously savaged with a knife. Fifteen months later, on September 9, 1983, the Monster of Florence made his first "mistake": instead of killing a man and woman, he shot two male tourists from Germany, Horst Meyer and Uwe Rusch Sens. (Public speculation that the victims might be gay was not substantiated and appears to have no bearing on the crime.) The lethal balance was restored on June 29, 1984, when Claudio Stefanacci and Pia Rontini were slain. Rontini had been stabbed more than 100 times, her genitals and left breast excised. On September 8, 1985, the stalker killed two French tourists, 25-year-old Jean-Michel Kraveichvili and 36-year-old Nadine Mauriot, claiming Mauriot's left breast and genitals as ghastly souvenirs. On the morning the bodies were found, a copper-jacketed Winchester bullet was also discovered, lying on the sidewalk in front of a hospital close to the crime scene. The next day, police received an envelope addressed with letters clipped from a newspaper; inside, they found part of Mauriot's genitalia, a mocking gift from their elusive quarry.

Recreation of the Monster's crimes revealed a striking similarity in every case. Each of the double murders occurred on moonless nights, between the hours of 10 P.M. and midnight. In each incident, authorities believe, the man was murdered first, the woman subsequently shot and mutilated as the killer exorcised his private frenzy. Fingerprint examinations of the murder scenes indicate that the gunman typically wore rubber surgical gloves, and that clue, coupled with the bullet found near the hospital and possible use of a scalpel to mutilate the female victims, led authorities to question hospital staffers. No suspects were identified, and homicide detectives freely admitted they had no leads in the baffling case. As described by Francisco Fleury, the district attorney in charge of the investigation, "The man could be your respectable next-door neighbor, a man above suspicion."

Three movies have been made, so far, about the Monster and his crimes, ranging from a pornographic feature to a documentary. One film was in production in September 1985, and members of the crew rushed to the latest murder site, shooting new scenes to update their story. Police, meanwhile, were fearful that increased publicity might prompt the killer to become more active or encourage "copycats" to emulate his crimes. In fact, however, the slayer appeared to have retired, with no confirmed kills since 1985.

Italian police questioned more than 100,000 persons and briefly charged six different suspects in the Florence case before they identified their best suspect yet. Arrested on January 17, 1993, 71-year-old Pietro Pacciani was a semiliterate farmhand and amateur taxidermist, who had been convicted in 1951 of murdering a traveling salesman caught "in an affectionate embrace" with Pacciani's girlfriend. (Following the murder, Pacciani made the woman lie beside the corpse and raped her there.) Paroled after 13 years in prison, Pacciani was later arrested for beating his wife and served four more years in prison (1987–91) for molesting his two daughters. Convicted of seven double murders in November 1994, Pacciani still maintained that he was "as innocent as Christ on the cross." An appellate court overturned his conviction on February 13, 1996.

Ironically, Pacciani's release from prison came within hours of police arresting his good friend, 70-year-old Mario Vanni, on charges of murdering victims Mauriot and Kraveichvili in 1985. Authorities soon revised their original theory, deciding that the crimes were committed by a gang of killers led by Pacciani, its members including Vanni, 77-year-old Giovanni Faggi, and 54-year-old Giancarlo Lotti. Ten months after Pacciani's release from custody, on December 12, 1996, Italy's Supreme Court reversed the appellate court's decision and ordered a new murder trial for Pacciani. His three alleged accomplices went to trial in Florence on May 21, 1997, charged with five double murders, while their supposed ringleader was confined to his home at Mercatale, watched by police as a "socially dangerous character." Pacciani died at home on February 22, 1998, one day before closing arguments began in the trial of his three alleged confederates. The final verdicts, on March 26, were a mixed bag: Faggi was acquitted on all counts; Lotti was sentenced to 30 years for his involvement in the deaths of eight victims; and Vanni drew a life sentence for participating in five of the Monster's double slayings. The remaining cases are officially unsolved.

The Monster's saga took another strange turn on August 14, 2000, when police in Florence arrested two 26-year-olds, Chiara Maggi and Massimo Marrazzo, on charges of kidnapping, extortion and attempted murder. The pair had snatched their victim, a 34-year-old merchant identified only as "Sandro," and held him for four days in a garage "transformed into a torture center," where they brutally abused him in a fruitless effort to extract confessions of participation in the Monster slayings. From jail, Maggi proclaimed suspicions that the victim—her former boyfriend—was a psychopath who had joined in the murder spree at age 13 (in 1978). Detective Michele Giuttari dismissed that assertion as groundless, maintaining that Pietro Pacciani committed the murders in concert with an unnamed "man of refined intelligence."

On April 5, 2001, the conservative *Times* of London reported police assertions that the Monster's crimes were planned and carried out by a cult of "high society Satanists" pursuing "weird rituals that beggar belief." The group's leader, "in light of new evidence," was thought to be a "distinguished doctor" driven by a "sick and twisted mind." Giancarlo Lotti, at trial in 1997, had proclaimed, "I don't know what this doctor is called, but I do know that it was he who ordered the 'jobs.'" Investigating magistrate Paolo Canessa also referred to "a mystery woman" who had drugged and beaten Pacciani's wife before ransacking the suspect's hovel. Financial records, lately uncovered, revealed cash deposits exceeding $550,000 into various bank accounts maintained by Pacciani through the years, while he worked as a common farm laborer. Canessa now regarded Pacciani himself as a murder victim, declaring, "It wasn't a violent death like those he inflicted on his victims, but it was a slow and certain death as a result of taking the wrong medication for his diabetic and heart complaints."

Indeed, police now believe that murders of accomplices who "knew too much" began in 1981, when a friend of Pacciani's named Renato Malatesta was hanged in a stable. Twelve years later, Malatesta's daughter Milva and her three-year-old son were found dead in a burned-out car. A few days after that grim discovery, police found another torched car containing the body of Francesco Vinci, Milva Malatesta's lover and another friend of Pacciani, who was once himself a Monster suspect. In 1994, persons unknown murdered and burned a local prostitute, Anna Mettei, who had been the lover of Francesco Vinci's son. "It can't be a coincidence," a detective told reporters. "We think these people not only knew the killers, but also knew who was acting in the shadows behind them." Authorities now suspect that Pacciani tried to blackmail the "evil mastermind" behind the murders, thus launching a purge of potential witnesses. Detectives had "a fair idea" of the leader's identity, they said, but large rewards—thus far unclaimed—were offered for further information.

On August 7, 2001, Detective Giuttari gave Florence prosecutors a dossier allegedly confirming that "a group of about a dozen Satanists, led by a distinguished surgeon, had commissioned the murders." Giuttari told reporters that he had compiled a list of suspects and "arrests would follow." A month later, police raided the homes and offices of Francesco Bruno, Italy's leading forensic psychologist, and Aurelio Mattei, another psychologist, employed by the Italian secret service. While denying that either man was a murder suspect, the police seized books, notes, and computer disks about

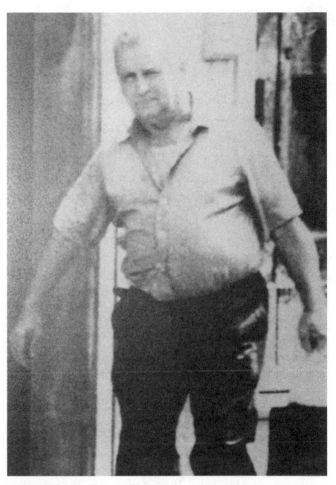

Suspect Pietro Pacciani was convicted, then freed on appeal. He died before his second trial. (Author's collection)

the Monster case. Press reports noted that Mattei had written a book on the case (*Rabbit on Tuesday*, 1992) which anticipated evidence uncovered by police in early 2001. Bruno, meanwhile, had regaled talk-show viewers with details of a secret service report prepared in early 1985 that suggested an occult link in the crimes. That report alleged that female genitalia and left breasts were prized for black magic rituals, and it went on to pinpoint a remote villa where the rituals may have occurred. Still, despite the promise of arrests in April 2001, no new charges were filed.

Rumors of the phantom slayer's return circulated through Florence in June 2002, after caretakers at Cappelle del Commiato (a cemetery in the hills outside town) reported five corpses mutilated by night-prowling vandals over a span of eight days. The first incident, involving an elderly woman's remains, was initially blamed on wild scavengers, but examination of the next two posthumous victims, one day later, revealed "careful removal of skin" in mutilations deemed "similar to those left on the victims of the Monster of Florence." Most troubling were reports that the final corpse, of yet another woman, had been mutilated while armed guards stood watch outside her tomb.

Rumors of a cult's involvement in the murders resurfaced in January 2004, with reports that four unnamed persons had been formally "cautioned" as suspects. Those under scrutiny included a lawyer, a retired pharmacist, and a former university professor specializing in dermatology and sexually transmitted diseases. On January 19, a police raid at dawn scoured one 60-year-old suspect's home for clues, but emerged without making arrests. Police also exhumed the body of Dr. Francesco Narducci, who drowned in Lake Trasimeno in 1985, and while the press claimed that Narducci had "dabbled" in occult rituals, no results of the belated autopsy were published.

Six months later, speaking as the chief of a 10-man "anti-Monster task force," Michele Giuttari told reporters, "These crimes are unique throughout the world for their cruelty and ferocity. They are black, brutal crimes. There are certainly ritualistic aspects, which seem to have a relevance: the fact that the same weapon was always used; the fact that the female bodies were never touched by a hand, but only by a blade— even the clothes were cut away with a knife; the fact that the tombs of the victims have frequently been defaced and commemorative crosses vandalized. All these things make an investigator curious." Giuttari predicted "a breakthrough" in the case, but none had occurred when this work went to press. Ironically, police in Lombardy arrested eight alleged Satanists in July 2004, charging them with a series of murders around Milan, dating from 1998.

"MOONLIGHT Murderer"

America was still recovering from the trauma of World War II and the euphoria of V-J Day when headlines focused national attention on the town of Texarkana, straddling the Texas-Arkansas border. There, between March 23 and May 4, 1946, an unknown slayer claimed at least five victims, surfacing at three-week intervals to murder when the moon was full. His rampage brought hysteria to Texarkana and environs, causing citizens to fortify their homes or flee the town entirely, sparking incidents of violence when a paperboy or salesman was mistaken for a lethal prowler in the night. Despite five decades of investigation and production of a feature film about the case, it stands officially unsolved today, the so-called phantom gunman unidentified.

The killer's first attack, unrecognized for several weeks, took place on February 23. Jimmy Hollis, age 24, was parked with his 19-year-old girlfriend, Mary Larey, on a lonely road near Texarkana when a tall, masked man approached their car with gun in hand. He ordered Hollis from the car and clubbed him to the ground, next turning on Larey and raping her with the gun barrel, tormenting her to the point that she begged him to kill her. Instead, he slugged her with the gun and turned back toward Hollis, allowing the young woman to escape on foot. Both victims managed to survive their ordeal, but the gunman would not be so lax a second time.

On March 23, 1946, 29-year-old Richard Griffin and 17-year-old Polly Ann Moore were killed on a lonely Texarkana lover's lane. Both victims were shot in the back of the head, Griffin found kneeling underneath the dashboard, and his girlfriend was sprawled in the back seat, but a blood-soaked patch of earth some 20 feet away suggested they had died outside the car. Both bodies were fully clothed, and recent reports deny any evidence of sexual assault, but contemporary rumors featured mention of rape, torture, and mutilation inflicted on Polly Moore.

Precisely three weeks later, on April 13, 17-year-old Paul Martin and 15-year-old Betty Jo Booker were ambushed in Spring Lake Park, following a late dance at the local VFW hall. Martin's lifeless body, shot four times, was found beside a rural highway on the morning of April 14. Booker's corpse was discovered six hours later and a mile away, shot in the face and heart. Again, the tales of fiendish torture spread through Texarkana, though a crop of modern journalists who have researched the case reject them as untrue.

The fanfare of publicity, complete with Texas Rangers on patrol and homicide detectives staked out in the guise of teenage lovers, caused the killer to adopt a new technique for what was said to be his last attack. On May 4, 1946, 36-year-old Virgil Starks was shot through the window of his farmhouse 10 miles from Texarkana as he read his evening paper after supper. Emerging from a bedroom at the sound of breaking glass, his wife was wounded twice before she managed to escape and summon help from neighbors. In her absence, the intruder prowled from room to room, leaving bloody footprints behind as he fled, dropping an untraceable flashlight in the bushes outside. Tracking dogs were hurried to the scene, but they lost their man at the point where he entered his car and drove off.

Two days after the Starks attack, with Texarkana living in a state of siege, a man's mangled body was found on the railroad tracks north of town. While some reporters have suggested that he may have been the killer capping off his murder spree with suicide, a coroner's report of May 7, 1946, reveals that victim Earl McSpadden had been stabbed to death before his body was dumped on the tracks, suffering further mutilation when a train passed over at 5:30 A.M. Today, it seems more likely that McSpadden was another victim of the "Moonlight Murderer," dispatched in an attempt to end the manhunt with a simulated suicide.

Arkansas lawman Max Tackett claimed to have captured the killer in the summer of 1946, basing his case on disjointed remarks from a convicted car thief and an inadmissible statement from the suspect's wife. At least one FBI agent also fingered the thief, later sentenced to life on unrelated charges, as a prime suspect in the murders, but he was never charged. If he *was* the killer, that fact somehow managed to elude Captain M. T. Gonzaullas, in charge of the Texas Rangers' investigation at Texarkana. As late as 1973, Gonzaullas listed the "moonlight" murders as his most baffling case, vowing that he would never stop hunting the killer as long as he lived. Today, the Ranger captain is no longer with us, and the case remains officially unsolved.

MOTIVES for Serial Murder

Serial killers in FICTION AND FILM are frequently portrayed as twisted geniuses, pursuing some gothic agenda that requires a modern Sherlock Holmes (or even psychic powers) to cut short the reign of terror. In real life, of course, the motives for serial murder are as diverse as those for any other type of crime—as varied, in fact, as the killers themselves. Some "experts" still insist that serial murder is "always sexual" in nature, but such broad generalization is no more valid than claims that serial killers are "always male" or "always white." In fact, there are no absolutes.

The FBI *Crime Classification Manual* (1992) presents four broad categories of homicide with 32 subcategories, nearly all of them applicable to some case of serial murder within recent years. Three are examined here, while the fourth—*group-cause homicide*—is discussed in the essay on TEAM KILLERS. The manual itself provides a number of examples, clearly demonstrating the diversity of motives for serial murder, and examination of the several categories readily brings other cases to mind.

CRIMINAL-ENTERPRISE HOMICIDE

The first category of murder, with 10 subheadings, is labeled by the Bureau as *criminal-enterprise homicide*—that is, any murder committed for personal gain. Some purists will contend that serial murderers "never kill for profit," but again, such absolutist claims will not survive close scrutiny.

The first subcategory of criminal-enterprise homicide is *contract* or *third-party murder*. While some theorists automatically exclude contract killers or "hit men"

from consideration as serial slayers, their argument becomes untenable when specific cases are examined. First, we know that some "dispassionate" assassins actually enjoy their work immensely, deriving both a psychological *and* a financial reward from their crimes. Likewise many contract killers—including the likes of "Iceman" Richard Kuklinski and Elmer "Trigger" Burke—have committed private, personally motivated murders in addition to their contract "hits." It is also well established that pathological slayers like Thomas Creech and Dennis Webb accept murder contracts on occasion, thus mixing business with pleasure.

A second type of criminal-enterprise slaying is the *gang-motivated murder*. Again, some purists will complain that no "gang-banger" should ever be counted as a "true" serial killer, no matter how many murders he commits . . . and again, the argument is weak. The aforementioned Thomas Creech and Dennis Webb both rode with "outlaw" motorcycle gangs on occasion, committing several murders each on behalf of those groups. In Canada, prolific slayer Yves "Apache" Trudeau killed many of his 42 known victims as a service to the Hell's Angels motorcycle gang, but an equal number were killed out of personal spite.

Criminal-competition homicide is a third form of criminal enterprise slaying, similar in many ways—if not indistinguishable—from gang-related slayings. The same arguments apply, and one need only recall the case of "Homicide Harry" Strauss, linked to over 100 slayings with Brooklyn's "Murder Incorporated," to see how prolific such killers may be.

Kidnap murder is the fourth type of criminal-enterprise homicide, assuming some sort of demand in exchange for the victim's return. William Hickman was one repeat killer who tried his hand at ransom kidnapping in 1927 to raise the tuition for college. He returned his 12-year-old victim on schedule, but she had been strangled, with her body hacked off at the waist, arms severed at the elbows, eyes stitched open to present a semblance of life at the ransom exchange.

The fifth type of criminal-enterprise slaying, *product-tampering homicide*, may—or may not—include a financial-extortion demand. No motive has yet been determined for the unsolved "TYLENOL MURDERS" of 1982, but those crimes inspired another practitioner, Stella Nickell, to poison her husband for his life insurance. As an adjunct to the scheme, she also killed a total stranger with poisoned Extra-Strength Excedrin capsules in an effort to divert police attention from herself.

Drug murder, the sixth type of criminal-enterprise killing, is typically—but not necessarily—related to organized gang activity. Once again, the distinction is blurred because many serial killers abuse drugs extensively, and some occasionally sell drugs to support themselves. Convicted killer William Mentzer, presently serving life in California, is known to have participated in cocaine smuggling and drug-related murders in Florida. That commercial activity did not prevent him from committing other homicides for personal motives, including alleged involvement in satanic human sacrifice.

The most common form of criminal-enterprise slaying linked to "bona fide" serial killers is doubtless the *insurance/inheritance-related* death. A majority of those who kill successive relatives and spouses, including both male "BLUEBEARD" slayers and female "BLACK WIDOWS," murder in anticipation of some financial reward. The FBI manual further subdivides this type of murder into *individual-profit* and *commercial-profit* slayings. In the first case, the killer hopes to profit financially, as through a life insurance payment; in the second, his-or-her desire is to achieve controlling interest in an active business concern (and the profits from same).

The last category of criminal-enterprise slaying, dubbed *felony murder*, refers to slayings that occur during commission of some other crime, such as robbery or burglary. Again, the FBI recognizes two subtypes. *Indiscriminate* felony murder refers to a homicide planned in advance but without specific victims in mind, as when a store is robbed and the customers killed to eliminate witnesses. Charles Sinclair, a nomadic killer linked to the murders of 10 coin shop proprietors, exemplifies such action. The flip side of the coin, *situational* felony murder, involves a murder spawned by panic, confusion, or impulse. Again, William Hickman provides a case in point, with his "accidental" murder of a Los Angeles druggist after police surprised him in an act of robbery.

PERSONAL-CAUSE HOMICIDE

The second broad classification of murder is *personal-cause homicide*, defined as "an act ensuing from interpersonal aggression [that] results in death to person(s) who may not be known to each other. The homicide is not motivated by personal gain or sex and is not sanctioned by a group. It is the result of an underlying emotional conflict that propels the offender to kill." Few students of crime would deny that these motives apply in many cases of serial murder.

The first subcategory listed in the Bureau manual is *erotomania-motivated killing*, wherein murder springs from the killer's fixation with his victim. A case in point is Nathan Trupp's murder of five total strangers in 1988, while stalking TV star Michael Landon (whom Trupp believed to be involved in a global fascist conspiracy).

Domestic homicide, another form of personal-cause murder, may be either *spontaneous* or *staged*. The killer in such cases has a familial or common-law relationship to his victim. *Spontaneous* domestic murder is essen-

tially a crime of passion, as when CARROLL EDWARD COLE strangled his second wife in a drunken rage. The *staged* domestic homicide may also spring from stress or anger, but an effort is made to deceive investigators, as when Paula Sims blamed a nonexistent "masked intruder" for the deaths of two successive children.

A third kind of personal-cause homicide is labeled *argument murder*, resulting from verbal disputes in the heat of the moment, distinguished from spontaneous domestic slayings by the FBI's insistence that victims exclude family or household members. This sounds like nitpicking until we recall the penchant for sudden violence among many serial killers, prepared to lash out on a whim, in response to real or imagined insults. Prolific slayer David Bullock shot one victim for laughing at him, another for the simple act of "messing with [a] Christmas tree, telling me how nice the Christmas tree was."

Conflict murders, in contrast to those arising from verbal arguments, spring from some ongoing tension between killer and victim. The circumstances may include anything from a feud between neighbors (which prompted DONALD HARVEY to poison one of his few victims not killed in hospitals) to a clash between criminal accomplices (as when Elmer Henley shot and killed DEAN CORLL in Houston, Texas).

A fifth kind of personal-cause homicide, labeled *authority killing* by the FBI, involves the murder of an actual or perceived authority figure in the killer's life. Prime examples may be found in the work of serial killers who, like HENRY LUCAS and EDMUND KEMPER, murdered abusive parents while simultaneously preying on strangers outside the home.

Revenge killing, yet another kind of personal-cause homicide, represents an act of retaliation for some real or perceived injury. The target, in turn, may be either symbolic or specific. Rudy Bladel, for instance, murdered a series of railroad employees after losing his job with the Rock Island Line, the killings cast in his mind as retribution against a heartless corporation.

A seventh type of personal cause homicide, dubbed *nonspecific-motive killing*, seems to be a catchall category for crimes without an apparent (or rational) motive. The acts of delusional psychotics fall into this category, and the FBI manual cites HERBERT MULLIN as an example, with his murders intended to prevent earthquakes in California.

Extremist homicide, the eighth class of personal murders, is subdivided by FBI analysts into *political*, *religious*, and *socioeconomic* murders, the latter spawned by hatred of specific ethnic, social, or religious groups. The sole example cited by the FBI is serial killer JOSEPH PAUL FRANKLIN, labeled a "political" killer despite his obsessive hatred of blacks and Jews. A case of religious extremism leading to murder is seen in

James and Susan Carson, self-styled "Muslim warriors" who killed three suspected "witches" in compliance with a verse from the Koran. Norman Bernard, who shot homeless transients as "a favor," offers an example of the socioeconomic killer.

"Mercy" homicides spring from a slayer's warped desire to end suffering by ending lives. It is a motive often seen in MEDICAL MURDERS, particularly in the case of homicidal nurses or nurse's aides. The FBI manual cites Donald Harvey as a case in point, with his confessions to murdering more than 50 hospital patients.

Closely related to "mercy" killing is another form of personal murder, *hero homicide*. In such cases, exemplified by killer nurses GENENE JONES and Richard Angelo, the slayer creates life-or-death situations while planning to "save the day" and garner adulation for himself, but death results from careless planning or technique.

The final type of personal-cause homicide, *hostage murder,* occurs most often with serial killers at the time of capture or when they are interrupted in commission of another crime. Fred Klenner and South African pedophile Gert Van Rooyen both took girlfriends hostage when authorities confronted them; each killed his hostage before committing suicide.

SEXUAL HOMICIDE

A third type of murder, *sexual homicide,* is clearly dominant in the realm of serial murder, where sexual motives are seen in two-thirds of all cases. The killer's expression of sexuality may be symbolic, even bizarre—as in cases of VAMPIRISM and CANNIBALISM—but it is there, all the same.

The FBI manual divides sexual murders into four broad categories. The "ORGANIZED" and "DISORGANIZED" types are discussed in separate entries, while the "mixed" category provides a convenient dump for lust killers who defy pigeonholing. The worst cases on record are those of *sadistic* sex murder, typically including prolonged torture and bizarre mutilation of victims. LAWRENCE ("Pliers") BITTAKER is a prime example, his practice of tape-recording torture sessions with his victims mimicked and improved upon by others like Canadian Paul Bernardo in this age of minicams.

In closing, it should never be assumed that all serial killers are one-dimensional drones, obsessed with a single motive to the exclusion of all other thoughts. The same offender who has raped and killed a dozen women in the past may brain his spouse tomorrow in the heat of a domestic argument or poison an aging parent to hasten a financial windfall. By all accounts, killing becomes easier with practice, over time. When it becomes habitual, a way of life, no one within the slayer's reach is ever truly safe.

See also MODUS OPERANDI; PARAPHILIA; PROFILING

MULLIN, Herbert William

Born in Salinas, California, in April 1947, Mullin was the son of Catholic parents, reared by his devout mother in an atmosphere that his own father regarded as oppressively religious. Still, Herbert seemed normal enough through his teens, participating in high school athletics and winning the class vote of confidence as "most likely to succeed." The June 1965 death of Mullin's best friend in a car crash appeared to change everything, producing a sudden and startling shift in Herb's personality. His bedroom was transformed into a shrine, with furniture arranged around the dead boy's photograph, and Mullin warned his girlfriend that he might be "turning gay."

By February 1969, Mullin seemed obsessed with Eastern religions, his family noting that he had become "more and more unrealistic" in daily behavior. A month later, they persuaded him to enter a mental institution, but he refused to cooperate with psychiatrists and was released after six weeks. October found him in the depths of full-blown paranoid schizophrenia, exacerbated by consumption of LSD and marijuana. Mullin heard "voices" commanding him to shave his head or burn his penis with a cigarette, and he obeyed their

Herbert Mullin killed to prevent catastrophic earthquakes. (Wide World API)

every order. Briefly returned to the hospital, he began writing letters to dozens of total strangers, signing them "a human sacrifice, Herb Mullin." An ill-advised trip to Hawaii in June 1970 resulted in Mullin's brief commitment to a mental institution there. Back in Santa Cruz, his odd behavior led to conflicts with police, and his problems were not erased by 15 months of hiding out in cheap San Francisco hotels. By the time he came home again in September 1972, the disembodied voices were commanding him to kill.

On October 13, 1972, while driving aimlessly through the Santa Cruz mountains, Mullin spotted elderly transient Lawrence White. Pulling his car to the side of the road, Mullin asked White to help him with some "engine trouble," then beat the old man to death with a baseball bat and left his body where it lay. Eleven days later, he picked up coed Mary Guilfoyle, stabbed her in the heart, then disemboweled her, scattering her organs on the shoulder of a lonely road, where skeletal remains were found in February 1973. On November 2, Mullin spoke too freely in the confessional at St. Mary's Church, afterward fatally stabbing Father Henry Tomei in a bid to protect himself from exposure.

Mullin's crimes coincidentally overlapped those of serial slayer EDMUND KEMPER, earning Santa Cruz an unwelcome reputation as "Murderville, USA." By November 1972, Herbert was hearing brand-new voices, emanating from prospective victims, begging him to kill them. He bought a pistol in December and resumed the hunt.

On January 25, 1973, Mullin went looking for Jim Gianera, the man who had "turned him on" to marijuana years earlier. Herb now regarded that act as part of a plot to destroy his mind, and he meant to avenge himself. Calling at Gianera's old address, he received new directions from 29-year-old Kathy Francis. Moving on, he found Gianera at home, shot the man to death, then knifed and shot Gianera's wife for good measure. From there, Mullin doubled back to kill Kathy Francis and her two small sons, shooting all three as they lay in bed.

On February 6, Mullin was hiking in a nearby state park when he met four teenage campers. Approaching the boys with casual conversation, he whipped out his gun and killed all four in a rapid burst of fire before they could react or flee. A week later, driving through Santa Cruz, Mullin pulled to the curb and fatally shot Fred Perez while the old man was working in his garden. This time, neighbors saw his license plate and Mullin was arrested by patrolmen moments later.

In custody, Mullin confessed to his crimes, insisting that the homicides were necessary to prevent cata-strophic earthquakes from destroying California. Charged and convicted in 10 of the murders (omitting White, Guilfoyle, and Tomei), Mullin was sentenced to life imprisonment. He will be eligible for parole in 2020.

MUNCHAUSEN'S Syndrome by Proxy

Named in 1951 for the legendary 18th-century purveyor of tall tales, Baron von Munchausen, Munchausen's syndrome is the psychiatric label for excessive hypochondria, a compulsive bid for sympathetic attention that includes false claims of illness and occasional self-injury. A curious parallel condition with relevance to serial murder, first described in 1977, is Munchausen's syndrome by proxy, wherein those responsible for care of children, invalids, and the like seek attention by harming their charges. A possible extension of the "hero" motive ascribed to some MEDICAL MURDERS in the FBI's *Crime Classification Manual* (1992), Munchausen's syndrome by proxy is also deemed responsible in certain cases where parents—always mothers, in the cases logged to date—kill their own children. MARYBETH TINNING is a prime example, described by psychoanalysts as a virtual sympathy junkie who murdered eight of her children between 1972 and 1985, all for the attention she received in periods of mourning. Such killers are often adept at covering their tracks, and cases like Tinning's and that of MARTHA WOODS (seven children slain between 1946 and 1969) have led to urgent reevaluation of families reporting multiple cases of SUDDEN INFANT DEATH SYNDROME.

See also MOTIVES

MYTHICAL Murders Reported in "Nonfiction" Sources

Serial killers at large are so frightening and fascinating—so "sexy," in media parlance—that some "nonfiction" authors seemingly cannot resist inventing cases of their own. Sometimes, the fudging amounts to simple exaggeration of known body counts for well-established slayers, while in other cases the reporters go all out, apparently manufacturing killers and victims out of thin air for the sake of "a good story." Unfortunately, those tales are proffered as fact and may lead the serious student astray. They are included here to set the record straight.

One of the earliest, most frequently exaggerated cases involves London's "JACK THE RIPPER" in 1888. Authorities involved in the manhunt generally agreed that Jack killed five women—and only five—between August and November of that fateful year. Still, speculation on additional victims, ranging in number from seven to 20 or more, continues in various published accounts to the present day. Some of the "extra" victims really *were* killed in London during the Ripper's heyday but in circumstances radically divergent from Red Jack's pattern; others—generally cited only as anonymous statistics—are apparently figments of the individual author's imagination.

Other examples of misstatement in the field include:

Salvatore Agron: Described in one text as a serial slayer who "dressed like Dracula" and drank the blood of "several" victims, this 16-year-old resident of New York City was in fact a street gang member, convicted (with others) in the routine 1959 murder of two rival gangsters.

SOURCE: J. Gordon Melton, *The Vampire Book* (1994).

Arizona ("Ma") Barker: The notorious mother of depression-era bank robbers appears in one strange account as a sadistic lesbian who kidnapped, tortured, and murdered countless young women, afterward ordering her outlaw sons to dump the bodies in various Minnesota lakes. No such corpses were ever found, and no evidence exists to support the story.

SOURCE: Jay Robert Nash, *Look for the Woman* (1981).

Australian "Ripper": An alleged series of mutilation-murders claiming at least seven victims between 1976 and 1979. While certainly plausible, no such crimes have been discovered through repeated queries to Australian police and journalists.

SOURCE: Jay Robert Nash, *Crime Chronology* (1984).

"Chicago Ripper": Presented as the unidentified mutilation-slayer of 20 women, the last killed in January 1906. (A second, garbled version claims all 20 murders occurred in 1906.) Chicago newspapers reveal that the victim in question was shot, with no reported mutilations, and that her death was speculatively linked to *one* other slaying. No trace of the elusive Ripper or his 20 victims is found in contemporary reports.

SOURCES: Nash, *Crime Chronology;* Eric Hickey, *Serial Murderers and Their Victims* (1997).

"Dunes case": Reported from Provincetown, Massachusetts, in the 1980s, where we are told that "police are investigating the serial killer who left the bodies of twelve young women in sand dunes." In fact, authorities confirm the occurrence of only one such murder, involving a woman found with her hands and feet severed.

SOURCE: Joel Norris, *Serial Killers* (1988).

"The Executioner": Described as an unidentified stalker who "killed at least nine transients" around Los Angeles in 1986, with the method of murder unstated, this "unsolved" case mirrors the crimes of "Skid Row Slayer" Michael Player, who shot nine men (eight of them homeless) before killing himself in October 1986. The case was closed in February 1987 after ballistics tests linked Player's weapon to the murders.

SOURCE: Hickey, *Serial Murderers and Their Victims.*

Joliet murders: Erroneously presented as the unsolved 1983 slayings of "fifteen victims" in Joliet, Illinois, this series actually included 17 deaths in two counties. Authorities consider at least 12 of the murders solved with the 1984 arrest of serial killer MILTON JOHNSON.

SOURCE: Hickey, *Serial Murderers and Their Victims.*

"Los Angeles Slasher": Vaguely described as the slayer of eight unspecified victims in 1974, this nonexistent UNSUB was apparently spawned by a hasty reading of inaccurate reports on the "Skid Row Slasher" case (see below).

SOURCE: Hickey, *Serial Murderers and Their Victims.*

"Midtown Slasher": A brief but notorious series of Manhattan stabbings, solved in July 1981 with the arrest of Charles Sears, but still sometimes erroneously cited as an unsolved case.

SOURCE: Norris, *Serial Killers.*

Moscow beheadings: An alleged series of decapitations claiming "several" female victims during 1979. No supporting evidence for this case has been found in the 15 years since its original publication.

SOURCE: Nash, *Crime Chronology.*

Joseph Mumfre: Named definitively in various accounts as the "AX MAN OF NEW ORLEANS," although he apparently never existed. One such report, by Jay Robert Nash, states that "Between 1916 and 1920 Mumfre . . . systematically murdered, according to reports, twelve members of the Pepitone family, using an axe to bash in each victim's head." No source is offered for said "reports," but they are clearly erroneous, since only one of the stalker's known victims—the last—was named Pepitone. Researcher William Kingman conclusively demonstrates that Mumfre's reported murder by one Ax Man victim's widow, cited as proof of his guilt, never occurred. Today, no record of Joseph Mumfre's life or death exists.

SOURCE: Jay Robert Nash, *Bloodletters and Badmen* (1973).

Edward Paisnal: A sadistic British pedophile who abused numerous children but never killed anyone, described erroneously in one text as a serial killer who buried victims at his home.

SOURCE: Norris, *Serial Killers.*

"Miguel Rivera": A pseudonym applied to New York City serial murder suspect ERNO SOTO in author Barbara Gelb's *On the Track of Murder* (1975). While Gelb informs her readers that an alias has been employed, "Rivera" still crops up as a flesh-and-blood killer in other nonfiction works.

SOURCE: Brian Lane and Wilfred Gregg, *The Encyclopedia of Serial Killers* (1992).

"Ralph Searl" and *"Tommy Searl":* Pseudonyms applied to real-life serial-killing brothers DANNY and LARRY RANES by author Conrad Hilberry in his book *Luke Karamazov* (1987). Once again, the original book acknowledges use of pseudonyms, but careless derivative works refer to the "Searl" brothers and list their several victims by fictional names.

SOURCE: Lane and Gregg, *The Encyclopedia of Serial Killers.*

"Skid Row Slasher": Described as an unsolved case, sometimes with incorrect dates and a mistaken tally of victims, in works published long after the arrest and conviction of perpetrator VAUGHN GREENWOOD.

SOURCES: Jay Robert Nash, *Open Files* (1984); Norris, *Serial Killers.*

"Mary Eleanor Smith" and *"Earl Smith":* An apparent effort to report the case of mother-son killing team Anne French and William Mayer, so garbled in transition that it becomes recognizable only through mention of French's nickname ("Shoebox Annie").

SOURCES: Eric Hickey, *Serial Murderers and Their Victims* (1991); Ronald Holmes and Stephen Holmes, *Serial Murder* (1998).

"Soda Pop Slasher": The alleged mutilation-slayer of 13 victims around New York City, still at large but "controlled" by the vigilance of his psychiatrist, who tells the tale. Admitted use of pseudonyms and altered dates makes the "notorious" case difficult to track. Suffice it to say that no case even vaguely similar has ever been reported in the *New York Times,* while various incidents and characters from the book mirror elements from such cinematic thrillers as *Final Analysis* and *Color of Night.*

SOURCE: Martin Obler and Thomas Clavin, *Fatal Analysis* (1997).

"Sunday Morning Slasher": A series of attacks on young women in Ann Arbor, Michigan, between April and July 1980, solved with the 1982 confession of CORAL WATTS. Years later, one account described the "unsolved" crimes occurring in Houston, Texas, during 1981.

SOURCE: Norris, *Serial Killers.*

"Suspect unknown": A series of unsolved murders from 1983, allegedly involving four women in White Plains, New York. Queries to police and journalists in White Plains have failed to discover any such crimes in 1983 or any other year.

SOURCE: Norris, *Serial Killers.*

"Suspect unknown": A report of alleged serial murders at a convalescent home in Galveston, Texas, with police "investigating the deaths of twenty-eight geriatric patients" in 1983. This case, apparently, *does* have some basis in reality, but it was not an example of serial murder. Rather, journalists in Galveston report that authorities investigated the "home" in question for chronic neglect of its inmates, resulting in several deaths.

SOURCE: Norris, *Serial Killers.*

"Texas Strangler": Reported as a series of 12 unsolved murders committed in the late 1960s and early 1970s, although several of the murders listed were solved in 1972, with the conviction of defendant Johnny Meadows.

SOURCES: Nash, *Open Files;* Hickey, *Serial Murderers and Their Victims.*

"3X": The unidentified New York gunman who killed two men and raped one woman in June 1930 unaccountably appears in some recent accounts as a "mad bomber" who "terrorized the city in the early 1930s."

SOURCES: Nash, *Open Files* and *Bloodletters and Badmen* (1996).

"Trailside Killer": The case of eight hikers murdered around Point Reyes, California, between August 1979 and March 1981, solved with the 1984 conviction of David Carpenter, erroneously described years later as involving "a cult killer of seven hitchhikers" in 1980, with the killer "still at large."

SOURCE: Norris, *Serial Killers.*

"Tulsa bludgeonings": The murders of four red-haired women between 1942 and 1948, solved with the arrest of Charles Floyd in 1949, is still presented as unsolved in some accounts.

SOURCE: Jay Robert Nash, *Encyclopedia of World Crime* (1992).

"ZODIAC": California's legendary one-that-got-away, cited in print as a killer who "murdered and

sexually assaulted several children in San Francisco" during 1974, and who was "[g]iven his name by the police because he carved the sign of the zodiac [*sic*] into the bodies of his victims." In

fact, "Zodiac" was active from 1966 to 1969, killed only adults, and coined his own nickname in letters to the press.

SOURCE: Norris, *Serial Killers.*

NASH, "Trigger"

An officer with the Atlanta, Georgia, Police Department in the 1940s, first name unknown, "Trigger" Nash (aka "Itchy Trigger Finger") earned his nickname by fatally shooting more than a dozen black men. Nash was also a member in good standing of the night-riding Ku Klux Klan, his cover blown in 1948 when infiltrator Stetson Kennedy began furnishing newspaper columnist Drew Pearson with minutes of meetings at Nathan Bedford Forest Klavern No. 1. Several Atlanta policemen addressed a Klan gathering on November 1, 1948, and Nash got a round of applause "for killing his thirteenth nigger in the line of duty." According to the minutes of that gathering,

> Trigger Nash, also a policeman, got up and made a talk and said he hoped he wouldn't have all the honor of killing the niggers in the South, and he hoped the people would do something about it themselves.

Today, in most jurisdictions, such a public statement would doubtless result in the patrolman being fired and most likely prosecuted under state or federal law. In 1948, however, ranking officers of the Klan-ridden Atlanta PD saw nothing unique or disturbing in Nash's behavior. (Kennedy also revealed that Atlanta's Klan "kops" had destroyed vital evidence in the case of a black taxi driver murdered by Klansmen.) Nash's ultimate fate is unknown, impossible to trace in the absence of cooperation from local authorities, but there is no record of prosecution for any of his multiple racist homicides.

NEELLEY, Alvin Howard and Judith Ann

Born June 7, 1964, in Murfreesboro, Tennessee, Judith Adams was the third of five children. She was nine years old when her father died in a motorcycle crash, barely 15 when she met the man who would irrevocably change her life. Alvin Neelley was a Georgia native, known to friends and family as a childhood prankster, "always smiling." Rejected by the navy for a minor heart condition, Alvin tried his hand at marriage, but it didn't take. He left three children when he hit the road and drifted through a string of odd jobs, winding up in Tennessee. Eleven years Judith's senior, Neelley dazzled her with his "sophistication," and they eloped to Georgia in the fall of 1979.

They settled briefly in Kennesaw, but Alvin's job at a roadside market offered no hope for advancement. Soon the lovers began to drift again, pulling small robberies and passing bad checks to support themselves on the road. Judith was five months pregnant when they finally married in Ringgold, Georgia, on July 14, 1980. Their honeymoon was an aimless trek through Alabama, Florida, Louisiana, and Texas, always winding back to Georgia when they tired of traveling.

On October 31, 1980, Judith robbed a woman at gunpoint in the parking lot of Riverbend Mall in Rome, Georgia. Arrested 10 days later as she tried to cash a rubber check, she steered police to the motel where Al sat waiting. Together, they faced one count of robbery and 15 counts of forgery. Judith delivered twins on November 12, and five days later she was transferred to a juvenile facility, the Rome Youth Development Center. For his role in the crime spree, Alvin drew a five-year prison term.

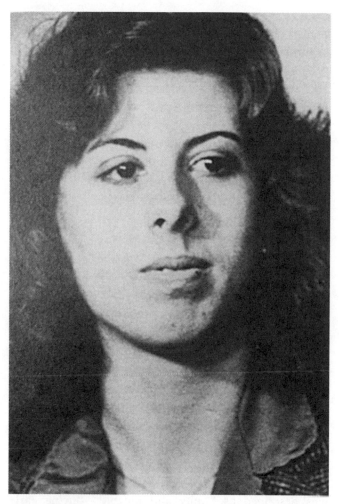

Judith Neelley (Author's collection)

The outlaw lovers kept in touch while they were locked away, some of the letters warm and loving, others jealous and accusatory. Alvin thought Judith was bedding black guards at the YDC; she threatened death to his imaginary girlfriends on the street. Released from custody in November 1981, Judith had to wait another five months for Alvin's parole. In the meantime, she played mother to her two children.

Money always seemed to be a problem for the transient lovers who saw themselves as latter-day outlaws. Sometimes they called each other "Boney and Claude," a joking reference to depression-era desperadoes Bonnie Parker and Clyde Barrow. On the highway, driving separate cars, they kept in touch with CB radios. Al Neelley called himself "The Nightrider," while Judith preferred "Lady Sundance." In case anyone missed the point, she was glad to explain: "You know, like *Butch Cassidy and the Sundance Kid.*" The cars were bought with $1,800 Alvin pilfered from the first job he obtained upon release from jail.

And when the thrill of stealing paled, they turned to random violence for the hell of it.

On September 10, 1982, four shots were fired into the home of Ken Dooley, a teacher at the Rome YDC. The following night, a Molotov cocktail damaged the house occupied by another YDC staffer, Linda Adair. At 1:41 A.M. on September 12, a female caller told police in Rome that the attacks were linked to "sex abuse that I went through in the YDC." She did not leave her name, but operators taped the call as a matter of routine.

Two weeks later, on September 25, 13-year-old Lisa Millican was abducted from the same Riverbend Mall where Judith had robbed her last victim in October 1980. A resident of Cedartown's home for neglected children, Lisa was enjoying a day's outing when she met Judith Neelley and was lured into Alvin's clutches. The couple held her prisoner for three days, repeatedly molesting her in seedy motel rooms while their own children watched. Finally tiring of the game, Judith tried injecting their victim with liquid drain cleaner, but she kept hitting muscle instead of a vein, reducing Lisa's flesh to what a coroner would call "the consistency of anchovy paste." Still Lisa lived, in agony, and she was driven to Alabama's Little River Canyon, where she was finished off with bullets after more injections failed to do the job. Back in Rome, Judith made several anonymous calls to police, directing them to the body, apparently unaware that her voice was being recorded for posterity.

Three days after Lisa's body was found, on October 3, 26-year-old John Hancock and his fiancée, 23-year-old Janice Chatman, were walking down Rome's Shorter Street when a flashy car pulled to the curb. Incredibly, when total stranger Judith Neelley asked them to a party, both agreed, climbing into her car for a drive to some nearby woods. En route, they played with Judith's children and eavesdropped on her CB conversation with "The Nightrider." Alvin was waiting when they reached their destination, but Hancock later fingered Judith as the one who drew a gun and marched them through the trees, shooting him once in the back and leaving him for dead. Janice Chatman, like the killer family, was gone without a trace when Hancock revived and staggered off in search of help.

Initially, police saw no connections in the string of recent crimes. That changed on October 12 with help from Linda Adair. The Hancock shooting had occurred near her home, and descriptions of the slender blond with two young children rang a bell. Adair supplied detectives with a snapshot of the Neelley twins, mug shots of Al and Judith quickly filling in the family album. Hancock recognized their faces in a photo lineup; so did two young women earlier approached by Judith on the street, both wise enough to turn her invitation down.

Police got a break on October 14 when the Neelleys were arrested for check fraud in Judith's hometown of Murfreesboro. Alvin initially denied raping Lisa Millican, but he finally caved in. Even so, he insisted, the crimes had been Judith's idea. She enjoyed rough sex with women, Alvin said, but the real turn-on was power—in this case, the literal power of life and death. Neelley fingered his wife for a minimum of eight murders, perhaps as many as 15, committed in her role as "enforcer" for an elusive white-slave ring. More to the point, he sketched and signed a map of rural Chattooga County, Georgia, where police found Janice Chatman's decomposing corpse.

The sketch sealed Alvin's fate in Georgia, but authorities in Alabama had no evidence to place him in the neighborhood of Little River Canyon where Lisa Millican was killed. Indicted for murder and aggravated assault in the Chatman-Hancock case, Alvin pled guilty and was sentenced to a double term of life imprisonment. He would not testify in Alabama when his helpmate went to trial.

And the wheels of justice were already turning for Judith across the border in DeKalb County. On December 17, she was denied youthful offender status and ordered to face trial as an adult on charges of first-degree murder, abduction with intent to harm, and abduction with intent to terrorize and sexually violate. It was a lethal combination, "special circumstances" that could send her off to the electric chair unless she beat the rap. Judith responded with a dual plea of not guilty and not guilty by reason of insanity, her trial set for March 7, 1983. Psychiatrists found her competent and legally sane, despite some evidence of "situational depression" and a vague personality disorder—"either of the passive-aggressive or dependent type."

Dependency, in fact, would be the key to Judith's defense, painting herself as a battered wife who followed Alvin's every command in fear of her life. Alabama detectives countered with descriptions of Judith as "one mean bitch" who "liked scaring people, dominating them."

Judith's trial opened in Fort Payne on schedule, with the defendant spending three days on the witness stand. Predictably, she blamed her husband for everything, describing a three-year ordeal of rapes and beatings. To each and every charge, the answer for her actions was the same: "Because Al told me to."

Alvin's first wife, Jo Ann Browning, also spoke for the defense, describing a similar pattern of spousal abuse, but her testimony was muddled and contradictory. At one point, she told the court she had never divorced Alvin; moments later she reversed herself, explaining that she had married Alvin before divorcing her first husband. Altogether, Browning's performance left much to be desired.

Jurors retired briefly before convicting Judith on all counts, but they were sympathetic enough to recommend life imprisonment over death. Judge Randall Cole disagreed, pronouncing a sentence of death on April 18, 1983. At 18, Judith Neelley became the youngest resident of Alabama's death row.

Police were still intrigued by Alvin's tale of other homicides, and while they found four Georgia cases between December 1981 and June 1982 still unsolved, no evidence connected either Neelley to the crimes. In August 1984, a young woman in Murfreesboro identified newspaper photos of Judith as the same "Casey" who lured her to a motel in October 1982, there pulling a gun and joining her husband in an all-night marathon of sexual assault. Between rapes, "Casey" had boasted of numerous murders, but again, no further evidence was found.

Judith Neelley's motion for a new trial was denied on September 6, 1983, and her conviction was later affirmed on appeal. Her death sentence was commuted to life imprisonment on January 8, 1999.

NELSON, Leonard Earle

Born in Philadelphia on May 12, 1897, Nelson was orphaned at nine months of age when his unmarried mother died of advanced venereal disease. Raised by an aunt whose religious zeal bordered on fanaticism, he was described as "quiet and morbid" during early childhood. At age 10, while playing in the street, he was struck by a trolley and dragged 50 feet; the accident left him comatose for six days with a hole in his temple, resulting in headaches and dizziness that grew progressively worse. Near the end of his life, Nelson suffered from pain so severe that he was sometimes unable to walk.

Aside from headaches, there were other side effects from Nelson's accident. His moods grew more oppressive, broken up by manic periods in which he took to walking on his hands or lifting heavy chairs with his teeth. He read the Bible compulsively, underlining numerous passages, but also shocked his aunt by talking "smut" and spying on his female cousin as she stripped for bed. When not preoccupied with voyeurism or the scriptures, Nelson spent his time in basements, relishing the solitude and darkness.

On May 21, 1918, Earle was charged with dragging a neighborhood girl into one of those basements and attempting to rape her. In court, it was revealed that Nelson had been called for military service and rejected as insane by the Naval Hospital Board, but he was convicted regardless and sentenced to two years on a penal farm. His third escape attempt was successful, on December 4, and Nelson would remain at large until the spring of 1921.

On August 5, 1919, posing as "Roger Wilson," Earle married a woman 36 years his senior. Their relationship was short lived, with Nelson's sexual perversions and obsessive jealousy driving his wife to the point of a nervous breakdown after six months. He called upon her in the hospital, there attempting to molest her in her bed before the staff responded to her screams and drove him off. Arrested as a fugitive, he escaped again in November 1923.

The next two years of Nelson's life are lost, but sometime in the interim between his flight and reappearance, Nelson made the jump from rape to homicide. In 16 months, from February 1926 to June 1927, he claimed at least 22 victims, preying chiefly on widows and spinsters who took him in, believing him to be a mild-mannered boarder, and were impressed by his charm and the Bible he carried.

On February 20, 1926, Earle rented rooms from 60-year-old Clara Newman in San Francisco; she was strangled and raped the same day. Following the identical murder of 65-year-old Laura Beale in San Jose, newsmen began writing stories about the "Dark Strangler," but their suspect remained elusive.

On June 10, Nelson was back in San Francisco, where he raped and strangled 63-year-old Lillian St. Mary, stuffing her body under a bed in her home. Ollie Russell was the next to die, in Santa Barbara on June 24. On August 16, Mary Nisbit suffered an identical fate in Oakland.

California had become too hot for Nelson, and he sought a change of scene, selecting Portland, Oregon, at random. On October 19, 32-year-old Beata Withers was raped and strangled, her body stashed in a trunk. The next day, Nelson killed Virginia Grant and left her corpse behind the furnace in a house she had advertised for rent. October 21 found Nelson in the company of Mable Fluke; her body, strangled with a scarf, was later found in the attic of her home.

Police in Portland finally identified their man, but finding him proved much more difficult. (Interviews with Nelson's aunt recalled his hand-walking exploits, prompting reporters to dub him "The Gorilla Murderer.") Nelson struck again in San Francisco on November 18, strangling the wife of William Edmonds. Six days later he strangled Blanche Myers in Oregon City, tucking her body beneath a bed in her boarding house.

As police dragnets swept the West Coast, Nelson moved eastward, hitchhiking and riding the rails. In Council Bluffs, Iowa, on December 23, he killed another landlady, Mrs. John Brerard. Settling in Kansas City for

Christmas, he strangled 23-year-old Bonnie Pace, rebounding on December 28 with the double murder of Germania Harpin and her eight-month-old son.

On April 27, 1927, Nelson strangled 53-year-old Mary McConnell in Philadelphia. A month later, in Buffalo, New York, the victim was 53-year-old Jennie Randolph. Moving on to Detroit, he murdered landlady Fannie May and one of her tenants, Maurene Oswald, on June 1. Two days later, he strangled 27-year-old Cecilia Sietsema in Chicago.

Nelson feared police were closing in on him by then and made a move to save himself that ultimately brought him to the gallows. Crossing the border into Winnipeg, Canada, he rented a room on June 8, 1927, and strangled Lola Cowan, a 13-year-old neighbor, the same day. On June 9, housewife Emily Patterson was found bludgeoned and raped in her home, her body hidden underneath a bed.

Hoping to cash in on his last crime, Nelson stole some clothing and sold it at a Winnipeg secondhand shop. Spending his cash on a haircut, he aroused further suspicion when the barber noticed flecks of dried blood in his hair. Recognized from a wanted poster in the local post office, Nelson was picked up and jailed in Killarney; he escaped after picking the lock on his cell with a nail file, but he was recaptured 12 hours later, trying to slip out of town.

Nelson's trial for the murder of Emily Patterson opened in Winnipeg on November 1, 1927. Only two witnesses—his aunt and ex-wife—were called by the defense in support of Nelson's insanity plea. Convicted and sentenced to die, he was hanged on January 13, 1928. Before the trap was sprung, he told spectators, "I am innocent. I stand innocent before God and man. I forgive those who have wronged me and ask forgiveness of those I have injured. God have mercy!"

In addition to his 22 confirmed murders, Nelson was also the prime suspect in a 1926 triple murder in Newark, New Jersey. The victims included Rose Valentine and Margaret Stanton, both strangled, along with Laura Tidor, shot when she tried to defend them from their killer.

NESSET, Arnfinn

Norway's premier serial killer was exposed in 1981 as a result of journalistic curiosity. The Orkdal Valley Nursing Home had opened for business in 1977, and its patients soon experienced a high rate of mortality. Considering their ages, this was not especially unusual; in early 1981, however, local journalists received a tip that hospital manager Arnfinn Nesset had ordered large quantities of curacit—a derivative of curare, the same poison used by South American Indians on the tips of their hunting arrows. Under questioning, Nesset first claimed he purchased the poison for use on a dog, then changed his story and confessed to the murders of 27 patients between May 1977 and November 1980.

At 46, Nesset had already cinched the Scandinavian record for serial murder, but he was not finished talking. "I've killed so many I'm unable to remember them all," he told police, prompting authorities to request lists of patients who had died in three institutions where Nesset had worked since 1962. In all, detectives were left with a list of 62 possible victims, but autopsies were futile, since curacit becomes increasingly difficult to trace with the passage of time.

Nesset offered a variety of MOTIVES for the murders—mercy killing, schizophrenia, simple morbid pleasure in the act itself—which led defense attorneys to suggest that he was mentally unbalanced. Four psychiatrists examined the balding, bespectacled killer, each pronouncing him sane and fit for trial. Before his day in court, the suspect proved his sanity by suddenly recanting his confessions, leaving prosecutors in a quandary.

Arnfinn Nesset (Author's collection)

He was finally charged with killing 25 of the established Orkdal Valley victims; five counts of forgery and embezzlement were added, based upon Nesset's theft of some $1,800 from those he killed.

Nesset pled innocent on all counts when his trial opened in October 1982. Five months later, on March 11, 1983, jurors convicted him on 22 counts of murder, one count of attempted murder, plus all five counts of forgery and embezzlement. Nesset was acquitted on the three remaining murder charges, but it scarcely mattered. Judges were unmoved by the defense plea that Nesset considered himself a "demigod," holding the power of life and death over his elderly patients. He was given the maximum sentence allowed under Norwegian law: 21 years in prison, with a possibility of 10 more years' preventive detention.

See also MEDICAL MURDERS

NILSEN, Dennis Andrew

Born in Scotland on November 23, 1945, Nilsen seldom saw his Norwegian father, who preferred strong drink and travel to the quiet life at home. Nilsen's parents were divorced when he was four years old, and his mother soon remarried. Joining the army in 1961, Nilsen remained in uniform for 11 years. Upon discharge, he moved to London and became a policeman, moving on from there through a series of government jobs. A closet homosexual, Nilsen would not kill for sex as did DEAN CORLL and JOHN GACY in the United States. Rather, his crimes appear to be the product of sheer loneliness, coupled with a morbid fascination for death. Keeping remains of his victims on hand for months at a time, Nilsen was (in the words of biographer Brian Masters), literally "killing for company."

Nilsen's loneliness was held at bay through 1976 and early 1977 by the presence of a live-in companion 10 years his junior. While they apparently never had sex, the younger man provided Nilsen with friendship and someone to talk to, sharing the daily grind of cooking, housework, and so forth. Nilsen was stricken by his roommate's departure in May 1977, and the pressures of a solitary life gradually mounted to the detonation point.

Nilsen's first victim, in December 1978, was an anonymous Irish youth whom he brought home and strangled with a necktie. Dennis later masturbated over the corpse, storing it beneath his floorboards until August 1979 when it was cremated on an outdoor bonfire. In November 1979, Nilsen tried to strangle Andrew Ho, a young Chinese man, but Ho escaped and summoned the police. Confronted with a former colleague, officers accepted Nilsen's story of attempted robbery by Ho and let the matter drop. A few days

Dennis Nilsen (Author's collection)

later, on December 3, Nilsen strangled Canadian Kenneth Ockendon with an electric cord and dissected his body, flushing parts down the toilet, while most of the butchered remains were stashed under his floor.

In May 1980, Nilsen murdered 19-year-old Martyn Duffey, hiding his corpse with the fragmentary Ockendon remains. That summer, 26-year-old Billy Sutherland joined the growing crowd, followed shortly by a victim who may have been Mexican or Filipino. "I can't remember the details," Nilsen said later. "It's academic. I put him under the floorboards."

Memories were vague about the next five victims, their names unknown, identified only by some physical trait or quirk of behavior that stuck in Nilsen's mind. A young Irishman and a malnourished transient were brought home in swift succession, and both were strangled to death in Nilsen's flat. Number eight was cut into three pieces, his remains hidden beneath the floor for two days before they were burned in another garden bonfire. Number nine was a young Scot, and his successor an unruly "Billy Sutherland type." Number 11 was a tough-talking skinhead, notable for the tattoo of a dotted line around his neck, with the instructions "Cut Here." Nilsen did, and the young man was incinerated on a bonfire during May of 1981.

In September of that year, Nilsen found epileptic Malcolm Barlow slumped against his garden wall and phoned for an ambulance. Barlow came back to see Nilsen the next day on his release from the hospital, and it proved a fatal mistake. A month later, when Nilsen found new lodgings, he cleaned house with one last bonfire, the blaze leaving police with no evidence of 12 murders spanning almost three years.

A month after settling in his new apartment, on November 25, 1981, Nilsen attempted to strangle Paul Nobbs with a necktie. Nobbs survived the attack, which took place as he slept, but he made no report to police. The next victim, John Howlett, fought bitterly for his life, forcing Nilsen to drown him in the bathtub when strangulation proved ineffective. Howlett's remains were hacked up in the tub, then boiled down in a kettle before they were flushed through the drains.

In May 1982, Nilsen tried to drown Carl Stottor in his bathtub, changing his mind in midstream, persuading Stottor the assault had been intended to "revive" him after he had nearly suffocated in his sleeping bag. Next day, while walking in the woods, Nilsen crept up behind Stottor and clubbed him to the ground, but again Stottor survived, shrugging off the attack and filing no complaint until after Nilsen was jailed for multiple murder.

Number 14 was alcoholic Graham Allen, killed and dissected in Nilsen's flat; portions of his body were bagged and stored in the cupboard, while other parts were boiled and flushed down the toilet. A local "punk" named Stephen Sinclair was the last to die, murdered on February 1, 1983; portions of his body were flushed down the toilet a week later.

It was finally too much for the plumbing, and Nilsen—like German JOACHIM KROLL before him—was betrayed by his pipes. Tenants of Nilsen's apartment building summoned a plumber to clear the clogged lines, and his discovery of human flesh brought police to the scene. In custody, Nilsen freely confessed his crimes and was sentenced to life imprisonment. Asked about the motive for his murders, he replied, "Well, enjoying it is as good a reason as any."

NORTHCOTT, Gordon Stewart

Canadian-born in 1908, Northcott would later claim that his father sodomized him at age 10, and his mother dressed him as a girl until he was 16. The old man finished his life in a lunatic asylum, and one of Northcott's paternal uncles died in San Quentin Prison years later, while serving a life term for murder. A homosexual sadist in the mold of DEAN CORLL and JOHN GACY, by age 21 Northcott was living on a poultry ranch near Riverside, California, sharing quarters with his mother and a 15-year-old nephew, Sanford Clark.

For years, Northcott mixed business with pleasure in Riverside, abducting boys and hiding them out on his ranch, renting his victims to wealthy southern California pedophiles. When he tired of the boys, they were shot or brained with an ax, their flesh dissolved in quicklime, and their bones transported to the nearby desert for disposal. Only one skeleton was ever found—a headless teenage Mexican, discovered near La Puente during February 1928—but homicide detectives identified three other victims. Walter Collins disappeared from home on March 10, 1928, and Northcott's mother was convicted of his death, but evidence suggests that she was acting under orders from her psychopathic son. Twelve-year-old Lewis Winslow and his 10-year-old brother Nelson vanished from Pomona on May 16, 1928, and Northcott was later condemned for their murders, despite the absence of bodies.

Gordon might have gone on raping and killing indefinitely, but in the summer of 1928, he visited the district attorney's office, complaining about a neighbor's "profane and violent" behavior. The outbursts reportedly upset his nephew, who was "training for the priesthood" by tending chickens at age 15. Questioned by sheriff's deputies, the neighbor recalled seeing Northcott beat Clark on occasion, and he urged detectives to "find out what goes on" at Gordon's ranch.

Immigration officials struck first, taking Clark into custody on a runaway complaint from his Canadian parents, and the boy regaled authorities with tales of murder, pointing out newly excavated "grave sites" on the ranch. Detectives dug up blood-soaked earth on September 17 revealing human ankle bones and fingers. They also found a bloodstained ax and hatchet on the premises, which Clark said had been used on human prey as well as chickens.

Northcott fled to Canada, but he was captured there and extradited back to Riverside in October. His mother claimed responsibility for slaying Walter Collins, but Clark fingered Gordon as the actual killer. Convicted on three counts of murder, including the Winslow brothers and the anonymous Mexican, Northcott was sentenced to hang. Spared by her age and gender, his mother received a life prison sentence in the Collins case.

Marking time at San Quentin, Northcott alternated between protestations of innocence and detailed confessions to the murders of "eighteen or nineteen, maybe twenty" victims. A pathological liar who cherished the spotlight, he several times offered to point out remains of more victims, always reneging at the last moment. (Northcott also named several of his wealthy "customers" at the ranch, but their identities were never published and no charges were filed.) Warden Clinton Duffy recalled his conversations with Northcott as "a lurid account of mass murder, sodomy, oral copulation and torture so vivid it made my flesh creep."

Northcott mounted the gallows on October 2, 1930, finally quailing in the face of death. Before the trap was sprung, he screamed, "A prayer! Please say a prayer for me!" His mother subsequently died in prison of natural causes.

OGORZOV, Paul

A German railroad worker and loyal Nazi Party member, Paul Ogorzov earned notoriety as the "S Bahn Murderer" in World War II. Stalking female victims around Rummelsberg on the Berlin line, he was a sadist who killed for sexual satisfaction, relishing the terror of his chosen prey. Between 1939 and 1941, he killed at least eight women, raping most of them before he beat them to death with a length of lead cable. Twenty-eight years old when his trial opened on July 24, 1941, Ogorzov received no sympathy from his fellow Nazis. Anxious to put the scandal behind them and get on with the business of murdering Jews, party leaders rushed through the proceedings in a single afternoon, sentencing Ogorzov to death. He was shot by a firing squad on July 26.

OKUBO Kiyoshi

Twenty-two years after the execution of KODAIRA YOSHIO, Japanese police found themselves in pursuit of another serial lust killer. Less adept than Kodaira at covering his tracks, the new practitioner was active for barely two months, but within that time he accosted at least 127 women (some reports say 150 or more), raped more than a dozen, and murdered eight. His capture, when it came, owed as much to personal negligence as to great detective work.

Born in January 1935, Okubo Kiyoshi was the third and youngest son in a family of eight children, on whom both parents lavished affection, and he was virtually immune to discipline. On one occasion, when a neighbor complained of Okubo knocking fruit from his persimmon trees, Kiyoshi's mother replied, "You shouldn't have planted those trees there."

Despite the coddling at home, Okubo was teased unmercifully at school over his "Western" appearance—the result of Russian blood in his mother's family. Resentful of the teasing and entirely undisciplined, Okubo was a problem student who received poor grades and frequent warnings about his poor attitude. A sixth-grade evaluation notes that he "engages in unseemly acts toward his superiors" and "is showing signs of maturity too early for his age." The latter complaint was a reference to his treatment of female classmates, including the incessant muttering of "words that shouldn't be said" in the company of girls.

In the summer of 1946, at age 11, Okubo was caught attempting to molest a neighbor's four-year-old daughter. Those who knew his family were only half joking when they began to describe Okubo as "little Kodaira" or the "son of Kodaira," comparing him to Tokyo's notorious rape-slayer. Nine years later, in July 1955, he raped a 17-year-old high school student in Maebashi and was sentenced to 18 months in prison, but the jail time was promptly commuted to three years' probation. Arrested for a second rape five months later, he found the judge less merciful and wound up serving three years in Matsumoto Prison.

Paroled at age 25, Okubo adopted the pseudonym of "Watanabe Kyoshi," posing as a student while he preyed on college coeds. Married in May 1962, he fathered two children before his next arrest for rape, in February 1967. Convicted of attacking two young women, he was sentenced to four and a half years in prison, winning provisional release on March 2, 1971. Ten days later, he paid ¥210,000 for the cream-colored Mazda sedan that would ultimately lead to his arrest and conviction for multiple murders.

Okubo's final rampage began on March 21, and lasted 64 days. Police were hot on his trail the whole time, furnished with descriptions of his Mazda and its license number by surviving victims, but Okubo still managed to claim eight lives before he was captured. A high school student, 17-year-old Tsuda Miyako, was the first to die, on March 31. Ten days later, Okubo killed Oikawa Mieko, a 17-year-old waitress. Ida Chieko, age 19, was murdered on April 17, while another student, 17-year-old Kawabata Shigeko, died the following day. Yet another 17-year-old student, Sato Akemi, met her death at Okubo's hands on April 27. Kawabo Kazuyo, an 18-year-old telephone operator, joined the list on May 3. Six days later, Okubo raped and murdered 21-year-old Takemura Reiko. His last murder victim, 21-year-old housemaid Takahashi Naoko, was slain the next day, May 10.

Okubo displayed no particular ingenuity in disposing of his victims: four were buried in a vacant lot adjacent to an industrial park near Takasaki City, and the others were simply discarded at rural dump sites. Repeated sightings of his Mazda in the Takasaki neighborhood inevitably led to Okubo's arrest on the evening of May 14. A girl was with him in the car when he was cornered by police, Okubo handing her some money and remarking that "You'd better take a taxi home."

Initially held on charges of abduction with intent to commit an immoral act, Okubo soon confessed his crimes and led police to the graves of several victims they had not yet discovered. Tried on eight counts of abduction, murder, and abandonment of corpses, Okubo told the court, "I became the brute that I am because of the police. During their investigation of the previous two cases in which I was involved, they treated me very badly. Their punishment was dealt out in a way that completely destroyed my humanity. It made me rebel against authority."

Asked for any final comments on his situation, Okubo went on to say, "If I could be reborn, I would like to come back as a weed. I was told by a woman I once knew that no matter how much weeds are tread upon, they snap back. That's the kind of existence I would like to have in the next life."

Convicted and sentenced to death on February 22, 1973, Okubo spent nearly three years at Tokyo's Kosuge Detention Center, appealing his sentence. The appeals were rejected, and he was finally hanged on January 23, 1976, six days after his 41st birthday.

OLAH, Susannah   *See* "ANGEL MAKERS OF NAGYREV"

OLSON, Clifford Robert

A native of Vancouver, British Columbia, born on New Year's Day, 1940, Olson spent most of his life in trouble with the police. Remembered as a bully in school, he logged 94 arrests between 1957 and 1981, serving time on charges that ranged from fraud to armed robbery and sexual assault. In prison, Olson was known as a homosexual rapist and sometime informer, once coaching fellow inmate Gary Marcoux into writing a detailed confession to the rape and mutilation-murder of a nine-year-old girl, then surfacing as a prosecution witness at the trial where the letters were used to convict Marcoux. Back on the street, Olson kept up his role as a police stool pigeon, moving in with the mother of his illegitimate son.

In November 1980, 12-year-old Christine Weller was abducted from her home in the Vancouver suburb of Surrey, her mutilated body found in the woods south of town on Christmas Day. Colleen Daignault, age 13, vanished from Surrey on April 16, and 16-year-old Darren Johnsrud was abducted from a Vancouver shopping mall less than a week later and found dead on May 2, his skull shattered by heavy blows.

Olson finally got around to marrying his girlfriend on May 15, 1981, and 16-year-old Sandra Wolfsteiner disappeared four days later, while hitchhiking through suburban Langley. On June 21, 13-year-old Ada Court was reported missing at Coquitlam when she failed to return home from a baby-sitting job. Judy Kozma, 14, disappeared on July 9, her mutilated body recovered from Lake Weaver near Agassiz in the Frazer Valley on July 25.

By that time, Olson was already considered a suspect in the various deaths and disappearances, his name first mentioned at a law enforcement conference on July 15. Despite sporadic surveillance of their man, police were unable to prevent him from claiming four more victims in the last week of July. Fifteen-year-old Raymond King disappeared from New Westminster on July 23, his body recovered from the shore of Lake Weaver two weeks later. On July 25, 18-year-old Sigrun Arnd was abducted and killed while thumbing rides near Vancouver, her remains finally identified through dental charts. Terri Carson vanished from the same Surrey housing complex where Christine Weller had lived, her corpse joining the list of those recovered from Lake Weaver. On July 30, 17-year-old Louise Chartrand disappeared while hitchhiking at Maple Ridge.

Officers tailing Olson arrested him days later, after he picked up two female hitchhikers on Vancouver

Island. The girls were unharmed, but a search of his van turned up an address book belonging to Judy Kozma. Formally charged with her murder six days later, Olson started dealing with the prosecution, striking a bargain that would pay his wife and child $10,000 per victim in return for information on four known murders and directions to six missing corpses. Olson made good on his part of the controversial deal, and the money was paid on schedule over furious public protest. On January 11, 1982, the self-described "Beast of British Columbia" pled guilty on 11 murder counts and was sentenced to 11 concurrent life terms.

In custody, Olson continues to provoke controversy with media forays reminiscent of CHARLES MANSON in the United States. In August 1997, in a bid for early parole, Olson claimed that he had earned $1.3 million in advances for three unpublished books and a collection of videotapes; the money, he said, would be placed in a trust fund for the benefit of his victims' families, should he be released. (At the same time, Olson also claimed he was responsible for a total of 143 murders, spanning the United States and Canada, a claim unlikely to win favor with parole boards.) Crown Prosecutor Joe Bellows denounced Olson's statements as "fantastic lies," predictably opposing the killer's bid for early release. On August 23, Olson addressed the jury that would rule on his petition for parole, asking them, "Do I look like some kind of raving lunatic?" The gallery of spectators exploded with shouts in the affirmative, and jurors deliberated less than 15 minutes before rejecting Olson's parole bid.

Barred from another parole bid until 2006, Olson sought other means to keep his name before the public. In 1999 he told Irish police that he had killed two women on a visit to their country in the 1980s, and that an unnamed personal friend was the still-at-large "South Dublin Killer," blamed for five disappearances. In a telephone interview with the *Irish Mirror*, Olson said, "All I am doing is trying to help authorities around the world to find the bodies of the dead men and women. I can find the bodies in Ireland without any problem. I know exactly where they are." Authorities passed on that offer, and likewise dismissed Olson's bid for a trip to Hawaii, where he allegedly claimed two victims during a 1980 vacation. In May 2003, Olson's ex-wife told reports that she had seen none of the infamous $100,000 payoff from 1982, which was eaten up instead by legal fees. The latest furor erupted in June 2004, when Olson and 12,500 other Canadian prisoners gained the right to vote in national elections. "It burns my ass," the father of one Olson victim said, "to know that he's going to cast a vote and cancel out my vote. It causes pain and suffering for all victims in Canada."

ONOPRIENKO, Anatoly

A native of Laski in the Zhitomirskaya Oblast district of the Ukraine, born in 1959, Anatoly Onoprienko was placed in an orphanage at the age of one year, following his mother's death. An older brother was kept at home with their father, and the fact of his abandonment apparently fueled a pathological hatred of families, erupting into a seven-year killing spree that would snuff out 52 lives.

A forestry student and sometime mental patient, Onoprienko got off to a slow start as a serial killer, claiming his first victim at age 30 in 1989. Eleven more would follow by 1995, but he had yet to hit his stride with a series of ultraviolent home invasions that would lead Ukrainian newspapers to dub him the Terminator. Prior to December 1995, his murders had gone virtually unnoticed, except by overworked police detectives and surviving loved ones of the victims, but Onoprienko was preparing to change his MODUS OPERANDI, venting his rage at whole families instead

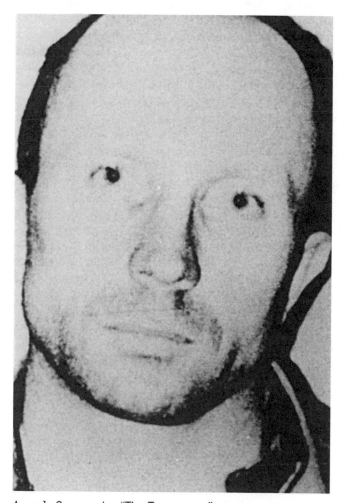

Anatoly Onoprienko, "The Terminator" (Author's collection)

of solitary targets. The massacres followed a pattern, Onoprienko invading isolated houses in the predawn hours, herding family members together and blasting them with a 12-gauge shotgun before looting and burning their homes. Frequently, police found family photos scattered at the crime scenes, torn and tossed about in the slayer's fury.

The first wholesale slaughter occurred on December 12, 1995, in Gamarnya, Zhitomirskaya Oblast, where a forestry teacher named Zaichenko, his wife, and two infant sons were killed in their home. Nine days later, four members of the Kryuchkov family were killed at Bratkovichi, their home set afirc. A passerby named Malinsky was also shot dead on the street outside when he glimpsed the fleeing gunman. On January 5, two businessmen named Odintsov and Dolinin were shot while sitting in their stalled car outside Energodar, Zaporozhskaya Oblast, and before the night was out, two more victims were killed at nearby Vasilyevka-Dnieprorudny, including a pedestrian named Garmasha and a policeman named Pybalko. The following day, three more men were shot and killed in a car parked on the Berdyansk-Dnieprovskaya highway.

The Terminator returned to Bratkovichi on January 17, butchering five members of the Pilat family and torching their home. Two apparent witnesses to the crime were also shot dead as the killer escaped. In Fastova, Kievskaya Oblast, four more victims were blasted on January 30, including a 28-year-old nurse, her two sons, and a male visitor. The Dubchak family was next, annihilated at home in Olevsk, Zhitomirskaya Oblast, on February 19. (The father and son were shot in that attack; the mother and daughter were beaten to death with a hammer.) Eight days later, in Malina, Lvivskaya Oblast, four members of the Bodnarchuk family were slain, the adults shot, their children hacked to death with an ax; within an hour, a male neighbor was also shot and mutilated in his home. Back in the Bratkovichi neighborhood on March 22, the Terminator shot and burned to death four members of the Novosad family.

Bratkovichi residents had seen enough. With the largest manhunt in Ukrainian history already under way, they demanded and received "an extreme response." A National Guard unit, complete with rocket launchers and armored vehicles, was sent to protect the village, while some 2,000 officers scoured the western Ukraine in search of their nameless, faceless quarry.

In the end, it was apparently a family quarrel that brought the reign of terror to a close. Anatoly Onoprienko was staying with a cousin's family when one of his hosts found weapons hidden in his room and a quarrel erupted, ending with Anatoly's ejection from the house. Before he left, the stalker vowed that his cousin's family would be "punished on Easter," a threat that was relayed to local authorities. On Easter Sunday, April 16, police traced Onoprienko to a girlfriend's home where he was arrested following a brief scuffle. A search of the premises revealed a tape deck stolen from the Novosad family, a pistol taken from a murder scene in Odessa, and a second firearm linked to several of the family massacres.

In custody, Onoprienko demanded to speak with "a general," and once the officer of proper rank arrived, he swiftly confessed a total of 52 murders, thus tying the official Russian record held by ANDREI CHIKATILO. The murders were compelled by "inner voices" emanating "from above," he claimed, though Anatoly wasn't sure if his orders came from God or aliens in outer space. Either way, the killer said, he was imbued with "strong hypnotic powers" and telepathic control over animals. The best thing, Anatoly said, would be for scientists to study him as "a phenomenon of nature."

Onoprienko was convicted on all counts and sentenced to death on April 1, 1999. There are still significant gaps in the time line of his movements between 1989 and 1995, although it is confirmed that Anatoly was expelled from both Austria and Germany during that period. Investigators are exploring possible links between their prisoner and other unsolved homicides in the Ukraine and elsewhere. Onoprienko's life was spared on March 22, 2000, when Ukrainian president Leonid Kuchma signed a new law abolishing capital punishment.

"ORANGE Coast Killer"

The latter 1970s were witness to a sudden rash of random, homicidal violence in America, alerting criminologists to a disturbing increase in the incidence of serial murders. Some regions of the country—Texas, Florida, New York—seemed bent on hogging headlines for their local maniacs, but none could hold a candle to the killing fields of southern California where the "Hillside Strangler," "Freeway Killer," "Sunset Slayer," "Skid Row Slasher," and a host of others plied their trade. One such—the "Orange Coast Killer"—went his ghoulish counterparts one better, slipping out of newsprint into legend as the one who got away.

In retrospect, detectives would agree the terror dated back to August 2, 1977, when Jane Bennington was slain in Corona Del Mar. Attacked in her home, the 29-year-old was raped, then beaten to death with a blunt instrument. Her killer left no clues for the police, and in the gap of 18 months before his next appearance, other homicides took precedence, demanding the attention of investigators.

The killer returned with a vengeance on April Fools' Day, 1979, raping Kimberly Rawlines in her Costa Mesa home before beating her to death. On May 14, Savannah Anderson, age 22, was assaulted and bludgeoned in Irvine. Ten days later, Kim Whitecotton, 20, survived an attack in her apartment in Santa Ana Heights, her graphic description of the incident spreading panic among her neighbors.

Overnight, there was a run on guns and guard dogs in the neighborhoods that seemed to mark the killer's chosen hunting ground. Publicity alerted women to the danger of an unlocked door or window, while composite sketches of the suspect—featuring a dark mustache and pock-marked cheeks—told women who to look for. Still, it seemed the slayer was invisible to everyone except his victims, free to come and go at will.

Jane Pettengill, age 24, was chosen on July 19, assaulted in her Costa Mesa home. She would survive, unlike her Costa Mesa neighbor, 30-year-old Marolyn Carleton, who was raped and bludgeoned on September 14. The killer moved to Tustin on September 30, administering a near-fatal beating to Diana Green. A week later, he killed 24-year-old Debra Jean Kennedy in Tustin. On December 21, the slayer claimed his only teenage victim, battering Debra Lynn Senior in Costa Mesa, afterward raping her corpse.

A special task force stalked the killer through a maze of clues and useless "tips" from frightened members of the public, all in vain. As summer faded into autumn, slowly giving way to winter, it became apparent that their man was gone. This time, the disappearance was no ruse, no holiday. The Orange Coast Killer, for whatever reason, had retired. As far as homicide detectives know, their man is still at large.

"ORGANIZED" Killers

In FBI parlance, for purposes of PROFILING, sexually motivated killers are divided into "organized," "DISORGANIZED," and "mixed" categories, based on personal characteristics and evidence found at crime scenes. In theory, such determinations aid police in tracking their quarry; in practice, however, there is no persuasive evidence of any recent profile leading to a murderer's arrest.

As outlined by FBI "mindhunters," a typical organized killer has good intelligence and is socially competent, tending toward skilled occupations. A review of the subject's childhood, if and when he is arrested, normally reveals a high birth-order status (the oldest or the only child), a father with stable employment, and a home life marked by inconsistent discipline, alternately harsh and lax. In adulthood, the organized killer often lives with a partner, frequently a legal spouse, and is sexually competent. Violence is precipitated by stress, including marital discord or loss of employment, and is often fueled by alcohol. The killer is mobile, maintaining one or more vehicles in good condition. His mood is controlled on the hunt, and he normally follows the progress of police investigations in the media. If pressed, the organized killer may find a new job or leave town to avoid apprehension.

Crime scene characteristics of the organized offender typically betray a murder planned well in advance, reflecting the killer's overall control of his environment. The victim is often a stranger (except in the case of stationary predators, killing in their homes or in the workplace). The hunter normally prefers submissive victims, often employing restraints to foil resistance during sexual assault or torture. The killer comes prepared with any necessary tools or weapons and removes them from the scene when he is done. He may personalize the victim through controlled (even scripted) conversation, thus feeding the ritualistic fantasies that dominate his life. When he is finished with his prey, the organized killer often transports the body to another location and hides it with care, taking pains to leave no useful evidence behind. So skillful are some predators, indeed, from London's "JACK THE RIPPER" to the present day, that they are never caught at all. Those who are captured by police more often come to grief through some careless mistake or dumb luck—a parking ticket foiled DAVID BERKOWITZ—than through brilliant detective work.

See also MODUS OPERANDI; MOTIVES; VICAP

OWEN, Duane Eugene

A home-invading thief and rapist in Palm Beach County, Florida, born February 13, 1961, Duane Owen murdered two victims and attempted to kill two more between February and May of 1984. His first known crime occurred on February 9 when he looted a local home and tried his best to murder the female inhabitant. Six weeks later, on March 24, he raped, robbed, and murdered a Palm Beach County woman in her home. Another burglary, on May 28, was accomplished without violence, but Owen rebounded with his second rape-murder the very next day.

Arrested in June, Owen escaped from the Palm Beach County jail on July 4 but was swiftly recaptured, a new charge filed against him for the jailbreak. With two counts of murder and sundry other felonies charged against him, bond was denied and Owen sat in jail until his trial in early 1986. Convicted on two

OWEN, Duane Eugene

counts of first-degree murder, one count of attempted murder, three counts of armed burglary, two counts of sexual battery with a deadly weapon, and one count of "regular" (i.e., unarmed) burglary, Owen received two death sentences, six life terms, plus 15 years when he faced the judge on March 13, 1986. A second trial, in July 1986, saw him convicted of escape and assault during a burglary (for the incident on May 24, 1984). On July 31, Owen was sentenced to another term of life imprisonment plus 15 years.

PACCIANI, Pietro   *See* "MONSTER OF FLORENCE"

PANDY, Andras

A Hungarian clergyman, Andras Pandy fled his homeland and emigrated to Belgium in 1956 during Hungary's abortive revolt against Russian control. Employed as a pastor and religious education teacher for the United Protestant Church, he made frequent visits to Hungary over the years and met his second wife—after the first allegedly deserted him—through "lonely-hearts" ads he placed in a Hungarian newspaper. Sadly, his second marriage was no more lasting than the first. By the time Pandy resigned from his church duties in 1992, his second spouse and four of Pandy's eight children were listed as missing.

None of those who "left" Pandy were ever seen again, although he claimed they were alive and well, living somewhere in Hungary. Daughter Agnes Pandy notified Belgian police of the disappearances in 1992, adding accusations that she and several stepsisters had been sexually abused by their father, but authorities were slow to act. While police dragged their feet, Rev. Pandy was busy concocting a hoax, inducing three unrelated children to join him on visits to kinfolk in Hungary, then asking his relatives to furnish written statements that his children were alive. The young stand-ins suspected nothing, trusting Pandy's explanation that their actions constituted "a rehearsal for a part in a movie about Pandy's life."

In fact, Pandy had protested too much, prompting police in Belgium and Hungary to launch a joint investigation of his case. Hungarian authorities had 60 missing-person cases on their books for the past decade, including many vanished women, and they wondered now if some may have answered Rev. Pandy's personal ads. Arrested in Belgium on October 20, 1997, the 71-year-old cleric was formally charged with killing two wives and four of his children. Pandy denied the charges, but Agnes was talking again while searchers in Brussels descended on several homes once occupied by Pandy's brood. By October 26, they had reported finding human bones and ashes, blood-spattered walls, and "large pieces of unspecified flesh" retrieved from a freezer. Five days later, detectives identified three children who had posed as Pandy's offspring during visits to Hungary.

Hungarian authorities, meanwhile, were busy searching the six interconnected basements of Pandy's former home at Dunakeszi, north of Budapest. They kept mum on their findings but suggested that an "old family tragedy" might be responsible for Pandy's killing spree. In fact, they suggested, the prisoner in Belgium might not be Andras Pandy at all, but rather a sibling of the *real* Andras Pandy, whose death had been officially recorded in 1956.

Police in Brussels weren't sure about that, but they tightened the case against their suspect—whoever he was—when Agnes Pandy was arrested on November 21, 1997, charged with playing an active role in the murders of the five missing Pandys. She confessed four days later, admitting that she and her father shot and/or sledgehammered to death her mother, two brothers, stepmother, and stepsister. Some of the corpses were dissolved in acid, Agnes said; others were hacked to bits and dumped with other meat, outside a Brussels slaughterhouse. Police also linked Agnes to the 1993 disappearance of a 12-year-old girl whose mother was romantically involved with Rev. Pandy.

The case took another bizarre turn on November 26, when the Hungarian newspaper *Nepsava* reported that Pandy had fostered an unknown number of Romanian children—orphan refugees from the 1989 revolution that toppled dictator Nicolae Ceaucescu—at his home in Brussels. The children were recruited by a charity called YDNAP (*Pandy* spelled backwards), and *Nepsava* reported that "nobody knows what happened to them or if they returned home" to Romania. There was more grim news on April 24, 1998, when Belgian police announced that teeth belonging to eight different people had been found in one of Pandy's former homes. Forensic tests indicated that the teeth came from seven women between the ages of 35 and 55, plus one man between 18 and 23, none of whom were related to Pandy. With 13 victims and counting, authorities refuse to speculate on the lethal pastor's final body count.

PANZRAM, Carl

A son of Prussian immigrants, born at Warren, Minnesota, in 1891, Panzram logged his first arrest at age eight for drunk and disorderly conduct. Three years later, a series of robberies landed him in reform school, and he set the place on fire at age 12, causing an estimated $100,000 damage. Paroled to his mother's custody in 1906, he ran away from home soon afterward. Life on the road meant more conflict with the law, and Panzram spent time in various juvenile institutions. He volunteered for the army while drunk but could not adapt to military discipline. Court-martialed for theft of government property in April 1907, he served 37 months in Leavenworth before his release from prison—and military service—in 1910. Upon discharge, Panzram described himself as "the spirit of meanness personified."

Back in civilian life, Panzram launched a career of robbery and indiscriminate murder spanning two continents. After one big score, he hired a yacht and lured several sailors out with promises of liquor; once aboard, the men were drugged and raped, then murdered, their bodies dumped into the sea. In Portuguese West Africa, Panzram hired eight blacks to help him hunt for crocodiles, then killed them, sodomized their corpses, and fed them to the hungry reptiles. Back in New York, he strangled a Kingston woman on June 16, 1923, "for the fun it gave me."

Five years later, on August 16, 1928, Panzram was arrested following a series of burglaries in Washington, D.C. Conviction earned him 20 years in Leavenworth,

where he promised to kill the first man who "crossed" him. His victim, selected without apparent motive, was Robert Warnke, a civilian laundry foreman. Panzram crushed his skull on June 20, 1929, and was promptly sentenced to hang.

From death row, the killer wrote: "In my lifetime I have murdered 21 human beings, I have committed thousands of burglaries, robberies, larcenies, arsons and last but not least I have committed sodomy on more than 1,000 male human beings. For all these things I am not in the least bit sorry." When opponents of CAPITAL PUNISHMENT fought for his life, Panzram responded with venomous letters. "I wish you all had one neck," he wrote, "and I had my hands on it." Mounting the scaffold on September 5, 1930, he seemed eager for death. "Hurry it up, you Hoosier bastard," he snapped at the executioner. "I could hang a dozen men while you're fooling around."

PARAPHILIA and Serial Murder

More commonly known as perversion or fetishism, paraphilia (from the Greek *para:* "beyond," "amiss"; and *philia:* "attachment to") describes the misdirection of sexual desire toward unusual or abnormal objects. Serial killers frequently suffer from sexual dysfunction that precludes normal relationships. Some of the pertinent paraphilias demonstrated in such cases include:

Anthropophagy—sexual fixation on eating human flesh in an act of CANNIBALISM. When applied specifically to corpses, often in advanced decomposition, the proper term is *necrophagia*. Cannibalism of young girls, as practiced by ALBERT FISH, is called *parthenophagy*.

Bestiality (or *zoophilia*)—sexual activity with animals, as practiced in childhood by HENRY LUCAS and others. Torture and mutilation of animals, seen as a childhood WARNING SIGN of future violence, is termed *bestial sadism*.

Bondage—the use of restraints in sexual activity may be harmless between consenting adults with established limits; when employed by murderous individuals such as Harvey Glatman in Los Angeles, it becomes a prelude to torture and death.

Coprophilia/coprolagnia—arousal sparked by feces, displayed in the writings of GERARD SCHAEFER, describing defecation by his female victims at the moment of death. When consumption of feces is involved, as with Albert Fish, the proper term is *coprophagia*.

Gerontophilia—sexual attraction to the elderly, seen in cases like that of ALBERT DESALVO, where a much younger killer preys on senior citizens for sex (as opposed to robbery of victims who are simply weaker and defenseless). Attraction to older men is termed *alphamegamia;* fixation on elderly women is called *graophilia* or *matronoloagnia.*

Hematophilia/hematomania—fixation on blood, commonly seen in cases of VAMPIRISM such as that of JOHN HAIGH.

Mutilation—often seen in sadistic or sexually motivated crimes. *Colobosis* refers specifically to mutilation of the male genitalia, *mazoperosis* to the female breasts, *perogynia* to mutilation of women (primarily the genitals), and *necrosadism* to mutilation of corpses (sometimes performed days or weeks after the murder as the killer revisits the crime scene).

Necrophilia—sexual fixation with death and corpses. When the obsession proceeds to intercourse, it is properly termed *necrocoitus. Necrochlesis* refers more specifically to sex with a female corpse.

Pedophilia—the proclivity for sex with children, seen in many serial child killers such as ARTHUR GOODE. Fixation on young boys is also called *pederasty.*

Pyromania/pyrophilia—sexual release obtained from setting and/or watching fires, a condition found in many cases of ARSON.

Sadism—arousal dependent on the suffering of others, named in the FBI *Crime Classification Manual* (1992) as one of the major motives for SEX CRIMES and serial murder.

Voyeurism—generally the passive act of watching others undress or have sex, typically accompanied by masturbation; spying sometimes turns deadly in the face of mounting frustration. Charles Floyd in Tulsa, Oklahoma, and Rickey Brogsdale in Washington, D.C, present two examples of voyeurs whose activities escalated to murder of those they secretly observed.

PARDO, Manuel, Jr.

Manny Pardo was 21 years old when he joined the Florida Highway Patrol in 1978, but his first stint in law enforcement was short lived. Accused of falsifying more than 100 traffic warnings and correction notices, he was allowed to resign a year after he joined the force in lieu of being fired. It seemed a small concession at the time, but it was all he needed: two months later, Pardo was hired by the Sweetwater Police Department to patrol a Miami suburb. Still, his problems continued, and in 1981, Pardo was one of four officers charged in a series of brutality cases filed by the state attorney general's office. Those charges were later dismissed, but Pardo was fired on January 21, 1985, after he flew to

the Bahamas to testify in defense of another ex-cop held for trial on drug-running charges.

Even then, the worst was yet to come. On May 7, 1986, Pardo and 25-year-old Roland Garcia were arrested on murder charges, accused in the execution-style slayings of drug dealer Ramon Alvero Cruz and his girlfriend, Daisy Ricard, who were shot and killed on April 23. Weeks later, on June 11, Metro Dade officials announced that Pardo and Garcia were linked to a total of nine murders—victims including six men and three women—dating back to January 1986. Detective Ted MacArthur told the press, "They were drug ripoffs, and quantities of cocaine were taken from the scene." The killing spree had ended with Ramon Alvero Cruz, alleged to be Pardo's underworld employer since he was fired by Sweetwater PD. As evidence against the killer cop, prosecutors cited Pardo's diary, which included written entries about the murders along with news clippings and photographs of several bloody corpses. Nazi memorabilia recovered from Pardo's home, together with the prisoner's own statements, revealed that he was also an ardent admirer of Adolf Hitler, believing that Jews and blacks were inferior species deserving of extermination.

Legal maneuvers delayed Pardo's trial for two years, but prosecutor David Waksman stood by the state's original theory of an ex-cop gone bad, addicted to cocaine and easy money, killing coke dealers to rip off their stashes, eliminating any witnesses who crossed his path. Pardo denied it, painting himself as a one-man vigilante squad committed to eliminating "parasites" and "leeches" from law-abiding society. His court-appointed lawyer, Ronald Guralnick, was committed to a different tack, presenting an INSANITY DEFENSE. "The man is crazy," Guralnick told reporters. "All you have to do is listen to him to know he's totally out of his mind."

And, indeed, Pardo seemed intent on proving that point when he took the witness stand in his own defense on April 13, 1988. Testifying against Guralnick's advice, Manny didn't bother to deny the killings; rather, he regretted that his final body count had been so low. "Instead of nine," he told the court, "I wish I could have been up here for ninety-nine." Furthermore, he declared, "I enjoyed what I was doing. I enjoyed shooting them. They're parasites and they're leeches, and they have no right to be alive. Somebody had to kill these people." He shot his victims multiple times after death, Manny said, to further "punish" them for their crimes, and he had taken Polaroid snapshots of the corpses, afterward burning some in an alabaster ashtray. "I sent their souls to the eternal fires of damnation of hell," he testified, "for the misery they caused."

Pardo staunchly denied the state's claim that he, himself, was a mercenary drug dealer. The very idea was "ludicrous" and "ridiculous," he said. Prosecutor Waksman asked about the $50,000 Pardo had earned from selling two kilos of stolen cocaine, the sum recorded in his diary, but Manny insisted that he had kept only $2,000 for himself—the bare minimum required to purchase guns and ammunition. After Pardo remarked that bullets cost him ten cents each, Waksman asked him whether it had cost him only $1.30 to kill two victims who were shot a total of 13 times. Pardo grinned as he replied, "That's a pretty good investment, isn't it?"

With Pardo's sanity at issue, both sides called psychiatrists to testify about his mental state. Syvil Marquit, appearing for the defense, reported that Pardo was insane and had been at the time of the nine murders. Manny was competent for trial, Marquit said, and understood the physical consequence of his actions, "but he doesn't know right from wrong." Court-appointed psychologist Leonard Haber, on the other hand, testified for the state that Pardo was "sane, but evil." Manny, for his part, agreed with the state, at least in regard to his sanity. As for psychologists, he told the court, "They're whores. Pay them enough money and they'll say anything."

Pardo's extreme racist views may have hurt him as much as the physical evidence of his guilt when he appeared before a jury that included five blacks and two Jews. Metro Dade detectives listed the Nazi paraphernalia found in his home and described the swastika tattoo worn by one of his dogs, a Doberman pinscher. Manny pitched in with testimony that Adolf Hitler was a "great man" whose activities had inspired Pardo to read more than 500 books on Nazism. The jury deliberated for six hours on April 15 before convicting Pardo of nine murders and nine other felony counts, including robbery and use of a firearm in commission of a crime.

Court reconvened five days later to consider Pardo's sentence. Attorney Guralnick and Manny's parents pleaded for leniency, citing his deranged mental state, while prosecutor Waksman argued the reverse. "He was weird, weird, weird," Waksman said, "but he was not insane." Pardo, meanwhile, was determined to remain the star performer in his own private drama. "I am a soldier," he told the court. "I accomplished my mission, and I humbly ask you to give me the glory of ending my life and not to send me to spend the rest of my life in state prison. I'm begging you to allow me to have a glorious end." The jury complied, and Judge Phillip Knight accepted their recommendation, handing down one death sentence for each of Pardo's nine murders, plus a term of 15 years in prison for the non-capital charges.

His commitment to death notwithstanding, Pardo made no objection when his conviction and sentence were automatically appealed to the Florida Supreme Court. There, on March 6, 1990, public defender Calianne Lantz told the assembled justices that Pardo was insane when he committed his nine murders. Assistant Attorney General Ralph Barreira disagreed, describing Manny as a brute who simply liked to kill. The court agreed with Barreira, affirming Pardo's conviction and the "special circumstances" which allowed his execution under Florida state law. A year later, on May 13, 1991, the US Supreme Court effectively upheld that decision, denying Pardo's plea for a writ of certiorari.

Pardo, meanwhile, had managed to attract at least a handful of admirers while his case was winding through the courts. One such, a self-described friend of the convicted serial killer, voiced his support in a letter to the *Orlando Sentinel Tribune*, published on April 22, 1990. It read, in part:

Manny was never accused of corruption. He was let go for his overzealousness in pursuit of criminals—no matter who they knew or whose relatives they were. And lest anyone get the idea that he just cruised around gunning people down, let me point out each of his victims was a thoroughly investigated, tried, convicted, and executed (by him) drug dealer whom Pardo had failed to get off the streets via the normal criminal justice system. Manny Pardo doesn't deserve condemnation, he deserves a commendation.

In fact, as even cursory research would have shown, Manny had been fired in Sweetwater for "showing a lack of good judgment and a habit of lying"—specifically in *defense* of an accused drug dealer—but the details hardly mattered. He was awaiting execution at Starke, the state's maximum-security prison . . . but he was not entirely out of action yet.

In March 1996 the *Miami Herald* revealed that Pardo, now christened the "Death Row Romeo," had been placing personal ads in tabloid newspapers, attracting lonely female pen pals who had mailed him thousands of dollars in return for hollow promises of love. The *Herald* reported that Manny had once accumulated some $3,530 in his prison canteen account, most of it sent to him by women, but prison officials declared that he had broken no rules, "although he may have broken several hearts." The lure was an ad that painted Manny in a near-heroic light. It read:

FLA. 116–156 CORRECTIONAL INSTITUTE INMATE. Ex-cop Vietnam vet. Took law into own hands and ended up on Death Row. He needs letters from sensitive-understanding female, for real-honest relationship.

One who responded was Barbara Ford, a 46-year-old cleaning woman from Findlay, Ohio. Three weeks after she answered Pardo's ad, Ford received a letter from Manny, along with several news clips describing his police career in a favorable light. The letter told her, "I want one special lady in my life. I don't play emotional games cause I hate emotional games. I also hate liars and users." From the beginning, Pardo's correspondence—always addressed to "the love of my life"—swiftly degenerated into a litany of complaints, invariably closing with mention of his need for "a few bucks a week to buy personal items like stamps, paper, shampoo, etc." One note described a tearful prison visit from his daughter, quoting her as saying, "Daddy, when I'm older and able to work, I will buy you a radio so you can listen to music and I will send you money from my weekly check so you can buy coffee, shampoo and your other needs."

In the meantime, Barbara Ford was happy to take up the slack, sending Pardo $430 from her yearly income of $7,500. Another "love of his life," mailing cash at the same time, was 54-year-old Betty Ihem from Oklahoma who began corresponding with Pardo 10 months before he hooked Barbara Ford. By the time Ford entered the picture, Pardo and Ihem were addressing each other as husband and wife, Betty collecting 275 letters from her incarcerated lover, sending him $1,200 over time from the salary she earned as a part-time Wal-Mart employee.

The correspondence was finally too much for Pardo, who tripped himself up with a clumsy mistake. On October 12, 1995, Betty Ihem received a letter meant for Barbara Ford. It read:

My Dearest Barb,

Hi. I hope this letter finds you in the best of health. You are all I want and need. I am not a dream and if my love interests you, well then it's yours.

I love you,
Manny

Predictably furious, Ihem sent the letter on to Ford, with her own explanatory note written on the back. Eight days later, Ford wrote to Pardo, addressing him as "Thief of Hearts" and enclosing photocopies of the money orders she had previously sent him.

You received the money under false pretenses [she wrote] which makes you a fake and not the "Man of Honor" which you professed to be. Needless to say, you are a liar and a hypocrite—the very things you said you hated in people. If you choose not to return the money, I will be your very worst nightmare and expose you for

the hypocrite you truly are. I'm not a very patient person so I hope you respond to my request immediately. The choice is yours.

Pardo replied on November 2, 1995, with all the arrogance of a condemned prisoner who knows he is; effectively untouchable.

Barb,

I hope you are in good health. I am reading your letter and am amazed you think your threats would affect me at all! You and your troubled life will also be exposed. In addition, my attorney will have a field day with you and that will be your nightmare lawsuit for slander, etc. You are a bitter and vindictive woman.

God bless,
Manny

Ford took her case to Florida governor Lawton Chiles on November 18, asking, "What kind of people are you in Florida? You have a guy on Death Row, and he still hurts people." Her reply came from Judy Belcher at the Florida Department of Corrections on November 29, advising Ford that no law forbade prisoners from placing personal ads or soliciting gifts from gullible pen pals. "On the contrary," Belcher wrote, "Florida Statutes have ruled it illegal to deny inmates that privilege because doing so would deny inmates access to the outside world. Many inmates, both male and female, have accumulated considerable amounts of money this way. They are convicts and some are experts at 'conning' honest people out of their hard earned dollars. Often, when we advise a person that an inmate is not being honest, the person will still choose to believe the inmate."

With that grudging seal of approval, Manny Pardo was free to pursue his career as a death-row swindler. Only the final, inevitable date with "Old Sparky" will curtail his correspondence with gullible women, and no final execution date has been set at this writing. With others who have killed repeatedly across the Sunshine State, Pardo takes his ease with pen in hand and plays the waiting game.

PAULIN, Thierry, and MATHURIN, Jean-Thierry

Between October 1984 and November 1987, elderly Parisian women lived in terror of a savage killer whom they dubbed the "Monster of Montmartre," after the neighborhood that was his favored hunting ground. The first victim, 83-year-old Anna Barbier-Ponthus, was found gagged, bound, and beaten to death in her apartment on October 5, 1984. Four days later, firefighters found 89-year-old Suzanne Foucault inside her burning flat, bound hand and foot, with a plastic bag pulled over her head. A third victim, 71-year-old Iona Seigaresco, was discovered on November 5, bound with electric cord and beaten to death in her small apartment on Boulevard de Clichy. If Parisian police had any doubts that a serial killer was at large in their city, those doubts were dispelled two days later with the discovery of two murdered women. Alice Benaim, age 84, and 80-year-old Marie Choy, next-door neighbors, were found slaughtered in their adjoining homes. (Choy had been bound with steel wire and forced to drink bleach before she was beaten to death.) On November 8, 75-year-old Maria Mico-Diaz was found in her flat, bound, gagged, and nearly hacked in two with 60 stab wounds.

Detectives didn't know it yet, but their quarry could hardly have been more flamboyant. A black transvestite drug addict who dyed his hair platinum blond, Thierry Paulin was a native of Martinique, born in 1963. A homosexual sadist, Paulin broke the usual mold of gay serial killers by preying on members of the opposite sex, sometimes accompanied on his raids by male lover Jean-Thierry Mathurin, a 19-year-old waiter from Martinique. Between them, they worked out a system of following old ladies home from the market, moving in to pounce as the victim unlocked her front door. The victims ranged in age from 60 years to 95, and the brutal violence they suffered told authorities the "Monster of Montmartre" had more on his mind than simple snatch-and-grab robbery.

Feeling the heat of public outrage, Parisian authorities swept the city for junkies and sexual deviates, grilling all they could find in hopes of turning up a lead. Paulin and Mathurin fled to Toulouse, killing time in gay bars and drug dens until they had a lovers' quarrel and parted company. Back in Paris, Paulin beat up a drug pusher who tried to swindle him, and the dealer surprised him by filing assault charges. Convicted at trial and sentenced to 16 months in jail, Paulin was paroled in 1987 and resumed his reign of terror as if the crime spree had never been interrupted. The violence peaked in November, with three victims killed on the weekend of Paulin's 24th birthday, but the Monster's time was running out. One of his victims had survived and offered a description to police. The gendarmes had no trouble locating a bleached-blond black man, arresting Paulin on December 1, but they were embarrassed to discover that his fingerprints—on file from previous arrests—matched those found at several murder scenes.

In custody, Paulin readily confessed to 21 murders, naming Mathurin as an accomplice in many cases. Jailed on nine counts of murder, Mathurin refused even to speak Paulin's name, habitually referring to him as "the other one." French abolition of CAPITAL PUNISH-

MENT would spare both killers from the guillotine, but Paulin's days were already numbered. Diagnosed as suffering from AIDS in 1985, he was still awaiting trial when he fell into a coma on March 10, 1989, and died of AIDS-related complications on April 16.

PETIOT, Marcel

A Frenchman born in 1897, Petiot first demonstrated criminal tendencies in public school by stealing from his classmates. He later moved on to looting mailboxes, and during military service, in 1917, he stole drugs from an army dispensary for sale to street addicts. Discharged with a pension and free treatment for psychoneurosis, Petiot went on to obtain a medical degree, despite spending part of his student days in an asylum. In 1928 he was elected mayor of Villanueve, while practicing medicine there, but his term was cut short by Petiot's conviction of theft in 1930. Whatever his sentence it did not hamper his continued criminal activity.

That same year, one of Dr. Petiot's patients—a Madame Debauve—was robbed and murdered in her home. Gossip blamed the doctor, but his chief accuser—another patient—was soon silenced by sudden death. A woman who accused Petiot of actively encouraging her daughter's drug addiction disappeared without a trace, but things were getting hot in Villanueve, and the good doctor struck off in search of a friendlier climate.

In Paris, he was convicted of shoplifting but was discharged on the condition that he seek psychiatric therapy. As World War II began, Petiot was convicted of drug trafficking and was alleged to be an addict himself, but the court released him after payment of a small fine. By early 1941, with Nazi occupation troops controlling much of France, he had devised a get-rich scheme that mirrored elements of Adolf Hitler's "final solution to the Jewish question."

Petiot bought a house on rue Lesueur in Paris, contracting for special modifications that were completed in September 1941. The revisions included raising garden walls to block his neighbors' view and construction of a triangular, windowless death chamber inside the house. As the war dragged on, Petiot made a fortune by posing as a member of the French resistance movement, offering to help Jews and other fugitives flee the country. Clients arrived at his house after dark, receiving an injection to guard against "foreign disease," and Petiot then led them to the chamber, watching their death throes through a hatch in one wall. Arrested by Gestapo agents in May 1943 on suspicion of aiding escapees, Petiot was released seven months later when the Nazis recognized a kindred spirit.

On March 11, 1944, neighbors on Rue Lesueur complained of rancid smoke pouring from Petiot's house,

Dr. Marcel Petiot at trial (Author's collection)

and police found the chimney on fire and no one at home. Firemen broke in and found 27 corpses in the basement, most in various stages of dismemberment. Held on suspicion of murder, Petiot was released after telling police that the dead men were Nazis, executed by the French resistance.

The doctor dropped out of sight in August 1944 when Paris was liberated, but two months later he fired off a letter to the press, claiming the Gestapo had tried to frame him for murder by dumping corpses at his home. The renewed investigation climaxed in Petiot's arrest on November 2, 1944, and while his rap sheet had mysteriously disappeared in Villanueve, authorities had ample evidence in hand. Formally charged with 27 murders, Petiot admitted 63 killings at his trial in March 1946, describing various homicides as the patriotic acts of a resistance fighter. The total may well have been higher, as one of Petiot's statements referred to 150 "liquidations," and 86 dissected bodies were pulled from the Seine between 1941 and 1943. Finally convicted on 26 counts, Petiot was guillotined on May 26, 1946.

PISTORIUS, Dr. Micki: Forensic profiler

A native of South Africa, born in 1971, Micki Pistorius worked as a journalist for eight years while completing her doctorate in psychology at the University of Pretoria. Even then, she told the press in 1996, "In my wildest dreams I never saw myself in the police force, but my interest in Freudian psychology led me to see a connection between the theory and serial killers. One thing led to another, and here I am."

"Here," for Dr. Pistorius is an unintended place in the spotlight, hailed as the leading practitioner of forensic PROFILING outside the United States. In fact, after a series of headline-grabbing cases in her native land, she is regarded by some observers as the most successful profiler in history, eclipsing such American colleagues as ROBERT RESSLER and JOHN DOUGLAS. Critics of profiling respond that while Pistorius has indeed described several fugitive serial killers with uncanny precision, profiling per se has yet to directly produce an arrest.

Dr. Pistorius received her first serial murder assignment within hours of joining the South African police, analyzing the brutal crimes of Cape Town's "Station Strangler," slayer of 22 boys between 1986 and 1994. That case was closed with the arrest and conviction of 28-year-old Norman Simons, an educated predator who spoke seven languages and claimed to be possessed by the spirit of his dead brother. (The claim did not protect him from a 25-year prison sentence.) Pistorius had been accurate in each particular of her profile on Simons—race, age, education, level of employment—but the arrest, as usual, came from another source: several acquaintances telephoned police to say that Simons resembled published suspect sketches of the Station Strangler.

Still, it was considered a victory for South Africa's fledgling profiler, and there has been little rest for Pistorius in the years since 1994, with postapartheid South Africa overrun by a veritable plague of serial killers. Pistorius quickly found herself caught up in the midst of simultaneous manhunts for such prolific slayers as "ABC Killer" MOSES SITHOLE (38 dead), "Phoenix Strangler" Sipho Thwala (18 killed), "Bootie Boer" Stewart Wilken (charged with 10 murders, including that of his own daughter), "Cleveland Strangler" David Selepe (killed in police custody), and "Donnybrook Killer" CHRISTOPHER ZIKODE. Meanwhile, even more random killers remain still at large: Johannesburg's "Nasrec Strangler" (15 dead and counting), the "Cape Town Ripper" (18 prostitutes butchered), the "Pine Town River Strangler" in KwaZulu, Natal (profiled as a black rape-slayer preying on white women), and others.

The incessant travel required by her job soon led Pistorius to divorce courts, and it has limited her prospects for a social life. "If I do meet a boyfriend," she has told the press, "he is more than likely to be in the same work as I am." That work in South Africa, as elsewhere, has traditionally been a male preserve, but Pistorius reports good progress with veteran detectives. "There was a lot of skepticism when I first arrived," she says, "but once I proved I could do the work, I was quite quickly accepted. Now, if anything, my male colleagues are very protective of me." Frequently compared to actress Jodie Foster in *The Silence of the Lambs,* Pistorius finds that her civilian friends "tend to ask me about the details of [a] case. When I tell them, they are shocked but fascinated. People are generally interested in horror." At the same time, she says, "Some people imagine I must be butch to be in this line of work, but I can assure you I am very feminine. I'm really just a normal girl at heart."

Pistorius has published two books on the problem of serial murder in modern South Africa, entitled *Catch Me a Killer* (2000) and *Strangers on the Street* (2002).

PROFILING of Unidentified Killers

Psychological "profiling" of unknown subjects at large—UNSUBs, in law-enforcement parlance—is a relatively new investigative tool, utilized for the first time in the mid-1950s; it is also one of the most controversial to date. In FICTION AND FILM, profilers are often depicted as psychics, picking up on "flashes" from an unknown killer's mind with every visit to a crime scene, tracking down their man (or woman) as inexorably as if they could read the subject's name and address in a crystal ball.

Unfortunately, nothing could be further from the truth.

Profiling, at the bottom line, is nothing more or less than educated guesswork. At its best, the guesswork may be *very* educated, drawing on experience from dozens (or hundreds) of previous cases, often assisted by computer analysis, refining the portrait of an UNSUB to the smallest detail. On the flip side, though, it may be worse than useless, leading homicide detectives down a false trail while the object of their manhunt watches from the sidelines and enjoys the show. In most cases, the reality of profiling falls somewhere in between the two extremes: experts are able to prepare a fair likeness of their subject without providing the essential details—name, address, and so forth—that would lead to an arrest.

Ironically, the first application of psychological profiling in a modern criminal case is also the only case to date where a profiler contributed directly to a subject's arrest. In 1956, forensic psychiatrist James Brussel prepared an amazingly accurate profile of New York's "Mad Bomber," deducing the subject's impotence from the phallic shape of his pipe bombs, generating a sketch

that could have passed for the bomber's photograph, even predicting—correctly—that the subject would be wearing a double-breasted suit (with the jacket buttoned!) at the time of his arrest. More to the point, an open letter from Dr. Brussel provoked bomber George Metesky to a written response, which in turn led police to his doorstep. No other profiler has yet rivaled Brussel's performance, and even where specific profiles are proved accurate in the wake of an arrest, apprehension itself is normally effected by routine police investigation.

Two cases often cited as profiling success stories clearly demonstrate the gap between publicity and reality. In Sacramento, California, sheriff's officers and FBI agents prepared a profile of an UNSUB blamed for six grisly murders during January 1978. At his arrest, defendant Richard Chase was found to match the profile in every respect; yet psychological analysis played no role whatsoever in his capture. Rather, Chase was spotted by a former high-school classmate wandering the streets in blood-soaked clothing and was turned in to the police, who picked him up for questioning and then discovered telling evidence inside his car. Six years later, Florida rape-slayer ROBERT LONG was the subject of another FBI profile, which again proved remarkably accurate once the suspect was in custody. Retired Gmen hail their achievement as if they had caught Long themselves, but in fact the killer sealed his own fate by releasing his penultimate victim alive, whereupon she provided authorities with a description of Long and his car.

When profilers miss their target, meanwhile, the results are sometimes truly bizarre. In 1963, a panel of psychiatrists—including the aforementioned Dr. Brussel—was convened to stalk the "Boston Strangler" from afar. The experts concluded that Boston was plagued by *two* killers, one who claimed elderly victims, and another—thought to be homosexual—who strangled younger women. Beyond that divergence, many similarities were postulated, including a suggestion that both men were teachers, living alone and killing on their scheduled holidays from school. Both UNSUBs were diagnosed as sexually inhibited, the products of traumatic childhoods featuring weak, distant fathers and cruel, seductive mothers. In fact, confessed strangler ALBERT DESALVO was a construction worker, living with his wife and two children, insatiably heterosexual. Examination of his background showed a brutal, domineering father and a mother who was weak and ineffectual. He *was* in his thirties, as projected for the two nonexistent teachers, but there the resemblance ended.

An even more dramatic failure came in early 1975, when another "expert panel" was assembled in Los Angeles to sketch a profile of the "Skid Row Slasher."

On January 30, the L.A. media broadcast descriptions of a "sexually impotent coward, venting his own feelings of worthlessness on hapless drifters and down-and-outers." The slasher was described as a friendless loner, probably a homosexual and possibly deformed, "driven by a frenzy to commit these murders as a substitute for normal heterosexual relations." His violence was most likely "spurred by an unresolved rage he feels toward his father, who could have been a brutal alcoholic." Sketches drawn to fit the profile showed a white male in his late twenties or early thirties, six feet tall, 190 pounds, with shoulder-length stringy blond hair framing an angular face. At his arrest, two days later, serial slayer VAUGHN GREENWOOD was revealed as a black man with no apparent deformities, whose murders smacked of ritual occultism, complete with blood-drinking and salt sprinkled around the corpses.

It is worth noting that even participating experts disagree on the value of criminal profiles. Dr. Norman Barr, one of the Skid Row Slasher panelists in California, belatedly admitted that "I don't think my statements would make any more sense than those of the average housewife." Across the continent, at Boston University, psychologist Russell Boxley declares: "I think the people who do profiles are bastardizing their discipline with a lot of mumbo-jumbo, without really knowing what they're doing. You know, it's a mystical thing, and people are very impressed. It's also a media thing." Boxley concludes that forensic psychologists tracking an UNSUB "can't do any better than a college student could with the same materials in front of him."

FBI "mindhunters," meantime, stand by their record and tactics, although some of their conclusions are vague, at best. Following protracted interviews with convicted serial killers in the 1980s, members of the Bureau's Behavioral Science Unit divided serial killers into "ORGANIZED" and "DISORGANIZED" subgroups. "Organized" killers are basically those who plan their crimes well in advance and take pains to avoid capture afterward, while "disorganized" slayers strike on a whim, leaving crime scenes littered with clues. The categories are deliberately broad, and while the fictional Dr. Hannibal Lecter was overly harsh in blaming the system's conception on "a real bottom feeder," FBI spokesmen have acknowledged its deficiency by creating an intermediate "mixed" category to accommodate troublesome cases.

While retired FBI agents JOHN EDWARD DOUGLAS and ROBERT K. RESSLER are probably the best-known profilers on Earth, other specialists also have trained themselves to cope with the worldwide occurrence of serial murder. Dr. MICKI PISTORIUS has established a reputation in South Africa, while Britain's Ian Stephen and Japan's Yuki Nishimura work against the rising tide in their respective nations. In the 1990s, Canadian criminologist Kim Rossmo created a software program for geographic profiling of killers at large, charting their crimes (and hopefully uncovering their lairs) via computer analysis of "spatial-temporal clusterings." The program serves not only to track transient slayers, but also to uncover those whom Rossmo calls "stealth predators"—the medical killers, "BLACK WIDOWS," and "BLUEBEARD KILLERS" whose crimes may be artfully disguised as natural or accidental deaths. "The challenge," Rossmo says, "is to determine that something is happening, even when no crimes have been reported." Official resistance to the newfangled software was shattered in Canada by the case of Robert Pickton, accused (but untried at press time) in the disappearances of more than 30 Vancouver prostitutes. Rossmo told reporters, "The data, if properly analyzed in that case, told us something. . . . And if people had faith in the [profiling] system, then it's like a fire alarm going off." In April 2000, authorities began testing Rossmo's system in Texas, where Houston investigator Cecil Wingo claimed "there are right now about 3,500 unsolved cases of serial killers."

"PSICÓPATA, El"

In 1997, Costa Rican authorities announced that some 31 victims may have been murdered over the course of a decade by an elusive slayer aptly dubbed the Psychopath. Previous estimates had been more modest, pegging the stalker's body count at 19 (including several victims who have not been found), but frustrated manhunters have added another dozen names to the list, all young men and women who vanished without a trace during 1996. Despite a recent plea for FBI assistance in tracking the killer, police in this Central American republic are no closer to their man today than when the string of grisly crimes began.

El Psicópata does his hunting, for the most part, in a rural area lately dubbed the "Triangle of Death," stretching from the southwestern quarter of Alajuela to the eastern part of Cartago, a few miles east of the nation's capital, at San José. Taking a cue from Italy's "MONSTER OF FLORENCE," the killer preys on young lovers, creeping up on couples as they have sex and shooting them to death with a large-caliber weapon, afterward mutilating the female's breasts and genitals. Occasional diversions from the pattern involve young women murdered on their own, the crime scenes including evidence of postmortem sexual assault.

Local authorities have drawn up several "profiles" of their unknown subject, all in vain. One theory blames the murders on a deranged ex-soldier or policeman, while another brands the killer as a child of wealthy stock—perhaps a politician's son or the offspring of a mighty landlord. Duration of the crime spree indicates a killer in his thirties, possibly his forties, and police believe he "could be" quite intelligent (presumably because they haven't caught him yet). It is believed by some investigators that El Psicópata follows and observes his chosen prey for several days before killing; yet one fact shines above all others in the case: whoever or whatever he turns out to be, at this writing, the Psychopath is still at large.

QUICK, Thomas

Sweden's most prolific serial killer to date was a sadistic necrophile who preferred children as victims, but that did not stop him from killing adults—or wiping out whole families—when the opportunity presented itself. Like GERARD SCHAEFER, Quick originally wanted to become a priest, but he drifted into random homicide instead, reportedly claiming his first victim at age 14. Arrested in 1996, he described a childhood fraught with physical and sexual abuse, then confessed to 15 homicides, including six in Norway.

Quick's confession solved the mystery of three Dutch tourists, murdered while vacationing in northern Sweden, and he was sentenced to life for those crimes. On May 28, 1997, Quick was also convicted of killing an Israeli tourist, one Yinon Levy, in 1988. Four months later, following Quick's directions, police unearthed what "could be a human finger bone" from the cellar of an abandoned farmhouse near Falun, but the victim was not identified, and no further charges were filed. In November 1997, Norwegian detectives found human bone fragments in a gravel pit near Drammen, where nine-year-old Therese Johannessen vanished in July 1988. Quick had confessed to her slaying and described the child's wristwatch in meticulous detail. Conviction in that case, on June 2, 1998, brought Quick's official tally to five victims.

Investigation into Quick's crimes and confessions continues at this writing, while Quick remains confined at Säters Sjukhus, Sweden's maximum-security institution for the criminally insane. In October 1999, authorities charged Quick with the 1985 murder of victim Gry Storvik. May 2000 brought charges in the slaying of two Norwegian girls. Further trials are unlikely, based on Quick's prognosis of incurable mental illness, but police are still pursuing allegations that he killed five other children in Finland, Norway, and Sweden between 1980 and 1989.

QUINN, Jane

Awakened by a gunshot in the predawn hours of November 2, 1911, John Miller scrambled out of bed and rushed to the apartment of his landlord, whence the sound had emanated. On arrival at the scene he found John Quinn, the landlord, lying in his bed, blood streaming from a fatal bullet wound. According to the dead man's wife, a prowler was responsible, though Miller saw no evidence of theft or any struggle. Jane Quinn declined to testify at the resulting inquest, and a Chicago coroner's jury deliberated for one hour on November 10 before ordering her arrest on murder charges.

By that time, police had learned a thing or two about the lethal Mrs. Quinn. They knew about her marriage to Canadian John MacDonald in October 1883 and his subsequent death from "alcohol poisoning" on September 28, 1901. A short month later, at Bass Lake, Michigan, the grieving widow had married Warren Thorpe—and he had later been shot to death in circumstances similar to those surrounding the Chicago case. Another death in bed, this time involving Jane's own mother, had occurred soon after in the house once occupied by Warren Thorpe.

The evidence was overwhelming, and Jane Quinn was speedily convicted at her trial on murder charges and sentenced to a term of life imprisonment. If nothing else, the verdict may have spared some future victims from the clutches of a bona fide "BLACK WIDOW."

QUINTILIANO, Matthew

A 14-year veteran of the Stratford, Connecticut, Police Department, Matt Quintiliano snapped one afternoon in May 1975 and accosted his wife outside the Bridgeport hospital where she worked, shooting her eight times with a pistol. Arrested for murder (and fired from his law enforcement job), Quintiliano spent three years in custody before a panel of judges found him innocent by reason of insanity. After three months of treatment, staff psychiatrists at a state hospital ordered his release, describing Quintiliano as "no longer a danger to himself or others."

Remarried by 1983, Quintiliano had no more luck with his second fling at matrimony than he had the first time around. Served with divorce papers on February 11 of that year, he murdered his wife the next day and was arrested on February 16, faced with another count of first-degree murder. Held in lieu of $750,000 bond, he was indicted, convicted on the charge, and confined to prison when psychiatrists agreed, this time, that he was sane.

RAGHAV, Raman

On August 13, 1969, officials in Bombay, India, announced that 40-year-old Raman Raghav had been sentenced to hang following his conviction of multiple murders. According to sketchy news reports, the defendant openly confessed to slaying 41 men, women, and children, his victims selected at random and slaughtered for the sheer pleasure of killing.

See also SHANKARIYA, KAMPATIMAR

RAIS, Gilles de

Born of French nobility in 1404, Gilles de Rais married a wealthy heiress at age 16, thus becoming the richest man in France—some say in all of Europe. He was known as "BLUEBEARD" for the glossy blue-black color of his whiskers, and he moved among the highest circles in the land. As Marshal of France, he fought beside Joan of Arc at Orléans, fielding a personal army of 200 knights against the English invaders. Following the coronation of Charles VII, at which he personally crowned the new king, Gilles retired from public life, dividing his time among five lavish country estates at Machecoul, Malemort, La Suze, Champtoce, and Triffauges.

In retirement, Gilles squandered his wealth in extravagant style, selling off some of his land to cover expenses before his heirs obtained a royal injunction barring further sales. On the side, he indulged a passion for sadistic pedophilia, molesting and murdering peasant children of both sexes to amuse himself. Gilles admittedly patterned his life after that of the Roman emperor Caligula, known for his debauchery and bloodlust in ancient times.

Still spending money by the cartload, Gilles de Rais turned to alchemy and black magic in hopes of producing gold from base metals. An aide, Gilles de Sille, conducted "scientific" experiments on the problem without success, and his master soon fell in with charlatans promising lavish rewards for a modest investment. Kidnapped children, once mere playthings in a game of life and death, now became sacrificial objects in the pursuit of boundless wealth. By 1439, Gilles de Rais was in league with Francisco Prelati, a defrocked Italian priest who guided him through ghoulish rituals, employing children's blood in vain attempts to conjure gold from common iron and lead.

A year later, Gilles ran afoul of the law on a trivial point when he sold his estate at Malemort to the treasurer of Brittany, Geoffroi le Ferron, in violation of the royal injunction. More to the point, Gilles barred the new owner's brother—a priest, Jean le Ferron—from the premises, beating and caging him when he demanded admission. Assaulting a priest left Gilles open to trial by the Catholic Church, which also filed charges of sorcery and sexual perversion with children. Torture was applied to Gilles de Rais, his servants, and four alleged accomplices in October 1440, producing a variety of confessions. Gilles himself confessed to numerous murders, begging forgiveness from the parents of his victims. On October 26, Gilles and two of his associates were strangled to death, the nobleman's body partially burned.

In retrospect, some historians regard the fate of Gilles de Rais as an ecclesiastical frame-up, noting that some of his lands were seized and sold by the church before his trial even began. Critics of this view point out that Gilles refused to confess under torture, pleading guilty on murder counts only when threatened with excommunication from the church. The conclusive evidence, however, lay with the dismembered remains of some 50 children found in a tower at Machecoul, and similar finds were reported from another of the defendant's estates. Published accounts of the case "credit" Gilles de Rais with at least 200 murders, some reports quadrupling that figure, and he certainly qualifies as a major serial killer.

RAMIREZ, Richard Leyva

Los Angeles is the serial murder capital of the world. It takes a special "twist" to capture headlines in a city where, by autumn 1983, five random slayers were at large and killing independently of one another. In the summer months of 1985, reporters found their twist and filled front pages with accounts of the sinister "Night Stalker," a sadistic home invader with a preference for unlocked windows and a taste for savage mutilation. As the story broke, the Stalker had three weeks of freedom left, but he was bent on making every moment count, and he would claim a minimum of 16 lives before the bitter end.

Unrecognized, the terror had begun a full year earlier with the murder of a 79-year-old woman at her home in suburban Glassell Park in June 1984. Police lifted fingerprints from a window screen at the site, but without a suspect for comparison, the clue led them nowhere.

By February 1985, police had two more murders on their hands, but they were keeping details to themselves. They saw no link, at first, with the abduction of a six-year-old Montebello girl, snatched from a bus stop near her school and carried away in a laundry bag, sexually abused before she was dropped off in Silver Lake on February 25. Two weeks later, on March 11, a nine-year-old girl was kidnapped from her bedroom in Monterey Park, raped by her abductor, and dumped in Elysian Park.

The Night Stalker reverted from child molestation to murder on March 17, shooting 34-year-old Dayle Okazaki to death in her Rosemead condominium and wounding roommate Maria Hernandez before he fled. Hernandez provided police with their first description of a long-faced intruder, notable for his curly hair, bulging eyes, and wide-spaced, rotting teeth.

Another victim on March 17 was 30-year-old Tsa Lian Yu, ambushed near her home in Monterey Park, dragged from her car, and shot several times by the attacker. She died the following day, and her killer celebrated his new score by abducting an Eagle Rock girl from her home on the night of March 20, sexually abusing her before he let her go.

The action moved to Whittier on March 27, with 64-year-old Vincent Zazzara beaten to death in his home. Zazzara's wife, 44-year-old Maxine, was fatally stabbed in the same attack, her eyes carved out and carried from the scene by her assailant. The Zazzaras had been dead two days before their bodies were discovered on March 29, and homicide detectives launched a futile search for clues.

On May 14, 65-year-old William Doi was shot in the head by a man who invaded his home in Monterey Park. Dying, Doi staggered to the telephone and dialed an emergency number before he collapsed, thus saving his wife from a lethal assault by the Stalker. Two weeks later, on May 29, 84-year-old Mabel Bell and her invalid sister, 81-year-old Florence Lang, were savagely beaten in their Monrovia home. The attacker paused to ink satanic pentagrams on Bell's body, drawing more on the walls before he departed. Found by a gardener on June 2, Lang survived her injuries, but Mabel Bell died on July 15.

In the meantime, the Night Stalker seemed intent on running up his score. On June 27, 32-year-old Patty Higgins was killed in her home at Arcadia, her throat slashed, and 77-year-old Mary Cannon was slain in identical style less than two miles away on July 2. Five days later, 61-year-old Joyce Nelson was beaten to death at her home in Monterey Park. The killer struck twice on July 20, first invading a Sun Valley home where he killed 32-year-old Chainarong Khovanath, beat and raped the dead man's wife, and battered their eight-year-old son before escaping with $30,000 worth of cash and jewelry. A short time later, 69-year-old Max Kneiding and his wife Lela, 66, were shot to death in their Glendale home.

"Night Stalker" Richard Ramirez in court (Wide World API)

218

Police were still maintaining silence on the subject of their latest maniac at large, but they began to feel the heat on August 6 after 38-year-old Christopher Peterson and his wife Virginia, age 27, were wounded by gunshots in their Northridge home. Descriptions matched the Stalker, and he struck again on August 8, shooting 35-year-old Elyas Abowath dead in his Diamond Bar home and brutally beating the victim's wife. That night, authorities announced their manhunt for a killer linked to a half-dozen recent homicides, a toll that nearly tripled in the next three weeks with fresh assaults and a new evaluation of outstanding cases.

On August 17, the Night Stalker deserted his normal hunting ground, gunning down 66-year-old Peter Pan at his home in San Francisco. Pan's wife was shot and beaten, but she managed to survive her wounds, identifying suspect sketches of the homicidal prowler.

By August 22, police had credited the Night Stalker with a total of 14 murders in California. Three weeks later, in Mission Viejo, he wounded 29-year-old Bill Carns with a shot to the head, then raped Carns's fiancée before escaping in a stolen car. The vehicle was recovered on August 28, complete with a clear set of fingerprints belonging to Richard Ramirez, a 25-year-old drifter from Texas whose Los Angeles rap sheet included numerous arrests for traffic and drug violations. Acquaintances described Ramirez as an ardent Satanist and longtime drug abuser, obsessed with the mock-satanic rock band AC/DC. According to reports, Ramirez had adopted one of the group's songs—"Night Prowler"—as his personal anthem, playing it repeatedly, sometimes for hours on end.

An all-points bulletin was issued for Ramirez on August 30, his mug shots were broadcast on TV, and he was captured by civilians in East Los Angeles the following day, mobbed and beaten as he tried to steal a car. Police arrived in time to save his life, and by September 29, Ramirez was facing a total of 68 felony charges, including 14 counts of murder and 22 counts of sexual assault. One of the murder counts was dropped prior to trial, but eight new felonies—including two more rapes and one attempted murder—were added to the list in December 1985.

A sister of Ramirez told the press he wanted to plead guilty, a desire frustrated by his attorneys, but the suspect made no public display of repentance. Sporting a pentagram on the palm of one hand, Ramirez waved to photographers and shouted "Hail Satan!" during a preliminary court appearance. Back in jail, he told a fellow inmate, "I've killed twenty people, man. I love all that blood."

The Night Stalker's trial was another Los Angeles marathon. Jury selection began on July 22, 1988, but it was September 20, 1989, before jurors convicted him on 13 murder counts and 30 related felonies. Two weeks later, on October 4, the panel recommended execution for Ramirez, and he was formally sentenced to death on November 7, 1989. "You maggots make me sick," he told the court. "You don't understand me. I am beyond good and evil. I will be avenged. Lucifer dwells in us all." Outside the courtroom, he told reporters, "Big deal. Death always went with the territory. I'll see you at Disneyland."

Subsequently shipped to San Francisco for trial in the Peter Pan slaying, Ramirez was besieged by female GROUPIES lining up to visit him in jail. The competition for his time, including brawls among his young admirers, so disrupted jailhouse routines that Ramirez was moved to San Quentin in September 1993, awaiting his trial on death row. Upon admission to "Q," Ramirez was found to have a metal canister hidden in his rectum containing a key and a needle and syringe. In June 1995, the San Francisco prosecution was postponed indefinitely, pending an appellate ruling on his prior conviction, expected sometime in the future.

RANES, Danny A. and Larry Lee

Homicidal siblings, cousins, even parent-child murder teams are found repeatedly in the annals of serial murder, but the Ranes brothers of Kalamazoo, Michigan, present an apparently unique case of serial-killing brothers who committed their crimes separately and independently of one another, with no contact or consultation while the murders were in progress. One brother robbed and shot five men in 1964; the other raped and killed four women eight years later. Ultimately, all they seemed to share in common was the CHILDHOOD TRAUMA of abusive violence, fierce sibling rivalry (including separate marriages to the same woman), and a taste for random murder.

Born a year apart on Kalamazoo's east side, Danny and Larry Ranes were the second and third of four children, battered incessantly by an alcoholic father who abandoned the family when they were 10 and nine years old, respectively. Before he finally left, their father never missed an opportunity to set the boys at odds with one another. On one occasion, Larry recalls, "He took out a quarter and threw it in the middle of the floor. He told us to fight, and whoever won got the quarter. We literally tried to kill each other, you know, over this damn quarter. Naturally, Danny won, and I detested him for it, even more so because the old man grabs him and pulls him down next to him, gives him the quarter, and I'm standing there crying." Even with their father gone, the battles continued. "I used to hit [Danny] with boards, throw knives at him, shoot him with bows and arrows, and shit like that," Larry said, in a prison interview.

As they grew up, the brutal competition extended to girls. Both ultimately married the same woman, first Danny, then Larry, catching her on the rebound after she and Danny were divorced. It made no difference to the younger Ranes that he was already in prison serving life when they tied the knot. It was still a victory of sorts over the brother he had simultaneously loved and hated all his life. Danny, for his part, calls Larry "the only companion I had most of my life. He's the only true foe I've ever had in my life. He's the only competition I've ever had in my life."

That twisted competition ultimately claimed at least nine lives. Larry, the younger brother, was first to turn homicidal. Discharged from the army in the fall of 1963 after spending his last 90 days of military service in the stockade, Larry drifted across country in April and May of 1964, thumbing rides, robbing at least five men, and killing them with point-blank gunshots to the head. Three of his victims were gas station attendants murdered during holdups: Vernon LaBenne in Battle Creek, Michigan; Charlie Sizemore in Lexington, Kentucky; and Charles Snider, in Elkhart, Indiana. The other two were motorists who picked Ranes up while he was hitchhiking: an unnamed victim in Nevada whose corpse was never found, and schoolteacher Gary Smock of Plymouth, Michigan, who offered Ranes a lift on Memorial Day. Larry was arrested at his girlfriend's house wearing Smock's shoes, and while he confessed to five murders, he was only charged in the latter case. At trial, supporting an INSANITY DEFENSE, psychologists testified that Ranes's crimes were acts of symbolic revenge against his father (a gas station worker like three of Larry's victims), but a jury shrugged it off and sentenced him to life imprisonment.

By that time, Danny Ranes had legal problems of his own, confined to state prison for assault and other charges. He was paroled on February 17, 1972—five days before his brother's retrial, ordered on appeal, was scheduled to begin in Kalamazoo. Legal maneuvers delayed those proceedings for nine months, and Larry pled guilty on November 2, receiving a new life sentence the following day. Meanwhile, Danny had stolen the local headlines with a series of brutal rape-slayings that marked him as the Ranes family's second serial killer.

Danny waylaid his first victim, 28-year-old Patricia Howk, on March 18, as she left a local discount store with her 17-month-old son. He kidnapped her and drove her to the outskirts of town, where he raped and stabbed her to death. Her child was found that night, wandering Kalamazoo's south side and crying for his mother; Howk's body was recovered the following day,

the community stunned by her death. Fifteen weeks later, on July 4, two 19-year-olds from Chicago—Linda Clark and Claudia Bidstrup—stopped for gas at the service station where 28-year-old Danny Ranes worked with Brent Koster, age 15. Ranes and Koster abducted the young women, drove them to a nearby lake in Danny's van, and raped them both repeatedly before they were strangled to death. The final victim, 18-year-old Patricia Fearnow of Kalamazoo, was kidnapped by Ranes and Koster on August 5, raped by both men, and suffocated with a plastic bag. A month later, Brent Koster broke down and confessed his role in the murders, leading police to Fearnow's corpse and naming Danny Ranes as his accomplice.

Arrested on Labor Day, Danny insisted he was innocent of any wrongdoing. Two separate juries disagreed, convicting him of Patricia Howk's murder in March 1973 and of Patricia Fearnow's four months later. Sentenced to life on each count, Ranes later pled no contest in the Clark-Bidstrup slayings and received yet another life sentence. Brent Koster, for all of his assistance to the state, still drew a life prison term in the Fearnow case.

As if the saga of these twisted brothers was not strange enough, Danny's ex-wife (divorced from him in July 1970) went on to wed brother Larry in prison. Larry Ranes, meanwhile, had legally changed his name to "Monk Steppenwolf," claiming some unspecified "significance" in Herman Hesse's novel of the same title. In 1987, Michigan author Conrad Hilberry presented the brothers as "Ralph and Tommy Searl" in his book *Luke Karamazov* (Hilberry's pseudonym for "Monk Steppenwolf"), a case study which has prompted certain careless writers to recount the bloody saga of the "Searl" brothers, complete with false names for their victims.

See also SOTO, ERNO

REES, Melvin David

A Maryland native born in 1933, Rees attended the state university at age 20, dropping out before graduation to pursue a career in music. On March 12, 1955, he was arrested on charges of assaulting a 36-year-old woman and dragging her into his car when she refused to enter voluntarily, but the case was dropped when his victim refused to press charges. Melvin's friends ignored the incident, if they were even conscious of it, viewing Rees as mild-mannered and intelligent, a talented artist who played the piano, guitar, clarinet, and saxophone with equal skill. He had a taste for modern jazz, and his employment often took him on the road.

On June 26, 1957, Margaret Harold was parked with her date, a young army sergeant, on a lonely lover's lane near Annapolis, Maryland, when a green

"Sex Beast" Melvin Rees is led to court in manacles. (Wide World API)

Chrysler pulled up in front of their car. A tall, thin-faced man approached, identified himself as the property's caretaker, then produced a gun, and climbed into the back seat. He demanded money from the couple, shooting Margaret in the head when she indignantly refused. Her date escaped on foot and called police, returning with an escort to discover that her body had been raped in death.

Nearby, the search team found a building made of cinder blocks with a broken basement window, and they crept inside. The inner walls were covered with a mix of pornographic photos and morgue shots of dead women; the only "normal" photo was a college yearbook picture that depicted Wanda Tipton, a 1955 graduate from the University of Maryland. Under questioning, she denied knowing anyone who fit the killer's description.

On January 11, 1959, a family of four disappeared while out for a drive near Apple Grove, Virginia. A relative found their abandoned car later that day, but no trace remained of Carroll Jackson, his wife Mildred, or their two daughters, five-year-old Susan and 18-month-old Janet. 'While police were beating the bushes in vain, a young couple reported that they had been forced off the road by an old blue Chevy that morning. The strange driver had climbed out and approached their car, at which time they made good their escape.

Two months later, on March 4, Carroll Jackson's body was discovered by two men whose car had bogged down in the mud near Fredericksburg, Virginia. Homicide detectives found the victim's hands were bound with a necktie, a single bullet in his head. When they removed his body from the roadside ditch, another corpse was found beneath it. Janet Jackson had been thrown alive into the ditch and suffocated by her father's weight.

On March 21, hunters stumbled across a grave site in Maryland, not far from the spot where Margaret Harold had been murdered in 1957. The bodies of Mildred and Susan Jackson were unearthed by investigators, both bearing signs of sexual assault and savage beatings with a blunt instrument. A stocking was knotted around Mildred's neck, but she had not been strangled, police surmising that the tourniquet had been applied to coerce her participation in oral sex. A quarter mile away, manhunters found a rundown shack with "fresh" tracks outside, a button from Mildred Jackson's dress lying on the floor.

The case was still unsolved in May when homicide detectives received an anonymous letter from Norfolk, naming Melvin Rees as the killer. A background search revealed his link to the University of Maryland—and a former close relationship with Wanda Tipton—but solid evidence was scarce, and no one seemed to know the traveling musician's whereabouts. In early 1960, the anonymous informant came forward with a recent letter from Rees, describing his latest job at a music store in West Memphis, Arkansas. FBI agents made the collar, and a search of Rees's home in Hyattsville turned up an instrument case with a pistol inside, plus various notes describing assorted sadistic acts. One such was clipped to a newspaper photo of Mildred Jackson. It read, in part: "Caught on a lonely road . . . Drove to a select area and killed husband and baby. Now the mother and daughter were all mine. . . ."

Maryland officers finally linked Rees to four other sex slayings. Schoolgirls Mary Shomette, 16, and 14-year-old Ann Ryan had each been raped and killed in College Park near the University of Maryland; 18-year-old Mary Fellers and 16-year-old Shelby Venable had been fished out of nearby rivers. Rees was not indicted for their deaths, but prosecutors felt they had enough to keep him off the streets. Convicted of Margaret Harold's murder in Baltimore, Rees was sentenced to life imprisonment, then handed over to Virginia authorities for trial. Upon conviction of multiple murder there, he was condemned, but the sentence was commuted to life imprisonment in 1972. Two decades later, still incarcerated, the "Sex Beast" died of natural causes.

RENCZI, Vera

Born to affluent parents in Bucharest in the early 1900s, Vera Renczi displayed a precocious interest in sex by age 10 when her family moved to Berkerekul. At age 15 she was found in the dormitory of a boy's school at midnight, and Vera afterward eloped with several lovers, coming home each time when she grew bored with their attentions. It was fine for Vera to desert a paramour, but none must ever try to turn the tables, as she had begun to demonstrate a pathological possessiveness.

Vera's first husband was a wealthy businessman, many years her senior, and she bore him a son before he disappeared one day without a trace. Declaring that her man had left without a word of explanation, Vera passed a year in mourning, finally reporting "news" of her husband's recent death in a car crash.

She soon remarried to a younger man, but he was flagrantly unfaithful, vanishing a few months later on what Vera described as "a long journey." Another year passed before she announced the receipt of a letter, penned by her spouse, declaring his intent of leaving her forever.

Vera Renczi would not wed again, but she had many lovers—32 in all—as years went by. They never seemed to stay around for long, and none were ever seen again once they "abandoned" Vera, but she always had an explanation for her neighbors . . . and another lover waiting in the wings. Police became involved when Vera's latest was reported missing by the wife he left at home; a search of Renczi's basement turned up 35 zinc coffins with the bodies of her missing husbands, son, and lovers tucked away inside.

Detained on murder charges, Vera made a full confession, stating that she killed her husbands and her lovers with arsenic when they began to stray, sometimes arranging a romantic "last supper" to climax a tryst. Her son's demise had been a different story, brought about by threats of blackmail when he stumbled on the basement crypt by accident. Some evenings, Vera liked to sit among the coffins in an armchair and enjoy the company of her adoring beaux. Convicted on the basis of her own confession, Vera drew a term of life imprisonment and subsequently died in custody.

RESSLER, Robert K.: FBI profiler

The son of a *Chicago Tribune* employee and born in 1937, Robert Ressler discovered his budding fascination with serial murder at age nine when the local case of WILLIAM HEIRENS received sensational newspaper coverage. A self-described "average student" in high school, Ressler joined the army after graduation and was stationed on Okinawa. Discharged after two years in uniform, he earned a degree in criminology and police administration at Michigan State University, then applied for a job with the Chicago Police Department. Rejected on grounds that recruits with "too much schooling" were likely to "make trouble" in the graft-ridden department, Ressler completed one semester of graduate study before he returned to the army, this time as a lieutenant.

For his second tour of duty, Ressler chose assignment to the military police and wound up commanding a platoon in Germany. Later, transferred stateside, he served as commander of the Criminal Investigative Division (CID) unit at Fort Sheridan near Chicago. Ressler was still on active duty when he returned to Michigan State for his master's degree; aside from classwork, he was also assigned to infiltrate the campus chapter of Students for a Democratic Society and report on the group's antiwar campaign. After Michigan State, he spent two more years as an army provost marshal, including one year of duty in Thailand.

Ressler's application to the FBI was accepted in 1970. Four years later, he was tapped for duty as a counselor for police officers training at the FBI National Academy in Quantico, Virginia. On the side, he became acquainted with the founders of the FBI's Behavioral Science Unit, learning as much as he could about abnormal psychology and criminal behavior. Soon, he was part of the BSU team, lecturing to police around the country and abroad. Ressler was visiting the British police academy at Barnshill in 1974 when he claims (incorrectly) to have coined the term SERIAL MURDER.

Ressler's primary field of expertise at the time was hostage negotiation, a subject he taught to various state and local police agencies through mid-1978. More road trips were involved, and he decided to use his spare time interviewing notorious murderers jailed in the states he visited, hoping to obtain information that would help the BSU solve crimes and identify unknown offenders. A California visit gave Ressler the chance to speak with EDMUND KEMPER, HERBERT MULLIN, JUAN CORONA, members of the MANSON "FAMILY," and other infamous slayers. A few months later, traveling with new BSU member JOHN DOUGLAS to West Virginia, Ressler interviewed Mansonites Lynette ("Squeaky") Fromme and Sandra Good, both serving time on federal charges.

Thus far, Ressler's FBI superiors had been reluctant to permit his prison interviews, but they had a change of heart in 1979, inaugurating the Criminal Personality Research Project. Ideally, it was hoped that understanding killers and rapists in custody would promote accurate PROFILING of those still at large. By 1983, interviews had been completed with 36 slayers, collectively responsible for 109 murders. The choice of subjects was skewed—all the subjects were male, all but three of them white—and those interviewed were not all serial killers, but the list did include such notorious names as THEODORE BUNDY, DAVID BERKOWITZ, JOHN GACY, Richard Speck, JEROME BRUDOS, Charles Davis, and Monte Rissell. Those interviews formed the hard core of an ever-expanding database, utilized today in profiling unknown offenders through the FBI's VICAP.

Retired from the FBI in 1990, Ressler has kept up a busy schedule of lectures and writing, police-training seminars, private consulting on criminal cases, and frequent appearances on TV talk shows. While he did not, in fact, coin the term *serial murder,* he remains a leading expert in the field today and has coauthored four books relevant to the subject. They include: *Sexual Homicide* (1988); the FBI *Crime Classification Manual* (1992); *Whoever Fights Monsters* (1992); and *I Have Lived in the Monster* (1997).

RIDGWAY, Gary Leon

For nearly two decades, between January 1982 and November 2001, police in Washington pursued an elusive predator who murdered girls and women along the seedy Sea-Tac Strip, between Seattle and Tacoma. Detectives dubbed their quarry the "Green River Killer," after his favorite dumping ground, and ultimately blamed him for the deaths or disappearances of 49 victims. Today, although a suspect has confessed and been imprisoned in that case, disturbing mysteries remain.

Published reports identify the killer's first known victim as Leann Wilcox, a 16-year-old Tacoma resident found strangled in a field near Federal Way, eight miles south of Seattle, on January 21, 1982. The absence of a pattern in that case prevented homicide detectives from establishing connections to the string of later deaths, and nearly two years would elapse before Wilcox was finally acknowledged as a "Green River" victim, in November 1983. Likewise, 36-year-old Amina Agisheff was simply a missing person when she vanished on July 7, 1982. Her skeletal remains were not recovered and identified until April 1984.

The first "official" victim, 16-year-old Wendy Coffield, was reported missing from her foster home on July 8, 1982, her body fished out of the Green River seven days later. Seventeen-year-old Gisele Lovvorn left home and vanished on July 17; she was found two months later, on September 25. On August 12, 23-year-old Deborah Bonner was dragged from the river, a half-mile upstream from where Coffield was found. On August 15 the Green River yielded three more victims: 31-year-old Marcia Chapman, 17-year-old Cynthia Hinds, and 16-year-old Opal Mills, all reported missing since August 1, 1982.

Police now realized they had a problem on their hands, and it was growing by the day. Two 17-year-olds, Kase Lee and Terri Milligan, went missing in late August 1982; Milligan's remains were identified on April 1, 1984. Eighteen-year-old Mary Meehan joined the missing list on September 15, 1982, followed by 15-year-old Debra Estes five days later. Their skeletal remains were found in November 1983 and May 1988, respectively. Linda Rule, age 16, disappeared on September 26, 1982; her remains were discovered on January 31, 1983.

FBI agent JOHN EDWARD DOUGLAS took a crack at PROFILING the Green River Killer in September 1982, and while the broad strokes of his 12-page assessment later proved correct—the killer was a white male from a troubled home who sought dominance over women—the fine points flew wide of the mark. As finally revealed in 2001, the slayer was not an unemployed outdoorsman who smoked and drank heavily, yet somehow remained in top physical form. The actual killer held one job for more than three decades, never smoked, drank only the occasional "lite" beer, and made no effort to remain in shape. His sole "outdoor activity" was hunting women. The case nearly killed Douglas, its stress producing a brain hemorrhage when he visited Seattle for a consultation on the crimes in December 1983.

According to police, the six known dead had all been prostitutes, but the killer also showed a taste for runaways and hitchhikers. Denise Bush, age 22, vanished on October 8, 1982; her skull surfaced in Oregon on June 12, 1985, while the rest of her remains were not found until February 1990. Seventeen-year-old Shawnda Summers disappeared one day after Bush, her remains identified by authorities in August 1983. Shirley Sherrill dropped from sight in late October; the 18-year-old's bones were found in June 1985. Rebecca Marrero, a 20-year-old friend of Debra Estes, was last seen alive on December 2, 1982. Fifteen-year-old Colleen Brockman vanished on Christmas Eve 1982; her bones were found in a ditch, 20 miles south of Seattle, on May 26, 1984.

Alma Smith, age 19, picked up her last "trick" in Seattle on March 3, 1983; her skeletal remains were found with Terri Milligan's in April 1984. Seventeen-year-old Delores Williams vanished on March 8 and was found dead on March 31, 1984. The killer's pace accelerated furiously during April, with 24-year-old Gail Matthews killed on April 10 (found September 18, 1983), 19-year-old Andrea Childers on April 16 (found October 11, 1983), 17-year-old Sandra Gabbert and 16-year-old Kimi-Kai Pitsor on April 17 (found in 1984 and 1986, respectively), and 18-year-old Marie Malvar on April 30 (found September 29, 2003).

May 1983 was equally lethal. Carol Christensen, age 19, vanished on May 3 and was found five days later. Sixteen-year-old Joanne Hovland also disappeared on May 3, shortly after her release from a juvenile detention facility in Everett; she remains missing today. Eighteen-year-old Martina Authorlee disappeared on May 22; her remains were found on November 14, 1984. On

May 23, 18-year-old Cheryl Wims dropped from sight, found dead on March 22, 1984. Two victims, 19-year-old Yvonne Antosh and 15-year-old Carrie Rois, disappeared on May 31; their remains were found in October 1983 and March 1985, respectively.

All the murders had a certain ritualistic quality. Like THEODORE ROBERT BUNDY before him, the Green River Killer preferred certain dump sites for multiple victims. At least eight such locations were used, the killer switching off despite police surveillance. Many victims were covered with loose brush and branches, and several were laid out beside fallen logs. Pathologists found small, pyramid-shaped stones inserted into the vaginas of several Green River victims; their significance is unknown to this day. At least one corpse was left by the killer with a dead fish draped across one thigh.

Police had two near-misses with the killer in spring 1983. On April 8, prostitute Gail Matthews climbed into a pickup truck on the Sea-Tac Strip, observed by her boyfriend as the vehicle pulled away. Her strangled body was found near Star Lake on September 18, 1983, but the boyfriend gave conflicting descriptions of the killer's vehicle and the search went nowhere. Meanwhile, on April 30, Marie Malvar worked the Strip near the spot where Matthews had vanished three weeks earlier. Malvar's pimp, Robert Woods, watched her enter a dark-colored pickup and followed the truck for several blocks before he lost it at a red light. Malvar never returned from her "date," but Woods described the pickup to her family and José Malvar went searching for his daughter. Finding the truck Woods had described, parked outside a house in Des Moines, Washington, Malvar directed police to the scene. Detective Robert Fox questioned the tenant, Gary Ridgway, on May 4 and accepted his denials at face value.

The interrogation solved nothing. Constance Naon, a 23-year-old prostitute, was reported missing on June 8, 1983; her bones were recovered in October. On June 12, the killer plucked 27-year-old Kimberly Reames from the Sea-Tac Strip. Her body was recovered the next afternoon. Kelly Ware, age 22, disappeared on July 19; her remains were found on October 29. Another 22-year-old, Tina Thompson, vanished on July 25 and was found dead on April 20, 1984. April Buttram, age 17, left home for the last time on August 4, 1983; her scattered remains were found in August and September 2003.

September 1983 was another busy month for the Green River Killer. He claimed 26-year-old Debbie Abernathy on the September 5; her skeletal remains were recovered on March 31, 1984. Nineteen-year-olds Tracy Winston and Maureen Feeney were reported missing on September 12 and 28, respectively; their remains were found in March and May 1986.

October's victims included 25-year-old Mary Bellow (killed October 11, found the next day), 16-year-old Pammy Avent (killed October 26, 1983, found August 16, 2003), and 22-year-old Delise Plager (killed October 30, 1983, found February 14, 1984). The slayer claimed 26-year-old Kimberly Nelson on November 1, 1983; her remains were found June 14, 1986. Lisa Yates, age 26, vanished on December 23 and was found dead on March 13, 1984.

A task force was organized to investigate the Green River murders in January 1984, but its formation failed to intimidate the killer. Relatives of Patricia Osborn, a 19-year-old prostitute, reported her missing on January 24, and her name made the Green River victims' list on February 11. Five days earlier, on February 6, 16-year-old Mary West was abducted en route to a neighborhood market; her skull was identified in September 1985. Seventeen-year-old Cindy Smith became the last official Green River victim on March 21, 1984; her remains were found on June 27, 1987.

Police reviewed their file on Gary Ridgway in spring 1984. By then, they knew that he had been arrested in July 1980, on suspicion of choking a hooker, but he was released without charges. In May 1982 he was jailed again, for soliciting sex from an undercover policewoman. That charge was apparently dropped, but two years later, on May 7, 1984, Ridgway agreed to task force requests that he sit for a polygraph test in the Green River case. The specific results of that session were never released, but court documents state that "Ridgway was considered to be cleared as a Green River suspect." Later, he bragged about the ease with which he fooled police. "I just relaxed and took the polygraph," he said. "I mean, I didn't practice or anything. Just relaxed and answered the questions and whatever came out, came out." That test was subsequently ruled "invalid," but at the time it diverted official attention from Ridgway toward other suspects.

Six months later, in November 1984, police discovered a survivor of the murder series. Rebecca Guay was 19 years old in November 1982, when she accepted $20 for a "car date" with the driver of a dark-colored pickup on Pacific Highway South. The "john" told Guay a sob story about his recent arrest in a prostitution sting, then drove her deep into the woods and tried to strangle her. She managed to escape, but waited two years to report the incident. When shown a photo lineup of six suspects, she immediately fingered Gary Ridgway's mug shot. This time, when questioned by police, Ridgway admitted paying Guay for sex, further granting that he choked her after she had bitten him. Detectives dropped the case.

Gary Ridgway was born in Salt Lake City in February 1949, an "average" child whose family moved to

Washington in 1960. They settled in McMicken Heights, near Seattle-Tacoma International Airport. Though courteous and friendly, Ridgway was a slow-witted student, 20 years old when he graduated from high school. By then, unknown to his parents or police, Ridgway had already attempted his first murder. In 1963 he stabbed a 6-year-old boy, lacerating his liver. When the child asked Ridgway, "Why did you kill me?" Ridgway paused, wiped the bloody knife on his victim's shirt, and replied, "I always wanted to know what it felt like to kill somebody." Forty years later, the victim recalled Ridgway walking away, "kinda putting his head in the air, you know, and laughing real loud."

Ridgway was not arrested for that crime, and it appeared to have no outward impact on his life. He married a high school classmate in August 1970, but discovery of his bride's adultery led Ridgway to brand her a "whore," and the couple divorced in January 1972. (Ironically, Ridgway himself was patronizing prostitutes at the same time.) Ridgway married his second wife in December 1973 and fathered a son who was born in September 1975. In the wake of that event, he reportedly became "fanatical" about religion, attending two different churches and leading his family on door-to-door prayer walks. Sometimes his wife found Ridgway sitting in front of the television, weeping with a Bible open on his lap. The couple separated in 1980 and divorced a year later, filing mutual restraining orders, though Ridgway retained visitation rights with his son.

Life was more stable for Ridgway on the work front, where he served for 32 years in the Kenworth Truck Company's paint shop and won awards for perfect attendance. In private, he was sexually insatiable, demanding intercourse from girlfriends two or three times per night, while keeping up his trysts with hookers on the side. Some partners, including Ridgway's third wife, later recalled his tastes as kinky, involving bondage, anal sex, and other "deviations" from the norm. On December 24, 1981, Ridgway told recent girlfriend Sharon Hebert that he had met a woman on the street and nearly killed her. He provided no details, and Hebert asked no questions, but she soon stopped dating Ridgway.

In July 1982, while riding with his seven-year-old son, Ridgway picked up a woman on the Sea-Tac Strip and drove to a wooded area, where he parked. Leaving his son behind, Ridgway went into the forest with his victim. He returned alone, explaining to his son that the woman had decided to "walk home." With three Green River victims slain that month, police remain uncertain of the vanishing woman's identity.

In contrast to such outrageous risks, Ridgway also took pains to cover his tracks and confuse investigators.

When one struggling victim scratched him, Ridgway clipped her fingernails to remove forensic evidence, then doused the scratches on his arm with acid to obscure them. He left gum and cigarettes beside some corpses, and once left an Afro hair-pick to incriminate the victim's pimp. In once case, Ridgway planted leaflets from an airport motel near a victim's body, then dropped her driver's license at Sea-Tac Airport, creating false trails. On occasions when he met a victim through her pimp, Ridgway phoned back after the murder to request another date, thus feigning ignorance about the crime. In January 1984, Ridgway drove with his son to a suburb of Portland, Oregon, dumping the remains of Denise Bush and Shirley Sherrill, then mailing a letter filled with false leads to the *Seattle Post-Intelligencer*. The ploy was successful, diverting task force detectives into Oregon for several months.

In early 1986, FBI agents focused their manhunt on Bill McLean, a trapper from Riverton Heights, Washington. He fit the white-outdoorsman profile, though he neither smoked nor drank, and did not frequent prostitutes. G-men arrested him on February 6, encouraged when he greeted them with a question: "What took you so long?" Still, a search of his home revealed nothing, and McLean passed multiple polygraph tests, emerging from jail to sue King County and a local newspaper for slander. A month later, agents requested another polygraph sitting from Gary Ridgway. He agreed on March 20, then changed his mind and refused on advice from a lawyer. Discouraged, the FBI "inactivated" its file on Ridgway.

The local task force took a different view, reopening its investigation of Ridgway on August 19, 1986. Interviews with his ex-wives and girlfriends collected tales of violence, aberrant sex, and venereal disease, together with Ridgway's fondness for pickup trucks and prostitutes. Police began to trail Ridgway, in hopes that he might lead them to a body dump, but the surveillance was haphazard. No officers were watching when he killed 19-year-old Patricia Barczak on October 17, 1986. No detectives were present when he kidnapped and strangled 21-year-old Roberta Hayes in February 1987.

Two months later, task force officers obtained a warrant to search Ridgway's body, home, vehicles, and his locker at work. Detective Matthew Haney's affidavit supporting the warrant declared: "It is highly probable that Gary Leon Ridgway is the Green River killer." Technicians swabbed Ridgway's mouth for DNA samples, plucking hairs from his head, chest and groin, while searchers confiscated various tools and articles of clothing. A backhoe was summoned to excavate Ridgway's backyard, all in vain. Aside from a pamphlet on marijuana, no evidence of any criminal activity was found. In 1988, while Ridgway wooed and wed his third wife, a forensic laboratory in New York compared his DNA samples with rape-kit evidence collected from victims Chapman, Christensen, and Mills. The current technology failed, forcing a judgment that the victim samples were too small for testing or comparison.

Task force investigators lost heart in the 1990s, convinced that their quarry had "retired" or moved on to some other hunting ground. Media reports quoted various detectives as believing the Green River Killer was responsible for unsolved prostitute murders in California and Missouri. Others thought their man was dead or locked up on some unrelated charge. Task force commander Robert Evans even questioned whether one man was responsible for all the listed murders. "It could be two, maybe even three separate serial murder cases," Evans told reporters. In fact, the stalker was neither absent nor inactive. He killed 31-year-old Marta Reeves in March 1990, her remains discovered six months later. Patricia Yellowrobe was murdered on August 4, 1998, her body found on August 6.

DNA technology caught up with Gary Ridgway in September 2001, as new procedures allowed definitive testing of samples deemed too small in 1988. On September 4, the Washington State Patrol's crime lab matched Ridgway's DNA to semen found on victims Chapman, Christensen, Hinds, and Mills. King County Sheriff Dave Reichert created a new "evidence review team" on September 11, designed to operate "under the radar" while perfecting the case against Ridgway. Two months later, on November 16, Ridgway was arrested in SeaTac, on a charge of loitering for purposes of prostitution. Still Reichert bided his time, delaying Ridgway's arrest on murder charges until November 30, 2001.

Gary Ridgway was formally charged with four counts of aggravated first-degree murder on December 5, 2001, but the case was far from closed. Sheriff Reichert told reporters that his office had reopened investigation of 80 cases involving women murdered or missing since 1984. The search also expanded into British Columbia, where 30-odd streetwalkers were reported missing from Vancouver and survivors recalled seeing Ridgway in the neighborhood. (That phase of the investigation led nowhere near Ridgway; Canadian suspect Robert Pickton was later charged in the Vancouver slayings.) Evidence collected after Ridgway's arrest included bone fragments found in his home and paint flecks from several bodies, matched at long last to the Kenworth plant where Ridgway worked. In March 2002, a friend of Ridgway's from the 1970s recalled the prisoner's remark that "prostitution is a terrible thing, and there ought to be a solution, and that solution was to terminate the prostitutes."

Police linked Ridgway to 100 different vehicles and began the arduous task of locating each one for a new forensic search.

Three more murder charges were filed against Ridgway on March 27, 2003, for victims Bonner, Coffield, and Estes. On April 10, Ridgway abandoned his claims of innocence and confessed responsibility for 25 of the Green River slayings, followed one day later by admission of many more crimes. A bargain was struck with the state, and Ridgway led police to the remains of victims Avent, Buttram, and Malvar, found between August 16 and September 29, 2003. On November 5, 2003, after Ridgway pleaded guilty to 48 murders, media reports spoke of 60 confessions and speculated that the final tally "might be closer to 70." In fact, police told journalists, Ridgway had "killed so many women he had a hard time keeping them straight." Ridgway's final statement to the court, before he vanished into prison, was brief and brought no solace to survivors of the dead. He said:

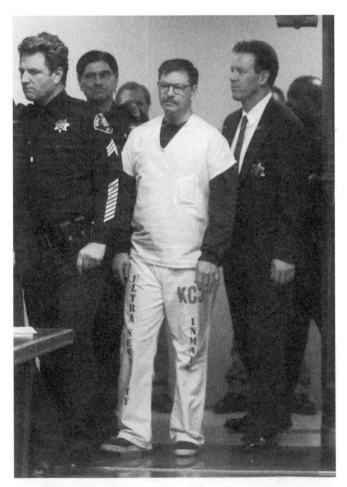

Gary Ridgway is escorted by guards to his sentencing. (AP Photo/Elaine Thompson)

226

I'm sorry for killing all those young ladies. I have tried to remember as much as I could to help the detectives to find and recover the ladies. I'm sorry for the scare I put into the communities. I want to thank the police, the prosecuting attorneys, my lawyers and all others that had the patience to work with me and to help me remember all the tragic things that I did and to be able to talk about them. I know the horrible things my acts were. I have tried for a long time to get these things out of my mind. I've tried for a long time to keep from killing any ladies. I'm sorry I put my wife, my son, my brothers and my family through this hell. I hope they can find a way to forgive me. I'm very sorry for the ladies that were not found. May they rest in peace. They need a better place than where I gave them. I'm sorry for killing these ladies. They had their whole lives ahead of them. I'm sorry for causing so much pain to so many families.

In addition to life imprisonment without parole, Ridgway was slapped with a $480,000 fine, which the state had no means to collect. On June 1, 2004, Judge Richard Jones compounded the absurdity by ordering Ridgway to pay $74,459 in restitution to survivors of his victims (specific stipends ranged from $300 to $6,500 per family). Like the state of Washington before them, mourners are unlikely to receive a penny of the court-ordered amount.

Gary Ridgway's confession left a nagging mystery behind in Seattle. He admitted slaying 42 of the "official" 49 Green River victims, plus six women not on the task force's list. None of the dead were personally known to their killer, and four remain unidentified today. "Green River" victims whose murders remain officially unsolved at press time for this work include Amina Agisheff, Joanne Hovland, Kase Lee, Keli McGuiness, Patricia Osborn, Kimberly Reames, and Leann Wilcox.

RIJKE, Sjef

Sjef Rijke seemed to have no luck at all with women. In January 1981, his 18-year-old fiancée, Willy Maas, experienced a week of racking stomach pains that climaxed in her death. The symptoms seemed to indicate food poisoning, though friends and relatives could never be precise about the suspect dish. At Willy's funeral in Utrecht, Holland, Sjef was visibly distraught.

His period of mourning was abbreviated by engagement of a female friend of several years, young Mientje Manders. Near the end of March, Sjef's second fiancée complained of nagging stomach pains that quickly proved debilitating. Rijke sat beside her bed and held her hand, tears streaming down his face when Manders died on April 2.

The authorities in Utrecht were concerned about the strange "coincidence," but Rijke seemed to have no motive for eliminating his fiancées. Flying in the face of grief, Sjef married only three weeks after Mientje's death. It was another star-crossed union, marred by Rijke's pathological jealousy; he quarreled bitterly with 18-year-old Maria, prompting her to leave him. Curious detectives asked about her health, and they discovered that Maria had been subject to repeated stomachaches throughout her short-lived marriage; change of domicile had cured the problem overnight.

A short time later, Sjef acquired a live-in lover who, in turn, began to suffer stomach problems. These were dutifully reported to her mother, who inquired about her diet. Sjef, the older woman learned, ate everything her daughter did, yet seemed to feel no ill effects. It was discovered that his latest paramour was fond of eating peanut butter as a snack between their normal meals, and samples from the jar were found to have a strange, metallic taste. Delivered to a chemist for analysis, the peanut butter was found to be laced with rat poison.

Still lacking any motive, homicide investigators searched for other suspects, grilling Rijke's cleaning lady. The investigation soon focused on Sjef, though, after a local merchant recalled selling him several boxes of poison in recent months. Under close questioning, Rijke broke down and confessed his crimes, describing the sadistic pleasure he obtained from watching women suffer. It was never his intention to kill his fiancées, he claimed; Sjef simply loved to see them squirm.

Found legally sane by court psychiatrists, Rijke was tried for the murder of Willy Maas in January 1972. Upon conviction he was sentenced to a double term of life imprisonment.

ROBINSON, John Edward, Sr.: First "Internet serial killer"

A native of Cicero, Illinois, born in 1943, John Robinson was well known in his community by age 13, an honor student at Quigley Preparatory Seminary and an Eagle Scout who led a troop of 120 other scouts in a command performance for Queen Elizabeth II. By 1961, he was enrolled at a local junior college, studying to become an X-ray technician. Three years later, he married Nancy Jo Lynch in Kansas City, Missouri.

Robinson was on the path to a solid middle-class life, but he somehow went astray. In June 1967, while working as a lab technician for a Kansas City doctor, he embezzled $33,000 and was placed on three years' probation. At his next job, as manager of a television rental company, Robinson stole merchandise and was fired, but his boss declined to prosecute. In 1969, he began work as a systems analyst for Mobil Oil. On August 27,

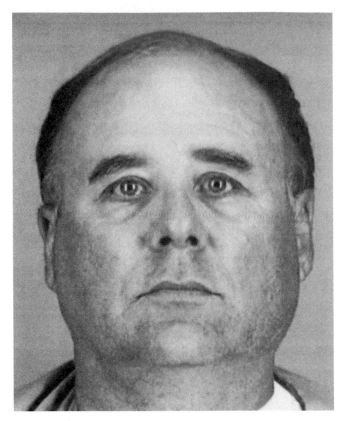

John E. Robinson (Corbis Sygma)

1970, exactly two weeks after his probation officer wrote that Robinson was "responding extremely well to probation supervision," Robinson stole 6,200 postage stamps from the company. This time, he was fired and charged with theft.

Moving on to Chicago in September 1970, Robinson embezzled $5,500 from yet another employer. He was fired again, but the victim waived prosecution when Robinson's father repaid the loss. Drifting back to Kansas City, Robinson was jailed for violating his probation and his term of supervised release was extended another five years, until 1976. A probation report from April 1973 records his "good prognosis," unaware that Robinson had recently swindled an elderly neighbor out of $30,000. His probation officer was so impressed with Robinson's improvement, in fact, that Robinson was discharged in 1974, two years ahead of schedule. It was not the system's first mistake with Robinson, nor would it be the last.

A free man once more, Robinson promptly created the Professional Service Association, ostensibly formed to provide financial counseling for Kansas City physicians. More embezzlement followed, prompting a federal grand jury to indict Robinson on four counts of securities and mail fraud. In June 1976, he was fined

$2,500 and placed on three years' probation—another wrist-slap that taught him precisely nothing.

In 1977, with his wife and four children, Robinson moved to Johnson County, Kansas, and took a fling at hydroponic farming behind the corporate facade of Hydro-Gro, Inc. A community activist who tackled multiple projects, Robinson was voted local "Man of the Year" in 1977 for his work with the handicapped. By 1980, Robinson had taken on a second job as personnel director for a local branch of Breeden Foods—where he promptly embezzled $40,000, financing a love nest for kinky liaisons with female bondage enthusiasts. Arrested in that case, he faced a seven-year prison term but spent only two months in jail, with five years' probation added to his tab.

Robinson's first known murder victim, 19-year-old Paula Godfrey, was employed by Robinson when she vanished in 1984. Police later received a letter, purportedly signed by Godfrey, insisting that she was "O.K." and that she did not wish to see her family. She remains among the missing to this day.

In December 1984, Robinson approached a Kansas City hospital and adoption agency, introducing himself as the spokesman for "Kansas City Outreach," allegedly a firm created to provide housing and job training for young unwed mothers. The hospital sent Robinson his first client, 19-year-old Linda Stasi, in January 1985. Stasi promptly vanished, leaving behind a typed letter explaining her urge to leave Missouri for parts unknown. Robinson's childless brother and sister-in-law took custody of Stasi's newborn daughter, paying Robinson $5,500 for a set of forged adoption papers.

Robinson's next brainstorm was the formation of a sadomasochistic prostitution ring for fun and profit. FBI agents learned of his venture and sent a female decoy around for a job interview, but the initial conversation proved so disturbing that G-men backed out, citing fear for their undercover agent's safety. Robinson's first known S&M employee was 21-year-old Theresa Williams, for whom he rented an apartment and arranged transportation on "dates." In May 1985, after less than a month on the job, Williams woke one morning to find Robinson raging through her apartment with a pistol, furious because she had invited a boyfriend to her flat. FBI agents relocated Williams, and Robinson was charged with assault. His probation was revoked for unauthorized firearms possession, but that decision was reversed on appeal, a higher court finding that the FBI had denied Robinson's constitutional right to confront his accuser in court.

The agents found some consolation in January 1986, when Kansas jurors convicted Robinson of another investment scam. Sentenced as a habitual offender,

Robinson drew a prison term of six to 19 years, but appeals stalled his incarceration until May 1987. In the meantime, 27-year-old Catherine Clampitt moved from Texas to Kansas, drawn by Robinson's promise of "a great job, a lot of traveling and a new wardrobe." She was never seen again.

In prison, Robinson quickly earned a reputation as a model inmate, using his time to develop a computer program that saved the Kansas penal system $100,000 yearly on administrative tasks. The cooperative attitude and a series of mild strokes earned Robinson the sympathy of prison psychologists. In November 1990 they described him as a "devoted family man" and a "nonviolent person [who] does not present a threat to society." Kansas paroled Robinson in January 1991, but he still owed time in Missouri, where he remained incarcerated until spring 1993.

Kansas prison librarian Beverly Bonner admired Robinson so much that she divorced her husband in 1993 and moved to Kansas City as the "president" of Hydro-Gro. She vanished in January 1994, after sending her family a letter explaining that her new job required extensive travel. Six months later, after prolonged correspondence, Sheila Faith left Colorado to join Robinson—her "dream man"—in Kansas City. Faith brought along her teenage daughter Debbie, who was confined to a wheelchair, and both soon disappeared.

By that time Robinson had discovered the Internet and begun trolling for fresh victims in cyberspace. One who survived told journalist David McClintock that she lost $17,000 to Robinson on a fraudulent investment scheme, arranged through e-mail correspondence. She was lucky, compared to Izabel Lewicka, a Polish immigrant and freshman at Indiana's Purdue University. Lewicka met Robinson on-line in early 1997, and that June she left home to serve an "internship" with Robinson in Kansas. Communication with her parents ceased abruptly, and they went looking for Izabel in August 1997, leaving Kansas empty-handed, without contacting police. Unknown to Lewicka's family, Robinson had coerced her into signing a six-page "slave contract," convincing her the document was legal while he kept her at an apartment in Olathe, Kansas. Lewicka survived in Robinson's clutches until August 1999, then dropped from sight. He told acquaintances that she had been deported for smoking marijuana.

Robinson's last known victim was 27-year-old Suzette Trouten, a Detroit nurse to whom Robinson offered a job in September 1999. The package was attractive: a $60,000 yearly salary, a company car, and wide-ranging travel. Trouten moved to Kansas City on February 13, 2000, and was last seen alive on March 1.

Kansas authorities, meanwhile, had been building a case against Robinson for sexual assault on yet another victim. They arrested him on June 2, 2000, and searched his Olathe home, seizing five computers and a host of other evidence, including a blank piece of stationery signed by Lisa Stasi 15 years earlier and her last motel receipt, dated January 10, 1985. Searchers visited a storage facility rented by Robinson and found a cache of S&M toys, along with various items related to Izabel Lewicka and Suzette Trouten: more blank stationery with signatures affixed, a birth certificate and Social Security card, Lewicka's slave contract, and sundry photographs (including bondage shots).

On June 3, 2000, police searched Robinson's 16-acre farm near La Cygne, Kansas, recovering two 55-gallon drums with women's corpses packed inside. The victims, both beaten to death with a hammer, were identified as Lewicka and Trouten. Two days later, another raiding party scoured a second storage facility rented by Robinson, this one in Cass County, Missouri. They found three more oil drums, sealed with duct tape and planted on mounds of cat litter to mask death's sickly odor. Inside the drums lay Betty Bonner, Sheila Faith, and Sheila's daughter Debbie. Like the rest, they had been hammered lifeless and entombed.

Robinson was charged in Kansas with two counts of capital murder (for victims Lewicka and Trouten), one count of first-degree murder (for Lisa Stasi), and various lesser charges. On October 28, 2003, jurors convicted him on all counts. The panel recommended execution, but formal sentencing was deferred pending Robinson's appeal of the verdict. That appeal was rejected on January 21, 2003, whereupon Judge John Anderson III sentenced Robinson to die by lethal injection for the Lewicka and Trouten murders, with a life prison term for Stasi's slaying.

Missouri authorities still awaited their turn with the defendant journalists dubbed the "Slavemaster" and America's "first Internet serial killer." On March 13, 2003, Kansas authorities approved Robinson's extradition to face trial for murdering Beverly Bonner, Sheila Faith, and Debbie Faith. Cass County formerly indicted Robinson on April 26, 2003, and while he initially pleaded not guilty on all counts, a plea bargain changed his mind six months later. On October 16, 2003, Robinson pleaded guilty as charged and accepted a sentence of life imprisonment. Waiver of Missouri's death penalty was contingent on Robinson's guilty plea in two additional cases, the murders of Catherine Clampitt and Paula Godfrey.

RODRIGUEZ VEGA, Jose Antonio

Spain's most prolific serial killer of modern times, bricklayer Jose Rodriguez murdered at least 16 elderly women between 1986 and 1988 in and around the northern coastal city of Santander. A paroled rapist, Rodriguez apparently suffered from impotence after leaving prison. In the new rash crimes, he typically charmed his victims into hiring him for some minor household repairs, then found himself "overcome with excitement" upon entering their homes. At that point, he swiftly strangled the women, removed their panties, and raped and molested them.

Rodriguez was fastidious in cleaning up his crime scenes—so cautious, in fact, that the first slayings were not recognized as homicides until he confessed. Victims were normally tucked in their beds when he finished amusing himself with their corpses, old age and tidy rooms encouraging authorities to write off any of the deaths as "natural." At the same time, Rodriguez habitually kept TROPHIES to commemorate his crimes, crafting an elaborate shrine for his mementos in the one-room, burgundy-draped apartment he shared with a female roommate. The full extent of his crime spree was only realized after Spanish police broadcast a videotape of Jose's apartment, prompting telephone calls from viewers who recognized possessions stolen from their murdered relatives.

At his trial, in 1991, Rodriguez seemed to enjoy the obvious grief of some observers, even relishing the threats against his life. Upon conviction he was sentenced to 440 years in prison, but the sentence meant little, despite its apparent severity. In fact, despite his sentence, Spanish law decreed that Rodriguez would serve no more than 30 years in custody, and authorities scheduled his tentative release for 2008. Before that happened, though, Rodriguez found himself in danger from fellow inmates, whose rough code of honor mandated summary punishment for rapists. After suffering multiple assaults at one prison, Rodriguez was transferred to the Topas jail, in western Salamanca Province, on October 22, 2002. Two days later, a pair of inmates armed with makeshift knives stabbed him to death in the prison exercise yard.

ROSS, Michael B.

Born in Brooklyn, Connecticut, where his parents ran an egg farm, Ross concentrated on animal science in high school, moving on the Cornell University in 1977 and earning a bachelor's degree in 1981. After graduation, he worked briefly at an egg farm near Columbus, Ohio, but Ross had trouble keeping his mind on the chickens. Bicycling through LaSalle City, Illinois, on September 28, 1981, he kidnapped a 16-year-old girl and dragged her into the woods, gagging her with a handkerchief and belt before police arrived. Charged with unlawful restraint, Ross pled guilty the following day and paid a $500 fine, drawing two years' probation before he returned to Connecticut.

On January 5, 1982, 17-year-old Tammy Williams disappeared in Brooklyn, while walking home from her boyfriend's house in broad daylight. Ross was not suspected in the case, but he had reason to be fearful, all the same. In February, he found employment at an Ohio egg farm, living peacefully for nearly three months before his next clash with the law.

On April 2, Ross turned up at a rural home in Licking County, Ohio, asking to borrow a flashlight. His car had broken down, he said, and when Ross came to return the light, he also asked to use the telephone. Inside the house, he tried to choke his benefactress—an off-duty policewoman—but she fought him off and gave a clear description to authorities, resulting in his swift arrest. Bailed out by his parents on May 11, Ross was sent home to Connecticut for 16 days of psychiatric study.

On June 15, 1982, Debra Taylor was riding with her husband when they ran out of gas near Danielson, Connecticut. They split up to find a filling station and Debra disappeared, her skeletal remains found by a jogger on October 30. In the meantime, Michael Ross pled guilty to assault charges in Ohio on August 4, paying a $1,000 fine and serving four months in jail before his release on December 22.

In May 1983, Ross was hired by a Connecticut insurance company, his application falsely denying any criminal convictions, and his work record was satisfactory until a slump in early November. On November 16, 19-year-old Robin Stravinsky was reported missing in Norwich, her body found by joggers a week later near a local hospital. Ross's employer was pleased to note an improvement in Michael's work through December and January, but by March 1984, the young man seemed to be entering another unexplained slump.

On April 22—Easter Sunday—14-year-old neighbors Leslie Shelley and April Brunais disappeared from Griswold, Connecticut, en route to a friend's house. Two months later, on June 13, Wendy Baribeault vanished in Lisbon on a short walk to the neighborhood store. Her body, raped and strangled, was found on June 15, and witnesses recalled seeing a blue subcompact car near the scene.

Police began working their way through a computer listing of 2,000 subcompact drivers, and they caught up with Ross on June 28. He swiftly confessed to the Baribeault murder, then directed authorities to a rural dump site where the bodies of Leslie Shelley and April Brunais were recovered. On June 30, officers followed Ross's directions to the shallow grave of Tammy Williams, and by July 5, he had been charged with a total of six homicides. Guilty pleas in the murders of Williams and Debra Taylor earned Ross a sentence of 120 years imprisonment. Convicted of four more slay-

Michael Ross, in manacles, is led from a police truck. (Wide World API)

ings on June 26, 1987, he was sentenced to death 10 days later.

In 1994, the state supreme court upheld Ross's murder conviction but overturned his death sentence on grounds that the trial judge wrongfully excluded portions of a psychiatric report that might have helped him escape the death penalty. A new penalty hearing was ordered, but Ross promptly fired his public defenders, collaborating with the prosecutor's office to expedite his own death. In March 1998, Ross signed an agreement with the prosecution acknowledging that his crimes were cruel and heinous, asking the court to order his immediate execution. Startled by this turn of events in a state where no condemned inmate has been executed since 1960, the court invalidated Ross's "death pact" on April 2, declaring such a bargain between prosecutors and defendant an illegal usurpation of judicial power. Jury selection for the new penalty hearing began on April 7, 1999, but another

year elapsed before that panel recommended execution on April 6, 2000. Judge Thomas Miano formally reinstated Ross's six death sentences on May 12, 2000.

Four months later, New York authorities sought to extradite Ross for trial in the 1982 rape-slaying of Paula Perrara, a high school cheerleader from Wallkill. Legal maneuvers stalled the transfer until August 2001, and while Ross initially entered a not guilty plea in that case, he changed his mind and admitted the slaying on September 24, 2001. That confession earned Ross a sentence of eight to 25 years in prison, effectively invalidated with his return to death row in Connecticut. Reversing his 1998 decision in September 2003, Ross hired a new team of lawyers to appeal his death sentence, thus ensuring further long-term delays in a state which has executed no condemned inmate since 1960. By 2005, Ross became determined to die, despite his lawyers' appeal. On May 13, he got his wish, when he was executed by lethal injection.

SCHAEFER, Gerard John

Gerard Schaefer was born in Wisconsin on March 26, 1946, the oldest of three children in a family he later described as "turbulent and conflictual." Years later, interviewed by court-appointed psychiatrists, he would refer to himself as "an illegitimate child," the product of a hasty shotgun wedding. He described his father as a verbally abusive alcoholic, flagrantly adulterous and often absent from home on business trips or otherwise. By 1960, Schaefer's family had settled in Fort Lauderdale, Florida. He graduated high school there in 1964, and he was working on the first of several college degrees when his parents divorced three years later.

By that time, if we accept Schaefer's statements to psychiatrists, he was well on the way to troubles of his own. "From an early age," Dr. R. C. Eaton recorded in 1973, "[Schaefer] has had numerous sexual hang-ups." Experiments with bondage and sadomasochism began around age 12. "I'd tie myself up to a tree," he told Dr. Mordecai Haber, "and I'd get excited sexually and do something to hurt myself." Around the same time he began to "masturbate and fantasize about hurting other people, women in particular." As if this weren't enough, Schaefer recalled, "I discovered women's underwear—panties. Sometimes I wore them. I wanted to hurt myself."

The violent self-loathing went back to his earliest childhood games. In those games, he told Dr. Haber, "I always got killed. I wanted to die. My father favored my sister, so I wanted to be a girl. I wanted to die. I was such a disappointment to my family as a kid, to my father—he loved my sister. I couldn't please my father, so in playing games I wanted to be killed."

Schaefer claimed to have visited a psychiatrist in 1966, seeking relief from his sexual deviance and homicidal fantasies, but therapy didn't help. If his later statements are credible, he kept on hearing voices "telling him to kill." That same year, he toured the South with Moral Rearmament, the cheery "Up With People" folks who sang that freedom isn't free. Schaefer thought about the priesthood as a calling, but he was turned away from St. John's Seminary, where, he recalled, "they said I didn't have enough faith." The rejection angered Schaefer so much that he quit the Catholic Church.

His next goal was a teaching job, through which he hoped to instill "American values" like "honesty, purity, unselfishness and love," but Schaefer was twice dropped from student-teaching programs for "trying to impose his own moral and political values on his students." The second time, supervisor Richard Goodhart recalls, "I told him when he left that he'd better never let me hear of his trying to get a job with any authority over other people, or I'd do anything I could to prevent it."

In 1968, Schaefer married Martha Fogg, but it didn't work out. Martha filed for divorce in May 1970, claiming "extreme cruelty." Schaefer took a few weeks to recuperate in Europe and North Africa that summer, coming home with a new goal in life. If he couldn't be a priest or a teacher, he would be a policeman. He applied to several departments and was rejected by the Broward County sheriff's office after failing a psychological test, but the small Wilton Manors Police Department hired him anyway. In March 1972, Schaefer earned a commendation for his role in a drug bust; one month later, on April 20, he was fired. Explanations vary: Chief Bernard Scott later said that Schaefer didn't have "an ounce of common sense," while ex-FBI Agent ROBERT RESSLER reports that Schaefer was disciplined for running female traffic violators through the department's computer, obtaining personal information, and later calling them for dates.

Whatever the cause of his firing, Schaefer needed a job. Near the end of June, he signed on with the Martin County Sheriff's Department, pulling up stakes and moving to Stuart, Florida. He had been on the job less than a month when he made a "dumb mistake" that would cost him his career and his freedom.

On July 21, 1972, Schaefer picked up two hitchhikers, 17-year-old Pamela Wells and 18-year-old Nancy Trotter, on the highway near a local beach. He told them (falsely) that hitchhiking was illegal in Martin County, then drove them back to a halfway house where they were staying. Schaefer offered to meet them next morning, off duty, and drive them to the beach himself. The girls agreed, but instead of taking them to the beach on July 22, Schaefer drove them to swampy Hutchinson Island off State Road A1A. There, he started making sexual remarks, then drew a gun and told the girls he planned to sell them as "white slaves" to a foreign prostitution syndicate. Forcing them out of the car, he bound both girls and left them balanced on tree roots with nooses around their necks, at risk of hanging if they slipped and fell. Schaefer left them then, promising to return shortly, but the girls escaped in his absence and reached the highway, where they flagged down a passing police car. They had no problem identifying their assailant, since Schaefer had told them his name.

By that time, Schaefer had discovered their escape and telephoned Sheriff Richard Crowder. "I've done something foolish," Schaefer told his boss. "You're going to be mad at me." He had "overdone" his job, Schaefer said, trying to "scare" the girls out of hitchhiking in the future for their own good. Fired on the spot, charged with false imprisonment and two counts of aggravated assault, Schaefer was released on $15,000 bond. At trial in November 1972, he pled guilty on one assault charge and the other counts were dropped. Judge D. C. Smith called Schaefer a "thoughtless fool" and sentenced him to a year in county jail to be followed by three years' probation. The ex-deputy began serving his sentence on January 15, 1973.

The most shocking revelations were yet to come, however. Two other girls were missing from the neighborhood, and they would not be as lucky as Trotter and Wells. On September 27, 1972, while Schaefer was free on bond pending trial, 17-year-old Susan Place and 16-year-old Georgia Jessup had vanished from Fort Lauderdale. Susan's parents said the girls were last seen at her house, leaving with an older man named "Gerry Shepherd" on their way to "play guitar" at a nearby beach. They never came back, but Lucille Place had noted Schaefer's license number, along with a description of his blue-green Datsun. It was March 25, 1973, before sluggish investigators traced the plate number back to Schaefer, by which time he was already in jail for assaulting teenage girls.

Schaefer denied any contact with Place and Jessup, but the case began unraveling on April 1, 1973, when skeletal remains were found on Hutchinson Island by three men collecting aluminum cans. Four days later, the victims were identified from dental records. Susan Place had been shot in the jaw, detectives remarking that evidence from the crime scene indicated the two girls were "tied to a tree and butchered." On April 7, police searched the home of Schaefer's mother, where Gerard had personal items stored in a spare bedroom. Evidence recovered in the search included a stash of women's jewelry, 100-plus pages of writing and sketches depicting mutilation-murders of young women, newspaper clippings about two women missing

Gerard Schaefer, the "Butcher of Blind Creek," poses for his police I.D. photo. (Author's collection)

since 1969, and pieces of I.D. belonging to vanished hitchhikers Collette Goodenough and Barbara Wilcox, both 19. The two girls had last been seen alive on January 8, a week before Schaefer was sent to jail in Martin County, and while their skeletal remains were found in early 1977, no cause of death could be determined; thus no charges were filed.

As for the news clips, one referred to the February 1969 disappearance of waitress Carmen Hallock, seemingly abducted from her home. Items of her jewelry were found in Schafer's hoard, along with a gold-filled tooth identified by Hallock's dentist, but once again no charges were filed. The second missing woman, Leigh Bonadies, had been a neighbor of Schaefer's when she disappeared in September 1969. He had complained of her "taunting" him by undressing with her curtains open, and a piece of her jewelry was found among his belongings, but no charges were filed when her skeletal remains were finally recovered in 1978. More jewelry linked Schaefer to the disappearance of 14-year-old Mary Briscolina, who vanished from Broward County with 13-year-old Elsie Farmer in October 1972. Their skeletons were found in early 1973, but once again no cause of death could be determined, and no charges were filed.

The list of suspected victims would grow over time, but Schaefer faced charges in only two murders. He was indicted on May 18, 1973, for the slayings of Jessup and Place. Held without bond pending trial, he was convicted on two counts of first-degree murder in October 1973, drawing concurrent terms of life imprisonment. Numerous appeals, some 20 in all, were uniformly rejected by various state and federal courts.

Schaefer was nearly forgotten by 1990, when former high school girlfriend Sondra London published a collection of his stories under the title *Killer Fiction*. More volumes followed, Schaefer insisting that his stories were art, police and prosecutors describing them as thinly veiled descriptions of actual crimes. In private letters to attorneys and acquaintances, Schaefer admitted as much, himself. Witness his reference to a story titled "Murder Demons," in a letter dated April 9, 1991: "What crimes am I supposed to confess? Farmer? Briscolina? What do you think ["Murder Demons"] is? You want confessions but don't recognize them when I anoint you with them and we've just gotten started."

Other correspondence swiftly raised the body count. "As you know," he wrote on January 20, 1991, "I've always harped on [District Attorney Robert] Stone's list of 34. In 1973 I sat down and drew up a list of my own. As I recall, my list was just over 80." The next day, given more time to reflect, Schafer went on: "I'm not claiming a huge number. . . . I would say it runs between 80 and 110. But over eight years and three

continents. . . . One whore drowned in her own vomit while watching me disembowel her girlfriend. I'm not sure that counts as a valid kill. Did the pregnant ones count as two kills? It can get confusing."

Years later, Schaefer's letters came back to haunt him when he was described in several true-crime books as a prolific serial killer. His response, a series of lawsuits filed against various authors for libel, were uniformly dismissed by the courts. In one such case, Judge William Steckler officially branded Schaefer a serial killer, finding him "undeniably linked" to numerous murders beyond the two for which he stood convicted. "He boasts of the private and public associations he has based on the reports that he is a serial killer of world-class proportions," Steckler wrote, "and it is only arrogant perversity which propels him toward this and similarly meritless lawsuits in which he claims otherwise."

Schaefer's luck ran out on December 3, 1995, when another inmate barged into his cell, slashed Schaefer's throat, and stabbed him in both eyes. Prison officials named the killer as inmate Vincent Rivera, serving life plus 20 years for two murders in Tampa, but no specific motive has been offered. It appears that Schaefer's reputation as a "rat" and troublemaker in the joint caught up with him at last.

And with the threat of nuisance litigation buried, gun-shy law enforcement officers felt free to air their views on Schaefer. Bill Hagerty, an ex-FBI agent who studied Schaefer for VICAP in the early 1980s, called him "one of the sickest. If I had a list of the top five, which would include all of the serial killers I have interviewed throughout the country, he would definitely be in the top five." For Shirley Jessup, still mourning her daughter, Schaefer's murder was simply a case of overdue justice. "I'd like to send a present to the guy who killed him," she told reporters. "I've always believed he was going to get his. I just wish it would have been sooner than later."

SELLS, Tommy Lynn

Transient serial killer Tommy Sells was born in Oakland, California, on June 28, 1964. With his twin sister, he brought to five the number of children borne by his unmarried mother, variously known as Nina Sells or Nina Lovins. Although he used the name Sells, Tommy grew up believing that his father was Joseph Lovins, a gambler who sometimes shared his mother's bed. Nina moved her children to Missouri a year after the twins were born. Six months later, both infants were stricken with spinal meningitis, which proved fatal for Tommy's sister. Later, he would wear a tombstone with her name tattooed on his left arm.

Life went from bad to worse for Tommy Sells after his brush with death. His mother left him in the care of an aunt for two years before taking him home. Sells began drinking liquor at age seven, was molested by a neighbor at eight, and smoked his first marijuana joint at age 10. Three years later, Sells climbed naked into his grandmother's bed while she slept, and was banned from the house. A short time later, his mother and siblings left town without notice, stranding him alone. Days later, Sells pistol-whipped his first female victim in a fit of rage. By age 14, in 1978, he was on the road, living the life of a permanent drifter.

By his own account, Sells committed his first murder in Port Gibson, Mississippi, on July 5, 1979. He shot 39-year-old John Cade Sr. with a .32-caliber pistol after Cade surprised Sells in the act of burglarizing his home. In 1980, he allegedly killed one man with an ice pick, outside a Chinese restaurant in Los Angeles, then moved north to Oakland and became embroiled in gang warfare. Sells stabbed another man "a bunch of times," while suffering a stab wound that barely missed his spine.

May 1981 found Sells reunited with his family in Little Rock, Arkansas, but Nina threw him out after he stripped and tried to join her in the shower. Sells checked into a mental health clinic at Jonesboro, telling staff psychologists, "I don't know who I am. I don't understand anything anymore." They had no help to offer, so he turned back to the bottle, logging his first arrest for public drunkenness at Little Rock in March 1982. Sells later confessed two Arkansas murders during the same period, but only one—the shooting of Hal Akins at his Saline County home—has been confirmed. The second case, Sells says, involved a woman kidnapped by himself and an unnamed accomplice. She was raped, murdered, and dumped into a flooded quarry in Pulaski County.

Sells moved to St. Louis in 1983. On July 31 of that year, Thomas Gill came home from work and glimpsed a man fleeing from his home. Inside, Gill found his wife Colleen and four-year-old daughter Tiffany beaten to death. Sells would confess to the murders 18 years later. Meanwhile, he was jailed for auto theft at Benton, Missouri, in May 1984 and pleaded guilty as charged, receiving a two-year prison term. Paroled in February 1985, Sells stole another car five months later. His mother reported Sells to police on July 22, and he fled a prison halfway house after being questioned by his parole officer. On July 26, Sells met 28-year-old Ena Cordt and her four-year-old son at a county fair in Forsyth, Missouri. The lonely divorcée invited Sells home, then made the fatal error of searching his knapsack. Sells caught her at it, and killed Ena and young Rory with a baseball bat. A drunken car wreck in September 1985 prompted authorities to revoke Sell's parole, and he finished his sentence in full, released once again on May 16, 1986.

Sells kept drifting, working odd jobs. In St. Louis, he shot a stranger and left him for dead, claiming self-defense in the face of an unprovoked assault. Sells was jailed for theft in a suburb of St. Louis, but the charge was dismissed. At Aransas Pass, Texas, he spent two days in the hospital for a near-fatal heroin overdose. The year 1986 took Sells to Fremont, California, where he is now suspected in the double murder of 20-year-old Jennifer Duey and 19-year-old Michelle Xavier. One victim was shot in the head and the other's throat was slashed. Susan Korcz vanished from Niagara, New York, on May 1, 1987, following a barroom spat with her boyfriend. Sells says he does not recall the crime per se, but claims he woke from an alcoholic blackout on May 3, to find himself aboard a freight train near the crime scene, wearing clothes stained with someone else's blood. Korcz's skeletal remains were found in a shallow grave at Lockport, New York, on September 5, 1995.

October 1987 found Sells in Winnemucca, Nevada, working for a roofing company. He bounced a worthless check on October 15, then compounded the problem two weeks later by stealing his boss's pistol, cash, and credit card. Sells used the card to rent a motel room, which he shared with new acquaintance Stefanie Stroh, a 20-year-old college student hitchhiking across the United States after 10 months in Europe. Sells later confessed to feeding Stroh a dose of LSD and strangling her, then weighting her feet with a tub of concrete and dropping her into a desert hot spring before he left Winnemucca on November 3.

On November 17, 1987, Keith Dardeen found Sells hitchhiking through Ina, Illinois, and took him home for dinner. Sells repaid the hospitality by shooting Dardeen in the head and severing his penis, then hammering young Peter Dardeen to death with a baseball bat. Finally, he attempted to rape Keith's pregnant wife Eileen, but the assault induced labor. In a frenzy, Sells clubbed both mother and newborn until they were lifeless, then left the bat protruding from Eileen's vagina.

Back in St. Louis, Sells was arrested for auto theft in January 1988, but he fled town in September, before the case went to trial. Days later, 11-year-old Melissa Trembley disappeared from Salem, New Hampshire. Last seen in the parking lot of a convenience store, talking to a man who resembled Sells, Trembley was found dead on September 12, raped and stabbed in a freight yard, where a train had run over her corpse.

Sells next roamed westward. He claims his next victims were an unnamed woman and her three-year-old son, whom he met in Salt Lake City, Utah. Sells put them to work begging cash on the street, then set off for Idaho in a stolen car. Along the way, Sells says he killed mother and child, dumping their bodies into the Snake River. Settled briefly in Tucson by December 1988, Sells fatally stabbed transient Kent Lauten, allegedly after a drug deal went sour. Lauten's body was found on December 18, and although Tucson police had no leads in that case, they jailed Sells for assault with a deadly weapon in a separate incident. That case was dismissed when the victim dropped from sight.

On January 27, 1989, Sells quarreled with a ticket agent on a train in Berkeley, California, then killed a streetwalker in another botched drug deal, dumping her body at Truckee, near Lake Tahoe. Police confirmed discovery of a "Jane Doe" corpse, still unidentified. In April 1989, Sells claims, he killed a woman in her twenties at Roseburg, Oregon. On May 9, he allegedly murdered a female hitchhiker who tried to steal his drug stash, dumping her body in a wooded area near the April victim. That same afternoon, Sells was jailed for theft after his employer at a Roseburg firewood stand caught him tapping the till. Sells served 15 days, then left town. Police in North Little Rock, Arkansas, charged Sells with theft on August 16, 1989, then released him one week later without prosecution. Oakland authorities placed him in detox for public drunkenness on October 18, 1989, and he logged an identical charge one month later, in Carson City, Nevada. December 1989 found Sells hospitalized in Phoenix, Arizona, for another heroin overdose. Police in Salt Lake City held Sells for cocaine possession on January 7, 1990, then released him on discovering that he had purchased harmless powder. Five days later, Sells was arrested for auto theft in Rawlings, Wyoming. Staffers at Wyoming State Hospital noted that he "looks much like CHARLES MANSON," with his matted hair and beard, but they found him competent for trial. Sells proved a model inmate at a rural prison camp and was released in January 1991.

As told by Sells, his next rampage began on December 9, 1991, when he invaded the Marianna, Florida, home of 28-year-old Teresa Hall. Sells ransacked the house, smashing a table and using one of its legs to fatally bludgeon Hall and her five-year-old daughter Tiffany. Drifting to Charleston, South Carolina, Sells was arrested twice for public drunkenness in March and April 1992. On May 13, in Charleston, West Virginia, a 20-year-old woman found Sells begging on the street and took him home. He raped, beat, and stabbed her, then looted the house, but his victim survived to summon police. Arrested on the strength of her description, Sells was convicted of malicious wounding on June 25, 1993, receiving a sentence of two to 10 years in prison. Authorities released him in May 1997.

Two months later, on July 29, Sells was ticketed for driving without a license in Cleveland, Tennessee. In October 1997 he left a pregnant girlfriend with his mother, in St. Louis, then moved on to Illinois alone. In Lawrenceville, on October 13, Sells invaded the home of Julie Rea, claiming that she insulted him at a nearby convenience store. Sells later confessed to punching and slashing Rea with a knife, then fatally stabbing her son, 10-year-old Joel Kirkpatrick. Surfacing next in Springfield, Missouri, Sells snatched teenager Stephanie Mahaney from her bedroom, then raped and strangled her, dumping her body in a farmer's pond where hunters found it on November 18, 1997. Sells returned briefly to St. Louis, then left again in January 1998, three months before his son was born.

In Texas, Sells joined the staff of a traveling carnival. He met a divorcée with three children in Del Rio, and married her in October 1998, but drink and drugs made the relationship a stormy one. Sells left alone for Florida in February 1999, then returned two weeks later, and was thrown out by his wife again on March 28. Two days later, he invaded the trailer home of 28-year-old Debbie Harris, raping and fatally stabbing her before he murdered 8-year-old Ambria Harris, leaving the knife in her chest. On April 18, Sells raped and strangled nine-year-old Mary Perez in San Antonio. One month later, on May 13, he repeated his crime with 13-year-old Haley McHone in Lexington, Kentucky. Sells hid her body in a park, where it remained concealed for 10 days, and sold her bicycle to a stranger for $20. Before McHone's body was found, Sells was jailed for drunk and disorderly conduct in Madison, Wisconsin. Released on June 24, he returned to Del Rio for another battle with his wife, quelled only when police were summoned to the scene.

Sells left Texas for Oklahoma on July 3, 1999. Two days later, he met 14-year-old Bobbie Lynn Wofford in Kingfisher, shooting her to death when she resisted rape. Sells stole her earrings and kept drifting, circling back to Del Rio in time for Christmas. On December 31, 1999, he invaded the Guajia Bay home of Terry and Crystal Harris, acquaintances Sells met through his employer. Creeping through the house with a knife, Sells murdered 13-year-old Kaylene Harris and left 10-year-old Krystal Surles for dead with her throat slashed. Almost miraculously, Surles survived to identify Sells, and he was arrested at home on January 2, 2000. He agreed to a search of his home, revealing bloody clothes and the 12-inch boning knife used in his latest crime. A short time later, Sells began his marathon confession, after remarking to Lieutenant Larry Pope, "I suppose you want me to tell you about the other one."

In the wake of those confessions, Texas Rangers flew Sells across country in a bid to clear outstanding cases. The effort mimicked tours with HENRY LEE LUCAS, almost 20 years earlier, but it failed to produce the same results. In Little Rock, police had no record of a 1982 murder at the house Sells pointed out, but investigators learned that the tenant had played dead after Sells fired a clumsy shot and missed him. Pulaski County officers refused to look for the woman Sells claimed to have killed in 1982, complaining that a search of flooded quarries was too costly. At Twin Falls, Idaho, Sells could not find the spot where he allegedly murdered another woman in 1997, afterward hacking her body apart with an ax and dropping it in the Snake River. In Nevada, Sells spoke to Winnemucca's sheriff and FBI agents about Stephanie Stroh, but her remains were not found.

Back in Texas, defense attorney Victor Garcia questioned his client's sanity, but Judge George Thurmond found Sells competent for trial on June 23, 2000. On September 12, Sells pleaded guilty to attempted murder in the case of Krystal Surles, while paradoxically pleading not guilty in the death of Kaylene Harris. That plea proved futile with a confession on record, and jurors convicted Sells of capital murder on September 18, 2000. Three days later, the panel sentenced Sells to death.

Investigation of the other slayings claimed by Tommy Sells continued as this volume went to press. On February 7, 2001, police in Texas announced their belief that Sells might be guilty of 70 murders across the United States, but authorities in other jurisdictions remain skeptical. Lawrenceville, Illinois, was a case in point, where Julie Rea-Harper was convicted in March 2002 for the murder of her son Joel Kirkpatrick in October 1997. Sentenced to 65 years in prison, Rea rejoiced when Sells confessed the crime, but prosecutor Todd Reitz demanded fresh DNA tests, dismissing Sells with the observation that "He has made false confessions before." An appellate court ordered Rea-Harper released from prison on July 9, 2004, pending results of the DNA test, but defiant prosecutors jailed her without bond in Lawrenceville. The troubling case was unresolved at press time for this volume.

On September 17, 2003, a grand jury in Greene County, Missouri, indicted Tommy Sells for the 1997 murder of Stephanie Mahaney. With Sells already facing death in Texas, some observers doubted that Sells would ever face trial in that case. Assistant prosecutor Dan Patterson told reporters, "We're pleased that he was indicted and hope this will bring some closure for the family. The good thing about the indictment is that we are in no rush to bring him back." No date has been scheduled for trial in that case.

"SERIAL Murder": Defined

Throughout most of human history, serial murder—that is, the consecutive killing of victims *in series*—was simply regarded and labeled as a form of "MASS MURDER." Only since the late 1950s have criminologists made a concerted effort to distinguish between different types of multiple murder, recognizing (however belatedly) that there may be method to the madness, as well as madness in the method. *How* a killer chooses, stalks and slays his victim may, in fact, help us determine *why* he kills. To that end if for no other reason, concise definitions are critical. Sadly, they are also hard to come by in a field where egos often count for more than understanding and needless debate over trivia serves to compound, rather than eliminate, confusion.

Criminologist James Reinhardt took the first major step toward disentangling serial murder from other types of multicide in 1957 when he coined the phrase "chain killers" in his book *Sex Perversions and Sex Crimes*. Simply stated, Reinhardt's chain killers were those who left a "chain" of victims behind them, slaughtered over time, and he went on to provide more examples five years later in *The Psychology of Strange Killers* (1962).

The term "serial murder" itself surfaced in 1961, according to author Harold Schechter and Jesse Sheidlower, editor of the *Oxford English Dictionary*. The quote, attributed to German critic Siegfried Kracauer in *Merriam-Webster's Third New International Dictionary* (1961) reads: "[He] denies that he is the pursued serial murderer." Five years later, in his book *The Meaning of Murder* (1966), British author John Brophy applied the label to "JACK THE RIPPER" and others. Another decade passed before forensic psychiatrist Donald Lunde mentioned "serial mass murder" in *Murder and Madness* (1976). Between those publications, FBI agent ROBERT K. RESSLER allegedly thought up the term on his own—coincidentally while visiting England in 1974, eight years after publication of Brophy's work—but he waited nearly two decades to claim credit for the brainstorm in *Whoever Fights Monsters* (1992).

The clamor for credit aside, self-styled "experts" on serial murder spend much of their time debating proper definitions and progress no further toward an understanding of the grim phenomenon itself. The FBI's *Crime Classification Manual* (1992) defines serial murder as "three or more separate events in three or more separate locations with an emotional cooling-off period between homicides." At first glance, the Bureau's definition seems clear and concise. A second look, however, reveals three built-in flaws that doom it from the start.

First, we have the requirement of "three or more" murders to make up a bona fide series. Unfortunately, the FBI's other "official" categories of murder—single, double, triple, mass, and SPREE MURDER—make no allowance for the slayer who claims only *two* victims with the requisite "cooling-off" period between crimes and who is then arrested prior to bagging number three. *Double* murder, in FBI parlance, describes two victims killed at the same time and place; *spree* murder, meanwhile, may have only two victims, but it is defined as "a single event with . . . no emotional cooling-off period between murders." Thus, the killer who waits months or even years between his first and second kill then finds himself in jail has no place whatsoever in the Bureau's scheme of things.

A second problem is the FBI's requirement that serial murders occur at "three or more separate locations." By that standard, some of the most prolific killers of modern times—including DEAN CORLL, JOHN GACY, DONALD HARVEY, and Britain's DENNIS NILSEN—do not qualify as serial murderers, since they killed most or all of their victims at a single location.

Finally, we run head-on into the elusive, undefined "cooling-off" period. No FBI spokesman has ever been able to pin down the time span; indeed, the *Crime Classification Manual* tells us that "[t]he cooling-off period can last for days, weeks, or months"—and, presumably, even for years. Various authors have tried to resolve the problem by suggesting arbitrary time limits: one suggests two weeks, another "more than thirty days," but none of their attempts to saddle unknown killers with a one-size-fits-all mandate stand up under close examination.

In terms of both utility and versatility, the best definition of serial murder on record—and the one applied throughout this book—was published by the National Institute of Justice (NIJ) in 1988. The NIJ defines serial killing as "a series of two or more murders, committed as separate events, usually, but not always, by one offender acting alone. The crimes may occur over a period of time ranging from hours to years. Quite often the motive is psychological, and the offender's behavior and the physical evidence observed at the crime scenes will reflect sadistic, sexual overtones."

By avoiding the rigid criteria of the FBI and other published definitions, the NIJ undoubtedly rankled some purists—and authors with textbooks to sell—but its broad definition at once closes all of the FBI's loopholes while providing coverage for cases otherwise denied any label at all. And thankfully, the NIJ's low-key approach has even breached the Bureau's bulwark of resistance to change. In November 1997, speaking to reporters in Milwaukee of a case in progress, FBI Special Agent Richard Eggleston defined serial murder as "two or more killings committed as separate events, usually by a lone offender."

See also MODUS OPERANDI; MOTIVES

SEX Crimes and Serial Murder

Seventy percent of all serial murders are sexually motivated. It comes as no surprise, therefore, that many repeat killers commit various other sex crimes through the years before they "graduate" to homicide. A pedophile or serial rapist may assault dozens—even hundreds—of victims before he starts killing. For some, murder is the pinnacle of "achievement," an end in itself and the only means of sexual release. Others, like Florida's ROBERT JOE LONG, add murder as an embellishment to their ongoing crimes, killing some victims and sparing others. In some cases, murder is simply expedient, a means of eliminating witnesses—particularly if the individual offender has a record of convictions for sex crimes and fears returning to prison.

In sexually motivated murder, the killer's personal fixation determines his (or her) choice of victims. Pedophiles hunt children (sometimes without regard to gender, more commonly preferring one sex or the other); "gay" killers typically (but not always) select same-sex victims; bisexual slayers may rape and kill victims of either sex, indiscriminately. Other sex-driven killers fixate on the elderly, on victims from a particular group or class (prostitutes, nurses, etc.), or those who possess specific physical traits (red hair, large breasts, tattoos).

Sex crimes may not be obvious at first glance. Indeed, there may be no sign whatsoever of a "normal" sexual assault. England's BRUCE LEE (born Peter Dinsdale), a prolific serial arsonist, achieved orgasm only when setting and watching fires, a pursuit that claimed 26 lives between 1973 and 1980. Forty years earlier, in Hungary, Sylvestre Matushke suffered a similar problem: in his case, the orgasmic trigger mechanism was train wrecks, prompting him to dynamite railroad tracks in the path of speeding passenger trains.

The most common sex crime—rape—is divided by the FBI's *Crime Classification Manual* (1992) into four broad categories with numerous subdivisions, as in the case of homicides. Generally, the Bureau recognizes "criminal enterprise rape," "personal cause sexual assault," "group cause sexual assault," and "sexual assault not classified elsewhere" (fittingly defined, without examples, as "those assaults that cannot be classified elsewhere").

Criminal-enterprise rape is rare among serial killers but cannot be ruled out in the case of those slayers committing criminal-enterprise murders. Subdivided into "primary felony rape" (where another crime such as burglary is intended and the victim is raped coincidentally) and "secondary felony rape" (where sexual assault is the primary goal, with robbery or some other crime committed as an afterthought), the FBI's classification oddly excludes the deliberate use of rape as a weapon of criminal enterprise. There are, for example, many cases on record of girls and women being raped as a "lesson" or warning to others—usually a husband, lover, or family member. Such incidents are most common among gangs and violent elements of organized crime.

Personal-cause assaults, the largest category in the Bureau manual, includes such diverse cases as *domestic* rape (victimizing a spouse, relative, or household member), *entitlement* rape (with victims including acquaintances, employees or subordinates, medical patients, etc.), *anger* rape (a sexual expression of rage targeting victims by age, gender, race, or some other specific criteria), *sadistic* rape (specifically intended to cause pain and fear), *abduction* rape (any case where the victim is transported to another crime scene), plus various types of sexual crimes against children.

Despite the numerous kinds of rape identified by Bureau analysts, the FBI contends that there are only four basic types of rapist. (In this context, "rape" includes any form of aggressive sexual assault without the limitations of restrictive legalese.) They include the *power-reassurance rapist*, whose crimes are "primarily an expression of his rape fantasies," commonly including the delusion that his victims enjoy the experience and will fall in love with their attacker; the *exploitative rapist*, with whom "sexual behavior is expressed as an impulsive predatory act," typically devoid of any intricate, long-running fantasy; the *anger rapist*, for whom "sexuality is in the service of a primary aggressive aim," frequently including misplaced notions of revenge against a hated class of persons (women, a particular race, some authority figure); and the *sadistic rapist*, whose crimes are once again the expression of fantasy, this time fueled by the victim's suffering rather than delusions of romance.

We often hear it said that "rape is not a sex crime; it's a crime of violence," a slogan initially adopted by feminists, perhaps in a laudable attempt to relieve rape victims of misplaced guilt or embarrassment. And, while the statement is true *to a point*, its very absolutism insures that it will often be wrong. There is, in fact, no division between "sex crimes" and "violent crimes"; indeed, a sexual assault is violent by definition—hence the term *assault*. Through the centuries, rape has been employed for many different purposes, including use as a weapon of genocide (in "ethnic cleansing" campaigns), as a form of punishment by gangs or individuals, even as a tool of police interrogation. (In one Latin American country, through the mid-1970s, police dogs were specially trained to rape female prisoners; the ancient Romans taught a wide variety of creatures, ranging from goats to giraffes, to perform similar acts in the Colosseum.)

On balance, it is both naive and dangerous to claim that while a wide variety of crimes—including ARSON, burglary, and murder—may be sexually motivated, rape never is. The notion is naive because it flies in the face of forensic psychology, blandly ignoring criminal motives; it is dangerous because, if applied literally, it would preclude authorities from examining probable suspects.

See also HOMOSEXUALITY; MOTIVES; PARAPHILIA

SHANKARIYA, Kampatimar

A naive of Jaipur, India, a 27-year-old Kampatimar Shankariya was convicted in early 1979 of using a hammer to kill at least 70 persons during the previous two years. In his detailed confession, Shankariya told police that he had killed his victims for the pleasure it provided. Hanged at Jaipur on May 16, 1979, the killer's last words were a gallows lament. "I have murdered in vain," he declared. "Nobody should become like me."

See also RAGHAV, RAMAN

SHIPMAN, Harold Frederick

The most prolific practitioner of MEDICAL MURDER since World War II was British physician Harold Shipman, who also holds the 20th-century record for serial murder in Europe. Official records show that 500 patients died in Shipman's care between 1977 and 1998, with at least 215 of those deaths now presumed to be homicides. Investigators admit that the full tally of Shipman's victims may never be known.

Harold Shipman—more commonly known as "Fred"—was the middle child of a working-class family, born on June 14, 1946. Classmates recall him as an academic plodder and accomplished athlete whose superior attitude kept him from forging close friendships. Shipman failed his first entry exam at Leeds University, but succeeded on his second try and maintained adequate grades to earn a medical degree. Contemporaries at Leeds remember Shipman as "pretentious" and "a bit strange," a loner who brought his sister to school dances in place of a date. At age 19, he surprised acquaintances by embarking on a romance with Primrose Oxtoby, three years his junior. She was barely 17, and five months pregnant, when they wed in 1966. Shipman's daughter was born in March 1967, followed by a son in 1971.

In March 1974, Shipman joined a medical practice in Todmorden, Yorkshire. While polite and cheerful with his colleagues and patients, Shipman was frequently rude to subordinates on staff, whom he belittled and dismissed as "stupid." In summer 1975, Shipman suffered a series of blackouts, medically inexplicable until

Dr. Harold Shipman (AP Photo/Manchester Police)

a partner in the practice discovered that Shipman had consumed huge doses of pethidine—"thousands and thousands of ampoules"—which he charged to the practice. His subterfuge was uncovered on September 25, 1975, and his partners fired Shipman on the spot, provoking a furious outburst. Shipman entered a drug rehab center, emerging in early 1976 to plead guilty on eight charges of forging prescriptions. The court dismissed 67 identical counts and fined him £600. In retrospect, authorities would question whether Shipman really used the vast amount of pethidine, a powerful narcotic, himself, or whether some was used to murder patients in his care. The question is still unresolved.

Despite his recent scandal, Dr. Shipman found work as a children's physician for the South West Durham Health Authority on September 12, 1977. Eighteen days later, he left that post to join a new medical practice, Donneybrook House, in Hyde. He bought a modest home in Mottram and sired two more sons, born in March 1979 and April 1982. Once again, partners and patients found Shipman cheerful enough, while staff members complained of his rudeness and sarcasm. In

1992, Shipman surprised his Donneybrook colleagues by quitting the practice to set up shop alone, absconding with 3,000 patients in the process. The betrayal proved doubly galling when Shipman opened his new office within yards of the Donneybrook center.

Many patients who followed Shipman to his new address were older women, who admired Shipman for his dedication, long hours, frequent house calls—and his generosity with drug prescriptions. Over time, Shipman ranked among the Tameside district's top five doctors (out of 104 in practice) with respect to numbers of prescriptions issued. During his last six years in practice, patients cheerfully donated £19,200 to purchase new equipment for his office, confident that Shipman would employ the tools in their best interest. Naturally, some of his patients died from time to time. Who could expect a man of medicine to save them all?

One such patient was Kathleen Grundy, who died under Shipman's care on June 24, 1998, eight days short of her 82nd birthday. Her death was not entirely unexpected, at that age, but her will took Grundy's children by surprise. Crudely typed on cheap paper, it read:

All my estate, money and house to my doctor. My family are not in need and I want to reward him for all the care he has given me and the people of Hyde. He is sensible enough to handle any problems this may give him. My doctor is H. F. Shipman.

While Grundy's affluent family truly did not need the £386,402 inheritance, they were suspicious of the will and her scrawled signature. Police shared those suspicions, heightened when a note arrived at her attorney's office, typed with the same machine on identical paper. It read: "I understand she lodged a will with you as I as a friend typed it out for her." The note bore no return address, and it was signed "S. Smith," a name unknown to Grundy's family and friends.

The witnesses to Mrs. Grundy's will were soon identified as two of Dr. Shipman's patients. Both had signed the document—folded to hide its text—while waiting in his office for appointments, on June 9, 1998. Further investigation led to Shipman's arrest on suspicion of murder, on September 7, 1998. Over the next three months, 17 of Shipman's former patients were exhumed for autopsy. All were women between the ages of 49 and 82 who had died in Shipman's care between April 1993 and June 1998. Post mortem examination revealed that 15 of the 18 suspected victims had died from overdoses of morphine. Shipman's trial on those charges convened at Preston, in northwestern England, on October 6, 1999. On January 31, 2000, he was convicted and sentenced to life imprisonment for the murders of Sarah Ashworth (April 17, 1993), Marie West

(March 6, 1995), Lizzie Adams (February 28, 1997), Jean Lilley (April 25, 1997), Ivy Lomas (May 29, 1997), Muriel Grimshaw (July 14, 1997), Marie Quinn (November 24, 1997), Kathleen Wagstaff (December 9, 1997), Bianka Pomfret (December 10, 1997), Norah Nuttall (January 26, 1998), Pamela Hillier (February 9, 1998), Maureen Ward (February 18, 1998), Winifred Mellor (May 11, 1998), Joan Melia (June 12, 1998), and Kathleen Grundy.

That grim tally was only the tip of the iceberg, however. By the time he went to trial in 1999, police were speculating publicly that Shipman might have murdered 75 to 100 patients. Old colleagues from Todmorden chimed in with accusations that their death rate during Shipman's tenure had numbered 30 to 40 above average, while Shipman's signature appeared on 22 death certificates. In July 2000, when Britain's High Court banned a secret government inquiry on Shipman's case in favor of public hearings, detectives suggested that "Dr. Death" may have claimed 192 lives. That inquiry examined 800 deaths and expected to report conclusions in 500 separate cases. In May 2001, police said they had conclusive evidence of 23 murders beyond the original 15, while speculating that Shipman murdered at least 297 victims and perhaps as many as 345. Relatives of one dead patient reported that her engagement ring was stolen, while another lost cash and her dentures. (With regard to the missing teeth, Shipman remarked, "She's probably swallowed them.") Patient Kenneth Smith, lost in December 1996, had begun calling Shipman the "Angel of Death" three weeks earlier, after neighbor Tommy Cheetham died in Shipman's care.

On July 19, 2002, High Court judge Dame Janet Smith declared that Dr. Shipman had murdered no less than 215 of his patients over a 23-year period; another 200 deaths were deemed "highly suspicious," while Smith harbored "real suspicion" in 45 outstanding cases. Of the 215 confirmed victims, 171 were women and 44 were men, ranging in age from 47 to 93 years. Officially, his first victim was Eva Lyons, killed at Todmorden in March 1975, but police harbored dark suspicions in the deaths of 62-year-old Robert Lingard and 84-year-old Elizabeth Pearce, who died at Todmorden within a five-hour span on January 21, 1975. Judge Smith charged that Shipman had murdered 71 patients at Donneybrook House and 143 while working alone in Hyde, during the period 1992–98. Smith called her report "as complete and accurate an account of Shipman's criminality as I believe it will be ever be possible for anyone other than Shipman himself to give."

No new charges were filed in the cases identified by Judge Smith, but it hardly mattered. At 6:20 A.M. on January 13, 2004, jailers found Shipman hanged in his cell at Wakefield Prison. Death was formally pronounced at 8:10 A.M., and the incident was recorded as a suicide. Kathleen Wood, daughter of 83-year-old victim Bessie Baddeley, spoke for most Shipman survivors when she told reporters, "I am not sorry he has gone, but it brings it all back and it stirs it all up for us again." Three months later, on April 12, Judge Smith announced that her inquiry would resume in order to decide if Shipman had murdered any victims between 1970 and 1974 when he was a resident at Pontefract General Infirmary. In August 2004, Smith recommended creation of a "drugs inspectorate" to monitor the quantity of drugs prescribed and stored by British doctors and pharmacists. No progress had been made in that direction when this volume went to press.

SITHOLE, Moses

South Africa's most prolific serial killer to date, Moses Sithole stands convicted of 38 slayings in a series of "ABC Murders" committed between January and October 1995. The crimes received their media nickname from the fact that they began in Atteridgeville (spawning ground for so many South African slayers), continued in Boksburg, and claimed more lives in Cleveland. The victims, all female, were apparently lured or transported to outlying fields where they were beaten, stripped, raped, and strangled with articles of their own clothing. Several victims were found with hands tied behind their backs, and one still wore a blindfold. Many were left with pieces of clothing draped across their faces as if to prevent them from staring at their killer in death.

South African authorities, virtually overrun by serial killers in the wake of apartheid's collapse, consulted ex-FBI Agent ROBERT RESSLER in their search for the "ABC" killer. Working in conjunction with DR. MICKI PISTORIUS, Ressler concluded that the murders in all three communities were linked. President Nelson Mandela was concerned enough about the crime wave to cancel a scheduled trip abroad, appearing in Boksburg with high-ranking justice officials, where he appealed for public help in tracking the strangler.

Police got their break in early October 1995 when a Cape Town newspaper, *The Star*, received an anonymous telephone call from the slayer. He identified himself as "the man that is so highly wanted," describing his murders as an act of revenge for a prior miscarriage of justice. As described by the caller, he had been arrested in 1978 for "a crime I didn't do"—specifically, a rape—and spent the next 14 years in prison, where he was "abused" and "tortured" by fellow inmates. To make matters worse, the caller said, his parents and sister had died while he was in prison. In retaliation for those wrongs, he explained, "I force a woman to go where I want, and when I go there I tell them, 'Do you know what? I was hurt, so I'm doing it now.' Then I kill them." When asked how many victims he had killed, the caller claimed 76—twice as many as police had found thus far. To verify his claim, he signed off with directions to the corpse of "a lady I don't think the police have discovered."

With so many clues in hand, police soon focused their search on Moses Sithole, a 31-year-old ex-convict and youth counselor who had suddenly dropped out of sight. Known to use as many as six pseudonyms, he proved an elusive quarry, but a tip directed them to his hideout in the Johannesburg slum of Benoni on October 18. Armed with a hatchet when officers approached him, Sithole wounded one policeman before he was shot and disarmed. He survived his wounds and was soon transferred from intensive care to a military hospital, where physicians diagnosed him as HIV-positive. In custody, he boasted of teaching his victims "a very good lesson" by killing them.

Robert Ressler's profile of the "ABC" killer had suggested the possibility of two TEAM KILLERS working together, and police initially suspected that Sithole might be an accomplice of David Selepe, linked to a half-dozen murders of women in Cleveland, but Sithole denied ever meeting Selepe, and no evidence has been found to connect the two men. (Selepe, for his part, had nothing to say on the subject. He was shot dead in December 1994, reportedly after attacking a policeman on a visit to one of his crime scenes. The officer who killed him was exonerated on a claim of self-defense.)

A full year passed before Moses Sithole made his first court appearance, on October 22, 1996, formally charged with 38 murders, 40 rapes, and six counts of robbery. His trial, scheduled to begin on November 14, was postponed when Sithole arrived in court that morning, his pants drenched in blood. He was rushed to a hospital, treated for an open knee wound apparently sustained at Pretoria Central Prison. When his trial finally convened in February 1997, an American voice expert identified Sithole as the caller who had boasted of his murders to reporters at *The Star*. Sithole had also confessed his crimes in detail to other inmates, some of whom were curiously equipped with both tape recorders and video cameras, capturing his boasts for posterity. The long-winded proceedings were delayed once again in August when Sithole started vomiting blood from a stomach ulcer, but there was no escaping justice. On December 5, 1997, jurors convicted Sithole on all counts; the following day, he was sentenced to a prison term of 2,410 years.

SNOWTOWN, Australia, murders

Snowtown is a small farming community located 93 miles north of Adelaide in the heart of South Australia's "wheat belt." Founded in 1878, it survives by hard work and iron will, its 520 year-round residents accustomed to hardship. Snowtown's only bank closed in the 1990s, and in January 1999 was rented out as storage space for $60 per month. If anyone had forecast possible locations for Australia's worst serial murders that year, it is unlikely Snowtown would have made the list—but small towns have their grisly secrets, too.

The nightmare began, unnoticed, with the August 1993 disappearance of Clinton Trezise, a 22-year-old homosexual known as "Happy Pants" to some of his acquaintances in Adelaide. An inveterate drifter, Trezise was barely missed until his skeletal remains were found buried at Lower Light, north of Adelaide, in 1995. In 1996, 47-year-old Suzanne Allen and 26-year-old Ray Davies vanished from the Adelaide's low-income district. In 1997, missing-persons reports were filed on 19-year-old Michael Gardiner, 18-year-old Thomas Trevilyan, and 40-year-old Barry Lane (a transvestite and twice-convicted pedophile). The missing list for 1998 included 37-year-old Elizabeth Haydon, her 18-year-old nephew Frederick Brooks, 29-year-old Garry O'Dwyer, 31-year-old Gavin Porter, and 21-year-old Troy Youde.

Police came close to cracking the case in November 1998, when Elizabeth Haydon vanished from home after a noisy dispute with her husband Mark. Later, detectives claimed that Elizabeth's remains and those of six other victims were stashed in a disabled Toyota Land Cruiser parked on the property in Smithfield Plains, but it was hauled off to a farm owned by friends, 90 miles from the scene, before officers examined it. Two months later, 40-year-old Mark Haydon and 32-year-old John Justin Bunting arrived in Snowtown, offering to rent the abandoned State Bank. The men told landlord Andrew Michael that they planned to store used parts for cars and motorcycles in the vault. A deal was struck, and the new renters soon delivered six black plastic vats to the bank. On Mother's Day, when a neighbor asked about the contents of the vats, Bunting replied, "You wouldn't want to know."

According to police, the last of 12 murders was carried out one day later, on May 9, 1999, inside the bank itself. The final victim, 24-year-old David Johnson, was lured to Snowtown by his 18-year-old half-brother James Spyridon Vlassakis (also a half-brother of victim Troy Youde). As later reconstructed by detectives, Vlassakis enticed Johnson with the offer of a cheap computer, then watched as he was tortured, strangled, and crudely dismembered by three confederates—Bunting, Haydon, and 27-year-old Robert Joe Wagner. Vlassakis later claimed that Wagner carved a slab of flesh from Johnson's corpse, then later fried and ate it.

A tangled web of personal relationships led police to Snowtown on May 20, 1999. Upon opening the bank's vault, heavy with the stench of death, they found six vats of acid haphazardly crammed with remains of eight corpses, identified as victims Brooks, Gardiner, Haydon, Johnson, Lane, O'Dwyer, Porter, and Youde. Also seized in the raid were ropes, handcuffs, knives, bone-crushing instruments, and an electric generator equipped with alligator clips. Pathologist John Gilbert later reported that at least two victims bore signs of torture, including burn marks on their torsos and scrotums.

John Bunting, Mark Haydon, and Robert Wagner were jailed on May 21 and charged with murder in Adelaide Magistrates Court. That afternoon, police armed with ground-penetrating radar visited the home in Salisbury North, where Bunting lived with James Vlassakis. Detective Bryan Hearn questioned Vlassakis, describing the fourth suspect as "overawed" by the display of police technology. More evidence was seized, and diggers unearthed two plastic bags filled with human remains, hidden beneath a concrete slab outside the house. Two days later, on May 23, further excavation revealed a skeleton buried 10 feet beneath the first set of remains. Those victims were identified as Suzanne Allen and Ray Davies.

The murders brought a short-lived economic boom to Snowtown, where residents cashed in with guided tours and hasty garage sales staged for the morbidly curious. Unsatisfied with local trade, the old bank's owner announced plans to auction its contents on the Internet. "There's been a lot of overseas interest," she told reporters, "so I figure I should give everyone a chance to buy significant pieces like the door." Police, meanwhile, were busy perfecting their case against Bunting, Haydon, Vlassakis, and Wagner. The story they pieced together was a grim mélange of sadism, perversity, and common greed.

John Bunting emerged as the ringleader and mastermind of the deadly quartet. Born in September 1966 in the Brisbane suburb of Inala, Bunting was sexually abused at some point in childhood. He would later describe the event to friends as "his accident." In a poor neighborhood awash with drugs and alcohol, Bunting stood out for his fanatical sobriety. He worked for a time in a slaughterhouse, regaling friends with his hatred of pedophiles, whom he dubbed "dirties." Mark Day, a teenage acquaintance, recalled Bunting's tales of assaulting child molesters, but dismissed the stories as "hot air." Associate Marcus Johnson recounted a "game" devised by Bunting and his friends, wherein they would "take care of" pedophiles by "burying them" or "throwing them off cliffs." At trial, Bunting

would tell the court, "Pedophiles were doing terrible things to children and innocent children were being damaged. The authorities did nothing about it, I was very angry. Someone had to do something about it. I decided to take action and I took that action." Police dismissed that claim, charging that Bunting killed most of his victims to steal their government welfare checks, torturing some to obtain the PIN numbers to their bank accounts.

Court-appointed psychologists struck a middle ground between Bunting's vigilante claims and bland police denials. In fact, they maintained, Bunting hated all those he regarded as "weak"—the unemployed, disabled, mentally defective—while reserving special anger for suspected pedophiles. He despised Elizabeth Haydon because she was unkempt, obese, and had eight children by multiple fathers. Bunting enjoyed a sexual relationship with Haydon's sister, Jodie Elliott, but dismissed her son (Fred Brooks) as "waste" because he had a learning disability. Bunting's torture of Brooks on the day he died included inserting a lit sparkler into the teenager's penis. Accomplice Robert Wagner had attempted suicide at age eight after he was molested by a family friend, and James Vlassakis also claimed a background of sexual abuse. Together, they made willing soldiers in Bunting's war against "dirties."

Barry Lane was a prime target for Bunting's homicidal rage, channeled through Wagner and Vlassakis. A flamboyant cross-dresser who called himself "Vanessa," twice convicted of molesting children, Lane met Robert Wagner soon after Wagner left school, still illiterate at age 14. Traumatized by sexual abuse and the beatings his father inflicted for trivial sins, Wagner fled home with Lane to live in New South Wales. They returned to Adelaide four years later, and settled in a house near Bunting's. Lane introduced Wagner to the neighbors as his fiancée. Their house was "putrid," friends recalled, because their four dogs defecated everywhere without restraint. Bunting befriended Wagner, tapping him as a source for names of pedophiles which Bunting posted on a "spider wall" at home. Their conversations soured Wagner's relationship with Lane, and Lane fled after violence erupted. The gang soon tracked him down and killed him at his new home in Hectorville.

Meanwhile, Bunting embarked on a relationship with Elizabeth Harvey, another unwed mother with children by multiple partners, whose sons included James Vlassakis, David Johnson, and Troy Youde. Vlassakis fell under Bunting's spell, and eventually sacrificed his two half-brothers to profitable war on "dirties." Mark Haydon was the odd man out, older than any of the rest, described in media reports as an ardent neo-Nazi who fell in line with Bunting's half-baked scheme to "purify" Adelaide while making a buck in the bargain.

The murders, as described in court, were both brutal and ritualized. Victims were beaten, shocked, and otherwise tortured, sometimes with fingers and toes crushed by pliers. Somber music set the tone. Victims were compelled to call Bunting "Lord Sir" and address Wagner as "God." Three early victims were buried, and parts of the rest were preserved for easy fetishistic access. Vlassakis gobbled drugs during the murders, but his three companions seemingly abstained. Wagner's detour into CANNIBALISM, following the Johnson murder, stood as grisly evidence that the crimes were never strictly a matter of profit.

In the wake of Johnson's death, Wagner visited the victim's father, claiming that Johnson had gone into hiding because he had been in a car accident and had impregnated a 13-year-old girl. Curious friends were treated to a tape recording, extracted from Johnson under torture, wherein he said, "I've got myself a real girlfriend. I don't need a whore." By that time, however, police were on the case, intercepting telephone calls between Bunting and Wagner, recording comments to support their search warrant in Snowtown.

Using fingerprints and dental records, police identified five victims from the bank vault on May 28, 1999. Three more were identified on June 12, and a total of 11 by September 1. Prosecutors presented more than 4,000 exhibits and 1,300 sworn declarations when they launched a committal hearing on December 12, 2000, required by Australian law to decide if the four suspects should be held for trial. That long-winded hearing was stalled in April 2001, permitting defense lawyers to review 6,000 hours of police wiretap recordings. Defendant Vlassakis provided another interruption on June 21, when he tearfully pleaded guilty to the murders of four victims (Brooks, Johnson, O'Dwyer, and Youde). Justice Kevin Duggan immediately sentenced Vlassakis to four life terms in prison, but his 42-year minimum without parole was later cut in half when Vlassakis turned state's evidence against his three confederates.

On July 3, 2001, Magistrate David Gurry confirmed that Bunting, Haydon, and Wagner should stand trial on 10 murder charges. Legal maneuvers severed Haydon's case from the others for separate trial, and the Bunting-Wagner trial was postponed until October 2002. A jury was empanelled on October 16, and testimony consumed the next 11 months. Both defendants were convicted in September 2003, Bunting on 11 murder counts, Wagner on 10. (Jurors deadlocked on the case of victim Suzanne Allen.) Judge Brian Martin sentenced both defendants to multiple life terms on October 29, 2003. While refusing to set a minimum sentence for either prisoner, Martin declared, "I make it plain

that I cannot envisage anything that would justify fixing a non-parole period. If I had the power to make an order for them never to be released, I would unhesitatingly make that order." In rejecting the strange vigilante defense, Martin added, "I am satisfied both of you derived pleasure from the physical act of killing and the violence and torture that preceded some of the killings. I am also satisfied you derived pleasure from the defleshing and dismembering of some of the bodies."

Even with that judgment rendered, the Snowtown case was not finished. Judge Martin ordered a retrial for the Allen murder, which—like Mark Haydon's trial—had not convened at press time for this volume. Bunting appealed his sentence in May 2004, claiming that prosecutors had obstructed his defense, but that assertion was rejected.

SOBHRAJ, Charles Gurmukh

Born Hotchand Bhawnani Gurmukh Sobhraj, in April 1944, Southeast Asia's most notorious serial killer was the illegitimate son of a Vietnamese peasant girl and a wealthy Indian merchant living in Saigon. Sobhraj's father married an Indian woman in Pooma, whereupon his mother retaliated by wedding a French military officer when Sobhraj was four years old. Indochina was in turmoil at the time, with French colonial troops fighting a hopeless rearguard action against Ho Chi Minh's rebels, and young Hotchand Sobhraj witnessed countless acts of violence before his stepfather took the family to France in 1953.

Sobhraj hated Europe and the Catholic boarding school in Paris where he soon became the butt of racial jokes and insults. (The school's main contribution to his future was a new name—"Charles"—appended in tribute to Sobhraj's clever impersonations of comedian Charlie Chaplin.) At first, he expressed his displeasure through tantrums and persistent bed-wetting, twice running away to Saigon in his teens. Sobhraj's father sent him back each time, but finally agreed to pay his passage for a trial visit home. The ticket never came, and Sobhraj turned to robbery, landing briefly in jail on his second attempt. He finally reached Vietnam on his own, but the family reunion was tense, and Sobhraj was soon packed off to live with relatives in India after wrecking his father's car. When he turned up in Saigon again, uninvited, Charles's father gave up and sent him back to France.

In Paris, Sobhraj was locked up twice for auto theft, emerging from custody the second time with a short-lived desire to "go straight." He married and found a job, but the workaday life quickly palled. Jailed again for writing bad checks on his sister's account, Sobhraj was freed when she dropped the charges. He continued bouncing checks, however, collecting some 30,000 francs before he fled with his wife to Bombay, there setting up shop as an international con man and smuggler, specializing in theft of passports from American and European tourists. Held for a jewel robbery in Delhi, Sobhraj was granted bail in spite of an escape attempt. He promptly fled to Kabul, Afghanistan, where police soon detained him for car theft and sundry lesser charges. Another jailbreak brought him back to France, where he kidnapped his infant daughter from his mother-in-law, leaving the woman drugged and locked in a closet.

Sobhraj's first known murder victim was a Pakistani chauffeur named Habib, hired by Sobhraj and a female companion in September 1972 for a trip between Rawalpindi and Peshawar. Along the way, for reasons still unclear, Sobhraj injected Habib with a drug that took his life, then dumped the victim's body in a river. Murder warrants were issued for suspect "Damon Seaman," but another year elapsed before Sobhraj was finally identified.

Arresting him was something else. November 1973 found Sobhraj in Istanbul, teaming with his brother Guy to drug and rob wealthy tourists. Both were arrested in Greece, but Charles managed another escape, leaving Guy to face charges while he fled back to India. In Delhi, he entered the heroin trade, gaining a foothold in the cutthroat business with inside information procured (via drugs and torture) from a local pusher, whom Sobhraj later killed.

Murder seemed to come easier each time, as Sobhraj established a lethal system. Often working with female accomplices, he ingratiated himself with tourists along Asia's "hippie trail," leaving corpses wherever he traveled. In time, police dubbed Sobhraj "The Serpent," for his skill at eluding capture and confinement. American reporters called him the "CHARLES MANSON of the East." He was a lethal customer by any name, claiming an estimated 20 lives between Turkey and Hong Kong.

The list of victims remains incomplete, but some have been identified. In October 1975, Sobhraj killed an American tourist, Teresa Knowlton, in his Delhi flat and had a cohort dump her corpse. A Turkish competitor in the drug trade, Vitali Hakim, was beaten, his neck snapped, his body doused with gasoline and set afire. In Bangkok, Sobhraj strangled Hakim's French contact, one Stephanie Parry. A month later, still in Bangkok, he strangled Dutch tourists Bintanja Henricus and Cornelia Hemker on December 16. Christmas found him in Nepal, where two more tourists were stabbed to death near Kathmandu, their bodies burned. Various published accounts identify the male victim, a Canadian, as either Laurent Carriere or Laddie du Parr, while his female traveling companion from California is

called either Connie Jo Bronzich or Annabella Tremont. Sobhraj—traveling as Bintanja Henricus, with the dead man's passport—was registered at the same hotel as his two latest victims, but he slipped out of Nepal after preliminary questioning.

Sobhraj continued his aimless trek across Asia, murdering Israeli Allen Jacobs for his passport at Varanasi, in northern India. (Accomplice Marie-Andrée Leclerc received a life sentence for the Jacobs murder. Diagnosed with cancer in 1983, she was released to her native Quebec and died there in 1984.) A few days later, on January 9, 1976, Sobhraj and two accomplices drugged a trio of Frenchmen at Goa, dumping their bodies at roadside, but all three survived the attack. In Hong Kong, victim Allen Gore was also lucky; he lost $8,000 but kept his life, despite a jolt of Sobhraj's chemical cocktail. Arrested with false passports in Bangkok, Sobhraj was released after bribing the local police. In Penang, he was detained for trying to cash stolen traveler's checks, but he managed to talk his way out of jail.

Back in Bombay, Sobhraj slipped a fatal mickey to French tourist Jean-Luc Solomon, moving on from there to more ambitious projects. He next drugged an entire class of 60 French engineering students, planning to rob them all, but miscalculation of the dosage sent 20 to a local hospital. This time police were ready, arresting Sobhraj on July 5, 1976. Although persuasive evidence linked him to at least 10 murders spanning half a dozen nations, he faced trial only for crimes in India. Convicted of "culpable homicide" in the Solomon case, Sobhraj was sentenced to seven years at hard labor, with two more years tacked on for drugging the French students. In 1982, he received a life sentence for murdering Allen Jacobs. Four years later, Sobhraj staged another jailbreak but was soon recaptured. Authors who interviewed The Serpent in prison contend that his escape was a deliberate ploy, planned to extend his Indian prison term beyond the statute of limitations for murder charges then pending in Thailand.

If true, the ploy worked. Sobhraj was paroled in 1997 and deported to France, where he settled into a comfortable existence as a celebrity rogue. Repudiating his various jailhouse confessions, Sobhraj granted interviews to journalists, filmmakers, and prospective biographers at $5,000 a session, providing rose-tinted glimpses of his life as an international man of mystery. In 2000, Sobhraj reportedly moved to London, but his Asian haunts exerted an irresistible allure. September 2003 found him back in Kathmandu, where Indian reporters tracked him down and published photos of him circulating on the streets. Police arrested him on September 19, citing open warrants in the 1975 murder case of victims Carriere-du Parr and Bronzich-Tremont.

Detectives claimed Sobhraj had once again entered Nepal as Bintjana Henricus, still milking the stolen identity of another former victim.

A judge denied bail to Sobhraj on October 20, 2003, and he sat in jail awaiting trial on immigration charges (including use of a false "Henricus" passport) while homicide investigators dusted off their 28-year-old murder case. Awaiting trial, Sobhraj airily dismissed the prosecution's "dubious writings" and other evidence from 1975, while staunchly maintaining his innocence. "If I am guilty," he asked a stringer from the *San Francisco Chronicle* in November 2003, "why didn't I run when the *Himalayan Times* said I was in Nepal? I have nothing to reproach myself for." A would-be prosecutor told the press, "There may not be much physical evidence against him, but eyewitness testimony is stronger than the documentary evidence. There are witnesses from the time who saw him, policemen and others."

Perhaps, but Sobhraj was still awaiting trial in June 2004, when court officials announced that his case would be postponed during Nepal's holiday festival season. Four days later, on June 29, spokesmen for Bakhtapur's district court informed the Kathmandu District Court that no trace could be found of Sobhraj's murder file from 1975. That news brought a solemn announcement from Balabhadra Bastola, administrative chief in Kathmandu, that trial could not proceed without the ancient evidence. Despite predictions from Sobhraj that he would soon be free once more, a Nepalese court convicted him of double murder on August 12, 2004. He was immediately sentenced to life imprisonment, whereupon Sobhraj told reporters, "I am shocked. I was found guilty without witnesses and evidence. I did not get a chance to defend myself. How can I defend on a case where there is no proper process? It was an unfair trial."

SOTO, Erno

Officially unsolved, the case of New York City's "Charlie Chopoff" murders occupied police for more than two years, from March 1972 through May 1974. The files are technically open today, despite the arrest of a promising suspect and his eventual commitment to a mental institution for the criminally insane. While he remains incarcerated, deemed incompetent for trial, the crimes may not be cleared, but lead investigators on the case are quick to note that "Charlie's" random depredations ended when their man was taken off the street.

Erno Soto's marriage seemed to be the root of all his problems. Separated from his wife for several years, he made a stab at reconciliation but was startled to discover that she had conceived a black child in his absence. (Soto and his wife are Puerto Ricans.) He pretended not to care, but as the boy's eighth birthday rolled around, Soto's behavior grew increasingly erratic, resulting in his commitment to Manhattan State Hospital in 1969 and 1970. He would return for further treatment at sporadic intervals thereafter, but the evidence suggests that Soto found his primary relief by stalking small, dark-skinned boys on New York's streets.

The first to die was Douglas Owens, black and eight years old, found murdered two blocks from his Harlem tenement on March 9, 1972. Discarded on a rooftop, Owens had been stabbed 38 times in the neck, chest, and back, his penis nearly severed from his body. An anonymous phone tip, received by police on March 23, fingered Erno Soto as a suspect in the case, but it was not pursued.

Another black boy, 10 years old, attacked on the city's Upper West Side on April 20. Stabbed in the neck and back, he was also sexually mutilated, his penis severed and carried away by the man who left him for dead. The boy survived his injuries and offered homicide detective a description of the suspect, but the trauma he had suffered limited his value as a witness.

On October 23, another black boy—nine-year-old Wendell Hubbard—was killed in East Harlem, six blocks from the site of the Owens murder. Hubbard was stabbed 17 times in the neck, chest, and abdomen, his penis removed by the killer and carried away from the scene. Five months later, on March 7, nine-year-old Luis Ortiz, a dark-skinned Puerto Rican, vanished on an errand to the corner store. His body—stabbed 38 times in the neck, chest, and back, penis severed and missing—was found in the basement of an apartment house along his route of travel.

Charles Sobhraj is guarded by police officers as he is taken into court in Kathmandu, Nepal. (AP Photo/Binod Joshi)

The death of Steven Cropper on August 17, 1973, appeared to break the killer's pattern. Cropper fit the victim profile perfectly—a black boy, eight years old—and while he had been murdered on a rooftop, he had not been stabbed. Instead, the fatal wounds were razor slashes, and his genitals were still intact. Police initially suspected that a second killer was responsible, but they later decided it was too coincidental for a pair of slashers to be stalking young black boys simultaneously around New York.

On May 15, 1974, Erno Soto was arrested after bungling the abduction of a nine-year-old Puerto Rican boy, being surrounded by neighbors and held for police after the child escaped his clutches. In custody, he confessed to the Cropper slaying, but "Charlie Chopoff's" sole surviving victim refused to pick Soto out of a lineup, saying only that the suspect's appearance was "similar." Officials at Manhattan State Hospital initially provided an alibi, stating that Soto had been confined on the date of Cropper's slaying, but they later admitted that he sometimes slipped away from the facility, unnoticed. Found to be insane, the suspect was returned to the hospital under closer guard, the "unsolved" murders terminating after he was locked away. Tagged with the pseudonym of "Miguel Rivera" when author Barbara Gelb described his case in *On the Track of Murder* (1975), Soto continues to confound some authors who report his crimes under the false name, instead of his own.

See also RANES, DANNY and LARRY

"SOUTHSIDE Slayer"

Unidentified at this writing, the "Southside Slayer" of Los Angeles is credited with at least 14 homicides between September 1983 and May 1987. At least three other victims are considered possible additions to the list, and three more managed to survive encounters with the stalker, offering police descriptions of a black man in his early thirties, sporting a mustache and baseball cap. The killer's chosen victims have been women, mostly black and mainly prostitutes, tortured with superficial cuts before they were strangled or stabbed to death in a grisly "pattern of overkill," their bodies dumped on residential streets, in alleyways, and in schoolyards.

Loletha Prevot was the killer's first known victim, found dead in Los Angeles on September 4, 1983. Four months passed before the killer struck again, on New Year's Day, dumping the corpse of Patricia Coleman in Inglewood. Another 10 months slipped away before discovery of a third victim, Sheila Burton—alias Burris—on November 18, 1984.

The elusive slayer adopted a regular schedule in 1985, beginning with the murder of Frankie Bell on January 1. Patricia Dennis was the next to fall, her mutilated body recovered on February 11. The first victim for March was Sheily Wilson, murdered in Inglewood on the 20th. Three days later, the stalker claimed Lillian Stoval in Los Angeles. Number eight was Patsy Webb, murdered on April 15, with Cathy Gustavson joining the list on July 28.

Thus far, the killer had missed only once, leaving one victim comatose after a savage beating. On August 6, his next intended target managed to escape by leaping from his moving car. She offered homicide detectives a description and assisted in the preparation of a widely published sketch, but officers appeared no closer to their suspect than they were in 1983.

Rebounding from his recent failure with another kill, the slayer dumped Gail Ficklin's body in Los Angeles on August 15. A 12-week lull was broken on November 6 with Gayle Rouselle's murder in Gardena, and the killer returned the next day to slaughter Myrtle Collier in L.A. Nesia McElrath, 23, was found slain on December 19, and Elizabeth Landcraft's mutilated corpse was found on December 22, 1985. The day after Christmas, Gidget Castro's body was discarded in the City of Commerce.

The new year was five days old when Tammy Scretchings met her killer in Los Angeles, becoming number 14 on the Southside Slayer's hit parade. On January 10, a 27-year-old prostitute was beaten and a male acquaintance stabbed when he attempted to restrain her violent customer. Their physical descriptions of the suspect tallied with reports from the survivor who escaped in August 1985.

The killer chalked up number 16, Lorna Reed, on February 11, 1986, discarding her corpse at San Dimas, 25 miles east of his usual hunting ground. Prostitute Verna Williams was found on May 26, her body slumped in the stairwell of a Los Angeles elementary school, and Trina Chaney joined the list November 3, in Watts. In January 1988, police announced that Carolyn Barney—killed May 29, 1987—was being added to the Southside list.

Three other victims have been unofficially connected to the Southside Slayer, though detectives hesitate to make a positive I.D. Loretta Jones, a 22-year-old coed with no criminal record, was murdered and dumped in a Los Angeles alley on April 15, 1986. A white "Jane Doe," age 25 to 30, was discovered strangled in a garbage dumpster three weeks later. Finally, Canoscha Griffin, 22, was stabbed to death on the grounds of a local high school, her body discovered on July 24.

By early 1988, police were backing off their initial body count, noting that defendant Charles Mosley had been convicted in one of the 1986 murders, while five more cases—involving victims Barney, Burris, Castro,

Ficklin, and McElrath—were considered "closed" with the arrest of two other serial slayers, Louis Craine and Daniel Siebert. Los Angeles police were less fortunate with their hasty arrest of an African-American L.A. County sheriff's deputy, Rickey Ross, as a suspect in the Southside case, when ballistics tests on the officer's pistol cleared him of involvement in the crimes. The case remains unsolved today.

"SPREE Murder": Defined

A prime example of FBI taxonomy refined to the point of inadvertent chaos, the term *spree murder* needlessly complicates classification of multiple homicides. According to the Bureau's *Crime Classification Manual* (1992), there are six kinds of murder: single, double, triple, mass, spree, and serial. The first three are self-explanatory, based on the number of victims killed at one time and place, while "MASS MURDER" involves the death of four or more victims. "SERIAL MURDER" logically involves the killing of successive victims over time—that is, *in series*—but FBI publicists could not resist adding a sixth category, which remains the topic of endless debate.

As defined by the Bureau, spree murder involves "a single event with two or more locations and no emotional cooling-off period between murders." The example cited is that of Howard Unruh, who in 1949 killed 13 victims in the space of 20 minutes, ambling through his neighborhood in Camden, New Jersey, shooting passers-by at random. Most criminologists regard Unruh as a *mass* murderer, based on the short time span and number of victims, but the FBI disagrees—illogically, it seems—based solely on the fact of his mobility.

Unfortunately, the FBI has not defined the requisite distance between murder scenes that shifts a bloodbath from mass to spree murder. Is it enough to have the killer run next door, or must he go around the block? Likewise, the elusive cooling-off period remains undefined and wholly subjective. How long must a slayer cool off between murders to graduate from spree to serial killing? One author proposes a minimum of 30 days between murders, without regard to the individual killer's state of mind, but such arbitrary deadlines are clearly absurd.

Our difficulty is further compounded when FBI Agents ROBERT RESSLER and JOHN DOUGLAS state in their book *Sexual Homicide* (1988) that a bona fide serial killer may switch to spree murders—and, presumably, back again—depending on his mood. They cite the case of CHRISTOPHER WILDER, acknowledged by the FBI as a serial killer in Florida before he was publicly identified in 1984, at which point he "went on a long-term killing spree throughout the country," ultimately dying in a shootout with police. The authors tell us that "Wilder's classification changed from serial to spree because of the multiple murders and the lack of a cooling-off period during his prolonged murder event, which lasted nearly seven weeks." Four years later in *Whoever Fights Monsters* (1992), Ressler further confused the issue by describing Richard Speck's massacre of eight student nurses in their shared living quarters as a spree murder (corrected in the paperback edition to read "mass murder").

Ultimately, such refinement of a term to the nth degree without defining the critical time spans involved or making allowance for individual cases, appears to serve no useful purpose. For that reason, as elsewhere explained, this book follows the definition of "serial murder" published by the National Institute of Justice in 1988, and disregards the "spree murder" classification as superfluous.

See also HISTORY OF SERIAL MURDER

SPREITZER, Edward   *See* "CHICAGO RIPPERS"

STANIAK, Lucian

As a young man in Warsaw, Staniak lost his parents and sister in a tragic automobile accident. The driver responsible—a young Polish Air Force captain's wife—was cleared of criminal responsibility, but Staniak remained obsessed with "justice" in the case, and over time he hatched a scheme to punish young blond women everywhere in Poland. He launched his campaign in 1964 with a letter to the Polish state newspaper. Writing in red ink with a peculiar style that earned him the nickname of the "Red Spider," Staniak warned: "There is no happiness without tears, no life without death. Beware! I am going to make you cry."

Employed as a translator for the official state publishing house, Staniak traveled widely in his profession, chalking up an estimated 20 female victims in the next two years. The first, a 17-year-old student, was raped and mutilated at Olsztyn on the anniversary of Polish liberation from Nazi occupation. The next day, one of Staniak's trademark letters declared, "I picked a juicy flower in Olsztyn and I shall do it again somewhere else, for there is no holiday without a funeral."

His next holiday victim was a blond 16-year-old who marched at the head of a student's parade on the day she died. An anonymous letter directed police to the body—ravaged, with a spike run through the genitals—in a factory basement not far from her home.

On All Saints' Day, Staniak murdered a blond hotel receptionist, mutilating her body with a screwdriver. Next day, he wrote the press that "Only tears of sorrow can wash out the stain of shame; only pangs of suffering can blot out the fires of lust." On May Day 1966, he raped and disemboweled a 17-year-old, dumping her body in a toolshed behind her home. Police were looking into 14 other cases when the killer left another victim raped and mutilated on a train that Christmas Eve. His letter to the press was simple and direct: "I have done it again."

An artist of sorts, Staniak was finally traced by police in 1967 after he slaughtered a fellow member of the Art Lovers Club. Police became suspicious when they viewed his paintings—mainly crimson, daubed on with a knife and focusing on scenes of mutilation—and they found that Staniak's itinerary for the past two years precisely coincided with the string of unsolved crimes. Arrested on the way home from his final murder, committed in a peevish bid for more publicity, Staniak readily confessed to 20 slayings and was sent to an asylum in Katowice for life.

STANO, Gerald Eugene

A native of Daytona Beach, Florida, born in 1951 and adopted as an infant, Stano suffered persistent learning and "adjustment" problems in his early school years, complicated by a lack of coordination that resulted in frequent falls. After several years in a Virginia military academy, he graduated from high school in Daytona Beach and went to work at his adoptive father's gas station, also holding jobs as a cook and waiter on the side. He met a lot of women, but they universally rejected him, increasing Stano's deep resentment toward a world of "bitches." Sometimes they laughed at him, but Stano also recalled that some "pulled my hair" or "threw beer bottles at me." Years later, after killing 41 women, Stano would confide to homicide detectives that "I hate a bitchy chick."

According to his own confession, Stano claimed his first two victims in New Jersey during 1969. He drifted into Pennsylvania in the early 1970s and murdered a half-dozen women there before returning to his native Florida, launching a one-man crime wave that would claim another 33 lives between 1973 and 1980. Devoted to the hunt, Stano preyed chiefly on prostitutes and hitchhikers, though one of his victims would be a high school cheerleader. They ranged in age from 13 to the mid-30s, dispatched by means of gunshots, knives, and strangulation. None were apparently raped, and state psychiatrists concluded that Stano drew his basic satisfaction from the simple act of murder. As one detective summed the killer up, "He thinks about three things: stereo systems, cars, and killing women."

Arrested in April 1980 after an intended victim managed to escape his clutches in Daytona Beach,

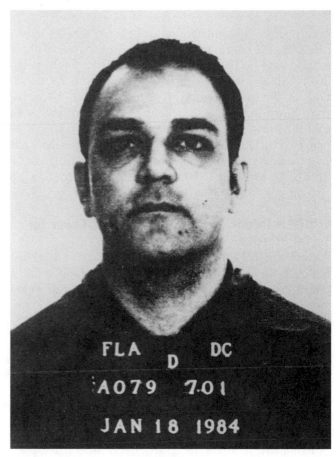

Gerald Stano (Author's collection)

Stano launched into a marathon confession, directing Florida police to the buried remains of 24 identifiable victims and two skeletal "Jane Does." By December 1983, Stano had provided details of 41 murders, though none of the cases from Pennsylvania or New Jersey were ever prosecuted. Even in Florida, with 27 corpses recovered, Stano faced trial in only a handful of cases. Life sentences were meted out for the murders of 17-year-old Barbara Bauer, kidnapped from Smyrna Beach and killed on September 6, 1973; 24-year-old Nancy Heard, found dead near Ormond Beach on January 3, 1975; 20-year-old Mary Maher, a coed stabbed to death in Daytona Beach on January 10, 1980; and 26-year-old Toni Van Haddocks, found at Holly Hill on February 15, 1980, with 51 stab wounds. Separate death sentences were imposed on Stano for the murders of 17-year-old Cathy Scharf, abducted from Port Orange and killed on December 17, 1973; 24-year-old Susan Bickrest, strangled and drowned in Spruce Creek on December 29, 1975; and 23-year-old Mary Muldoon, shot and drowned at New Smyrna Beach on November 12, 1977.

Stano came within moments of execution on July 2, 1986, before an appellate court granted him an indefinite stay. He continued to play the legal system like a master until his luck ran out 12 years later, finally keeping his date with "Old Sparky" on March 23, 1998. One of the investigators active on his case, Detective John Carlton, witnessed Stano's execution and later told the press, "It wasn't traumatic for me to see someone who had killed forty-one people put to death. What was traumatic for me was that we had to wait from the time of his arrest in 1980 to 1998, for his execution."

SUDDEN Infant Death Syndrome as Cover for Serial Murder

A catchall label for the otherwise inexplicable deaths of babies (also known as "cot death" in Britain), sudden infant death syndrome (SIDS) has apparently provided a convenient cover for those serial-killing parents who murder their own children, either for profit (as from life insurance) or some morbid compulsion to kill. An average 7,000 to 8,000 babies die from SIDS in the United States each year with no symptoms of any recognizable illness, and while such deaths have been routinely ignored for decades, authorities now believe that as many as 20 percent of alleged SIDS victims may in fact have been murdered by parents or other caretakers.

Ironically, it was a 1972 article on SIDS itself, published in the medical journal *Pediatrics,* which prompted the reversal opinion among physicians and law enforcement officers. The article's author, Dr. Alfred Steinschneider—later president of the Sudden Infant Death Syndrome Institute in Atlanta—profiled one anonymous family with five children lost to SIDS, using the case to support his theory that a genetic defect may produce prolonged apnea (disruption of an infant's breathing during sleep), and so cause death. District Attorney William Fitzpatrick of Onondaga, New York, read the article in 1986 as background material for an unrelated infanticide case and instantly suspected foul play in the family identified only as "H." Years of detective work in public records finally identified Waneta Hoyt, a Berkshire, New York, housewife convicted in 1995 of murdering five babies and sentenced to a prison term of 75 years to life.

Hoyt's case, sadly, is far from unique. Another New Yorker, MARYBETH TINNING, is suspected of killing eight children, but was convicted on one murder count. Diana Lumbrera lost seven children before authorities intervened; she now stands convicted of murdering two, in Texas and Kansas. MARTHA WOODS also lost seven infants before she was sentenced to life on one count of first-degree murder in Maryland. DEBRA SUE TUGGLE claimed at least five tiny victims before she was con-

victed of murder in 1984; even then, a sympathetic jury recommended the minimum 10-year sentence. In 1994, Illinois resident Gail Savage pleaded guilty to smothering three of her children, and Debra Gedzius Fornuto—suspected of killing six children and her husband between 1972 and 1989—escaped prosecution thanks to confusion of "expert" opinions on SIDS. (Fornuto died in a Las Vegas car crash on July 8, 2002, leaving the mystery forever unsolved.)

Today, most pediatricians dismiss the notion of "hereditary" SIDS, agreeing with San Antonio medical examiner Vincent Di Maio that "two SIDS deaths [in one family] is improbable, but three is impossible." Even so, at this writing only 10 states routinely autopsy all alleged SIDS victims. Too many hospitals and prosecutors still apply what Di Maio calls the Three-Baby Rule. "You wait until they kill the third kid," he explains, before exhumations and court-ordered autopsies begin. Even then, there may be no conclusive evidence of homicide, with "gentle" suffocation the method of choice among serial baby-killers. Yet another problem with some physicians is the application of SIDS diagnoses to unexplained deaths of children age two years and older. Majority opinion now concurs that SIDS should *never* be listed as a cause of death for children more than 12 months old.

Analysis of SIDS cases in Britain, where they are known as "cot deaths," created a furor in January 2004, with the announcement that a legal review of 258 infant deaths without apparent cause would be severely curtailed. That decision emerged from the case of defendant Angela Cannings, whose murder conviction was overturned on appeal. Britain's Appeal Court ruled on January 19 that medical study of SIDS was "still at the frontiers of knowledge," dictating that in cases where trial depended "almost exclusively on a serious disagreement between distinguished and reputable experts, it will often be unwise, and therefore unsafe, to proceed." The Cannings decision followed a 2003 appellate decision reversing Sally Clarke's conviction for killing two young sons, and the acquittal of pharmacist Trupti Patel on charges that she murdered three infants.

See also "BLACK WIDOWS"; MUNCHAUSEN'S SYNDROME BY PROXY

SURADJI, Ahmad

An Indonesian cattle breeder and self-styled sorcerer, Ahmad Suradji was 36 years old in 1986 when his late father appeared to him in a dream, commanding him to increase his occult powers by killing 70 women in black magic rituals. According to his later confessions, Suradji—aka Nasib Kelawang or Datuk Mariniggi—wasted no time in following the old man's orders.

It was easy enough to find victims, since local women often visited his home outside Medan, the capital of North Sumatra, to purchase love charms and similar items. Each sacrifice followed the same pattern: after charging his victim a fee that ranged from $200 to $400, Suradji led the unsuspecting female to a nearby sugar plantation, where he dug a hole and buried her up to the waist, supposedly as part of a ritual designed to ensure her lover's fidelity. Once the victim was effectively immobilized, Suradji then strangled her with an electric cord, drank the victim's saliva, stripped the corpse, and buried it with the head pointed toward his home to channel the spirit's mystical powers. If all else failed and willing customers ran short, Suradji would hire prostitutes and murder them instead.

Suradji was still short of his 70-victim goal on April 28, 1997, when three bodies were found on the plantation and police arrested him for questioning. In custody, he initially confessed to killing 16 victims over the past five years, but a search of his home turned up clothing and personal items linked to 25 missing women, and Suradji finally confessed to a total of 42 murders spanning 11 years. His three wives, all sisters, were jailed as accomplices, but two were later released, with only the oldest—38-year-old Tumini—charged after confessing her role in the crimes.

Police unearthed 40 corpses on the plantation, victims ranging in age from 12 to 30 years, and while some 80 local families had reported missing females during the span of Suradji's rampage, Ahmad and Tumini were charged with only 42 counts of murder when their trial began on December 21, 1997. By that time, both defendants had recanted their confessions, claiming they were tortured by police, but no denials could explain the corpses unearthed near Suradji's home. On April 27, 1998, Suradji was convicted and sentenced to death by firing squad. Tumini was also convicted and sentenced to life imprisonment. Suradji's lawyers have announced that they will appeal his conviction.

SUTCLIFFE, Peter William

A long-haul trucker and "harlot killer" who proved rather indiscriminate in choosing victims was Great Britain's "Yorkshire Ripper," Peter Sutcliffe. While residing in apparent harmony with his beloved wife—herself a diagnosed schizophrenic who spent time in institutions—Sutcliffe waged a five-year war against the female population of England's northern counties. With his ball-peen hammer, chisel, and assorted other implements of slaughter, Sutcliffe claimed a minimum of 13 victims killed and seven wounded. In addition to the documented body count, he is believed by some to be responsible for other unsolved murders on the European continent.

The roots of Sutcliffe's homicidal rage are difficult to trace. His family appears to have been torn by dark suspicions on his father's part of infidelity by Peter's mother, and the boy's opinion of all women may have suffered in an atmosphere of brooding doubt. As a young man, he found employment with a local mortuary and was prone to "borrow" jewelry from the corpses; in his comments, easily dismissed as "jokes" by coworkers at the time, there is a hint of budding necrophilia, more disturbing than the strain of larceny. A favorite outing for the would-be Ripper was a local wax museum, where he lingered by the hour over torsos that depicted the results of gross venereal disease. Before his marriage, Sutcliffe frequently expressed his fears of having caught "a dose" from contact with the prostitutes of Leeds and Birmingham.

Sutcliffe's first attacks on women, in July and August 1975, were unsuccessful in that both his victims managed to survive the crushing blows of hammers to their skulls and the slashes he inflicted on their torsos after they were down. October was a better month for Peter: on the 29th he slaughtered prostitute Wilma McCann in Leeds and thus officially began the Ripper's reign of terror.

There seemed to be no schedule for his crimes. On January 20, 1976, housewife/hooker Emily Jackson was bludgeoned to death in Leeds, her prostrate body bearing 50 stab wounds. Sutcliffe did not strike again for 13 months, attacking Irene Richardson, another prostitute, again in Leeds. He move to Bradford for the April butchery of Tina Atkinson, another prostitute, found murdered in her own apartment, mutilated after death.

On June 16, the Ripper struck again, but his selection of a victim made the slaying different, more appalling to the populace at large. At 16 years of age, Jane MacDonald was an "innocent," the perfect girl next door, cut down while strolling to a relative's house, almost within sight of home. Her murder put the Ripper on a different plane, immediately serving notice that no girl or woman in the northern counties was safe.

Maureen Long was assaulted on the streets of Bradford in July, but she survived the blows that Sutcliffe rained upon her skull. In October, he crossed the Pennines to murder Jean Jordan in Manchester, crushing her skull with 11 hammer strokes, stabbing her 24 times after death. When she had not been found within a week, he would return to move the body and slash it further, making its location more apparent to police.

In January 1978, Sutcliffe killed a prostitute named Helen Rytka in the town of Huddersfield. In April 1979, another "innocent," 19-year-old Josephine Whittaker, was butchered in Halifax. A civil servant, Marguerite Walls, was murdered at Pudsley in August, and 12 days later Sutcliffe slaughtered coed Barbara Leach, in Bradford.

In the middle of their manhunt, homicide investigators were bedeviled by a mocking tape and several letters from "the Ripper." Later, with their man in custody, they learned that all were hoaxes, perpetrated by another twisted mind that found vicarious release in toying with detective. Countless hours were wasted by police and independent searchers, looking for a man whose penmanship and accent bore no smallest similarity to Sutcliffe's own. The charlatan responsible—suspected in two unrelated homicides—remains at large today.

The Ripper had two more near misses in October and November, wounding victims in the towns of Leeds and Huddersfield. Both would survive their wounds, and Sutcliffe took a year's vacation prior to killing coed Jacqueline Hill at Leeds in November 1980. The latest victim's mutilations were familiar to police, but Sutcliffe also stabbed her in the eye, unsettled by the corpse's "reproachful stare."

On January 2, 1981, police arrested Sutcliffe with a prostitute in one of several areas that had been subject to surveillance through the manhunt. Even so, they almost let him slip the net by stepping out of sight to urinate behind some shrubbery, there dropping the incriminating weapons he carried beneath his jacket. At the station, Sutcliffe finally broke down, confessing everything. Detectives noted that their subject seemed relieved to have it all behind him. So he seemed, as well, to spectators in court when he received a term of life imprisonment for 13 homicides and various assaults. (Author David Yallop, in *Deliver Us from Evil* [1982], links the Ripper to four additional murders and seven nonfatal assaults, including crimes in France and Sweden.) From the cab of Sutcliffe's truck, detectives had retrieved a written statement that appeared to summarize the Ripper's twisted view of life:

In this truck is a man whose latent genius, if unleashed, would rock the nation, whose dynamic energy would overpower those around him. Better let him sleep?

Shortly after his conviction, Sutcliffe was examined by prison psychiatrists and pronounced insane, whereupon he was transferred to Broadmoor Hospital. On March 10, 1997, he was attacked by another homicidal inmate and stabbed in both eyes. Emergency surgery saved the sight in his right eye, but Sutcliffe was permanently blinded in the left. Public outrage erupted in April 1999, with tabloid revelations that authorities planned to let Sutcliffe visit his dying father, and the mercy excursion was promptly canceled. In November 2002, Yorkshire police announced preparation of new charges against Sutcliffe, on the chance that he someday requested parole, but the Ripper showed no desire for freedom. In April 30, 2003, members of parliament from Leeds alleged that Sutcliffe had deceived psychiatrists and they requested his transfer from Broadmoor hospital to a normal maximum-security prison. No action had been taken on that effort when this volume went to press.

TEAM Killers: Serial murder by groups

Contrary to popular belief, serial killers are not always loners, brooding in seclusion between their violent outbursts. In fact, some 13 percent of American cases involve multiple killers. Of those, 56 percent find two killers working together, while the remaining 44 percent include groups ranging in size from three slayers to a dozen or more.

Demographically, male pairs (like killing cousins KENNETH BIANCHI and ANGELO BUONO) are the most common team slayers, representing 30 percent of the American total. Male-female couples, typified by GERALD and CHARLENE GALLEGO account for another 25 percent, with the male partner generally (sometimes inaccurately) presumed to be dominant. All-male "wolf packs," ranging in number from three to a half-dozen members, represent 10 percent of America's identified team killers. Larger groups, particularly cults like the MANSON "FAMILY," sometimes find male and female killers cooperating toward a common goal, however bizarre. The rarest grouping of killers is found in the all-female team, ranging in size from occasional couples (e.g., GWENDOLYN GRAHAM and CATHERINE WOOD) to larger groups like the Austrian "ANGELS OF DEATH" or Hungary's "ANGEL MAKERS OF NAGYREV."

The FBI's *Crime Classification Manual* (1992) recognizes three types of "group cause homicide," including *cult, extremist,* and *group-excitement* murders. CULT killers sometimes prey on strangers, as in the case of the "CHICAGO RIPPERS" but may also turn upon their own, as seen in several of the Manson murders. Extremist homicides, according to the FBI, break down into the same general MOTIVES as those of individual murders—that is, political, religious, and socioeconomic. (The Bureau further subdivides extremist murders by a group into *paramilitary* and *hostage* killings.) No apparent distinction is made in the FBI manual between cult murders and those committed by a religious extremist group, which also fits the basic definition of a "cult." The so-called ZEBRA MURDERS, for example, were committed by members of a Black Muslim splinter group that aimed to exterminate "white devils," thus making the crimes both religious *and* racial in motive. Finally, group-excitement murders—vaguely defined by the FBI as a case involving "two or more persons who cause the death of an individual"—apparently result form some emotional and chaotic confrontation. A case in point is the murder of a member of the Hebrew Israelites (a black cult that is not connected in any way to Israel or Judaism) in Florida, beaten to death by fellow cultists after accusations of "heresy."

A glaring omission from the FBI's list of group homicide motives is any reference to *criminal enterprise* murders. Despite the manual's inclusion of individual gang-motivated murders, contract killings and murders spawned by criminal competition, the Bureau strangely makes no allowance for financial motives in group-caused homicides. This oversight is all the more surprising since contract murders, by definition, involve at least two parties, while the vast majority of gang- and drug-related murders involve organized groups. There is also well-established evidence of group involvement in insurance/inheritance-related murders (e.g., the BOLBER-PETRILLO-FAVATO MURDER RING) and in sexual or sadistic crimes (e.g., the Gallego case and others). In short, any motive capable of driving one person to kill may also be shared by a group.

TERRELL, Bobbie Sue

A native of tiny Woodlawn, Illinois, the future "Death Angel" of Florida grew up overweight, myopic, and painfully shy. Her seven siblings included four brothers afflicted with muscular dystrophy, two of whom would die from the disease before Bobbie Sue reached her mid-thirties. Above-average grades in school were countered by an outspoken religious fervor that amused or embarrassed Bobbie's classmates. Only in church did she shine, playing the organ for Sunday services and displaying a fine singing voice.

Graduating high school in 1973, Bobbie Sue was doubtless influenced by family illness in her choice of a nursing career. By 1976, she was a registered nurse, ready to take her place in the medical community. Married to Danny Dudley a short time later, Bobbie was despondent at learning she could not bear children. The couple adopted a son, but their marriage collapsed when the boy was hospitalized for a drug overdose. Dudley accused his wife of feeding the boy tranquilizers prescribed for her own schizophrenia, a charge that led to Bobbie being stripped of custody in the divorce.

Alone again, Bobbie Sue's health and mental state swiftly declined. She was hospitalized five times in short order—for fibroid stomach tumors, for a hysterectomy and removal of her ovaries, for surgery on a broken arm that failed to heal properly, for gall bladder problems, for ulcers and pneumonia. Bobbie voluntarily committed herself to a state mental hospital, spending more than a year under psychiatric treatment. On release, she held several short-term nursing jobs before she was hired to work at Hillview Manor, a rest home in Greenville, Illinois.

It wasn't long before the staff at Hillview Manor started to record bizarre events surrounding Bobbie Sue. She fainted frequently on duty without apparent cause, and twice she intentionally slashed her own vagina with scissors. The second wound required emergency surgery at Barnes Hospital in St. Louis where Bobbie told a counselor she stabbed herself in rage and frustration over her infertility.

Discharged from her job at the rest home, Bobbie Sue moved to St. Petersburg in July 1984, obtaining a Florida nursing license that August. Drifting from job to job in the Tampa Bay area, she was still dogged by mysterious ailments, including a bout of rectal bleeding that led to an emergency colostomy. In spite of everything, October found her employed as a shift supervisor at St. Petersburg's North Horizon Health Center, assigned to work from 11:00 P.M. to 7:00 A.M.

With Bobbie Sue in charge, the late-night "graveyard shift" soon lived up to its sinister nickname. Aggie Marsh, age 97, was the first to die, on November 13, 1984. Advanced age made her death seem commonplace, but questions were raised a few days later, when 94-year-old Anna Larson nearly died from an insulin overdose. The riddle: Mrs. Larson wasn't diabetic, and insulin was kept in a locked cabinet with Nurse Dudley holding the only key. Despite this, the matter was not seriously investigated.

The grim toll continued. On November 23, 85-year-old Leathy McKnight died from an insulin overdose on Dudley's shift; the same night, an unexplained fire broke out in a linen closet, with arson suspected. Two more patients, 79-year-old Mary Cartwright and 85-year-old Stella Bradham, died on the night of November 25. The next day, a Monday dubbed The Holocaust by worried staffers, five more patients died in quick succession.

Matters went from bad to worse after that, including an anonymous call to the rest home, a woman's voice whispering that five patients had been murdered in their beds. Police were called to North Horizon in the predawn hours of November 27, finding Nurse Dudley with a stab wound in her side. Bobbie Sue blamed a prowler for the assault, and detectives were further concerned by reports of 12 patient deaths in the past 13 days.

A full-scale investigation was launched, leading to Bobbie Sue's December dismissal "for the good of the facility." When she filed a $22,000 claim for workman's compensation based on her stabbing, the hospital countered with psychiatric reports branding Dudley a "borderline schizophrenic" who suffered from Munchausen's Syndrome (a mental condition characterized by false claims of illness and self-inflicted wounds). Reports of Bobbie's Illinois self-mutilations were obtained, and her claim was rejected.

On January 31, 1985, Dudley entered a Pinellas County hospital for medical and psychiatric treatment. By that time she was already a prime suspect in several deaths at North Horizon, and detectives had obtained exhumation orders for nine patients—including bodies buried in Wisconsin, Pennsylvania, and Texas. Bobbie Sue was still hospitalized on February 12 when Florida's Department of Professional Regulation issued an emergency order suspending her nurse's license. DPR spokesmen further asked the state's Board of Nursing for a permanent revocation order, calling Dudley "an immediate, serious danger to the public health, safety, and welfare."

Bobbie Sue demanded a formal hearing, and while waiting for her day in court she married 38-year-old Ron Terrell, a plumber from Tampa. Matrimony failed to do the trick where Bobbie's mental problems were concerned, and she soon found herself in another psycho ward, this time committed against her will. She was still inside when the Board of Nursing announced a five-year suspension of her license, with reinstatement conditional upon successful psychiatric treatment.

Licensing became the least of Bobbie's problems on March 17, when she was formally charged with attempting to murder Ann Larson in November 1984. Arresting officers found the Terrells living in a roadside tent, recently evicted from their small apartment, but a search of the former residence turned up sufficient evidence to support indictments on four counts of first-degree murder. Bobbie Sue was held without bond pending trial in the deaths of Aggie Marsh, Leathy McKnight, Stella Bradham, and Mary Cartwright.

The trial was scheduled to begin on October 20, 1985, but legal maneuvers and psychiatric tests repeatedly postponed the starting date. At last, in February 1988, Bobbie Sue pled guilty to reduced charges of second-degree murder and was sentenced to a term of 60 years imprisonment.

See also MEDICAL MURDERS

TINNING, Marybeth Roe

For a devoted mother, Marybeth Tinning seemed to have no luck at all raising children. In the 13 years from 1972 to 1985, she lost nine infants in Schenectady, New York. Police would later charge that eight of those were slain deliberately for MOTIVES so bizarre they challenge credibility.

The first to go was daughter Jennifer, a mere eight days old when she died on January 3, 1972. An autopsy listed the cause of death as acute meningitis, and since the baby never left St. Clare's Hospital after her birth, authorities consider her death the only case above suspicion. We may never know what emotional shock waves were triggered in Marybeth Tinning's mind by the death of her newborn daughter, but more of their children soon joined the casualty list.

Less than three weeks later, on January 20, two-year-old Joseph Tinning Jr. was pronounced dead on arrival at Ellis Hospital in Schenectady. Doctors blamed his death on a viral infection and "seizure disorder," but no autopsy was performed to verify those findings. Four-year-old Barbara Tinning died six weeks later, on March 20, and autopsy surgeons, lacking an obvious cause of death, attributed her passing to "cardiac arrest." Barbara's death as the first reported to police, but officers closed their file on the case after a brief consultation with hospital physicians.

And the deaths continued.

When two-week-old Timothy died at Ellis Hospital, doctors were once more unable to determine a cause, listing the case under the umbrella of SUDDEN INFANT DEATH SYNDROME (SIDS). On September 2, 1975, Nathan Tinning died at the age of five months, an autopsy blaming his case on "pulmonary edema." SIDS was the culprit again on February 2, 1979, when Mary Tinning died six months short of her third birthday, but no cause was ever determined in the death of three-month-old Jonathan, on March 24, 1980. Three-year-old Michael Tinning was still in the process of being adopted when he was rushed to St. Clare's Hospital on August 2, 1981. Physicians could not save his life, and while they viewed his passing with a "high level of suspicion," the cause of death was listed as bronchial pneumonia.

The real questions began on December 20, 1985, when three-month-old Tammi Lynne Tinning was found unconscious in bed, blood staining her pillow. Rushed to St. Clare's Hospital, she was beyond help, and while doctors ascribed her death to SIDS, they also telephoned the state police. An investigation led to Marybeth Tinning's arrest on February 4, 1986, after she confessed to pressing a pillow over Tammi Lynne's face when the child "fussed and cried." In custody, she also confessed to murdering Timothy and Nathan but staunchly denied killing any of the others. "I smothered them with a pillow," she told detectives, "because I'm not a good mother."

In fact, psychiatrists decided, the problem ran deeper than that. Marybeth Tinning was diagnosed as suffering from a condition called MUNCHAUSEN'S SYNDROME BY PROXY, in which those responsible for the care of children, invalids, and the like sometimes seek attention by harming their charges. Friends and relatives recalled Marybeth preening at funerals, basking in the spotlight of sympathy, playing her role of grieving mother to hilt. It was suggested that the outpouring of condolence following her first baby's death in 1972 had become addictive, driving Marybeth to kill one child after another in pursuit of the sympathy "fixes" she craved.

On July 17, 1987, Tinning was convicted of second-degree murder in Tammi Lynne's death, jurors acquitting her of "deliberately" killing the child, blaming her for a lesser degree of homicide through her "depraved indifference to human life." It was a compromise verdict—more sympathy for Marybeth—but it carried a prison sentence of 20 years to life. Husband Joseph Tinning seemed bewildered by the whole affair. In newspaper interviews, he admitted occasional suspicion of his wife but had managed to push it aside. "You have to trust your wife," he said. "She has her things to do, and as long as she gets them done, you don't ask questions."

TOOLE, Ottis Elwood

A native of Jacksonville, Florida, Toole was born on March 5, 1947. His alcoholic father soon took off for parts unknown, leaving Toole in the care of a religious fanatic mother and a sister who dressed him in girl's clothes "to play." Toole's confusion was exacerbated by his grandmother, an alleged Satanist, who branded Ottis "the devil's child" and sometimes took him on the graveyard runs that yielded human body parts for use in "magic" charms. Toole ran away from home repeatedly but always drifted back again. He suffered from seizures and derived satisfaction from torching vacant houses in his neighborhood. Questioned later about his choice of targets, Toole replied, "I just hated to see them standing there."

By his own admission, Toole committed his first murder at age 14. The victim, a traveling salesman, picked him up outside town and drove him into the woods for sex. Afterward, Toole "got nervous" and ran the man down with his own car.

Classified as retarded with an IQ of 75, Toole dropped out of school in the eighth grade. His first arrest, for loitering, was logged in August 1964, and others followed, building up a rap sheet filled with counts of petty theft and lewd behavior. He married briefly, but his bride departed after three days' time, repulsed by Toole's overt homosexuality. By 1974, Toole was drifting and touring the western states in an

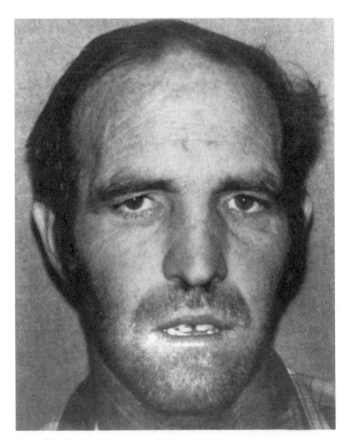

Ottis Toole (Author' collection)

old pickup truck. Acquaintances thought nothing of it, but later evidence suggests he may have claimed at least four victims in a six-month period.

Police suspect Toole in the death of 24-year-old Patricia Webb, shot in Lincoln, Nebraska, on April 18, 1974. Five months later, on September 19, a lone gunman invaded a massage parlor in Colorado Springs; employee Yon Lee was stabbed, her throat slashed, before the attacker moved on to rape, shoot, and stab coworker Sun Ok Cousin. Both women were set on fire, but Lee survived to describe her assailant as clean-shaven, six feet two, and 195 pounds, driving a white pickup truck. Police, for reasons yet unclear, arrested—and ultimately convicted—Park Estep, a mustachioed soldier who stood five feet ten, tipped the scales at a mere 150 pounds, and owned a *red* pickup truck. Meanwhile, on October 10, 31-year-old Ellen Holman was abducted from Pueblo, Colorado, shot three times in the head, and dumped near the Oklahoma border. Homicide investigators now believe Toole also pulled the trigger in that crime.

Two years later, Toole met killer HENRY LUCAS at a Jacksonville soup kitchen, taking him home for a night of drinking, conversation, and sex. The men had much in common, sharing memories of murder, looking forward to a time when they might hunt together. By 1983, according to police, they had traversed the continent together several times, annihilating random victims at a dizzying pace.

On January 14, 1977, Toole startled relatives by marrying a woman 24 years his senior. The relationship was curious from day one, and Novella Toole soon found herself sharing Ottis with Henry Lucas and other strangers. "A few nights after we were married," she said, "he told me he got nervous a lot, especially if he couldn't get a man. He'd get angry, he said, and then he couldn't get excited with a women." They were separated by 1978, Lucas and Toole moving in with Toole's mother, sharing quarters with sister Drusilla Powell and her children, Frank and Frieda.

The homicidal soul mates found work with a Jacksonville roofing company, Southeast Color Coat, but office manager Eileen Knight recalls that they disappeared frequently, sometimes for weeks at a stretch. "Ottis would come and go," she told Jacksonville newsmen. "We'd hire him whenever he came back because he was a good worker." Toole's landlord, Betty Goodyear, said of Ottis and Henry, "They went out of town, always disappearing. All [Toole] cared about was that old car. I think they were using it for robbing people because they always seemed to have a lot of money." Along the way, Toole allegedly introduced Lucas to a satanic cult, the "Hand of Death," that kidnapped children, practiced human sacrifice, and cranked out snuff films on a secret ranch in Mexico.

Toole's mother died in May 1981, following surgery, and the loss hit him hard. Ottis haunted the cemetery, sometimes at night, stretching out on the ground by her grave, supposedly feeling the earth move beneath him. A short time later, sister Drusilla died of a drug overdose, considered a probable suicide, and her children were packed off to juvenile homes. Alone for once with Lucas off on his own or in jail, Toole brooded, drinking heavily and popping pills. It was around this time—on July 27—that six-year-old Adam Walsh disappeared from a Hollywood, Florida, shopping mall, and his severed head was later recovered from a Vero Beach canal on August 10.

Lucas returned in October, discharged from a Maryland jail, and together the men contrived Frieda Powell's escape from a Polk County juvenile home. By January 1982, authorities were looking for the girl in Jacksonville, and she fled westward with Lucas, They were gone two days before Toole learned of their departure, and he lapsed into "a world of his own," pacing the floor and muttering over Henry's betrayal. He wandered to forget and killed along the way, reportedly claiming nine victims in six states between January 1982 and February 1983.

On May 23 and 31, 1983, two houses were burned in Toole's Jacksonville neighborhood. Teenage accomplices fingered Toole on June 6, and he freely confessed to setting an estimated 40 fires over the past two decades. Convicted of second-degree ARSON on August 5, he drew a term of 20 years in prison.

By that time, Lucas was singing in Texas, and Toole backed his partner up with more confessions. Toole's statements "cleared" 25 murders in 11 states, and he admitted participating with Lucas in another 108 homicides. A practicing cannibal, Toole also dropped hints about his interest in Satanism but stopped short of naming alleged fellow cult members.

On October 21, 1983, Toole confessed to the murder of Adam Walsh, startling Assistant Police Chief Leroy Hessler with details that were "grisly beyond belief." As Hessler told the media, "There are certain details only he could know. He did it. I've got details that no one else would know. He's got me convinced." In spite of that endorsement, officers reversed their stance a few weeks later, issuing statements that Toole was "no longer a suspect" in the crime.

Another troubling case harked back to 1974 and the carnage in Colorado Springs. Toole confessed to the massage parlor attack in September 1984, again providing details of the crime, but embarrassed prosecutors swiftly mounted their counterattack. After hours of hostile grilling, Toole threw in the towel. "Okay," he told authorities, "If you say I didn't kill her, maybe I didn't." (In a strange, unsatisfying compromise, Park

Estep was later released—on his first paroled bid—though his name was not formally cleared. The curious display of mercy by Colorado's parole board convinced some observers that the state accepted Toole's guilt but refused to publicly acknowledge a mistake.)

On April 28, 1984, Toole was convicted in Jacksonville of setting the fire that killed 64-year-old George Sonnenberg in January 1982. Sentenced to death for that crime, he was indicted one month later for the murder of 19-year-old Ada Johnson in Tallahassee, during February 1983. Conviction on that charge brought a second death sentence, but both were commuted to life imprisonment on appeal. In 1991, Toole pled guilty to four more slayings in Florida, receiving a superfluous quartet of new life sentences. Police in Hollywood, Florida, were reviewing the Adam Walsh case when Toole died of cirrhosis in September 1996, and authorities were embarrassed to learn that all traces of critical DNA evidence had vanished from their files. The case remains officially unsolved, though Adam's parents (and a number of police investigators) are convinced of Toole's guilt.

Ironically, Toole's name was seldom mentioned in the controversy over Henry Lucas's confessions and his later change of heart in April 1985. No effort has been made to challenge Toole's involvement in at least a score of homicides from coast to coast, and it is just as well, considering his dialogue with Lucas, taped by Texas Rangers in November 1983.

TOOLE: *Remember that one time I said I wanted me some ribs? Did that make me a cannibal?*

LUCAS: *You wasn't a cannibal, It's the force of the devil, something forced on us that we can't change. There's no reason denying what we become. We know what we are.*

TOOLE: *Remember how I liked to pour some blood out of them?*

LUCAS: *Ottis, you and I have become something people look on as an animal. There's no way of changing what we done, but we can stop it and not allow other people to become what we have. And the only way to do that is by honesty.*

TRIAL of Serial Killers

Our legal system guarantees the basic right of every criminal, no matter how sadistic or depraved, to mount a competent defense. In practice, it is only since the 1960s, with the liberal rulings of the U.S. Supreme Court under chief Justice Earl Warren, that suspect rights have been enforced with any uniformity. Before that era, "third-degree" tactics were commonplace if not routine and clearly produced miscarriages of justice, as when suspect Frank Dolezal was beaten into confessing the crimes of Cleveland's "MAD BUTCHER OF KINGSBURY RUN."

Defending serial killers in court is an arduous, unpopular, and sometimes hazardous occupation. While some defendants waive their right to an attorney, in a few—like THEODORE BUNDY—exercise their egos by defending themselves, most random slayers welcome the advice of counsel. Few are affluent enough to spring for big-name talent, though famous attorneys sometimes attach themselves to a high-profile case for publicity's sake. Boston attorney F. Lee Bailey inflated his reputation in the 1960s by defending serial slayers Charles Schmid and ALBERT DESALVO, while across the continent, Melvin Belli offered his services to the elusive "ZODIAC" as part of a vain effort to induce the killer's surrender. More often, public defenders or court-appointed lawyers inherit such cases, and a losing verdict is sometimes the least of their problems. Los Angeles attorney Ronald Hughes died mysteriously in November 1970 shortly after quarreling with client CHARLES MANSON, and some authorities still believe he was murdered by the drifter's homicidal "family." In other cases, lawyers defending a serial killer have more to fear from the public at large, as when New York attorneys Frank Armani and Francis Belge were threatened—and Belge was assaulted on the street—while defending three-time killer Robert Garrow.

As a practical matter, few serial killers are punished for all of their crimes. Some, like JOHN GACY and JUAN CORONA, plant their victims in close proximity, facilitating multiple convictions, but most are less considerate of the authorities. Where evidence is weak or nonexistent—as in many of the crimes attributed to Ted Bundy—prosecutors play their strongest hand, often settling for one or two murder charges in lieu of 15 or 20. Some jurisdictions stubbornly deny a killer's guilt for reasons best known to themselves, as in the case of San Diego's willful blindness to the crimes of CARROLL COLE. In other cases, politics and economics override the quest for justice, prosecutors ever mindful of the fact that trials cost money and taxpayers vote. Public opinion may demand indictment in a sensational case, but if the trial runs over budget—or results in an acquittal—every prosecutor understands the risk of backlash at the ballot box.

Prosecution, like politics, makes for strange bedfellows. Negotiations is part of the game, and a shortage of physical evidence sometimes mandates unsavory bargains for testimony. Child-slayer CLIFFORD OLSON holds the record for audacity, persuading the Royal Canadian Mounted Police to pay him $10,000 each for the bodies of 10 missing victims, but most such bargains are trade-offs, swapping reduced prison time—or complete immunity—for a guilty plea or testimony from a criminal accomplice. In San Francisco, Anthony Harris faced prosecution on two murder counts when he turned state's evidence against his fellow "Death Angels" in the notorious "ZEBRA" case in return for immunity. CHARLENE GALLEGO drew a lenient 16-year sentence (and is now at liberty) for helping place her husband on death row, while Linda Kasabian earned total immunity with her testimony in the Mason murder trial.

Dramatic trials make headlines, but 90 percent of American felony cases are settled with negotiated plea bargains, and serial murders are no exception. Few citizens complain when murderers are jailed for life, but cries of outrage are routine when a negotiated plea reduces or eliminates a first-degree murder charge, sometimes returning a compulsive killer to the street. In Florida, James Pough's first homicide was booked as manslaughter and bargained down to aggravated assault, earning Pough five years' probation; at the end of that term, his criminal record was expunged, allowing Pough to purchase legally the firearms with which he killed eight other victims. Nurse Mary Robaczynski admitted the slayings of four Maryland patients, but prosecutors threw in the towel after a mistrial, dropping all charges in return for the surrender of Robaczynski's nursing license. In Boston, attorney F. Lee Bailey negotiated a classic plea bargain for strangler Albert DeSalvo, 13 counts of murder lost in the shuffle as DeSalvo accepted a life term on rape and burglary charges.

Serial murder trials are often long and costly, particularly in California, where lawyers pride themselves on billing by the hour and moving with glacial speed. Charles Manson's first trial required a month of jury selection and eight months of testimony to land four defendants on death row. In the case of "Night Stalker" RICHARD RAMIREZ, jury selection took over three months, with nearly 3,000 interviews, while another nine months were consumed by the trial. RANDY KRAFT's Orange County murder trial lasted 13 months, costing the taxpayers more than $10 million. These cases pale, however, in comparison to the Los Angeles trial of "Hillside Strangler" ANGELO BUONO, with its 10-month preliminary hearing and two full years of testimony, dragging on from November 1981 through November 1983. The hands-down champion of delay and evasion, sadist CHARLES NG, was arrested by Canadian authorities in June 1985 on suspicion of killing more than a dozen victims in northern California. He stalled extradition until 1991 and managed to postpone his trial with a series of legal maneuvers; it finally commenced in September 1998, concluding with Ng's conviction in April 1999 and a death sentence in June

1999—more than 15 years after the discovery of his crimes.

Outright acquittals in cases of serial murder are rare but not unknown. Boston attorneys scored a surprise victory for defendant Mary Kelliher in 1908, persuading jurors that six of her close relatives had absorbed lethal doses of arsenic from a "contaminated mattress" over a three-year period. In New Jersey, Dr. Mario Jascalevich was acquitted of using curare to poison six patients, but adverse publicity surrounding the 12-year investigation drove him back to his native Argentina, where he died of a cerebral hemorrhage in 1984. Los Angeles jurors acquitted VAUGHN GREENWOOD of two murder counts in 1976, but conviction in nine other cases sent him to prison for life without parole. Eight years later, in another "Skid Row" case, Bobby Maxwell was convicted of two murders and acquitted of three more, while a hung jury left five counts unresolved. A similar compromise verdict in Indiana condemned shotgun slayer Christopher Peterson in four of seven "identical" slayings, while acquitting him of three. In Georgia, nurse Terri Rachals confessed three murders and was charged with six, but her precarious mental state prompted jurors to acquit on most of the charges, finding her guilty but mentally ill on one count of aggravated assault.

With 50 states and countless local jurisdictions trying murder cases every day, it is perhaps too much to hope for any semblance of consistency in sentencing. Since 1900, 68 percent of America's convicted serial killers been sentenced to varying prison terms; another 25 percent have been sentenced to die for their crimes, and 40 percent of those condemned have actually been executed.

California, boasting more serial killers than any other U.S. state and most foreign countries, moved to mitigate the cost of separate, repetitive trials in September 1998, with passage of a new "Serial Killer, Single Trial" statute. In an age when long-winded serial murder trials cost taxpayers an average of $1.5 million per victim, lawmakers viewed consolidation as the fiscal cure. Defense attorneys loudly disagreed, complaining that the single-trial requirement imposed crushing burdens on lawyers and placed their clients on a fast track to death row. "It allows district attorneys to pile on a lot of cases into one," said San Francisco public defender Jeff Brown, "and really undercuts the ability to mount a defense. It's not fair." To that, state senator Richard Rainey replied, "Serial killers who go on brutal killing rampages do so without consideration for county lines. The current system is not only a waste of time and money, but it causes unnecessary pain for victims and their loved ones." As for potential errors, district attorney Art Danner of Santa Cruz told reporters,

"There are enough safeguards in the language [of the statute] to protect any defendant."

See also CAPITAL PUNISHMENT; INCARCERATION; INSANITY DEFENSE

TROPHIES and Souvenirs Kept by Serial Killers

It has long been recognized that some killers, especially those driven by sexual or sadistic MOTIVES, retain personal objects taken from their victims as mementos of the event. In such cases, FBI analysts distinguish between *trophies* (collected by "ORGANIZED" KILLERS to commemorate a successful hunt) and *souvenirs* (kept by "DISORGANIZED" KILLERS as fuel for their fantasies), but since the items and their method of collection are identical, the distinction is largely semantic.

Items collected by serial slayers range from the mundane—snapshots, a driver's license, jewelry, or some article of clothing—to ghoulish and bizarre, including amputated body parts. Author Joel Norris labels such behavior as the "totem phase" of serial murder, wherein killers cling to symbols of their momentary triumph, hoping to prolong a satisfaction that evades them in reality. Other slayers strive for the same result by following their cases in the media, saving press clips or jotting their thoughts in a diary, even revisiting crime scenes despite the great personal risk.

For sheer outrageousness, no case to date can match ED GEIN's Wisconsin house of horrors—with skulls mounted on bedposts, skinned-out faces hanging on the walls, and dangling mobiles made from female body parts—but serial killers display no end of variety in their selections. JEROME BRUDOS photographed his victims and preserved one severed breast as a paperweight. Cannibal Stanley Baker carried the knuckle bones of one victim in a pouch on his belt, while Alex Mengel scalped a woman and wore her hair as a disguise in his next attempted kidnapping. Sadists LAWRENCE BITTAKER and Ian Brady recorded the screams of their tormented victims, while LEONARD LAKE and others have preserved their crimes on videotape. In Egypt, a prolific "BLUE BEARD" caught in April 1920 kept the severed heads of 20 women in his home.

An interesting (if inconclusive) aspect of the FBI's research suggests that random shooters are more prone to certain types of follow-up behavior than are hands-on killers. Bureau analysts divided their captive subjects into two groups, one for killers who used firearms exclusively, the other limited to slayers with a preference for sharp or blunt instruments. Eighty-two percent of the gunmen admitted following their cases in the press, while only 50 percent of the hands-on killers were interested. Of the shooters, 64 percent saved clippings about themselves and 56 percent kept diaries, versus 26 percent of the clubbers and hackers on both questions. Twenty-one percent of the gunmen photographed their victims, while only 11 percent of the manual killers brought cameras along. Gunmen were also marginally more likely to revisit crime scenes, 44 percent to 34 percent, but no significant difference was seen in collection of physical trophies. FBI spokesmen stop short of drawing conclusions from their data, but logic dictates that gunmen crave reaffirmation of their crimes since shooting is a more remote act, lacking the physical contact—and thus, satisfaction—of beating, stabbing, or strangling their victims to death.

See also MODUS OPERANDI; WEAPONS

TUGGLE, Debra Sue

The case of Debra Tuggle perfectly exemplifies how loopholes in "The System" may allow determined murderers to roam at large for years. As the rarest of predators—a black female serial killer of children—she fell through the cracks of a government network designed to protect those she killed, claiming at least five victims before she was brought to a semblance of justice. Sadly, even when her crimes had been revealed, the very agencies that should have stopped her killing spree a decade earlier were more concerned with bad publicity than human lives.

With 20/20 hindsight, it is easy to declare that Debra Tuggle never should have been allowed to have a child, much less the five she ultimately bore to different fathers in 11 years. She clearly lacked the temperament for motherhood, but there was something else at work in Tuggle's mind as well, beyond mere rage or boredom with the drudgery of her maternal role: a dark and deadly "something" that compelled her to eliminate the very lives she brought into the world.

Debra's first child, William Henry, was born in 1972. Eighteen months later he had a half-brother, Thomas Bates, and the pressure of raising them was mounting on Debra, pushing her over the edge. Both children died suddenly in 1974, Thomas barely two months old, William three months short of his second birthday. Physicians in Debra's hometown of Little Rock, Arkansas, were sympathetic to the grieving mother's plight. In the absence of physical symptoms, they blamed William's death on pneumonia, listing Thomas as a victim of SUDDEN INFANT DEATH SYNDROME (SIDS).

A third son, Ronald Johnson, was nine months old when he suddenly stopped breathing in 1976. Again, Debra's public display of grief was convincing; once again, SIDS was blamed for the death. Two years later, Tuggle shot herself in the abdomen, an apparent suicide attempt, and was briefly committed to a state hospital for treatment. The doctors there pronounced her "cured," and she was on the street in time to bear and kill her fourth child—Terranz Tuggle—at Malvern, Arkansas, in 1979. As far as Malvern's finest could determine, it was simply one more SIDS-related death.

For all her aversion to children, Debra seemed to enjoy men and sex. Gravitating back to Little Rock, she met George Paxton, 10 years her senior, on a blind date. They hit it off at once, and by early 1982, Paxton had asked Tuggle to share his home. If anyone asked, she was there to care for Paxton's three children, but Debra's duties were not limited to housekeeping. By the spring of 1983, she would herself be carrying a Paxton child.

But first, she had an urge to thin the herd.

On June 23, 1982, Paxton was out at the movies when Debra had him paged, sobbing out the news that his daughter, two-year-old Tomekia, was dead. She had no explanation, and the hospital demanded none. It was stretching credibility to blame SIDS for the death of a child Tomekia's age, but stranger things have happened in the world of pediatric medicine. Case closed.

Almost.

The news that she was pregnant in the spring of 1983 knocked Debra for a loop. That May, she tried to give herself a coat-hanger abortion, but she bungled the attempt. George Paxton's family doctor tried to have her booked for psychiatric treatment by the state, but his petition was denied. A healthy girl, G'Joy Paxton, was born in October 1983 . . . but Debra's time was swiftly running out.

It took an employee of the state mental health department, Dr. Alexander Merrill, to finally see through Tuggle's years of "bad luck" in November 1983. Merrill was the first to analyze a list of unrelated victim surnames, recognizing that a single woman had been linked to five child deaths within a decade. Pulaski County's coroner, Steve Nawajoczyk, was interested, and so were the police. On March 20, 1984, Debra was jailed on four counts of first-degree murder; Terranz Tuggle's case, in Malvern, remained "open." Two days later, the court set her bond at a prohibitive $750,000.

Little Rock physicians and Arkansas public health officials were quick to absolve themselves of any negligence in Tuggle's case. Debra's children each had different fathers, after all—and besides, her explanations of the sudden deaths were "credible." In retrospect, we know that "normal" SIDS does not haunt any given mother, claiming the lives of child after child, but Arkansas doctors appeared to be learning their craft by trial and error.

In custody, Tuggle admitted pressing a pillow over Tomekia's face to "stop her crying" while Debra watched television. She held the pillow in place for some two minutes with the desired result but claimed she still "didn't think Tomekia was dead." Only later—presumably when her program was finished—did the murderess realize her "mistake."

Skeptical jurors convicted Tuggle of first-degree murder on September 18, 1984, but they dredged up sympathy enough to recommend the statutory minimum sentence of 10 years in prison. Sentenced accordingly, Debra still faced one more trial, on charges of murdering her first three sons. Conviction on those charges could bring a death sentence, but Tuggle's luck had finally begun to change.

On December 7, 1984, Circuit Judge Floyd Lofton dismissed all three outstanding murder counts. There was no scientific evidence to indicate a homicide in Ronald Johnson's death, the judge declared, and state law barred the prosecution from using Tuggle's prior conviction on an identical crime to make the case. As far as Thomas Bates and William Henry were concerned, Judge Lofton ruled that the statute of limitations had run out on their deaths after 10 years of official inaction. Prosecutors vowed to appeal the ruling, but their efforts were futile, leaving Tuggle with the prospect of mandatory release at age 36 in 1994.

Dr. Merrill, meanwhile, had established a system for tracking suspicious SIDS deaths in Arkansas. He was hot on the trail of another sinister case—four deaths in one family—when his superiors fired him in January 1985. Officially, Merrill was canned for airing "unwarranted criticism" of state health officials. In his view, the doctor had been punished for "making waves" and exposing the foibles of a negligent bureaucracy.

No motive was advanced by prosecutors in the Tuggle case, but her behavior—including the bungled suicide attempt—points toward another case of MUNCHAUSEN'S SYNDROME BY PROXY, in which unstable mothers or other caregivers deliberately harm their charges, thriving on the resultant sympathy and attention. Then again, perhaps she simply hated children.

"TYLENOL Murders"

The unsolved "Tylenol murders" are unique among serial killings in that the slayer never actually saw his victims and had no idea of their identity or number until he (or she) was advised of the deaths by media reports. Perhaps predictably, by its very nature, the case has also had a greater impact on American society—and beyond—than any other case of serial murder in history.

The terror began on September 29, 1982, when 12-year-old Mary Kellerman, a resident of suburban Elks Grove Village near Chicago complained to her parents of a scratchy throat and sniffles. Treated with an Extra-Strength Tylenol capsule, Mary was found unconscious

on the bathroom floor next morning at 7:00 A.M. and she died three hours later at a local hospital. Autopsy results determined that the capsule Mary Kellerman ingested had contained a lethal mix of normal Tylenol and deadly cyanide.

Those results had yet to be reported on the afternoon of September 29 when three members of the Janus family, residing in another Chicago suburb, swallowed Extra-Strength Tylenol capsules and shortly collapsed. None of the three was saved, despite best efforts of physicians working around the clock.

With the body count at four and holding for the moment, a local firefighter, Lieutenant Phillip Cappitelli, began putting two and two together in his mind. He was aware of Mary Kellerman's death from conversations with a relative; now, with reports of the Janus triple poisoning on his police scanner, he huddled with coworkers, soon making the link between Extra-Strength Tylenol and four victims to date. Warnings were issued throughout greater Chicago on September 30, but three more victims had already been poisoned in the meantime, none of whom survived.

On October 1, 1982, the manufacturers of Extra-Strength Tylenol recalled some 264,000 bottles of their product from stores in Chicago and environs, while the U.S. Food and Drug Administration broadcast warnings for consumers to avoid the drug until such time as an investigation was completed. Four days later, the recall went nationwide after police in Oroville, California, blamed Tylenol laced with strychnine for the near-fatal convulsions suffered by victim Greg Blagg. By October 6, authorities in Canada, Great Britain, Norway, Italy, the Philippines, and South Korea were also taking steps to clear the suspect bottles from their shelves. The following day, authorities in Philadelphia retracted their suicide verdict in the April 3 death of a student, William Pascual, deciding the incident "might have been connected" to poisoned Tylenol capsules. A fresh examination of Extra-Strength Tylenol capsules found in Pascual's apartment found them contaminated with cyanide.

Back in Chicago, meanwhile, investigators traced the deadly capsules to the stores where they were purchased. On October 4, it was announced that one additional tainted bottle of Extra-Strength Tylenol had been found at each of five stores examined. Because of the small number found citywide, police concluded that the Tylenol was bought or stolen, "spiked" with poison by a lurking killer, then surreptitiously returned to store shelves. That judgment was buttressed on October 5 after medical examiners toured the Tylenol plant in Fort Washington, Pennsylvania. Cyanide *was* used at the plant, but security measures were tight, and the odds against in-house contamination were pegged at "a million to one."

The immediate result of the scare was a call for new and stricter safety features in the packaging of patent medicines. In Illinois, Cook County's board of supervisors passed an ordinance on October 4, 1982, requiring that all such containers sold within the county must have "tamper-proof" seals. The very next day, a federal task force convened to address the problem on a national basis. By October 6, Secretary of Health and Human Services Richard Schweiker had issued executive orders requiring tamper-resistant seals on all patent medicines and similar items designed for human consumption. Another step toward safety from random poisoning followed with invention of the "caplet"—that is, capsule-shaped (but solid) tablets that cannot be opened and contaminated.

Still, prevention was easier than punishment in this troubling case, where the lurking killer (or killers) left no clues behind. It is a testament to human nature that, with the Tylenol scare at its height, certain opportunistic felons tried to jump on the bandwagon, demanding cash to avert future poisonings, but while they went to prison on extortion charges, none was ever linked to the actual murders. There was also a brief rash of "copycat" crimes, with victims in Colorado and Florida injured, respectively, by eye drops and mouthwash tainted with acid. In the final analysis, homicide investigators in Illinois, California, and Pennsylvania could never decide if their poisoning cases were linked. Officially, the unknown "Tylenol killer" faces seven counts of murder for the crimes around Chicago, if and when police are able to identify a suspect. But at 23 years and counting since the crimes, it seems unlikely that the case will ever actually be solved.

UNSOLVED Murders

Apprehension of serial killers is not a foregone conclusion, by any means. In this century, 18 percent of all recognized repeat slayers have given detectives the slip, including at least four—BELLE GUNNESS, BELA KISS, Carl Menarik, and Randolph Dial—who eluded police *after* their identities and crimes were publicized. More common, by far, are stalkers like London's "JACK THE RIPPER" or the American "ZODIAC" and "MOONLIGHT MURDERER," whose crimes excite the public for a time before they simply fade from public consciousness, forever unidentified.

Various reasons typically advanced for the cessation of unsolved serial murders include speculation on the killer's death, imprisonment on unrelated charges, or commitment to a mental institution. In the absence of a name, however (and conclusive evidence connecting any given suspect to the crimes in question) such theories are nothing more than idle mind games. A more troubling notion—that certain serial killers voluntarily "retire" from the hunt—is less welcome to police and civilians alike, since it implies the slayer may resume his homicidal acts at any time as he or she sees fit.

FBI spokesmen are frequently asked to speculate on the number of unidentified serial killers at large in America. Their estimates typically range from 35 to 50, sometimes as high as 100, while critics claim the figures thus elicited are too conservative. The plain truth is that *no one knows* how many homicidal stalkers are at large on any given day. Police can only tabulate the cases they have recognized—that is, the ones in which repeated murders have been linked by circumstantial evidence. Another breed of killer, those who hide their victims well and leave no tracks behind, are automatically omitted from such estimates, since law enforcement has no clue that they exist.

JOHN GACY is a case in point, along with DEAN CORLL, JUAN CORONA, and Milwaukee's JEFFREY DAHMER. By themselves, these four men collectively claimed more than 100 victims without arousing police suspicion and were betrayed in the end by some careless mistake or a fluke of circumstance. Less prolific but luckier in the end, Eugene Butler spent the last seven years of his life in a North Dakota mental institution; he had been dead two years before construction workers razed his former home and found six corpses buried in the crawl space.

Author Carl Sifakis, in his *Encyclopedia of American Crime* (1982), speculates that the true American murder rate may be double the figure recorded each year if we consider MISSING PERSONS plus homicides disguised as accidental deaths or suicides. MEDICAL MURDERS are also sometimes difficult to recognize, certified as "natural" deaths by inexperienced doctors . . . or by the killer himself if he happens to be the attending physician. Homicide statistics are further skewed by the fact that victims discovered years after death—as with the 29 discovered on Gacy's property in 1978—are logged in the year of discovery, rather than the years in which they were murdered.

See also PROFILING

UNTERWEGER, Jack

A native of Styria, in southeastern Austria, Unterweger was the illegitimate son of an American soldier and an

Austrian prostitute. Born in 1951, he was raised among hookers and pimps, growing up wild with an unpredictable temper. He was a chronic truant by age nine and logged his first arrest at 16 for assaulting a prostitute. Over the next nine years, he accumulated 16 convictions—mostly for sexual attacks on women—and spent all but 12 months of that time behind bars. Briefly freed in 1976, he was charged with murder after he bludgeoned another streetwalker with an iron bar, then strangled her with her own brassiere. In court, he admitted his crime, telling the judge, "I envisioned my mother in front of me, and I killed her."

Sentenced to life imprisonment, Unterweger followed the lead of certain American convicts, reinventing himself as an author of "important" literature. Over the next 14 years, he produced various poems, plays, short stories, and an autobiography that made him the toast of Viennese café society. Influential Austrians petitioned the government for his release, and the "rehabilitated" killer was paroled on May 23, 1990. "That life is over now," he told the press. "Let's get on with the new."

And so he did. Overnight, Jack become a fixture on television talk shows, posing as a model of prison rehabilitation, enjoying most-favored-guest status at high-society cocktail parties. Money follows celebrity, and Unterweger sported designer clothes, drove a Ford Mustang with the license tag reading "Jack 1," and acquired a blond girlfriend the same age as his last victim. Unfortunately, Jack's "new life" was a charade. Austrian police report that Unterweger killed at least six prostitutes within his first 12 months of freedom.

In June 1991, Jack got a chance to take his show on the road. An Austrian magazine commissioned him to write about crime in Los Angeles. Winging off to L.A. with his lover, Unterweger wangled several ride-alongs with local police. He wrote a couple of articles, focusing primarily on Hollywood prostitutes, but Jack also had a more personal interest in his subject. The first victim, 35-year-old Shannon Exley, was found in Boyle Heights on June 20. Number two, 33-year-old Irene Rodriguez, was found in the same neighborhood 10 days later. Peggy Booth, age 26, was found dead in a Malibu canyon on July 10. All three women were hookers, all three had been savagely beaten before they were strangled with their own bras, and all three bodies were sexually violated with tree branches. (Some accounts refer vaguely to a fourth, unnamed victim in San Diego, but no charges were ever filed in that case.)

Unterweger was safely back in Austria by the time Interpol officials recognized descriptions of the L.A. killer's MODUS OPERANDI in February 1992. An Austrian SWAT team raided Unterweger's Vienna apartment, but their suspect was already gone, embarked

Jack Unterweger poses with a hangman's noose. (Author's collection)

with his teenage lover on a jaunt that would take them through Switzerland, France, and Canada and back once more to the United States. Along the way, he paused for telephone calls to the Austrian media, alternately taunting police and proclaiming his innocence. A trail of credit card receipts led manhunters to Miami, Florida, where Unterweger was captured without resistance. (His girlfriend told police they had chosen Miami as their refuge because she "liked Don Johnson," star of the *Miami Vice* TV series.)

In custody once more, Unterweger was accused of killing 11 prostitutes since his release from prison—six in Austria, three in Los Angeles, and two more in Czechoslovakia. The Czechs didn't want him, but Austria and the United States squabbled over jurisdiction, Jack's homeland winning out when Austrian officials agreed to try Unterweger for five foreign murders as well as the six committed on their own soil. Extradition was thereby approved, and Los Angeles authorities packed up their forensic evidence for shipment across the Atlantic.

Back home in Graz, Unterweger was indicted on 11 murder counts in August 1992, but legal maneuvers delayed his trial for nearly two years. The proceedings finally began on April 20, 1994, and lasted for two months, including testimony by FBI experts imported from Quantico, Virginia. Unterweger seemed confident throughout the trial, never failing to smile for the cameras, but evidence was mounting up against him. A bomb blast at the courthouse failed to disrupt jury deliberations on June 28, and Unterweger was convicted that afternoon on nine murder counts and acquitted of two others. The judge promptly sentenced him to life imprisonment in maximum security, but Unterweger had the last laugh. At 3:40 A.M. on June 29, jailers found him hanging from a curtain rod in his cell, the drawstring from his sweatpants looped around his neck. Several audio cassettes were recovered from his cell, but their content has never been divulged.

URDIALES, Andrew

Chicago native Andrew Urdiales was 13 years old in June 1978, when he beat the family dog to death with a baseball bat, then persuaded his parents the animal had broken its neck in an accidental fall. After high school, Urdiales joined the U.S. Marine Corps and was stationed at Camp Pendleton, in southern California, from 1984 to 1991. While still in uniform, he used his combat training to commit a string of gruesome murders that baffled Golden State authorities for a decade.

The first victim was 23-year-old Robbin Brandley, a fine arts student at Saddleback Community College in Mission Viejo, California. On the night of January 18, 1986, following a concert on campus, Urdiales attacked Brandley in a dimly lit parking lot, stabbing her 41 times in the back, neck, chest, and hands. Police were still puzzling over that crime in July 1988, when Urdiales claimed his second victim. Julie McGhee was a 29-year-old prostitute whom Urdiales shot repeatedly with a .45-caliber pistol, leaving her corpse near Cathedral City, in Riverside County. Two months later, on September 25, police found 31-year-old Mary Ann Wells, another prostitute, shot with the same pistol at an abandoned industrial complex in San Diego. The same gun was used again, on April 17, 1989, to kill 18-year-old streetwalker Tammy Erwin at Palm Springs.

After the Erwin slaying, Urdiales dismantled his pistol to scatter its parts far and wide. He left the Marine Corps with an honorable discharge in 1991, returning home to his parents in Chicago, but September 1992 found him back in southern California for a holiday. Nineteen-year-old Jennifer Asbenson accepted a ride to work from Urdiales, after he found her waiting at a bus stop, but she spurned his romantic advances. Returning at the end of her shift, he lured Asbenson with the offer of another ride, then held a knife to her throat and bound her hands, proceeding to the nearby desert where he raped Asbenson and choked her unconscious. Reviving in the trunk of her kidnapper's rented car, Asbenson managed to open the lid and escape on foot. Urdiales returned the car and flew home the same day.

Chicago acquaintances, unfamiliar with his history of adolescent sadism toward animals, described Urdiales as "different" after his stint in the Marine Corps. His childhood friend Gary Zabala later told reporters, "I think the Marines changed his life." Be that as it may, Urdiales took a hiatus from murder after Asbenson's escape. He would not kill again until March 1995, on another California visit. There, he met 32-year-old prostitute Denise Maney working the streets of Cathedral City and drove her to the desert. As Urdiales later described the event to police, he bound Maney and raped her, then stuck a .45-caliber pistol in her mouth and "blew the back of her head off." He then stripped the corpse of all clothing and possessions, leaving it for desert scavengers.

Andrew Urdiales (AP Photo/Illinois Dept. of Corrections)

Success in far-off California seemingly persuaded Urdiales that it would be safe to hunt at home. While working as a security guard at a store in downtown Chicago, Urdiales spent his free time trolling for prostitutes in suburban Hammond, Indiana. His first home-town victim was 25-year-old Laura Uylaki, a Hammond resident found floating in Cook County's Wolf Lake on April 14, 1996. Uylaki had been shot twice in the head with a .38-caliber pistol. Exactly two months later, on July 14, police hauled 21-year-old Cassandra Corum from the Vermillion River in Livingston County, 90 miles south of Chicago. The Hammond woman had been shot and stabbed repeatedly. On August 2, 1996, the action shifted back to Wolf Lake, with discovery of 22-year-old Lynn Huber.

Later in 1996, Chicago police detained Urdiales for a weapons violation involving that same .38, but he was released without charges. In April 1997, a Hammond prostitute fled screaming from his car after Urdiales flashed a gun and tried to handcuff her. Police arrested Urdiales on April 23, and ballistics tests on his weapon were still in progress when he confessed eight murders and the rape of Jennifer Asbenson. Lab reports confirmed that the .38 registered to Urdiales had indeed killed victims Uylaki, Corum, and Huber. His confessions were chilling, including admissions that Urdiales "was turned on by watching women suffer." Often, he said, victims begged for their lives, saying things like " 'Please don't kill me' and the usual babbling." Palm Springs detective John Booth described his conversation with Urdiales as "the worst interview I've ever had. He just sat there and said things like, 'Then I blew her head off,' like it was no big deal."

Despite that calm facade, Urdiales was placed on a round-the-clock suicide watch following his formal arraignment on April 29, 1997. Chicago authorities filed two murder counts against him (Uylaki and Huber), while prosecutors in California and downstate Illinois prepared other cases. Formal Cook County indictments followed on May 13, while Urdiales was held without bail. A new arraignment followed on June 13, 1997, at which time Urdiales pleaded not guilty. Legal wrangling over capital punishment in Illinois state courts postponed further progress in the case until April 30, 2001, when prosecutors filed a notice of intent to seek the death penalty against Urdiales. His trial for the murders of Lynn Huber and Laura Uylaki began on April 8, 2002, including reports from one psychiatrist that Urdiales claimed a history of childhood molestation. Siblings refuted that story, and jurors convicted Urdiales of both murder counts on May 23. The same panel imposed a death sentence on May 30, 2002.

The story might have ended there, bogged down in long-winded appeals spanning years or decades, but Illinois was rocked by a series of scandals at the turn of the new millennium, involving gross misconduct by police and prosecutors in high-profile capital cases. In the 1990s, private investigators from Northwestern University's Center on Wrongful Convictions revealed evidence of coerced confessions and suppressed exculpatory evidence that freed 17 Illinois inmates from death row. Finally, on January 11, 2003, outgoing governor George Ryan proclaimed that "the Illinois capital punishment system is broken." By executive order, he commuted all death sentences still pending in the state—167 condemned men and women in all, including Andrew Urdiales.

Angry appeals of Ryan's decision proved fruitless in court, but Illinois prosecutors still had another shot at Urdiales, for the murder of Cassandra Corum in Livingston County. Facing another death sentence under revised rules of procedure, Urdiales changed his game plan on April 24, 2004, revising his INSANITY DEFENSE to a plea of "guilty but mentally ill." Prosecutor Michael Hood denigrated that claim while branding Urdiales "a cold, calculated killing machine" who had "honed his craft" through successive murders. Defense attorney Stephen Richards told reporters, "Any serial-killer case is going to be used as a poster child for the death penalty. However, [Urdiales] has serious mental health issues and suffered abuse. You can't just look at what the number of murders is." Judge Harold Frobish disagreed, rejecting the defendant's plea and convicting Urdiales of first-degree murder on May 10, 2004. Two weeks later, a jury chosen for the trial's penalty phase imposed a new death sentence. California prosecutors have suggested that they may wish to try Urdiales for his murders in that state, but no extradition requests had been filed when this work went to press.

VACHER, Joseph

Known to history as the "French Ripper," Vacher was one of the few serial killers on record who looked and acted the part in daily life. Born in 1869, the last of 15 children in a poor farming family in southeastern France, Vacher was known throughout his life for erratic fits of temper. He joined the French army in 1890, published accounts disagreeing on whether he was drafted or enlisted voluntarily. In any case, Vacher seemed to enjoy military service at first, striving hard to earn the rank of corporal. When his promotion was delayed—unjustly, in his view—Vacher attempted suicide by slashing his throat with a razor. The wound was not fatal, and his superiors were so impressed with Vacher's dedication to the service that they hastened his promotion.

It soon became apparent that Corporal Vacher had serious problems. He intimidated his fellow soldiers, eyeing their throats and mumbling comments about "flowing blood," to the point that some of them complained and Vacher was sent to the infirmary for observation. Out on sick leave, he met a young woman at Baumes-des-Dames and fell in love at first sight. The lady did not spurn him outright, but her response was cool enough to provoke one of Vacher's tantrums. Whipping out a pistol in the midst of an argument, he shot the woman three times (she survived) and then turned the gun on himself. No great marksman, even at point-blank range, Vacher survived his second suicide attempt with a damaged right eye and a partially paralyzed face. Committed to the Asylum of Saint-Ylle, Vacher behaved in such outrageous style that even the most violent of his fellow inmates gave him a wide

berth. Transferred to the Asylum of Saint-Robert in 1893, he seemed to improve dramatically—so much so, in fact, that doctors released him as "cured" on April 1, 1894.

Vacher started drifting, adopting a vagrant lifestyle, hiking from one town to the next with no clear destination in mind. What he *did* have in mind was the sadistic rape and murder of anyone who caught his fancy, a homicidal compulsion which claimed at least 11 lives (some accounts say 14; one claims 26) before his next arrest, in August 1897. Gender seemed irrelevant to Vacher, though he apparently murdered more women than men. His first known victim was 21-year-old Eugénie Delhomme, a factory girl Vacher stabbed, disemboweled, and raped after death near Vienne in June 1894. Most of the victims that followed were farm workers, each in turn stabbed to death, then raped and grossly mutilated after death, some of the bodies bearing human bite marks. Authorities discerned a pattern from descriptions of a filthy, scar-faced tramp seen in the neighborhood of several homicides, but no one seemed to know the drifter's name and tracing him took time.

On August 4, 1897, Vacher spied a woman collecting pine cones in the Bois des Pelleries and attacked her, but she fought back with surprising strength, screaming for help. Her husband, children, and several neighbors rushed to the scene, overpowered Vacher, and dragged him to the local inn, where he entertained his captors with accordion music while waiting for police to arrive. Charged with the relatively minor crime of offending public decency, Vacher was sentenced to three months in jail. For reasons yet unknown, he then wrote a confession to 11 homicides and mailed it to the court, explaining that his crimes were committed "in a moment of frenzy." Vacher blamed his bloodlust on the bite of a rabid dog, allegedly suffered when he was eight years old. Prolonged examination by psychiatrists determined that he was mentally fit to stand trial for murder.

Despite Vacher's written confession, he was charged with only one slaying—that of Victor Portalier, a young shepherd killed at Tournon in 1895. Vacher's trial was held at the Ain Assizes in October 1898, highlighted by his outbursts and posturing in court. At one point, he lurched erect from his seat, shouting, "Glory to Jesus! Long live Joan of Arc! Glory to the great martyr of our time! Glory to the great savior!" Despite his performance, jurors found him sane and guilty as charged. Vacher was sentenced to die and was dragged kicking and screaming to the guillotine on December 31, 1898.

VAKRINOS, Dimitris

A quick-tempered Greek who stopped growing at five feet four inches, taxi driver Dimitris Vakrinos was arrested on April 9, 1997, at the climax of a one-man crime spree that had spanned the best part of a decade. In custody, he confessed to five murders, six attempted murders, one attempted rape, four armed robberies, and one attempted robbery. His victims were to blame, Vakrinos told police, for having mocked his sawed-off stature. Held without bail pending trial, Vakrinos committed suicide on May 12, using his own shoelaces to hang himself from a showerhead in the prison's isolation ward—a trick, ironically, that might have proven unsuccessful for a taller man.

"VALLEY Killer"

The scenic Connecticut River Valley forms a natural border between the states of New Hampshire and Vermont—a generally quiet, peaceful place in which to live. And yet, since 1978, the region has been terrorized by two vicious serial killers. One was captured and incarcerated for his crimes in 1983; the other—and more lethal of the two—remains at large today.

The first confirmed victim of the faceless stalker known to locals as the "Valley Killer" was 26-year-old Cathy Millican, an enthusiastic birdwatcher, last seen alive on September 24, 1978, when she drove to a wetlands preserve at New London, New Hampshire, to practice her hobby. She failed to return home that night, and her body was found the next day, sprawled near a path through the wetlands, her clothing disarranged, her belongings scattered along the trail as if she had been dragged for some distance. Millican was killed by stab wounds to the throat, after which her slayer drove

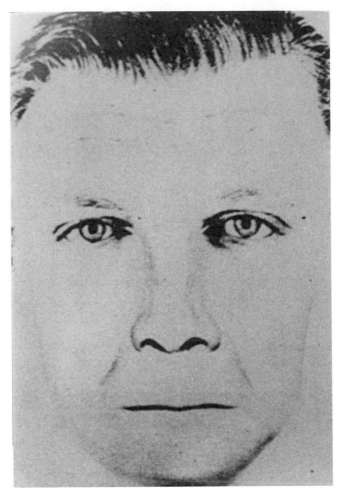

Police sketch of the "Valley Killer" (Author's collection)

the knife repeatedly into her lower body, clearly a sadistic sexual attack.

Police were still puzzling over that case a year later when 13-year-old Sherry Nastasia was reported missing in Springfield, Vermont. Skeletal remains, found on December 13, included a broken leg and fractured ribs, but the cause of death was tentatively fixed as strangulation. Twelve-year-old Theresa Fenton, who was abducted while riding her bike in Springfield on August 29, 1981, was found alive the next day. Hopelessly injured by a savage beating, she died on August 31. The next victim, 11-year-old Caty Richards, was kidnapped on April 9, 1983, and found beaten to death the next day, but this time a witness was able to describe the killer and his car. Suspect Gary Schaefer was quickly arrested and later confessed to the murders of Fenton and Richards, plus the abduction of a female hitchhiker who managed to escape his clutches in November 1982. In December 1983, he pled no contest to one murder count (Richards) and one charge of kidnapping (the survivor). Schaefer never admitted involvement in

Sherry Nastasia's death, but most investigators think he is responsible for that crime as well.

The other "Valley Killer," meanwhile, seems to have gone on hiatus while Schaefer was playing his cat-and-mouse game with police around Springfield. His next presumed victim was 17-year-old Bernice Courtemanche, last seen alive on May 30, 1984, when she left her job as a nurse's aide at the Sullivan County Nursing Home, in Beauregard Village, New Hampshire. A coworker drove Bernice to nearby Claremont, where she announced her intention of hitchhiking to Newport for a visit with her boyfriend. Bernice never arrived; authorities feared that she may have drowned in the flood tide of a nearby river. Their hopes for a "natural" solution to the mystery were dashed on April 19, 1986, when skeletal remains were found by two fishermen near Kellyville, New Hampshire. Bernice was identified from dental records three days later, knife marks on her cervical vertebrae indicating she was stabbed to death.

In the two years between Bernice's disappearance and the discovery of her remains, the Valley Killer had already claimed three more victims. Ellen Fried, a 26-year-old nurse, was last seen alive on the night of July 10, 1984, and reported missing after she missed two days of work at Valley Regional Hospital in Claremont. Her car was found soon after, parked on a narrow forest lane nearby, but it was September 19, 1985, before her skeleton was found at Newport, New Hampshire. Fried was identified on October 1, and while the first autopsy failed to note a cause of death, subsequent reexamination found apparent knife wounds, listing her death as a homicide by stabbing.

Eva Morse, a single mother with one 10-year-old daughter, arrived at her regular job in Charlestown, New Hampshire, at 7:00 A.M. on July 10, 1985, but never punched in. Instead, she lingered barely long enough to make a telephone call, then told her supervisor that she was going home sick. A coworker who spoke with Morse before she left would later tell police that Eva was bound for Claremont, hitchhiking to visit her one-time lesbian lover. As word of her disappearance spread, a motorist reported giving Morse a lift to the Charlestown-Claremont line, and there she vanished—until loggers found her skeleton on April 25, 1986, the skull nearly severed by stab wounds.

Lynda Moore was the next to die, found stabbed to death in the kitchen of her home at Saxtons River, Vermont—south of Springfield—when her husband came home from work on April 15, 1986. The medical examiner counted more than two dozen stab wounds to her throat and abdomen, plus defensive cuts on both hands and arms. Moore's husband was initially suspected by police, as every spouse is suspect in such cases, but investigation swiftly cleared him of involvement in the crime.

The Valley Killer's apparent medical fetish resurfaced in January 1987 when he chose another nurse as his next victim. Barbara Agnew, 36, lived in Norwich, Vermont, and worked part-time at Mary Hitchcock Memorial Hospital across the river in Hanover, New Hampshire. She was last seen alive on January 10 after a day of skiing with a friend near Winhall, Vermont. Three days later, her wallet and a woman's blood-stained clothing were found in the dumpster at a gas station south of White River Junction, Vermont, and a call to Agnew's workplace confirmed that she was missing. Her car was found abandoned on January 14 at a highway rest stop in Hartford, Vermont; police noted that her skis were missing, although her poles and boots were left behind. Agnew's remains, preserved intact by frigid weather, were found by hikers near Hartland, Vermont, on March 28. An autopsy revealed multiple stab wounds to the neck, apparently inflicted from behind, plus gashes to the lower abdomen that had become the Valley Killer's signature.

By this time, homicide investigators had their eyes on two more unsolved murders from the area, one dating back to June 11, 1968, when 15-year-old Jo Anne Dunham vanished from Claremont, New Hampshire. Found strangled the next day, her death bore no resemblance to the unknown slasher's crimes, but police noted that her corpse was found within a mile of the point where Eva Morse was last seen alive.

Another victim, 25-year-old Elizabeth Critchley, had disappeared on July 25, 1981, while hitchhiking from Massachusetts to her home in Vermont. Found two weeks later at Unity, New Hampshire, she had not been stabbed, but neither could the coroner determine any other cause of death. Her body had been found three miles from Gary Schaefer's home, and while authorities had questioned him about the case, he was never positively linked to Critchley's death. In fact, police now saw that her body had been dumped within two miles of the point where Eva Morse and Jo Anne Dunham were slain.

To this day, authorities cannot agree on whether victims Dunham and Critchley belong on the Valley Killer's hit list. They feel more confidence concerning Jane Boroski, a pregnant 22-year-old who was attacked at a country store on Route 9, south of Keene, New Hampshire, on the night of August 6, 1988. An unknown man approached Boroski in the parking lot, dragging her out of her car, and pulled a knife when she fought back. At one point in their scuffle, when she asked why he had chosen her, the man replied, "You beat up my girlfriend." Boroski denied it, and the man appeared confused. "Isn't this a Massachusetts car?" he asked. Boroski pointed out New Hampshire license plates, and the stranger hesitated, began to turn away, then rushed her with the knife again. Boroski was stabbed before approaching headlights caused her attacker to flee, but she survived her wounds and gave birth to a healthy daughter two months later.

Boroski also described her assailant for police, assisting in the preparation of a sketch that was widely published throughout the Connecticut River Valley. In 1991, the crime was reenacted—and the sketch displayed for a national audience—on TV's *Unsolved Mysteries*, hosted by Robert Stack. The program had a history of clearing unsolved crimes, but there were no leads generated in Boroski's case. The Valley Killer, though apparently "retired" since August 1988, is unidentified and still at large today.

VAMPIRISM and Serial Murder

"Blood sports" are a fairly common form of sexual activity in modern society, with certain nightclubs and role-playing games devoted to make-believe vampires. The wise practitioners of such pastimes are frugal in consumption and take care with hygiene in this age of AIDS, but serial killers with a literal lust for blood (hematomania) predictably take the game to fatal extremes.

There have probably always been flesh-and-blood vampires among us throughout history. If Countess ERZSEBET BÁTHORY's infamous bloodbaths belong more to fable than fact, still it is known that she and her aristocratic predecessor GILLES DE RAIS used blood spilled from their victims as a prime ingredient for pagan rituals and alchemy. More recently, FRITZ HAARMANN killed more than tow dozen German youths by biting out their throats, and Britain's JOHN HAIGH claimed to drink the blood of victims whom he robbed and murdered, prior to dunking them in acid baths. Wayne Boden, the Canadian "Vampire Rapist," also tapped his female victims as a source of blood, his crimes mimicked by Marcelo de Andrade in Brazil and John Crutchley in Florida.

Some delusional subjects regard themselves as literal vampires, requiring periodic blood infusions to survive. One such was California's Richard Trenton Chase: convinced that some unspecified disease was "drying up" his blood, he killed repeatedly for refills to replenish his supply. More often, though, the thirst for blood is sexual in nature, akin to CANNIBALISM in that it allows the vampire to "possess"—indeed, consume—his victim on the most intimate possible terms.

Curiously, there may also be an occasional profit motive for vampirism, as suggested in a case reported from Colombia. There, in the city of Cali, 10 adolescent boys were found dead between October 1963 and February 1964, their bodies drained of blood and dumped in vacant lots. Pathologists blamed the deaths on deliberate exsanguination, suggesting that a black-market "blood ring" was killing children and selling their blood for $25 per quart. Two surviving victims, a pair of 12-year-old twins, went missing for four days in December 1963; found in badly weakened condition, they described a house where they and other boys were held against their will and injected with drugs to make them sleep. What happened next is anybody's guess, however, since the house was never found and the Cali "vampire" murders remain unsolved.

See also PARAPHILIA

VANNI, Mario   *See* "MONSTER OF FLORENCE"

VICAP: Law enforcement tool

While FICTION AND FILM have wildly exaggerated the role of FBI agents in pursuing and capturing serial killers, the Bureau *does* play a part in tracking such predators. The "chase" is typically a mental exercise of PROFILING unknown subjects, with most of the work done in basement quarters at the FBI Academy in Quantico, Virginia, by members of the Bureau's Investigative Support Unit (formerly Behavioral Science). Accurate profiling requires input from detectives working on the case, wherever they may be, and that information is collected through VICAP—the FBI's Violent Criminal Apprehension Program.

VICAP was the brainchild of retired Los Angeles police commander Pierce Brooks, a veteran of serial murder investigations dating from the 1950s, who recognized the glaring lack of any information network geared to track nomadic killers on the move. In Brooks's day, the only antidote to "LINKAGE BLINDNESS" in such cases was exhaustive study of long-distance news reports or steady correspondence with other (sometimes hostile) law enforcement agencies. Computers offered the obvious solution, and Brooks told anyone who would listen of his plans for a nationwide network designed to collect and compare details of unsolved crimes, thus charting patterns that might otherwise be missed.

Retained by the FBI in 1981, Brooks and former Seattle detective Robert Keppel began hammering out the VICAP framework, drafting an investigating questionnaire for local officers, but they still had far to go, in terms of winning over the Washington bureaucracy. Best-selling author Ann Rule beat the drum of VICAP with a series of editorials in 1982, joining Brooks and others to plead the FBI's case in July 1983 Senate hearings. A year later, in June 1984, President Ronald Reagan announced the creation of a National Center for Analysis of Violent Crime, charged with the primary goal of tracking repeat killers. The VICAP computer network, based at the FBI Academy, went on-line in May 1985, accepting reports of murders and MISSING PERSONS and discarded corpses from across the nation.

Unlike fictional G-men and -women, members of the VICAP team and ISU are paid to analyze crimes rather than to conduct active field investigations. With fewer than a dozen full-time agents, ISU is not equipped for staging manhunts, crashing into suspect hideouts, or gunning down desperate killers. On the rare occasions when VICAP agents *do* visit a crime scene, their function is purely advisory, reviewing local task force operations and suggesting more efficient means of handling information. The national program's success or failure ultimately hinges on cooperation from local agencies, where jealousy, resentment, or simple fatigue sometimes conspire to frustrate VICAP.

Six months of operation was enough to highlight VICAP's problems in the field. Overworked police considered the 44-page federal questionnaire too cumbersome and time consuming. If a killer picked off 10 or 15 victims and the FBI required a separate questionnaire for each, some locals opted to ignore the federal team and spare themselves a case of writer's cramp. The current VICAP forms are two-thirds shorter than their predecessors, but reduced paperwork has not solved all the Bureau's problems in coordinating manhunts. For many local officers, the FBI is still J. Edgar Hoover once removed, a headline-grabbing agency more interested in claiming credit for recovery of stolen cars and the arrest of "Top Ten" fugitives than helping out the average working cop. Some Bureau spokesmen are still too quick to shoot from the lip—as when an agent in Atlanta blamed anonymous black parents for the deaths of several murdered children—and many police departments still view the feds as rank interlopers, their very presence a tacit indictment of local methods.

A VICAP case where everything apparently worked out as planned occurred in Wilmington, Delaware, where five young prostitutes were tortured to death between November 1987 and October 1988. FBI profilers reviewed the case evidence, sketching a portrait of a suspect who was white, a local resident employed in the construction trade, age 25 to 35, fascinated with police work, and using a van for transport and disposal of his victims. Fiber samples taken from bodies narrowed down the range of carpeting inside the van, and VICAP agents recommended a decoy operation to lure the killer with policewomen disguised as hookers. One such decoy managed to obtain some carpet fibers and a license number for the "creepy" trick whose manner-

isms set alarm bells ringing in her mind, and surveillance was established on suspect Steven Pennell. A 31-year-old white man, Pennell was a professional electrician, with two college semesters of criminology behind him. His applications to local police departments had all been rejected, but he clearly fit the VICAP profile as a "police buff." Scientific analysis of hairs, fibers, and bloodstains from his van convinced a jury of Pennell's guilt in two murders, and he was executed by lethal injection on March 14, 1992.

VICAP spokesmen often cite Pennell's case as proof positive of their success in profiling killers, but Delaware authorities—while grateful for the FBI's help—are more reserved. The fiber evidence was critical, they grant, but it had not connection to the suspect profile, which local investigators now describe as "most general stuff." The decoy operation was standard police work, they say, and would have caught Pennell regardless of his occupation, race, or age.

Sour grapes? A touch of jealousy, perhaps? In any case, while many frontline homicide investigators readily acknowledge VICAP's value in connecting far-flung crimes, some still insist that the program (in their opinion) has yet to prove itself capable of identifying a specific predator and bringing him to justice.

ViCLAS: Law enforcement tool

ViCLAS—the Violent Crime Analysis Linkage System—was the brainchild of Canada's first criminal profiler, Sergeant Ron MacKay. Assigned to the General Investigative Section of the Royal Canadian Mounted Police (RCMP) in North Vancouver, MacKay envisioned a system that would improve on the FBI's VICAP program for linking unsolved homicides and sexual assaults across the country. When MacKay conceived his idea in August 1990, the RCMP already maintained its Major Case File at headquarters in Ottawa, but most local police departments refused to submit the voluminous paperwork required for case submissions. MacKay and colleague Keith Davidson sought to remedy that problem with computers, recruiting two students at Ottawa's Algonquin College—Paul Leury and John Ripley—to write the necessary software programs.

Although actively employed from 1992, ViCLAS was formally unveiled on December 16, 1993, with a press conference held at the Ontario Provincial Police Academy outside Toronto. Present for the system's public launch were various RCMP leaders, together with officers from 23 Canadian law enforcement agencies, the FBI, New York State Police, New Jersey State Police, and members of Iowa's Sex Crimes Analysis Section. Administration of ViCLAS was assigned to the new

Canadian Association of Violent Crime Analysts (CAVCA).

Like VICAP, the ViCLAS program requires submission of detailed questionnaires from field investigators. Submission forms consist of a 36-page booklet with 245 questions (cut from an original 262 in 1995) or a shorter eight-page form with 83 questions. Within 18 months of its launch, ViCLAS had drawn 57 links among 584 unsolved cases on file. By the end of 1995, the system permitted MacKay to estimate that Canada hosted 12 to 20 active serial killers at large. While some resistance lingers, voluntary ViCLAS submissions increased from 124 cases in 1992 (the year before its formal launch) to 120,362 cases by September 2001.

Since its inception, interest in ViCLAS has spread rapidly around the world. Authorities in Austria and the Netherlands committed to its use on February 9, 1995, four days before MacKay presented the system at an international conference in China. Since then, ViCLAS has been adopted in Australia, Sweden, and several U.S. states. FBI agent Mike Cryan, assigned to the VICAP program at Quantico, Virginia, described ViCLAS as "the Cadillac system in the world," and VICAP pioneer David Cavanaugh (at Harvard University) was equally impressed. "The Canadians," Cavanaugh said, "have done to automated case linkage what the Japanese did with assembly line auto production. They have taken a good American idea and transformed it into the best in the world." On December 13, 1995, summarizing police failures in the case of Ontario TEAM KILLERS Paul Bernardo and Karla Homolka, Justice Archie Campbell recommended that ViCLAS submissions should be mandatory throughout the province. He wrote:

> Experience shows that it is not enough merely to encourage ViCLAS reporting by means of the standard policies and procedures of individual forces. Encouragement is not enough. Unless the entry of information into ViCLAS is centrally mandated and enforced throughout Ontario, and its operation supported through training and strong reinforcement of the reporting requirement, its power to link predatory serial crimes is greatly weakened.

Despite such widespread praise and multiple requests from its own analysts, FBI headquarters remains stubbornly opposed to adoption of ViCLAS in place of VICAP. Given the bureau's history and elitist attitudes, that resistance is unlikely to subside in the near future.

VICTIMOLOGY of Serial Murder

While serial killers in FICTION AND FILM are often depicted as twisted geniuses or mute, unfeeling beasts, selecting their prey by means so convoluted that it takes a psychic or computer wizard to unravel their design, the truth is rather different. In fact, the real-life victims of random slayers are as ordinary as their killers first appear to be. Their ranks include male and female, young and old, all races, affluent and destitute, well-educated and illiterate. They are drifters and debutantes, housewives and hookers, retirees and runaways, with the occasional celebrity thrown in. Some are aware of the risk when they take to the streets; others are hopelessly blind to their danger when murder comes calling at home. Indeed, the only trait they share in common is their moment in the spotlight of a killer's twisted fantasy.

Male murder victims in America normally outnumber females three to one, but serial killers nearly reverse that trend, claiming 65 percent female victims and 35 percent male. Victims both sexes range from infants to the elderly, depending on the killer's personal quirk. In terms of ethnic breakdown, American serial murder victims are 89 percent Caucasian and 10 percent black; Asians and Native Americans divide the other one percent. Forty-two percent of America's serial slayers target victims of the opposite sex exclusively, while 16 percent kill only same-sex victims; 39 percent kill at least one victim of each sex, and the offender's sex remains unknown in 3 percent of all cases, with the killers still at large, unseen by living witnesses. Ninety-four percent of America's "normal" murders involve killers and victims of the same race, but serial slayers fall below the norm, with 65 percent of their recorded murders in the same-race category; another 10 percent kill only members of a different race, while 11 percent cross the color line impartially, from one crime to the next. (A lack of evidence leaves the killer's race unknown in 14 percent of American cases.)

In terms of selection, some 40 percent of America's serial stalkers choose their prey on the basis of gender, with female victims outnumbering males by a ratio of 10-to-1. (Male victims selected by gender alone normally fall prey to homosexual killers, a group outnumbered 6-to-1 by "straight" serial slayers.) Potential profit ranks second on the list of criteria for victim selection in serial murder, accounting for 7 percent of American cases. "BLUEBEARD" killers and "BLACK WIDOWS" are especially prone to kill for cash, but the FBI's *Crime Classification Manual* (1992) presents a wide range of "criminal enterprise" MOTIVES, all founded in greed, which may apply to serial killers.

Age is the next most common factor in serial victim selection, with 6 percent of America's random killers preying on children or the elderly. A victim's health or physical condition is the killer's prime consideration in 3 percent of American serial murders, generally involving MEDICAL MURDERS. Race is the dominant factor in victim selection for 2 percent of America's predators, while another 2 percent apparently choose victims on the basis of their residence (or lack of same, where killers like VAUGHN GREENWOOD prey on homeless targets).

A victim's specific appearance—as opposed to general characteristics of sex, race, or age—seems to be the prime criterion for selection in 1 percent of American serial murders. (William Hanson, San Francisco's "Paper Bag Killer," shot only middle-aged men who walked with a limp, mistaking each in turn for the man who once raped his sister.) Occupations doom another 1 percent of American serial victims, with prostitutes of both sexes dominating the list of job-related murders. (College coeds and exotic dancers also rank significantly among victims of choice.) Finally, 13 percent of American serial killers appear to change their criteria for victim selection over time—as when Robert Shawcross switched from killing children in the early 1970s to prostitutes in 1989—while the basis for selection is unknown in 12 percent of all reported cases.

Except in contract murders, where a victim is selected for the killer by third parties, serial killers generally seek out "targets of opportunity," taking victims as they come to minimize personal risk. This trait, at least to some degree, accounts for the frequent victimization of prostitutes and hitchhikers, both of whom (although for very different reasons) specialize in catching rides with total strangers. Other "easy marks" include the homeless, couples parked in a secluded lover's lane, patients in hospitals or rest homes, and victims surprised in their own beds by lethal home invaders. Wherever they strike, psychologists and law enforcement officers agree, serial killers behave much like predators in the wild, stalking the weak and unwary, lying in wait for their prey as they thin out the herd.

See also MODUS OPERANDI

VLASSAKIS, John   *See* SNOWTOWN

WAGNER, Robert   *See* SNOWTOWN

WANG Ganggang

Little background information is available today on China's most prolific serial killer, since state security forces imposed a gag rule on his case in 2003. Officials say that Wang Ganggang was born in Henan Province in July 1968, and ran away from home in 1985. Wang's parents described him as an introverted and studious child who did well in a village boarding school before he left at age 17 to work in a coal mine. His last known residence in Zhengyang County was a thatched hut with one piece of furniture, a 20-year-old bed, illuminated by a single 15-watt lightbulb. He traveled widely as a rootless drifter, known by a list of pseudonyms, including Yang Liu, Yang Xinhai, and Yang Zhiya. Traversing four provinces on a bicycle, Wang worked odd jobs to survive, employed most often as a cook at various construction sites. In 1996, he received a five-year sentence for attempted rape at Zhumadian, in Henan Province.

Following his release from custody in 1999 or 2000 (reports differ), Wang was abandoned by his girlfriend. That rejection sparked an epic killing spree, beginning in winter 2000, as Wang invaded rural homes and slaughtered whole families in the style of Ukrainian "Terminator" ANATOLY ONOPRIENKO. Variously armed with a hammer, meat cleaver, or shovel, Wang claimed at least 67 lives and raped an estimated 25 women during a two-year rampage, including 26 attacks in Anhui, Hebei, Henan, and Shandong Provinces. Several crime scenes revealed evidence of necrophilia. Wang typically wore gloves, leaving a bloodied white pair at one crime scene, and he often donned oversized clothing and shoes to confuse witnesses. Police captured him on November 3, 2003, during "a routine inspection of entertainment venues" in Hebei Province.

While most details of Wang's crime spree were suppressed by official order, the *Guangzhou Daily* told its readers: "His methods were extremely cruel—he didn't leave survivors, and more than a few families were exterminated by his hand." Conflicting reports claimed that five or 10 victims survived with serious head wounds. Authorities described the MOTIVES for Wang's crimes as rape and robbery, involving detailed surveillance of potential victims as he roamed from town to town. In at least one case, Wang burglarized a home, then returned the next night to kill its inhabitants and rape a teenage girl. Wang's last raid claimed five victims in Dongliangxiang, on August 8, 2003, with two teenage girls raped after death.

Wang's murder trial in Henan Province, at Luohe City Intermediate People's Court, consumed all of one hour on February 1, 2004. Wang declined to appeal his sentence, and he was shot by a military firing squad on February 14. His case, coinciding with the prosecution of serial killer HUANG YONG in Henan Province, brought unwelcome attention to China's modern rash of serial murders. In both cases, police failed to broadcast alerts while the crimes were in progress.

"WANNA-BES": Would-be serial killers

In a society that often grants celebrity—even "folk hero" status—to violent felons, it should come as no surprise that certain twisted individuals admire and seek to emulate infamous killers. As with Wild West outlaws, Prohibition bootleggers, Depression-era bank robbers, and modern ghetto "gang bangers," so notorious serial killers also have a fringe-dwelling cult of rapt admirers. Most such "fans" never progress beyond the stage of being GROUPIES, spending their hard-earned (or stolen) money on ARTWORK AND MEMORABILIA related to serial murder. Some correspond with caged killers directly; a smaller number visit their idols in person or accept collect phone calls from prison; a tiny handful "fall in love" and marry slayers sentenced to death or a life behind bars.

And some—thankfully a minuscule percentage—physically imitate the deeds of their "heroes" in real life.

Contrary to the expressed fears of law enforcement personnel and the plot devices of FICTION AND FILM, there seems to be no case on record where an individual has consciously, precisely acted out a series of "copycat" murders (although one Maryland defendant, arrested for beheading his mother in 1989, initially identified himself to the arresting officers as "Hannibal Lecter," psycho-psychiatrist from *Red Dragon* and *The Silence of the Lambs*). The closest thing yet to a series of "copycat" crimes was reported from Georgia in the late 1970s, where sex slayer WILLIAM HANCE masqueraded briefly as a racist vigilante, his letters to police alleging (falsely) that his crimes against black women were a response to "Stocking Strangler" CARLTON GARY's murder of elderly whites. (Hance himself was black, the notes an effort to divert suspicion form himself to a nonexistent "Chairman of the Forces of Evil.")

Elsewhere, we know that serial killers including CARROLL EDWARD COLE, British gay-slayer COLIN IRELAND, and New York "Zodiac" killer Heriberto Seda collected books and/or newspaper clippings about other serial slayers before they embarked on their own killing sprees. Cole especially admired "Boston Strangler" ALBERT DESALVO, while Ireland studied "the FBI manual" for details on how to succeed at his game. When asked why he had killed five victims, Ireland told police, "I have got the book; I know how many you have to do." Other practitioners—the frustrated "wanna-bes" examined here—apparently set out to murder a series of victims but somehow fell short of their goal, either through clumsiness or pure bad luck. This list includes:

- *Robert Vannatta:* Vannatta, of Mr. Vernon, Illinois, was sentenced to 199 years in August 1943 for the July sex-murder of local waitress Norma Bradford. Prior to the killing, Vannatta raped a 19-year-old girl and burglarized local shops, stealing money and weapons. At his arrest, police seized Vannatta's "Diary of Revenge," including a hit list of eight intended victims. "I promised myself to kill all of these low-downs," Vannatta wrote, "and I'll get them all. No stopping until the last one is dead." The list included a local judge and prosecutor, plus six members of Vannatta's family, his stepmother's name heavily underlined. "I'll get her last," Vannata wrote, "for in that way, the old witch will suffer more from the suspense of waiting for her just deserts."

- *William Hollenbaugh:* Hollenbaugh tried his best to commit serial murder in Franklin County, Pennsylvania, between April 1964 and May 1966, but the ex-convict and sometime mental patient was continually frustrated by poor marksmanship in his sniping attacks on local residents and motorists. For two years, the elusive "Mountain Man of Shade Gap" terrorized his chosen hunting ground, but his sole fatality was FBI Agent Terry Anderson, shot from ambush on May 17, 1966, near the end of an eight-day manhunt. By that time, Hollenbaugh had been identified, and he was killed while resisting arrest the following day.

- *Rodney Gene Beeler:* A fetish burglar and rapist in Orange County, California, Beeler was—like at least seven serial killers before him—forced to wear girls' clothing as a child. That may (or may not) help to explain his habit of stealing women's underwear from homes and laundromats and masturbating into the bras and panties. Later, following a burglary conviction, Beeler was examined by psychiatrists, one of whom wrote in his report: "Beeler is naturally evil, as some men are naturally passionate or bellicose, tender or weak." A second analyst went so far as to call him "soulless" and "a natural enemy of mankind." In July 1985, Beeler raped and robbed a 53-year-old woman; five months later, he shot and killed 23-year-old Anthony Stevenson, apparently during a bungled robbery attempt. Convicted of murder in July 1988, he was sentenced to death on May 4, 1989.

- *Michael Sams:* A British felon known as "Metal Mickey" for the artificial leg he wore, Sams abducted 18-year-old prostitute Julie Dart from Leeds on July 9, 1991, demanding $280,000 ransom in a series of letters Dart was forced to write. (One note threatened that a local department store would be firebombed if police ignored the demands.) The ransom was never paid, but it made no difference to Dart, who was murdered as soon as she had finished writing the letters. Her body was found July 14. A final note from the killer warned that "Prostitutes are easy to pick up and I won't spend any more time in prison for killing two instead of one!" His second victim, abducted from Birmingham on January 22, was not a hooker, though: 25-year-old Stephanie Slater was a real estate agent. Sams demanded $300,000 for her safe return, and this time the ransom was paid, his victim released unharmed. Detectives tracked Sams to his home in Newark, arresting him in January 1992; he subsequently confessed to Julie Dart's murder, whereupon he was sentenced to life imprisonment.

- *Todd Everett Fluette* and *David Allen Kring:* This pair may actually have achieved serial-killer status in San Diego, California, but since they were charged with and convicted of only one murder, they officially rank as "wannabes." Between November 4 and December 8, 1991, three men were stabbed to death in the vicinity of Balboa Park, their bodies hacked and mutilated in a grisly pattern of overkill. Investigation led detectives to US Navy seamen Fluette and Kring, who had boasted to fellow sailors of "rolling bums" and "killing faggots" in Balboa Park. Their "jokes" included references to "skinning the skin off the faggots like you would skin a potato," and while other seamen did not take the conversations seriously, they described Kring and Fluette as "serial killer nuts" who openly admired JOHN GACY, THEODORE BUNDY, and the unidentified "ZODIAC." Indicted for the murder of 48-year-old Michael Hamilton (the third victim), Kring pled guilty in July 1992; on August 13, he was sentenced to a prison term of 25 years to life. Fluette went on trial five days later, was convicted of the same murder on August 31, and was sentenced to life imprisonment without parole. Both defendants deny any role in the other two murders, and those cases remain officially unsolved.

- *Jason Massey:* Another fan of Ted Bundy and of "Night Stalker" RICHARD RAMIREZ, Massey recorded his ghoulish aspirations in a 500-page diary he titled "Slayer's Book of Death." He also kept a cooler filled with rotting animal heads at his home in Ennis, Texas, 60 miles southwest of Dallas. On the night of July 26, 1993, Massey began his campaign by murdering 14-year-old James King and his 13-year-old stepsister Christina Benjamin from Garrett, Texas. Both were shot, then decapitated, with their hands and feet severed and further mutilations inflicted on their torsos. Local police had a record of complaints against Massey dating back to 1987 when he was 15 years old. Investigators turned up evidence linking him to the murders, and he was indicted on August 11, 1993. At trial, his diary helped the prosecution, with its frank admission

that "It makes me happy to think of all the hurt I can cause." Massey hoped to murder 700 victims before he died, thus achieving the "greatest slaughter and carnage wrought upon the earth by one man." Convicted on all counts at trial, he was sentenced to death on October 12, 1994. Massey was executed by lethal injection on April 3, 2001.

- *Todd Rizzo:* An 18-year-old resident of Waterbury, Connecticut, Rizzo was yet another avid fan of infamous serial killers, citing JEFFREY DAHMER as his personal favorite. Discharged from the Marine Corps after less than a year in uniform, Rizzo set about emulating his hero in October 1997. Luring a 13-year-old neighbour into his back yard "to hunt snakes," Rizzo then knocked the boy down, "sat on him like a horse and hit him a bunch of times in the head" with a sledgehammer. Linked to the murder by a witness who saw his car near the spot where the body was dumped, Rizzo told police the murder was committed for "no good reason. It was like a sort of urge, I guess."

- *Aida Nourredin Mohammed Abu Zeid:* A 25-year-old Egyptian nurse at a Cairo hospital, Abu Zeid was arrested on December 17, 1997, charged with killing one patient and attempting to murder 29 others. Her MOTIVE was revenge against a hospital physician who shunned her romantic overtures. After confessing the crimes, Abu Zeid attempted suicide by leaping from a third-story window.

- *Hayward Bissell:* A 37-year-old Ohio resident, Bissell went berserk in DeKalb County, Alabama, on January 23, 2000, ramming one man with his car and stabbing another, then knifing the second victim's dogs to death before he fled the scene. When police stopped Bissell's car, they found a woman's headless body strapped in the passenger seat. In addition to beheading girlfriend Patricia Booher, Bissell also cut out her heart, then severed one hand and one leg. Arresting officers removed her larynx from his pocket. Police subsequently determined that Bissell killed Booher at a rest stop in Georgia. At trial in February 2002, Bissell pled "guilty but insane" and received a life prison term.

- *John Allan:* British slayer John Allan poisoned girlfriend Cheryl Lewis with cyanide in October 1998, while the couple was on holiday in Luxor, Egypt. One year earlier, the 48-year-old industrial chemist had forged a will in Lewis's name, making himself the beneficiary of her £460,000 estate. When police arrested Allan in February 1999, they found enough cyanide in his car to kill 600 people—some of it allegedly carmarked for current girlfriend Jennifer Hughes. Detectives dubbed Allan a profit-motivated "BLUEBEARD KILLER," and while they also suspected him of shooting his second wife in Zambia (she survived), no charges were filed in that case. Jurors convicted Allan of murdering Lewis on March 8, 2000, and he received a life sentence.

- *Patrick Lee Harned:* Seventeen-year-old Patrick Harned was living with a convicted sex offender in February 1999, when he strangled a seven-year-old girl and hid her corpse under the floorboards of his parents' home in Astoria, Oregon. Jailed pending trial on aggravated murder charges, Harned penned a letter asking imprisoned "Happy Face Killer" KEITH JESPERSON for advice on his legal defense. Defense attorneys cited Harned's correspondence with dozens of convicted felons as evidence of mental illness. Harned received a sentence of life imprisonment without parole on November 9, 2000.

- *Michael Leopold:* Following his arrest for aggravated assault on a streetwalker, this 38-year-old resident of Vancouver, British Columbia, informed psychiatrists of his longstanding desire to torture and kill prostitutes. He received an 11-year prison sentence in that case, on August 25, 2000. Police briefly considered Leopold a suspect in the disappearance of more than 20 Vancouver hookers, but that case was apparently resolved with the arrest of suspect Robert Pickton.

- *Mathew Hardman:* On July 16, 2002, police in Llanfair, Wales, reported the arrest of a 17-year-old art student for the November 2001 mutilation-slaying of 94-year-old Mabel Leyshon. Evidence produced at trial revealed that Hardman was obsessed with VAMPIRISM and drank Leyshon's blood in a quest for immortality. He also removed the victim's heart, wrapped it in newspaper, and placed it in a saucepan on a silver platter. Convicted of murder on August 2, 2002, Hardman was sentenced to a minimum of 12 years in prison.

- *Name withheld:* On March 26, 2003, a judge in Oslo, Norway, sentenced an unnamed 21-year-old ballet dancer to 15 years in prison for strangling a prostitute. Evidence presented in court revealed the defendant as a devotee of serial murder who hallucinated a personal friendship with British slayer DENNIS NILSEN. In passing sentence, Judge Gudrun Andvord declared, "The court finds that since his interest in death, murder, mutilation of corpses, necrophilia, serial killers, violent pornography and more continues, and if he does not develop or change his personality, then there is a present danger of the repetition of serious criminal acts from which society must be protected by placing him in preventative custody."

- *Michael Hernandez:* Before fatally stabbing an eighth-grade classmate on February 3, 2004, 14-year-old Michael Hernandez filled a notebook with doodles and jottings that revealed his fascination with violent crime. One note, released to the press by police in Palmetto Bay, Florida, disclosed Hernandez's plan for life: "You will be a serial killer and mass murderer, stay alone, never forget God ever, have a cult and plan a mass kidnapping for new world . . . be an expert thief etc." Authorities charged Hernandez as an adult, with first-degree murder. Trial in his case was pending when this volume went to press.

WARNING Signs of Violent Tendencies

While generalizations are admittedly hazardous, psychologists have long recognized certain childhood or adolescent behaviors as symptoms of violence to come in adulthood. The often-cited "triad" of warning signs, including ARSON, cruelty toward animals, and persistent adolescent enuresis (bed-wetting) was originally identified from a single anonymous case in the 1940s, but time has proved at least the general validity of all three symptoms as indicators of a child with serious mental/emotional problems.

The FBI elaborated on those very basic guidelines with its study of 36 sexually motivated killers conducted between 1979 and 1983. Questions of the study's validity to serial murder in general arise from the fact that all of those questioned were male, all but three of them white, and no killer with other than sexual MOTIVES was included for study, but the results are still instructive. According to the Bureau's published results, 43 percent of the killers were sexually abused in childhood; 73 percent reported "sexually stressful events"; 72 percent admitted childhood fetishism; 68 percent suffered from enuresis as children (60 percent lasting into adolescence); 56 percent set fires in childhood (52 percent in their teens); 36 percent tortured animals as children (46 percent in adolescence); 54 percent were cruel to childhood peers (64 percent as adolescents); 71 percent were chronic liars; and 38 percent assaulted adults (up to a whopping 84 percent in adolescence).

In addition to behavioral traits, analysts have also compiled lists of medical or genetic symptoms displayed by so-called BAD SEEDS, allegedly predestined to violence. While such diagnoses dating from the moments after birth (or even from prenatal tests) are perilous, potentially branding innocuous children as "violence prone," it is equally clear that behavioral indicators, especially those involving violent or destructive activity in childhood, should be viewed with grave concern by parents, counselors, and teachers.

See also JUVENILE KILLERS; PARAPHILIAS

WATERFIELD, Fred   *See* GORE, DAVID ALLAN

WATTS, Coral Eugene

Born at Fort Hood, Texas, in 1953, Coral Watts grew up on the move, attending public schools in Texas, West Virginia, and Michigan before finishing high school—after a fashion—in Inkster, a Detroit suburb. Despite a tested IQ of 75, he was admitted to Western Michigan University at Kalamazoo and was enrolled there when he started acting out his violent fantasies against women in October 1974.

His first two victims managed to survive when Watts came knocking on the doors of their apartments, starting on October 25. Watts choked them both unconscious, leaving them for dead with not attempt at rape or robbery, but he was disappointed when the press reported both of them were still alive. He found knives more efficient, claiming his first fatality on October 30 when 19-year-old Gloria Steele was stabbed 33 times and discarded near campus.

Identified as a suspect in the nonfatal assaults, Watts had himself committed to a state hospital on the advice of his attorney, refusing to answer any questions about the Steele murder case. Fourteen months after the fact, he struck a bargain with Kalamazoo prosecutors, pleading guilty to one assault in return for dismissal of another similar charge, accepting a one-year sentence in the county jail. Upon release, he moved to Ann Arbor, marrying long enough to father a child, but his deep-seated hatred of women made the relationship untenable, and he was divorced in May 1980.

Meanwhile, Watts was hunting. When his marriage started showing signs of strain, he spent some time with relatives in the Detroit suburb of Grosse Pointe Farms, jogging by night to keep himself in shape. On October 31, 1979, he invaded the home of 35-year-old Jeanne Clyne, slashing her to death—again without attempting rape or robbery—before he fled. Eyewitnesses described an African-American man jogging near the scene, but homicide detectives had no way of linking their case with a five-year-old series of crimes against women in Kalamazoo.

Back in Ann Arbor, Watts entered criminal history as the "Sunday Morning Slasher," claiming at least three victims in motiveless, random attacks committed between 3:00 and 5:00 A.M. on peaceful Sunday mornings. In April 1980, 18-year-old Shirley Small was hacked to death in her apartment, followed by 20-year-old Glenda Richmond in July and 29-year-old Rebecca Huff in September. Canadian authorities believe Watts may have crossed the border into Windsor that October, assaulting 20-year-old Sandra Dalpe outside her apartment, leaving her near death with multiple stab wounds to the face and throat.

By that time, Watts had fallen under scrutiny from local homicide investigators. A task force was organized in July 1980 to probe the Sunday slashings, and Watts was placed under sporadic surveillance, a November court order permitting officers to plant a homing device in his car. Despite pursuit by squad cars and a helicopter, though, Watts managed to commit at least one murder while police were on his trail. Fired from his job as a diesel mechanic in March 1981, he moved south to Houston, leaving the murder investigation at loose ends. Michigan authorities alerted their Texas counterparts, but Watts was accustomed to living under surveillance. He found a new mechanic's job and started visiting a local church, sometimes living with relatives, other times out of his car.

And the murders continued.

Coral Watts (Author's collection)

On March 27, 1981, Edith Ledet, a 34-year-old medical student, was stabbed to death while jogging in Houston. Six months later, on September 12, 25-year-old Elizabeth Montgomery was attacked while walking her dog at midnight, staggering into her nearby apartment before she collapsed. Two hours later, 21-year-old Susan Wolfe was knifed to death outside her apartment, nearby, presumed to be a victim of the same assailant.

The new year brought no respite from horrors in Houston. In January, 27-year-old Phyllis Tamm was found on the campus of Rice University, hanged with an article of her own clothing; another Rice student, 25-year-old Margaret Fossi, was killed that same month, found in the trunk of her car, her larynx crushed by a powerful blow that produced death by asphyxiation. On February 7, Elena Semander, a 20-year-old coed, was found strangled and partially nude in a trash bin, not far from a tavern where she had spent the evening.

In March 1982, Emily LaQua was reported missing from Brookshire, Texas, 40 miles north of Houston, but authorities drew no immediate connection with the spate of unsolved murders. On March 31, 20-year-old Mary Castillo was found, strangled and seminude, in a Houston ditch. Three nights later, 19-year-old Christine McDonald vanished while hitchhiking home from a party on the Rice campus. Suzanne Searles, 25, joined the missing list on April 5, her shoes and broken spectacles recovered from her car in the parking lot of her apartment complex. Carrie Mae Jefferson, age 32, vanished after working the night shift on April 15, and 26-year-old Yolanda Degracia was killed the following night, stabbed six times in her home. High school student Sheri Strait disappeared with her mother's car on May 1, the car and her body recovered together on May 4. Two weeks later, Gloria Cavallis, a 32-year-old exotic dancer, was found dead in a trash dumpster, her body wrapped in cast-off curtains.

On the morning of May 23, 1982—a Sunday—Watts was caught while fleeing from the Houston apartment where he had assaulted tenants Lori Lister and Melinda Aguilar. Lister was half-drowned in the bathtub, while Aguilar escaped by leaping from the balcony and calling for help. Held in lieu of $50,000 bond, Watts was charged with two counts of attempted murder, plus burglary and aggravated assault. On the day of his arrest, another victim, 20-year-old Michelle Maday, was found strangled to death in the bathtub of her Houston apartment.

Psychiatrists declared Watts sane but noted his pathological hatred of women, whom he regarded as evil incarnate. The feelings dated back to childhood, Watts said, when a favorite uncle was allegedly killed by female relatives. Diagnosed as a paranoid schizophrenic, Watts was said to view the world around him "as pure fantasies which resolve to a large extent around the struggle against the 'evil' he sees everywhere."

On August 9, 1982, with jury selection under way for his trial, Watts struck a controversial bargain with the prosecutor's office. In return for his guilty plea on burglary charges and acceptance of a 60-year prison sentence—the equivalent of life imprisonment in Texas—Watts would clear the books on several unsolved Houston murders while escaping trial for homicide.

With the deal complete and Watts compelled to serve a minimum of 20 years before consideration for parole, he confessed to 10 Houston murders, including those of victims Wolfe, Jefferson, Montgomery, Fossi, Semander, Searles, Garcia, Tamm, Ledet, and Maday. He also threw in some surprises, including the nonfatal slashing of a Galveston 19-year-old, attacked on January 30, 1982, and the "accidental" death of 22-year-old Linda Tilley, found floating in an Austin, Texas, swimming pool on September 5, 1981. Other nonfatal assaults were also cleared in Austin, Galveston, and Seabrook, Texas.

Watts led authorities to the remains of victims Searles and Jefferson in Houston, directing other searchers to the body of Emily LaQua, near Brookshire, and he was still talking when Michigan weighed in with charges in the murder of Jeanne Clyne. Swapping testimony for immunity, Watts ran his score up to 13 confessed murders with the Clyne case, but detectives suggest that his actual body count includes a minimum of 22 victims. On September 3, 1982, Watts received his 60-year sentence, the judge declaring, "I hope they put you so deep in the penitentiary that they'll have to pipe sunlight to you."

Tough talk aside, Watts remained eligible for parole, and Texas residents were outraged in July 2002 when they learned that his release had been scheduled for May 2006. Ex-judge Doug Shaver, who sentenced Watts in 1982, told reporters, "It makes me kind of sick. It's the most unforgettable case I ever had before me, and he's the most dangerous person I've ever come face to face with. When he gets out, some woman is going to die." Texas authorities denied Watts's fifth parole bid in November 2002, repeating that the law required them to free him in 2006, at age 52. Relief came from Michigan, where prosecutors announced a new murder indictment in March 2004. The victim in that case, 36-year-old Helen Dutcher, was slain in the Detroit suburb of Ferndale on December 1, 1979. Police initially lacked evidence to charge Watts with the crime, so Dutcher's murder was excluded from the list of homicides for which Watts had immunity. Extradited to Michigan in April 2004, Watts filed a not guilty plea at his arraignment on June 17. Michigan jurors convicted Watts of first-degree murder on November 17, 2004, in the December 1979 slaying of Helen Fuchter. He received a mandatory sentence of life imprisonment.

WEAPONS Preferred by Serial Killers

When it comes to choice of weapons, American serial killers defy all national norms. In 1996, according to the FBI's *Uniform Crime Report,* 68 percent of American murders were committed with firearms, 26 percent were the result of hands-on violence—stabbing, beating, strangulation—and another 6 percent were committed by other means, including ARSON, BOMBS and poison. Serial slayers, by contrast, prefer the personal touch: 51 percent kill manually, versus 22 percent who rely exclusively on guns and 10 percent who utilized "other" means; another 14 percent alternate between shooting and manual attacks, and 3 percent—including killers like HENRY LUCAS and OTTIS TOOLE—use anything and everything available as homicidal tools. (Lucas once bragged that he had murdered using "everything but poison," including victims who were crucified, run down with cars, and burned alive.)

In classifying sexually motivated killers as "ORGANIZED" and "DISORGANIZED," FBI analysts determined that the first group normally planned their crimes in detail, procuring any necessary weapons well ahead of time, and the latter type more often killed on impulse, thus arriving unprepared, and found their weapons waiting for them at the murder scene. "Disorganized" offenders also have a tendency to leave their tools behind, often with useful fingerprints, while their "organized" competitors keep (or dispose of) their weapons in an effort to avoid detection.

A significant break from the serial-killing "norm" is seen when drugs and poisons are employed. Aside from MEDICAL MURDERS wherein both male and female killers display a fondness for lethal injections, the great majority of poisoners are women, typically "BLACK WIDOWS" who spice their home cooking with unorthodox ingredients ranging from arsenic to antifreeze. This tendency of female slayers to avoid the use of shotguns, axes, and piano wire has prompted some authors to dub them "gentle" killers, but that designation fails to recognize the suffering endured by many victims of successive deadly doses that result in blindness, seizures, hemorrhages, and a protracted, agonizing death.

By the later 1990s, human bodily fluids themselves were sometimes considered weapons of multiple murder, as authorities worldwide pursued individuals accused of deliberately infecting multiple sex partners with HIV (the incurable virus that causes AIDS). In Finland, Stephen Thomas reportedly had unprotected

Murder tools of Britain's "Yorkshire Ripper" (Author's collection)

sex with more than 100 prostitutes after learning that he was HIV positive. Italian police published photos of prostitute Giuseppina Barbieri in February 1998, declaring that the HIV positive woman had engaged in unsafe sex with a staggering 5,000 clients. The same month brought announcements that Darnell McGee, a Missouri AIDS carrier murdered in January 1997, had infected at least 18 of his 100-plus sex partners since his illness was diagnosed in 1992. The first U.S. criminal charges on record were filed against Nushawn Williams, jailed on a New York drug charge in September 1997, who later admitted seducing girls with crack cocaine and having unprotected sex with his sedated victims. At least a dozen teenage girls were thus infected, resulting in a February 1999 guilty plea on charges of reckless endangerment and statutory rape. (He received a sentence of four to 12 years in prison.) Tennessee divorcée Pamela Wiser cited revenge as a motive for exposing 50 men to her disease. In December 1998 she pled guilty on 22 counts of criminal exposure and received a 26-year prison term.

The first case of an HIV-positive defendant charged with deliberate murder was reported from Hamilton, Ontario, in February 2005. Johnson Aziga, 48 years old, was initially indicted in 2004 for endangering the lives of 13 women, with whom he had unprotected sex despite his knowledge that he carried AIDS. Seven of Aziga's unknowing partners later tested positive for HIV, and two died from AIDS-related illnesses, in December 2003 and May 2004. Nine months after the second death, Canadian prosecutors charged Aziga with two counts of first-degree murder. No trial date had been scheduled for Aziga's case at press time for this volume.

See also MODUS OPERANDI; MOTIVES

WEST, Frederick and Rosemary

In August 1992, police in Gloucester, England, launched an investigation of child-abuse charges filed against local contractor Frederick West and his wife Rosemary. Both suspects were arrested on August 6, Fred charged with rape and sodomy of a minor, his wife held as an accomplice to the crime. Large quantities of pornography were seized from the family home at 25 Cromwell Street, but the case collapsed when two young witnesses refused to testify. Still, detectives and social workers continued their investigation of the strange family, and that persistence revealed a festering nightmare.

The abortive case against Fred and Rosemary West was not their first brush with the law. Twenty years earlier, they had been charged with assaulting another young victim, 16-year-old Caroline Raine. Raine was pregnant when the Wests picked her up in September 1972, hitchhiking from Tewksbury to Cinderford in search of work. They hired Raine on the spot, to serve as nanny for their children, but she soon grew nervous in their company. Fred West incessantly discussed her pregnancy, offering an amateur abortion if Raine changed her mind about keeping the child. She soon left their home, but met the Wests again in December, once again while thumbing rides. Raine was barely in the car before Fred beat her unconscious, bound her, and drove her home for a sadistic "genital examination" that included flogging Raine's vagina with a belt. They threatened to kill Raine and bury her "under the paving stones of Gloucester," but she screamed for help when a visitor came to the door, landing the Wests in jail. Rape charges were dismissed, but the Wests pled guilty to indecent assault with bodily harm, paying a £100 fine.

The new investigation cost Fred and Rosemary the custody of their six youngest children, as new details of kinky sex and violence emerged from 25 Cromwell Street. Worse yet, the children sent to foster care voiced fears of being planted "under the patio like Heather" if they spoke against their parents. Sixteen-year-old Heather West had dropped from sight in June 1987, without benefit of a missing-person report from her parents. When questioned, Fred and Rosemary insisted that Heather had left school and home for a job at a holiday camp in Devon. Searchers arrived to dig up the Wests' garden on February 24, 1994. The search was still in progress on February 25, when Fred confessed to killing Heather and burying her in the garden. By then, police had found sufficient evidence to know that she was not alone.

Fred West was born in 1941, the first of seven children born within a decade to Walter and Daisy West at Much Marcle, 120 miles west of London. A poor student who was frequently punished for misbehavior at school, Fred also displayed a perverse sexual interest in his younger sisters. One later claimed to have carried his child, though Fred blamed the pregnancy on his father. At age 17, a motorcycle crash left Fred comatose for a week. He woke to find a thick metal plate in his skull and one leg permanently shorter than the other. Disfigurement did not prevent him from romancing 16-year-old prostitute Catherine "Rena" Costello, but she soon moved to Scotland, leaving Fred to play the field. One target pushed him from a fire escape after Fred thrust a hand up her skirt, resulting in another head wound.

In 1961, Fred and a friend were fined for shoplifting. Later that year, he was accused of impregnating a 13-year-old neighbor. At his trial for statutory rape, a physician testified that West suffered from epileptic seizures. The news saved him from jail, but not from conviction. The jury's vote left West a convicted child molester at age 20. Rena Costello returned to pick up their relationship in summer 1962, bringing word that she was pregnant by an Asian bus driver. Fred told his parents that the child was his and married Rena in November 1962, embarking on a life in Scotland. When daughter Charmaine was born in March 1963, Fred wrote his mother that the child had been stillborn, prompting him to adopt a mixed-race replacement.

Despite her background as a streetwalker, Rena soon balked at Fred's nonstop demands for sex, including sodomy and bondage. Dissatisfied, Fred sated his desires with young girls he met on his job as driver of an ice cream truck. Rena bore a second daughter, Anne-Marie, in 1964, around the same time that Fred struck and killed a young boy with his truck. Fearing that he would lose his job, he moved the family to Gloucester and found work in a slaughterhouse, where he developed (in the words of British author Colin Wilson) "a morbid obsession with corpses and blood and dismemberment." Rena went back to Scotland in 1965, leaving both children with Fred, and in her absence Gloucester recorded eight rapes by a man matching West's description. When Rena returned in July 1966, she found Fred living with another woman, Anna McFall. That sight prompted a visit to police, where Rena denounced Fred as a pervert unfit to raise children.

Anna announced her own pregnancy in early 1967, but Fred took the news badly. He killed Anna that July and dismembered her body, retaining her fingers and toes as grim TROPHIES of the act when he buried her (and her unborn child) in a field near Much Marcle. Rena soon rejoined the dysfunctional family, turning tricks in her free time while Fred openly fondled daughter Charmaine. Some investigators now believe he murdered 15-year-old Mary Bastholm in January 1968, after snatching her from a Gloucester bus stop. As evidence, investigators note that West patronized a market where Bastholm worked, and that one witness claims to have seen the girl in his car. West later admitted grabbing other victims from bus stops, but he was never charged with Bastholm's murder. Daisy West died in February 1968, and Fred soon embarked on a series of workplace petty thefts that cost him one job after another. November 1968 found him driving a bakery truck, when he met teenage prostitute Rosemary Letts.

Rosemary was born in November 1953, the daughter of a violent schizophrenic father and a clinically depressed mother who endured sessions of electroshock therapy while pregnant with her daughter. Household punishments included frequent beatings, marathon gardening sessions, and dousings with buckets of cold water when the children overslept. Slow-witted and afflicted with nervous tics, Rosemary was nicknamed "Dozy Rosie" for her habit of lapsing into semiconscious dream states. Obesity made matters worse, subjecting her to constant ridicule from peers. Forbidden to date by her father, she fondled her brother and teased older men on the sly, at least one of whom raped her. Soon Rosemary began selling sex on the streets. Her parents separated in early 1969, and Rosemary startled neighbors by moving in with her father. Their odd relationship fueled rumors of incest that remain unsubstantiated.

Bill Letts opposed his daughter's relationship with Fred West, but his threats proved ineffective. West was sentenced to prison in 1969 for his till-tapping exploits, but Rosemary stood by him; the couple were already expecting their first child. Heather West was born in 1970, increasing Rosemary's resentment of the burden posed by Charmaine and Anne-Marie. Eight-year-old Charmaine disappeared in June 1971, with Fred still in jail, Rosemary explaining that mother Rena had come to claim her eldest child while leaving Anne-Marie behind. Rosemary committed the murder, but Fred left prison on June 24, in time to bury the small corpse beneath their home at 25 Midland Road. Before planting the child and pouring concrete over her grave, he removed her fingers, toes, and kneecaps.

Despite the birth of her child, Rosemary's parents still tried to reclaim her from West, but she balked at leaving her married lover. Her passion was tempered with fear, it seemed. Rosemary once told her parents, "You don't know him. There's nothing he wouldn't do—even murder." Fred also invited various men to the Midland Road house, where he watched them have sex with Rosemary. Rena, meanwhile, had returned to investigate Charmaine's disappearance, prompting Fred to strangle her in August 1971. Once again he dismembered the body, retaining its fingers and toes before he buried the rest in a field near Much Marcle. Fred and Rosemary married in January 1972 and continued their

kinky sex life. They put ads in swingers' newspapers and hired babysitters to watch their children while they scoured Gloucester for "young virgins." At least one of those babysitters was also drugged and raped.

In June 1972, Rosemary bore another daughter, named Mae. That arrival prompted a move to larger quarters, at 25 Cromwell Street, boasting a garage and large basement. The Wests took in boarders to cover their bills, while Fred converted the cellar into a private torture chamber. Daughter Anne-Marie was its first victim, raped repeatedly by Fred with the advice that he was preparing her for marriage. As with Rosemary, Fred also invited strange men to molest his daughter. (Fred impregnated his daughter once, then procured an abortion when the fetus developed in her fallopian tube.) The assault on Caroline Raine followed in December 1972, while Rosemary was pregnant once again, and the Wests escaped with a small fine in January 1973 after persuading the court that Raine had consented to rough sex.

Lynda Gough, a 21-year-old seamstress, joined the Wests as a live-in nanny in 1973, but the relationship soon soured. Fred murdered and dismembered her, removing Gough's fingers, toes, and kneecaps before he buried her remains in the basement. Son Stephen was born in August, but his arrival failed to halt the progress of a grisly pattern at 25 Cromwell Street. Two months later, the Wests kidnapped 15-year-old Carol Cooper, abused her sexually, then strangled and dismembered her before burying her in their cellar. On December 27, 1973, Fred snatched Lucy Partington, a 21-year-old college student, from a Gloucester bus stop. She was raped and tortured for a week before she joined the other victims in a basement grave. Fred clumsily cut himself while truncating Lucy's remains and was forced to visit a hospital emergency room for stitches on January 13, 1974.

The latest victims were reported missing by their families, but police had no clue to their whereabouts for nearly two decades. Meanwhile, the Wests continued their experiments in bondage, rape, and murder. A Swiss hitchhiker, 21-year-old Thérèsa Siegenthaler, joined the growing list of victims on April 16, 1974. Fifteen-year-old Shirley Hubbard was kidnapped on November 14, 1974, followed by 19-year-old Juanita Mott on April 11, 1975. All found their way to the basement graveyard, dismembered and buried with no public link to the Wests. At least one victim beside Anne-Marie survived the basement dungeon. Known only as "Miss A" in court documents, she was lured home by the Wests sometime in 1976, then raped by Fred and sexually assaulted by Rosemary. Reporting the incident to police years after the fact, Miss A also described two other naked female victims in the cellar, neither of whom is publicly identified.

Rosemary produced another daughter, Tara, in December 1977. A short time later, Shirley Robinson, an 18-year-old bisexual prostitute, moved into 25 Cromwell Street, cheerfully accommodating the desires of both Fred and Rosemary. Fred soon impregnated Robinson, while Rosemary carried the child of a West Indian visitor. Fred was proud of the double pregnancy, but Rosemary grew jealous of Robinson and demanded her removal. Fred complied, slaying Robinson in June 1978, dismembering her and the fetus she carried. Deeming the basement plot full to capacity, Fred buried his latest victims in the garden outside. Rose delivered her mixed-race daughter, named Louise, in November 1978, bringing the total number of children at home to six.

The next known victim on Cromwell Street, 17-year-old Alison Chambers, was tortured, murdered, and dismembered in September 1979. She joined Shirley Robinson and her unnamed child in the garden graveyard. Anne-Marie soon left home to live with a boyfriend, whereupon Fred shifted his incestuous attentions to Heather and Mae, beating them when they resisted. He still had time for Rosemary, as well, siring another son, Barry, born in June 1980. Two more children followed—Rosemary Jr. in April 1982 and Lucyanna in July 1983—but neither was Fred's biological offspring. No further victims are identified from that period, though police believe the Wests probably continued their predatory lifestyle. At home, Rose grew increasingly violent and irrational, raging and beating the children without apparent cause.

Heather West spilled details of her sordid life to friends in 1986, but no one thought to notify police about the ghoulish goings-on. Fred and Rosemary silenced Heather forever on June 19, 1987, adding her dismembered remains to the garden boneyard while informing the rest of their children that Heather had left home. Unknowingly, son Stephen helped to dig his sister's grave. That secret remained inviolate until February 1994, when police arrived with excavating tools and carried Fred away to jail.

In custody, on February 25, Fred West admitted killing Heather and burying her in the garden. "The thing I'd like to stress," he said, "is that Rose knew nothing at all." Discovery of a third human leg in the garden brought detectives back to question Fred again. He pointed out the graves of Shirley Robinson and Alison Chambers, then reluctantly directed searchers to his basement body cache. In some cases, West had not bothered to learn his victims' names. He called Thérèsa Siegenthaler "Tulip," in the mistaken belief she was Dutch, and dubbed another victim "Scar Hand," for a burn that caught his eye. As talks proceeded, Fred sent officers to the Much Marcle fields where Rena West and Ann McFall were buried, then on to his former Midland Road home. In time, he spoke of 20 other unnamed victims, taunting police with an offer to reveal their corpses at a rate of one per year.

Rose feigned shock at Fred's confessions, but police believed she had full knowledge of the crimes and may have been a willing participant. The strongest case was that of Charmaine West, murdered while Fred was serving time in jail. Initially charged with sex crimes on April 18, 1994, Rosemary maintained a pose of outraged innocence. At their first joint hearing, she shied from Fred's touch and told police he sickened her. Although Fred had started the charade, public rejection wounded him. Charged with 12 murders on December 13, 1994, he wrote to Rosemary: "We will always be in love. You will always be Mrs. West, all over the world. That is important to me and to you." She failed to answer, and Fred grew despondent. On January 1, 1995, he hanged himself in prison, using strips of bedsheet as a noose.

Robbed of their prime suspect, prosecutors charged Rosemary with 10 counts of murder (excluding victims Rena West and Ann McFall). Her trial convened on October 3, 1995, with prosecution witnesses including Caroline Raine, "Miss A," and daughter Anne-Marie. Their testimony established Rosemary's sexual sadism beyond reasonable doubt, though none had witnessed any homicides. Still, Raine's memory of threatened burial on Cromwell Street made the link, supporting prosecutor Brian Leveson's contention that Rosemary could not have been oblivious while Fred filled their basement and garden with corpses. Rosemary's plea of monumental ignorance fell on deaf ears, as the court convicted her on all counts, imposing 10 life sentences. The "House of Horrors" on Cromwell Street was demolished in October 1996, paved over in July 1997 as an unassuming pedestrian walkway. (Plans for a memorial garden were rejected, in fear that the place might attract murder GROUPIES.) On July 30, 1997, Home Secretary Jack Straw rejected Rosemary's appeal, decreeing that she should remain in prison for the rest of her life.

Elsewhere, grim tragedy stalked other members of the West family. Fred's brother, 54-year-old John, was jailed in autumn 1996 on charges of raping a niece more than 300 times. On November 29, he followed Fred's lead, hanging himself in jail. Anne-Marie West attempted suicide in November 1999, leaping from a bridge near Gloucester, but bystanders pulled her from the river in time to save her life. Brother Stephen, jilted by a girlfriend, tried to hang himself in January 2002, but the rope snapped and spared him.

On March 5, 2000, Rosemary West launched a new appeal, claiming to possess photographic proof that Fred had killed alone, without her help. Those pictures never surfaced, but police raided the home of a London pedophile on March 17, 2000, seizing pornographic videotapes that included footage of Rosemary sexually abusing children. One investigator called the tapes "the grossest and vilest type you can imagine. It features Rose committing grossly indecent acts on young girls. Several are under age and one of them looks to be only about five." Detectives labored in vain to identify those victims, one Scotland Yard spokesman telling reporters, "They may have been murdered. Fred West spoke of more than 20 before he killed himself, so it is important to find out who the girls are on the film. Most of their victims were in their teens but we are now wondering if they could have been involved in the abduction and murder of small children."

That mystery remains unsolved today, but Rosemary gave up the last of her appeals on September 30, 2001. A formal statement, issued via her attorney, declared: "I do not believe that even if I was released that I could ever relax or feel free, be left alone or have any peace of mind. More importantly, I would not be able to resume a normal relationship with my family." Rosemary apologized to Anne-Marie, claiming that "I would love to be reconciled and have contact with her." In respect to a planned TV documentary on her case, Rosemary said, "It can only open old wounds or delay any healing process for the victims' families."

"WEST Side Rapist"

Within a single year, between November 1974 and October 1975, a vicious prowler terrorized the west side of Los Angeles, raping 33 women and killing at least 10. While all of his victims were elderly, ranging in age from 63 to 92 years, the incessant attacks spread an aura of fear citywide, boosting gun sales and turning neighbor against neighbor as dark suspicions flourished. In the end, he slipped away without a trace and left police to search in vain for clues to his identity.

The first to die, on November 7, 1974, was 72-year-old Mary Scialese, followed the next day by Lucy Grant, age 92. On November 14, the slayer claimed Lillian Kramer, 67, rebounding on the night of December 4 to kill 74-year-old Ramona Gartner. A new year brought no respite from the violence, with 71-year-old Sylvia Vogal murdered on March 22, 1975. Una Cartwright, age 78, was slaughtered on April 8; 75-year-old Olga Harper was killed two weeks later. Murdered on May 22, 86-year-old Effie Martin was the eighth fatality in 23 attacks. Her death was the eighth fatality in 23 attacks. Her death was followed by the September homicide of Cora Perry, 79, and the slaying of 63-year-old Leah Leshefsky on October 28.

By New Year's Day, two months had passed without a new assault, and residents of West L.A. began to breathe a little easier. In time, they would forget, but homicide detectives would continue searching for their man across a decade, covering the same ground endlessly without result. A possible solution to the case has been suggested in the person of Brandon Tholmer, confined for three years to a state mental hospital after raping a 79-year-old woman in October 1975. Tholmer lived in the area and committed home invasion crimes similar to those of the West Side Rapist. Eleven years later, in 1986, Tholmer—then 37—was sentenced to life in prison for the rape-slayings of four elderly women since 1981. To date, no evidence has been produced connecting Tholmer with the earlier series of murders, and the West Side Rapist remains officially unidentified.

WILDER, Christopher Bernard

Born March 13, 1945, Christopher Wilder was the product of an international marriage between an American naval officer and an Australian native. A sickly child from the beginning, Wilder was given last rites as an infant. Two years later, he nearly drowned in a swimming pool; at age three, he suffered convulsions while riding with his parents in the family car and had to be resuscitated.

By his teens, the boy had problems of a different sort. At 17, in Sydney, Wilder and a group of friends were charged with gang-raping a girl on the beach. He pled guilty to carnal knowledge and received one year's probation, with a provision for mandatory counseling. The program included group therapy and electroshock treatments, but it seemed to have little effect.

Wilder married at age 23, but the union lasted only a few days. His bride complained of sexual abuse and finally left him after finding panties (not her own) and photographs of naked women in a briefcase Wilder carried in his car. In November 1969, he used nude photographs to extort sex from an Australian student nurse; she complained to the police, but charges were ultimately dropped when she refused to testify in court.

Australia was growing too hot for Wilder, so he moved to the United States. Settling in southern Florida, he prospered in the fields of construction and electrical contracting, earning (or borrowing) enough money to finance fast cars and a luxurious bachelor pad, complete with hot tub and a private photographic studio. The good life visibly agreed with Wilder, but it did not fill his other, hidden needs.

In March 1971 at Pompano Beach, Wilder was picked up on a charge of soliciting women to pose for nude photos; he plea-bargained down to disturbing the peace and paid a small fine. Six years later, in October 1977, he coerced a female high school student into oral sex, threatening to beat her if she refused, and he was jailed a second time. Wilder admitted the crime to his therapist, but confidential interviews are inadmissible in court, and he was later acquitted. On June 21, 1980, he lured a teenage girl into his car with promises of a modeling job and then drove her to a rural area where she was raped. Another plea bargain to charges of attempted sexual battery earned him five years' probation, with further therapy ordered by the court. Following his last arrest in Florida, the self-made man complained of suffering from blackouts.

Visiting his parents in Australia, Wilder was accused of kidnapping two 15-year-old girls from a beach in New South Wales on December 28, 1982, and forcing them to pose for pornographic snapshots. Traced through the license number of his rented car, Wilder was arrested on December 29, charged with kidnapping and indecent assault. His family posted $350,000 bond, and Wilder was permitted to return to the United States, his trial scheduled for May 7, 1983. Legal delays postponed the case, but Wilder was scheduled to appear in court for a hearing on April 3, 1984.

He never made it.

On February 6 Rosario Gonzalez, 20, disappeared from her job at the Miami Grand Prix. Chris Wilder was driving as a contestant that day, and witnesses recall her leaving with a man who fit Wilder's description. Her body has never been found.

On March 4, 23-year-old Elizabeth Kenyon vanished after work from the school where she taught in Coral Gables. She was seen that afternoon with Wilder at a local gas station, and his name was found in her address book. Kenyon's parents remembered her speaking of Wilder as "a real gentleman," unlike the various photographers who asked if she would model in the nude. As in the February case, no trace of Kenyon has been found.

Wilder celebrated his 39th birthday on March 13, treating himself to the peculiar gift of a 1973 Chrysler. Three days later, the *Miami Herald* reported that a Boynton Beach race driver was wanted for questioning in the disappearance of two local women. Wilder was not named in the story, but he got the point. Missing his scheduled therapy session on March 17, he met with his business partner the following night. "I am not going to jail,' he vowed, tearfully. "I'm not going to do it." Packing his car, Wilder dropped off his dogs at a kennel and drove out of town, heading north.

Indian Harbour lies two hours north of Boynton Beach. On March 19, 21-year-old Terry Ferguson disappeared from a local shopping mall where witnesses remembered seeing Wilder. Her body was recovered four days later from a Polk County canal.

On March 20 Wilder abducted a university coed from a shopping mall in Tallahassee, driving her across the state line to Bainbridge, Georgia. There, in a cheap motel, he raped her repeatedly and tortured her with electric shocks, smearing her eyelids with Super Glue. Wilder fled after his captive managed to lock herself in the bathroom, screaming and pounding on the walls to draw attention from the other motel guests.

The killer touched down next in Beaumont, Texas. Terry Walden, 24, informed her husband on March 21 that a bearded man had approached her between classes at the local university, soliciting her for a modeling job. She thanked him and declined the offer, but the conversation struck a chord of memory when Terry disappeared two days later. Her body, torn by multiple stab wounds, was dragged from a canal on March 26.

One day earlier, 21-year-old Suzanne Logan disappeared from a shopping mall in Oklahoma City. Her body was found on March 26, floating in Milford Reservoir near Manhattan, Kansas. Raped and stabbed, she had apparently been tortured prior to death.

Sheryl Bonaventura was the next to die, abducted from a mall in Grand Junction, Colorado, on March 29. Another shopper placed Wilder in the mall, soliciting women for modeling jobs, and he had been seen with Sheryl at a nearby restaurant that afternoon. She joined the missing list as Wilder worked his way across the country, killing when he paused to rest.

On April 1, 17-year-old Michelle Korfman vanished from a fashion show at the Meadows Mall in Las Vegas, Nevada. Snapshots taken at the time show Wilder smiling from the sidelines, watching as the teenage girls paraded past him in their miniskirts.

At last, it was enough. Linked to three murders, one kidnapping, and four disappearances, Wilder was described by FBI spokesmen as "a significant danger" to the public at large. His name was added to the Bureau's "Ten Most Wanted" list on April 3, 1984.

The following day, he abducted 16-year-old Tina Marie Risico in Torrance, California, raping her that night and through successive evenings as they stayed in various motels, working their way eastward. Subjected to threats and abuse, living constantly in the shadow of death, Risico agreed to help Wilder find other victims as he continued his long flight to nowhere.

On April 10, Dawnette Wilt was lured away from a shopping mall in Merrillville, Indiana, raped and tortured through the course of that day and the next. Wilder tried to murder her on April 12, stabbing Dawnette and leaving her for dead outside Rochester, New York, but she managed to survive and staggered to the nearest highway, where a passing motorist discovered her and drove her to a hospital.

Wilder's final victim was Beth Dodge, abducted near Victor, New York, on April 12 and shot to death in a nearby gravel pit. Following the murder, Wilder drove his teenage captive to Boston's Logan Airport, purchasing a one-way ticket to Los Angeles and seeing her off at the gate.

Wilder's sudden attack of compassion remains unexplained, but he wasted no time in searching out another victim. On April 13 he brandished his gun at a woman near Beverly, Massachusetts, but she fled on foot, unharmed. Continuing his aimless hunt, the killer stopped for gas that afternoon in Colebrook, New Hampshire, unaware that he had reached the end of his run.

Passing by the service station, state troopers Wayne Fortier and Lco Jellison recognized Wilder's car from FBI descriptions. Approaching the vehicle, they called out to Wilder and saw him break for the car, diving inside as he went for his pistol. Jellison leaped on the fugitive's back, struggling for the .357 magnum, and two shots rang out. The first passed through Wilder and pierced Jellison's chest, lodging in his liver; the second snuffed out Wilder's life, resulting in what a pathologist termed "cardiac obliteration."

Wilder's death, ironically, did not resolve the tangled case. Sheryl Bonaventura's body was discovered in Utah on May 3, the victim of a point-blank gunshot wound. Michelle Korfman was found in the Angeles National Forest on May 11, but another month would pass before she was identified, her family's worst fears confirmed. No trace has yet been found of Wilder's early victims in Miami and environs.

With his death, Chris Wilder was inevitably linked to other unsolved crimes. A pair of girls, aged 10 and 12, identified his mug shot as the likeness of a man who snatched them from a park in Boynton Beach in June of 1983 and forced them to fellate him in the nearby woods. His name was likewise linked with other deaths and disappearances across two decades in Australia and America.

In 1965, Marianne Schmidt and Christine Sharrock accompanied a young man matching Wilder's description into the beachfront dunes near Sydney; strangled, raped, and stabbed, their bodies were discovered in a shallow grave, but no one has been charged to date. In 1981, teenagers Mary Hare and Mary Optiz were abducted from a mall in Lee County, Florida; Hare was later found stabbed to death, while Optiz remains among the missing. During 1982, skeletal remains of unidentified women were unearthed on two separate occasions near property owned by Wilder in Loxahatchee; one victim had been dead for several years, the other for a period of months.

And the list goes on: Tammi Leppert, teenage model, kidnapped from her job at a convenience store on Merritt Island, July 6, 1983; Melody Gay, 19, abductcd on the graveyard shift at an all-night store in Collier

County, Florida, on March 7, 1984, her body pulled from a rural canal three days later; Colleen Osborne, 15, missing from her bedroom in Daytona Beach, March 15, 1984. Chris Wilder was seen in Daytona that day, propositioning "models."

There was a final ghoulish twist to Wilder's story. Following an autopsy on April 13, 1984, New Hampshire pathologist Dr. Robert Christie received a telephone call from a man claiming to represent Harvard University. Wilder's brain was wanted for study, the caller explained, in order to determine whether defect or disease had sparked his killing spree. Dr. Christie agreed to deliver the brain on receipt of a written request. Two weeks later he was still waiting, and spokesmen for Harvard's medical school denied making any such request.

WILLIAMS, Wayne Bertram *See* ATLANTA "CHILD MURDERS"

WOMEN as Serial Killers

It is often said—or was, until very recently—that "serial killers are always men." So entrenched was that belief by 1990 that the arrest of man-killer AILEEN WUORNOS in Florida prompted journalists to report the earth-shaking discovery of "the first female serial killer."

In fact, nothing could be further from the truth.

Indeed, the earliest recorded serial killer was a woman, identified in the history of ancient Rome simply as Locusta the Poisoner. Contemporary accounts describe her as "notorious" in first-century Rome, but little is known of her handiwork today, except that she murdered both Emperor Claudius and his heir before her luck ran out and she was publicly executed in A.D. 69.

Female offenders *do* represent a minority in serial murder as in all other forms of homicide, with women charged in some 12 percent of cases where serial killers are identified. (Overall, female killers account for 10 percent of American murders in any given year.) In terms of MODUS OPERANDI, women typically reverse the trends of male serial killers: while *stationary* killers average barely 8 percent of the American total, a significant 29 percent of female slayers fall into that category, including the bulk of "BLACK WIDOWS" and nurses or nurse's aides involved in MEDICAL MURDERS. In terms of MOTIVE, although only 14 percent of American serial slayers kill strictly for cash, a whopping 41 percent of female practitioners murder for money. The rest share other motives with their male counterparts, including "mercy" or "hero" homicides, murder for revenge, and the occasional case of sexual sadism.

When women emerge as TEAM KILLERS, they most often murder in conjunction with a male accomplice and are frequently assumed (sometimes in rank defiance of the evidence) to be the willing tools of dominant males. That attitude, redolent of sexism, has prompted several female team killers to defend themselves in court with pleas of "battered wife syndrome," but juries disgusted with spiraling crime rates are increasingly prone to discount such arguments, meting out long prison terms—or capital sentences—without regard to gender. Condemned female killers *do* benefit, it would seem, from chivalry or simple squeamishness as they approach an execution date. While 49 American women stood sentenced to die in January 2005—including six serial killers among them—only 10 females (versus 906 men) have been executed since CAPITAL PUNISHMENT was restored in 1976. Significantly, three of the 10 were convicted "black widows" (Velma Barfield, Betty Beets, and Judias Buenoaño). A fourth was Florida "Damsel of Death" AILEEN WUORNOS, and a fifth was two-time lesbian killer Wanda Jean Allen.

See also WEAPONS

WOOD, Catherine   *See* GRAHAM, GWENDOLYN

WOODS, Martha

An army wife who followed her husband around the country from one military base to the next, Martha Woods also suffered from the bizarre mental illness dubbed "MUNCHAUSEN'S SYNDROME BY PROXY." Victims of this rare condition are driven to seek attention or sympathy by fabricating ailments for their loved ones, sometimes inflicting deliberate harm to support their claims of mysterious illness. In this case, the quirk cost seven children their lives.

Martha's victims included three of her own children, a nephew, a niece, a neighbor's child, and the son she adopted when targets grew scarce. The cross-country killing spree lasted most of a quarter-century from 1946 to 1969. Geography was Martha's friend, preventing medical examiners in various locations from connecting her several crimes until her luck ran out at last, in Baltimore.

Martha's pattern was always the same, involving a rush to the nearest hospital with an unconscious baby in her arms. Each time, the infant was alone in Martha's care when it abruptly, inexplicably "stopped breathing." The children were revived and sent home with Woods, but they inevitably suffered more attacks within a span of hours or days. Altogether, police calculated in hindsight, nine children had suffered a total of 27 life-threatening respiratory attacks, with seven resulting in

death. The first six deaths were listed as "natural," though symptoms were consistent with deliberate suffocation.

Aside from her penchant for smothering infants, Woods also displayed the typical Munchausen's trait of pathological lying. Following the adoption of daughter Judy, she complained of threats from the girl's real parents. They had turned up on her doorstep, Martha claimed, demanding their daughter back, threatening her life when she refused. Faceless strangers were circling her home in a car at odd hours, and someone had tried to burn the house. In fact, army investigators found flammable liquid splashed on one wall of Martha's home, but they suspected her of staging the scene herself. Judy's biological parents were far away, in another state, and officers finally dismissed the whole story as a hoax.

Time ran out for Woods in Baltimore when authorities finally turned up evidence of murder in the death of her adopted son, seven-month-old Paul. Intensive psychiatric testing found her sane and fit for trial. The judge admitted evidence from other deaths to prove the case on Paul, and Martha was convicted after five months of testimony and sentenced to life imprisonment on one count of first-degree murder.

WUORNOS, Aileen Carol

She has been heralded in tabloid headlines and on television talk shows as America's "first female serial killer." In fact, Aileen Wuornos was neither the first nor the worst, although she did display a curiously "masculine" approach to homicide. Suspected of at least seven murders, sentenced to die in four of the six cases she confessed to police, Wuornos insisted that some or all of her admitted killings were performed in self-defense, resisting violent assaults by men whom she solicited while working as a prostitute. Ironically, information uncovered by journalists in November 1992 suggests that in one case, at least, her story may well be true.

America's future media monster was born Aileen Pittman in Rochester, Michigan, on February 29, 1956. Her teenage parents separated months before she was born, father Leo Pittman moving on to serve time in Kansas and Michigan mental hospitals as a deranged child molester. Mother Diane Pratt recalls Aileen and her older brother Keith as "crying, unhappy babies," and their racket prompted her to leave them with her parents in early 1960. On March 18 of that year, maternal grandparents Lauri and Britta Wuornos legally adopted the children as their own.

Aileen's childhood showed little improvement from there. At age six she suffered scarring facial burns while she and Keith were setting fires with lighter fluid. Aileen later told police that she had sex with Keith at an early age, but acquaintances doubt the story and Keith is unable to speak for himself, having died of throat cancer in 1976. At any rate, Aileen was clearly having sex with *someone,* for she turned up pregnant in her 14th year, delivering her son at a Detroit maternity hospital on March 23, 1971. Grandmother Britta died on July 7, and although her death was blamed on liver failure, Diane Pratt suspected her father of murder, claiming he threatened to kill Aileen and Keith if they were not removed from his home.

In fact, they became wards of the court, Aileen soon dropping out of school to work the streets full-time, earning her way as a teenage hooker, drifting across country as the spirit moved her. In May 1974, using the alias "Sandra Kretsch," she was jailed in Jefferson County, Colorado, for disorderly conduct, drunk dri-

Aileen Wuornos stands before the judge at her trial. (Wide World API)

ving, and firing a .22-caliber pistol from a moving vehicle. Additional charges of failure to appear were filed when she skipped town ahead of her trial. Back in Michigan on July 13, 1976, Aileen was arrested in Antrim County for simple assault and disturbing the peace after she lobbed a cue ball at a bartender's head. Outstanding warrants from Troy, Michigan, were also served on charges of driving without a license and consuming alcohol in a motor vehicle. On August 4, Aileen settled her debt to society with a $105 fine.

The money came, at least indirectly, from her brother. Keith's death on July 17 surprised her with a life insurance payment of $10,000, squandered within two months on luxuries including a new car, which Aileen promptly wrecked. In late September, broke again, she thumbed a ride to Florida, anxious to sample a warmer climate, hoping to practice her trade in the sun. It was a change of scene, but Aileen's attitude was still the same, and she inevitably faced more trouble with the law.

On May 20, 1981, Wuornos was arrested in Edgewater, Florida, for armed robbery of a convenience store. Sentenced to prison on May 4, 1982, she was released 13 months later, on June 30, 1983. Her next arrest, on May 1, 1984, was for trying to pass forged checks at a bank in Key West. On November 30, 1985, named as a suspect in the theft of a pistol and ammunition in Pasco County, Aileen borrowed the alias "Lori Grody" from an aunt in Michigan. Eleven days later, the Florida Highway Patrol cited "Grody" for driving without a valid license. On January 4, 1986, Aileen was arrested in Miami under her own name, charged with auto theft, resisting arrest, and obstruction by false information; police found a .38-caliber revolver and a box of ammunition in the stolen car. On June 2, 1986, Volusia County deputies detained "Lori Grody" for questioning after a male companion accused her of pulling a gun in his car and demanding $200. In spite of her denials, Aileen was carrying spare ammunition on her person, and a .22 pistol was found beneath the passenger seat she occupied. A week later, using the new alias "Susan Blahovec," she was ticketed for speeding in Jefferson County, Florida. The citation includes a telling observation: "Attitude poor. Thinks she's above the law."

A few days after that incident, Aileen met lesbian Tyria Moore in a Daytona gay bar. They soon became lovers, and while the passion faded after a year or so, they remained close friends and traveling companions, more or less inseparable for the next four years. On July 4, 1987, police in Daytona Beach detained "Tina Moore" and "Susan Blahovec" for questioning, on suspicion of slugging a man with a beer bottle. "Blahovec" was alone on December 18 when highway patrolmen cited her for walking on the interstate and possessing a suspended driver's license. Once again, the citation noted "Attitude poor," and "Susan" proved it over the next two months with threatening letters mailed to the circuit court clerk on January 11 and February 9, 1988.

A month later, Wuornos was trying a new approach and a new alias. On March 12, 1988, "Cammie Marsh Greene" accused a Daytona Beach bus driver of assault, claiming he pushed her off his buss following an argument; Tyria Moore was listed as a witness to the incident. On July 23, a Daytona Beach landlord accused Moore and "Susan Blahovec" of vandalizing their apartment, ripping out carpets, and painting the walls dark brown without his approval. In November 1988, "Susan Blahovec" launched a six-day campaign of threatening calls against a Zephyrhills supermarket, following an altercation over lottery tickets.

By 1989, Aileen's demeanor was increasingly erratic and belligerent. Never one to take an insult lightly, she now went out of her way to provoke confrontations, seldom traveling without a loaded pistol in her purse. She worked the bars and truck stops, thumbing rides to snag a trick when all else failed, supplementing her prostitute's income with theft when she could. Increasingly, with Moore, she talked about the many troubles in her life and a yearning for revenge.

Richard Mallory, a 51-year-old electrician from Palm Harbor, was last seen alive by coworkers on November 30, 1989. His car was found abandoned at Ormond Beach the next day, his wallet and personal papers scattered nearby, along with several condoms and a half-empty bottle of vodka. On December 13, his fully dressed corpse was found in the woods northwest of Daytona Beach, shot three times in the chest with a .22 pistol. Police searching for a motive in the murder learned that Mallory had been divorced five times, earning a reputation as a "heavy drinker" who was "very paranoid" and "very much into porno and the topless bar scene." A former employee described him as "mental," but police came up empty in their search for a criminal record. They could find "nothing dirty" on the victim, finally concluding that he was just a paranoid womanizer.

The investigation was stalled at that point on June 1, 1990, when a nude "John Doe" victim was found, shot six times with a .22 and dumped in the woods 40 miles north of Tampa. By June 7, the corpse had been identified from dental records as 43-year-old David Spears, last seen leaving his Sarasota workplace on May 19. Spears had planned to visit his ex-wife in Orlando that afternoon, but he never made it. Ironically, his boss had spotted the dead man's missing pickup truck on May 25, parked along I-75 south of Gainesville, but there the trail went cold.

By the time Spears was identified, a third victim had already been found. Charles Carskaddon, age 40, was a part-time rodeo worker from Booneville, Missouri, missing since May 31. He had vanished somewhere along I-75, en route to meet his fiancée in Tampa, his naked corpse found 30 miles south of the Spears murder site on June 6. Carskaddon had been shot nine times with a .22-caliber weapon, suggesting a pattern to officers who still resisted the notion of a serial killer at large. On June 7, Carskaddon's car was found in Marion County, a .45 automatic and various personal items listed as stolen from the vehicle.

Peter Siems, a 65-year-old merchant seaman turned missionary, was last seen on June 7, 1990, when he left his Jupiter, Florida, home to visit relatives in Arkansas. Siems never arrived, and a missing-person report was filed with police on June 22. No trace of the man had been found by July 4 when his car was wrecked and abandoned in Orange Springs, Florida. Witnesses described the vehicle's occupants as two women, one blond and one burnette, providing police sketch artists with a likeness of each. The blond was injured and bleeding. Police lifted a bloody palmprint from the vehicle's trunk.

Eugene Burress, age 50, left the Ocala sausage factory where he worked to make his normal delivery rounds on July 30, 1990. A missing-person report was filed when he had not returned by 2:00 A.M. the next day, and his delivery van was found two hours later. On August 4, his fully dressed body was found by a family picnicking in the Ocala National Forest. Burress had been shot twice with a .22-caliber pistol in the back and chest. Nearby, police found his credit cards, business receipts, and an empty cash bag from a local bank.

Fifty-six-year-old Dick Humphreys was a retired Alabama police chief, lately employed by the Florida Department of Health and Rehabilitative Services to investigate child abuse claims in Ocala. His wife reported him missing when he failed to return home from work on the night of September 11, 1990, and Humphreys was found the next day in an undeveloped subdivision, shot seven times with a .22 pistol, his pants pockets turned inside out. On September 19, his car was found abandoned and stripped of license plates behind a defunct service station in Live Oak. Impounded on September 25, the car was not traced to Humphreys until October 13, the same day his discarded badge and other personal belongings were found in Lake County, 70 miles southeast of the murder scene.

Victim number seven was 60-year-old Walter Antonio, a trucker from Merritt Island who doubled as a reserve police officer for Brevard County. Found in the woods northwest of Cross City on November 19, 1990, he had been shot three times in the back and once in the head. Antonio was nude but for socks, his clothes later found in a remote area of neighboring Taylor County. His car, meanwhile, was found back in Brevard County on November 24. Police determined that Antonio's killer had stolen a distinctive gold ring along with his bagde, nightstick, handcuffs, and flashlight.

By that time, journalists had noted the obvious pattern detectives were reluctant to accept, and media exposure forced authorities to go public with their suspect sketches on November 30, 1990. Over the next three weeks, police received four calls identifying the suspects as Tyria Moore and "Lee Blahovec." Their movements were traced through motel receipts, detectives learning that "Blahovec" also liked to call herself "Lori Grody" and "Cammie Marsh Greene." Fingerprint comparisons did the rest, naming "Blahovec/Grody/Greene" as Aileen Wuornos, placing her at the scene where Peter Siems's car was wrecked in July, but it still remained for officers to track the women down.

Meanwhile, "Cammie Greene" was busy pawning items stolen from her victims and pocketing some extra cash. On December 6, she pawned Richard Mallory's camera and radar detector in Daytona, moving on to Ormond Beach with a box of tools stolen from David Spears. (She also left a thumbprint behind in Ormond Beach, identical to that of "Lori Grody.") The next day, in Volusia County, "Greene" pawned Walter Antonio's ring, later identified by his fiancée and the jeweler who sized it.

With mug shots and a list of names in hand, it was a relatively simple matter to trace Aileen Wuornos, though her rootless lifestyle delayed the arrest for another month. On January 9, 1991, she was seized at the Last Resort, a biker bar in Harbor Oaks, detained on outstanding warrants for "Lori Grody" while police finished building their murder case. A day later, Tyria Moore was traced to her sister's home in Pennsylvania, where she agreed to help police. Back in Florida, detectives arranged a series of telephone conversations between Moore and Wuornos. Tyria begged Aileen to confess for Moore's sake and spare her from prosecution as an accomplice. One conversation led police to a storage warehouse Aileen had rented, a search revealing tools stolen from David Spears, the nightstick taken from Walter Antonio, another camera, and an electric razor belonging to Richard Mallory.

On January 16, 1991, Wuornos summoned detectives and confessed to six killings, all allegedly performed in self-defense. She denied killing Peter Siems, whose body was still missing, and likewise disclaimed any link to the murder of a "John Doe" victim shot to death with a .22-caliber weapon in Brooks County, Georgia, and found in an advanced state of decay on May 5, 1990. (No charges were filed in that case.) "I

shot 'em 'cause to me it was like a self-defending thing," she told police, "became I felt if I didn't shoot 'em and I didn't kill 'em, first of all . . . if they survived, my ass would be gettin' in trouble for attempted murder, so I'm up shit's creek on that one anyway, and if I didn't kill 'em, you know, of course, I mean I *had* to kill 'em . . . or, it's like retaliation, too. It's like, 'You bastards, you were going to hurt me.' "

Within two weeks of her arrest, Aileen and her attorney had sold movie rights to her story. At the same time, three top investigators on her case retained their own lawyer to field offers from Hollywood, cringing with embarrassment when their unseemly haste was publicly revealed. In self-defense, the officers maintained that they were moved to sell their version of the case by "pure intentions," planning to put the money in "a victim's fund." To a man, they denounced exposure of their scheme as the malicious work of brother officers, driven by their jealousy at being cut out of the deal.

A bizarre sideshow to the pending murder trial began in late January 1991 with the appearance of Arlene Pralle as Aileen's chief advocate. A 44-year-old rancher's wife and "born-again" Christian, Pralle advised Wuornos in her first letter to prison that "Jesus told me to write you." Soon, they were having daily telephone conversations at Pralle's expense, Arlene arranging interviews for Wuornos and herself and becoming a fixture on tabloid talk shows from coast to coast. In Pralle's words, their relationship was "a soul binding. We're like Jonathan and David in the Bible. It's as though part of me is trapped in jail with her. We always know what the other is feeling and thinking. I just wish I was Houdini. I would get her out of there. If there was a way, I would do it, and we could go and be vagabonds forever." Instead, Pralle did the next best thing, legally adopting Wuornos as her "daughter."

Aileen's trial for the murder of Richard Mallory opened on January 13, 1992. Eleven days later, Wuornos took the stand as the only defense witness, repeating her tale of a violent rape and beating at Mallory's hands, insisting that she shot him dead in self-defense, using her pistol only after he threatened her life. With no hard evidence to support her claim, jurors rejected the story, deliberating a mere 90 minutes before they convicted Aileen of first-degree murder on January 27. "I'm innocent!" she shouted when the verdict was announced. "I was raped! I hope you get raped! Scumbags of America!" The jury recommended death on January 29, and the following day Aileen was formally sentenced to die. In April, she pled guilty to the murders of victims Burress, Humphreys, and Spears, with a second death sentence imposed on May 7, 1992.

Around the same time, Aileen offered to show police where the corpse of Peter Siems was hidden near Beaufort, South Carolina. Authorities flew her to the Piedmont State, but nothing was found at the designated site, Daytona police insisting that Wuornos created the ruse to get a free vacation from jail. They speculate that Siems was dumped in a swamp near I-95 north of Jacksonville, but his body has never been found.

The Wuornos case took an ironic twist on November 10, 1992, with reporter Michele Gillen's revelations on *Dateline NBC*. Thus far, Aileen's defenders and Florida prosecutors alike had failed to unearth any criminal record for Richard Mallory that would substantiate Aileen's claim of rape and assault. In the official view, Mallory was "clean," if somewhat paranoid and oversexed. Gillen, though, had no apparent difficulty finding out that Mallory had served 10 years for violent rape in another state, facts easily obtained by running his name through the FBI's computer network.

"The fascinating part about this," Gillen said, "is here is a woman who for the past year has been screaming that she didn't get a fair trial and that everyone was rushing to make a TV movie about her—and in reality that comes true." (The first TV movie depicting Aileen aired on a rival network one week to the day after Gillen's report.) Even so, Gillen stopped short of calling for Aileen's release. "She's a sick woman who blew those men away," Gillen said, "but that's no reason for the state to say, 'She's confessed to killing men; we don't have to do our homework.' "

After nine years on death row, Wuornos decided to abandon her appeals. In April 2001 she asked Florida's supreme court to expedite her execution, "since I'm one who seriously hates life and would kill again." In a July 2001 interview with the *Ocala Star-Banner*, Wuornos recanted her claim that her victims were shot in self-defense. "I just flat robbed, killed them," she declared, "and there was a lot of hatred behind everything." Wuornos added that before the first shooting, she had "always wanted to kill somebody." At a special hearing convened on July 20, 2001, she told Judge Michael Hutchenson, "I will kill again. I've got hate crawling through my system. There is no point in sparing me. I'm a waste of the taxpayers' money." Hutchenson deemed Wuornos competent, and the state supreme court approved the inmate's decision to fire her attorneys on April 1, 2002. Wuornos was executed by lethal injection six months later, on October 9, 2002.

XITAVHUDZI, Elias

One of half a dozen serial killers spawned by the South African township of Atteridgeville in modern times, Elias Xitavhudzi was nicknamed "Pangaman" prior to capture, after the long, broad-bladed knife he used to kill and mutilate his 16 female victims. Occurring in the 1960s, Xitavhudzi's crimes were doubly traumatic for strictly segregated Atteridgeville, since the victims were white and their killer turned out to be black. Upon capture, Xitavhudzi was swiftly tried and sentenced to death, but his spirit lives on in Atteridgeville, which continues to produce vicious stalkers on a regular basis—most recently, the still-unidentified "Atteridgeville Mutilator."

YAKIMA Reservation Murders

Authorities are divided in their opinions as to whether a serial killer is responsible for the murders of at least 13 women committed since 1980 on the 1.3 million-acre Yakima Indian Reservation in Washington State. Eleven of the 13 victims were Native American, most of them born and raised on the reservation, many with histories of alcohol abuse. Most of the victims were in their twenties; at least eight left children behind. Some were stabbed to death, while others were beaten, shot, or strangled; two were apparently drowned, and one was run down by a car. The bodies have typically been dumped in remote, wooded areas where decomposition and exposure to the elements or scavengers erases evidence, leaving the cause of death unknown in several cases. At least two other Indian women—Karen Louise Johnly and Daisey May Tallman, both in their twenties—were also reported missing between 1987 and 1992, but their names have not been added to the "official" Yakima victims list.

One lawman who believes a serial killer *is* responsible for the murders, Melford Hall, retired in 1989 after 22 years as a criminal investigator for the Bureau of Indian Affairs, citing the homicides as part of his reason for leaving the job. As Hall told reporters in January 1993, "They'll probably say, 'He doesn't know what he's talking about. But then you look at all these names.'" Hall links the murders to rampant alcoholism, so prominent at Yakima and other reservations. "My own opinion," he explains, "is this guy sits at a tavern someplace and waits for an intoxicated woman and grabs her."

Yakima's Tribal Police Department, meanwhile, refuses all requests for interviews on the murders, but agents from the FBI's Seattle field office fulfilled Hall's prediction, calling it "extremely unlikely" that one killer was responsible for all 13 of the Yakima murders. FBI spokesman William Gore referred to "significant evidence" and "logical suspects" in three of the cases, although no charges were filed. On January 27, 1993, the FBI declared that 12 of the Yakima murders "are closed, though they could be reopened if new information surfaced."

But the question remains: Is anybody looking? Melford Hall, for one, was bitter toward the FBI. "A lot of times we would call them," he told reporters, "and they'd say, 'Just send over a report.' They spent millions of dollars over there [i.e., on the GREEN RIVER murders], and wouldn't spend anything here." It is a further point of bitter irony, Hall noted, that the FBI has direct responsibility for all murders committed on Indian reservations, but none at all in local murders, like Seattle's infamous "Green River" case.

Another lawman who compared the two unsolved cases was Yakima County Sheriff's Deputy Dave Johnson, who complained that murder investigations are hampered by the tendency of some tribal members to leave the reservation without informing friends or family. "It's kind of like the Green River victims, many of whom were prostitutes," Johnson said. "You have individuals with no permanent address." One who resented the comparison was Johnnie Wyman, whose sister—44-year-old Jo Anne Betty Wyman—was found dead on the reservation in 1991, three years after she disappeared. "The authorities take the attitude that it's just a bunch of drunken Indian women," Wyman told the press. "It's just another slap in the face. I can't candy-coat it for anybody. She was my sister, and she meant something to me."

The most recent slaying—and that which finally brought national publicity to the murders—was that of Shari Dee Sampson Ewell, found strangled and sexually mutilated on December 30, 1992, in a section of the reservation closed to non-Indians. Sufficient media attention was generated by Ewell's death that the Yakima Indian Nation offered a $1,000 reward for information leading to the killer's arrest, the fund increased by $5,000 from the FBI on May 14, 1993. Thus far, the money has not helped. The murders on the Yakima reservation remain unsolved.

YATES, Robert Lee, Jr.

The U.S. Pacific Northwest has produced many serial killers, but none in modern times has proved as effective at dodging police as Robert Yates Jr. His 23-year killing spree is presently unrivaled in American history. Today, with Yates awaiting execution in Washington State, authorities still puzzle over what it was that drove him to the brink of madness and beyond.

In October 1945, nine years before Yates was born, his paternal grandmother killed her sleeping husband with an ax. She was indicted for murder but never stood trial, and relatives dismiss any suggestion that the crime may have influenced her grandson. Yates entered the world on May 27, 1952, as a breech baby (born feet first). He was sexually molested by an older boy at age six. His family brands those events as irrelevant. Raised in Oak Harbor, Washington, Yates graduated from high school in 1970 and moved on to Walla Walla Community College, where he met his future wife. Claims that he earned a degree in biology remain unverified, but today we know that Yates claimed his first two victims a year before his marriage, in July 1975.

Twenty-one-year-old Patrick Oliver and 22-year-old Susan Savage were picnicking beside Mill Creek, 10 miles east of Walla Walla, when Yates arrived and shot them both. A quarter-century later, Yates explained that he often went target shooting in the area on days off from his job as a guard at Walla Walla's state prison. He shot the two strangers on a whim, covered their bodies with brush, and left a mystery that remained unsolved until he confessed the crime in October 2000. Yates married in July 1976 and joined the army two years later, serving 18 years in uniform as a helicopter pilot. His tour of duty included stints in Somalia (where Yates was reprimanded for shooting wild pigs from the air) and Haiti, but he spent most of his military career in the United States. Upon discharge from the army, in April 1996, Yates moved his wife and five children to

Spokane, where he worked at a Kaiser Aluminum plant and spent weekends flying with the Air National Guard.

None of it kept him from killing. On July 7, 1988, he picked up Stacy Hawn, a 23-year-old drug-addicted prostitute, in Shoreline, Washington. Yates drove her to a site near Mount Vernon and shot her once in the head. Her skeletal remains were found on December 28, but Hawn's boyfriend did not report her missing until February 1989. She was identified the following month. In the first half of 1990, three women were shot and discarded along the Spokane River. Yolanda Sapp, age 26, was found on February 22, followed by 34-year-old Nickie Lowe (March 25) and 38-year-old Kathy Brisbois (May 15). Lowe and Brisbois were killed with the same .22-caliber weapon. Sherry Palmer, age unknown, was found shot to death outside Tacoma on May 13, 1992. Another shooting victim, 60-year-old Patricia Barnes from Port Orchard, was discovered in rural Kitsap County on August 25, 1995.

Although Yates maintained a busy schedule after April 1996, juggling family, work, and the National Guard, he still found time to hunt. At the same time, he developed a ritualized "signature," leaving victims with plastic trash bags pulled over their heads, several dumped in the same area. Thirty-eight-year-old Shannon Zielinski was discarded near Tacoma on June 14, 1996. On August 16, 1997, 16-year-old runaway Jennifer Joseph was last seen alive as she entered a white Chevrolet Corvette driven by a white man in his forties. She was found 10 days later, hooded with trash bags and shot through the head with a .22-caliber pistol. The same day brought discovery of another woman's decomposing body, in a different Spokane neighborhood. The second victim was identified as Heather Hernandez, a 20-year-old drifter. Investigators found semen on Joseph's body, along with a brown hair from a Caucasian male. The bullet that killed Joseph bore "insufficient characteristics" for comparison with the .22 slugs extracted from victims Brisbois and Lowe.

On September 24, 1997, a Spokane patrolman stopped Robert Yates, at the wheel of a white 1977 Chevrolet Corvette, for a minor traffic violation. Yates received a citation, which correctly recorded his license plate number but misidentified his vehicle as a Camaro. It was a small but critical mistake, corrected long after the fact when detectives double-checked the car's registration. In the meantime, detectives seeking a Corvette from the Joseph murder knew nothing of Yates.

Six weeks later, on November 5, a man walking his dog spotted a shallow grave near Spokane's Hangman Valley Road. Police found 29-year-old Darla Scott, another prostitute, buried with two trash bags over her head, shot twice in the brain with a .25-caliber weapon. Again, semen was found that later matched the DNA of

Robert Yates Jr. On December 7, 1997, pedestrians in Tacoma found the nude body of 24-year-old Melinda Mercer discarded in a vacant lot. Four trash bags covered her head, ventilated with three .25-caliber bullets. Less than two weeks elapsed before the next murder in Spokane. On December 18 a workman found 36-year-old Shawn Johnson's body on Hangman Valley Road, masked with two trash bags, shot twice in the head, her body stained with semen. The year ended badly, with discovery of two more victims on December 26. Both lay in a gravel pit near Hangman Valley Road, each shot twice, both hooded with three plastic bags. Thirty-one-year-old Laurel Wason was partially covered with foreign debris later traced to Yates's backyard, and semen on her body matched his DNA. Shawn McClenahan, age 39, also bore semen traces, and a fingerprint from Yates marked one of the trash bags covering her head.

Police failed to identify their man from evidence collected during 1997, since Yates had no criminal record and his DNA was not on file. Investigators could have found his fingerprints in military dossiers, but their search was limited to known felons. Yates suffered his first brush with the law in 1998, on a count of domestic violence against his wife, but the charge was dismissed without trial and detectives assigned to the ongoing murders made no connection between the dissimilar cases.

On February 8, 1998, the semen-stained body of 41-year-old Sunny Oster was found in a wooded area of western Spokane County. Three trash bags covered her head, drilled with two gunshot wounds, but only one slug was recovered. Spokane residents held a candlelight vigil for the murdered women four days later, while police announced ongoing investigation of 17 unsolved murders reported in the area since 1984. Theoretical links were drawn to the "Green River Killer" (later identified as GARY LEON RIDGWAY), although that stalker never used firearms. Another victim was found on April 1, 1998, dumped within 50 yards of the pit where McClenahan and Wason were discovered. Linda Maybin, a 34-year-old prostitute and drug addict, had been shot once in the head, shrouded with two plastic bags. Semen from her body matched Yates's DNA, while plant clippings strewn across her body were traced to the killer's backyard.

Those discoveries took time, however, and police had few viable leads as they added the latest murder to their growing list. By April 14, detectives knew that victims Maybin, McClenahan, and Scott had all worked for the same escort service, but that clue failed to identify their killer. Melody Murfin's name made the serial murder list when she dropped from sight in May 1998, but her corpse was not recovered until Yates led

searchers to her grave—beneath his bedroom window—in October 2000. More remains were found in the killer's favored hunting ground on June 10, 1998, but missing pieces and advanced decomposition left even the victim's gender in doubt. Police had better luck on July 7, when a transient found 47-year-old Michelyn Derning in Spokane's East Central neighborhood. Concealed beneath a discarded hot-tub cover, Derning had been stripped and shot once in the head. No bullet was found, but officers recovered a .25-caliber cartridge at the scene. Unlike most of the victims, missing long before their bodies were uncovered, Derning had been seen alive one short week earlier.

Yates logged his first failure on August 1, 1998, with 32-year-old Christine Smith. He paid Smith $40 for oral sex, performed in the back of his van, then shot her in the head when she proved unable to arouse him. Dazed from the bullet's impact, believing that she had been punched by her "john," Smith survived to file a police report on the incident. Complaining of assault and robbery, she described her assailant as a 50-year-old white man (Yates was 46), five feet, 10 inches tall, with sandy blond hair. His van was black, a 1970s model with an orange exterior stripe, bucket seats, wood paneling inside, and raised bed in back. Ironically, Smith had asked the man if he was Spokane's "psycho killer," whereupon he replied that "he had five kids and would not do that." Smith remained unaware of her gunshot wound until recurring headaches sent her to the emergency room, where X-rays revealed bullet fragments in her face and skull.

Despite Smith's clear description, detectives were no closer to their man. On September 3, 1998, they added 43-year-old Melody Murfin to the presumed victims' list. Missing since May 13, Murfin was another drug-addicted prostitute, whose disappearance caused alarm. Her body was not found until October 2000, when Robert Yates directed searchers to a flowerbed outside his home. Meanwhile, in October 1998, police in Lewiston announced a new investigation into the murders of three more victims. The trio—18-year-old Jacqueline Miller, 21-year-old Kristina Nelson, and 35-year-old Steven Pearsall—vanished together from the Lewiston Civic Theater in September 1982. Pearsall was still missing, but the women's bodies had been found together on a hillside near Kendrick, in 1984. Authorities suspected one killer at work in those murders, in the 1979 disappearance of 12-year-old Christina White from the Asotin County Fair, and in the mutilation-slaying of 22-year-old Kristen David. David had vanished on a bike ride from Moscow to Lewiston in 1981; her headless torso, with one leg attached, was found eight days later, on the north shore of the Snake River near Clarkston; her head, arms and part of one leg were found farther downstream the next day. (None of the latter crimes were ultimately linked to Robert Yates.)

Police questioned various subjects, including an unnamed "prime suspect" in the Lewiston murders, without result as the manhunt continued. The next bona fide victim, 35-year-old Connie Ellis, was found in Tacoma on October 13, 1998. One bullet was extracted from her head, which was swaddled in three trash bags. Eight days later, Pierce County detectives voiced fears that a corpse in Parkland "could have been dumped there by the Spokane killer," but no further details were released.

Robert Yates survived another near miss with the law on November 10, 1998. He was driving a 1985 Honda Civic when police stopped him at 1:25 A.M. in a neighborhood notorious for streetwalkers. More to the point, a known prostitute—one Jennifer Robinson—was riding with Yates in the car. Yates claimed that Robinson's father had asked him to find her and bring her home, an improbable story that Robinson confirmed to avoid spending more time in jail. Stymied, the officer released them and filed a report on the incident which vanished into police files.

Spring 1999 brought a flurry of news in the case. On March 9, a dog retrieved a human hand from woodland south of Snoqualmie, then led searchers to the skeleton of Jennifer Justus. Although she matched the Spokane victim profile, police quickly dismissed Justus as a possible victim of the region's elusive killer. On April 15, sheriff's deputies visited a physician at home in Spokane's affluent South Hill district, deemed a "person of interest" in the February rape of a downtown prostitute, but they found no link to the serial murders. Two days later, Spokane police investigating another "high-risk" victim's disappearance found charred human bones in the furnace of a downtown apartment building. Scandal erupted on May 6, after police chief Alan Chertok said informers had named his predecessor, Chief Terry Mangan, as a suspect in the slayings. Cornered by reporters, Chertok said that Mangan—subsequently hired by the FBI—was not suspected of the crimes "and never would be." His previous comment, Chertok claimed, "wasn't meant to be taken seriously." The denial was too little and too late. Chertok resigned from the police department on May 27, 1999.

Two years after the fact, task force investigators discovered the error on Robert Yates's traffic citation from September 1997, drawing the obvious link between his white Corvette and the murder of Jennifer Joseph. Detectives interviewed Yates for the first time on September 14, 1999, recording a list of his vehicles and pursuing further details of his encounter with Jennifer Robinson. Yates repeated his lie from November 1998

Robert Lee Yates is escorted into court in Spokane, Washington, on May 31, 2000. (Reuters/Corbis)

and declined to provide blood samples for DNA comparison. Robinson, in a separate interview, admitted that Yates had paid $20 for oral sex, and further confirmed that her father lived outside Spokane and had never met Yates.

Deception focused suspicion more sharply on Yates. Detectives learned that he had been grounded as a military helicopter pilot pending medical evaluations during 1997 and 1998, when many of the victims were killed. Interrogation of his wife revealed that Yates once came home from a late-night drive with bloodstains in the rear of his van. (Yates claimed he had struck a dog, then drove it to a veterinary clinic.) Yates had destroyed the bloody fabric from the van, but police traced his vintage Corvette to its new owner in April 2000 and matched its carpet fibers to those found on Jennifer Joseph's body. Bloodstains from the car's floorboard matched Joseph's DNA, and a button found in the car proved identical to those on Joseph's blouse.

Police arrested Yates on April 18, 2000, and subsequently matched his DNA to that found in semen recovered from six murder victims around Spokane. Publication of his mug shot in a local newspaper brought confirmation from Christine Smith that Yates was the man who shot her in August 1998. Yates was formally charged with Joseph's murder on April 19, held in lieu of $1.5 million bail. One day later, debris from his yard was matched to the grave sites of victims Maybin, McClenahan, and Wason. That afternoon, Sheriff Sterk told reporters, "We have Mr. Yates tied to at least 12 of the homicides, possibly 18." Announcement of Yates's arrest renewed scrutiny of unsolved murders in Germany, New York, and Alabama, where he had served at various times with the U.S. Army, but thus far no charges have been filed outside of Washington. New indictments in Spokane, filed on May 18,

2000, charged Yates with the murders of victims Dern-ing, Johnson, Maybin, McClenahan, Oster, and Wason, plus attempted murder in the case of Christine Smith. Exactly two months later, Pierce County prosecutors charged Yates with the murders of Connie Ellis and Linda Mercer.

Yates initially pled not guilty on all counts, then changed his mind in October 2000 and directed police to the remains of two victims buried at his home, over-looked in previous searches. Newspapers announced a plea bargain on October 16, whereby Yates escaped the death penalty while confessing 13 homicides in Skagit, Spokane, and Walla Walla Counties. The deal was for-malized in court on October 26, and Yates received a sentence of 408 years in prison. Dissatisfied with that bargain, Pierce County authorities pressed for capital punishment in the Ellis and Mercer slayings; Yates responded on November 1 with twin not guilty pleas. Jurors convicted him of those crimes on September 19, 2002, then recommended execution on October 3. Judge John McCarthy formally sentenced Yates to death on October 9, 2002.

YERSHOV, Vadim

A Siberian army deserter, 24-year-old Vadim Yershov went to trial in October 1997 on charges of raping, rob-bing, and fatally stabbing 19 victims in the months after his unscheduled departure from military service. As a soldier of sorts, he pled his case before a military tri-bunal in the Siberian city of Krasnoyarsk, where he was convicted and sentenced to death on June 9, 1998. Yer-shov reportedly fainted as the sentence was pronounced, but the dramatic gesture may have been in vain. Russia has suspended execution of death sentences in recent years, although CAPITAL PUNISHMENT remains part of the nation's legal code. The Council of Europe has urged Russia to abolish the death penalty as a condition of its membership in the group, and it seems likely that eco-nomic interests will spare Vadim Yershov from the firing squad. At that, considering the state of prisons in Siberia, he may eventually wish he *had* been shot.

YORK, George R., and LATHAM, James D.

George York, 18, and James Latham, 19, were privates in the U.S. Army when they met at Fort Hood, Texas, in the early part of 1959. Something clicked between them as it has with other lethal soul mates, and they privately decided on a course of robbery and murder that would carry them—almost—from coast to coast.

That May, the friends went AWOL from Fort Hood, making York's hometown of Jacksonville, Florida, the first stop on their itinerary. On May 29 in Jacksonville,

they met Althea Ottavio and Patricia Hewitt, who were visiting from Georgia, and strangled both women, steal-ing their money and car. Their bonus was a loaded pis-tol, found inside the glove compartment.

On June 7, the pair stopped briefly in Tulahoma, Tennessee, where they murdered elderly John Whit-taker, swapping the new victim's car for their hot set of wheels. Whittaker's vehicle brought them to Edwardsville, Illinois, where they murdered 35-year-old Albert Reed for the hell of it. Seven miles down the road, they looted a gas station and killed the attendant, Martin Drenovac, age 69.

By June 9, the lethal nomads were cruising through Kansas, pausing at Wallace long enough to murder Otto Ziegler, a 62-year-old road master for the Union Pacific railroad. In Craig, Colorado, they offered 18-year-old Rachel Moyer a ride to California, dumping her corpse in a riverbed outside town, where it would be found on June 11.

By that time, York and Latham were in custody. The FBI had started tracking them for violation of the Dyer Act, prohibiting transportation of a stolen car across state lines, and federal bulletins kept local law enforce-ment agencies apprised of the duo's westward progress. On June 10, they were captured by a Utah sheriff and lodged in jail at Salt Lake City for interrogation.

On June 12, after 24 hours of stone silence, the pris-oners cracked, relating details of their rampage with a kind of twisted pride. They boasted of eight or nine murders, and eight notches had been carved into the handle of their stolen gun, but in fact there were only seven dead. (The FBI later reported that two unnamed victims had survived their wounds.) Convicted in Kansas of the Ziegler slaying, York and Latham were sentenced to death on December 19, 1962. Addressing the court, they declared, "We killed together, so we expect to die together." They got their wish two and a half years later, mounting the gallows on June 22, 1965. Their deaths wrote finis to an era, since Kansas—while maintaining CAPITAL PUNISHMENT—has executed no more inmates to this day.

YOUNG, Lila Gladys

Lila Coolen, the daughter of devout Seventh-Day Adventist parents, was born at Fox Point, Nova Scotia, in 1899. At age 26 she met and married William Peach Young, an Oregon native transplanted to New Brunswick, where he aspired to the role of an Adventist "medical missionary" without benefit of ordination or medical training. Soon after their marriage, with Lila expecting the first of five children, the Youngs moved to Chicago, where William was licensed as a chiropractor in December 1927. Two months later they moved back to Nova Scotia, opening the Life and Health Sanitarium in East Chester, 40 miles southwest of Halifax. Lila entered service as a professional midwife, and their establishment was soon rechristened the Ideal Maternity Home and Sanitarium, with William acting as superintendent and Lila as managing director. Clients flocked to the "home" in response to newspaper advertisements that read:

IDEAL MATERNITY HOME "Mothers Refuge" also department for girls. NO PUBLICITY INFANTS home in connection. Write for literature. East Chester, N.S.

Brochures for the home promised to shield "Expectant Mothers from gossip," but every service has its price. Married women seeking refuge with the Youngs paid an average $75 each for delivery and two weeks of convalescence in the early days of operation, but unwed mothers, frightened of scandal, faced a stiffer price. The Youngs demanded an average $100 or $200 in advance for room and board, delivery of the infant, and arranging subsequent adoption, plus another $12 for diapers and supplies, with an average two-dollar weekly maintenance fee for warehousing infants between delivery and adoption. If a baby died at the home, the mother was changed $20 for a funeral—performed by the Youngs' handyman at a standing rate of 50 cents per corpse, with white pine butterboxes standing in for coffins.

In short, it was the classic "BABY FARMING" racket, elevated to an art form. Girls without the ready cash in hand were sometimes allowed to work off their debts at the home, thus providing the Youngs with a steady stream of unpaid domestic help. Medical care was another realm open to shortcuts, with Lila and William each billing themselves as "doctors" on their letterheads. In fact, Lila delivered the babies herself, while William knelt at the bedside in prayer, but some clients saw a more ruthless side of the Youngs, complaining of Lila's rough—even brutal—handling. "She was physically immense," one client recalled. "She had an overpowering presence and a great sense of power. She could strike terror into people. No one dared to challenge her."

In short order, the Ideal Maternity Home became a virtual baby factory, hosting scores of unwed mothers averaging age 17. Between 1928 and 1935, Lila reported 148 births and 12 infants deaths at the home, a mortality rate of 8.1 percent that nearly tripled Nova Scotia's 3.1 percent average. On March 4, 1936, Lila and William were changed with two counts of manslaughter in the January deaths of Eva Nieforth and her newborn child, allegedly caused by negligence and unsanitary conditions at the home. Both were acquitted

at a three-day trial in May 1936, but the Royal Canadian Mounted Police adopted a policy of investigating each reported death at the home in years to come.

One problem, of course, was the issue of unreported infant deaths. Handyman Glen Shatford would later admit burying between 100 and 120 babies in a field owned by Lila's parents near Fox Point, adjoining the Adventist cemetery. "We buried them in rows," he said, "so it was easy to see how many there were." In a typical case, recalled by Shatford from April 1938, an unnamed infant lay in the Youngs' tool shed for five days, covered by a box, before it was driven to Fox Point for burial. A motive for the surreptitious disposal may be found in Lila's standard charge of $300 to board a baby "for the rest of its natural life." Some were farmed out to a neighbor who cared for their needs at a cost of three dollars a week, while others reached the end of their "natural lives" in record time. Some adoption "rejects"—including children of mixed race or those with physical defects—were reportedly starved to death on a diet of water and molasses.

For all the money paid to Lila and her husband by their pregnant clients, the Youngs made their greatest profit from adoptive parents, charging an average of $800 to $1,000 per infant in the 1930s, escalating to an average $5,000 per head during World War II. In the 1940s, Ideal Maternity earned $60,000 per year from its live-in clients, including a special $50 fee from any mother who specified adoptive parents of a particular religion. On the flip side, Lila and William banked at least $3.5 million from the "adoption"—that is, sale—of infants between 1937 and 1947. One client who changed her mind in 1946 and sought to get her child back was told the boy had already been placed for adoption, but he might be retrieved . . . if the mother could come up with $10,000 in cash.

By 1943, the Youngs were housing 70 infants on any given day. Their original cottage had grown to a sprawling complex of 54 rooms, 14 bathrooms, and multiple nurseries, valued at $40,000 with no outstanding mortgage. Clients could reserve private or semiprivate rooms, if they were put off by the thought of sleeping on a common ward. Business was so good, in fact, that Lila began to brag . . . and thereby caused herself no end of grief.

Public health officials had been watching the Youngs for a decade, but they found their first concrete evidence of neglect in 1945, inspectors reporting squalid conditions, swarming flies and filthy bedding, some infants weighing 50 percent of the norm for their age. Lila fired back with charges of harassment, but her time was running out. A new amendment to the Maternity Boarding House Act of 1940 broadened licensing requirements to incorporated companies, and the

Youngs' license application was swiftly rejected, Ideal Maternity ordered shut down in November 1945.

It was not that simple to close a multimillion-dollar business, of course, and the Youngs continued to operate without a license while their case was appealed. U.S. Immigration officers joined the chorus of complaints in early 1946, citing evidence that Lila had smuggled black-market babies into the United States. In March, the Youngs were arraigned on eight counts, including violation of the Maternity Boarding House Act and practicing medicine without a license, but their conviction on three counts on March 27 resulted in a piddling fine of $150. On June 4, 1946, they were convicted of illegally selling babies to four American couples and fined a total of $428.90. William, drinking heavily by now, was later convicted of perjury based on his testimony at the June trial, but babies were still being born at Ideal Maternity in early 1947.

The end, when it came, was as much a result of Lila's arrogance as any official action. Fuming at media coverage of her case, she filed a $25,000 libel suit against a local newspaper, thereby opening the floodgates of damning testimony from all sides. Jurors dismissed her suit after brief deliberation, and the trial exposed her operation for the brutal, mercenary sham it was. Ideal Maternity was closed before year's end, the Youngs bankrupt and debt-ridden, finally selling off their property and moving to Quebec. The "home," scheduled for conversion into a resort hotel, burned to the ground on September 23, 1962. Cancer had claimed William's life by year's end, and Lila died of leukemia in 1967 after moving back to Nova Scotia. Her tombstone bears the legend: "till we meet again."

YUKL, Charles William

A child of divorce, Charles Yukl was 31 years old and married, self-employed as a piano teacher in New York City, when he claimed his first victim in 1966. On October 24 of that year, police responded to a homicide report at Yukl's apartment house, where they discovered the body of 25-year-old Suzanne Reynolds. A student of Yukl's, she had been beaten, stripped, and stabbed to death before the teacher "found" her in a vacant flat, investigating after he "noticed" the open door on his way upstairs.

Arrested and charged with the murder the next morning, Yukl confessed under questioning, before his attorney arrived at the jail. Months of wrangling over constitutional issues led to a plea bargain in February 1968, with reduced charges of manslaughter earning Yukl a sentence of seven to 15 years in prison. A model inmate, Yukl was released on parole in June 1973, two years before the expiration of his "guaranteed minimum" sentence. Objections from the state were overruled, with Yukl cited as "a good risk for parole." He waited all of 14 months before he killed again.

On August 20, 1974, the nude and strangled body of Karen Schlegel, an aspiring actress, was discovered on the rooftop of an apartment house in Greenwich Village. She had been dead 12 hours when a janitor discovered her remains, but authorities had no difficulty selecting a suspect. Charles Yukl was a tenant of the house where Schlegel died, and he confessed to luring his victim with an advertisement placed in a theatrical magazine. Upon arrival, Karen Schlegel had been strangled with a necktie, stripped, and carried to the roof where she was found.

Psychiatrists found Yukl competent for trial, and he was formally indicted on September 6. On June 3, 1976, he managed to strike another bargain with the state, accepting a sentence of 15 years to life in return for his guilty plea. This time, however, there would be no premature parole. On August 22, 1982, the killer hanged himself in prison with a shredded mattress cover, and his death was ruled a suicide.

ZARINSKY, Robert

Born in New Jersey during 1941, Robert Zarinsky exhibited signs of mental instability in adolescence. By the early 1960s he was calling himself "Lt. Schaefer, leader of the American Republican Army." Convicted of ARSON and grave desecration after he torched five lumberyards and vandalized Jewish cemeteries in Monmouth and Union Counties, the one-man army spent 13 months in Trenton State Psychiatric Hospital. Despite his daily contact with psychiatrists, Zarinsky still slipped through the net, his lethal quirks unrecognized by trained professionals. Settling in Linden upon his release, Zarinsky opened a wholesale produce business, but his darker fantasies cried out for satisfaction.

In April 1969, 17-year-old Linda Balbanow was kidnapped on the short walk home from her job at a drugstore in Union County, New Jersey. Her lifeless body was recovered soon thereafter, floating in the Raritan River near Woolbridge. When 16-year-old Rosemary Calandriello disappeared from Atlantic Highlands later that year, Zarinsky was charged with her kidnapping. Authorities delayed prosecution while the futile search for her body continued, and Zarinsky's attorney won dismissal of the charge on grounds that his client was denied a speedy trial.

In December 1974, police had their eyes on Zarinsky again, this time investigating the murders of 14-year-old Doreen Carlucci and 15-year-old Joanne Delardo in Middlesex Country. The victims were kidnapped together, their bodies discarded in Manalapan Township, half naked, each strangled with electric cord. Detectives were still seeking positive links in the two recent crimes when they got a fresh break on the Calan-

driello abduction. According to acquaintances, Zarinsky had been boasting of the murder, confident that he could not be prosecuted in the absence of a corpse.

Authorities felt otherwise. On February 25, 1975, Zarinsky was charged with the murder of Rosemary Calandriello and held in lieu of $125,000 bond. His trial in April ended with Zarinsky's conviction of first-degree murder, and he was sentenced to life imprisonment. The verdict was affirmed on appeal in July 1976, the appellate court ruling that failure to produce a victim's body was no bar to prosecution in a murder case—particularly when the suspect brags about the killing to his friends.

Zarinsky made headlines again in August 1999, when FBI agents and officers from seven other law enforcement agencies scoured his former home in Linden, Pennsylvania, seeking traces of four additional victims. Zarinsky inherited the house from his mother, and after his arrest it had acquired a local reputation for being "haunted." At the same time, Zarinsky's sister implicated Zarinsky and cousin Theodore Schiffer in the 1958 murder of Rahway, New Jersey, police officer Charles Bernoskie. Schiffer pled guilty in that case and turned state's evidence against Zarinsky, but a jury acquitted Zarinsky of Bernoskie's murder. Undeterred, Bernoskie's widow filed a civil suit against Zarinsky for wrongful death, and a second jury found him liable on August 21, 2003, awarding the plaintiff an uncollectable $9.5 million in damages.

"ZEBRA" Murders

For a period of 179 days, between October 1973 and APril 1974, white residents of San Francisco were terrorized by a series of random, racially motivated attacks that claimed 15 lives, leaving another eight victims wounded or raped. By January 1974, authorities knew with fair certainty that the killers were members of a Black Muslim splinter group, the "Death Angels," that required the murder of "blue-eyed devils" as a form of initiation. By their very nature—and the form of the police response—the "Zebra" murders (so called after a police code name for the case) heightened racial tension by the Bay and left a legacy of doubt that time has failed to dissipate.

The first known "Zebra" victims were Richard and Quita Hague, abducted by blacks in a van as they walked down the street on October 19, 1973. Richard Hague was hacked about the head and face with a machete, stunned and left for dead before the attackers raped his wife and finished her with the same machete, leaving her nearly decapitated. By some miracle, Richard survived the ordeal.

Three days later, gunman Jessie Lee Cooks abducted a young white woman, holding her captive for two hours while he raped her repeatedly and forced her to perform oral sex. Arrested on this and other charges prior to the conclusion of the "Zebra" case, Cooks—a psychopathic ex-convict—pled guilty to one count of murder in return for dismissal of other counts. By the time the "Zebra" case broke in 1974, he was already serving his sentence.

On October 29, 28-year-old Frances Rose was shot and killed by a black man who tried to invade her moving car on a San Francisco street. A month later, on November 25, 53-year-old Saleem Erakat was tied up and shot execution-style in his small grocery store. Paul Dancik died on December 11, shot three times in the chest while walking to a corner phone booth. Two days later, 35-year-old Arthur Agnos was wounded and Marietta Di Girolamo was killed in separate, random shooting incidents. The use of a similar (or identical) weapon in each of the crimes suggested one triggerman or a group of killers sharing lethal hardware.

Things went from bad to worse near Christmas. On December 20, 81-year-old Ilario Bertuccio was killed while walking home from work, and Angela Roselli was wounded three times as she left a Christmas party. Neal Moynihan, 19, and 50-year-old Mildred Hosler died six minutes apart on December 22, cut down in random attacks. On December 23, a gathering of Death Angels tortured and dismembered an unknown transient in their San Francisco loft, dumping his mangled remains on a beach where they were found next morning. Never identified, he is listed in homicide files as "John Doe #169" for 1973.

The killers celebrated the New Year with a freewheeling rampage on January 28, killing four persons and wounding a fifth in the space of two hours. The dead included 32-year-old Tana Smith, shot down on her way to a fabric store; Vincent Wollin, killed on his 69th birthday; 54-year-old John Bambic, shot repeatedly at point-blank range; and 45-year-old Jane Holly, fatally wounded by a gunman who approached her on the street. Survivor Roxanne Miller, age 23, recalled that her assailant smiled and said "Hi" before he opened fire.

On April 1, 19-year-old Thomas Rainwater and 21-year-old Linda Story were gunned down while walking to a neighborhood store. Rainwater was killed outright, while Story survived with permanent nerve damage. Two weeks later, on Easter Sunday, Ward Anderson and Terry White were wounded by black gunmen at a San Francisco bus stop. The last victim, Nelson Shields, was shot three times in the back and killed on April 16, 1974.

Police response to the "Zebra" murders was almost as controversial as the crimes themselves. A policy of stopping blacks at random on the street and frisking them for weapons produced cries of racism and civil rights violations, while producing no viable suspects. The case was broken in late April when gunman Anthony Cornelius Harris surrendered voluntarily and made a full confession to authorities. Turning state's evidence, he named eight Death Angel killers aside from himself, and seven of the suspects were picked up in raids on May 1. (Jessie Cooks was already in prison.)

Four of the suspects were ultimately freed for lack of solid evidence, and they remain at large today. Indicted for the "Zebra" crimes were Jessie Cooks, J. C. Simon, Larry Craig Green, and Manuel Leonard Moore. Harris, Moore, and Cooks had met while serving time in San Quentin on various felony charges, and they had joined the Black Muslim movement while still behind bars.

The "Zebra" trial set a new record for California criminal proceedings, lasting from March 3, 1975 to March 9, 1979. Three of the four defense attorneys were provided and paid by the Nation of Islam in a demonstration of solidarity with the accused murderers. At the end of the marathon trial, jurors took barely 18 hours to convict all defendants on all counts, and the four gunmen were sentenced to life imprisonment.

As for the Death Angels, their existence has never been publicly acknowledged by American law enforcement, and the results of confidential investigations into the cult remain classified. According to author Clark Howard, there were 15 "accredited" Death Angels—those who had earned their "wings" by killing a specified numbers of white—at large in California during 1973. None of them were swept up in the "Zebra" dragnet, which bagged only prospective members, still short of their tally for final qualification. They and their brethren in the cult are presumably still at large and possibly still hunting.

ZIKODE, Christopher Mhlengwa

A South African predator known as the "Donnybrook Serial Killer," after the rural Natal midlands town where his crimes were committed, Zikode murdered 18 victims and attempted to kill 11 more between 1993 and 1995. Launching his rampage at age 19, Zikode followed the same MODUS OPERANDI in most of his attacks: choosing a likely house, he kicked the door in, gunned down any men or boys on hand, then dragged the females off to nearby plantations where they were raped repeatedly—for up to five hours at a stretch—before they, too, were killed. If the women resisted his assault, Zikode was not above shooting them first and then raping their corpses. An alternative technique, employed with several victims, involved ambushing women or girls on lonely footpaths, carrying them off to be raped and killed.

Zikode was arrested for the first time in July 1995 for the attempted murder of a female victim named Beauty Zulu. Granted bail on that charge, he committed at least five more offenses—including one murder, one rape, two attempted murders, and one housebreaking with intent to rape—before he was jailed again in September. Held this time without bond, Zikode went to trial in late 1996, the proceedings highlighted by South Africa's star forensic profiler, DR. MICKI PISTORIUS. Finally convicted on 21 charges including eight murders, five rapes, five attempted murders, and one indecent assault—all committed between April and September 1995—Zikode was sentenced on January 7, 1997, to a prison term of 140 years. The High Court judge who sentenced him avoided comment on the "gory details" of the case but did remark specifically on Zikode's "contemptible" attitude toward women.

"ZODIAC"

California's most elusive serial killer claimed his first confirmed victim on October 30, 1966, in Riverside. That evening, Cheri Jo Bates, an 18-year-old freshman at Riverside City College, emerged from the campus library to find her car disabled, the distributor coil disconnected. Police theorize that her killer approached with an offer of help, then dragged her behind some nearby shrubbery where a furious struggle ended with Cheri stabbed in the chest and back, her throat slashed so deeply that she was nearly decapitated.

In November 1966, a letter to the local press declared that Cheri "is not the first and she will not be the last." Following publication of an article about the

case on April 30, 1967, identical letters were posted to the newspaper, police, and to the victim's father. They read: "Bates had to die. There will be more."

On December 20, 1968, 17-year-old David Faraday was parked with his date, 16-year-old Betty Lou Jensen, on a rural road east of the Vallejo city limits in northern California. A night-stalking gunman found them there and killed both teenagers, shooting Faraday in the head as he sat behind the wheel of his car. Betty Lou ran 30 feet before she was cut down by a tight group of five shots in the back, fired from a .22-caliber automatic pistol.

On July 4, 1969, Michael Mageau, 19, picked up his date, 22-year-old Darlene Ferrin, for a night on the town. At one point, Mageau believed they were being followed, but Darlene seemed to recognize the other motorist, telling Mageau, "Don't worry about it." By midnight, they were parked at Blue Rock Springs Park when a familiar vehicle pulled alongside and the driver shined a bright light in their eyes, opening fire with a 9mm pistol. Hit four times, Mageau survived; Darlene, with nine wounds, was dead on arrival at a local hospital.

Forty minutes after the shooting, Vallejo police received an anonymous call, directing officers to the murder scene. Before hanging up, the male caller declared, "I also killed those kids last year."

In retrospect, friends and relatives recalled that Darlene Ferrin had been suffering harassment through anonymous phone calls and intimidating visits by a heavyset stranger in the weeks before her death. She called the strange man Paul and told one girlfriend that he wished to silence her because she had seen him commit a murder. Police searched for "Paul" in the wake of Darlene's slaying, but he was never located or identified.

"Zodiac" cryptogram, decoded by a California high school teacher (Author's collection)

Threatening "Zodiac" letter addressed to a San Francisco newspaper (Author's collection)

On July 31, 1969, the killer mailed letters to three Bay Area newspapers, each containing one-third of a cryptic cipher. Ultimately broken by a local high school teacher, the message began: "I like killing people because it is so much fun." The author explained that he was killing in an effort to "collect slaves," who would serve him in the afterlife. Another correspondence, mailed on August 7, introduced the "Zodiac" name and provided details of the latest murder, leaving police in no doubt its author was the killer.

On September 27, 20-year-old Bryan Hartnell and Cecilia Shepherd, 20, were enjoying a picnic at Lake Berryessa near Vallejo when they were accosted by a hooded gunman. Covering them with a pistol, the stranger described himself as an escaped convict who needed their car "to go to Mexico." Producing a coil of clothesline, he bound both victims before drawing a long knife, stabbing Hartnell five times in the back. Cecilia Shepherd was stabbed 14 times, including four in the chest as she twisted away from the plunging blade.

Departing the scene, their assailant paused at Hartnell's car to scribble on the door with a felt-tipped pen. He wrote:

Vallejo
12-20-68
7-4-69
Sept 27-69-6:30
by knife

A phone call to police reported the crime, but by that time, a fisherman had already discovered the victims. Brian Hartnell survived his wounds, but Cecilia Shepherd was doomed, another victim for the man who called himself the Zodiac.

On October 11, San Francisco cab driver Paul Stine was shot in the head and killed with a 9mm automatic pistol. Witnesses saw the gunman escape on foot toward the Presidio, and police descended on the neighborhood in force. At one point in the search, two patrolmen stopped a heavyset pedestrian and were directed in pursuit of their elusive prey, not realizing that the "tip" had been provided by the very man they sought.

In the wake of Stine's murder, the Zodiac launched a new barrage of letters, some containing swatches of the cabbie's bloodstained shirt. Successive messages claimed seven victims, instead of the established five, and the killer threatened to "wipe out a school bus some morning." He also vowed to change his method of "collecting souls": "They shall look like routine robberies, killings of anger, & a few fake suicides, etc." Five days before Christmas, he wrote to prominent attorney Melvin Belli, pleading for help with the chilling remark that "I cannot remain in control for much longer."

On March 22, 1970, Kathleen Johns was driving with her infant daughter near Modesto, California, when another motorist pulled her over, flashing his headlights and beeping his horn. The man informed her that a rear tire on her car seemed dangerously loose; he worked on it briefly with a lug wrench, but when she tried to drive away, the wheel fell off. Her benefactor offered a lift to the nearest garage, then took Kathleen on an aimless drive through the countryside, threatening her life and that of her child before she managed to escape from the car, hiding in a roadside irrigation ditch. Reporting the abduction at a local police station, Johns noticed a wanted poster bearing sketches of the Zodiac, and she identified the man as her attacker.

Nine more letters were received from Zodiac between April 1970 and March 1971, but police were unable to trace further crimes in the series. On January 30, 1974, a San Francisco newspaper received the first authentic Zodiac letter in nearly three years, signing off with the notation: "Me-37; SFPD-0."

One officer who took the estimated body count seriously was Sheriff Don Striepke of Sonoma County. In a 1975 report, Striepke referred to a series of 40 unsolved murders in four western states, which seemed to form a giant Z when plotted on the map. While tantalizing, Striepke's theory seemed to fall apart with the identification of THEODORE BUNDY as a prime suspect in several of the homicides.

On April 24, 1978, the Zodiac mailed his 21st letter, chilling Bay Area residents with the news that "I am back with you." No traceable crimes were committed, however, and Homicide Inspector Dave Toschi was later removed from the Zodiac detail on suspicion of writing the letter himself. In fact, while Toschi confessed to writing several anonymous letters to the press, praising his own performance on the case, expert analysts agree that the April note was, in fact, written by the killer.

Theories abound in the Zodiac case. One was aired by author "George Oakes" (a pseudonym) in the November 1981 issue of *California* magazine, based on a presumption of the killer's obsession with water, clocks, binary mathematics, and the writings of Lewis Carroll. Oakes claimed to know the Zodiac's identity and says the killer telephoned him several times at home. He blames the Zodiac for an ARSON fire that ravaged 25,000 acres near Lake Berryessa in June 1981, but *California* editors acknowledged that FBI agents "weren't very impressed" with the theory. Spokesmen for the California state attorney general's office went further, describing the tale as "a lot of bull."

Despite collection of 30 or 40 fingerprints allegedly belonging to the Zodiac (reports vary on the total number), the killer remains unidentified today. Hundreds of suspects were questioned, their fingerprints compared to those on file, but all in vain. Zodiac suspects publicly identified to date include:

Bruce Davis: A one-time member of the Charles MANSON "FAMILY," presently serving a life sentence for two counts of first-degree murder in California, Davis lived in San Francisco prior to joining Manson's tribe and moving south. Although a proven killer with a fascination for occult symbolism, Davis did not fit descriptions of the crew-cut Zodiac and no evidence exists to link him with the slayer's crimes. His fingerprints do not match those alleged to be the Zodiac's, and Davis was in custody by mid-1970, thus ruled out as a source of Zodiac letters mailed after that time. Finally, researcher Tom Voigt cites a 1970 report from the California Bureau of Criminal Identification and Investigation, noting that "All male members of the Manson family have been investigated and eliminated as Zodiac suspects."

Theodore Kaczynski: The elusive "Unabomber," presently serving life without parole in federal prison on three counts of first-degree murder, Kaczynski was named as a Zodiac suspect after FBI agents arrested him in 1998. The "evidence" usually cited in support of his candidacy includes Kaczynski's residency in the San Francisco area during the late 1960s, his penchant for writing to the press after various criminal acts, and his demonstrated expertise at building bombs. (The Zodiac never used explosives, but one of his letters included a crude diagram of a bomb.) Unfortunately for proponents of this theory, Kaczynski has been cleared of involvement in the Zodiac murders by both the FBI and the San Francisco Police Department. According to official reports, Kaczynski was exonerated of the murders by fingerprint and handwriting comparison, and by proof of his absence from California on five specific dates of known Zodiac activity.

Lawrence Kane: Profiled as a Zodiac suspect by the *America's Most Wanted* TV show on November 14, 1998, Kane was 38 years old in 1962, when he suffered brain damage in an automobile accident. Three years later, a psychologist declared that Kane was "losing the ability to control self-gratification." Darlene Ferrin's sister reportedly named Kane as the man who followed and harassed Ferrin over several weeks before her murder, and Kane disposed of his car five days after the Mageau-Ferrin shooting in July 1969. Kathleen Johns also reportedly identified Kane as the man who abducted her in March 1970. Researcher Tom Voigt claims that Kane's surname "can be easily seen" in a Zodiac cipher mailed to police on April 20, 1970 (though other students of the correspondence disagree). Voigt also reports that Kane was living in Nevada "as of early 1999," a fact apparently unknown to producers of *America's Most Wanted* when they broadcast pleas for viewers to locate him three months earlier. Kane's present whereabouts are unknown, but since no charges have been filed against him, he is free to travel where he will.

Rick Marshall: A Texas native, 38 years old at the time of the Zodiac's first known murder in 1966, Marshall seems to be linked with the crimes more by geographic coincidence than anything resembling solid evidence. Tom Voigt reports that Marshall "is still considered a strong Zodiac suspect by several investigators," but his fingerprints match none of those collected from the Zodiac's crime scenes or letters. In place of evidence, we are told that Marshall lived in Riverside "at the approximate time" of the Bates murder, but later resided in San Francisco from 1969 to 1989. His apartment stood "within a few miles" of the Stine murder scene, and the call letters of a radio station (KTIM) where Marshall worked in the early 1970s allegedly "resemble" cryptic symbols from one of the Zodiac's letters. On balance, it is something less than a compelling case.

Michael O'Hare: Initially named as a Zodiac suspect by author Gareth Penn in his book *Times 17* (1987), later featured as one of several Zodiac prospects on the Learning Channel's review of the case, O'Hare is linked to the crimes only by an ephemeral web of conjecture involving Morse code and binary mathematics. Penn also flies in the face of established evidence, blaming the Zodiac for homicides committed in Massachusetts as late as 1981. Most students of the case dismiss his theory as implausible; a notation on Tom Voigt's Zodiac Web site goes further, asserting that "it is the opinion of more than one researcher that Penn himself makes a much better candidate to be the Zodiac than does O'Hare."

Charles Clifton Collins: Named publicly as a suspect for the first time in October 2002, Collins was fingered by his son, New York journalism student William Collins, in a report aired by television's *Primetime Live.* As the younger Collins explained, he was reading a book on the Zodiac murders sometime in the 1990s, when he saw photocopies of the killer's letters and thought, "Oh my God, that's my dad's handwriting." Further research persuaded Collins that his father (deceased in 1993) resembled suspect sketches of the Zodiac, that his shoe size matched the killer's, and that he lived in San Francisco when the murders were committed. The suspect's initials—"CCC"—were also penned on one of the cards Zodiac sent police in his heyday. William Collins appealed to the producers for help, saying, "I need to know if Charles Clifton Collins, my father, the guy who held me when I was a baby—was a serial killer. I have to know. I have to know." Subsequent DNA testing on an envelope licked by Collins's father formally excluded him as a suspect.

Arthur Leigh Allen: The most widely known Zodiac suspect, named during his lifetime by several California investigators and after his death by author Robert Graysmith (among others) in his book *Zodiac Unmasked* (2002). Allen was investigated by various law enforcement agencies from October 1969 until the week after his death in August 1992, and although he pleaded guilty to child molestation in March 1975, serving 29 months in a California state hospital, no charges were ever filed against him in connection with the Zodiac case. Arguments for and against Allen's guilt in the Zodiac murders include the following points:

(1) While employed as a schoolteacher in Calaveras County, California, Allen missed work on Tuesday, November 1, 1966, first claiming the time off as "school business," later changing his story to make it a sick day. Accusers suggest that he took the day off to recuperate from hypothetical "facial wounds" inflicted by Riverside murder victim Cherry Bates on October 30. However, Bates was killed on Sunday night, some 350 miles south of Calaveras County, and Allen taught classes the following day without incident.

(2) A Royal typewriter with Elite type, the same kind used to write the anonymous letters following Cherry Bates's murder, was seized in a search of Allen's home on February 14, 1991. Although police specifically listed the typewriter on their search warrant, Zodiac researcher Jake Wark reports that no effort had been made as of 2002 to match the machine with the Bates correspondence. Until a match is made, Allen's possession of the typewriter proves nothing.

(3) Sometime in late 1968 or early 1969 (reported dates vary), Allen allegedly told acquaintance Don Cheney that he planned to commit a series of random murders, shooting couples in lover's lanes and taunting police with letters signed "Zodiac." Allen's offhand discussion of his planned crimes supposedly included specific descriptions of his intended weapons and plans to attack a school bus (threatened in one of the Zodiac's subsequent letters). Cheney's credibility suffers from the fact that he first revealed the alleged conversation in July 1971, nearly two years after the last known Zodiac murder made international headlines. Even then, he told an employer, rather than contacting police directly, and important details of his story changed over time. Critics note that Cheney once complained of Allen attempting to molest his (Cheney's) daughter on a camping trip, and Vallejo detectives acknowledged that "This might be a motive why Cheney would make such an accusation against Arthur Allen."

(4) On October 6, 1969, Allen was questioned by Vallejo police concerning the Lake Berryessa attack. In that interview, he reportedly told authorities that he "was going to go to Berryessa" on the day of the crime, but changed his mind and "went up the coast instead." Allen cited a couple from Treasure Island as alibi witnesses but never supplied police with their names, address, or telephone number. Accusers note that Allen's shoe size

was identical to that of footprints left by the Lake Berryessa killer (though the prints were never matched to shoes owned by Allen). Survivor Bryan Hartnell allegedly viewed Allen at work, sometime in the mid-1970s, reportedly telling police that Allen's "physical appearance and voice were the same as Zodiac's." While the date of the viewing is uncertain, we must recall that several years (at least) had passed since the attack, and furthermore that Hartnell never saw the killer's face. A foot-long knife was seized at Allen's home during the police search of February 14, 1991, but again researcher Jake Wark reports that no efforts have yet been made (as of September 2002) to match the knife with wounds suffered by the Lake Berryessa victims.

(5) Four days after the Vallejo police interview, on October 10, 1969, Allen allegedly told acquaintance Ralph Spinelli that he was "going to San Francisco to kill a cabbie." The Paul Stine murder occurred one day later and was reported throughout the United States and around the world. Nonetheless, Spinelli made no report of the conversation until December 1990, when he (Spinelli) was charged with armed robbery in Nevada, facing a 30-year-prison term. As in the case of Don Cheney, Spinelli also had a prior history of conflict with Allen: Allen had been arrested in Vallejo on June 15, 1958, after a fistfight with Spinelli, and the charges were dismissed three weeks later.

(6) In July 1992, Zodiac survivor Michael Mageau allegedly picked Allen's mug shot from a police photo lineup, telling detectives, "That's him! He's the man who shot me!" True or not, the fact remains that no charges were filed against Allen prior to his death from natural causes on August 26, 1992.

Despite the allegations against Arthur Leigh Allen, certain facts remain undisputed. A report to Vallejo police from the California Department of Justice, dated July 29, 1971, states clearly that Allen's handwriting had been compared to that of all Zodiac letters received thus far, and none were found to match. A year later, Vallejo police sought a second opinion from FBI handwriting experts, whereupon Allen was "dismissed as a suspect" in the Zodiac correspondence. A search of Allen's home on September 14, 1972, "found nothing that would incriminate Allen in the Zodiac crimes," and he subsequently passed a 10-hour polygraph examination. His fingerprints were also compared with all those collected in the Zodiac case and produced no matches. On balance, Jake Wark is probably correct in his judgment that Allen "was simply one of dozens of Vallejo locals who had been fingered by a friend, an enemy, an acquaintance, or a relative based on little more than a hunch."

Police took what may be their last stab at solving the case in October 2002, when they submitted envelopes from various Zodiac correspondence for DNA testing. Their hope: If the killer licked a stamp or envelope flap, saliva traces might contain enough genetic material to identify the killer once and for all. In fact, Dr. Cydne Holt, supervisor of the San Francisco Police Department's DNA laboratory, did recover DNA samples from one stamp on a Zodiac card, mailed on November 8, 1969, but the test results were disappointing to many investigators. When compared to brain tissue preserved from Arthur Allen's 1992 autopsy, the DNA conclusively eliminated Allen as the man who licked the stamp. The same test also excluded suspect Charles Clifton Collins and an unnamed "prominent San Francisco lawyer who is still living."

But does DNA in fact clear Allen as the killer? Dr. Holt equivocated, noting that the stamp sample contained only four of a possible nine DNA markers, plus gender indicators proving that the subject was male. "It's not enough to positively identify anyone as Zodiac," Holt told reporters, "but it is enough to narrow suspicions, or perhaps even eliminate suspects." Journalist Robert Graysmith, author of two books touting Arthur Allen as the slayer, hedged his bets in an interview with the *San Francisco Chronicle*. "I've always wondered if there wasn't more than one person involved," Graysmith said. "Someone running interference for Allen. It's what makes it one of the great mysteries of all times."

Appendixes

The following appendix of cases not detailed in the main text is divided into three parts, dealing respectively with solo murderers, team killers, and unsolved cases. Information provided for each includes the name, sex, race, and age of perpetrator(s), where known; the approximate date(s) and venue of homicidal activity; the killer's type and motivation; plus a brief description of the case and disposition (where available). Abbreviations used throughout include the following: **AKA** = also known as; **d.** = died (followed by date); **MO** = modus operandi. Gender abbreviations are standard: **M** = male; **F** = female. (In cases of team killers, both genders may appear—for example, a killing team consist- ing of two men and a woman would show "2 M/1 F.") Races are abbreviated as: **W** = white; **B** = black; **H** = Hispanic; **A** = Asian; **NA** = Native American (including Inuit). Types of serial murder are abbreviated as: **N** = nomadic; **T** = territorial; **S** = stationary. Motives are abbreviated as: **CE** = criminal enterprise: **PC** = personal cause; **Sex.** = sexual; **Sad.** = sadistic; **GC** = group cause. (Since motives often vary, more than one may be listed—for example, PC/CE describes a killer who acts on occasion from personal motives, at other times for criminal gain.) Unsolved cases in Appendix C are listed chronologically.

Appendix A: Solo Killers

Abbandando, Frank (1910–42)   AKA: Dasher
SEX: M   RACE: W   TYPE: T   MOTIVE: CE
DATE(S): 1931–40   VENUE: N.Y./N.J.   VICTIMS: 40+
MO: Contract killer for "MURDER, INC."
DISPOSITION: Executed at Sing Sing, Feb. 19, 1942

Abdelali (1962–   )
SEX: M   RACE: A   TYPE: T   MOTIVE: Sex./Sad.
DATE(S): 2001–04   VENUE: Taroudant, Morocco
   VICTIMS: Nine confessed
MO: Pedophile torture-slayer of children whose bodies were found near his home
DISPOSITION: Confessed in custody; disposition unknown

Abdelhaq, Dina (1964–   )
SEX: F   RACE: Unk.   TYPE: S   MOTIVE: CE
DATE(S): 1994–95   VENUE: Chicago, Ill.   VICTIMS: Two suspected
MO: Smothered seven-week-old daughter for $200,000 life insurance; previous death of 18-week-old daughter from SIDS considered suspicious by police
DISPOSITION: Convicted of mail fraud in federal court, received 21-year prison term in Sept. 1999; affirmed on appeal in April 2001

Adam, Scotty R. (1974–   )
SEX: M   RACE: W   TYPE: T   MOTIVE: PC
DATE(S): 1993/1998   VENUE: Kansas   VICTIMS: Two

MO: Stabbed unarmed college student in fight; fatally beat infant boy
DISPOSITION: Convicted of second-degree murder, July 1993, sentenced 15 years to life; new trial in 1996 reduced verdict to involuntary manslaughter, sentenced 3–10 years; paroled April 1996; convicted of felony murder on Sept. 24, 1999, sentenced 42 years

Adams, Jeff (?–   )   AKA: Incubus
SEX: M   RACE: W   TYPE: T   MOTIVE: Sex./Sad.
DATE(S): 1988   VENUE: San Gabriel, Calif.   VICTIMS: Three
MO: Tortured wealthy housewives to death in their homes
DISPOSITION: Life sentence

Adolfo, Gustavo (1982–   )
SEX: M   RACE: H   TYPE: T   MOTIVE: Sex.
DATE(S): 1996–99   VENUE: San Miguel, El Salvador
   VICTIMS: 17 alleged
MO: Rape-mutilation slayings of young women
DISPOSITION: Convicted as a juvenile on seven murder counts; sentenced to seven years

Adorno, George (1959–   )
SEX: M   RACE: H   TYPE: T   MOTIVE: CE
DATE(S): 1974/1977   VENUE: New York City   VICTIMS: Four
MO: Committed triple murder during robbery; killed again after 19 days on parole
DISPOSITION: 15 years to life, 1977

Akin, Joe Dewey (1956–   )
SEX:M   RACE: W   TYPE: N: MOTIVE: PC
DATE(S):1990–91   VENUE: Ala./Ga.   VICTIMS: 18
   suspected
MO:Hospital nurse who killed patients
DISPOSITION:Convicted on one count in Ala., 1992

Akinmurele, Stephen (1978–99)
SEX: M   RACE: B   TYPE: N   MOTIVE: Unk.
DATE(S): 1995–98   VENUE: Isle of Man and Black-
   pool, England   VICTIMS: Five
MO: Three elderly women killed in arson fires; elderly
   couple bludgeoned during home invasion
DISPOSITION: Suicide by hanging prior to trial,
   August 1999

Albanese, Charles (1946–95)
SEX: M   RACE: W   TYPE: T   MOTIVE: CE
DATE(S): 1980–81   VENUE: Ill.   VICTIMS: Three
MO:Poisoned father, mother-in-law, and grandmother
   to inherit family business
DISPOSITION: Condemned, 1982; executed Sept. 20,
   1995

Albani, Adil (1983–2005)
SEX: M   RACE: A   TYPE: T   MOTIVE: PC-nonspe-
cific
DATE(S): 2004   VENUE: Zamboanga, Philippines
   VICTIMS: More than four
MO: Stabbed several fishermen; shot 50-year-old Chi-
nese woman
DISPOSITION: Killed by vigilante gunman on Feb. 15,
   2005, while hiding from police

Albright, Charles (1934–   )   AKA: Dallas Ripper
SEX: M   RACE: W   TYPE: T   MOTIVE: Sex./Sad.
DATE(S): 1990–91   VENUE: Dallas, Tex.   VIC-
   TIMS: Three
MO: Shot female prostitutes and cut out their eyes
DISPOSITION: Life sentence on one count, 1991

Alderisio, Felix Anthony (1912–71)
SEX: M   RACE: W   TYPE: T   MOTIVE: CE/PC
DATE(S): 1930s–65   VENUE:Chicago, Ill.   VIC-
   TIMS: 13+
MO: Syndicate "enforcer" and hit man
DISPOSITION: Convicted of extortion, 1966; died in
   prison, 1971

Alegre, Patrice (1969–   )
SEX: M   RACE: W   TYPE: T   MOTIVE: Sex.
DATE(S): 1989–97   VENUE: Toulouse, France   VIC-
   TIMS: 30+ alleged

MO: Rape-slayer of women, including neighbors and
   prostitutes; claims he arranged S&M orgies for
   prominent citizens and killed at their request to prevent blackmail
DISPOSITION: Life sentence on five murder counts,
   Feb. 24, 2002

al-Hubal, Abdallah (d. 1998)
SEX: M   RACE: A   TYPE: T   MOTIVE: PC-nonspe-
cific
DATE(S): 1989–98   VENUE: Ymen   VICTIMS: 13
MO: Motive unclear in nine-year series of slayings
DISPOSITION: Killed in shoot-out with police, Aug.
   15, 1998

Allam, Ibrahim Hamza   DOB: Unknown
SEX: M   RACE: A   TYPE: N   MOTIVE: PC/CE
DATE(S): 1977–83   VENUE: Germany/Austria/France
   VICTIMS: Four to six
MO: Killed twice from anger/jealousy; others for trans-
   portation
DISPOSITION: 20 years in Austria, 1986

Allen, Bill (d. 1882)
SEX: M   RACE: B   TYPE: T   MOTIVE: PC
DATE(S): 1882   VENUE: Chicago, Ill.   VICTIMS:
   Four
MO: Shot two men in argument and two policemen
   during manhunt
DISPOSITION: Killed while resisting arrest, Dec. 1882

Allen, Billy (?–?)
SEX: M   RACE: W   TYPE: N   MOTIVE: PC
DATE(S): 1880s   VENUE: S. Dak./ N. Mex.   VIC-
   TIMS: "Several"
MO: Old West gunfighter
DISPOSITION: Unknown

Allen, David Michael [See MU'MIN, DAWUD MAJID]

Allen, Quincy (1980–   )
SEX: M   RACE: B   TYPE: N   MOTIVE: PC
DATE: 2002   VENUE: NC/SC   VICTIMS: Four
MO: Random thrill-killer, shot one woman and three
   men; burned woman's body
DISPOSITION: Pleaded guilty on two counts in North
   Carolina, received life prison term on Feb. 28, 2004

Allen, Shirley Goude (1941–   )
SEX: F   RACE: W   TYPE: T   MOTIVE: CE
DATE(S): 1978/82   VENUE: St. Louis, Mo.   VIC-
   TIMS: Two
MO: "Black widow" poisoner of husbands for life
   insurance

DISPOSITION: Life term with 50-year minimum, 1984

Allen, Wanda Jean (1959–2001)
SEX: F RACE: B TYPE: T MOTIVE: PC
DATE(S): 1981/1988 VENUE: Oklahoma City, Okla.
  VICTIMS: Two
MO: Shot her lesbian lovers during arguments
DISPOSITION: Convicted of manslaughter in 1981,
  subsequently paroled; executed for second killing on
  Jan. 11, 2001

Allison, Robert A. (1840–87) AKA: Clay
SEX: M RACE: W TYPE: N MOTIVE: PC
DATE(S): 1870–87 VENUE: Tex./N. Mex. VIC-
  TIMS: 15–21
MO: Alcoholic "shootist" and diagnosed "maniac";
  killed one victim for snoring
DISPOSITION: Killed in freak accident with wagon,
  1887

Allitt, Beverly (1968–) AKA: Angel of Death
SEX: F RACE: W TYPE: S MOTIVE: PC
DATE(S): 1991 VENUE: Grantham, England VIC-
  TIMS: Three
MO: Munchausen's syndrome by proxy; killed hospital
  patients
DISPOSITION: 13 life terms on various charges, 1992

Alterie, Louis [*See* VERAIN, LELAND]

Alston, Robert Sylvester (1969–)
SEX: M RACE: Unk. TYPE: T MOTIVE: Sex.
DATE(S): 1990s VENUE: Greensboro, N.C. VIC-
  TIMS: Four
MO: Dismembered young women
DISPOSITION: Pleaded guilty in 1998 and received
  four life terms

Alton (?–?)
SEX: M RACE: W TYPE: T MOTIVE: Sex.
DATE(S): 1880s VENUE: London, England VIC-
  TIMS: "Several"
MO: "Ripper" of young women
DISPOSITION: Hanged, date unknown

Alves, Raymond (1941–)
SEX: M RACE: H TYPE: T MOTIVE: Sex.
DATE(S): Late 1960s/early 1970s VENUE: Bergen
  County, N.J. VICTIMS: 12+
MO: Violent rapist of young females; after 1977 arrest
  for two rapes, he confessed the murders of more
  than a dozen women

DISPOSITION: Sentenced to 48 years on two rape
  counts, 1978; paroled in 1992 and again in 2000,
  returned to prison each time for parole violations

Amati, Tony Ray (1977–)
SEX: M RACE: W TYPE: T MOTIVE: PC/CE
DATE(S): 1996 VENUE: Las Vegas, Nev. VIC-
  TIMS: Three alleged
MO: "Thrill-killer" of male victims shot during petty
  robberies
DISPOSITION: Sentenced to life on one count, Decem-
  ber 1999; acquitted on a second count by same jury,
  though police found the murder weapon in his
  home; third murder count dismissed

Amberg, Louis (1898–1935) AKA: Pretty
SEX: M RACE: W TYPE: T MOTIVE: CE/PC
DATE(S): 1918–35 VENUE: New York City VIC-
  TIMS: "At least 100"
MO: Psychopathic Brooklyn racketeer
DISPOSITION: Murdered by gangland rivals, Oct.
  1935

Amos, Lowell (1944–)
SEX: M RACE: W TYPE: T MOTIVE: CE
DATE(S): 1979–87 VENUE: Detroit, Mich. VIC-
  TIMS: Four suspected
MO: "Bluebeard" slayer of wives and mother for
  insurance
DISPOSITION: Life without parole on one count,
  1996

Anastasio, Umberto (1903–57) AKA: Albert Anasta-
  sia; "Mad Hatter"; Lord High Executioner
SEX: M RACE: W TYPE: T MOTIVE: PC/CE
DATE(S): 1920–57 VENUE: New York City VIC-
  TIMS: 20+ personal
MO: Psychopathic mafioso and leader of "MURDER,
  INC."; besides personal killings, estimates of "con-
  tracts" ordered range from 100 to 400+
DISPOSITION: Condemned for murder of a long-
  shoreman, 1920; acquitted at second trial in 1922
  after witnesses vanished; murdered by rival mob-
  sters, Oct. 25, 1957

Andermatt, Roger (1968–)
SEX: M RACE: W TYPE: S MOTIVE: PC-non-
  specific
DATE(S): 1995–2001 VENUE: Lucerne, Switzerland
  VICTIMS: 22
MO: Nurse who killed Alzheimer's patients aged
  66–95 by suffocation and lethal injections; Five
  other victims survived.

DISPOSITION: Received life prison term on Jan. 28, 2005

Anderson, Allen Leroy (1942–)
SEX: M   RACE: W   TYPE: N   MOTIVE: CE
DATE(S): 1976   VENUE: USA, nationwide   VICTIMS: Eight definite
MO: Robbery-murders in transit cross-country
DISPOSITION: 40 years in Minn.; Fla. death sentence commuted to life

Anderson, Curtis Dean (1961–)
SEX: M   RACE: W   TYPE: T   MOTIVE: Sex.
DATE(S): 1990s   VENUE: Northern California   VICTIMS: 10 suspected
MO: Convicted kidnapper, described by police as prime suspect in murders and disappearances of girls aged four to seven; confessed one murder and 10 abductions to police in May 2001, saying, "This is gonna go down like ZODIAC"
DISPOSITION: Imprisoned from 1992 to 1999 for the 1991 kidnapping of a 25-year-old woman; received life term in July 2001 for kidnapping an eight-year-old girl who escaped alive

Anderson, Dale R. (1952–)
SEX: M   RACE: W   TYPE: T   MOTIVE: Sex.
DATE(S): 1978–89   VENUE: St. Clair County, Ill.   VICTIMS: More than seven alleged
MO: Profiler ROBERT RESSLER names Anderson as the strangler of six females aged 14–24, and one young boy; Anderson denies any murders but admits, "These cases and a lot of others you don't know about are related."
DISPOSITION: Life prison term in 1989, on two murder counts; two suspects serving time for three other killings are deemed innocent by Ressler

Anderson, Richard Harold (1948–)
SEX: M   RACE: W   TYPE: N   MOTIVE: PC
DATE(S): 1972/87   VENUE: Fla.   VICTIMS: Two
MO: Murders in Hillsborough and Pinellas counties; one victim was man who propositioned Anderson's girlfried
DISPOSITION: 20-year term, 1974; condemned, 1988

Anderson, Robert Leroy (1969–)
SEX: M   RACE: W   TYPE: T   MOTIVE: Sex.
DATE(S): 1994–96   VENUE: Sioux Falls, S. Dak.   VICTIMS: Two
MO: Rape-slayer of women aged 28 and 29; victims strangled or suffocated

DISPOSITION: Convicted of kidnapping one victim, 1997; condemned on two murder counts, April 7, 1999

Anderson, Russell (?–)
SEX: M   RACE: W   TYPE: T   MOTIVE: PC-non-specific
DATE(S): 1987   VENUE: Salt Lake City, Utah   VICTIMS: Three
MO: Execution-style shootings of mentally retarded adults
DISPOSITION: Pleaded guilty; three consecutive terms of five years to life

Anderson, William L. (d. 1864)   AKA: Bloody Bill
SEX: M   RACE: W   TYPE: N   MOTIVE: PC/CE
DATE(S): 1850s–64   VENUE: Kans./Mo.   VICTIMS: 54 admitted
MO: Career criminal and member of "QUANTRILL'S RAIDERS"
DISPOSITION: Killed in Union ambush, Oct. 26, 1864

Andrade, Marcel de (1966–)   AKA: Nitteroi vampire
SEX: M   RACE: H   TYPE: T   MOTIVE: Sex./Sad.
DATE(S): 1991   VENUE: Rio de Janeiro, Brazil   VICTIMS: 14
MO: Raped/killed boys, age six to thirteen, and drank their blood
DISPOSITION: Confined to lunatic asylum; escaped/recaptured, 1997

Andrews, Ralph Raymond (1945–)
SEX: M   RACE: W   TYPE: N   MOTIVE: Sex./Sad.
DATE(S): 1972–91   VENUE: Ill./Ind./Mich./Wisc.   VICTIMS: 20–40 estimated
MO: Rape-slayer of females, stabbed and eviscerated victims, usually teens; boasted in prison of "many" murders
DISPOSITION: Acquitted of attempted murder after stabbing two 15-year-olds, 1973; life sentence for a 1991 murder, in 1993; second life term for a 1977 murder in April 2003

Angeline, Betty Jean (1942–)
SEX: F   RACE: W   TYPE: T   MOTIVE: PC
DATE(S): 2001   VENUE: Independence, Va.   VICTIMS: Two
MO: Shot female acquaintances aged 59 and 62 in their homes
DISPOSITION: Pleaded guilty on both counts and received life sentence, Nov. 2001

Angelo, Richard (1962–)
SEX: M   RACE: H   TYPE: S   MOTIVE: PC-hero

DATE(S): 1987   VENUE: West Islip, N.Y.   VICTIMS: 10+ estimated

MO: "Hero" murders of hospital patients by male nurse

DISPOSITION: 50 years to life on four counts

Anh, The Duong (1975–   )
SEX: M   RACE: A   TYPE: N   MOTIVE: CE-felony
DATE(S): 1998–99   VENUE: California   VICTIMS: 10

MO: Gang leader who shot male victims during robberies, including four killed in one incident

DISPOSITION: Convicted in January 2003 on three counts of first-degree murder and one count second-degree; condemned in February 2003 on three counts

Ankers, Winifred (?–   )
SEX: F   RACE: W   TYPE: S   MOTIVE: PC-revenge
DATE(S): 1911–12   VENUE: Brooklyn, N.Y.   VICTIMS: Eight confessed

MO: Hospital employee; killed infants in maternity ward out of spite for nurses

DISPOSITION: Confessed, Feb. 1912; disposition unreported

Anthony, Michael Lee (1947–   )
SEX: M   RACE: B   TYPE: S   MOTIVE: PC
DATE(S): 2001   VENUE: Highland Park, Mich.   VICTIMS: Two

MO: Habitual sex offender and self-styled "black Jesus," found with remains of murdered women in his basement

DISPOSITION: Received a prison term of 15–30 years for rape and robbery in 1991, mistakenly paroled in 1996 (instead of 2011); returned to prison on that charge while awaiting trial on two murder counts

Archambault, Serge (1956–   )
SEX: M   RACE: W   TYPE: T   MOTIVE: Sex.
DATE(S): 1989–92   VENUE: Montreal, Quebec   VICTIMS: Three

MO: Traveling salesman and lust-killer of women

DISPOSITION: 25 years on three counts of first-degree murder, 1993

Archer, Gerald Thomas (1932–95)
SEX: M   RACE: W   TYPE: T   MOTIVE: Sex.
DATE(S): 1969–71   VENUE: Chatham and London, Ontario   VICTIMS: Three

MO: Females in their 50s and 60s beaten and stabbed

DISPOSITION: Life sentence on one count, 1972; died in prison 1995; publicly blamed for two more murders in February 2000

Archerd, William Dale (1912–   )
SEX: M   RACE: W   TYPE: N   MOTIVE: PC
DATE(S): 1947–66   VENUE: Calif./Nev.   VICTIMS: Six suspected

MO: "Bluebeard" slayer of wives/others, via insulin injections

DISPOSITION: Condemned on three counts, 1968; commuted to life, 1972

Ardison, Victor (?–?)
SEX: M   RACE: W   TYPE: T   MOTIVE: Sex.
DATE(S): 19th century   VENUE: France   VICTIMS: "Several"

MO: Necrophile who slept with severed heads of his victims

DISPOSITION: Guillotined, date unknown

Arguelles, Roberto (1962–2003)
SEX: M   RACE: W   TYPE: T   MOTIVE: Sex.
DATE(S): 1992   VENUE: Salt Lake City, Utah   VICTIMS: Four confessed

MO: Lust killer of three teenage girls and 42-year-old woman

DISPOSITION: Pleaded guilty and requested execution, 1997; died in prison of "unknown causes," Nov. 13, 2003

Arinaitwe, Richard (1977–   )
SEX: M   RACE: B   TYPE: T   MOTIVE: Unk.
DATE(S): 1998   VENUE: Kampala, Uganda   VICTIMS: Eight

MO: Strangled women, including a 35-year-old American tourist; tried to kill the magistrate who took his confession in March 1999

DISPOSITION: 48-month sentence for attempted murder, 1999; condemned for murder in December 2003

Armstrong, John Eric (1974–   )
SEX: M   RACE: W   TYPE: T   MOTIVE: Sex.
DATE(S): 1999–2000   VENUE: Detroit, Mich.   VICTIMS: Six

MO: Strangler of female prostitutes; confessed murders of 11 women and one man, allegedly committed in the United States, Hong Kong, Singapore, and Thailand while a U.S. Navy seaman, 1993–99; authorities discount those claims but blamed Armstrong for six murders in Michigan

DISPOSITION: Life sentence without parole on one count, April 2001; pleaded guilty on three counts of second degree murder and received a 31-year sentence in July 2001

Arnold, Herbert (1944–   )
SEX: M   RACE: W   TYPE: T   MOTIVE: PC/Sex.

DATE(S): 1965/70   VENUE: New York City   VICTIMS: Three

MO: Rape-slayer of two female neighbors; killed kidnap victim

DISPOSITION: Ruled insane, 1965 (later released); incompetent for trial, 1970; convicted on one count, 1973 (paroled 1983); back to asylum on rape charge, 1991

Arnold, Terry (1962–   )
SEX: M   RACE: W   TYPE: N   MOTIVE: Sex.
DATE(S): 1981–87   VENUE: North America   VICTIMS: "Several" suspected
MO: Rape-slayer of girls and young women killed while he worked for a traveling carnival
DISPOSITION: Life sentence in Canada, 1991, for the 1987 murder of a 16-year-old girl; named as prime suspect in three more Canadian murders, plus others in Mexico and five U.S. states (Fla., N.Y., Okla., Tex., and Va.)

Arrington, Marie Dean (1933–   )
SEX: F   RACE: B   TYPE: T   MOTIVE: PC/CE
DATE(S): 1964/68   VENUE: Fla.   VICTIMS: Two
MO: Shot husband; killed female victim kidnapped to extort son's release from prison
DISPOSITION: 20 years for manslaughter, 1965; condemned, 1969; sentence commuted to life, 1972

Artieda, Ramiro (d. 1939)
SEX: M   RACE: H   TYPE: T   MOTIVE: CE/PC
DATE(S): 1930s   VENUE: La Paz, Bolivia   VICTIMS: Eight
MO: Killed brother for inheritance, then strangled seven 18-year-old girls resembling lover who jilted him
DISPOSITION: Shot by firing squad, July 3, 1939

Askeborn, Glenn (1944–   )
SEX: M   RACE: W   TYPE: N   MOTIVE: Sex.
DATE(S): 1975/84   VENUE: Conn./Maine   VICTIMS: Two suspected
MO: Women bound/killed in identical circumstances
DISPOSITION: Imprisoned on one count, in Maine

Atkins, Benjamin (1968–   )   AKA: Woodward Corridor Killer
SEX: M   RACE: B   TYPE: T   MOTIVE: Sex.
DATE(S): 1991–92   VENUE: Detroit, Mich.   VICTIMS: 11
MO: Strangler of female prostitutes
DISPOSITION: Life imprisonment, 1994

Atkins, Joseph Ernest (1947–99)
SEX: M   RACE: W   TYPE: T   MOTIVE: PC

DATE(S): 1970/85   VENUE: North Charleston, S.C.   VICTIMS: Three
MO: Shot his brother, adoptive father, and a teenage neighbor
DISPOSITION: Life term for brother's death, 1970 (paroled 1980); executed on two counts Jan. 22, 1999

Avinain, Charles (1799–1867)
SEX: M   RACE: W   TYPE: T   MOTIVE: CE
DATE(S): 1867   VENUE: Paris, France   VICTIMS: "Several"
MO: Butcher who robbed/dismembered male customers
DISPOSITION: Guillotined, 1867

Bailey, Leslie (1950–93)   AKA: Catweazle
SEX: M   RACE: W   TYPE: T   MOTIVE: Sex.
DATE(S): 1980s   VENUE: England   VICTIMS: Three+
MO: Pedophile slayer of boys age six to 14; police suggest 25 possible victims; alleged accomplices in second and third murders never charged
DISPOSITION: 15 years for manslaughter (with three accomplices), 1989; life term on second count, 1991; life term on third count, 1992; found dead in cell "under suspicious circumstances," Oct. 1993
ACCOMPLICES: Stephen Barrell (?–   ), 15 years in 1989; Sidney Cooke (1928–   ), 19 years in 1989; Robert Oliver (1955–   ), 15 years in 1989

Bajramovic, Miro (?–   )
SEX: M   RACE: W   TYPE: T   MOTIVE: PC-extremist
DATE(S): 1991   VENUE: Croatia   VICTIMS: 86 confessed
MO: Croat soldier who killed Serbs during "ethnic cleansing"
DISPOSITION: Confessed in open court; outcome unknown

Baker, Cullen Montgomery (1836–68/69)
SEX: M   RACE: W   TYPE: N   MOTIVE: PC/CE
DATE(S): 1861–68   VENUE: Ark./Tex.   VICTIMS: 12+
MO: Old West outlaw and murderer
DISPOSITION: Killed by posse in Dec. 1868 or Jan. 1869

Baker, Stanley Dean (1948–   )
SEX: M   RACE: W   TYPE: N   MOTIVE: PC-extremist
DATE(S): 1970   VENUE: Mont./Calif.   VICTIMS: Two confessed

MO: Mutilation/cannibal murders influenced by Satanism
DISPOSITION: Mont. life sentence (paroled 1985)

Balaam, Anthony (1966–)
SEX: M RACE: Unk. TYPE: T MOTIVE: Sex.
DATE(S): 1994–96 VENUE: Trenton, N.J. VICTIMS: Four
MO: Raped/strangled four female prostitutes aged 27–41 within a two-mile radius of his home; fifth victim escaped to notify police
DISPOSITION: Convicted on four counts; received life prison terms, June 16, 2000

Baldi, Joseph (1941–)
SEX: M RACE: W TYPE: T MOTIVE: Sex.
DATE(S): 1970–72 VENUE: Queens, N.Y. VICTIMS: Four
MO: Home invader, stabbed young women in bed
DISPOSITION: 25 years to life, 1975; parole denied 1997

Ballard, Billy Ray, Jr. (?–)
SEX: M RACE: W TYPE: N MOTIVE: Sex./Sad.
DATE(S): 1985 VENUE: Wash./Wyo. VICTIMS: Two confessed
MO: Rape-torture slayer of victims chosen at random; arrested for two rapes in Wyoming, linked by fingerprints to the murders of two Seattle victims dumped in Grant County, Wash.
DISPOSITION: Life prison term in Wyoming

Baltis, Yiannis (1970–)
SEX: M RACE: W TYPE: T MOTIVE: PC-nonspecific
DATE(S): 1995–2004 VENUE: Salonika, Greece VICTIMS: Four
MO: Killed three Albanian immigrants he employed as shepherds, 1995–96; kidnapped a girlfriend and shot her two brothers, killing one, 2004
DISPOSITION: Confessed four murders; disposition unknown

Bankston, Clinton, Jr. (1971–)
SEX: M RACE: B TYPE: T MOTIVE: Sex.
DATE(S): 1987 VENUE: Athens, Ga. VICTIMS: Five
MO: Killed/mutilated five victims in two home invasions
DISPOSITION: Five life terms, May 1988

Banovic, Predrag (1970–)
SEX: M RACE: W TYPE: T MOTIVE: PC-extremist

DATE(S): 1992 VENUE: Keraterm, Bosnia VICTIMS: Five
MO: Bosnian Serb concentration camp guard who killed five inmates and injured at least 27 others in "ethnic cleansing"
DISPOSITION: Pleaded guilty and received an eight-year prison term, Oct. 29, 2003

Baptistella, Dr. Sergio Luiz (1955–)
SEX: M RACE: H TYPE: T MOTIVE: PC
DATE(S): 1998 VENUE: Rio de Janeiro, Brazil VICTIMS: Four alleged
MO: Physician who shot six other doctors in personal disputes, killing four; one victim was his former lover from medical school
DISPOSITION: Confessed three murders in custody; disposition unknown

Barbeault, Marcel (1941–) AKA: Killer from the Shadows
SEX: M RACE: W TYPE: T MOTIVE: PC-nonspecific
DATE(S): 1969–76 VENUE: Nogent, France VICTIMS: Eight
MO: Random shooter of victims age 20–49, mostly female
DISPOSITION: Life term, 1982; reduced to 20 years on appeal

Barber, Danny Lee (1956–99)
SEX: M RACE: W TYPE: T MOTIVE: Sex./PC
DATE(S): 1978–79 VENUE: Dallas, Tex. VICTIMS: Four suspected
MO: Thrill-killer of victims including both genders; tried to rape corpses of two female victims; shot a man "just to have some fun with him"
DISPOSITION: Executed on Feb. 11, 1999

Barbosa, Daniel Camargo (1941–)
SEX: M RACE: H TYPE: N MOTIVE: Sex./Sad.
DATE(S): 1974–88 VENUE: Colombia/Ecuador VICTIMS: 72
MO: Pedophile "ripper" of young girls
DISPOSITION: 16-year term in Ecuador, 1989 (the legal maximum)

Barboza, Joseph (1932–76) AKA: The Animal
SEX: M RACE: W TYPE: N MOTIVE: CE-felony
DATE(S): 1950s–1971 VENUE: New England/Calif. VICTIMS: 27 confessed
MO: Mafia contract killer who turned state's evidence in 1968
DISPOSITION: Confessed 26 murders and received a one-year prison term in exchange for testimony in

various trials; helped frame four innocent men for one of his own murders in Boston; released in March 1969; pleaded guilty to second-degree murder in California, 1971, and received a five-year sentence; murdered in San Francisco soon after his release, on Feb. 11, 1976

Barfield, Margie Velma (1932–84)
SEX: F   RACE: W   TYPE: T   MOTIVE: CE
DATE(S): 1969–78   VENUE: N.C.   VICTIMS: Five
MO: "Black widow" slayer of husbands/others, mostly by poison
DISPOSITION: Executed Nov. 2, 1984

Barker, Glenn (1959–   )
SEX: M   RACE: ?   TYPE: N   MOTIVE: Sex.
DATE(S): 1982/96   VENUE: Va.   VICTIMS: Three suspected
MO: Killed 12-year-old girl; named by police as prime suspect in murders of his girlfriend and her daughter (child raped)
DISPOSITION: 18 years on one count, 1982 (paroled 1991); no charges filed in later crimes despite police announcement

Barone, Cesar Francesco (1960–   )   BORN: Rode, Adolph James
SEX: M   RACE: W   TYPE: N   MOTIVE: Sex./Sad.
DATE(S): 1979–80/91–92   VENUE: Fla./Wash./Ore.
VICTIMS: Seven+ suspected
MO: Rape-slayer of women
DISPOSITION: Condemned on two counts in Ore. + 45 years on third count, 1995

Barrera, Marco (1963–   )
SEX: M   RACE: H   TYPE: S   MOTIVE: PC/Sad.
DATE(S): 1997–98   VENUE: San Bernardino, Calif.
VICTIMS: Two
MO: Fathered 14 children by two sisters, fatally torturing two of them
DISPOSITION: Condemned on two counts, July 2001; one "wife" received 12-year sentence for child abuse, Aug. 2001; second "wife" turned state's evidence

Barron, Jack (1961–   )
SEX: M   RACE: W   TYPE: T   MOTIVE: CE-felony
DATE(S): 1992–95   VENUE: Sacramento, Calif.
VICTIMS: Three or four
MO: Profit-motivated slayer of his wife, son and mother for life insurance payments; only suspect in death of his four-year-old daughter
DISPOSITION: Convicted of killing his wife (1992), son (1993), and mother (1995), but acquitted of

killing his daughter (1994); received three consecutive life terms on April 15, 2000

Barton, "Kid" (?–?)
SEX: M   RACE: W   TYPE: T   MOTIVE: CE
DATE(S): 1860s   VENUE: N. Mex.   VICTIMS: "Several"
MO: Old West outlaw leader
DISPOSITION: Hanged "in late 1860s"

Bartsch, Juergen (1950–76)
SEX: M   RACE: W   TYPE: T   MOTIVE: Sex./Sad.
DATE(S): 1967   VENUE: Bonn, Germany   VICTIMS: Four
MO: Pedophile who tortured young boys to death
DISPOSITION: Life sentence, 1967; died Apr. 28, 1976, during voluntary surgical castration

Bashor, Donald (1929–57)
SEX: M   RACE: W   TYPE: T   MOTIVE: Sex.
DATE(S): 1955–56   VENUE: Los Angeles, Calif.
VICTIMS: Two
MO: Home invader; bludgeoned women
DISPOSITION: Executed Oct. 11, 1957

Bateson, Paul (1939–   )
SEX: M   RACE: W   TYPE: T   MOTIVE: Sex./Sad.
DATE(S): 1977–78   VENUE: New York City   VICTIMS: Seven confessed
MO: Dismembered gay men "for fun"
DISPOSITION: 20 years to life on one count, 1979

Batten, William (?–   )
SEX: M   RACE: W   TYPE: T   MOTIVE: Sex.
DATE(S): 1969–75   VENUE: Aberdeen, Wash.   VICTIMS: Three
MO: Confined to asylum as a child molester, 1967; linked to disappearance of a girlfriend, 1969; stabbed two teenage hitchhikers in 1975
DISPOSITION: Two consecutive life terms for murder, with additional prison time for use of a deadly weapon in his crimes

Baughman, John Earl (1942–   )
SEX: M   RACE: W   TYPE: N   MOTIVE: PC-domestic
DATE(S): 1970–95   VENUE: Ill./Antigua   VICTIMS: Three
MO: Ex-cop; killed wives and one wife's lover
DISPOSITION: Condemned in Antigua, 1996

Baumeister, Herbert Richard (1947–95)
SEX: M   RACE: W   TYPE: N   MOTIVE: Sex.

DATE(S): 1980–95   VENUE: Ind./Ohio   VICTIMS: 16 suspected
MO: Lust killer of gay men; some buried near his home, others dumped in rural areas spanning two states
DISPOSITION: Suicide while a fugitive, July 2, 1995

Baxter, Patrick (1969–   )
SEX: M   RACE: Unk.   TYPE: T   MOTIVE: Sex.
DATE(S): 1987–90   VENUE: White Plains, N.Y.   VICTIMS: Three
MO: Rape slayer of females aged 14–25
DISPOSITION: Convicted on three counts, 2002; received three consecutive terms of 75 years to life

Beach, Gary (1942–   )
SEX: M   RACE: Unk.   TYPE: S   MOTIVE: PC-non-specific
DATE(S): 1999   VENUE: Kansas City, Mo.   VICTIMS: Five
MO: Shot victims, including a step-nephew, and left their decomposing bodies at his home
DISPOSITION: Pleaded guilty on five murder counts; received life sentence, March 2002

Beagle, Billy Ray (1947–98)
SEX: M   RACE: W   TYPE: T   MOTIVE: PC-non-specific
DATE(S): 1993   VENUE: Baker Country, Fla.   VICTIMS: Two
MO: Shot sportsmen in random attacks
DISPOSITION: Suicide during shoot-out with police, Mar. 25, 1998

Beardslee, Donald Jay (1943–2005)
SEX: M   RACE: W   TYPE: N   MOTIVE: Sex./CE
DATES: 1969/1981   VENUE: Mo./Calif.   VICTIMS: Three
MO: Fatally stabbed a 52-year-old woman after sex; killed two women aged 19 and 23 in a bungled drug transaction
DISPOSITION: Served seven years of an 18-year sentence in Missouri for first murder; condemned on two counts in 1984; executed Jan. 19, 2005

Beck, Dieter (?–   )
SEX: M   RACE: W   TYPE: MOTIVE: Sex./Sad.
DATE(S): 1961–68   VENUE: Rehme, Germany   VICTIMS: Three
MO: Rape-slayer of women
DISPOSITION: Life sentence, 1969

Becker, Marie Alexandrine (1877–194?)
SEX: F   RACE: W   TYPE: T   MOTIVE: PC/CE

DATE(S): 1932–36   VENUE: Liege, Belgium   VICTIMS: 12+ estimated
MO: Poisoned husband, male lover, and female customers (who were also robbed)
DISPOSITION: Life sentence, 1936; died in prison during World War II

Beets, Betty Lou (1937–2002)
SEX: F   RACE: W   TYPE: T   MOTIVE: CE
DATE(S): 1981/83   VENUE: Dallas County, Tex.   VICTIMS: Two
MO: "Black widow" slayer of husbands for life insurance
DISPOSITION: Condemned on one count, 1985; executed Feb. 24, 2000

Beggs, William (1963–   )
SEX: M   RACE: W   TYPE: N   MOTIVE: Sex./Sad.
DATE(S): 1987–99   VENUE: England/Scotland   VICTIMS: Three suspected
MO: Mutilation-slayer of gay men, using razors
DISPOSITION: Three convictions for assaults with razors; cleared of one murder count on a legal technicality; convicted on a second count, 1987; life sentence on a third count, October 2001

Belcastro, James (?–?)   AKA: King of the Bombers
SEX: M   RACE: W   TYPE: T   MOTIVE: CE
DATE(S): 1918–29   VENUE: Chicago, Ill.   VICTIMS: 100+ suspected
MO: "Black Hand" extortionist; later chief bomber for ALPHONSE CAPONE gang
DISPOSITION: Acquitted on one count, 1927; died of natural causes

Bell, Larry Eugene (d. 1996)
SEX: M   RACE: W   TYPE: T   MOTIVE: Sex.
DATE(S): 1985   VENUE: Lexington County, S.C.   VICTIMS: Three
MO: Lust killer of girls age nine to 17
DISPOSITION: Condemned on two counts, 1986; executed Oct. 4. 1996

Bell, Mary Flora (1957–   )
SEX: F   RACE: W   TYPE: T   MOTIVE: Sad.
DATE(S): 1968   VENUE: Newcastle, England   VICTIMS: Two
MO: Killed/mutilated boys age three and four
DISPOSITION: Imprisoned as juvenile on two manslaughter counts

Bell, Michael Bernard (1970–   )
SEX: M   RACE: W   TYPE: T   MOTIVE: PC

DATE(S): 1989–93   VENUE: Duval County, Fla.
VICTIMS: Five suspected
MO: Killed in personal disputes; victims included
mother's boyfriend, his own lover, and their child
DISPOSITION: Condemned on two counts + 25 years
on third count, 1995

Bellen, Michel (1946–)
SEX: M   RACE: W   TYPE: N   MOTIVE: Sex.
DATE(S): 1964/82   VENUE: Belgium   VICTIMS:
Three
MO: Rape-strangler of nurses attacked in their homes
DISPOSITION: Condemned, 1965 (commuted to life);
paroled 1982; condemned 1983 (commuted to life,
1984)

Beniquez, Jorge Adam (1969–)
SEX: M   RACE: H   TYPE: N   MOTIVE: CE
DATE(S): 1990–91   VENUE: Puerto Rico/N.Y.   VIC-
TIMS: Nine suspected
MO: Career criminal; "most wanted man in Puerto
Rico"
DISPOSITION: Convicted on one count of second-
degree murder in N.Y., 1992

Bennet, Robert Eugene (1938–)
SEX: M   RACE: W   TYPE: N   MOTIVE: PC
DATE(S): 1978/89   VENUE: Ore./Utah   VICTIMS:
Two
MO: Wife killed in Ore.; male victim dismembered in
Utah
DISPOSITION: Pleaded guilty to second degree in
Utah; five years to life

Berdella, Robert A. (1949–)
SEX: M   RACE: W   TYPE: T   MOTIVE: Sex./Sad.
DATE(S): 1984–87   VENUE: Kansas City, Mo.   VIC-
TIMS: Seven suspected
MO: Gay torturer-slayer of men age 19–23
DISPOSITION:Life term on five counts, 1988; died
Oct. 8, 1992

Bergamo, Marco (?–)   AKA: Monster of Bolzano
SEX: M   RACE: W   TYPE: T   MOTIVE: Sex.
DATE(S): 1985–92   VENUE: Bergamo, Italy   VIC-
TIMS: Five
MO: Stabbed young women in random attacks
DISPOSITION: Life sentence

Berk, Lucia Isabella Quirina de (1961–)
SEX: F   RACE: W   TYPE: T   MOTIVE: PC-mercy
DATE(S): 1997–2001   VENUE: The Hague, Nether-
lands   VICTIMS: More than four

MO: Nurse charges with killing or attempting to kill
18 patients at three area hospitals
DISPOSITION: Convicted of four murders and three
attempted murders; life sentence imposed, March
24, 2003

Bermudez, Manuel Octavio (?–)
SEX: M   RACE: H   TYPE: T   MOTIVE: Sex./Sad.
DATE(S): 2002–03   VENUE: Valle del Cauca
Province, Colombia   VICTIMS: More than 30
MO: Ice cream vendor linked by police to slayings of
numerous young boys; 12-year-old victim found
dead at his home, with evidence of other slayings
DISPOSITION: Unknown

Bernard, Norman (1951–)
SEX: M   RACE: B   TYPE: N   MOTIVE: PC
DATE(S): 1983   VENUE: N.C./Calif.   VICTIMS:
Three
MO: "Mercy" shootings of homeless men
DISPOSITION: Life without parole in Calif., 1984

Bernson, Stanley (?–)
SEX: M   RACE: W   TYPE: N   MOTIVE: Sex.
DATE(S?) 1970s   VENUE: U.S. Pacific Northwest
VICTIMS: 30 alleged
MO: Rape-slayer of females, charged with murders in
Washington and Oregon
DISPOSITION: Life prison term for stabbing a 15-
year-old girl at Richland, Wash.; charges filed but
never prosecuted for the slaying of a teenager at
Umatilla, Ore.

Besnard, Marie (1896–?)   AKA: Queen of poisoners
SEX: F   RACE: W   TYPE: T   MOTIVE: CE/PC
DATE(S): 1927–49   VENUE: Loudon, France   VIC-
TIMS: 13
MO: Poisoned husbands and relatives for inheritance
DISPOSITION: Acquitted despite confessions, Dec. 1961

Bessarabo, Marie-Louise Victorine (1868–?)   AKA:
Hera Myrtle
SEX: F   RACE: W   TYPE: N   MOTIVE: PC
DATE(S): 1892/1914/20   VENUE: Mexico/France
VICTIMS: Three
MO: "Black widow" slayer of husband and lovers
DISPOSITION: Life term on one count, 1920

Bey, Marko (1965–)
SEX: M   RACE: B   TYPE: T   MOTIVE: Sex.
DATE(S): 1983–84   VENUE: Monmouth County, N.J.
VICTIMS: Two
MO: Juvenile rape-slayer of women
DISPOSITION: Condemned, 1989

Bible, Danny Paul (1951–   )
SEX: M   RACE: W   TYPE: N   MOTIVE: Sex./PC
DATE(S): 1979/83   VENUE: Tex.   VICTIMS: Four
   confessed
MO: Raped/stabbed woman (1979); killed sister-in-
   law, her infant child, and roommate
DISPOSITION: 25 years on one count in Tex. plus 20
   years concurrent for kidnapping in Montana, 1984
   (paroled 1992); confessed three more after arrest for
   rape in Louisiana, 1998; convicted and condemned,
   June 2003

Bichel, Andreas (1770–1808)   AKA: Bavarian Ripper
SEX: M   RACE: W   TYPE: T   MOTIVE: CE/Sex.
DATE(S): 1790s–1808   VENUE: Bavaria   VICTIMS:
   50+ suspected
MO: Fortune-teller who stabbed/robbed female clients
DISPOSITION: Beheaded for two murders, 1808

Biegenwald, Richard (1940–   )
SEX: M   RACE: W   TYPE: N   MOTIVE:
   CE/PC/Sex.
DATE(S): 1958–82   VENUE: N.J./N.Y.   VICTIMS:
   Seven
MO: Shot victims during robberies and after rape
DISPOSITION: Jailed 1958–75; 1983 death sentence
   commuted to life

Bijeh, Mohammed (1980–2005)
SEX: M   RACE: A   TYPE: T   MOTIVE: Sex.
DATE(S): 2003–04   VENUE: Pakdasht, Iran   VIC-
   TIMS: 22+
MO: Lured children to desert with aid from accomplice
   Ali Baghi, then raped and killed them; confessed 22
   murders in custody but suspected of more
DISPOSITION: Flogged and hanged on March 16,
   2005; Baghi received 15-year prison term

Bilancia, Donato (1950–   )
SEX: M   RACE: W   TYPE: T   MOTIVE: PC-nonspecific
DATE(S): 1997–98   VENUE: Italian Riviera   VIC-
   TIMS: 14–17
MO: Shot/strangled strangers in fits of blind rage; identified victims include six female prostitutes; a newlywed couple; two jewelers; two security guards; and
   two women shot in restrooms aboard trains in transit
DISPOSITION: Received 13 life terms "for 17 murders," April 14, 2000

Billik, Herman [*See* VAJICEK, HERMAN]

Bird, Jake (1901–49)
SEX: M   RACE: B   TYPE: N   MOTIVE: Sex.

DATE(S): 1930s–47   VENUE: USA nationwide   VIC-
   TIMS: 44 confessed
MO: Rape-slayer of females during home invasions,
   often used ax
DISPOSITION: Hanged in Wash., July 15, 1949

Birt, Billy Sunday (1938–   )
SEX: M   RACE: W   TYPE: N   MOTIVE: CE/PC
DATE(S): 1960s–1973   VENUE: Georgia   VICTIMS:
   56 alleged
MO: "Dixie Mafia" member who killed rival gang-
   sters, robbery victims, and personal enemies
DISPOSITION: Condemned on three murder counts,
   May 1975; sentence commuted to life imprisonment
   on appeal, 1988

Bischoff, Charles (1886–1947)
SEX: M   RACE: W   TYPE: T   MOTIVE: Sex.
DATE(S): 1915–31   VENUE: Cincinnati, Ohio   VIC-
   TIMS: Four
MO: Pedophile slayer of children
DISPOSITION: Ruled insane; died in asylum Apr. 10,
   1947

Bishop, Arthur Gary (d. 1988)
SEX: M   RACE: W   TYPE: T   MOTIVE: Sex.
DATE(S): 1979–83   VENUE: Salt Lake City, Utah
   VICTIMS: Five
MO: Pedophile slayer of children
DISPOSITION: Executed June 9, 1988

Bishop, Jesse Walter (d. 1979)
SEX: M   RACE: W   TYPE: N   MOTIVE: CE
DATE(S): 1970s   VENUE: Western U.S.   VICTIMS:
   19 confessed
MO: Armed robber and confessed hit man
DISPOSITION: Executed on one count in Nev., Oct.
   22, 1979

Black, Robert (1947–   )   AKA: Smelly Bob
SEX: M   RACE: W   TYPE: N   MOTIVE: Sex.
DATE(S): 1969–90   VENUE: England   VICTIMS:
   Five to eight+
MO: Pedophile slayer of girls age nine to 16
DISPOSITION: 105 years minimum on three counts,
   1994

Bladel, Rudy (1971–   )
SEX: M   RACE: W   TYPE: N   MOTIVE: PC-
   revenge
DATE(S): 1963–78   VENUE: Ind./Mich.   VICTIMS:
   Seven
MO: Shot railroad employees to avenge loss of job
DISPOSITION: three consecutive life terms

Blair, Robert (?–)
SEX: M   RACE: W   TYPE: N   MOTIVE: PC
DATE(S): 1983–95   VENUE: Vt./N.H.   VICTIMS:
Four
MO: Killed his wife and son with a hammer at Concord, N.H.; later confessed to killing a woman and her child at Rutland, Vt., with an accomplice who died in 1987
DISPOSITION: Life prison term on two counts in New Hampshire, 1996

Bland, Warren James (1936–)
SEX: M   RACE: W   TYPE: T   MOTIVE: Sex./Sad.
DATE(S): 1986   VENUE: Southern Calif.   VICTIMS:
Three+ suspected
MO: Career sex offender; torture slayer of girls age seven to 14
DISPOSITION: Condemned on one count, 1993

Blank, Daniel (1962–)
SEX: M   RACE: Unk.   TYPE: T   MOTIVE: CE-felony
DATE(S): 1997   VENUE: Ascension Parish, La.
VICTIMS: Six
MO: Killed five women and one man during home invasions staged to finance his compulsive gambling
DISPOSITION: Condemned on one count, Sept. 1999; condemned on second count, Oct. 2000

Blaunsteiner, Ilfriede (1932–)   AKA: Black Widow
SEX: F   RACE: W   TYPE: T   MOTIVE: CE
DATE(S): 1981–95   VENUE: Austria   VICTIMS:
Five confessed
MO: Profit-motivated poisoner of husband and others
DISPOSITION: Life term on one count, 1997

Bobbitt, Jerry Dale (1962–)   AKA: Scissors Man
SEX: M   RACE: W   TYPE: T   MOTIVE: CE/Sad.
DATE(S): 1994   VENUE: Orlando, Fla.   VICTIMS:
Two
MO: Women age 34 and 53 stabbed in their places of business
DISPOSITION: Life + 25 years on two counts, 1996

Boczkowski, Timothy (1955–)
SEX: M   RACE: W   TYPE: N   MOTIVE: CE
DATE(S): 1990/94   VENUE: N.C./Pa.   VICTIMS:
Two
MO: "Bluebeard" slayer of wives for insurance
DISPOSITION: Life term in N.C., 1996; condemned in Pennsylvania, 1999

Boden, Wayne Clifford (?–)   AKA: Vampire Rapist
SEX: M   RACE: W   TYPE: N   MOTIVE: Sex./Sad.

DATE(S): 1968–71   VENUE: Montreal/Calgary, Canada   VICTIMS: Five
MO: Rape-murders of women, with gnawing on bodies
DISPOSITION: 1972 life sentence

Bolder, Martsay L. (1957–93)
SEX: M   RACE: B   TYPE: N   MOTIVE: CE/PC
DATE(S): 1973/79   VENUE: Mo.   VICTIMS: Two
MO: Killed burglary victim; stabbed prison cellmate
DISPOSITION: Life on one count, 1973; condemned, 1980; executed Jan. 27, 1993

Bolin, Oscar Ray (1962–)
SEX: M   RACE: W   TYPE: N   MOTIVE: Sex.
DATE(S): 1986–90   VENUE: USA nationwide   VICTIMS: 30+ suspected
MO: Long-haul trucker; rape-slayer of women
DISPOSITION: Condemned in three Fla. cases, 1991–92; indicted on one count in Tex. (trial unlikely)

Bolton, Darren Lee (1967–96)
SEX: M   RACE: W   TYPE: T   MOTIVE: Sex.
DATE(S): 1982/86   VENUE: Tucson, Ariz.   VICTIMS: Two
MO: Pedophile slayer of girls age two and seven
DISPOSITION: Condemned on one count, 1993; executed June 19, 1996

Bomar, Arthur (1959–)
SEX: M   RACE: W   TYPE: T   MOTIVE: Sex.
DATE(S): 1993–97   VENUE: Philadelphia, Pa.   VICTIMS: Three+
MO: Rape-slayer of young women
DISPOSITION: Condemned, 1998

Bombeek, Cecile (1933–)   AKA: Sister Godfrida
SEX: F   RACE: W   TYPE: S   MOTIVE: PC/Sad.
DATE(S): 1976–77   VENUE: Wetteren, Belgium
VICTIMS: Three to 21
MO: Injected rest home patients with insulin
DISPOSITION: Confessed three murders; life term, 1978

Bonny, Anne (1700–?)
SEX: F   RACE: W   TYPE: N   MOTIVE: CE
DATE(S): 1714–20   VENUE: Caribbean   VICTIMS:
"Numerous"
MO: Fatally stabbed family maid; afterward joined pirate crew and "never flinched from murder" during raids
DISPOSITION: Escaped from prison, 1721; never recaptured

Boost, Werner (1928–   )   AKA: Doubles Killer
SEX: M   RACE: W   TYPE: T   MOTIVE: Sad.
DATE(S): 1945–56   VENUE: Dusseldorf, Germany
   VICTIMS: Five+
MO: Lover's-lane slayer of couples
DISPOSITION: Life sentence, 1959

Borgia, Cesare (1476–1507)
SEX: M   RACE: W   TYPE: T   MOTIVE: CE/PC
DATE(S): c. 1495–1507   VENUE: Italy   VICTIMS:
   "Dozens"
MO: Aristocratic poisoner of relatives and enemies
   alike; also ordered many slayings by his henchmen
DISPOSITION: Killed in Spain after fleeing an Italian
   prison

Bosket, Willie James, Jr. (1962–   )
SEX: M   RACE: B   TYPE: T   MOTIVE: PC/CE
DATE(S): 1978   VENUE: New York City   VICTIMS:
   Three
MO: Killed teenage boy in fight; shot men in petty robberies
DISPOSITION: Pleaded guilty on two counts as juvenile, 1978 (released 1983); three to seven years for
   attempted robbery, 1984; 25 years to life for arson
   and assaults in prison, 1987; 25 years to life for
   stabbing fellow inmate, 1989

Bottaro, Angelo (1939–88)
SEX: M   RACE: W   TYPE: T   MOTIVE: CE
DATE(S): 1970s–80s   VENUE: Siracusa, Sicily   VIC-
   TIMS: 20+
MO: Mafia executioner
DISPOSITION: Stabbed to death in hospital, Dec. 3,
   1988

Bouchana, José Lazaro (1958–   )
SEX: M   RACE: H   TYPE: S   MOTIVE: Sex.
DATE(S): 1997–98   VENUE: Mexico City   VIC-
   TIMS: More than three
MO: Subway driver who raped/murdered women at his
   home, arrested after one victim escaped; police
   found "at least three" bodies buried under his patio,
   plus videotapes of women being tortured
DISPOSITION: Unknown

Boucher, Maurice (1953–   )   AKA: Mom
SEX: M   RACE: W   TYPE: T   MOTIVE: CE-felony
DATE(S): 1990s   VENUE: Montreal, Quebec   VIC-
   TIMS: 13
MO: Local leader of Hells Angels motorcycle gang
   who killed and ordered slayings of criminal rivals
   and other victims

DISPOSITION: Convicted of murdering two prison
   guards; received life prison term on May 5, 2002

Bourassa, Richard A. (1973–   )
SEX: M   RACE: W   TYPE: S   MOTIVE: PC-non-
   specific
DATE(S): 1986/90   VENUE: Anaheim Hills, Calif.
   VICTIMS: Two
MO: "Accidentally" shot two male friends at his home
DISPOSITION: 18 years to life, 1991, on guilty plea to
   one count

Bowles, Gary Ray (1962–   )
SEX: M   RACE: W   TYPE: N   MOTIVE: CE
DATE(S): 1994   VENUE: Md./Ga./Fla.   VICTIMS:
   Six suspected
MO: Robbed/murdered gay men
DISPOSITION: Condemned on one count + life
   terms on two more, 1996; two life terms for rob-
   bery/burglary; five years grand theft; death sen-
   tence overturned on appeal; condemned again,
   May 1999

Bowlind, Ronnie Lee (?–   )
SEX: M   RACE: W   TYPE: T   MOTIVE: CE
DATE(S): 1989   VENUE: London, Ky.   VICTIMS:
   Two
MO: Shot gas station attendants in robberies
DISPOSITION: Condemned, 1992

Boyd, Lucious (1958–   )
SEX: M   RACE: B   TYPE: T   MOTIVE: Sex.
DATE(S): 1998   VENUE: Ft. Lauderdale, Fla.   VIC-
   TIMS: Four alleged
MO: Mortuary employee and rape-slayer of women
   aged 19–25
DISPOSITION: Condemned on one murder count,
   June 21, 2002; also received a life term for kidnap-
   ping and 15 years for sexual battery in same case

Boykin, Clover (1975–   )
SEX: F   RACE: W   TYPE: S   MOTIVE: PC-nonspe-
   cific
DATE(S): 1993/95   VENUE: West Palm Beach, Fla.
   VICTIMS: Two confessed
MO: Killed her infant children, allegedly inspired by
   dreams
DISPOSITION: Life term + 40 years on two counts,
   1996

Boyle, Benjamin Herbert (1943–97)
SEX: M   RACE: W   TYPE: N   MOTIVE: Sex./Sad.
DATE(S): 1979–85   VENUE: Calif./Tex.   VICTIMS:
   Two confirmed

MO: Trucker who beat/strangled women after rape
DISPOSITION: Executed in Tex., Apr. 29, 1997

Brady, Roger Hoan (1966–)
SEX: M   RACE: W   TYPE: N   MOTIVE: CE-felony
DATE(S): 1994–95   VENUE: Calif./Ore.   VICTIMS: Two
MO: Armed robber; killed policeman and female holdup victim
DISPOSITION: Life term in Ore.; condemned in Calif., 1998

Branch, Eric Scott (1972–)
SEX: M   RACE: W   TYPE: T   MOTIVE: Sex.
DATE(S): 1993   VENUE: Pensacola, Fla.   VICTIMS: ?
MO: Ted Bundy "WANNA-BE"; named by authorities as serial murder suspect
DISPOSITION: Condemned on one murder count, 1994

Brandt, Carl (1956–2004)
SEX: M   RACE: W   TYPE: N   MOTIVE: PC-nonspecific
DATE(S): 1971–2004   VENUE: U.S./Europe   VICTIMS: More than seven suspected
MO: Shot both parents at age 13, killing his pregnant mother; fatally stabbed his wife and 37-year-old niece at age 47, decapitating and disemboweling one victim; suspected of two similar murders in Florida (1989 and 1995), plus others in Germany and Holland
DISPOSITION: No charges filed in first case; spent one year in a psychiatric hospital; suicide by hanging at the second crime scene, on Sept. 15, 2004

Bratislav, Vladimir (?–)   AKA: Beast of Lysva
SEX: M   RACE: W   TYPE: T   MOTIVE: Sex./Sad.
DATE(S): 1997–98   VENUE: Lysva, Russia   VICTIMS: 30
MO: Rape-mutilation slayer of young women
DISPOSITION: Sentenced to life imprisonment

Braun, Gregory Francis (1961–)
SEX: M   RACE: W   TYPE: N   MOTIVE: CE-felony
DATE(S): 1989   VENUE: Kans./Tex./N. Mex./Okla.   VICTIMS: Five
MO: Shot female clerks during robberies of stores in three states; compared murder to "shooting craps in Vegas"
DISPOSITION: Life prison terms imposed in Kansas, Texas, and New Mexico; executed in Oklahoma, July 20, 2000

Breedlove, McArthur (1947–)
SEX: M   RACE: B   TYPE: N   MOTIVE: CE
DATE(S): 1974–78   VENUE: Fla.   VICTIMS: Two
MO: Murders in Broward and Dale Counties
DISPOSITION: Condemned, 1979; 25 years on second count, 1982

Breslin, Joseph Franklin (1943–82)
SEX: M   RACE: W   TYPE: N   MOTIVE: PC-nonspecific
DATE(S): 1968/82   VENUE: Calif.   VICTIMS: Three
MO: Mental patient who killed a fellow inmate and two victims outside the asylum
DISPOSITION: Shot dead during armed robbery, July 1982

Breton, Robert, Sr. (1946–)
SEX: M   RACE: W   TYPE: T   MOTIVE: PC-domestic
DATE(S): 1966/86   VENUE: Waterbury, Conn.   VICTIMS: Three
MO: Stabbed father (1966), son, and ex-wife
DISPOSITION: Suspended sentence for manslaughter, 1966; condemned, 1989

Brewer, James D. (1955–)
SEX: M   RACE: W   TYPE: T   MOTIVE: PC/CE
DATE(S): 1977–78   VENUE: Indianapolis, Ind.   VICTIMS: Two
MO: Shot female holdup victim; killed man in rage over gay encounter
DISPOSITION: 60-year term on one count, 1993; reduced to 50 years, 1995

Brice, Greg, Jr. (?–)
SEX: M   RACE: B   TYPE: T   MOTIVE: PC
DATE(S): 1994–96   VENUE: Washington, D.C.   VICTIMS: Four
MO: Shot male victims in personal arguments
DISPOSITION: Confined as a juvenile on his first murder charge, 1994; indicted as an adult for second slaying, October 1994; escaped from jail in May 1995; still at large when he killed two more victims in May 1996; convicted on one count and received a term of 30 years to life, Jan. 17, 1997; pleaded guilty to one count of manslaughter in 1998 and received a term of five to 15 years; two other counts dropped in plea bargain

Bridges, Tyearone (1958–87)
SEX: M   RACE: B   TYPE: T   MOTIVE: CE-felony
DATE(S): 1987   VENUE: New Orleans, La.   VICTIMS: Two
MO: Middle-aged women shot in robbery attempts
DISPOSITION: Killed resisting arrest, Dec. 7, 1987

Briggen, Joseph (1850–1903)
SEX: M   RACE: W   TYPE: S   MOTIVE: CE
DATE(S): 1880s–1902   VENUE: Northern Calif.
   VICTIMS: 12+
MO: Rancher who fed farmhands to his prize hogs
DISPOSITION: Life sentence, 1902; died in prison

Brinvilliers, Marie de (1630–1676)
SEX: F   RACE: W   TYPE: T   MOTIVE: CE
DATE(S): 1665–73   VENUE: Paris, France   VIC-
   TIMS: 54 confessed
MO:Poisoned 50 hospital patients as "practice" for
   profit-motivated murders of her father, brothers, and
   lover
DISPOSITION: Beheaded July 17, 1676

Brisbon, Henry (1956–   )
SEX: M   RACE: B   TYPE: T   MOTIVE: CE/PC
DATE(S): 1973/82   VENUE: Chicago/Menard, Ill.
   VICTIMS: Three
MO: Killed two in robbery, one in prison
DISPOSITION: 1,000–3,000 years, 1973; condemned,
   1982

Britt, Eugene V. (1957–   )
SEX: M   RACE: B   TYPE: T   MOTIVE: Sex./Sad.
DATE(S): 1995   VENUE: Lake/Porter counties, Ind.
   VICTIMS: 11 confessed
MO: Random slayer of victims age eight to 51, all but
   one female
DISPOSITION: Life without parole for guilty plea on
   one count, 1996; trial on six more counts scheduled
   for 2005

Brogsdale, Rickey Henry (1963–   )   AKA: Peeping
   Tom Killer
SEX: M   RACE: W   TYPE: T   MOTIVE: Sex.
DATE(S): 1987   VENUE: Washington, D.C.   VIC-
   TIMS: Four
MO: Homicidal voyeur; shot 11 women, killing four
DISPOSITION: 63 years to life on four counts, 1989

Broni, Milena Quaglini da (1957–   )
SEX: F   RACE: W   TYPE: T   MOTIVE: PC
DATE(S): 1995–98   VENUE: Pavia, Italy   VICTIMS:
   Three confessed
MO: Slayer of men aged 53–83 who "wanted to have
   sex"; beat her husband to death as he slept; drugged
   and drowned another victim in his bathtub
DISPOSITION: Convicted of her husband's murder,
   December 1999; confessed two more murders in court

Bronshtein, Antuan (1972–   )
SEX: M   RACE: W   TYPE: T   MOTIVE: CE-felony

DATE(S): 1991   VENUE: Philadelphia, Pa.   VIC-
   TIMS: Two
MO: Shot male jewelers during holdups
DISPOSITION: Life term on one count, 1992; con-
   demned on second count, 1993

Brooks, John (1966–   )
SEX: M   RACE: B   TYPE: T   MOTIVE: CE-felony
DATE(S): 1986   VENUE: New Orleans, La.   VIC-
   TIMS: Nine
MO: Victims shot in street robberies
DISPOSITION: Convicted/condemned for six murders

Bropst, Tony (1953–   )
SEX: M   RACE: W   TYPE: N   MOTIVE: CE-felony
DATE(S): 1986   VENUE: Ariz./Colo.   VICTIMS:
   Two
MO: Victims shot for cars
DISPOSITION: 40 years in Ariz.; 40 years to life in
   Colo.

Brown, Barry Austin (?–   )
SEX: M   RACE: W   TYPE: T   MOTIVE: CE-felony
DATE(S): 1974   VENUE: Santa Cruz/San Mateo,
   Calif.   VICTIMS: Three
MO: Robbery murders of two men and a woman
DISPOSITION: Guilty plea on three counts; consecu-
   tive life terms, 1974

Brown, Charles Noel (1933–   )
SEX: M   RACE: W   TYPE: N   MOTIVE: CE-felony
DATE(S): 1961   VENUE: Minn./Iowa   VICTIMS:
   Three
MO: Men shot in robberies/abductions
DISPOSITION: Condemned in Iowa, Sept. 1961

Brown, Henry Newton (1857–84)
SEX: M   RACE: W   TYPE: N   MOTIVE: CE/PC
DATE(S): 1870s–84   VENUE: Tex./N. Mex./Kans.
   VICTIMS: Six
MO: Old West outlaw and occasional lawman
DISPOSITION: Shot while attempting to rob bank,
   May 1, 1884

Brown, Raymond Eugene (1946–   )
SEX: M   RACE: W   TYPE: T   MOTIVE: CE/Sex.
DATE(S): 1960/87   VENUE: Clay-Russell counties,
   Ala.   VICTIMS: Five
MO: Stabbed three relatives; raped/stabbed mother-
   daughter
DISPOSITION: Life, 1960 (paroled 1973); returned to
   prison as parole violator (for rape), 1973 (released
   again, 1986); condemned 1987

Brown, Vernon (?–)
SEX: M   RACE: B   TYPE: N   MOTIVE: Sex.
DATE(S): 1980–86   VENUE: Ind./Mo.   VICTIMS: Five+
MO: Killer pedophile; blamed crimes on drug addiction
DISPOSITION: Condemned in Mo.

Brown, Willie (1957–)
SEX: M   RACE: B   TYPE: T   MOTIVE: Sex.
DATE(S): 1979/1999   VENUE: Detroit, Mich.   VICTIMS: More than two
MO: Strangler of black gay men, killed exactly 20 years apart; suspected in a string of similar murders
DISPOSITION: Convicted on one count, 1979; paroled 1994; convicted on second count, November 1999

Broyles, James (1968–)
SEX: M   RACE: W   TYPE: T   MOTIVE: PC-domestic
DATE(S): 1984/96   VENUE: Edmonton, Alberta   VICTIMS: Two
MO: Strangled grandmother and girlfriend for "nagging" him
DISPOSITION: Confined as juvenile, 1984; 20 years for second-degree murder, 1998

Bryan, Joseph Francis, Jr. (1939–)
SEX: M   RACE: W   TYPE: N   MOTIVE: Sex./Sad.
DATE(S): 1964   VENUE: S.C./Fla./N.J.   VICTIMS: Three
MO: Sadistic pedophile, abducted/tortured young boys
DISPOSITION: Federal life sentence for kidnapping, 1965

Bryan, Peter (1969–)   AKA: "The Cannibal"
SEX: M   RACE: W   TYPE: T   MOTIVE: PC-nonspecific
DATE(S): 1993/2004   VENUE: London, England   VICTIMS: Three
MO: Bludgeoned 20-year-old woman with a hammer; killed a 43-year-old male friend and cooked his brain; murdered a 59-year-old fellow patient at Broadmoor asylum
DISPOSITION: Detained in mental hospital, 1994–2001; pleaded guilty with diminished responsibility on two counts voluntary manslaughter, March 15, 2005; returned to asylum indefinitely

Brydges, Ralph Lionel (d. 1927)   AKA: Monster of Rome
SEX: M   RACE: W   TYPE: T   MOTIVE: Sex.
DATE(S): 1924–27   VENUE: Rome, Italy   VICTIMS: Six+

MO: Pedophile strangler of children
DISPOSITION: Convicted; sentence unknown

Brumfitt, Paul (1956–)
SEX: M   RACE: W   TYPE: N   MOTIVE: Sex./PC
DATE(S): 1980/2000   VENUE: England   VICTIMS: Three
MO: Beat a tailor to death and strangled a bus driver, 1980; stabbed a 19-year-old female prostitute to death and burned her body, then raped another streetwalker, 2000
DISPOSITION: Received three life terms for manslaughter and wounding, 1980; released July 1993; convicted of murder and sentenced to life, July 22, 2000

Buccieri, Fiore (1904–73)   AKA: Fifi
SEX: M   RACE: W   TYPE: T   MOTIVE: PC-revenge
DATE(S): 1924–72   VENUE: Chicago, Ill.   VICTIMS: "Numerous"
MO: Mafia executioner; labeled lord high executioner of the Chicago syndicate by FBI agents, 1966
DISPOSITION: Died of cancer, 1973

Buchanan, Denise (?–)
SEX: F   RACE: W   TYPE: T   MOTIVE: PC-nonspecific
DATE(S): 1989–94   VENUE: Reno, Nev.   VICTIMS: Three
MO: Mother who killed her children in the guise of SIDS
DISPOSITION: Convicted on two counts, April 1999; received two consecutive life sentences without parole

Buenoaño, Judias (1943–98)   AKA: The Black Widow
SEX: F   RACE: W   TYPE: N   MOTIVE: CE-inheritance
DATE(S): 1971–80   VENUE: Fla./Colo.   VICTIMS: Three
MO: "Black widow" slayer of husband, son, and lover
DISPOSITION: Executed in Fla., Mar. 30, 1998

Buenrostro, Dora Luz (1960–)
SEX: F   RACE: H   TYPE: S   MOTIVE: PC
DATE(S): October 1994   VENUE: San Jacinto, Calif.   VICTIMS: Three
MO: Killed her children over a three-day period
DISPOSITION: Condemned on Oct. 2, 1998

Bullock, David (1960–)
SEX: M   RACE: W   TYPE: T   MOTIVE: CE/PC

DATE(S): 1981–82   VENUE: New York City   VIC-
   TIMS: Six confirmed
MO: Confessed shooting 10 victims "to amuse myself"
DISPOSITION: six terms of 25 years to life

Burchart, Leslie Leon (1949–2002)
SEX: M   RACE: Unk.   TYPE: T   MOTIVE: PC-nonspecific
DATE(S): 1994–96   VENUE: Richmond, Va.   VIC-
   TIMS: Seven suspected
MO: Schizophrenic with history of voyeurism and
   "flashing" who assaulted four men, killing three,
   aged 35–46; suspected of strangling four women
   aged 55–84 in their homes
DISPOSITION: Confessed murders of male victims
   while jailed for trespassing, in 1996; received 105
   years for murder and malicious wounding; died in
   prison, Aug. 16, 2002

Burke, Elmer (1917–58)   AKA: Trigger
SEX: M   RACE: W   TYPE: N   MOTIVE: CE/PC
DATE(S): 1946–54   VENUE: Eastern USA   VIC-
   TIMS: "Numerous"
MO: Career criminal and contract killer
DISPOSITION: Executed at Sing Sing, Jan. 9, 1958

Burke, Frederick R. (1893–1940)   AKA: Killer
SEX: M   RACE: W   TYPE: N   MOTIVE: CE
DATE(S): 1920–31   VENUE: Ill./N.Y./Mich.   VIC-
   TIMS: "Numerous"
MO: Career criminal and contract killer; prime suspect
   in 1929 St. Valentine's Day massacre
DISPOSITION: Life term in Mich. on one count, 1931;
   died in prison of heart attack, July 10, 1940

Burke, James (1931–   )   AKA: Jimmy the Gent
SEX: M   RACE: W   TYPE: T   MOTIVE: CE/PC
DATE(S): 1949–80   VENUE: N.Y./N.J.   VICTIMS:
   "Numerous"
MO: Syndicate mobster and hit man
DISPOSITION: Life term on one count in N.Y., 1985

Burrows, Albert Edward (1861–1923)
SEX: M   RACE: W   TYPE: T   MOTIVE: PC/Sex.
DATE(S): 1920/23   VENUE: Cheshire, England
   VICTIMS: Four
MO: "Bluebeard" slayer of wife and two children
   (1920); molested and killed a four-year-old boy
   (1923); bodies dumped in mine shaft
DISPOSITION: Hanged, Aug. 1923

Burtsev, Roman (1971–   )
SEX: M   RACE: W   TYPE: T   MOTIVE: Sex.

DATE(S): 1995–96   VENUE: Rostov-on-Don, Russia
   VICTIMS: Six
MO: Pedophile who killed child victims to avoid prose-
   cution
DISPOSITION: Confessed in custody; disposition
   unknown

Busch, Henry Adolph (1931–62)
SEX: M   RACE: W   TYPE: T   MOTIVE: PC-non-
   specific
DATE(S): 1960   VENUE: Hollywood, Calif.   VIC-
   TIMS: Three
MO: "Zombie-like" strangler of women who attacked
   six, killing three aged 53–72 (including his aunt) in
   their homes
DISPOSITION: Condemned on one count, with life
   terms on two others; executed in June 1962

Buse, William H. (d. 1858)
SEX: M   RACE: W   TYPE: T   MOTIVE: Sex.
DATE(S): 1857–58   VENUE: Miss.   VICTIMS: "Sev-
   eral"
MO: Lust killer of women
DISPOSITION: Hanged on one count, Nov. 1858

Bushara, Wilson (1959–   )
SEX: M   RACE: B   TYPE: S   MOTIVE: Cult
DATE(S): 1999   VENUE: Kampala, Uganda   VIC-
   TIMS: 24 alleged
MO: "Prophet" of the World Last Message Warning
   Church, identified as killer of 24 cult members;
   arrested July 2000
DISPOSITION: Unknown

Buss, Timothy (1969–   )
SEX: M   RACE: ?   TYPE: T   MOTIVE: Sex.
DATE(S): 1981/95   VENUE: Kankakee County, Ill.
   VICTIMS: Two
MO: Killed five-year-old girl and 10-year-old boy
DISPOSITION: 25-year term, 1981 (paroled 1993);
   condemned, 1996

Butler, Eugene (d. 1913)
SEX: M   RACE: W   TYPE: S   MOTIVE: Unk.
DATE(S): 1900s   VENUE: Niagara, N. Dak.   VIC-
   TIMS: Six
MO: Male skeletons found buried under home
DISPOSITION: Died in asylum before crimes were dis-
   covered

Caifano, John Michael (1911–   )   AKA: Marshall
   Caifano
SEX: M   RACE: W   TYPE: N   MOTIVE: CE
DATE(S): 1929–64   VENUE: Ill./Nev.   VICTIMS: 10+

MO: Syndicate enforcer and hit man
DISPOSITION: Various federal prison terms since 1964

Calo, Giuseppe (1955–)
SEX: M   RACE: W   TYPE: N   MOTIVE: CE
DATE(S): 1988–89   VENUE: Ariz.   VICTIMS: Seven confessed
MO: Killed business associates in drug deals and contract hits
DISPOSITION: 10 life terms + 140 years, 1993

Camacho, Genaro Ruiz (1955–)
SEX: M   RACE: H   TYPE: N   MOTIVE: CE/PC
DATE(S): 1987–89   VENUE: Dallas, Tex.   VICTIMS: Five
MO: Drug dealer whose victims included his own girlfriend
DISPOSITION: Condemned

Campagna, Louis (1900–55)   AKA: Little New York
SEX: M   RACE: W   TYPE: N   MOTIVE: CE
DATE(S): c. 1917–41   VENUE: N.Y./Ill.   VICTIMS: "Numerous"
MO: Syndicate enforcer and hit man
DISPOSITION: 10 years for extortion, 1943 (paroled 1946); died of heart attack, 1955

Campanella, Vincenzo (1973–)   AKA: Monster of Palermo
SEX: M   RACE: W   TYPE: T   MOTIVE: PC-nonspecific
DATE(S): 1990   VENUE: Palermo, Italy   VICTIMS: Two
MO: Slayer of victims in random attacks
DISPOSITION: Confined as juvenile offender

Campbell, Henry Colin (1896–1930)
SEX: M   RACE: W   TYPE: T   MOTIVE: CE-inheritance
DATE(S): 1928–29   VENUE: N.J.   VICTIMS: Two
MO: "Bluebeard" bigamist, shot two wives
DISPOSITION: Executed Apr. 17, 1930

Campbell, James (1969–)
SEX: M   RACE: W   TYPE: T   MOTIVE: Sex.
DATE(S): 1987–88   VENUE: Beenham, England   VICTIMS: Two
MO: Rape-slayer of young women
DISPOSITION: Life sentence on one count, 1988

Canady, James Dwight (?–)
SEX: M   RACE: W   TYPE: T   MOTIVE: Sex.

DATE(S): 1969   VENUE: Seattle, Wash.   VICTIMS: Two
MO: Serial rapist who killed two of four known victims
DISPOSITION: Life prison term

Candle, Arrigo (?–)   AKA: Monster of the Wedge
SEX: M   RACE: W   TYPE: T   MOTIVE: Sex.
DATE(S): 1991–93   VENUE: Italy   VICTIMS: "Several"
MO: Shot female prostitutes with .357 Magnum
DISPOSITION: Convicted; sentence unknown

Cannan, John (1953–)
SEX: M   RACE: W   TYPE: N   MOTIVE: Sex.
DATE(S): 1978–87   VENUE: England   VICTIMS: Three suspected
MO: Rape-slayer of young women
DISPOSITION: Life sentence on one count, 1988

Cannon, Lucretia Patricia (1783–1829)
SEX: F   RACE: W   TYPE: S   MOTIVE: CE/Sad.
DATE(S): 1802–29   VENUE: Reliance, Del.   VICTIMS: 24 confessed
MO: Killed husband and child prior to entering slave trade and operating a tavern where patrons were robbed and killed; slaves and servants tortured/killed for amusement
DISPOSITION: Condemned, Apr. 1829; suicide by poison in jail

Canonico, Frank Anthony (1938–)
SEX: M   RACE: W   TYPE: N   MOTIVE: Sex.
DATE(S): 1970s–80s   VENUE: Eastern USA   VICTIMS: 25 confessed
MO: Shot "loose women" met in bars while traveling
DISPOSITION: Two life terms in Fla., May 1982

Capone, Alphonse (1899–1947)   AKA: Scarface
SEX: M   RACE: W   TYPE: N   MOTIVE: CE
DATE(S): 1919–29   VENUE: N.Y./Ill.   VICTIMS: Five+ personal
MO: Prohibition mobster; ordered hundreds of murders besides those committed personally
DISPOSITION: 11 years for tax evasion, 1932; died from tertiary syphilis, Jan. 25, 1947

Caputo, Ricardo (1950–)
SEX: M   RACE: H   TYPE: N   MOTIVE: PC
DATE(S): 1971–83   VENUE: USA/Mexico   VICTIMS: Five
MO: "Bluebeard" slayer of lovers
DISPOSITION: 25 years to life in N.Y., 1995

Carawan, George Washington (d. 1852)
SEX: M   RACE: W   TYPE: T   MOTIVE: PC
DATE(S): 1840s–52   VENUE: Goose Creek, N.C.
   VICTIMS: Three
MO: Killed first wife, second wife's suspected lover,
   and a male neighbor
DISPOSITION: Suicide by gunshot during murder
   trial, 1852

Cardinella, Salvatore (1880–1921)   AKA: The Devil
SEX: M   RACE: W   TYPE: T   MOTIVE: CE
DATE(S): c. 1910–21   VENUE: Chicago, Ill.   VIC-
   TIMS: 20+
MO: "Black Hand" extortionist and killer
DISPOSITION: Hanged on one count, 1921

Carpenter, David Joseph (1930–   )   AKA: Trailside
   Killer
SEX: M   RACE: W   TYPE: T   MOTIVE: Sex./sad.
DATE(S): 1979–80   VENUE: San Francisco, Calif.
   VICTIMS: 10
MO: Shot/stabbed hikers in local parks
DISPOSITION: Condemned

Carpenter, Joseph (1933–   )
SEX: M   RACE: B   TYPE: T   MOTIVE: PC/Sex.
DATE(S): 1963/86   VENUE: France   VICTIMS:Two
MO: Killed wife, 1965; raped/killed woman in 1986
DISPOSITION: 1965 life sentence (paroled 1980); life
   term, 1987

Carr, Hank Earl (d. 1998)
SEX: M   RACE: W   TYPE: N   MOTIVE: PC/Sad.
DATE(S): 1997–98   VENUE: Fla.   VICTIMS: Four+
   suspected
MO: Shot three lawmen in May 1998; previously
   boasted of beating an unknown man to death
DISPOSITION: Suicide by gunshot, May 19, 1998

Carr, John Dell (1962–   )
SEX: M   RACE: W   TYPE: T   MOTIVE: PC
DATE(S): 1990–91   VENUE: Shelby/Hamilton coun-
   ties, Ind.   VICTIMS: Two
MO: Killed mother-in-law and a female acquaintance
DISPOSITION: 80 years on one count, 1992; 60 years
   concurrent on second count, 1997

Carr, Robert Frederick, III (1943–   )
SEX: M   RACE: W   TYPE: N   MOTIVE: Sex./Sad.
DATE(S): 1972–76   VENUE: Fla./Conn.   VICTIMS:
   Four
MO: Rapist who killed one woman and three children
DISPOSITION: Three life terms + 360 years in Fla.,
   Sept. 1976

Carr, Thomas (d. 1870)
SEX: M   RACE: W   TYPE: T   MOTIVE: Sex.
DATE(S): 1869–70   VENUE: Ohio   VICTIMS: 14
   suspected
MO: Lust killer of women
DISPOSITION: Hanged on one count, 1870

Carraher, Patrick (d. 1946)
SEX: M   RACE: W   TYPE: T   MOTIVE: PC-argu-
   ment
DATE(S): 1934/45   VENUE: Glasgow, Scotland
   VICTIMS: Two
MO: Killed soldiers in drunken brawls
DISPOSITION: three years for manslaughter (1934);
   hanged Apr. 4, 1946

Carrington, Celeste Simone (1961–   )
SEX: F   RACE: B   TYPE: N   MOTIVE: CE
DATE(S): 1991–92   VENUE: San Carlos and Palo
   Alto, Calif.   VICTIMS: Two
MO: Killed two men during burglaries
DISPOSITION: Condemned on Nov. 23, 1994

Carroll, Robert Lee (?–   )
SEX: M   RACE: W   TYPE: N   MOTIVE: PC
DATE(S): 1970/89   VENUE: Ohio/Ala.   VICTIMS:
   Two
MO: Drug-related murder in Ohio; stabbed Ala. jail
   inmate
DISPOSITION: Convicted in Ohio (sentence
   unknown); condemned in Ala.

Carter, Dean Phillip (1957–   )
SEX: M   RACE: W   TYPE: N   MOTIVE: Sex.
DATE(S): 1984   VENUE: Calif.   VICTIMS: Five
MO: Strangled women in three cities
DISPOSITION: Condemned

Carter, Jonathan Erik (1980–99)
SEX: M   RACE: W   TYPE: T   MOTIVE:
   Unknown
DATE(S): 1999   VENUE: Miami, Fla.   VICTIMS:
   Five alleged
MO: Career thief who shot four victims, killing three,
   in a December shooting spree; posthumously named
   as the killer of two other victims
DISPOSITION: Suicide by gunshot prior to capture,
   Dec. 28, 1999

Carter, Frank (1881–1926)   AKA: Phantom Sniper
SEX: M   RACE: W   TYPE: T   MOTIVE: PC-non-
   specific
DATE(S): 1926   VENUE: Omaha, Nebr./Council
   Bluffs, Iowa   VICTIMS: Three

MO: Random shootings of three men and a girl
DISPOSITION: Hanged

Carter, Horace (1918–)
SEX: M   RACE: W   TYPE: N   MOTIVE: PC-nonspecific
DATE(S): 1951   VENUE: England   VICTIMS: Three
MO: Strangler of young girls; no sexual assault
DISPOSITION: Declared legally insane; confined to asylum

Carter, Robert Anthony (1964–98)
SEX: M   RACE: B   TYPE: T   MOTIVE: CE
DATE(S): 1981   VENUE: Houston, Tex.   VICTIMS: Two
MO: Killed robbery victims
DISPOSITION: Executed May 18, 1998

Casablanca, John (1943–)
SEX: M   RACE: W   TYPE: T   MOTIVE: CE/PC
DATE(S): 1965/81   VENUE: New York City   VICTIMS: Five
MO: Three contract murders; two killings in personal disputes
DISPOSITION: Plea bargain to three counts of manslaughter, 1965 (paroled 1982); ruled insane on two counts, 1981

Cassandra, Simone (?–)   AKA: Monster of Norma
SEX: M   RACE: W   TYPE: T   MOTIVE: Sex.
DATE(S): 1992–95   VENUE: Norma, Italy   VICTIMS: "Several"
MO: Confessed 11 rapes, with "several" victims strangled
DISPOSITION: Pled guilty; sentence unknown

Cassimiro, Andre Luiz (1965–)
SEX: M   RACE: H   TYPE: T   MOTIVE: Sex./Sad./CE
DATE(S): 1995–96   VENUE: Juiz de Fora, Brazil   VICTIMS: Five
MO: Burglar who raped/tortured/strangled women age 58–77
DISPOSITION: Confessed 1996; sentence unknown

Castro, Edward (1950–)
SEX: M   RACE: H   TYPE: N   MOTIVE: CE
DATE(S): 1987   VENUE: Fla.   VICTIMS: Two
MO: Robbed/stabbed men met in Pinellas and Marion county bars
DISPOSITION: Condemned 1988 + five years for robbery; life on second count, 1991

Catlin, Steven David (1944–)
SEX: M   RACE: W   TYPE: N   MOTIVE: CE-inheritance
DATE(S): 1976–84   VENUE: Calif./Nev.   VICTIMS: Four
MO: Poisoned parents and two wives with herbicide
DISPOSITION: Condemned

Cavaness, Dr. John Dale (1925–86)
SEX: M   RACE: W   TYPE: N   MOTIVE: CE
DATE(S): 1977/84   VENUE: Ill./Mo.   VICTIMS: Two
MO: Shot his own sons for life insurance
DISPOSITION: Condemned, 1985; suicide in prison, Nov. 17, 1986

Chabakwenzi, Chamwinu (?–)
SEX: M   RACE: B   TYPE: N   MOTIVE: PC/CE
DATE(S): 2002   VENUE: Zambia   VICTIMS: "Several"
MO: Hired killer of elderly suspected "witches" in two provinces, whose employers included several children; self-styled "savior of the young ones"
DISPOSITION: Unknown

Chacon, Augustin (d. 1902)   AKA: The Hairy One
SEX: M   RACE: H   TYPE: N   MOTIVE: CE/Sad.
DATE(S): 1895–1901   VENUE: Ariz. Territory   VICTIMS: Eight+
MO: Sadistic outlaw; slayer of holdup victims and lawmen
DISPOSITION: Hanged, Nov. 1902

Chadd, Billy (1954–)
SEX: M   RACE: W   TYPE: N   MOTIVE: Sex.
DATE(S): 1974–78   VENUE: Calif./Nev.   VICTIMS: Three confessed
MO: Stabbed two women and one man in sexual assaults
DISPOSITION: Nev. life sentence; 13 years for rape in Calif.

Chanal, Pierre (1946–2003)
SEX: M   RACE: W   TYPE: T   MOTIVE: Sex./Sad.
DATE(S): 1980–88   VENUE: Marne region, France   VICTIMS: Eight
MO: Sadistic rape-slayer of young men
DISPOSITION: Served seven years for torture-rape of a surviving victim, 1988–95; committed suicide by slashing an artery in his left leg on eve of trial on three murder counts, Oct. 14, 2003

Chapman, George [*See* KLOSOWSKI, SEVERIN]

Chapman, Glenn Edward (1967–)
SEX: M   RACE: B   TYPE: T   MOTIVE: Sex.

DATE(S): 1992   VENUE: Hickory, N.C.   VICTIMS: Two
MO: Rape-slayer of female addicts
DISPOSITION: Condemned on one count, 1994

Charleston, Shavonda (1979–   )
SEX: F   RACE: B   TYPE: S   MOTIVE: PC-nonspecific
DATE(S): 1999–2000   VENUE: Louisville, Ky.   VICTIMS: Four
MO: Mother who murdered her own children, aged two weeks, 17 months, two years, and five years, staging the deaths as SIDS
DISPOSITION: Pleaded guilty on four counts and received a life term without parole, June 19, 2001

Chase, Richard Trenton (1950–   )   AKA: Sacramento Vampire
SEX: M   RACE: W   TYPE: T   MOTIVE: PC-nonspecific
DATE(S): 1977–78   VENUE: Sacramento, Calif.   VICTIMS: Six
MO: Killed random victims to drink their blood
DISPOSITION: Condemned, 1979; prison suicide, Dec. 26, 1980

Chavez, Francisco de (d. 1541)
SEX: M   RACE: H   TYPE: N   MOTIVE: PC-extremist
DATE(S): 1532–33   VENUE: Peru   VICTIMS: 600+
MO: Spanish conquistador and associate of Hernando Pizarro; killed at least 600 young Inca children, with an uncertain number of adults
DISPOSITION: Killed by a mob in Spain, 1541

Chavez, Juan (1964–   )
SEX: M   RACE: H   TYPE: T   MOTIVE: PC
DATE(S): 1986–89   VENUE: Los Angeles, Calif.   VICTIMS: Five
MO: Killed gay men aged 46–57 in "effort to stop the spread of AIDS"
DISPOSITION: Confessed murders while imprisoned for a 1996 kidnapping; received five consecutive life terms without parole, June 21, 1999

Chavez, Juan Rodriguez (1968–2003)   AKA: Thrill Killer
SEX: M   RACE: H   TYPE: T   MOTIVE: PC/CE-felony
DATE(S): 1985/1995   VENUE: Dallas, Tex.   VICTIMS: 11 confessed
MO: Shot male victim in 1985; shot others during a three-month crime spree, during robberies and for the "thrill of killing"

DISPOSITION: Received 15-year sentence for murder in 1987; paroled 1994; executed on one count, April 22, 2003

Chermukhin, Konstantin (?–   )   AKA: The Barbarian
SEX: M   RACE: W   TYPE: T   MOTIVE: Sex.
DATE(S): 1990s   VENUE: Rostov-on-Don, Russia   VICTIMS: Four confessed
MO: Killed three young children and one child's mother
DISPOSITION: Unknown

Chiatti, Luigi (?–   )   AKA: Monster of Foligno
SEX: M   RACE: W   TYPE: T   MOTIVE: Sex.
DATE(S): 1992–93   VENUE: Foligno, Italy   VICTIMS: Two
MO: Pedophile slayer of children
DISPOSITION: Life sentence

Chilala, Bernard Gilbert (?–   )
SEX: M   RACE: B   TYPE: T   MOTIVE: PC-nonspecific
DATE(S): 1989–99   VENUE: Lusaka, Zambia   VICTIMS: 30–70
MO: Ex-soldier who killed random victims with axes and hoes
DISPOSITION: Condemned on four counts, Dec. 1, 2000

Choate, Pearl (1907–   )
SEX: F   RACE: W   TYPE: N   MOTIVE: CE-inheritance
DATE(S): 1930s–65   VENUE: England   VICTIMS: Seven suspected
MO: "Black widow" slayer of elderly millionaire husbands
DISPOSITION: Served 12 years on one murder count

Christenson, William Dean (1945–   )
SEX: M   RACE: W   TYPE: N   MOTIVE: Sex./PC-argument
DATE(S): 1981–82   VENUE: Canada/Eastern U.S.   VICTIMS: Five to 30
MO: At least four women stabbed/dismembered; one man shot
DISPOSITION: Life + 20 years for two Pa. murders

Christian, James Edward (1944–   )   AKA: Black Satin Killer
SEX: M   RACE: W   TYPE: N   MOTIVE: Sex./Sad.
DATE(S): 1970   VENUE: Canada/eastern U.S.   VICTIMS: Three
MO: Mutilation-slayer of young women
DISPOSITION: Plea bargain for two life terms

Christiansen, Thor Nis (1945–)
SEX: M   RACE: W   TYPE: T   MOTIVE: Sex.
DATE(S): 1976–77   VENUE: Santa Barbara, Calif.
   VICTIMS: Four
MO: Execution-style shootings of young women
DISPOSITION: Life term, 1980; murdered in prison
   Mar. 30, 1981

Christofi, Styllou (1900–54)
SEX: F   RACE: W   TYPE: N   MOTIVE: PC-conflict
DATE(S): 1925/53   VENUE: Cyprus/England   VIC-
   TIMS: Two
MO: Killed mother and daughter-in-law
DISPOSITION: Hanged in England

Christopher, Joseph G. (1955–)
SEX: M   RACE: W   TYPE: N   MOTIVE: PC-
   extremist
DATE(S): 1980   VENUE: N.Y.   VICTIMS: 13 admit-
   ted
MO: Racist who shot/stabbed black and Hispanic men
DISPOSITION: Life sentence, 1985

Chung Doo-Young (1967–)
SEX: M   RACE: A   TYPE: T   MOTIVE: CE-felony
DATE(S): 1985–2000   VENUE: Pusan, South Korea
   VICTIMS: Ten
MO: Killed a security guard in 1985; killed nine more
   victims in 13 robberies between June 1999 and April
   2000
DISPOSITION: Served 12 years (1985–97) for first
   murder; paroled from a theft conviction, March
   1999; confessed nine murders, April 2000; final disposition unknown

Cianculli, Leonarda (d. 1970)   AKA: Witch of Corregio
SEX: F   RACE: W   TYPE: S   MOTIVE: PC-nonspe-
   cific
DATE(S): 1939–40   VENUE: Corregio, Italy   VIC-
   TIMS: Three
MO: Killed female acquaintances, cooking their bodies
   to produce "magic" potions and candles to defeat a
   "family curse"
DISPOSITION: Committed to asylum for 30 years,
   1946; died of stroke in custody, Oct. 15, 1970

Clarey, Richard N., Jr. (1961–)
SEX: M   RACE: W   TYPE: N   MOTIVE: PC-non-
   specific
DATE(S): 1970s–84   VENUE: Germany/Mich.   VIC-
   TIMS: Three confirmed
MO: Confessed random murders of "more than 100,
   less than 150"
DISPOSITION: Two Mich. terms of life without parole

Clark, Hadden (1952–)
SEX: M   RACE: W   TYPE: N   MOTIVE: PC-non-
   specific
DATE(S): 1980s–1990s   VENUE:
   Md./Mass./Conn./R.I./Vt.   VICTIMS: 11 confessed
MO: Discharged from U.S. Navy as a paranoid schizo-
   phrenic, 1984; killed women and girls and cannibal-
   ized them in an effort to "become" his victims
DISPOSITION: Serving 70 years in Maryland for mur-
   ders of a 23-year-old woman (1992) and a six-year-
   old girl (1996); confessed other slayings in four New
   England states but failed to locate graves

Clark, Dr. Roland E. (d. 1972)
SEX: M   RACE: W   TYPE: S   MOTIVE: PC-non-
   specific
DATE(S): 1954–67   VENUE: Detroit, Mich.   VIC-
   TIMS: Five
MO: Physician linked to deaths of three patients and
   two employees
DISPOSITION: Three to 15 years for manslaughter;
   died in prison, 1972

Clark, Ronald Wayne, Jr. (1968–)
SEX: M   RACE: W   TYPE: N   MOTIVE: CE
DATE(S): 1989–90   VENUE: Fla.   VICTIMS: Two
MO: Holdup-murders in Nassau and Duval counties
DISPOSITION: Life terms for murder and robbery,
   1990; condemned on second count, 1991

Clements, Archie (1843–66)
SEX: M   RACE: W   TYPE: N   MOTIVE: CE/PC
DATE(S): 1861–66   VENUE: Kans./Mo.   VICTIMS:
   "Numerous"
MO: Notorious member of "QUANTRILL'S RAIDERS"
DISPOSITION: Killed by Union troops, Dec. 13, 1866

Clements, Dr. Robert George (1890–1947)
SEX: M   RACE: W   TYPE: T   MOTIVE: CE-inheri-
   tance
DATE(S): 1920-47   VENUE: England   VICTIMS:
   Four
MO: Medical "Bluebeard," killed wives with morphine
   injections
DISPOSITION: Suicide to avoid arrest

Clepper, Gregory (1967–)
SEX: M   RACE: B   TYPE: T   MOTIVE: Sex.
DATE(S): 1995–96   VENUE: Chicago, Ill.   VIC-
   TIMS: 40 confessed
MO: Rape-strangler of female prostitutes who insisted
   that he pay for sex

DISPOSITION: Pleaded guilty on one count and received an 80-year prison term, March 20, 2001; 12 other counts dismissed in plea bargain

Click, Franklin (1919–50)
SEX: M RACE: W TYPE: T MOTIVE: Sex./Sad./PC-extremist
DATE(S): 1944 VENUE: Fort Wayne, Ind. VICTIMS: Three
MO: Rape-slayer of women age 17–38
DISPOSITION: Executed, Dec. 1950

Cline, Alfred L. (1888–1948)
SEX: M RACE: W TYPE: T MOTIVE: CE-inheritance
DATE(S): 1930–45 VENUE: Western U.S. VICTIMS: Nine
MO: "Bluebeard" slayer of eight wives and one male friend
DISPOSITION: 126-year sentence in Calif.; died in prison, Aug. 1948

Cloutier, Robert (1964–)
SEX: M RACE: W TYPE: T MOTIVE: Sex.
DATE(S): 1990 VENUE: Chicago, Ill. VICTIMS: Two
MO: Rape-slayer of women
DISPOSITION: Condemned on one count, 1991; life + 146 years on second count, 1991

Cobb, Hoyt Budd (1931–)
SEX: M RACE: W TYPE: N MOTIVE:CE-felony
DATE(S): 1960s VENUE: Ga./Fla. VICTIMS: Two
MO: Bludgeoned two victims in robberies
DISPOSITION: Concurrent life terms in Ga. and Fla. (paroled 1989)

Coddington, Herbert James (1959–)
SEX: M RACE: W TYPE: N MOTIVE: Sex./Sad.
DATE(S): 1981–87 VENUE: Nev/Calif. VICTIMS: Three
MO: Rape-slayer of female victims
DISPOSITION: Condemned in Calif., 1987

Code, Nathaniel Robert, Jr. (1956–)
SEX: M RACE: B TYPE: T MOTIVE: Sex./Sad./PC-domestic
DATE(S): 1984–86 VENUE: Shreveport, La. VICTIMS: 13
MO: Bisexual home invader, killed six men, three women, and four children
DISPOSITION: Condemned

Coffey, Fred Howard, Jr. (1945–)
SEX: M RACE: ? TYPE: N MOTIVE: Sex.

DATE(S): 1975–86 VENUE: Md./N.C./Va. VICTIMS: Five+ suspected
MO: Pedophile slayer of children aged 8–12
DISPOSITION: 50 years for molestation in North Carolina, 1986; condemned on one count, 1987 (commuted to life on appeal, 1995)

Cohen, Charles Mark (1954–)
SEX: M RACE: W TYPE: N MOTIVE: PC/CE
DATE(S): 1988–89 VENUE: Del./Calif. VICTIMS: Three
MO: Stabbed/bludgeoned parents; stabbed/robbed gay man
DISPOSITION: Life term for killing parents in Del., 1992

Coit, Jill (c. 1943–)
SEX: F RACE: W TYPE: N MOTIVE: CE
DATE(S): 1969–76 VENUE: Tex./Colo. VICTIMS: Two
MO: "Black widow" slayer of husbands for profit
DISPOSITION: Life without parole + 48 years on one count in Colo., 1996

Coleman, Charles Troy (1947–90)
SEX: M RACE: W TYPE: N MOTIVE: PC/CE
DATE(S): 1976–79 VENUE: Calif./Okla. VICTIMS: Four
MO: Bludgeoned an acquaintance; shot three robbery victims
DISPOSITION: Executed in Okla., Sept. 10, 1990

Coll, Vincent (1909–32) AKA: "Mad Mick"; Mad Dog
SEX: M RACE: W TYPE: T MOTIVE: CE/PC
DATE(S): 1920s–32 VENUE: New York City VICTIMS: Seven+
MO: Psychopathic racketeer involved in Prohibition gang wars
DISPOSITION: Murdered by rival gangster, Feb. 9, 1932

Collins, Darnell (d. 1995)
SEX: M RACE: ? TYPE: N MOTIVE: CE-felony
DATE(S): 1995 VENUE: N.Y./N.J. VICTIMS: Five
MO: Shot victims during two-state crime spree
DISPOSITION: Killed while resisting arrest, June 21, 1995

Collins, John Norman (1947–) AKA: Ypsilanti Ripper
SEX: M RACE: W TYPE: N MOTIVE: Sex./Sad.
DATE(S): 1967–69 VENUE: Mich./Calif. VICTIMS: Eight

MO: Mutilation-slayer of young women
DISPOSITION: Mich. life sentence on one murder count

Colwell, Lawrence (1969–)
SEX: M RACE: W TYPE: N MOTIVE: Sex./Sad./CE
DATE(S): 1994 VENUE: Nev./Calif. VICTIMS: Three
MO: Beat/strangled one woman and two men "for fun"; one victim robbed
DISPOSITION: Condemned in Nev.

Comer, Chester (d. 1935)
SEX: M RACE: W TYPE: N MOTIVE: PC-non-specific
DATE(S): 1934–35 VENUE: Kans./Okla. VICTIMS: Five
MO: Shot wife, ex-wife, three male strangers in unexplained rampage
DISPOSITION: Died Nov. 27, 1935, after shoot-out with police

Commander, Charles J., IV (1968–)
SEX: M RACE: W TYPE: N MOTIVE: PC-non-specific
DATE(S): 1989–90 VENUE: Fla./N.J. VICTIMS: Two suspected
MO: Shot/dismembered women, one of them his roommate
DISPOSITION: 22 years on one count, second degree + five years for possession of concealed firearm in Fla.

Conahan, Daniel Owen, Jr. (1954–) AKA: Hog Trail Killer
SEX: M RACE: W TYPE: T MOTIVE: Sex./Sad.
DATE(S): 1994–97 VENUE: Punta Gorda, Fla. VICTIMS: Six
MO: Gay mutilation-slayer of young men dumped in rural settings
DISPOSITION: Condemned on one count with 15 years for kidnapping, Dec. 10, 1999

Conde, Rory Enrique (1965–) AKA: Tamiami Strangler
SEX: M RACE: H TYPE: T MOTIVE: Sex.
DATE(S): 1994–95 VENUE: Dade County, Fla. VICTIMS: Six
MO: Rape-strangler of female prostitutes
DISPOSITION: Received 18-year terms on each of four felony counts (armed robbery, burglary, kidnapping, and sexual assault), Feb. 13, 1998; condemned on one murder count, March 7, 2000; received five life terms for other slayings, April 3, 2001

Conz, Gianni (?–) AKA: Strangler of the Hills
SEX: M RACE: W TYPE: T MOTIVE: Sex.
DATE(S): 1975 VENUE: Veronisi Hills, Italy VICTIMS: Three
MO: Lust killer of women
DISPOSITION: Died of natural causes, 1980

Cook, William (1929–52)
SEX: M RACE: W TYPE: N MOTIVE: PC-non-specific
DATE(S): 1950–51 VENUE: Mo./Calif. VICTIMS: Six
MO: Shot two men one woman and three children kidnapped while traveling
DISPOSITION: Executed in Calif., Dec. 12, 1952

Cooke, Eric Edgar (1929–64)
SEX: M RACE: W TYPE: T MOTIVE: PC-non-specific
DATE(S): 1959–61 VENUE: Perth, Australia VICTIMS: Six
MO: Stabbed/shot two men and three women in random attacks
DISPOSITION: Hanged Oct. 24, 1964

Cooke Sidney (1928–)
SEX: M RACE: W TYPE: N MOTIVE: Sex.
DATE(S): 1970s–80s VENUE: England VICTIMS: "Several" suspected
MO: Fairgrounds worker and pedophile child-slayer
DISPOSITION: 16 years on one count, 1988 (paroled 1998)

Copeland, David (1976–)
SEX: M RACE: W TYPE: T MOTIVE: PC-extremist
DATE(S): 1999 VENUE: London, England VICTIMS: Three
MO: White-supremacist engineer who planted nail bombs in pubs, including one gay bar, killing three persons and wounding 129
DISPOSITION: Pled guilty to manslaughter on June 5, 2000, and received a life prison term

Coppola, Michael (1904–66)
SEX: M RACE: W TYPE: N MOTIVE: CE/Sad.
DATE(S): 1920s–60 VENUE: N.Y./Ky. VICTIMS: "Numerous"
MO: Sadistic Mafia "enforcer"; killed for pleasure and profit; performed kitchen-table abortions on wife
DISPOSITION: Convicted of extortion, 1960 (paroled 1963)

Corbett, Tammy (1965–)
SEX: F RACE: W TYPE: S MOTIVE: PC-nonspecific
DATE(S): 1987–89 VENUE: Carlinsville, Ill. VICTIMS: Four
MO: Killed her own young children
DISPOSITION: Life term on four counts, 1993

Corcoran, Joseph (1975–)
SEX: M RACE: W TYPE: T MOTIVE: PC
DATE(S): 1992/1997 VENUE: Kokomo, Ind. VICTIMS: Six
MO: Killed his parents in 1992; later shot his brother and three other men for "talking about him"
DISPOSITION: Acquitted of killing his parents, though relatives now admit his guilt; condemned on four counts, May 1999

Corio, Pier Luigi (?–) AKA: Monster of Leffe
SEX: M RACE: W TYPE: T MOTIVE: PC
DATE(S): 1987–89 VENUE: Leffe, Italy VICTIMS: Three+ suspected
MO: Victims shot, some buried in his garden
DISPOSITION: Life sentence

Corliss, Charles (1940–)
SEX: M RACE: W TYPE: N MOTIVE: Sex.
DATE(S): 1960/90 VENUE: Mont./Wash. VICTIMS: Two
MO: Slayer of women; one victim shot
DISPOSITION: Jailed in Mont., 1965–85; 74 years in Wash. on one murder count and two counts attempted murder, 1991

Corner, Mark (1977–)
SEX: M RACE: W TYPE: T MOTIVE: Sex.
DATE(S): 2003 VENUE: Liverpool, England VICTIMS: Two
MO: Killed and dismembered two female prostitutes
DISPOSITION: Pled guilty with diminished capacity on two counts, Oct. 24, 2003; confined to Ashworth Hospital

Cortez, Gregorio (1875–1916)
SEX: M RACE: H TYPE: N MOTIVE: PC
DATE(S): 1901 VENUE: Tex. VICTIMS: Three
MO: Suspected livestock rustler; killed lawmen while a fugitive
DISPOSITION: 50 years on two counts, 1901 (pardoned, 1913)

Cortez, Manuel Trinidad (1955–)
SEX: M RACE: H TYPE: N MOTIVE: Sex.
DATE(S): 1978–79 VENUE: Ore. VICTIMS: Three

MO: Mutilation-slayer of girls age 11–16
DISPOSITION: Life sentence on two counts, 1980

Corvin, Mendum Paul (1934–)
SEX: M RACE: W TYPE: N MOTIVE: CE-felony
DATE(S): 1968–70 VENUE: Fla./Pa. VICTIMS: Two
MO: Twice impregnated his adolescent daughter, killing newborns to avoid prosecution for incest
DISPOSITION: Pleaded guilty; two concurrent life terms

Corwin, Daniel Lee (1959–98)
SEX: M RACE: W TYPE: N MOTIVE: Sex.
DATE(S): 1987 VENUE: Tex. VICTIMS: Three
MO: Rape-slayer of women age 26 to 72
DISPOSITION: Executed Dec. 7, 1998

Costa, Antone Charles (1945–74)
SEX: M RACE: W TYPE: N MOTIVE: Sex./Sad.
DATE(S): 1966–69 VENUE: Calif./N.Y./Mass. VICTIMS: Eight
MO: Sadistic necrophile/cannibal-slayer of young women
DISPOSITION: Mass. life sentence, 1970; prison suicide May 12, 1974

Cota, Fernando Velazco (1946–84)
SEX: M RACE: H TYPE: T MOTIVE: Sex.
DATE(S): 1966–69 VENUE: San Jose, Calif. VICTIMS: Seven
MO: Convicted rapist, preyed on women ages 20–57
DISPOSITION: Suicide to avoid arrest, Oct. 14, 1984

Cottingham, Richard Francis (1946–)
SEX: M RACE: W TYPE: T MOTIVE: Sex./Sad.
DATE(S): 1977–80 VENUE: N.Y./N.J. VICTIMS: Five
MO: "Ripper" of female prostitutes
DISPOSITION: Multiple life terms, 1981–84

Cotton, Mary Ann (1832–73)
SEX: F RACE: W TYPE: N MOTIVE: CE/Sad.
DATE(S): 1857–72 VENUE: England VICTIMS: 21+
MO: "Black widow" poisoner of family members
DISPOSITION: Hanged Mar. 24, 1873

Courtwright, Timothy Isaiah (1848–87) AKA: Longhair Jim
SEX: M RACE: W TYPE: N MOTIVE: PC
DATE(S): 1883–87 VENUE: Tex./N. Mex./Kans. VICTIMS: Four+
MO: Hired gunman, "regulator," and sometime lawman

DISPOSITION: Killed in shoot-out with LUKE SHORT, Feb. 8, 1887

Cowans, Jesse James (1960–)
SEX: M   RACE: W   TYPE: T   MOTIVE: CE/Sad.
DATE(S): 1977/96   VENUE: Monroe County, Ohio   VICTIMS: Two
MO: Strangled paraplegic man (1977) and elderly woman (1996)
DISPOSITION: Condemned, 1997

Cox, Frederick Pete (1953–)
SEX: M   RACE: B   TYPE: T   MOTIVE: Sex.
DATE(S): 1997   VENUE: Orlando, Fla.   VICTIMS: Three
MO: Violently attacked five women, killing three; all but one victim were prostitutes
DISPOSITION: Three life terms for murder, January 2003; also received two 30-year terms for attempted murder in nonfatal assaults

Cox, Scott William (1962–)
SEX: M   RACE: W   TYPE: N   MOTIVE: Sex.
DATE(S): 1980s–92   VENUE: USA/Canada   VICTIMS: 20+ suspected
MO:Long-haul trucker; confessed slayer of female prostitutes in western U.S. and Canada
DISPOSITION: Consecutive 12.5-year terms on two counts, 1993

Coyner, James [*See* ROBINSON, ALONZO]

Craig, Donnie Gene (1965–)
SEX: M   RACE: W   TYPE: N   MOTIVE: CE
DATE(S): 1987–88   VENUE: Fla.   VICTIMS: Two
MO: Gay males robbed/killed at home
DISPOSITION: 25-year sentence on one murder count

Craig, Eric Roland (1932–)
SEX: M   RACE: W   TYPE: T   MOTIVE: Sex./Sad.
DATE(S): 1932   VENUE: Sydney, Australia   VICTIMS: Three
MO: Bludgeoned females age 14–30
DISPOSITION: Condemned, 1933 (commuted to life on appeal)

Craine, Louis (1957–)
SEX: M   RACE: B   TYPE: T   MOTIVE: Sex.
DATE(S): 1985–87   VENUE: Los Angeles, Calif.   VICTIMS: Five
MO: Rape-slayer of black prostitutes
DISPOSITION: Condemned

Crawford, Charles L. (1939–)
SEX: M   RACE: W   TYPE: N   MOTIVE: PC
DATE(S): 1964   VENUE: Mo./Ind.   VICTIMS: Three confessed
MO: Shot/hacked male victims to death
DISPOSITION: Life term in Mo., 1965 (paroled 1990); convicted on one count in Ind., 1994

Crawford, John (?–)
SEX: M   RACE: Unk.   TYPE: T   MOTIVE: Sex.
DATE(S): 1981/1992   VENUE: Alberta, Canada   VICTIMS: Four
MO: Sex-slayer of Aboriginal women
DISPOSITION: Convicted of first murder, 1982; paroled 1989; received three life terms in 1993

Cream, Dr. Thomas Neill (1850–92)
SEX: M   RACE: W   TYPE: N   MOTIVE: CE/Sad.
DATE(S): 1880–92   VENUE: Canada/USA/England   VICTIMS: Seven
MO: "Bluebeard" physician and sadistic poisoner of prostitutes
DISPOSITION: Hanged Nov. 15, 1892

Creech, Thomas Eugene (1950–)
SEX: M   RACE: W   TYPE: N   MOTIVE: CE/PC
DATE(S): 1967–75   VENUE: Western U.S.   VICTIMS: 42 confessed
MO: Claims gang-related kills, contract "hits," human sacrifice
DISPOSITION: Condemned for two Idaho murders

Creighton, Mary Frances (d. 1936)
SEX: F   RACE: W   TYPE: N   MOTIVE: CE
DATE(S): 1923–35   VENUE: N.J./N.Y.   VICTIMS: Three
MO: "Black widow" poisoner of brother, mother-in-law, and lover's wife
DISPOSITION: Executed July 19, 1936
ACCOMPLICE: Earl Applegate (1898–1936) executed July 19, 1936 for participation in his wife's murder

Cross, Theresa Jimmie Francine (1946–)
SEX: F   RACE: W   TYPE: S   MOTIVE: PC/Sad.
DATE(S): 1964/1985   VENUE: Sacramento County, Calif.   VICTIMS: Three
MO: Shot her husband in an argument; shot and starved one of her daughters and fatally beat another
DISPOSITION: Acquitted in her husband's death; pled guilty on two murder counts regarding her daughters and received two life terms, October 1995

Crump, Michael Wayne (1960–)
SEX: M   RACE: B   TYPE: T   MOTIVE: PC

DATE(S): 1985–86   VENUE: Hillsborough, Fla.
   VICTIMS: Two
MO: Killed victims in personal altercations
DISPOSITION: Life term on one count, 1987; condemned on second count, 1989

Crump, Thomas Wayne (1940–   )
SEX: M   RACE: W   TYPE: T   MOTIVE: CE/PC
DATE(S): 1970s–80   VENUE: N. Mex./Nev.   VICTIMS: 11 confessed
MO: Killed his wife, a prostitute, and various strangers.
DISPOSITION: N. Mex. life sentence; condemned in Nev.

Crutchley, John Brennan (1946–2002)
SEX: M   RACE: W   TYPE: N   MOTIVE: Sex./Sad.
DATE(S): 1977–85   VENUE: Va./Fla.   VICTIMS: Seven suspected
MO: "Vampire" rapist linked to deaths/disappearances of women
DISPOSITION: 25-year sentence for sexual assault in Fla., 1986 (paroled, Aug. 1996); returned to prison three days later for using illegal drugs; suicide in prison, April 1, 2002

Cruz, James Robert, Jr. (1957–   )
SEX: M   RACE: W   TYPE: N   MOTIVE: Sex.
DATE(S): 1980s–93   VENUE: Midwest U.S.   VICTIMS: "Several"
MO: Trucker; rape-strangler of women, mostly prostitutes
DISPOSITION: Life term on one count in Pa., 1994

Cullen, Charles (1960–   )
SEX: M   RACE: W   TYPE: N   MOTIVE: PC-mercy
DATE(S): 1987–2003   VENUE: N.J./Pa.   VICTIMS: 40 confessed
MO: Nurse who killed patients at 10 hospitals and nursing homes
DISPOSITION: Pleaded guilty to 17 murders on Oct. 8, 2004; received multiple life terms with 127 years minimum

Cummins, Gordon Frederick (1914–42)   AKA: Blackout Ripper
SEX: M   RACE: W   TYPE: T   MOTIVE: Sex./Sad.
DATE(S): 1941–42   VENUE: London, England   VICTIMS: Four to six
MO: Mutilation-murders of women
DISPOSITION: Hanged for four murders, June 25, 1942

Cunanan, Andrew Philip (1970–97)
SEX: M   RACE: A   TYPE: N   MOTIVE: PC-nonspecific

DATE(S): 1997   VENUE: Minn./Ill./N.J./Fla.   VICTIMS: Five
MO: Random murders of men by gay "thrill killer"
DISPOSITION: Suicide in Fla. to avoid capture

Cunningham, Anna (1873–   ?)
SEX: F   RACE: W   TYPE: S   MOTIVE: PC-nonspecific
DATE(S): 1918–25   VENUE: Gary, Ind.   VICTIMS: Five
MO: "Black widow" poisoner of husband and children
DISPOSITION: Life sentence on one count, 1925

Curreli, Sergio (?–   )   AKA: Monster of Arbus
SEX: M   RACE: W   TYPE: T   MOTIVE: PC-nonspecific
DATE(S): 1982–90   VENUE: Arbus, Italy   VICTIMS: Five
MO: Random victims shot/hanged/burned
DISPOSITION: Life sentence

Cutro, Gail (1960–   )
SEX: F   RACE: W   TYPE: S   MOTIVE: PC-nonspecific
DATE(S): 1993   VENUE: Columbia, S.C.   VICTIMS: Two
MO: Day-care provider who murdered two four-month-old infants left in her home
DISPOSITION: Convicted on one murder count and sentenced to life imprisonment, 1994; verdict overturned on appeal, 1998; convicted on two counts and sentenced to life, July 2, 2000; acquitted of injuring a third four-month-old at second trial

Cutter, Larry M. (1966–   )
SEX: M   RACE: W   TYPE: T   MOTIVE: Sex.
DATE(S): 1991–92   VENUE: Indianapolis, Ind.   VICTIMS: Four suspected
MO: Rape-slayer of women age 18–37
DISPOSITION: 110 years on one count, 1995

Cvjetan, Sasa (1974–   )
SEX: M   RACE: W   TYPE: T   MOTIVE: PC-extremist
DATE(S): 1999   VENUE: Kosovo, Serbia   VICTIMS: 14
MO: Policeman who murdered Albanians, mostly women and children, during "ethnic cleansing"
DISPOSITION: Received life sentence, March 16, 2004

Daddano, William, Sr. (1912–75)   AKA: Willie Potatoes
SEX: M   RACE: W   TYPE: T   MOTIVE: CE/Sad.

DATE(S): 1930s–60s   VENUE: Chicago, Ill.   VICTIMS: "Numerous"
MO: Syndicate torture-slayer
DISPOSITION: Convicted of conspiracy, 1969; died in prison, 1975

Dalton, Lawrence N. (1945–   )
SEX: M   RACE: W   TYPE: N   MOTIVE: Sex.
DATE(S): 1977–78   VENUE: Wisc./Ill.   VICTIMS: More than three
MO: Rape-slayer of at least two women and a 12-year-old girl
DISPOSITION: Life term on one count in Wisc., 1984

Damren, Floyd William (1951–   )
SEX: M   RACE: W   TYPE: N   MOTIVE: CE
DATE(S): 1994   VENUE: Fla.   VICTIMS: Two
MO: Killed burglary victim and a criminal accomplice, in Clay and Putnam counties
DISPOSITION: Condemned on one count + life for burglary, 1995; life term on second count, 1996

Daniels, Robert Wayne, Jr. (?–   )
SEX: M   RACE: W   TYPE: N   MOTIVE: CE-felony
DATE(S): 1977–78   VENUE: Ore./Ariz./Calif.   VICTIMS: Six
MO: Victims shot/robbed, often while camping
DISPOSITION: Life prison term in Ore.

Danks, Joseph (1961–   )   AKA: Koreatown Slasher
SEX: M   RACE: W   TYPE: T   MOTIVE: PC-nonspecific
DATE(S): 1987/90   VENUE: Los Angeles/Tehachapi, Calif.   VICTIMS: Six
MO: Stabbed homeless transients (1987); killed cellmate (1990)
DISPOSITION: Life term, 1988; condemned, 1991

Danos, Abel (d. 1952)
SEX: M   RACE: W   TYPE: N   MOTIVE: Sad./CE/PC-extremist
DATE(S): 1940–48   VENUE: France/Italy   VICTIMS: 110+
MO: Career criminal; Gestapo executioner in World War II; shot police during postwar robberies
DISPOSITION: Executed in France, Mar. 1952

Daugherty, Jeffrey Joseph (1955–88)
SEX: M   RACE: W   TYPE: N   MOTIVE: CE-felony
DATE(S): 1976   VENUE: Eastern U.S.   VICTIMS: Four
MO: Robbed/shot four women on trip from Mich. to Fla.
DISPOSITION: Executed in Fla., Nov. 7, 1988

Daughtrey, Earl Llewellyn, Jr. (1949–   )
SEX: M   RACE: W   TYPE: N   MOTIVE: Sex.
DATE(S): 1971–85   VENUE: Ala./Ga.   VICTIMS: Three alleged by FBI
MO: Ex-con/mental patient publicly named as probable murderer
DISPOSITION: Served time in Fla. and Ga. for attacks on women

Davey, Margaret (d. 1542)
SEX: F   RACE: W   TYPE: N   MOTIVE: PC-nonspecific
DATE(S): 1530s–1542   VENUE: England   VICTIMS: "Several"
MO: Domestic cook who poisoned various employers and their families
DISPOSITION: Boiled alive, 1542

Davis, Arlie Ray (1955–2002)
SEX: M   RACE: Unk.   TYPE: T   MOTIVE: Sex.
DATE(S): 1994–96   VENUE: Central Illinois   VICTIMS: More than four suspected
MO: Rape-slayer of female prostitutes; victims beaten and strangled
DISPOSITION: Condemned for killing a woman in Kewanee, 1999; sentence commuted to life on appeal; prime suspect in several Peoria disappearances

Davis, Bruce A. (1948–   )
SEX: M   RACE: W   TYPE: N   MOTIVE: CE/PC
DATE(S): 1969–82   VENUE: USA, nationwide   VICTIMS: 33 confessed
MO: Killed 32 gay men and one prison guard
DISPOSITION: Five to 15 years in D.C.; life + 45 years in Ill.

Davis, Cecil Emile (1960–   )
SEX: M   RACE: ?   TYPE: T   MOTIVE: Sex.
DATE(S): 1997   VENUE: Tacoma, Wash.   VICTIMS: Three suspected
MO: Rape-slayer of elderly women in their homes
DISPOSITION: Condemned on one count, 1998

Davis, Charles (?–   )
SEX: M   RACE: W   TYPE: T   MOTIVE: Sex.
DATE(S): 1970s   VENUE: Md.   VICTIMS: Five
MO: Ambulance driver and rape-slayer of women; dumped victims on his own route and phoned in reports; then retrieved bodies
DISPOSITION: Life imprisonment

Davis, Frank (1953–   )
SEX: M   RACE: W   TYPE: T   MOTIVE: Sex./Sad.

DATE(S): 1971/83   VENUE: La Porte County, Ind.
   VICTIMS: Three
MO: Pedophile slayer of teenage boys
DISPOSITION: 1984 death sentence commuted to life,
   July 1997

Davis, Gregory (1966–   )
SEX: M   RACE: B   TYPE: N   MOTIVE: Sex./Sad.
DATE(S): 1986–87   VENUE: Ga./Miss.   VICTIMS:
   Four
MO: Home invader who preyed on elderly women
DISPOSITION: Condemned in Miss.

Davis, Richard Allen (1954–   )
SEX: M   RACE: W   TYPE: N   MOTIVE: Sex.
DATE(S): 1973–93   VENUE: Calif.   VICTIMS: Two
   suspected
MO: Suspect in shotgun "suicide" of girlfriend; rape-
   slayer of 12-year-old girl
DISPOSITION: Condemned on one count

Dawson, Timothy Carl (1961–   )
SEX: M   RACE: Unk.   TYPE: T   MOTIVE: PC/CE-
   felony
DATE(S): 1998   VENUE: Atlanta, Ga.   VICTIMS:
   Four
MO: Shot male victims at two downtown hotels, rob-
   bing those killed in the second incident
DISPOSITION: Convicted on four counts of murder
   and sentenced to life in prison, Nov. 14, 2002

Day, William Scott (1951–   )
SEX: M   RACE: B   TYPE: N   MOTIVE: CE-felony
DATE(S): 1986–87   VENUE: Tenn./Ariz./Fla./Tex.
   VICTIMS: Five
MO: Escaped convict from Michigan who
   robbed/killed random victims
DISPOSITION: Received three consecutive life terms in
   Tennessee

Dean, Williamina (1847–95)
SEX: F   RACE: W   TYPE: S   MOTIVE: CE-felony
DATE(S): 1890–95   VENUE: Invercargill, New
   Zealand   VICTIMS: More than Five
MO: "Baby farmer" who killed infants left in her care
DISPOSITION: Hanged on April 12, 1895

DeBardeleben, James Mitchell, II (1940–   )
SEX: M   RACE: W   TYPE: N   MOTIVE:
   CE/Sex./Sad.
DATE(S): 1965–83   VENUE: USA nationwide   VIC-
   TIMS: Eight+ suspected
MO: Career criminal and sexual sadist active in 44
   American states, with victims of both sexes

DISPOSITION: 375 years cumulative time from six
   separate trials

Deeming, Frederick Bailey (1853–92)
SEX: M   RACE: W   TYPE: N   MOTIVE: CE
DATE(S): 1891–92   VENUE: England/Australia
   VICTIMS: Six
MO: "Bluebeard" slayer of wives and children for
   profit
DISPOSITION: Hanged in Australia, May 23, 1892

DeJesus, Carmello (1934–73)
SEX: M   RACE: H   TYPE: N   MOTIVE: Sex.
DATE(S): 1971–73   VENUE: N.Y./N.J./Fla.   VIC-
   TIMS: Four confessed
MO: Stabbed/shot women in three states
DISPOSITION: Suicide in N.Y., Sept. 8, 1973; left
   written confession

Delage, Richard Tobias (1945–   )
SEX: M   RACE: W   TYPE: N   MOTIVE: PC-non-
   specific
DATE(S): 1960–75   VENUE: N.Y./Pa./Conn.   VIC-
   TIMS: Two to four+
MO: Shot women in random, motiveless attacks
DISPOSITION: Plea bargained for 20-year maximum,
   Sept. 1976

del Junco, Francisco (1957–   )
SEX: M   RACE: H   TYPE: T   MOTIVE: Sex./Sad.
DATE(S): 1995–96   VENUE: Miami, Fla.   VICTIMS:
   Four
MO: Slayer of black female drug addicts who burned
   his victims' bodies
DISPOSITION: Sentenced to four life terms, June 4,
   2003

Delpino, Jesus Carmenate (1960–   )
SEX: M   RACE: H   TYPE: T   MOTIVE: Sex./PC
DATE(S): 1982   VENUE: South Florida   VICTIMS:
   Four confessed
MO: Killed his 14-year-old girlfriend and her mother in
   May 1982, wounding a third victim at the same
   time; subsequently confessed the murders of two
   women on Key West
DISPOSITION: Received three life terms for murder
   and attempted murder, Feb. 28, 1993; received a
   one-year sentence for escape, Aug. 27, 1993;
   received a sentence of three years and nine months
   for conspiracy to escape, July 5, 2000

De Melker, Daisy Louisa (1886–1932)
SEX: M   RACE: W   TYPE: T   MOTIVE: CE-insur-
   ance

DATE(S): 1909–31   VENUE: South Africa   VICTIMS: Six
MO: "Black widow" poisoner of husband and children
DISPOSITION: Hanged Dec. 30, 1932

Demps, Bennie E. (1950–2000)
SEX: M   RACE: B   TYPE: T   MOTIVE: CE/PC
DATE(S): 1971/76   VENUE: Fla.   VICTIMS: Three
MO: Killed two robbery victims in St. Johns County; murdered a fellow prison inmate
DISPOSITION: Life + 20 years on two counts, 1971; condemned, 1978; executed June 7, 2000

Dennis, Jerome (1967–   )
SEX: M   RACE: B   TYPE: T   MOTIVE: Sex.
DATE(S): 1991–92   VENUE: East Orange, N.J.   VICTIMS: Five
MO: Rape-slayer of females age 16 to 41
DISPOSITION: Life sentence with 60-year minimum, 1993

Denyer, Paul (1972–   )
SEX: M   RACE: W   TYPE: T   MOTIVE: Sex./Sad.
DATE(S): 1993   VENUE: Frankston, Australia   VICTIMS: Three
MO: Hater of women who claimed he "always wanted to kill" from age 14; stabbed/strangled three females aged 17–22
DISPOSITION: Life term with no minimum sentence

Deshayes, Catherine (d. 1680)   AKA: La Voisin
SEX: F   RACE: W   TYPE: T   MOTIVE: CE
DATE(S): 1660s–78   VENUE: Paris, France   VICTIMS: 2,500 confessed
MO: "Witch" and "seer" who sacrificed infants in satanic rituals for wealthy clients
DISPOSITION: Burned at the stake, Feb. 22, 1680
ACCOMPLICE: Abbé Guibourg (1612–82), renegade priest who assisted in black masses; died in prison

DeSimone, Thomas (d. 1979)
SEX: M   RACE: W   TYPE: T   MOTIVE: CE/PC
DATE(S): 1960s–70s   VENUE: N.Y./N.J.   VICTIMS: Six+
MO: Syndicate mobster and hit man
DISPOSITION: Murdered in gangland reprisal, Jan. 1979

DeStefano, Sam (1909–73)   AKA: Mad Sam
SEX: M   RACE: W   TYPE: T   MOTIVE: CE/Sad.
DATE(S): 1927–71   VENUE: Chicago, Ill.   VICTIMS: "Numerous"
MO: Syndicate hit man, rapist, sexual psychopath; murder victims included his own brother

DISPOSITION: Convicted of intimidating witnesses, 1972; murdered at home while the case was on appeal, 1973

Dial, Randolph Franklin (1944–   )
SEX: M   RACE: W   TYPE: N   MOTIVE: CE
DATE(S): 1979–83   VENUE: Okla./Nev.   VICTIMS: "Numerous" confessed
MO: Alcoholic sculptor and confessed contract killer; also claimed antidrug vigilante murders
DISPOSITION: Life term on one count in Okla., 1986; escaped from prison with deputy warden's wife (presumed kidnap victim), 1989; still at large

Diamond, John, Jr. (1896–1931)   AKA: Legs
SEX: M   RACE: W   TYPE: T   MOTIVE: CE/PC
DATE(S): 1920–31   VENUE: New York City   VICTIMS: 12+
MO: Independent racketeer; engaged in Prohibition gang wars
DISPOSITION: Murdered by rival gangsters, Dec. 17, 1931

Diao Ruiying (1954–98)
SEX: F   RACE: A   TYPE: T   MOTIVE: PC-nonspecific
DATE(S): 1997–98   VENUE: Shangqiu, China   VICTIMS: Five
MO: Poisoned neighborhood children aged four to six
DISPOSITION: Executed Jan. 18, 1999

Diaz, Robert Rubane (1938–   )
SEX: M   RACE: H   TYPE: T   MOTIVE: PC
DATE(S): 1981   VENUE: Southern Calif.   VICTIMS: 12–50
MO: Male nurse; killed patients age 52–89 by injection
DISPOSITION: Condemned on 12 counts, 1984

Diederich, Klaus (1946–   )
SEX: M   RACE: W   TYPE: Y   MOTIVE: Sex.
DATE(S): 1984   VENUE: Kassel, Germany   VICTIMS: Three
MO: Rape-slayer of women age 22–77
DISPOSITION: Life sentence

Dillbeck, Donald David (1963–   )
SEX: M   RACE: W   TYPE: N   MOTIVE: CE-felony
DATE(S): 1979/90   VENUE: Fla.   VICTIMS: Two
MO: Killed policeman (1979); kidnapped and stabbed female motorist after escape from prison
DISPOSITION: Life term, 1979 (escaped 1990); condemned, 1991

Dillon, Thomas (1951–)
SEX: M   RACE: W   TYPE: N   MOTIVE: PC-non-specific
DATE(S): 1989–90   VENUE: Ohio/Ind./Mich.   VICTIMS: Five to 11
MO: Shot outdoorsmen in random, motiveless attacks
DISPOSITION: 165 years for five Ohio murders, 1993

Dobbert, Ernest John, Jr. (d. 1984)
SEX: M   RACE: W   TYPE: S   MOTIVE: PC-domestic
DATE(S): 1972   VENUE: Fla.   VICTIMS: Two
MO: Abusive father; beat/strangled children age seven and 11
DISPOSITION: Executed Sept. 7, 1984

Dodd, Westley Allan (1961–93)
SEX: M   RACE: W   TYPE: T   MOTIVE: Sex./Sad.
DATE(S): 1989   VENUE: Vancouver, Wash.   VICTIMS: Three
MO: Pedophile and Satanist; torture-slayer of young boys
DISPOSITION: Hanged Jan. 5, 1993

Doss, Nannie Hazel (1905–65)   AKA: Giggling Grandma
SEX: F   RACE: W   TYPE: N   MOTIVE: CE/PC
DATE(S): 1923–54   VENUE: N.C./Ala./Okla.   VICTIMS: 10 confessed
MO: "Black widow" slayer of four husbands, four children, and two sisters; small insurance payments received in some cases; husbands killed in quest for "romance"
DISPOSITION: Received life prison term in 1955; died in custody, 1965

Dowler, David A. (1967–)
SEX: M   RACE: W   TYPE: T   MOTIVE: PC-non-specific
DATE(S): 1983–87   VENUE: Odessa, Tex.   VICTIMS: Three
MO: Killed three acquaintances with cyanide/chloroform after having "premonitions" of their deaths
DISPOSITION: Life sentence, 1988

Downing, William (d. 1900/08)
SEX: M   RACE: W   TYPE: T   MOTIVE: CE
DATE(S): 1890s   VENUE: Ariz. Territory   VICTIMS: 30+
MO: Old West lawman/outlaw
DISPOSITION: Killed resisting arrest, 1900 or 1908 (reports vary)

Doyle, Daniel Lee (1959–)
SEX: M   RACE: W   TYPE: T   MOTIVE: CE-felony

DATE(S): 1981   VENUE: Broward County, Fla.   VICTIMS: Two
MO: Killed kidnap/robbery victims
DISPOSITION: Condemned on one count, 1982; life on second count + five years for kidnapping, 1982

Drew, Carl H. (?–)
SEX: M   RACE: W   TYPE: T   MOTIVE: CE/Sad./PC-extremist
DATE(S): 1979–80   VENUE: Fall River, Mass.   VICTIMS: Three suspected
MO: Occultist and pimp who organized his "stable" as a satanic coven; "sacrificed" young women who displeased him
DISPOSITION: Life without parole on one count, 1981

Drinkwater, Dr. Peter (?–)
SEX: M   RACE: W   TYPE: T   MOTIVE: PC
DATE(S): 1966/72   VENUE: England   VICTIMS: Two
MO: Ran down elderly man with his car; murdered his wife
DISPOSITION: Three-year driver's license suspension in first case; 12 years for manslaughter, 1972

Duan Guocheng (1973–)   AKA: Red Dress Killer; Psycho Killer
SEX: M   RACE: A   TYPE: N   MOTIVE: Sex.
DATE(S): 1999–2001   VENUE: China   VICTIMS: 19 suspected
MO: Mutilation-slayer of women in Hubei and Hunan Provinces; most victims wore red dresses when attacked
DISPOSITION: Sentenced to seven years detention as a juvenile at age 13; served five years for robbery, mid-1990s; convicted of multiple murders, Jan. 30, 2003; sentence unknown

Dufour, Donald William (1956–)
SEX: M   RACE: W   TYPE: N   MOTIVE: CE/Sex.
DATE(S): 1982   VENUE: Miss./Fla.   VICTIMS: Five to 12
MO: Robbed and murdered gay men in their homes
DISPOSITION: Condemned in Miss., 1983; condemned in Fla., 1984

Dugan, Brian (1957–)
SEX: M   RACE: W   TYPE: N   MOTIVE: Sex.
DATE(S): 1983–84   VENUE: Ill.   VICTIMS: Three confessed
MO: Rape-slayer of female victims age seven to 27
DISPOSITION: Life term on two counts, 1985

Dumollard, Martin (d. 1862)   AKA: Monster of
Montluel
SEX: M   RACE: W   TYPE: T   MOTIVE: CE/Sad.
DATE(S): 1855–61   VENUE: Lyons, France   VIC-
TIMS: 30–40 estimated
MO: Killed/robbed young women; one victim buried
alive; later reports of cannibalism/vampirism unsub-
stantiated
DISPOSITION: Guillotined, 1862; wife Marie sen-
tenced to 20 years as accomplice

Dunbar, Jerry Lee (1961–   )
SEX: M   RACE: B   TYPE: T   MOTIVE: Sex.
DATE(S): 1989   VENUE: Fairfax/Alexandria, Va.
VICTIMS: Two
MO: Strangled women after sex; kept decomposing
bodies in his motel rooms
DISPOSITION: Convicted on two counts, 1990

Dunkle, Jon Scott (1961–   )
SEX: M   RACE: W   TYPE: N   MOTIVE: PC-non-
specific
DATE(S): 1981–85   VENUE: Calif.   VICTIMS:
Three
MO: "Thrill killer" of adolescent boys
DISPOSITION: Condemned, 1990

Dunlap, Timothy (1969)
SEX: M   RACE: W   TYPE: N   MOTIVE: PC/CE
DATE(S): 1991   VENUE: Ohio/Idaho   VICTIMS: Two
MO: Killed girlfriend with crossbow; shot bank teller
in robbery
DISPOSITION: Condemned in Idaho (1992) and Ohio
(1993)

Dupas, Peter Norris (1953–   )
SEX: M   RACE: W   TYPE: T   MOTIVE: Sex.
DATE(S): 1985–99   VENUE: Victoria, Australia
VICTIMS: Four suspected
MO: Sex offender with convictions dating from 1972,
who stabbed female victims
DISPOSITION: Life term on one count, Aug. 16, 2000;
life term on second count, Aug. 15, 2004

Duquette, James (1959–   )
SEX: M   RACE: W   TYPE: N   MOTIVE: Sex.
DATE(S): 1987–87   VENUE: Wis./Ill.   VICTIMS:
Four+ suspected
MO: Rape-slayer of teenage girls
DISPOSITION: Multiple life terms in Wis. and Mass.
(for rape)

Durand, Earl (1913–39)
SEX: M   RACE: W   TYPE: T   MOTIVE: CE

DATE(S): 1939   VENUE: Park County, Wyo.   VIC-
TIMS: Five
MO: Poacher; killed two officers in jailbreak, two more
in ambush of posse, and one bank teller in abortive
robbery
DISPOSITION: Killed in shoot-out during bank robbery

Durkin, Martin James (1900–?)
SEX: M   RACE: W   TYPE: T   MOTIVE: CE
DATE(S): 1925   VENUE: Chicago, Ill.   VICTIMS:
Two
MO: Career criminal; killed two lawmen in separate
incidents
DISPOSITION: 35 years for murder + 15 years on fed-
eral charges, 1926 (paroled 1954)

Durocher, Michael A. (1960–93)
SEX: M   RACE: W   TYPE: T   MOTIVE: PC-non-
specific
DATE(S): 1983–88   VENUE: Jacksonville, Fla.   VIC-
TIMS: Five
MO: Killed his lover, her two children, and two men
DISPOSITION: Executed Aug. 25, 1993

Dyer, Albert (d. 1938)
SEX: M   RACE: W   TYPE: T   MOTIVE: Sex.
DATE(S): 1937   VENUE: Los Angeles, Calif.   VIC-
TIMS: Three
MO: Pedophile slayer who prayed over bodies of his
victims
DISPOSITION: Hanged at San Quentin, 1938

Dyer, Amelia (1839–96)
SEX: F   RACE: W   TYPE: N   MOTIVE: CE
DATE(S): 1880–96   VENUE: England   VICTIMS:
Six in 1896 alone
MO: "Baby farmer" who killed infants of unwed
mothers
DISPOSITION: Hanged June 10, 1896

Dzhumagliev, Nikolai (?–   )   AKA: Metal Fang
SEX: M   RACE: W   TYPE: N   MOTIVE: PC/Sex.
DATE(S): 1970s–91   VENUE: Russia   VICTIMS:
Seven to 100 (reports vary)
MO: Cannibal "ripper" of women; fed human flesh to
friends at dinner parties
DISPOSITION: Served time for manslaughter in 1970s;
ruled insane 1980; escaped from asylum, 1989;
recaptured 1991

Earp, Wyatt Berry Stapp (1848–1929)
SEX: M   RACE: W   TYPE: N   MOTIVE: PC

DATE(S): 1878–82   VENUE: Kans./Ariz.   VICTIMS: Seven+

MO: Old West gambler/pimp and occasional lawman; killed personal enemies for various reasons, including revenge

DISPOSITION: Died of natural causes, Jan. 13, 1929

Eastman, Edward (1873–1920)   AKA: Monk

SEX: M   RACE: W   TYPE: T   MOTIVE: CE

DATE(S): 1890s–1920   VENUE: New York City   VICTIMS: 50+

MO: Career criminal and street gang leader

DISPOSITION: Murdered Dec. 26, 1920

Eaton, Dennis Wayne (1957–)

SEX: M   RACE: W   TYPE: T   MOTIVE: PC

DATE(S): 1989   VENUE: Shenandoah County, Va.   VICTIMS: Four

MO: Shot victims, including girlfriend and a policeman

DISPOSITION: Life without parole on three counts; condemned on one count; executed June 18, 1998

Eberling, Richard George (1930–98)

SEX: M   RACE: W   TYPE: N   MOTIVE: Sex./PC

DATE(S): 1956–83   VENUE: Ohio/Mich.   VICTIMS: Five suspected

MO: Female victims bludgeoned; some raped

DISPOSITION: Life term on one count in Ohio, 1989; died in prison July 25, 1998

Edel, Frederick W. (?–)

SEX: M   RACE: W   TYPE: N   MOTIVE: CE

DATE(S): 1926–27   VENUE: Conn./N.Y.   VICTIMS: Three alleged

MO: Petty criminal; shot an innkeeper and a male acquaintance; bludgeoned/robbed a wealthy divorcée

DISPOSITION: Acquitted on one count, 1926; condemned 1930 (commuted to life, 1931); deported to Germany on parole; died there at age 72

Edelin, Thomas (1968–)

SEX: M   RACE: B   TYPE: T   MOTIVE: CE-felony

DATE(S): 1990s   VENUE: Washington, D.C.   VICTIMS: 11

MO: Drug dealer who murdered and ordered slayings of various rivals

DISPOSITION: Life prison term

Edwards, Delory (1959–)   AKA: Uzi

SEX: M   RACE: W   TYPE: N   MOTIVE: CE

DATE(S): 1985–88   VENUE: N.Y./D.C./Md./Pa.   VICTIMS: Six+

MO: Sadistic Jamaican drug dealer; alleged to be first dealer of "crack" cocaine in USA

DISPOSITION: seven consecutive life terms + 15 years, 1989, on 42 counts including six murders

Edwards, Robert Mark (1952–)

SEX: M   RACE: W   TYPE: N   MOTIVE: Sex./Sad.

DATE(S): 1986/93   VENUE: Calif./Hawaii   VICTIMS: Two

MO: Torture-slayer of women age 55 and 67

DISPOSITION: Life term in Hawaii, 1995; condemned in Calif., 1998

Edwards, Vernon David, Jr. (1938–)

SEX: M   RACE: W   TYPE: T   MOTIVE: Sex./Sad.

DATE(S): 1954–59   VENUE: Miami, Fla.   VICTIMS: Two

MO: Rape-slayer of seven-year-old girl and 55-year-old woman

DISPOSITION: Life sentence, 1972

Elledge, James Homer (1943–2001)

SEX: M   RACE: W   TYPE: T   MOTIVE: Sex.

DATE(S): 1975/1998   VENUE: Seattle, Wash.   VICTIMS: Three

MO: While on parole from a 1975 bludgeon-murder conviction, Elledge attacked at least four women, strangling one in the church where he served as janitor

DISPOSITION: Life sentence for first murder; paroled 1995; executed for second killing, Aug. 28, 2001

Elledge, William Duane (1950–)

SEX: M   RACE: W   TYPE: N   MOTIVE: Sex./CE

DATE(S): 1974   VENUE: Broward/Duval Counties, Fla.   VICTIMS: Three

MO: Raped/strangled woman; shot two robbery victims

DISPOSITION: Life term on one count, 1974; condemned on second count, 1977; life term on third count + 50 years for sexual assault, 1977

Elton, Dwayne (?–)

SEX: M   RACE: W   TYPE: T   MOTIVE: Sex.

DATE(S): 1984   VENUE: Fort Lewis, Wash.   VICTIMS: Two

MO: Shot one female prostitute, strangled and slashed another, dumping their bodies near Madigan Army Hospital

DISPOSITION: Pleaded guilty at court-martial to avoid execution; received a life term in military prison

E., Nandor (?–)

SEX: M   RACE: W   TYPE: T   MOTIVE: CE-felony

DATE(S): 1998   VENUE: Budapest, Hungary   VICTIMS: Three
MO: Yugoslavian soldier who deserted to Hungary in 1991; shot store clerks
DISPOSITION: 35-year sentence for desertion, in absentia; confessed three murders in March 1998; disposition unknown

Engelenhoven, Kely Van (1963–   )
SEX: M   RACE: W   TYPE: T   MOTIVE: Sex.
DATE(S): 1990–91   VENUE: Sioux Falls, S. Dak
VICTIMS: Two suspected
MO: Pedophile slayer of girls age nine and 11
DISPOSITION: Life sentence, 1991

Engelman, Dr. Glennon E. (1927–   )   AKA: Killing Dentist
SEX: M   RACE: W   TYPE: T   MOTIVE: CE/PC-revenge
DATE(S): 1954–80   VENUE: St. Louis, Mo.   VICTIMS: Seven
MO: Seduced female patients, then murdered their husbands for insurance; killed female plaintiff in a civil lawsuit filed against him with car bomb
DISPOSITION: Five life terms + 60 years

Entratta, Charles (d. 1931)
SEX: M   RACE: W   TYPE: T   MOTIVE: CE
DATE(S): 1920s–31   VENUE: New York City   VICTIMS: Five+
MO: Contract killer for JOHN DIAMOND in various gang wars
DISPOSITION: Murdered by rival gangsters, 1931

Erskine, Scott (1963–   )
SEX: M   RACE: W   TYPE: N   MOTIVE: Sex./Sad.
DATE(S): 1989–93   VENUE: Fla./Calif.   VICTIMS: Three confessed
MO: Torture-slayer of two San Diego boys aged nine and 13; confessed the murder of a woman at Palm Beach, Florida, while imprisoned for those crimes
DISPOSITION: Serving a 70-year term for rape in California when DNA linked him to child murders; condemned on two counts, June 2, 2002; confessed Florida slaying, August 2002

Escamilla Gonzalez, Martin (?–   )
SEX: M   RACE: H   TYPE: T   MOTIVE: PC
DATE(S): 1987–98   VENUE: Mexico/Tex.   VICTIMS: More than four
MO: Mexican national, convicted of murder in his homeland; later killed his wife and two girlfriends in Texas, dumping remains near his home; some

reports mention a fourth woman's body recovered by police
DISPOSITION: Convicted of murder in Mexico, 1987; subsequently released and moved to Austin, Texas; convicted on three counts of murder in Texas and sentenced to life imprisonment, Sept. 8, 2000

Estrada, Enrique (1941–   )
SEX: M   RACE: H   TYPE: T   MOTIVE: CE/Sad.
DATE(S): 1976   VENUE: Los Angeles, Calif.   VICTIMS: Two
MO: Residential burglar; bound/bludgeoned elderly women
DISPOSITION: Life sentence, 1978

Etheridge, Ellen (1938–   )
SEX: M   RACE: W   TYPE: S   MOTIVE: PC-domestic
DATE(S): 1913   VENUE: Bosque County, Tex.   VICTIMS: Four
MO: "Black widow" poisoner of stepchildren
DISPOSITION: Life sentence after guilty plea

Evans, David (1957–   )
SEX: M   RACE: W   TYPE: N   MOTIVE: Sex./Sad.
DATE(S): 1977–88   VENUE: England   VICTIMS: Two suspected
MO: Rape-slayer of teenage girls
DISPOSITION: 30 years on plea bargain to manslaughter, 1989

Evans, Donald Leroy (1957–99)
SEX: M   RACE: W   TYPE: N   MOTIVE: Sex.
DATE(S): 1975–91   VENUE: USA   VICTIMS: 60+ confessed
MO: Rape-slayer of females, age 10 and up
DISPOSITION: Condemned in Miss. on one count, 1993; murdered in prison, Jan. 5, 1999

Evans, Gary (1955–98)
SEX: M   RACE: W   TYPE: N   MOTIVE: CE
DATE(S): 1985–97   VENUE: N.Y.   VICTIMS: Five
MO: Jewel thief; killed three accomplices and two robbery victims
DISPOSITION: Died in leap from police van, attempting escape en route to trial, Aug. 14, 1998

Evonitz, Richard Marc (1963–2002)
SEX: M   RACE: W   TYPE: N   MOTIVE: Sex.
DATE(S): 1996–97   VENUE: Md./Va.   VICTIMS: Four confirmed
MO: Rape slayer of a 25-year-old woman in Baltimore and three girls aged 12–16 at Spotsylvania, Va.; also

raped a 15-year-old girl in Columbia, South Carolina; other rapes and murders suspected in several states

DISPOSITION: Suicide by gunshot following police pursuit in Sarasota, Florida, on June 27, 2002; DNA and other evidence closed four murder cases

Ewen, Gunter Hermann (1962–1999)

SEX: M   RACE: W   TYPE: N   MOTIVE: PC-non-specific

DATE(S): 1999   VENUE: Germany/France   VICTIMS: Five

MO: Shot five victims in Dillingen, Germany, and three in Sierck-les-Bains, France, killing 5; police blamed the rampage on attempts to kill a prosecution witness in a theft case

DISPOSITION: Suicide by gunshot as police stormed his hotel room in Luxembourg on May 16, 1999

Ezerski, Adam Joseph (1982–   )

SEX: M   RACE: W   TYPE: T   MOTIVE: PC/CE

DATE(S): 2001   VENUE: Ft. Lauderdale, Fla.   VICTIMS: Two alleged

MO: Drifter linked to assaults on gay men, including two victims murdered in Florida and another who survived in San Francisco

DISPOSITION: Pleaded guilty in one case, receiving 25 years for second-degree murder and 15 years for robbery

Fain, Roger Eugene (1954–   )

SEX: M   RACE: W   TYPE: T   MOTIVE: Sex.

DATE(S): 1994   VENUE: Austin, Tex.   VICTIMS: Two

MO: Rape-slayer of women

DISPOSITION: Life term on one count, 1995

Faludi, Timea (1977–   )   AKA: Black Angel

SEX: F   RACE: W   TYPE: S   MOTIVE: PC-"mercy"

DATE(S): 2000–01   VENUE: Budapest, Hungary   VICTIMS: 30–35 confessed

MO: Nurse who admitted killing patients at Gyula Nyiro Hospital; charged with eight murders but boasted of 30–35 at trial

DISPOSITION: Despite murder confession in court, received a nine-year sentence on reduced charges of attempted murder, Dec. 1, 2002; also banned from nursing for life

Fautenberry, John Joseph (1965–   )

SEX: M   RACE: W   TYPE: N   MOTIVE: CE

DATE(S): 1982–91   VENUE: USA nationwide   VICTIMS: Six+

MO: Cross-country trucker; killed robbery victims

DISPOSITION: 99-year term on one count in Ark., 1991; condemned on one count in Ohio, 1992; charges filed on four counts in N.J. and Ore.

Fayne, Lorenzo (1971–   )

SEX: M   RACE: B   TYPE: T   MOTIVE: Sex./Sad.

DATE(S): 1989–93   VENUE: East St. Louis, Ill.   VICTIMS: Five

MO: Rape slayer of a six-year-old boy and four girls aged 9–17; victims beaten, strangled, and stabbed, with evidence of necrophilia

DISPOSITION: Received life prison term for boy's murder; condemned for killings of four girls, Nov. 15, 2001

Feldman, Douglas Alan (1958–   )

SEX: M   RACE: W   TYPE: T   MOTIVE: PC

DATE(S): 1998   VENUE: Dallas, Tex.   VICTIMS: Two

MO: Motorcyclist who shot three truck drivers, killing two, in "road rage" incidents

DISPOSITION: Condemned, Sept. 1, 1999

Feltner, Jeffrey Lynn (1962–93)

SEX: M   RACE: W   TYPE: S   MOTIVE: PC-"mercy"

DATE(S): 1988–89   VENUE: Melrose, Fla.   VICTIMS: Eight confessed

MO: Hospital nurse who smothered patients

DISPOSITION: Pled guilty on two counts, receiving life term + 17 years, 1991; died of AIDS in prison, Mar. 17, 1993

Ferguson, Darrell Wayne (1978–   )   AKA: Gator

SEX: M   RACE: W   TYPE: T   MOTIVE: PC-cult

DATE(S): 2000–01   VENUE: East Dayton, Ohio   VICTIMS: 11

MO: Satanist who robbed and murdered three victims aged 61–69; in custody, confessed eight more slayings

DISPOSITION: Pleaded guilty on three counts; condemned Sept. 12, 2003

Ferguson, John Errol (1948–   )

SEX: M   RACE: W   TYPE: T   MOTIVE: CE/PC

DATE(S): 1977   VENUE: Dade County, Fla.   VICTIMS: Eight

MO: Massacred six victims (with two accomplices) in home invasion; kidnapped/killed two teenagers

DISPOSITION: Condemned on eight counts, 1978

ACCOMPLICES: Marvin Francois executed May 29, 1995; Beauford J. White executed Aug. 28, 1987

Ferrell, Jack Dempsey (1940–   )

SEX: M   RACE: B   TYPE: T   MOTIVE: PC-argument

DATE(S): 1981/92   VENUE: Orange County, Fla.
VICTIMS: Two
MO: Shot women during arguments
DISPOSITION: 15 years to life, 1982 (paroled 1987);
condemned, 1993

Field, Frederick Herbert Charles (1905–36)
SEX: M   RACE: W   TYPE: T   MOTIVE: PC-non-specific
DATE(S): 1931/36   VENUE: London, England   VICTIMS: Two
MO: Strangled women in their homes "because I wanted to murder someone"
DISPOSITION: Hanged May 11, 1936

Figueroa, Danny (1960–   )
SEX: M   RACE: H   TYPE: T   MOTIVE: PC-non-specific
DATE(S): 1986   VENUE: Riveriside County, Calif.
VICTIMS: Four
MO: Retarded "thrill killer" of victims shot in random snipings
DISPOSITION: 66 years to life, 1987

Fisher, John King (1854–84)
SEX: M   RACE: W   TYPE: T   MOTIVE: CE/PC
DATE(S): 1871–84   VENUE: Tex.   VICTIMS: Four+
MO: Outlaw-turned-lawman on Tex-Mex border
DISPOSITION: Killed in saloon ambush, March 1884

Fitzsimmons, George Kearon Joseph (1937–   )   AKA: Buffalo Ripper; Karate Chop Killer
SEX: M   RACE: W   TYPE: N   MOTIVE: PC-non-specific
DATE(S): 1969/73   VENUE: N.Y./Pa.   VICTIMS: Four
MO: Killed parents (1969) and elderly caretakers (1973)
DISPOSITION: Ruled insane, 1969; released from asylum 1973; two concurrent life terms, 1976

Flanagan, Sean (1961–89)
SEX: M   RACE: W   TYPE: T   MOTIVE: PC-non-specific
DATE(S): 1987   VENUE: Las Vegas, Nev.   VICTIMS: Two
MO: Gay hustler; killed other gay men to "help society"
DISPOSITION: Executed June 23, 1989

Flannery, Christopher (d. 1985)   AKA: Mr. Rent-a-Kill
SEX: M   RACE: W   TYPE: N   MOTIVE: CE-felony

DATE(S): 1970s–1985   VENUE: Australia   VICTIMS: "Numerous"
MO: Freelance gangland contract killer active in Melbourne and Sydney
DISPOSITION: Vanished on May 9, 1985; presumed murder victim

Flegenheimer, Arthur (1902–35)   AKA: Dutch Schultz
SEX: M   RACE: W   TYPE: T   MOTIVE: CE/PC
DATE(S): 1921–35   VENUE: N.Y./N.J.   VICTIMS: "Numerous"
MO: Psychopathic racketeer; often killed in a rage; ordered more homicides during gang wars and extortion campaigns
DISPOSITION: Murdered by rival mobsters, Oct. 29, 1935

Fletcher, John Bill, Jr. (?–   )
SEX: M   RACE: W   TYPE: T   MOTIVE: Sex.
DATE(S): 1987   VENUE: Yakima, Wash.   VICTIMS: Two
MO: Serial rapist who fatally stabbed at least two victims
DISPOSITION: Serving a 46-year term for a rape in 1986, when he confessed two slayings from 1987; received a new life prison term

Flowers, John (1970–   )
SEX: M   RACE: W   TYPE: T   MOTIVE: PC-non-specific
DATE(S): 1997   VENUE: Las Vegas, Nev.   VICTIMS: Two
MO: Kidnap-slayer of women picked at random
DISPOSITION: Pleaded guilty but mentally ill on one count, receiving a life prison term on May 17, 2003; police "misplaced" second victim's body, resulting in dismissal of that case

Floyd, Cecil Henry (?–   )
SEX: M   RACE: ?   TYPE: N   MOTIVE: CE
DATE(S): 1973–74   VENUE: Kans./Nev./Ind./Fla.
VICTIMS: Six
MO: Shot robbery victims
DISPOSITION: Life terms in Ind. and Nev. (one count each); pled guilty on third count in Kans.

Floyd, Charles (?–   )
SEX: M   RACE: W   TYPE: T   MOTIVE: Sex.
DATE(S): 1942–48   VENUE: Tulsa, Okla.   VICTIMS: Five to six
MO: Voyeur rape-slayer of redhaired females attacked in homes; authorities counted death of a nine-month pregnant victim as a double murder

DISPOSITION: Declared insane; committed to asylum, 1949

Floyd, Charles Arthur (1904–34) AKA: Pretty Boy
SEX: M RACE: W TYPE: N MOTIVE: CE/PC
DATE(S): 1926–34 VENUE: Okla./Mo./Ohio VICTIMS: Seven+
MO: Career criminal; shot lawmen to avoid arrest; allegedly killed at least three men from personal spite
DISPOSITION: Killed by FBI agents in Ohio, Oct. 22, 1934

Floyd, John (1949–) AKA: Crazy Johnny
SEX: M RACE: W TYPE: T MOTIVE: PC
DATE(S): 1980 VENUE: New Orleans, La. VICTIMS: Two
MO: Violent alcoholic/addict; stabbed men in fits of rage
DISPOSITION: Life term with 40-year minimum on one count, 1982

Folbigg, Kathleen (1967–)
SEX: F RACE: W TYPE: S MOTIVE: PC-nonspecific
DATE(S): 1989–99 VENUE: Newcastle, Australia VICTIMS: Four
MO: Mother who suffocated her young children at her home
DISPOSITION: Convicted on three murder counts and one count manslaughter; received a 40-year prison term with 30 years minimum, Oct. 24, 2003

Fornuto, Debbie (d. 2002)
SEX: F RACE: W TYPE: T MOTIVE: PC
DATE(S): 1972–87 VENUE: Cook County, Ill. VICTIMS: Seven suspected
MO: Accused of killing her ex-husband and six of her children, the latter deaths staged as SIDS
DISPOSITION: Died in a car crash on July 11, 2002, in Las Vegas, Nev.

Forrest, Warren (?–)
SEX: M RACE: W TYPE: T MOTIVE: Sex.
DATE(S): 1972–75 VENUE: Vancouver, Wash. VICTIMS: Seven suspected
MO: Rape-slayer of women
DISPOSITION: Found guilty but mentally ill on one count; confined to mental institution

Fortmeyer, Julia (?–?)
SEX: F RACE: W TYPE: T MOTIVE: CE
DATE(S): 1870s VENUE: St. Louis, Mo. VICTIMS: Four+

MO: Abortionist and murderer; three corpses and "dozens" of bones found in her home
DISPOSITION: five years for manslaughter, 1875

Fotopolous, Konstantino X. (1959–)
SEX: M RACE: W TYPE: T MOTIVE: CE
DATE(S): 1989 VENUE: Volusia County, Fla. VICTIMS: Two
MO: Greek national; killed burglary victims
DISPOSITION: Condemned on two counts + life terms on five related felonies

Fox, Richard E. (1956–)
SEX: M RACE: W TYPE: T MOTIVE: PC/Sex.
DATE(S): 1983/89 VENUE: Bowling Green, Ohio VICTIMS: Two suspected
MO: Wife smothered: teenage girl kidnapped/murdered
DISPOSITION: Condemned on one count, 1990

Frampton, Morris John (?–)
SEX: M RACE: W TYPE: 2 MOTIVE: Sex./Sad.
DATE(S): 1977 VENUE: Seattle, Wash. VICTIMS: Two alleged
MO: Beat female prostitutes
DISPOSITION: Condemned on one murder count, with prison time for two nonlethal assaults; death sentence commuted on appeal, 1981

Francois, Kendall (1971–)
SEX: M RACE: B TYPE: T MOTIVE: Sex.
DATE(S): 1996–98 VENUE: Poughkeepsie, N.Y. VICTIMS: Eight
MO: HIV-positive slayer who murdered drug-addicted female prostitutes and hid their bodies at the home he shared with his parents and sister
DISPOSITION: Pleaded guilty on 17 felony counts, June 21, 2000; received eight consecutive terms of 25 years to life, plus 18 months for assault on a surviving victim, Aug. 9, 2000

Franqui, Leonardo (1970–)
SEX: M RACE: W TYPE: T MOTIVE: CE
DATE(S): 1991–92 VENUE: Dade Company, Fla. VICTIMS: Two
MO: Italian national; killed robbery victims
DISPOSITION: Condemned on one count, 1993; condemned on second count with three life terms + 80 years on lesser charges, 1994

Fraser, Leonard John (1952–)
SEX: M RACE: W TYPE: T MOTIVE: Sex.
DATE(S): 2000 VENUE: Rockhampton, Australia VICTIMS: Five

MO: Rape-slayer of three women and a nine-year-old girl

DISPOSITION: Served 19 years on two convictions for rape and attempted rape; received indefinite term for murder of nine-year-old girl; life term with 30-year minimum imposed for three murders of women, June 12, 2000; life term for a fourth woman's murder, Sept. 7, 2000

Frasson, Renato (?–)   AKA: Caretaker of Vincenza
SEX: M   RACE: W   TYPE: T   MOTIVE: Sex.
DATE(S): 1991–92   VENUE: Vincenza, Italy   VICTIMS: Two
MO: "Ripper" of women; victims sexually mutilated
DISPOSITION: Convicted; sentence unknown

Fratianno, Aladena (1913–)   AKA: Jimmy the Weasel
SEX: M   RACE: W   TYPE: N   MOTIVE: CE
DATE(S): 1930s–50s   VENUE: Ohio/Calif./Nev.
VICTIMS: 11+ suspected
MO: Mafia contract killer
DISPOSITION: Admitted nine murders on entry to federal witness program, 1970

Frederick, Earl Alexander (1951–2002)
SEX: M   RACE: W   TYPE: T   MOTIVE: PC-non-specific
DATE(S): 1970s–1980s   VENUE: Oklahoma   VICTIMS: More than two
MO: Confessed the beating to death of a 41 year-old man at Noble and the shotgun slaying of a 77-year-old woman at Texline, blaming the crimes on multiple personality disorder; some accounts claim up to 16 suspected murders
DISPOSITION: Executed on July 30, 2002

Freeman, John Dwayne (1962–)
SEX: M   RACE: W   TYPE: T   MOTIVE: CE
DATE(S): 1986   VENUE: Duval County, Fla.   VICTIMS: Two
MO: Beat/stabbed burglary victims
DISPOSITION: Life term plus 34 years on one count, 1987; condemned, 1988

Freeney, Ray MacArthur (1973–)
SEX: M   RACE: B   TYPE: T   MOTIVE: Sex.
DATE(S): 2002   VENUE: Houston, Tex.   VICTIMS: Two
MO: Diagnosed schizophrenic in 1995; confessed sexually motivated stabbings of five prostitutes, including two fatalities
DISPOSITION: Condemned on Aug. 28, 2003

French, James (d. 1966)
SEX: M   RACE: W   TYPE: N   MOTIVE: PC-non-specific
DATE(S): 1958   VENUE: Stroud, Okla.   VICTIMS: Two
MO: Violent drifter who killed a motorist he met while hitchhiking; later killed cellmate while awaiting trial for first slaying
DISPOSITION: Executed on Aug. 10, 1966

Frost, Samuel (d. 1793)
SEX: M   RACE: W   TYPE: T   MOTIVE: PC-non-specific
DATE(S): 1783/93   VENUE: Princeton, Mass.   VICTIMS: Two
MO: Drove stake through father's head; killed landlord with hoe
DISPOSITION: Hanged, Oct. 1793

F., Timea (1977–)   AKA: Black Angel
SEX: F   RACE: W   TYPE: S   MOTIVE: PC
DATE(S): 1994–2001   VENUE: Budapest, Hungary   VICTIMS: 21
MO: Nurse who admitted killing patients at Gyula Nyiroe Hospital with tranquilizer injections; also claimed victims at a clinic in the Netherlands
DISPOSITION: Unknown

Fuchs, Franz (?–)
SEX: M   RACE: W   TYPE: N   MOTIVE: PC extremist
DATE(S): 1995   VENUE: Austria   VICTIMS: Four
MO: White supremacist who killed four persons and wounded 12 with 29 letter and pipe bombs targeting ethnic minorities
DISPOSITION: Life prison term imposed, March 10, 1999

Fyfe, William Patrick (1955–)
SEX: M   RACE: W   TYPE: T   MOTIVE: Sex.
DATE(S): 1979–89   VENUE: Montreal, Quebec   VICTIMS: Nine confessed
MO: Rape-slayer of women aged 26–59, who killed his first victim while on a day pass from jail
DISPOSITION: Pleaded guilty to five murders committed since 1981, receiving a life prison term in September 2001; subsequently confessed four more slayings; no further charges filed

Gabrion, Marvin Charles, II (1954–)
SEX: M   RACE: W   TYPE: T   MOTIVE: PC-felony
DATE(S): 1997   VENUE: Ottawa County, Mich.   VICTIMS: Four alleged

MO: Raped an 18-year-old woman in August 1996, then killed the victim and her 11-month-old daughter in June 1997, after she filed charges; following arrest, Gabrion was named prime suspect in the murders of three men
DISPOSITION: Condemned in federal court, on March 5, 2002, for killing one victim in a national park

Galan, Alfredo (1977–)   AKA: Playing Card Killer
SEX: M   RACE: H   TYPE: T   MOTIVE: PC-nonspecific
DATE(S): 2003   VENUE: Madrid, Spain   VICTIMS: Nine
MO: Ex-soldier and mental patient, shot 11 victims, aged 18–50, in random attacks, killing nine; left playing cards on victims' bodies
DISPOSITION: Surrendered on July 3, 2003, and confessed a compulsion to kill; admitted eight shootings; ballistics matched his weapon to three other slayings; disposition unknown

Gallego, Gerald Albert (d. 1955)
SEX: M   RACE: W   TYPE: T   MOTIVE: PC
DATE(S): 1954   VENUE: Jackson County, Miss.   VICTIMS: Two
MO: Cop-hating father of GERALD ARMAND GALLEGO; murdered lawmen out of spite for a previous beating by police
DISPOSITION: Executed Mar. 3, 1955

Gamper, Ferdinand (d. 1996)   AKA: Monster of Merano
SEX: M   RACE: W   TYPE: T   MOTIVE: PC-nonspecific
DATE(S): 1996   VENUE: Merano, Italy   VICTIMS: Six
MO: Shepherd who shot five victims in random attacks and killed policeman while resisting arrest
DISPOSITION: Suicide during police shoot-out, Mar. 1, 1996

Garcia, Guinevere Falakassa (1959–)
SEX: F   RACE: H   TYPE: T   MOTIVE: PC-domestic
DATE(S): 1977/91   VENUE: Chicago, Ill.   VICTIMS: Two
MO: Killed her daughter (1977) and elderly husband (1991)
DISPOSITION: 20 years on guilty plea to daughter's death, 1982 (paroled 1991); condemned, 1992 (commuted to life)

Garnier, Gilles (d. 1573)
SEX: M   RACE: W   TYPE: T   MOTIVE: PC-nonspecific

DATE(S): 1572   VENUE: Dôle, France   VICTIMS: Four confessed
MO: "Werewolf" cannibal-killer of children
DISPOSITION: Burned at the stake, Jan. 1573

Garr, Kevin George (1964–)
SEX: M   RACE: ?   TYPE: T   MOTIVE: CE
DATE(S): 1989/91   VENUE: Madison/Orange Counties, Va.   VICTIMS: Two
MO: Women aged 46 and 66 abducted from parking lots
DISPOSITION: Convicted on one count in Madison County, second-degree murder

Garrison, Wayne Henry (1959–)
SEX: M   RACE: W   TYPE: T   MOTIVE: Sex.
DATE(S): 1973–89   VENUE: Tulsa, Okla.   VICTIMS: Three
MO: Strangled his four-year-old cousin at age 13; killed a three-year-old boy while on furlough from a psychiatric hospital, 1975; strangled and dismembered a 13-year-old boy in 1989
DISPOSITION: Committed to asylum after first murder; pleaded guilty to voluntary manslaughter after second killing, sentenced to four years; released in 1977; received three and a half-year sentence in 1997, for drugging and kidnapping a 15-year-old victim in North Carolina; condemned for his third murder, Dec. 19, 2001

Garrow, Robert F. (1937–78)
SEX: M   RACE: W   TYPE: T   MOTIVE: Sex./Sad.
DATE(S): 1973   VENUE: N.Y.   VICTIMS: Four
MO: Stabbed/bludgeoned two men and two women
DISPOSITION: 25 years to life on one count, 1974; shot dead in prison break Sept. 11, 1978

Garza, Juan Raul (1957–2001)
SEX: M   RACE: H   TYPE: T   MOTIVE: CE
DATE(S): 1990–91   VENUE: Brownsville, Tex.   VICTIMS: Three
MO: Shot male associates in the narcotics trade
DISPOSITION: Executed on June 19, 2001

Garza Hoth, Gabriel (?–)   AKA: Black Widower
SEX: M   RACE: H   TYPE: T   MOTIVE: CE-felony
DATE(S): 1991–97   VENUE: Mexico City   VICTIMS: Three
MO: Profit motivated killer who collected life insurance payments on his wife and lovers
DISPOSITION: Life prison term and a $2,200 fine imposed on Nov. 10, 2000, for the murder 1997 of a girlfriend he insured for $400,000

Gaskin, Louis Bernard (1967–)
SEX: M RACE: B TYPE: N MOTIVE: CE
DATE(S): 1986/89 VENUE: Fla. VICTIMS: Seven
MO: Killed robber/ burglar victims in Flagler and
  Volusia counties
DISPOSITION: Multiple trials in 1990; condemned on
  four counts; life terms on three counts; six life terms
  for robbery/burglary

Gasser, John R. (?–)
SEX: M RACE: W TYPE: N MOTIVE: Sex.
DATE(S): 1948/1982 VENUE: Washington State
  VICTIMS: Two
MO: Rape-strangler of women aged 22 and 49
DISPOSITION: Imprisoned for first crime as a college
  student, 1948–62, 1964–69; received life term for
  second murder

Gates, Anne (1949–)
SEX: F RACE: W TYPE: N MOTIVE: CE
DATE(S): 1978/87 VENUE: Ind./La. VICTIMS:
  Two suspected
MO: "Black widow" slayer of husbands for profit
DISPOSITION: Pled "no contest" on one count in La.,
  1989; received $25,000 from victim's estate, 1992

Gaynor, Alfred (1967–)
SEX: M RACE: B TYPE: T MOTIVE: Sex.
DATE(S): 1997–98 VENUE: Springfield, Mass.
  VICTIMS: Four
MO: Rape-slayer of drug-addicted black women lured
  with cocaine
DISPOSITION: Received four consecutive life terms,
  May 19, 2000

Geary, Melvin (1931–)
SEX: M RACE: W TYPE: N MOTIVE: Sex./PC
DATE(S): 1973/92 VENUE: Nev. VICTIMS: Two
MO: Stabbed 38-year-old woman and a 71-year-old
  man
DISPOSITION: Life term on one count, 1973 (paroled
  1986); condemned on second count

Geist, Joseph (1956–)
SEX: M RACE: W TYPE: T MOTIVE: PC-
  extremist
DATE(S): 1986 VENUE: Chicago, Ill. VICTIMS:
  Two
MO: Neo-Nazi cab driver; shot adult male victims at
  random
DISPOSITION: 65 years on one count, 1989; 18 years
  for attempted murder of victim who survived, 1990;
  condemned on second count, 1991 (commuted to
  life on appeal, 1992)

Genrich, Jimmy (1961–) AKA: Mad Bomber
SEX: M RACE: W TYPE: T MOTIVE: PC-non-
  specific
DATE(S): 1991 VENUE: Grand Junction, Colo.
  VICTIMS: Two
MO: Serial bomber of random targets
DISPOSITION: Life sentence, 1992

Georges, Guy (1962–) AKA: Beast of the Bastille;
  East Paris Killer
SEX: M RACE: B TYPE: T MOTIVE: Sex./CE-
  felony
DATE(S): 1991–97 VENUE: Paris, France VIC-
  TIMS: Seven
MO: Raped, robbed and slashed throats of 11 young
  women, killing seven
DISPOSITION: Confessed murders at trial; received a
  life term with 22-year minimum, April 5, 2001

Geralds, Hubert, Jr. (1964–)
SEX: M RACE: B TYPE: T MOTIVE: Sex.
DATE(S): 1995 VENUE: Chicago, Ill. VICTIMS:
  Six
MO: Slayer of drug-addicted prostitutes
DISPOSITION: Convicted Nov. 13, 1997

Ghanam, Mohamed Elsayed (1964–)
SEX: M RACE: B TYPE: T MOTIVE: CE-felony
DATE(S): 1998–99 VENUE: Bangkok, Thailand
  VICTIMS: Six
MO: Unlicensed tour guide who stabbed and robbed
  foreign male tourists aged 32–64
DISPOSITION: Unknown

Giancana, Sam (1908–75) AKA: Momo
SEX: M RACE: W TYPE: T MOTIVE: CE/Sad.
DATE(S): 1925–57 VENUE: Chicago, Ill. VIC-
  TIMS: "Numerous"
MO: Mafia hit man before he assumed leadership of
  the Chicago "family," three victims known before
  age 20; ordered at least 79 murders, 1957–66
DISPOSITION: Murdered at home, June 19, 1975

Gibaldi, Vincenzo (1903–36) AKA: "Machine Gun"
  Jack McGurn
SEX: M RACE: W TYPE: N MOTIVE: PC/CE
DATE(S): 1933–51 VENUE: Ill./N.Y. VICTIMS:
  22+
MO: Contract killer for ALPHONSE CAPONE gang;
  prime suspect in 1929 St. Valentine's Day massacre
DISPOSITION: Murdered Feb. 14, 1936

Gibbs, Charles (1800–31)
SEX: M RACE: W TYPE: N MOTIVE: CE

DATE(S): c. 1820–30   VENUE: At sea   VICTIMS: 400 claimed

MO: Sea-going pirate; signed on as crewman of small vessels, then murdered other crewmen and stole cargoes

DISPOSITION: Hanged in N.Y., Apr. 22, 1831

Gibbs, Janie Lou (1932–)
SEX: F   RACE: W   TYPE: T   MOTIVE: CE
DATE(S): 1966–67   VENUE: Cordele, Ga.   VICTIMS: Five

MO: "Black widow" poisoner of husband, children, and grandchild, killed for life insurance

DISPOSITION: Committed to asylum, 1968; deemed competent for trial in 1974; five consecutive life terms, 1976

Gibson, Gregory (1978–)
SEX: M   RACE: ?   TYPE: T   MOTIVE: CE
DATE(S): 1992/98   VENUE: Durham, N.C.   VICTIMS: Two

MO: Killed robbery victims, one of them a 90-year-old man

DISPOSITION: Convicted on one count in juvenile court, 1992; confined until age 18 (1996); jailhouse suicide by hanging, Nov. 13, 1998

Gilbert, Kristen (1966–)   AKA: Angel of Death
SEX: F   RACE: W   TYPE: S   MOTIVE: PC-nonspecific
DATE(S): 1995–96   VENUE: Northampton, Mass.   VICTIMS: Four

MO: Thrill-killing nurse who used drugs to kill patients at a veterans' hospital; two of six known victims survived

DISPOSITION: Convicted on three counts first-degree murder, one count second-degree, and two counts attempted murder; received four consecutive life terms without parole plus 20 years on lesser charges, March 26, 2001

Giles, Bernard E. (1953–)
SEX: M   RACE: W   TYPE: T   MOTIVE: Sex.
DATE(S): 1973   VENUE: Brevard County, Fla.   VICTIMS: Four

MO: Necrophile slayer of female victims

DISPOSITION: Life terms on three counts, 1974; life term on fourth count + 15 years on lesser felonies, 1977

Gillis, Lester M. (1908–34)   AKA: George ("Baby Face") Nelson
SEX: M   RACE: W   TYPE: N   MOTIVE: CE

DATE(S): 1926–34   VENUE: Ill./Minn./Calif.?/Wash.?   VICTIMS: Four+

MO: Career criminal and alleged part-time hit man; confirmed victims killed during robberies or shootouts with lawmen

DISPOSITION: Killed in shoot-out with FBI agents, Nove. 27, 1934

Gilmore, Gary Mark (1940–77)
SEX: M   RACE: W   TYPE: T   MOTIVE: CE
DATE(S): 1976   VENUE: Salt Lake City, Utah   VICTIMS: Two

MO: Executed male victims in petty robberies

DISPOSITION: Executed by firing squad, Jan. 17, 1977

Girard, Henri (1875–1921)
SEX: M   RACE: W   TYPE: T   MOTIVE: CE
DATE(S): 1912/1918   VENUE: Paris, France   VICTIMS: Two

MO: Poisoned acquaintances for life insurance

DISPOSITION: Suicide in jail, awaiting trial, May 1921

Giri, Laxman (1911–80)
SEX: M   RACE: A   TYPE: T   MOTIVE: PC-nonspecific
DATE(S): 1970s   VENUE: India   VICTIMS: "Several"

MO: Cult leader; sacrificed children to make followers immortal

DISPOSITION: Died in jail, Mar. 5, 1980

Girts, Robert (1953–)
SEX: M   RACE: W   TYPE: N   MOTIVE: PC-domestic
DATE(S): 1977–92   VENUE: Ohio   VICTIMS: Two suspected

MO: "Bluebeard" slayer of wives

DISPOSITION: 20 years to life on one count, 1993

Giudice, Giancarlo (1953–)   AKA: Devil of Turin
SEX: M   RACE: W   TYPE: T   MOTIVE: Sex./Sad.
DATE(S): 1984–87   VENUE: Turin, Italy   VICTIMS: Seven

MO: Torture-slayer of prostitutes

DISPOSITION: Life sentence, 1987

Giugliano, Maurizio (?–)   AKA: Monster of Rome
SEX: M   RACE: W   TYPE: T   MOTIVE: Sex./PC
DATE(S): 1983–84/92   VENUE: Rome, Italy   VICTIMS: Eight

MO: Strangled/stabbed/shot women; smothered cellmate with pillow after capture

DISPOSITION: Confined to lunatic asylum, 1984

Glanton, John Joel (1815–50)
SEX: M   RACE: W   TYPE: N   MOTIVE: CE
DATE(S): 1841–50   VENUE: Tex./Mexico   VICTIMS: 100+
MO: Ex-convict and gunman for hire; later led scalp-hunting gang that often murdered Mexicans and sold their hair as "Apache" scalps
DISPOSITION: Killed by Indians, with most of his gang, Apr. 1850

Glatman, Harvey Murray (1928–59)
SEX: M   RACE: W   TYPE: T   MOTIVE: Sex.
DATE(S): 1957–58   VENUE: South Calif.   VICTIMS: Three
MO: Rape-murders of young women
DISPOSITION: Executed Sept. 18, 1959

Glaze, Billy Richard (1953–)
SEX: M   RACE: W   TYPE: T   MOTIVE: Sex./Sad.
DATE(S): 1986–87   VENUE: Minneapolis, Minn.   VICTIMS: Three
MO: Bludgeon slayer of Native American women
DISPOSITION: Life term with 50-year minimum, 1989

Glover, John Wayne (1932–)   AKA: Granny Killer
SEX: M   RACE: W   TYPE: T   MOTIVE: Sex./Sad.
DATE(S): 1989–90   VENUE: Sydney, Australia   VICTIMS: Six
MO: Bludgeoned elderly women with hammers in public places, then strangled them with their own underwear
DISPOSITION: Pleaded guilty in November 1991 and received a life prison term

Goble, Sean Patrick (1967–)
SEX: M   RACE: W   TYPE: N   MOTIVE: Sex.
DATE(S): 1980s–95   VENUE: Southern U.S.   VICTIMS: "Dozens" suspected
MO: Long-haul trucker; rape-slayer of women
DISPOSITION: Two consecutive life terms in Tenn., 1995

Goebbels, Peter (1961–)
SEX: M   RACE: W   TYPE: T   MOTIVE: Sex.
DATE(S): 1984–85   VENUE: Berlin, Germany   VICTIMS: Four
MO: Rape-slayer of females age 17–22
DISPOSITION: Life sentence, 1985

Goetz, Fred (1897–1934)
SEX: M   RACE: W   TYPE: N   MOTIVE: CE
DATE(S): 1920s–34   VENUE: Midwestern U.S.   VICTIMS: 12+

MO: Career criminal and contract killer; possible participant in 1929 St. Valentine's Day massacre
DISPOSITION: Murdered by BARKER-KARPIS GANG, Mar. 22, 1934

Goldstein, Martin (?–1941)   AKA: Buggsy
SEX: M   RACE: W   TYPE: T   MOTIVE: CE
DATE(S): 1930s–40   VENUE: N.Y./N.J.   VICTIMS: 30+
MO: Contract killer for "MURDER, INC."
DISPOSITION: Executed at Sing Sing, June 12, 1941

Golovkin, Anatoly (?–)
SEX: M   RACE: W   TYPE: T   MOTIVE: Sex./Sad.
DATE(S): 1986–94   VENUE: Moscow, Russia   VICTIMS: 11
MO: "Straightforward maniac" who killed boys
DISPOSITION: Condemned, 1994

Gomez, Lloyd (d. 1953)
SEX: M   RACE: H   TYPE: N   MOTIVE: CE
DATE(S): 1949–51   VENUE: Calif.   VICTIMS: Nine
MO: Killed/robbed hoboes
DISPOSITION: Executed Oct. 17, 1953

Goodin, Anthony J. (1965–)
SEX: M   RACE: W   TYPE: N   MOTIVE: CE
DATE(S): 1982–87   VENUE: Okla./Ala./Ga./Fla.   VICTIMS: Seven suspected
MO: Drifter linked to random murders; three identified victims were male, including two gays
DISPOSITION: Life sentence on one count in Ga., 1988

Gore, Marshall Lee (1963–)
SEX: M   RACE: W   TYPE: N   MOTIVE: CE/Sex.
DATE(S): 1988   VENUE: Fla.   VICTIMS: Two
MO: Killed robber/kidnap victims in Columbia and Dade Countries; child victim raped
DISPOSITION: Condemned on two counts, 1990 and 1995; seven life terms + 110 years on other felony counts.

Gorobets, Paval (?–)
SEX: M   RACE: W   TYPE: T   MOTIVE: PC-nonspecific
DATE(S): 1997–98   VENUE: Bishkek, Kyrgyzstan   VICTIMS: Two
MO: Killed a male tenant and his own girlfriend, dismembering and cannibalizing their bodies
DISPOSITION: Condemned on March 5, 1999

Gorton, Jeffrey W. (?–)
SEX: M   RACE: W   TYPE: N   MOTIVE: Sex.

DATE(S): 1986/1991   VENUE: Eastern Michigan
  VICTIMS: Two
MO: Rape-slayer of women in Flint and Wayne
  County
DISPOSITION: Three life terms in Wayne County,
  August 2002; pleaded guilty in Flint on second
  count, 2003

Goss, Dean Neel (1936–92)
SEX: M   RACE: W   TYPE: T   MOTIVE: CE/PC-
  domestic
DATE(S): 1982–85   VENUE: Houston, Tex.   VIC-
  TIMS: Three suspected
MO:Alleged "Bluebeard" slayer of two wives and male
  employee
DISPOSITION: Shot dead in disputed circumstances,
  Nov. 1992

Gossman, Klaus (1941–   )
SEX: M   RACE: W   TYPE: T   MOTIVE: CE/Sad.
DATE(S): 1960–64   VENUE: Nuremburg, Germany
  VICTIMS: Six
MO: Self-proclaimed "death's agent"; shot victims in
  holdups and random street attacks
DISPOSITION: Life sentence, 1965

Gottfried, Gessina Margaretha (1798–1828)
SEX: F   RACE: W   TYPE: T   MOTIVE: PC-domes-
  tic/CE
DATE(S): 1822–25   VENUE: Bremen, Germany
  VICTIMS: 16 confessed
MO: "Black widow" poisoner of relatives and
  acquaintances
DISPOSITION: Beheaded, 1828

Grace, James Willie (1946–   )
SEX: M   RACE: W   TYPE: T   MOTIVE: PC-non-
  specific
DATE(S): 1976   VENUE: Durham, N.C.   VICTIMS:
  More than two suspected
MO: Schizophrenic sniper; shot men in random attacks
DISPOSITION: Three consecutive 10-year terms for
  attempted murder and assault with deadly weapon,
  1977 (released 1993)

Graham, Harrison (1959–   )
SEX: M   RACE: W   TYPE: S   MOTIVE: Sex.
DATE(S): 1983–87   VENUE: Philadelphia, Pa.   VIC-
  TIMS: Seven
MO: Retarded addict; strangled prostitutes and kept
  the remains in his apartment
DISPOSITION: Convicted on all counts, 1988: life
  term followed by six death penalties (to prevent
  parole)

Graham, William Brocius (1857–82)   AKA: Curly Bill
SEX: M   RACE: W   TYPE: N   MOTIVE: CE/PC
DATE(S): 1870s–82   VENUE: Mexico/Ariz.   VIC-
  TIMS: "Numerous"
MO: Old West outlaw and feudist
DISPOSITION: Killed by WYATT EARP, Mar. 24, 1882

Grant, Gary G. (?–   )
SEX: M   RACE: W   TYPE: T   MOTIVE: PC-non-
  specific
DATE(S): 1971   VENUE: Renton, Wash.   VICTIMS:
  Four
MO: U.S. Navy enlistee who stabbed/strangled two six-
  year-old boys and two teenage girls, all dumped in
  woods near his home
DISPOSITION: Life prison term

Grant, Sam (d. 1876)
SEX: M   RACE: B   TYPE: N   MOTIVE: CE
DATE(S): 1870s   VENUE: Western U.S.   VICTIMS:
  "Numerous"
MO: Hired killer and scalp hunter
DISPOSITION: Killed by JOHN JOHNSTON, 1876

Granviel, Kenneth (1950–   )
SEX: M   RACE: W   TYPE: N   MOTIVE: Sex./Sad.
DATE(S): 1976   VENUE: Tex.   VICTIMS: Four
MO: Stabbed two women and two children in random
  attacks
DISPOSITION: Executed Feb. 27, 1996

Grasso, Thomas Joseph (1962–95)
SEX: M   RACE: W   TYPE: N   MOTIVE: PC-non-
  specific
DATE(S): 1990–91   VENUE: Okla. N.Y.   VICTIMS:
  Two
MO: "Thrill killer" of 87-year-old woman (Okla.) and
  84-year-old man (N.Y.)
DISPOSITION: Executed in Okla., Mar. 20, 1995

Gravano, Salvatore (1945–   )   AKA: Sammy the Bull
SEX: M   RACE: W   TYPE: T   MOTIVE: CE/PC
DATE(S): 1970–90   VENUE: N.Y./N.J.   VIC-
  TIMS:19–36 admitted
MO: Mafia "enforcer" and hit man
DISPOSITION: Granted immunity in return for testi-
  mony, 1990; 19-year sentence for drug offenses,
  Oct. 30, 2002

Gray, Dana Sue (1958–   )
SEX: F   RACE: W   TYPE: T   MOTIVE: CE
DATE(S): 1977–78   VENUE: Riverside County, Calif.
  VICTIMS: Three

MO: Ex-nurse; robbed/strangled women aged 66–87; one victim also stabbed
DISPOSITION: Life term without parole, 1998

Gray, Josephine (1946–) AKA: Black Widow
SEX: F RACE: W TYPE: T MOTIVE: CE-felony
DATE(S): 1974–96 VENUE: Maryland VICTIMS: Three alleged
MO: Named by police and prosecutors as the slayer of two husbands and a cousin-lover, shot for life insurance payments
DISPOSITION: Charged with murders of both husbands in 1991, charges dismissed when witnesses vanished or recanted testimony; convicted of mail fraud in federal court, August 2002; received the maximum 40-year sentence on Dec. 2, 2002, with an order to repay $170,000 in life insurance proceeds

Gray, Marvin (1955–)
SEX: M RACE: Unk. TYPE: T MOTIVE: PC
DATE(S): 1980s–1993 VENUE: Denver, Colo. VICTIMS: 23 confessed
MO: Random slayer of victims in personal confrontations
DISPOSITION: Received life sentence as habitual criminal in 1993, for a 1992 armed robbery; received life term with 30 years minimum in 2000, for a 1984 murder; confessed 23 murders in court, June 2001, while on trial for a second murder; convicted and received two more life terms, June 6, 2001

Gray, Ronald Adrian (1966–)
SEX: M RACE: B TYPE: T MOTIVE: Sex.
DATE(S): 1986–87 VENUE: Fayetteville, N.C. VICTIMS: Four
MO: Soldier at Fort Bragg; rape-slayer of women age 18–24
DISPOSITION: Three consecutive life terms after guilty plea, 1987; condemned by military court-martial, 1988

Green, Cleo Joel, III (1958–) AKA: Red Demon
SEX: M RACE: B TYPE: T MOTIVE: Sex.
DATE(S): 1983 VENUE: Louisville, Ky. VICTIMS: Three
MO: "Possessed" home-invader; rape-slayer of elderly women
DISPOSITION: Ruled incompetent for trial, 1984

Green, Malcolm (1946–)
SEX: M RACE: W TYPE: N MOTIVE: PC-nonspecific
DATE(S): 1971/90 VENUE: Wales VICTIMS: Two

MO: Killed female prostitute (1971) and male stranger (1990)
DISPOSITION: Life term, 1971 (paroled 1989); life term, 1991

Green, Ricky Lee (1960–97)
SEX: M RACE: W TYPE: T MOTIVE: Sex./Sad.
DATE(S): 1985–86 VENUE: Fort Worth, Tex. VICTIMS: Four
MO: Bisexual torture-slayer of two men and two women
DISPOSITION: Executed Oct. 9, 1997

Green, Samuel (d. 1822)
SEX: M RACE: W TYPE: N MOTIVE: CE/Sex.
DATE(S): 19th century VENUE: New England VICTIMS: "Numerous"
MO: Career criminal; killed rape and robbery victims
DISPOSITION: Hanged in Mass., Apr. 1822

Greenawalt, Randy (1949–97)
SEX: M RACE: W TYPE: N MOTIVE: PC/CE
DATE(S): 1973–74/78 VENUE: Ariz./Colo. VICTIMS: Nine suspected
MO: Shot sleeping truckers for personal amusement; helped TISON family kill five victims after prison break
DISPOSITION: Life term for death of one trucker, 1974 (escaped 1978); condemned, 1979; executed in Ariz. Jan. 23, 1997

Greenberg, Bertram (d. 1971)
SEX: M RACE: W TYPE: N MOTIVE: Sex./CE-felony
DATE(S): 1971 VENUE: Calif./Ariz. VICTIMS: Three
MO: Raped/strangled woman; shot policemen during manhunt
DISPOSITION: Killed running police roadblock in N. Mex.

Greeson, Lloyd Donald, Jr. (1924–)
SEX: M RACE: W TYPE: N MOTIVE: CE
DATE(S): 1964 VENUE: Fla./Pa. VICTIMS: Two
MO: Robbed/murdered women age 37 and 44
DISPOSITION: 20 years on one count of second degree in Fla., 1964

Grenier, Jean (?–?)
SEX: M RACE: W TYPE: T MOTIVE: PC-nonspecific
DATE(S): 1603 VENUE: Landes, France VICTIMS: "Several"
MO: Deranged "werewolf" slayer of children
DISPOSITION: Confined to monastery for life, 1603

Gribble, Timothy Lane (1964–2000)
SEX: M RACE: W TYPE: T MOTIVE: Sex.
DATE(S): 1985–87 VENUE: Galveston, Tex. VICTIMS: Three confessed
MO: Rape-slayer of women aged 23–36
DISPOSITION: Executed on one count, March 15, 2000

Grieveson, Steven (1970–)
SEX: M RACE: W TYPE: T MOTIVE: Sex./Sad.
DATE(S): 1993–94 VENUE: Sunderland, England VICTIMS: Three
MO: Repressed homosexual who raped, murdered, and burned three teenage male students from the same school in separate incidents
DISPOSITION: Received three life prison terms, Feb. 28, 1996

Grills, Caroline (1885–?) AKA: Aunt Thally
SEX: F RACE: W TYPE: T MOTIVE: PC/CE
DATE(S): 1947–48 VENUE: Sydney, Australia VICTIMS: Four
MO: "Black widow" poisoner of relatives (with thallium)
DISPOSITION: Life sentence, 1949

Grimson, Allan (1958–)
SEX: M RACE: W TYPE: N MOTIVE: PC
DATE(S): 1980s VENUE: England and at sea VICTIMS: More than three
MO: Royal Navy seaman who killed shipmates and a bartender
DISPOSITION: Once investigated in the disappearances of 20 sailors worldwide, Grimson confessed the murders of one shipmate and a British bartender in 2001, receiving a life prison term; prime suspect in the disappearance of another shipmate at Gibraltar, 1986

Grinder, James B. (1945–)
SEX: M RACE: W TYPE: N MOTIVE: Sex.
DATE(S): 1976–84 VENUE: Ark./Mo. VICTIMS: Four
MO: Rape-slayer of females in their teens and twenties
DISPOSITION: Life sentence after guilty plea to one count in Missouri, June 1999; admits sexual contact with two Arkansas victims

Grissom, Richard (1960–)
SEX: M RACE: B TYPE: T MOTIVE: Sex.
DATE(S): 1989 VENUE: Kansas City, Mo. VICTIMS: Three
MO: Rape-slayer of young women abducted from homes
DISPOSITION: three consecutive life terms

Gross, Dr. Heinrich (1916–)
SEX: M RACE: W TYPE: S MOTIVE: PC-extremist
DATE(S): 1930s VENUE: Austria VICTIMS: More than nine
MO: Nazi physician who killed "defective" children under state euthanasia program
DISPOSITION: Murder trial aborted on March 2, 2000, due to defendant's advanced senile dementia

Grossmann, Georg Karl (1863–1921)
SEX: M RACE: W TYPE: S MOTIVE: Sex./CE
DATE(S): 1910–21 VENUE: Berlin, Germany VICTIMS: 50+ suspected
MO: Paroled pedophile and child killer; murdered prostitutes after sex and sold their flesh in his butcher shop
DISPOSITION: Jailhouse suicide by hanging

Groves, Vincent Darrell (1953–)
SEX: M RACE: B TYPE: T MOTIVE: Sex./Sad.
DATE(S): 1973–81/88 VENUE: Denver, Colo. VICTIMS: 14 suspected
MO: Rape-slayer of street prostitutes
DISPOSITION: 12 years on one count, 1982 (paroled 1987); life term, 1989; 20 years on plea to third count, 1990; died in prison, Oct. 31, 1996

Guatney, William (1922–) AKA: Freight Train
SEX: M RACE: W TYPE: N MOTIVE: PC-non-specific
DATE(S): 1975–79 VENUE: Nebr./Kans./Ill. VICTIMS: Five suspected
MO: Transient linked to murder to boys age nine to 13
DISPOSITION: Ruled incompetent for trial, 1980; murder confessions suppressed; committed to mental institution

Guerrero, Francisco (?–?) AKA: Slitter of Women's Throats
SEX: M RACE: H TYPE: N MOTIVE: Sex./Sad.
DATE(S): 1880s VENUE: Mexico VICTIMS: "Several"
MO: Mutilation-slayer of women
DISPOSITION: Executed, date unknown

Gufler, Max (1910–)
SEX: M RACE: W TYPE: N MOTIVE: PC
DATE(S): 1946–58 VENUE: Austria VICTIMS: 18 suspected
MO: "Bluebeard" slayer of wives/fiancées
DISPOSITION: Confessed four murders; life sentence, May 1961

Guimaraes, Edson Isadora (1957–   )   AKA: Angel of Death
SEX: M   RACE: H   TYPE: S   MOTIVE: PC-"mercy"
DATE(S): 1998–99   VENUE: Rio de Janeiro, Brazil
VICTIMS: 150 suspected
MO: Male nurse accused of killing patients in ICU at Salgado Filho Hospital by turning off their oxygen supplies; 131 died in his care between Jan. 1 and May 4, 1999, with unspecified others during 1998
DISPOSITION: Unknown

Gunning, James D. (1971–   )
SEX: M   RACE: Unk.   TYPE: N   MOTIVE: Sex.
DATE(S): 1990s   VENUE: Eastern United States
VICTIMS: 10 suspected
MO: Jailed for attempted murder of three New Jersey women, suspected of raping and strangling 10 women in three states
DISPOSITION: Pleaded guilty on one murder count and received a 17-year sentence with 14 years minimum, March 28, 2003

Gurino, Vito (1907–?)   AKA: Socko; Chicken Head
SEX: M   RACE: W   TYPE: T   MOTIVE: CE
DATE(S): 1931–40   VENUE: N.Y./N.J.   VICTIMS: Eight+
MO: Contract killer for "MURDER, INC."
DISPOSITION: 80 years to life on three counts, 1940; died in prison

Gurule, Raymond Anthony (1958)
SEX: M   RACE: NA   TYPE: T   MOTIVE: PC
DATE(S): 1982/84   VENUE: Redwood City, Calif.
VICTIMS: Two
MO: Killed 15-year-old boy and 81-year-old woman
DISPOSITION: Condemned on one count, 1990

Guy, Martin G. (1962–   )
SEX: M   RACE: W   TYPE: T   MOTIVE: Sex.
DATE(S): 1998–99   VENUE: Norfolk County, Mass.
VICTIMS: Three suspected
MO: Prime suspect in stabbings of women aged 25–82
DISPOSITION: Life sentence on one murder count

Guzman, James (1964–   )
SEX: M   RACE: W   TYPE: N   MOTIVE: CE
DATE(S): 1982/91   VENUE: Fla.   VICTIMS: Two
MO: Killed robbery/kidnap victims in Dade and Volusia counties
DISPOSITION: 30 years on one count, 1982 (paroled 1991); condemned + life term for armed robbery, 1996

Hadley, Paul (d. 1923)   AKA: The Claw
SEX: M   RACE: W   TYPE: N   MOTIVE: CE/Sex.
DATE(S): 1916–21   VENUE: Okla./Ariz.   VICTIMS: Three
MO: Killed a sheriff (Okla.) and married couple (Ariz.); several rapes
DISPOSITION: 99 years (Okla.), 1916; escaped 1921; hanged Apr. 13, 1923

Hahn, Anna Marie (1906–38)
SEX: F   RACE: W   TYPE: N   MOTIVE: CE-inheritance
DATE(S): 1932–37   VENUE: Ohio/Colo.   VICTIMS: Five
MO: Self-styled nurse and "black widow" poisoner of elderly men
DISPOSITION: Executed in Ohio June 20, 1938

Haigh, Paul Steven (1957–   )
SEX: M   RACE: W   TYPE: T   MOTIVE: Sex./Sad.
DATE(S): 1977–78   VENUE: Victoria, Australia
VICTIMS: Seven
MO: Slayer of young women; stabbed one victim 157 times; attended funerals of four victims as a mourner
DISPOSITION: Seven consecutive life terms

Halabi, Mohammed (1957–   )   AKA: Tel Aviv Strangler
SEX: M   RACE: A   TYPE: T   MOTIVE: PC-extremist
DATE(S): 1989   VENUE: Tel Aviv/Jaffa, Israel   VICTIMS: Seven
MO: Palestinian strangler of four Jews and three Israeli Arabs
DISPOSITION: Confessed all counts; sentence unknown

Hall, Archibald Thompson (1924–   )   AKA: Monster Butler
SEX: M   RACE: W   TYPE: N   MOTIVE: CE
DATE(S): 1978   VENUE: Scotland/England   VICTIMS: Five
MO: Robbed/murdered employers and a criminal accomplice
DISPOSITION: Two life terms, 1978

Hall, Dewain (1964–90)
SEX: M   RACE: B   TYPE: T   MOTIVE: Sex.
DATE(S): 1989   VENUE: Oakland, Calif.   VICTIMS: Two
MO: Shot female prostitutes
DISPOSITION: Jailhouse suicide by drowning, Nov. 23, 1990

Hall, James Waybern (1906–46)   AKA: Big Jim
SEX: M   RACE: W   TYPE: T   MOTIVE: PC/CE

DATE(S): 1944–45   VENUE: Ark.   VICTIMS: Four
MO: Murdered his wife, followed by three men in
  apparent robberies
DISPOSITION: Executed Jan. 4, 1946

Hanaei, Saeed (1963–2002)
SEX: M   RACE: A   TYPE: T   MOTIVE: PC-extrem-
  ist
DATE(S): 2000–02   VENUE: Mashhad, Iran   VIC-
  TIMS: 16–19
MO: Strangled female prostitutes aged 25–50, with
  their own headscarves; killed "for the sake of God"
  to "purify" Muslim society
DISPOSITION: Hanged on 16 counts, April 17, 2002

Hand, Gerald (1949–)
SEX: M   RACE: W   TYPE: T   MOTIVE: CE-felony
DATE(S): 1976–2002   VENUE: Ohio   VICTIMS:
  Four
MO: Murdered three wives for insurance money; also
  shot his alleged accomplice in the first two slayings
DISPOSITION: Condemned on two counts, June 4,
  2003, for killing his third wife and a male acquain-
  tance in 2002

Hankins, Terry Lee (1975–)
SEX: M   RACE: Unk.   TYPE: T   MOTIVE: PC
DATE(S): 2000   VENUE: Arlington, Tex.   VICTIMS:
  Five confessed
MO: Shot his wife and two stepchildren; in custody,
  confessed the earlier bludgeon murders of his father
  and half-sister
DISPOSITION: Condemned on two counts of killing
  his stepchildren, May 2002

Hanson, William P. (1949–)   AKA: Paper Bag Killer
SEX: M   RACE: W   TYPE: T   MOTIVE: PC-
  revenge
DATE(S): 1973   VENUE: San Francisco, Calif.   VIC-
  TIMS: Two
MO: Shots/stabbed middle-aged men resembling his
  sister's rapist
DISPOSITION: Declared insane, 1974; confined to
  state hospital

Hardin, John Wesley (1853–95)
SEX: M   RACE: W   TYPE: N   MOTIVE: PC
DATE(S): 1868–78   VENUE: Tex./Kans.   VICTIMS:
  40+
MO: Racist gunfighter; killed blacks, Mexicans, Indi-
  ans, Union soldiers, and personal enemies
DISPOSITION: 25 years for murder, 1878 (paroled
  1894); murdered by JOHN SELMAN, Aug. 19, 1895

Harding, Donald Eugene (1949–92)
SEX: M   RACE: W   TYPE: N   MOTIVE: CE
DATE(S): 1882   VENUE: Ark./Tex./Calif./Ariz.   VIC-
  TIMS: Seven
MO: Robbed/murdered victims in cross-country ram-
  page
DISPOSITION: Condemned on three counts in Ariz.;
  executed Apr. 6, 1992

Hardy, Anthony John (1949–)   AKA: Camden Ripper
SEX: M   RACE: W   TYPE: T   MOTIVE: PC-nonspecific
DATE(S): 2002   VENUE: London, England   VIC-
  TIMS: Three
MO: Mental patient who killed a female prostitute in
  his apartment, then beheaded two more women in
  separate attacks; heads still missing
DISPOSITION: Pleaded guilty on three murder counts;
  received three life prison terms, Nov. 25, 2003

Harper, Robert (?–)
SEX: M   RACE: ?   TYPE: N   MOTIVE: PC
DATE(S): 1931   VENUE: Mich.   VICTIMS: Five
MO: Escaped convict (murder); killed two victims
  while at large; murdered warden and deputy warden
  after recapture
DISPOSITION: Condemned

Harrington, Paul L. (1946–)
SEX: M   RACE: W   TYPE: T   MOTIVE: PC-nonspecific
DATE(S): 1975/1999   VENUE: Detroit, Mich.   VIC-
  TIMS: Five
MO: Shot his wife and two daughters, 1975; shot second wife and his three-month-old son, 1999
DISPOSITION: Acquitted on grounds on insanity in
  first case, 1977; released from asylum after two
  months' treatment; received life term without parole
  in second case, Nov. 2, 2000

Harris, Dewayne Lee (1971–)   AKA: Khalil Iman
  Muhammad
SEX: M   RACE: B   TYPE: T   MOTIVE: Sex.
DATE(S): 1997–98   VENUE: Seattle, Wash.   VIC-
  TIMS: Three
MO: Strangler of female prostitutes who were bound,
  gagged with their own underwear, and dumped in
  vacant lots
DISPOSITION: Life prison term on one count

Harris, Ralph (1972–)
SEX: M   RACE: Unk.   TYPE: T   MOTIVE: CE/Sex.

DATE(S): 1992–95 VENUE: Chicago, Ill. VICTIMS: Six
MO: Drug addict who robbed and killed elderly men, raped women
DISPOSITION: Condemned on one count, March 24, 1999; also received 75 years in prison for attempted murder and robbery of a second victim

Harris, Richard Eugene (?–)
SEX: M RACE: W TYPE: T MOTIVE: Sex.
DATE(S): 1970s–80s VENUE: Tulsa, Okla. VICTIMS: Three suspected
MO: Gay slayer of men; victims shot/stabbed
DISPOSITION: Served five years for manslaughter on first killing; 10 years to life for slaying committed two years after parole

Harris, Robert Alton (1953–)
SEX: M RACE: W TYPE: T MOTIVE: CE
DATE(S): 1975/78 VENUE: San Diego County, Calif. VICTIMS: Three
MO: Killed brother's teenage roommate; robbed/shot two teens
DISPOSITION: Five years for manslaughter, 1973 (paroled 1978); executed on two counts, Apr. 21, 1992

Harrison, Lester (1933–)
SEX: M RACE: B TYPE: T MOTIVE: Sex./Sad.
DATE(S): 1951/1970–73 VENUE: Menard/Chicago, Ill. VICTIMS: Seven
MO: Murdered fellow prison inmate, 1951; killed women in/around Grant Park; mutilations included cannibalism
DISPOSITION: Incompetent for trial, 1951; acquitted as insane in 1978, but confined indefinitely as sexual predator

Hatcher, Charles Ray (1929–84)
SEX: M RACE: W TYPE: N MOTIVE: Sex./Sad.
DATE(S): 1978–82 VENUE: Mo./Ill./Calif. VICTIMS: 16 confessed
MO: Transient pedophile; killed children of both sexes
DISPOSITION: Mo. life sentence, 1984; prison suicide, Dec. 7, 1984

Hawkins, Samuel (1943–95) AKA: Traveling Rapist
SEX: M RACE: B TYPE: N MOTIVE: Sex.
DATE(S): 1976–77 VENUE: Tex. VICTIMS: Two
MO: Raped/killed 12-year-old girl; stabbed pregnant housewife
DISPOSITION: Condemned on two counts; executed Feb. 21, 1995

Hawkins, Thomas W., Jr. (1964–)
SEX: M RACE: B TYPE: T MOTIVE: PC-nonspecific
DATE(S): 1980/89 VENUE: Berks County, Pa. VICTIMS: Three suspected
MO: Rape-slayer of girlfriend (1980) and other women (1989)
DISPOSITION: Six to 15 years as juvenile, 1980; condemned, 1990

Hayes, Daryl (1960–)
SEX: M RACE: W TYPE: T MOTIVE: Sex.
DATE(S): 1975–76 VENUE: Bergen County, N.J. VICTIMS: Two
MO: Rape-slayer of women age 36 and 62 in their homes
DISPOSITION: Life on one murder count plus 37 years for rape, 1978

Haynes, Jonathan Preston (1953–)
SEX: M RACE: W TYPE: N MOTIVE: PC-extremist
DATE(S): 1987–93 VENUE: Calif./Ill. VICTIMS: Two
MO: Shot beautician and surgeon for "helping blacks look white"
DISPOSITION: Condemned in Ill., 1994

Heath, Neville George Clevely (1917–46)
SEX: M RACE: W TYPE: T MOTIVE: Sex./Sad.
DATE(S): 1946 VENUE: London/Bournemouth, England VICTIMS: Two
MO: Torture-slayer of women age 21 and 32
DISPOSITION: Hanged Oct. 16, 1946

Heath, Ronald Palmer (1961–)
SEX: M RACE: W TYPE: N MOTIVE: PC
DATE(S): 1977/89 VENUE: Fla. VICTIMS: Two
MO: Murdered victims in Duval and Alachua counties
DISPOSITION: 30 years, 1977 (paroled 1988); condemned, 1990

Heaulme, Francis (1959–)
SEX: M RACE: W TYPE: N MOTIVE: Sex.
DATE(S): 1984–92 VENUE: France VICTIMS: 11 confessed
MO: Alcoholic transient rape-slayer of women and children (both sexes); victims ranged in age from nine to 60 years
DISPOSITION: Convicted in five separate murder trials, 1992-99; sentences tally two life terms plus 65 years

Hein, Juergen (1939–)
SEX: M RACE: W TYPE: N MOTIVE: Sex./Sad.

DATE(S): 1967/1985   VENUE: Germany   VICTIMS: Three

MO: Strangled wife, 1967; killed/mutilated two women age 50 and 55, 1985

DISPOSITION: Eight years for manslaughter, 1976 (paroled 1972); 10 years for rape of 6-year-old girl, 1973 (paroled 1985); 2 consecutive life terms, 1986

Henderson, Jacob (1971–   )

SEX: M   RACE: Unk.   TYPE: T   MOTIVE: PC/Sad.

DATE(S): 1990   VENUE: San Diego, Calif.   VICTIMS: Three

MO: Bludgeoned and sexually mutilated a male transient; later stabbed two male roommates

DISPOSITION: Received two consecutive life terms plus 15 years at second trial, April 2002

Henderson, Robert Dale (1946–93)

SEX: M   RACE: W   TYPE: N   MOTIVE: PC-nonspecific

DATE(S): 1980–82   VENUE: Ohio/La./Miss./Fla.   VICTIMS: 12 confessed

MO: Transient impulse-killer; victims included three in-laws and nine strangers selected at random

DISPOSITION: Executed in Fla., Apr. 23, 1993

Henriquez, Alejandro (1961–   )

SEX: M   RACE: H   TYPE: T   MOTIVE: Sex.

DATE(S): 1989–90   VENUE: New York City   VICTIMS: Four suspected

MO: Sex-slayer of three females age 10–21 and a 15-year-old boy

DISPOSITION: 25 years to life for one murder, 1992

Henry, John Ruthell (1951–   )

SEX: M   RACE: B   TYPE: N   MOTIVE: PC

DATE(S): 1975/85   VENUE: Fla.   VICTIMS: Three

MO: Killed victims in Hillsborough and Pasco counties

DISPOSITION: 15 years, 1976 (paroled 1983); condemned on two counts, 1992

Hensley, Lawrence Michael (1969–   )

SEX: M   RACE: W   TYPE: T   MOTIVE: PC-nonspecific

DATE(S): 1999   VENUE: Sidney, Ohio   VICTIMS: Four

MO: Satanist who killed three teenagers at his home, then shot a Bible teacher

DISPOSITION: Life sentence following guilty plea, March 7, 2000

Henson, Rhea R. (?–   )

SEX: F   RACE: W   TYPE: S   MOTIVE: PC-mercy

DATE(S): 1999   VENUE: Fairfax, Va.   VICTIMS: Two

MO: Nurse who gave terminal patients lethal injections at Inova Fair Oaks Hospital

DISPOSITION: Pleaded guilty on one count in 2000; received two-year suspended sentence

Hernandez Chavez, Noe (1979–   )

SEX: F   RACE: H   TYPE: T   MOTIVE: Sex./Sad.

DATE(S): 1998   VENUE: Pachuca, Mexico   VICTIMS: Two

MO: Raped and beheaded a six-year-old boy; strangled a three-year-old girl "for pure pleasure" in prison visiting room

DISPOSITION: Unknown

Hernandez, Francis G. (1963–   )

SEX: M   RACE: H   TYPE: T   MOTIVE: Sex./Sad.

DATE(S): 1981   VENUE: Long Beach, Calif.   VICTIMS: Two

MO: Rape-slayer of women age 18 and 21

DISPOSITION: Condemned, 1983

Hernandez, Rodolfo Baiza (1949–2002)

SEX: M   RACE: H   TYPE: T   MOTIVE: CE-felony

DATE(S): 1970s–1980s   VENUE: San Antonio, Tex.   VICTIMS: 13

MO: Shot five illegal migrant workers during robbery, killing one; later confessed 12 additional murders while awaiting execution

DISPOSITION: Executed on one count, March 21, 2002

Herrington, Michael Lee (1943–   )

SEX: M   RACE: W   TYPE: T   MOTIVE: Sex./Sad.

DATE(S): 1966   VENUE: Milwaukee, Wis.   VICTIMS: Three

MO: Raped/stabbed females age 10–19

DISPOSITION: Two consecutive life terms plus 32 years

Hey, Susan (1959–   )

SEX: F   RACE: W   TYPE: S   MOTIVE: PC-"mercy"

DATE(S): 1996   VENUE: Austin, Tex.   VICTIMS: Two

MO: Nurse at rest home; injected elderly men with potassium

DISPOSITION: Pled guilty, 1998; 50-year term with 25-year minimum

Hickock, James Butler (1837–76)   AKA: Wild Bill

SEX: M   RACE: W   TYPE: N   MOTIVE: PC

DATE(S): 1861–75   VENUE: Nebr./Kans./Mo.   VICTIMS: 11+

MO: Gunfighter and occasional lawman; shot personal enemies

DISPOSITION: Murdered while playing poker, Aug. 2, 1876

Hickman, William Edward (1908–28)
SEX: M   RACE: W   TYPE: N   MOTIVE: CE/PC
DATE(S): 1926–27   VENUE: Los Angeles, Calif.
   VICTIMS: Two to five
MO: Shot druggist in holdup; dismembered 12-year-old kidnap victim; suspected in other deaths from Calif. to Pa.
DISPOSITION: Hanged on one count, Oct. 16, 1928

Hicks, James (1951–)
SEX: M   RACE: W   TYPE: T   MOTIVE: PC/Sex.
DATE(S): 1977–96   VENUE: Maine   VICTIMS:
   Three to five
MO: Killed his wife in 1977; prime suspect in murder/disappearances of four other women during 1977, 1982, and 1996
DISPOSITION: Convicted of fourth-degree murder in wife's death, 1984; received 10-year sentence, paroled 1990; received 55-year term for armed robbery of a 67-year-old woman at Lubbock, Tex., Sept. 29, 2000; confessed two murders in Maine to avoid prison in Texas; pleaded guilty on both counts and received life sentence, Nov. 17, 2000

Hickson, Monroe (1909–67)   AKA: Blue Boy
SEX: M   RACE: B   TYPE: T   MOTIVE: CE
DATE(S): 1946   VENUE: Aiken, S.C.   VICTIMS:
   Four
MO: Killed three merchants and a housewife during robberies
DISPOSITION: Life + 20 years, 1957; escaped from prison 1966; died of natural causes while a fugitive, Dec. 29, 1967

Higgenbotham, Chester L. (1965–)
SEX: M   RACE: W   TYPE: T   MOTIVE: Sex./Sad.
DATE(S): 1994–95   VENUE: Newton, Kans.   VICTIMS: Two
MO: Rape-slayer of women in crimes with a common "signature of bondage"
DISPOSITION: Received separate 40-year prison terms on two counts, 1998 and 1999

Hill, Clarence (1929–84)
SEX: M   RACE: B   TYPE: T   MOTIVE: PC-nonspecific
DATE(S): 1938–40   VENUE: Hamilton Township, N.J.   VICTIMS: Six
MO: Shot couples parked in a local lover's lane
DISPOSITION: Life sentence on one count, 1944

Hill, Donetta Marie (1966–)
SEX: F   RACE: B   TYPE: T   MOTIVE: PC
DATE(S): 1990–91   VENUE: Philadelphia, Pa.   VICTIMS: Two
MO: Killed 2 men, ages 21 and 74, in personal altercations
DISPOSITION: Condemned, April 9, 1992

Hill, Dr. John (1931–72)
SEX: M   RACE: W   TYPE: T   MOTIVE: PC
DATE(S): 1950s–69   VENUE: Houston, Tex.   VICTIMS: Five admitted
MO: Boasted to second wife of killing five victims, including first wife, his father, brother, and a fellow physician
DISPOSITION: Mistrial in wife's death, 1971; shot in apparent contract murder with second trial pending, Sept. 24, 1972

Hill, Walter (1935–97)
SEX: M   RACE: B   TYPE: N   MOTIVE: PC
DATE(S): 1951–77   VENUE: Ga./Ala.   VICTIMS: Five
MO: First murder, 1951; next killed fellow inmate in Atlanta Federal Penitentiary; shot three members of his teenage girlfriend's family when they refused to let him marry the girl, 1977
DISPOSITION: 10 years for first kill (paroled 1961); paroled on second count, 1975; condemned 1980 in Ala.; executed May 1997

Hilley, Audrey Marie (1933–87)
SEX: F   RACE: W   TYPE: T   MOTIVE: PC-nonspecific
DATE(S): 1975–79   VENUE: Anniston, Ala.   VICTIMS: Four
MO: "Black widow" poisoner of relatives and others
DISPOSITION: 1983 life term for murdering her husband + 20 years for attempted murder of daughter; escaped prison in 1987 and died of natural causes while at large

Hines, Douglas (1948–)
SEX: M   RACE: B   TYPE: N   MOTIVE: CE
DATE(S): 1973/91   VENUE: Tex/Calif.   VICTIMS: Two
MO: Burglar targeting older women; stabbed two who surprised him
DISPOSITION: 15 years to life in Tex., 1973; Calif. life term, 1993

Hiroaki Hidaka (1962–)
SEX: M   RACE: A   TYPE: T   MOTIVE: CE-felony

DATE(S): 1996   VENUE: Hiroshima, Japan   VICTIMS: Four
MO: Taxi driver who robbed and killed female fares aged 16–45; victims stabbed and strangled
DISPOSITION: Condemned on Feb. 9, 2000

Hiroaki Nishijima (1976–)
SEX: M   RACE: A   TYPE: T   MOTIVE: CE-felony
DATE(S): 2002   VENUE: Kyoto, Japan   VICTIMS: Two
MO: Robbed and strangled two women, aged 19 and 28, whom he met through a cell phone dating service
DISPOSITION: Received life prison term, Nov. 10, 2002

Hittle, Daniel Joe (1966–)
SEX: M   RACE: W   TYPE: N   MOTIVE: PC
DATE(S): 1979/89   VENUE: Minn./Tex.   VICTIMS: Seven
MO: Shot adoptive parents; killed five, including a policeman and a four-year-old girl, soon after parole
DISPOSITION: 30 years in Minn, 1979 (paroled 1988); condemned in Tex.

Hofmann, Kuno (1931–)
SEX: M   RACE: W   TYPE: N   MOTIVE: Sex.
DATE(S): 1971   VENUE: Germany   VICTIMS: Three
MO: Satanist and necrophile; shot three victims and drank their blood
DISPOSITION: Life sentence, 1972

Hohenberger, Robert Carl (d. 1978)
SEX: M   RACE: W   TYPE: N   MOTIVE: Sex.
DATE(S): 1978   VENUE: Fla./La.   VICTIMS: Seven suspected
MO: Ex-convict rape-slayer of teenage girls
DISPOSITION: Suicide by gunshot to avoid arrest, June 1978

Holliday, Dr. John Henry (1852–87)   AKA: Doc
SEX: M   RACE: W   TYPE: N   MOTIVE: PC
DATE(S): 1866–85   VENUE: Ga./Tex./Colo./Wyo./N.Mex./Ariz.   VICTIMS: 16–35
MO: Dentist turned gambler/gunfighter in Old West
DISPOSITION: Died of tuberculosis, Nov. 8, 1887

Holman, George (?–)
SEX: M   RACE: W   TYPE: T   MOTIVE: PC-nonspecific
DATE(S): 1944   VENUE: Oakland/San Francisco   VICTIMS: 22

MO: Serial arsonist; 11 fires claimed 22 lives
DISPOSITION: 22 consecutive life terms

Holmes, Darryl (?–)
SEX: M   RACE: Unk.   TYPE: T   MOTIVE: CE-felony
DATE(S): 1999   VENUE: Greenville, S.C.   VICTIMS: Two confessed
MO: Shot victims in armed robberies
DISPOSITION: Convicted of murder in one case; overturned on appeal; pleaded guilty to manslaughter in September 2001, receiving sentence of 25–30 years in return for details of a second crime

Holmes, Henry Howard [*See* MUDGETT, HERMAN]

Honka, Fritz (?–)
SEX: M   RACE: W   TYPE: S   MOTIVE: Sex.
DATE(S): 1971–74   VENUE: Hamburg, Germany   VICTIMS: Four
MO: Strangled prostitutes and kept bodies in his apartment
DISPOSITION: Life sentence, 1975

Hooijaijers, Frans (?–)
SEX: M   RACE: W   TYPE: S   MOTIVE: PC
DATE(S): 1960s–71   VENUE: Netherlands   VICTIMS: 264 suspected
MO: Nursing home attendant; killed patients with insulin
DISPOSITION: 13 years on five counts, 1971

Hopper, Vernon Lynn (1960–)
SEX: M   RACE: W   TYPE: N   MOTIVE: Sex.
DATE(S): 1992   VENUE: Tex.   VICTIMS: Two
MO: Nomadic rapist; killed two 11-year-old girls
DISPOSITION: Two life terms + 198 years

Horton, Wayne Donald (1956–)
SEX: M   RACE: W   TYPE: N   MOTIVE: PC/CE
DATE(S): 1972–76   VENUE: Las Vegas, Nev.   VICTIMS: Four
MO: Impulsive killer of victims in arguments and holdups
DISPOSITION: Four terms of life without parole, 1976

Housel, Tracey Lee (1960–)
SEX: M   RACE: W   TYPE: N   MOTIVE: CE/Sex.
DATE(S): 1984–85   VENUE: Tex/Ga.   VICTIMS: Two
MO: Killed two motorists for their cars, raping the female
DISPOSITION: Condemned in Ga., 1986

Howard, Ronnie (?–   )
SEX: M   RACE: B   TYPE: T   MOTIVE: Sex./Sad.
DATE(S): 1985   VENUE: S.C.   VICTIMS: Two
MO: Suffocated women with plastic bags over their heads
DISPOSITION: Life term on one count; condemned on second count
ACCOMPLICES: Two other men sentenced to life terms, one for each death

Hoyt, Waneta Ethel (1943–   )
SEX: F   RACE: W   TYPE: S   MOTIVE: PC-nonspecific
DATE(S): 1965–71   VENUE: Oswego, N.Y.   VICTIMS: Five
MO: Killed her own children, disguised as SIDS
DISPOSITION: 75 years to life on five counts, 1995; died in prison, Aug. 13, 1998

Hubbard, Randall L. (1960–   )
SEX: M   RACE: ?   TYPE: T   MOTIVE: CE
DATE(S): 1995–96   VENUE: Morgan County, Ind.   VICTIMS: Three suspected
MO: Shot male robbery victims
DISPOSITION: 120 years on two counts, 1998

Hullett, Johnny (?–   )
SEX: M   RACE: W   TYPE: T   MOTIVE: Sex.
DATE(S): 1981   VENUE: Clover, S.C.   VICTIMS: Three
MO: Rape slayer of women aged 57–81, strangled in their homes; two victims left in bathtubs; the third had no bathtub but was drenched in fruit juice
DISPOSITION: Life term on one murder count

Hume, Brian Donald (1919–   )   AKA: Flying Smuggler
SEX: M   RACE: W   TYPE: N   MOTIVE: PC/CE
DATE(S): 1949/59   VENUE: England/Switzerland   VICTIMS: Two
MO: Killed a personal enemy (1949) and robbery victim (1959)
DISPOSITION: 12 years as "accessory," 1950 (paroled 1958); life sentence, 1959; ruled insane, 1976

Hunt, Brian Alpress (1950–   )
SEX: M   RACE: W   TYPE: N   MOTIVE: PC-nonspecific
DATE(S): 1992–99   VENUE: Fla./Tenn.   VICTIMS: Four
MO: Homeless transient who beat a male acquaintance to death in 1992; stabbed another man to death in a quarrel over money; from jail, directed police to the graves of two male victims in Tennessee

DISPOSITION: Received a four-year term for manslaughter in Florida, Dec. 1992; paroled May 1994; life term in Florida, April 17, 1999; active detainer from Tennessee if paroled

Hunt, Henry Lee (1944–2003)
SEX: M   RACE: NA   TYPE: T   MOTIVE: CE
DATE(S): 1984   VENUE: Robeson County, N.C.   VICTIMS: Three
MO: Carried out the contract murder of a male victim, then killed a police informant 6 days later
DISPOSITION: Executed on Sept. 12, 2003

Hunt, Kenneth Dean (1966–   )
SEX: M   RACE: Unk.   TYPE: T   MOTIVE: Sex./CE-felony
DATE(S): 1988/1998   VENUE: Los Angeles, Calif.   VICTIMS: Three
MO: Registered sex offender who killed and raped two women, aged 60 and 71, in residential burglaries; killed a third victim in a fight
DISPOSITION: Served time for voluntary manslaughter on one count; condemned on two counts, March 21, 2001

Hunter, Birt Leroy (1947–2000)
SEX: M   RACE: W   TYPE: T   MOTIVE: CE-felony
DATE(S): 1968/1989   VENUE: Jefferson City, Mo.   VICTIMS: Three
MO: Career criminal who killed victims during robberies
DISPOSITION: Imprisoned for the murder of a blind bartender, 1968–80; executed on two counts of murder, June 28, 2000; accomplice Tomas Grant Ervin executed for the latter crime on March 28, 2001

Hunter, Lendell (?–   )
SEX: M   RACE: Unk.   TYPE: T   MOTIVE: Sex.
DATE(S): 1971/1975   VENUE: Atlanta, Ga.   VICTIMS: Two suspected
MO: Serial rapist who bludgeoned female victims during home invasions
DISPOSITION: Received three consecutive life terms plus 95 years for various felony counts, Jan. 1972; escaped in Dec. 1972 and killed another woman; recaptured Aug. 1974

Huntley, Ian (?–   )
SEX: M   RACE: W   TYPE: T   MOTIVE: Sex.
DATE(S): 2002   VENUE: Soham, England   VICTIMS: Two
MO: Pedophile with record of convictions dating from 1995; kidnapped and murdered two schoolgirls

DISPOSITION: Life sentence imposed, Dec. 17, 2003; fiancée Maxine Carr received 42-month term for conspiracy to obstruct justice

Husereau, Philip (d. 1988)
SEX: M RACE: W TYPE: N MOTIVE: Sex./Sad.
DATE(S): 1983–84 VENUE: Nev./N.Y. VICTIMS: Five
MO: Strangled girlfriends during sex; confessed to sister
DISPOSITION: Accidental death during autoerotic asphyxia, Feb. 18, 1988

Huskey, Thomas Dee (1960–) AKA: Zoo Man
SEX: RACE: Unk. TYPE: T MOTIVE: Sex.
DATE(S): 1991–92 VENUE: Knoxville, Tenn. VICTIMS: Four confessed
MO: Serial rapist of female prostitutes, nicknamed from his preference for sex assaults near the Knoxville Zoo; blamed his crimes on multiple personality disorder
DISPOSITION: Confessed four murders in custody; mistrial on those charges, February 1999, when the jury deadlocked on sanity issues; convicted in multiple rape trials, 2000–04, presently serving 66 years in prison; new trial for murder pending

Huster, Karen Lee (1959–)
SEX: F RACE: W TYPE: N MOTIVE: PC
DATE(S): 1996–2000 VENUE: Ore./Calif. VICTIMS: Three suspected
MO: Murdered her 10-year-old daughter in 1996; arrested in 2000 at a Los Angeles apartment whose 73-year-old tenant is still missing; human remains found in freezer at the scene
DISPOSITION: Convicted of her daughter's murder, Feb. 8, 2002; received a term of 25 years to life

Hu Wanlin (1948–)
SEX: M RACE: A TYPE: N MOTIVE: Unk.
DATE(S): 1982/97–98 VENUE: China VICTIMS: 210+
MO: "Spirit doctor" who administered herbal "medicine" at unlicensed clinics, resulting in numerous deaths
DISPOSITION: Served 14 years for killing 20 patients in Shaanxi Province(paroled 1997); sentenced to 15 years on Jan. 16, 2001

Ingle, Phillip Lee (1961–)
SEX: M RACE: W TYPE: T MOTIVE: PC-nonspecific
DATE(S): 1991 VENUE: N.C. VICTIMS: Four
MO: Home invader who bludgeoned elderly couples
DISPOSITION: Four death sentences + one life term, 1994

Ireland, Jack (?–?) AKA: Hatchet Jack
SEX: M RACE: W TYPE: N MOTIVE: PC
DATE(S): 1840s–70s VENUE: Rocky Mountains VICTIMS: 100+
MO: "Mountain man" who killed numerous Indians; also killed whites who traded with Indians
DISPOSITION: Unknown

Irtyshov, Igor (?–)
SEX: M RACE: W TYPE: T MOTIVE: Sex.
DATE(S): 1994–96 VENUE: St. Petersburg, Russia VICTIMS: "Several"
MO: Pedophile slayer of boys; some disemboweled
DISPOSITION: Condemned, 1996

Irvin, Marvin Lee (1950–)
SEX: M RACE: W TYPE: T MOTIVE: PC
DATE(S): 1979–90 VENUE: St. Joseph, Mo. VICTIMS: Five suspected
MO: Shot/bludgeoned women during arguments
DISPOSITION: 100-year. minimum on plea to three counts, 1991

Ishaak, Mohammed Adam Omar (1952–2001) AKA: Sana Ripper
SEX: M RACE: A TYPE: T MOTIVE: Sex.
DATE(S): 1999–2000 VENUE: Sana, Yemen VICTIMS: 50 confessed
MO: Sudanese morgue attendant who raped, killed, and dismembered women
DISPOSITION: Publicly flogged for drinking alcohol, then shot for murder, on June 22, 2001

Ivery, Samuel (1957–)
SEX: M RACE: B TYPE: N MOTIVE: PC-nonspecific
DATE(S): 1992 VENUE: Calif./Ariz./Ill./Ala. VICTIMS: Four+
MO: "Ninja of God"; beheaded females age 17–27
DISPOSITION: Condemned in Ala., 1994

Jablonski, Philip Carl (1946–)
SEX: M RACE: W TYPE: N MOTIVE: Sex./Sad.
DATE(S): 1979/91 VENUE: Calif./Utah VICTIMS: Five
MO: Sadistic rape-slayer and necrophile; victims include two wives and a mother-in-law
DISPOSITION: 13 years eight months, 1979 (paroled 1990); condemned in Calif., 1994

Jackson, Calvin (1948–)
SEX: M RACE: B TYPE: S MOTIVE: Sex./CE
DATE(S): 1973–74 VENUE: New York City VICTIMS: Nine

MO: Addict rape-slayer of women age 39–79, all but one killed at hotel where he worked as a janitor
DISPOSITION: 18 consecutive life terms, 1975

Jackson, Charles (1937–2002)
SEX: M   RACE: Unk.   TYPE: T   MOTIVE: Sex.
DATE(S): 1980–82   VENUE: Oakland, Calif.   VICTIMS: Seven
MO: Rape-slayer of women during home invasions; also stabbed one victim's husband
DISPOSITION: Life sentence imposed on one count, for a 1982 murder; died of heart attack in prison, Feb. 15, 2002; DNA posthumously proved links to six other slayings

Jackson, Elton Manning (1956–   )   AKA: Hampton Roads Killer
SEX: M   RACE: ?   TYPE: T   MOTIVE: Sex.
DATE(S): 1990s   VENUE: Chesapeake, Va.   VICTIMS: 12 suspected
MO: Lust strangler of gay men
DISPOSITION: Life term on one count,1998

Jackson, Mary Jane (1836–?)   AKA: Brick Top
SEX: F   RACE: W   TYPE: T   MOTIVE: PC-argument
DATE(S): 1856–61   VENUE: New Orleans, La.   VICTIMS: Four
MO: Prostitute with violent temper; stabbed male acquaintances
DISPOSITION: 10 years for one count, 1861; reprieved by new governor when Union troops occupied New Orleans nine months later

Jackson, Michael Wayne (1945–86)
SEX: M   RACE: W   TYPE: N   MOTIVE: PC-non-specific
DATE(S): 1986   VENUE: Ind./Ky.   VICTIMS: Three
MO: Shot h is probation officer and two other men
DISPOSITION: Suicide by gunshot to avoid arrest, Oct. 2, 1986

Jackson, Patricia (1949–   )
SEX: F   RACE: B   TYPE: T   MOTIVE: PC-argument
DATE(S): 1966/81   VENUE: Tuscaloosa, Ala.   VICTIMS: Two
MO: Slashed boyfriend with razor; stabbed female bartender
DISPOSITION: 12 years for second-degree, 1966 (paroled 1970); condemned 1981 (commuted to life on appeal)

Jackson, Ray Shawn (1968–   )   AKA: Gilham Park Strangler
SEX: M   RACE: B   TYPE: T   MOTIVE: Sex.
DATE(S): 1989–90   VENUE: Kansas City   VICTIMS: Six
MO: Rape-slayer of street prostitutes
DISPOSITION: Six consecutive life terms without parole, 1991

Jackson, Robin (1949–98)   AKA: The Jackal
SEX: M   RACE: W   TYPE: T   MOTIVE: PC-extremist
DATE(S): 1973–98   VENUE: Northern Ireland   VICTIMS: 100+
MO: Protestant terrorist and contract killer who shot, stabbed, and bombed Catholic Republican victims and suspected police informers
DISPOSITION: Died of lung cancer, January 1998

Jacobs, Clawvern (1947–   )
SEX: M   RACE: W   TYPE: T   MOTIVE: CE/Sex.
DATE(S): 1974/86   VENUE: Knott County, Ky.   VICTIMS: Two
MO: Robbed/killed woman (1974); killed/mutilated second woman
DISPOSITION: Condemned, 1989

James, Eugene H. (?–   )
SEX: M   RACE: W   TYPE: T   MOTIVE: PC-non-specific
DATE(S): 1948   VENUE: Baltimore/Washington, D.C.   VICTIMS: Two
MO: Stabbed two girls, both age 11, in municipal parks
DISPOSITION: Life sentence, 1948

Jameswhite, Richard (1974–   )   AKA: Babyface
SEX: M   RACE: ?   TYPE: N   MOTIVE: CE
DATE(S): 1993–94   VENUE: N.Y./Conn./Pa./Ga.   VICTIMS: 15 suspected
MO: Victims killed in armed robberies
DISPOSITION: Life term on one count in Ga., 1994

Jasinskyj, Tony (1959–   )
SEX: M   RACE: W   TYPE: N   MOTIVE: Sex.
DATE(S): 1980s   VENUE: England   VICTIMS: "Several"
MO: British soldier who raped and strangled a 14-year-old girl near his base at Aldershot; linked to that crime and unspecified others by DNA evidence in 2001
DISPOSITION: Received a life term on one murder count plus 10 years for rape, May 2002

Jeanneret, Marie (1836–84)
SEX: F   RACE: W   TYPE: T   MOTIVE: PC-nonspecific
DATE(S): 1866–67   VENUE: Lausanne, Switzerland
   VICTIMS: Eight
MO: Self-styled "nurse" who poisoned patients and
   employer
DISPOSITION: Life sentence on six counts; died in
   prison, 1884

Jebson, Ronald (1939–   )
SEX: M   RACE: W   TYPE: T   MOTIVE: Sex.
DATE(S): 1970–74   VENUE: England   VICTIMS:
   Three
MO: Pedophile slayer of children aged 8–12
DISPOSITION: Received life sentence for the 1974
   murder of an eight-year-old girl; subsequently con-
   fessed two previous slayings

Jeffries (?–?)   AKA: Jeffries the Monster
SEX: M   RACE: W   TYPE: N   MOTIVE: PC/CE
DATE(S): 19th century   VENUE: Australia   VIC-
   TIMS: "Several"
MO: Escaped convict, rapist, and cannibal
DISPOSITION: Killed by posse

Jegado, Helene (1803–51)
SEX: F   RACE: W   TYPE: N   MOTIVE: CE
DATE(S): 1833–51   VENUE: France   VICTIMS: 23+
MO: Thieving servant; poisoned employers and
   coworkers
DISPOSITION: Beheaded in Dec. 1851

Jelisic, Goran (1968–   )   AKA: Adolf
SEX: M   RACE: W   TYPE: S   MOTIVE: PC-
   extremist
DATE(S): 1992   VENUE: Brcko, Bosnia   VICTIMS:
   100+ suspected
MO: Serb slayer of Muslims in Luka concentration
   camp
DISPOSITION: Pled guilty to 12 murders, 1998

Jenkins, Cecil (1965–   )
SEX: M   RACE: Unk.   TYPE: T   MOTIVE: Sex.
DATE(S): 1997–98   VENUE: Indianapolis, Ind.
   VICTIMS: Four alleged
MO: Serial rapist of at least seven women, killing four;
   two victims left in cars
DISPOSITION: Received 130-year term for rape and
   kidnapping of one victim, March 2, 1999; received
   78 years on second rape conviction, March 11,
   1999; received 65-year sentence on one murder
   count, Nov. 28, 2001

Jenkins, James Gilbert (1834–64)
SEX: M   RACE: W   TYPE: N   MOTIVE: CE
DATE(S): 1840s–1864   VENUE: Mo./Tex./Iowa/Calif.
   VICTIMS: 18
MO: Murdered robbery victims (eight whites and 10
   Indians)
DISPOSITION: Hanged on one count in Calif., 1864

Jennings, Desmond Dominique (1971–99)
SEX: M   RACE: B   TYPE: T   MOTIVE: CE-felony
DATE(S): 1992–93   VENUE: Fort Worth, Tex.   VIC-
   TIMS: 5–20
MO: Shot prostitutes and addicts during crack house
   robberies; police proved five slayings and suspect 15
   more
DISPOSITION: Executed on two counts, Nov. 16,
   1999

Jennings, Wilbur Lee (1941–   )   AKA: Ditchbank
   Murders
SEX: M   RACE: B   TYPE: T   MOTIVE: Sex.
DATE(S): 1984–86   VENUE: Fresno, Calif.   VIC-
   TIMS: Four
MO: Slayer of female prostitutes; bodies dumped in
   canals
DISPOSITION: Condemned with additional sentence
   of life + 64 years on lesser charges, 1986

Jensen, Richard Allen (1947–   )
SEX: M   RACE: W   TYPE: T   MOTIVE: Sex./Sad.
DATE(S): 1990–91   VENUE: Grand Rapids, Mich.
   VICTIMS: Three
MO: "Ripper" of street prostitutes
DISPOSITION: Life term on one count, 1991

Johns, Alis Ben (1974–   )
SEX: M   RACE: W   TYPE: N   MOTIVE: PC
DATE(S): 1996   VENUE: Ozarks region, Mo.   VIC-
   TIMS: Three suspected
MO: Mentally retarded suspect in series of shooting
   deaths
DISPOSITION: Condemned on one count, 1999

Johns, Ronnie (?–   )
SEX: M   RACE: B   TYPE: T   MOTIVE: CE
DATE(S): 1991   VENUE: Flint, Mich.   VICTIMS:
   Four
MO: Victims shot in robbery attempts
DISPOSITION: 15 years to life on one count, 1992;
   life without parole on second count, 1992

Johnson, Alison (1966–   )
SEX: F   RACE: W   TYPE: S   MOTIVE: PC-nonspecific

DATE(S): 1996–2000 VENUE: Doncaster, England
VICTIMS: Three
MO: Mother who killed her newborn children; two found at her home; one still missing
DISPOSITION: Pleaded guilty to manslaughter by negligence, June 12, 2002; received a sentence of three years community rehabilitation

Johnson, Emanuel (1963–)
SEX: M RACE: B TYPE: T MOTIVE: CE
DATE(S): 1988 VENUE: Sarasota County, Fla.
VICTIMS: Two
MO: Killed burglary/holdup victims
DISPOSITION: Condemned on two counts, 1991; five life terms + 30 years on lesser charges

Johnson, James Rodney (?–)
SEX: M RACE: W TYPE: T MOTIVE: PC-nonspecific
DATE(S): 1990 VENUE: Cooper/Moniteau Counties., Mo. VICTIMS: Four
MO: Shot three police officers and a sheriff's wife in separate attacks
DISPOSITION: Condemned, 1991

Johnson, Jay Thomas (1968–)
SEX: M RACE: Unk. TYPE: T MOTIVE: PC
DATE(S): 1991 VENUE: Minneapolis, Minn. VICTIMS: Two
MO: AIDS victim who killed gay men aged 21 and 48
DISPOSITION: Pleaded guilty on both counts, receiving two consecutive life terms plus 15 years on lesser charges

Johnson, Martha (1955–)
SEX: F RACE: F TYPE: T MOTIVE: PC-nonspecific
DATE(S): 1977–82 VENUE: GA. VICTIMS: Four suspected; two confessed
MO: Smothered her own children; deaths mistaken for SIDS
DISPOSITION: Condemned, 1990 (commuted on appeal)

Johnson, Matthew Steven (1963–)
SEX: M RACE: W TYPE: T MOTIVE: Sex.
DATE(S): 1996–2000 VENUE: Hartford, Conn.
VICTIMS: Seven alleged
MO: Drifter with history of violent crimes and felony convictions dating from age 19, including four-year terms for assault (1982–86) and robbery (1992–96); rape-slayer of women aged 28–37, in Hartford's North End

DISPOSITION: Convicted on three murder counts; received life term, April 1, 2004

Johnson, Paul David (1945–)
SEX: M RACE: W TYPE: N MOTIVE: PC-domestic
DATE(S): 1984/89 VENUE: Tenn./Fla. VICTIMS: Two
MO: "Bluebeard" slayer of wives
DISPOSITION: Convicted on one count in Tenn., 1984; life term in Fla., 1990

Johnson, Ronnie (1961–)
SEX: M RACE: B TYPE: T MOTIVE: CE
DATE(S): 1989 VENUE: Miami, Fla. VICTIMS: Two
MO: Robbery-murders of two victims
DISPOSITION: Condemned on first count, Dec. 13, 1991; condemned on second count, July 16, 1992

Johnson, Tivian (1970–)
SEX: M RACE: B TYPE: T MOTIVE: CE
DATE(S): 1991 VENUE: Dade County, Fla. VICTIMS: Two
MO: Killed robbery victims
DISPOSITION: Triple life sentence, 1993; death + two life terms, 1995

Johnston, John (1850–1900) AKA: Crow Killer; Liver-eating Johnson
SEX: M RACE: W TYPE: N MOTIVE: PC
DATE(S): 1843–78 VENUE: Rocky Mountains
VICTIMS: Hundreds
MO: "Mountain man" and prolific killer of Indians for revenge or racism; killed 300 Crows, plus numerous Utes, Blackfeet, Cheyenne, Sioux, Nez Perce, etc.; relieved of duty in Civil War for killing Indians allied with his own (Union) side
DISPOSITION: Died of natural causes, Jan. 21, 1900

Jones, Bryan (1957–) AKA: Dumpster Killer
SEX: M RACE: B TYPE: T MOTIVE: Sex.
DATE(S): 1985–86 VENUE: San Diego, Calif. VICTIMS: Four
MO: Rape-slayer of prostitutes; bodies left in dumpsters
DISPOSITION: Condemned on two counts, 1994

Jones, Daniel Steven (1961–)
SEX: M RACE: W TYPE: N MOTIVE: CE
DATE(S): 1980s VENUE: Nev./Fla. VICTIMS: Three suspected
MO: Killed one Nev. man for his trailer; others suspected in Fla.
DISPOSITION: Condemned on one count in Nev.

Jones, Harold (1906–)
SEX: M   RACE: W   TYPE: T   MOTIVE: Sex.
DATE(S): 1921   VENUE: Abertillery, Wales   VIC-
    TIMS: Two
MO: Rape-slayer of girls age eight and 11
DISPOSITION: Indeterminate prison sentence, 1921

Jones, Jeffrey Gerard (1960–)
SEX: M   RACE: B   TYPE: T   MOTIVE: PC-nonspe-
    cific
DATE(S): 1985–86   VENUE: Sacramento, Calif.
    VICTIMS: Four
MO: Bludgeoned male victims with hammer in public
    restrooms
DISPOSITION: Condemned, 1987

Jones, Sydney (d. 1915)
SEX: M   RACE: B   TYPE: N   MOTIVE: PC-non-
    specific
DATE(S): 1900s   VENUE: U.S. nationwide   VIC-
    TIMS: 13 confessed
MO: Random murders of men (11 blacks, two
    whites)
DISPOSITION: Hanged in Ala. on June 25, 1915

Jordan, Keydrick Deon (1972–)
SEX: M   RACE: B   TYPE: T   MOTIVE: CE/SEx.
DATE(S): 1991–92   VENUE: Orange County, Fla.
    VICTIMS: Two
MO: Shot woman in robbery; raped/killed another and
    burned her home
DISPOSITION: Life on one count, 1993; condemned
    on second count, 1994

Joyner, Anthony (1961–)
SEX: M   RACE: B   TYPE: S   MOTIVE: Sex.
DATE(S): 1983   VENUE: Philadelphia, Pa.   VIC-
    TIMS: Six
MO: Rape-slayer of elderly women at rest home where
    he worked
DISPOSITION: Life sentence, 1984

Judge, Giancarlo (?–)   AKA: Monster of Torino
SEX: M   RACE: W   TYPE: T   MOTIVE: Sex.
DATE(S): 1983–86   VENUE: Torino, Italy   VIC-
    TIMS: Nine
MO: Shot/strangled female prostitutes
DISPOSITION: 30 years in lunatic asylum

Judy, Steven Timothy (1956–81)
SEX: M   RACE: W   TYPE: N   MOTIVE: Sex./Sad.
DATE(S): 1970s   VENUE: Ind./Tex./La./Calif.   VIC-
    TIMS: 11 confessed

MO: Rape-slayer of women; also drowned three chil-
    dren of one victim
DISPOSITION: Executed in Ind., Mar. 9, 1981

Junco, Francisco del (1958–)
SEX: M   RACE: H   TYPE: T   MOTIVE: PC
DATE(S): 1995–96   VENUE: Miami, Fla.   VICTIMS:
    Four confessed
MO: Cuban immigrant; killed and set afire female
    addicts, age 37–44
DISPOSITION: Confessed June 1996; sentence
    unknown

Jurkiewicz, Thomas [*See* YORK, THOMAS]

Justus, Buddy Earl (1953–90)
SEX: M   RACE: W   TYPE: N   MOTIVE: Sex.
DATE(S): 1978   VENUE: Ga./Fla./Va.   VICTIMS:
    Three
MO: Transient rape-slayer of women
DISPOSITION: Executed in Va., Dec. 13, 1990

Kaczynski, Theodore John (1942–)   AKA:
Unabomber
SEX: M   RACE: W   TYPE: N   MOTIVE: PC-non-
    specific
DATE(S): 1978–93   VENUE: USA nationwide   VIC-
    TIMS: Three
MO: Serial bomber; 17 blasts in seven states
DISPOSITION: Life without parole on 1998 guilty plea

Kahl, Gordon (d. 1984)
SEX: M   RACE: N   TYPE: N   MOTIVE: PC-
    extremist
DATE(S): 1983–84   VENUE: N.Dak./Ark.   VIC-
    TIMS: Three
MO: Neo-Nazi tax-evader; killed lawmen while a fugi-
    tive
DISPOSITION: Killed in shoot-out with police, June 3,
    1984

Kalejs, Konrad (1913–2001)
SEX: M   RACE: W   TYPE: N   MOTIVE: PC-
    extremist
DATE(S): 1941–45   VENUE: Latvia VICTIMS:
    30,000
MO: Nazi collaborator and member of roving murder
    squad
DISPOSITION: Died Nov. 12, 2001, while fighting
    extradition to Latvia on war crimes charges

Kalichuk, Alexander (d. 1975)
SEX: M   RACE: W   TYPE: T   MOTIVE: Sex.

DATE(S): 1950s   VENUE: London, Ontario   VICTIMS: Two alleged
MO: Sergeant in Canadian air force, posthumously identified as pedophile slayer of young girls
DISPOSITION: Died before evidence of guilt was collected

Kappen, Paul (1941–91)   AKA: Saturday Night Strangler
SEX: M   RACE: W   TYPE: T   MOTIVE: Sex.
DATE(S): 1973   VENUE: Llandarcy, Wales   VICTIMS: Three
MO: Rape-strangler of female hitchhikers, all 16 years old
DISPOSITION: Died before new DNA techniques linked him to crimes

Kaprat, Edwin Bernard, III (1964–95)   AKA: Granny Killer
SEX: M   RACE: W   TYPE: T   MOTIVE: Sex./Sad.
DATE(S): 1991/93   VENUE: Hernando County, Fla.   VICTIMS: Five
MO: Beat man to death, 1991; rape-slayer of women age 72–87, killed/burned in their homes, 1993
DISPOSITION: two years house arrest for using dead man's credit cards, 1991; condemned, 1995; murdered in prison Apr. 20, 1995

Kasler, Steven L. (?–   )
SEX: M   RACE: W   TYPE: N   MOTIVE: Sex./CE
DATE(S): 1980s–1990s   VENUE: United States   VICTIMS: 34 confessed
MO: Drifter who implicated himself in 34 murders, then recanted
DISPOSITION: Received a 99-year sentence for kidnapping and robbing a woman in Louisiana; pleaded no contest to an Ohio murder and received a life sentence on Dec. 14, 1999

Katsumi Hoshinois (1976–   )
SEX: M   RACE: H   TYPE: T   MOTIVE: CE-felony
DATE(S): 1999   VENUE: Tokyo, Japan   VICTIMS: Two
MO: Thief who drugged, robbed, and dumped 11 women he met through a dating service; two victims died of hypothermia
DISPOSITION: Unknown

Kee, Ahron (1973–   )
SEX: M   RACE: B   TYPE: T   MOTIVE: Sex.
DATE(S): 1991–98   VENUE: Harlem, New York City   VICTIMS: Three
MO: Rape-slayer of petite females aged 13–19

DISPOSITION: Received life prison term for three murders and five rapes at trial in 2000; received 20 years for a sixth rape, Aug. 12, 2004

Keene, John (d. 1865)
SEX: M   RACE: W   TYPE: N   MOTIVE: CE
DATE(S): 1861–65   VENUE: Tenn./Utah   VICTIMS: Five+
MO: Confederate navy deserter and outlaw during Civil War
DISPOSITION: Hanged on one count in Salt Lake City, 1865

Kelley, Doyle (?–   )
SEX: M   RACE: W   TYPE: T   MOTIVE: CE
DATE(S): 1981–93   VENUE: Joplin, Mo.   VICTIMS: Three suspected
MO: Suspected as accomplice in robbery-slaying of young woman, 1981; "Bluebeard" slayer of wives in staged "accidents," 1990/93
DISPOSITION: Life term on two counts, 1994

Kelliher, Mary (?–?)
SEX: F   RACE: W   TYPE: S   MOTIVE: PC-domestic
DATE(S): 1905–8   VENUE: Boston, Ma.   VICTIMS: Six
MO: "Black widow" poisoner of husband and relatives
DISPOSITION: Escaped conviction by blaming deaths on a mattress contaminated with arsenic

Kelly, Horace Edward (1959–   )
SEX: M   RACE: B   TYPE: T   MOTIVE: Sex.
DATE(S): 1984   VENUE: San Bernardino, Calif.   VICTIMS: Three
MO: Necrophile rape-slayer of two women; also shot 11-year-old boy while trying to abduct the victim's female cousin
DISPOSITION: Condemned 1986

Kelly, Kieron (1928–   )
SEX: M   RACE: W   TYPE: T   MOTIVE: PC-extremist
DATE(S): 1975–83   VENUE: London, England   VICTIMS: Five confessed
MO: Homophobobic slayer of gay males
DISPOSITION: Life term on one count, 1984

Kennedy, Edward Dean (d. 1992)
SEX: M   RACE: B   TYPE: N   MOTIVE: CE
DATE(S): 1978/81   VENUE: Fla.   VICTIMS: Three
MO: Killed motel clerk (1978); shot policeman and male civilian after prison break

DISPOSITION: Life term, 1978 (escaped 1981); condemned, 1981; executed July 21, 1992

Kennedy, Julian (1943–)
SEX: M   RACE: W   TYPE: N   MOTIVE: PC/CE
DATE(S): 1958–73   VENUE:
   Fla./Ark./Ga./N.Mex./Tex.   VICTIMS: 9+ confessed
MO: Outlaw biker and career criminal; confessed murders during holdups, jail breaks, drug deals, and personal arguments
DISPOSITION: Life term on one count in Ga., 1973

Ketchum, Tom (1862–1901)   AKA: Black Jack
SEX: M   RACE: B   TYPE: T   MOTIVE: Sex.
DATE(S): 1880s–1901   VENUE:
   Tex./N.Mex./Colo./Ariz.   VICTIMS: "Several"
MO: "Wild Bunch" outlaw and murderer
DISPOSITION: Hanged in Ariz., Apr. 26, 1901

Keyes, Russell (1957–98)
SEX: M   RACE: W   TYPE: N   MOTIVE: PC/CE
DATE(S): 1990s   VENUE: Portugal/France/Morocco
   VICTIMS: Five
MO: British national; killed women who spurned marriage proposals in his pursuit of altered citizenship
DISPOSITION: Shot by American bride in Ariz. after he confessed five murders, July 21, 1998

Khan, Dr. Sohrab Aslam (1944–)
SEX: M   RACE: A   TYPE: T   MOTIVE: PC-nonspecific
DATE(S): 1986   VENUE: Lahore, Pakistan   VICTIMS: 13
MO: Thrill-killer of male victims in random shootings
DISPOSITION: Unreported by Pakistani authorities

Kibbe, Roger Reece (1941–)   AKA: I-5 Killer
SEX: M   RACE: W   TYPE: N   MOTIVE: Sex.
DATE(S): 1986–88   VENUE: Calif./Nev.   VICTIMS:
   Seven+ suspected
MO: Rape-strangler of females age 17–26
DISPOSITION: Life term with 18-year minimum on one count, 1991

Kilgore, Dean (1950–)
SEX: M   RACE: B   TYPE: T   MOTIVE: CE/PC
DATE(S): 1978/89   VENUE: Polk County, Fla.   VICTIMS: Two
MO: Killed kidnap victim; murdered prison inmate
DISPOSITION: two life terms, 1978; condemned, 1990

Kim, Hyu Soo (1971–)
SEX: M   RACE: A   TYPE: T   MOTIVE: Sad.

DATE(S): 2001   VENUE: London, England   VICTIMS: Two
MO: Landlord who killed female tenants, aged 21 and 22, by binding and suffocating them with ornate giftwrap tape; nude corpses were hidden on his property
DISPOSITION: Life sentence on guilty plea to one count, March 25, 2003

Kimbrough, Petrie [*See* LOCKETT, WILL]

Kinne, Sharon (1940–)
SEX: F   RACE: W   TYPE: N   MOTIVE: PC/CE
DATE(S): 1960–62   VENUE: Mo./Mexico   VICTIMS: Three
MO: "Black widow" slayer of husband, lover's wife, and boyfriend
DISPOSITION: 13 years on one count in Mexico, 1963

Kinney, James Allen (1948–)
SEX: M   RACE: ?   TYPE: N   MOTIVE: Sex.
DATE(S): 1980s–90s   VENUE:
   Mich./Minn./Iowa/Idaho/Oreg./Wash.   VICTIMS:
   More than six suspected
MO: Transient rape-slayer of young women
DISPOSITION: Pleaded guilty on one murder count in Washington, Dec. 12, 2001; received life prison term without parole, Jan. 14, 2002

Kipp, Martin James (1952–85)   AKA: Dr. Crazy
SEX: M   RACE: NA   TYPE: N   MOTIVE: PC
DATE(S): 1983–84   VENUE: Los Angeles/Orange counties, Calif.   VICTIMS: Two
MO: Rape-strangler of teenage girls
DISPOSITION: Condemned, 1987

Kiyotaka Katsuta (1948–2000)
SEX: M   RACE: A   TYPE: N   MOTIVE: PC/CE
DATE(S): 1972–82   VENUE: Japan   VICTIMS: Eight confessed
MO: Japan's "most evil" criminal, arrested after a 10-year rampage; strangled four Kyoto women, 1972–77, then switched to shooting men in robberies at Kobe and Nagoya
DISPOSITION: Condemned, 1986; hanged on Nov. 30, 2000

Klenner, Frederick Robert, Jr. (1956–)
SEX: M   RACE: W   TYPE: N   MOTIVE: PC
DATE(S): 1984–85   VENUE: Ky./N.C.   VICTIMS: Eight
MO: Stabbed/shot five relatives of his girlfriend; later murdered the girlfriend and her two children

DISPOSITION: Suicide by bomb to avoid arrest, June 3, 1985

Klimek, Tillie (1865–?)
SEX: F   RACE: W   TYPE: T   MOTIVE: CE
DATE(S): 1914–20   VENUE: Chicago, Ill.   VICTIMS: Six
MO: "Black widow" poisoner of husbands and a female neighbor
DISPOSITION: Life sentence, 1921

Klosowski, Severin Antoniovitch (1865–1903)   AKA: George Chapman
SEX: M   RACE: W   TYPE: N   MOTIVE: CE
DATE(S): 1897—1902   VENUE: England   VICTIMS: Three
MO: Profit-motivated poisoner of common-law wives; suspect in 1888 "JACK THE RIPPER" case
DISPOSITION: Hanged April 7, 1903

Knight, Thomas (1951–   )
SEX: M   RACE: B   TYPE: T   MOTIVE: PC
DATE(S): 1974/1980   VENUE: Miami, Fla.   VICTIMS: Three
MO: Killed two victims in personal altercations, then murdered another inmate
DISPOSITION: Condemned on two counts, April 21, 1975; condemned on third count, Jan. 20, 1983

Kock, Eugene de (1949–   )   AKA: Prime Evil
SEX: M   RACE: W   TYPE: T   MOTIVE: PC-extremist
DATE(S): 1970s–80s   VENUE: South Africa   VICTIMS: "Numerous"
MO: Policeman who murdered black antiapartheid activists
DISPOSITION: 212 years for six murders and 83 lesser counts, 1996

Koedatich, James J. (1948–   )
SEX: M   RACE: W   TYPE: N   MOTIVE: PC/Sex.
DATE(S): 1971/82–83   VENUE: Fla./N.J.   VICTIMS: Three+
MO: Killed male roommate (1971) and at least two females
DISPOSITION: Condemned on one count, 1984 (commuted to life on appeal); life term on second count, 1985

Koltun, Julian (1950–   )
SEX: M   RACE: W   TYPE: T   MOTIVE: Sex.
DATE(S): 1980–81   VENUE: Eastern Poland   VICTIMS: Two
MO: "Vampire" rape-slayer of women
DISPOSITION: Life sentence, 1981

Komar, Janusz (1963–   )
SEX: M   RACE: W   TYPE: N   MOTIVE: Sad./CE
DATE(S): 1983   VENUE: Germany   VICTIMS: Two
MO: Czech immigrant; beat/stomped women age 26 and 68, also robbing second victim
DISPOSITION: 10 years maximum sentence due to age

Komaroff, Vasili (1871–1923)   AKA: Wolf of Moscow
SEX: M   RACE: W   TYPE: T   MOTIVE: CE
DATE(S): 1921–23   VENUE: Moscow, Russia   VICTIMS: 33 confessed
MO: Horse dealer who robbed/killed customers at his stable
DISPOSITION: Executed with wife (convicted as accomplice), June 18, 1923

Komin, Alexander (1953–   )
SEX: M   RACE: W   TYPE: N   MOTIVE: CE/Sex.
DATE(S): 1971/82   VENUE: Fla./N.J.   VICTIMS: Three confirmed
MO: Killed male roommate (1971); raped stabbed female victims
DISPOSITION: Convicted of murder/robbery in Fla., 1971 (paroled 1982); condemned on one count in N.J., 1984 (reduced on appeal); life term for second count, 1985

Kondro, Joseph (?–   )
SEX: M   RACE: NA   TYPE: N   MOTIVE: Sex.
DATE(S): 1982–97   VENUE: Washington State   VICTIMS: "Dozens"
MO: Rapist and strangler of young girls, suspected in disappearances and deaths spanning 15 years
DISPOSITION: Confessed two murders and two rapes to avoid execution; received 55-year prison term in 1999

Koudri, Mohammed (?–   )
SEX: M   RACE: A   TYPE: T   MOTIVE: Sex.
DATE(S): 1994   VENUE: Milan, Italy   VICTIMS: Two
MO: Slayer of gay men
DISPOSITION: Convicted; sentence unknown

Krebs, Rex Allen (1966–   )
SEX: M   RACE: W   TYPE: T   MOTIVE: Sex.
DATE(S): 1999   VENUE: San Luis Obispo, Calif.   VICTIMS: Two
MO: Convicted sex offender and self-described "monster" who killed two 20-year-old coeds, hiding bodies on his property
DISPOSITION: Condemned on two counts, May 11, 2001

Krist, Gary Steven (1945–)
SEX: M   RACE: W   TYPE: N   MOTIVE: PC-nonspecific
DATE(S): 1959–64   VENUE: Alaska/Calid./Utah   VICTIMS: Four confessed
MO: Confessed slayer of two gay men, one girl, and an unidentified victim
DISPOSITION: Ga. life term for kidnapping, 1969; never charged with murder

Krueger, David Michael (1918–)
SEX: M   RACE: W   TYPE: T   MOTIVE: Sex.
DATE(S): 1956–57/91   VENUE: Ontario, Canada   VICTIMS: Four confessed
MO: Pedophile slayer of children; killed/sodomized 27-year-old man
DISPOSITION: Ruled insane, 1957; committed fourth murder on day pass from asylum; ruled insane again 1992

Kuklinski, Richard (1935–)
SEX: M   RACE: W   TYPE: T   MOTIVE: PC/CE
DATE(S): 1949–86   VENUE: N.J./N.Y.   VICTIMS: 100+
MO: Beat personal enemy to death in fight, age 14; adult career criminal and contract killer; also killed for pleasure and revenge
DISPOSITION: Consecutive life terms with 60-year minimums on each of four counts, 1988; indicted in February 2003 for the 1979 murder of a New York City policeman, confessed during a TV interview; trial pending

Kulaxides, Peter (?–?)
SEX: M   RACE: W   TYPE: T   MOTIVE: PC-domestic
DATE(S): 1920s   VENUE: Greece   VICTIMS: Six suspected
MO: "Bluebeard" slayer of wives
DISPOSITION: Confessed one count, Sept. 1930; sentence unknown

Kutzner, Richard William (1942–2002)
SEX: M   RACE: W   TYPE: T   MOTIVE: CE-felony
DATE(S): 1996   VENUE: Harris County, Tex.   VICTIMS: Two
MO: Women aged 54 and 59, bound and strangled during robberies
DISPOSITION: Executed on Aug. 7, 2002

Kuzikov, Ilshat (1959–)
SEX: RACE: W   TYPE: T   MOTIVE: PC-nonspecific
DATE(S): 1992–96   VENUE: St. Petersburg, Russia   VICTIMS: Three
MO: Alcoholic cannibal who murdered and devoured male drinking cronies, keeping blood and body parts in his flat
DISPOSITION: Convicted on three murder counts, March 19, 1997

Kuznetsof (d. 1929)
SEX: M   RACE: W   TYPE: T   MOTIVE: CE-felony
DATE(S): 1920s   VENUE: Russia   VICTIMS: Six+
MO: Alleged leader of "Volga pirates"; killed two relatives and at least four others in various robberies
DISPOSITION: Executed by firing squad, 1929

Kyte, Alun (1967–)   AKA: Midlands Ripper
SEX: M   RACE: W   TYPE: T   MOTIVE: Sex.
DATE(S): 1984–96   VENUE: British Midlands   VICTIMS: 19 suspected
MO: Raped and strangled female prostitutes and hitchhikers
DISPOSITION: Life sentence on two counts, 2000

Kyteler, Alice (?–?)
SEX: F   RACE: W   TYPE: T   MOTIVE: CE/Cult
DATE(S): 1300s   VENUE: Kilkenny, Ireland   VICTIMS: More than four
MO: Black widow slayer of four husbands; also accused of witchcraft and human sacrifice
DISPOSITION: Convicted and condemned in absentia but never captured; her maid, Petronella de Meath, was convicted as an accomplice and burned at the stake on Nov. 3, 1324

L., Thomas (1969–)
SEX: M   RACE: W   TYPE: T   MOTIVE: PC-extremist
DATE(S): 1995–96   VENUE: Germany   VICTIMS: Five confessed
MO: Nazi skinhead; shot political opponents and a gang defector
DISPOSITION: Confessed, Mar. 1996; sentence unknown

Lacenaire, Pierre François (d. 1835)
SEX: M   RACE: W   TYPE: T   MOTIVE: CE
DATE(S): 1834   VENUE: Paris, France   VICTIMS: Three confessed
MO: Killed robbery victims
DISPOSITION: Guillotined, 1835

LaFerte, Georges (1952–)
SEX: M   RACE: W   TYPE: T   MOTIVE: Sex.
DATE(S): 1983–84   VENUE: Nantes, France   VICTIMS: Two

MO: Alcoholic lust-killer of young women
DISPOSITION: Life sentence, 1987

Landau, Abraham (d. 1935)   AKA: Misfit
SEX: M   RACE: W   TYPE: T   MOTIVE: CE
DATE(S): 1920s–35   VENUE: N.Y./N.J.   VICTIMS:
   "Numerous"
MO: Contract killer for ARTHUR FLEGENHEIMER gang
DISPOSITION: Murdered with Flegenheimer, Oct. 23,
   1935

Landzo, Esad (?–)
SEX: M   RACE: W   TYPE: S   MOTIVE: PC-
   extremist
DATE(S): 1992   VENUE: Celibici, Bosnia   VICTIMS:
   Three+
MO: Raped/killed Serbs in concentration camp
DISPOSITION: 15 years on three murder counts, 1998

Lane, Doyle Edward (1961–)
SEX: M   RACE: W   TYPE: N   MOTIVE: Sex.
DATES(S): 1980/90   VENUE: Tex./Kans.   VICTIMS:
   Two suspected
MO: Pedophile slayer of girls age eight and nine
DISPOSITION: Condemned on one count in Tex.,
   1992

Lang, Donald (1945–)   AKA: Dummy
SEX: M   RACE: B   TYPE: T   MOTIVE: PC-nonspe-
   cific
DATES(S): 1965/72   VENUE: Chicago, Ill.   VIC-
   TIMS: Two
MO: Illiterate deaf-mute slayer of women
DISPOSITION: Ruled incompetent for trial, 1965;
   released from asylum, 1971; life sentence, 1972
   (overturned on appeal; remanded to asylum)

Langley, Robert P., Jr. (1959–)
SEX: M   RACE: W   TYPE: T   MOTIVE: PC-non-
   specific
DATES(S): 1987–89   VENUE: North Salem, Ore.
   VICTIMS: Two
MO: Parolee; killed woman (1987) and fellow ex-con-
   vict (1989), planting bodies near his halfway house
   residence
DISPOSITION: Condemned in two separate trials,
   1989

LaPage, Joseph (d. 1878)
SEX: M   RACE: W   TYPE: N   MOTIVE: Sex./Sad.
DATES(S): c. 1870–73   VENUE: Mass./Canada
   VICTIMS: Two

MO: French-Canadian trapper; donned bearskin and
   mask to rape and mutilate young women around
   Halloween season
DISPOSITION: Hanged in Quebec, Mar. 15, 1878

Lara, Mario (1955–)
SEX: M   RACE: H   TYPE: T   MOTIVE: CE/Sex.
DATES(S): 1981   VENUE: Dade County, Fla.   VIC-
   TIMS: Two
MO: Serial rapist; killed female prosecution witness in
   upcoming trial; stabbed teenage rape victim
DISPOSITION: Condemned on one count + life with
   25-year minimum on second count, 1982

LaRette, Anthony Joe, Jr. (1962–95)
SEX: M   RACE: W   TYPE: N   MOTIVE: Sex./Sad.
DATES(S): 1977–80   VENUE: Kans./Mo.   VICTIMS:
   Three confessed
MO: Young women killed with multiple stab wounds
DISPOSITION: Executed in Mo., Nov. 29, 1995

Laskey, Posteal (1937–)   AKA: Cincinnati Strangler
SEX: M   RACE: B   TYPE: T   MOTIVE: Sex.
DATES(S): 1965–66   VENUE: Cincinnati, Ohio
   VICTIMS: Seven
MO: Rape-slayer of women age 51–81
DISPOSITION: Convicted on one count, 1967

Lawrence, Michael Alan (1955–)
SEX: M   RACE: W   TYPE: N   MOTIVE: CE
DATES(S): 1976/90   VENUE: Fla.   VICTIMS: Two
MO: Killed robbery victims in Santa Rosa and Escam-
   bia Counties
DISPOSITION: Life term, 1976 (paroled 1985); con-
   demned, 1990

Laws, Keith Richard (?–)
SEX: M   RACE: W   TYPE: N   MOTIVE: CE
DATES(S): 1970/89   VENUE: Va./Netherlands   VIC-
   TIMS: Two
MO: Profit-motivated slayer of wife (1970) and elderly
   male acquaintance (1989)
DISPOSITION: Imprisoned for wife's murder,
   1970–87; life term in Amsterdam, 1991

Lawson, Bennie L. (d. 1994)
SEX: M   RACE: ?   TYPE: T   MOTIVE: PC
DATES(S): 1994   VENUE: Washington, D.C.   VIC-
   TIMS: Six suspected
MO: Suspected of a triple murder; opened fire in police
   station, killing three lawmen and wounding two
   more
DISPOSITION: Killed in shoot-out with police, Nov.
   22, 1994

Lear, Tuhran (?–)
SEX: M RACE: B TYPE: T MOTIVE: CE
DATES(S): 1980s VENUE: Chicago, Ill. VICTIMS: Two
MO: Killed teenager as juvenile; shot robbery victim
DISPOSITION: Condemned

Leasure, William Ernest (1946–) AKA: Mild Bill
SEX: M RACE: W TYPE: T MOTIVE: CE
DATES(S): 1977–81 VENUE: Los Angeles County, Calif. VICTIMS: Three
MO: Corrupt policeman and contract killer
DISPOSITION: 15 years to life on two counts, 1991

Lee, Derrick Todd (1969–)
SEX: M RACE: B TYPE: T MOTIVE: Sex.
DATE(S): 1998–2003 VENUE: Baton Rouge, La. VICTIMS: Seven
MO: Attacked 8 women, killing seven, in four parishes surrounding Baton Rouge
DISPOSITION: Received life term without parole on one count of second-degree murder, Aug. 16, 2004; convicted on second count, Oct. 12, 2004

Leger, Antoine (d. 1824)
SEX: M RACE: W TYPE: T MOTIVE: Sex./Sad.
DATES(S): 1820s VENUE: France VICTIMS: "Several"
MO: Cannibal "ripper" or young women who also drank blood of his victims, sometimes removing and devouring hearts
DISPOSITION: Guillotined, 1824

Legere, Allan Joseph (1948–) AKA: Madman of Miramichi
SEX: M RACE: W TYPE: N MOTIVE: Sad.
DATES(S): 1986/89 VENUE: New Brunswick, Canada VICTIMS: Five+
MO: Tortured first victim to death; others stabbed, bludgeoned, strangled, asphyxiated
DISPOSITION: Life term, 1986 (escaped 1989); second life term, 1991

Lehman, Christa (1922–)
SEX: F RACE: W TYPE: S MOTIVE: PC
DATES(S): 1952–54 VENUE: Worms, Germay VICTIMS: Three
MO: "Black widow" poisoner of husband, father-in-law, and a female neighbor
DISPOSITION: Life sentence, 1954

Lemieux, Joseph A. (1908–50)
SEX: M RACE: W TYPE: T MOTIVE: PC-nonspecific

DATES(S): 1943/50 VENUE: Lawrence, Mass. VICTIMS: Two
MO: Strangler of women; one victim mutilated
DISPOSITION: Convicted of manslaughter, 1943 (paroled 1948); suicide after second murder, Nov. 17, 1950

Lent, Lewis, Jr. (1950–)
SEX: M RACE: W TYPE: N MOTIVE: Sex.
DATES(S): 1983–90 VENUE: Eastern U.S. VICTIMS: Eight suspected
MO: Lust killer of five females (age 10–21) and three males (age 12–15)
DISPOSITION: Life without parole in Mass., 1995; 25 years to life in N.Y., 1997

Leonard, Eric Royce (1969–) AKA: Thrill Killer
SEX: M RACE: W TYPE: T MOTIVE: PC-nonspecific
DATES(S): 1991 VENUE: Sacramento, Calif. VICTIMS: Six
MO: Shot victims/witnesses in petty robberies
DISPOSITION: Condemned

Leonski, Edward Joseph (1917–42) AKA: Singing Strangler
SEX: M RACE: W TYPE: T MOTIVE: PC-nonspecific
DATES(S): 1919–42 VENUE: Melbourne, Australia VICTIMS: Three
MO: Alcoholic American soldier, killed women "for their voices"
DISPOSITION: Hanged Nov. 9, 1942

Leroy, Francis (1943–) AKA: The Werewolf
SEX: M RACE: W TYPE: T MOTIVE: PC-nonspecific
DATES(S): 1961/83 VENUE: Bergerac, France VICTIMS: Two
MO: Donned costumes to attack victims during full moons
DISPOSITION: 20 years, 1963 (paroled 1972); life without parole, 1989

Leslie, Nashville Franklin (1842–1925)
SEX: M RACE: W TYPE: T MOTIVE: PC
DATES(S): 1880s VENUE: Ariz. Territory VICTIMS: 13 claimed
MO: Old West gunman; victims included his live-in lover
DISPOSITION: 25 years for murder of his girlfriend, 1889; pardoned and released, 1897

Le Thanh Van (1956–)
SEX: F RACE: A TYPE: T MOTIVE: CE-felony

DATE(S): 1998–2001   VENUE: Ho Chi Minh City, Vietnam   VICTIMS: 13
MO: Poisoned acquaintances, then stole their cash and other valuables; unnamed boyfriend charged as an accomplice
DISPOSITION: Arrested in August 2004; disposition unknown

Lewis, Gerald Patrick (1965–)
SEX: M   RACE: Unk.   TYPE: N   MOTIVE: Sex.
DATE(S): 1980s–1990s   VENUE: Ala./Ga./Mass. VICTIMS: Seven confessed
MO: Transient rape-slayer of women
DISPOSITION: Condemned on two counts in Alabama, Dec. 10, 1999; received life prison term on one count in Massachusetts, Aug. 8, 2000

Libmann, Achim (1946–)
SEX: M   RACE: W   TYPE: T   MOTIVE: PC-revenge
DATES(S): 1986   VENUE: Frankfurt, Germany VICTIMS: Two
MO: Strangled prostitutes after his wife became one
DISPOSITION: Pled guilty; life sentence, 1987

Lightbourne, Wendell (1940–)
SEX: M   RACE: B   TYPE: T   MOTIVE: Sex.
DATES(S): 1959   VENUE: Bermuda   VICTIMS: Two
MO: Rape-slayer of female tourists; bite marks on bodies
DISPOSITION: Death sentence commuted to life imprisonment

Lindsey, William Darrell (1935–)
SEX: M   RACE: W   TYPE: N   MOTIVE: Sex.
DATE(S): 1988–97   VENUE: Fla./N.C.   VICTIMS: More than seven
MO: Rape-slayer of women; victims beaten and shot; prime suspect in seven Florida murders and the death of an Asheville, N.C., prostitute
DISPOSITION: Pleaded guilty to four counts of second-degree murder in Florida, receiving 30-year terms for each count, May 21, 1999; pled guilty on two more counts and received 30-year terms on both in Florida, July 8, 1999

Lineveldt, Gamal Salie (1919–42)
SEX: M   RACE: W   TYPE: T   MOTIVE: Sex.
DATES(S): 1940–41   VENUE: Cape Town, South Africa   VICTIMS: Four
MO: Raped/bludgeoned women
DISPOSITION: Confessed all counts; hanged, 1942

Lin Lai-Fu (1960–91)
SEX: M   RACE: A   TYPE: T   MOTIVE: CE

DATES(S): 1986–91   VENUE: Taiwan   VICTIMS: 24
MO: Career criminal; killed victims in gang warfare, kidnappings, and robberies
DISPOSITION: Executed July 25, 1991

Li Pingping (1960–2004)
SEX: M   RACE: A   TYPE: T   MOTIVE: PC/Sex
DATE(S): 1995–2003   VENUE: Beijing, China   VICTIMS: Six
MO: Taxi driver who killed his ex-employer's wife and 12-year-old daughter after being fired; subsequently killed and dismembered female prostitutes
DISPOSITION: Executed, June 2004; wife Dong Meirong received 15-year prison term, March 2004, as an accessory to murder and for harboring stolen money

Lisemba, Raymond (d. 1942)
SEX: M   RACE: W   TYPE: N   MOTIVE: CE
DATES(S): 1930s–40s   VENUE: Colo./Calif.   VICTIMS: Three
MO: "Bluebeard" slayer of wives and a male friend for insurance
DISPOSITION: Hanged in Calif., May 1942

Little, Dwain Lee (1947–)
SEX: M   RACE: W   TYPE: N   MOTIVE: Sex.
DATES(S): 1964/75 VENUE: Ore.   VICTIMS: Five
MO: Raped/stabbed 16-year-old girl; shot family of four
DISPOSITION: Life term, 1966 (paroled 1974); returned as parole violator, 1975 (released 1977); three consecutive life terms for rape + attempted murder, 1980

Liu Jun (1971–)
SEX: M   RACE: A   TYPE: N   MOTIVE: CE/Sex
DATE(S): 1997–99   VENUE: China   VICTIMS: 22
MO: Posed as repairman to invade and rob homes in five Chinese provinces, killing 22 victims, wounding six others and raping several women
DISPOSITION: Unknown

Liu Mingwu (1961–)
SEX: M   RACE: A   TYPE: N   MOTIVE: PC-non-specific
DATE(S): 2001   VENUE: Anhui Province, China VICTIMS: 29
MO: Stabbed and bludgeoned homeless victims in several cities, afterward setting their bodies afire
DISPOSITION: Unknown

Li Yuhui (1970–99)
SEX: M   RACE: A   TYPE: T   MOTIVE: CE-felony

DATE(S): 1998   VENUE: Hong Kong, China   VICTIMS: Five

MO: Fortune-teller who poisoned three women and two teenage girls, robbing them of $150,000

DISPOSITION: Executed on April 20, 1999

Lockett, Will (d. 1920)   AKA: Petrie Kimbrough

SEX: M   RACE: B   TYPE: N   MOTIVE: Sex.

DATES(S): 1912–15   VENUE: Ill./Ind./Ky.   VICTIMS: Four confessed

MO: Rape-slayer of women and a 10-year-old girl

DISPOSITION: Executed in Ky. on one count, Mar. 11, 1920

Lockhart, Michael Lee (1945–97)

SEX: M   RACE: W   TYPE: N   MOTIVE: Sex./CE

DATES(S): 1987   VENUE: Ind./Tex./Fla./Tenn.   VICTIMS: Six+ suspected

MO: Rape-slayer of girls; killed police officer resisting arrest

DISPOSITION: Condemned on two counts in Ind. and one in Tex.; executed in Tex., Dec. 9, 1997

Locusta (d. 69 A.D.)

SEX: F   RACE: W   TYPE: T   MOTIVE: CE-felony

DATE(S): 54–68   VENUE: Rome   VICTIMS: More than three

MO: Hired poisoner of royal victims

DISPOSITION: Executed in the Colosseum, Jan. 9, 1969

Long, David (1953–99)

SEX: M   RACE: W   TYPE: N   MOTIVE: PC

DATE(S): 1978–86   VENUE: Calif./Tex.   VICTIMS: Five

MO: Killed three roommates with a hatchet (1986); subsequently confessed the murders of a gas station attendant (1978) and former employer (1983)

DISPOSITION: Executed on three counts, Dec. 8, 1999

Long, Neal Bradley (1927–)

SEX: M   RACE: W   TYPE: T   MOTIVE: PC-extremist

DATES(S): 1972–75   VENUE: Dayton, Ohio   VICTIMS: Seven

MO: Random shootings motivated by racism

DISPOSITION: Consecutive life terms on two counts, 1975

Long, Steven (d. 1868)

SEX: M   RACE: W   TYPE: N   MOTIVE: PC

DATES(S): 1860s   VENUE: Wyo.   VICTIMS: Eight+

MO: Gunfighter, outlaw, and occasional lawman

DISPOSITION: Lynched by vigilantes, Oct. 1868

Longley, William P. (1851–78)

SEX: M   RACE: W   TYPE: N   MOTIVE: PC

DATES(S): 1867–77   VENUE: Tex./Kans.   VICTIMS: 32 admitted

MO: Racist gunfighter; shot blacks, Mexicans, Union soldiers, and personal enemies

DISPOSITION: Hanged Oct. 11, 1878

Lopes, Edmund (1935–)

SEX: M   RACE: W   TYPE: T   MOTIVE: PC-domestic

DATES(S): 1966/70   VENUE: Bloomingdale, Ill.   VICTIMS: Two

MO: Baptist minister; "Bluebeard" slayer of wife and girlfriend

DISPOSITION: 20 years for attempted murder, 1971; 50–99 years for murder, 1972 (paroled, 1983); arrested as parole violator, Jan. 1992 (released again, May 1992)

Lord, Brian Keith (1961–)

SEX: M   RACE: W   TYPE: N   MOTIVE: PC/Sex

DATE(S): 1975/1986   VENUE: Calif./Wash.   VICTIMS: Two

MO: Shot a family friend at age 14; kidnapped his sister-in-law at 20; raped and murdered a teenage girl in 1986

DISPOSITION: Detained as a juvenile, 1975–76; imprisoned for kidnapping, 1980–83; condemned in 1987; death sentence commuted, 1997; conviction overturned on appeal, 1999; convicted second time, April 30, 2003; received life prison term

Lott, Ronald C. (1961–)

SEX: M   RACE: B   TYPE: T   MOTIVE: Sex.

DATE(S): 1986–87   VENUE: Oklahoma City, Okla.   VICTIMS: Two

MO: Serial rapist of women aged 74–92; two of four known victims suffocated in their homes; innocent suspect Robert Lee Miller Jr. served 11 years for the murders before DNA linked Lott to the slayings

DISPOSITION: 25 years for guilty plea on two rapes, 1987; condemned on two murder counts, January 2002

Louis, Emile (1934–)

SEX: M   RACE: W   TYPE: T   MOTIVE: Sex.

DATE(S): 1977–79   VENUE: Rouvray, France   VICTIMS: Seven confessed

MO: Ex-soldier and serial rapist of females, various ages; suspected of 11 murders; confessed seven in police custody; all known victims were mentally disabled

DISPOSITION: Served two terms for child abuse, 1979–83 and 1989–93; on March 26, 2004 received a 20-year sentence for repeatedly drugging and raping his wife and stepdaughter in the 1990s; 10-year statute of limitations on murder precluded prosecution despite confession of seven homicides, made to police in 2000

Loutriotis, Sotiria (1939–)
SEX: F   RACE: W   TYPE: T   MOTIVE: PC-nonspecific
DATE(S): 198?/2000   VENUE: Kalambaka, Greece   VICTIMS: Two
MO: Killed her son and husband with axes in separate incidents
DISPOSITION: Life prison term for son's murder; released Oct. 1999; killed husband in June 2000; returned to asylum on new charge

Lovett, William (1892–1923)   AKA: Wild Bill
SEX: M   RACE: W   TYPE: T   MOTIVE:CE
DATES(S): c. 1916–23   VENUE: New York City   VICTIMS: "Numerous"
MO: Violent leader of Irish "White Hand" racketeers
DISPOSITION: Murdered by rival thugs, Oct. 31, 1923

Lowe, Joseph (1846–99)   AKA: Rowdy Joe
SEX: M   RACE: W   TYPE: N   MOTIVE: CE
DATES(S): 1860s–99   VENUE: Kans./Tex./Ariz./Colo.   VICTIMS: "Several"
MO: Alleged member of "QUANTRILL'S RAIDERS" during Civil War; later pimp/gambler/gunman
DISPOSITION: Killed in gunfight, Denver, Colo., 1899

Lucas, David Allen (1956–)
SEX: M   RACE: W   TYPE: T   MOTIVE: Sex.
DATES(S): 1979–84   VENUE: San Diego, Calif.   VICTIMS: Six suspected
MO: Rape-slayer of women and children
DISPOSITION: Condemned on three counts, 1989

Ludke, Bruno (1909–44)
SEX: M   RACE: W   TYPE: N   MOTIVE: Sex.
DATES(S): 1928–43   VENUE: Germany   VICTIMS: 85 confessed
MO: Rape-slayer of females
DISPOSITION: Died under Nazi experimentation, Apr. 8, 1944

Luft, Lothar (1941–)
SEX: M   RACE: W   TYPE: T   MOTIVE: PC
DATES(S): 1986   VENUE: Germany   VICTIMS: Three

MO: Killed his wife, mother-in-law, and girlfriend
DISPOSITION: Life sentence, 1986 (escaped 1993)

Lumbrera, Diana (1957–)
SEX: F   RACE: H   TYPE: N   MOTIVE: PC-nonspecific
DATES(S): 1976–90   VENUE: Tex./Kans.   VICTIMS: Seven
MO: Mother who killed her own children
DISPOSITION: Life terms in Kans. and Tex., 1990

Lusk, Bobby E. (1951–)
SEX: M   RACE: W   TYPE: N   MOTIVE: CE
DATES(S): 1976–78   VENUE: Fla.   VICTIMS: Two
MO: Suffocated holdup victim; murdered fellow inmate
DISPOSITION: Two life terms, 1977; life term on second count, 1980

Luther, Thomas Edward (1957–)
SEX: M   RACE: W   TYPE: N   MOTIVE: Sex.
DATES(S): 1970s–94   VENUE: Vt./Colo./W.Va./Pa.   VICTIMS: 9+ suspected
MO: Rape-slayer of women
DISPOSITION: 15–35 years for rape in W. Va., 1995; 48 years for one count of murder in Colo., 1996; two 50-year terms for assault and attempted murder in Colo., 1996

Lyles, Anjette Donovan (1917–77)
SEX: F   RACE: W   TYPE: T   MOTIVE: PC-nonspecific
DATES(S): 1952–57   VENUE: Macon, Ga.   VICTIMS: Four
MO: Voodoo practitioner and "black widow" poisoner of two husbands, mother-in-law, and a daughter
DISPOSITION: Condemned on one count, 1958; ruled insane and sent to state hospital in 1960; died there in Dec. 1977

Lynch, John (1813–42)   AKA: Berrima Ax Murderer
SEX: M   RACE: W   TYPE: T   MOTIVE: CE/PC
DATE(S): 1835/1841–42   VENUE: Berrima, Australia   VICTIMS: Ten
MO: Career criminal who killed at least one man while riding with a gang of bush rangers; subsequently killed nine neighbors with an ax
DISPOSITION: Acquitted of murder despite his confession in 1835 (two other gang members were hanged for the crime); hanged for later slayings on April 22, 1842

M., Henryk (1943–?)
SEX: M   RACE: W   TYPE: T   MOTIVE: CE

DATES(S): 1986/92   VENUE: Piotrkow Trybunalski, Poland   VICTIMS: Seven
MO: Shot robbery victims in cold blood
DISPOSITION: Condemned, 1993

Maake, Maupa Cedric (1963–   )   AKA: Wemmer Pan Killer
SEX: M   RACE: B   TYPE: T   MOTIVE: Sex/CE
DATE(S): 1995–97   VENUE: Wemmer Pan, South Africa   VICTIMS: 34
MO: Attacked couples making love in rural areas, robbing them and raping the women before killing both; ultimately charged with 24 murders, 28 attempted murders, 15 rapes, 46 robberies, and various lesser charges
DISPOSITION: Received prison terms totaling 1,340 years on March 14, 2000, for 27 murders and 88 lesser charges

MacDonald, William (1926–   )   AKA: Sydney Mutilator
SEX: M   RACE: W   TYPE: T   MOTIVE: Sad./PC-revenge
DATES(S): 1961–62   VENUE: Sydney, Australia   VICTIMS: Four
MO: "Ripper" of gay males; allegedly sought revenge for homosexual rape in his teens
DISPOSITION: Life sentence, 1962; later ruled insane and moved to an asylum

Macek, Richard O. (1948–   )   AKA: Mad Biter
SEX: M   RACE: W   TYPE: N   MOTIVE: Sex./Sad.
DATES(S): 1974–75   VENUE: Wis./Ill.   VICTIMS: Three
MO: Rape-slayer and mutilator of females age three to 26
DISPOSITION: Indefinite sentence to Wis. asylum as deranged sex offender, 1976; 50–75 years in Ill. on one count, 1976; Wis. life term on guilty plea to one count, 1977; 30 years for rape in Wis. and 200–400 years for two Ill. murder counts, 1980

MacGregor, Dr. Robert (1879–1928)
SEX: M   RACE: W   TYPE: S   MOTIVE: CE
DATES(S): 1909–11   VENUE: Ubly, Mich.   VICTIMS: Three
MO: Killed his lover's husband and two sons for insurance
DISPOSITION: Life sentence, 1912 (pardoned by governor, 1916); remained as prison physician until his death

Mackay, Patrick David (1952–   )
SEX: M   RACE: W   TYPE: T   MOTIVE: PC-non-specific
DATES(S): 1974–75   VENUE: Middlesex, England   VICTIMS: 11 suspected
MO: Psychopath obsessed with Nazism; stabbed/axed victims of both sexes, age 17–89
DISPOSITION: Life sentence following guilty plea on three counts of manslaughter; two other counts dropped in plea bargain

Macon, Ronald (1964–   )
SEX: M   RACE: Unk.   TYPE: T   MOTIVE: Sex.
DATE(S): 1999   VENUE: Chicago, Ill.   VICTIMS: Three
MO: While jailed for the rape of his former babysitter, DNA evidence linked Macon to the rape-murders of three South Side women
DISPOSITION: Pleaded guilty on three counts; received three life terms, September 2003

Madden, Owen (1892–1965)   AKA: Owney the Killer
SEX: M   RACE: W   TYPE: T   MOTIVE: CE
DATES(S): 1909–32   VENUE: New York City   VICTIMS: "Numerous"
MO: British-born gangster of Prohibition era
DISPOSITION: Eight years for one count in N.Y., 1915–23; retired from mob in 1940s; died in Ark., 1965

Magliolo, Michael Scott (1960–   )
SEX: M   RACE: W   TYPE: N   MOTIVE: Sex.
DATES(S): 1977–91   VENUE: Tenn./Ohio/Tex./Pa./La./Ark.   VICTIMS: 10+ suspected
MO: Transient rape-slayer of young women; also suspected of killing his half-brother
DISPOSITION: Life + 50 years in Tenn., 1993; 15 years to life in Ohio, 1993

Magoon, Seymour (?–?)   AKA: Blue Jaw
SEX: M   RACE: W   TYPE: T   MOTIVE: CE
DATES(S): 1931–40   VENUE: N.Y./N.J.   VICTIMS: "Numerous"
MO: Contract killer for "Murder, Inc."
DISPOSITION: Immunity granted in return for testimony

Mahlanga, David (1957–   )
SEX: M   RACE: B   TYPE: T   MOTIVE: Sex.
DATE(S): 2002–03   VENUE: Malkerns, Swaziland   VICTIMS: 34
MO: Decapitated 33 women and one child as revenge for conviction on a previous rape charge; rural

graves found during police search for serial killer Bongani Vilakati
DISPOSITION: Unknown

Maione, Harry (d. 1942)   AKA: Happy
SEX: M   RACE: W   TYPE: N   MOTIVE: CE
DATES(S): 1931–40   VENUE: Eastern USA   VICTIMS: 12+
MO: Contract killer for "MURDER, INC."
DISPOSITION: Executed at Sing Sing, Feb. 19, 1942

Majors, Orvill Lynn, Jr. (1961–   )
SEX: M   RACE: W   TYPE: S   MOTIVE: Unk.
DATE(S): 1994   VENUE: Linton, Ind.   VICTIMS: More than six
MO: Nurse who killed patients at Vermillion County Hospital with lethal injections; indicted for murdering six of 120 who died in his care
DISPOSITION: Convicted on six counts; received 65-year sentence on Nov. 15, 1999

Malarkey, Johnnie (1970–   )
SEX: M   RACE: Unk.   TYPE: T   MOTIVE: CE/PC
DATE(S): 1993–98   VENUE: Fresno, Calif.   VICTIMS: 11
MO: Jailed in 1998 for helping his sister commit a murder, he confessed 10 more slayings from 1993: seven victims shot during a bar robbery, three others killed in separate attacks
DISPOSITION: Life prison term

Malevre, Christine (1970–   )
SEX: F   RACE: W   TYPE: S   MOTIVE: PC-"mercy"
DATE(S): 1997–98   VENUE: Mantes-la-Jolie, France   VICTIMS: 30 confessed
MO: Nurse who euthanized elderly patients at François-Quesnay Hospital, allegedly complying with requests from the patients or their families
DISPOSITION: Received 10-year prison term for six slayings, Jan. 31, 2003

Malone, Victor (?–   )
SEX: M   RACE: Unk.   TYPE: T   MOTIVE: Sex.
DATE(S): 1980s   VENUE: Detroit, Mich.   VICTIMS: Three
MO: Rape-slayer of female prostitutes
DISPOSITION: Life terms imposed on three murder counts

Mansfield, William, Jr. (1956–   )
SEX: M   RACE: W   TYPE: N   MOTIVE: Sex.
DATES(S): 1980–81   VENUE: Fla./Calif.   VICTIMS: five+

MO: Son of convicted molester; rape-slayer of females age 15–30
DISPOSITION: Concurrent life terms in Calif. and Fla.

Manso, Gerardo Marten (1957–   )
SEX: M   RACE: H   TYPE: T   MOTIVE: PC
DATES(S): 1991/93   VENUE: Dade County, Fla.   VICTIMS: Two
MO: Shot wife's suspected lover; shot employees at his job
DISPOSITION: 22 years on one count, 1994; condemned on second count + four life terms for attempted murder, 1995

Manuel, Peter Thomas Anthony (1927–58)
SEX: M   RACE: W   TYPE: N   MOTIVE: CE/Sad.
DATES(S): 1956–58   VENUE: Scotland/England   VICTIMS: 9–12
MO: Career criminal; murdered victims during robberies
DISPOSITION: Hanged in Glasgow, July 11, 1958

Marbley, Odell (1955–   )
SEX: M   RACE: B   TYPE: T   MOTIVE: PC
DATES(S): 1977/80   VENUE: Indianapolis, Ind.   VICTIMS: Two
MO: Bludgeoned girlfriend's four-year-old son; shot male acquaintance
DISPOSITION: Served 15 years on murder convictions

Marcus, Jerry (1951–   )
SEX: M   RACE: B   TYPE: N   MOTIVE: Sex.
DATES(S): 1971–87   VENUE: Ala./Miss./Tenn./Ga.   VICTIMS: 15 suspected
MO: Transient rape-slayer of women
DISPOSITION: Confessed seven murders; life term on one count in Ala., 1988

Marek, Marthe (1904–38)
SEX: F   RACE: W   TYPE: T   MOTIVE: CE
DATES(S): 1920–37   VENUE: Vienna, Austria   VICTIMS: Four
MO: "Black widow" poisoner of husbands and others, for insurance
DISPOSITION: Beheaded, Dec. 6, 1938

Marjek, Ali (1958–77)
SEX: M   RACE: A   TYPE: T   MOTIVE: Sex.
DATES(S): 1976–77   VENUE: Syria   VICTIMS: Three
MO: Pedophile rape-slayer of young boys
DISPOSITION: Hanged Mar. 27, 1977

Marquette, Richard Lawrence (1935–   )
SEX: M   RACE: W   TYPE: N   MOTIVE: Sex./Sad.

DATES(S): 1961/75   VENUE: Portland/Salem, Ore.
   VICTIMS: Three
MO: Dismembered adult female victims
DISPOSITION: Life sentence on first count (paroled
   1975); life term on second count, 1975

Marshall, Robert Wayne (1955–92)
SEX: M   RACE: W   TYPE: T   MOTIVE: Sex.
DATES(S): 1988–92   VENUE: Pittsbugh, Pa.   VIC-
   TIMS: Two
MO: Gay alcoholic; dismembered male victims
DISPOSITION: Suicide to avoid arrest, May 15, 1992

Martin, James Lindsay (1955–)
SEX: M   RACE: W   TYPE: N   MOTIVE: CE-felony
DATES(S): 1991–92   VENUE: Nev./Calif.   VICTIMS:
   Two
MO: Career criminal; shot 68-year-old woman and 91-
   year-old man in holdups
DISPOSITION: Life term in Calif., 1993

Martin, Lee Roy (1937–72)
SEX: M   RACE: W   TYPE: T   MOTIVE: Sex.
DATES(S): 1967–68   VENUE: Gaffney, S.C.   VIC-
   TIMS: Four
MO: Strangled females age 14–32
DISPOSITION: Four life terms; murdered in prison,
   May 1972

Martin, Rhonda Belle (1907–57)
SEX: F   RACE: W   TYPE: T   MOTIVE: PC-domestic
DATES(S): 1934–55   VENUE: Ubly, Mich.   VIC-
   TIMS: Seven confessed
MO: "Black widow" poisoner of husbands, mother,
   children
DISPOSITION: Executed Oct. 11, 1957

Martino, Alfonso de (?–)
SEX: M   RACE: W   TYPE: S   MOTIVE: PC-non-
   specific
DATES(S): 1993–94   VENUE: Frosinone, Italy   VIC-
   TIMS: Four
MO: Nurse who killed hospital patients with curare
DISPOSITION: Convicted; sentence unknown

Martorano, John (1941–)
SEX: M   RACE: W   TYPE: N   MOTIVE: CE-felony
DATE(S): 1981–99   VENUE: Mass./Fla./Okla.   VIC-
   TIMS: 20 confessed
MO: Contract killer for Boston's Winter Hill Gang
   who turned state's evidence in 1995; pled guilty to
   10 murders and various lesser charges in October
   1999; in exchange for testimony, received a 12½-

year sentence with credit for four years already
served

Mashiane, Johannes (d. 1989)   AKA: Beast of
   Atteridgeville
SEX: M   RACE: B   TYPE: T   MOTIVE: PC/Sex.
DATES(S): 1982/88–89   VENUE: Atteridgeville,
   South Africa   VICTIMS: 13
MO: Killed girlfriend (1982); sodomized and
   stoned/strangled young boys
DISPOSITION: Five years for first murder; killed by
   bus fleeing scene of attack on 13th child (possible
   suicide)

Mashowo, Lanelo (?–)
SEX: M   RACE: B   TYPE: N   MOTIVE: Unk.
DATE(S): 1996–98   VENUE: Zambia   VICTIMS: 30
   suspected
MO: Killed family of three in 1996; other crimes
   unspecified
DISPOSITION: Convicted of triple murder, 1996; sent
   to asylum (escaped days after arrival); arrested for
   later crimes on Feb. 12, 1999; disposition unknown

Maslich, Andrei (?–)
SEX: M   RACE: W   TYPE: T   MOTIVE: PC
DATES(S): 1990s   VENUE: Siberia, Russia   VIC-
   TIMS: Four
MO: Imprisoned for two murders; killed/cannibalized
   cellmates in two separate incidents
DISPOSITION: Condemned 1995 for killing one cell-
   mate; condemned on second count, 1996

Mason, David Edwin (1957–93)
SEX: M   RACE: W   TYPE: N   MOTIVE: CE/Sad.
DATES(S): 1980/82   VENUE: Calif.   VICTIMS: Five
MO: Robbed/bludgeoned elderly women (1980); killed
   cellmate while awaiting trial
DISPOSITION: Executed Aug. 24, 1993

Matajke, Dorothy (?–)
SEX: F   RACE: W   TYPE: N   MOTIVE: CE
DATES(S): 1972–86   VENUE: Iowa/Ark.   VICTIMS:
   Three+
MO: Live-in "nurse" who robbed and poisoned elderly
   clients
DISPOSITION: Life + 60 years on two counts in Ark.,
   1987.

Matenjwa, Elvis (d. 2004)
SEX: M   RACE: B   TYPE: N   MOTIVE: PC-non-
   specific
DATE(S): 2003   VENUE: Esikhawini, South Africa
   VICTIMS: Two

MO: Cannibal slayer of women, arrested when remains of a missing 46-year-old victim were found cooking at his home

DISPOSITION: Arrested in September 2003, then released on bail pending further investigation; died of gastroenteritis at local hospital, Sept. 27, 2004

Mateo, Angel (?–)
SEX: M   RACE: H   TYPE: T   MOTIVE: CE/PC
DATE(S): 1995–96   VENUE: Rochester, N.Y.   VICTIMS: Four
MO: Shot male victims, including two drug dealers and two personal enemies
DISPOSITION: Condemned on one count, 1999; sentence reduced to life on appeal, August 2004

Mather, David (1845–?)   AKA: Mysterious Dave
SEX: M   RACE: W   TYPE: N   MOTIVE: PC/CE
DATES(S): 1970s–80s   VENUE: Kans./N. Mex./Tex.
VICTIMS: 14+
MO: Outlaw, gunfighter, and occasional lawman
DISPOSITION: Allegedly returned to native Canada, late 1880s

Matta, Chander (1969–)
SEX: M   RACE: ?   TYPE: T   MOTIVE: Sex.
DATES(S): 1989–90   VENUE: D.C./Va.   VICTIMS: Three confessed
MO: Shot/bludgeoned/strangled blond female prostitutes
DISPOSITION: Life term without parole, 1991

Matteucci, Andrea (?–)   AKA: Monster of Aosta
SEX: M   RACE: W   TYPE: T   MOTIVE: Sex.
DATES(S): 1980–95   VENUE: Aosta/Puglia, Italy
VICTIMS: Six+
MO: Lust slayer of female prostitutes and one gay man; bodies burned
DISPOSITION: Pled guilty on four counts; sentence unknown

Matthews, Ynobe Katron (1976–2004)
SEX: M   RACE: B   TYPE: T   MOTIVE: Sex.
DATE(S): 1999–2000   VENUE: Brazos County, Tex.
VICTIMS: Two
MO: Sexually assaulted several females, killing two whose bodies were dumped in rural areas
DISPOSITION: Executed on one count, Jan. 6, 2004

Mattson, Michael Dee (1953–)
SEX: M   RACE: W   TYPE: T   MOTIVE: Sex.
DATES(S): 1978   VENUE: Los Angeles area   VICTIMS: Two
MO: Strangled girls age nine and 16
DISPOSITION: Condemned

Maturino Resendiz, Angel (1959–)
SEX: M   RACE: H   TYPE: N   MOTIVE: Sex/CE-felony
DATE(S): 1997–99   VENUE: Tex./Ky./Ill.
VICTIMS: 11
MO: Mexican national deported from the United States at least 10 times between 1985 and 1999; traveled widely by train, killing random victims who lived near railroad lines; identified victims include six in Texas, two in Florida, two in Illinois, and one in Kentucky
DISPOSITION: Received 20-year sentence for burglary in Miami, 1979; paroled September 1985; condemned on one murder count in Texas, May 22, 2000; immunity granted upon confession of two Florida slayings

Maudsley, Robert (1953–)
SEX: M   RACE: W   TYPE: N   MOTIVE: CE/PC
DATE(S): 1974–78   VENUE: England   VICTIMS: Four
MO: Killed and robbed a gay man in London for drug money, while working as a male prostitute (1974); subsequently murdered fellow inmates at a mental hospital (1977) and prison (1978)
DISPOSITION: Committed to Broadsmoor asylum in 1974; transferred to Wakefield prison after second murder; sentenced to indefinite solitary confinement after last two murders

Maury, Robert Edward (1956–)
SEX: M   RACE: W   TYPE: N   MOTIVE: Sex./CE
DATES(S): 1985–87   VENUE: Redding, Calif.   VICTIMS: Three
MO: Strangled women and collected "secret witness" rewards for directing police to their corpses
DISPOSITION: Condemned, 1989

Maxwell, Bobby Joe (1945–)   AKA: Skid Row Stabber
SEX: M   RACE: B   TYPE: T   MOTIVE: PC-nonspecific
DATES(S): 1978   VENUE: Los Angeles, Calif.   VICTIMS: 10
MO: Occultist and ritual slayer of homeless men
DISPOSITION: Life term on two counts, 1984

May, Cheryl (1965–)
SEX: F   RACE: W   TYPE: S   MOTIVE: PC-"mercy"
DATE(S): 1997   VENUE: Fort Wayne, Ind.   VICTIMS: Six suspected
MO: Nurse accused of killing comatose/terminal patients with morphine

DISPOSITION: Pleaded guilty to reckless endangerment in the death of one patient who died following a morphine overdose; maximum sentence eight years; prosecutors dismissed one murder count and closed other homicide investigations as part of plea bargain

Mazurkiewicz, Wladislaw (1911–57)   AKA: Gentleman Murderer
SEX: M   RACE: W   TYPE: T   MOTIVE: CE
DATES(S): 1950s   VENUE: Cracow, Poland   VICTIMS: 30 confessed
MO: Home-invading robber who murdered victims of both sexes
DISPOSITION: Hanged Jan. 31, 1957

McCaffery, Archibald Beattie (1949–)   AKA: Mad Dog
SEX: M   RACE: W   TYPE: T   MOTIVE: PC-non-specific
DATE(S): 1973   VENUE: Sydney, Australia   VICTIMS: Three
MO: Career criminal who plotted seven murders to resurrect his dead infant son; arrested after killing three men selected at random
DISPOSITION: Received three life terms at trial, 1974; paroled 1993; after further legal problems, deported to his native Scotland on May 1, 1997; charged with abduction, assault, and breach of peace at Hawick, Scotland, in April 2004

McCarty, Henry (1859–81)   AKA: William H. Bonney
SEX: M   RACE: W   TYPE: N   MOTIVE: CE/PC
DATES(S): 1877–81   VENUE: Ariz./N. Mex.   VICTIMS: Four to 10
MO: Old West gunfighter, outlaw, and feudist in range wars
DISPOSITION: Shot July 10, 1881

McDuff, Kenneth Allen (1946–98)
SEX: M   RACE: W   TYPE: N   MOTIVE: Sex./Sad.
DATES(S): 1966/1991–92   VENUE: Tex.   VICTIMS: Nine suspected
MO: Killed three teens, 1966; rape slayer of women, 1991–92
DISPOSITION: Condemned, 1966 (commuted to life, 1972; paroled 1990); condemned on one count, 1993; executed Nov. 17, 1998
ACCOMPLICES: Roy Dale Green (1948–), served 13 years of 31-year sentence for his part in 1966 triple murder; Alva Hank Worley (1958–), confessed participation in one 1992 kidnapping, granted immunity for turning state's evidence.

McErlane, Frank (d. 1932)
SEX: M   RACE: W   TYPE: T   MOTIVE: CE/PC
DATES(S): 1920–32   VENUE: Chicago, Ill.   VICTIMS: 15+
MO: Psychotic racketeer; introduced the tommy gun to gangland warfare in 1925
DISPOSITION: Died of pneumonia, 1932

McFadden, Jerry Walter (1948–99)
SEX: M   RACE: W   TYPE: T   MOTIVE: Sex.
DATE(S): 1986   VENUE: Hawkins, Tex.   VICTIMS: Three
MO: Serial rapist on parole from multiple convictions when he killed three female victims
DISPOSITION: Executed on one count, Oct. 14, 1999

McFadden, Reginald (1954–)
SEX: M   RACE: Unk.   TYPE: N   MOTIVE: Sex.
DATE(S): 1970/1994   VENUE: Pa./N.Y.   VICTIMS: Four alleged
MO: Rape-slayer of women and one woman's male companion
DISPOSITION: Served 24 years on first murder conviction (1970–94); received two life terms for subsequent slayings, plus consecutive terms for rape and robbery

McGinlay, Joseph (1955–)
SEX: M   RACE: W   TYPE: N   MOTIVE: Sex.
DATES(S): 1973/96   VENUE: Scotland   VICTIMS: Two
MO: Lust killer of females age 16 and 23
DISPOSITION: Life term, 1973 (paroled 1996); life term, 1997

McGinnis, Virginia [See REARDEN, VIRGINIA]

McGown, Dr. Richard (1937–)
SEX: M   RACE: W   TYPE: S   MOTIVE: PC
DATES(S): 1986–92   VENUE: Harare, Zimbabwe   VICTIMS: Five alleged
MO: Overdosed hospital patients with morphine in "experiments"
DISPOSITION: Six-month sentence for two "negligent" deaths, 1995

McGray, Michael Wayne (1964–)
SEX: M   RACE: W   TYPE: N   MOTIVE: Sex/CE/PC
DATE(S): 1983–98   VENUE: Canada/Wash.   VICTIMS: 16 confessed
MO: Drifter who killed victims of both sexes in random violent encounters

DISPOSITION: Convicted of six murders in separate trials across Canada during 2000–01; received concurrent terms of 25 years to life in each case

McGurn, Jack [*See* GIBALDI, VINCENZO]

McKinney, James (1861–1902)
SEX: M   RACE: W   TYPE: N   MOTIVE: CE/Sad.
DATES(S): 1880s–1902   VENUE: Colo./Calif.   VICTIMS: "Several"
MO: Psychopathic outlaw/gunman
DISPOSITION: Killed in shoot-out with authorities, Apr. 18, 1902

McKnight, Anthony (1954–   )
SEX: M   RACE: B   TYPE: T   MOTIVE: Sex.
DATES(S): 1984–86   VENUE: Oakland, Calif.   VICTIMS: Seven suspected
MO: Rape slayer of women, including several prostitutes
DISPOSITION: Never charged with murder; 63 years for rape and attempted murder of six women who survived attacks, 1987

McKoy, Lamon (1988–   )
SEX: M   RACE: W   TYPE: T   MOTIVE: Sex.
DATE(S): 2004   VENUE: Geneva, N.Y.   VICTIMS: Two
MO: Rape-slayer of females age 14 and 18; one victim was his cousin
DISPOSITION: Pleaded guilty and accepted sentence of 20 years to life, Dec. 17, 2004

McLean, Ralph (1966–95)
SEX: M   RACE: ?   TYPE: N   MOTIVE: PC
DATES(S): 1995   VENUE: Md./D.C.   VICTIMS: Two
MO: "Cop hater" who shot lawmen from ambush
DISPOSITION: Killed resisting arrest, May 29, 1995

McManus, Fred (1935–   )
SEX: M   RACE: W   TYPE: N   MOTIVE: CE/PC
DATES(S): 1953   VENUE: N.Y./Ill./Iowa/Minn.   VICTIMS: Five
MO: Thrill-killer of holdup victims in four states
DISPOSITION: Life sentence in N.Y. on one count, 1953

McRae, John Rodney (1935–   )
SEX: M   RACE: ?   TYPE: N   MOTIVE: Sex.
DATES(S): 1950–87   VENUE: Mich./Fla.   VICTIMS: Four suspected
MO: Convicted pedophile slayer of two boys; suspected of two more

DISPOSITION: Served 21 years in Mich. for murder of eight-year-old boy (paroled 1971); convicted on second count in Mich., 1998; life sentence in Fla., Jan. 4, 1999

McSparen, Mildred (d. 1988)
SEX: F   RACE: W   TYPE: S   MOTIVE: PC-nonspecific
DATES(S): 1981   VENUE: Lomax, Ill.   VICTIMS: Two
MO: "Black widow" poisoner of two young children
DISPOSITION: Attempted jailhouse suicide by hanging, Dec. 4, 1981; comatose from hanging until death in hospital from pneumonia, Nov. 4, 1988

Meach, Charles L., III (?–   )
SEX: M   RACE: W   TYPE: T   MOTIVE: PC/CE
DATES(S): 1973–82   VENUE: Anchorage, Alaska   VICTIMS: Five
MO: Bludgeoned man in park; shot four teen campers who caught him stealing from their tent
DISPOSITION: Acquitted on grounds of insanity, 1973; 396 years without parole four counts, 1983

Meade, Harold (1948–   )
SEX: M   RACE: W   TYPE: T   MOTIVE: PC-nonspecific
DATE(S): 1969/1992   VENUE: New Haven, Conn.   VICTIMS: Four suspected
MO: Bludgeon slayer of three mentally retarded youths, suspected of a fourth killing while on work furlough from prison
DISPOSITION: Life term on three counts; no charges filed in fourth case

Meadows, Johnny (1937–   )
SEX: M   RACE: W   TYPE: T   MOTIVE: Sex.
DATES(S): 1968–71   VENUE: Tex.   VICTIMS: Four confessed
MO: Lust killer of adult females
DISPOSITION: 99 years on guilty plea to one count, 1972

Medina, Teofilo, Jr. (1943–   )
SEX: M   RACE: H   TYPE: T   MOTIVE: CE
DATES(S): 1984   VENUE: Orange County, Calif.   VICTIMS: Three
MO: Paroled rapist; shot three young men in holdups
DISPOSITION: Condemned, 1987

Medley, Joseph D. (1903–48)
SEX: M   RACE: W   TYPE: N   MOTIVE: CE
DATES(S): 1940s   VENUE: D.C./Midwest   VICTIMS: Three+ suspected

MO: Robbed/murdered women
DISPOSITION: Executed in Washington, D.C., on one count, Dec. 20, 1948

Medrano, Juan Martin (1955–) AKA: The Jackal
SEX: M RACE: H TYPE: N MOTIVE: CE-felony
DATE(S): 1970s VENUE: U.S./Mexico VICTIMS: 32 confessed
MO: Contract killer for Mexican crime syndicates who admitted 25 murders in Mexico and seven in three U.S. states
DISPOSITION: Life sentence in Texas, 1978, after confessing seven murders in Texas, Alabama, and Mexico; transferred to Mexico in a Dec. 1980 prisoner exchange; released in Mexico, 1984; arrested for drugs in Texas, Dec. 2001; received a life prison term after confessing 25 more slayings, including 23 in Mexico and two in Florida

Meeks, Douglas Ray (1953–)
SEX: M RACE: B TYPE: T MOTIVE: PC
DATES(S): 1974 VENUE: Taylor County, Fla. VICTIMS: Two
MO: Killed two victims in personal disputes
DISPOSITION: Condemned on two counts, 1975

Melton, Antonio Lebaron (1972–)
SEX: M RACE: B TYPE: T MOTIVE: CE
DATES(S): 1990–91 VENUE: Escambia County, Fla. VICTIMS: Two
MO: Killed holdup victims
DISPOSITION: Life term on one count, 1991; condemned on second, 1992

Menarik, Carl (1889–?)
SEX: M RACE: W TYPE: S MOTIVE: PC-nonspecific
DATES(S): 1914 VENUE: Yonkers, N.Y. VICTIMS: Eight confessed
MO: Austrian immigrant, poisoned patients at rest home where he worked
DISPOSITION: Confined to asylum, 1915; escaped 1916; never found

Mendoza, Ivan (1966–)
SEX: M RACE: H TYPE: T MOTIVE: Sex.
DATES(S): 1981–82 VENUE: New York City VICTIMS: Two
MO: Stabbed women during robberies
DISPOSITION: Convicted on both counts, 1983

Mengel, Alex J. (1955–85)
SEX: M RACE: W TYPE: N MOTIVE: Sex./CE
DATES(S): 1985 VENUE: N.Y. VICTIMS: Two

MO: Killed/scalped woman; shot policeman who stopped his car
DISPOSITION: Killed while attempting escape from custody, Apr. 26, 1985

Mengele, Dr. Josef (1911–79?)
SEX: M RACE: W TYPE: S MOTIVE: Sad./PC-extremist
DATES(S): 1943–45 VENUE: Auschwitz, Poland VICTIMS: Dozens
MO: Nazi physician who murdered concentration camp inmates in personal fits of rage, killing others in the course of weird medical experiments; personally ordered execution of hundreds more, including 300 children burned alive in one incident
DISPOSITION: Fled to South America after World War II; allegedly suffered heart attack while swimming and drowned, 1979

Mentzer, William (?–)
SEX: M RACE: W TYPE: T MOTIVE: CE
DATES(S): 1974–88 VENUE: Calif./N.Y./Fla. VICTIMS: Five+ suspected
MO: Contract killer with ties to drug syndicates; also named by DAVID BERKOWITZ as participant in satanic cult murders
DISPOSITION: Life without parole on two counts in Calif., 1991

Menzi, Kurt (1962–)
SEX: M RACE: W TYPE: T MOTIVE: Sex.
DATES(S): 1983–84 VENUE: St. Gallen, Switzerland VICTIMS: Two
MO: Rape-slayer of girls age 10 and 18
DISPOSITION: Life sentence on one count, 1985

Merrett, John Donald (1908–54)
SEX: M RACE: W TYPE: N MOTIVE: CE/PC
DATES(S): 1926/54 VENUE: Scotland/England VICTIMS: Three confessed
MO: Smuggler who killed his mother (1926); later killed his estranged wife and mother-in-law (1954)
DISPOSITION: Acquitted, 1926; suicide by gunshot on Feb. 17, 1954

Mesa, Joseph, Jr. (1980–)
SEX: M RACE: W TYPE: S MOTIVE: CE-felony
DATE(S): 2000–01 VENUE: Washington, D.C. VICTIMS: Two
MO: Deaf student at Gallaudet University, who beat/stabbed two male fellow students, both age 19, in their dormitory rooms during attempted robberies
DISPOSITION: Convicted on two counts in May 2002; received life prison term

Metheny, Joe Roy (1955–)
SEX: M   RACE: W   TYPE: T   MOTIVE: Sex./Sad.
DATES(S): 1976–95   VENUE: Baltimore, Md.   VICTIMS: 10 confessed
MO: Admitted mutilation-murders of men and women
DISPOSITION: Life term on one count, 1997; condemned on second count, 1998; death sentence overturned on appeal, July 2000

Meyer, Thomas (1961–)
SEX: M   RACE: W   TYPE: T   MOTIVE: Sex.
DATES(S): 1986–87   VENUE: Bonna, Germany   VICTIMS: Three
MO: Home invader; killed females age 13–37 and set fires
DISPOSITION: Life sentence on three counts, 1988

Mfeka, Samuel Bongani (?–)
SEX: M   RACE: B   TYPE: T   MOTIVE: Sex.
DATES(S): 1993–96   VENUE: KwaZulu Natal, South Africa   VICTIMS: Six
MO: Rape-slayer of women; also suspect in "NASREC STRANGLER" case
DISPOSITION: Confessed six counts at arrest, Sept. 1996

Middleton, David (1961–)
SEX: M   RACE: B   TYPE: N   MOTIVE: Sex./Sad.
DATES(S): 1993–95   VENUE: Colo./Nev.   VICTIMS: Three
MO: Ex-cop and paroled rapist; sex-slayer of women age 18–45; torture devices found in his home
DISPOSITION: Condemned on two counts in Nev., 1997

Miller, Donald Gene (1955–)
SEX: M   RACE: W   TYPE: T   MOTIVE: Sex.
DATES(S): 1978   VENUE: Lansing, Mich.   VICTIMS: Four confessed
MO: Rapist who killed his fiancée and three other women
DISPOSITION: 30–50 years for rape and attempted murder of surviving victims, 1978; 15 years on plea bargain to voluntary manslaughter, 1979

Miller, George Thaxton (1900–)
SEX: M   RACE: W   TYPE: T   MOTIVE: PC-extremist
DATES(S): 1926   VENUE: Crenshaw County, Ala.   VICTIMS: Two admitted
MO: Ku Klux Klansman; shot black men "in self-defense"
DISPOSITION: Claimed acquittals by all-white juries (records lost)

Miller, Gerald Wesley (1936–)
SEX: M   RACE: W   TYPE: T   MOTIVE: PC-domestic
DATES(S): 1984/89   VENUE: Salem, Ore.   VICTIMS: Two
MO: "Bluebeard" slayer of wives
DISPOSITION: Life term on two counts, 1993

Miller, Hugh (1969–)
SEX: M   RACE: W   TYPE: T   MOTIVE: PC
DATES(S): 1995   VENUE: Burlington City, N.J.   VICTIMS: Three
MO: Shot his mother, ex-girlfriend, and a male acquaintance
DISPOSITION: Three consecutive life terms, 1998

Miller, James B. (1861–1909)   AKA: Killin' Jim
SEX: M   RACE: W   TYPE: N   MOTIVE: PC/CE
DATES(S): 1883–1909   VENUE: Ark./Tex./N. Mex./Okla.   VICTIMS: 40–50 claimed
MO: Gunfighter and hired killer; occasional lawman
DISPOSITION: Lynched in Okla., Apr. 19, 1909

Miller, John Lawrence (1942–)
SEX: M   RACE: W   TYPE: T   MOTIVE: PC-non-specific
DATES(S): 1957/75   VENUE: Los Angeles County, Calif.   VICTIMS: Three
MO: Bludgeoned an infant, 1957; shot his parents, 1975
DISPOSITION: Convicted of murder, 1958 (paroled 1975); life term, 1975

Miller, Joseph D. (1965–)
SEX: M   RACE: W   TYPE: T   MOTIVE: Sex.
DATE(S): 1987–90   VENUE: Dauphin and Perry Counties, Pa.   VICTIMS: Four
MO: Rape-slayer of women discarded at local trash dumps; led police to graves and confessed four slayings after arrested for assault in 1992
DISPOSITION: Condemned on two counts; life term on a third count; death sentence commuted on appeal, Dec. 18, 2002

Miller, Joseph Robert (1954–)
SEX: M   RACE: W   TYPE: T   MOTIVE: Sex.
DATES(S): 1976–77/1993   VENUE: Ill.   VICTIMS: Four
MO: Strangler of prostitutes in Chicago (1970s) and Peoria
DISPOSITION: Served 15 years for first two kills; condemned, 1994; sentence commuted to life, 2003

Miller, Vernon C. (d. 1933)
SEX: M   RACE: W   TYPE: N   MOTIVE: CE

DATES(S): 1925–33   VENUE: Midwest USA   VIC-
TIMS: "Numerous"
MO: War-hero lawman turned contract killer
DISPOSITION: Murdered by gangland associates,
Nov. 28, 1933

Miller, Walter (d. 1870)
SEX: M   RACE: W   TYPE: T   MOTIVE: CE
DATES(S): 1870   VENUE: Chelsea, England   VIC-
TIMS: Two
MO: Robbed/killed elderly victims in their homes
DISPOSITION: Confessed two counts and was hanged

Minghella, Maurizio (?–)   AKA: Strangler of
Valpocevera
SEX: M   RACE: W   TYPE: T   MOTIVE: Sex.
DATES(S): 1978   VENUE: Valpocevera, Italy   VIC-
TIMS: Four
MO: Rape-slayer of young women
DISPOSITION: Life sentence

Minow, Paul (?–?)
SEX: M   RACE: W   TYPE: S   MOTIVE: PC-non-
specific
DATES(S): 1907   VENUE: Berlin, Germany   VIC-
TIMS: Three
MO: Epileptic "ripper" of girls, all under five years old
DISPOSITION: Confessed, Nov. 1907; sentence
unknown

Mirabella, John (1905–55)
SEX: M   RACE: W   TYPE: N   MOTIVE: CE
DATES(S): 1920s–40s   VENUE: Mich./Ohio   VIC-
TIMS: "Numerous"
MO: Alcoholic Mafia hit man
DISPOSITION: Died of cirrhosis, 1955

Mirshekari, Yaghoub Ali (1957–2005)   AKA: Yellow
Scorpion
SEX: M   TYPE: T   MOTIVE: CE-felony
DATE(S): 2003–04   VENUE: Zahedan, Iran   VIC-
TIMS: 10
MO: Shot and stabbed truck drivers, then stole and
sold their trucks
DISPOSITION: Hanged on June 12, 2005; five accom-
plices, all members of his immediate family, were
sentenced to prison for lesser offenses

Mitchell, Jason (1972–)
SEX: M   RACE: W   TYPE: T   MOTIVE: PC-non-
specific
DATE(S): 1995   VENUE: Bramford, England   VIC-
TIMS: Three

MO: Schizophrenic released from mental hospital three
days before he killed a married couple in their home;
later strangled and dismembered his father
DISPOSITION: Life sentence reduced to 10-year minimum on appeal; attempted to strangle fellow
inmate, April 2000

Mitchell, Roy (1892–1923)
SEX: M   RACE: B   TYPE: T   MOTIVE: CE/Sex.
DATES(S): 1909–11   VENUE: Waco, Tex.   VIC-
TIMS: Five confessed
MO: Killed constable with an ax; attacked couples in
lover's lane; at least one rape
DISPOSITION: Hanged July 30, 1923

Mitchell, Tony Garrett (1979–)
SEX: M   RACE: B   TYPE: T   MOTIVE: Sex.
DATE(S): 2002   VENUE: Mt. Pleasant, Tenn.   VIC-
TIMS: Two
MO: Kidnapped and shot three black women, killing
two; bodies dumped within a one-mile radius in
wooded area
DISPOSITION: Pled guilty on two murder counts to
avoid death sentence, Nov. 4, 2002; received two
consecutive life terms; pled guilty on one count of
attempted murder, Jan. 3, 2003

Mmbengwa, David (?–)
SEX: M   RACE: B   TYPE: T   MOTIVE: CE-felony
DATE(S): 1991/1996   VENUE: Pietersburg, South
Africa   VICTIMS: Eight
MO: Armed robber who preyed on couples making
love in wooded areas outside town
DISPOSITION: Convicted of culpable homicide,
December 1991; served four years of a six-year
term; on Aug. 2, 2001 received seven life terms for
murder plus 46 years on various lesser charges

Modeno, Mariano (d. 1878)
SEX: M   RACE: W   TYPE: N   MOTIVE: PC
DATES(S): 1830s–78   VENUE: Rocky Mountains
VICTIMS: 100+
MO: "Mountain man" and "endless killer" of Indians
DISPOSITION: Died of natural causes, 1878

Modzieliewski, Stanislav (?–)
SEX: M   RACE: W   TYPE: T   MOTIVE: Sex.
DATES(S): 1960s   VENUE: Lødz, Poland   VICTIMS:
Seven
MO: "Vampire" slayer of women; six other victims
survived
DISPOSITION: Convicted of seven murders and six
attempted murders, 1969

Moffett, Jessie Ray (1959–98)
SEX: M   RACE: B   TYPE: T   MOTIVE: Sex./CE
DATES(S): 1979/87   VENUE: San Diego, Calif.
  VICTIMS: Two
MO: Bludgeoned young woman (1979); shot security
  guard in holdup
DISPOSITION: Condemned, 1992; died in prison May
  2, 1998

Mofokeng, Sylvester (1972–   )
SEX: M   RACE: W   TYPE: T   MOTIVE: CE
DATES(S): 1990s   VENUE: Johannesburg, South
  Africa   VICTIMS: 13
MO: Escaped inmate with prior murder conviction;
  killed 12 more victims during home invasions while
  at large
DISPOSITION: Life + 70 years for first murder; 10 life
  terms + 145 years, 1997

Molinari, Robert Joseph (1958–   )
SEX: M   RACE: W   TYPE: N   MOTIVE: PC
DATE(S): 1990s   VENUE: United States   VICTIMS:
  More than five suspected
MO: Drifter who stabbed, strangled and bludgeoned
  male acquaintances
DISPOSITION: Life sentence on one count from
  Miami, Fla., on Feb. 11, 2000; charges pending on a
  Pennsylvania case if paroled

Monahan, Annie (?–?)
SEX: F   RACE: W   TYPE: T   MOTIVE: CE
DATES(S): 1906–17   VENUE: New Haven, Conn.
  VICTIMS: Four
MO: "Black widow" poisoner of husbands and niece,
  for insurance
DISPOSITION: Life sentence, 1919

Montgomery, William David (1963–   )
SEX: M   RACE: W   TYPE: T   MOTIVE: Sex.
DATES(S): 1992–93   VENUE: Bensalem Township,
  Pa.   VICTIMS: Two
MO: Bludgeoned a stripper and a prostitute with claw
  hammer
DISPOSITION: Pled guilty and received life term, 1994

Moody, Kenneth (1975–   )
SEX: M   RACE: Unk.   TYPE: T   MOTIVE: PC/Sex
DATE(S): 1995   VENUE: Perry County, Miss.   VIC-
  TIMS: Three
MO: With 14-year-old cousin David Moody, killed a
  27-year-old man, then raped and killed the victim's
  21-year-old girlfriend; later the same month, with
  another cousin, stabbed a male stranger in an
  argument

DISPOSITION: Received life terms without parole on
  two counts, April 2001; Donald Moody received a
  life term on one count, plus five years as an accessory on a second count

Moody, Robert Joe (1959–   )
SEX: M   RACE: W   TYPE: T   MOTIVE: CE
DATE(S): 1993   VENUE: Tucson, Ariz.   VICTIMS:
  Two
MO: Killed and robbed women during home invasions,
  to support drug habit
DISPOSITION: Condemned on two counts, June 1995;
  retried with same result, May 2001; sentence com-
  muted on appeal, Aug. 9, 2004

Moody, Walter Leroy, Jr. (1945–   )
SEX: M   RACE: W   TYPE: N   MOTIVE: PC-
  extremist
DATES(S): 1989   VENUE: Ala./Ga.   VICTIMS: Two
MO: Racist mail bomber; killed a judge and an attorney
DISPOSITION: Life without parole in federal prison;
  condemned in Ala., 1997

Moore, Blanche Taylor (1933–   )
SEX: M   RACE: H   TYPE: T   MOTIVE: PC/CE
DATES(S): 1966–   VENUE: Burlington, N.C.   VIC-
  TIMS: Four
MO: "Black widow" poisoner of father, husband,
  mother-in-law, and boyfriend
DISPOSITION: Condemned, 1991

Moore, Douglas Donald (1967–2004)
SEX: M   RACE: W   TYPE: T   MOTIVE: Sex.
DATE(S): 2003   VENUE: Montreal, Quebec   VIC-
  TIMS: Three
MO: Convicted pedophile, charged with 11 new counts
  of child molestation involving three victims, March
  2004; DNA subsequently linked him to the murders
  of three male victims aged 15–22, found in wooded
  areas around Montreal
DISPOSITION: Suicide in jail, April 2, 2004; links to
  homicides were discovered posthumously

Moore, Ernest (1973–98)
SEX: M   RACE: ?   TYPE: T   MOTIVE: PC/CE
DATES(S): 1998   VENUE: Cameron County, Tex.
  VICTIMS: Four
MO: Shot two women at girlfriend's house; later killed
  two policemen
DISPOSITION: Killed resisting arrest, July 7, 1998

Moore, Henry Lee (?–?)
SEX: M   RACE: W   TYPE: N   MOTIVE: PC-nonspecific

DATE(S): 1911–12   VENUE:
Kans./Ill./Iowa/Colo./Mo.   VICTIMS: 26 suspected
MO: Transient home invader, slaughtered whole families with axes
DISPOSITION: Life sentence in Mo. for ax murder of his mother and grandmother, 1912

Moore, Peter (1940–)
SEX: M   RACE: W   TYPE: T   MOTIVE: PC-nonspecific
DATE(S): 1995   VENUE: North Wales, United Kingdom   VICTIMS: Four
MO: Theater owner and mutilation-slayer of adult males; blamed his crimes on "Jason" from *Friday the 13th* movie series
DISPOSITION: Life term without parole, 1996

Moorehead, Steven (1962–)
SEX: M   RACE: Unk.   TYPE: T   MOTIVE: Sex.
DATE(S): 1990s   VENUE: Steubenville, Ohio   VICTIMS: Six confessed
MO: Shot female victims after sex; admitted six murders, but local sheriff estimated dead at eight
DISPOSITION: Accomplice Fred Horner pleaded guilty to three felony counts and received a three-year sentence, July 2002; prosecutors waived the death penalty for Moorehead in favor of life imprisonment without parole

Moran, Richard Allen (1954–96)
SEX: M   RACE: W   TYPE: T   MOTIVE: CE/PC
DATE(S): 1984–91   VENUE: Las Vegas, Nev.   VICTIMS: Three
MO: Murdered holdup victims and his ex-wife
DISPOSITION: Executed on three counts, March 30, 1996

Morandini, Vitaline (?–)   AKA: Monster of Portoglio
SEX: F   RACE: W   TYPE: T   MOTIVE: PC-nonspecific
DATE(S): 1955–56   VENUE: Portoglio, Italy   VICTIMS: 10
MO: Staged "accidents" for selected victims
DISPOSITION: Convicted; sentence unknown

Moreau, Pierre-Desiré (d. 1874)
SEX: M   RACE: W   TYPE: T   MOTIVE: PC/CE
DATE(S): 1870s   VENUE: Paris, France   VICTIMS: Two
MO: Bluebeard pharmacist who poisoned his wives, the first in order to marry a rich woman, the second for her money
DISPOSITION: Guillotined on Oct. 4, 1874

Morello, Peter (1880–1930)   AKA: The Clutching Hand
SEX: M   RACE: W   TYPE: T   MOTIVE: CE
DATE(S): 1920s   VENUE: New York City   VICTIMS: "Numerous"
MO: Mafia "enforcer" and hit man
DISPOSITION: Killed by a man known only as "BUSTER FROM CHICAGO," 1930

Morgan, Daniel (1830–65)   AKA: Mad Dan; Mad Dog
SEX: M   RACE: W   TYPE: N   MOTIVE: CE-felony
DATE(S): 1863–65   VENUE: Australia   VICTIMS: Three
MO: Bandit who shot policemen and suspected informers
DISPOSITION: Ambushed and killed by police on April 9, 1865

Morgan, John (d. 1869)   AKA: Mad Mose
SEX: M   RACE: W   TYPE: N   MOTIVE: PC/Sad.
DATE(S): 1840s–69   VENUE: Rocky Mountains   VICTIMS: 100+
MO: Revenge-motivated slayer of Indians; enjoyed dismembering his victims while they lived
DISPOSITION: Killed in battle with Indians, 1869

Morris, Major, Jr. (1954–)
SEX: M   RACE: W   TYPE: N   MOTIVE: Sex.
DATE(S): 1972–76   VENUE: Ill.   VICTIMS: Six suspected
MO: Lust killer of girls age 15–18
DISPOSITION: Confessed one murder; 100–200 years, 1996

Morris, Cory (1978–)
SEX: M   RACE: W   TYPE: S   MOTIVE: Sex
DATE(S): 2002–03   VENUE: Phoenix, Ariz.   VICTIMS: 5–6
MO: Strangled female victims during sex at his home, then dumped bodies nearby. Caught when a relative smelled a corpse in his trailer.
DISPOSITION: Condemned on five counts, July 19, 2005. No charge filed in a sixth suspected case.

Morris, Raymond Leslie (1929–)   AKA: Monster of Cannock Chase
SEX: M   RACE: W   TYPE: T   MOTIVE: Sex.
DATE(S): 1965–67   VENUE: England   VICTIMS: Four suspected
MO: Pedophile who strangled girls age five to 10
DISPOSITION: Life sentence on one count, 1969

Mors, Frederick [*See* MENARIK, CARL]

Morse, Hugh Bion (1930–   )
SEX: M   RACE: W   TYPE: N   MOTIVE: Sex.
DATE(S): 1959–61   VENUE: Wash./Ala./Minn.
   VICTIMS: Four
MO: Rape-slayer of women age 28–69; also molested
   children
DISPOSITION: Double life term in Minn., 1961

Morse, Joseph (?–   )
SEX: M   RACE: ?   TYPE: T   MOTIVE: PC-nonspe-
cific
DATE(S): 1960s   VENUE: Calif.   VICTIMS: Three
MO: Killed mother, sister, and stranger selected at ran-
dom
DISPOSITION: Condemned (commuted to life, 1972)

Moseley, Carl Stephen (1966–   )
SEX: M   RACE: W   TYPE: T   MOTIVE: Sex.
DATE(S): 1991   VENUE: Stokes/Forsyth Counties,
   N.C.   VICTIMS: Two
MO: Raped/stabbed women age 35 and 38
DISPOSITION: Condemned, 1993

Moseley, Eddie Lee (1947–   )
SEX: M   RACE: B   TYPE: N   MOTIVE: Sex.
DATE(S): 1973–87   VENUE: Florida   VICTIMS: 12+
alleged
MO: Rape slayer of females aged eight to 54, linked to
   various murders and nonlethal rapes by DNA evidence
DISPOSITION: Confined to state hospital as a dangerous offender since 1988; ruled incompetent for trial
   on murder charges, Nov. 20, 2001

Moseley, Winston (1935–   )
SEX: M   RACE: B   TYPE: T   MOTIVE: PC-nonspe-
cific
DATE(S): 1963–64   VENUE: Queens, N.Y.   VIC-
TIMS: Three confessed
MO: Thrill-killer of females age 15–29
DISPOSITION: Condemned on one count, 1964 (com-
   muted to life, 1972)

Motto, Alberto (?–   )   AKA: Monster of Vimercate
SEX: M   RACE: W   TYPE: T   MOTIVE: Sex.
DATE(S): 1992–95   VENUE: Vimercate, Italy   VIC-
TIMS: "Several"
MO: Confessed 11 sexual assaults; "several" victims
   strangled
DISPOSITION: Pled guilty; sentence unknown

Mount, Kenneth Eugene (?–   )
SEX: M   RACE: W   TYPE: T   MOTIVE: CE

DATE(S): 1985/88   VENUE: Bakersfield, Calif.   VIC-
TIMS: Three charged
MO: Shot/stabbed/bludgeoned men age 29–73, in their
   homes
DISPOSITION: Life without parole on one count, 1989

Msomi, Elifasi (d. 1956)   AKA: Axe Killer
SEX: M   RACE: B   TYPE: T   MOTIVE: Sad./PC-
nonspecific
DATE(S): 1950s   VENUE: Natal, South Africa   VIC-
TIMS: 15
MO: Hacked victims to death, allegedly on orders of
   tokoloshe spirit that possessed him
DISPOSITION: Hanged, Jan. 1956

Msundwana, Mtimane (d. 1937)   AKA: Loskop Killer
SEX: M   RACE: B   TYPE: T   MOTIVE: PC/CE
DATE(S): 1929–36   VENUE: Natal, South Africa
   VICTIMS: Eight confessed
MO: Shotgun slayer of merchants, mostly Indian
DISPOSITION: Hanged, 1937

Mudgett, Herman Webster (1860–96)   AKA: Henry
   Howard Holmes
SEX: M   RACE: W   TYPE: N   MOTIVE:
CE/Sex./Sad.
DATE(S): 1869–95   VENUE: N.H./Ill.   VICTIMS: 27
confessed
MO: Suspected of killing childhood playmate; later
   medical student and career criminal specializing in
   insurance scams; constructed boarding house in
   Chicago, robbing/killing various tenants (mostly
   female), selling some corpses to medical schools for
   dissection; estimates of final body count range from
   50 to 200+
DISPOSITION: Hanged in Ill., May 7, 1896

Mughal, Muhammad Sarwar (?–   )
SEX: M   RACE: A   TYPE: T   MOTIVE: PC-extremist
DATE(S): 2002–03   VENUE: Gujranwala, India
   VICTIMS: Three confessed
MO: Religious fanatic who murdered female prosti-
   tutes in protest of police inaction against vice
DISPOSITION: Unknown

Mukhankin, Vladimir (1960–   )
SEX: M   RACE: W   TYPE: T   MOTIVE: Sex.
DATE(S): 1995–96   VENUE: Rostov-on-Don, Russia
   VICTIMS: Eight
MO: Lust killer of women
DISPOSITION: Condemned after guilty plea, 1997

Mu'Min, Dawud Majid (1952–97)
SEX: M   RACE: B   TYPE: N   MOTIVE: CE/Sex.

DATE(S): 1973/88   VENUE: Va.   VICTIMS: Two
MO: Killed cab driver in holdup; raped/stabbed woman
DISPOSITION: 48-year sentence, 1973 (escaped 1988); condemned, 1989; executed Nov. 13, 1997

Murdock, Kenneth (1963)
SEX: M   RACE: W   TYPE: T   MOTIVE: CE
DATE(S): 1985–97   VENUE: Ontario, Canada   VICTIMS: Three+
MO: Contract killer for Canadian Mafia family
DISPOSITION: Life term with 13-year minimum on three counts, 1998

Murphy, Charles (1887–?)
SEX: M   RACE: W   TYPE: N   MOTIVE: CE
DATE(S): 1921/30   VENUE: Wash.   VICTIMS: Two
MO: Bludgeoned/robbed employer (1921); murdered wife (1930)
DISPOSITION: Confessed wife's murder; 60–75 years, 1931

Murphy, Donald (1944–   )
SEX: M   RACE: B   TYPE: T   MOTIVE: Sex.
DATE(S): 1980   VENUE: Detroit, Mich.   VICTIMS: Five confessed
MO: Lust killer of black prostitutes
DISPOSITION: Pled guilty on two counts, 1982; two concurrent 30-year terms

Murrell, John A. (1794–?)
SEX: M   RACE: W   TYPE: T   MOTIVE: CE
DATE(S): c. 1815–35   VENUE: Southern USA   VICTIMS: 500+
MO: Southern planter who stole/resold slaves, killing hundreds in the process; victims often disemboweled and weighted with stones, then sunk in rivers; also plotted slave revolt as diversion for looting of major southern cities
DISPOSITION: Served 10 years in Tenn. for fomenting slave revolt, c. 1835–45

Myers, Karl Lee (1957–   )
SEX: M   RACE: W   TYPE: N   MOTIVE: Sex./CE
DATE(S): 1976–96   VENUE: Kans./Okla.   VICTIMS: Five suspected
MO: Rape-slayer of women; self-described contract killer
DISPOSITION: Condemned on one count, 1998

Myrtel, Hera [See BESSARABO, MARIE-LOUISE]

Najma
SEX: M   RACE: A   TYPE: T   MOTIVE: Sex.

DATE(S): 1999–2000   VENUE: Takhar, Afghanistan   VICTIMS: Three
MO: Kidnapped and raped four women, killing three
DISPOSITION: Hanged on Aug. 27, 2000

Nance, Wayne Nathan (1955–85)
SEX: M   RACE: W   TYPE: T   MOTIVE: Sex./Sad.
DATE(S): 1974–86   VENUE: Mont.   VICTIMS: Six suspected
MO: Shot/stabbed females age 15–39
DISPOSITION: Fatally shot during home invasion, Sept. 4, 1986

Napoletano, Eric Ernest (1965–   )
SEX: M   RACE: W   TYPE: N   MOTIVE: Sex./Sad.
DATE(S): 1984–90   VENUE: Pa./N.Y./Del.   VICTIMS: Three alleged
MO: Prime suspect in mutilation-slaying of his 15-year-old girlfriend; shot his mother-in-law; murdered his second wife
DISPOSITION: Convicted of wife's murder in Delaware, received a 35-year prison term on June 25, 1993; pleaded guilty to second-degree murder in New York on condition that conspiracy charges filed against his mother were dismissed; received a consecutive term of 15 years to life on June 20, 1996

Nash, Stephen A. (?–   )
SEX: M   RACE: W   TYPE: N   MOTIVE: Sex./Sad.
DATE(S): 1950s   VENUE: Los Angeles, Calif.   VICTIMS: 11 confessed
MO: Stabbed random victims, children and adults
DISPOSITION: Condemned on two counts, 1957

Nash, Viva Leroy (1916–   )
SEX: M   RACE: W   TYPE: N   MOTIVE: CE
DATE(S): 1977/82   VENUE: Utah/Ariz.   VICTIMS: Two
MO: Killed holdup victims
DISPOSITION: Two terms of five years to life for murder/robbery in Utah, 1978 (escaped 1982); condemned in Ariz., 1983

Nassar, George (1932–   )
SEX: M   RACE: A   TYPE: T   MOTIVE: PC/CE
DATE(S): 1948/1964   VENUE: Mass.   VICTIMS: Two
MO: Shot a Lawrence store clerk at age 15; later shot a gas station attendant and attempted to kill two female bystanders, age 32; also considered a prime suspect in the "Boston Strangler" murders
DISPOSITION: Confined as a juvenile for first murder, 1948–61; admitted to state hospital for the criminally insane in October 1964

Natale, Ralph (1934–)
SEX: M   RACE: W   TYPE: T   MOTIVE: CE-felony
DATE(S): 1970s–1990s   VENUE: Philadelphia, Pa.
   VICTIMS: Seven confessed
MO: Mafia soldier and later boss who killed criminal
   rivals
DISPOSITION: Pleaded guilty on seven murder counts
   and other felonies, May 5, 2000; received life term
   and a $250,000 fine

Ncama, Nicholas Lungisa (1968–)
SEX: M   RACE: B   TYPE: T   MOTIVE: Sex./CE-
felony
DATE(S): 1996–97   VENUE: Port Elizabeth, South
   Africa   VICTIMS: Four alleged
MO: Serial rapist of females, including his teenage
   stepdaughter, and murderer of victims aged 15–26
DISPOSITION: Convicted on three of four murder
   charges, plus one rape, one attempted rape, and one
   indecent assault; received three life terms plus 42
   years on Dec. 18, 1998

Ndlangamandla, Velaphi (1966–)   AKA: Saloon
Killer
SEX: M   RACE: B   TYPE: T   MOTIVE: CE/Sex.
DATE(S): 1998   VENUE: Piet Retief, South Africa
   VICTIMS: 19
MO: Armed robber who killed victims and raped at least
   one, during a five-month series of home invasions
DISPOSITION: Received a 137-year prison term on
   Sept. 18, 2002, on charges including 19 murder
   counts, nine attempted murders, six robberies, five
   housebreakings, two firearms violations, one
   attempted robbery, and one indecent assault

Neal, William Lee "Cody" (1956–)
SEX: M   RACE: W   TYPE: T   MOTIVE: Sex./Sad.
DATE(S): 1998   VENUE: Denver, Colo.   VICTIMS:
   Three
MO: Rape-slayer of three women tortured and killed
   with an ax, while a fourth victim was forced to
   watch
DISPOSITION: Condemned in 1999, after pleading
   guilty to three counts of murder, three sexual
   assaults, and seven other counts, including kidnapping and felony menacing; sentence commuted to
   life on appeal, Dec. 2003

Neilson, Donald (1937–)   AKA: Black Panther
SEX: M   RACE: W   TYPE: N   MOTIVE: CE
DATE(S): 1974–75   VENUE: England   VICTIMS:
   Four

MO: Armed robber and kidnappers; shot three postal
   employees and "accidentally" killed teenage kidnap
   victim
DISPOSITION: Five life terms, 1976

Nelson, George [*See* GILLIS, LESTER]

Nemechek, Francis (1951–)
SEX: M   RACE: W   TYPE: T   MOTIVE: Sex.
DATE(S): 1974–76   VENUE: Graham/Trego coun-
   ties., Kans.   VICTIMS: Five
MO: Rape-slayer of females age 16–21; also killed
   three-year-old boy
DISPOSITION: Five consecutive life terms, 1977

Neu, Kenneth (1910–35)
SEX: M   RACE: W   TYPE: N   MOTIVE: CE
DATE(S): 1933   VENUE: N.Y./La.   VICTIMS: Two
MO: Gay drifter; robbed/killed two male sex partners
DISPOSITION: Hanged in N.Y., Feb. 1, 1935

Neumann, Alwin (?–)
SEX: M   RACE: W   TYPE: T   MOTIVE: Sex./PC-
argument
DATE(S): 1983–87   VENUE: Kiel, Germany   VIC-
TIMS: Four
MO: Strangled women age 19–40, including three
   prostitutes at the same brothel (1983–86), after they
   "insulted" him
DISPOSITION: Life sentence, 1998

Neuschafer, Jimmy (1953–98)
SEX: M   RACE: W   TYPE: T   MOTIVE: Sex./PC
DATE(S): 1976/?   VENUE: Carson City, Nev.   VIC-
TIMS: Three
MO: Rape-slayer of teenage girls; strangled prison
   inmate
DISPOSITION: Two consecutive life terms for rape-
   murders; condemned for murder in prison; executed
   July 26, 1998

Newman, Sarah Jane (1813–?)   AKA: Sally Skull
SEX: F   RACE: W   TYPE: T   MOTIVE: PC-domestic
DATE(S): c. 1830–64   VENUE: Tex.   VICTIMS: Five
MO: "Black widow" slayer of husbands
DISPOSITION: Disappeared with latest husband, 1867

Nickell, Stella Maudine (1944–)
SEX: F   RACE: W   TYPE: T   MOTIVE: CE
DATE(S): 1986   VENUE: King County, Wash.   VIC-
TIMS: Two
MO: Inspired by Ill. "TYLENOL MURDERS," poisoned
   husband for insurance, also total stranger to divert
   police suspicion

DISPOSITION: 90-year terms on each of two murder counts; concurrent 10-year terms on three counts of product tampering

Nicolai, Anne M. (1963–)
SEX: F   RACE: W   TYPE: T   MOTIVE: PC-nonspecific
DATE(S): 1999–2000   VENUE: Saginaw, Mich.
MO: Nurse, hospitalized five times for psychiatric treatment, who confessed killing three elderly patients with morphine
DISPOSITION: Prosecutor waived charges in April 2001, despite confession

Nicolaus, Robert Henry (1933–)
SEX: M   RACE: W   TYPE: T   MOTIVE: PC-domestic
DATE(S): 1964/85   VENUE: Sacramento, Calif.   VICTIMS: Four
MO: Shot his children, age two to seven (1964) and ex-wife (1985)
DISPOSITION: Condemned on three counts, 1964 (reduced to life on appeal, 1967; paroled 1977); condemned 1987

Nicoletti, Charles (1916–77)
SEX: M   RACE: W   TYPE: T   MOTIVE: CE/PC
DATE(S): 1940s–77   VENUE: Chicago, Ill.   VICTIMS: "At least 40"
MO: Mafia enforcer and hit man
DISPOSITION: Fatally wounded by unknown gunmen, Mar. 30, 1977

Nisby, Marcus [*See* PLAYER, MICHAEL]

Nixon, Robert (1920–39)   AKA: Brick Moron
SEX: M   RACE: W   TYPE: N   MOTIVE: PC-nonspecific
DATE(S): 1936–38   VENUE: Chicago/Los Angeles   VICTIMS: Five
MO: Victims bludgeoned with bricks in their homes or hotel rooms
DISPOSITION: Executed in Ill., June 1939

Nobles, Jonathan Wayne (1962–)
SEX: M   RACE: W   TYPE: T   MOTIVE: Sex.
DATE(S): 1986   VENUE: Tex.   VICTIMS: Two
MO: Stabbed women
DISPOSITION: Condemned

Noe, Marie (1929–)
SEX: F   RACE: W   TYPE: S   MOTIVE: PC-nonspecific
DATE(S): 1946–68   VENUE: Kensington, Pa.   VICTIMS: 8–10

MO: Mother whose 10 children died sequentially before attaining 15 months of age; eight cases subsequently blamed on suffocation; two cases remain uncertain
DISPOSITION: Pleaded guilty on eight counts, June 28, 1999; received 20 years probation beginning with five years house arrest; violated probation in November 2000; close supervision extended indefinitely

Nolan, Dempsey, Jr. (1967–)
SEX: M   RACE: B   TYPE: N   MOTIVE: CE
DATE(S): 1996–97   VENUE: Ind./Calif.   VICTIMS: Five suspected
MO: Slayer of male robbery victims
DISPOSITION: Life term with 25-year minimum on one count in Calif., 1997

Norio Nagayama (1949–97)
SEX: M   RACE: A   TYPE: N   MOTIVE: CE
DATE(S): 1968   VENUE: Japan   VICTIMS: Four
MO: Killed robbery victims
DISPOSITION: Executed Aug. 1997

Norris, Melissa (?–)
SEX: F   RACE: W   TYPE: T   MOTIVE: PC-nonspecific
DATE(S): 197?/86   VENUE: Gaithersburg, Md.   VICTIMS: Three confessed
MO: Set house fire that killed mother and brother; bludgeoned infant son in "exorcism" ritual
DISPOSITION: Escaped punishment on grounds of temporary insanity

Nuss, Ralph (?–)
SEX: M   RACE: W   TYPE: N   MOTIVE: Sex.
DATE(S): 1966   VENUE: Mich./Ohio   VICTIMS: Two confessed; three suspected
MO: Psychiatric social worker and gay necrophile slayer of male sex partners
DISPOSITION: Life sentence on two counts, in Mich.

Oates, Reginald Vernon (1950–)
SEX: M   RACE: W   TYPE: T   MOTIVE: Sex./Sad.
DATE(S): 1968   VENUE: Baltimore, Md.   VICTIMS: Four
MO: Cannibal pedophile, bludgeoned four boys age five to 10, mutilating bodies and drinking their blood
DISPOSITION: Declared insane; confined to state hospital

O'Bannion, Charles Dion (1892–1924)
SEX: M   RACE: W   TYPE: T   MOTIVE: CE/Sad.

DATE(S): 1920–24   VENUE: Chicago, Ill.   VICTIMS: 25–60
MO: Sadistic bootlegger and racketeer
DISPOSITION: Murdered by rival mobsters, Nov. 10, 1924

Obremski, Russell Loren (1945–   )
SEX: M   RACE: W   TYPE: T   MOTIVE: PC
DATE(S): 1969   VENUE: Jackson County, Ore.
   VICTIMS: Two
MO: Killed two women during a violent drug binge
DISPOSITION: Received two consecutive life terms, 1969; paroled 1993; parole revoked 1994

O'Connor, Raymond (1938–67)   AKA: Ducky
SEX: M   RACE: W   TYPE: T   MOTIVE: CE-felony
DATE(S): 1960s   VENUE: Sydney, Australia   VICTIMS: More than six
MO: Underworld contract killer
DISPOSITION: Shot by gangland rivals, May 26, 1967

Odell, Diane (1953–   )
SEX: M   RACE: W   TYPE: S   MOTIVE: PC-non-specific
DATE(S): 1982–85   VENUE: Kauneonga Lake, N.Y.
   VICTIMS: Three
MO: Mother who killed her infant children at home; hid mummified remains in a storage shed
DISPOSITION: Convicted on three counts of second-degree murder, Dec. 6, 2003; received prison term of 25 years to life, Jan. 27, 2004

Oken, Steven Howard (1962–   )
SEX: M   RACE: W   TYPE: N   MOTIVE: Sex.
DATE(S): 1987   VENUE: Md./Maine
   VICTIMS:Three
MO: Lust killer of women age 20–43
DISPOSITION: Life without parole in Maine, 1988; condemned in Md.

Okev, Daniel (?–   )   AKA: Negev Desert Psychopath
SEX: M   RACE: W   TYPE: T   MOTIVE: PC-non-specific
DATE(S): 1997   VENUE: Negev Desert, Israel   VICTIMS: Several
MO: Former Israeli soldier who blamed multiple personality disorder for his shooting of two foreign tourists (killing one); named as prime suspect in a series of local rape-murders
DISPOSITION: Received a 20-year sentence for one murder and one attempted murder, May 3, 1999

Olson, Clifford Robert (1940–   )
SEX: M   RACE: W   TYPE: T   MOTIVE: Sex./Sad.

DATE(S): 1980–81   VENUE: British Columbia, Canada   VICTIMS: 11
MO: Stabbed/bludgeoned victims of both sexes, age nine to 18
DISPOSITION: 11 life terms, 1982

O'Neal, Robert Earl, Jr. (1961–95)
SEX: M   RACE: W   TYPE: T   MOTIVE: CE/PC-extremist
DATE(S): 1978/84   VENUE: Mo.   VICTIMS: Two
MO: Neo-Nazi; killed elderly man in burglary; stabbed black prison inmate
DISPOSITION: Life term on first count; condemned, 1983; executed Dec. 6, 1995

O'Neall, Darren Dee (1960–   )
SEX: M   RACE: W   TYPE: N   MOTIVE: Sex.
DATE(S): 1987   VENUE: Wash./Idaho/Utah   VICTIMS: Six+ suspected
MO: Transient rape-slayer of young women
DISPOSITION: 27 years with 18.5-year minimum on one count, in Wash., 1989

Orpinelli, Larete Patrocinio (1952–   )
SEX: M   RACE: H   TYPE: N   MOTIVE: Sex./Sad.
DATE(S): 1993–2000   VENUE: Eastern Brazil   VICTIMS: 10
MO: Pedophile with long history of psychiatric treatment, 1967–93; slayer of children aged 5–11
DISPOSITION: Confessed 10 murders; disposition unknown

Outlaw, Bass (d. 1894)
SEX: M   RACE: W   TYPE: N   MOTIVE: PC
DATE(S): 1880s–94   VENUE: Ga./Tex.   VICTIMS: "Several"
MO: Alcoholic lawman who became "homicidal maniac" when drunk
DISPOSITION: Killed in shoot-out with JOHN SELMAN, Apr. 5, 1894

Owens, John F. (?–   )
SEX: M   RACE: Unk.   TYPE: T   MOTIVE: Sex.
DATE(S): 1999–2000   VENUE: Rochester, N.Y.
   VICTIMS: Two
MO: Kidnapped and raped four women, killing two
DISPOSITION: Received life term without parole on two counts of murder and one count of rape, May 2001; convicted of another nonfatal rape in September 2001

Pace, Lyndon Fitzgerald (?–   )
SEX: M   RACE: Unk.   TYPE: T   MOTIVE: Sex.

DATE(S): 1988–89   VENUE: Atlanta, Ga.   VICTIMS: Four
MO: Rape-slayer of women aged 42–56
DISPOSITION: Condemned on four counts, March 1996

Padhi, Maheshwar (1973–)   AKA: Stoneman
SEX: M   RACE: A   TYPE: T   MOTIVE: Unknown
DATE(S): 1999   VENUE: Berhampur, India   VICTIMS: Seven
MO: Killed seven victims in four months, crushing their skulls with stones
DISPOSITION: Unknown

Palmer, Dr. William (1824–56)
SEX: M   RACE: W   TYPE: T   MOTIVE: CE/PC
DATE(S): 1890s–1908   VENUE: Staffordshire, England   VICTIMS: 13+
MO: Poisoner of relatives and acquaintances
DISPOSITION: Hanged June 14, 1856

Panchenko, Dr. Dimitri (?–?)
SEX: M   RACE: W   TYPE: T   MOTIVE: CE
DATE(S): 1890s–1911   VENUE: Russia   VICTIMS: "Several"
MO: Physician who disposed of unwanted relatives for a price
DISPOSITION: 15 years on one count, 1911

Parker, Calvin (1969–)
SEX: M   RACE: Unk.   TYPE: T   MOTIVE: Sex./Sad.
DATE(S): 2000   VENUE: San Diego, Calif.   VICTIMS: Two alleged
MO: Raped, tortured and dismembered 29-year-old female roommate; prime suspect in the mutilation-murder of a 30-year-old woman found burned on a downtown streetcorner
DISPOSITION: Condemned on one count, Aug. 12, 2002

Parker, Gerald (1955–)   AKA: Bedroom Basher
SEX: M   RACE: B   TYPE: T   MOTIVE: Sex.
DATE(S): 1978–79   VENUE: Orange County, Calif.   VICTIMS: Six
MO: Home-invading rapist; bludgeoned females age 17–31, also killing a pregnant sixth victim's full-term fetus
DISPOSITION: Confessed to rape, 1996; convicted on six murder counts, Oct. 1998; condemned, 1999

Parker, Norman, Jr. (1944–)
SEX: M   RACE: B   TYPE: N   MOTIVE: PC/CE

DATE(S): 1966/78   VENUE: Fla./D.C.   VICTIMS: Three
MO: Stabbed teenage boy; shot one man in drug rip-off and another barroom argument
DISPOSITION: Life term in Fla., 1966 (escaped 1978); life on second count in D.C., 1979; condemned on third count in Fla. + multiple life terms for robbery and rape, 1981

Parker, Robert Lee (?–)
SEX: M   RACE: W   TYPE: N   MOTIVE: PC-non-specific
DATE(S): 1995–96   VENUE: Ga./Wash.   VICTIMS: Four suspected
MO: Killed female neighbors and set fire to their apartments; also shot a male motorist chosen at random
DISPOSITION: Received life term without parole on two counts in Washington on Feb. 13, 1999

Parks, Larry James (1954–)
SEX: M   RACE: W   TYPE: T   MOTIVE: PC
DATE(S): 1996–99   VENUE: Manatee County, Fla.   VICTIMS: Four
MO: Murdered a 35-year-old woman and her two daughters, aged four and seven; suspected in the fatal shooting of a man at his home
DISPOSITION: Three life prison terms

Paul, James Allen (?–)
SEX: M   RACE: W   TYPE: N   MOTIVE: PC/CE
DATE(S): 1984   VENUE: N.J./Conn./Vt.   VICTIMS: Three
MO: Shot two women and a 45-year-old man in separate incidents; at least one victim robbed
DISPOSITION: Life with 30-year minimum on guilty plea to one count in N.J., 1984

Pavlovich, Milka (d. 1935)
SEX: M   RACE: W   TYPE: T   MOTIVE: PC-domestic
DATE(S): 1935   VENUE: Belovar, Yugoslavia   VICTIMS: Six
MO: "Black widow" poisoner of husband and other relatives
DISPOSITION: Hanged, May 1935

Payne, Eric Christopher (1973–)
SEX: M   RACE: W   TYPE: T   MOTIVE: Sex./CE
DATE(S): 1997   VENUE: Henrico County, Va.   VICTIMS: Two
MO: Women age 51 and 63 raped/bludgeoned/robbed in their homes
DISPOSITION: Twice condemned, 1997–98

Peace, Charles Frederick (1832–79)
SEX: M   RACE: W   TYPE: T   MOTIVE: CE-felony
DATE(S): 1876   VENUE: Sheffield, England   VIC-
TIMS: Two
MO: Burglar who killed a woman in her home; in cus-
tody, he confessed the slaying of a policeman three
months earlier
DISPOSITION: Hanged on Feb. 25, 1879

Peeler, Russell, Jr. (1972–   )
SEX: M   RACE: Unk.   TYPE: T   MOTIVE: CE
DATE(S): 1998   VENUE: Bridgeport, Conn.   VIC-
TIMS: Three
MO: Killed a man in drug dispute, May 1998; subse-
quently killed a woman and her daughter scheduled
to testify in that case
DISPOSITION: Received a 105-year prison term on
one count, December 1999

Peete, Lofie Louise Preslar (d. 1947)
SEX: F   RACE: W   TYPE: N   MOTIVE: CE-felony
DATE(S): 1910–44   VENUE: Tex./Calif.   VICTIMS:
Five
MO: Profit-motivated slayer of husband, lovers,
coworker and employer
DISPOSITION: Acquitted of first killing on plea of
self-defense; received life prison term for second
murder, January 1921; paroled 1939; executed on
April 11, 1947

Peiry, Michel (1959–   )
SEX: M   RACE: W   TYPE: N   MOTIVE: Sex./Sad.
DATE(S): 1981–87   VENUE: Fla./Switzerland   VIC-
TIMS: Three
MO: Gay lust killer of teenage boys; bodies burned
DISPOSITION: Declared insane and confined to asy-
lum, 1988

Pekalski, Leszek (?–   )
SEX: M   RACE: W   TYPE: T   MOTIVE: Sex.
DATE(S): 1984–92   VENUE: Poland   VICTIMS: 70
confessed
MO: Random slayer; attacked victims of both sexes
DISPOSITION: Convicted on one count, 1996; sen-
tenced to 25 years in psychiatric institution

Pennell, Steven Brian (1957–92)   AKA: Corridor
Killer
SEX: M   RACE: W   TYPE: T   MOTIVE: Sex./Sad.
DATE(S): 1987–88   VENUE: New Castle County,
Del.   VICTIMS: Five
MO: Torture-slayer of female prostitutes
DISPOSITION: Executed Mar. 14, 1992

Penton, David Elliott (1958–   )
SEX: M   RACE: Unk.   TYPE: N   MOTIVE: Sex.
DATE(S): 1985–88   VENUE: Tex./Ohio   VICTIMS:
Four alleged
MO: Pedophile slayer of girls aged 4–9
DISPOSITION: Life prison term in Ohio for one mur-
der committed in 1988; trial pending on three
counts in Texas

Peoples, Louis James (1962–   )
SEX: M   RACE: Unk.   TYPE: T   MOTIVE: CE-
felony
DATE(S): 1997   VENUE: Stockton, Calif.   VIC-
TIMS: Four
MO: Stole pistol and badge from a policeman, used the
gun in a series of armed robberies and killed four
male victims aged 29–56
DISPOSITION: Condemned on four murder counts,
June 6, 2000

Pereira, Francisco de Assis (1967–   )   AKA: Park
Maniac
SEX: M   RACE: H   TYPE: T   MOTIVE: Sex.
DATE(S): 1998   VENUE: São Paulo, Brazil   VIC-
TIMS: 11
MO: Rape-slayer of petite brunette females who lured
victims by posing as a fashion photographer
DISPOSITION: Erroneous media report of Dec. 18,
2000 claimed Pereira was killed by fellow inmates
while awaiting trial; convicted on 11 murder counts
in three separate trials, 2001–02, receiving a total of
268 years in prison

Perkins, Reginald W. (?–   )
SEX: M   RACE: Unk.   TYPE: N   MOTIVE: Sex./PC
DATE(S): 1982/2000   VENUE: Ohio/Tex.   VIC-
TIMS: Two suspected
MO: Serial rapist suspected of killing one teenage victim's mother; later robbed and strangled his stepmother
DISPOSITION: Received life term plus 6–25 years, all
concurrent, for raping an Ohio minor in 1982;
paroled February 2000; condemned for his stepmother's murder, March 19, 2002

Perry, Calvin, III (1965–84)
SEX: M   RACE: B   TYPE: T   MOTIVE: Sex./Sad.
DATE(S): 1983   VENUE: Ft. Wayne, Ind.   VICTIMS:
Five suspected
MO: Rapist home invader; bludgeoned victims age
11–78
DISPOSITION: Confessed prior to jailhouse suicide,
Jan. 1984

Perry, George W. E. (1892–1950)
SEX: M   RACE: W   TYPE: N   MOTIVE: CE
DATE(S): 1929–30   VENUE: Wis./Calif./La./Maine
   VICTIMS: Four
MO: "Bluebeard" slayer of wives for profit
DISPOSITION: Life term in Wisc., 1931; died in
   prison, Mar. 1950

Pesquet, Bernard (1922–)
SEX: M   RACE: W   TYPE: S   MOTIVE: CE
DATE(S): 1941/74–76   VENUE: Rouen/Paris, France
   VICTIMS: Six
MO: Bludgeoned man in robbery, 1941; killed victims
   for profit, 1974–76, cementing corpses inside stair-
   case of his home
DISPOSITION: Life term, 1956 (paroled 1961); life
   term, 1984

Peters, Damien Anthony (1969–)
SEX: M   RACE: W   TYPE: S   MOTIVE: PC-revenge
DATE(S): 2001   VENUE: Perth, Australia   VIC-
   TIMS: Two
MO: Dismembered gay lovers aged 27 and 50 at his
   flat following his HIV-positive diagnosis
DISPOSITION: Life prison term, December 2002

Peterson, Christopher Dwayne (1968–)
SEX: M   RACE: B   TYPE: T   MOTIVE: PC
DATE(S): 1990   VENUE: Porter/Lake Counties., Ind.
   VICTIMS: Seven confessed
MO: Shotgun slayer of white victims in random attacks
DISPOSITION: Condemned on four counts, 1991–92
ACCOMPLICE: Ronald J. Harris (1969–) convicted
   in 1991 as shooter in one of seven murders and
   accomplice in a second

Peterson, Davie Elliott (1958–)
SEX: M   RACE: W   TYPE: N   MOTIVE: Sex.
DATE(S): 1988–97   VENUE: Ohio/Tex.   VICTIMS:
   Four suspected
MO: Drifter who kidnapped and murdered children
DISPOSITION: Life term in Ohio for the 1988 murder
   of a nine-year-old girl; trial pending in Texas on three
   murder counts, including a three-year-old victim

Petrov, Dr. Maxim (1964–)
SEX: M   RACE: W   TYPE: T   MOTIVE: CE-felony
DATE(S): 2000–02   VENUE: St. Petersburg, Russia
   VICTIMS: Ten
MO: Physician who drugged 50 elderly victims before
   looting their apartment, killing those who awoke
   prematurely
DISPOSITION: Life sentence imposed, December 2002

Petrovs, Kaspars (1975–)
SEX: M   RACE: W   TYPE: T   MOTIVE: CE-felony
DATE(S): 2001–04   VENUE: Riga, Latvia   VIC-
   TIMS: More than 38
MO: Befriended, robbed, and murdered older women
DISPOSITION: Confessed 38 murders, Jan. 2005; life
   sentence imposed May 12, 2005

Pheach Phen (1979–)
SEX: M   RACE: A   TYPE: T   MOTIVE: PC
DATE(S): 1999   VENUE: Kompong Cham, Cambodia
   VICTIMS: Five
MO: HIV-positive killer who drank the blood of vic-
   tims as a "cure," on the advice of native healers
DISPOSITION: Unknown

Philipe, Joseph (d. 1866)   AKA: Terror of Paris
SEX: M   RACE: W   TYPE: T   MOTIVE: Sex./Sad.
DATE(S): 1861–66   VENUE: Paris, France   VIC-
   TIMS: Eight
MO: "Ripper" of female prostitutes and a 10-year-old
   child
DISPOSITION: Guillotined, July 1866

Phillips, Cindy (1966–)
SEX: F   RACE: W   TYPE: N   MOTIVE: CE
DATE(S): 1981–98   VENUE: Kan./Tex./Colo.   VIC-
   TIMS: Three suspected
MO: Alleged "black widow" slayer of husbands and
   lovers for profit
DISPOSITION: Convicted on Jan. 26, 1999 of hiring a
   hit man to kill her husband in Colorado; charges
   pending in Kansas and Texas

Phillips, John Paul (?–)
SEX: M   RACE: W   TYPE: T   MOTIVE: Sex.
DATE(S): 1975–81   VENUE: Carbondale, Ill.   VIC-
   TIMS: Four suspected
MO: Rape-slayer of women age 21–30
DISPOSITION: Condemned on one count

Picchioni, Ernesto (?–)   AKA: Monster of Nerola
SEX: M   RACE: W   TYPE: T   MOTIVE: Sex.
DATE(S): 1946–47   VENUE: Nerola, Italy   VIC-
   TIMS: 16
MO: Lust killer of women; buried victims in his garden
DISPOSITION: Convicted; sentence unknown

Pierce, Alexander (?–?)
SEX: M   RACE: W   TYPE: N   MOTIVE: PC-non-
   specific
DATE(S): 19th century   VENUE: Australia   VIC-
   TIMS: Five

MO: Escaped convict; killed/cannibalized fellow fugitives
DISPOSITION: Hanged

Pierce, Charles E. (d. 1999)
SEX: M   RACE: Unk.   TYPE: N   MOTIVE: Sex.
DATE(S): 1960s–1970s   VENUE: New England
   VICTIMS: Three confessed
MO: Pedophile employed with a traveling carnival, imprisoned for the 1969 murder of a 13-year-old girl; subsequently confessed murders of two more girls
DISPOSITION: Life sentence on one count, 1980; died in prison, Feb. 13, 1999

Pietrzak, Stanley (1954–   )
SEX: M   RACE: W   TYPE: N   MOTIVE: Sex./PC
DATE(S): 1976–98   VENUE: Calif./Wash.   VICTIMS: Three
MO: Convicted sex offender whose wife and girlfriends died or vanished in his company; charred bones of last victim found in furnace at an apartment building where Pietrzak served as custodian
DISPOSITION: Convicted of molesting two girls aged five and nine in 1990; received 40-year term for murder of his second missing lover, November 2000

Pinkerton, Jay Kelly (1969–86)
SEX: M   RACE: W   TYPE: T   MOTIVE: Sex./Sad.
DATE(S): 1969/80   VENUE: Amarillo, Tex.   VICTIMS: Two
DISPOSITION: Executed May 15, 1986

Piper, Donald (1963–   )
SEX: M   RACE: W   TYPE: T   MOTIVE: Sex.
DATE(S): 1997–98   VENUE: Des Moines, Iowa
   VICTIMS: Two
MO: Stabbed/strangled female guest and maid at local hotels
DISPOSITION: Convicted on one murder count, June 4, 2001; convicted on second count, June 2002; life terms imposed in both cases

Piper, Thomas W. (1849–76)   AKA: Boston Belfry Murderer
SEX: M   RACE: W   TYPE: T   MOTIVE: Sex.
DATE(S): 1873–76   VENUE: Boston, Mass.   VICTIMS: Four confessed
MO: Rape-slayer of young girls, one in the church where he served as sexton
DISPOSITION: Hanged, 1876

Pirrera, Samuel (1967–   )
SEX: M   RACE: W   TYPE: T   MOTIVE: Sex./PC
DATE(S): 1991/1999   VENUE: Hamilton, Ontario
   VICTIMS: Two
MO: Murdered his first wife in 1991; dismembered a 34-year-old woman in 1999; arrested when his second wife found body parts at home
DISPOSITION: Died in jail of a drug overdose, February 2000, while negotiating a plea bargain on two murder counts

Pitchfork, Colin (1960–   )
SEX: M   RACE: W   TYPE: T   MOTIVE: Sex.
DATE(S): 1983/86   VENUE: Leicester, England   VICTIMS: Two
MO: Rape-slayer of 15-year-old girls
DISPOSITION: Double life term on guilty plea, 1988

Pizzuto, Gerald Ross (1973–   )
SEX: M   RACE: W   TYPE: N   MOTIVE: CE
DATE(S): 1985   VENUE: Idaho/Wash.   VICTIMS: Four
MO: Victims of both sexes shot/bludgeoned in robberies
DISPOSITION: Condemned on two counts, 1986; also convicted of grand theft and robbery

Player, Michael (1960–86)   AKA: Skid Row Slayer
SEX: M   RACE: B   TYPE: T   MOTIVE: PC-nonspecific
DATE(S): 1986   VENUE: Los Angeles, Calif.   VICTIMS: 10
MO: Shot homeless men, age 23–66
DISPOSITION: Suicide by gunshot, Oct. 10, 1986

Pleil, Rudolf (d. 1958)
SEX: M   RACE: W   TYPE: T   MOTIVE: Sex./Sad.
DATE(S): 1946–50   VENUE: Germany   VICTIMS: 25 confessed
MO: Mutilation-slayer of random victims, mostly women
DISPOSITION: 12 years for manslaughter in ax murder of a salesman, 1947; life for nine rape-murders, 1950; suicide by hanging in prison, Feb. 1958
ACCOMPLICES: Karl Hoffman (1914–   ) sentenced to life on six counts, 1950; Konrad Schuessler (1928–   ) sentenced to life for two murders and one attempted murder

Poehlke, Norbert Hans (d. 1985)
SEX: M   RACE: W   TYPE: N   MOTIVE: CE/PC
DATE(S): 1984–85   VENUE: Germany/Italy   VICTIMS: Six
MO: Police inspector who shot men age 36–47, using their stolen cars in robberies; also shot his wife and two sons
DISPOSITION: Suicide by gunshot, Oct. 23, 1985

Pomeroy, Jesse Harding (1860–1932)
SEX: M   RACE: W   TYPE: T   MOTIVE: PC/Sad.
DATE(S): 1870s–80s   VENUE: Boston, Mass.   VIC-
TIMS: 20+ alleged
MO: Sadistic slayer of street children; set prison fire
that killed three fellow inmates
DISPOSITION: Condemned on two counts, 1876
(commuted to life, 1878); spent 41 years in solitary;
died in prison, 1932

Pommerais, Dr. Edmund de la (1836–63)
SEX: M   RACE: W   TYPE: T   MOTIVE: CE
DATE(S): 1862–63   VENUE: France   VICTIMS: Two
MO: Compulsive gambler; poisoned female victims for
insurance
DISPOSITION: Guillotined, 1863

Pommerenke, Heinrich (1937–)   AKA: Beast of the
Black Forest
SEX: M   RACE: W   TYPE: T   MOTIVE: Sex.
DATE(S): 1959–60   VENUE: Germany   VICTIMS:
10 confessed
MO: Religious fanatic rape-slayer of women
DISPOSITION: Six life terms with 140-year minimum,
1960

Pool, Dave (?–?)
SEX: M   RACE: W   TYPE: N   MOTIVE: CE/PC
DATE(S): 1861–65   VENUE: Kans./Mo.   VICTIMS:
"Numerous"
MO: Notorious member of "QUANTRILL'S RAIDERS"
DISPOSITION: Surrendered May 22, 1865; no prose-
cution

Popova, Madame (d. 1909)
SEX: F   RACE: W   TYPE: T   MOTIVE: PC/CE
DATE(S): 1880s–1900s   VENUE: Samara, Russia
VICTIMS: 300 confessed
MO: Poisoner for hire, specializing in abusive husbands
DISPOSITION: Executed in Mar. 1909

Porter, Ronald Elliot (1947–)
SEX: M   RACE: W   TYPE: T   MOTIVE: Sex.
DATE(S): 1984–85   VENUE: San Diego, Calif.   VIC-
TIMS: 14 alleged
MO: Rape-slayer of women
DISPOSITION: 15 years on one count, with eight years
consecutive for sex offenses, 1993

Potts, Frank (1944–)
SEX: M   RACE: W   TYPE: N   MOTIVE: Sex.
DATE(S): 1977–89   VENUE: Ala.   VICTIMS: 15
alleged; one confessed

MO: Paroled pedophile; linked to death/disappearance
of three named teenagers and 12 unspecified victims;
one skeleton found on his property in Ala.
DISPOSITION: Life term with 25-year minimum for
Fla. sex crimes, 1994; indicted on one murder count
in Ala.

Pough, James Edward (1948–90)   AKA: Pops
SEX: M   RACE: B   TYPE: T   MOTIVE: PC-nonspe-
cific
DATE(S): 1971/90   VENUE: Jacksonville, Fla.   VIC-
TIMS: 11
MO: Shot male friend (1971); shot strangers at random
(1990)
DISPOSITION: 1971 murder charge reduced to aggra-
vated assault (five years probation); suicide by gun-
shot, June 18, 1990

Powers, Harry F. (1889–32)   AKA: Mail-order Blue-
beard
SEX: M   RACE: W   TYPE: S   MOTIVE: CE
DATE(S): 1920s–31   VENUE: Quiet Dell, W. Va.
VICTIMS: 50 alleged
MO: Profit-motivated "Bluebeard" slayer of prospec-
tive fiancées lured with lonely-hearts ads
DISPOSITION: Confessed five murders; hanged for
one on Mar. 19, 1932

Poyner, Syvasky L. (d. 1993)
SEX: M   RACE: B   TYPE: T   MOTIVE: CE/Sex.
DATE(S): 1984   VENUE: Hampton/Newport News,
Va.   VICTIMS: Five
MO: Shot female robbery victims, stripping one body
DISPOSITION: Executed Mar. 18, 1993

Prada, Hernando Arturo (1973–2000)
SEX: M   RACE: H   TYPE: N   MOTIVE: CE-felony
DATE(S): 1990s   VENUE: Colombia   VICTIMS: 10
MO: Bandit imprisoned for murders of robbery victims
DISPOSITION: Received a 60-year sentence; escaped
during a prison transfer in February 2000; captured
and executed by vigilante death squad on Feb. 22

Prejean, Dalton (d. 1990)
SEX: M   RACE: B   TYPE: T   MOTIVE: CE
DATE(S): 1974/77   VENUE: La.   VICTIMS: Two
MO: Robbed/killed taxi driver; shot policeman
DISPOSITION: Imprisoned, 1974 (paroled 1978); exe-
cuted May 18, 1990

Presenti, Valentino (?–)   AKA: Monster of Genoa
SEX: M   RACE: W   TYPE: T   MOTIVE: Sex.
DATE(S): 1976–91   VENUE: Genoa, Italy   VIC-
TIMS: Four+

MO: Lust killer of women
DISPOSITION: Life sentence

Presnell, Virgil Delano, Jr. (1954–)
SEX: M   RACE: W   TYPE: T   MOTIVE: Sex.
DATE(S): 1976   VENUE: Atlanta, Ga.   VICTIMS:
   Two suspected
MO: Pedophile slayer of preadolescent girls
DISPOSITION: Condemned, 1976

Price, Craig Chandler (1974–)   AKA: Iron Man
SEX: M   RACE: B   TYPE: T   MOTIVE: PC/Sad.
DATE(S): 1987/89   VENUE: Warwick, R.I.   VIC-
   TIMS: Four
MO: Home invader; beat/stabbed females age eight to
   39
DISPOSITION: Pled guilty in juvenile court; confined
   until age 21

Price, Ricky Lee (?–)
SEX: M   RACE: W   TYPE: N   MOTIVE: Sex.
DATE(S): 1980s   VENUE: Va./N.C.   VICTIMS: Two
MO: Strangler of women
DISPOSITION: Life term + 58 years in Va., 1985; con-
   demned in N.C., 1987; died in prison on Nov. 23,
   1998

Pries, Dieter (1956–)
SEX: M   RACE: W   TYPE: T   MOTIVE: CE/Sex.
DATE(S): 1974/84–97   VENUE: Germany   VIC-
   TIMS: Two+
MO: Robbed/killed grandmother (1974); rape slayer of
   women
DISPOSITION: Eight years for murder as juvenile (con-
   fined to asylum); judged insane and committed, 1978

Prince, Cleophus, Jr. (1967–)   AKA: Clairemont Killer
SEX: M   RACE: B   TYPE: T   MOTIVE: Sex./Sad.
DATE(S): 1990   VENUE: San Diego, Calif.   VIC-
   TIMS: Six
MO: Home-invading "ripper" of women age 18–42
DISPOSITION: Condemned, 1993

Prince, Hamisi (1990–)
SEX: M   RACE: B   TYPE: T   MOTIVE: PC-nonspecific
DATE(S): 1998–99   VENUE: Cyangusu Prefecture,
   Rwanda   VICTIMS: More than three
MO: Nine-year-old son of man imprisoned for genocide; arrested for beating a three-year-old girl to
   death, whereupon he confessed killing "many children in the past"
DISPOSITION: Sent to a reeducation camp, Nov. 11,
   1999

Prince, Walter (1902–34)
SEX: M   RACE: W   TYPE: N   MOTIVE: PC
DATE(S): 1928/34   VENUE: Manchester/Retford,
   England   VICTIMS: Two
MO: Murdered one man and one woman in personal
   disputes
DISPOSITION: Hanged, 1934

Pritchard, Dr. Edward William (d. 1865)
SEX: M   RACE: W   TYPE: T   MOTIVE: PC-domes-
   tic
DATE(S): 1863–65   VENUE: Glasgow, Scotland
   VICTIMS: Four
MO: "Bluebeard" poisoner of wife, mother-in-law, and
   children
DISPOSITION: Hanged, July 28, 1865

Profit, Mark Antonio (1964–)
SEX: M   RACE: B   TYPE: T   MOTIVE: Sex.
DATE(S): 1996   VENUE: Minneapolis, Minn.   VIC-
   TIMS: Four suspected
MO: Slayer of female prostitutes in/around Wirth Park
DISPOSITION: Two consecutive life terms, 1997, on
   one count of murder and two counts of rape

Protopappas, Dr. Tony (1945–)
SEX: M   RACE: W   TYPE: S   MOTIVE: PC-non-
   specific
DATE(S): 1982–83   VENUE: Costa Mesa, Calif.
   VICTIMS: Three
MO: Dentist who deliberately overdosed three female
   patients, age 13–31, with anesthetic
DISPOSITION: three concurrent terms of 15 years to
   life, 1984

Prudom, Barry Peter (1944–82)   AKA: Cop Killer
SEX: M   RACE: W   TYPE: N   MOTIVE: CE-felony
DATE(S): 1982–83   VENUE: England   VICTIMS:
   Three
MO: Fatally shot two policemen and a male robbery
   victim
DISPOSITION: Suicide during shoot-out with police,
   July 4, 1982

Pruett, Marion Albert (1949–99)   AKA: Mad Dog
SEX: M   RACE: W   TYPE: N   MOTIVE: PC/CE-
   felony
DATE(S): 1981   VENUE: Ark./Colo./Miss./N. Mex.
   VICTIMS: Five
MO: Serving time for a Georgia bank robbery when he
   killed his cellmate, framing another inmate for the
   crime; testimony in that case earned him release in
   1979, with placement in the witness protection program; Pruett soon developed a $4,000-per-week

drug habit and turned to violence; bludgeoned his common-law wife with a hammer and burned her body, then embarked on an interstate crime spree, shooting three male victims in armed robberies
DISPOSITION: Received life terms for three murders in Colorado, Mississippi, and New Mexico; executed in Arkansas, April 13, 1999

Pruett, Mark David (1949–93)
SEX: M   RACE: W   TYPE: T   MOTIVE: Sex.
DATE(S): 1975–85   VENUE: Va.   VICTIMS: Five+
MO: Rape-slayer of women
DISPOSITION: Executed on two counts, Dec. 16, 1993

Puente, Dorothea Helen (1929–   )
SEX: F   RACE: W   TYPE: S   MOTIVE: CE
DATE(S): 1982–88   VENUE: Sacramento, Calif.
   VICTIMS: Nine
MO: "Black widow" landlady; poisoned tenants for pension checks
DISPOSITION: Life without parole on three counts, 1993

Putt, George Howard (1946–   )
SEX: M   RACE: W   TYPE: N   MOTIVE: Sex./Sad.
DATE(S): 1969   VENUE: Miss./Tenn.   VICTIMS: Five
MO: Home-invading mutilation-slayer of men and women
DISPOSITION: Condemned, 1970 (sentence commuted to 99 years, 1972)

Quansah, Charles Papa Kwabena Ebo (1964–   )
SEX: M   RACE: B   TYPE: T   MOTIVE: Sex.
DATE(S): 1999–2000   VENUE: Accra, Ghana   VICTIMS: 34 confessed
MO: Rape slayer of women
DISPOSITION: Confessed, then recanted; condemned at trial, July 2002

Quantrill, William Clarke (1837–65)
SEX: M   RACE: W   TYPE: N   MOTIVE: PC/CE
DATE(S): 1855–65   VENUE: Ill./Mo./Kans./Tex./Ky.
   VICTIMS: "Numerous"
MO: Psychopathic career criminal; leader of outlaw "QUANTRILL'S RAIDERS" during Civil War; ordered hundreds of murders besides those committed personally
DISPOSITION: Shot by Union soldiers, May 10, 1865; died June 6

Raby, Clarence Leon (1933–60)
SEX: M   RACE: ?   TYPE: T   MOTIVE: CE

DATE(S): 1960   VENUE: Tenn.   VICTIMS: Two
MO: Career criminal; shot holdup victim and policeman
DISPOSITION: Killed in escape attempt, Oct. 24, 1960

Rachals, Terri Eden Maples (1962–   )
SEX: F   RACE: W   TYPE: S   MOTIVE: PC-nonspecific
DATE(S): 1985   VENUE: Albany, Ga.   VICTIMS: Six confessed
MO: Hospital nurse who poisoned intensive-care patients
DISPOSITION: Found guilty but mentally ill on one count aggravated assault; 17-year prison term plus three years probation; released April 2003

Racine, Steven (1964–   )
SEX: M   RACE: Unk.   TYPE: T   MOTIVE: CE-felony
DATE(S): 1990–2001   VENUE: Montreal, Quebec
   VICTIMS: Six
MO: Career criminal who bound and strangled victims in drug-related killings
DISPOSITION: Pleaded guilty to all counts on Sept. 25, 2002, receiving a life prison term with a 25-year minimum

Rahman, Yusef Abdullah (1968–   )
SEX: M   RACE: B   TYPE: N   MOTIVE: PC-nonspecific
DATE(S): 1987–88   VENUE: Kans./N.Y.   VICTIMS: Four confessed
MO: Shot men in random sniping attacks
DISPOSITION: 42 years to life on one count, 1990; concurrent life term on second count, 1992

Raies, Jean (?–?)
SEX: F   RACE: W   TYPE: T   MOTIVE: CE
DATE(S): 1880   VENUE: Geneva, Switzerland   VICTIMS: 12
MO: Nurse who killed patients to collect "bounty" offered by local mortician for new clients
DISPOSITION: Life sentence; died in prison

Raj, Subbah (1949–   )
SEX: M   RACE: A   TYPE: T   MOTIVE: PC-nonspecific
DATE(S): 2002   VENUE: Kamakshipuram, India
   VICTIMS: Eight
MO: Thrill-killer of beggars, slain by stones dropped on heads as they slept; captured in attack on decoy mannequins; confessed to police that he "found happiness in killing stranded persons"
DISPOSITION: Unknown

Ralston, Larry (1949–)
SEX: M   RACE: ?   TYPE: T   MOTIVE: Sex.
DATE(S): 1975–77   VENUE: Clermont/Clinton Counties, Ohio   VICTIMS: Five
MO: Rape-slayer of females aged 15–23
DISPOSITION: Four life terms, 1978; fifth life term, 1984

Ramirez Sánchez, Ilich (1949–)   AKA: Carlos the Jackal
SEX: M   RACE: H   TYPE: N   MOTIVE: CE/PC-extremist
DATE(S): 1974–82   VENUE: France/Austria   VICTIMS: 12+
MO: Left-wing terrorist for hire; victims murdered by gunshot and bombing
DISPOSITION: Life sentence for three counts in Paris, 1997

Rand, Andre (1943–)   AKA: Pied Piper of Staten Island
SEX: M   RACE: W   TYPE: T   MOTIVE: Sex.
DATE(S): 1972–87   VENUE: New York City   VICTIMS: Five suspected
MO: Pedophile slayer of girls aged 5–12
DISPOSITION: Convicted of kidnapping, 1989, while jury deadlocked on murder charge in case of girl still missing; received prison term of 25 years to life; trial on second kidnapping case in progress at press time

Randall, James Michael (1954–)
SEX: M   RACE: W   TYPE: T   MOTIVE: Sex./Sad.
DATE(S): 1995–96   VENUE: Pinellas County, Fla.   VICTIMS: Two
MO: Rape-strangler of female prostitutes left in dumpsters
DISPOSITION: Condemned in 1997; sentence reduced to life on appeal, April 2000

Rardon, Gary Duane (1944–)
SEX: M   RACE: W   TYPE: N   MOTIVE: PC/CE
DATE(S): 1962/74   VENUE: Indianapolis/Chicago   VICTIMS: Four
MO: Jailed for manslaughter at 18; later shot three men in holdups
DISPOSITION: Four years for manslaughter, 1962; 40–100 years, Feb. 1977

Rath, Thomas (1959–)
SEX: M   RACE: W   TYPE: T   MOTIVE: Sex.
DATE(S): 1981–83   VENUE: Bremen, Germany   VICTIMS: Four suspected
MO: Rapist and "ripper" of females age 17–20
DISPOSITION: Life sentence for sexual assault, 1985

Rathbun, Charles Edgar (1957–)
SEX: M   RACE: W   TYPE: N   MOTIVE: Sex.
DATE(S): 1989–95   VENUE: Mich./Ohio/Calif.   VICTIMS: Six suspected
MO: Convicted rapist; photographer and lust-killer of women
DISPOSITION: Life without parole on one count in Calif., 1996

Razaq, Abdul (1944–)
SEX: M   RACE: A   TYPE: T   MOTIVE: Sex.
DATE(S): 2001–02   VENUE: Bahawalpur, India   VICTIMS: Eight
MO: Rape-strangler of elderly women
DISPOSITION: Unknown

Read, Mark Brandon (1955–)   AKA: Chopper
SEX: M   RACE: W   TYPE: T   MOTIVE: PC
DATE(S): 1979–91   VENUE: Melbourne, Australia   VICTIMS: 19 confessed
MO: Self-described vigilante slayer of criminals
DISPOSITION: Served 20+ years for assault and other felony counts; released from prison July 1997

Read, Mary (d. 1721)
SEX: F   RACE: W   TYPE: N   MOTIVE: CE
DATE(S): 1719–20   VENUE: Caribbean   VICTIMS: "Several"
MO: Abducted by pirates; joined the crew on various raids
DISPOSITION: Died in prison, Apr. 1721

Rearden, Virginia (1932–)   AKA: Virginia McGinnis
SEX: F   RACE: W   TYPE: N   MOTIVE: CE
DATE(S): 1972–87   VENUE: Ky./Calif.   VICTIMS: Three
MO: "Black widow" slayer of husband, daughter, and female friend for insurance
DISPOSITION: Life without parole in Calif., 1992

Red Dog, James Allen (1954–93)
SEX: M   RACE: NA   TYPE: T   MOTIVE: PC
DATE(S): 1990–91   VENUE: Del.   VICTIMS: Five suspected
MO: Killed acquaintances in personal disputes
DISPOSITION: Condemned on one count, 1992; executed Mar. 3, 1993

Reed, Todd Alan (1967–)   AKA: Forest Park Serial Killer
SEX: M   RACE: W   TYPE: T   MOTIVE: Sex.
DATE(S): 1987/1999   VENUE: Portland, Ore.   VICTIMS: Three to five

MO: Rape-slayer of three women strangled in Forest
Park, 1999; prime suspect in murders of two teenage
girls 12 years earlier
DISPOSITION: Pleaded guilty on three counts and
received three consecutive life terms, Feb. 24, 2001

Reeves, Jack Wayne (1940–)
SEX: M   RACE: W   TYPE: N   MOTIVE: PC-
domestic
DATE(S): 1967/78/94   VENUE: Italy/Tex.   VIC-
TIMS: Three
MO: Shot male victim in Italy; "Bluebeard" slayer of
wives in U.S.
DISPOSITION: 1967 manslaughter conviction
(released after four months.); 35 years on one count,
1995; 99 years with 40-year minimum, 1996

Regan, John (1945–74)   AKA: Nano the Magician
SEX: M   RACE: W   TYPE: T   MOTIVE: CE-felony
DATE(S): 1960s–1970s   VENUE: Sydney, Australia
VICTIMS: "Multiple"
MO: Underworld contract killer nicknamed for his
ability to make victims disappear
DISPOSITION: Shot by gangland rivals in September
1974

Register, Glen Randall (1959–)
SEX: M   RACE: W   TYPE: N   MOTIVE: PC/CE
DATE(S): 1998–99   VENUE: Colo./Fla.   VICTIMS:
Two suspected
MO: Drifter who bludgeoned and robbed three male
victims aged 26–57, killing two; two victims beaten
with toilet tank lids
DISPOSITION: Life sentence for a Florida murder plus
30 years for robbery, on Sept. 26, 2001; detainer
from Colorado in case of parole

Reid, Paul Dennis (1956–)
SEX: M   RACE: W   TYPE: N   MOTIVE: CE-felony
DATE(S): 1996–97   VENUE: Tenn./Ill.   VICTIMS:
12+ suspected
MO: Shot victims in armed robberies of various restaurants
DISPOSITION: Condemned on two counts for Feb.
1997 holdup-murders in Tennessee, April 15, 1999;
condemned on two counts for April 1997 holdup-
murders in Tennessee, Sept. 9, 1999; condemned on
three counts for March 1997 holdup-murders in
Tennessee, May 28, 2000

Reinbold, William (?–)   AKA: The Hammer
SEX: M   RACE: W   TYPE: T   MOTIVE: Sex./Sad.
DATE(S): 1983–88   VENUE: Farmington, Ill.   VIC-
TIMS: Three suspected

MO: Abducted a woman from a local laundromat and
beat her to death; prime suspect in the disappearance of another woman and a pregnant 17-year-old
girl
DISPOSITION: Life term received for one murder at
trial in 1991; overturned on appeal; received
another life term at second trial; eligible for parole
in 2019

Reldan, Robert R. (1940–)
SEX: M   RACE: W   TYPE: T   MOTIVE: Sex.
DATE(S): 1974–75   VENUE: Northern N.J.   VIC-
TIMS: Eight suspected
MO: Slayer of females age 14–26
DISPOSITION: Life sentence on two counts, 1979

Reles, Abraham (1970–41)   AKA: Kid Twist
SEX: M   RACE: W   TYPE: T   MOTIVE: CE/PC
DATE(S): 1930–40   VENUE: N.Y./N.J.   VICTIMS:
30+
MO: Contract killer for "MURDER, INC."
DISPOSITION: Murdered in police custody after turn-
ing state's evidence, Nov. 12, 1941

Remeta, Daniel Eugene (1958–98)
SEX: M   RACE: W   TYPE: N   MOTIVE: CE
DATE(S): 1985   VENUE: Fla./Ark./Kans.   VICTIMS:
Five
MO: Robbed/shot victims in cross-country rampage;
wife called him a "warrior who stood up for his
beliefs"
DISPOSITION: Executed in Fla., Mar. 30, 1998

Rendall, Martha (d. 1909)
SEX: F   RACE: W   TYPE: S   MOTIVE: Sad.
DATE(S): 1907–8   VENUE: Australia   VICTIMS:
Three
MO: Killed three stepchildren by feeding them
hydrochloric acid
DISPOSITION: Hanged, Oct. 6, 1909

Rezala, Sid Ahmed (1979–2000)
SEX: M   RACE: B   TYPE: N   MOTIVE: PC-nonspecific
DATE(S): 1999   VENUE: France   VICTIMS: Three
confessed
MO: Stabbed his 20-year-old girlfriend and two other
women, aged 20 and 36, after "seeing flashes"
DISPOSITION: Arrested in Lisbon; suicide by fire in
his Lisbon jail cell, on June 29, 2000

Rhoades, Paul Ezra (1957–)
SEX: M   RACE: W   TYPE: N   MOTIVE: Sex./CE

DATE(S): 1985–87   VENUE: Utah/Idaho   VICTIMS: Six suspected
MO: Shot females age 16–34, some robbed and raped
DISPOSITION: Condemned in Idaho, 1988

Rich, Darrell Keith (1955–2000)   AKA: Hilltop Rapist
SEX: M   RACE: W   TYPE: T   MOTIVE: Sex.
DATE(S): 1978   VENUE: Redding, Calif.   VICTIMS: Four
MO: Rape-slayer of females aged 11–26; two victims bludgeoned with stones, one shot, one thrown from bridge
DISPOSITION: Executed on March 15, 2000

Richards, Robert McKinley (d. 1989)
SEX: M   RACE: W   TYPE: N   MOTIVE: Sex.
DATE(S): 1986–87   VENUE: Tenn.   VICTIMS: Two confessed
MO: Self-declared rape-slayer of teenage girls
DISPOSITION: Strangled by cellmate in jail, at his request, 1989

Richards, Stephen Lee (d. 1879)   AKA: Nebraska Fiend
SEX: M   RACE: W   TYPE: N   MOTIVE: PC/CE
DATE(S): 1879   VENUE: Lincoln/Minden, Nebr.   VICTIMS: Nine +
MO: Random "thrill" killings; victims include a family of five
DISPOSITION: Hanged, Apr. 1879

Richmond, Earl, Jr. (1961–   )
SEX: M   RACE: B   TYPE: N   MOTIVE: CE/Sex.
DATE(S): 1990–91   VENUE: N.J./N.C.   VICTIMS: Five
MO: Home invader, killed victims age 11–68
DISPOSITION: Life + six years in N.J. on one count, 1993; condemned in N.C. on three counts, 1995

Rifkin, Joel (1959–   )
SEX: M   RACE: W   TYPE: T   MOTIVE: Sex./Sad.
DATE(S): 1991–92   VENUE: New York City area   VICTIMS: 18
MO: Slayer of female prostitutes
DISPOSITION: Multiple life terms, 1994–95

Ringgold, John Peter (1844–82)   AKA: Johnny Ringo
SEX: M   RACE: W   TYPE: N   MOTIVE: CE/PC
DATE(S): 1870s–82   VENUE: Tex./Mexico/Ariz.   VICTIMS: "Numerous"
MO: Old West outlaw, gunfighter, and feudist
DISPOSITION: Found murdered in Ariz., July 14, 1882

Rissell, Monte Ralph (1959–   )
SEX: M   RACE: W   TYPE: T   MOTIVE: Sex.
DATE(S): 1976–77   VENUE: Alexandria, Va.   VICTIMS: Five
MO: Rape-slayer of women age 22–34
DISPOSITION: Life terms on five counts

Rivera Benitez, Martin (?–   )   AKA: Big Soul
SEX: M   RACE: H   TYPE: T   MOTIVE: CE-felony
DATE(S): 1969–72   VENUE: Jasatipan, Mexico   VICTIMS: 50+
MO: Contract killer operating from a mortuary where police found 12 headless corpses in 1972; later confessed "more killings than I can remember"
DISPOSITION: Life prison term

Rivera, Reinaldo (1963–   )
SEX: M   RACE: H   TYPE: N   MOTIVE: Sex.
DATE(S): 1999–2000   VENUE: S.C./Ga.   VICTIMS: Four
MO: Kidnapped and raped seven females aged 17–21, killing four
DISPOSITION: Condemned on one count in Georgia, Jan. 26, 2004; received 105 years for three Georgia rapes and other felonies, Feb. 12, 2004

Rivera, Vincent Faustino (1963–   )
SEX: M   RACE: H   TYPE: T   MOTIVE: PC
DATE(S): 1990/95   VENUE: Fla.   VICTIMS: Three
MO: Killed two victims in Hillsborough County; named as slayer of GERARD SCHAEFER in prison at Starke, Gainesville, Florida
DISPOSITION: Life + 20 years on two counts, 1990

Robaczynski, Mary Rose (?–   )
SEX: F   RACE: W   TYPE: S   MOTIVE: PC-"mercy"
DATE(S): 1977–78   VENUE: Baltimore, Md.   VICTIMS: Four confessed
MO: Nurse who disconnected intensive-care patients from life-support devices
DISPOSITION: Mistrial with hung jury, 1979; charges dropped in bargain to permanently revoke nursing license

Robbins, Gary A. (1935–88)
SEX: M   RACE: W   TYPE: N   MOTIVE: Sex./Sad.
DATE(S): 1981–88   VENUE: Mich./Ohio/Md./Pa.   VICTIMS: Four+
MO: Traveling salesman; rape-slayer of women in homes advertised for sale; some victims tortured
DISPOSITION: Suicide after shoot-out with Pa. police, Apr. 14, 1988

Roberts, Andrew L. (d. 1878)   AKA: Buckshot
SEX: M   RACE: W   TYPE: S   MOTIVE: PC/Sad.

DATE(S): 1870s   VENUE: N. Mex.   VICTIMS: "Numerous"
MO: Prolific Old West gunman and hired killer
DISPOSITION: Killed in shoot-out with "regulators," Apr. 4, 1878

Roberts, David James (1944–   )
SEX: M   RACE: B   TYPE: T   MOTIVE: Sex./PC-revenge
DATE(S): 1974   VENUE: Indianapolis, Ind.   VICTIMS: Four
MO: Serial rapist who killed one victim's infant; also burned home of a man who reported him for theft, killing three
DISPOSITION: Condemned, 1975

Robinson, Alonzo (?–?)
SEX: M   RACE: B   TYPE: N   MOTIVE: Sex.
DATE(S): 1926–34   VENUE: Mich./Miss.   VICTIMS: Six suspected
MO: Necrophile mutilation-slayer of one man and five women; kept heads and other body parts as souvenirs
DISPOSITION: Confessed in Miss., 1934; sentence unreported

Robinson, Harvey (1974–   )
SEX: M   RACE: W   TYPE: T   MOTIVE: Sex.
DATE(S): 1992–93   VENUE: Allentown, Pa.   VICTIMS: Three
MO: Rape-slayer of females age 13–47
DISPOSITION: Three death sentences + 157 years for rape

Robinson, Maxine (1968–   )
SEX: F   RACE: W   TYPE: S   MOTIVE: PC-nonspecific
DATE(s): 1989/1993 VENUE: Chester-le-Street, England   VICTIMS: Three
MO: Mother who killed her children, ages nine months to five years
DISPOSITION: Convicted of killing her 19-month old daughter and 5-year-old son, 1995; received life prison term; pleaded guilty to murdering her nine-month-old daughter, April 22, 2004; received consecutive life sentences

Robinson, Sarah Jane (d. 1905)
SEX: F   RACE: W   TYPE: S   MOTIVE: CE
DATE(S): 1880s   VENUE: Boston, Mass.   VICTIMS: Six
MO: "Black widow" poisoner of relatives/friends for insurance

DISPOSITION: Condemned (commuted to life term on appeal); died in prison, 1905

Robison, Larry Keith (1957–2000)
SEX: M   RACE: W   TYPE: T   MOTIVE: PC-nonspecific
DATE(S): 1982   VENUE: Fort Worth, Tex.   VICTIMS: Five
MO: Paranoid schizophrenic who beheaded his gay lover, then killed four others in a psychotic murder spree
DISPOSITION: Executed on Jan. 21, 2000

Roche, Charles, Jr. (1964–   )
SEX: M   RACE: ?   TYPE: T   MOTIVE: PC
DATE(S): 1980s   VENUE: Ind.   VICTIMS: Eight confessed
MO: Killed two men in Hammond; other murders confessed
DISPOSITION: Condemned on two counts, 1990; confessed six more, 1998

Roche, John Francis (1927–54)
SEX: M   RACE: W   TYPE: T   MOTIVE: Sex./CE
DATE(S): 1953–54   VENUE: Queens, New York   VICTIMS: Six confessed
MO: Bludgeoned/stabbed/robbed two men and four females age 13–85; at least one female victim also raped
DISPOSITION: Executed Jan. 27, 1956

Rode, Adolph James [*See* BARONE, CESAR]

Rodrigues de Brito, Francisco das Chagas (?–   )
SEX: M   RACE: H   TYPE: N   MOTIVE: Sex./Sad.
DATE(S): 1980s–1990s   VENUE: Northern Brazil   VICTIMS: 38
MO: Mutilation-slayer of young boys who castrated his victims; arrested in March 2004, with remains of two victims found in his home at São Luiz; confessed 14 murders in Pará State during the 1980s and 24 in Maranhão State since 1991
DISPOSITION: Unknown

Rodriguez, Robert Neal (1950–92)
SEX: M   RACE: H   TYPE: T   MOTIVE: Sex.
DATE(S): 1984/92   VENUE: Tallahassee, Fla.   VICTIMS: Three
MO: Shot females age 16–22, when rape plans went awry
DISPOSITION: Suicide by cyanide to avoid arrest, May 15, 1992

Roeder, Michaela (1950–   )   AKA: Angel of Death
SEX: F   RACE: W   TYPE: S   MOTIVE: PC-"mercy"

DATE(S): 1980s   VENUE: Wuppertal-Barmen, Germany   VICTIMS: 10–17
MO: Hospital nurse who killed intensive-care patients
DISPOSITION: Confessed 10 murders; life sentence, 1989

Rogers, Bob (1873–95)
SEX: M   RACE: W   TYPE: N   MOTIVE: CE
DATE(S): 1892–95   VENUE: Okla. Territory   VICTIMS: Two
MO: Outlaw "wanna-be"; stabbed/shot peace officers
DISPOSITION: Killed resisting arrest, Mar. 13, 1895

Rogers, David Keith (1947–   )
SEX: M   RACE: W   TYPE: T   MOTIVE: Sex.
DATE(S): 1986   VENUE: Kern County, Calif.   VICTIMS: Three suspected
MO: Sheriff's deputy who shot prostitutes age 15 and 21
DISPOSITION: Condemned, 1987

Rogers, Dayton Leroy (1953–   )   AKA: Molalla Forest Killer
SEX: M   RACE: W   TYPE: T   MOTIVE: Sex./Sad.
DATE(S): 1987   VENUE: Portland, Ore.   VICTIMS: Eight
MO: Torture-slayer and "ripper" of female prostitutes
DISPOSITION: Life with 20-year minimum on one count, 1988; condemned on seven counts, 1989; sentence reversed again, May 4, 2000

Rogers, George White (1898–1958)
SEX: M   RACE: W   TYPE: N   MOTIVE: PC/CE
DATE(S): 1934/1953   VENUE: Atlantic Ocean/N.J.   VICTIMS: 135 suspected
MO: Radio operator aboard the cruise ship *Morro Castle,* now prime suspect in the shipboard fire that killed 133 passengers and crew on Sept. 8, 1934 (possibly set to conceal one homicide aboard)
DISPOSITION: Imprisoned for attempted murder while serving as a policeman in Bayonne, N.J.; after parole, killed two robbery victims and received a life term; died in prison, 1958

Rogers, Glen Edward (1962–   )   AKA: Cross-Country Killer
SEX: M   RACE: W   TYPE: N   MOTIVE: Sex.
DATE(S): 1992–96   VENUE: United States   VICTIMS: 70+ confessed
MO: Transient rape-mutilation slayer of women in various states; confessed 70+ murders to relatives
DISPOSITION: Condemned on one count in Florida, July 11, 1997; condemned on one count in California, June 21, 1999

Rogers, Kenneth Paul (1943–   )
SEX: M   RACE: ?   TYPE: T   MOTIVE: Sex.
DATE(S): 1969   VENUE: Ill.   VICTIMS: Three
MO: Rape-strangler of females, including his wife
DISPOSITION: Two concurrent 75–100-year terms, 1969; third concurrent 75–100-year term, 1970

Rogers, Ramon Jay (1959–   )
SEX: M   RACE: W   TYPE: N   MOTIVE: PC
DATE(S): 1977/1993–94   VENUE: Idaho/Calif.   VICTIMS: Four suspected
MO: Suspected of wife's murder (1977); dismembered a male friend and two women
DISPOSITION: Condemned on one count in Calif., 1996

Rollack, Peter (1974–   )
SEX: M   RACE: B   TYPE: T   MOTIVE: CE-felony
DATE(S): 1990s   VENUE: New York City   VICTIMS: Eight
MO: Leader of gang called Sex, Money, and Murder; ordered and participated in eight murders and one attempted murder related to drug trafficking
DISPOSITION: Pleaded guilty on all counts in January 2000, accepting a sentence of life without parole in solitary confinement

Rolle, Randal (1918–49)
SEX: M   RACE: W   TYPE: S   MOTIVE: PC-non-specific
DATE(S): 1940s   VENUE: Miss.   VICTIMS: "At least nine"
MO: Skeletal remains found at home after suicide
DISPOSITION: Suicide by gunshot, Oct. 14, 1949

Rolling, Danny Harold (1954–   )   AKA: Gainesville Ripper
SEX: M   RACE: W   TYPE: N   MOTIVE: Sex./Sad.
DATE(S): 1989–90   VENUE: La./Fla.   VICTIMS: Eight confessed
MO: Mutilation slayer of victims in random home invasions
DISPOSITION: Condemned in Fla., 1994

Ronghi, Frank (1965–   )
SEX: M   RACE: W   TYPE: N   MOTIVE: Sex.
DATE(S): 1991/2000   VENUE: Iraq/Yugoslavia   VICTIMS: More than two confessed
MO: U.S. soldier and rape-slayer of an 11-year-old Albanian girl in Kosovo; boasted of killing other victims "in the desert," presumably a reference to the first Gulf War

DISPOSITION: Pleaded guilty to murder and forcible sodomy, receiving a term of life imprisonment without parole, Aug. 1, 2000

Ronning, Michael (?–)
SEX: M   RACE: W   TYPE: N   MOTIVE: Sex.
DATE(S): 1982–86   VENUE: Miss./Ark./Tex.   VICTIMS: Six confessed
MO: Rape slayer of females aged 17–20
DISPOSITION: Convicted on one count and sentenced to life in Arkansas, 1986; confessed additional murders in Michigan, 1992; passed polygraph on one Michigan case for which another man is imprisoned, 1996; plea bargain on three Michigan murders rejected, 1997

Rooyen, Gert van (d. 1990)
SEX: M   RACE: W   TYPE: T   MOTIVE: Sex.
DATE(S): 1988–89   VENUE: South Africa   VICTIMS: Seven
MO: Pedophile slayer of young girls; also shot his adult female lover
DISPOSITION: Suicide by gunshot to avoid arrest, 1990

Rosenfeld, Brian Kevin (1958–)
SEX: M   RACE: W   TYPE: S   MOTIVE: PC-"mercy"
DATE(S): 1990   VENUE: Pinellas County, Fla.   VICTIMS: 23 confessed
MO: Nurse who murdered elderly rest home patients
DISPOSITION: Three life terms with 25 years minimum, 1992

Rosenkrantz, Bernard (d. 1935)   AKA: Lulu
SEX: M   RACE: W   TYPE: T   MOTIVE: CE
DATE(S): 1920s–35   VENUE: N.Y./N.J.   VICTIMS: "Numerous"
MO: Contract killer for ARTHUR FLEGENHEIMER gang
DISPOSITION: Murdered with Flegenheimer, Oct. 23, 1935

Roth, Randolph Gordon (1954–)
SEX: M   RACE: W   TYPE: T   MOTIVE: CE
DATE(S): 1981/90   VENUE: Seattle, Wash., area   VICTIMS: Two
MO: "Bluebeard" slayer of wives for insurance
DISPOSITION: 50 years on one count, 1992

Roulet, Jacques (?–?)
SEX: M   RACE: W   TYPE: N   MOTIVE: Sex./Sad.
DATE(S): 1590s   VENUE: France   VICTIMS: "Many" confessed

MO: "Werewolf" cannibal-slayer of victims slain at random
DISPOSITION: Condemned, 1598; later committed to asylum as insane

Rowland, Walter Graham (d. 1947)
SEX: M   RACE: W   TYPE: T   MOTIVE: PC
DATE(S): 1930s–46   VENUE: Manchester, England   VICTIMS: Two
MO: Killed a child and a 40-year-old woman
DISPOSITION: Imprisoned on first counts; hanged on second count, Feb. 27, 1947

Rowles, "Snowy" (d. 1932)   AKA: John Thomas Smith
SEX: M   RACE: W   TYPE: N   MOTIVE: CE
DATE(S): 1929–30   VENUE: Australia   VICTIMS: Two+
MO: Robbed/murdered male acquaintances in Australian desert
DISPOSITION: Hanged June 13, 1932

Rowntree, Mark (1957–)
SEX: M   RACE: W   TYPE: T   MOTIVE: PC-nonspecific
DATE(S): 1976   VENUE: Leeds, England   VICTIMS: Four
MO: Stabbed strangers age three to 85 in random attacks, directed by "voices"
DISPOSITION: Ruled insane; indefinite committal to asylum, 1976

Rozier, Robert (1956–)
SEX: M   RACE: B   TYPE: N   MOTIVE: PC/Cult
DATE(S): 1981–86   VENUE: Fla./Mo./N.J./N.Y.   VICTIMS: More than seven
MO: Enforcer for the Hebrew Israelite cult; killed cult defectors and opponents; at least one victim killed from personal spite
DISPOSITION: 22-year prison term in Florida, 1987; later turned state's evidence against cult leader Yahweh Ben Yahweh and entered witness protection program as "Robert Ramses"; convicted in July 2000 of check fraud in California; charges dismissed in a New Jersey cult murder, September 2000

Rudabaugh, Dave (1841–86)
SEX: M   RACE: W   TYPE: N   MOTIVE: PC/CE
DATE(S): 1876–86   VENUE: Tex./N. Mex./Mexico   VICTIMS: "Several"
MO: Old West outlaw and gunman; victims included one lawman
DISPOSITION: Beheaded by friends of his last two victims, in Mexico, Feb. 1886

Rudloff, Fritz (1904–54)
SEX: M   RACE: W   TYPE: S   MOTIVE: PC-revenge
DATE(S): 1954   VENUE: Walterhausen, East Germany   VICTIMS: Three
MO: Hospital nurse who killed three patients to spite their doctor, a personal enemy
DISPOSITION: Executed, 1954

Rulloffson, Edward Howard (d. 1871)   AKA: Edward Ruloff
SEX: M   RACE: W   TYPE: N   MOTIVE: PC/CE
DATE(S): 1870–71   VENUE: N.Y.   VICTIMS: Four+
MO: "Herb healer" who killed patients (including his wife and daughter), selling bodies for dissection; also killed male burglary victim
DISPOSITION: Hanged on one count, May 1871

Runge, Paul Frederick (1970–)
SEX: M   RACE: Unk.   TYPE: T   MOTIVE: Sex.
DATE(S): 1995–97   VENUE: Chicago, Ill.   VICTIMS: Eight confessed
MO: Rape-slayer of female victims aged 10–43; confessed murders on video tape; additional DNA links found to several victims
DISPOSITION: Confessed in custody, then pleaded not guilty; received 90-year prison term for an October 2000 jailbreak, July 25, 2002; murder trial pending at press time

Rush, James Blomfield (d. 1849)
SEX: M   RACE: W   TYPE: T   MOTIVE: PC
DATE(S): 1848   VENUE: Norwich, England   VICTIMS: Three alleged
MO: Tried for murdering his landlord in a personal dispute; also accused of killing his own parents
DISPOSITION: Hanged on April 21, 1849

Rust, Mark Erin (1965–)
SEX: M   RACE: W   TYPE: T   MOTIVE: Sex.
DATE(S): 1999   VENUE: South Australia   VICTIMS: Two
MO: Rape slayer of women in their 20s and 30s
DISPOSITION: Pleaded guilty on one count in December 2002; pleaded guilty on second count in April 2003; received life term without parole, April 2004

Russell, George Waterfield (1958–)
SEX: M   RACE: B   TYPE: T   MOTIVE: Sex.
DATE(S): 1990   VENUE: Seattle, Wash.   VICTIMS: Three
MO: Raped/bludgeoned/strangled women age 24–36
DISPOSITION: Two consecutive life terms plus 28 years, 1991

Ruzicka, James (1950–)
SEX: M   RACE: W   TYPE: T   MOTIVE: Sex.
DATE(S): 1973   VENUE: Seattle, Wash.   VICTIMS: Two
MO: Serial rapist who killed girls age 14 and 16
DISPOSITION: Two consecutive life terms, 1974

Ryakhovsky, Sergei (1963–)   AKA: The Hippopotamus
SEX: M   RACE: W   TYPE: T   MOTIVE: Sex./Sad.
DATE(S): 1991–93   VENUE: Moscow, Russia   VICTIMS: 19
MO: Obese necrophile; victims raped/mutilated after death
DISPOSITION: Condemned, 1995

Saietta, Ignazio (1877–1944)   AKA: Lupo the Wolf
SEX: M   RACE: W   TYPE: T   MOTIVE: CE
DATE(S): 1899–1920   VENUE: New York City   VICTIMS: 60+
MO: "Black Hand" extortionist and killer; victims slaughtered at "murder stable" in Italian Harlem
DISPOSITION: Served prison terms for extortion and counterfeiting

Saldivar, Efren (1970–)   AKA: Angel of Death
SEX: M   RACE: H   TYPE: S   MOTIVE: PC-"mercy"
DATE(S): 1989–97   VENUE: Glendale, Calif.   VICTIMS: 60+ confessed
MO: Respiratory therapist at Glendale Adventist Medical Center who killed patients by suffocation and injection; confessed 60 murders through 1994 but "lost count" over the next three years
DISPOSITION: Pleaded guilty on six counts and received life prison term without parole, March 12, 2002

Sampson, Gary Lee (1960–)
SEX: M   RACE: Unk.   TYPE: N   MOTIVE: CE-felony
DATE(S): 2001   VENUE: Mass./N.H.   VICTIMS: Three
MO: Hitchhiker who murdered those who offered rides and stole their cars
DISPOSITION: Condemned under federal carjacking statute, Dec. 27, 2003

Samuels, Mary Ellen (1948–)
SEX: F   RACE: W   TYPE: T   MOTIVE: PC
DATE(S): 1988–89   VENUE: Southern California   VICTIMS: Two
MO: Arranged the contract murder of her husband, then killed the gunman
DISPOSITION: Condemned on Sept. 16, 1994

Sanchez, Ted Brian (1964–)
SEX: M   RACE: H   TYPE: T   MOTIVE: CE
DATE(S): 1987   VENUE: Bakersfield, Calif.   VIC-
  TIMS: Three
MO: Beat/stabbed robbery victims
DISPOSITION: Condemned

Sanchez-Velasco, Rigoberto (1959–)
SEX: M   RACE: H   TYPE: T   MOTIVE: Sex./PC
DATE(S): 1986/1995   VENUE: Florida   VICTIMS:
  Three
MO: Rape-slayer of an 11-year-old girl in Miami; later
  killed two death row inmates at state prison
DISPOSITION: Condemned on one count, plus life for
  sexual battery on a child and five years for theft;
  received two terms of 15 years to life for prison slay-
  ings, June 1998

Sanders, Martin Lee (?–)
SEX: M   RACE: W   TYPE: N   MOTIVE: Sex.
DATE(S): 1980–90   VENUE: Washington State   VIC-
  TIMS: Four alleged
MO: Long-haul trucker and rape-slayer of teenaged
  girls
DISPOSITION: Arrested 1990; confessed two murders
  to avoid execution; received life prison term

Santo, Anthony (1894–)
SEX: M   RACE: H   TYPE: N   MOTIVE: PC-non-
  specific
DATE(S): 1908   VENUE: N.Y./Mass.   VICTIMS:
  Three
MO: Murdered younger children during "mad spells"
DISPOSITION: Ruled insane; committed to asylum for
  life

Santonastaso, Peter (?–)   AKA: Monster of Caserta
SEX: M   RACE: W   TYPE: T   MOTIVE: Sex.
DATE(S): 1994–95   VENUE: Caserta, Italy   VIC-
  TIMS: Four suspected
MO: Slayer of female prostitutes
DISPOSITION: Pled guilty on one count; sentence
  unknown

Santos, José Augusto dos (1960–)
SEX: M   RACE: H   TYPE: T   MOTIVE: Cult
DATES(S): 1995–2000   VENUE: São Paulo, Brazil
  VICTIMS:Two
MO: Priest of Candomblé religion, linked to human
  sacrifice and grave robberies; 16 human skulls and
  other bones found at his home; formally charged
  with killing a child and a man whose remains were
  recovered
DISPOSITION: Unknown

Santos, Steven (1982–)
SEX: M   RACE: Unk.   TYPE: T   MOTIVE: CE-
  felony
DATE(S): 2002   VENUE: New York City   VICTIMS:
  Three
MO: Burglar who shot three victims aged 49–88, in the
  same apartment house
DISPOSITION: Convicted and sentenced to life impris-
  onment, November 2003

Sapp, John (1949–)
SEX: M   RACE: W   TYPE: N   MOTIVE: PC
DATE(S): 1975–86   VENUE: Calif.   VICTIMS:
  Four+ suspected
MO: Drifter linked to the deaths of his mother, girl-
  friend, and two male victims
DISPOSITION: Condemned, 1987

Sappington, Marc V. (1979–)
SEX: M   RACE: W   TYPE: T   MOTIVE: PC-nonspecific
DATE(S): 2001   VENUE: Kansas City, Kan.   VIC-
  TIMS: Three
MO: Drug addict who heard voices predicting his
  death if he did not kill various neighbors; cannibalized the youngest of his victims, also kidnapping a
  fourth, who survived
DISPOSITION: On Sept. 4, 2004 received a life term
  with 75-year minimum for three murders, plus six
  and a half years for kidnapping and two and a half
  years for carjacking

Sarmento, William (1966–)
SEX: M   RACE: W   TYPE: T   MOTIVE: PC-non-
  specific
DATE(S): 1987   VENUE: Providence, R.I.   VIC-
  TIMS: Two
MO: Killed two young boys, blaming orders from
  Satan
DISPOSITION: Ruled incompetent; committed to asy-
  lum, 1989

Sarwar, Maulvi Gulam (?–)
SEX: M   RACE: A   TYPE: T   MOTIVE: PC-
  extremist
DATE(S): 2001   VENUE: Lahore, Pakistan   VIC-
  TIMS: Four confessed
MO: Religious fanatic who attacked five prostitutes,
  killing four
DISPOSITION: Confessed his crimes in custody, then
  recanted; charges dismissed when witnesses refused
  to testify

Savage, Gail (1963–)
SEX: F   RACE: W   TYPE: S   MOTIVE: PC-nonspecific
DATE(S): 1991–93   VENUE: Waukegan, Ill.   VICTIMS: Three
MO: Killed her own children; deaths blamed on SIDS
DISPOSITION: 20 years on guilty plea to three manslaughter counts, 1994

Savini, Paul (?–)   AKA: Monster of St. Remo
SEX: M   RACE: W   TYPE: T   MOTIVE: Sex.
DATE(S): 1991–92   VENUE: St. Remo, Italy   VICTIMS: Four suspected
MO: Smothered middle-aged prostitutes
DISPOSITION: Suicide to avoid arrest, 1992

Schaefer, Gary Lee (1951–)
SEX: M   RACE: W   TYPE: T   MOTIVE: Sex.
DATE(S): 1979–83   VENUE: Springfield, Vt.   VICTIMS: Three
MO: Rape-slayer of young girls
DISPOSITION: 30 years to life in plea bargain on one count

Scheanette, Dale Devon (1973–)
SEX: M   RACE: W   TYPE: T   MOTIVE: Sex.
DATE(S): 1996   VENUE: Arlington, Tex.   VICTIMS: Two
MO: Raped five women during home invasions, killing two aged 22 and 25; victims left nude in their bathtubs
DISPOSITION: Condemned on two counts, January 2003

Schlatter, Darrell (1952–)
SEX: M   RACE: W   TYPE: T   MOTIVE: CE
DATE(S): 1985–92   VENUE: Tulsa, Okla.   VICTIMS: Three
MO: Swindler who murdered his victims
DISPOSITION: Suicide by hanging in jail, June 30, 1993

Schmid, Charles Howard, Jr. (1942–75)   AKA: Pied Piper of Tucson
SEX: M   RACE: W   TYPE: T   MOTIVE: PC-nonspecific
DATE(S): 1964–65   VENUE: Tucson, Ariz.   VICTIMS: Three
MO: Thirll killer of girls age 15–19
DISPOSITION: Condemned, 1966 (commuted, 1972); murdered in prison, Mar. 1975

Schmidt, Helmuth (d. 1918)   AKA: American Bluebeard
SEX: M   RACE: W   TYPE: N   MOTIVE: CE
DATE(S): 19??–18   VENUE: Mich./N.Y./N.J./Mo.
VICTIMS: "Dozens" suspected
MO: Profit-motivated "Bluebeard" slayer of immigrant women, lured with ads in newspaper "lonely-hearts" columns
DISPOSITION: Jailhouse suicide in Mich. prior to trial on one count, 1918

Schmidt, William Cecil, Jr. (1933–89)
SEX: M   RACE: W   TYPE: N   MOTIVE: PC-nonspecific
DATE(S): 1987–89   VENUE: Ga./Ariz.   VICTIMS: Three suspected
MO: "Survivalist" gunrunner and occultist; linked to beating/strangulation of three women, including his wife
DISPOSITION: Suicide in Ariz. to avoid capture, Jan. 1990

Schrott, Ernest (?–)   AKA: Monster of Bolzano
SEX: M   RACE: W   TYPE: T   MOTIVE: Sex.
DATE(S): 1993–95   VENUE: Bolzano, Italy   VICTIMS: Two confessed
MO: Rape-slayer of women
DISPOSITION: Pled guilty; sentence unknown

Schultz (1870–21)
SEX: M   RACE: W   TYPE: T   MOTIVE: PC
DATE(S): 1894–1920   VENUE: Spandau, Germany   VICTIMS: 11
MO: Random slayer of men, women, and children, including two brothers-in-law
DISPOSITION: Executed, 1921

Scieri, Antoinette (?–?)
SEX: F   RACE: W   TYPE: T   MOTIVE: CE
DATE(S): 1924–26   VENUE: St. Gilles, France   VICTIMS: 12
MO: "Nurse" who robbed/killed elderly patients
DISPOSITION: Condemned, 1926 (sentence commuted to life on appeal)

Scott, Kody (1963–)   AKA: Monster
SEX: M   RACE: B   TYPE: T   MOTIVE: CE/PC
DATE(S): 1975–85   VENUE: Los Angeles, Calif.   VICTIMS: 12+ admitted
MO: Violent member of Crips street gang
DISPOSITION: Seven years for attempted murder, 1985 (paroled 1988); seven years for assault and auto theft, 1991

Scripps, John Martin (d. 1996)
SEX: M   RACE: W   TYPE: N   MOTIVE: CE

DATE(S): 1994–95   VENUE: Central America/Southeast Asia   VICTIMS: Four+

MO: Trained butcher and British escaped convict; victims robbed and dismembered during global flight from justice

DISPOSITION: Hanged in Singapore, Apr. 19, 1996

Scully, Anthony (1944–)

SEX: M   RACE: W   TYPE: T   MOTIVE: CE/Sex.

DATE(S): 1983   VENUE: Oakland/San Francisco, Calif.   VICTIMS: Seven

MO: Ex-cop who killed prostitutes and a drug dealer, sealing some bodies in oil drums, left in Golden Gate Park

DISPOSITION: Life without parole, 1986

Seager, Monte (1962–)

SEX: M   RACE: W   TYPE: T   MOTIVE: Sex.

DATE(S); 1987–79   VENUE: Mt. Pleasant, Iowa   VICTIMS: Three

MO: Shot a woman before raping and shooting her 12-year-old daughter; later beat a second woman to death

DISPOSITION: Charged with double murder in 1981, dismissed due to improper search; convicted of 1979 murder and sentenced to a life term, completed in February 2000; convicted of double murder in 1999, overturned on appeal in 1999; convicted of double murder at second trial, Aug. 2000, receiving two consecutive life terms

Sears, Charles (1949–)

SEX: M   RACE: W   TYPE: T   MOTIVE: PC-nonspecific

DATE(S): 1981   VENUE: New York City   VICTIMS: Two

MO: Slashed male vagrants with razor in random street assaults

DISPOSITION: Ruled incompetent and committed to asylum, 1982

Seda, Heriberto (1970–)   AKA: Zodiac

SEX: M   RACE: H   TYPE: T   MOTIVE: PC-nonspecific

DATE(S): 1990–94   VENUE: New York City   VICTIMS: Three

MO: Random street shootings of nine victims; three died

DISPOSITION: 83 years on three counts, 1998

Seefeld, Adolf (1871–1936)

SEX: M   RACE: W   TYPE: N   MOTIVE: Sex.

DATE(S): 1908–35   VENUE: Germany   VICTIMS: 12 confessed

MO: Pedophile poisoner of prepubescent boys

DISPOSITION: Executed May 23, 1936

Segee, Robert Dale (1930–)

SEX: M   RACE: W   TYPE: N   MOTIVE: Sad./Pyearomania

DATE(S): 1938–50   VENUE: New England/Japan   VICTIMS: 173 confessed

MO: Murdered children in individual assaults; set many fires, including one that killed 169 victims

DISPOSITION: Confessed in 1950; never charged with murder; four to 40 years for arson in Conn.; released from supervision, May 1959

Seiha Fujima (1961–)

SEX: M   RACE: A   TYPE: N   MOTIVE: PC

DATE(S): 1981–82   VENUE: Japan   VICTIMS: Four

MO: Killed a 21-year-old man in dispute over money (Yokohama); next stabbed a 45-year-old woman and her two teenage daughters (Fujisawa); finally killed his 19-year-old accomplice in those murders (Amagasaki)

DISPOSITION: Condemned; death sentence upheld on appeal, June 17, 2004

Selepe, David (d. 1994)   AKA: Cleveland Strangler

SEX: M   RACE: B   TYPE: T   MOTIVE: Sex.

DATE(S): 1990s   VENUE: Cleveland, South Africa   VICTIMS: 11 alleged

MO: Rape-strangler of women

DISPOSITION: Shot by policeman he attacked during tour of murder sites, Dec. 17, 1994

Sellers, Sean Richard (1969–)

SEX: M   RACE: W   TYPE: T   MOTIVE: PC-extremist

DATE(S): 1985–86   VENUE: Oklahoma City   VICTIMS: Three

MO: Shot his parents and a store clerk as satanic sacrifices

DISPOSITION: Condemned, 1986; executed Feb. 4, 1999

Selman, John (1839–96)

SEX: M   RACE: W   TYPE: N   MOTIVE: PC/CE

DATE(S): 1880–96   VENUE: Tex.   VICTIMS: 20

MO: Renegade lawman and outlaw; victims included BASS OUTLAW and JOHN WESLEY HARDIN

DISPOSITION: Killed in shootout with fellow lawman, Apr. 1, 1896

Serviatti, Cesar (?–)   AKA: Monster of the Railway Line

SEX: M   RACE: W   TYPE: N   MOTIVE: PC-nonspecific

DATE(S): 1988   VENUE: Italy   VICTIMS: Seven
MO: Killed victims along Railroad line between Rome and La Spezia
DISPOSITION: Convicted; sentence unknown

Sexton, Eddie Lee (1942–   )
SEX: M   RACE: W   TYPE: T   MOTIVE: PC-domestic
DATE(S): 1993   VENUE: Hillsborough County, Fla.   VICTIMS: Two
MO: Abusive/incestuous father who commanded his children to kill; daughter smothered her infant child on his orders; son strangled the child's father (Sexton's son-in-law)
DISPOSITION: Condemned + 15 years for conspiracy, 1995; death sentence overturned with new trial ordered, 1997

Shah, Abdullah (1965–   )   AKA: Zavad's Dog
SEX: M   RACE: A   TYPE: T   MOTIVE: PC-extremist
DATE(S): 1992–96   VENUE: Afghanistan   VICTIMS: Hundreds
MO: Served under commander Zavad during civil war, slaughtering numerous civilian victims en route between Kabul and Jalalabad during Afghan civil war; also killed four of his five wives, one scalded with boiling oil
DISPOSITION: First murder trial imposed a 20-year sentence; trial judge dismissed and replaced for second trial; executed on conviction of 20 murders, April 20, 2004

Shapiro, Jacob (1899–1947)   AKA: Gurrah
SEX: M   RACE: W   TYPE: T   MOTIVE: CE
DATE(S): 1920s–36   VENUE: N.Y./N.J.   VICTIMS: "Numerous"
MO: Labor racketeer and sadistic gangland killer
DISPOSITION: Life term in N.Y., 1936; died in prison, 1947

Sharafudin (?–?)   AKA: Butcher of Hooshiarpore
SEX: M   RACE: A   TYPE: N   MOTIVE: CE
DATE(S): 1850s–60s   VENUE: India   VICTIMS: 14+
MO: "Notorious poisoner" of intended robbery victims; one report by British officer alludes to "hundreds" poisoned, though a majority of those poisoned apparently survived
DISPOSITION: "Baffled pursuit"; never captured

Shawcross, Arthur John (1945–   )
SEX: M   RACE: W   TYPE: T   MOTIVE: Sex.
DATE(S): 1972/1988–89   VENUE: Rochester, N.Y.   VICTIMS: 13
MO: Sex slayer of two children (1972) and 11 female prostitutes
DISPOSITION: 25 years on one count, 1972 (paroled 1987); 250 years on 10 counts, 1991

Shaw, Gary A. (?–   )
SEX: M   RACE: W   TYPE: T   MOTIVE: Sex.
DATE(S): 1985   VENUE: Tacoma, Wash.   VICTIMS: Two
MO: Rape-slayer of women who were dumped in the woods outside town
DISPOSITION: Life prison term

Shaw, Sebastian Alexander (1967) Born: Chau Quong Ho
SEX: M   RACE: A   TYPE: T   MOTIVE: PC/Sex.
DATE(S): 1991–92   VENUE: Portland, Ore.   VICTIMS: Three
MO: Enraged at coworkers, killed total strangers to vent anger while avoiding suspicion; also raped one male victim's girlfriend and another woman, who survived; DNA linked him to a second woman's rape-slaying
DISPOSITION: Pleaded guilty on two murder counts and received a life sentence in 2000; charged with second killing in 2004; judge issued rare pretrial acquittal on grounds of "inexcusable neglect" by prosecution

Shearing, David William (1959–   )
SEX: M   RACE: W   TYPE: T   MOTIVE: Sex./Sad.
DATE(S): 1983   VENUE: British Columbia   VICTIMS: Six
MO: Killed four adult campers aged 40–66; took two of their daughters, aged 11 and 13, as sex slaves, then murdered them later
DISPOSITION: Received six concurrent life terms with a 25-year minimum, April 17, 1984

Shekhar, Shashi (1976–   )
SEX: M   RACE: A   TYPE: N   MOTIVE: CE-felony
DATE(S): 1995–96   VENUE: India   VICTIMS: Four
MO: Strangled household maids and robbed the homes of their employers
DISPOSITION: Received four consecutive life terms in two murder trials, the second completed on April 30, 2004

Shepherd, Joseph (?–   )
SEX: M   RACE: ?   TYPE: T   MOTIVE: PC
DATE(S): 1992/94   VENUE: Tenn.   VICTIMS: Two
MO: Killed first victim in 1992; teen girl killed in 1994
DISPOSITION: Convicted on first count (overturned on appeal); condemned, 1994 (commuted, 1995)

Sherman, Lydia (1825–79)   AKA: Queen Poisoner
SEX: F   RACE: W   TYPE: N   MOTIVE: CE
DATE(S): 1864–71   VENUE: N.Y./Conn.   VICTIMS: 10
MO: "Black widow" poisoner of husbands and children for life insurance
DISPOSITION: Life sentence; died in prison May 16, 1879

Shikder, Ershad (d. 2004)
SEX: M   RACE: A   TYPE: T   MOTIVE: PC/CE-felony
DATE(S): 1984–2004   VENUE: Khulna, Bangladesh VICTIMS: 79+
MO: Criminal "godfather" and enforcer for political interests who also killed personal enemies; bodyguards report that he committed at least 20 murders personally and ordered 59; arrested after he killed a member of the ruling political clique
DISPOSITION: Hanged on conviction of seven murders, May 11, 2004

Shipin, Sergei (1975–   )
SEX: M   RACE: W   TYPE: T   MOTIVE: Sex./Sad.
DATE(S): 1998–99   VENUE: St. Petersburg, Russia VICTIMS: 10
MO: Serial rapist who attacked 12 women, killing 10; several murder victims were cannibalized
DISPOSITION: Confessed his crimes in November 1999; sentence unknown

Shobek, Michiah (1954–76)
SEX: M   RACE: B   TYPE: T   MOTIVE: PC-nonspecific
DATE(S): 1976   VENUE: Nassau, Bahamas   VICTIMS: Three
MO: Stabbed male American tourists, describing them as "angels of Lucifer"
DISPOSITION: Hanged Oct. 19, 1976

Short, Luke (1854–93)   AKA: Understaker's Friend
SEX: M   RACE: W   TYPE: N   MOTIVE: PC
DATE(S): 1876–90   VENUE: Kans./Colo./Tex.   VICTIMS: 10+
MO: Bootlegger, gambler, and gunfighter
DISPOSITION: Died of dropsy at age 39

Shreeves, Bruce Henderson (1951–   )
SEX: M   RACE: W   TYPE: T   MOTIVE: PC-nonspecific
DATE(S): 1973   VENUE: Montgomery County, Md. VICTIMS: Two

MO: AWOL sailor; shot male adults in unprovoked attacks
DISPOSITION: Life sentence, 1973

Shulman, Robert (1954–   )
SEX: M   RACE: W   TYPE: T   MOTIVE: Sex.
DATE(S): 1998   VENUE: New York City   VICTIMS: Five
MO: Dismembered female prostitutes from Queens, leaving remains in trash bins throughout Brooklyn and Westchester County
DISPOSITION: Condemned on three counts, May 7, 1999

Sides, Mervin (?–   )
SEX: M   RACE: W   TYPE: N   MOTIVE: CE
DATE(S): 1989   VENUE: Nev./Okla.   VICTIMS: Eight confessed; three confirmed
MO: Executed victims of kidnap-robberies
DISPOSITION: Life without parole on two counts in Okla., 1990; life with 15 years minimum in Nev., 1993; accomplice Bill Harris sentenced to life without parole in Okla.

Sidyno, Samuel (1962–   )   AKA: Capital Park Killer
SEX: M   RACE: B   TYPE: T   MOTIVE: Sex.
DATE(S): 1998–99   VENUE: Pretoria, South Africa VICTIMS: Seven
MO: Alleged strangler of two females and five males aged 12–25; female victims were raped
DISPOSITION: Received seven life terms on Sept. 6, 2000

Siebert, Daniel Lee (1955–   )
SEX: M   RACE: W   TYPE: N   MOTIVE: Sex./Sad.
DATE(S): 1979/85–86   VENUE: Nev./N.J./Calif./Ala. VICTIMS: 11+
MO: Stabbed gay man (1979); strangled women and children
DISPOSITION: Convicted of manslaughter, 1979 (paroled 1985); condemned in Ala., 1987

Siegel, Benjamin (1905–47)   AKA: Bugsy
SEX: M   RACE: W   TYPE: N   MOTIVE: CE/PC
DATE(S): 1920s–40s   VENUE: N.Y./N.J./Calif.   VICTIMS: "Numerous"
MO: Psychopathic racketeer; insisted on personal involvement in murders even after elevation to "boss" status
DISPOSITION: Murdered for embezzling mob money, June 20, 1947

Sigsbee, Donald M. (1935–   )
SEX: M   RACE: Unk.   TYPE: T   MOTIVE: Sex.

DATE(S): 1973–76   VENUE: Madison County, N.Y.
   VICTIMS: Five alleged
MO: Rape-slayer of female hitchhikers aged 12–21
DISPOSITION: Received sentence of 25 years to life on
   one murder count, April 20, 2004

Silva, Mauricio Rodriguez (1960–   )
SEX: M   RACE: H   TYPE: T   MOTIVE: PC
DATE(S): 1978/84   VENUE: Los Angeles, Calif.
   VICTIMS: Four
MO: Shot three teenagers and strangled his own half-
   sister
DISPOSITION: Convicted of manslaughter, 1978
   (paroled 1984); condemned on three counts, 1985;
   commuted to life, April 2001

Silveria, Robert Joseph (1958–   )   AKA: Boxcar Killer
SEX: M   RACE: W   TYPE: N   MOTIVE: PC/CE
DATE(S): 1980s–96   VENUE:
   Ore./Mont./Utah/Wash./Calif./Ariz./Kans./Fla.
   VICTIMS: 14+
MO: Transient who murdered other hoboes
DISPOSITION: Two consecutive life terms in Ore.,
   1998

Simmons, Beoria Abraham, III (1954–   )
SEX: M   RACE: B   TYPE: T   MOTIVE: Sex.
DATE(S): 1981–83   VENUE: Louisville, Ky.   VIC-
   TIMS: Three
MO: Rape-slayer of white women kidnapped and shot
DISPOSITION: Condemned

Simmons, Willie (1964–   )
SEX: M   RACE: B   TYPE: T   MOTIVE: PC-nonspe-
   cific
DATE(S): 1987   VENUE: St. Louis, Mo.   VICTIMS:
   Two
MO: Bludgeoned/strangled women during home inva-
   sions
DISPOSITION: Condemned, 1989

Simon, Robert R. (1950–   )   AKA: Mudman
SEX: M   RACE: W   TYPE: N   MOTIVE: CE/Sex.
DATE(S): 1971–95   VENUE: Pa./N.J./Va.   VICTIMS:
   Seven+ suspected
MO: Outlaw biker and career criminal; shot woman
   who resisted sex (1974); killed police officer follow-
   ing robbery (1995)
DISPOSITION: 10–20 years in Pa., 1982 (paroled
   1995); condemned in N.J., 1997

Simons, Norman Afzal (1974–   )   AKA: Station
   Strangler
SEX: M   RACE: W   TYPE: T   MOTIVE: Sex.

DATE(S): 1986–94   VENUE: Cape Town, South
   Africa   VICTIMS: 22
MO: Gay slayer of young boys; chose mixed-race victims
DISPOSITION: 25 years on one count; increased to life
   term on appeal

Sims, Paula Marie (1959–   )
SEX: F   RACE: W   TYPE: T   MOTIVE: PC-nonspe-
   cific
DATE(S): 1986/89   VENUE: Ill.   VICTIMS: Two
MO: Killed her own infant children, blaming "masked
   intruders"
DISPOSITION: Life without parole, 1990

Sinclair, Angus (1945–   )
SEX: M   RACE: W   TYPE: N   MOTIVE: Sex.
DATE(S): 1977–80   VENUE: Scotland   VICTIMS:
   12+ alleged
MO: Rape slayer of young women abducted from or
   near urban bars
DISPOSITION: Received life sentence in 1982 for 14
   sexual assaults on girls aged 6–14 during 1978–79;
   received second life term on one count of murder,
   2001; DNA links him to other slayings

Sinclair, Charles T. (d. 1990)
SEX: M   RACE: W   TYPE: N   MOTIVE: CE-felony
DATE(S): 1980–90   VENUE: U.S./Canada   VIC-
   TIMS: 12
MO: Executed coin shop proprietors in robberies
   across seven U.S. states and British Columbia
DISPOSITION: Died of heart attack in jail before trial,
   Aug. 1990

Singh, Dara (?–   )
SEX: M   RACE: A   TYPE: N   MOTIVE: PC-
   extremist
DATE(S): 1999   VENUE: Eastern India   VICTIMS:
   Three
MO: Hindu extremist who led mobs against spokes-
   men for other religions in the Keonihar and
   Mayurbhani districts; burned to death an Australian
   missionary and his two young sons; later lynched a
   Muslim merchant and torched his store
DISPOSITION: Singh condemned on three counts,
   Sept. 22, 2003; 12 unnamed accomplices received
   life prison terms at the same time

Siswanto (?–   )   AKA: Robot Gedek
SEX: M   RACE: A   TYPE: N   MOTIVE: Sex./Sad.
DATE(S): 1994–96   VENUE: Indonesia   VICTIMS:
   12 confessed
MO: Pedophile mutilator of boys age nine to 15
DISPOSITION: Condemned, 1997

Smallwood, Frederick Baker, Sr. (1944–)
SEX: M   RACE: W   TYPE: N   MOTIVE: CE
DATE(S): 1991/95   VENUE: Ga./Va.   VICTIMS: Two
MO: Baptist minister and "Bluebeard" slayer of women for profit
DISPOSITION: Life sentence in Va., 1995

Smith, Benjamin Nathaniel (1978–99)
SEX: M   RACE: W   TYPE: N   MOTIVE: PC-extremist
DATE(S): 1999   VENUE: Ill./Ind.   VICTIMS: Two
MO: Neo-Nazi cultist who targeted racial/ethnic minorities in drive-by shootings; shot 10 victims, killing two
DISPOSITION: Suicide by gunshot during police pursuit near Salem, Ill., on July 3, 1999

Smith, Charles (?–)
SEX: M   RACE: W   TYPE: T   MOTIVE: PC-nonspecific
DATE(S): 1958   VENUE: Miami, Fla.   VICTIMS: Two
MO: Shot male victims without apparent motive
DISPOSITION: Life sentence, 1958

Smith, Frank Lee (1947–)
SEX: M   RACE: B   TYPE: T   MOTIVE: PC/CE/Sex.
DATE(S): 1960/65/85   VENUE: Broward County, Fla.   VICTIMS: Three
MO: Stabbed boy in argument; shot holdup victim; raped/killed eight-year-old girl
DISPOSITION: 11 months juvenile detention, ⸝ 1960–61; life term, 1966; condemned, 1985

Smith, George Joseph (1872–1915)   AKA: Brides-in-the-bath Murderer
SEX: M   RACE: W   TYPE: T   MOTIVE: CE
DATE(S): 1912–14   VENUE: England   VICTIMS: Three
MO: "Bluebeard" slayer of wives for profit, drowning each in the bathtub as staged "accidents"
DISPOSITION: Hanged Aug. 13, 1915

Smith, Gerald (d. 1990)
SEX: M   RACE: W   TYPE: T   MOTIVE: PC
DATE(S): 1980s   VENUE: Mo.   VICTIMS: Two
MO: Beat ex-girlfriend to death, 1980; stabbed prison inmate
DISPOSITION: Condemned on both counts; executed Jan. 18, 1990

Smith, John David (1950–)
SEX: M   RACE: W   TYPE: N   MOTIVE: PC

DATE(S): 1974/1994   VENUE: Ohio/N.J.   VICTIMS: Two
MO: Bluebeard slayer of wives reported missing 20 years apart; remains of first wife found 1980, identified in 2000; second wife still missing
DISPOSITION: Convicted of first wife's murder in Ohio; received a term of 15 years to life on July 19, 2001; held responsible for second wife's death in a New Jersey civil lawsuit, Dec. 21, 2000

Smith, Joseph Clarence, Jr. (1949–)
SEX: M   RACE: W   TYPE: T   MOTIVE: Sex.
DATE(S): 1975–76   VENUE: Phoenix, Ariz.   VICTIMS: Two
MO: Stabbed/suffocated teenage female hitchhikers
DISPOSITION: Condemned on one count, pled guilty on second, 1977

Smith, Lemuel Warren (?–)
SEX: M   RACE: ?   TYPE: N   MOTIVE: CE-felony
DATE(S): 1976–81   VENUE: N.Y.   VICTIMS: Three
MO: Shot two holdup victims; beat/strangled female prison guard
DISPOSITION: three life terms, 1977; condemned 1983; sentence commuted

Smith, Mark Alan (1949–)
SEX: M   RACE: W   TYPE: N   MOTIVE: Sex.
DATE(S): 1966–70   VENUE: South Korea/Germany/U.S.   VICTIMS: 15–20
MO: Rape-slayer of young women on three continents
DISPOSITION: 500 years for three counts in Ill., 1971

Smith, Ned (?–)
SEX: M   RACE: W   TYPE: T   MOTIVE: PC/CE
DATE(S): 1981–1990   VENUE: Sydney, Australia   VICTIMS: More than seven
MO: Syndicate mobster who killed a trucker in a road-rage incident; later confessed six other slayings to a prison cellmate
DISPOSITION: Life sentence for the trucker's murder, 1990; turned state's evidence against fellow gangsters, 1993; indicted on four additional murder counts, 1995; received another life prison term, September 1998

Smith, Philip John (1966–)   AKA: Big Foot
SEX: M   RACE: W   TYPE: N   MOTIVE: Sex./Sad.
DATE(S): 1985–2000   VENUE: U.K./Ireland   VICTIMS: 40 suspected
MO: Traveling fair worker who bludgeoned women in random attacks throughout England, Scotland, Wales, and Ireland

DISPOSITION: Received life prison term for murders of three women at Birmingham, England, July 18, 2001

Smith, Stephen Richard (?–86)
SEX: M   RACE: W   TYPE: T   MOTIVE: PC
DATE(S): 1982–86   VENUE: San Antonio, Tex.
VICTIMS: Three+ suspected
MO: Vigilante cop linked to shootings of suspected criminals
DISPOSITION: Killed by fellow officer, Aug. 17, 1986

Smith, William Scott (?–   )
SEX: M   RACE: W   TYPE: N   MOTIVE: Sex.
DATE(S): 1981/84   VENUE: Idaho/Ore.   VICTIMS: Three suspected
MO: Lust killer of females age 14–21
DISPOSITION: Life term with 40-year minimum on two counts in Ore., 1984

Smithers, Samuel Lee (1953–   )
SEX: M   RACE: W   TYPE: T   MOTIVE: PC
DATE(S): 1996   VENUE: Hillsborough Co., Fla.
VICTIMS: Two
MO: Murders committed in personal altercations, 16 days apart
DISPOSITION: Condemned on two counts, June 25, 1999

Smyth, Evan (1964–   )
SEX: M   RACE: W   TYPE: T   MOTIVE: PC-non-specific
DATE(S): 2003   VENUE: Wheaton, Md.   VICTIMS: Four
MO: Over a two-week period, stabbed a 20-year-old man, shot a 21-year-old man, then beat and strangled a 17-year-old girl in her home; flesh found at the third crime scene matched DNA of a 43-year-old man still missing.
DISPOSITION: Pleaded guilty on four counts and received four consecutive life terms, July 2004

Snell, Richard Wayne (1930–95)
SEX: M   RACE: W   TYPE: N   MOTIVE: PC-extremist
DATE(S): 1994   VENUE: Ark.   VICTIMS: Two
MO: Neo-Nazi; shot black policeman and pawnbroker thought to be Jewish
DISPOSITION: Executed Apr. 19, 1995

Snow, David Alexander (1955–   )
SEX: M   RACE: W   TYPE: T   MOTIVE: Sex.
DATE(S): 1991–92   VENUE: Ontario, Canada   VICTIMS: Four suspected

MO: Killed a married couple and two women; female victims raped
DISPOSITION: Life term on two counts, 1997

Snyder, David E., Jr. (1963–   )
SEX: M   RACE: W   TYPE: TN   MOTIVE: Sex.
DATE(S): 1982–84   VENUE: Fla./Md.   VICTIMS: Four suspected
MO: Rape-slayer of girls age 14–17
DISPOSITION: Life sentence on one count in Md., 1985

Snyder, Leroy (1931–   )
SEX: M   RACE: ?   TYPE: T   MOTIVE: CE/Sex.
DATE(S): 1969   VENUE: Camden, N.J.   VICTIMS: Seven confessed
MO: Robbed/beat/stabbed seven acquaintances, raping two of the females
DISPOSITION: three consecutive life terms, 1970

Sobig, Klaus Peter (1957–   )
SEX: M   RACE: W   TYPE: T   MOTIVE: Sex./Sad./CE
DATE(S): 1976/84   VENUE: Bielfeld, Germany   VICTIMS: Two
MO: Stabbed male robbery victim (1976); raped/strangled elderly woman during residential burglary (1984)
DISPOSITION: Nine and one-half years on one count, 1977 (paroled 1983); life term, 1985

Sodeman, Arnold Karl (1900–36)
SEX: M   RACE: W   TYPE: T   MOTIVE: Sex.
DATE(S): 1930–35   VENUE: Victoria, Australia   VICTIMS: Four
MO: Alcoholic strangler of girls age six to 16
DISPOSITION: Hanged, June 1936

Sokichi Furuya (1914–85)
SEX: M   RACE: A   TYPE: N   MOTIVE: CE
DATE(S): 1965   VENUE: Japan   VICTIMS: 10
MO: Robbed/killed elderly victims in their homes
DISPOSITION: Hanged, May 31, 1985

Sokolowski, David Allen (1957–   )
SEX: M   RACE: W   TYPE: S   MOTIVE: PC-conflict
DATE(S): 1992   VENUE: Schley, N.C.   VICTIMS: Two
MO: Dismembered female lover and male friend at his home
DISPOSITION: Life term with 20-year minimum, 1994

Solomon, Morris, Jr. (1944–   )
SEX: M   RACE: B   TYPE: T   MOTIVE: Sex.

DATE(S): 1986–87   VENUE: Sacramento, Calif.
   VICTIMS: Seven
MO: Rape-slayer of women in his neighborhood
DISPOSITION: Condemned, 1988

Somkid, Pumpuang
SEX: M   TYPE: N   MOTIVE: Sex
DATE(S): 2005   VENUE: Thailand   VICTIMS: 4–5
MO: Rape-strangler of female prostitutes
DISPOSITION: Arrested June 29, 2005; found with
   items stolen from various victims and confessed in
   custody to four murders. Police claim a fifth victim,
   whom Somkid denied killing. Trial pending at press
   time.

Sommer, Fred, Jr. (?–)
SEX: M   RACE: W   TYPE: T   MOTIVE: CE
DATE(S): 1957   VENUE: Cameron Mills, N.Y.   VIC-
   TIMS: Two
MO: Killed motorists to use cars in armed robberies
DISPOSITION: Life sentence, 1958

Sonner, Michael H. (1968–)
SEX: M   RACE: W   TYPE: N   MOTIVE: CE-felony
DATE(S): 1993   VENUE: Tex./Nev.   VICTIMS:
   Three
MO: Shot two robbery victims (Tex.) and police officer
   (Nev.)
DISPOSITION: Condemned in Nev., 1994

Sorenson, Della (1897–?)
SEX: F   RACE: W   TYPE: N   MOTIVE: PC-domes-
   tic
DATE(S): 1918–25   VENUE: Nebr.   VICTIMS: Seven
MO: "Black widow" poisoner of family members "to
   get even"
DISPOSITION: Ruled insane and committed to asy-
   lum, 1925

Soulakiotis, Mariam (1900–?)
SEX: F   RACE: W   TYPE: S   MOTIVE: PC-extremist
DATE(S): 1940–50   VENUE: Keratea, Greece   VIC-
   TIMS: 177
MO: Calendarist cult leader whose followers died from
   beatings, torture, and starvation
DISPOSITION: Two years for illegally detaining a
   child, 1951; 14 years for additional felonies, 1953;
   no murder charges

Sovdat, Matija (1975–)
SEX: M   RACE: W   TYPE: T   MOTIVE: PC-non-
   specific
DATE(S): 1994–96   VENUE: Stockholm, Sweden
   VICTIMS: Seven confessed

MO: Violent drug addict who confessed seven murders
   after police found effects of a missing 74-year-old
   woman in his home; other victims, of both sexes,
   ranged in age from 16 to 60; one victim mutilated
   with hands severed
DISPOSITION: Unknown

Spanbauer, David F. (1940–2002)
SEX: M   RACE: W   TYPE: T   MOTIVE: Sex.
DATE(S): 1994   VENUE: Wisc.   VICTIMS: Three
MO:Rape-slayer of females age 10–21
DISPOSITION: 403 years on three counts, 1994; died
   in prison, July 29, 2002

Spangler, Robert M. (1933–2001)
SEX: M   RACE: W   TYPE: N   MOTIVE: PC-nonspecific
DATE(S): 1978–94   VENUE: Colo./Ariz.   VICTIMS:
   Five
MO: Bluebeard killer of wives and children; shot first
   wife and two children in 1978, staging the scene as a
   murder-suicide by wife; pushed second wife into
   Grand Canyon, 1992; third wife died of drug overdose, 1994
DISPOSITION: Confessed four murders (excluding
   third wife) after diagnosis of cancer in 2000; died
   with trial pending, 2001

Spara, Hieronyma (d. 1659)
SEX: F   RACE: W   TYPE: T   MOTIVE: CE
DATE(S): 1650s   VENUE: Italy   VICTIMS:
   "Numerous"
MO: "Witch" and poisoner-for-hire of husbands
DISPOSITION: Hanged with one accomplice and three
   clients, 1659

Spaziano, Joseph Robert (1944–)   AKA: Crazy Joe
SEX: M   RACE: W   TYPE: T   MOTIVE: Sex./Sad.
DATE(S): 1973   VENUE: Altamonte Springs, Fla.
   VICTIMS: Two suspected
MO: Outlaw biker; alleged rape-slayer of young
   women left in dumpsters
DISPOSITION: Life + five years for rape/assault, 1975
   (victim blinded with a knife); condemned on one
   count, 1976 (death sentence overturned on appeal,
   new trial pending)

Speck, Richard Franklin (1941–91)
SEX: M   RACE: W   TYPE: N   MOTIVE: Sex.
DATE(S): 1966   VENUE: Ind./Ill.   VICTIMS: 12 suspected
MO: Linked to four random murders of women before
   he massacred eight student nurses in their Chicago
   rooming house

DISPOSITION: Condemned, 1966 (commuted 1972); died in prison Dec. 5, 1991

Spencer, Anthony (1947–   )
SEX: M   RACE: B   TYPE: T   MOTIVE: Sex.
DATE(S): 1964   VENUE: New York City   VICTIMS: Two
MO: Serial rapist; killed two of 14 known victims
DISPOSITION: Life sentence, 1965

Spencer, Diane (1968–   )
SEX: F   RACE: W   TYPE: N   MOTIVE: PC-nonspecific
DATE(S): 1983–90   VENUE: Mich./Pa.   VICTIMS: Three suspected
MO: Suffocated her young children, blaming SIDS
DISPOSITION: Life term on one count in Mich., 1992

Spencer, Timothy Wilson (1962–94)
SEX: M   RACE: B   TYPE: T   MOTIVE: Sex./Sad.
DATE(S): 1987   VENUE: Arlington County, Va.   VICTIMS: Four
MO: Serial rapist who tortured his victims, killing some
DISPOSITION: Executed Apr. 27, 1994

Spillman, Jack Owen, III (?–   )
SEX: M   RACE: W   TYPE: T   MOTIVE: Sex./Sad.
DATE(S): 1994–95   VENUE: Okanogan County, Wash.   VICTIMS: Three
MO: Rape-mutilation slayer of female victims, one nine years old; aspired to be the "world's greatest serial killer"
DISPOSITION: Confessed three counts to avoid death sentence; received life prison term, 1996

Spilotro, Anthony (1938–86)   AKA: Tony the Ant
SEX: M   RACE: W   TYPE: N   MOTIVE: CE/PC
DATE(S): 1960s–86   VENUE: Ill./Nev./Calif.   VICTIMS: 16–18 personal
MO: Mafia "enforcer" and hit man; ordered various murders aside from those committed personally
DISPOSITION: Murdered by gangland rivals in Ind., June 1986

Spisak, Frank G., Jr. (1950–   )
SEX: M   RACE: W   TYPE: T   MOTIVE: PC-extremist
DATE(S): 1982   VENUE: Cleveland, Ohio   VICTIMS: Four
MO: Transvestite Nazi; shot blacks and suspected Jews
DISPOSITION: Condemned, 1983

Spotz, Mark Newton (1972–   )
SEX: M   RACE: W   TYPE: N   MOTIVE: PC-nonspecific

DATE(S): 1995   VENUE: Pa.   VICTIMS: Four
MO: Shot brother and three women age 41–71, in four-county rampage
DISPOSITION: 17–30 years for manslaughter on one count; condemned on three others

Spraggins, Jerry Jerome (1955–   )
SEX: M   RACE: W   TYPE: S   MOTIVE: CE/Sex.
DATE(S): 1981–83   VENUE: Montclair, N.J.   VICTIMS: Three suspected
MO: Burglar-rapist linked to deaths of three women in the same apartment over two-year period
DISPOSITION: 30-year sentence on one count, 1985

Stafford, Roger Dale (1951–95)
SEX: M   RACE: W   TYPE: N   MOTIVE: CE
DATE(S): 1978   VENUE: Okla.   VICTIMS: Nine suspected
MO: Murdered a family of three in June 1978; shot six victims in a restaurant holdup three weeks later
DISPOSITION: Executed July 1, 1995

Stager, Barbara (1948–   )
SEX: F   RACE: W   TYPE: T   MOTIVE: CE
DATE(S): 1977/96   VENUE: Monroe County, Ohio   VICTIMS: Two
MO: "Black widow" slayer of husbands for insurance, in staged firearms "accidents"
DISPOSITION: Condemned on one count, 1989 (commuted on appeal)

Stapleburg, Marthinus Jakobus (1974–   )
SEX: M   RACE: W   TYPE: T   MOTIVE: PC-extremist/CE
DATE(S): 1995–96   VENUE: South Africa   VICTIMS: Five
MO: Racist gunman; shot blacks, robbing several victims
DISPOSITION: Life term, 1997

Starrett, Richard Daniel (1960–   )
SEX: M   RACE: W   TYPE: N   MOTIVE: Sex.
DATE(S): 1988–89   VENUE: S.C./Ga.   VICTIMS: Two
MO: Rapist/slayer of girls and young women met through newspaper classified ads
DISPOSITION: Five life terms in S.C., 1991; five life terms in Ga., 1993

Stefano, Raffaele de (?–   )   AKA: Vampire of Aversa
SEX: M   RACE: W   TYPE: T   MOTIVE: Sex.
DATE(S): 1992   VENUE: Aversa, Italy   VICTIMS: Two
MO: Victims gassed and stabbed to death
DISPOSITION: Life sentence

Stephani, Paul Michael (1944–) AKA:Weepy-voiced killer
SEX: M   RACE: W   TYPE: T   MOTIVE: PC-nonspecific
DATE(S): 1981–82   VENUE: Minneapolis/St. Paul
   VICTIMS: Three
MO: Stabbed women age 18–33 in random attacks
DISPOSITION: 40 years on one count, 1982; confessed two more from prison, 1997

Stevanin, Gianfranco (?–)
SEX: M   RACE: W   TYPE: T   MOTIVE: Sex./Sad.
DATE(S): 1990s   VENUE: Verona, Italy
   VICTIMS:Six
MO: Farmworker; raped/mutilated women
DISPOSITION: Life sentence, 1998

Stevens, Alan Michael (1942–) AKA: Buzzard
SEX: M   RACE: W   TYPE: T   MOTIVE: Sex.
DATE(S): 1985–90   VENUE: San Diego, Ca.   VICTIMS: Three to four suspected
MO: Drifter and rape-slayer of young women
DISPOSITION: 25 years to life on one count, 1991

Stevens, Charles Arnett (1960–)
SEX: M   RACE: B   TYPE: T   MOTIVE: PC-nonspecific
DATE(S): 1969–76   VENUE: Oakland, Calif.   VICTIMS: Three
MO: Shot freeway motorists in random drive-by attacks
DISPOSITION: Condemned

Stevens, Walter (1867–1939)   AKA: Dean of Chicago Gunmen
SEX: M   RACE: W   TYPE: T   MOTIVE: CE
DATE(S): c. 1900–29   VENUE: Chicago, Ill.   VICTIMS: 60+
MO: Syndicate hit man
DISPOSITION: Retired from mob involvement; died of natural causes

Stewart, Kenneth Allen (1963–)
SEX: M   RACE: B   TYPE: T   MOTIVE: CE
DATE(S): 1984–85   VENUE: Hillsborough County, Fla.   VICTIMS: Two
MO: Killed robbery victims and torched their homes
DISPOSITION: Condemned on two counts + 141 years, 1986

Stewart, Ray Lee (1942–86)
SEX: M   RACE: W   TYPE: T   MOTIVE: PC-nonspecific
DATE(S): 1981   VENUE: Rockford, Ill., and Beloit, Wisc.   VICTIMS: Six

MO: Shot male victims during a month-long murder spree
DISPOSITION: Executed on three counts in Illinois, Sept. 16, 1986

Stiles, Billie (d. 1908)
SEX: M   RACE: W   TYPE: N   MOTIVE: PC/CE
DATE(S): 1880s–1908   VENUE: Ariz./Nev.   VICTIMS: "Several"
MO: Outlaw and occasional lawman; killed own father at age 12
DISPOSITION: Shot from ambush by 12-year-old son of last victim, Jan. 1908

Stokes, Winford Lavern (1951–90)
SEX: M   RACE: B   TYPE: N   MOTIVE: PC-nonspecific
DATE(S): 1969–78   VENUE: Mo.   VICTIMS: Three
MO: Psychotic slayer of women
DISPOSITION: Ruled insane on two counts; escaped from asylum, 1978; executed on third count, May 12, 1990

Stone, Michael Anthony (1955–)
SEX: M   RACE: W   TYPE: T   MOTIVE: PC-extremist
DATE(S): 1984–88   VENUE: Belfast, North Ireland   VICTIMS: Six
MO: Sectarian assassin of Catholics and Republicans
DISPOSITION: Life term for six murders and five attempted murders, 1989

Stoudenmire, Dallas (1845–82)   AKA: Stoudenmire the Butcher
SEX: M   RACE: W   TYPE: T   MOTIVE: PC
DATE(S): 1881   VENUE: El Paso, Tex.   VICTIMS: Four+
MO: Quick-trigger renegade lawman
DISPOSITION: Killed in personal quarrel, Sept. 18, 1882

Straffen, John Thomas (1930–)
SEX: M   RACE: W   TYPE: T   MOTIVE: PC-nonspecific
DATE(S): 1951–52   VENUE: Bath/Farley Hill, England   VICTIMS: Three
MO: Deranged child killer; bludgeoned/stabbed girls age five to nine
DISPOSITION: Condemned, 1952; commuted to life the same year.

Strauss, Harry (1908–41)   AKA: Pittsburgh Phil; Pep
SEX: M   RACE: W   TYPE: N   MOTIVE: CE

DATE(S): 1932–40 VENUE: USA nationwide VICTIMS: 100+ suspected
MO: Premier killer of "MURDER, INC."
DISPOSITION: Executed at Sing Sing, June 12, 1941

Stroud, Robert Franklin (1887–1963) AKA: Bird Man of Alcatraz
SEX: M RACE: W TYPE: N MOTIVE: PC
DATE(S): Killed a personal enemy in Alaska; later murdered a prison guard
DISPOSITION: Received two consecutive life terms

Stuard, James William (1937–) AKA: Senior Citizen Killer
SEX: M RACE: B TYPE: T MOTIVE: Sex.
DATE(S): 1989 VENUE: Phoenix, Ariz. VICTIMS: Three
MO: Home-invading rape-slayer of women age 74–81
DISPOSITION: Convicted on three counts, 1990

Stuchberry, David (1948–97)
SEX: M RACE: W TYPE: N MOTIVE: Sex.
DATE(S): 1979–97 VENUE: England VICTIMS: Four suspected
MO: Ex-convict linked to beating deaths of women
DISPOSITION: Fatally stabbed by woman attacked in her home

Stuller, Nicklaus (d. 1577)
SEX: M RACE: W TYPE: T MOTIVE: Sex./Sad.
DATE(S): 1570s VENUE: Germany VICTIMS: Four
MO: "Ripper" who disemboweled pregnant women and a soldier
DISPOSITION: Publicly tortured to death, 1577

Stumpe (or Stubbe), Peter (d. 1589)
SEX: M RACE: W TYPE: T MOTIVE: Sex./Sad.
DATE(S): 1564–89 VENUE: Bedburg, Germany VICTIMS: 15+
MO: "Werewolf" cannibal-killer of numerous victims, including his own incestuous offspring
DISPOSITION: Beheaded and burned, Oct. 28, 1589; daughter Beell and mistress Katherine Trompin burned as accomplices

Stutzman, Eli E., Jr. (1950–)
SEX: M RACE: W TYPE: N MOTIVE: Sex.
DATE(S): 1977–85 VENUE: Ohio/Tex./Neb. VICTIMS: Five suspected
MO: Gay drifter; killed his wife, young son, and three men
DISPOSITION: 40 years on guilty plea to one count, in Tex.; HIV positive

Subbiah, Arulraj (1977–)
SEX: M RACE: A TYPE: T MOTIVE: PC-nonspecific
DATE(S): 1998–2001 VENUE: Palayamkottai, India VICTIMS: Three
MO: Stabbed his brother-in-law, bludgeoned a male coworker, then stabbed a male witness to the second killing; drank blood in each case
DISPOSITION: Granted bail on first and second cases; final disposition unknown

Succo, Robert (d. 1988)
SEX: M RACE: W TYPE: N MOTIVE: PC-nonspecific
DATE(S): 1988 VENUE: France VICTIMS: Six
MO: Paranoid schizophrenic slayer of three policemen and three civilians
DISPOSITION: Suicide in Italian jail, May 23, 1988

Suff, William Lester (1950–)
SEX: M RACE: W TYPE: N MOTIVE: PC/Sex./Sad.
DATE(S): 1973/85–92 VENUE: Tex./Calif. VICTIMS: 13–35
MO: Killed infant daughter; "ripper" of female prostitutes
DISPOSITION: 70 years in Tex., 1973 (paroled 1983); condemned, 1995

Sullivan, John Joseph (1939–) AKA: Mad Dog
SEX: M RACE: W TYPE: N MOTIVE: CE
DATE(S): 197?–81 VENUE: N.Y. VICTIMS: 23 suspected
MO: Career criminal; armed robber and contract killer
DISPOSITION: Life terms with 100-year minimum on three counts, 1982

Swango, Dr. Michael (1954–)
SEX: M RACE: W TYPE: N MOTIVE: PC-nonspecific
DATE(S): 1978–97 VENUE: U.S./Africa VICTIMS: "Dozens" suspected
MO: Named by FBI as probable serial killer of hospital patients in Ill., Ohio, Va., Namibia, Zambia, and Zimbabwe
DISPOSITION: Five-year term for poisoning Ill. paramedics, 1985 (paroled 1987); plea-bargained for 42-month sentence in N.Y. on charges of illegally prescribing drugs, 1998

Swann, James Edward, Jr. (1964–) AKA: Shotgun Stalker
SEX: M RACE: B TYPE: T MOTIVE: PC-nonspecific

DATE(S): 1993   VENUE: Washington, D.C.   VIC-
TIMS: Three
MO: "Possessed" drive-by slayer of victims shot at ran-
dom
DISPOSITION: Not guilty by reason of insanity, 1994

Swann, Lucas (1960–)
SEX: M   RACE: W   TYPE: T   MOTIVE: PC-non-
specific
DATE(S): 1987–88   VENUE: Stockport, England
VICTIMS: Two
MO: Stabbed man and woman in random attacks
DISPOSITION: 20 years to life on guilty plea, both
counts, 1988

Swearingen, Larry Ray (1971–)
SEX: M   RACE: W   TYPE: N   MOTIVE: Sex.
DATE(S): 1994/1998   VENUE: Ark./Tex.   VICTIMS:
Two
MO: Strangler of teenage girls who resembled each
other, both dumped in national forests within 50
miles of where they were kidnapped
DISPOSITION: Condemned on one count in Texas,
July 2000

Sweeney, John (1956–)
SEX: M   RACE: W   TYPE: N   MOTIVE: PC-nonspecific
DATE(S): 1994–2001   VENUE: London and Amsterdam   VICTIMS: Four
MO: Attacked five female lovers with axes and knives,
killing four
DISPOSITION: Convicted of a 1994 attempted murder, 2001; received four life terms for a second ax
attack and firearms violations, March 2002

Sweet, William Earl (1967–)
SEX: M   RACE: B   TYPE: T   MOTIVE: CE
DATE(S): 1990   VENUE: Duval County, Fla.   VIC-
TIMS: Two
MO: Home-invader; killed holdup victims
DISPOSITION: Condemned on one count, 1991; 35
years on second count, 1994

Swiatek (d. 1850)
SEX: M   RACE: W   TYPE: N   MOTIVE: PC-nonspecific
DATE(S): 1840s   VENUE: Austria   VICTIMS: Six+
confessed
MO: Transient cannibal-killer whose family shared the
meat
DISPOSITION: Jailhouse suicide by hanging, prior to
trial

Swindler, John E. (1944–90)
SEX: M   RACE: W   TYPE: N   MOTIVE: CE
DATE(S): ?   VENUE: Ark./S.C./Fla.   VICTIMS:
Four
MO: Killed victims in three states, including a police-
man in Ark.
DISPOSITION: Convicted on three counts in two
states; executed in Ark., June 18, 1990

Tadik, Dusko (1956–)
SEX: M   RACE: W   TYPE: T   MOTIVE: PC-
extremist
DATE(S): 1992   VENUE: Bosnia   VICTIMS: 123
alleged
MO: Bosnian Serb pub owner; tortured/killed Croatian
and Muslim neighbors during "ethnic cleansing"
DISPOSITION: Convicted on 11 counts of war crimes,
1997

Tannenbaum, Albert (1906–)   AKA: Allie; Tick-
Tock
SEX: M   RACE: W   TYPE: T   MOTIVE: CE
DATE(S): 1925–40   VENUE: N.Y./N.J.   VICTIMS:
Six+
MO: Contract killer for "MURDER, INC."
DISPOSITION: Immunity granted in exchange for tes-
timony

Tannenbaum, Gloria (d. 1971)
SEX: F   RACE: W   TYPE: T   MOTIVE: PC-nonspe-
cific
DATE(S): 1969   VENUE: Boulder, Colo.   VICTIMS:
Three suspected
MO: Poisoned two neighbors; linked to disappearance
of her lover
DISPOSITION: Committed to mental hospital, 1969;
suicide by poison while confined there, Mar. 9,
1971

Tanzi, Michael Anthony (1977–)
SEX: M   RACE: W   TYPE: N   MOTIVE: Sex.
DATE(S): 1999   VENUE: Fla./Mass.   VICTIMS:
Three suspected
MO: Kidnapped and strangled a 49-year-old woman;
prime suspect in murders of two more women at the
laundries where they worked alone
DISPOSITION: Condemned on one count in Florida
on April 11, 2003; also received three life terms
for kidnapping, armed robbery and armed carjacking

Tapson, Floyd (1960–)
SEX: M   RACE: W   TYPE: N   MOTIVE: Sex.

DATE(S): 1987–96   VENUE: Min./N. Dak./Mont.
VICTIMS: Three alleged
MO: Former group home employee, named by police
as sexual predator of mentally retarded women;
alleged victims include one killed in 1994; two missing in 1987 and 1996; one raped, shot, and left for
dead in 1998
DISPOSITION: Received life sentence with 30-year
minimum for nonfatal attack in Montana, Aug. 10,
1999; overturned on appeal, 2001; accepted plea
bargain in same case with two concurrent 75-year
terms for attempted murder and aggravated kidnapping, Nov. 22, 2003

Taylor, Blake Raymond (1966–   )
SEX: M   RACE: W   TYPE: T   MOTIVE: Sex.
DATE(S): 1985–88   VENUE: San Diego, Calif.   VIC-
TIMS: Three alleged
MO: Named by police as rape-slayer of prostitutes
DISPOSITION: Nine years for attempted murder of a
prostitute

Taylor, Gary Addison (1936–   )
SEX: M   RACE: W   TYPE: N   MOTIVE: Sex./Sad.
DATE(S): 1972–76   VENUE: Mich./Tex./Wash.
VICTIMS: 20 suspected
MO: Rape-slayer of women in at least three states
DISPOSITION: Life term on one count in Wash., Apr.
1976

Taylor, Kenneth Gordon (1941–   )
SEX: M   RACE: W   TYPE: N   MOTIVE: PC-non-
specific
DATE(S): 1977–78   VENUE: Tenn./Ohio/Pa.   VIC-
TIMS: 17 confessed
MO: Thrill-killer of victims selected at random
DISPOSITION: 30 years on one count of second
degree in Ohio, 1979

Taylor, Michael (1979–   )
SEX: M   RACE: Unk.   TYPE: T   MOTIVE: Sex./PC
DATE(S): 1995/1999   VENUE: Missouri   VICTIMS:
Two
MO: Murdered a teenaged girl; later strangled prison
cellmate
DISPOSITION: Life term on first murder; condemned
on second count, Jan. 19, 2003

Tcaiuc (1917–?)
SEX: M   RACE: W   TYPE: T   MOTIVE: PC-nonspecific
DATE(S): 1935   VENUE: Jasi, Romania   VICTIMS:
21 confessed

MO: Thrill-killer of men lured to the woods by his girlfriend, allegedly at her insistence
DISPOSITION: Unknown; probably executed

Tenneson, Michael (1960–   )
SEX: M   RACE: W   TYPE: N   MOTIVE: CE
DATE(S): 1987   VENUE: Wis./Colo.   VICTIMS: Five
MO: Escaped convict who killed/robbed victims of
both sexes
DISPOSITION: two life terms + 48 years in Colo.,
1988; three life terms in Wis., 1988

Tenney, Edward L. (1959–   )
SEX: M   RACE: W   TYPE: T   MOTIVE: PC-non-
specific
DATE(S): 1993   VENUE: Aurora, Ill.   VICTIMS:
Three
MO: Man and two women shot in/near their homes
DISPOSITION: Condemned on two counts, 1998

Terry, Charles E. (d. 1981)
SEX: M   RACE: ?   TYPE: N   MOTIVE: Sex.
DATE(S): 1962–63   VENUE: N.Y./La.   VICTIMS:
Two+ suspected
MO: Rape-strangler of women
DISPOSITION: Confessed one count in N.Y., 1963;
died in prison, 1981

Terry, Michael (?–   )
SEX: M   RACE: B   TYPE: T   MOTIVE: Sex.
DATE(S): 1985–86   VENUE: Atlanta, Ga.   VIC-
TIMS: Six
MO: Shot/stabbed gay men after sex
DISPOSITION: Life without parole on two counts,
1987

Teruhiko Masue (1963–   )
SEX: M   RACE: A   TYPE: T   MOTIVE: Sex./PC
DATE(S): 1987–89   VENUE: Kitagata, Japan   VIC-
TIMS: Three
MO: Killed a female acquaintance after rape, a girlfriend who dated other men, and a woman who
accused him of damaging her car
DISPOSITION: Confessed three murders while serving
time for attempted robbery, then recanted; DNA
linked him to the crimes in 2002; final disposition
unknown

Thacker, Steven Ray (1970–   )
SEX: M   RACE: W   TYPE: N   MOTIVE: CE-felony
DATE(S): 1999–2000   VENUE: Mo./Okla./Tenn.
VICTIMS: Three
MO: Stabbed an Oklahoma woman to death for her
credit cards; stabbed a man in Missouri while stealing

his car; killed the tow truck driver who stopped to help him when the stolen car ran out of gas
DISPOSITION: Condemned in Oklahoma and Tennessee; life sentence in Missouri

Thanos, John Frederick (1949–94)
SEX: M   RACE: W   TYPE: T   MOTIVE: CE-felony
DATE(S): 1990   VENUE: Md.   VICTIMS: Three
MO: Shot robbery victims age 14–18
DISPOSITION: Condemned on three counts; executed May 17, 1994

Theron, John (?–)
SEX: M   RACE: W   TYPE: T   MOTIVE: PC-extremist
DATE(S): 1979–80   VENUE: Namibia   VICTIMS: 200 confessed
MO: South African special forces officer who murdered black prisoners of war by strangulation and lethal injection; also "experimented" on black taxi drivers with poisoned beer
DISPOSITION: Absolved by South Africa's Truth and Reconciliation Commission in return for confession

Tholmer, Brandon (1949–)
SEX: M   RACE: W   TYPE: T   MOTIVE: Sex./CE
DATE(S): 1981–84   VENUE: Los Angeles, Calif.   VICTIMS: 34 suspected
MO: Rape-slayer of elderly women; victims also robbed
DISPOSITION: Four consecutive life terms, 1986

Thomas, Ed Clifford (1960–)
SEX: M   RACE: W   TYPE: T   MOTIVE: PC
DATE(S): 1980   VENUE: Dade County, Fla.   VICTIMS: Two
MO: Killed victims in personal disputes
DISPOSITION: Two life terms, 1981

Thomas, Renard Carlos (1962–)
SEX: M   RACE: Unk.   TYPE: T   MOTIVE: PC
DATE(S): 1981–98   VENUE: DeKalb County, Calif.   VICTIMS: Three suspected
MO: Named as prime suspect in the murders of two wives and a girlfriend
DISPOSITION: Received life sentence on April 9, 2003, for the 1998 murder of his second wife; identified by prosecutors as the probable killer in two other cases

Thomas, William Gregory (1960–)
SEX: M   RACE: W   TYPE: T   MOTIVE: CE
DATE(S): 1991/93   VENUE: Duval County, Fla.   VICTIMS: Two

MO: "Bluebeard" slayer of ex-wife and mother
DISPOSITION: Condemned on one count + life terms for second count, burglary and kidnapping, 1994

Thompson, Ben (1843–84)
SEX: M   RACE: W   TYPE: N   MOTIVE: PC
DATE(S): 1863–84   VENUE: La./Tex.   VICTIMS: Eight+
MO: "Shootist" and occasional lawman; shot various personal enemies, including a Union soldier
DISPOSITION: Killed in gunfight at San Antonio, Mar. 11, 1884

Thompson, Jerry K. (1961–)
SEX: M   RACE: W   TYPE: T   MOTIVE: CE
DATE(S): 1991   VENUE: Indianapolis, Ind.   VICTIMS: Three
MO: Career criminal; shot two men and one woman in holdups
DISPOSITION: Condemned

Thompson, Kelly Ray (1968–)
SEX: M   RACE: W   TYPE: N   MOTIVE: Sex.
DATE(S): 1990s   VENUE: Wash./Colo.   VICTIMS: Eight confessed
MO: Stabbed women in random attacks
DISPOSITION: 31 years on one count in Wash., 1998

Thompson, Raymond Michael (1930–)
SEX: M   RACE: W   TYPE: T   MOTIVE: CE-felony
DATE(S): 1980–82   VENUE: Broward County, Fla.   VICTIMS: Two
MO: Killed robbery/kidnap victims
DISPOSITION: Condemned on one count + life for kidnapping, 1986; 17 years six months on second count, 1987

Thompson, Robert J. (1909–)
SEX: M   RACE: W   TYPE: T   MOTIVE: Sex./CE
DATE(S): 1958   VENUE: Mexico   VICTIMS: Two
MO: American expatriate; raped/robbed/bludgeoned female tourists
DISPOSITION: Life sentence, Nov. 1958

Thompson, William (1845–88?)   AKA: Texas Billy
SEX: M   RACE: W   TYPE: N   MOTIVE: PC
DATE(S): 1973   VENUE: Kans./Colo./Tex.   VICTIMS: "Several"
MO: Psychotic brother of BEN THOMPSON; victims included at least one lawman
DISPOSITION: Reportedly killed in Laredo, Tex.

Thompson, William Paul (1937–89)
SEX: M   RACE: W   TYPE: N   MOTIVE: CE/PC

DATE(S): 1980s   VENUE: N.Y./Kans./Calif./Nev.
  VICTIMS: Six confessed
MO: Shot men in personal conflicts and contract murders
DISPOSITION: Convicted on two counts in Calif.; executed in Nev. on one count, June 19, 1989

Thorpe, Scott Harlan (1960–)
SEX: M   RACE: W   TYPE: T   MOTIVE: PC
DATE(S): 2001   VENUE: Nevada City, Calif.   VICTIMS: Three
MO: Delusional paranoid who shot five victims, killing three
DISPOSITION: Pleaded guilty to three murder counts, March 24, 2003; found to be insane and committed to an asylum for life

Threinen, David (1947–)
SEX: M   RACE: W   TYPE: T   MOTIVE: Sex.
DATE(S): 1975   VENUE: Saskatoon, Canada   VICTIMS: Four
MO: Pedophile slayer of two boys aged nine and 12, and two girls aged seven and eight
DISPOSITION: Pled guilty on four counts and received life term, 1975; rejected all further parole bids, August 2000

Thwala, Sipho Agmatir (1967–)   AKA: Phoenix Strangler
SEX: M   RACE: B   TYPE: T   MOTIVE: Sex.
DATE(S): 1994–98   VENUE: Phoenix, South Africa   VICTIMS: 16–19
MO: Rape-slayer of black women aged 20–30, strangled with their own underwear
DISPOSITION: Acquitted of a rape-murder in 1994; received 506-year sentence on March 31, 1999 for 16 murders and various lesser felonies

Tilley, Joe Vance (1974–)
SEX: M   RACE: W   TYPE: T   MOTIVE: Sad.
DATE(S): 1990   VENUE: Johnson/Marshall counties, Okla.   VICTIMS: Three
MO: Thrill-killer of elderly man and two 15-year-old girls
DISPOSITION: Life without parole on one count, 1993; condemned on second count

Tingler, Richard Lee, Jr. (1940–)
SEX: M   RACE: W   TYPE: N   MOTIVE: CE-felony
DATE(S): 1968   VENUE: Cleveland/Columbus, Ohio   VICTIMS: Six
MO: Executed victims of both sexes during robberies
DISPOSITION: Condemned, 1969 (sentence commuted to life, 1972)

Tipton, John Calvin (1936–58)
SEX: M   RACE: W   TYPE: T   MOTIVE: Sex.
DATE(S): 1956   VENUE: Orange County, Calif.   VICTIMS: Two
MO: Home-invader; stabbed 18-year-old girls in breasts
DISPOSITION: Executed on one count, Sept. 27, 1958

Tipton, Richard (1971–)
SEX: M   RACE: B   TYPE: T   MOTIVE: CE-drugs
DATE(S): 1992   VENUE: Richmond, Va.   VICTIMS: 11
MO: Led drug gang in series of murders
DISPOSITION: Condemned under federal law

Todd, George (1841–64)
SEX: M   RACE: W   TYPE: N   MOTIVE: PC/CE
DATE(S): 1861–64   VENUE: Kans./Mo.   VICTIMS: "Numerous"
MO: Member of "QUANTRILL'S RAIDERS"
DISPOSITION: Killed by Union sniper, Oct. 22, 1864

Todd, Sweeney (1756–1802)   AKA: Human Ghoul
SEX: M   RACE: W   TYPE: S   MOTIVE: CE
DATE(S): 1784–1801   VENUE: London, England   VICTIMS: 160 alleged
MO: Real-life "demon barber of Fleet Street" who robbed/killed patrons of both sexes; flesh of victims processed and sold as "veal pies" by lover/accomplice Margery Lovett
DISPOSITION: Hanged on one count, Jan. 25, 1802; Lovett committed suicide in prison after confessing, Dec. 1801

Toffania (1653–1723)
SEX: F   RACE: W   TYPE: T   MOTIVE: CE/Sad.
DATE(S): 1670–1719   VENUE: Naples, Italy   VICTIMS: 600 estimated
MO: Extreme feminist; poisoner-for-hire of unwanted husbands
DISPOSITION: Executed by garrote, 1723

Tolerton, Kenyon (?–)
SEX: M   RACE: B   TYPE: N   MOTIVE: Sex.
DATE(S): 1976–80   VENUE: Colo.   VICTIMS: Four suspected
MO: Sex slayer of petite white females aged 14–21; victims stabbed
DISPOSITION: Life without parole plus 48 years on two counts, 1993; new DNA evidence under investigation in two more cases

Toppan, Jane (1854–1938)
SEX: M   RACE: W   TYPE: T   MOTIVE: PC-nonspecific

DATE(S): 1880–1901   VENUE: New England   VIC-
   TIMS: 70–100 suspected
MO: Live-in "nurse" who poisoned patients and their
   relatives
DISPOSITION: Confessed 31 counts, 1901; confined
   to insane asylum where she died, in Aug. 1938

Torres, Leslie (1971–   )
SEX: M   RACE: H   TYPE: T   MOTIVE: CE
DATE(S): 1988   VENUE: New York City   VICTIMS:
   Five
MO: Victims shot in robberies staged to support drug
   addiction
DISPOSITION: Life term with 60-year minimum, Apr.
   1989

Torres Hernandez, Ramon (1971–   )   AKA: The
   Razor
SEX: M   RACE: H   TYPE: T   MOTIVE: Sex.
DATE(S): 1991   VENUE: San Antonio, Tex.   VIC-
   TIMS: Five alleged
MO: Rape-slayer of young women, sometimes operat-
   ing with accomplices
DISPOSITION: Condemned on one count, Oct. 2002;
   named as prime suspect in four additional rape-
   murders

Toshihiko Haseqawa (1951–2001)
SEX: M   RACE: A   TYPE: N   MOTIVE: CE-felony
DATE(S): 1979–83   VENUE: Japan   VICTIMS:
   Three
MO: Killed two men, aged 20 and 30, for insurance
   payments; murdered a 39-year-old money broker
   during robbery
DISPOSITION: Hanged on Dec. 27, 2001

Totia, Hiralal (?–   )
SEX: M   RACE: A   TYPE: T   MOTIVE: PC
DATE(S): 2004   VENUE: Shankarpur, India   VIC-
   TIMS: Three
MO: Vampire killer of a policeman, a cab driver, and a
   woman; drank blood of victims to prevent their spir-
   its from haunting him
DISPOSITION: Unknown

Townser, Anthony (1975–   )
SEX: M   RACE: B   TYPE: N   MOTIVE: CE
DATE(S): 1993   VENUE: Ill./Mo.   VICTIMS: Three
   suspected
MO: Home invader; killed/robbed elderly whites
DISPOSITION: 75-year term on one count, 1995

Tracy, Harry (1876–1902)
SEX: M   RACE: W   TYPE: N   MOTIVE: CE

DATE(S): 1897–1902   VENUE: Colo./Wyo./Utah
   VICTIMS: "Several"
MO: "Wild Bunch" outlaw known for his murderous
   temper
DISPOSITION: Suicide by gunshot to avoid arrest,
   Aug. 6, 1902

Traore, Mamadou (1973–   )
SEX: M   RACE: B   TYPE: T   MOTIVE: PC
DATE(S): 1997   VENUE: Paris, France   VICTIMS:
   Two
MO: Senegal native who blamed demonic possession
   for violent assaults on six women, including two
   fatalities
DISPOSITION: Life sentence with 22-year minimum,
   February 2000

Trapishkin, Nicholas (d. 1926)
SEX: M   RACE: W   TYPE: N   MOTIVE: CE
DATE(S): 1920-26   VENUE: Russia   VICTIMS: 100
   alleged
MO: Apparent outlaw; several robbery charges also
   included
DISPOSITION: Executed, 1926

Travis, Maury Troy (1966–2002)
SEX: M   RACE: W   TYPE: T   MOTIVE: Sex.
DATE(S): 2001–02   VENUE: St. Louis, Mo.   VIC-
   TIMS: 10–20 alleged
MO: Black female prostitutes beaten and strangled
DISPOSITION: Arrested June 7, 2002; suicide by
   hanging in his cell, June 10

Trawick, Jack Harrison (1946–   )
SEX: M   RACE: W   TYPE: N   MOTIVE: Sex./Sad.
DATE(S): 1972–92   VENUE: Ala./Ore./at sea   VIC-
   TIMS: Five confessed
MO: Rape-strangler of women, including one thrown
   overboard on cruise ship sailing from Seattle to Alaska
DISPOSITION: Condemned in Ala., 1994

Trillo, Martin (?–   )
SEX: M   RACE: ?   TYPE: T   MOTIVE: Sex.
DATE(S): 1981   VENUE: Sacramento, Calif.   VIC-
   TIMS: Two
MO: Lust strangler of women
DISPOSITION: Two life terms without parole, 1984

Troppmann, Jean-Baptiste (1848–70)   AKA: Human
   Tiger
SEX: M   RACE: W   TYPE: T   MOTIVE: CE
DATE(S): 1869   VENUE: France   VICTIMS: Eight
MO: Murdered entire family during prolonged swindle
DISPOSITION: Guillotined Jan. 19, 1870

Troyer, Daniel Ray (1960–)
SEX: M   RACE: W   TYPE: T   MOTIVE: Sex./CE-felony
DATE(S): 1985–88   VENUE: Salt Lake City, Utah
VICTIMS: 13 suspected
MO: Robbed, beat and sexually assaulted women, aged 69–88, in their homes
DISPOSITION: Received sentence of 1–15 years for attacking a 71-year-old paraplegic in 1978; paroled 1982; received 15 years for a 1982 burglary; paroled in 1985; 1988 murder charge dismissed on technical grounds; pled guilty on two murder counts and received consecutive life terms (one without parole), June 1999; confessed three more murders with prosecution waived, October 1999

Trueblood, Lydia (?–?)
SEX: F   RACE: W   TYPE: N   MOTIVE: CE-inheritance
DATE(S): 1915–19   VENUE: Mo./Mont./Idaho
VICTIMS: Five
MO: "Black widow" poisoner of husbands and a brother-in-law for life insurance
DISPOSITION: Life sentence in Idaho, 1921

Trupp, Nathan (1947–)
SEX: M   RACE: W   TYPE: N   MOTIVE: PC-nonspecific
DATE(S): 1988   VENUE: N. Mex./Calif.   VICTIMS: Five
MO: Shot random victims while stalking actor Michael Landon
DISPOSITION: Declared insane; confined to state hospital

Tsuiman, Yuri (?–)   AKA: Beast of Taganrog
SEX: M   RACE: W   TYPE: T   MOTIVE: Sex.
DATE(S): 1990s   VENUE: Rostov-on-Don, Russia
VICTIMS: Four
MO: Pedophile slayer of young girls
DISPOSITION: Unknown

Tsutomu Miyazaki (1963–)
SEX: M   RACE: A   TYPE: N   MOTIVE: Sex.
DATE(S): 1988–89   VENUE: Japan   VICTIMS: Four confessed
MO: Kidnapped/killed girls age four to seven; necrophile
DISPOSITION: Condemned, 1997

Tucker, James Neil (1957–2004)
SEX: M   RACE: W   TYPE: T   MOTIVE: CE
DATE(S): 1992   VENUE: Midlands, S.C.   VICTIMS: Two
MO: Shot women aged 54 and 21, during residential burglaries; formerly served 17 years for rape in Utah
DISPOSITION: Executed on May 28, 2004

Tuggle, Lem Davis, Jr. (d. 1996)
SEX: M   RACE: W   TYPE: T   MOTIVE: Sex.
DATE(S): 1971/83   VENUE: Smyth County, Va.
VICTIMS: Two
MO: Rape-slayer of women
DISPOSITION: Life term, 1971 (paroled 1983); executed Dec. 12, 1996

Tullis, Patrick (1959–)
SEX: M   RACE: W   TYPE: T   MOTIVE: PC
DATE(S): 1987   VENUE: Chicago, Ill.   VICTIMS: Two
MO: Homophobic slayer of gay men; victims stabbed/strangled
DISPOSITION: 60 years on two counts, 1989

Ture, Joseph Donald, Jr. (1950–)
SEX: M   RACE: W   TYPE: N   MOTIVE: Sex.
DATE(S): 1978–80   VENUE: Minn.   VICTIMS: Six suspected
MO: Rape-slayer of females and three children of one victim shot during home invasion
DISPOSITION: Convicted and sentenced to life on two murder counts for killing a 19-year-old waitress in Afton (1978) and an 18-year-old waitress in West St. Paul (1980)

Turner, Julia Lynn Womack (1968–)
SEX: F   RACE: W   TYPE: T   MOTIVE: PC/CE
DATE(S): 1995–2001   VENUE: Cumming, Ga.   VICTIMS: Three alleged
MO: "Black widow" who poisoned husband and common-law husband with antifreeze; male employer also died under mysterious circumstances, with $40,000 missing from his office
DISPOSITION: Convicted on May 14, 2004 of poisoning husband in 1995; received life prison term; charged pending in second case

Turner, Lise Jane (1956–)
SEX: M   RACE: W   TYPE: T   MOTIVE: PC-nonspecific
DATE(S): 1980–82   VENUE: Christchurch, New Zealand   VICTIMS: Four
MO: Killed young children, two of them her own
DISPOSITION: Life term + 10 years for attempted murders, 1984 (paroled 1997)

Ulayuk, Eli (1968–)
SEX: M   RACE: NA   TYPE: T   MOTIVE: Sex.

DATE(S): 1988/2004   VENUE: Yellowknife, Northwest Territories, Canada   VICTIMS: Two

MO: Necrophile slayer of a female friend and his female parole officer; both victims stabbed/strangled prior to sex

DISPOSITION: Convicted of manslaughter in first case, 1992; paroled June 2004; charged with second murder, Oct. 7, 2004; trial pending

Underwood, L. C. (1948–   )

SEX: M   RACE: W   TYPE: T   MOTIVE: PC

DATE(S): 1993   VENUE: Salisbury, N.C.   VICTIMS: Two suspected

MO: Ex-cop and obsessive stalker; killed ex-girlfriend's elderly mother and her new lover in separate attacks

DISPOSITION: Life + 40 years on one count, 1997

Undisclosed (?–   )

SEX: M   RACE: ?   TYPE: S   MOTIVE: CE

DATE(S): 1920   VENUE: Tanta, Egypt   VICTIMS: 20

MO: "Bluebeard" slayer of women for profit; kept severed heads in his home

DISPOSITION: Unreported

Undisclosed (?–   )

SEX: M   RACE: H   TYPE: T   MOTIVE: Unk.

DATE(S): 1920–21   VENUE: Mexico City, Mexico   VICTIMS: Four

MO: "Bluebeard" slayer of female lovers

DISPOSITION: Convicted Feb. 18, 1922; sentence unknown

Undisclosed (d. 1942)   AKA: The Ghoul

SEX: M   RACE: W   TYPE: T   MOTIVE: PC

DATE(S): 1942   VENUE: Guadalcanal   VICTIMS: "Several"

MO: Deranged U.S. Marine stabbed fellow soldiers in nocturnal attacks

DISPOSITION: Shot by sentry while fleeing last crime scene

Undisclosed (1932–   )   AKA: Harry Brown

SEX: M   RACE: Unk.   TYPE: T   MOTIVE: PC

DATE(S): 1980s   VENUE: Melbourne, Australia   VICTIMS: Six

MO: "Deeply religious" man identified in 2001 as the prime suspect in murders of six females aged 14–73, who were kidnapped from streets and suburban bus stops, with bodies dumped outside town

DISPOSITION: Unknown

Undisclosed (?–   )

SEX: M   RACE: A   TYPE: S   MOTIVE: Unk.

DATE(S): 1952   VENUE: Quezon City, Philippines   VICTIMS: Four+

MO: Skeletal remains found by police in home of unidentified man

DISPOSITION: Unknown

Undisclosed (1950–   )

SEX: M   RACE: A   TYPE: T   MOTIVE: Sex./PC-extremism

DATE(S): 1966–67   VENUE: Tokyo, Japan   VICTIMS: Three

MO: Rape-slayer of young women who mocked his biracial origins

DISPOSITION: Life sentence, 1967

Undisclosed (1944–   )

SEX: M   RACE: A   TYPE: S   MOTIVE: Undisclosed

DATE(S): 1985–86   VENUE: Xidan, China   VICTIMS: Three

MO: Restaurant owner; killed three teens and served their flesh as pork

DISPOSITION: Undisclosed

Undisclosed (1944–   )

SEX: F   RACE: A   TYPE: S   MOTIVE: PC

DATE(S): 1980s–1990s   VENUE: Tokyo, Japan   VICTIMS: Six

MO: Decomposed remains of newborn infants found in plastic bags in an apartment closet; 58-year-old tenant admitted the babies were hers

DISPOSITION: No charges filed

Undisclosed (1948–   )

SEX: F   RACE: B   TYPE: T   MOTIVE: GC alleged

DATE(S): 1985–99   VENUE: KwaZulu-Natal, South Africa   VICTIMS: 20+ alleged

MO: Children abducted and killed in *muti* magic rituals; suspect arrested in Sept. 1999 with two children missing since 1996; later led police to several graves; identified as black-magic "healer"

DISPOSITION: Unknown

Undisclosed (1968–   )

SEX: M   RACE: Unk.   TYPE: T   MOTIVE: Sex.

DATE(S): 1987   VENUE: Thunder Bay, Ontario   VICTIMS: Two

MO: Rape-slayer of 16-year-old girls

DISPOSITION: Arrested, July 2000; disposition unknown

Undisclosed (1968–   )

SEX: F   RACE: W   TYPE: S   MOTIVE: PC

DATE(S): 1992–97   VENUE: Norway   VICTIMS: Four

MO: Mother who killed four of her children, ranging in age from two days to six weeks, staged as SIDS cases
DISPOSITION: Unknown

Undisclosed
SEX: M   RACE: W   TYPE: N   MOTIVE: Sex./Sad.
DATE(S): 1994–99   VENUE: Germany/Holland   VICTIMS: Three confessed
MO: Mutilation-slayer of women; who beheaded and dismembered his victims
DISPOSITION: Unknown; confessed three murders to police in November 1999

Undisclosed (1988–   )
SEX: F   RACE: B   TYPE: T   MOTIVE: Cult
DATE(S): 1994–2001   VENUE: Maiduguri, Nigeria   VICTIMS: 48 confessed
MO: Girl arrested at age 13, suspected of killing a two-year-old boy and cutting out his heart; she confessed participation in 48 human sacrifices since age seven and led police to the home of her cult leader
DISPOSITION: Unknown

Undisclosed (?–   )
SEX: M   RACE: Unk.   TYPE: T   MOTIVE: Sex./CE
DATE(S): 1996–97   VENUE: Johannesburg, South Africa   VICTIMS: 14
MO: Rape-slayer of women beaten or shot; some victims also robbed
DISPOSITION: Unnamed subject charged with 23 offenses in December 1997; counts include murder, rape, and robbery; disposition unknown

Undisclosed (1975–   )
SEX: M   RACE: Unk.   TYPE: T   MOTIVE: Unk.
DATE(S): 1994–98   VENUE: Stockholm, Sweden   VICTIMS: Eight
MO: "Signature" killer of victims stabbed in their homes after visits to communal laundries
DISPOSITION: Unknown

Undisclosed
SEX: Unk.   RACE: Unk.   TYPE: S   MOTIVE: Unk.
DATE(S): 1997–98   VENUE: Dayton, Ohio   VICTIMS: Four
MO: Unnamed minor, identified as prime suspect in the suffocation of four children, aged one to three years, who died at the home of Regina Moreland over a seven-month period; victims included two of Moreland's grandsons, one granddaughter, and a great-niece
DISPOSITION: Child subject submitted for psychiatric testing/treatment, July 1998

Undisclosed (1962–   )
SEX: F   RACE: Unk.   TYPE: S   MOTIVE: PC-non-specific
DATE(S): 1997–2001   VENUE: The Hague, Netherlands   VICTIMS: 14
MO: Nurse who killed patients with lethal injections at four local hospitals; victims primarily infants, young children, and seniors
DISPOSITION: Unknown

Undisclosed (?–   )
SEX: M   RACE: Unk.   TYPE: T   MOTIVE: PC
DATE(S): 1998   VENUE: Overton, Tex.   VICTIMS: Two
MO: Beat and stabbed women aged 75 and 89 in their bathrooms at home
DISPOSITION: In Nov. 1999, police chief Ed Williams announced that the unnamed killer was imprisoned on other charges

Undisclosed (?–   )   AKA: Cannibal of Kosovo
SEX: M   RACE: W   TYPE: T   MOTIVE: PC-non-specific
DATE(S): 1997–99   VENUE: Kosovo, Yugoslavia   VICTIMS: "Several"
MO: Serbian policeman arrested by UN peacekeepers who found human limbs and organs in his refrigerator
DISPOSITION: Arrested June 28, 1999; outcome unknown

Undisclosed (1959–   )
SEX: M   RACE: W   TYPE: S   MOTIVE: Sex.
DATE(S): 1999   VENUE: Velsk, Siberia   VICTIMS: Eight
MO: Rape-slayer of women aged 16–49, killed at his rural cabin and buried in nearby woods; confessed and revealed bodies after charged with rape
DISPOSITION: Unknown

Undisclosed (d. 2000)   AKA: Bas Congo Throatcutter
SEX: M   RACE: B   TYPE: T   MOTIVE: Sex.
DATE(S): 1999–2000   VENUE: Democratic Republic of Congo   VICTIMS: 12
MO: Slayer who slashed throats of female victims in Bas Congo Province
DISPOSITION: Killed by a victim's husband, May 2, 2000

Undisclosed (?–   )
SEX: M   RACE: B   TYPE: T   MOTIVE: Sex./Sad.
DATE(S): 2000   VENUE: Chiradzulu, Malawi   VICTIMS: Eight

MO: Killed and dismembered women, keeping partial remains of several at his home
DISPOSITION: Arrested in March 2000; disposition unknown

Undisclosed (1966–)
SEX: M   RACE: Unk.   TYPE: S   MOTIVE: PC-"mercy"
DATE(S): 2000–01   VENUE: Lucerne, Switzerland   VICTIMS: 27 confessed
MO: Nurse who admits killing victims aged 66–95 at five area nursing homes; methods included suffocation and drug overdoses
DISPOSITION: Police confirm 24 deaths as homicides; trial scheduled for early 2005

Undisclosed (1972–)
SEX: F   RACE: Unk.   TYPE: S   MOTIVE: PC-"mercy"
DATE(S): 2001   VENUE: Melbourne, Australia   VICTIMS: More than two
MO: Nurse linked to unnatural deaths of two patients aged 63 and 89; 80 similar deaths under ongoing investigation
DISPOSITION: Unknown

Undisclosed (1973–)
SEX: M   RACE: W   TYPE: T   MOTIVE: Sex.
DATE(S): 2002–03   VENUE: Rostov-on-Don, Russia   VICTIMS: 25+
MO: Rape-slayer of women
DISPOSITION: Unknown

Undisclosed (1979–)
SEX: M   RACE: Unk.   TYPE: S   MOTIVE: PC-mercy
DATE(S): 2003–04   VENUE: Sonthofen, Germany   VICTIMS: 16 confessed
MO: Hospital nurse who confessed killing patients aged 60–89 with lethal injections; 64 other "suspicious" deaths under review
DISPOSITION: Unknown

Undisclosed (?–)
SEX: F   RACE: A   TYPE: S   MOTIVE: PC-"mercy"
DATE(S): 2003–04   VENUE: Japan   VICTIMS: Four alleged
MO: Doctor accused of killing elderly and comatose patients at hospitals in Haborocho, Hokkaido, and Nayoro
DISPOSITION: Unknown

Undisclosed (1983–)   AKA: School Killer
SEX: M   RACE: A   TYPE: T   MOTIVE: PC-nonspecific
DATE(S): 1997   VENUE: Kobe, Japan   VICTIMS: Two
MO: 14-year-old who attacked five younger children, killing two; one victim beheaded
DISPOSITION: Indefinite sentence to juvenile prison, 1997

Unknown (d. 1598)   AKA: Werewolf of Châlons
SEX: M   RACE: W   TYPE: T   MOTIVE: Sex./Sad.
DATE(S): 1590s   VENUE: Châlons, France   VICTIMS: "Dozens"
MO: "Demon tailor" who killed/cannibalized patrons of his shop and rural victims ambushed in the nearby forest
DISPOSITION:Burned at the stake, Dec. 1598

Unknown (?–?)   AKA: Bald Head Pete
SEX: M   RACE: W   TYPE: N   MOTIVE: PC
DATE(S): 1840s–70s   VENUE: Rocky Mountains   VICTIMS: 100+
MO: "Mountain man" and scalp hunter, prolific slayer of Indians
DISPOSITION: Unknown

Unknown (?–?)   AKA: Arkansas Bill
SEX: M   RACE: W   TYPE: T   MOTIVE: PC
DATE(S): 1870s   VENUE: Dodge City, Kans.   VICTIMS: 22 claimed
MO: Old West gunman
DISPOSITION: Unknown

Unknown (d. 1931)   AKA: Buster from Chicago
SEX: M   RACE: W   TYPE: N   MOTIVE: CE
DATE(S): 1920–31   VENUE: Ill./N.Y.   VICTIMS: "Numerous"
MO: "Most prolific hit man of the entire [1920s] underworld"
DISPOSITION: Murdered in New York City poolhall, Sept. 1931

Ursinus, Sophie Charlotte Elizabeth (1760–1836)
SEX: F   RACE: W   TYPE: T   MOTIVE: PC/CE
DATE(S): 1785–1801   VENUE: Berlin, Germany   VICTIMS: Three
MO: "Black widow" poisoner of her lover, husband, and aunt for personal gain
DISPOSITION: Convicted on one count and sentenced to life; died in prison on April 4, 1836

Vajicek, Herman (?–?)   AKA: Herman Billik
SEX: M   RACE: W   TYPE: T   MOTIVE: CE-inheritance
DATE(S): 1905   VENUE: Chicago, Ill.   VICTIMS: Six
MO: Poisoned six members of one family over eight months
DISPOSITION: 1907 death sentence commuted; released Jan. 1917

Valenti, Richard Raymond (1943–   )
SEX: M   RACE: W   TYPE: T   MOTIVE: Sex.
DATE(S): 1973–74   VENUE: Charleston County, S.C.   VICTIMS: Three
MO: Rape-slayer of teenage girls
DISPOSITION: Consecutive life terms on two counts, 1974

Valenti, Rocco (d. 1922)
SEX: M   RACE: W   TYPE: T   MOTIVE: CE
DATE(S): 1920s   VENUE: N.Y./N.J.   VICTIMS: 20
MO: Underworld contract killer
DISPOSITION: Killed in gangland shoot-out, New York City, Aug. 9, 1922

Valera, Mark (1980–   )   AKA: Van Krevel
SEX: M   RACE: W   TYPE: T   MOTIVE: PC
DATE(S): 1998   VENUE: Wollongong, Australia   VICTIMS: Two
MO: Mutilation-slayer of men who scrawled satanic graffiti at crime scenes; at arrest, claimed sexual advances from both victims triggered memories of childhood molestation by his father.
DISPOSITION: Convicted on two counts and sentenced to life, Sept. 7, 2000

Valkenburgh, Elizabeth Van (d. 1846)
SEX: F   RACE: W   TYPE: T   MOTIVE: PC-domestic
DATE(S): 1840s   VENUE: Fulton, N.Y.   VICTIMS: Two
MO: "Black widow" poisoner of husbands
DISPOSITION: Hanged, Jan. 24, 1846

Van der E., M. (1946–   )
SEX: F   RACE: W   TYPE: S   MOTIVE: Unknown
DATE(S): 1996   VENUE: Anjum, Netherlands   VICTIMS: Two
MO: Killed men aged 26 and 38 with a hammer at her boardinghouse and buried the corpses in the garden
DISPOSITION: Convicted on two manslaughter counts, June and December 1997; received eight-year sentence in July 1998; unnamed male accomplice sentenced to three years on one manslaughter count

Van Schoor, Louis (?–   )
SEX: M   RACE: W   TYPE: T   MOTIVE: PC-extremist
DATE(S): 1988–92   VENUE: East London, South Africa   VICTIMS: 39
MO: Ex-cop turned security guard who shot 101 unarmed blacks and mixed-race victims "in the line of duty," killing 39
DISPOSITION: Convicted of seven murders and two attempted murders in 1992; received 20-year prison term

Vargas, Dorangel (?–   )   AKA: Hannibal Lecter of the Andes
SEX: M   RACE: H   TYPE: T   MOTIVE: PC
DATE(S): 1997–98   VENUE: San Cristobal, Venezuela   VICTIMS: 10 confessed
MO: Cannibal killer who admitted devouring 10 men over two years; remains found at his rural home; released from prison, Oct. 31, 2004, after serving 12 years
DISPOSITION: Unknown

Veerappan, Munusamy (1945–2004)
SEX: M   RACE: A   TYPE: N   MOTIVE: CE-felony
DATE(S): 1984–2004   VENUE: India   VICTIMS: 150+
MO: Bandit, kidnapper, and poacher who killed policemen, game wardens, and others, plus more than 2,000 elephants
DISPOSITION: Killed in police ambush with three cohorts, Oct. 18, 2004

Velten, Maria (1916–   )
SEX: F   RACE: W   TYPE: T   MOTIVE: PC/CE
DATE(S): 1963–80   VENUE: Kempten, Germany   VICTIMS: Five confirmed
MO: "Black widow" poisoner of father, aunt, husbands/lovers; "mercy" motive claimed in first two deaths; others killed for money
DISPOSITION: Life sentence, 1983

Verain, Leland (1892–1935)   AKA: Louis "Two Gun" Alterie
SEX: M   RACE: W   TYPE: T   MOTIVE: CE/PC
DATE(S): 1922–25   VENUE: Chicago, Ill.   VICTIMS: "Numerous"
MO: Psychopathic Prohibition-era gangster; alleged "inventor" of machine-gun ambush murders
DISPOSITION: Shot by rival mobsters, July 18, 1935

Vermilyea, Louise (d. 1910)
SEX: F   RACE: W   TYPE: N   MOTIVE: CE/PC-nonspecific

DATE(S): 1893–1910   VENUE: Ill.   VICTIMS: Nine
MO: "Black widow" poisoner of husbands and children for life insurance; also poisoned lodgers in her rooming house without apparent motive
DISPOSITION: Suicide by poison following arrest

Vernage, Nicholas (1965–)
SEX: M   RACE: B   TYPE: T   MOTIVE: CE/PC
DATE(S): 1991   VENUE: East London, Ontario   VICTIMS: Three
MO: Fatally stabbed two burglary victims and a policeman
DISPOSITION: Five life terms for three murders and two attempts, 1992

Verzeni, Vincenzo (1849–?)
SEX: M   RACE: W   TYPE: T   MOTIVE: Sex.
DATE(S): 1869–72   VENUE: Bottamuco, Italy   VICTIMS: "Probably 12"
MO: Strangled/disemboweled women; drank their blood
DISPOSITION: Life sentence, 1873

Viana, Nicholas (1903–21)
SEX: M   RACE: W   TYPE: T   MOTIVE: CE
DATE(S): 1920–21   VENUE: Chicago, Ill.   VICTIMS: "Several"
MO: "Black Hand" extortionist and killer
DISPOSITION: Hanged on one count, 1921

Vick, Tony (?–)
SEX: M   RACE: W   TYPE: N   MOTIVE: CE
DATE(S): 1993–96   VENUE: Tenn.   VICTIMS: Four suspected
MO: "Bluebeard" slayer of wife, fiancée, and others, for insurance
DISPOSITION: Life term on one count, 1997; second life term, 1998

Vickers, Robert Wayne (1958–)   AKA: Bonzai Bob
SEX: M   RACE: W   TYPE: S   MOTIVE: PC-argument
DATE(S): 1978/82   VENUE: Florence, Ariz.   VICTIMS: Two
MO: Slayer of fellow prison inmates in separate incidents
DISPOSITION: Condemned, 1978; condemned 1982

Vilakati, Bongani (d. 2003)
SEX: M   RACE: B   TYPE: T   MOTIVE: PC
DATE(S): 2002   VENUE: Malkerns, Swaziland   VICTIMS: Six
MO: Slayer of victims found buried at his home
DISPOSITION: Killed by police while resisting arrest, March 29, 2003

Villareal, David (1955–)
SEX: M   RACE: H   TYPE: N   MOTIVE: Sad./CE
DATE(S): 1974–81   VENUE: Tex.   VICTIMS: Seven suspected
MO: Bludgeoned/stabbed male victims aged 18–72; some robbed
DISPOSITION: Life term on one count plus two years for assault, 1979; life plus five years on second count, 1981; five years for aggravated assault on prison guard, 1987

Vizzardelli, George William (?–)   AKA: Monster of Sarzana
SEX: M   RACE: W   TYPE: T   MOTIVE: PC/CE
DATE(S): 1937–39   VENUE: Sarzana, Italy   VICTIMS: Five
MO: Vendetta and holdup murders by juvenile offender
DISPOSITION: Life sentence, 1940 (pardoned, 1968)

Voirbo, Pierre (d. 1869)
SEX: M   RACE: W   TYPE: T   MOTIVE: CE
DATE(S): 1860s   VENUE: Paris, France   VICTIMS: 10+ suspected
MO: Killed creditors and robbery victims
DISPOSITION: Confessed one count; suicide prior to trial, 1869

Wable, John Wesley (1929–54)
SEX: M   RACE: W   TYPE: N   MOTIVE: PC-nonspecific
DATE(S): 1953   VENUE: Pa./Ohio   VICTIMS: Two
MO: Shot sleeping truckers in random, motiveless attacks
DISPOSITION: Executed on one count in Pa., Sept. 26, 1954

Waddingham, Dorothea Nancy (1899–1936)
SEX: F   RACE: W   TYPE: S   MOTIVE: CE
DATE(S): 1935–36   VENUE: Nottingham, England   VICTIMS: Two
MO: Killed nursing home patients with morphine, for inheritance
DISPOSITION: Hanged, Apr. 1936

Wainewright, Thomas Griffiths (?–?)
SEX: M   RACE: W   TYPE: T   MOTIVE: CE/PC
DATE(S): 1828–37   VENUE: England   VICTIMS: Four
MO: Poisoner of relatives (for profit) and a male acquaintance
DISPOSITION: Transported to Australian penal colony

Waite, Dr. Arthur Warren (1889–1917)
SEX: M RACE: W TYPE: T MOTIVE: CE
DATE(S): 1916 VENUE: Mich. VICTIMS: Two
MO: Dentist who killed his in-laws for inheritance
DISPOSITION: Executed, May 1917

Walden, Robert Lee, Jr. (?–)
SEX: M RACE: W TYPE: T MOTIVE: Sex./CE
DATE(S): 1990–92 VENUE: Tucson, Ariz. VICTIMS: Two
MO: Home-invading rape-slayer; victims also robbed
DISPOSITION: Condemned on one count, 1992; 28 years each on six other felony counts

Waldon, Billy Ray (1952–)
SEX: M RACE: W TYPE: N MOTIVE: PC-nonspecific/CE
DATE(S): 1985 VENUE: Okla./Calif. VICTIMS: Four
MO: Apparent thrill-killer on motiveless rampage; some victims robbed incidentally
DISPOSITION: Condemned, 1987

Walker, Clarence (1929–)
SEX: M RACE: B TYPE: N MOTIVE: PC/Sex./Sad.
DATE(S): 1945–66 VENUE: Tenn./Ohio/Mich./Ill./Ind. VICTIMS: 14 suspected
MO: Shot 14-year-old boy; "ripper" of females age seven to 60
DISPOSITION: seven years for manslaughter in Tenn., 1945; 320 years in Ill. for attempted murder, rape, and robbery, 1968

Walker, Dorna Diane (1949–)
SEX: F RACE: W TYPE: T MOTIVE: PC
DATE(S): 1969/1999 VENUE: Winston-Salem, N.C. VICTIMS: Three
MO: Stabbed husband during argument; shot boyfriend who planned to leave her
DISPOSITION: Life sentence without parole on one murder count, April 2002; also 21–26 months for firearms possession by convicted felon

Walker, Gary Alan (d. 2000)
SEX: M RACE: W TYPE: T MOTIVE: Sex./CE
DATE(S): 1984 VENUE: Tulsa, Okla., area VICTIMS: Five
MO: Rape-slayer of women; also robbed/killed a 63-year-old man
DISPOSITION: Condemned on one count in 1985; condemned on second count, 1985 (overturned on appeal); received life without parole plus 500 years at new trial; executed on first count, Jan. 13, 2000

Wallace, George Kent (1941–2000) AKA: Mad Paddler
SEX: M RACE: W TYPE: N MOTIVE: Sex./Sad.
DATE(S): 1976/87–90 VENUE: N.C./Ark./Okla. VICTIMS: five suspected
MO: Torture-slayer of young boys
DISPOSITION: Three life terms plus 60 years on 1991 guilty plea in Arkansas; condemned in Oklahoma, April 1991; executed Aug. 10, 2000

Waqanivalu, Waisale (1979–)
SEX: M RACE: Polynesian TYPE: T MOTIVE: PC-nonspecific
DATE(S): 2004 VENUE: Fiji VICTIMS: Five
MO: Victims bludgeoned with metal pipes or stones in rural lover's lanes
DISPOSITION: Confessed five murders and one attempted murder; received life prison term on Feb. 26, 2005

Wallace, Henry Louis (1941–)
SEX: M RACE: B TYPE: T MOTIVE: Sex.
DATE(S): 1993–94 VENUE: Charlotte, N.C. VICTIMS: 11
MO: Rape-slayer of female acquaintances age 18–35
DISPOSITION: Condemned, 1995

Walls, Frank Athen (1967–)
SEX: M RACE: W TYPE: T MOTIVE: CE
DATE(S): 1987 VENUE: Okaloosa County, Fla. VICTIMS: Three
MO: Killed burglary/kidnap victims
DISPOSITION: Condemned on one count, with life term + 40 years on second count, 1992; life term on third count, 1994

Walls, Samuel Cornelius (1939–)
SEX: M RACE: W TYPE: T MOTIVE: PC/Sex.
DATE(S): 1959–88 VENUE: N.J. VICTIMS: Two
MO: Beat man to death (1959); rape-slayer of woman (1988)
DISPOSITION: 20-year sentence, 1959 (paroled 1974); 25-year term , 1989

Walraven, James Samuel (1949–) AKA: Bathtub Killer
SEX: M RACE: W TYPE: T MOTIVE: Sex.
DATE(S): 1981 VENUE: Atlanta, Ga. VICTIMS: Three
MO: Female victims, all age 22, raped and strangled in their homes, left in bathtubs filled with hot water
DISPOSITION: Condemned on one count, 1982; commuted to life in prison on appeal

Walton, Edward (d. 1908)
SEX: M RACE: B TYPE: N MOTIVE: PC-non-specific
DATE(S): 1896–1908 VENUE: Ala./Ill./Pa./Ohio/W.Va. VICTIMS: Five
MO: Confessed slayer of two men and three women, including his common-law wife; no motive cited
DISPOSITION: Hanged in W.Va. on one count, July 17, 1908

Walton, Vernon (1950–)
SEX: M RACE: W TYPE: T MOTIVE: PC-non-specific
DATE(S): 1972/91 VENUE: La Jolla/San Diego, Calif. VICTIMS: Two
MO: Accused slayer of women age 22 and 50
DISPOSITION: Acquitted on one count (police maintain guilt), 1972; 20 years for manslaughter, 1992

Wang Huaiyi (1968–2004)
SEX: M RACE: A TYPE: T MOTIVE: Sex./CE-felony
DATE(S): 2003–04 VENUE: Zhengshou, China VICTIMS: Six
MO: Police officer who raped, robbed, and murdered women
DISPOSITION: Condemned on six counts, Oct. 1, 2004

Wardell, Gordon (1952–)
SEX: M RACE: W TYPE: T MOTIVE: PC-domestic/Sex.
DATE(S): 1991–94 VENUE: West Midlands, England VICTIMS: Three+ suspect
MO: Killed wife; prime suspect in deaths of several prostitutes
DISPOSITION: Life term for wife's murder, 1995

Warder, Dr. Alfred William (d. 1866)
SEX: M RACE: W TYPE: N MOTIVE: PC/CE
DATE(S) 1820–66 VENUE: England VICTIMS: Three
MO: Bluebeard physician who poisoned successive wives
DISPOSITION: Charged with third wife's death in 1866; committed suicide during trial

Wardrip, Faryion Edward (1959–)
SEX: M RACE: Unk. TYPE: T MOTIVE: Sex.
DATE(S): 1985–86 VENUE: North Texas VICTIMS: Five
MO: Rape-slayer of women in their 20s
DISPOSITION: Confessed one count in 1986 and served 11 years in prison, paroled 1997; condemned on second count, November 1999

Warner, Karl F. (1950–)
SEX: M RACE: W TYPE: T MOTIVE: Sex./Sad.
DATE(S): 1969–70 VENUE: San Jose, Calif. VICTIMS: Three
MO: Mutilation-slayer of girls age 14–18
DISPOSITION: Life sentence, Sept. 1971

Warren, Leslie Eugene (?–)
SEX: M RACE: W TYPE: N MOTIVE: Sex.
DATE(S): 1986–90 VENUE: N.Y./N.C./S.C. VICTIMS: Six+ suspected
MO: Rape-slayer of women
DISPOSITION: Life term on one count in S.C., 1993; condemned in N.C.

Washington, Allen (1948–)
SEX: M RACE: W TYPE: T MOTIVE: Sad.
DATE(S): 1969–78 VENUE: Chicago, Ill. VICTIMS: Three suspected
MO: Bludgeoned three of his own young children in separate incidents
DISPOSITION: 10 years for involuntary manslaughter, 1971 (paroled in 1974); 40 years for murder, July 1980

Washington, Annette (1958–)
SEX: F RACE: B TYPE: T MOTIVE: CE
DATE(S): 1986 VENUE: New York City VICTIMS: Two
MO: Health-care worker; robbed/stabbed elderly women in homes
DISPOSITION: 50 years to life, 1987

Waters, David Roland (1947–2003)
SEX: M RACE: W TYPE: N MOTIVE: PC/CE
DATE(S): 1964–95 VENUE: Ill./Tex. VICTIMS: Six suspected
MO: Killed a teenage acquaintance in 1964; murdered another male acquaintance in 1984; participated in a triple kidnap-murder in Texas, 1995; prime suspect in a sixth killing, also in Texas
DISPOSITION: Convicted of murder at age 18; received a prison term of 30–60 years; received 20-year term in Texas, April 2, 2001; died in prison, Jan. 31, 2003

Waters, Margaret (1835–70)
SEX: F RACE: W TYPE: T MOTIVE: CE
DATE(S): 1866–70 VENUE: Brixton, England VICTIMS: 19+
MO: "Baby farmer"; drugged/starved infants
DISPOSITION: Hanged, Oct. 11, 1870

Watson, James B. (1870–1939)
SEX: M   RACE: W   TYPE: N   MOTIVE: PC-
domestic
DATE(S): 1918–20   VENUE: Idaho/Wash./Calif.
VICTIMS: 25+ alleged
MO: Hermaphrodite "Bluebeard" slayer of wives
DISPOSITION: Life term on confession of seven
counts, 1920; died in prison Oct. 15, 1939

Weaver, Steven (1955–)   AKA: Weed
SEX: M   RACE: W   TYPE: T   MOTIVE: CE/PC
DATE(S): 1987   VENUE: Indianapolis, Ind.   VIC-
TIMS: Four confessed
MO: Outlaw biker, killed fellow gang members
DISPOSITION: 135-year sentence for two murders and
one attempted

Weaver, Ward (1963–)
SEX: M   RACE: W   TYPE: T   MOTIVE: Sex.
DATE(S): 2002   VENUE: Oregon City, Ore.   VIC-
TIMS: Two
MO: Raped and murdered two female neighbors aged
12 and 13 and hid their bodies at his home; also
raped his son's girlfriend, who escaped alive
DISPOSITION: Pled guilty on two murder counts and
five lesser felonies, with a "no contest" plea on 10
additional charges; received two consecutive life
terms without parole, Sept. 23, 2004

Webb, Dennis Duane (1952–)
SEX: M   RACE: W   TYPE: N   MOTIVE:
PC/Sex./CE
DATE(S): 1973–1987   VENUE: Tex./Calif.   VIC-
TIMS: Eight+ confessed
MO: Outlaw biker; killed robbery victims, also blacks
and gays from personal spite; contract killer; raped
victims of both sexes
DISPOSITION: Condemned in Calif., 1988

Weber, Jeanne (1875–1910)
SEX: F   RACE: W   TYPE: N   MOTIVE: Sad.
DATE(S): 1905–08   VENUE: Northern France   VIC-
TIMS: 10
MO: Strangled young children for the thrill of killing;
victims included three of her own children, two
nephews, a niece, and four children left in her care
by friends of employers
DISPOSITION: Acquitted at first murder trial, Feb. 6,
1906; released in second case for lack of evidence,
December 1907; ruled insane on third charge and
committed to asylum, May 1908; suicide by manual
strangulation in 1910

Webster, Robert (1922–)
SEX: M   RACE: W   TYPE: T   MOTIVE: Sex.
DATE(S): 1946/63   VENUE: Northern Calif.   VIC-
TIMS: Two
MO: Rape-slayer of women age 19 (1946) and 38
(1963)
DISPOSITION: 1946 life term (paroled 1954); second
life term, 1963

Weeks, Robert (1929–)
SEX: M   RACE: W   TYPE: N   MOTIVE: PC-
domestic
DATE(S): 1968/80–81   VENUE: Nev./Calif.   VIC-
TIMS: Three
MO: "Bluebeard" slayer of wife and fiancées who left
him
DISPOSITION: Life without parole on two counts in
Nev., 1988

Weidenbroeker, Helmut (1965–)
SEX: M   RACE: W   TYPE: T   MOTIVE: Sex.
DATE(S): 1982–86   VENUE: Aachen, Germany
VICTIMS: Three to five
MO: Lust murders of women
DISPOSITION: Life sentence on one murder count,
1987

Weidmann, Eugen (1915–39)
SEX: M   RACE: W   TYPE: N   MOTIVE: CE
DATE(S): 1935–37   VENUE: France   VICTIMS: Six
confessed
MO: German immigrant; killed victims in robberies
and ransom kidnappings
DISPOSITION: Guillotined May 18, 1939

Weinberg, Abraham (d. 1935)   AKA: Bo
SEX: M   RACE: W   TYPE: T   MOTIVE: CE
DATE(S): 1920s–35   VENUE: N.Y./N.J.   VICTIMS:
"Numerous"
MO: Chief contract killer of ARTHUR FLEGENHEIMER
gang
DISPOSITION: Murdered by Flegenheimer, Aug. 1935

Weiss, Emmanuel (d. 1944)
SEX: M   RACE: W   TYPE: T   MOTIVE: CE
DATE(S): 1931–40   VENUE: N.Y./N.J.   VICTIMS:
"Numerous"
MO: Contract killer for "MURDER, INC."
DISPOSITION: Executed at Sing Sing, Mar. 2, 1944

Wenzinger, Gerd (1944–97)
SEX: M   RACE: W   TYPE: N   MOTIVE: Sad.
DATE(S): 1990s   VENUE: Germany/Brazil   VIC-
TIMS: 17

MO: "Torture doctor" who dissected women on two continents; at least one murder videotaped
DISPOSITION: Suicide by hanging in Brazil, June 16, 1997

West, Ronald Glenn (1947–)
SEX: M   RACE: W   TYPE: T   MOTIVE: Sex.
DATE(S): 1970   VENUE: Toronto, Canada   VICTIMS: More than two
MO: Policeman who raped and shot two nurses in separate attacks; prime suspect in eight robbery-slayings, including the Ottawa Valley Killer's crimes (1975–87) and a 1991 double murder near Sault Ste. Marie
DISPOSITION: Pled guilty on two counts and received a life sentence, Aug. 7, 2001

Wheat, Clarence (d. 1980)
SEX: M   RACE: W   TYPE: S   MOTIVE: PC
DATE(S): 1979–80   VENUE: Miss.   VICTIMS: Three
MO: Killed policeman in domestic dispute; pardoned eight months later due to terminal cancer; killed wife, son, and self
DISPOSITION: Suicide by gunshot, June 1980

Whisenhant, Thomas (?–)
SEX: M   RACE: W   TYPE: T   MOTIVE: Sex./CE
DATE(S): 1963–76   VENUE: Mobile, Ala.   VICTIMS: Four
MO: Shot women in robberies; one raped, two mutilated postmortem
DISPOSITION: Condemned on one count, 1997; life terms on two counts

White, Nathaniel (1960–)
SEX: M   RACE: B   TYPE: T   MOTIVE: Sex./Sad.
DATE(S): 1991–92   VENUE: Orange County, N.Y.   VICTIMS: Six
MO: Women raped/stabbed by paroled rapist
DISPOSITION: 150 years in prison on six counts

White, Richard Paul (1965–)
SEX: M   RACE: W   TYPE: N   MOTIVE: Sex./PC
DATE(S): 2002–03   VENUE: Col.   VICTIMS: Six confessed
MO: Kidnapped and raped eight women, killing five, in three counties; also murdered a 27-year-old male coworker in a fourth county
DISPOSITION: Pleaded guilty to coworker's murder in Arapahoe County and received a life term without parole, Sept. 7, 2004; pled guilty on two murder counts and charges of using weapons to sexually assault three other women in Jefferson County, receiving another life term on Sept. 16, 2004; 28

additional felony counts were dismissed in that deal, with murder charges waived in Costilla and Otero Counties; White also directed police to bodies of three additional victims

White, Robert Excell (1938–99)   AKA: Excell the Executioner
SEX: M   RACE: W   TYPE: T   MOTIVE: CE-felony
DATE(S): 1974   VENUE: Waco, Tex.   VICTIMS: Four
MO: Stabbed gun collector and stole weapons; used stolen guns to kill three men in a commercial robbery
DISPOSITION: Condemned on three counts, August 1974; sentence overturned on appeal, 1997; condemned at second trial, June 1997; executed March 30, 1999

White, Ronald Lee (1956–)
SEX: M   RACE: Unk.   TYPE: T   MOTIVE: PC
DATE(S): 1987–88   VENUE: Southern Colorado   VICTIMS: Three
MO: Killed two men in personal disputes, at Pueblo and Colorado Springs; later shot his roommate, dismembering the body to delay identification
DISPOSITION: Life sentence imposed on two counts, 1990; condemned for roommate's murder, 1991; death sentence overturned on appeal, 1998; received life term at new trial, Aug. 27, 2001

White Shirley (1932–)
SEX: F   RACE: W   TYPE: T   MOTIVE: CE
DATE(S): 1971–92   VENUE: Kinston, N.C.   VICTIMS: Three suspected
MO: "Black widow" slayer of husbands and stepchild
DISPOSITION: Life term on one count, 1992

Whiteway, Alfred C. (1931–54)
SEX: M   RACE: W   TYPE: T   MOTIVE: Sex.
DATE(S): 1953   VENUE: London, England   VICTIMS: Two
MO: Lust killer of teenage girls bludgeoned in parks
DISPOSITION: Hanged, 1954

Whitney, Dennis (1943–)
SEX: M   RACE: W   TYPE: N   MOTIVE: CE-felony
DATE(S): 1960   VENUE: Calif./Ariz./Fla.   VICTIMS: Seven
MO: Shot robbery victims; kidnapped and bludgeoned one woman
DISPOSITION: Condemned on two counts in Fla., 1960; commuted, 1972

Whitt, Jimmy Earl (1971–94)
SEX: M   RACE: ?   TYPE: N   MOTIVE: CE-felony

DATE(S): 1994   VENUE: Ala./Miss.   VICTIMS: Four
MO: Killed one holdup victim and three policemen in
   three-week rampage
DISPOSITION: Suicide to avoid arrest, June 28, 1994

Wilcox, Donald (1968–2003)
SEX: M   RACE: Unk.   TYPE: T   MOTIVE: CE-
felony
DATE(S): 2003   VENUE: Nueces County, Tex.   VIC-
TIMS: Three
MO: Killed a married couple, aged 79 and 77, with
   their own pistol during a home-invasion robbery;
   later killed a 61-year-old man with same gun
DISPOSITION: Suicide by gunshot after wounded in a
   shootout with police, Feb. 13, 2003

Wilken, Stewart (1964–   )   AKA: Bootie Boer
SEX: M   RACE: W   TYPE: T   MOTIVE: Sex.
DATE(S): 1990–97   VENUE: Port Elizabeth, South
   Africa   VICTIMS: 11+
MO: Sex slayer and cannibal; victims included prosti-
   tutes, young boys, and his own daughter
DISPOSITION: Seven life terms, 1998

Wille, John Francis (1964–   )
SEX: M   RACE: W   TYPE: N   MOTIVE:
PC/Sex./Sad.
DATE(S): 1980–85   VENUE: La./Fla./Tex./Ala.   VIC-
TIMS: Six suspected
MO: Drifter linked to murders of four men (including
   one sexually mutilated) and two females (an elderly
   woman burned in her home; an eight-year-old girl
   raped/strangled)
DISPOSITION: Life term with 25-year minimum in
   Fla., 1985; later condemned in La.

Williams, Dorothy (1952–   )
SEX: F   RACE: B   TYPE: T   MOTIVE: CE-felony
DATE(S): 1989   VENUE: Chicago, Ill.   VICTIMS:
Three confessed
MO: Strangled/robbed elderly shut-ins to support her
   drug habit
DISPOSITION: Condemned on one count, with two
   life terms for other slayings; death sentence com-
   muted to life imprisonment, 2003

Williams, George E. (1943–   )
SEX: M   RACE: W   TYPE: T   MOTIVE: Sex.
DATE(S): 1983–84   VENUE: Chicago, Ill.   VIC-
TIMS: Seven suspected
MO: Home invader who raped/strangled elderly
   women
DISPOSITION: Life term without parole on two
   counts

Williams, Henry Robert (?–   )
SEX: M   RACE: W   TYPE: T   MOTIVE: Sex.
DATE(S): 1972–73   VENUE: Mississauga, Ontario
   VICTIMS: Two
MO: Rape-slayer of girls age 16 and 19
DISPOSITION: Life term on one count; chose volun-
   tary castration in lieu of additional prison time,
   upon second conviction

Williams, John (d. 1811)   AKA: Ratcliff Highway
   Demon
SEX: M   RACE: W   TYPE: T   MOTIVE: CE
DATE(S): 1811   VENUE: London, England   VIC-
TIMS: Five
MO: Home invader who slashed/bludgeoned robbery
   victims
DISPOSITION: Suicide by hanging prior to trial, 1811

Williams, John, Jr. (1961–   )
SEX: M   RACE: B   TYPE: T   MOTIVE: Sex.
DATE(S): 1996–97   VENUE: Raleigh, N.C.   VIC-
TIMS: Five suspected
MO: Rape-slayer of black women chosen at random
DISPOSITION: Condemned on two murder counts,
   March 1998

Williams, John S. (1863–1932)
SEX: M   RACE: W   TYPE: T   MOTIVE: CE
DATE(S): c. 1910–21   VENUE: Jasper County, Ga.
   VICTIMS: 18 suspected
MO: Enslaved blacks, killing those who fled or
   "caused trouble"
DISPOSITION: Life term on one count, 1921; life term
   on second count, 1922; killed in prison, Jan. 26,
   1932

Williams, Kenneth D. (1979–   )
SEX: M   RACE: W   TYPE: N   MOTIVE: CE
DATE(S): 1998–99   VENUE: Ark.   VICTIMS: Two
MO: Robbed/killed a 19-year-old woman at Pine Bluff;
   later shot a 57-year-old man after a prison break
DISPOSITION: Life term for first murder, September
   1999; escaped from prison in October 1999; recap-
   tured the following day

Williams, Laron Ronald (1949–85)
SEX: M   RACE: B   TYPE: N   MOTIVE: Sex./CE
DATE(S): 197?/81   VENUE: Tenn.   VICTIMS: Three
MO: Killed a prostitute; murdered priest and police-
   man while a fugitive from prison on that charge
DISPOSITION: 10 years for first count (escaped Apr.
   1981); condemned on two counts, 1981; fatally
   beaten by other inmates, July 7, 1985

Williams, Leslie Allen (1953–   )
SEX: M   RACE: W   TYPE: T   MOTIVE: Sex.
DATE(S): 1991–92   VENUE: Oakland/Genessee
   Counties, Mich.   VICTIMS: Four
MO: Rape-slayer of teenage girls
DISPOSITION: Life without parole on one count,
   1992

Williams, Robert (1936–97)
SEX: M   RACE: B   TYPE: N   MOTIVE: PC/Sex.
DATE(S): 1977   VENUE: Nebr./Iowa   VICTIMS:
   Three confessed
MO: Killed sister and two other women; raped/shot
   one who survived
DISPOSITION: Executed in Nebr., Dec. 2, 1997

Williams, Ronald Turney (d. 1981)
SEX: M   RACE: W   TYPE: N   MOTIVE: CE
DATE(S): 1975/79   VENUE: W.Va./Ariz.   VICTIMS:
   Three
MO: Career criminal; victims included two policemen
DISPOSITION: Life term on one count, 1975 (escaped
   1979); killed by FBI in N.Y. while resisting arrest,
   June 8, 1981

Williams, Ronnie Keith (1962–   )
SEX: M   RACE: B   TYPE: T   MOTIVE: Sex.
DATE(S): 1984/93   VENUE: Broward County, Fla.
   VICTIMS: Two
MO: Pedophile lust killer
DISPOSITION: 17 years for second-degree + seven
   years for child molesting, 1984 (paroled, 1992);
   condemned, 1996

Williams, Sidney (1972–89)
SEX: M   RACE: B   TYPE: T   MOTIVE: PC
DATE(S): 1989   VENUE: New Orleans, La.   VIC-
   TIMS: Three
MO: Shot male victims in personal confrontations
DISPOSITION: Fatally shot by an acquaintance, Oct.
   3, 1989

Williamson, Stella (1904–80)
SEX: F   RACE: W   TYPE: S   MOTIVE: PC
DATE(S): 1923–33   VENUE: Gallitzin, Pa.   VIC-
   TIMS: Five
MO: Unwed mother who killed five infants, storing the
   corpses in a suitcase in the attic of her home
DISPOSITION: Died of natural causes, Aug. 1980,
   leaving directions to the remains with an explana-
   tory letter

Willis, Fred (1951–   )
SEX: M   RACE: B   TYPE: T   MOTIVE: Sex.

DATE(S): 1984/97   VENUE: Las Vegas, Nev.   VIC-
   TIMS: Two
MO: Rape-slayer of female prostitutes age 24 and 25
DISPOSITION: Imprisoned, 1985 (paroled 1995); life
   term, 1998

Willoughby, John R. (?–   )
SEX: M   RACE: ?   TYPE: T   MOTIVE: PC
DATE(S): 1975/83   VENUE: Indianapolis, Ind.   VIC-
   TIMS: Two
MO: Killed teenage girl and off-duty policewoman
DISPOSITION: 130 years on one count

Wilson, Brandon (1978–   )
SEX: M   RACE: W   TYPE: N   MOTIVE: PC
DATE(S): 1998   VENUE: Calif./Utah   VICTIMS: two
   suspected
MO: Deranged drug abuser convinced that God
   ordered him to kill as a means of ending the world;
   stabbed a young boy in a public restroom; arrested
   after wounding a woman; suspected of killing
   another child in Utah
DISPOSITION: Condemned in California, Oct. 6, 1999

Wilson, Catherine (1822–62)
SEX: F   RACE: W   TYPE: N   MOTIVE: CE
DATE(S): 1854–62   VENUE: England   VICTIMS:
   Five
MO: Transient poisoner of acquaintances for profit
DISPOSITION: Hanged, Oct. 20, 1862

Wilson, Mary Elizabeth (1891–1961)
SEX: F   RACE: W   TYPE: T   MOTIVE: CE
DATE(S): 1956–57   VENUE: Windy Hook, England
   VICTIMS: Four
MO: "Black widow" poisoner of husbands/lovers for
   profit
DISPOSITION: Condemned, 1958 (commuted on
   appeal); died in prison, 1961

Wilson, Otto (1911–46)
SEX: M   RACE: W   TYPE: T   MOTIVE: Sex./Sad.
DATE(S): 1944   VENUE: Los Angeles, Calif.   VIC-
   TIMS: Two
MO: Women dismembered in hotel rooms
DISPOSITION: Executed Sept. 20, 1946

Wimberly, Anthony (1961–   )
SEX: M   RACE: B   TYPE: T   MOTIVE: CE/Sex.
DATE(S): 1984–85   VENUE: Oakland, Calif.   VIC-
   TIMS: Three
MO: Burglar who raped/killed female victims in
   homes/stores
DISPOSITION: Three life terms without parole, 1994

Winkles, James Deland (1940–   )
SEX: M   RACE: W   TYPE: T   MOTIVE: CE
DATE(S): 1980–81   VENUE: Pinellas Company, Fla.
VICTIMS: Two
MO: Victims shot during robberies
DISPOSITION: Condemned on two counts, April 14, 2003

Wirth, Robert (1960–   )
SEX: M   RACE: W   TYPE: T   MOTIVE: CE/Sad.
DATE(S): 1987–88   VENUE: Milwaukee, Wis.   VICTIMS: Six to eight
MO: Elderly victims beaten/stabbed in their homes
DISPOSITION: Four consecutive life terms + 20 years, 1991

Wise, Martha Hasel (1883–?)   AKA: Borgia of America
SEX: F   RACE: W   TYPE: T   MOTIVE: PC-nonspecific
DATE(S): 1924–25   VENUE: Medina County, Ohio
VICTIMS: Three
MO: "Black widow" poisoner of relatives; also prolific arsonist
DISPOSITION: Life term, 1925; died in prison

Wittman, Manfred (1945–   )   AKA: Beast of Oberfranken
SEX: M   RACE: W   TYPE: T   MOTIVE: Sex.
DATE(S): 1959–60   VENUE: Germany   VICTIMS: Three confessed
MO: Impotent "ripper" of young women
DISPOSITION: Life term on guilty plea

Wolter, Michael (1972–89)
SEX: M   RACE: W   TYPE: N   MOTIVE: Sex.
DATE(S): 1980–83   VENUE: Germany   VICTIMS: Eight suspected
MO: Rape-slayer of females age 25; victims stabbed/strangled
DISPOSITION: Life term on confession to five counts

Wongsin, Sila (d. 1959)
SEX: M   RACE: A   TYPE: T   MOTIVE: PC-extremist
DATE(S): 1958–59   VENUE: Korat, Thailand   VICTIMS: Five+
MO: "Devil-worship" cult leader linked to human sacrifices
DISPOSITION: Executed, June 26, 1959

Wood, David Leonard (1951–   )   AKA: Desert Killer
SEX: M   RACE: W   TYPE: T   MOTIVE: Sex./Sad.
DATE(S): 1987–88   VENUE: El Paso, Tex.   VICTIMS: 15 confessed
MO: Rape-slayer of young women
DISPOSITION: Condemned on six murder counts

Wood, Frederick G. (1912–   )
SEX: M   RACE: W   TYPE: T   MOTIVE: PC
DATE(S): 1926–60   VENUE: N.Y.   VICTIMS: Five confessed
MO: Beat male victims to death in personal confrontations
DISPOSITION: Life term on one count, 1942 (paroled 1960); condemned on two counts, 1962 (commuted to life, 1972)

Wood, Isaac (d. 1858)
SEX: M   RACE: W   TYPE: N   MOTIVE: CE
DATE(S): 1858   VENUE: N.Y./N.J.   VICTIMS: Seven
MO: Poisoned wife, child, and other relatives for inheritance
DISPOSITION: Hanged, July 1858

Wood, James Edward (1947–   )
SEX: M   RACE: W   TYPE: N   MOTIVE: Sex.
DATE(S): 1967–92   VENUE: La./Ark./Idaho   VICTIMS: Seven+ suspected
MO: Rape-slayer of girls and women
DISPOSITION: Condemned in Idaho on one count, 1994

Woodfield, Randall Brent (1950–   )   AKA: I-5 Killer
SEX: M   RACE: W   TYPE: N   MOTIVE: Sex./CE
DATE(S): 1961   VENUE: Ore./Wash./Calif.   VICTIMS: 12+ suspected
MO: Raped/robbed/shot females age 14–37 in random attacks
DISPOSITION: Life + 90 years in Ore., 1981; 35 years more in second trial for sex crimes in Ore. 2003

Wooten, Charles (1949–   )
SEX: M   RACE: Unk.   TYPE: N   MOTIVE: CE/PC
DATE(S): 1968/93   VENUE: Ft. Worth, Tex.   VICTIMS: Three
MO: Killed two holdup victims; killed/dismembered father
DISPOSITION: four life terms on two counts, 1970 (paroled 1991); life term, 1995

Workman, Charles (1908–   )   AKA: The Bug
SEX: M   RACE: W   TYPE: T   MOTIVE: CE
DATE(S): 1926–41   VENUE: N.Y./N.J.   VICTIMS: "Numerous"
MO: Contract killer for "MURDER, INC."
DISPOSITION: Life term in N.J. for murder of ARTHUR FLEGENHEIMER, 1941 (paroled 1964)

Wright, Douglas Franklin (1940–96)
SEX: M   RACE: W   TYPE: T   MOTIVE: PC
DATE(S): 1991   VENUE: Ore.   VICTIMS: Six+
MO: Lured homeless men from Portland; shot them in
  Wasco County
DISPOSITION: Executed on Sept. 6, 1996

Wright, Dwayne Allen (1972–   )
SEX: M   RACE: B   TYPE: N   MOTIVE: PC
DATE(S): 1989   VENUE: Md./Va./D.C./   VICTIMS:
  Three
MO: Drug addict; shot male victims in personal dis-
  putes
DISPOSITION: Condemned on one count in Va., 1992

Wright, William (d. 1997)   AKA: King Rat
SEX: M   RACE: W   TYPE: T   MOTIVE: PC-
  extremist
DATE(S): 1980s–1997   VENUE: Northern Ireland
  VICTIMS: Dozens
MO: Leader of Protestant terrorist "rat pack" that
  killed Catholics, Republicans, and suspected police
  informers
DISPOSITION: Murdered by Republican rivals, Dec.
  27, 1997

Wyatt, "Señor" (d. 1864)
SEX: M   RACE: W   TYPE: M   MOTIVE: PC
DATE(S): 1840s–64   VENUE: Rocky Mountains
  VICTIMS: 100+
MO: "Mountain man" and prolific racist slayer of
  Indians; also kidnapped Mexican girls to serve as
  concubines, murdering male relatives who pursued
  him
DISPOSITION: Killed by Mexicans in revenge for kid-
  nap/rape

Wyatt, Thomas Anthony (1964–   )
SEX: M   RACE: W   TYPE: T   MOTIVE: Sex./PC
DATE(S): 1988 venue: Indian River Company, Fla.
  VICTIMS: Two
MO: One victim killed after kidnap-rape, second killed
  in personal altercation
DISPOSITION: Condemned on one count, Feb. 22,
  1991; condemned on second count, Dec. 20, 1991

Yaddav, Akku (d. 2004)
SEX: M   RACE: A   TYPE: T   MOTIVE: Sex.
DATE(S): 2002–03   VENUE: Nagpur, India   VIC-
  TIMS: "Several"
MO: Bandit and serial rapist accused of multiple mur-
  ders
DISPOSITION: Mobbed and killed by 200+ women
  during a pretrial hearing

Yang Zinhai *See* WANG GANGGANG

Yasutoshi Kamata (1940–   )
SEX: M   RACE: A   TYPE: T   MOTIVE: Sex.
DATE(S): 1985–94   VENUE: Osaka, Japan   VIC-
  TIMS: Five
MO: Rape-strangler of females aged 9–46; demanded
  ransom for his youngest victim prior to murder
DISPOSITION: Condemned on five counts, March 25,
  1999

Yates, Daniel (?–   )
SEX: M   RACE: W   TYPE: N   MOTIVE: Sad.
DATE(S): 1985–87   VENUE: Wash./Okla.   VIC-
  TIMS: Two
MO: Kidnapped, tortured and shot three hitchhikers,
  aged 12 and 13, at Silverdale, Wash. (killing one);
  prime suspect in the murder of a 35-year-old woman
  in Oklahoma
DISPOSITION: 60 years for murder and attempted
  murder in Washington

Yeo, Jonathan (1959–91)
SEX: M   RACE: W   TYPE: T   MOTIVE: Sex.
DATE(S): 1991   VENUE: Hamilton, Ontario   VIC-
  TIMS: Two
MO: Lust killer of women age 19 and 28
DISPOSITION: Suicide by gunshot to avoid arrest,
  Aug. 1991

Yershov, Vadim (1973–   )
SEX: M   RACE: W   TYPE: T   MOTIVE: Sex./CE
DATE(S): 1997   VENUE: Siberia, Russia   VIC-
  TIMS: 19
MO: Rape/robbed/stabbed victims in random attacks
DISPOSITION: Condemned, 1998

York, Thomas (?–   )   AKA: Thomas Jurkiewicz
SEX: M   RACE: W   TYPE: T   MOTIVE: CE
DATE(S): 1978/81   VENUE: Chicago, Ill.   VICTIMS:
  Two
MO: Slayer of wife and female business partner for
  insurance
DISPOSITION: 40 years on federal conspiracy charges,
  1989

Yoo Young-chul (1971–   )
SEX: M   RACE: A   TYPE: S   MOTIVE: Sex./CE
DATE(S): 2003–04   VENUE: Seoul, South Korea
  VICTIMS: 31 confessed
MO: Lured victims to his home, killed them with ham-
  mers, then dismembered and concealed the bodies

DISPOSITION: 14 convictions for rape and theft, paroled last time in 2003; boasted of 31 murders in court, on Sept. 21, 2004; disposition unknown

Young, David Franklin (1960–)
SEX: M   RACE: W   TYPE: N   MOTIVE: Sex.
DATE(S): 1987   VENUE: Utah/Ind.   VICTIMS: Two
MO: Rape slayer of women; victims stabbed/bludgeoned
DISPOSITION: 35 years to life in Ind., 1987; condemned in Utah, 1988

Young, Graham Frederick (1947–90)
SEX: M   RACE: W   TYPE: S   MOTIVE: PC/Sad.
DATE(S): 1962/71   VENUE: London/Bovington, England   VICTIMS: Three
MO: Poisoned stepmother (1962) and various others (1971)
DISPOSITION: 1972 life sentence; died in prison, Aug. 1, 1990

Youngblood, Herbert (1899–1934)
SEX: M   RACE: B   TYPE: N   MOTIVE: CE
DATE(S): 1933–34   VENUE: Ind./Mich.   VICTIMS: Two
MO: Killed merchant in robbery; shot deputy sheriff
DISPOSITION: Killed resisting arrest, Mar. 16, 1934

Zamastil, William Floyd (1952–)
SEX: M   RACE: W   TYPE: N   MOTIVE: Sex./PC
DATE(S): 1974–78   VENUE: Ariz./Calif./Wisc.   VICTIMS: Seven suspected
MO: Drifter who killed victims of both sexes in random encounters; some female victims were raped
DISPOSITION: Surrendered and confessed rape-murder of a 23-year-old woman in Dane County, Wisc., 1978; received life prison term; on May 28, 2004 pleaded guilty to 1978 beating deaths of an 18-year-old woman and her 17-year-old brother at Canoga Park, Calif.; received 25 years to life, concurrent with his Wisconsin sentence

Zani, Robert Joseph (1944–)
SEX: M   RACE: W   TYPE: N   MOTIVE: PC/CE
DATE(S): 1969–79   VENUE: Okla./Tex./Ark.   VICTIMS: Six+ suspected
MO: Killed his mother and multiple robbery victims, with a preference for real estate agents
DISPOSITION: 99 years on one count in Tex., 1981; 99 years for mother's murder in Okla., 1982 (overturned on appeal, 1986)

Zayas, Carlos (1948–)
SEX: M   RACE: H   TYPE: N   MOTIVE: Sex.

DATE(S): 1980–87   VENUE: Pa./N.J.   VICTIMS: Two
MO: Strangled girlfriends after sex
DISPOSITION: Life term on one court, 1989; second (consecutive) life term, 1990

Zeck, Michael Duane, III (1969–)
SEX: M   RACE: W   TYPE: T   MOTIVE: CE/Sex.
DATE(S): 1996   VENUE: Fla.   VICTIMS: Two
MO: Raped/robbed/killed women in Okaloosa and Santa Rosa counties.
DISPOSITION: two trials in 1997: condemned on one count; life term without parole on second count

Zeid, Aida Nourre din Mohammed Abu (1973–)
SEX: F   RACE: A   TYPE: S   MOTIVE: PC
DATE(S): 1996–97   VENUE: Alexandria, Egypt   VICTIMS: 18 confessed
MO: Nurse who killed hospital patients so she could sleep
DISPOSITION: Condemned on one count, 1998; sentence overturned on appeal

Zhang Haiguan (d. 1999)
SEX: M   RACE: A   TYPE: T   MOTIVE: CE
DATE(S): 1999   VENUE: Shanghai, China   VICTIMS: Three
MO: A member of the criminal "Concrete Head Black Gun Gang," who used a female victim's severed head to extort money
DISPOSITION: Killed in shootout with police, Nov. 5, 1999

Zhang Lisong (1968–98)   AKA: Monster Murderer
SEX: M   RACE: A   TYPE: T   MOTIVE: Sex.
DATE(S): 1997–98   VENUE: Hubei Province, China   VICTIMS: Nine
MO: Rape-slayer of women
DISPOSITION: Shot Sept. 24, 1998

Zhou Wen (1965–)   AKA: Taxi Devil
SEX: M   RACE: A   TYPE: T   MOTIVE: PC
DATE(S): 2003   VENUE: Anshan, China   VICTIMS: Six confessed
MO: Taxi driver enraged by his wife's secret abortion, who killed female fares and dumped their bodies outside town; confessed in custody and produced a diary of his crimes
DISPOSITION: Unknown

Zon, Hans von (1942–)
SEX: M   RACE: W   TYPE: T   MOTIVE: Sex./CE
DATE(S): 1964–67   VENUE: Amsterdam, Netherland   VICTIMS: Five

MO: Bisexual slayer; killed two female lovers, one gay man, and two male robbery victims

DISPOSITION: Lif term, 1967; robbery accomplice Oude Nol drew a seven-year term

Zu Shenatir (?–?)
SEX: M   RACE: A   TYPE: S   MOTIVE: Sex.
DATE(S): Fifth century   VENUE: Yemen   VICTIMS: "Numerous"
MO: Pedophile slayer of boys at his home
DISPOSITION: Fatally stabbed by last intended victim

Zurwehm, Dieter (1942–   )
SEX: M   RACE: W   TYPE: T   MOTIVE: Sex./CE-felony
DATE(S): 1972/1999   VENUE: Germany   VICTIMS: Five
MO: Murdered a woman at Dueren, 1972; escaped from prison December 1998; killed two elderly couples during a home-invasion robbery at Remagen; DNA evidence linked him to two attempted rapes

DISPOSITION: Convicted on four murder counts, plus kidnapping, robbery, and attempted rape; received life prison term, June 8, 2000

Zwanziger, Anna Maria (1760–1811)
SEX: F   RACE: W   TYPE: N   MOTIVE: PC-nonspecific
DATE(S): 1806–09   VENUE: Germany   VICTIMS: Four
MO: Household servant who poisoned employers and coworkers, including wives and children of men she hoped to marry, as well as the men themselves when no proposals were forthcoming
DISPOSITION: Beheaded in July 1811

Zwerbach, Maxwell (1882–1908)   AKA: Kid Twist
SEX: M   RACE: W   TYPE: T   MOTIVE: CE/PC
DATE(S): 1890s–1908   VENUE: New York City   VICTIMS: 20+
MO: Street gang "enforcer" and contract killer
DISPOSITION: Killed in gangland ambush, May 14, 1908

Appendix B: Team Killers

Abel, Wolfgang (1959–   ); **Furlan, Mario** (1960–   )
SEX: 2 M   RACE: W   TYPE: N   MOTIVE: GC-extremist
DATE(S): 1977–84   VENUE: Italy   VICTIMS: 14
MO: Methods varied from individual kills to arson-mass murder
DISPOSITION: 30 years each, 1987; released to "open custody" on appeal, based on time served prior to trial

Adams, Charles (?–   ); **Bruintjies, Johannes** (?–   ); **Chavulla, Laston** (?–   ); **Ruiters, Dawid** (?–   ); **Solomon, André Douglas** (?–   )   AKA: Flower Gangsters
SEX: 5 M   RACE: B   TYPE: N   MOTIVE: PC
DATE(S): 1996–97   VENUE: Northern Cape, South Africa   VICTIMS: Eight
MO: Escaped convicts and gang members who murdered a male acquaintance and seven strangers while still at large
DISPOSITION: All five convicted on three counts of murder and various lesser offenses, receiving life terms; two convicted on two additional murder counts, receiving 25-year terms

Allen, Michael (1972–   )   AKA: Fat Rat; **Johnson, Cleamon** (1969–   )   AKA: Big Evil
SEX: 2 M   RACE: B   TYPE: T   MOTIVE: GC-gang
DATE(S): 1990s   VENUE: Los Angeles, Calif.   VICTIMS: 60+ suspected
MO: Homicidal members of the "Bloods" street gang
DISPOSITION: Both condemned on two counts, 1997

Alves, Joaquim (1929–   ); **Ferreira, Priscilla Souza** (1978–   )
SEX: M/F   RACE: H   TYPE: T   MOTIVE: Cult
DATE(S): 1999–2000   VENUE: Victoria da Conquista, Brazil   VICTIMS: "Several"
MO: Self-styled sorcerer and his girlfriend, found with ritual implements and a murdered six-year-old boy in their home; each accused the other of murder; police link other child sacrifices to the couple
DISPOSITION: Unknown

Andrade, Valentina de (1928–   ); **Caldas Brandão, Dr. Césio** (?–   ); **Ferreira de Souza, Dr. Anísio** (?–   ); **Madeira Gomes, Amailton** (?–   ); **Santos Lima, Carlos Alberto dos** (?–   )   AKA: Superior Universal Enlightenment
SEX: 1 F/4 M   RACE: H   TYPE: T   MOTIVE: GC-cult
DATE(S): 1989–93   VENUE: Altamira, Brazil   VICTIMS: 14
MO: Satanic UFO cult that believed all children born after 1981 are evil and must be eliminated; members included two physicians, an ex-policeman, and a wealthy businessman, led by a self-styled clairvoyant; kidnapped, tortured and castrated 19 boys aged 8–13, killing 14
DISPOSITION: Santos received a 35-year term for one murder and two attempted murders, Aug. 30, 2003; Madeira received 57 years for three murders in separate trial, Aug. 30, 2003; Dr. Ferreira received 77 years for three murders and one attempted murder, Sept. 4, 2003; leader Andrade was acquitted of three murders and two attempted murders, Dec. 6, 2003

Anselmi, Albert (1884–1929); **Scalise, John** (1900–29)
SEX: 2 M   RACE: W   TYPE: N   MOTIVE: CE
DATE(S): 1920s   VENUE: Sicily/U.S.   VICTIMS: "Numerous"
MO: Prolific Mafia assassins during Prohibition era, suspected of participation in Chicago's St. Valentine's Day massacre and many other gangland murders
DISPOSITION: Beaten to death by ALPHONSES CAPONE on May 7, 1929

Asahara, Shoko (1955–) et al.   AKA: "Aum Shinrikyo" (Supreme Truth)
SEX: c. 5,000 M/F   RACE: A   TYPE: N   MOTIVE: GC-cult
DATE(S): 1989–96   VENUE: Japan   VICTIMS: 20+
MO: Doomsday cult whose leader ordered murders of defecting members, cult associates, and perceived enemies; cultists also committed mass murder via release of nerve gas on crowded subway trains
DISPOSITION: Eight members ordered to pay ¥100 million to families of four victims killed in subway gas attack, 1996; one cult member sentenced to 15 years for two counts of murder and gassing of victims who survived, 1997; one member condemned on four counts, three sentenced to terms from 6 1/2 years to life on charges of murder and kidnapping, 1998; further trials ongoing

Assassins, Order of   AKA: *Hashishin*
SEX: M   RACE: A   TYPE: N   MOTIVE: GC-cult/CE
DATE(S): 1092–1260   VENUE: Middle East/Europe   VICTIMS: Thousands
MO: Muslim splinter sect whose members hired out as professional killers during the Crusades; self-interest prevailed, and assassins frequently served Christian masters.
DISPOSITION: Members scattered or exterminated when Mongol raiders overran the cult stronghold in Persia

Aung Kyau Saw (?–); **Picherd Saenko** (1980–)
SEX: 2 M   RACE: A   TYPE: T   MOTIVE: CE-felony
DATE(S): 2001–02   VENUE: Bangkok, Thailand   VICTIMS: Three confessed
MO: Unlicensed tour guides who killed and robbed tourists, including one Canadian and two Japanese
DISPOSITION: Unknown

Baninzi, Asande (1983–); **Nombewu, Mtutuzeli** (d. 2001)
SEX: 2 M   RACE: B   TYPE: T   MOTIVE: CE/Sex.

DATE(S): 2001   VENUE: Gugulethu, South Africa   VICTIMS: 18
MO: Armed robbers and rapists who killed robbery victims and suspected police informers during four-month crime spree
DISPOSITION: Nombewu killed by police while resisting arrest; on May 5, 2004 Baninzi received 19 life terms plus 189 years on conviction of 14 murders, four rapes, and two armed robberies; additional life terms were imposed at a separate trial for four other slayings

Barker, Arthur (1899–1939), **Fred** (1901–35), and **Herman** (1893–1927); **Karpis, Alvin** (1908–79); et al.
SEX: 4+ M   RACE: W   TYPE: N   MOTIVE: CE/PC
DATE(S): 1920–34   VENUE: Okla./Kans./Mo./Ark./Minn./Ill.   VICTIMS: 11+
MO: Career criminals allegedly led by mother of the Barker brothers; killed lawmen, holdup victims, and gangland associates
DISPOSITION: Herman killed in Kans. shoot-out with police, Aug. 29, 1972; Fred and "Ma" Barker killed by FBI in Fla., Jan. 20, 1935; Arthur sentenced to life for kidnapping, 1935 (killed in prison break attempt, Jan. 13, 1939); Karpis sentenced to life, 1936 (paroled and deported to Canada, 1969); various peripheral gang members killed or imprisoned

Barrow, Clyde Chestnut (1909–34); **Parker, Bonnie** (1910–34); **Barrow, Ivan** (c. 1901–33); **Hamilton, Raymond** (d. 1935); **Jones, William Daniel** (1915–?)
SEX: 4 M/1 F   RACE: W   TYPE: N   MOTIVE: CE-felony
DATE(S): 1930–34   VENUE: Tex./Okla. Mo.   VICTIMS: 12
MO: Nomadic bandits; shot holdup victims and lawmen
DISPOSITION: Ivan Barrow fatally wounded by posse, July 1933; Bonnie and Clyde killed in police ambush, May 1934; Hamilton executed, May 1935; Jones sentenced to life

Beane, Sawney (d. 1435), et al.
SEX: 27 M/21 F   RACE: W   TYPE: T   MOTIVE: CE/PC
DATE(S): c. 1410–35   VENUE: County Galway, Scotland   VICTIMS: 1,000 est.
MO: Incestuous cave-dwelling family; ambushed, robbed, and cannibalized travelers along Scottish coast
DISPOSITION: Captured in 1435 and executed without trial; male members of the clan were drawn and quartered; females were burned alive

Bemore, Terry Douglas (1956–); **Cosby, Keith** (1959–)
SEX: 2 M   RACE: B   TYPE: T   MOTIVE: CE/Sad.
DATE(S): 1985   VENUE: San Diego, Calif.   VICTIMS: Two
MO: Beat/stabbed victims in liquor store robberies
DISPOSITION: Bemore condemned, 1989; life without parole for Cosby, 1989

Bender, William, "Ma," John, Kate (DOBs unk.)
SEX: 2 M/2 F   RACE: W   TYPE: T   MOTIVE: CE
DATE(S): 1872–73   VENUE: Cherryvale, Kans.   VICTIMS: 11 confirmed
MO: Homicidal family; robbed/killed boarders in their roadside inn
DISPOSITION: Unknown; rumors of vigilante lynching unsubstantiated

Bernardo, Paul (1964–); **Homolka, Karla** (1970–)
SEX: M/F   RACE: W   TYPE: T   MOTIVE: Sex./Sad.
DATE(S): 1990–92   VENUE: Ontario, Canada   VICTIMS: Three
MO: Lust killers of three young women, including Karla's sister
DISPOSITION: Homolka turned state's evidence, receiving 10–12 years in return for testimony, 1994; Bernardo sentenced to life with 25-year minimum, 1995; Homolka released on July 4, 2005

Birnie, David and Catherine (both 1951–)
SEX: M/F   RACE: W   TYPE: T   MOTIVE: Sex./Sad.
DATE(S): 1986   VENUE: Freemantle, Australia   VICTIMS: Five
MO: Rape-murders of young women
DISPOSITION: Life sentences for both 1987

Bijeh, Mohammed (?–); **Baghi, Ali** (?–)   AKA: Vampires of the Tehran Desert
SEX: 2 M   RACE: A   TYPE: T   MOTIVE: Sex./Sad.
DATE(S): 2003–04   VENUE: Tehran, Iran   VICTIMS: 20 alleged
MO: Rape-slayers of victims lured to the desert on hunting expeditions; those killed included 17 children, two men, and one woman
DISPOSITION: On Oct. 14, 2004, Bijeh was condemned on two counts of rape, also receiving 15 years for kidnapping, three years for seven counts of murder, and 100 lashes for crimes against the dead; Baghi was acquitted of murder but received 15 years for kidnapping and 100 lashes

Blakely, Falicia (1979–); **Ervin, Ameshia** (1982–)
SEX: 2 F   RACE: B   TYPE: T   MOTIVE: CE-felony
DATE(S): 2002   VENUE: Atlanta, Ga.   VICTIMS: Four
MO: Prostitutes who robbed and shot male victims lured from bars for sex
DISPOSITION: Blakely pleaded guilty on three counts, Jan. 16, 2004; Ervin pleaded guilty on three counts, June 9, 2004; both received life prison terms

Brady, Al (d. 1937); **Dalhover, James** (d. 1938); **Shaffer, Clarence** (d. 1937)
SEX: 3 M   RACE: W   TYPE: N   MOTIVE: CE
DATE(S): 1930s   VENUE: Midwest U.S.   VICTIMS: Five
MO: Armed robbers; shot lawmen and bank tellers
DISPOSITION: Brady and Shaffer killed by FBI in Maine, Oct. 12, 1937; Dalhover subsequently executed

Brady, Ian Duncan (1938–); **Hindley, Myra** (1942–2002)
SEX: M/F   RACE: W   TYPE: N   MOTIVE: Sex./Sad.
DATE(S): 1963–65   VENUE: Scotland/England   VICTIMS: 10 suspected
MO: "Thrill killers" of male and female victims, various ages
DISPOSITION: Life sentences for both on three counts, 1966; Hindley died in prison on Nov. 15, 2002

Braun, Thomas Eugene; Maine, Leonard (both 1951–)
SEX: 2 M   RACE: W   TYPE: N   MOTIVE: CE/Sex.
DATE(S): 1967   VENUE: Wash./Ore.   VICTIMS: Three
MO: Victims shot for their vehicles; one woman raped
DISPOSITION: Life terms for both

Brooks, Benjamin H. (1967–); **Treesh, Frederick J.** (1964–)
SEX: 2 M   RACE: W   TYPE: N   MOTIVE: CE
DATE(S): 1994   VENUE: Mich./Ohio   VICTIMS: Two
MO: Killed holdup victims
DISPOSITION: Treesh condemned in Ohio; 56 years to life to Brooks, 1996

Brown, John (1800–59), **Frederick⁻** (1827–56), **Jason** (1823–?), **Oliver** (c. 1838–59), et al.
SEX: 15 M   RACE: W/B   TYPE: N   MOTIVE: GC-extremist
DATE(S): 1855–59   VENUE: Kans./Va.   VICTIMS: 12+

MO: Religious fanatic abolitionist, his sons, and assorted other followers; murdered advocates of slavery in Kans. and in later raid on U.S. arsenal at Harper's Ferry, Va.; several victims dismembered
DISPOSITION: Frederick killed in battle, Aug. 18, 1856; Oliver and 11 others killed at Harper's Ferry; John Brown hanged, Dec. 2, 1859

Brown, John Frank (1963–); **Coetzee, Samuel Jacques** (1967–97)
SEX: 2 M   RACE: W   TYPE: T   MOTIVE: Sex./Sad./CE
DATE(S): 1993–95   VENUE: South Africa   VICTIMS: Five
MO: Gay lovers who robbed/killed/mutilated men met in gay bars
DISPOSITION: Coetzee, suicide during trial, May 1997; life term Brown on guilty plea, 1997

Buck, Rufus (d. 1896); **Davis, Lewis** (d. 1896); **Davis, Lucky** (d. 1896); **July, Maomi** (d. 1896); **Sampson, Sam** (d. 1896)
SEX: 5 M   RACE: NA   TYPE: T   MOTIVE: GC
DATE(S): 1895   VENUE: Okla. Territory   VICTIMS: Two
MO: Killed two white victims; robbed/raped others in two-week "war"
DISPOSITION: All five hanged together on July 1, 1896

Burke, Peter (1959–); **Crawford, Cody Vernon** (1958–); **Thacker, Oren** (1958–)
SEX: 3 M   RACE: W   TYPE: T   MOTIVE: Sad./GC-extremist
DATE(S): 1974   VENUE: Farmington, N. Mex.   VICTIMS: Three
MO: Teenage racists who beat/burned Navajo men to death
DISPOSITION: Each sentenced to indefinite juvenile confinement, 1974; release mandatory at age 21

Burke, William (1792–1829); **Hare, William** (?–?)
SEX: 2 M   RACE: W   TYPE: T   MOTIVE: CE
DATE(S): 1827–28   VENUE: Edinburgh, Scotland   VICTIMS: 12 minimum
MO: Sold corpses of victims for medical dissection
DISPOSITION: Burke hanged, 1829; Hare immunized for testimony

Burse, Nathaniel (1955–79); **Clark, Michael** (1957–); **Jackson, Garland** (1956–); **Moran, Edward, Jr.** (1955–79); **Patry, Darrell** (1958–); **Taylor, Donald** (1957–); **Taylor, Reuben** (1956–); **Wilson, Robert** (1960–)   AKA: De Mau Mau
SEX: 8 M   RACE: B   TYPE: N   MOTIVE: GC-extremist
DATE(S): 1978   VENUE: Ill./Nebr.   VICTIMS: 12
MO: Black racists; shot whites in home invasions
DISPOSITION: Burse and Moran murdered in jail, June 1979; life terms for their accomplices

Burrows, Erskine Durrant (d. 1973); **Tacklyn, Larry Winfield** (d. 1973)
SEX: 2 M   RACE: B   TYPE: T   MOTIVE: GC-extremist
DATE(S): 1972–73   VENUE: Bermuda   VICTIMS: Five
MO: Black power activists; shot five white men (including governor)
DISPOSITION: Both hanged, 1973

Bux, Jose Miculax (d. 1946); **Macu, Mariano** (?–)
SEX: 2 M   RACE: H   TYPE: T   MOTIVE: Sex.?
DATE(S): 1946   VENUE: Colombia   VICTIMS: 12
MO: Killed boys age 10–16; details withheld by police
DISPOSITION: Bux executed July 18, 1946; life term for Macu

Carr, Jonathan (1980–); **Carr, Reginald** (1978–)
SEX: 2 M   RACE: B   TYPE: T   MOTIVE: CE/Sex.
DATE(S): 2000   VENUE: Wichita, Kan.   VICTIMS: Five
MO: Fatally shot a 55-year-old woman, then invaded a home with five persons present, raped two women, and shot all five victims, killing four
DISPOSITION: Both condemned in November 2002

Carrion, Christopher Alan (1971–); **Zaepfel, Leigh Ann** (1973–)
SEX: M/F   RACE: W   TYPE: N   MOTIVE: CE
DATE(S): 1990   VENUE: Ind./Okla.   VICTIMS: Three
MO: Holdup victims shot execution-style
DISPOSITION: Dual life terms for both in Okla., 1991

Carson, James Michael (1950–), **Susan** (1941–)
AKA: Michael and Suzan Bear
SEX: M/F   RACE: W   TYPE: N   MOTIVE: PC-extremist
DATE(S): 1981–83   VENUE: California   VICTIMS: Three
MO: Self-styled "Muslim warriors"; killed three suspected "witches"
DISPOSITION: 25 years to life for both on each of three counts, 1984

Chan Ka-chun (1972–); **Chan Ki-nang** (1969–); **Leung Sze-lai** (1975–)

SEX: 3 M   RACE: A   TYPE: T   MOTIVE: Sex./CE
DATE(S): 1996–97   VENUE: China   VICTIMS:
   Three
MO: Raped/robbed women; victims suffocated and
   stabbed
DISPOSITION: All three convicted, 1999: three life
   terms plus 26 years for Chan Ka-chun; two life
   terms for Chan Ki-nang; 12 years for Leung Sze-lai
   on guilty plea to manslaughter and rape

Chaney, Ben, Jr. (1953–   ); **Rutrell, Martin** (1955–   );
   Thompson, L. L. (1950–70)
SEX: 3 M   RACE: B   TYPE: N   MOTIVE: GC-
   extremist
DATE(S): 1970   VENUE: Fla./S.C.   VICTIMS: Four
MO: Young blacks who robbed/shot whites to "get
   even" for racism in the South
DISPOSITION: Thompson killed in shoot-out with
   S.C. victims, May 20, 1970; Chaney and Rutrell
   imprisoned in S.C.

Chen Chin-hsing (d. 1999); **Kao Tien-men** (d. 1997);
   Lin Chun-sheng (d. 1997)
SEX: 3 M   RACE: A   TYPE: T   MOTIVE: CE/Sex.
DATE(S): 1997   VENUE: Taiwan   VICTIMS: 12
MO: Shot nine political victims "gangland style";
   killed a doctor and his nurse after plastic surgery on
   Chen; kidnapped and killed the teenage daughter of
   a TV celebrity; several surviving female victims
   raped
DISPOSITION: Lin killed in shootout with police,
   August 1997; Kao committed suicide when cornered
   by police, November 1997; Chen executed by firing
   squad, Oct. 6, 1999

"Chijon Family"
SEX: 7 M   RACE: A   TYPE: N   MOTIVE: GC-
   extremist
DATE(S): 1993–94   VENUE: South Korea   VIC-
   TIMS: Five
MO: Cannibal ex-convicts driven by hatred of the
   wealthy
DISPOSITION: All condemned, 1994

Childs, John (?–   ); **MacKenny, Henry** (1936–   ); **Pinfold, Terence** (?–   )
SEX: 3 M   RACE: W   TYPE: T/N   MOTIVE: CE-
   felony
DATE(S): 1965–79   VENUE: London, England   VIC-
   TIMS: 11 confessed
MO: Freelance contract killers who murdered five men
   and a 10-year-old boy, 1974–78; in 1998 Childs
   confessed five other slayings, both personal and

gang-related, committed at various sites throughout
England between his teenage years and 1979
DISPOSITION: Pinfold received a 10-year sentence for
   robbery in 1977; Childs confessed contract murders
   after he was jailed for hijacking in June 1979; Childs
   testified against his two accomplices at trial in
   December 1979; Pinfold convicted on one count,
   receiving life prison term; MacKenny convicted on
   two counts, receiving life term with 25 years minimum; Childs also received a life term

Clanton, Newman Haynes (d. 1881), **Joseph Isaac**
   (1847–87), **Phineas Fay** (1845–?), **William Harrison**
   (1862–81)
SEX: 4+ M   RACE: W   TYPE: N   MOTIVE: CE/PC
DATE(S): 1873–87   VENUE: Ariz./Mexico   VIC-
   TIMS: 60+
MO: Old West outlaw family whose gang also included
   WILLIAM BROCIUS GRAHAM, JOHN RINGGOLD, and
   others; staged murderous raids into Mexico for loot
   and livestocks; engaged in bloody feud with WYATT
   EARP, his brothers, and JOHN HOLLIDAY around
   Tombstone, Ariz.
DISPOSITION: Newman killed with five associates in
   Mexico, following massacre of 19 Mexicans, July
   1881; William killed at O.K. Corral gunfight with
   two associates, Oct. 26, 1881; Joseph killed by
   posse, June 1887; Phineas sent to Yuma prison,
   1887 (paroled 1897)

Clark, Henry Lovell William (1868–1913); **Fullam,
   Augusta Fairfield** (1875–1914)
SEX: M/F   RACE: W   TYPE: T   MOTIVE: PC-
   domestic
DATE(S): 1911–12   VENUE: Agra, India   VICTIMS:
   Two
MO: Adulterous lovers; killed Clark's wife and Ful-
   lam's husband
DISPOSITION: Both condemned; Clarke hanged Mar.
   26, 1913; Fullam died of heatstroke in prison, May
   28, 1914

Clopton, Phillip (1951–90); **Cable, James Ray**
   (1949–   )
SEX: 2 M   RACE: W   TYPE: T   MOTIVE: Sex.
DATE(S): 1989–90   VENUE: Ky.   VICTIMS: Three
   suspected
MO: Kidnappers and rape-slayers of female victims
DISPOSITION: Clopton shot dead by teenage victim,
   Apr. 1990; three consecutive 100-year terms (with
   150-year minimum) for Cable on kidnap, rape, and
   sodomy charges, 1991

Coleman, Alton (1955–2002); **Brown, Debra Denise** (1959–)
SEX: M/F   RACE: B   TYPE: N   MOTIVE: Sex./CE
DATE(S): 1984   VENUE: Ill./Ind./Ohio   VICTIMS: Eight
MO: "Thrill killers" of victims age 7–77
DISPOSITION: Both condemned (Coleman in all three states); Coleman executed in Ohio, April 26, 2002

Cook, Anthony (1948–); **Cook, Nathaniel** (1957–)
SEX: 2 M   RACE: B   TYPE: T   MOTIVE: Sex./CE-felony
DATE(S): 1973–80   VENUE: Toledo, Ohio   VICTIMS: Nine
MO: Brothers who preyed chiefly on couples, robbing and murdering four men aged 21–43, raping and killing five females aged 12–22; a sixth rape victim survived multiple stab wounds
DISPOSITION: Anthony received a term of 15 years to life for one murder in 1999; Anthony pleaded guilty to a second murder, rape, and attempted murder in April 2000, receiving another sentence of 15 years to life, while seven murder counts were dismissed; Nathaniel pleaded guilty on one murder charge and two kidnapping counts in April 2000, receiving a term of 21–75 years with release scheduled for 2020

Cooper, Robert W. (1979–); **MacKay, Charles** (1973–)
SEX: 2 M   RACE: W   TYPE: N   MOTIVE: Sex.
DATE(S): 1999   VENUE: Ohio/Mich.   VICTIMS: Four
MO: Rape-slayers of female prostitutes aged 36–43; survivors also raped
DISPOSITION: MacKay pleaded guilty on one count in Toledo, Ohio, February 2000; Cooper pleaded guilty to one murder and a separate rape in Monroe County, Mich., March 2000; received life term plus seven years (27 years minimum); Cooper received 10–15 years for rape-murders of two Toledo victims, September 2000; MacKay received life plus eight years for murder and a separate rape in Michigan, October 2000

Copeland, Ray (1913–93); **Copeland, Faye** (1920–2003)
SEX: M/F   RACE: W   TYPE: S   MOTIVE: CE
DATE(S): 1986–89   VENUE: Mooresville, Mo.   VICTIMS: Five
MO: Married couple who killed hired hands on their farm
DISPOSITION: Both condemned, 1991; Ray died in prison, October 1993; Faye's sentence commuted to life, August 1999; died in prison Dec. 18, 2003

Couvrette, Annette (?–); **Gravel, Germaine** (?–); **Lapierre, Imelda** (?–); **Lemire, Elizabeth** (?–); **Tanuay, Germaine** (?–)
SEX: 5 F   RACE: W   TYPE: S   MOTIVE: PC/CE
DATE(S): 1950–51   VENUE: Canton, China   VICTIMS: 2,116
MO: French Canadian Catholic nuns who ran the Holy Child Orphanage, killing most of their charges and illegally selling infants who survived; 2,116 of 2,251 inmates died between October 1950 and February 1951; no body count before that time is available
DISPOSITION: All five nuns were convicted of murder in 1951; Couvrette and Gravel received five-year prison terms, while the other three were deported

Dalton, Emmett (1871–?), **Grattan** (1865–92), **Robert** (1868–92), **William** (1866–93)
SEX: 4 M   RACE: W   TYPE: N   MOTIVE: CE
DATE(S): 1891–92   VENUE: Calif./Okla./Kans.   VICTIMS: Eight+
MO: Old West outlaw brothers; killed lawmen and robbery victims
DISPOSITION: Grattan and Robert killed in Kans. robbery, Oct. 4, 1892; Emmett sentenced to life for same holdup (paroled 1907); William killed by posse, Sept. 25, 1893

Daniels, Murl (1924–49); **West, John Coulter** (d. 1948)
SEX: 2 M   RACE: W   TYPE: N   MOTIVE: PC/CE
DATE(S): 1948   VENUE: Ohio   VICTIMS: Six
MO: Escaped convicts; killed various victims while at large
DISPOSITION: West killed by posse, July 1948; Daniels executed, Jan. 3, 1949

Daveggio, James (1961–); **Michaud, Michelle** (1959–)
SEX: M/F   RACE: W   TYPE: N   MOTIVE: Sex./Sad.
DATE(S): 1990s   VENUE: Calif./Nev.   VICTIMS: Six suspected
MO: Kidnapped, tortured, and raped female victims of various ages; Daveggio also molested and tortured various members of his family
DISPOSITION: Both condemned on Sept. 25, 2002, for the 1997 torture-slaying of a 22-year-old woman; in August 1999 Daveggio received a 24-year prison term and $500,000 fine for kidnapping and raping a victim in Reno; Michaud also received a 12-year sentence and $175,000 fine in that case; Daveggio received additional prison time for molesting his daughter; he remains suspect in the California murders of a woman and four young girls

DeMeo, Roy Albert (1941–83); **Borelli, Henry** (1948–); **Gaggi, Anthony Frank** (1926–); **Testa, Joseph, Jr.** (1955–) AKA: The Murder Machine
SEX: 4 M RACE: W TYPE: T MOTIVE: CE/PC
DATE(S): 1975–82 VENUE: N.Y. VICTIMS: 75–100
MO: Contract killers for Gambino Mafia "family"
DISPOSITION: DeMeo murdered, Jan. 10, 1983; life term + 160 years for Borelli, 1986; multiple life terms for Gaggi and Testa, 1989

Dingum (?–?); **Cornerford** (d. 1837)
SEX: 2 M RACE: W TYPE: N MOTIVE: PC
DATE(S): 1837 VENUE: Port Phillip, Australia VICTIMS: Seven+
MO: "Bush rangers" who cannibalized fellow outlaws
DISPOSITION: Cornerford lynched; life term for Dingum

Dirlewanger, Oskar-Paul (1895–1945) et al. AKA: Sonderkommando Dirlewanger
SEX: 854 M RACE: W TYPE: N MOTIVE: GC-extremist
DATE(S): 1940–45 VENUE: East Europe/Russia VICTIMS: Thousands
MO: Nazi mobile death squad led by convicted sex offender, composed entirely of ex-convicts; killed Jews and other civilians, including participation in suppression of Warsaw Ghetto revolt
DISPOSITION: Dirlewanger died in Allied detention camp, June 7, 1945; no postwar charges were filed on assumption that all active members died in action

Dohmeyer, Juergen (1948–); **Leuking, Kurt** (1953–) AKA: The Mad Dogs
SEX: 2 M RACE: W TYPE: T MOTIVE: CE
DATE(S): 1983 VENUE: Hannover, Germay VICTIMS: Three
MO: Shot robbery victims, one male and two female
DISPOSITION: Life terms for both, 1988

Doorbal, Noel Alexander (1971–); **Lugo, Danial** (1963–)
SEX: 2 M RACE: H TYPE: T MOTIVE: CE
DATE(S): 1995 VENUE: Miami, Fla. VICTIMS: Two
MO: Career criminals, killed victims during robberies
DISPOSITION: Both condemned July 17, 1998

Dotson, James Erwin (1975–); **Labore, Kimberly Lee** (1971–)
SEX: M/F RACE: W TYPE: T MOTIVE: PC-nonspecific
DATE(S): 2000 VENUE: Watsonville, Calif. VICTIMS: Two
MO: Beat and slashed a male drifter and the owner of a rest home
DISPOSITION: Dotson received two terms of life without parole, January 2001; Labore received a term of 60 years to life, April 2001

Dudley, Kenneth Edwin (?–), **Irene Gwyn** (?–)
SEX: M/F RACE: W TYPE: N MOTIVE: PC/Sad.
DATE(S): 1946/1958–61 VENUE: N.Y./Fla./Ariz./Ky./Va. VICTIMS: Six
MO: Brutal parents whose children died from abuse and hunger on a rambling cross-country trek
DISPOSITION: Kenneth served one year in N.Y. for "improper burial" of first child

Duffy, John Francis (1956–); **Mulcahy, David** (1959–) AKA: Railway Murderers
SEX; 2 M RACE: W TYPE: N MOTIVE: Sex.
DATE(S): 1985–86 VENUE: England VICTIMS: Three
MO: Serial rapists who attacked female victims in or near British railway stations, 1982–86, killing three of an estimated 15 victims
DISPOSITION: Duffy received three life terms plus 30 years for multiple rapes, 1988; named Mulcahy as his accomplice in October 2000; Mulcahy received three life terms for murder on Feb. 2, 2001; also received concurrent 24-year terms for each of seven rapes and 18-year terms on each of five conspiracy charges

Dvoracek, Mrs., and unnamed male accomplices
SEX: 1 F/7 M RACE: W TYPE: S MOTIVE: CE
DATE(S): 1918–25 VENUE: Iglau, Czechoslovakia VICTIMS: Four+
MO: Robbed/murdered Polish refugees at Mrs. Dvoracek's home
DISPOSITION: All condemned, 1925

Einsatzgruppen
SEX: Approximately 3,000 M RACE: W TYPE: N MOTIVE: GC-extremist
DATE(S): 1941–45 VENUE: USSR VICTIMS: Two million est.
MO: Mobile Nazi murder squads in occupied Russia; killed an estimated 1.5 million Jews and 500,000 Russian civilians
DISPOSITION: 24 senior officers tried at Nuremburg, July 1947 to Apr. 1948; one suicide; 14 condemned (four executed, 10 commuted); eight imprisoned; one convicted but not sentenced due to poor health

Ellebracht, Walter Wesley, Sr. (?–); **Walter Wesley, Jr.** (?–); **Caldwell, Robert, Carlton** (?–)
SEX: 3 M   RACE: W   TYPE: S   MOTIVE: CE/Sad.
DATE(S): 1980s   VENUE: Kerr County, Tex.   VICTIMS: "Several" suspected
MO: Father-son ranchers and their foreman; enslaved/tortured male drifters; tape-recorded torture sessions and boasted to captives of multiple murders
DISPOSITION: All three convinced on one count, 1986; 15 years for William Jr.; 14 years for Caldwel; seven years probation for William Sr.

Elliott, Eric (1978–); **Gilbert, Lewis Eugene, III** (1971–)
SEX: 2 M   RACE: W   TYPE: N   MOTIVE: CE
DATE(S): 1994   VENUE: Ohio/MO/Okla.   VICTIMS: Four
MO: Shot robbery victims including an 86-year-old man and three women aged 37–79
DISPOSITION: Elliott pleaded guilty on one count and received a life prison term without parole in Ohio; Gilbert was executed on one count in Oklahoma, July 2, 2003

Espinosa, Felipe (d. 1863), **Julian** (d. 1863), **Victorio** (d. 1863)
SEX: 3 M   RACE: H   TYPE: N   MOTIVE: PC-extremist
DATE(S): 1861–63   VENUE: Colo.   VICTIMS: 26
MO: Mexican brothers; sought to kill 100 Anglos in revenge for the earlier U.S. war with Mexico
DISPOSITION: Victorio lynched by vigilantes; Julian and Victorio killed by U.S. Army scout Tom Tobin

Esposito, John (1971–); **Woodward, Alicia** (1978–)
SEX: M/F   RACE: W   TYPE: N   MOTIVE: CE
DATE(S): 1996   VENUE: Ga./Okla.   VICTIMS: Three confessed
MO: "Thrill killers" of robbery victims
DISPOSITION: Esposito condemned on one count in Ga., 1998; trial pending for Woodward

Evans, Paul, Jr. (1980–); **Townsend, Nathan** (1980–)
SEX: 2 M   RACE: W   TYPE: N   MOTIVE: PC-nonspecific
DATE(S): 1999–2000   VENUE: Ala./Miss.   VICTIMS: Four suspected
MO: Thrill killers of two teenage girls shot in Jones County, Miss.; prime suspects in a similar murder at Ozark, Ala.
DISPOSITION: Townsend pleaded no contest and testified against Evans; Evans received two life terms in Mississippi

Fernandez, Raymond Martinez (1914–51); **Beck, Martha Julie** (1920–51)   AKA: Lonely Hearts Killers
SEX: M/F   RACE: W   TYPE: N   MOTIVE: CE
DATE(S): 1948–49   VENUE: Ill./N.Y./Mich.   VICTIMS: Five+
MO: Homicidal swindlers of women seduced by Fernandez
DISPOSITION: Both executed in N.Y., Mar. 8, 1951

Freight Train Riders of America
SEX: ?M   RACE: W   TYPE: N   MOTIVE: CE/PC
DATE(S): 1970s–90s   VENUE: Western USA   VICTIMS: "Hundreds"
MO: "Hobo" fraternity blamed by law enforcement for scores of random murders spanning two decades
DISPOSITION: Several professed members convicted of individual murders; ROBERT SILVERIA convicted on multiple counts

French, Anne (?–?)   AKA: Shoebox Annie Mayer; **William Donald** (?–?)
SEX: F/M   RACE: W   TYPE: N   MOTIVE: CE
DATE(S): 1920s   VENUE: Mont./Wash.   VICTIMS: Seven suspected
MO: Mother-son career criminals; killed robbery victims
DISPOSITION: Life for Mayer in Wash. as habitual criminal, 1928; five to 10 years for French in Wash., 1928; both died in prison

Genna, Angelo (d. 1925), **James** (d. 1925), **Michael** (d. 1925), **Peter** (?–?), **Sam** (?–?), **Tony** (?–?)   AKA: The Terrible Gennas
SEX: 6M   RACE: W   TYPE: T   MOTIVE: CE
DATE(S): c. 1910–25   VENUE: Chicago, Ill.   VICTIMS: Dozens
MO: Sicilian immigrants; "Black Hand" extortionists and bootleggers; killed extortion victims, rival gangsters, and lawmen
DISPOSITION: Angelo murdered by rival thugs, May 25, 1925; Mike killed in shoot-out with police, June 13, 1925; James murdered by rivals, July 8, 1925; surviving brothers fled to Sicily, 1925; returned to Chicago after repeal of Prohibition as "legitimate" businessmen

Ghira, Andrea (?–); **Guido, Giovanni** (?–); **Izzo, Angelo** (?–)   AKA: Monster of Circeo
SEX: 3 M   RACE: W   TYPE: T   MOTIVE: Sex.
DATE(S): 1975   VENUE: Circeo, Italy   VICTIMS: Two+ suspected
MO: Gang rapists who murdered their female victims
DISPOSITION: Convicted; sentences unk.

Gonzales, Delfina (?–); **Maria de Jesus** (?–)
SEX: 2 F   RACE: H   TYPE: S   MOTIVE: CE
DATE(S): 1950s–63   VENUE: Guanajuato, Mexico
   VICTIMS: 100+
MO: Sisters and white-slavers; killed prostitutes, their
   babies, and male customers (who were also robbed)
DISPOSITION: 40 years each, 1964

Goodman, Keith Eugene (1959–); **Holland, Tracy
   Lynn** (1968–); **Mead, Jon Christopher** (1967–)
SEX: 2 M/1 F   RACE: W   TYPE: N   MOTIVE: CE
DATE(S): 1989–90   VENUE: N.Y./Miss.   VICTIMS:
   Four
MO: Slayers of random holdup victims
DISPOSITION: Goodman, life + 20 years in N.Y.,
   1990; Mead, life + 20 years in N.Y., 1991; Holland
   turned state's evidence; Goodman and Mead con-
   victed on one count of homicide Mass., 1992

Gray, Kevin L. (1971–); **Moore, Rodney L.** (1965–)
SEX: 2 M   RACE: B   TYPE: T   MOTIVE: CE-
felony
DATE(S): 1990s   VENUE: Washington, D.C.   VIC-
TIMS: 29
MO: Drug dealers who murdered competitors and per-
   sonal enemies
DISPOSITION: Both convicted in January 2003, Gray
   on 19 counts of murder, Moore on 10; both con-
   demned

Gusenberg, Frank (1892–1929), **Peter** (1888–1929)
SEX: 2 M   RACE: W   TYPE: T   MOTIVE: CE
DATE(S): 1920–29   VENUE: Chicago, Ill.   VIC-
TIMS: "Numerous"
MO: Brothers and contract killers for a bootleg syndi-
cate
DISPOSITION: Murdered together in St. Valentine's
   Day massacre

Haerm, Dr. Teet (1953–); **Allgen, Dr. Thomas Lars**
   (1949–)
SEX: 2 M   RACE: W   TYPE: T   MOTIVE: Sex./Sad.
DATE(S): 1982–87   VENUE: Stockholm, Sweden
   VICTIMS: 10+
MO: Torture-slayers of women, mostly prostitutes;
   cannibalized victims and drank their blood; Haerm,
   as Stockholm's medical examiner, misdirected investigation for five years; Haerm also suspected in his
   wife's 1982 "suicide"
DISPOSITION: Both sentenced to life on one count,
   1988, after Allgen confessed; Allgen also convicted
   of incest with his five-year-old daughter; convictions
   overturned on a legal technicality, whereupon Allgen
   recanted confessions; both acquitted at second trial,

1989, although the court cited "reasonable cause"
to believe they were guilty

Hale, Steven (1977–); **Wessell, Chalk** (d. 1998)
SEX: 2 M   RACE: W   TYPE: N   MOTIVE: PC-non-
specific
DATE(S): 1998   VENUE: Ill./Ind.   VICTIMS: Five
MO: Thrill killers who shot victims of both sexes in
   random attacks
DISPOSITION: Wessell shot himself prior to arrest, in
   April 1998; Hale received life terms in Illinois (June
   1999) and Indiana (March 2000)

Haley, Kevin Bernard (1964–), **Reginald** (1960–)
SEX: 2 M   RACE: B   TYPE: T   MOTIVE:
CE/Sex./Sad.
DATE(S): 1983–84   VENUE: Los Angeles, Calif.
VICTIMS: Seven
MO: Career criminals, serial rapists, and random slay-
   ers of females age 15 to 89
DISPOSITION: Life + 60 years for Reginald, 1987;
   Kevin condemned, 1988

Halstead, Dennis (1955–); **Kogut, John** (1964–);
   Restivo, John (1959–)
SEX: 3 M   RACE: W   TYPE: T   MOTIVE:
Sex./CE
DATE(S): 1984–85   VENUE: Long Island, N.Y.
VICTIMS: Four suspected
MO: Rape-slayers of teenage girls; also suspected in
   bizarre "suicide" of a potential state witness
DISPOSITION: Life terms for all three on one count,
   1986

Harpe, Micajah (1768–99)   AKA: Big Harpe   **Harpe,
   Wiley** (1770–1804)   AKA: Little Harpe
SEX: 2 M   RACE: W   TYPE: N   MOTIVE: PC/CE
DATE(S): 1798–1804   VENUE: Tenn./Ill./Ky./Miss.
VICTIMS: 40+
MO: Career criminals and mutilation-slayers of victims
   ranging from total strangers to their own children
DISPOSITION: Micajah killed by posse in Ky., Aug.
   1799; Wiley hanged in Miss., Feb. 8, 1804

Harrelson, Sharon Lynn (1945–); **Adams, Gary Starr**
   (1943–)
SEX: F/M   RACE: W   TYPE: T   MOTIVE: CE
DATE(S): 1976/88   VENUE: Colo.   VICTIMS: Two
MO: Lovers who killed Sharon's husbands for life
   insurance
DISPOSITION: Life terms for both on guilty plea, two
   counts

Helzer, Glenn (1970–); **Helzer, Justin** (1972–);
Godman, Dawn (1974–)
SEX: 2 M/1 F   RACE: W   TYPE: T   MOTIVE:
PC/CE-felony
DATE(S): 2000   VENUE: Concord, Calif.   VICTIMS:
Five
MO: Christian fanatics who financed a "war against
Satan" by means of extortion; killed two kidnap vic-
tims aged 85 and 78; also killed Glenn's girlfriend
(who delivered ransom note), her mother and
mother's boyfriend (to eliminate witnesses)
DISPOSITION: Glenn pleaded guilty on five counts in
2004, penalty phase pending at press time; Godman
turned states evidence, receiving a sentence of 38
years to life; Justin condemned on three counts with
life terms on two others, Aug. 4, 2004

Hernandez, Cayetano (?–), **Santos** (d. 1963); **Solis
Magdalena** (?–)
SEX: 2 M/1 F   RACE: H   TYPE: T   MOTIVE: GC-
cult
DATE(S): 1963   VENUE: Tamaulipas, Mexico   VIC-
TIMS: 12
MO: Rural cult leaders and con artists; sacrificed 10
disciples; also killed a policeman and civilian witness
DISPOSITION: Santos killed in shoot-out with police
raiding party; Cayetano, Solis, and 12 disciples
imprisoned

Herrera, Tony (1969–) **et al.**
SEX: 5 M   RACE: H   TYPE: T   MOTIVE: PC-non-
specific
DATE(S): 1984–85   VENUE: Dallas, Tex.   VIC-
TIMS: Seven suspected
MO: Teenage "thrill killers" of random victims; some
also robbed
DISPOSITION: 30 years for Herrera on one count,
1986; other juvenile suspects remain unidentified,
dispositions unknown

Herzog, Loren Joseph (1965–); **Shermantine, Wesley
Howard, Jr.** (1965–)
SEX: 2 M   RACE: W   TYPE: T   MOTIVE: Sex./CE
DATE(S): 1984–98   VENUE: San Joaquin County,
Calif.   VICTIMS: Five
MO: Shot three male victims; raped and murdered two
females, aged 16 and 25
DISPOSITION: Shermantine condemned on three
counts, May 2001; Herzog received prison term of
50 years to life on three counts, Oct. 23, 2001

Hobbs, James (1819–79); **Kirker, James** (1810–1852)
SEX: 2 M   RACE: W   TYPE: N   MOTIVE: CE

DATE(S): 1830s–70s   VENUE: Mexico   VICTIMS:
1,000+
MO: Professional scalp hunters; Kirker killed at least
300 Indians before teaming with Hobbs, and they
killed many more together, including 300 slaughtered in a single village
DISPOSITION: Kirker died of alcoholism in Calif.,
1852; Hobbs kept up sporadic scalping (and ironically joined in some Indian raids on whites, including destruction of JOHN GLANTON gang) until his
natural death in 1879

Hottle, Billy Joe (1973–); **Swick, Craig S.** (1970–)
SEX: 2 M   RACE: W   TYPE: N   MOTIVE: CE
DATE(S): 1993   VENUE: West Virginia   VICTIMS:
Three
MO: Cousins who escaped from prison together, rob-
bing and killing random victims while at large
DISPOSITION: Both convicted of murder, attempted
murder, kidnapping, attempted kidnapping and lar-
ceny; sentences include three life terms plus 15–50
years on lesser charges

Howell, Michael Wayne (1959–); **Watson, Mona
Lisa** (1960–)
SEX: M/F   RACE: W   TYPE: N   MOTIVE: CE
DATE(S): 1987   VENUE: Ala./Tenn./Okla.   VIC-
TIMS: Four suspected
MO: Murdered holdup/carjack victims
DISPOSITION: Howell condemned in Okla. (1988)
and Tenn. (1989); Watson turned state's evidence in
exchange for life term

Hubbard, Vincent (1965–); **Huber, Eileen** (1971–);
Lewis, John Irvin (1970–); **Machuca, Robin**
(1965–)
SEX: 3 M/F   RACE: B   TYPE: T   MOTIVE: CE
DATE(S): 1991   VENUE: Los Angeles County, Calif.
VICTIMS: Three
MO: Kidnapped/shot robbery victims
DISPOSITION: Life terms for Hubbard, Huber, and
Machuca, 1993; Irvin condemned, 1993

Hurd, Steven Craig (1950–); **Giboney, Christopher**
(1953–); **Hulse, Arthur** (1964–); **Taylor, Herman** (1963–)
SEX: 4 M   RACE: W   TYPE: T   MOTIVE: GC-cult
DATE(S): 1970   VENUE: Los Angeles/Orange Counties, Calif.   VICTIMS: Two
MO: Satanists who mutilated/cannibalized one man
and one woman
DISPOSITION: Hurd ruled insane, confined to state
hospital; accomplices processed as juvenile offenders

Inderjeet, et al.
SEX: 6M   RACE: A   TYPE: T   MOTIVE: CE-felony
DATE(S): 2004   VENUE: Delhi, India   VICTIMS: Three
MO: Kidnapped, robbed, and murdered taxi drivers
DISPOSITION: Unknown

Infante Jimenez, Rudolfo (1963–   ); **Villeda, Anna Maria Ruiz** (1971–   )
SEX: M/F   RACE: H   TYPE: T   MOTIVE: Sex./Sad.
DATE(S): 1991   VENUE: Matamoros, Mexico   VICTIMS: Eight
MO: Lust killers of young women lured with employment offers
DISPOSITION: 40 years each, 1993

Isaac, Tommy Lee (1976–   ); **Johnson, Roderick** (1975–   ); **Jones, Aubrey** (1976–   ); **Whaley, Michael** (1974–   ); **Whaley, Terrell** (1975–   )
SEX: 5 M   RACE: B   TYPE: T   MOTIVE: Group excitement
DATE(S): 1992   VENUE: Richardson, Tex.   VICTIMS: Three
MO: "Thrill-killers" of white teenagers
DISPOSITION: Life terms for Jones and T. Whaley, 1993; 40 years for M. Whaley, 1993; 20 years for Johnson, 1993; 10 years for Isaac, 1993

Jackson, Peyton; Jackson, O'Delle; Jackson, Pearl; Reed, John; Glover, Fred (DOBs: Unk.)
SEX: 4 M/1 F   RACE: B   TYPE: T   MOTIVE: CE
DATE(S): 1919–23   VENUE: Birmingham, Ala.   VICTIMS: 15+
MO: White merchants killed with axes during robberies
DISPOSITION: Confessions reported, Jan. 1924; sentences unknown

James, Alexander Franklin (1843–1915); **Jesse Woodson** (1847–82); **Younger, Coleman** (1844–1916); **James** (1848–1903); **John** (1851–74); **Robert** (1853–89)
SEX: 6M   RACE: W   TYPE: N   MOTIVE: CE/PC
DATE(S): 1862–76   VENUE: Kans./Mo./Ky./Iowa/Minn.   VICTIMS: 14+ after war
MO: Members of "QUANTRILL'S RAIDERS" during Civil War; later killed lawmen and holdup victims in bank and train robberies
DISPOSITION: John Younger killed by Pinkerton detective, Mar. 16, 1874; Jesse James murdered, Apr. 3, 1882; other three Younger brothers sentenced to life terms in Minn., 1876

Janin (d. 1919); **Moujot** (d. 1919)
SEX: 2 M   RACE: W   TYPE: T   MOTIVE: CE-felony
DATE(S): 1919   VENUE: France   VICTIMS: Two
MO: French soldiers; killed female restaurant proprietors during robberies
DISPOSITION: Shot by firing squad, Aug. 1919

Johnson, Steven J. (1970–   ); **Hunter, Earnest** (1970–   ); **Jones, Robert** (1971–   )
SEX: 3 M   RACE: One W/Two B   TYPE: T
MOTIVE: CE
DATE(S): 1993   VENUE: Jacksonville, N.C.   VICTIMS: Two
MO: "Enforcers" for prostitution ring; killed hookers
DISPOSITION: Two life terms for Johnson, 1994; 13 years for Jones, 1994; 10 years for Hunter, 1994

Johnston, Bruce, Sr. (1939–   ); **David** (?–   ); **Norman** (?–   ); **Hamm, Ancell Eugene** (1946–   ); **et al.**
SEX: 4+M   RACE: W   TYPE: T   MOTIVE: CE
DATE(S): 1970–78/85   VENUE: Chester County, Pa.   VICTIMS: Nine+
MO: Career criminal brothers, with accomplices; specialized in theft of farm equipment over tristate area; killed police and suspected informers; Bruce killed fellow prison inmate, 1985
DISPOSITION: Hamm sentenced to life for killing two policemen, 1974; six consecutive life terms for Bruce, 1980; four consecutive life terms for David and Norman, 1980; Bruce died in prison, August 2002

Jones, John Ray (1971–   ); **Rose, Jason Wayne** (1968–   )
SEX: 2 M   RACE: W   TYPE: T   MOTIVE: GC-cult
DATE(S): 1988   VENUE: Springfield, Ore.   VICTIMS: Two suspected
MO: Satanists who videotaped sacrifice of one teenage girl; prime suspects in second case with "certain similarities"
DISPOSITION: Rose condemned, 1989; life term with 25-year minimum for Jones, 1989

Jones, Milton (1970–   ); **Simmons, Theodore** (1969–   )
SEX: 2 M   RACE: B   TYPE: T   MOTIVE: CE
DATE(S): 1987   VENUE: Buffalo, N.Y.   VICTIMS: Two
MO: Robbed/killed Catholic priests in their rectories
DISPOSITION: Two consecutive terms of 25 years to life for each defendant, 1988

Kauffman, Christopher (1979–); **McMahan, Jamie** (1975–)
SEX: 2 M   RACE: W   TYPE: T   MOTIVE: CE
DATE(S): 1997   VENUE: Iowa   VICTIMS: Two
MO: Shot elderly holdup victims in Mahaska and Poweshiek counties
DISPOSITION: Life without parole for both, 1998

Keene, Marvallous (1933–); **Smith, Demarcus** (1975–); **Matthews, Heather** (1972–); **Taylor Laura** (1976–)
SEX: 2 M/2 F   RACE: 2B/2W   TYPE: T   MOTIVE: CE
DATE(S): 1992   VENUE: Dayton, Ohio   VICTIMS: Five
MO: "Thrill-killers" of victims in petty robberies
DISPOSITION: Keene condemned; life term for Matthews on plea bargain; Smith and Taylor confined as juveniles until age 21

Kelbach, Walter (1938–); **Lance, Myearon** (1941–)
SEX: 2 M   RACE: W   TYPE: T   MOTIVE: CE/Sex./Sad.
DATE(S): 1966   VENUE: Salt Lake City, Utah   VICTIMS: Five
MO: Homosexual slayers of five men and one woman during robberies; two male victims also raped
DISPOSITION: Both condemned, 1967; commuted to life terms, 1972

Kelley, Edward "Ned" (1855–80); **Kelly, Daniel** (1863–80); **Hart, Steven** (1859–80); **Byrne, Joseph** (1857–80)
SEX: 4 M   RACE: W   TYPE: N   MOTIVE: CE
DATE(S): 1874–80   VENUE: Australia   VICTIMS: Four
MO: Rural bandits who killed policemen and an informer
DISPOSITION: Byrne fatally shot by police on July 27, 1880; Hart and Dan Kelly shot themselves during the same battle; Ned Kelly hanged on Nov. 11, 1880

Kimes, Sante (1934–); **Kimes, Kenneth** (1975–)
SEX: F/M   RACE: W   TYPE: N   MOTIVE: CE-felony
DATE(S): 1990s   VENUE: US/Bahamas   VICTIMS: more than six alleged
MO: Mother and son swindlers linked to multiple deaths and disappearances of fraud victims, including a man in Los Angeles and an 82-year-old millionaire in New York City
DISPOSITION: Convicted in New York on 113 felony counts, including one murder, May 18, 2000; Sante received a prison term of 120 years and four

months; Kenneth received 125 years and eight months

Knighton, Robert Wesley (1942–); **Brittain, Lawrence Lingle** (1973–); **Williams, Ruth Renee** (?–)
SEX: 2 M/1 F   RACE: W   TYPE: N   MOTIVE: CE
DATE(S): 1990   VENUE: Mo./Okla.   VICTIMS: Four
MO: Killed robbery victims in their homes
DISPOSITION: Knighton condemned in Okla., 1990; life term for Brittain in Mo., 1990; 15 years for Williams in Mo., 1990

Knoppa, Antony Michael (1948–); **Lanham, Harry** (?–)
SEX: 2 M   RACE: W   TYPE: N   MOTIVE: Sex./Sad.
DATE(S): 1971   VENUE: Tex.   VICTIMS: Four
MO: Lust killers of girls and young women
DISPOSITION: Life terms for both, 1972

Knotek, David (1952–); **Knotek, Michelle** (1954–)
SEX: M/F   RACE: W   TYPE: S   MOTIVE: PC
DATE(S): 1994–2003   VENUE: South Bend, Wash.   VICTIMS: Four
MO: Killed three lodgers at their home, including one relative; two victims burned, their ashes scattered on a nearby beach; suspected in the beating death of an 81-year-old man who hired Michelle as a caregiver
DISPOSITION: Michelle pleaded no contest on two murder counts and received a 15-year sentence on June 21, 2004; David pleaded guilty on two counts of second-degree murder, receiving a 15-year sentence on Aug. 26, 2004

LeBaron, Ervil Morrell (1925–81), **et al.**   AKA: Church of the Lamb of God
SEX: ?M/?W   RACE: W   TYPE: N   MOTIVE: GC-cult
DATE(S): 1966–88   VENUE: Mexico/Utah/Calif./Tex.   VICTIMS: 22+
MO: Polygamous cult of excommunicated Mormons; murdered cult defectors and rival polygamists in acts of "blood atonement"; victims included Ervil's brother and pregnant daughter; cultists support themselves via odd jobs, bank robberies, and organized auto theft
DISPOSITION: Ervil sentenced to 12 years in Mexico for brother's death, 1973 (reversed on appeal, 1974); life term in Utah, 1980 (died in prison, July 1981); son Aaron LeBaron (1968–) sentenced to 45 years on three counts in Tex., 1997; three other

cultists serving life for murders in Tex.; five pled guilty to auto theft in Ariz.

Lee, James (?–?), **Pink** (d. 1885), **Tom** (d. 1885)
SEX: 3 M   RACE: W   TYPE: T   MOTIVE: CE
DATE(S): 1880s   VENUE: Cooke County, Tex.   VICTIMS: 40+ alleged
MO: Outlaw brothers blamed for numerous holdups and murders
DISPOSITION: Pink and Tom killed by posse Dec. 1885; James disappeared after surprise acquittal on charges of killing four lawmen

LeGrand, Devernon (1925–   ), **Steven** (1950–   )
SEX: 2 M   RACE: B   TYPE: N   MOTIVE: PC/CE
DATE(S): 1963–75   VENUE: N.Y.   VICTIMS: Six+
MO: Cult leader and his son; killed two of Devernon's wives, two teen sisters, and two male cohorts in prostitution ring
DISPOSITION: 25 years to life for both, 1977

Lelièvre, André (?–   ), **Yvette** (?–   )
SEX: M/F   RACE: W   TYPE: S   MOTIVE: PC-domestic
DATE(S): 1950s–60s   VENUE: France   VICTIMS: Seven
MO: Married couple; in lieu of practicing birth control, drowned newborn infants and buried them at home
DISPOSITION: Life sentences for both, 1969

Liao Chang-Shin (d. 1945); **Hsui Chang-Shan** (d. 1945)
SEX: 2 M   RACE: A   TYPE: S   MOTIVE: CE
DATE(S): 1945   VENUE: Changzhou, China   VICTIMS: 79 confessed
MO: Robbed/killed guests at their inn
DISPOSITION: Both executed

Lippard, Christopher (?–   ); **Roache, Charles Wesley** (1974–   )
SEX: 2 M   RACE: W   TYPE: T   MOTIVE: CE-felony
DATE(S): 1999   VENUE: Haywood County, N.C.   VICTIMS: Six
MO: Bludgeoned a male acquaintance to steal his car; massacred a family of five when the car broke down near their home
DISPOSITION: On July 28, 2000, Lippard received four consecutive life terms on four counts of first-degree murder, plus 18–26 years on one count of second degree murder; on April 21, 2001, Roache was condemned on two counts and received life terms on three more

Lovett, Michael (1959–   ); **Wyatt, Thomas Anthony** (1964–   )
SEX: 2 M   RACE: W   TYPE: N   MOTIVE: CE/Sex.
DATE(S): 1988   VENUE: Indian River County, Fla.   VICTIMS: Two
MO: Escaped convicts from N.C., killing on the run; victims kidnapped/robbed/raped
DISPOSITION: Both condemned, 1991

Ma Yong (1960–   ); **Duan Zhiqun** (1983–   )
SEX: M/F   RACE: A   TYPE: T   MOTIVE: CE
DATE(S): 2003   VENUE: Shenzhen, China   VICTIMS: 12
MO: Posed as employment brokers, robbing and killing young women who applied for jobs
DISPOSITION: Both condemned after pleading guilty, Nov. 25, 2003

Majola, Simon (1968–   ); **Nikosi, Themba** (1979–   )
SEX: 2 M   RACE: B   TYPE: T   MOTIVE: CE-felony
DATE(S): 2000–01   VENUE: Johannesburg, South Africa   VICTIMS: Eight
MO: Robbed male victims of cash, jewelry, and cell phones before drowning them in Bruma Lake
DISPOSITION: Both received 13 life terms plus 797 years on March 23, 2003

Marlow, James Gregory (1956–   ); **Coffman, Cynthia Lynn** (1962–   )
SEX: M/F   RACE: W   TYPE: N   MOTIVE: CE/Sex.
DATE(S): 1986   VENUE: Calif./Ariz.   VICTIMS: Three
MO: Robbed/murdered women age 18–35; at least one victim raped
DISPOSITION: Both condemned in Calif., 1989

Martin, Bradley A. (1972–   ); **King, Carolyn A.** (1966–   )
SEX: M/F   RACE: W/B   TYPE: N   MOTIVE: CE
DATE(S): 1993   VENUE: Pa./N.Dak./Nev.   VICTIMS: Three
MO: Killed robbery/kidnap victims
DISPOSITION: Martin condemned + 31–61 years in Pa., 1994; King condemned + 34–68 years in Pa., 1994

Mazikane, Lazarus Tshidiso (1973–   ); **Motshegwa, Kaizer** (1973–   )
SEX: 2 M   RACE: B   TYPE: T   MOTIVE: Sex./CE-felony
DATE(S): 1993–98   VENUE: Nasrec/Soweto, South Africa   VICTIMS: 51

MO: Robbed and murdered victims of both sexes; all 32 female victims were raped, regardless of age; victims include 17 children, aged five to eight (11 of them female)

DISPOSITION: Charges against Motshegwa dismissed on grounds of terminal illness; at trial he testified against Mazikane and denied any wrongdoing; Mazikane convicted on 74 felony counts, including 16 murders; received 17 life terms plus 738 years for other felonies on Dec. 3, 2003

McCrary, Sherman Ramon (1925–88), **Carolyn Elizabeth** (1928–), **Danny Sherman** (1952–); **Taylor, Carl Robert** (1938–), **Ginger McCrary** (1949–)

SEX: 3 M/2 F   RACE: W   TYPE: N
MOTIVE: CE/Sex.
DATE(S): 1971–72   VENUE: USA nationwide   VICTIMS: 22 suspected

MO: Nomadic criminal family subsisting by armed robbery; also kidnapped/raped/murdered female holdup victims

DISPOSITION: Sherman sentenced to life terms in Colo. and Tex. (suicide by hanging in Colo. prison, Oct. 9, 1988); consecutive life terms for Carl in Colo., Tex. and Fla.; Carolyn served two years in Colo. as accessory to murder (died of natural causes after parole); Ginger turned state's evidence to escape prosecution for murder, serving eight years in Colo. for check fraud; Danny sentenced to life on two counts in Tex., 1973 (paroled 1983); 12-year sentence in Tex. for parole violation and child molestation, 1986

Millardo, José (d. 1864)   AKA: Apache Joe; **Sepulveda, Anton** (d. 1869)

SEX: Two M   RACE: H   TYPE: N   MOTIVE: PC
DATE(S): 1840s–60s   VENUE: Rocky Mountains
VICTIMS: 100+

MO: "Mountain men" and prolific killers of Indians; tally unk., but Sepulveda bragged of killing 26 to avenge Millardo's death, 1864–69

DISPOSITION: Both killed by Indians in separate battles

Miller, James William (1938–); **Worrell, Christopher Robin** (1954–77)

SEX: 2 M   RACE: W   TYPE: T   MOTIVE: Sex.
DATE(S): 1976–77   VENUE: Adelaide, Australia
VICTIMS: Seven

MO: Bisexual lovers who stabbed young women after sex

DISPOSITION: Worrell killed in car crash, Feb. 19, 1977; Miller sentenced to life on six counts, 1980

Movement for the Restoration of the Ten Commandments

SEX: Mixed   RACE: B   TYPE: T   MOTIVE: GC-cult
DATE(S): 1998–99   VENUE: Uganda   VICTIMS: 979+

MO: Cult murders of numerous victims buried in mass graves at several sites; victims hacked, strangled, and poisoned

DISPOSITION: Unknown

Munoz, Jose (1970–); **Romero, Orlando Gene** (1968–); **Self, Christopher** (1971–)

SEX: 3 M   RACE: H   TYPE: T   MOTIVE: CE
DATE(S): 1992   VENUE: Riverside County, Calif.
VICTIMS: Three

MO: Shot male victims in robberies

DISPOSITION: Romero and Self condemned on three counts, 1995; life term for Munoz on plea bargain

"Murder, Inc."

SEX: M   RACE: W   TYPE: N   MOTIVE: CE
DATE(S): 1931–40   VENUE: USA nationwide   VICTIMS: 1,000 est.

MO: "Enforcement" arm of national crime syndicate; dispatched contract killers nationwide from New York City

DISPOSITION: Exposed by gunman ABRAHAM RELES, 1940; seven killers executed in N.Y., 1941–42; several others sentenced to long prison terms; larger crime syndicate undamaged

Murphy, Hugh Leonard Thompson (1952–82), **et al.** AKA: Shankill Butchers

SEX: 12 M   RACE: W   TYPE: T   MOTIVE: GC-extremist
DATE(S): 1972–82   VENUE: Belfast, North Ireland
VICTIMS: 34

MO: Sectarian torture-slayers of Catholic victims chosen at random; others killed in bombings and driveby shootings

DISPOSITION: Murphy executed Nov. 16, 1982, as a result of ironic collaboration between Catholic and Protestant guerrillas; 11 other gang members received 42 life terms in series of trials, 1977–79

Musa, Bilal (1966–); **Ibrahim, Susan** (1969–)

SEX: M/F   RACE: A   TYPE: N   MOTIVE: CE-felony
DATE(S): 1994–98   VENUE: Jordan   VICTIMS: 12

MO: Husband-wife team who posed as journalists or vendors to enter homes, then robbed and killed the occupants

DISPOSITION: Musa condemned on seven counts, executed Dec. Dec. 7, 2000; Ibrahim condemned on one count, commuted to life sentence on appeal

Nash, Glenn (1925–); **Freshwater, Margo** (1948–)
SEX: M/F   RACE: W   TYPE: N   MOTIVE: PC/CE
DATE(S): 1966   VENUE: Tenn./Miss./Fla.   VICTIMS: Three
MO: Mentally unbalanced attorney and his teenage client-lover who embarked on a tristate crime spree, shooting victims in armed robberies
DISPOSITION: Nash was ruled insane by courts in three states, confined to a psychiatric hospital until 1983; Freshwater received a 99-year term on one count, in Tennessee, but escaped from prison in October 1970; she remained at large until May 2002, when she was captured in Ohio and returned to prison

Nicklasson, Allen L. (1972–); **Skillicorn, Dennis J.** (1960–)
SEX: 2 M   RACE: W   TYPE: N   MOTIVE: CE
DATE(S): 1994   VENUE: Mo./Ariz.   VICTIMS: Three
MO: Shot robbery victims
DISPOSITION: Both condemned on one count, in Mo.

Okpara, Odoh, et al.
SEX: 31 M/2 F   RACE: B   TYPE: T   MOTIVE: GC
DATE(S): 2001–02   VENUE: Neke, Nigeria   VICTIMS: 36+
MO: Police investigating ritual murders seized 36 human skulls in raids on cult shrines, arresting 33 magic practitioners; press reports state that "only strangers are sacrificed" to local deities
DISPOSITION: Defendants charged with unlawful possession of human remains; trial results unreported

Orji, Clifford (?–); **Tahiru** (?–)
SEX: 2 M   RACE: B   TYPE: T   MOTIVE: PC-nonspecific
DATE(S): 1998–99   VENUE: Lagos, Nigeria   VICTIMS: Several
MO: Cannibals arrested in the act of cooking a murdered woman at their home beneath an urban bridge; remains of other victims found at the scene
DISPOSITION: Unknown

Penn, Thomas Lee (1948–), **William** (1941–)
SEX: Two M   RACE: B   TYPE: T   MOTIVE: CE-felony
DATE(S): 1966   VENUE: Richmond, Va.   VICTIMS: Six confessed

MO: Shot robbery victims of both sexes, age 16–78
DISPOSITION: Life sentence for both on one count

"Quantrill's raiders"
SEX: M   RACE: W   TYPE: N   MOTIVE: PC/CE
DATE(S): 1861–65   VENUE: Kans./Mo./Tex./Ky.   VICTIMS: 700+
MO: Group of "irregulars" led by WILLIAM QUANTRILL during Civil War; robbed/raped/murdered citizens of both sides
DISPOSITION: 70+ members killed in battle or executed; many survivors pursued postwar careers of robbery and murder

Ramone, Merle (1974–); **Apachito, Lyle** (1983–); **Scatero, Dion** (1983–)
SEX: 3 M   RACE: NA   TYPE: T   MOTIVE: CE-felony
DATE(S): 2001   VENUE: Albuquerque, N. Mex.   VICTIMS: Two
MO: Killed victims in armed robberies
DISPOSITION: Apachito and Scatero pled guilty on reduced charges, May 25, 2003; Ramone convicted on two murder counts, June 17, 2003; all received life terms on Aug. 22, 2003

Ray, David Parker (1939–); **Hendy, Cindy Lee** (1959–); **Yancy, Dennis Roy** (1972–)
SEX: M/F   RACE: W   TYPE: T   MOTIVE: Sex./Sad.
DATE(S): 1996–99   VENUE: Elephant Butte, N. Mex.   VICTIMS: 14+ alleged
MO: Kidnapped and sexually abused women in a private torture chamber; Hendy accused Ray of 14 murders; Ray also suspected of killing male coworker in Arizona, in 1988; Yancy confessed strangling a 22-year-old woman in the torture chamber
DISPOSITION: Yancy pleaded guilty on one count of second-degree murder and received a 20-year sentence, December 1999; Hendy received a 36-year term as Ray's accomplice, May 12, 2000; Ray received a 224-year sentence for abducting and torturing two women in 1996 and 1999, Sept. 20, 2001; Ray's daughter Glenda received two and a half years as accomplice to her father, December 2001

Reserve Police Battalion 101
SEX: 550M   RACE: W   TYPE: T   MOTIVE: GC-extremist
DATE(S): 1942–43   VENUE: Poland   VICTIMS: 38,000+

MO: Mobile Nazi murder squad operating as "police"; casualty figures represent bare minimum officially acknowledged

DISPOSITION: Two executed and two imprisoned for 3–8 years, 1958; five more imprisoned for 5–8 years, 1968; six others convicted without being sentenced; additional cases dismissed

Romano, John Joseph (1958–2002); **Woodruff, David Wayne** (1959–2002)
SEX: 2 M RACE: 2H TYPE: T MOTIVE: CE/PC
DATE(S): 1985–86 VENUE: Oklahoma City, Okla.
 VICTIMS: Two
MO: Fatally stabbed a 52-year-old jeweler during robbery and a 63-year-old personal acquaintance
DISPOSITION: Romano executed Jan. 29, 2002; Woodruff executed Jan. 31, 2002

Ruiz, Paul (1948–97); **Denton, Earl Van** (1950–97)
SEX: 2 M RACE: W TYPE: N MOTIVE: CE
DATE(S): 1977 VENUE: Ark. VICTIMS: Six
MO: Escaped convicts; shot male victims while at large
DISPOSITION: Both condemned, 1980; both executed Jan. 8, 1997

Sach, Amelia (1873–1902); **Walters, Annie** (d. 1902)
SEX: 2 F RACE: W TYPE: T MOTIVE: CE
DATE(S): 189?–1902 VENUE: London, England
 VICTIMS: "Numerous"
MO: "Baby farmers" who killed infants of unwed mothers
DISPOSITION: Hanged together, 1902

Schaeffer, Gerrit C. (?–) wife (?–)
SEX: M/F RACE: W TYPE: S MOTIVE: PC-domestic
DATE(S): 1951–58 VENUE: Rotterdam, Netherland
 VICTIMS: Four
MO: Married couple; killed newborn infants at home
DISPOSITION: Life sentences for both, 1959

Sifrit, Benjamin (1978–); **Sifrit, Erika** (1978–)
SEX; M/F RACE: W TYPE: N MOTIVE: CE-felony
DATE(S): 2001–02 VENUE: Pa./Md. VICTIMS: Three alleged
MO: Husband-wife team who robbed and murdered a couple in Ocean City, Md.; prime suspects in the slaying of a woman and beating of her boyfriend in Bedford County, Pa.
DISPOSITION: Benjamin received a 38-year term on one count of second-degree murder, plus burglary, assault and other charges, July 2003; Eric received a

life term plus 20 years on two murder counts, plus assorted lesser charges, August 2003

Sims, Mitchell Carlton (1960–); **Padgett, Ruby Carolyn** (1965–) AKA: The Killing Team
SEX: M/F RACE: W TYPE: N MOTIVE: Sad./CE
DATE(S): 1985 VENUE: S.C./Calif. VICTIMS: Three
MO: Torture-slayers of Domino's Pizza employees in robberies
DISPOSITION: Sims condemned in both Calif. and S.C.; Padgett imprisoned

Smith, Harold Glenn (1966–); **Cravey, Michael Gene** (1967–); **Rivera, Shannon** (1969–); **Tosh, Martin Wayne** (1969–); **Trimmer, John-Michael Alexander** (?–)
SEX: 4 M/1 F RACE: W TYPE: T MOTIVE: GC-cult
DATE(S): 1985 VENUE: Houston, Tex. VICTIMS: Four suspected
MO: Satanists who committed sadistic human sacrifice
DISPOSITION: Life term for Smith on one count, 1986; 60 years for Trimmer, 1986; life term for Cravey, 1987; 25 years for Tosh, 1987; 15 years for Rivera, 1987

Spesivtsev, Sasha (1970–); **Spesivtsev, Lyudmilla** (?–)
SEX: M/F RACE: W TYPE: S MOTIVE: Sex./Sad.
DATE(S): 1991–97 VENUE: Novosibirsk, Siberia
 VICTIMS: 80 alleged
MO: Mother-son cannibal team; Sasha raped/killed underage girls to "cleanse" society; mother lured victims to their apartment and helped him cook/eat the victims
DISPOSITION: Sasha ruled insane and committed to asylum for life, Oct. 4, 1999; Lyudmilla sentenced to 13 years as accomplice to murder and for forcing some victims to eat human flesh

Starkweather, Charles Raymond (1938–59); **Fugate, Caril Ann** (1943–)
SEX: M/F RACE: W TYPE: N MOTIVE: PC-nonspecific
DATE(S): 1957–58 VENUE: Nebr./Wyo. VICTIMS: 11
MO: Teenage thrill killers on Midwest rampage
DISPOSITION: Starkweather executed in Nebr., June 25, 1959; Fugate sentenced to life, 1958 (paroled 1976)

Taborsky, Joseph L. (1924–); **Culombe, Arthur** (1923–)
SEX: 2 M RACE: W TYPE: N MOTIVE: CE-felony

DATE(S): 1951/55   VENUE: Conn.   VICTIMS: Seven

MO: Taborsky killed his first holdup victim in 1951; teamed with Culombe four years later for a series of robbery-murders

DISPOSITION: Taborsky condemned, 1951; acquitted at retrial after chief witness went insane; life terms for both, 1956

"Taxhali Hotel Gang"

SEX: 5 M   RACE: A   TYPE: T   MOTIVE: Sex./Sad.

DATE(S): 2000   VENUE: Lahore, Pakistan   VICTIMS: "Several"

MO: Gay killers lured men to isolated sites, then murdered them

DISPOSITION: Unknown

Thugs   AKA: Sons of Death

SEX: M   RACE: A   TYPE: N   MOTIVE: GC-cult

DATE(S): c. 1250–1852   VENUE: India   VICTIMS: Two to four million

MO: Worshippers of Kali; robbed/murdered male victims throughout India, typically strangling and mutilating chosen prey; British authorities claimed 40,000 victims in 1812 alone; one Thug, Buhram, confessed 931 murders at his 1840 arrest

DISPOSITION: 4,500 cultists convicted of various crimes, 1830–48, with 110 condemned for murder; cult allegedly defunct in 1852, although occasional reports of "thuggee" were logged as late as 1867

Tison, Gary Gene (1936–78); **Donald** (1958–78), **Raymond** (1959–   ), **Ricky** (1958–   )

SEX: 4 M   RACE: W   TYPE: N   MOTIVE: CE

DATE(S): 1967/78   VENUE: Ariz./Colo.   VICTIMS: Seven

MO: Career criminal and convicted cop-killer who escaped from prison with aid of three sons and fellow inmate RANDY GREENAWALT, killing seven hostages while at large

DISPOSITION: Donald killed in shoot-out with police, Aug. 7, 1978; Gary found dead in Ariz. desert, Aug. 22, 1978; Raymond and Ricky condemned, 1979 (commuted to multiple life terms on appeal, 1992)

Undisclosed

SEX: 16M   RACE: A   TYPE: T   MOTIVE: CE

DATE(S): 1996–98   VENUE: Jinzhong, China   VICTIMS: 28

MO: Gang murdered migrant workers and concealed corpses in staged mine cave-ins; collected $62,000 in fraudulent life insurance claims

DISPOSITION: Ten defendants condemned, June 2000; five others received life prison terms; one sentenced to 15 years

Undisclosed

SEX: 3 M   RACE: Unk.   TYPE: T   MOTIVE: PC-nonspecific

DATE(S): 2000   VENUE: Germany   VICTIMS: Two

MO: Sons of U.S. soldiers stationed in Germany, aged 14, 17, and 18 at the time of their murder spree in February 2000; dropped stones on passing cars from highway bridges, killing two persons and injuring four

DISPOSITION: All three convicted of murder on Dec. 22, 2000; received prison terms ranging from seven to eight and a half years, based on age at time of murders

Undisclosed

SEX: 4 M   RACE: A   TYPE: T   MOTIVE: CE-felony

DATE(S): 2000–01   VENUE: Yunan Province, China   VICTIMS: Nine

MO: Robbed 10 women, killing nine

DISPOSITION: All executed on June 5, 2001

Undisclosed

SEX: 3 M   RACE: A   TYPE: T   MOTIVE: CE-felony

DATE(S): 2001   VENUE: Sichuan Province, China   VICTIMS: 15

MO: Robbed 17 taxis, killing 15 drivers

DISPOSITION: All three executed, June 5, 2001

Undisclosed

SEX: 3 M/1 F   RACE: W   TYPE: T   MOTIVE: CE/PC

DATE(S): 2001–02   VENUE: Zhytomyr, Ukraine   VICTIMS: Six

MO: Husband and wife, with wife's brother and a male friend, who robbed, tortured, and cannibalized women in woods outside town; arrested while trying to collect ransom on their last victim

DISPOSITION: Charged with six murders and 20+ robberies; disposition unknown

Undisclosed

SEX: 30M/F   RACE: B   TYPE: T   MOTIVE: GC

DATE(S): 2003–04   VENUE: Anambra State, Nigeria   VICTIMS: 50+

MO: Police raids on local magic shrines in August 2004 reveal 20 human skulls and 50 corpses, many with genitals and other "magic" organs missing

DISPOSITION: Unknown

Wardlaw, Virginia (?–?); **Martin, Caroline Wardlaw** (d. 1913); **Sneyd, Mary Wardlaw** (?–?)
SEX: 3 F   RACE: W   TYPE: N   MOTIVE: CE
DATE(S): 1900s   VENUE: South U.S.   VICTIMS: Three
MO: Sisters who killed family members for insurance
DISPOSITION: Mary acquitted at trial; Virginia died in jailhouse hunger strike; Catherine ruled insane, died in asylum, 1913

Wells, Roland (1971–   ); **Wells, Angela** (1972–   )
SEX: M/F   RACE: W   TYPE: T   MOTIVE: CE-felony
DATE(S): 1997–2001   VENUE: Peoria, Ill.   VICTIMS: Three suspected
MO: Husband-wife team who killed a 20-year-old acquaintance for his $1,800 tax refund check; in prison, Roland confessed the murder of another man in 1997; suspected of a third man's death in 1998
DISPOSITION: Angela pleaded guilty and turned state's evidence on Oct. 29, 2001, receiving a 40-year sentence; Roland convicted on her testimony and sentenced to life imprisonment

Yahweh Ben Yahweh (1935–   ) et al.   AKA: Hebrew Israelites
SEX: ?M/?W   RACE: B   TYPE: N   MOTIVE: GC-cult
DATE(S): 1981–90   VENUE: Fla./Ill./Mich./N.J.
VICTIMS: 25+ suspected
MO: Black racist cult; alleged victims include cult defectors and opponents, "white devils" killed at random, and at least two children dead from abuse/neglect within cult
DISPOSITION: Member ROBERT ROZIER confessed multiple murders in Fla.; Yahweh and six disciples convicted on federal conspiracy charges, 1992

Young, Robert (d. 1980); **Wright, Blanche** (1959–   )
SEX: M/F   RACE: B   TYPE: T   MOTIVE: Sex./CE
DATE(S): 1974/80   VENUE: New York City   VICTIMS: Four
MO: Young raped/killed female burglary victim; on parole, teamed with Wright as contract killers
DISPOSITION: Young killed in shootout with intended victim, Feb. 1980; Wright drew 18 years to life on one count + 15 years to life for two additional murders

Zhang Jun, et al.
SEX: 10 M/4 F   RACE: A   TYPE: N   MOTIVE: CE-felony
DATE(S): 2000   VENUE: China   VICTIMS: 28
MO: Criminal gang that killed 28 victims in 20+ armed robberies; female gang members were all lovers of leader Zhang Jun; one confessed killing a man to prove her love
DISPOSITION: All executed in May 2001

Appendix C: Unresolved Cases

Unknown   AKA: "Servant Girl Annihilator"
SEX: Unk.   TYPE: T   MOTIVE: Unk.
DATES: 1884–85   VENUE: Austin, Tex.   VICTIMS: 8
MO: Police and reporters credited one unknown killer for the Ripper-style murders of six blacks and two whites. Despite the killer's nickname, not all victims were servants—or females
DISPOSITION: Unsolved

Unknown
SEX: Unk.   RACE: Unk.   TYPE: T   MOTIVE: Sex./Sad.
DATE(S): 1885   VENUE: Moscow, Russia   VICTIMS: "Several"
MO: "Ripper" of prostitutes
DISPOSITION: Unsolved

Unknown
SEX: Unk.   RACE: Unk.   TYPE: T   MOTIVE: Sex./Sad.
DATE(S): 1887   VENUE: Tex.   VICTIMS: "Several"
MO: "Ripper" of black prostitutes
DISPOSITION: Unsolved

Unknown   AKA: Servant Girl Annihilator
SEX: M   RACE: Unk.   TYPE: T   MOTIVE: Unk.
DATE(S): 1884–85   VENUE: Austin, Tex.   VICTIMS: Eight
MO: Home invader who attacked nine victims, killing seven women and one man; axes used in all but one case, where an 11-year-old girl was raped and stabbed in the ear with an iron bar
DISPOSITION: Unsolved

Unknown
SEX: Unk.   RACE: Unk.   TYPE: T   MOTIVE: Unk.
DATE(S): 1888–89   VENUE: London, England   VICTIMS: Two
MO: Mutilation-slayer of women, presumed prostitutes, whose torsos were found in or near the Thames
DISPOSITION: Unsolved

Unknown
SEX: Unk.   RACE: Unk.   TYPE: T   MOTIVE: Sex./Sad.
DATE(S): 1889   VENUE: Nicaragua   VICTIMS: "Several"
MO: "Ripper" of prostitutes
DISPOSITION: Unsolved

Unknown   AKA: Jack the Strangler
SEX: Unk.   RACE: Unk.   TYPE: T   MOTIVE: Sex./Sad.
DATE(S): 1894/1903   VENUE: Denver, Colo.   VICTIMS: Four
MO: Strangled/bludgeoned prostitutes
DISPOSITION: Unsolved

Unknown
SEX: Unk.   RACE: Unk.   TYPE: T   MOTIVE: Unk.
DATE(S): 1904–10   VENUE: Cumminsville, Ohio   VICTIMS: Five
MO: Women bludgeoned to death
DISPOSITION: Unsolved

Unknown   AKA: Shotgun Man
SEX: M   RACE: W   TYPE: T   MOTIVE: CE

DATE(S): 1910–11   VENUE: Chicago, Ill.   VICTIMS: 15
MO: Unidentified "Black Hand" assassin
DISPOSITION: Unsolved

Unknown
SEX: Unk.   RACE: Unk.   TYPE: T   MOTIVE: Unk.
DATE(S): 1910–46   VENUE: Northwest Territories, Canada   VICTIMS: 10+
MO: Trappers/prospectors beheaded in Nahanni Valley
DISPOSITION: Unsolved

Unknown
SEX: Unk.   RACE: W   TYPE: S   MOTIVE: Unk.
DATE(S): 1911   VENUE: Lancaster, England   VICTIMS: Three
MO: Members of Bingham family poisoned at home
DISPOSITION: Family member acquitted; unsolved

Unknown
SEX: M   RACE: B   TYPE: N   MOTIVE: PC-extremist
DATE(S): 1911–12   VENUE: Tex./La.   VICTIMS: 49
MO: Home invader slaughters black families with ax
DISPOSITION: Unsolved

Unknown   AKA: Jack the Ripper
SEX: M   RACE: B   TYPE: T   MOTIVE: Sex./Sad.
DATE(S): 1911–12   VENUE: Atlanta, Ga.   VICTIMS: 20
MO: Mutilation-slayer of black women, some prostitutes
DISPOSITION: Unsolved

Unknown
SEX: Unk.   RACE: Unk.   TYPE: N   MOTIVE: Sad.?
DATE(S): 1911–12   VENUE: Colo.   VICTIMS: Four to seven
MO: Women bludgeoned in Denver and Colorado Springs
DISPOSITION: Unsolved

Unknown   AKA: Jack the Ripper
SEX: Unk.   RACE: Unk.   TYPE: T   MOTIVE: Unk.
DATE(S): 1915   VENUE: New York City   VICTIMS: Two
MO: Mutilation-slayer of five-year-old girl and four-year-old boy
DISPOSITION: Unsolved

Unknown
SEX: Unk.   RACE: Unk.   TYPE: T   MOTIVE: Possible "BABY FARMING
DATE(S): 1915   VENUE: New York City   VICTIMS: 14

MO: Newborn infants drowned in Hudson River
DISPOSITION: Unsolved

Unknown
SEX: Unk.   RACE: Unk.   TYPE: T   MOTIVE: Unk.
DATE(S): 1921   VENUE: Austria   VICTIMS: Six
MO: Hikers missing, presumed murdered in separate incidents
DISPOSITION: Unsolved

Unknown
SEX: F   RACE: W   TYPE: S   MOTIVE: PC-domestic?
DATE(S): 1921–22   VENUE: Cleveland, Ohio   VICTIMS: Five
MO: Alleged "black widow" slayer of husbands/children
DISPOSITION: Unknown; files "lost"; no media follow-up

Unknown
SEX: Unk.   RACE: Unk.   TYPE: T   MOTIVE: Unk.
DATE(S): 1922   VENUE: Warsaw, Poland   VICTIMS: 11
MO: Mutilation-slayer of women found in nearby woods
DISPOSITION: Unsolved

Unknown   AKA: Headless Murders
SEX: Unk.   RACE: Unk.   TYPE: T   MOTIVE: Unk.
DATE(S): 1924–39   VENUE: Lawrence County, Pa.   VICTIMS: Five+
MO: Victims beheaded, dumped in local "murder swamp"
DISPOSITION: Unsolved; possible link to Cleveland's "MAD BUTCHER"

Unknown   AKA: Toledo Clubber
SEX: M   RACE: W   TYPE: T   MOTIVE: Sex./Sad.
DATE(S): 1925–26   VENUE: Toledo, Ohio   VICTIMS: Five or six
MO: Women bludgeoned and raped
DISPOSITION: Unsolved

Unknown
SEX: Unk.   RACE: Unk.   TYPE: S   MOTIVE: Unk.
DATE(S): 1928–29   VENUE: South Croydon, England   VICTIMS: Three
MO: Members of one family poisoned over time
DISPOSITION: Unsolved

Unknown   AKA: 3X
SEX: M   RACE: W   TYPE: T   MOTIVE: Unk.

DATE(S): 1930   VENUE: Queens, N.Y.   VICTIMS: Two
MO: Men shot in lover's lane attacks; one woman raped; letters to the press hint at international political intrigue
DISPOSITION: Unsolved

Unknown
SEX: Unk.   RACE: Unk.   TYPE: T   MOTIVE: Unk.
DATE(S): 1930   VENUE: Mexico City   VICTIMS: Five
MO: Male victims apparently hanged, then buried on Pachuca Road
DISPOSITION: Unsolved

Unknown   AKA: Mad Trapper
SEX: Unk.   RACE: Unk.   TYPE: T   MOTIVE: Unk.
DATE(S): 1930–31   VENUE: Ark.   VICTIMS: 15
MO: Sportsmen killed at random
DISPOSITION: Unsolved

Unknown
SEX: M   RACE: Unk.   TYPE: T   MOTIVE: Sex./Sad.
DATE(S): 1931–36   VENUE: San Diego, Calif.   VICTIMS: Seven
MO: Rape/torture slayer of females age 10–22
DISPOSITION: Unsolved

Unknown
SEX: Unk.   RACE: Unk.   TYPE: T   MOTIVE: Unk.
DATE(S): 1935   VENUE: Berlin, Germany   VICTIMS: "Several"
MO: Steel cables strung across highways, causing fatal accidents
DISPOSITION: Unsolved

Unknown
SEX: Unk.   RACE: Unk.   TYPE: T   MOTIVE: Unk.
DATE(S): 1942   VENUE: Hamamatsu City, Japan   VICTIMS: Nine
MO: Deaf-mutes killed between Oct. and Dec.
DISPOSITION: Unsolved

Unknown (Town Hospital)
SEX: Unk.   RACE: Unk.   TYPE: S   MOTIVE: Unk.
DATE(S): 1944–47   VENUE: Macon, France   VICTIMS: 17
MO: Female patients killed with lethal injections
DISPOSITION: Unsolved

Unknown
SEX: Unk.   RACE: Unk.   TYPE: N   MOTIVE: Unk.
DATE(S): 1948   VENUE: Sweden   VICTIMS: Four

MO: Weekend passengers shoved from moving trains
DISPOSITION: Unsolved

Unknown
SEX: F   RACE: W   TYPE: T   MOTIVE: Unk.
DATE(S): 1949–52   VENUE: Somersworth, N.H.   VICTIMS: Four
MO: Mummified newborns found in suitcase, 1982
DISPOSITION: Unnamed female suspect deceased

Unknown
SEX: Unk.   RACE: Unk.   TYPE: S   MOTIVE: Unk.
DATE(S): 1950s   VENUE: Adelaide, Australia   VICTIMS: Three
MO: Skeletal remains of infants found under house in 2000
DISPOSITION: Unsolved

Unknown   AKA: Atteridgeville Mutilator
SEX: Unk.   RACE: Unk.   TYPE: T   MOTIVE: Unk.
DATE(S): 1956   VENUE: Atteridgeville, South Africa   VICTIMS: Six
MO: Young boys castrated, with tongues removed
DISPOSITION: Unsolved

Unknown
SEX: Unk.   RACE: Unk.   TYPE: T   MOTIVE: Sex./Sad.
DATE(S): 1956–57   VENUE: Chicago, Ill.   VICTIMS: Three
MO: Slayer of teenage girls; one victim dismembered
DISPOSITION: Unsolved

Unknown
SEX: Unk.   RACE: Unk.   TYPE: T   MOTIVE: Unk.
DATE(S): 1963–64   VENUE: Cali, Colombia   VICTIMS: 10
MO: Boys age 10–18 found drained of blood
DISPOSITION: Unsolved

Unknown
SEX: Unk.   RACE: Unk.   TYPE: T   MOTIVE: CE?
DATE(S): 1965–66   VENUE: Columbus, Ohio   VICTIMS: Three
MO: Three men shot, two in apparent robberies
DISPOSITION: Unsolved

Unknown (Riverdell Hospital)
SEX: Unk.   RACE: Unk.   TYPE: T   MOTIVE: Unk.
DATE(S): 1965–66   VENUE: Oradell, N.J.   VICTIMS: Nine
MO: Patients killed with curare injections
DISPOSITION: Unsolved; Dr. Mario Jascalevich acquitted, 1978

Unknown
SEX: M   RACE: Unk.   TYPE: T   MOTIVE: Sex./Sad.
DATE(S): 1965–66   VENUE: Monmouth/Ocean
   counties, N.J.   VICTIMS: Six
MO: Lust murders of victims age five to 44, both sexes
DISPOSITION: Unsolved

Unknown
SEX: Unk.   RACE: Unk.   TYPE: T   MOTIVE: Unk.
DATE(S): 1967–69   VENUE: London, Ontario   VIC-
   TIMS: Three to five
MO: Murders of unnamed women linked in official
   reports
DISPOSITION: Unsolved

Unknown
SEX: M   RACE: Unk.   TYPE: T   MOTIVE: Sex.
DATE(S): 1967–69   VENUE: London, Ontario   VIC-
   TIMS: 10
MO: Rape-murders of women linked by crime scene
   evidence
DISPOSITION: Unsolved

Unknown   AKA: Four P Movement or Four Pi
SEX: Mixed   RACE: W   TYPE: N   MOTIVE: Cult
DATE(S): 1967–??   VENUE: USA nationwide   VIC-
   TIMS: "Numerous"
MO: Satanic cult practitioners of human sacrifice;
   alleged to deal narcotics and "snuff" films; accept
   murder contracts
DISPOSITION: Confessed member STANLEY BAKER
   convicted of murder in Mont., 1970; links to MAN-
   SON "FAMILY"; confessed member DAVID BERKOWITZ
   convicted of six N.Y. murders, 1978; alleged member WILLIAM MENTZER convicted of one Calif. murder, 1991; other cultists still at large

Unknown   AKA: Bible John
SEX: M   RACE: W   TYPE: T   MOTIVE: Sex./Sad.
DATE(S): 1968–69   VENUE: Glasgow, Scotland
   VICTIMS: Three
MO: Women picked up at dance halls and strangled
DISPOSITION: Unsolved

Unknown
SEX: M   RACE: Unk.   TYPE: N   MOTIVE: Sex.
DATE(S): 1969   VENUE: Conn./N.Y.   VICTIMS:
   Three
MO: Young girls bludgeoned; at least one raped
DISPOSITION: Unsolved

Unknown
SEX: Unk.   RACE: Unk.   TYPE: N   MOTIVE: PC
DATE(S): 1969–73   VENUE: Calif.   VICTIMS: 15

MO: Victims killed on/near dates of astrological significance
DISPOSITION: Unsolved

Unknown   AKA: Death Angels
SEX: M   RACE: B   TYPE: N   MOTIVE: Cult/PC-
   extremist
DATE(S): 1969–??   VENUE: Calif. (and beyond?)
   VICTIMS: 64+ by 1974
MO: Black racist cult, kills whites at random to earn
   "wings"
DISPOSITION: Four prospects convicted of "ZEBRA"
   murders

Unknown   AKA: Truckstop Killer
SEX: M   RACE: Unk.   TYPE: N   MOTIVE: Sex./Sad.
DATE(S): 1969–92   VENUE: Eastern USA   VIC-
   TIMS: 27+
MO: Stalker of truckstop hookers and stranded female
   motorists
DISPOSITION: Unsolved; probably involves several
   killers

Unknown (Salem Veterans Medical Center)
SEX: Unk.   RACE: Unk.   TYPE: S   MOTIVE: Unk.
DATE(S): 1970s   VENUE: Roanoke, Va.   VICTIMS:
   Three reported
MO: Skeletal remains of missing patients found on
   hospital grounds, 1992
DISPOSITION: Results of investigation unreported

Unknown   AKA: Maxwell's Silver Hammer
SEX: Unk.   RACE: Unk.   TYPE: T   MOTIVE: Cult
DATE(S): 1970–??   VENUE: Santa Barbara, Calif.
   VICTIMS: Five
MO: Campers stabbed/hacked to death on beach by
   robed attackers
DISPOSITION: Unsolved; cult name revealed by MAN-
   SON "FAMILY"

Unknown
SEX: M   RACE: Unk.   TYPE: T   MOTIVE: Sex.
DATE(S): 1970–86   VENUE: Wildwood, N.J.   VIC-
   TIMS: Three
MO: Rape-murders of women, bodies left under local
   boardwalk
DISPOSITION: Unsolved

Unknown
SEX: M   RACE: W   TYPE: T   MOTIVE: Unk.
DATE(S): 1971   VENUE: Washington, D.C.   VIC-
   TIMS: 10
MO: Gay men stabbed/slashed in their homes
DISPOSITION: Unsolved; photo of suspect unidentified

Unknown
SEX: M   RACE: B   TYPE: T   MOTIVE: GC/CE
DATE(S): 1971–72   VENUE: Chicago, Ill.   VIC-
   TIMS: Six
MO: Black men robbed/shot, apparently by several
   offenders
DISPOSITION: Unsolved

Unknown
SEX: Unk.   RACE: Unk.   TYPE: T   MOTIVE: Unk.
DATE(S): 1971–76   VENUE: Tex. Gulf coast   VIC-
   TIMS: 21
MO: Females age 12–21 killed in three counties, by
   various means
DISPOSITION: Unsolved

Unknown   AKA: Alphabet Murders
SEX: Unk.   RACE: Unk.   TYPE: T   MOTIVE: Unk.
DATE(S): 1971–73   VENUE: Rochester, N.Y.   VIC-
   TIMS: Three
MO: Young Catholic girls with matching initials killed
DISPOSITION: Unsolved; KENNETH BIANCHI sus-
   pected, not charged

Unknown
SEX: Unk.   RACE: Unk.   TYPE: N   MOTIVE: Unk.
DATE(S): 1972–75   VENUE: Northern Calif.   VIC-
   TIMS: 14
MO: Slayer of females age 12–22, mostly
   strangled/smothered
DISPOSITION: Unsolved

Unknown
SEX: M   RACE: Unk.   TYPE: T   MOTIVE: Sex.
DATE(S): 1973   VENUE: Prince Georges County, Md.
   VICTIMS: Five
MO: Black women from Washington, D.C., sodomized
   and murdered
DISPOSITION: Unsolved

Unknown
SEX: Unk.   RACE: Unk.   TYPE: N   MOTIVE: Unk.
DATE(S): 1973   VENUE: Mich.   VICTIMS: "At least
   20"
MO: Prostitutes murdered; details withheld by police
DISPOSITION: Unsolved

Unknown
SEX: Unk.   RACE: Unk.   TYPE: T   MOTIVE: CE
DATE(S): 1973   VENUE: Mobile/Baldwin Counties,
   Ala.   VICTIMS: Three
MO: Shotgun slayings of gas station attendants in
   holdups

DISPOSITION: Suspect Michael Pardue convicted on
   basis of coerced confession, 1973; murder charges
   subsequently dropped, though Pardue continues
   serving life term for a 1987 escape. Murders
   unsolved.

Unknown
SEX: Unk.   RACE: Unk.   TYPE: T   MOTIVE: Unk.
DATE(S): 1973   VENUE: New York City   VICTIMS:
   Seven
MO: "Ripper" of gay males
DISPOSITION: Unsolved

Unknown
SEX: Unk.   RACE: Unk.   TYPE: T   MOTIVE: Unk.
DATE(S): 1973–74   VENUE: Gallup, N.Mex.   VIC-
   TIMS: Three
MO: Navajo men beaten/slashed to death in separate
   attacks
DISPOSITION: Unsolved

Unknown
SEX: Unk.   RACE: Unk.   TYPE: T   MOTIVE: Unk.
DATE(S): 1973–77   VENUE: Zephyrhills, Fla.   VIC-
   TIMS: Eight
MO: Prostitutes and strippers killed; details withheld
   by police
DISPOSITION: Unsolved

Unknown   AKA: Highway murders
SEX: M   RACE: Unk.   TYPE: N   MOTIVE:
   Sex./Sad.
DATE(S): 1973–81   VENUE: Western Canada   VIC-
   TIMS: 28 suspected
MO: Women (and one transvestite) killed along Trans-
   Canada Highway.
DISPOSITION: Unsolved

Unknown
SEX: Unk.   RACE: Unk.   TYPE: T   MOTIVE: Unk.
DATE(S): 1973–80   VENUE: New South Wales, Aus-
   tralia   VICTIMS: 20
MO: Backpackers and hitchhikers missing
DISPOSITION: Unsolved; police deem cases unrelated
   to convicted killer IVAN MILAT

Unknown   AKA: The Family
SEX: 9M   RACE: W   TYPE: T   MOTIVE: Sex./Sad.
DATE(S): 1973–83   VENUE: Adelaide, Australia
   VICTIMS: More than five
MO: Alleged gang of homosexual men who kidnapped,
   raped, and tortured 200 male victims, killing at least
   five, aged 14–25

DISPOSITION: Alleged "Family" member Bevan Spencer Von Einem convicted of murdering a 15-year-old boy, sentenced to 36 years without parole in 1984; other cases remain unsolved

Unknown
SEX: Unk.   RACE: Unk.   TYPE: T   MOTIVE: Unk.
DATE(S): 1973–2001   VENUE: Auxerre, France
   VICTIMS: 17–30
MO: Young women murdered and missing; most were mentally handicapped
DISPOSITION: Unsolved

Unknown
SEX: Unk.   RACE: Unk.   TYPE: T   MOTIVE: Unk.
DATE(S): 1974   VENUE: Rawlins, Wyo.   VICTIMS: Four
MO: Girls age 10–19 vanish from local rodeo; one found bludgeoned
DISPOSITION: Unsolved

Unknown
SEX: Unk.   RACE: Unk.   TYPE: T   MOTIVE: CE
DATE(S): 1974   VENUE: St. Louis, Mo.   VICTIMS: Four
MO: Victims kidnapped/shot after store robberies
DISPOSITION: Unsolved

Unknown   AKA: The Doodler
SEX: M   RACE: W   TYPE: T   MOTIVE: Sex./Sad.
DATE(S): 1974–75   VENUE: San Francisco, Calif.
   VICTIMS: 14
MO: "Ripper" of gay men
DISPOSITION: Allegedly identified, but never charged

Unknown
SEX: Unk.   RACE: Unk.   TYPE: S   MOTIVE: PC-mercy?
DATE(S): 1975   VENUE: Ann Arbor, Mich.   VICTIMS: 11
MO: Patients killed in VA hospital
DISPOSITION: Unsolved (two nurses convicted, freed on appeal)

Unknown   AKA: Bigfoot
SEX: M   RACE: Unk.   TYPE: T   MOTIVE: Sex.
DATE(S): 1975   VENUE: Detroit, Mich.   VICTIMS: Seven
MO: Women (mostly prostitutes) raped and bludgeoned in Cass Corridor area; UNSUB (police jargon for "Unknown Subject") nicknamed for large footprints
DISPOSITION: Unsolved

Unknown
SEX: Unk.   RACE: Unk.   TYPE: T   MOTIVE: Sex.
DATE(S): 1975   VENUE: Southern Fla.   VICTIMS: Five
MO: Women kidnapped after killer disabled their cars in mall parking lots
DISPOSITION: Unsolved

Unknown   AKA: Ottawa Valley Killer
SEX: M   RACE: W   TYPE: T   MOTIVE: CE-felony
DATE(S): 1975–87   VENUE: Ottawa Valley, Ontario
   VICTIMS: Six
MO: Victims slain in home-invasion robberies, with houses burned to hide evidence; the dead include four men, aged 48–71 and two women aged 59 and 83
DISPOSITION: Unsolved; rape-slayer Ronald Glenn West suspected but never charged

Unknown   AKA: San Mateo Slasher
SEX: M   RACE: Unk.   TYPE: T   MOTIVE: Sex./Sad.
DATE(S): 1976   VENUE: San Mateo County, Calif.
   VICTIMS: Five
MO: "Ripper" of young brunette women
DISPOSITION: Unsolved; suspect jailed for rape, paroled 1981

Unknown   AKA: The Babysitter
SEX: M   RACE: W   TYPE: T   MOTIVE: Sex.
DATE(S): 1976–77   VENUE: Oakland County, Mich.
   VICTIMS: Four to seven
MO: Killed children of both sexes; molested male victims
DISPOSITION: Unsolved

Unknown
SEX: M   RACE: W.   TYPE: T   MOTIVE: Sex.
DATE(S): 1976–77   VENUE: Washington County, Pa.
   VICTIMS: Five
MO: Young women strangled/beaten after rape
DISPOSITION: Unsolved

Unknown
SEX: Unk.   RACE: Unk.   TYPE: T   MOTIVE: Unk.
DATE(S): 1976–78   VENUE: New Haven, Conn.
   VICTIMS: Four+
MO: Targets black women, including at least three prostitutes
DISPOSITION: Unsolved

Unknown   AKA: I-35 murders
SEX: M   RACE: Unk.   TYPE: N   MOTIVE: Sex./Sad.

DATE(S): 1976–81   VENUE: Tex.   VICTIMS: 22
MO: Victims of both sexes killed along Interstate
   Highway 35
DISPOSITION: Unsolved; several cases blamed on
   HENRY LUCAS

Unknown
SEX: M   RACE: Unk.   TYPE: T   MOTIVE: Sex.
DATE(S): 1976–85   VENUE: Butler County, Ohio
   VICTIMS: Four
MO: Women aged 18–41 strangled; DNA evidence
   links the crimes; police blame unspecified "other
   murders" on the same unknown killer, spanning
   Butler and Hamilton Counties during 1977–82
DISPOSITION: Unsolved

Unknown   AKA: East Area Rapist
SEX: M   RACE: Unk.   TYPE: N   MOTIVE: Sex.
DATE(S): 1976–86   VENUE: California   VICTIMS:
   10 killed, 40+ raped
MO: Raped 40+ victims in Northern California home
   invasions, 1976–78; DNA links the rapist to four
   murders in Southern California during 1978 and six
   more in the period 1980–86
DISPOSITION: Unsolved

Unknown   AKA: Ironman
SEX: Unk.   RACE: Unk.   TYPE: T   MOTIVE: Unk.
DATE(S): late 1970s   VENUE: Atteridgeville, South
   Africa   VICTIMS: Seven
MO: Nocturnal strollers bludgeoned with iron bar
DISPOSITION: Unsolved

Unknown   AKA: Hammer Group
SEX: Unk.   RACE: Unk.   TYPE: T   MOTIVE: Unk.
DATE(S): late 1970s   VENUE: Lahore, Pakistan
   VICTIMS: 17
MO: Bludgeon murders of 17 night watchmen
DISPOSITION: Unsolved

Unknown
SEX: Unk.   RACE: Unk.   TYPE: T   MOTIVE: Unk.
DATE(S): 1976–95   VENUE: Oklahoma City   VIC-
   TIMS: Four to five
MO: Women dismembered
DISPOSITION: Unsolved

Unknown
SEX: M   RACE: B   TYPE: T   MOTIVE: Unk.
DATE(S): 1977   VENUE: Atlanta, Ga.   VICTIMS:
   Three
MO: Couples shot in lover's lane attacks
DISPOSITION: Unsolved

Unknown
SEX: M   RACE: Unk.   TYPE: N   MOTIVE: Sex.
DATE(S): 1977–80   VENUE: Scotland   VICTIMS:
   Seven
MO: DNA evidence links cases of female victims aged
   17–36 raped, beaten, and strangled in Edinburgh
   and Glasgow
DISPOSITION: Unsolved

Unknown
SEX: Unk.   RACE: Unk.   TYPE: T   MOTIVE: Unk.
DATE(S): 1977–93   VENUE: Dallas, Tex. area   VIC-
   TIMS: Eight
MO: Seven girls, age two to 14, and one eight-year-old
   boy murdered
DISPOSITION: Unsolved

Unknown
SEX: Unk.   RACE: Unk.   TYPE: T   MOTIVE: Unk.
DATE(S): 1978–79   VENUE: Newcastle, Australia
   VICTIMS: Four
MO: Female victims aged 14–20 missing
DISPOSITION: Unsolved

Unknown
SEX: M   RACE: Unk.   TYPE: N   MOTIVE:
   Sex./Sad.
DATE(S): 1978–79   VENUE: La./Miss.   VICTIMS:
   Three
MO: Male victims aged 17–22 hog-tied to strangle in
   fetal positions; DNA evidence links the cases
DISPOSITION: Unsolved

Unknown
SEX: Unk.   RACE: Unk.   TYPE: N   MOTIVE: Sex.?
DATE(S): 1978–84   VENUE: England   VICTIMS:
   Seven to 13
MO: Children of both sexes killed; "at least seven"
   cases linked
DISPOSITION: Unsolved

Unknown
SEX: Unk.   RACE: Unk.   TYPE: T   MOTIVE:
   Unk.
DATE(S): 1979   VENUE: Houston, Tex.   VICTIMS:
   Four
MO: Three women beheaded; boyfriend of one victim
   shot
DISPOSITION: Unsolved

Unknown (Good Samaritan Hospital)
SEX: Unk.   RACE: Unk.   TYPE: S   MOTIVE: Unk.
DATE(S): 1979–80   VENUE: Downer's Grove, Ill.
   VICTIMS: Two

MO: Elderly women killed by insulin injection
DISPOSITION: Nurse suspended without charges; unsolved

Unknown
SEX: Unk.   RACE: Unk.   TYPE: T   MOTIVE: Unk.
DATE(S): 1979–80   VENUE: Mandurah, Australia   VICTIMS: Three
MO: Mutilation-murders of two young women; 12-year-old girl missing
DISPOSITION: Unsolved

Unknown   AKA: Lewiston Valley Killer
SEX: Unk.   RACE: Unk.   TYPE: N   MOTIVE: Unk.
DATE(S): 1979–82   VENUE: Idaho/Wash.   VICTIMS: Five
MO: Three victims dismembered and two missing between Lewiston, Idaho, and Clarkston, Wash.; victims include three young women, one girl, and one man
DISPOSITION: Unsolved

Unknown
SEX: Unk.   RACE: Unk.   TYPE: N   MOTIVE: Unk.
DATE(S): 1979–82   VENUE: Ohio   VICTIMS: Eight
MO: Four young couples killed while out on dates
DISPOSITION: Unsolved

Unknown   AKA: Original Nightstalker
SEX: M   RACE: Unk.   TYPE: T   MOTIVE: Sex./Sad.
DATE(S): 1979–84   VENUE: Orange and Ventura Counties, Calif.   VICTIMS: 10
MO: Victims, usually couples, bludgeoned during home invasions; female victims raped; crimes linked by DNA evidence
DISPOSITION: Unsolved

Unknown
SEX: Unk.   RACE: Unk.   TYPE: T   MOTIVE: GC-cult
DATE(S): 1980s   VENUE: Yunguyo, Peru   VICTIMS: "Numerous"
MO: Seasonal human sacrifices; victims painted/mutilated
DISPOSITION: Unsolved

Unknown
SEX: Unk.   RACE: Unk.   TYPE: T   MOTIVE: Sex./Sad.
DATE(S): 1980   VENUE: Detroit, Mich.   VICTIMS: 18

MO: Street murders of black women, including some prostitutes
DISPOSITION: Conflicting confessions of two suspects leave at least 13 cases unsolved

Unknown
SEX: Unk.   RACE: Unk.   TYPE: T   MOTIVE: CE-felony
DATE(S): 1980   VENUE: Dorchester County, S.C.   VICTIMS: Three
MO: Male gas station employees abducted/shot after holdups
DISPOSITION: Unsolved

Unknown
SEX: Three M   RACE: H   TYPE: T   MOTIVE: CE/Sad.
DATE(S): 1980   VENUE: Los Angeles, Calif.   VICTIMS: Three reported
MO: Victims stabbed after surrendering money in holdups
DISPOSITION: Unsolved

Unknown
SEX: Unk.   RACE: Unk.   TYPE: T   MOTIVE: Unk.
DATE(S): 1980   VENUE: Buffalo, N.Y.   VICTIMS: Two
MO: Black taxi drivers found with hearts excised
DISPOSITION: Unsolved; JOSEPH CHRISTOPHER suspected

Unknown
SEX: Unk.   RACE: Unk.   TYPE: T   MOTIVE: Unk.
DATE(S): 1980–81   VENUE: Jesup, Ga.   VICTIMS: Four
MO: Unexplained deaths of half-siblings with same father
DISPOSITION: Unsolved

Unknown
SEX: M   RACE: Unk.   TYPE: T   MOTIVE: Sex./Sad.
DATE(S): 1980–82   VENUE: Atlanta, Ga.   VICTIMS: Seven+
MO: Black women stabbed repeatedly after sex
DISPOSITION: Unsolved

Unknown
SEX: Unk.   RACE: Unk.   TYPE: T   MOTIVE: Sex./Sad.
DATE(S): 1980–83   VENUE: Adelaide, Australia   VICTIMS: Six
MO: Sex slayer of teenage males; two victims dismembered
DISPOSITION: Unsolved

Unknown   AKA: I-10 Killer
SEX: M   RACE: Unk.   TYPE: N   MOTIVE: Sex.
DATE(S): 1980–90   VENUE: United States   VICTIMS: 20
MO: Female prostitutes and hitchhikers buried in shallow graves along Interstate Highway 10, between California and Florida
DISPOSITION: Unsolved; police suspect long-haul trucker

Unknown
SEX: M   RACE: Unk.   TYPE: T   MOTIVE: Sex.
DATE(S): 1980–98   VENUE: County Wicklow, Ireland   VICTIMS: Six to nine
MO: Six women aged 17–26 missing within a 30-mile area, 1995–98; police theorize links to three rape-murders of women aged 23–30 in same region between 1980 and 1992.
DISPOSITION: Unsolved

Unknown
SEX: Unk.   RACE: Unk.   TYPE: T   MOTIVE: Unk.
DATE(S): 1981   VENUE: Ft. Lauderdale, Fla.   VICTIMS: Three
MO: Murder of black females, age 13–30; at least one bludgeoned
DISPOSITION: Unsolved

Unknown
SEX: M   RACE: W   TYPE: T   MOTIVE: Unk.
DATE(S): 1981   VENUE: Oklahoma City, Ok.   VICTIMS: Four
MO: Girls age 13–16 vanished from Okla. State Fair
DISPOSITION: Unsolved

Unknown
SEX: Unk.   RACE: Unk.   TYPE: T   MOTIVE: Unk.
DATE(S): 1981–82   VENUE: Richland, Ga.   VICTIMS: Three
MO: Teenage girls abducted/killed by nocturnal home invader
DISPOSITION: Unsolved

Unknown
SEX: Unk.   RACE: Unk.   TYPE: T   MOTIVE: Unk.
DATE(S): 1981–83   VENUE: Salem, Ore.   VICTIMS: Six
MO: Random murders of females age nine to 32; at least three shot
DISPOSITION: Unsolved

Unknown
SEX: Unk.   RACE: Unk.   TYPE: T   MOTIVE: Unk.

DATE(S): early 1980s   VENUE: Lahore, Pakistan   VICTIMS: 10
MO: Night watchmen killed with lethal injections
DISPOSITION: Unsolved

Unknown
SEX: Unk.   RACE: Unk.   TYPE: N   MOTIVE: Unk.
DATE(S): 1981–86   VENUE: Utah/Pa./Conn.   VICTIMS: Three
MO: Young men shot; genitals severed and missing
DISPOSITION: Unsolved

Unknown
SEX: M   RACE: Unk.   TYPE: N   MOTIVE: Sex.
DATE(S): 1981–1999   VENUE: Ohio/Pa.   VICTIMS: 27
MO: Female prostitutes, 21 black and six white, killed and dumped nude along isolated roads between Geauga County, Ohio, and Crawford County, Pa.
DISPOSITION: Unsolved

Unknown
SEX: Unk.   RACE: Unk.   TYPE: T   MOTIVE: Unk.
DATE(S): 1982   VENUE: Hollywood, Calif.   VICTIMS: Two
MO: Teenage boys strangled, dumped beside Hollywood Freeway
DISPOSITION: Unsolved

Unknown
SEX: M   RACE: Unk.   TYPE: T   MOTIVE: Sex.
DATE(S): 1980s–2002   VENUE: Northwest Territories, Canada   VICTIMS: 78
MO: Murdered and missing women, cases jointly investigated by Project Kare
DISPOSITION: Unsolved

Unknown
SEX: M   RACE: Unk.   TYPE: T   MOTIVE: Sex.
DATE(S): 1982   VENUE: Toronto, Canada   VICTIMS: Four
MO: Rape-slayer of women age 19–38
DISPOSITION: Unsolved

Unknown
SEX: M   RACE: Unk.   TYPE: T   MOTIVE: Sex.
DATE(S): 1982   VENUE: New York City   VICTIMS: Five
MO: Women age 21–41 strangled; at least one raped
DISPOSITION: Unsolved

Unknown
SEX: M   RACE: Undisclosed   TYPE: T   MOTIVE: Unk.

DATE(S): 1982   VENUE: Los Angeles, Calif.   VICTIMS: Two killed
MO: Random street shootings
DISPOSITION: Unsolved

Unknown
SEX: M   RACE: Unk.   TYPE: T   MOTIVE: Unk.
DATE(S): 1982–83   VENUE: Battle Creek, Mich. VICTIMS: Three
MO: Young women murdered; police suspect Satanists
DISPOSITION: Unsolved

Unknown   AKA: Prostitute Hunter
SEX: Unk.   RACE: Unk.   TYPE: T   MOTIVE: Sex./Sad.
DATE(S): 1982–83   VENUE: Lisbon, Portugal   VICTIMS: Two
MO: Torture-slayer of young female prostitutes
DISPOSITION: Unsolved

Unknown   AKA: Mad Killers of Brabant
SEX: M   RACE: Unk.   TYPE: T   MOTIVE: CE-felony
DATE(S): 1982–85   VENUE: Brabant, Belgium   VICTIMS: 28
MO: Holdup gang; victims killed in supermarket robberies
DISPOSITION: Unsolved

Unknown
SEX: Unk.   RACE: Unk.   TYPE: N   MOTIVE: Unk.
DATE(S): 1982–89   VENUE: N.Mex./Mnt./Okla./Ala. VICTIMS: Four
MO: Roman Catholic priests abducted and murdered
DISPOSITION: Unsolved

Unknown
SEX: Unk.   RACE: Unk.   TYPE: T   MOTIVE: Unk.
DATE(S): 1982–92   VENUE: Ontario, Canada   VICTIMS: Six
MO: Women killed, dumped in rural lover's lanes
DISPOSITION: Unsolved

Unknown
SEX: Unk.   RACE: Unk.   TYPE: T   MOTIVE: Sex.?
DATE(S): 1983–84   VENUE: Alameda County, Calif. VICTIMS: Four
MO: Teenage girls murdered
DISPOSITION: Unsolved

Unknown   AKA: .25-caliber Killer; Penn Station Sniper
SEX: Unk.   RACE: Unk.   TYPE: T   MOTIVE: Unk.

DATE(S): 1983–84   VENUE: New York City   VICTIMS: Seven
MO: Adult males shot with same weapon in/around Pennsylvania Railroad Station in apparently random attacks
DISPOSITION: Unsolved

Unknown
SEX: Unk.   RACE: Unk.   TYPE: T   MOTIVE: Unk.
DATE(S): 1983–84   VENUE: Portland, Ore.   VICTIMS: Four
MO: Stalker of black prostitutes
DISPOSITION: Unsolved

Unknown
SEX: M   RACE: W   TYPE: T   MOTIVE: Sex.?
DATE(S): 1983–91   VENUE: San Francisco area   VICTIMS: Five
MO: Girls age four to 13 abducted and murdered
DISPOSITION: Unsolved (suspect named, but not charged)

Unknown   AKA: Great Basin Killer
SEX: M   RACE: Unk.   TYPE: N   MOTIVE: Sex./Sad.
DATE(S): 1983–97   VENUE: Idaho/Nev./Utah/Wyo. VICTIMS: "At least nine"
MO: Female motorists and hitchhikers stripped, raped, and murdered in patterns of "overkill"; several shot repeatedly with small-caliber firearms; many corpses ritually posed near highways
DISPOSITION: Unsolved

Unknown
SEX: Unk.   RACE: Unk.   TYPE: T   MOTIVE: Unk.
DATE(S): 1983–2004   VENUE: Edmonton, Canada VICTIMS: 18+
MO: Female prostitutes murdered and missing
DISPOSITION: Unsolved

Unknown
SEX: Unk.   RACE: Unk.   TYPE: T   MOTIVE: Unk.
DATE(S): 1984–85   VENUE: Ft. Worth, Tex.   VICTIMS: Five
MO: Females age 15–23 abducted/killed; at least one shot
DISPOSITION: Unsolved

Unknown (Prince Georges Hospital)
SEX: Unk.   RACE: Unk.   TYPE: S   MOTIVE: Unk.
DATE(S): 1984–85   VENUE: Prince Georges County, Md.   VICTIMS: 22–50+

MO: Patients killed with potassium injections
DISPOSITION: Unsolved; nurse Jane Bolding confessed one murder, then recanted; charges dismissed

Unknown
SEX: Unk. RACE: Unk. TYPE: T MOTIVE: Unk.
DATE(S): 1984–85 VENUE: El Paso, Tex. VICTIMS: Three
MO: Taxi drivers killed (one) or missing (two)
DISPOSITION: Unsolved

Unknown
SEX: M RACE: Unk. TYPE: T MOTIVE: Sex.
DATE(S): 1984–85 VENUE: Montreal, Canada VICTIMS: Four
MO: Boys age four to 12 molested, then stabbed, beaten, or drowned
DISPOSITION: Unsolved

Unknown (Gilmore Lane Convalescent Hospital)
SEX: Unk. RACE: Unk. TYPE: S MOTIVE: Unk.
DATE(S): 1984–85 VENUE: Oroville, Calif. VICTIMS: 49 suspected
MO: "Suspicious" deaths of elderly patients
DISPOSITION: Results of investigation unpublished; no charges

Unknown
SEX: Unk. RACE: Unk. TYPE: T MOTIVE: Unk.
DATE(S): 1984–91 VENUE: Galveston County, Tex. VICTIMS: Six
MO: Females aged 16–23 beaten, strangled, and dumped within a one-mile radius
DISPOSITION: Unsolved

Unknown
SEX: M RACE: Unk. TYPE: N MOTIVE: Sex.
DATE(S): 1984–92 VENUE: Ark./Pa./Tenn./Miss./Ky. VICTIMS: Six to 12
MO: Redheaded women strangled/suffocated, dumped along highways
DISPOSITION: Unsolved

Unknown AKA: Bergie Killings
SEX: Unk. RACE: Unk. TYPE: T MOTIVE: Unk.
DATE(S): Mid-1980s VENUE: Cape Town, South Africa VICTIMS: Three+
MO: Male vagrants shot in alleys with same pistol
DISPOSITION: Unsolved

Unknown
SEX: Unk. RACE: Unk. TYPE: T MOTIVE: Unk.

DATE(S): 1985 VENUE: New York City VICTIMS: Two
MO: Older women killed with ax in hotel rooms
DISPOSITION: Unsolved

Unknown
SEX: Unk. RACE: Unk. TYPE: T MOTIVE: Unk.
DATE(S): 1985–86 VENUE: Queens, N.Y. VICTIMS: Three
MO: Hispanic gay males robbed/beaten/strangled in their homes
DISPOSITION: Unsolved

Unknown
SEX: Unk. RACE: Unk. TYPE: T MOTIVE: Unk.
DATE(S): 1985–86 VENUE: Salt Lake City, Utah VICTIMS: Three
MO: Women in their 20s killed stabbed and shot
DISPOSITION: Unsolved

Unknown
SEX: M RACE: Unk. TYPE: T MOTIVE: Sex.
DATE(S): 1985–86 VENUE: Honolulu, Hawaii VICTIMS: 5
MO: Rape-strangler of women
DISPOSITION: Unsolved

Unknown
SEX: Unk. RACE: Unk. TYPE: T MOTIVE: Unk.
DATE(S): 1985–87 VENUE: British Columbia/Alberta, Canada VICTIMS: Five
MO: Murders of female prostitutes and strippers
DISPOSITION: Unsolved

Unknown
SEX: M RACE: Unk. TYPE: T MOTIVE: Unk.
DATE(S): 1985–88 VENUE: San Diego, Calif. VICTIMS: 10+
MO: Slayer of females age 19–36, mostly strangled
DISPOSITION: Unsolved; speculative link to "GREEN RIVER KILLER"

Unknown
SEX: Unk. RACE: Unk. TYPE: T MOTIVE: Sex.?
DATE(S): 1985–90 VENUE: Inkster, Mich. VICTIMS: Six
MO: Black female prostitutes murdered
DISPOSITION: Unsolved

Unknown AKA: Snohomish Valley Killer
SEX: Unk. RACE: Unk. TYPE: N MOTIVE: Unk.
DATE(S): 1985–93 VENUE: Snohomish County, Wash. VICTIMS: 41 suspected

MO: Young women dead and missing, including many prostitutes
DISPOSITION: Unsolved; link to "GREEN RIVER" case possible

Unknown
SEX: M   RACE: Unk.   TYPE: T   MOTIVE: Unk.
DATE(S): 1985–96   VENUE: Atlanta, Ga.   VICTIMS: 10
MO: Female prostitutes murdered
DISPOSITION: Unsolved

Unknown   AKA: Negev Desert Psychopath
SEX: M   RACE: Unk.   TYPE: T   MOTIVE: Unk.
DATE(S): 1985–97   VENUE: Negev Desert, Israel   VICTIMS: Nine +
MO: Hikers shot, apparently at random
DISPOSITION: Unsolved

Unknown
SEX: Unk.   RACE: Unk.   TYPE: N   MOTIVE: Unk.
DATE(S): 1985–2004   VENUE: British Columbia, Canada   VICTIMS: More than six
MO: Six aboriginal women murdered along Highway 16; Native spokesmen accuse police of ignoring 500 disappearances in 20 years
DISPOSITION: Unsolved

Unknown
SEX: M   RACE: Unk.   TYPE: T   MOTIVE: Sex.
DATE(S): 1986   VENUE: Wiltshire/Portsmouth, England   VICTIMS: Three
MO: Strangler of females age 17–36; at least one raped
DISPOSITION: Unsolved

Unknown
SEX: M   RACE: Unk.   TYPE: T   MOTIVE: Sex.
DATE(S): 1986   VENUE: Wiltshire, England   VICTIMS: Three
MO: Rape-slayer of women age 24–45
DISPOSITION: Unsolved

Unknown
SEX: M   RACE: Unk.   TYPE: T   MOTIVE: Sex.
DATE(S): 1986–87   VENUE: Suitland, Md.   VICTIMS: Five
MO: Young black women raped/stabbed
DISPOSITION: Unsolved

Unknown   AKA: Colonial Parkway Killer
SEX: Unk.   RACE: Unk.   TYPE: T   MOTIVE: Unk.
DATE(S): 1986–88   VENUE: Virginia   VICTIMS: Eight
MO: Abducts/kills couples from lover's lanes
DISPOSITION: Unsolved

Unknown   AKA: Twin Cities Killer
SEX: M   RACE: Unk.   TYPE: T   MOTIVE: Sex./Sad.
DATE(S): 1986–94   VENUE: Minneapolis/St. Paul, Minn.   VICTIMS: 34
MO: Murders of women, mostly prostitutes; some mutilated
DISPOSITION: Unsolved

Unknown   AKA: Last Call Killer
SEX: M   RACE: W   TYPE: T   MOTIVE: Sex./Sad.
DATE(S): 1986–94   VENUE: New York City   VICTIMS: Six
MO: Gay men aged 26–57 lured from New York City gay bars, murdered, and dismembered; remains dumped in New York, New Jersey, and Connecticut
DISPOSITION: Suspect Richard W. Rogers Jr. charged with two of six murders in the series; trial pending at press time

Unknown
SEX: M   RACE: Unk.   TYPE: N   MOTIVE: Sex.
DATE(S): 1987   VENUE: London/Colchester, England   VICTIMS: Two
MO: Rape-murders of women age 20 and 25
DISPOSITION: Unsolved

Unknown
SEX: Unk.   RACE: Unk.   TYPE: T   MOTIVE: Unk.
DATE(S): 1987–88   VENUE: Bell, Calif.   VICTIMS: Five
MO: Random shootings of homeless men, age 52–66
DISPOSITION: Unsolved

Unknown
SEX: Unk.   RACE: Unk.   TYPE: T   MOTIVE: Unk.
DATE(S): 1987–88   VENUE: New Orleans, La.   VICTIMS: Five
MO: Women in their twenties strangled or asphyxiated
DISPOSITION: Unsolved

Unknown
SEX: Unk.   RACE: Unk.   TYPE: T   MOTIVE: Cult
DATE(S): 1987–89   VENUE: Mexico   VICTIMS: 70+
MO: Sacrificial murders in Mexico City and Veracruz
DISPOSITION: Unsolved

Unknown
SEX: M   RACE: Unk.   TYPE: T   MOTIVE: Sex.
DATE(S): 1987–91   VENUE: Hartford, Conn.   VICTIMS: 11
MO: Lust killer of women
DISPOSITION: Unsolved

Unknown
SEX: Unk.   RACE: Unk.   TYPE: T   MOTIVE: CE?
DATE(S): 1987–91   VENUE: Snohomish County, Wash.   VICTIMS: Three
MO: Victims dismembered and dumped in rural areas include a Bulgarian crime boss, a Korean female prostitute, and an unidentified male
DISPOSITION: Unsolved

Unknown
SEX: Unk.   RACE: Unk.   TYPE: T   MOTIVE: Unk.
DATE(S): 1987–92   VENUE: Atlanta, Ga.   VICTIMS: Six
MO: Transvestite "drag queens" murdered
DISPOSITION: Unsolved

Unknown
SEX: Unk.   RACE: Unk.   TYPE: T   MOTIVE: Unk.
DATE(S): 1987–96   VENUE: London, England   VICTIMS: Nine
MO: Female prostitutes beaten/strangled
DISPOSITION: Unsolved

Unknown
SEX: M   RACE: Unk.   TYPE: T   MOTIVE: Sex.
DATE(S): 1987–2000   VENUE: Fayetteville, N.C.   VICTIMS: 7–12
MO: Rape-murders of women aged 21–37, most beaten and strangled; at least seven of the victims were prostitutes
DISPOSITION: Unsolved.

Unknown
SEX: M   RACE: Unk.   TYPE: T   MOTIVE: Sex.
DATE(S): Late 1980s–1999   VENUE: Pittsburgh, Pa.   VICTIMS: 12+
MO: Rape-murders of drug-addicted prostitutes blamed on one offender
DISPOSITION: Unsolved

Unknown   AKA: Index Killer
SEX: M   RACE: Unk.   TYPE: T   MOTIVE: Sex.
DATE(S): 1988   VENUE: Seattle, Wash.   VICTIMS: Two to five
MO: Two female prostitutes stabbed in the Index district; two others killed and a missing 14-year-old girl last seen with one victim may be linked.
DISPOSITION: Unsolved

Unknown
SEX: M   RACE: Unk.   TYPE: T   MOTIVE: Sex.
DATE(S): 1988   VENUE: Northern Virginia   VICTIMS: Three
MO: Rape-murders of women in their 20s, linked by DNA evidence
DISPOSITION: Unsolved

Unknown
SEX: Unk.   RACE: Unk.   TYPE: T   MOTIVE: Unk.
DATE(S): 1988   VENUE: San Diego, Calif.   VICTIMS: Three
MO: Gay males killed by multiple head shots
DISPOSITION: Unsolved

Unknown
SEX: M   RACE: Unk.   TYPE: T   MOTIVE: Unk.
DATE(S): 1988   VENUE: Washington, D.C.   VICTIMS: Three
MO: Women beaten/strangled at three-week intervals
DISPOSITION: Unsolved

Unknown   AKA: Highway Killer
SEX: M   RACE: Unk.   TYPE: T   MOTIVE: Sex./Sad.
DATE(S): 1988   VENUE: New Bedford, Mass.   VICTIMS: Nine to 11
MO: Lust killer of women, mainly prostitutes and drug addicts
DISPOSITION: Unsolved

Unknown
SEX: M   RACE: Unk.   TYPE: T   MOTIVE: Unk.
DATE(S): 1988–89   VENUE: Newcastle, Australia   VICTIMS: Two
MO: Female prostitutes strangled
DISPOSITION: Unsolved

Unknown
SEX: M   RACE: Unk.   TYPE: T   MOTIVE: Sex.
DATE(S): 1988–90   VENUE: Ft. Wayne, Ind.   VICTIMS: Two
MO: "Identical" rape-murders of girls age seven and eight
DISPOSITION: Unsolved

Unknown
SEX: Unk.   RACE: Unk.   TYPE: T   MOTIVE: Sex.?
DATE(S): 1988–92   VENUE: Union County, N.J.   VICTIMS: Four
MO: Black female prostitutes killed
DISPOSITION: Unsolved

Unknown
SEX: Unk.   RACE: Unk.   TYPE: N   MOTIVE: Sex.?
DATE(S): 1988–92   VENUE: Fla./Ill./Ky./Minn./Ohio   VICTIMS: Nine+
MO: Women dismembered in at least five states
DISPOSITION: Unsolved

Unknown   AKA: Strangler of Milan
SEX: M   RACE: Unk.   TYPE: T   MOTIVE: Sex.
DATE(S): 1988–92   VENUE: Milan, Italy   VICTIMS:
   Four+
MO: Female prostitutes stabbed/strangled
DISPOSITION: Unsolved

Unknown
SEX: Unk.   RACE: Unk.   TYPE: T   MOTIVE: Unk.
DATE(S): 1988–93   VENUE: Montreal, Canada
   VICTIMS: 11
MO: "Ripper" of gay males killed in their homes
DISPOSITION: Unsolved

Unknown
SEX: Unk.   RACE: Unk.   TYPE: T   MOTIVE: Unk.
DATE(S): 1988–95   VENUE: Southeastern Va.   VIC-
   TIMS: 10
MO: "Ripper" of gay males
DISPOSITION: Unsolved

Unknown   AKA: Happy Loving Couples Killer
SEX: M   RACE: Unk.   TYPE: T   MOTIVE: Unk.
DATE(S): 1988–2000   VENUE: New York City
   VICTIMS: 22–24
MO: Ritual murders of newlywed couples, with throats
   and wrists slashed; victims are bound back-to-back
   in a seated position, each wearing the other's clothes
   backward. Police call the 12th crime, in August
   2000, a copycat's "pale, uninspired imitation" of the
   other 11 attacks
DISPOSITION: Unsolved

Unknown
SEX: M   RACE: B   TYPE: T   MOTIVE: CE
DATE(S): 1989   VENUE: Brooklyn, N.Y.   VICTIMS:
   Two
MO: Elderly women killed in daylight robberies
DISPOSITION: Unsolved

Unknown
SEX: Unk.   RACE: Unk.   TYPE: T   MOTIVE: Unk.
DATE(S): 1989   VENUE: Washington, D.C.   VIC-
   TIMS: Two
MO: Young female prostitutes shot
DISPOSITION: Unsolved

Unknown
SEX: Unk.   RACE: Unk.   TYPE: T   MOTIVE: Unk.
DATE(S): 1989   VENUE: Princeton, N.J.   VICTIMS:
   Two
MO: Women stabbed in apparently random attacks
DISPOSITION: Unsolved

Unknown
SEX: Unk.   RACE: Unk.   TYPE: T   MOTIVE: Unk.
DATE(S): 1989   VENUE: New York City   VICTIMS:
   Four
MO: Hispanic men bludgeoned, left in trash bags
DISPOSITION: Unsolved

Unknown
SEX: Unk.   RACE: Unk.   TYPE: T   MOTIVE: Cult?
DATE(S): 1989   VENUE: Fla. Keys   VICTIMS: Two
MO: Women found with hearts excised; apparent rit-
   ual murders
DISPOSITION: Unsolved

Unknown
SEX: Unk.   RACE: Unk.   TYPE: T   MOTIVE: CE?
DATE(S): 1989   VENUE: Ind.   VICTIMS: Two
MO: Days Inn motel clerks shot with same pistol
DISPOSITION: Unsolved

Unknown
SEX: Unk.   RACE: Unk.   TYPE: T   MOTIVE: Unk.
DATE(S): 1989–90   VENUE: Ala./Fla.   VICTIMS:
   Four
MO: Couples shot by home invader with same gun
DISPOSITION: Unsolved

Unknown
SEX: M   RACE: Unk.   TYPE: T   MOTIVE: Sex.
DATE(S): 1989–90   VENUE: Kansas City, Mo.   VIC-
   TIMS: Six
MO: Slayer of female prostitutes
DISPOSITION: Unsolved

Unknown
SEX: Unk.   RACE: Unk.   TYPE: T   MOTIVE: PC-
   extremism?
DATE(S): 1989–90   VENUE: Lawrence, Kans.   VIC-
   TIMS: Four
MO: Native American victims; further details withheld
DISPOSITION: Unsolved

Unknown
SEX: M   RACE: Unk.   TYPE: T   MOTIVE: Sex.
DATE(S): 1989–90   VENUE: Washington, D.C.
   VICTIMS: Five
MO: Slayer of female prostitutes
DISPOSITION: Unsolved

Unknown
SEX: Unk.   RACE: Unk.   TYPE: T   MOTIVE: GC
   suspected
DATE(S): 1989–91   VENUE: Pará State, Brazil   VIC-
   TIMS: 26

MO: Ritualistic mutilation-murders of boys
DISPOSITION: Unsolved; police blame cultists

Unknown
SEX: Unk. RACE: Unk. TYPE: T MOTIVE: Unk.
DATE(S): 1989–92   VENUE: Monroe County, N.Y.
  VICTIMS: Four
MO: Slayer of female prostitutes and addicts
DISPOSITION: Unsolved

Unknown
SEX: M RACE: Unk. TYPE: T MOTIVE: Unk.
DATE(S): 1989\#208>92   VENUE: Rochester, N.Y.
  VICTIMS: 14–16
MO: Prostitutes murdered and missing
DISPOSITION: Unsolved

Unknown
SEX: Unk. RACE: Unk. TYPE: N MOTIVE:
  Unk.
DATE(S): 1989–99   VENUE:
  Fla./Iowa/La./Minn./Wis./Wyo.   VICTIMS: Eight
MO: Kidnap-murders of females aged 12–52, all with
  blond shoulder-length hair; four found bludgeoned,
  four still missing; five vanished while jogging or
  skating; five kidnapped in proximity to Civil War
  battle reenactments
DISPOSITION: Unsolved

Unknown   AKA: .22-Caliber Killer
SEX: Unk. RACE: Unk. TYPE: T MOTIVE: Unk.
DATE(S): 1990   VENUE: Spokane, Wash. VIC-
  TIMS: Three
MO: Female prostitutes shot with .22-caliber pistol
  and dumped along the Spokane River
DISPOSITION: Unsolved

Unknown
SEX: Unk. RACE: Unk. TYPE: T MOTIVE: Unk.
DATE(S): 1990   VENUE: New York City VICTIMS:
  Four to seven
MO: Taxi drivers shot by apparent "thrill killer"
DISPOSITION: Unsolved

Unknown
SEX: Unk. RACE: Unk. TYPE: T MOTIVE: Unk.
DATE(S): 1990   VENUE: Richmond, Va. VICTIMS:
  "Several"
MO: Black women stabbed
DISPOSITION: Unsolved

Unknown
SEX: Unk. RACE: Unk. TYPE: T MOTIVE: Unk.

DATE(S): 1990–91   VENUE: Oakland, Calif.   VIC-
  TIMS: Two
MO: "Jane Doe" victims dismembered, dumped in
  Oakland Estuary
DISPOSITION: Unsolved

Unknown
SEX: Unk. RACE: Unk. TYPE: T MOTIVE: Unk.
DATE(S): 1990–91   VENUE: Woonsocket, R.I.   VIC-
  TIMS: Three
MO: Female prostitutes strangled
DISPOSITION: Unsolved

Unknown
SEX: Unk. RACE: Unk. TYPE: S MOTIVE:
  Sex./Sad.
DATE(S): 1990–92   VENUE: Houston, Tex.   VIC-
  TIMS: Two
MO: Men bound and murdered S/M-style in same
  vacant house
DISPOSITION: Unsolved

Unknown
SEX: Unk. RACE: Unk. TYPE: T MOTIVE: Sex.?
DATE(S): 1990–93   VENUE: Stockholm, Sweden
  VICTIMS: Seven
MO: Gay males killed; details withheld by police
DISPOSITION: Unsolved

Unknown
SEX: Unk. RACE: Unk. TYPE: T MOTIVE: Unk.
DATE(S): 1990–94   VENUE: Lombardy region, Italy
  VICTIMS: Three
MO: Slayer of three-year-old children between Como
  and Swiss border
DISPOSITION: Unsolved

Unknown   AKA: Golden Years Killer
SEX: Unk. RACE: Unk. TYPE: T MOTIVE:
  Sex./Sad.
DATE(S): 1990–97   VENUE: Richmond, Va.   VIC-
  TIMS: 24
MO: Home invader; beat/stabbed women age 55–90
DISPOSITION: Unsolved

Unknown
SEX: Unk. RACE: Unk. TYPE: T MOTIVE: Sex.
DATE(S): 1990–97   VENUE: Rome, Italy VICTIMS:
  19
MO: Murders of gay men in their homes
DISPOSITION: Unsolved

Unknown
SEX: Unk. RACE: Unk. TYPE: N MOTIVE: Sex.

DATE(S): 1990–97   VENUE: Mich.   VICTIMS: 20+
MO: Murders of female prostitutes
DISPOSITION: Unsolved

Unknown   AKA: Eighth Street Killer
SEX: M   RACE: B   TYPE: T   MOTIVE: Sex.
DATE(S): 1990s   VENUE: Miami, Fla.   VICTIMS: 31
MO: Black prostitutes murdered
DISPOSITION: Unsolved

Unknown   AKA: Monster of the SS 10
SEX: M   RACE: Unk.   TYPE: T   MOTIVE: Sex.
DATE(S): 1990s   VENUE: Piedmont region, Italy   VICTIMS: Seven
MO: Women stabbed/strangled along highway
DISPOSITION: Unsolved

Unknown   AKA: South-Side Rapist
SEX: M   RACE: Unk.   TYPE: T   MOTIVE: Sex.
DATE(S): 1990s   VENUE: St. Louis, Mo.   VICTIMS: Five to 10 (reports vary)
MO: Rape-slayer of women
DISPOSITION: Unsolved

Unknown
SEX: M   RACE: Unk.   TYPE: N   MOTIVE: Sex.
DATE(S): 1990s   VENUE: Idaho/Utah/Nev./Wyo.   VICTIMS: Eight
MO: "Similar" or "identical" murders of women
DISPOSITION: Unsolved

Unknown
SEX: M   RACE: Unk.   TYPE: T   MOTIVE: Sex.
DATE(S): 1990s   VENUE: Aosta, Italy   VICTIMS: "Several"
MO: Female prostitutes murdered
DISPOSITION: Unsolved

Unknown
SEX: M   RACE: Unk.   TYPE: T   MOTIVE: Sex.
DATE(S): 1990s   VENUE: Turin, Italy   VICTIMS: "Numerous"
MO: Slayer of gay men
DISPOSITION: Unsolved

Unknown
SEX: M   RACE: Unk.   TYPE: T   MOTIVE: Sex.
DATE(S): 1990s   VENUE: Turin, Italy   VICTIMS: "Several"
MO: Elderly victims stabbed, one while riding city bus
DISPOSITION: Unsolved

Unknown
SEX: Unk.   RACE: Unk.   TYPE: T   MOTIVE: PC-extremist?
DATE(S): 1990s   VENUE: Turin, Italy   VICTIMS: Seven
MO: Blacks stabbed by apparent racist killer
DISPOSITION: Unsolved

Unknown
SEX: 2 M   RACE: Unk.   TYPE: T   MOTIVE: Unk.
DATE(S): 1991   VENUE: Porterville, Calif.   VICTIMS: Three
MO: Deliberate hit-and-run attacks on joggers and bicyclists
DISPOSITION: Unsolved

Unknown
SEX: Unk.   RACE: Unk.   TYPE: T   MOTIVE: Unk.
DATE(S): 1991   VENUE: Cleveland, Ohio   VICTIMS: Four
MO: Arab-American grocers killed in their stores
DISPOSITION: Unsolved

Unknown
SEX: Unk.   RACE: Unk.   TYPE: N   MOTIVE: Sad.
DATE(S): 1991   VENUE: Ohio/Calif./Va./Md./Pa./Canada   VICTIMS: "At least nine"
MO: Victims burned alive in cars; details withheld by police
DISPOSITION: Unsolved

Unknown
SEX: M   RACE: B   TYPE: T   MOTIVE: Sex.
DATE(S): 1991–92   VENUE: Union County, N.J.   VICTIMS: Eight
MO: Black women strangled
DISPOSITION: Unsolved

Unknown
SEX: Unk.   RACE: Unk.   TYPE: T   MOTIVE: Sex.?
DATE(S): 1991–92   VENUE: Detroit, Mich.   VICTIMS: Nine
MO: Black, drug-addicted prostitutes murdered
DISPOSITION: Unsolved

Unknown
SEX: Unk.   RACE: Unk.   TYPE: T   MOTIVE: Sex.
DATE(S): 1991–92   VENUE: Macon, Ga.   VICTIMS: Five
MO: Lust killer of women
DISPOSITION: Unsolved

Unknown
SEX: Unk.   RACE: Unk.   TYPE: T   MOTIVE: Unk.
DATE(S): 1991–93   VENUE: Marion County, Fla.
   VICTIMS: 18
MO: Women killed, dumped in remote areas
DISPOSITION: Unsolved

Unknown
SEX: M   RACE: Unk.   TYPE: T   MOTIVE: Sex.
DATE(S): 1991–93   VENUE: Calgary, Canada   VICTIMS: Five
MO: Female victims aged 16–29 bludgeoned and stabbed, dumped on city outskirts; four were prostitutes
DISPOSITION: Unsolved

Unknown
SEX: M   RACE: B   TYPE: T   MOTIVE: Unk.
DATE(S): 1991–94   VENUE: Kansas City, Mo.   VICTIMS: 10
MO: Female victims dumped in Missouri River, "many" with legs severed
DISPOSITION: Unsolved

Unknown
SEX: Unk.   RACE: Unk.   TYPE: T   MOTIVE: Unk.
DATE(S): 1991–94   VENUE: Bridgeport, Conn.
   VICTIMS: Four
MO: Adult males dismembered
DISPOSITION: Unsolved

Unknown
SEX: M   RACE: Unk.   TYPE: T   MOTIVE: Sex.
DATE(S): 1991–96   VENUE: New Orleans, La.
   VICTIMS: 26
MO: Women raped, strangled, and dumped in rural areas of several parishes surrounding the city; most victims were black prostitutes
DISPOSITION: Unsolved; suspect Russell Ellwood, once suspected of more than eight murders and charged with two, received a life sentence on one count, Aug. 17, 1999

Unknown
SEX: M   RACE: B   TYPE: T   MOTIVE: CE/PC
DATE(S): 1991–99   VENUE: Columbus, Ohio   VICTIMS: 13
MO: Police link 16 shootings (13 fatal) in one east-side neighborhood; some cases involved robbery and/or drugs
DISPOSITION: Unsolved

Unknown   AKA: "Black Magic Murders"
SEX: Unk.   RACE: Unk.   TYPE: T   MOTIVE: GC suspected
DATE(S): 1991–2002   VENUE: São Luís, Brazil
   VICTIMS: 22
MO: Boys castrated, mutilated, sometimes drained of blood
DISPOSITION: Conviction of two men in separate cases failed to stop the killing; human sacrifice suspected but unverified

Unknown (Truman Memorial Veterans Hospital)
SEX: Unk.   RACE: Unk.   TYPE: S   MOTIVE: Unk.
DATE(S): 1992   VENUE: Columbia, Mo.   VICTIMS: 48
MO: Suspicious deaths of male patients, allegedly injected with muscle relaxants
DISPOSITION: Unsolved; nurse Richard Allen Williams charged with 10 counts of murder in June 2002; exonerated 14 months later when lab tests proved inaccurate

Unknown
SEX: M   RACE: W   TYPE: T   MOTIVE: Sex.
DATE(S): 1992   VENUE: Rostov-on-Don, Russia
   VICTIMS: 8
MO: Lust killer of women; details withheld by police
DISPOSITION: Unsolved

Unknown
SEX: Unk.   RACE: Unk.   TYPE: T   MOTIVE: Unk.
DATE(S): 1992–95   VENUE: Portland, Ore.   VICTIMS: Two
MO: Random shootings wound three, killing two
DISPOSITION: Unsolved

Unknown
SEX: Unk.   RACE: Unk.   TYPE: T   MOTIVE: Unk.
DATE(S): 1992–95   VENUE: Denver, Colo.   VICTIMS: Four
MO: "Ripper" of gay men
DISPOSITION: Unsolved

Unknown
SEX: M   RACE: B   TYPE: T   MOTIVE: CE
DATE(S): 1992–95   VENUE: Chicago, Ill.   VICTIMS: Four
MO: Black men shot in daylight holdups at their homes
DISPOSITION: Unsolved

Unknown   AKA: I-70 Killer
SEX: M   RACE: W   TYPE: N   MOTIVE: CE/PC

DATE(S): 1992–94   VENUE: Ind./Kans./Mo./Tex.
VICTIMS: Six to 10
MO: Victims shot in petty robberies; all but one female
DISPOSITION: Unsolved

Unknown
SEX: Unk.   RACE: Unk.   TYPE: T   MOTIVE: Unk.
DATE(S): 1992/94   VENUE: Milan, Italy   VICTIMS:
Two
MO: Elderly women, stabbed, left in open fields
DISPOSITION: Unsolved

Unknown
SEX: Unk.   RACE: Unk.   TYPE: T   MOTIVE: Unk.
DATE(S): 1992/94   VENUE: Lombardy region, Italy
VICTIMS: Two
MO: Men dismembered and left in trash bags in Milan
and Novara; both victims found on Feb. 17.
DISPOSITION: Unsolved

Unknown
SEX: M   RACE: Unk.   TYPE: T   MOTIVE: Sex.
DATE(S): 1992–95   VENUE: Houston, Tex.   VIC-
TIMS: "Several"
MO: Rape-murders of Hispanic females aged 9–21;
victims left nude
DISPOSITION: Unsolved

Unknown
SEX: Unk.   RACE: Unk.   TYPE: T   MOTIVE: Unk.
DATE(S): 1992–96   VENUE: Charlotte/Mecklenburg,
Va.   VICTIMS: Four
MO: Black women dead or missing; task force organized
DISPOSITION: Unsolved

Unknown   AKA: Lisbon Ripper
SEX: M   RACE: Unk.   TYPE: N   MOTIVE:
Sex./Sad.
DATE(S): 1992–97   VENUE: Europe   VICTIMS: 18
alleged
MO: "Nearly identical" murders of prostitutes in five
nations
DISPOSITION: Unsolved

Unknown
SEX: M   RACE: Unk.   TYPE: T   MOTIVE: Sex.
DATE(S): 1992–97   VENUE: Galveston County, Tex.
VICTIMS: Four
MO: Females aged 17–23 missing and presumed mur-
dered, cars found abandoned
DISPOSITION: Unsolved

Unknown
SEX: Unk.   RACE: Unk.   TYPE: N   MOTIVE: Unk.

DATE(S): 1992–98   VENUE: Ireland   VICTIMS: 12
MO: Disappearance without a trace of women age
18–26
DISPOSITION: Unsolved

Unknown
SEX: M   RACE: W   TYPE: T   MOTIVE: PC-
extremist?
DATE(S): 1993   VENUE: Los Angeles, Calif.   VIC-
TIMS: Three
MO: Street shootings of black/Hispanic males by white
stranger
DISPOSITION: Unsolved

Unknown
SEX: Unk.   RACE: Unk.   TYPE: T   MOTIVE: Unk.
DATE(S): 1993   VENUE: Warsaw, Poland   VIC-
TIMS: Three+
MO: Women bludgeoned in random attacks
DISPOSITION: Unsolved

Unknown
SEX: Unk.   RACE: Unk.   TYPE: T   MOTIVE: Unk.
DATE(S): 1993   VENUE: Chino, Calif.   VICTIMS:
Five
MO: Black females strangled
DISPOSITION: Unsolved

Unknown
SEX: Unk.   RACE: Unk.   TYPE: T   MOTIVE: CE
DATE(S): 1993   VENUE: Cairo, Ga.   VICTIMS:
Two
MO: Store clerks stabbed in robberies
DISPOSITION: Unsolved

Unknown
SEX: M   RACE: Unk.   TYPE: T   MOTIVE: Sex.
DATE(S): 1993   VENUE: St. Louis County, Mo.
VICTIMS: Two
MO: Girls age nine and 10 beaten to death
DISPOSITION: Unsolved

Unknown
SEX: Unk.   RACE: Unk.   TYPE: T   MOTIVE: CE
DATE(S): 1993   VENUE: Indianapolis, Ind.   VIC-
TIMS: Two
MO: Taxi drivers shot in apparent robbery attempts
DISPOSITION: Unsolved

Unknown
SEX: Unk.   RACE: Unk.   TYPE: T   MOTIVE: Unk.
DATE(S): 1993   VENUE: Waycross, Ga.   VICTIMS:
Three

MO: Teen couple and 40-year-old woman shot with
.22-cal. weapon
DISPOSITION: Unsolved

Unknown
SEX: Unk.   RACE: Unk.   TYPE: T   MOTIVE: Unk.
DATE(S): 1993–94   VENUE: Turin, Italy   VICTIMS:
Three+
MO: Teenage girls murdered or missing
DISPOSITION: Unsolved

Unknown
SEX: Unk.   RACE: Unk.   TYPE: T   MOTIVE: CE
DATE(S): 1993–94   VENUE: Washington, D.C.
VICTIMS: 13
MO: Same pistol used in multiple shootings
DISPOSITION: Unsolved

Unknown
SEX: M   RACE: B   TYPE: T   MOTIVE: CE-drugs
DATE(S): 1993–94   VENUE: Indianapolis, Ind.
VICTIMS: Three
MO: Police publicly link multiple shootings
DISPOSITION: Unsolved

Unknown   AKA:Pomona Strangler
SEX: M   RACE: Unk.   TYPE: T   MOTIVE: Sex.
DATE(S): 1993–95   VENUE: Los Angeles County,
Calif.   VICTIMS: Six
MO: Strangler of female prostitutes
DISPOSITION: Unsolved

Unknown
SEX: M   RACE: Unk.   TYPE: T   MOTIVE: Sex.
DATE(S): 1993–95   VENUE: Somerset County, N.J.
VICTIMS: Five
MO: Female prostitutes murdered
DISPOSITION: Unsolved

Unknown (4)
SEX: M   RACE: Unk.   TYPE: T   MOTIVE: Sex.
DATE(S): 1993–99   VENUE: England   VICTIMS: 14
MO: "Operation Enigma" task force studied 207
unsolved murders of women from 1986 to 1999,
concluding in that four unknown serial killers were
responsible for "cluster" slayings of 14 women since
1993 in different parts of England; no further details
presently available
DISPOSITION: All four cases remain unsolved

Unknown
SEX: Unk.   RACE: Unk.   TYPE: T   MOTIVE: Unk.
DATE(S): 1993–2001   VENUE: Bayview, Calif.   VIC-
TIMS: 50

MO: Black women apparently killed at random
DISPOSITON: Unsolved

Unknown
SEX: Unk.   RACE: Unk.   TYPE: T   MOTIVE: Unk.
DATE(S): 1994   VENUE: Irving, Tex.   VICTIMS:
Three
MO: Gay men stabbed
DISPOSITION: Unsolved

Unknown
SEX: Unk.   RACE: Unk.   TYPE: T   MOTIVE: Unk.
DATE(S): 1994   VENUE: Gary, Ind.   VICTIMS: Five
MO: Police report victims killed, then set on fire
DISPOSITION: Unsolved

Unknown
SEX: M   RACE: Unk.   TYPE: T   MOTIVE: Sex.
DATE(S): 1994–95   VENUE: Jackson, Miss.   VIC-
TIMS: Four
MO: Prostitutes strangled after sex
DISPOSITION: Unsolved

Unknown
SEX: M   RACE: Unk.   TYPE: T   MOTIVE: Sex.?
DATE(S): 1994–96   VENUE: Grand Rapids, Mich.
VICTIMS: 11
MO: Slayings of nine prostitutes and two "Jane Does"
DISPOSITION: Unsolved

Unknown
SEX: M   RACE: Unk.   TYPE: T   MOTIVE: Sex.
DATE(S): 1994–97   VENUE: Kent County, Mich.
VICTIMS: 11
MO: Lust murders of women, including eight prosti-
tutes
DISPOSITION: Unsolved

Unknown
SEX: Unk.   RACE: Unk.   TYPE: T   MOTIVE:
Sex./Sad.
DATE(S): 1994–97   VENUE: Maranháo, Brazil
VICTIMS: Seven
MO: Young boys killed, with genital mutilation
DISPOSITION: Unsolved

Unknown
SEX: Unk.   RACE: Unk.   TYPE: T   MOTIVE: Sex.?
DATE(S): 1994–98   VENUE: Essex County, N.J.
VICTIMS: 16
MO: Murders of black women age 19–37, mostly pros-
titutes
DISPOSITION: Unsolved

Unknown
SEX: Unk.   RACE: Unk.   TYPE: T   MOTIVE: CE/PC
DATE(S): 1994–98   VENUE: Albuquerque, N. Mex.
   VICTIMS: Five
MO: Gay men killed by various means, robbed of cash and cars; one victim dumped in Iowa; serial murder "not ruled out"; speculative link to sixth case in Santa Fe
DISPOSITION: Unsolved

Unknown
SEX: M   RACE: Unk.   TYPE: T   MOTIVE: Sex.
DATE(S): 1994–2001   VENUE: Hartford, Conn.
   VICTIMS: 5–11
MO: "Similar" beating deaths of five female transients aged 28–41, found partly nude; three killed in June of different years; police say six other murders of women are "unrelated"
DISPOSITION: Unsolved

Unknown
SEX: M   RACE: W   TYPE: T   MOTIVE: Sex.
DATE(S): 1994–2005   VENUE: Toronto, Ontario
   VICTIMS: Four
MO: Rape-slayer of female prostitutes aged 23–35, bodies discarded in or near Lake Ontario; in 1998 police released sketch of white male suspect who assaulted another prostitute in the same area
DISPOSITION: Unsolved

Unknown
SEX: Unk.   RACE: Unk.   TYPE: T   MOTIVE: Unk.
DATE(S): 1995   VENUE: Shoreline, Wash.   VICTIMS: Two
MO: Female health care workers bound, stabbed, homes set afire
DISPOSITION: Unsolved

Unknown   AKA: Nasrec Strangler
SEX: M   RACE: Unk.   TYPE: T   MOTIVE: Unk.
DATE(S): 1995–96   VENUE: South Africa   VICTIMS: 15
MO: Rape-slayings of women between Johannesburg and Soweto
DISPOSITION: Samuel Mfeka suspected; not charged

Unknown
SEX: Unk.   RACE: Unk.   TYPE: T   MOTIVE: Unk.
DATE(S): 1995–96   VENUE: Las Vegas, Nev.   VICTIMS: Three
MO: Asian women sealed in plastic bags, buried in desert
DISPOSITION: Unsolved

Unknown
SEX: Unk.   RACE: Unk.   TYPE: T   MOTIVE: Unk.
DATE(S): 1995–96   VENUE: Greene County, Ind.
   VICTIMS: Five
MO: Women age 32–88 murdered or missing
DISPOSITION: Unsolved

Unknown
SEX: Unk.   RACE: Unk.   TYPE: T   MOTIVE: Unk.
DATE(S): 1995–97   VENUE: Bothell, Wash.   VICTIMS: Two+
MO: Unidentified human skeletal remains found near town
DISPOSITION: Unsolved

Unknown
SEX: Unk.   RACE: Unk.   TYPE: T   MOTIVE: GC alleged
DATE(S): 1995–97   VENUE: Jalpaigur district, India
   VICTIMS: 100+
MO: Infants and young children abducted and murdered in ritual fashion; 60+ women lynched in retaliation, suspected of surrendering children to cults
DISPOSITION: Unsolved; police blame Tantric ritual practitioners

Unknown   AKA: Latin Jack the Ripper
SEX: Unk.   RACE: Unk.   TYPE: T   MOTIVE: Unk.
DATE(S): 1995–98   VENUE: Perpignan, France
   VICTIMS: Three
MO: Women aged 19 and 22 mutilated near local railway station, with wounds resembling those portrayed in Salvador Dalí paintings; a 17-year-old victim is missing and presumed dead
DISPOSITION: Unsolved; suspect in one case released when crimes continued

Unknown
SEX: M   RACE: Unk.   TYPE: T   MOTIVE: Sex.
DATE(S): 1995–99   VENUE: Chicago, Ill.   VICTIMS: 6–11
MO: DNA evidence links murders of six female prostitutes found in abandoned South Side buildings; in July 1999 police blamed "four predators" for the deaths of 12 local women; three suspects were charged in one case, in Sept. 1999, but initial reports of a DNA link in two other cases proved erroneous
DISPOSITION: Unsolved

Unknown
SEX: Unk.   RACE: Unk.   TYPE: T   MOTIVE: Unk.
DATE(S): 1995–2003   VENUE: Philadelphia, Pa.
   VICTIMS: Four

MO: Suspicious deaths of four children fathered by same man with different women; two daughters, aged 18 months and five months, asphyxiated together in June 1995, ruled homicide without suspects; a three-year-old son allegedly died of SIDS in October 2002, followed by a three-month-old son in December 2003
DISPOSITION: Unsolved; police deny that the father is a suspect

Unknown
SEX: M RACE: Unk. TYPE: T MOTIVE: Sex.
DATE(S): 1996 VENUE: Arlington, Tex. VICTIMS: Two
MO: Female teachers raped and strangled at home, left in bathtubs bound with duct tape; DNA links their killer to a nonfatal rape in Feb. 1999
DISPOSITION: Unsolved

Unknown
SEX: M RACE: B TYPE: T MOTIVE: Unk.
DATE(S): 1996 VENUE: Minneapolis, Minn. VICTIMS: Three
MO: Two prostitutes and one transvestite beaten/stabbed, then burned
DISPOSITION: Unsolved

Unknown
SEX: Unk. RACE: Unk. TYPE: T MOTIVE: Unk.
DATE(S): 1996 VENUE: Estonia VICTIMS: Unk.
MO: Police say serial killer "terrorizing" northeast section of the country; no details released
DISPOSITION: Unsolved

Unknown
SEX: Unk. RACE: Unk. TYPE: T MOTIVE: Sex.?
DATE(S): 1996 VENUE: Johannesburg, South Africa VICTIMS: Two
MO: Elementary school teachers killed, posed "identically"
DISPOSITION: Unsolved

Unknown AKA: Werewolf Killer
SEX: Unk. RACE: Unk. TYPE: T MOTIVE: Unk.
DATE(S): 1996 VENUE: India VICTIMS: 16
MO: Children killed/mutilated
DISPOSITION: Unsolved

Unknown
SEX: Unk. RACE: Unk. TYPE: T MOTIVE: Unk.
DATE(S): 1996 VENUE: Toronto, Ontario VICTIMS: Three
MO: Female prostitutes shot in head with the same gun
DISPOSITION: Unsolved

Unknown
SEX: M RACE: Unk. TYPE: T MOTIVE: Unk.
DATE(S): 1996 VENUE: Perm, Russia VICTIMS: Seven
MO: Rape-slayer of women; at least one stabbed
DISPOSITION: Unsolved

Unknown
SEX: Unk. RACE: Unk. TYPE: T MOTIVE: Unk.
DATE(S): 1996 VENUE: Toronto, Canada VICTIMS: Three
MO: Prostitutes shot on city streets
DISPOSITION: Unsolved

Unknown AKA: Prostitute Killer
SEX: Unk. RACE: Unk. TYPE: T MOTIVE: Unk.
DATE(S): 1996 VENUE: Cape Town, South Africa VICTIMS: "About 20"
MO: Slayer of female prostitutes
DISPOSITION: Unsolved

Unknown
SEX: Unk. RACE: Unk. TYPE: T MOTIVE: Unk.
DATE(S): 1996 VENUE: Malden, Mo. VICTIMS: Four
MO: Two double murders by unknown home invader
DISPOSITION: Unsolved

Unknown
SEX: Unk. RACE: Unk. TYPE: T MOTIVE: Unk.
DATE(S): 1996 VENUE: Hammond, Ind. VICTIMS: Four
MO: Female prostitutes shot with same gun
DISPOSITION: Unsolved

Unknown
SEX: Unk. RACE: Unk. TYPE: T MOTIVE: Unk.
DATE(S): 1996–97 VENUE: Md. VICTIMS: Five
MO: Black gay males stabbed/shot in their homes
DISPOSITION: Unsolved

Unknown
SEX: Unk. RACE: Unk. TYPE: T MOTIVE: GC-cult
DATE(S): 1996–97 VENUE: Siberia, Russia VICTIMS: Five
MO: Authorities blame satanic cult for suffocation/hangings teen males, described as ritual killings
DISPOSITION: Unsolved

Unknown
SEX: Unk. RACE: Unk. TYPE: T MOTIVE: Unk.

DATE(S): 1996–97   VENUE: Perth, Australia   VICTIMS: Three
MO: Women abducted from or near the Continental Hotel
DISPOSITION: Unsolved

Unknown
SEX: Unk.   RACE: Unk.   TYPE: T   MOTIVE: Unk.
DATE(S): 1996–97   VENUE: Brest, Belarus   VICTIMS: Four
MO: Taxi drivers and gas station attendant shot
DISPOSITION: Unsolved

Unknown
SEX: Unk.   RACE: Unk.   TYPE: N   MOTIVE: Unk.
DATE(S): 1996–98   VENUE: Ohio/Ky./Ind.   VICTIMS: 12
MO: Women of "similar age and appearance" killed in tristate area surrounding Cincinnati; 10 counties involved
DISPOSITION: Unsolved

Unknown
SEX: Unk.   RACE: Unk.   TYPE: N   MOTIVE: Unk.
DATE(S): 1996–98   VENUE: Queensland/New South Wales, Australia   VICTIMS: More than three
MO: Slayer of female hitchhikers
DISPOSITION: Unsolved

Unknown   AKA: Claremont Killer
SEX: M   RACE: Unk.   TYPE: T   MOTIVE: Sex.
DATE(S): 1996–98   VENUE: Claremont, Australia   VICTIMS: Four
MO: Blond female prostitutes murdered and dumped in the desert
DISPOSITION: Unsolved

Unknown
SEX: Unk.   RACE: Unk.   TYPE: T   MOTIVE: Unk.
DATE(S): 1996–98   VENUE: Columbus, Miss.   VICTIMS: Five
MO: Elderly victims stabbed and strangled in their homes
DISPOSITION: Unsolved

Unknown
SEX: Unk.   RACE: Unk.   TYPE: N   MOTIVE: Unk.
DATE(S): 1996/1999   VENUE: Mass./Fla.   VICTIMS: Two
MO: Women cut in half "with surgical precision" and left in dumpsters in Boston and Hollywood, Fla.; lower half of Boston victim never found
DISPOSITION: Unsolved; police blame a single killer

Unknown
SEX: M   RACE: Unk.   TYPE: N   MOTIVE: Sex.
DATE(S): 1996–99   VENUE: New England   VICTIMS: Three
MO: Rape-murders of women, dumped nearly nude along rural highways; first two victims were dropped at Norwich and Waterford, Conn.; the third was abducted in Massachusetts and dumped at Vernon, Vt.
DISPOSITION: Unsolved

Unknown
SEX: M   RACE: Unk.   TYPE: T   MOTIVE: Sex.
DATE(S): 1996–99   VENUE: Queensland, Australia   VICTIMS: Three
MO: Female hikers aged 16–20 kidnapped and murdered; police blame "a new IVAN MILAT"
DISPOSITION: Unsolved

Unknown
SEX: M   RACE: Unk.   TYPE: T   MOTIVE: Sex.
DATE(S): 1997   VENUE: Houston, Tex.   VICTIMS: Two
MO: Girls aged nine and 12 killed and dumped naked in local waterways
DISPOSITION: Unsolved; suspect named but never charged in those crimes was later imprisoned for a nonfatal abduction

Unknown
SEX: Unk.   RACE: Unk.   TYPE: T   MOTIVE: Sex./Sad.
DATE(S): 1997   VENUE: Apulia, Italy   VICTIMS: Seven
MO: Elderly women stabbed in their homes
DISPOSITION: Unsolved

Unknown
SEX: M   RACE: B   TYPE: N   MOTIVE: GC-extremist
DATE(S): 1997   VENUE: South Africa   VICTIMS: 13+
MO: White farmers killed by roving black gang
DISPOSITION: Unsolved

Unknown
SEX: Unk.   RACE: Unk.   TYPE: T   MOTIVE: Unk.
DATE(S): 1997   VENUE: Dunbar, South Africa   VICTIMS: "Several"
MO: Police report murder series; all details withheld
DISPOSITION: Unsolved

Unknown
SEX: Unk.   RACE: Unk.   TYPE: T   MOTIVE: Sex./Sad.

DATE(S): 1997 VENUE: Cape Town, South Africa
VICTIMS: Two
MO: Barmaid and prostitute killed/mutilated at Devil's Peak
DISPOSITION: Unsolved

Unknown
SEX: Unk. RACE: Unk. TYPE: T MOTIVE: Unk.
DATE(S): 1997 VENUE: Cape Town, South Africa
VICTIMS: Two
MO: Male vagrants bludgeoned with stones while sleeping
DISPOSITION: Unsolved

Unknown
SEX: M RACE: Unk. TYPE: T MOTIVE: Sex.
DATE(S): 1997 VENUE: Mpumalanga district, South Africa VICTIMS: Two
MO: "Identical" rape-strangulation of women
DISPOSITION: Unsolved

Unknown
SEX: Unk. RACE: Unk. TYPE: N MOTIVE: Unk.
DATE(S): 1997 VENUE: Rome/Florence, Italy VICTIMS: Two
MO: Older, affluent gay males bludgeoned in their homes
DISPOSITION: Unsolved

Unknown AKA: Butcher of Mons
SEX: M RACE: Unk. TYPE: T MOTIVE: Sex./Sad.
DATE(S): 1997 VENUE: Mons, Belgium VICTIMS: Four
MO: Women dismembered, dumped along highways
DISPOSITION: Unsolved

Unknown
SEX: Unk. RACE: Unk. TYPE: T MOTIVE: Unk.
DATE(S): 1997–98 VENUE: Toronto, Canada VICTIMS: reports vary
MO: Six+ victims shoved onto subway tracks; at least one survived
DISPOSITION: Unsolved

Unknown
SEX: Unk. RACE: Unk. TYPE: T MOTIVE: Unk.
DATE(S): 1997–98 VENUE: Humberside, England
VICTIMS: Three
MO: Female prostitutes killed; one dismembered
DISPOSITION: Unsolved

Unknown
SEX: 2 M RACE: Unk. TYPE: T MOTIVE: Unk.

DATE(S): 1997–98 VENUE: South Africa VICTIMS: Five
MO: Six-year-old girls killed and mutilated in small towns south of Johannesburg; police blame a two-man serial-killing team
DISPOSITION: Unsolved

Unknown
SEX: M RACE: W TYPE: T MOTIVE: Sex.
DATE(S): 1997–98 VENUE: Cornwall/Devon, England VICTIMS: Two
MO: Random stabber of females aged 14–42; four attacked, two fatally
DISPOSITION: Unsolved

Unknown
SEX: Unk. RACE: Unk. TYPE: T MOTIVE: Unk.
DATE(S): 1997–98 VENUE: New York City VICTIMS: Four
MO: White male college students aged 19–22 dumped in local rivers (two at the same Hudson River site, five months apart); all were over 6'1" tall, with brown hair and eyes; cause of death undetermined
DISPOSITION: Unsolved

Unknown
SEX: M RACE: Unk. TYPE: T MOTIVE: Sex.
DATE(S): 1997–98 VENUE: Hull, England VICTIMS: Four
MO: Three prostitutes strangled; one missing and presumed dead
DISPOSITION: Unsolved

Unknown
SEX: M RACE: Unk. TYPE: T MOTIVE: Sex.
DATE(S): 1997–99 VENUE: Broward County, Fla. VICTIMS: Five
MO: Women aged 30–44 beaten, strangled, and dumped in public places
DISPOSITION: Unsolved

Unknown
SEX: M RACE: W TYPE: T MOTIVE: Unk.
DATE(S): 1997–99 VENUE: Yorkshire, England VICTIMS: Two
MO: Two women fatally stabbed; two others abducted while walking a dog, escaped with minor knife wounds
DISPOSITION: Unsolved; supporters of defendant Derek Christian, convicted on thin evidence of a similar murder from February 1995, blame one killer for all three slayings

Unknown
SEX: Unk.   RACE: Unk.   TYPE: T   MOTIVE: Unk.
DATE(S): 1997–99   VENUE: San Luis Obispo, Calif.
  VICTIMS: Three
MO: College co-eds missing, presumed murdered
DISPOSITION: Unsolved

Unknown
SEX: M   RACE: W   TYPE: T   MOTIVE: Sex.
DATE(S): 1997–2001   VENUE: Erie, Pa.   VICTIMS:
  Eight
MO: Women aged 18–35 strangled with their own
  underwear and dumped at isolated sites
DISPOSITION: Unsolved

Unknown
SEX: M   RACE: Unk.   TYPE: T   MOTIVE: Sex.
DATE(S): 1997–99   VENUE: Pittsburg, Calif.   VIC-
  TIMS: Four
MO: Female prostitutes killed, dumped beside major
  highways
DISPOSITION: Unsolved

Unknown
SEX: M   RACE: Unk.   TYPE: T   MOTIVE: PC-
  extremist
DATE(S): 1997–98   VENUE: Jerusalem, Israel   VIC-
  TIMS: Two
MO: Seven Arabs stabbed, two fatally; Jewish nation-
  alist suspected
DISPOSITION: Unsolved

Unknown
SEX: Unk.   RACE: Unk.   TYPE: T   MOTIVE: Sex.?
DATE(S): 1997–98   VENUE: Irving/East Orange, N.J.
  VICTIMS: Five
MO: Slayer of black women, mostly prostitutes; offi-
  cially unrelated to similar murders in Newark
DISPOSITION: Unsolved

Unknown
SEX: Unk.   RACE: Unk.   TYPE: T   MOTIVE: Unk.
DATE(S): 1997–98   VENUE: Glasgow, Scotland
  VICTIMS: Seven
MO: Slayer of female prostitutes; at least one bludgeoned
DISPOSITION: Unsolved

Unknown   AKA: River Monster
SEX: Unk.   RACE: Unk.   TYPE: T   MOTIVE: Unk.
DATE(S): 1997–98   VENUE: Transkei, South Africa
  VICTIMS: Seven
MO: Mutilation-murders; victims found in/near Mzint-
  lava River
DISPOSITION: Unsolved

Unknown
SEX: Unk.   RACE: Unk.   TYPE: T   MOTIVE: Cult?
DATE(S): 1997–98   VENUE: Johannesburg, South
  Africa   VICTIMS: 16
MO: Children dead/missing in apparent ritual murders
DISPOSITION: Unsolved

Unknown
SEX: M   RACE: Unk.   TYPE: T   MOTIVE: Sex.
DATE(S): 1997–2001   VENUE: West Country, Scot-
  land   VICTIMS: Three
MO: Police blame one offender for stabbing deaths of
  female victims aged 14–41, killed at Exeter (1997),
  Falmouth (1998), and Dundee (2001)
DISPOSITION: Unsolved

Unknown
SEX: Unk.   RACE: Unk.   TYPE: N   MOTIVE: Unk.
DATE(S): 1997/2003   VENUE: Penn.   VICTIMS:
  Three
MO: 76-year-old woman found in basement of her
  home at Meadville, missing cervical vertebrae and
  internal organs; six years later, Philadelphia police
  find woman and man, aged 64 and 60, with throats
  cut in separate incidents; male victim's heart, lung
  and liver missing
DISPOSITION: Unsolved

Unknown
SEX: Unk.   RACE: Unk.   TYPE: T   MOTIVE: Unk.
DATE(S): 1997–2003   VENUE: Long Island, N.Y.
  VICTIMS: Four
MO: Women left nude, with heads and hands severed;
  three victims found near Long Island Expressway,
  one in Hempstead Lake State Park
DISPOSITION: Unsolved

Unknown
SEX: Unk.   RACE: Unk.   TYPE: T   MOTIVE:
  Unk.
DATE(S): 1997–2004   VENUE: La Crosse, Wis.
  VICTIMS: Seven
MO: White males aged 19–28 drowned in local rivers;
  one victim found with fractured skull
DISPOSITION: Unsolved

Unknown
SEX: Unk.   RACE: Unk.   TYPE: T   MOTIVE: GC
DATE(S): 1998   VENUE: Delmas, South Africa
  VICTIMS: Four
MO: Children beheaded, various organs missing
DISPOSITION: Unsolved; Dr. MICKI PISTORIUS blames
  muti—magic trade in human organs

Unknown
SEX: Unk.   RACE: Unk.   TYPE: T   MOTIVE: GC
DATE(S): 1998   VENUE: Banyuwangi, Java, Indonesia   VICTIMS: 153
MO: Nocturnal home invaders target suspected witchcraft practitioners, slashing their throats and mutilating corpses
DISPOSITION: Unsolved

Unknown
SEX: Unk.   RACE: Unk.   TYPE: T   MOTIVE: PC
DATE(S): 1998   VENUE: Philippines   VICTIMS: Seven
MO: Men beheaded and dumped in rural locations
DISPOSITION: Unsolved; police suggest revenge against alleged rapists

Unknown
SEX: M   RACE: H   TYPE: S   MOTIVE: Sex.
DATE(S): 1998   VENUE: São Paulo, Brazil   VICTIMS: Six
MO: Rape-murders of young women in the Heavenly Garden, near São Paulo's zoo; a seventh victim who survived was lured to the park by a man posing as a professional photographer
DISPOSITION: Unsolved

Unknown
SEX: Unk.   RACE: Unk.   TYPE: T   MOTIVE: PC
DATE(S): 1998   VENUE: Nmadolo, South Africa   VICTIMS: Three
MO: Elderly women suspected of witchcraft, shot in their homes
DISPOSITION: Unsolved

Unknown
SEX: Unk.   RACE: Unk.   TYPE: T   MOTIVE: Unk.
DATE(S): 1998   VENUE: Los Angeles County, Calif.   VICTIMS: Three
MO: Freeway motorists shot in random attacks, two with same gun
DISPOSITION: Unsolved

Unknown
SEX: Unk.   RACE: Unk.   TYPE: T   MOTIVE: Unk.
DATE(S): 1998   VENUE: Indianapolis, Ind.   VICTIMS: Four
MO: Women age 29–40 found killed in same neighborhood
DISPOSITION: Unsolved

Unknown
SEX: Unk.   RACE: Unk.   TYPE: T   MOTIVE: Unk.

DATE(S): 1998   VENUE: Albuquerque, N. Mex.   VICTIMS: Five
MO: Gay men murdered; speculative link to sixth case in Santa Fe
DISPOSITION: Unsolved

Unknown
SEX: Unk.   RACE: Unk.   TYPE: T   MOTIVE: Unk.
DATE(S): 1998   VENUE: Anchorage, Ark.   VICTIMS: Six
MO: Slayer of women; one dead and five missing
DISPOSITION: Unsolved

Unknown
SEX: Unk.   RACE: Unk.   TYPE: T   MOTIVE: Unk.
DATE(S): 1998   VENUE: Woolongong, Australia   VICTIMS: Two
MO: Vigilante killer of convicted pedophiles; victims mutilated
DISPOSITION: Unsolved

Unknown
SEX: M   RACE: W   TYPE: T   MOTIVE: Unk.
DATE(S): 1998   VENUE: Budapest, Hungary   VICTIMS: Three
MO: Men shot at close range in random street attacks
DISPOSITION: Unsolved

Unknown
SEX: Unk.   RACE: Unk.   TYPE: T   MOTIVE: Unk.
DATE(S): 1998   VENUE: London, England   VICTIMS: Two
MO: Women age 30 and 35 bound, shot execution-style
DISPOSITION: Unsolved

Unknown
SEX: Unk.   RACE: Unk.   TYPE: T   MOTIVE: Unk.
DATE(S): 1998   VENUE: Dallas, Tex.   VICTIMS: Two
MO: Truckers shot; attacks linked by police
DISPOSITION: Unsolved

Unknown
SEX: M   RACE: Unk.   TYPE: T   MOTIVE: CE
DATE(S): 1998   VENUE: Moscow, Russia   VICTIMS: 10
MO: Victims killed in carjackings; bodies found buried at a commercial garage
DISPOSITION: Unsolved

Unknown   AKA: Devon Slasher
SEX: Unk.   RACE: Unk.   TYPE: T   MOTIVE: Unk.
DATE(S): 1998   VENUE: Devon, England   VICTIMS: Two

MO: "Ripper" of female victims killed while walking dogs
DISPOSITION: Unsolved

Unknown
SEX: Unk.   RACE: Unk.   TYPE: T   MOTIVE: Unk.
DATE(S): 1998   VENUE: Miami, Fla.   VICTIMS: Two
MO: Gay men shot in their homes
DISPOSITION: Unsolved

Unknown
SEX: M   RACE: Unk.   TYPE: T   MOTIVE: Sex.
DATE(S): 1998–99   VENUE: Charlotte, N.C.   VICTIMS: Five
MO: Black women aged 24–39 murdered and missing
DISPOSITION: Unsolved

Unknown
SEX: M   RACE: Unk.   TYPE: T   MOTIVE: Sex.
DATE(S): 1998–99   VENUE: Campbell County, Tenn. VICTIMS: Two
MO: Female victims stabbed repeatedly, one also shot; bodies dumped along Stinking Creek Road
DISPOSITION: Unsolved; police blame serial killer

Unknown
SEX: Unk.   RACE: Unk.   TYPE: T   MOTIVE: Unk.
DATE(S); 1998–99   VENUE: Norfolk County, Mass. VICTIMS: Three
MO: Two women and one man aged 58–82 beaten and stabbed in separate attacks, in parks and wooded areas of Walpole, Wellesley, and Westwood; all attacked in morning hours
DISPOSITION: Unsolved; suspect in one case released when DNA failed to match saliva from bite mark on a female victim's breast

Unknown
SEX: M   RACE: B   TYPE: T   MOTIVE: Unk.
DATE(S): 1998–99   VENUE: Lusaka, Zambia   VICTIMS: 30–70
MO: Farm residents hacked to death with axes and hoes; victims include the deputy speaker of the National Assembly and his wife
DISPOSITION: Unsolved

Unknown
SEX: Unk.   RACE; Unk.   TYPE: T   MOTIVE: Unk.
DATE(S): 1998–99   VENUE: Rapid City, S. Dak. VICTIMS: Eight
MO: Homeless men drowned
DISPOSITION: Unsolved

Unknown
SEX: Unk.   RACE: Unk.   TYPE: T   MOTIVE: Unk.
DATE(S): 1998–99   VENUE: Sydney, Australia   VICTIMS: Four
MO: Homeless transients bludgeoned while sleeping
DISPOSITION: Unsolved

Unknown
SEX: M   RACE: Unk.   TYPE: T   MOTIVE: Sex.
DATE(S): 1998–2000   VENUE: Boise, Idaho   VICTIMS: Three
MO: Rape-murders of Caucasian women in their 20s
DISPOSITION: Unsolved

Unknown
SEX: M   RACE: W   TYPE: T   MOTIVE: Sex.
DATE(S): 1998–2000   VENUE: Barnaul, Siberia   VICTIMS: 10+
MO: "Several" bodies of female victims discarded in rural areas outside town; at least five college-age victims remain missing; police blame a "maniac" active in the area "for several years"
DISPOSITION: Unsolved

Unknown
SEX: Unk.   RACE: Unk.   TYPE: T   MOTIVE: Unk.
DATE(S): 1998–99   VENUE: Perth, Australia   VICTIMS: Two
MO: Female prostitutes missing, presumed dead
DISPOSITION: Unsolved; task force officers deny any link to the murders of four prostitutes in suburban Claremont during the period 1996–98

Unknown
SEX: Unk.   RACE: Unk.   TYPE: T   MOTIVE: Unk.
DATE(S): 1998–99   VENUE: New Orleans, La.   VICTIMS: Eight
MO: Black males in teens and 20s strangled and left barefoot in garbage bins or beside roads; two victims were neighbors; all were involved with drugs
DISPOSITION: Unsolved

Unknown
SEX: M   RACE: Unk.   TYPE: T   MOTIVE: Sex.
DATE(S): 1998–99   VENUE: Pietermaritzburg, South Africa   VICTIMS: Six
MO: Police blame one man for rape-murders of local women
DISPOSITION: Unsolved

Unknown
SEX: Unk.   RACE: Unk.   TYPE: T   MOTIVE: GC alleged

DATE(S): 1998–99   VENUE: Sundra, South Africa
VICTIMS: Four
MO: Children decapitated over seven months; four
skulls, and three bodies found
DISPOSITION: Unsolved; police blame *muti* practitioners

Unknown   AKA: "Jack the Butcher"
SEX: M   RACE: Unk.   TYPE: N   MOTIVE: Sex./Sad.
DATE(S): 1998–2000   VENUE: Belize   VICTIMS:
Eight
MO: Rape-mutilation murders of girls aged 9–15; a
ninth victim survived in 1999; arrest of a suspect in
the third case failed to stop the killings
DISPOSITION: Unsolved

Unknown
SEX: M   RACE: Unk.   TYPE: T   MOTIVE: Sex.
DATE(S): 1998–2000   VENUE: Accra, Ghana   VIC-
TIMS: 25
MO: Rape-murders of women; bodies left nude and
supine
DISPOSITION: Unsolved

Unknown
SEX: M   RACE: Unk.   TYPE: T   MOTIVE: Sex.
DATE(S): 1998/2003   VENUE: Anne Arundel County,
Md.   VICTIMS: Two
MO: DNA evidence links murders of females aged 37
and 14, killed five years apart at Odenton and
Millersville; one victim raped and stabbed
DISPOSITION: Unsolved

Unknown
SEX: Unk.   RACE: Unk.   TYPE: T   MOTIVE: Unk.
DATE(S): 1998–99   VENUE: Rockhampton, Australia
VICTIMS: Four
MO: Female victims aged 9–39, missing and presumed
dead in four cases
DISPOSITION: Unsolved

Unknown
SEX: Unk.   RACE: Unk.   TYPE: T   MOTIVE: Unk.
DATE(S): 1999   VENUE: Buffalo, N.Y.   VICTIMS:
Two
MO: Female prostitutes aged 32 and 39 stabbed and
strangled on consecutive February days in the same
West Side neighborhood
DISPOSITION: Unsolved

Unknown
SEX: M   RACE: Unk.   TYPE: T   MOTIVE: Sex.
DATE(S): 1999   VENUE: Itabuna, Brazil   VICTIMS:
Four

MO: Women raped, bound, stabbed, and dumped
beside highways
DISPOSITION: Unsolved

Unknown
SEX: M   RACE: A   TYPE: T   MOTIVE: Unk.
DATE(S): 1999   VENUE: Los Angeles, Calif.   VIC-
TIMS: Three
MO: Asian male in early 20s shot eight victims, killing
three, in two different auto accessory stores, in June
and August 1999; nothing stolen in either case
DISPOSITION: Unsolved

Unknown
SEX: M   RACE: Unk.   TYPE: T   MOTIVE: Sex.
DATE(S): 1999   VENUE: Flint, Mich.   VICTIMS:
Seven
MO: Rape-murders of black female prostitutes
DISPOSITION: Unsolved

Unknown
SEX: Unk.   RACE: Unk.   TYPE: T   MOTIVE: Unk.
DATE(S): 1999   VENUE: Anniston, Ala.   VICTIMS:
Five
MO: Three women and two men killed; three victims
shot by home invaders; two dumped outdoors (one
shot, one bludgeoned)
DISPOSITION: Unsolved

Unknown
SEX: Unk.   RACE: Unk.   TYPE: T   MOTIVE: Unk.
DATE(S): 1999   VENUE: Brisbane, Australia   VIC-
TIMS: Four
MO: Four females missing over four months, ages nine
to adult
DISPOSITION: Unsolved

Unknown
SEX: Unk.   RACE: Unk.   TYPE: T   MOTIVE:
Sex./Sad.
DATE(S): 1999   VENUE: Bangkok, Thailand   VIC-
TIMS: Four
MO: Women murdered; three found wrapped in plastic
bags, one in river; police blame "foreign serial killer"
DISPOSITION: Unsolved

Unknown
SEX: Unk.   RACE: Unk.   TYPE: T   MOTIVE: Unk.
DATE(S): 1999   VENUE: Kent, England   VICTIMS:
Three
MO: Police link the double murder of a man and
woman, killed with a shotgun in their Kemsing
home, to the earlier slaying of a man in Durham
DISPOSITION: Unsolved

481

Unknown
SEX: M   RACE: Unk.   TYPE: T   MOTIVE: Sex.
DATE(S): 1999   VENUE: Bahia State, Brazil   VIC-
TIMS: Four
MO: Women aged 19–36 bound, raped, stabbed
repeatedly
DISPOSITION: Unsolved

Unknown
SEX: M   RACE: W   TYPE: N   MOTIVE: Sex.
DATE(S): 1999–2000   VENUE: Calif./Nev.   VIC-
TIMS: Two
MO: Seven-year-old girls murdered in Vallejo, Calif.,
and Las Vegas, Nev.; eight-year-old girl escaped kid-
napper in Vallejo, Aug. 2000
DISPOSITION: Unsolved

Unknown
SEX: M   RACE: Unk.   TYPE: T   MOTIVE: Sex.
DATE(S): 1999–2000   VENUE: Baton Rouge, La.
VICTIMS: Five
MO: Black women aged 33–44 killed and dumped
around town; police withhold cause of death
DISPOSITION: Unsolved; suspect charged in a sixth
similar case reportedly cleared in the other five

Unknown
SEX: Unk.   RACE: Unk.   TYPE: T   MOTIVE: GC
alleged
DATE(S): 1999–2000   VENUE: London, England
VICTIMS: Two
MO: Black men from the same family hanged in
apparent suicides, later deemed racist murders;
both had been harassed by the neo-Nazi group
Combat 18
DISPOSITION: Unsolved

Unknown
SEX: Unk.   RACE: Unk.   TYPE: T   MOTIVE: Unk.
DATE(S): 1999–2000   VENUE: London, England
VICTIMS: Three
MO: Police blame one offender for the disappearance
of three women aged 19–27 apparently snatched
from the street during an 18-month period; one vic-
tim was Vietnamese, one Nigerian, and one Polish
DISPOSITION: Unsolved

Unknown
SEX: M   RACE: Unk.   TYPE: T   MOTIVE: Sex.
DATE(S): 1999–2000   VENUE: Hawaii   VICTIMS:
Three to five
MO: White females aged 38–52 raped and stabbed
repeatedly on Kaua'i; victims include two dead, one

missing, and one survivor; police see possible link to
two similar murders on Oahu in 1999
DISPOSITION: Unsolved

Unknown
SEX: M   RACE: Unk.   TYPE: T   MOTIVE: CE
DATE(S): 1999–2000   VENUE: Washington, D.C.
VICTIMS: Two
MO: Five taxi drivers shot in robberies, two fatally
DISPOSITION: Unsolved

Unknown
SEX: M   RACE: Unk.   TYPE: T   MOTIVE: Sex.
DATE(S): 1999–2000   VENUE: Baton Rouge, La.
VICTIMS: Five
MO: Black prostitutes murdered, bodies discarded in
public places.
DISPOSITION: Unsolved

Unknown
SEX: Unk.   RACE: Unk.   TYPE: S   MOTIVE: PC
DATE(S): 1999–2000   VENUE: Evry, France   VIC-
TIMS: 20–40
MO: "Suspicious" deaths at a medical clinic, described
by officials in April 2001 as "killing for convenience
by overworked staff"
DISPOSITION: No suspects publicly identified

Unknown
SEX: M   RACE: Unk.   TYPE: T   MOTIVE: Sex.
DATE(S): 1999–2000   VENUE: Lipetsk, Russia
VICTIMS: 14
MO: Women raped, beaten, and stabbed, bodies
dumped in nearby forest
DISPOSITION: Unsolved

Unknown
SEX: M   RACE: Unk.   TYPE: T   MOTIVE: Sex.
DATE(S): 1999–2001   VENUE: Moscow, Russia
VICTIMS: Eight
MO: Gay men stabbed repeatedly; victims include four
Russians and four tourists
DISPOSITION: Unsolved

Unknown   AKA: River Man
SEX: M   RACE: Unk.   TYPE: T   MOTIVE: Sex.
DATE(S): 1999–2001   VENUE: Newlands East, South
Africa   VICTIMS: 13
MO: Rape-murders of women, all dumped in the Umh-
langeni River
DISPOSITION: Unsolved

Unknown
SEX: M   RACE: Unk.   TYPE: T   MOTIVE: Sex.

DATE(S): 1999–2002 VENUE: Lawton, Okla. VICTIMS: Four
MO: Women aged 25–29 killed and dumped in creeks or ditches
DISPOSITION: Unsolved

Unknown
SEX: M RACE: Unk. TYPE: T MOTIVE: Sex.
DATE(S): 1999–2003 VENUE: Dade County, Fla. VICTIMS: 13
MO: Murders of female prostitutes aged 21–35
DISPOSITION: Unsolved

Unknown
SEX: M RACE: Unk. TYPE: N MOTIVE: Sex.
DATE(S): 1999–2004 VENUE: Ark./La./Miss./Okla./Tenn./Tex. VICTIMS: 10
MO: Truckstop prostitutes murdered and dumped along interstate highways
DISPOSITION: Unsolved

Unknown
SEX: Unk. RACE: Unk. TYPE: T MOTIVE: Unk.
DATE(S): 1999–2004 VENUE: Lubbock, Tex. VICTIMS: Three
MO: Female prostitutes fatally beaten; two were friends and former roommates
DISPOSITION: Unsolved

Unknown
SEX: M RACE: Unk. TYPE: S MOTIVE: Unk.
DATE(S): 2000 VENUE: Ashfield, Australia VICTIMS: 16 suspected
MO: "Baffling" deaths of 16 patients at Allara Nursing Home in two months
DISPOSITION: Unsolved; coroner's report in May 2003 found "no explanation"

Unknown
SEX: Unk. RACE: Unk. TYPE: T MOTIVE: Unk.
DATE(S): 2000 VENUE: Atlanta, Ga. VICTIMS: Four
MO: Victims shot with same gun along Martin Luther King, Jr., Drive during summer months
DISPOSITION: Unsolved

Unknown
SEX: Unk. RACE: Unk. TYPE: T MOTIVE: Unk.
DATE(S): 2000 VENUE: West Philadelphia, Pa. VICTIMS: Five
MO: Victims of both genders killed and burned in one neighborhood during a five-month period
DISPOSITION: Unsolved

Unknown
SEX: Unk. RACE: Unk. TYPE: T MOTIVE: Unk.
DATE(S): 2000 VENUE: Granite City, Ill. VICTIMS: Two
MO: 21-year-old woman and 46-year-old man found dead in same approximate location over a two-day span in August; both classified as homicides with undetermined cause of death
DISPOSITION: Unsolved

Unknown
SEX: M RACE: Unk. TYPE: T MOTIVE: Sex./Sad.
DATE(S): 2000 VENUE: Budapest, Hungary VICTIMS: Four
MO: Middle-aged prostitutes stabbed
DISPOSITION: Unsolved

Unknown
SEX: M RACE: Unk. TYPE: T MOTIVE: Sex.
DATE(S): 2000 VENUE: Baton Rouge, La. VICTIMS: Six
MO: Rape-murders of six women in three months; at least three victims were prostitutes
DISPOSITION: Unsolved

Unknown
SEX: Unk. RACE: Unk. TYPE: T MOTIVE: Unk.
DATE(S): 2000 VENUE: Baia Mare, Romania VICTIMS: Seven
MO: Homeless transients killed during July and August; six bludgeoned, one drowned
DISPOSITION: Suspect Grigore Bota reportedly confessed two murders in Aug. 2000; disposition of case unknown

Unknown
SEX: M RACE: Unk. TYPE: T MOTIVE: Sex./Sad.
DATE(S): 2000 VENUE: Cape Town, South Africa VICTIMS: Six
MO: Five children murdered and one missing in the Cape Flats district within a month; two girls dismembered
DISPOSITION: Unsolved

Unknown
SEX: Unk. RACE: Unk. TYPE: T MOTIVE: Unk.
DATE(S): 2000 VENUE: Denver, Colo. VICTIMS: Seven
MO: Homeless men beaten to death in Lower Downtown district
DISPOSITION: Unsolved

Unknown
SEX: M   RACE: Unk.   TYPE: N   MOTIVE: Sex.
DATE(S): 2000   VENUE: Norway/Sweden   VIC-
   TIMS: Three
MO: Two girls aged eight and 10 stabbed to death at a
   lake near Kristiansand, Norway, with evidence of
   molestation; three knives found at scene; one week
   later, a similar attack on several girls at Orrefors,
   Sweden, killed one
DISPOSITION: Unsolved

Unknown
SEX: Unk.   RACE: Unk.   TYPE: T   MOTIVE: PC/CE
DATE(S): 2000   VENUE: Houston, Tex.   VICTIMS:
   Six
MO: Immigrant convenience store clerks robbed/shot
   in apparent hate crimes; victims included two Indi-
   ans, two Pakistanis, two Lebanese, and two Viet-
   namese
DISPOSITION: Unsolved

Unknown
SEX: Unk.   RACE: Unk.   TYPE: T   MOTIVE: Unk.
DATE(S): 2000   VENUE: Nairobi, Kenya   VICTIMS:
   Three
MO: Girls, aged 6–10, kidnapped and killed in local
   slum neighborhood; rumors (denounced by United
   Nations) claim 30–50 victims in 12 months; lynch
   mobs killed three suspects in October 2000
DISPOSITION: Unsolved; true number of victims
   uncertain

Unknown
SEX: Unk.   RACE: Unk.   TYPE: T   MOTIVE: Unk.
DATE(S): 2000   VENUE: Houston, Tex.   VICTIMS: 2
MO: Two victims named Mary Morris killed three days
   apart; both left in their cars, parked at isolated sites
DISPOSITION: Unsolved; police blame "a clumsy hit
   man"

Unknown
SEX: Unk.   RACE: Unk.   TYPE: S   MOTIVE: Unk.
DATE(S): 2000   VENUE: Mbabane, Swaziland   VIC-
   TIMS: Five
MO: Corpses found buries at an abandoned homestead
   in July; three identified as an Indian businessman
   and his children, missing for a month; police call it
   the work of a serial killer
DISPOSITION: Unsolved

Unknown
SEX: M   RACE: Unk.   TYPE: T   MOTIVE: Sex.
DATE(S): 2000   VENUE: Durban, South Africa
   VICTIMS: Five

MO: Rape-murders of black women aged 30–40
DISPOSITION: Unsolved

Unknown   AKA: The Ripper
SEX: Unk.   RACE: Unk.   TYPE: T   MOTIVE:
   Sex./Sad.
DATE(S): 2000–01   VENUE: San José, Costa Rica
   VICTIMS: Two
MO: Teenage female prostitutes dismembered, dumped
   in or near the Agres River
DISPOSITION: Unsolved; considered unrelated to "EL
   PSICÓPATA"

Unknown
SEX: Unk.   RACE: Unk.   TYPE: T   MOTIVE: Unk.
DATE(S): 2000–01   VENUE: Broward and Dade
   Counties, Fla.   VICTIMS: Four
MO: Female prostitutes found nude in luggage left
   beside highways or canals
DISPOSITION: Unsolved

Unknown
SEX: M   RACE: Unk.   TYPE: T   MOTIVE: Sex.
DATE(S): 2000–01   VENUE: East St. Louis, Ill.
   VICTIMS: 13
MO: Black female prostitutes and addicts murdered,
   several covered with plastic trash bags
DISPOSITION: Unsolved

Unknown
SEX: Unk.   RACE: Unk.   TYPE: T   MOTIVE: Unk.
DATE(S): 2000–01   VENUE: Dade County, Fla.
   VICTIMS: Two or three
MO: Two female prostitutes stabbed repeatedly and
   dumped in local waterways; a third prostitute stran-
   gled and left on land may be linked
DISPOSITION: Unsolved

Unknown
SEX: M   RACE: Unk.   TYPE: T   MOTIVE: Sex.
DATE(S): 2000–02   VENUE: Norwich, England
   VICTIMS: Four
MO: Three female prostitutes strangled, one missing
DISPOSITION: Unsolved

Unknown
SEX: M   RACE: Unk.   TYPE: T   MOTIVE:
   Sex./Sad.
DATE(S): 2000–04   VENUE: Chihuahua City, Mexico
   VICTIMS: 16
MO: Ten teenage females raped and strangled, with at
   least six others missing
DISPOSITION: Unsolved; some observers suspect a
   link to ongoing murders in CIUDAD JUÁREZ

Unknown
SEX: M   RACE: Unk.   TYPE: T   MOTIVE: Sex.
DATE(S): 2000–04   VENUE: Peoria, Ill.   VICTIMS:
  Six
MO: Rape-slayer of black female prostitutes
DISPOSITION: Unsolved

Unknown   AKA: Blanco
SEX: M   RACE: Unk.   TYPE: T/N   MOTIVE:
  PC/Sex.
DATE(S): 2001   VENUE: Guatemala City, Guatemala
  VICTIMS: Five to seven
MO: Prostitutes smothered with sheets of plastic; mes-
  sages written on bodies claim seven dead and
  describe the killer's "pact with Lucifer"
DISPOSITION: Unsolved; some officials suspect the
  same UNSUB of one killing in El Salvador; police in
  Los Angeles deny published reports of two similar
  murders there

Unknown
SEX: Unk.   RACE: Unk.   TYPE: N   MOTIVE: GC
  suspected
DATE(S): 2001   VENUE: Honduras   VICTIMS: Six
MO: Young boys abducted from rural towns, one
  found beheaded; police blame a gang, "Los
  Rockeros," alleged to practice Satanism
DISPOSITION: Unsolved

Unknown
SEX: Unk.   RACE: Unk.   TYPE: T   MOTIVE: Unk.
DATE(S): 2001   VENUE: Pierce County, Wash.   VIC-
  TIMS: Two
MO: Women aged 73 and 77 fatally beaten in their
  homes, one month apart
DISPOSITION: Unsolved

Unknown
SEX: Unk.   RACE: Unk.   TYPE: T   MOTIVE: Unk.
DATE(S): 2001   VENUE: Durban, South Africa
  VICTIMS: Seven
MO: Skeletal remains of six women in their 30s and
  one infant found in sugarcane fields; some bodies
  burned
DISPOSITION: Unsolved

Unknown
SEX: Unk.   RACE: Unk.   TYPE: T   MOTIVE:
  Sex./Sad.
DATE(S): 2001   VENUE: London, England   VIC-
  TIMS: Two
MO: Female prostitutes aged 24 and 31 dismembered
  and dumped in rivers
DISPOSITION: Unsolved

Unknown
SEX: Unk.   RACE: Unk.   TYPE: T   MOTIVE: Unk.
DATE(S): 2001   VENUE: Lombata, Swaziland   VIC-
  TIMS: 24–33
MO: Women and children found in shallow graves out-
  side town; official reports differ on the total number
  of victims
DISPOSITION: Unsolved

Unknown
SEX: Unk.   RACE: Unk.   TYPE: N   MOTIVE:
  GC?
DATE(S): 2001   VENUE: India   VICTIMS: 586
MO: Two caches of skeletal remains found in June and
  July include 500 skulls and other bones at an aban-
  doned house in Calcutta, with 86 skulls found in
  Siliguri, 375 miles farther north
DISPOSITION: Unsolved; police blame Tantric ritual
  practitioners

Unknown   AKA: Anthrax Killer
SEX: Unk.   RACE: Unk.   TYPE: N   MOTIVE: Unk.
DATE(S): 2001   VENUE: Eastern United States   VIC-
  TIMS: Five
MO: Anthrax spores mailed to various targets along
  the Eastern Seaboard between Oct. 4 and Nov. 21,
  2001; 46 persons infected, five fatally
DISPOSITION: Unsolved

Unknown
SEX: M   RACE: Unk.   TYPE: T   MOTIVE:
  Sex./Sad.
DATE(S): 2001–02   VENUE: Boston, Mass.   VIC-
  TIMS: Two
MO: "Similar" murders of prostitutes aged 17 and 19
DISPOSITION: Unsolved

Unknown
SEX: Unk.   RACE: Unk.   TYPE: T   MOTIVE: Unk.
DATE(S): 2001–02   VENUE: Boston, Mass.   VIC-
  TIMS: Two
MO: Teenage female prostitutes, throats slashed
DISPOSITION: Unsolved

Unknown
SEX: Unk.   RACE: Unk.   TYPE: T   MOTIVE:
  Sex./Sad.
DATE(S): 2001–02   VENUE: Moscow, Russia   VIC-
  TIMS 12+
MO: Official reports from November 2002 mention
  "at least a dozen" women murdered, either stran-
  gled or with throats slashed
DISPOSITION: Unsolved

Unknown

SEX: Unk. RACE: Unk. TYPE: T MOTIVE: Sex. assumed

DATE(S): 2001–03 VENUE: Worcester, Mass. VICTIMS: Three

MO: Kidnap-murders of petite female Hispanic prostitutes, dumped along I-290; two victims were acquainted from a drug rehab program

DISPOSITION: Unsolved

Unknown

SEX: M RACE: W TYPE: T MOTIVE: Sex.

DATE(S): 2001/2004 VENUE: Port Elizabeth, South Africa VICTIMS: Four

MO: Four black women strangled in 2001, one in April 2004; at least four were known prostitutes

DISPOSITION: Unsolved; police blame a serial killer

Unknown

SEX: M RACE: Unk. TYPE: T MOTIVE: Sex.

DATE(S): 2002 VENUE: Houston, Tex. VICTIMS: Three

MO: DNA links rape-murders of Hispanic females, aged 15–38, in the same East End neighborhood

DISPOSITION: Unsolved

Unknown

SEX: M RACE: W TYPE: T MOTIVE: Unk.

DATE(S): 2002 VENUE: Botshabelo, South Africa VICTIMS: Three

MO: Young boys strangled, dumped at different sites in same general area; all last seen with tall, thin man with dark complexion

DISPOSITION: Unsolved

Unknown

SEX: Unk. RACE: Unk. TYPE: N MOTIVE: Unk.

DATE(S): 2002 VENUE: Minn./Wisc. VICTIMS: Four

MO: College students aged 20–22 missing from four separate towns during October and November; victims include three men and one woman; all still missing

DISPOSITION: Unsolved

Unknown

SEX: Unk. RACE: Unk. TYPE: T MOTIVE: Unk.

DATE(S): 2002 VENUE: Maricopa County, Ariz. VICTIMS: Eight

MO: Male Mexican migrants handcuffed and shot execution style in serial attacks, March to October; bodies left exposed in the desert

DISPOSITION: Unsolved

Unknown

SEX: Unk. RACE: Unk. TYPE: T MOTIVE: Unk.

DATE(S): 2002 VENUE: Southern Florida VICTIMS: Four

MO: Decomposed bodies found in coastal waters near Key Largo and Palm Beach County, with no evidence of boat mishaps; all unidentified

DISPOSITION: Unsolved

Unknown

SEX: Unk. RACE: Unk. TYPE: T MOTIVE: Unk.

DATE(S): 2002–03 VENUE: Ahmedabad, India VICTIMS: 35–40

MO: Street children murdered and missing; some victims last seen entering a white van at the town's railroad depot

DISPOSITION: Unsolved

Unknown

SEX: Unk. RACE: Unk. TYPE: T MOTIVE: Unk.

DATE(S): 2002–03 VENUE: Phoenix, Ariz. VICTIMS: Six

MO: Women aged 32–46 killed and dumped in Garfield neighborhood; all but one found nude; four with evidence of drugs

DISPOSITION: Unsolved

Unknown

SEX: 2 M RACE: Unk. TYPE: T MOTIVE: CE-felony

DATE(S): 2002–04 VENUE: Ngong, Kenya VICTIMS: 20

MO: Victims shot in nocturnal armed robberies; police blame a two-man team for the crimes

DISPOSITION: Unsolved

Unknown

SEX: Unk. RACE: Unk. TYPE: T MOTIVE: Unk.

DATE(S): 2003 VENUE: White River, South Africa VICTIMS: Two

MO: Girls aged 12 and 15 found beside a local railroad line two days apart, in January; throats cut with "the same instrument"

DISPOSITION: Unsolved

Unknown

SEX: Unk. RACE: Unk. TYPE: T MOTIVE: Unk.

DATE(S): 2003 VENUE: Jacksonville, Fla. VICTIMS: Two

MO: Teenage females vanished 10 days apart in January; found together at a construction site on Feb. 5

DISPOSITION: Unsolved

Unknown

SEX: M RACE: W TYPE: T MOTIVE: CE

DATE(S): 2003   VENUE: Samara, Russia   VICTIMS: 15

MO: Women aged 35–50 bludgeoned and robbed of their handbags; two victims survived, describing a long-faced man with a black hat

DISPOSITION: Unsolved

Unknown   AKA: Saturday Slayers
SEX: 2 M   RACE: B   TYPE: T   MOTIVE: PC
DATE(S): 2003   VENUE: Brooklyn, N.Y.   VICTIMS: Five

MO: Male victims shot execution-style in public places; police call the crimes "thrill killings" with robbery "as an afterthought"; all but one crime committed on Saturday

DISPOSITION: Unsolved

Unknown
SEX: Unk.   RACE: Unk.   TYPE: T   MOTIVE: PC/CE
DATE(S): 2003   VENUE: Lahore, Pakistan   VICTIMS: Six

MO: "Identical" bludgeon murders of male victims sleeping outside, attacked between 2 and 3 A.M., with petty robbery in some cases. Victims include night watchmen, vendors, and truckers, killed within a one-mile radius on Ravi Road

DISPOSITION: Unsolved

Unknown
SEX: Unk.   RACE: Unk.   TYPE: T   MOTIVE: Unk.
DATE(S): 2003   VENUE: Charleston, W. Va.   VICTIMS: Three

MO: Sniper slayings of two men and one woman aged 26–34 in public places; same weapon used in all three crimes

DISPOSITION: Unsolved

Unknown
SEX: Unk.   RACE: Unk.   TYPE: T   MOTIVE: Unk.
DATE(S): 2003   VENUE: Anchorage, Ak.   VICTIMS: Two

MO: Torsos of women washed ashore in June and November; one victim identified

DISPOSITION: Unsolved

Unknown
SEX: Unk.   RACE: Unk.   TYPE: T   MOTIVE: CE/PC
DATE(S): 2003   VENUE: Indianapolis, Ind.   VICTIMS: Two

MO: Immigrant grocers robbed/shot, a week apart
DISPOSITION: Unsolved

Unknown
SEX: M   RACE: Unk.   TYPE: T   MOTIVE: Sex.
DATE(S): 2003   VENUE: Moscow, Russia   VICTIMS: 12

MO: Women beaten and strangled during July, left nude in a north-side neighborhood; several sexually assaulted without actual rape; no robberies

DISPOSITION: Unsolved; police deem the 30-day rash of identical slayings "coincidental"

Unknown
SEX: M   RACE: Unk.   TYPE: T   MOTIVE: Sex.
DATE(S): 2003   VENUE: Edmonton, Canada   VICTIMS: Two

MO: Prostitutes murdered one week apart
DISPOSITION: Unsolved

Unknown
SEX: M   RACE: Unk.   TYPE: T   MOTIVE: Sex./Sad.
DATE(S): 2003   VENUE: Guatemala City, Guatemala   VICTIMS: 10

MO: Young girls tortured to death; two bodies left together in each case

DISPOSITION: Unsolved

Unknown
SEX: Unk.   RACE: Unk.   TYPE: T   MOTIVE: Unk.
DATE(S): 2003   VENUE: Marlboro, England   VICTIMS: Two

MO: Skeletal remains of two adults (one female) found at a boarding school within a week; date and cause of death undetermined

DISPOSITION: Unsolved

Unknown
SEX: Unk.   RACE: Unk.   TYPE: T   MOTIVE: PC/CE
DATE(S): 2003   VENUE: New York City   VICTIMS: "At least five"

MO: Arab merchants shot in bodega robberies; police blame at least three crimes on one killer

DISPOSITION: Unsolved

Unknown
SEX: Unk.   RACE: Unk.   TYPE: T   MOTIVE: Unk.
DATE(S): 2003   VENUE: Galfingue Forest, France   VICTIMS: Four

MO: Newborn infants found dead in trash bags
DISPOSITION: Unsolved

Unknown
SEX: Unk.   RACE: Unk.   TYPE: T   MOTIVE: CE
DATE(S): 2003–04   VENUE: Mexico City, Mexico   VICTIMS: Three

MO: Elderly women robbed, strangled in their homes
DISPOSITION: Unsolved

Unknown
SEX: Unk.　RACE: Unk.　TYPE: N　MOTIVE: Unk.
DATE(S): 2003–04　VENUE: Ariz./Calif.　VICTIMS: Four
MO: Camping couples shot execution-style in their sleeping bags, with no signs of robbery or struggle; first murder at Bumble Bee, Ariz. (Oct. 2003); second crime in Sonoma County, Calif. (Aug. 2004)
DISPOSITION: Unsolved

Unknown
SEX: M　RACE: Unk.　TYPE: T　MOTIVE: Sex.
DATE(S): 2003–04　VENUE: Worcester, Mass.　VICTIMS: Four
MO: Rape-murders of petite Hispanic prostitutes, all drug addicts; bodies dumped in wooded areas, one in Maine
DISPOSITION: Unsolved

Unknown
SEX: M　RACE: Undisclosed　TYPE: T　MOTIVE: Sex.
DATES: 2003–04　VENUE: Baltimore, Md.　VICTIMS: Three
MO: Rapist of female prostitutes; attacked 15 victims, killing three aged 19–32; slain victims beaten and strangled
DISPOSITION: Unsolved

Unknown　AKA: Little Old Lady Killer
SEX: Unk.　RACE: Unk.　TYPE: T　MOTIVE: Unk.
DATE(S): 2003–04　VENUE: Mexico City　VICTIMS: 18
MO: Women aged 65–80 beaten and strangled in their homes, with no signs of forced entry to houses
DISPOSITION: Unsolved

Unknown
SEX: M　RACE: Unk.　TYPE: T　MOTIVE: Sex.
DATE(S): 2004　VENUE: Philadelphia, Pa.　VICTIMS: Three
MO: Females "known to police" aged 24–31 strangled and left nude, two bodies in trash bins, during January and February
DISPOSITION: Unsolved

Unknown
SEX: Unk.　RACE: Unk.　TYPE: T　MOTIVE: GC alleged

DATE(S): 2004　VENUE: Muridke, Pakistan　VICTIMS: Three
MO: Children aged five to eight stabbed repeatedly; a fourth victim survived
DISPOSITION: Unsolved; police blame black-magic practitioners

Unknown
SEX: M　RACE: Unk.　TYPE: T　MOTIVE: Sex.
DATE(S): 2004　VENUE: Bronx, N.Y.　VICTIMS: Two
MO: Hispanic women in their 30s stripped and strangled in abandoned buildings
DISPOSITION: Unsolved

Unknown
SEX: Unk.　RACE: Unk.　TYPE: T　MOTIVE: GC alleged
DATE(S): 2004　VENUE: Marowa, Zimbabwe　VICTIMS: "Several"
MO: Mutilation-murders of young children, with some victims raped
DISPOSITION: Unsolved; locals blame black-magic practitioners

Unknown
SEX: Unk.　RACE: Unk.　TYPE: T　MOTIVE: Unk.
DATE(S): 2004　VENUE: Kansas City, Mo.　VICTIMS: Six
MO: Black women aged 25–45 killed in the same neighborhood, cause of death undisclosed; police blame one offender for all six cases
DISPOSITION: Suspect Terry Blair, charged in one case, previously served 21 years for the 1983 murder of his pregnant ex-girlfriend; trial pending

Unknown
SEX: Unk.　RACE: Unk.　TYPE: T　MOTIVE: Unk.
DATE(S): 2004　VENUE: London, England　VICTIMS: Two
MO: Hammer attacks on five women, killing two on public streets
DISPOSITION: Unsolved

Unknown
SEX: Unk.　RACE: Unk.　TYPE: T　MOTIVE: Unk.
DATE(S): 2004　VENUE: Caracas, Venezuela　VICTIMS: Nine
MO: Homeless victims, including eight men and one woman, beaten to death with large stones as they slept
DISPOSITION: Unsolved

Bibliography

Ablow, Keith. *Without Mercy.* New York: Free Press, 1994.

Abrahamsen, David. *Confessions of Son of Sam.* New York: Columbia University Press, 1985.

———. *Murder and Madness.* London: Robson Books, 1992.

———. *The Murdering Mind.* New York: Harper & Row, 1973.

Adam, H. L. *Trial of George Chapman.* London: William Hodge, 1930.

Adams, Terry. *Eye of the Beast.* New York: St. Martin's Press, 1998.

Adleman, Robert. *The Bloody Benders.* New York: Stein & Day, 1970.

Adams, Terry, Mary Brooks-Mueller, and Scott Shaw. *Eye of the Beast.* Omaha: Addicus Books, 1998.

Alibrandi, Tom, and Frank Armani. *Privileged Information.* New York: HarperCollins, 1984.

Allen, William. *Starkweather.* Boston, Houghton Mifflin, 1967.

Altman, Jack, and Martin Ziporyn. *Born to Raise Hell.* New York: Grove, 1967.

Anderson, Chris, and Sharon McGehee. *Bodies of Evidence.* New York: Lyle Stuart, 1991.

Anderson, Frank. *The Dark Strangler.* Calgary: Frontier, 1974.

Angelella, Michael. *Trail of Blood.* New York: New American Library, 1979.

Anonymous. *Compulsion to Kill.* Arlington, Va.: Time-Life Books, 1993.

———. *Gary Ridgway.* Bellevue, Wa.: King County Journal, 2003.

———. *Murder and Mayhem.* New York: Signet, 1991.

———. *Narrative and Confession of Lucretia P. Cannon.* New York: n.p., 1841.

———. *The Poison Fiend.* Philadelphia: Barclay & Co., 1872.

———. *Serial Killers.* Arlington, Va.: Time-Life Books, 1992.

———. *Truth Stranger than Fiction: Lydia Sherman.* Philadelphia: T. R. Callenden, 1873.

———. *Unsolved Crimes.* Arlington, Va.: Time-Life Books, 1993.

Appleton, Arthur. *Mary Ann Cotton.* London: Michael Joseph, 1973.

Apsche, Jack. *Probing the Mind of a Serial Killer.* Morrisville, Penn.: International Information Associates, 1993.

Aronson, Theo. *Prince Eddy and the Homosexual Underworld.* New York: Barnes & Noble, 1994.

Badal, James. *In the Wake of the Butcher.* Kent, Ohio: Kent State University Press, 2001.

Baden, Michael. *Unnatural Death.* New York: Ivy Books, 1989.

Baer, Rosemary. *Reflection on the Manson Trial.* Waco, Tx.: Word, 1972.

Bakos, Susan. *Appointment for Murder.* New York: Putnam, 1989.

Baldwin, James. *The Evidence of Things Not Seen.* New York: Holt, 1995.

Ball, Pamela. *Jack the Ripper: A Psychic Investigation.* Leicester: Arcturus Publishing, 1998.

Banks, Harold. *The Strangler!* New York: Avon, 1967.

Bardens, Dennis. *The Ladykiller.* London: P. Davies, 1972.

Barer, Burl. *Body Count.* New York: Pinnacle, 2002.

Barnard, Allan. *The Harlot Killer.* New York: Dodd, Mead, 1953.

Bartlett, Evan. *Love Murders of Harry F. Powers.* New York: Sheftel Press, 1931.

Bataille, Georges. *The Trial of Gilles de Rais.* Paris: Jean-Jacques Pauvert, 1965.

Baumann, Ed. *Step Into My Parlor.* Chicago: Bonus Books, 1991.

Beadle, William. *Jack the Ripper: Anatomy of a Myth.* Dagenham, England: Wat Tyler Books, 1995.

Beattie, John. *The Yorkshire Ripper.* London: Quartet/Daily Star, 1981.

Becker, Audrey. *Dying Dreams.* New York: Pocket Books, 1993.

Bedford, Sybille. *The Trial of Dr. Adams.* New York: Time, 1958.

Begg, Paul. *Jack the Ripper.* London: Robson Books, 1988.

———. *Jack the Ripper: The Definitive History.* Harlow, England: Longman, 2002.

Begg, Paul, Martin Fido, and Keith Skinner. *The Jack the Ripper A–Z.* London: Headline, 1996.

Bellini, John. *The Babyface Killer.* New York: Pinnacle, 2002.

Benedetti, Jean. *The Real Bluebeard.* New York: Stein & Day, 1972.

Berg, Karl. *The Sadist.* London: Heinemann, 1932.

Berkowitz, David. *The "Son of Sam."* Edison, N.J.: American Focus Publishing, 1998.

Berry-Dee, Christopher. *Talking with Serial Killers.* London: Blake, 2002.

Bilton, Michael. *Wicked Beyond Belief.* London: HarperCollins, 2002.

Bingham, John, and William Muncie. *The Hunting Down of Peter Manuel, Glasgow Multiple Murderer.* London: Macmillan, 1971.

Biondi, Ray, and Walt Hecox. *All His Father' Sins.* New York: Pocket Books, 1988.

———. *The Dracula Killer.* New York: Pocket Books, 1992.

Bishop, George. *Witness to Evil.* Los Angeles: Nash Publishing, 1971.

Blackburn, Daniel. *Human Harvest.* Los Angeles: Knightsbridge, 1990.

Blandford, Neil, and Bruce Jones. *The World's Most Evil Men.* New York: Berkley, 1990.

Bledsoe, Jerry. *Before He Wakes.* New York: Onyx, 1994.

———. *Bitter Blood.* New York: E. P. Dutton, 1988.

———. *Death Sentence.* New York: Dutton, 1998.

Blundell, Nigel. *Encyclopedia of Serial Killers.* London: J. G. Press, 1996.

Boar, Roger, and Nigel Blundell. *The World's Most Infamous Murderers.* New York: Exeter Books, 1983.

Bortnick, Barry. *Deadly Urges.* New York: Pinnacle, 1997.

Boswell, Charles, and Lewis Thompson. *The Girls in Nightmare House.* New York: Gold Medal, 1955.

Bowe, Barry. *Born to Be Wild.* New York: Warner, 1994.

Bradlee, Ben, Jr., and Dale Van Atta. *Prophet of Blood.* New York: Putnam, 1981.

Brady, Ian. *The Gates of Janus.* London: Turnaround, 2001.

Braidhill, Kathy. *Evil Secrets.* New York: Pinnacle, 1996.

———. *To Die For.* New York: St. Martin's Press, 2000.

Bravin, Jess. *Squeaky.* New York: Buzz Books, 1997.

Breo, Dennis, and William Martin. *The Crime of the Century.* New York: Bantam, 1993.

Briffett, David. *The Acid Bath Murders.* Sussex, England: Field Place Press, 1988.

Brinck, Gretchen. *The Boy Next Door.* New York: Kensington, 1999.

Brown, Pat. *Killing for Sport.* Beverly Hills, Calif.: New Millennium Press, 2003.

Brown, Wenzell. *Introduction to Murder.* New York: Greenberg, 1952.

Bruno, Anthony. *The Ice Man.* New York: Dell, 1993.

Brussel, James. *Casebook of a Crime Psychiatrist.* New York: Bernard Geis, 1968.

Bryne, Gerald. *John George Haigh, Acid Killer.* London: J. Hill, 1954.

Buck, Pearl. *The Honeymoon Killers.* London: Sphere Books, 1970.

Bugliosi, Vincent, and Curt Gentry. *Helter Skelter.* New York: Norton, 1974.

Burn, Gordon. *Happy Like Murderers.* London: Faber & Faber, 1999.

———. *Somebody's Husband, Somebody's Son.* New York: Viking, 1984.

Burnside, Scott, and Alan Cairns. *Deadly Innocence.* New York: Warner Books, 1995.

Busch, Alva. *Roadside Prey.* New York: Pinnacle, 1996.

Byrne, Gerald. *Borstal Boy.* London: J. Hill, 1954.

———. *John George Haigh, Acid Killer.* London: J. Hill, 1954.

Cahill, Bette. *Butterbox Babies.* Toronto: McClelland-Bantam, 1992.

Cahill, Tim. *Buried Dreams.* New York: Bantam, 1985.

Call, Max. *Hand of Death.* Lafayette, La.: Prescott Press, 1985.

Calohan, George. *My Search for the "Son of Sam."* New York: Universe.com, 2001.

Canter, David. *Criminal Shadows.* Irving, Tx.: Authorlink Press, 2000.

Carlo, Phillip. *The Night Stalker.* New York: Kensington Books, 1996.

Carpozi, George. *Son of Sam.* New York: Manor Books, 1977.

Cartel, Michael. *Disguise of Sanity: Serial Mass Murder.* Toluca Lake, Calif.: Pepperbox Books, 1985.

Castel, Albert, and Thomas Goodrich. *Bloody Bill Anderson.* Mechanicsburg, Pa.: Stackpole Books, 1998.

Cauffiel, Lowell. *Forever and Five Days.* New York: Zebra, 1992.

———. *House of Secrets.* New York: Pinnacle, 1997.

Cavanaugh, Mary. *Mommy's Little Angels.* New York: Onyx, 1995.

Cawthorne, Nigel. *Satanic Murder.* London: True Crime, 1995.

Chafe, Linda, and Elliott Leyton. *Serial Murder: Modern Scientific Perspectives.* Aldershot: Ashgate, 1999.

Chapman, Ivan. *Private Eddie Leonski.* Sydney, N.S.W. Hale & Ironmonger, 1982.

Cheney, Margaret. *The Co-Ed Killer.* New York: Walker, 1976.

Chase, Alston. *Harvard and the Unabomber.* New York: W. W. Norton, 2003.

Christie, Trevor. *Etched in Arsenic.* Philadelphia: J. B. Lippincott, 1968.

Chynoweth, Rena, and Dean Shapiro. *The Blood Covenant.* Austin, Tex.: Diamond Books, 1990.

Clark, Doug. *Dark Paths, Cold Trails.* Toronto: HarperCollins, 2002.

Clark, Tim, and John Penycate. *Psychopath.* London: Routledge & Kegan Paul, 1976.

Clarke, James. *Last Rampage.* New York: Houghton Mifflin, 1988.

Clarkson, Wensley. *Death at Every Stop.* New York: St. Martin's Press, 1997.

———. *The Good Doctor.* London: Blake Publishing, 2001.

———. *The Railroad Killer.* New York: St. Martin's Press, 1999.

———. *Whatever Mother Says.* New York: St. Martin's Press, 1995.

Colby-Newton, Katie. *Jack the Ripper: Opposing Viewpoints.* San Diego: Greenhaven Press, 1990.

Conover, Jim. *Slayer of Innocence.* Pekin, Ill.: Lynch Law Productions, 2003.

Conradi, Peter. *The Red Ripper.* New York: Dell, 1992.

Cook, Thomas. *Early Graves.* New York: Dutton, 1990.

Cooper, Cynthia, and Sam Sheppard. *Mockery of Justice.* New York: Onyx, 1997.

Copeland, James. *The Butler.* London: Granada, 1981.

Cornwell, Patricia. *Portrait of a Killer.* New York: G. P. Putnam's Sons, 2002.

Cory, Patricia. *An Eye to the Future.* Norwich, England: D&P Cory, 1993.

Coston, John. *Sleep, My Child, Forever.* New York: Onyx, 1995.

Coston, John. *To Kill and Kill Again.* New York: Onyx, 1992.

Coville, Gary, and Patrick Luciano. *Jack the Ripper.* Jefferson, N.C.: McFarland Publishing, 1999.

Cox, Bill. *Born Bad.* New York: Pinnacle, 1996.

Cox, Mike. *The Confessions of Henry Lee Lucas.* New York: Ivy Books, 1991.

Cox, Robert. *Deadly Pursuit.* New York: Ballantine, 1977.

Cray, Ed. *Burden of Proof.* New York: Macmillan, 1973.

Cross, Roger. *The Yorkshire Ripper.* London: Granada, 1981.

Crow, Alan, and Peter Damson. *Bible John.* New York: First Press Publishing, 1997.

Cullen, Robert. *The Killer Department.* New York: Pantheon Books, 1993.

Cullen, Tom. *Autumn of Terror.* London: Bodley Head, 1965.

Cunningham, Eugene. *Triggernometry.* Norman: University of Oklahoma Press, 1941.

Curtis, L. Perry. *Jack the Ripper and the London Press.* New Haven, Conn.: Yale University Press, 2001.

Dahmer, Lionel. *A Father's Story.* New York: Morrow, 1994.

Damio, Ward. *Urge to Kill.* New York: Pinnacle, 1974.

Damore, Leo. *In His Garden.* New York: Arbor House, 1981.

Davey, Frank. *Karla's Web.* Toronto: Penguin, 1995.

Davis, Carol. *Women Who Kill.* London: Allison & Busby, 2001.

Davis, Don. *The Milwaukee Murders.* New York: St. Martin's Press, 1991.

Dawkins, Vickie, and Nina Higgins. *Devil's Child.* New York: St. Martin's Press, 1989.

De La Torre, Lillian. *The Truth About Belle Gunness.* New York: Gold Medal, 1955.

De Locksley, John. *The Enigma of Jack the Ripper.* London: The Author, 1995.

———. *Jack the Ripper Unveiled.* London: The Author, 1995.

———. *A Ramble with Jack the Ripper.* London: The Author, 1996.

DeNevi, Don, and John Campbell. *Into the Minds of Madmen.* Amherst, N.Y.: Prometheus Books, 2004.

Dettlinger, Chet, and Jeff Pugh. *The List.* Atlanta: Philmay, 1983.

Devlin, Patrick. *Easing the Passing*. London: Bodley Head, 1985.

Dew, Walter. *The Hunt for Jack the Ripper*. Birmingham, England: Dave Froggatt, 1998.

Dickson, Grierson. *Murder by Numbers*. London: Robert Hale, 1958.

Dillman, John. *Blood Warning*. New York: G. P. Putnam's Sons, 1990.

Dillon, Martin. *The Shankill Butchers*. London: Hutchinson, 1989.

———. *Stone Cold*. London: Hutchinson, 1992.

Dillon, Richard. *The Hatchet Men*. Sausalito, Calif.: Comstock, 1962.

Disbury, David. *The Watchfield Horror*. Egham, England: Roberts G. Disbury, 2001.

Dodd, Westley, Lori Steinhorst, and John Rose. *When the Monster Comes out of the Closet*. Salem, Ore.: Rose Publications, 1994.

Douglas, Arthur. *Will the Real Jack the Ripper*. Chorley, England: Countryside Publications, 1979.

Douglas, John; Ann Burgess; Allen Burgess; and Robert Ressler. *Crime Classification Manual*. San Francisco: Jossey-Bass, 1992.

Douglas, John, and Mark Olshaker. *The Cases That Haunt Us*. New York: Scribner, 2000.

Douglas, John, and Mark Olshaker. *Journey Into Darkness*. New York: Pocket Books, 1997

———. *Mind Hunter*. New York: Scribner, 1995.

———. *Obsession*. New York: Scribner, 1998.

Douglas, John, and Stephen Singular. *Anyone You Want Me to Be*. New York: Scribner, 2003.

Downs, Thomas. *The Door-to-Door Killer*. New York: Dell, 1984.

———. *Murder Man*. New York: Dell, 1984.

Du Clos, Bernard. *Fair Game*. New York: St. Martin's Press, 1993.

Dunboyne, Lord. *The Trial of John George Haigh*. London: William Hodge, 1953.

Dvorchak, Robert, and Lisa Holewa. *Milwaukee Murders*. New York: Dell, 1991.

Eddowes, John. *The Man On Your Conscience*. London: Cassell, 1955.

———. *The Two Killers of Rillington Place*. London: Little, Brown, 1994.

Edwards, Ivor. *Jack the Ripper's Black Magic Rituals*. London: John Blake, 2002.

Edwards, Owen. *Burke & Hare*. Edinburgh: Mercat Press, 1980.

Eftimiades, Maria. *Garden of Graves*. New York: St. Martin's Press, 1993.

Egger, Steven. *The Killers Among Us*, Second Edition. Upper Saddle River, N.J.: Prentice Hall, 2002.

———. *Serial Murder: An Elusive Phenomenon*. New York: Praeger, 1990.

Egginton, Joyce. *From Cradle to Grave*. New York: William Morrow, 1989.

Eggleston, John. *Jack the Ripper: An Encyclopedia*. Santa Barbara, Calif.: ABC-Clio, 2001.

Elkind, Peter. *The Death Shift*. New York: Viking, 1989.

Emmons, Nuel, and Charles Manson. *Manson in His Own Words*. New York: Grove, 1986.

Englade, Ken. *Cellar of Horror*. New York: St. Martin's Press, 1988.

Evans, Stewart, and Paul Gainey. *The Lodger*. London: Century, 1995.

Evans, Stewart, and Keith Skinner. *Jack the Ripper: Letters from Hell*. Phoenix Mill, England: Sutton Publishing, 2001.

———. *The Ultimate Jack the Ripper Companion*. New York: Carroll & Graf, 2000.

Everitt, David. *Human Monsters*. Chicago. Contemporary Books, 1993.

Ewing, Charles. *Kids Who Kill*. Lexington, Mass.: Lexington Books, 1990.

Fairclough, Melvyn, and Joseph Sickert. *The Ripper and the Royals*. London: Duckworth, 1991.

Fanning, Diane. *Into the Water*. New York: St. Martin's Press, 2004.

———. *Through the Window*. New York: St. Martin's Press, 2003.

Farr, Louise. *The Sunset Murders*. New York: Pocket Books, 1992.

Farson, Daniel. *Jack the Ripper*. London: Michael Joseph, 1972.

Fawkes, Sandy. *Killing Time*. London. Hamlyn, 1978.

Feldman, Paul. *Jack the Ripper: The Final Chapter*. London: Virgin, 1997.

Fero, Kelly. *The Zani Murders*. Austin, Tex.: Texas Monthly Press, 1990.

Ferry, Jon, and Damian Inwood. *The Olson Murders*. Langley, B.C.: Cameo Books, 1982.

Fido, Martin. *The Crimes Detection and Death of Jack the Ripper*. London: Weidenfeld and Nicolson, 1987.

———. *A History of British Serial Killing*. London: Carlton Books, 2001.

Fielder, Jim. *Slow Death*. New York: Kensington, 2003.

Firstman, Richard, and Jamie Talan. *The Death of Innocents*. New York: Bantam, 1997.

Fisher, Joseph. *Killer Among Us*. Westport, Conn.: Praeger, 1997.

Fisher, Peter. *An Illustrated Guide to Jack the Ripper*. Cheshire, England: P&D Riley, 1996.

Fletcher, Jaye. *Deadly Thrills*. New York: Onyx, 1995.

Flowers, Anna. *Blind Fury*. New York: Pinnacle, 1993.

———. *Bound to Die*. New York: Pinnacle, 1995.

Flowers, R. Barri. *The Sex Slave Murders*. New York: St. Martin's Press, 1996.

Follain, John. *Jackal*. New York: Arcade, 1998.

Fortune, Jan. *The True Story of Bonnie and Clyde*. New York: Signet, 1968.

Fox, James. *Serial Killers*. London: Time-Life, 2000.

Fox, James, and Jack Levin. *Killer on Campus*. New York: Avon, 1996.

——. *Overkill*. New York: Plenum Press, 1994.

Frank, Gerald. *The Boston Strangler*. New York: New American Library, 1967.

Franke, David. *The Torture Doctor*. New York: Hawthorn Books, 1975.

Frasier, David. *Murder Cases of the Twentieth Century*. Jefferson, N.C.: McFarland, 1996.

Freedberg, Sydney. *Brother Love*. New York: Pantheon, 1994.

Freeman, Lucy. *"Before I Kill More . . ."* New York: Crown, 1955.

Frisbe, Thomas, and Randy Garrett. *Victims of Justice*. New York: Avon, 1998.

Fuhrman, Mark. *Murder in Spokane*. New York: Cliff Street Books, 2001.

Fuller, Jean. *Sickert and the Ripper Crimes*. Oxford: Mandrake Press, 1990.

Furio, Jennifer. *The Serial Killer Letters*. Philadelphia: Charles Press, 1998.

Furneaux, Rupert. *The Two Stranglers of Rillington Place*. London: Panther, 1961.

Gacy, John. *A Question of Doubt*. New York: Craig Bowley Consultants, 1991.

Gaddis, Thomas, and James Long. *Killer*. New York: Macmillan, 1970.

Ganey, Terry. *St. Joseph's Children*. New York: Lyle Stuart, 1989.

Gaskins, Donald, and Wilton Earle. *Final Truth*. New York: Pinnacle, 1993.

Gaute, J. H. H., and Robin Odell. *Murder "Whatdunnit."* London: Harrap, 1982.

——. *Murder Whereabouts*. London: Harrap, 1986.

——. *The New Murderers' Who's Who*. New York: International Polygonics, 1989.

Geberth, Vernon. *Sex-Related Homicide and Death Investigations*. Boca Raton, Fla.: CRC Publications, 2003.

Gekowski, Anna. *Murder by Numbers*. London: André Deutsch, 1998.

George, Edward, and Dary Matera. *Taming the Beast*. New York: St. Martin's Press, 1998.

Gerdes, Louise. *Serial Killers*. San Diego: Greenhaven Press, 2000.

Gibbs, Nancy, et al. *Mad Genius*. New York: Warner Books, 1996.

Gilmore, John. *Cold-Blooded*. Portland, Ore.: Feral House, 1996.

Gilmore, John, and Ron Kenner. *The Garbage People*. Los Angeles: Amok Books, 1996.

Gilmore, Mikal. *Shot in the Heart*. New York: Doubleday, 1994.

Gilmour, Walter, and Leland Hale. *Butcher, Baker*. New York: Onyx, 1991.

Ginsburg, Philip. *Poisoned Blood*. New York: Warner, 1987.

——. *The Shadow of Death*. New York: Jove Books, 1993

Gibney, Bruce. *The Beauty Queen Killer*. New York: Pinnacle, 1984.

Glatt, John. *Cradle of Death*. New York: St. Martin's Press, 2000.

——. *Internet Slavemaster*. New York: St. Martin's Press, 2001.

Godwin, George. *Peter Kurten*. London: Acorn, 1938.

Godwin, Grover. *Hunting Serial Predators*. Boca Raton, Fla.: CRC Press, 2000.

Godwin, John. *Murder USA*. New York: Ballantine, 1978.

Gollmar, Robert. *Edward Gein*. New York: Charles Hallberg, 1981.

Goodman, Jonathan. *Medical Murders*. New York: Lyle Stuart, 1991.

——. *Trial of Ian Brady and Myra Hindley*. London: David & Charles, 1973.

Goodrich, Thomas. *Black Flag*. Bloomington: Indiana University Press, 1995.

Gordon, R. Michael. *Alias Jack the Ripper*. Jefferson, N.C.: McFarland, 2001.

——. *The American Murders of Jack the Ripper*. Westport, Conn.: Praeger, 2003.

——. *The Thames Torso Murders of Victorian London*. Jefferson, N.C.: McFarland, 2002.

Goulding, Warren. *Just Another Indian*. Calgary, Alberta: Fifth House, 2001.

Gray, Philip. *Ghoulies and Ghosties and Long-leggety Beasties*. Bozeman: Badger Press of Montana, 1998.

Grayham, Anne, and Carol Emmas. *The Last Victim*. London: Headline, 1999.

Graysmith, Robert. *The Bell Tower*. Washington, D.C.: Regnery, 1999.

——. *The Sleeping Lady*. New York: Dutton, 1990.

——. *Unabomber*. Washington, D.C.: Regnery, 1997.

——. *Zodiac*. New York: St. Martin's Press, 1986.

——. *Zodiac Unmasked*. New York: Berkley, 2002.

Green, Jonathon. *The Greatest Criminals of All Time*. New York: Stein & Day, 1982.

Greene, Trevor. *Bad Date*. Toronto: ECW Press, 2001.

Gregory, Roy. *Jack the Ripper and Victorian London*. Cambridgeshire, England: Elm Publications, 1995.

Gribble, Leonard. *The Hallmark of Horror*. London: John Long, 1973.

———. *Sisters of Cain*. London: John Long, 1972.

Grombach, John. *The Great Liquidator*. New York: Doubleday, 1980.

Gurwell, John. *Mass Murder in Houston*. Houston: Cordovan Press, 1974.

Haines, Max. *Canadian Crimes*. Toronto: Signet Books, 1998.

———. *Doctors Who Kill*. Toronto: Sun Publishing, 1993.

———. *Unnatural Causes*. Toronto: Penguin, 2002.

Haining, Peter. *Sweeney Todd*. New York: Barnes & Noble, 1993.

Hallworth, Rodney, and Mark Williams. *Where There's a Will—*. Jersey, England: Capstans Press, 1983.

Hanna, David. *Harvest of Horror*. New York: Belmont Tower, 1975.

Hardy, Allison. *Kate Bender*. Girard, Kans.: Haldeman-Julius, 1944.

Harrington, Joseph, and Robert Burger. *Eye of Evil*. New York: St. Martin's Press, 1993.

———. *Justice Denied*. New York: Plenum Press, 1999.

Harris, Melvin. *Jack the Ripper: The Bloody Truth*. London: Columbus Books, 1987.

———. *The Ripper File*. London: W. H. Allen, 1988.

———. *The True Face of Jack the Ripper*. London: Michael O'Mara, 1994.

Harrison, Fred. *Brady & Hindley*. London: Ashgrove Press, 1986.

Harrison, Michael. *Clarence*. London: W. H. Allen, 1972.

Harrison, Paul. *Jack the Ripper: The Mystery Solved*. London: Robert Hale, 1991.

Harrison, Shirley. *The Diary of Jack the Ripper*. London: Smith Gryphon, 1993.

———. *Jack the Ripper: The American Connection*. London: Blake, 2003.

Harrison, Shirley, and David Canter. *Jack the Ripper: The American Connection*. London: John Blake, 2003.

Hartman, Mary. *Victorian Murderesses*. New York: Schocken Books, 1977.

Havill, Adrian. *Born Evil*. New York: St. Martin's Press, 2001.

———. *The Mother, the Son, and the Socialite*. New York: St. Martin's Press, 1999.

Hawkes, Harry. *The Capture of the Black Panther*. London: Harrap, 1978.

———. *Murder on the A34*. London: John Long, 1970.

Hazelwood, Roy, and Stephen Michaud. *Dark Dreams*. New York: St. Martin's Press, 2001.

Headley, Bernard. *The Atlanta Youth Murders and the Politics of Race*. Carbondale: Southern Illinois University Press, 1998.

Heilbroner, David. *Death Benefit*. New York: Crown, 1993.

Heimer, Mel. *The Cannibal*. New York: Lyle Stuart, 1971.

Helmer, William, and Rick Mattix. *Public Enemies*. New York: Checkmark Books, 1998.

Henderson, Bruce. *Trace Evidence*. New York: Penguin, 1998.

Hickey, Charles, Todd Lighty, and John O'Brien. *Goodbye, My Little Ones*. New York: Onyx, 1996.

Hinton, Bob. *From Hell*. Gwent, Wales: Old Bakehouse Publications, 1998.

Holden, Anthony. *The St. Albans Poisoner*. London: Hodder & Stoughton, 1974.

Horwitz, Sari, and Michael Ruane. *Sniper*. New York: Random House, 2003.

Howard, Clark. *Zebra*. New York: Berkley, 1980.

Howells, Martin, and Keith Skinner. *The Ripper Legacy*. London: Sidgwick & Jackson, 1987.

Hoyt, Olga. *Lust for Blood*. Lanham, Md.: Scarborough House, 1984.

Humes, Edward. *Buried Secrets*. New York: Dutton, 1991.

Humphries, William. *Profile of a Psychopath*. Batavia, Ill.: Flinn, 1999.

Indiana, Gary. *Three Month Fever*. New York: Cliff Street Books, 1999.

Iserson, Kenneth. *Demon Doctors: Physicians as Serial Killers*. Tucson, Az.: Galen Press, 2002.

Jackman, Tom, and Troy Cole. *Rites of Burial*. New York: Pinnacle, 1998.

Jackson, Steve. *Monster*. New York: Kensington, 1998.

Jacobs, David, ed. *Sex Sadists*. New York: Pinnacle, 1995.

Jaeger, Richard, and M. William Balousek. *Massacre in Milwaukee*. Oregon, Wisc.: Waubesa Press, 1991.

Jakubowski, Maxim, and Nathan Braund, eds. *The Mammoth Book of Jack the Ripper*. New York: Carroll & Graf, 1999.

James, John. *The Benders of Kansas*. Wichita: Kan-Okla Publishing, 1913.

James, P. D., and T. A. Crutchley. *The Maul and the Pear Tree*. London: Constable & Co., 1971.

Jeffers, H. Paul. *Who Killed Precious?* New York: Pharos Books, 1991.

Johnson, Pamela. *On Iniquity*. New York: Scribner, 1967.

Jones, Ann. *Women Who Kill*. New York: Holt, Rinehart & Winston, 1980.

Jones, Barbara. *Evil Beyond Belief*. London: Blake, 1992.

———. *Voices from an Evil God*. London: 1993.

Jones, Elwyn, and John Lloyd. *The Ripper File*. London: Arthur Baker, 1975.

Jones, Frank. *Trail of Blood*. Toronto: McGraw-Hill Ryerson, 1981.

Jones, Janie, and Carol Clerk. *The Devil and Miss Jones*. London: Smith Gryphon, 1993

Jones, Richard, ed. *Killer Couples*. Secaucus, N.J.: Lyle Stuart, 1987.

Jouve, Nicole. *"The Street Cleaner."* London: Marion Boyers, 1986.

Kallio, Lauri. *Confess or Die*. New York: Minerva Press, 1999.

Keers, Christine, and Dennis St. Pierre. *The Riverside Killer*. New York: Pinnacle, 1996.

Kelleher, Michael, and C. L. Kelleher. *Murder Most Rare*. Westport, Conn.: Praeger, 1998.

Kelleher, Michael, and David Van Nuys. *"This Is the Zodiac Speaking."* Westport, Conn.: Praeger, 2002.

Kelly, Alexander. *Jack the Ripper: A Bibliography and Review of the Literature*. London: Association of Assistant Librarians, 1984.

Kelly, Greg. *Killer on the Loose*. Rockford, Ill.: Paperboy Press, 1998.

Kelly, Susan. *The Boston Stranglers*. New York: Birch Lane, 1995.

Kendall, Elizabeth. *The Phantom Prince*. Seattle: Madrona, 1981.

Kennedy, Dolores. *William Heirens: His Day in Court*. Chicago: Bonus Books, 1991.

Kennedy, Dolores, and Robert Nolin. *On a Killing Day*. Chicago: Bonus Books, 1992.

Kennedy, Ludovic. *10 Rillington Place*. London: Gollancz, 1961.

Keppel, Robert. *The Psychology of Serial Killer Investigations*. Amsterdam: Academic Press, 2003.

———. *The Riverman*. New York: Pocket Books, 1995.

———. *Serial Murder*. Cincinnati: Anderson Publishing, 1989.

———. *Signature Killers*. London: Arrow, 1997.

Keyes, Daniel. *Unveiling Claudia*. New York: Bantam, 1986.

Keyes, Edward. *The Michigan Murders*. New York: Pocket Books, 1976.

Kidder, Tracy. *The Road to Yuba City*. New York: Doubleday, 1974.

Kilroy, Jim, and Bob Stewart. *Sacrifice*. Dallas: Word Publishing, 1990.

King, Brian, ed. *Lustmord*. Burbank, Calif.: Bloat, 1996.

King, Gary. *Blind Rage*. New York: Onyx, 1995.

———. *Blood Lust*. New York: Onyx, 1992.

———. *Driven to Kill*. New York: Windsor, 1993.

Klausner, Lawrence. *Son of Sam*. New York: McGraw-Hill, 1981.

Knight, Stephen. *Jack the Ripper: The Final Solution*. London: George Harrap, 1976.

Kolarik, Gera-Lind, and Wayne Klatt. *Freed to Kill*. Chicago: Chicago Review Press, 1990.

Kozenczak, Joseph, and Karen Hendrikson. *A Passing Acquaintance*. New York: Carlton Press, 1992.

Krivich, Mikhail, and Olgert Olgin. *Comrade Chikatilo*. Fort Lee, N.J.: Barricade Books, 1993.

Kuncl, Tom. *Death Row Women*. New York: Pocket Books, 1994.

Kuncl, Tom, and Paul Eisenstein. *Ladies Who Kill*. New York: Pinnacle, 1985.

La Bern, Arthur. *Haigh: The Mind of a Murderer*. London: W. H. Allen, 1973.

Lane, Brian. *The Butchers*. London: True Crime, 1991.

———. *Chronicle of 20th Century Murder*. London: Virgin, 1993.

———. *The Encyclopedia of Women Killers*. London: Headline, 1994.

Lane, Brian, and Wilfred Greg. *The Encyclopedia of Mass Murder*. London: Headline, 1994.

———. *The Encyclopedia of Serial Killers*. London: Headline, 1992.

Lane, Brian Alan. *Cat and Mouse*. Los Angeles: Dove Books, 1997.

Lang, Denise. *A Call for Justice*. New York: Avon, 2000.

Langlois, Janet. *Belle Gunness*. Bloomington: Indiana University Press, 1985.

Larsen, Richard. *The Deliberate Stranger*. Englewood Cliffs, N.J.: Prentice-Hall, 1980.

Larson, Erik. *The Devil in the White City*. New York: Crown, 2003.

Lasseter, Don. *Body Double*. New York: Kensington, 2002.

———. *Dead of Night*. New York: Onyx, 1997.

———. *Die for Me*. New York: Pinnacle, 2000.

———. *Property of the Folsom Wolf*. New York: Pinnacle, 1995.

Lasseter, Don, and Dana Holliday. *Zodiac of Death*. New York: Berkley, 1999.

Lavelle, Patrick. *Shadow of the Ripper*. London: John Blake, 2003.

Lavergne, Gary. *Bad Boy from Rosebud*. Denton: University of North Texas Press, 1999.

Leith, Rod. *The Prostitute Murders*. New York: Lyle Stuart, 1983.

Lester, David. *Serial Killers*. Philadelphia: The Charles Press, 1995.

Levin, Jack, and James Fox. *Mass Murder*. New York: Plenum, 1985.

Levine, Richard. *Bad Blood*. New York: Random House, 1982.

Lewis, Bernard. *The Assassins*. New York: Oxford University Press, 1967.

Lindberg, Richard. *Return to the Scene of the Crime*. Nashville, Tn.: Cumberland House, 1999.

Linder, Seth, Caroline Morris, and Keith Skinner. *Ripper Diary: The Inside Story*. Stroud, England: Sutton, 2003.

Linedecker, Clifford. *Death of a Model*. New York: St. Martin's Press, 1997.

———. *Hell Ranch*. Austin, Tex.: Diamond Books, 1989.

———. *The Man Who Killed Boys*. New York: St. Martin's Press, 1980.

———. *Night Stalker*. New York: St. Martin's, 1991.

———. *Prison Groupies*. New York: Pinnacle, 1993.

———. *Serial Thrill Killers*. New York: Knightsbridge, 1990.

———. *Smooth Operator*. New York: St. Martin's Press, 1997.

———. *Thrill Killers*. New York: Paperjacks, 1987.

Linedecker, Clifford, and William Burt. *Nurses Who Kill*. New York: Pinnacle, 1990.

Livsey, Clara. *Tha Manson Women*. New York: Marek, 1980.

London, Sondra. *True Vampires*. Los Angeles: Feral House, 2004.

Louderback, Lew. *The Bad Ones*. New York: Fawcett, 1968.

Lourie, Richard. *Hunting the Devil*. New York: HarperCollins, 1993.

Lucas, Norman. *The Sex Killers*. London: W. H. Allen, 1974.

Lucas, Norman, and Phil Davies. *The Monster Butler*. London: Arthur Barker, 1979.

Lunde, Donald. *Murder and Madness*. San Francisco: San Francisco Book Company, 1976.

———. *The Die Song*. New York: W. W. Norton, 1980.

MacLean, Rick, and André Veniot. *Terror*. Toronto: McClelland & Stewart, 1990.

———. *Terror's End*. Toronto: McClelland & Stewart, 1992.

Maeder, Thomas. *The Unspeakable Crimes of Dr. Petiot*. Boston: Little, Brown, 1980.

Mair, George. *Angel of Death*. New York: Chamberlain Bros., 2004.

Manners, Terry. *Deadlier Than the Male*. London: Pan, 1995.

Marchbanks, David. *The Moors Murders*. London: Frewin, 1966.

Markman, Ronald, and Dominic Bosco. *Alone with the Devil*. New York: Doubleday, 1989.

Marks, Paula. *And Die in the West*. Norman: University of Oklahoma Press, 1989.

Marriner, Brian. *On Death's Bloody Trail*. New York: St. Martin's Press, 1991.

Marsh, Rob. *With Criminal Intent: The Changing Face of Crime in South Africa*. Kenilworth: Ampersand Press, 1999.

Martin, John. *Butcher's Dozen*. New York: Harper & Brothers, 1950.

Martingale, Moira. *Cannibal Killers*. New York: St. Martin's, 1993.

Master, R. E. L., and Eduard Lea. *Perverse Crimes in History*. New York: Julian, 1963.

Masters, Brian. *Killing for Company*. London: Jonathan Cape, 1985.

———. *She Must Have Known*. London: Transworld Publishers, 1996.

———. *The Shrine of Jeffrey Dahmer*. London: Hodder & Stoughton, 1993.

Matters, Leonard. *The Mystery of Jack the Ripper*. London: Hutchinson and Co., 1928.

Matthews, John, and Christine Wicker. *The Eyeball Killer*. New York: Pinnacle, 1996.

McAdams, Frank, and Timothy Carney. *Final Affair*. New York: Berkley, 2002.

McConnell, Brian. *Found Naked and Dead*. London: New English Library, 1974.

McConnell, Brian, and Douglas Bence. *The Nilsen File*. London. Futura, 1983.

McCormick, Donald. *The Identity of Jack the Ripper*. London: Great Pan Books, 1962.

McDonald, R. Robin. *Black Widow*. New York: St. Martin's Press, 1986.

McDougal, Dennis. *Angel of Darkness*. New York: Warner, 1991.

———. *Mother's Day*. New York: Fawcett Gold Medal, 1995.

———. *The Yosemite Murders*. New York: Ballantine, 2000.

McIntyre, Tommy. *Wolf in Sheep's Clothing*. Detroit: Wayne State University Press, 1988.

McLaren, Angus. *A Prescription for Murder*. Chicago: University of Chicago Press, 1993.

McNally, Raymond. *Dracula Was a Woman*. New York: McGraw-Hill, 1983.

McPhilemy, Sean. *The Committee*. Boulder, Colo.: Roberts Rinehart, 1999.

McQuillan, Alice. *They Call Them Grifters*. New York: Onyx, 2000.

Mendoza, Antonio. *Killers on the Loose*. London: Virgin, 2000.

Metz, Leon. *The Shooters*. New York: Berkley, 1976.

Meyer, Gerald. *The Memphis Murders*. New York: Seabury, 1974.

Michaud, Stephen. *Lethal Shadow*. New York: Onyx, 1994.

Michaud, Stephen, and Hugh Aynesworth. *Murderers Among Us*. New York: Signet, 1991.

———. *The Only Living Witness*. New York: Simon & Schuster, 1983.

———. *Ted Bundy. Conversations with a Killer.* New York: New American Library, 1989.

Michaud, Stephen, and Roy Hazelwood. *The Evil That Men Do.* New York: St. Martin's Press, 1998.

Mitchell, Corey. *Dead and Buried.* New York: Pinnacle, 2003.

Mitchell, Sandra. *The Miramichi Axe Murder.* Halifax, N.S.: Nimbus, 1992.

Mitrione, Dan. *Suddenly Gone.* New York: St. Martin's Press, 1995.

Mladinich, Robert. *From the Mouth of the Monster.* New York: Pocket Books, 2001.

Monaco, Richard, and Bill Burt. *The Dracula Syndrome.* New York: Avon, 1993.

Mones, Paul. *Stalking Justice.* New York: Pocket Books, 1995.

Moore, Kelly, and Dan Reed. *Deadly Medicine.* New York: St. Martin's, 1988.

Moose, Charles. *Three Weeks in October.* New York: Dutton, 2003.

Morlin, Bill, and Jeanette White. *Bad Trick.* Spokane, Wa.: New Media Ventures, 2001.

Morrison, Helen, and Harold Goldberg. *My Life Among the Serial Killers.* New York: William Morrow, 2004.

Morton, James. *Gangland International.* London: Warner, 1999.

Moser, Don, and Jerry Cohen. *The Pied Piper of Tucson.* New York: New American Library, 1967.

Moss, Jason. *The Last Victim.* New York: Warner Books, 1999.

Mulgrew, Ian. *Final Payoff.* Toronto: McClelland-Bantam, 1990.

Murphy, Dennis, and Patrick Kennedy. *Incident, Homicide.* Boston: Quimby World Headquarters Publications, 1992.

Mustain, Gene, and Jerry Capeci. *Murder Machine.* New York: Onyx, 1993.

Myers, John. *Doc Holliday.* Lincoln: University of Nebraska Press, 1955.

Naifeh, Steven, and Gregory Smith. *Stranger in the Family.* New York: Onyx, 1996.

Nelson, Mark, and Gerald Oswald. *The 34th Victim.* Westmont, Ill.: Fortune Productions, 1986.

Nelson, Polly. *Defending the Devil.* New York: William Morrow, 1994.

Nerad, Jack. *Fatal Photographs.* New York: Avon, 1998.

Neville, Richard, and Julie Clark. *The Life and Crimes of Charles Sobhraj.* London: Jonathan Cape, 1979.

Newton, Michael. *Hunting Humans.* Port Townsend, Wash.: Loompanics Unlimited, 1990.

———. *Raising Hell.* New York: Avon, 1993.

———. *Rope.* New York: Pocket Books, 1998.

———. *Serial Slaughter.* Port Townsend, Wash.: Loompanics Unlimited, 1992.

———. *Silent Rage.* New York: Dell, 1994.

———. *Still at Large.* Port Townsend, Wash.: Loompanics Unlimited, 1998.

———. *Waste Land.* New York: Pocket Books, 1998.

Newton, Michael, and Judy Ann Newton. *The FBI Most Wanted.* New York: Garland, 1989.

Nickel, Steven. *Torso.* Winston-Salem, N.C.: J. F. Blair, 1989.

Norris, Joel. *Arthur Shawcross.* New York: Pinnacle, 1992.

———. *Henry Lee Lucas.* New York: Zebra, 1991.

———. *Jeffrey Dahmer.* New York: Windsor, 1992.

———. *Serial Killers: The Growing Menace.* New York: Dolphin, 1988.

———. *Walking Time Bombs.* New York: Bantam, 1992.

Norton, Carla. *Disturbed Ground.* New York: Morrow, 1994.

Obler, Martin, and Thomas Clavin. *Fatal Analysis.* New York: Dell, 1998.

O'Brien, Darcy. *Murder in Little Egypt.* New York: Morrow, 1989.

———. *Two of a Kind: the Hillside Stranglers.* New York: New American Library, 1985

Odell, Robin. *Jack the Ripper in Fact and Fiction.* London: Harrap and Co., 1965.

———. *Landmarks in 20th Century Murder.* London: Headline, 1995.

O'Donnell, Elliot. *Women Bluebeards.* London: Stanley Paul, n.d.

O'Donnell, Jeff. *Starkweather.* Lincoln, Neb.: J&L Lee Publications, 1993.

O'Donnell, Kevin. *The Jack the Ripper Whitechapel Murders.* Essex, England: Ten Bells Publishing, 1997.

O'Hagan, Andrew. *The Missing.* New York: New Press, 1995.

Olsen, Gregg. *Abandoned Prayers.* New York: Warner, 1990.

———. *Bitter Almonds.* New York: Warner, 1993.

———. *The Confessions of an American Black Widow.* New York: St. Martin's Press, 1998.

Olsen, Jack. *Charmer.* New York: Avon, 1994.

———. *Hastened to the Grave.* New York: St. Martin's Press, 1998.

———. *"I": The Creation of a Serial Killer.* New York: St. Martin's Press, 2002.

———. *The Man with the Candy.* New York: Simon & Schuster, 1974.

———. *The Misbegotten Son.* New York: Delacorte Press, 1993.

O'Neal, Bill. *The Pimlico Encyclopedia of Western Gunfighters*. London: Pimlico, 1998.

Orth, Maureen. *Vulgar Favors*. New York: Delacorte Press, 1999.

Owens, Greg, and Darcy Henton. *No Kill, No Thrill*. Calgary, Alberta: Red Deer Press, 2001.

Paley, Bruce. *Jack the Ripper: The Simple Truth*. London: Headline, 1995.

Palmer, Scott. *Jack the Ripper: A Reference Guide*. Folkstone, England: Scarecrow Press, 1995.

Palermo, George. *The Faces of Violence*. Springfield, Ill.: Charles C. Thomas, 2004.

Papa, Juliet. *Lady Killer*. New York: St. Martin's Press, 1995.

Penrose, Valentine. *The Bloody Countess*. London: Calder & Boyars, 1970.

Petit, Mark. *A Need to Kill*. New York: Ivy Books, 1990.

Philpin, John. *Stalemate*. New York: Bantam, 1997.

Philpin, John, and John Donnelly. *Beyond Murder*. New York: Onyx, 1994.

Pienciak, Richard. *Mama's Boy*. New York: Onyx, 1997.

Pistorius, Micki. *Catch Me a Killer*. Johannesburg: Penguin, 2000.

———. *Strangers on the Street: Serial Homicide in South Africa*. Sandton, South Africa: Penguin, 2002.

Plaidy, Jean. *A Triptych of Poisoners*. London: Robert Hale, 1958.

Plimmer, John. *In the Footsteps of the Whitechapel Murders*. Sussex: Book Guild Ltd., 1998.

Posner, Gerald, and John Ware. *Mengele*. New York: McGraw-Hill, 1986.

Potter, J. D. *The Monsters of the Moors*. New York: Ballantine, 1966.

Pron, Nick. *Lethal Marriage*. New York: Bantam, 1996.

Provost, Gary. *Across the Border*. New York: Pocket Books, 1989.

Pulitzer, Lisa, and Joan Swirsky. *Crossing the Line*. New York: Berkley, 1994.

Quimby, Myron. *The Devil's Emissaries*. New York: Curtis Books, 1969.

Rae, George. *Confessions of the Boston Strangler*. New York: Pyramid, 1967.

Raper, Michell. *Who Was Jack the Ripper?* London: Tabaret Press, 1974.

Reichert, Dave. *Chasing the Devil*. New York: Little, Brown, 2004.

Reinhardt, James. *The Murderous Trail of Charles Starkweather*. Springfield, Ill.: C. C. Thomas, 1960.

———. *The Psychology of Strange Killers*. Springfield, Ill.: C. C. Thomas, 1962.

Ressler, Robert; Ann Burgess; and John Douglas. *Sexual Homicide*. Lexington, Mass.: Lexington Books, 1988.

Ressler, Robert, and Tom Schachtman. *I Have Lived in the Monster*. New York: St. Martin's Press, 1997.

———. *Whoever Fights Monsters*. New York: St. Martin's Press, 1994.

Reynolds, Michael. *Dead Ends*. New York: Warner, 1992.

Reynolds, Richard. *Cry for War*. San Francisco: Squibob Press, 1987.

Rignall, Jeff. *29 Below*. Chicago: Wellington Press, 1979.

Ritchie, Jean. *Myra Hindley*. London: Angus & Robertson.

Robinson, Tim. *The Whitechapel Horrors*. Manchester: Daisy Bank Publishing, n.d.

Roemer, William. *The Enforcer*. New York: Ivy Books, 1994.

Rogers, Brian, ed. *Reflections on Jack the Ripper*. Brighton, England: The Author, 1999.

Rolling, Danny, and Sondra London. *The Making of a Serial Killer*. Portland, Ore.: Feral House, 1996.

Rosen, Fred. *Body Dump*. New York: Pinnacle, 2002.

Rothert, Otto. *The Outlaws of Cave-in-Rock*. Carbondale: Southern Illinois University Press, 1996.

Rule, Ann. *The I-5 Killer*. New York: New American Library, 1984.

———. *Lust Killer*. New York: New American Library, 1983.

———. *The Stranger Beside Me*. New York: New American Library, 1980.

———. *The Want-Ad Killer*. New York: New American Library, 1983.

Rumbelow, Donald. *The Complete Jack the Ripper*. London: Penguin, 1975.

———. *Jack the Ripper: the Complete Casebook*. New York: Berkley, 1988.

Russell, Sue. *Damsel of Death*. London: True Crime, 1992.

Russell, Sue. *Lethal Intent*. New York: Pinnacle, 2002.

Ryder, Stephen, ed. *The First Fifty Years of Jack the Ripper*. 2 vols. Paramus, N.J.: Ripperological Preservation Society, 1998.

Ryzuk, Mary. *The Gainesville Ripper*. New York: St. Martin's Press, 1995.

Sanders, Ed. *The Family*. New York: Dutton, 1971.

Sasser, Charles. *At Large*. New York: St. Martin's Press, 1998.

———. *Homicide!* New York: Pocket Books, 1990.

Schaefer, G. J. *Killer Fiction*. Los Angeles: Feral House, 1995.

Schechter, Harold. *Bestial*. New York: Pocket Books, 1998.

———. *Deranged*. New York: Pocket Books, 1990.

———. *Depraved*. New York: Pocket Books, 1998.

———. *Deviant*. New York: Pocket Books, 1989.

———. *Fatal*. New York: Pocket Books, 2004.

———. *Fiend*. New York: Simon & Schuster, 2000.

———. *The Serial Killer File*. New York: Ballantine Books, 2003.

Schechter, Harold, and David Everitt. *The A to Z Encyclopedia of Serial Killers*. New York: Pocket Books, 1996.

Schiller, Lawrence, and Susan Atkins. *The Killing of Sharon Tate*. New York: New American Library, 1970.

Schreck, Nikolas. *The Manson File*. New York: Amok Press, 1988.

Schreiber, Flora. *The Shoemaker*. New York: Simon & Schuster, 1983.

Schreiber, Mark. *Shocking Crimes of Postwar Japan*. Tokyo: Yenbooks, 1996.

Schultz, Duane. *Quantrill's War*. New York: St. Martin's Press, 1996.

Schutze, Jim. *Cauldron of Blood*. New York: Avon, 1989.

———. *Preacher's Girl*. New York: William Morrow, 1993.

Schwartz, Ann. *The Man Who Could Not Kill Enough*. Secaucus, N.J.: Carol, 1992.

Schwartz, Ted. *The Hillside Strangler*. New York: Doubleday, 1981.

Scott, Robert. *Savage*. New York: Pinnacle, 2002.

Sears, Donald. *To Kill Again*. Wilmington, Del.: Scholarly Resources, 1991.

Segrave, Kerry. *Women Serial and Mass Murderers*. Jefferson, N.C.: McFarland, 1992.

Seltzer, Mark. *Serial Killers*. New York: Routledge, 1998.

Selwyn, Francis. *Rotten to the Core?* London: Routledge, 1988.

Sereny, Gitta. *The Case of Mary Bell*. London: Methuen, 1972.

Sharkey, Terrence. *Jack the Ripper*. London: Wardlock, 1987.

Shay, Jack. *Blood in the Wilderness*. Princeton, N.J.: The Author, 1998.

Shepherd, Sylvia. *The Mistress of Murder Hill*. Bloomington, Ind.: 1st Books, 2001.

Shipley, Stacey, and Bruce Arrigo. *The Female Homicide Offender*. Upper Saddle River, N.J.: Pearson Prentice Hall, 2004.

Singular, Stephen. *Charmed to Death*. New York: Pinnacle, 1995.

Sitford, Mikaela. *Addicted to Murder*. London: Virgin Publishing, 2000.

Skelton, Douglas. *Blood on the Thistle*. London: HarperCollins, 1994.

Smith, Carlton. *Dying for Daddy*. New York: St. Martin's Press, 1998.

———. *Fatal Charm*. New York: Onyx, 1993.

———. *Killing Season*. New York: Onyx, 1994.

———. *Murder at Yosemite*. New York: St. Martin's Press, 1999.

Smith, Carlton, and Thomas Guillen. *The Search for the Green River Killer*. New York: Onyx, 1991.

———. *Shadows of Evil*. New York: St. Martin's Press, 2001.

Smithkey, John. *Jack the Ripper*. North Canton, Ohio: Key Publications, 1998.

Sohail, Khalid. *The Myth of the Chosen One*. Toronto: White Knight Publications, 2002.

Sounes, Howard. *Fred and Rose*. London: Warner, 1995.

Sparrow, Gerald. *Satan's Children*. London: Odhams. 1966.

———. *Women Who Murder*. London: Arthur Baker, 1970.

Speare, D. *Jack the Ripper: Crime Scene Investigation*. Philadelphia: Xlibris, 2003.

Spiering, Frank. *Prince Jack*. New York: Doubleday, 1978.

Spinks, Sarah. *Cardiac Arrest*. Toronto: Doubleday, 1985.

Spizer, Joyce. *The Cross Country Killer*. Dallas: Top Publications, 2001.

Springer, Patricia. *Blood Rush*. New York: Pinnacle, 1994.

———. *Blood Stains*. New York: Pinnacle, 2002.

———. *Mail Order Murder*. New York: Pinnacle, 1999.

Steele, Phillip, and Marie Scoma. *The Family Story of Bonnie and Clyde*. Gretna, La.: Pelican, 2000.

Stewart, Bob. *No Remorse*. New York: Pinnacle, 1996.

Stewart, James. *Blind Eye*. New York: Simon & Schuster, 1999.

Stewart, William. *Jack the Ripper: A New Theory*. London: Quality Press, 1939.

Stoddart, Charles. *Bible John*. Edinburgh: Paul Harris, 1980.

Stokes, Hugh. *Madame de Brinvilliers*. London: Thomas Nelson, 1912.

Stowers, Carlton. *Scream at the Sky*. New York: St. Martin's Press, 2003.

Strachan, Ross. *The Jack the Ripper Handbook*. Irvine, Scotland: Great Scot Services, 1999.

Strean, Herbert, and Lucy Freeman. *Our Wish to Kill*. New York: Avon, 1991.

Sugden, Philip. *The Complete History of Jack the Ripper*. New York: Carroll & Graf, 1995.

Sugden, Peter. *The Life and Times of Jack the Ripper*. Bristol, England: Sienna/Paragon, 1996.

Sullivan, Terry, and Peter Maiken. *Killer Clown*. New York: Grosset & Dunlap, 1983.

Symons, Mitchell. *The Man Who Shorted Out the Electric Chair*. New York: Avon, 1994.

Tailbitzer, Bill. *Too Much Blood*. New York: Vantage Press, 1978.

Tannenbaum, Robert, and Peter Greenberg. *The Piano Teacher.* New York: New American Library, 1987.

Tatar. *Lustmord.* Princeton, N.J.: Princeton University Press, 1995.

Terry, Maury. *The Ultimate Evil.* New York: Doubleday, 1987.

Thomas, Donald. *Dead Giveaway.* London: Michael O'Mara Books, 1993.

Thompson, Thomas. *Serpentine.* New York: Dell, 1979.

Thorp, Raymond, and Robert Bunker. *Crow Killer.* Bloomington: Indiana University Press, 1958.

Tidyman, Ernest. *Dummy.* Boston: Little, Brown, 1974.

Tithecott, Richard. *Of Men and Monsters.* Madison: University of Wisconsin Press, 1997.

Treherne, John. *The Strange History of Bonnie and Clyde.* New York: Cooper Square Press, 1984.

Trotter, William, and Robert Newsom III. *Deadly Kin.* New York: St. Martin's Press, 1988.

Trow, M. J. *The Many Faces of Jack the Ripper.* West Sussex, England: Summersdale Publishers, 1997.

Tullett, Tom. *Portrait of a Bad Man.* London: Evans Brothers, 1956.

Tully, James. *The Secret of Prisoner 1167.* London: Robinson Publishing, 1997.

Turkus, Burton, and Sid Feder. *Murder, Inc.* New York: Da Capo Press, 1951.

Turnbull, Peter. *The Killer Who Never Was.* Hull, England: Clark, Lawrence, 1996.

Ubelaker, Douglas, and Henry Scammel. *Bones.* New York: HarperPaperbacks, 1992.

Underwood, Peter. *Jack the Ripper.* London: Blandford, 1987.

U.S. Senate Judiciary Committee. *Serial Murders.* Washington, D.C.: U.S. Government Printing Office, 1984.

Utley, Robert. *Billy the Kid.* Lincoln: University of Nebraska Press, 1989.

Valentine, Steven. *The Black Panther Story.* London: New English Library, 1976.

Van Hoffman, Eric. *A Venom in the Blood.* New York: Donald I. Fine, 1990.

Villasenor, Victor. *Jury.* Boston: Little, Brown, 1977.

Vorpagel, Russell. *Profiles in Murder.* New York: Plenum, 1998.

Wagner, Margaret. *The Monster of Düsseldorf.* London: Faber, 1932.

Waits, Chris, and Dave Shors. *Unabomber.* Helena, Mont.: Helena Independent Record, 1999.

Wakefield, H. Russell. *Landru.* London: Duckworth, 1936.

Wallace, Richard. *Jack the Ripper.* London: Gazelle, 1997.

Walsh, John. *Tears of Rage.* New York: Pocket Books, 1997.

Walsh, Mike. *Fallen Son.* New York: Onyx, 1994.

Wansell, Geoffrey. *An Evil Love.* London: Headline, 1996.

Ward, Bernie. *Bobby Joe: In the Mind of a Monster.* Boca Raton, Fla.: Cool Hand Communications, 1995.

———. *Families Who Kill.* New York: Pinnacle, 1993.

———. *Innocent Prey.* New York: Pinnacle, 1994.

Watkins, Paul, and Guillermo Soledad. *My Life with Charles Manson.* New York: Bantam, 1979.

Waumbaugh, Joseph. *The Blooding.* New York: Perigord Press, 1989.

Weber, Don, and Charles Bosworth. *Precious Victims.* New York: Signet, 1991.

Weinstein, Fannie, and Ruth Schumann. *Please Don't Kill Mommy!* New York: St. Martin's Press, 2001.

Weinstein, Fannie, and Melinda Wilson. *Where the Bodies Are Buried.* New York: St. Martin's Press, 1998.

Wellman, Joy, Lisa McVey, and Susan Replogle. *Smoldering Embers.* Far Hills, N.J.: New Horizon Press, 1997.

Wertham, Frederic. *The Show of Violence.* Garden City, N.Y.: Doubleday, 1949.

West, Anne. *Out of the Shadows.* London: Pocket Books, 1996.

West, Donald. *Sacrifice Unto Me.* New York: Pyramid, 1974.

West, Stephen, and Mae West. *Inside 25 Cromwell St.* London: Peter Grose, 1995.

Whitechapel, Simon. *Crossing to Kill.* London: Virgin, 2000.

Whitehead, Tony. *Mary Ann Cotton.* London: Whitehead, 2000.

Whittaker, Mark, and Les Kennedy. *Sins of the Brother.* Sydney, Australia: McMillan, 1998.

Whittington-Egan, Richard. *A Casebook on Jack the Ripper.* London: Wildy and Sons, 1975.

Whittle, Brian, and Joan Ritchie. *Prescription for Murder.* New York: Warner Books, 2000.

Wick, Steve. *Bad Company.* New York: St. Martin's Press, 1990.

Wilcox, Robert. *The Mysterious Deaths at Ann Arbor.* New York: Popular Library, 1977.

Wilding, John. *Jack the Ripper Revealed.* London: Constable/Volcano Books, 1993.

Williams, Emlyn. *Beyond Belief.* New York.

Williams, Stephen. *Invisible Darkness.* New York: Bantam, 1996.

Wilson, Colin. *A Casebook of Murder.* London: Leslie Frewin, 1969.

———. *The Corpse Garden.* London: True Crime Library, 1998.

———. *Order of Assassins.* London: Hart-Davis, 1972.

———. *Written in Blood.* 3 vols. New York: Warner, 1989.

Wilson, Colin, and Robin Odell. *Jack the Ripper: Summing Up the Evidence.* London: Bantam, 1987.

Wilson, Colin, and Patricia Pitman. *The Encyclopedia of Murder.* London: Barker, 1961.

Wilson, Colin, and Donald Seaman. *The Encyclopedia of Modern Murder.* London: Barker, 1983.

———. *The Serial Killers.* New York: Carol, 1990.

Wilson, Colin, and Damon Wilson. *The Killers Among Us.* 2 vols. New York: Warner, 1995.

Wilson, John. *The Trial of Peter Manuel.* London: Secker and Warburg, 1959.

Wilson, Patrick. *Murderess.* London: Joseph, 1971.

Wilson, Robert, *Devil's Disciples.* Poole, England: Javelin Books, 1986.

———. *Return to Hell.* London: Javelin Books, 1988.

Winn, Steven, and David Merrill. *Ted Bundy: the Killer Next Door.* New York: Bantam, 1979.

Winne, Mark. *Priority Mail.* New York: Scribner, 1995.

Winwar, Frances. *The Saint and the Devil.* New York: Harper, 1948.

Witzig, Eric. *Observations on the Serial Killer Phenomenon.* Quantico, Va.: FBI Academy, 1999.

Wizinski, Sy. *Charles Manson: Love Letters to a Secret Disciple.* Terre Haute, Ind.: Moonmad Press, 1976.

Wolf, A. P. *Jack the Myth: A New Look at the Ripper.* London: Robert Hale, 1993.

Wolf, Leonard. *Bluebeard.* New York: Clarkson N. Potter, 1980.

Wolfe, Linda. *Love Me to Death.* New York: Pocket Books, 1998.

Wolff, Camille. *Who Was Jack the Ripper?* London: Grey House, 1995.

Wood, William. *The Bone Garden.* New York: Pocket Books, 1994.

Woodhall, Edwin. *Jack the Ripper.* London: Mellifont Press, 1937.

Woods, Paul. *Ed Gein—Psycho!* London: Annihilation Press, 1992.

Wright, Stephen. *Jack the Ripper: An American View.* New York: Mystery Notebook Editions, 1999.

Wyre, Ray, and Tim Tate. *The Murder of Childhood.* London: Penguin, 1995.

Yallop, David. *Deliver Us From Evil.* New York: Coward, McCann, 1982.

Yerrington, J. M. W. *The Official Report of the Trial of Sarah Jane Robinson.* Boston: Wright & Potter, 1888.

York, Mary. *The Bender Tragedy.* Mankato, Kans.: George W. Neff, 1875.

Young, Winifred. *Obsessive Poisoner.* London: Hale, 1973.

Zierold, Norman. *Three Sisters in Black.* Boston: Little, Brown, 1968.

Index